Pbig/123RF

Stephen VanHorn/Shutterstock

FuzzBones/Shutterstock

Accounting Information Systems

Ppbig/123RF

Stephen VanHorn/Shutterstock

FuzzBones/Shutterstock

Accounting Information Systems

FIFTEENTH EDITION

Marshall B. Romney
Professor Emeritus, Brigham Young University

Paul John Steinbart
Professor Emeritus, Arizona State University

Scott L. Summers
Brigham Young University

David A. Wood
Brigham Young University

Pearson

Please contact https://support.pearson.com/getsupport/s/contactsupport with any queries on this content.

Cataloging-in-Publication Data is available on file at the Library of Congress.

6 2022

Pearson

ISBN 10: 0-13-557283-5
ISBN 13: 978-0-13-557283-2

Brief Contents

Preface xix

PART I Conceptual Foundations of Accounting Information Systems 1

CHAPTER 1 **Accounting Information Systems: An Overview 2**

CHAPTER 2 **Overview of Transaction Processing and Enterprise Resource Planning Systems 30**

CHAPTER 3 **Systems Documentation Techniques 58**

PART II Data Analytics 91

CHAPTER 4 **Relational Databases 92**

CHAPTER 5 **Introduction to Data Analytics in Accounting 136**

CHAPTER 6 **Transforming Data 162**

CHAPTER 7 **Data Analysis and Presentation 188**

PART III Control of Accounting Information Systems 221

CHAPTER 8 **Fraud and Errors 222**

CHAPTER 9 **Computer Fraud and Abuse Techniques 256**

CHAPTER 10 **Control and Accounting Information Systems 296**

CHAPTER 11 **Controls for Information Security 334**

CHAPTER 12 **Confidentiality and Privacy Controls 368**

CHAPTER 13 **Processing Integrity and Availability Controls 396**

PART IV Accounting Information Systems Applications 425

CHAPTER 14 **The Revenue Cycle: Sales to Cash Collections 426**

CHAPTER 15 **The Expenditure Cycle: Purchasing to Cash Disbursements 468**

CHAPTER 16 **The Production Cycle 506**

CHAPTER 17 The Human Resources Management and Payroll Cycle 536

CHAPTER 18 General Ledger and Reporting System 566

PART V The REA Data Model 599

CHAPTER 19 Database Design Using the REA Data Model 600

CHAPTER 20 Implementing an REA Model in a Relational Database 634

CHAPTER 21 Special Topics in REA Modeling 658

PART VI The Systems Development Process 691

CHAPTER 22 Introduction to Systems Development and Systems Analysis 692

CHAPTER 23 AIS Development Strategies 728

CHAPTER 24 Systems Design, Implementation, and Operation 758

Glossary 786

Index 803

Contents

Preface xix

PART I Conceptual Foundations of Accounting Information Systems 1

CHAPTER 1 Accounting Information Systems: An Overview 2

Introduction 3

Information Needs and Business Processes 5

Information Needs 6

Business Processes 7

Accounting Information Systems 10

How an AIS Can Add Value to an Organization 11

An AIS Can Use Artificial Intelligence and Data Analytics to Improve Decision Making 12

The AIS and Blockchain 14

Cloud Computing, Virtualization, and the Internet of Things 18

The AIS and Corporate Strategy 18

The Role of the AIS in the Value Chain 19

Summary and Case Conclusion 20 ■ Key Terms 21

AIS IN ACTION: Chapter Quiz 21 ■ Discussion Questions 22 ■ Problems 23 ■

AIS IN ACTION SOLUTIONS: Quiz Key 27

CHAPTER 2 Overview of Transaction Processing and Enterprise Resource Planning Systems 30

Introduction 31

Transaction Processing: The Data Processing Cycle 32

Data Input 32

Data Storage 33

Data Processing 39

Information Output 39

Transaction Processing: Blockchain 41

Enterprise Resource Planning (ERP) Systems 42

Summary and Case Conclusion 45 ■ Key Terms 45

AIS IN ACTION: Chapter Quiz 45 ■ Discussion Questions 46 ■ Problems 47

CASE 2-1 Bar Harbor Blueberry Farm 52

CASE 2-2 SDC 54

AIS IN ACTION SOLUTIONS: Quiz Key 54

CHAPTER 3 **Systems Documentation Techniques 58**

Introduction 59

Business Process Diagrams 60

Flowcharts 63

Types of Flowcharts 65

Program Flowcharts 68

Data Flow Diagrams 69

Subdividing the DFD 71

Summary and Case Conclusion 74 ■ Key Terms 74

AIS IN ACTION: Chapter Quiz 75 ■ Comprehensive Problem 76 ■ Discussion Questions 76 ■ Problems 76

CASE 3-1 Dub 5 82

AIS IN ACTION SOLUTIONS: Quiz Key 83 ■ Comprehensive Problem Solution 85

PART II **Data Analytics 91**

CHAPTER 4 **Relational Databases 92**

Introduction 92

Databases and Files 93

Using Data Warehouses for Data Analytics 95

The Advantages of Database Systems 95

The Importance of Good Data 96

Database Systems 96

Logical and Physical Views of Data 96

Schemas 97

The Data Dictionary 98

DBMS Languages 100

Relational Databases 100

Types of Attributes 101

Designing a Relational Database for S&S, Inc. 101

Basic Requirements of a Relational Database 103

Two Approaches to Database Design 105

Creating Relational Database Queries 105

Query 1 105

Query 2 108

Query 3 111

Query 4 111

Query 5 113

Database Systems and the Future of Accounting 114

Summary and Case Conclusion 116 ■ Key Terms 116

AIS IN ACTION: Chapter Quiz 116 ■ Comprehensive Problem 117 ■ Discussion Questions 118 ■ Problems 119

CASE 4-1 Research Project 127

AIS IN ACTION SOLUTIONS: Quiz Key 128 ■ Comprehensive Problem Solution 129

Appendix: Data Normalization 132 ■ Summary 135

CHAPTER 5 **Introduction to Data Analytics in Accounting 136**

Introduction 137

Ask the Right Questions 139

Extract, Transform, and Load Relevant Data 139

Extracting Data 140

Transforming Data 143

Loading Data 144

Apply Appropriate Data Analytic Techniques 145
Interpret and Share the Results with Stakeholders 146
Interpreting Results 146
Sharing Results 147
Additional Data Analytics Considerations 148
Automation 148
Data Analytics Is Not Always the Right Tool 150
Summary and Case Conclusion 150 ■ Key Terms 150
AIS IN ACTION: Chapter Quiz 151 ■ Discussion Questions 152 ■ Problems 152
CASE 5-1 Robotic Process Automation—Wood's Amazing Woods Inc. 157
AIS IN ACTION SOLUTIONS: Quiz Key 159

CHAPTER 6 Transforming Data 162
Introduction 163
Attributes of High-Quality Data 164
Data Structuring 165
Aggregate Data 165
Data Joining 166
Data Pivoting 166
Data Standardization 167
Data Parsing and Data Concatenation 167
Cryptic Data Values 169
Misfielded Data Values 170
Data Formatting and Data Consistency 170
Data Cleaning 172
Data De-Duplication 172
Data Filtering 172
Data Contradiction Errors 173
Data Threshold Violations 173
Violated Attribute Dependencies 174
Data Entry Errors 174
Data Validation 174
Visual Inspection 175
Basic Statistical Tests 175
Audit a Sample 175
Advanced Testing Techniques 176
Summary and Case Conclusion 176 ■ Key Terms 176
AIS IN ACTION: Chapter Quiz 177 ■ Discussion Questions 178 ■ Problems 178
CASE 6-1 Hotel Data Cleaning Case 183
AIS IN ACTION SOLUTIONS: Quiz Key 184

CHAPTER 7 Data Analysis and Presentation 188
Introduction 189
Data Analysis 189
Descriptive Analytics 189
Diagnostic Analytics 191
Predictive Analytics 193
Prescriptive Analytics 194
Common Problems with Data Analytics 194
Data Presentation 196
Choosing the Right Visualization 196
Designing High-Quality Visualizations 199
Summary and Case Conclusion 209 ■ Key Terms 209

AIS IN ACTION: Chapter Quiz 210 ■ Discussion Questions 211 ■ Problems 211
CASE 7-1 Analyzing Gamified Training 215
CASE 7-1 Appendix 216
ANALYTICS MINDSET Gamification 217
AIS IN ACTION SOLUTIONS: Quiz Key 218

PART III Control of Accounting Information Systems 221

CHAPTER 8 Fraud and Errors 222
Introduction 223
AIS Threats 223
Natural and Political Disasters 223
Software Errors and Equipment Malfunctions 225
Unintentional Errors 225
Intentional Acts 226
Introduction to Fraud 227
Misappropriation of Assets 228
Fraudulent Financial Reporting 229
SAS No. 99 (AU-C Section 240): The Auditor's Responsibility to Detect Fraud 229
Who Perpetrates Fraud and Why 230
The Fraud Triangle 230
Computer Fraud 235
The Rise in Computer Fraud 235
Computer Fraud Classifications 236
Preventing and Detecting Fraud and Abuse 238
Using Data Analytics to Prevent and Detect Fraud 240
Summary and Case Conclusion 242 ■ Key Terms 243
AIS IN ACTION: Chapter Quiz 243 ■ Discussion Questions 244 ■ Problems 245
CASE 8-1 David L. Miller: Portrait of a White-Collar Criminal 250
CASE 8-2 Heirloom Photo Plans 251
AIS IN ACTION SOLUTIONS: Quiz Key 253

CHAPTER 9 Computer Fraud and Abuse Techniques 256
Introduction 256
Computer Attacks and Abuse 257
Social Engineering 266
Malware 270
Summary and Case Conclusion 279 ■ Key Terms 280
AIS IN ACTION: Chapter Quiz 280 ■ Discussion Questions 281 ■ Problems 282
CASE 9-1 Shadowcrew 292
AIS IN ACTION SOLUTIONS: Quiz Key 293

CHAPTER 10 Control and Accounting Information Systems 296
Introduction 297
Why Threats to Accounting Information Systems Are Increasing 297
Overview of Control Concepts 298
The Foreign Corrupt Practices and Sarbanes–Oxley Acts 299
Control Frameworks 300
COBIT Framework 300
COSO'S Internal Control Framework 302
The Control Environment 304
Management's Philosophy, Operating Style, and Risk Appetite 305
Commitment to Integrity, Ethical Values, and Competence 305
Internal Control Oversight by the Board of Directors 306

Organizational Structure 306
Methods of Assigning Authority and Responsibility 306
Human Resources Standards That Attract, Develop, and Retain Competent Individuals 307
External Influences 308

Risk Assessment and Risk Response 309
Estimate Likelihood and Impact 309
Identify Controls 309
Estimate Costs and Benefits 309
Determine Cost/Benefit Effectiveness 310
Implement Control or Accept, Share, or Avoid the Risk 311

Control Activities 311
Proper Authorization of Transactions and Activities 311
Segregation of Duties 312
Project Development and Acquisition Controls 315
Change Management Controls 316
Design and Use of Documents and Records 316
Safeguard Assets, Records, and Data 316
Independent Checks on Performance 317

Communicate Information and Monitor Control Processes 318
Information and Communication 318
Monitoring 319

Summary and Case Conclusion 321 ■ Key Terms 322
AIS IN ACTION: Chapter Quiz 322 ■ Discussion Questions 323 ■ Problems 324
CASE 10-1 The Greater Providence Deposit & Trust Embezzlement 330
AIS IN ACTION SOLUTIONS: Quiz Key 331

CHAPTER 11 Controls for Information Security 334

Introduction 335

Three Fundamental Information Security Concepts 336
1. Security Is a Management Issue, Not Just a Technology Issue 336
2. People: The Critical Factor 338
3. The Time-Based Model of Information Security 339

Protecting Information Resources 341
Physical Security: Access Controls 341
Process: User Access Controls 342
IT Solutions: Antimalware Controls 346
IT Solutions: Network Access Controls 346
IT Solutions: Device and Software Hardening Controls 351
IT Solutions: Encryption 353

Detecting Attacks 353
Log Analysis 353
Intrusion Detection Systems 354
Honeypots 354
Continuous Monitoring 354

Responding to Attacks 355
Computer Incident Response Team (CIRT) 355
Chief Information Security Officer (CISO) 355

Monitor and Revise Security Solutions 356
Penetration Testing 356
Change Controls and Change Management 356

Security Implications of Virtualization, Cloud Computing, and the Internet of Things 357

Summary and Case Conclusion 358 ■ Key Terms 358

AIS IN ACTION: Chapter Quiz 359 ■ Discussion Questions 360 ■ Problems 360
CASE 11-1 Assessing Change Control and Change Management 365
CASE 11-2 Research Project 365
AIS IN ACTION SOLUTIONS: Quiz Key 365

CHAPTER 12 Confidentiality and Privacy Controls 368
Introduction 369
Protecting Confidentiality and Privacy 369
Identify and Classify Information to Be Protected 370
Protecting Sensitive Information with Encryption 370
Controlling Access to Sensitive Information 370
Training 372
Privacy Regulations and Generally Accepted Privacy Principles 372
The EU's GDPR and U.S. Laws 372
Generally Accepted Privacy Principles 373
Encryption 376
Factors That Influence Encryption Strength 377
Types of Encryption Systems 377
Virtual Private Networks (VPNs) 379
Hashing 380
Digital Signatures 381
Digital Certificates and Public Key Infrastructure 382
Blockchain 383
Summary and Case Conclusion 386 ■ Key Terms 386
AIS IN ACTION: Chapter Quiz 386 ■ Discussion Questions 388 ■ Problems 388
CASE 12-1 Protecting Privacy of Tax Returns 392
CASE 12-2 Generally Accepted Privacy Principles 393
AIS IN ACTION SOLUTIONS: Quiz Key 393

CHAPTER 13 Processing Integrity and Availability Controls 396
Introduction 396
Processing Integrity 397
Input Controls 397
Processing Controls 399
Output Controls 400
Illustrative Example: Credit Sales Processing 401
Processing Integrity Controls in Spreadsheets 403
Availability 403
Minimizing Risk of System Downtime 403
Recovery and Resumption of Normal Operations 404
Summary and Case Conclusion 409 ■ Key Terms 410
AIS IN ACTION: Chapter Quiz 410 ■ Discussion Questions 411 ■ Problems 412
CASE 13-1 Ensuring Systems Availability 420
CASE 13-2 Ensuring Process Integrity in Spreadsheets 421
AIS IN ACTION SOLUTIONS: Quiz Key 422

PART IV Accounting Information Systems Applications 425

CHAPTER 14 The Revenue Cycle: Sales to Cash Collections 426
Introduction 428
Revenue Cycle Information System 430
Process 430
Threats and Controls 430

Sales Order Entry 433
Taking Customer Orders 434
Credit Approval 436
Checking Inventory Availability 438
Responding to Customer Inquiries 439
Shipping 441
Pick and Pack the Order 441
Ship the Order 443
Billing 445
Invoicing 446
Maintain Accounts Receivable 448
Cash Collections 451
Process 451
Threats and Controls 452
Summary and Case Conclusion 454 ■ Key Terms 455
AIS IN ACTION: Chapter Quiz 455 ■ Discussion Questions 456 ■ Problems 456
CASE 14-1 Research Project: How CPA Firms Are Leveraging New Developments in IT 465
AIS IN ACTION SOLUTIONS: Quiz Key 465

CHAPTER 15 The Expenditure Cycle: Purchasing to Cash Disbursements 468
Introduction 469
Expenditure Cycle Information System 470
Process 470
Threats and Controls 473
Ordering Materials, Supplies, and Services 477
Identifying What, When, and How Much to Purchase 477
Choosing Suppliers 479
Receiving 483
Process 484
Threats and Controls 485
Approving Supplier Invoices 486
Process 486
Threats and Controls 489
Cash Disbursements 489
Process 489
Threats and Controls 489
Summary and Case Conclusion 492 ■ Key Terms 493
AIS IN ACTION: Chapter Quiz 493 ■ Discussion Questions 494 ■ Problems 494
CASE 15-1 Group Case Analysis: School District Expenditure Fraud 503
CASE 15-2 Anatomy of a Multi-Million Dollar Embezzlement at ING Bank 503
AIS IN ACTION SOLUTIONS: Quiz Key 504

CHAPTER 16 The Production Cycle 506
Introduction 507
Production Cycle Information System 509
Process 510
Threats and Controls 510
Product Design 511
Process 511
Threats and Controls 513
Planning and Scheduling 513
Production Planning Methods 513

Key Documents and Forms 513
Threats and Controls 517
Production Operations 518
Threats and Controls 518
Cost Accounting 520
Process 520
Threats and Controls 521
Summary and Case Conclusion 526 ■ Key Terms 527
AIS IN ACTION: Chapter Quiz 527 ■ Discussion Questions 528 ■ Problems 529
CASE 16-1 The Accountant and CIM 533
AIS IN ACTION SOLUTIONS: Quiz Key 533

CHAPTER 17 The Human Resources Management and Payroll Cycle 536
Introduction 537
HRM/Payroll Cycle Information System 538
Overview of HRM Process and Information Needs 538
Threats and Controls 540
Payroll Cycle Activities 543
Update Payroll Master Database 544
Validate Time and Attendance Data 545
Prepare Payroll 547
Disburse Payroll 551
Calculate and Disburse Employer-Paid Benefits, Taxes, and Voluntary Employee Deductions 553
Outsourcing Options: Payroll Service Bureaus and Professional Employer Organizations 553
Summary and Case Conclusion 554 ■ Key Terms 555
AIS IN ACTION: Chapter Quiz 555 ■ Discussion Questions 556 ■ Problems 557
CASE 17-1 Excel Project: Sorting and Grouping Data 563
AIS IN ACTION SOLUTIONS: Quiz Key 563

CHAPTER 18 General Ledger and Reporting System 566
Introduction 567
General Ledger and Reporting System 568
Process 569
Threats and Controls 569
Update General Ledger 571
Process 571
Threats and Controls 572
Post Adjusting Entries 574
Process 575
Threats and Controls 576
Prepare Financial Statements 576
Process 576
Threats and Controls 583
Produce Managerial Reports 584
Process 584
Threats and Controls 584
Summary and Case Conclusion 588 ■ Key Terms 588
AIS IN ACTION: Chapter Quiz 589 ■ Discussion Questions 590 ■ Problems 590
CASE 18-1 Exploring iXBRL Viewers 596
CASE 18-2 Evaluating a General Ledger Package 596
AIS IN ACTION SOLUTIONS: Quiz Key 596

PART V The REA Data Model 599

CHAPTER 19 Database Design Using the REA Data Model 600
Introduction 600
Database Design Process 601
Entity-Relationship Diagrams 602
The REA Data Model 603
Three Basic Types of Entities 604
Structuring Relationships: The Basic REA Template 604
Developing an REA Diagram 607
Step 1: Identify Relevant Events 607
Step 2: Identify Resources and Agents 609
Step 3: Determine Cardinalities of Relationships 610
What an REA Diagram Reveals About an Organization 614
Business Meaning of Cardinalities 614
Uniqueness of REA Diagrams 615
Summary and Case Conclusion 616 ■ Key Terms 617
AIS IN ACTION: Chapter Quiz 617 ■ Comprehensive Problem 620 ■ Discussion Questions 620 ■ Problems 621
CASE 19-1 REA Data Modeling Extension 625
AIS IN ACTION SOLUTIONS: Quiz Key 626 ■ Comprehensive Problem Solution 630

CHAPTER 20 Implementing an REA Model in a Relational Database 634
Introduction 635
Integrating REA Diagrams Across Cycles 635
Merging Redundant Resource Entities 638
Merging Redundant Event Entities 639
Validating the Accuracy of Integrated REA Diagrams 640
Implementing an REA Diagram in a Relational Database 640
Step 1: Create Tables for Each Distinct Entity and M:N Relationship 640
Step 2: Assign Attributes to Each Table 642
Step 3: Use Foreign Keys to Implement 1:1 and 1:N Relationships 643
Completeness Check 644
Using REA Diagrams to Retrieve Information from a Database 645
Creating Journals and Ledgers 645
Generating Financial Statements 646
Creating Managerial Reports 647
Summary and Case Conclusion 647 ■ Key Term 648
AIS IN ACTION: Chapter Quiz 648 ■ Comprehensive Problem 649 ■ Discussion Questions 649 ■ Problems 650
CASE 20-1 Practical Database Design 652
AIS IN ACTION SOLUTIONS: Quiz Key 653 ■ Comprehensive Problem Solution 655

CHAPTER 21 Special Topics in REA Modeling 658
Introduction 659
Additional Revenue and Expenditure Cycle Modeling Topics 659
Additional Revenue Cycle Events and Attribute Placement 659
Additional Expenditure Cycle Events and Attribute Placement 661
Sale of Services 664
Acquisition of Intangible Services 664
Digital Assets 665
Rental Transactions 665

Additional REA Features 667
Employee Roles 667
M:N Agent–Event Relationships 667
Locations 667
Relationships Between Resources and Agents 667
Production Cycle REA Model 668
Additional Entities—Intellectual Property 668
Production Cycle Events 670
New REA Feature 670
Combined HR/Payroll Data Model 671
HR Cycle Entities 671
Tracking Employees' Time 672
Financing Activities Data Model 673
Summary and Case Conclusion 674
AIS IN ACTION: Chapter Quiz 677 ■ Discussion Questions 678 ■ Problems 679
CASE 21-1 Practical Database Assignment 684
AIS IN ACTION SOLUTIONS: Quiz Key 684
Appendix: Extending the REA Model to Include Information About Policies 688

PART VI The Systems Development Process 691

CHAPTER 22 Introduction to Systems Development and Systems Analysis 692
Introduction 693
Systems Development 695
The Systems Development Life Cycle 695
The Players 696
Planning Systems Development 697
Planning Techniques 699
Feasibility Analysis 699
Capital Budgeting: Calculating Economic Feasibility 700
Behavioral Aspects of Change 701
Why Behavioral Problems Occur 702
How People Resist Change 702
Preventing Behavioral Problems 703
Systems Analysis 704
Initial Investigation 704
Systems Survey 706
Feasibility Study 707
Information Needs and Systems Requirements 707
Systems Analysis Report 709
Summary and Case Conclusion 710 ■ Key Terms 711
AIS IN ACTION: Chapter Quiz 712 ■ Comprehensive Problem 713 ■ Discussion Questions 713 ■ Problems 714
CASE 22-1 Audio Visual Corporation 722
AIS IN ACTION SOLUTIONS: Quiz Key 723 ■ Comprehensive Problem Solution 725

CHAPTER 23 AIS Development Strategies 728
Introduction 729
Purchasing Software 729
Selecting a Vendor 730

Acquiring Hardware and Software 730
Evaluating Proposals and Selecting a System 731
Development by In-House Information Systems Departments 733
End-User-Developed Software 733
Advantages and Disadvantages of End-User Computing 734
Managing and Controlling End-User Computing 735
Outsourcing the System 736
Advantages and Disadvantages of Outsourcing 736
Methods for Improving Systems Development 737
Business Process Management 738
Prototyping 739
Agile Methodologies 741
Computer-Aided Software Engineering 744
Summary and Case Conclusion 745 ■ Key Terms 745
AIS IN ACTION: Chapter Quiz 746 ■ Comprehensive Problem 747 ■ Discussion Questions 747 ■ Problems 748
CASE 23-1 Wong Engineering Corp. 752
AIS IN ACTION SOLUTIONS: Quiz Key 753 ■ Comprehensive Problem Solution 756

CHAPTER 24 **Systems Design, Implementation, and Operation 758**
Introduction 759
Conceptual Systems Design 759
Evaluate Design Alternatives 759
Prepare Design Specifications and Reports 761
Physical Systems Design 761
Output Design 762
File and Database Design 762
Input Design 763
Program Design 764
Procedures and Controls Design 765
Systems Implementation 766
Implementation Planning and Site Preparation 766
Selecting and Training Personnel 767
Complete Documentation 768
Testing the System 768
Systems Conversion 769
Operation and Maintenance 770
Summary and Case Conclusion 771 ■ Key Terms 772
AIS IN ACTION: Chapter Quiz 772 ■ Comprehensive Problem 773 ■ Discussion Questions 774 ■ Problems 775
CASE 24-1 Citizen's Gas Company 781
AIS IN ACTION SOLUTIONS: Quiz Key 781 ■ Comprehensive Problem Solution 783

Glossary 786
Index 803

Preface

New to This Edition

INTRODUCING TWO NEW CO-AUTHORS

Scott L. Summers and David A. Wood, both from Brigham Young University, joined as new co-authors. Scott and David created the new section on data analytics (Part II), consisting of four chapters. The first chapter is an update of Chapter 4 that discusses relational databases not only as the basis for transaction processing systems, but also as one of the sources of Big Data and Analytics. The next three chapters (Chapters 5–7) discuss the Extract, Transfer, and Load (ETL) process and various data analytic techniques. This new content covers an extremely important topic that affects all aspects of designing, using, managing, and auditing an AIS.

ENHANCEMENTS IN THE FIFTEENTH EDITION

We made extensive revisions to the content of the material to incorporate recent developments while retaining the features that have made prior editions easy to use. Every chapter has been revised to include up-to-date examples of important concepts. Specific changes include the following:

1. Introduced several new topics in Chapter 1. The chapter discusses how an AIS can use artificial intelligence and data analytics to improve decision making, how the AIS is affected by blockchain technology, and the use of cloud computing, virtualization, and the internet of things.
2. Shortened and simplified the discussion of computer fraud and abuse techniques by eliminating many of the less frequently used techniques.
3. Simplified the discussion of control and the AIS by using the COSO Internal Control framework instead of the COSO Enterprise Risk Management framework as the structure for discussing controls.
4. Updated the discussion of information security countermeasures.
5. Updated the discussion of transaction processing and encryption to include blockchain technology.
6. Updated the discussion of privacy to include the EU's General Data Privacy Regulation (GDPR).
7. Updated the end-of-chapter discussion questions and problems, including Excel exercises that are based on articles from the *Journal of Accountancy* so that students can develop the specific skills used by practitioners. Most chapters also include a problem that consists of multiple-choice questions we have used in our exams to provide students with an additional chance to check how well they understand the chapter material.
8. Moved the topic of auditing (Chapter 11 in the fourteenth edition) to a web-only appendix because most of that material is covered in other courses.

Solving Learning and Teaching Challenges

STRUCTURED LEARNING

KEY LEARNING OBJECTIVES When you finish reading this text, you should understand the following key concepts:

- Basic activities performed in major business cycles.
- What data needs to be collected to enable managers to plan, evaluate, and control an organization's business activities.
- How to extract, transfer, and load (ETL) data from both the organization's AIS and other sources into a common repository that can be used for data analytics.
- How IT developments can improve the efficiency and effectiveness of business processes.
- How to design an AIS to provide the information needed to make key decisions in each business cycle.
- Risk of fraud and motives and techniques used to perpetrate fraud.
- COSO's models (Internal Control and ERM) for internal control and risk management as well as specific controls used to achieve these objectives.
- Control Objectives for Information and Related Technology (COBIT) framework for the effective governance and control of information systems and how IT affects the implementation of internal controls.
- AICPA's Trust Services framework for ensuring systems reliability by developing procedures to protect the confidentiality of proprietary information, maintain the privacy of personally identifying information collected from customers, assure the availability of information resources, and provide for information processing integrity.
- Fundamentals of information security.
- Fundamental concepts of database technology and data modeling and their effect on an AIS.
- Tools for documenting AIS work, such as REA diagrams, business processing diagrams, data flow diagrams, and flowcharts.
- Basic steps in the system development process to design and improve an AIS.

FEATURES TO FACILITATE LEARNING To help students understand these concepts, the text includes the following features:

1. **Each chapter begins with an integrated case that introduces key chapter concepts and topics and identifies several key issues or problems that students should be able to solve after mastering the material presented in that chapter.** The case is referenced throughout the chapter, and the chapter summary presents solutions to the problems and issues raised in the case.
2. **Focus boxes and real-world examples** to help students understand how companies use the latest IT developments to improve their AIS.
3. **Hands-on Excel exercises in many chapters** to help students hone their computer skills. Many of these exercises are based on "how-to" tutorials that appeared in recent issues of the *Journal of Accountancy*. Some of those articles discuss older versions of Excel, thereby giving students practice in developing the important life-long learning skill of adapting older instructions to updated versions of software.
4. **Numerous discussion questions and problems in every chapter** provide additional opportunities for students to demonstrate mastery of key concepts. Many problems were developed from reports in current periodicals. Other problems were selected from various professional examinations, including the CPA, CMA, CIA, and SMAC exams. One problem in every chapter consists of a set of multiple-choice questions to provide practice in answering exam-style questions. One or more problems where students are asked to match terms with their definitions to help students learn the terminology introduced in that chapter. **Each chapter also has one or more cases** that require more extensive exploration of specific topics.

5. **Quizzes** at the end of each chapter enable students to self-assess their understanding of the material. We also provide detailed explanations about the correct answer to each quiz question.
6. A number of chapters have a **comprehensive problem** in the AIS in Action section at the end of the chapter with the solution to the problem provided after quiz question solutions and explanations at the very end of the chapter.
7. **Extensive use of full-color graphics.** The text contains hundreds of figures, diagrams, flowcharts, and tables that illustrate chapter concepts, and color is used to highlight key points.
8. Definitions of key terms are repeated in the **glossary margins** in each chapter. In addition, a **comprehensive glossary** located at the back of the book makes it easy to look up the definition of the various technical terms used in the text.

CONTENT AND ORGANIZATION

Part I: Conceptual Foundations of Accounting Information Systems Part I consists of three chapters that present the underlying concepts fundamental to an understanding of AIS.

Chapter 1 introduces basic terminology and provides an overview of AIS topics. It discusses how an AIS can add value to an organization and how it can be used to help organizations implement corporate strategy. It also discusses the types of information companies need to successfully operate and introduces the basic business processes that produce that information. It concludes by describing the role of the AIS in an organization's value chain. It also introduces several new topics in the text: artificial intelligence, data analytics, blockchain, virtualization, cloud computing, and the Internet of Things.

Chapter 2 introduces transaction processing in automated systems and presents basic information about input/output, processing, and data storage concepts as well as the wide range of data that must be collected by the AIS. This information helps students understand what an AIS does; throughout the remainder of the book, we discuss advances in IT and how it affects the manner in which those functions are performed. The chapter discusses the impact of blockchain on transaction processing. Chapter 2 also introduces Enterprise Resource Planning (ERP) systems and their importance and uses in modern business.

Chapter 3 covers three of the most important tools and techniques used to understand, evaluate, design, and document information systems: business process diagrams, flowcharts, and data flow diagrams. Students will learn how to read, critique, and create systems documentation using these tools.

Part II: Data Analytics Part II consists of four chapters about relational databases, the ETL process, and various data analytics techniques.

Chapter 4 describes the principles of relational database design and how to use SQL to analyze the data. It also discusses how an organization's relational database used for transaction processing provides one important source of data for advanced data analytics.

Chapter 5 introduces the topic of data analysis and begins by stressing the importance of formulating and asking the right questions to obtain useful insights. It then explains the basic steps of extracting, transforming, and loading (ETL) data to be used for analytics. Next, it discusses how to choose appropriate analytic techniques and how to interpret and share the results. A discussion about the potential for automating analytics and a word of caution about the limits of what analytics can and cannot do concludes the chapter.

Chapter 6 delves into more detail about the different steps in the ETL process, focusing on how to transform data. It begins by describing the attributes that make data useful for analytics and then discusses techniques for structuring data, standardizing data being consolidated from multiple sources, cleaning data, and validating data.

Chapter 7 discusses the differences between descriptive, diagnostic, predictive, and prescriptive analytic techniques. It also describes how to choose the right visualization tools to aid in analysis and presents best practices for designing high-quality visualizations.

Part III: Control of Accounting Information Systems The six chapters in Part III focus on threats to the reliability of the AIS and applicable controls for addressing and mitigating the risks associated with those threats.

Chapter 8 introduces students to the different kinds of threats faced by information systems, primarily focusing on the threats of fraud and errors. The chapter describes the different types of fraud and explains how fraud is perpetrated, who perpetrates it, and why it occurs.

Chapter 9 discusses computer fraud and abuse techniques. Three major types of computer fraud are discussed: computer attacks and abuse, social engineering, and malware. The chapter explains the dozens of ways computer fraud and abuse can be perpetrated.

Chapter 10 uses the COSO Internal Control framework, to discuss the basic concepts of internal control. It introduces the expanded enterprise risk management (COSO-ERM) model and compares it with the COSO Internal Control framework. It also introduces the COBIT framework which applies those concepts to IT, thereby providing a foundation for effective governance and control of information systems.

Chapter 11 focuses on information security. It introduces the fundamental concepts of defense-in-depth and the time-based approach to security. The chapter provides a broad survey of a variety of security topics, including access controls, firewalls, encryption, and incident detection and response.

Chapter 12 discusses the many specific computer controls used in business organizations to achieve the objectives of ensuring privacy and confidentiality and discusses the implications of new regulations such as the EU's General Data Privacy Regulation (GDPR) and similar laws enacted by California and other states. The chapter also provides a detailed discussion of blockchain technology.

Chapter 13 addresses the controls necessary to achieve the objectives of accurate processing of information and ensuring that information is available to managers whenever and wherever they need it. It also discusses how virtualization and cloud technology are changing the methods used for backup and recovery.

Part IV: Accounting Information Systems Applications Part IV focuses on how a company's AIS provides critical support for its fundamental business processes. Most large and many medium-sized organizations use enterprise resource planning (ERP) systems to collect, process, and store data about their business processes as well as to provide information reports designed to enable managers and external parties to assess the organization's efficiency and effectiveness. To make it easier to understand how an ERP system functions, Part III consists of five chapters, each focusing on a particular business process.

Chapter 14 covers the revenue cycle (also referred to as the sales-to-cash business process), describing all the activities involved in taking customer orders, fulfilling those orders, and collecting cash.

Chapter 15 examines the expenditure cycle (also referred to as the purchase-to-pay business process), describing all the activities involved in ordering, receiving, and paying for merchandise, supplies, and services.

Chapter 16 reviews the production (manufacturing) cycle, with a special focus on the implications of recent cost accounting developments, such as activity-based costing, for the design of the production cycle information system.

Chapter 17 explains the human resources management/payroll cycle, focusing primarily on the activities involved in processing payroll.

Chapter 18 explores the general ledger and reporting activities in an organization, discussing topics such as XBRL, the balanced scorecard, and the switch from GAAP to IFRS.

Each of these five chapters explains the three basic functions performed by the AIS: efficient transaction processing, provision of adequate internal controls to safeguard assets (including data), and preparation of information useful for effective decision making.

Part V: The REA Data Model Part V consists of three chapters that focus on the REA data model, which provides a conceptual tool for designing and understanding the database underlying an AIS.

Chapter 19 introduces the REA data model and how it can be used to design an AIS database. The chapter focuses on modeling the revenue and expenditure cycles. It also demonstrates how the REA model can be used to develop an AIS that can not only generate traditional financial statements and reports but can also more fully meet the information needs of management.

Chapter 20 explains how to implement an REA data model in a relational database system. It also shows how to query a relational database to produce various financial statements and management reports.

Chapter 21 explains how to develop REA data models of the production, HR/payroll, and financing cycles. It also discusses a number of advanced modeling issues such as the acquisition and sale of intangible products and services and rental transactions.

Part VI: The Systems Development Process Part VI consists of three chapters that cover various aspects of the systems development process.

Chapter 22 introduces the systems development life cycle and discusses the introductory steps of this process (systems analysis, feasibility, and planning). Particular emphasis is placed on the behavioral ramifications of change.

Chapter 23 discusses an organization's many options for acquiring or developing an AIS (e.g., purchasing software, writing software, end-user-developed software, and outsourcing) and for speeding up or improving the development process (business process management, prototyping, agile methodologies, and computer-assisted software engineering).

Chapter 24 covers the remaining stages of the systems development life cycle (conceptual design, physical design, implementation, and operation and maintenance) and emphasizes the interrelationships among the phases.

SUPPLEMENTAL RESOURCES For more information and resources, visit www.pearson.com.

TECHNOLOGY-REINFORCED LEARNING

REVEL™

Educational Technology Designed for the Way Today's Students Read, Think, and Learn When students are engaged deeply, they learn more effectively and perform better in their courses. This simple fact inspired the creation of REVEL: an interactive learning environment designed for the way today's students read, think, and learn.

REVEL enlivens course content with media interactives and assessments—integrated directly within the authors' narrative—that provide opportunities for students to read, practice, and study in one continuous experience. This immersive educational technology replaces the print textbook and is designed to measurably boost students' understanding, retention, and preparedness. Learn more about REVEL http://www.pearsonhighered.com/revel/

EXCEL HOMEWORK PROBLEMS Accountants need to become proficient with Excel because it is a useful tool for tasks related to every business process. That is why each of the chapters in the business process section contains several homework problems designed to teach new Excel skills in a context related to one of the business processes discussed in the chapter.

As with any software, Microsoft regularly releases updates to Microsoft Office, but not everyone always immediately switches. During your career you will periodically move to a newer version of Excel. When you do, you will find that sometimes you need to make only minor changes to existing spreadsheets, but other times you may have to make more significant changes because the newer version of Excel now incorporates different features and functions.

So how do you keep abreast of changes? And how can you learn new Excel skills "on the job" to simplify tasks that you now find yourself doing repeatedly? You could pay to take a course, but that can be costly, time-consuming and not always timely. Alternatively, you can develop life-long learning skills to continuously update your knowledge. One important way to do this is to begin now to save copies of two types of articles that regularly appear in the *Journal of Accountancy*. The first is the monthly column, "Technology Q&A," which often contains answers to questions about how do you do something in a newer version of Excel that you know how to do in an older version. The second type of article is a complete tutorial about a powerful way to use one or more Excel functions to automate a recurring task. Often, this second type of article has an online spreadsheet file that you can download and use to follow along with the example and thereby teach yourself a new skill.

The *Journal of Accountancy* website maintains an archive of these articles that you can search to see if there is one that addresses a task that is new for you. Even if the article explains how to do something (such as create a pivot table) in an older version of Excel, in most cases you will find that many of the steps have not changed. For those that have, if you read the old way to do it as described in the article, you can then use Excel's built-in help feature to see how to do the same task in the newer version that you are now using.

The ability to learn how to use new versions of software on your own is an important lifelong learning skill. Indeed, recruiters are looking for evidence that a job candidate not only has acquired a body of knowledge but also knows how to research and learn new versions of existing software tools. The various Excel homework problems in this text help you learn how to do this.

From the Authors

TO THE INSTRUCTOR

This book is intended for use in a one-semester course in accounting information systems at either the undergraduate or graduate level. Introductory financial and managerial accounting courses are suggested prerequisites, and an introductory information systems course that covers a computer language or software package is helpful, but not necessary.

The book can also be used as the main text in graduate or advanced undergraduate management information systems courses.

The topics covered in this text provide information systems students with a solid understanding of transaction processing systems that they can then build on as they pursue more in-depth study of specific topics such as databases, data analytics, networks, systems analysis and design, cloud computing, virtualization, blockchain, artificial intelligence, Internet of Things, computer security, and information system controls.

TO THE STUDENT

As in previous editions, the fifteenth edition of *Accounting Information Systems* is designed to prepare you for a successful accounting career whether you enter public practice, industry, or government. All of you will be users of accounting information systems. In addition to being users, some of you will become managers. Others will become internal and external auditors, and some of you will become consultants. Regardless of your role, you will need to understand how accounting information systems work in order to effectively measure how cost-effectively they perform, to assess their reliability and that of the information produced, or to lead the redesign and implementation of new and better systems. Mastering the material presented in this text will give you the foundational knowledge you need to excel at all those tasks.

This text discusses important new IT developments, such as blockchain and data analytics, because such developments affect business processes and often cause organizations to redesign their accounting systems to take advantage of new capabilities. The focus, however, is not on IT for the sake of IT, but on how IT affects business processes and controls. Indeed, new IT developments not only bring new capabilities, but also often create new threats and affect the overall level of risk. This text will help you understand these issues so that you can properly determine how to modify accounting systems controls to effectively address those new threats and accurately assess the adequacy of controls in those redesigned systems. We also discuss the effect of recent regulatory developments, such as the EU's General Data Privacy Regulation (GDPR) and similar legislation in California and other states, on the design and operation of accounting systems.

In addition to technology- and regulatory-driven changes, companies are responding to the increasingly competitive business environment by reexamining every internal activity to reap the most value at the least cost. As a result, accountants are asked to do more than simply report the results of past activities. They must take a more proactive role in both providing and interpreting financial and nonfinancial information about the organization's activities. Therefore, throughout this text, we discuss how accountants can improve the design and functioning of the accounting information system (AIS) so that it truly adds value to the organization by providing management with the information needed to effectively run an organization.

Acknowledgments

We wish to express our appreciation to all supplements authors for preparing the various supplements that accompany this edition. We thank Martha M. Eining of the University of Utah and Carol F. Venable of San Diego State University for preparing the comprehensive cases included on our website. We are also grateful to Iris Vessey for her contributions to the problem material. We thank Bill Heninger of Brigham Young University for allowing us to use portions of his database normalization tutorial to create the appendix to Chapter 4.

Perhaps most importantly, we are indebted to the numerous faculty members throughout the world who have adopted the earlier editions of this book and who have been generous with their suggestions for improvement. We are especially grateful to the following faculty who participated in reviewing the fifteenth edition throughout various stages of the revision process:

A. Faye Borthick, *Georgia State University*
Gerald Childs, *Waukesha County Technical College*
Steven Johnson, *Minnesota State University, Mankato*
Stanley X Lewis, *Troy University*
Andrew B. Nyaboga, *William Paterson University*
Magdy Roufaiel, *Empire State College*
Milton Shen, *University of Alabama - Huntsville*
Jennifer Tseng, *Mission College*
Thomas L. Zeller, *Loyola University Chicago*

We are grateful for permission received from four professional accounting organizations to use problems and unofficial solutions from their past professional examinations in this book. Thanks are extended to the American Institute of Certified Public Accountants for use of CPA Examination materials, to the Institute of Certified Management Accountants for use of CMA Examination materials, to the Institute of Internal Auditors for use of CIA Examination materials, and to the Society of Management Accountants of Canada for use of SMAC Examination materials. We also wish to thank Netsuite, Inc., for providing permission to use screenshots of their software throughout the text.

Of course, any errors in this book remain our responsibility. We welcome your comments and suggestions for further improvement.

Finally, we want to thank our wives and families for their love, support, and encouragement. We also want to thank God for giving us the ability to start and complete this book.

—Marshall B. Romney
Springville, Utah

—Paul John Steinbart
Apache Junction, Arizona

—Scott L. Summers
Provo, Utah

—David A. Wood
Provo, Utah

Conceptual Foundations of Accounting Information Systems

PART I

Kheng Guan Toh/Shutterstock

CHAPTER 1
Accounting Information Systems: An Overview

CHAPTER 2
Overview of Transaction Processing and Enterprise Resource Planning Systems

CHAPTER 3
Systems Documentation Techniques

CHAPTER

1

Accounting Information Systems: An Overview

LEARNING OBJECTIVES

After studying this chapter, you should be able to:

1. Distinguish data from information, discuss the characteristics of useful information, and explain how to determine the value of information.
2. Explain the decisions an organization makes, the information needed to make them, and the major business processes present in most companies.
3. Explain how an accounting information system (AIS) adds value to an organization, how it affects and is affected by corporate strategy, and its role in a value chain.

INTEGRATIVE CASE S&S

After working for years as a regional manager for a retail organization, Scott Parry opened his own business with Susan Gonzalez, one of his district managers, as his partner. They formed S&S to sell appliances and consumer electronics. Scott and Susan pursued a "clicks and bricks" strategy by renting a building in a busy part of town and adding an electronic storefront.

Scott and Susan invested enough money to see them through the first six months. They will hire 15 employees within the next two weeks—three to stock the shelves, four sales representatives, six checkout clerks, and two to develop and maintain the electronic storefront.

Scott and Susan will host S&S's grand opening in five weeks. To meet that deadline, they have to address the following important issues:

1. What decisions do they need to make to be successful and profitable? For example:
   a. How should they price products to be competitive yet earn a profit?
   b. Should they extend credit, and, if so, on what terms? How can they accurately track what customers owe and pay?
   c. How should they hire, train, and supervise employees? What compensation and benefits package should they offer? How should they process payroll?
   d. How can they track cash inflows and outflows to avoid a cash squeeze?
   e. What is the appropriate product mix? What inventory quantities should they carry, given their limited showroom space?

Ndul/123RF

2. What information do Scott and Susan need to make those decisions?
    a. What information do the external entities they interact with need?
    b. What information do management and other employees need?
    c. How can they gather, store, and disseminate that information?
3. What business processes are needed, and how should they be carried out?
4. What functionality should be provided on the website?

Although Scott and Susan could use an educated guess or "gut feeling" to make these decisions, they know they can make better decisions if they obtain additional information. A well-designed AIS can solve these issues and provide the information they need to make any remaining decisions.

Introduction

We begin this chapter by explaining important terms and discussing the kinds of information organizations need and the business processes used to produce that information. We continue with an exploration of what an accounting information system (AIS) is, how an AIS adds value to an organization, how an AIS and corporate strategy affect each other, and the role of the AIS in the value chain.

A **system** is a set of detailed methods, procedures, and routines that carry out specific activities, perform a duty, achieve goals or objectives, or solve one or more problems. Most systems are composed of smaller subsystems that support the larger system. For example, a college of business is a system composed of various departments, each of which is a subsystem. Moreover, the college itself is a subsystem of the university.

system - Detailed methods, procedures, and routines that carry out activities, perform a duty, achieve goals or objectives, or solve problems.

Each subsystem is designed to achieve one or more organizational goals. Changes in subsystems cannot be made without considering the effect on other subsystems and on the system as a whole. **Goal conflict** occurs when a subsystem's goals are inconsistent with the goals of another subsystem or with the system as a whole. **Goal congruence** occurs when a subsystem achieves its goals while contributing to the organization's overall goal. The larger the organization and the more complicated the system, the more difficult it is to achieve goal congruence.

goal conflict - When a subsystem's goals are inconsistent with the goals of another subsystem or the system as a whole.

goal congruence - When a subsystem achieves its goals while contributing to the organization's overall goal.

Data are facts that are collected, recorded, stored, and processed by an information system. Businesses need to collect several kinds of data such as the activities that take place, the resources affected by the activities, and the people who participate in the activity. For example, the business needs to collect data about a sale (date, total amount), the resource sold (good or service, quantity sold, unit price), and the people who participated (customer, salesperson).

data - Facts that are collected, recorded, stored, and processed by an information system.

Information is data that have been organized and processed to provide meaning and context that can improve the decision-making process. As a rule, users make better decisions as the quantity and quality of information increase. Table 1-1 presents 14 characteristics that make information useful and meaningful.

information - Data that have been organized and processed to provide meaning and improve decision making.

TABLE 1-1 Characteristics of Useful Information

Access restricted	Able to limit access to authorized parties
Accurate	Correct; free of error; accurately represents events and activities
Available	Available to users when needed; in a format that can be easily and quickly used
Reputable	Perceived as true and credible due to highly regarded source or content
Complete	Does not omit aspects of events or activities; of enough breadth and depth
Concise	Clear, succinct; appropriate volume presented briefly but comprehensively
Consistent	Presented in same format over time
Current	Includes event and activity data up to the present date and time
Objective	Unbiased; unprejudiced; impartial
Relevant	Reduces uncertainty; improves decision making; applicable and helpful
Timely	Provided in time for decision makers to make decisions
Useable	Easy to use for different tasks; human and machine readable
Understandable	Presented in a useful and intelligible format; easily comprehended and interpreted
Verifiable	Same information produced by two independent, knowledgeable people

machine-readable - Data in a format that can be processed by a computer.

Data is most useful when it is in a **machine-readable** format that can be read and processed by a computer. This processing may involve data collection, recording, storage, updating, and data dissemination. For example, public companies are now required to code their financial statements using XBRL (eXtensible Business Reporting Language)—a programming language designed specifically to facilitate the communication of financial and other business information. Without XBRL, electronic documents are digital versions of paper reports. Humans can read the data, but computers cannot automatically process the data until a person manually enters it in the appropriate format. XBRL changes that by encoding information about what a particular data item means so that other computer programs can understand what to do with it. XBRL is discussed more fully in Chapter 16.

Using machine readable formats like XBRL improves many of the other 14 characteristics that make information useful. For example, XBRL improves:

- Reliability by reducing human error and using standard taxonomies.
- Relevance by assigning relevant meaning to data so it can be compared to similar data from other organizations.
- Accessibility by enabling the automatic importing of data into decision models and other computer systems.
- Understandability and usability by making the data readable to both humans and computers.
- Timeliness by reducing the time needed to import, produce, and distribute information.

Machine readable data also facilitates newer technologies such as artificial intelligence and data analytics, which are discussed later in the chapter.

information overload - Exceeding the amount of information a human mind can absorb and process, resulting in a decline in decision-making quality and an increase in the cost of providing information.

information technology (IT) - The computers and other electronic devices used to store, retrieve, transmit, and manipulate data.

value of information - The benefit provided by information minus the cost of producing it.

However, there are limits to the amount of information the human mind can absorb and process. **Information overload** occurs when those limits are passed, resulting in a decline in decision-making quality and an increase in the cost of providing that information. Information system designers use **information technology (IT)** to help decision makers more effectively filter and condense information. For example, Walmart has invested heavily in IT so that every day it can collect and process almost 50 petabytes of transaction data and mine more than 200 internal and external databases to produce valuable information.

The **value of information** is the benefit produced by the information minus the cost of producing it. Benefits of information include reduced uncertainty, improved decisions, and improved ability to plan and schedule activities. The costs include the time and resources spent to produce and distribute the information. Information costs and benefits can be difficult to quantify, and it is difficult to determine the value of information before it has been produced and utilized. Nevertheless, the expected value of information should be calculated as effectively as possible so that the costs of producing the information do not exceed its benefits.

To illustrate the value of information, consider the case of 7-Eleven. When a Japanese company licensed the very successful 7-Eleven name from Southland Corporation, it invested heavily in IT. However, the U.S. stores did not. Each 7-Eleven store in Japan was given a computer that:

- Keeps track of the 3,000 items sold in each store and determines what products are moving, at what time of day, and under what weather conditions.
- Keeps track of what and when customers buy to make sure it has in stock the products most frequently purchased.
- Orders sandwiches and rice dishes from suppliers automatically. Orders are placed and filled three times a day so that stores always have fresh food. In addition, suppliers can access 7-Eleven sales data electronically so that they can forecast demand.
- Coordinates deliveries with suppliers. This reduces deliveries from 34 to 12 a day, resulting in less clerical receiving time.
- Prepares a color graphic display that indicates which store areas contribute the most to sales and profits.

Average daily sales of 7-Eleven Japan were 30% higher and its operating margins almost double those of its closest competitor. What happened to Southland and its 7-Eleven stores in the United States? Profits declined, and Southland eventually had to file for bankruptcy. 7-Eleven Japan came to the company's rescue and purchased 64% of Southland.

As shown in Figure 1-1, an **information system** is the combination of the people and the technologies in an organization that collect, record, store, and process data to produce the information needed to make informed decisions.

information system - The people and technologies in an organization that produce information.

Information Needs and Business Processes

All organizations need information in order to make effective decisions. In addition, all organizations have certain business processes in which they are continuously engaged. A **business process** is a set of related, coordinated, and structured activities and tasks that are performed by a person, a computer, or a machine, and that help accomplish a specific organizational goal.

business process - A set of related, coordinated, and structured activities and tasks, performed by a person, a computer, or a machine, that helps accomplish a specific organizational goal.

To make effective decisions, organizations must decide what decisions they need to make, what information they need to make the decisions, and how to gather and process the data needed to produce the information. This data gathering and processing is often tied to the

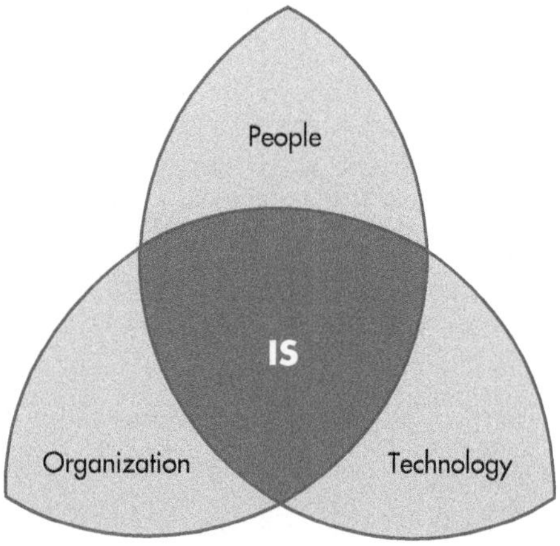

FIGURE 1-1
The Components of an Information System

basic business processes in an organization. To illustrate the process of identifying information needs and business processes, let's return to our S&S case study.

INFORMATION NEEDS

Scott and Susan decide they must understand how S&S functions before they can identify the information they need to manage S&S effectively. Then they can determine the types of data and procedures they will need to collect and produce that information. They created Table 1-2

TABLE 1-2 Overview of S&S's Business Processes, Key Decisions, and Information Needs

Business Processes	Key Decisions	Information Needs
Acquire capital	How much	Cash flow projections
	Find investors or borrow funds	Pro forma financial statements
	If borrowing, how to obtain best terms	Loan amortization schedule
Acquire building and equipment	Size of building	Capacity needs
	Amount of equipment	Building and equipment prices
	Rent or buy	Market study
	Location	Tax tables and depreciation regulations
	How to depreciate	
Hire and train employees	Experience requirements	Job descriptions
	How to assess integrity and competence of applicants	Applicant job history and skills
	How to train employees	
Acquire inventory	What models to carry	Market analyses
	Optimal level of inventory to carry	Sales and inventory turnover forecasts
	How much to purchase	Inventory status reports
	How to manage inventory (store, control, etc.)	Vendor performance
	Which vendors; best quality, prices	
Advertising and marketing	Which media	Cost analyses
	Content	Market coverage
Sell merchandise	What is optimal price for each product	Product costs; desired margins
	How to customize products for customers	Customer needs and preferences
	How to deliver products to customer	Customer delivery preferences
	Offer in-house credit; determine credit limits	Credit card costs; company policies
	Which credit cards to accept	Customer credit status
Collect payments from customers	If offering credit, what terms	Customer account status
	How to effectively handle cash receipts	Accounts receivable aging report
		Accounts receivable records
Pay employees	Amount to pay	Sales (for commissions)
	Deductions and withholdings	Time worked (hourly employees)
	Process payroll in-house or use outside service	W-4 forms
		Costs of external payroll service
Pay taxes	Payroll tax requirements	Government regulations
	Sales tax requirements	Total wage expense
		Total sales
Pay vendors	Whom to pay	Vendor invoices
	When to pay	Accounts payable records
	How much to pay	Payment terms

to summarize part of their analysis. It lists S&S's basic business processes, some key decisions that need to be made for each process, and information they need to make the decisions.

Scott and Susan realize that the list is not exhaustive, but they are satisfied that it provides a good overview of S&S. They also recognize that not all the information needs listed in the right-hand column will be produced internally by S&S. Information about payment terms for merchandise purchases, for example, will be provided by vendors. Thus, S&S must effectively integrate external data with internally generated data so that Scott and Susan can use both types of information to run S&S.

S&S will interact with many external parties, such as customers, vendors, and governmental agencies, as well as with internal parties such as management and employees. To get a better handle on the more important interactions with these parties, they prepared Figure 1-2.

BUSINESS PROCESSES

Scott decides to reorganize the business processes listed in Table 1-2 into groups of related transactions. A **transaction** is an agreement between two entities to exchange goods or services or any other event that can be measured in economic terms by an organization. Examples include selling goods to customers, buying inventory from suppliers, and paying employees. The process that begins with capturing transaction data and ends with informational output, such as the financial statements, is called **transaction processing**. Transaction processing is covered in more depth in Chapter 2.

Many business activities are pairs of events involved in a **give-get exchange**. Most organizations engage in a small number of give-get exchanges, but each type of exchange happens many times. For example, S&S will have thousands of sales to customers every year in exchange for cash. Likewise, S&S will continuously buy inventory from suppliers in exchange for cash.

These exchanges can be grouped into five major **business processes or transaction cycles**:

- The **revenue cycle**, where goods and services are sold for cash or a future promise to receive cash. This cycle is discussed in Chapter 14.

transaction - An agreement between two entities to exchange goods or services, such as selling inventory in exchange for cash; any other event that can be measured in economic terms by an organization.

transaction processing - Process of capturing transaction data, processing it, storing it for later use, and producing information output, such as a managerial report or a financial statement.

give-get exchange - Transactions that happen a great many times, such as giving up cash to get inventory from a supplier and giving employees a paycheck in exchange for their labor.

business processes or transaction cycles - The major give-get exchanges that occur frequently in most companies.

revenue cycle - Activities associated with selling goods and services in exchange for cash or a future promise to receive cash.

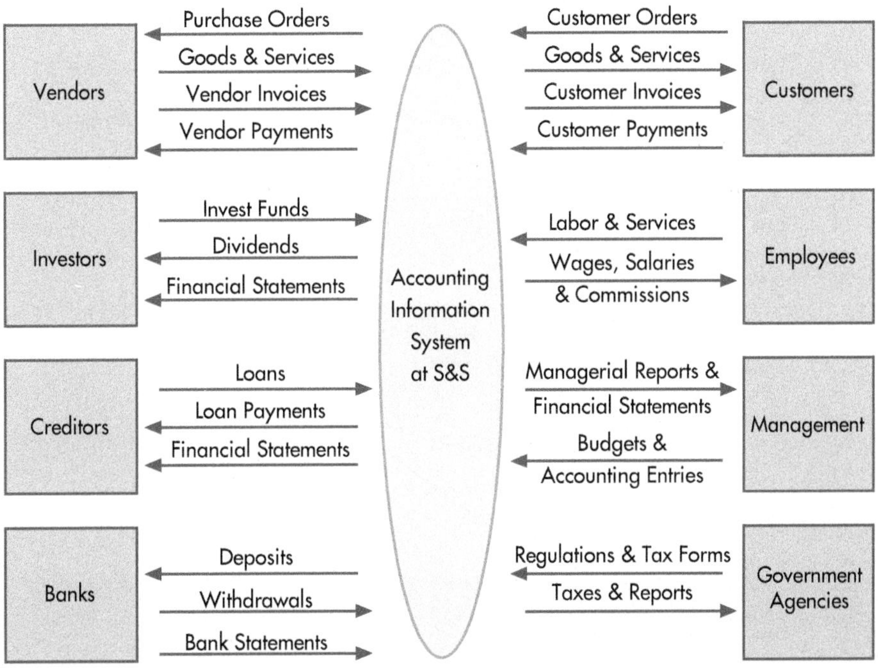

FIGURE 1-2
Interactions between S&S and External and Internal Parties

expenditure cycle - Activities associated with purchasing inventory for resale or raw materials in exchange for cash or a future promise to pay cash.

production cycle - Activities associated with using labor, raw materials, and equipment to produce finished goods. Also called conversion cycle.

human resources/payroll cycle - Activities associated with hiring, training, compensating, evaluating, promoting, and terminating employees.

financing cycle - Activities associated with raising money by selling shares in the company to investors and borrowing money as well as paying dividends and interest.

- The **expenditure cycle**, where companies purchase inventory for resale or raw materials to use in producing products in exchange for cash or a future promise to pay cash. This cycle is discussed in Chapter 15.
- The **production cycle**, or conversion cycle, where raw materials are transformed into finished goods. This cycle is discussed in Chapter 16.
- The **human resources/payroll cycle**, where employees are hired, trained, compensated, evaluated, promoted, and terminated. This cycle is discussed in Chapter 17.
- The **financing cycle**, where companies sell shares in the company to investors and borrow money, and where investors are paid dividends and interest is paid on loans.

These cycles process a few related transactions repeatedly. For example, most revenue cycle transactions are either selling goods or services to customers or collecting cash for those sales. Figure 1-3 shows the main transaction cycles and the give-get exchange inherent in each cycle.

These basic give-get exchanges are supported by a number of other business activities. For example, S&S may need to answer a number of customer inquiries and check inventory levels before it can make a sale. Likewise, it may have to check customer credit before a credit sale is made. Accounts receivable will have to be increased each time a credit sale is made and decreased each time a customer payment is received. Table 1-3 lists the major activities in each transaction cycle.

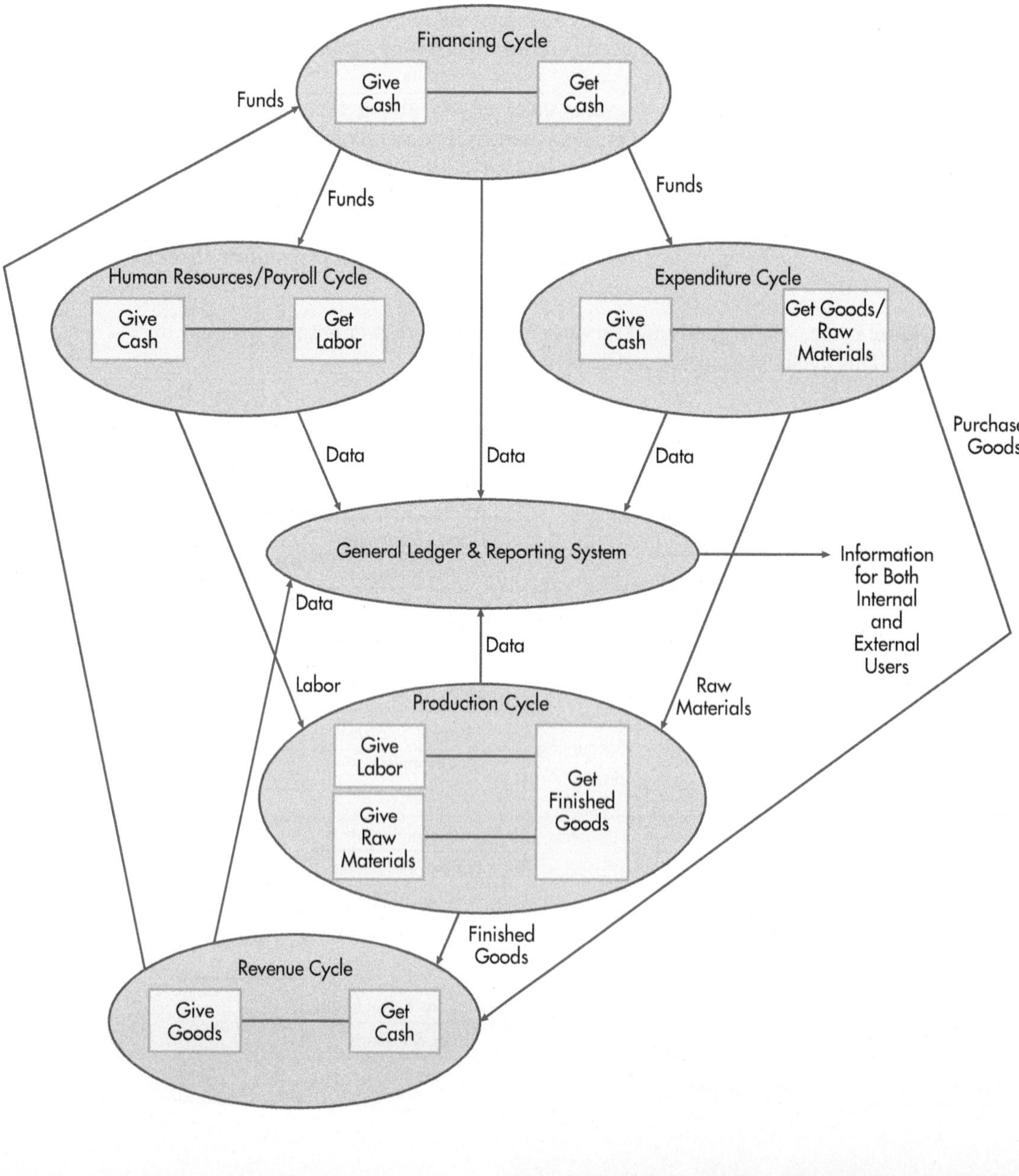

FIGURE 1-3
The AIS and Its Subsystems

Notice that the last activity listed in Table 1-3 for each transaction cycle is "Send appropriate information to the other cycles." Figure 1-3 shows how these various transaction cycles relate to one another and interface with the **general ledger and reporting system**, which is used to generate information for both management and external parties. The general ledger and reporting system is discussed in more depth in Chapter 18.

general ledger and reporting system - Information-processing operations involved in updating the general ledger and preparing reports for both management and external parties.

In many accounting software packages, the various transaction cycles are implemented as separate modules. Not every organization needs to implement every module. Retail stores like S&S, for example, do not have a production cycle and would not implement that module. Moreover, some organizations have unique requirements. Financial institutions, for example, have demand deposit and installment-loan cycles that relate to transactions involving customer accounts and loans. In addition, the nature of a given transaction cycle differs across different types of organizations. For example, the expenditure cycle of a service company,

TABLE 1-3 Common Cycle Activities

Transaction Cycle	Major Activities in the Cycle
Revenue	Receive and answer customer inquiries
	Take customer orders and enter them into the AIS
	Approve credit sales
	Check inventory availability
	Initiate back orders for goods out of stock
	Pick and pack customer orders
	Ship goods to customers or perform services
	Bill customers for goods shipped or services performed
	Update (increase) sales and accounts receivable
	Receive customer payments and deposit them in the bank
	Update (reduce) accounts receivable
	Handle sales returns, discounts, allowances, and bad debts
	Prepare management reports
	Send appropriate information to the other cycles
Expenditure	Request goods and services be purchased
	Prepare, approve, and send purchase orders to vendors
	Receive goods and services and complete a receiving report
	Store goods
	Receive vendor invoices
	Update (increase) accounts payable
	Approve vendor invoices for payment
	Pay vendors for goods and services
	Update (reduce) accounts payable
	Handle purchase returns, discounts, and allowances
	Prepare management reports
	Send appropriate information to the other cycles
Human Resources/Payroll	Recruit, hire, and train new employees
	Evaluate employee performance and promote employees
	Discharge employees
	Update payroll records
	Collect and validate time, attendance, and commission data
	Prepare and disburse payroll
	Calculate and disburse taxes and benefit payments

TABLE 1-3 Continued

Transaction Cycle	Major Activities in the Cycle
Human Resources/Payroll	Prepare employee and management reports
	Send appropriate information to the other cycles
Production	Design products
	Forecast, plan, and schedule production
	Request raw materials for production
	Manufacture products
	Store finished products
	Accumulate costs for products manufactured
	Prepare management reports
	Send appropriate information to the other cycles
Financing	Forecast cash needs
	Sell stock/securities to investors
	Borrow money from lenders
	Pay dividends to investors and interest to lenders
	Retire debt
	Prepare management reports
	Send appropriate information to the other cycles

such as a public accounting or a law firm, does not normally involve processing transactions related to the purchase, receipt, and payment for merchandise that will be resold to customers.

Each transaction cycle can include many different business processes or activities. Each business process can be relatively simple or quite complex.

After preparing Tables 1-2 and 1-3 and Figures 1-2 and 1-3, Scott and Susan believe they understand S&S well enough to begin shopping for an information system. Susan recalled a previous employer that had several separate information systems because its software was not designed to accommodate the information needs of all managers. She also vividly recalled attending one meeting where she witnessed the negative effects of having multiple systems. The head of marketing had one report on year-to-date sales by product, the production manager had a different report that contained different sales figures, and the controller's report, which was produced by the general ledger system, had yet a third version of year-to-date sales. Over an hour was wasted trying to reconcile those different reports! Susan vowed to ensure that S&S did not ever find itself in such a mess. She would make sure that any system selected would have the capability to integrate both financial and nonfinancial data about S&S's various business processes so that everyone could pull information from the same system.

Accounting Information Systems

accounting information system (AIS) - A system that collects, records, stores, and processes data to produce information for decision makers. It includes people, procedures and instructions, data, software, information technology infrastructure, and internal controls and security measures.

accounting - The systematic and comprehensive recording of an organization's financial transactions, including summarizing, analyzing, and reporting these transactions to all users.

It has often been said that accounting is the language of business. If that is the case, then an **accounting information system (AIS)** is the intelligence—the information-providing vehicle—of that language.

Accounting is the systematic and comprehensive recording of an organization's financial transactions. It also includes summarizing, analyzing, and reporting these transactions to management, owners/investors, oversight agencies, and tax collection entities. That means accounting is a data identification, collection, and storage process as well as an information development, measurement, and communication process. By definition, accounting is an information system, since an AIS collects, records, stores, and processes accounting and other data to produce information for decision makers. This is illustrated in Figure 1-4.

An AIS can be a paper-and-pencil manual system, a complex system using the latest in IT, or something in between. Regardless of the approach taken, the process is the same. The

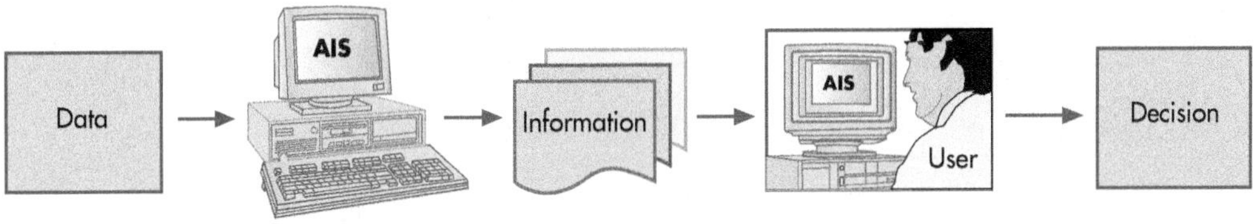

FIGURE 1-4
An AIS Processes Data to Produce Information for Decision Makers

AIS must collect, enter, process, store, and report data and information. The paper and pencil or the computer hardware and software are merely the tools used to produce the information.

This text does not distinguish an AIS from other information systems. Instead, our viewpoint is that the AIS can and should be the organization's primary information system and that it provides users with the information they need to perform their jobs.

There are six components of an AIS:

1. The *people* who use the system.
2. The *procedures and instructions* used to collect, process, and store data.
3. The *data* about the organization and its business activities.
4. The *software* used to process the data.
5. The *information technology infrastructure*, including the computers, peripheral devices, and network communications devices used in the AIS.
6. The *internal controls and security measures* that safeguard AIS data.

These six components enable an AIS to fulfill three important business functions:

1. Collect and store data about organizational activities, resources, and personnel. Organizations have a number of business processes, such as making a sale or purchasing raw materials, which are repeated frequently.
2. Transform data into information so management can plan, execute, control, and evaluate activities, resources, and personnel. Decision making is discussed in detail later in this chapter.
3. Provide adequate controls to safeguard the organization's assets and data. Control concepts are discussed in detail in Chapters 8–13.

Since accounting data comes from an AIS, AIS knowledge and skills are critical to an accountant's career success. Interacting with an AIS is one of the most important activities accountants perform. Other important AIS-related activities include designing information systems and business process improvements, as discussed in Chapters 22 to 24. Focus 1-1 explains a specialty to designate that certain CPAs (Certified Public Accountants) have an in-depth knowledge of AIS topics.

HOW AN AIS CAN ADD VALUE TO AN ORGANIZATION

A well-designed AIS can add value to an organization by:

1. ***Improving the quality and reducing the costs of products or services.*** For example, an AIS can monitor machinery so operators are notified immediately when performance falls outside acceptable quality limits. This helps maintain product quality, reduces waste, and lowers costs.
2. ***Improving efficiency.*** For example, timely information makes a just-in-time manufacturing approach possible, as it requires constant, accurate, up-to-date information about raw materials inventories and their locations.
3. ***Sharing knowledge.*** Sharing knowledge and expertise can improve operations and provide a competitive advantage. For example, CPA firms use their information systems to share best practices and to support communication between offices. Employees can search the corporate database to identify experts to provide assistance for a particular client; thus, a CPA firm's international expertise can be made available to any local client.
4. ***Improving the efficiency and effectiveness of its supply chain.*** For example, allowing customers to directly access inventory and sales order entry systems can reduce sales and marketing costs, thereby increasing customer retention rates.

FOCUS 1-1 CITP—An IT Specialty Designation for CPAs

The American Institute of Certified Public Accountants (AICPA) offers several specialty designations for CPAs. The CITP (Certified Information Technology Professional) designation reflects the AICPA's recognition of the importance of IT and its interrelationship with accounting. A CITP possesses a broad range of business, managerial, and technological knowledge, making it possible for the CITP to understand how organizations use IT to achieve their business objectives. To obtain a CITP certification, a person must demonstrate a mastery of the following topics: information system management, business intelligence, fraud, risk assessment, internal control concepts, and how to test and evaluate an information system.

There are many reasons to earn the CITP certification:

- Because only CPAs can be CITPs, this certification further differentiates you from others in the marketplace.
- It affirms your value as an IT specialist and increases your value to your employer or clients.
- It is a great "calling card" for IT people who want to be leaders in industry, public practice, government, or academia.
- It opens the doors to new technology-related roles and opportunities.
- Automatic membership in the IT Section, which allows you to meet, share best practices, network, and communicate with other CITPs. You can also receive CITP newsletters and other communications, attend CITP Webinars, receive CITP member discounts, and access exclusive CITP resources and content on the CITP website.

To qualify for the CITP designation, you must:

- Be a CPA and a member of the AICPA
- Pass the CITP exam
- In the five years preceding your application, meet the 1,000-hour experience and the 75-hour continuing professional education requirements

Based on information from http://www.aicpa.org.

5. ***Improving the internal control structure.*** An AIS with the proper internal control structure can help protect systems from fraud, errors, system failures, and disasters.
6. ***Improving decision making.*** Improved decision making is vitally important and is discussed below in more detail.

AN AIS CAN USE ARTIFICIAL INTELLIGENCE AND DATA ANALYTICS TO IMPROVE DECISION MAKING

Decision making is a complex, multistep activity that involves identifying a problem, collecting and interpreting data, evaluating ways to solve the problem, selecting a solution methodology, and determining and implementing the solution. An AIS can help in the decision-making process by providing the information to reduce uncertainty, providing feedback about the effectiveness of prior decisions, providing information in a timely manner, and identifying situations that require management action.

Artificial intelligence and data analytics tools can be used in each of these decision-making activities to help improve decision making.

artificial intelligence (AI) - The use of computer systems to simulate human intelligence processes such as learning, reasoning, and self-improvement.

Artificial intelligence (AI) uses computer systems to simulate human intelligence processes such as learning (acquiring information and rules for using it), reasoning (interpreting data and using its rules to arrive at conclusions), and self-improvement (learning from the information and past experiences to improve its rules).

The AI field draws from many disciplines, including computer science, information engineering, linguistics, mathematics, philosophy, and psychology. Some popular AI applications include expert systems, intelligent routing of delivery vehicles, machine vision (used in self-driving cars), and speech recognition. Some popular AI cloud offerings include Amazon AI, Google AI, IBM Watson, and Microsoft Cognitive Services.

Here are a few examples of the fields where AI is used:

- **Business.** AI-driven robots now perform many highly repetitive tasks, especially in manufacturing. AI algorithms determine how to better serve customers. Website chatbots provide immediate customer service.

- **Education.** AI software automatically grades student work, assesses student performance and progress, and provides additional support as needed.
- **Finance.** Robo-based stock picking algorithms give advice on what stocks to buy and sell. Software executes most stock market trades. Personal finance applications use AI to advise their users and keep track of their finances.
- **Healthcare.** AI can make better and faster diagnoses than humans, thereby improving patient outcomes and reducing costs. For example, doctors can use IBM Watson to mine patient data, evaluate their symptoms, access external databases, communicate a diagnosis and how confident Watson is in the diagnosis, and receive and answer doctor questions.

Data analytics is the use of software and algorithms to discover, describe, interpret, communicate, and apply meaningful patterns in data to improve business performance. Data analytics tools draw from many disciplines, including computer programming, mathematics, operations research, and statistics. Companies have long analyzed their past performance. Data analytics is a more recent development and is designed to focus on the future and answer questions such as why something happened, what will happen next, and how performance can be improved. Analytics tools are most efficient when there are abundant computational resources and there is a large quantity of data from multiple internal or external databases.

data analytics - Use of software and algorithms to find and solve problems and improve business performance.

An essential part of most analytic tools is a **data dashboard** that displays important data points, metrics, and key performance indicators in the form of line or bar charts, tables, or gauges. A dashboard provides a central location for businesses to monitor performance. The dashboard is connected to internal and external data sources, analyzes the data, and displays it visually in an easy-to-understand format. Dashboards are usually customized to meet the specific needs of a business process, department, or the entire company.

data dashboard - A display of important data points, metrics, and key performance indicators in easily understood line or bar charts, tables, or gauges.

There are many different types of analytics, including predictive, prescriptive, descriptive, and cognitive. Some analytics are named after their usage such as retail, supply chain, store optimization, sales force optimization, marketing optimization, call center optimization, web, social media, speech, credit risk, and fraud analytics. Analytics are also categorized by their use and characteristics such as actionable, visual, embedded, automated, and operational analytics.

Analytics can help improve decision making in many ways. At the most basic level, analytics can identify a problem or issue for management to resolve. At an intermediate level, analytics can also collect the data needed to solve the problem, analyze it, and make recommendations to management on how to resolve it. At an advanced level, actionable insights can be integrated into the systems used to make decisions. That is, the analytics can be embedded into AIS components, such as databases, applications, and devices, and operationalized to automatically resolve problems that occur and communicate solutions to management.

The data analytics market is estimated to exceed $50 billion and is growing rapidly. Businesses use analytics to increase sales, create products and services to meet new customer needs, reduce costs, and improve decision making. Here are just a few ways data analytics are used:

- Cargill has developed an analytics platform that allows dairy farmers to use a tablet or computer to analyze large quantities of data about their cows' living conditions, diet, and milk productivity. When cows are happier and more comfortable, they produce more milk.
- Under Armour uses data from MapMyFitness to determine popular running routes and times so it knows when to advertise sneakers, energy drinks, and other products. Research shows that when an advertiser sells repeat-purchase products, ads sent at the right time to consumers will generate up to 16 times more sales than when sent at other times.
- Most web-based retailers such as Amazon use their sales database to suggest additional products and services for its customers to purchase.
- A technician at a support center uses key words from a caller, as well as a database of past problems and solutions, to quickly solve technical issues. In time, when the data and analytics are robust enough, the process will be automated; customers will visit the company's website and diagnose most problems themselves, with the most complex issues handed off to a human technician.

- An airline embeds sensors in all important airplane components, continuously monitors them, automatically schedules preventive maintenance, and provides a detailed list of what needs to be done.

Focus 1-2 explains how Walmart uses data analytics to improve their business.

FOCUS 1-2 Data Analytics at Walmart

Walmart, the world's biggest retailer, has more than 245 million customers who shop at more than 20,000 stores in 28 countries. Walmart tracks individual customers, gathering data on what customers like and what they buy. Every hour, more than 1 million customers purchase something, which generates 2.5 petabytes (a quadrillion bytes) of unstructured data. The 2.5 petabytes are roughly 167 times the books contained in America's Library of Congress.

To make use of this data, Walmart spent considerable resources to become a leader in big data analytics. In fact, Walmart's data analytics efforts started before the term *big data* became popular. Walmart's analytics systems analyze millions of products and hundreds of millions of customers using data gathered from many different internal and external data sources.

Data analytics support several Walmart goals. First, they optimize and personalize customers' shopping experiences, whether they are in a store, shopping online via a computer or a mobile device, or browsing Walmart's website. They analyze customer data and buying behaviors to better anticipate customer needs. Walmart also uses analytics to improve the store checkout experience.

Second, data analytics optimize operational efficiency, including increasing sales and profits, facilitating better and quicker decision making, improving store and employee efficiency, improving product assortment, managing the supply chain, and locating distribution centers and stores. Analytics helped Walmart (1) develop smarter stocking, pricing, merchandising, and marketing solutions in real time and (2) make its pharmacies more efficient.

Walmart analyzed sales before and after big data analytics were used to change their e-commerce strategy and found that online sales increased 10% to 15%, resulting in $1 billion in incremental revenue.

The data analytics team at Walmart Labs monitors Walmart.com and analyzes every clickable action to determine what consumers buy online and how to improve their online experience. The Lab also monitors what is trending on Twitter, local events such as sports activities and concerts that affect sales, and local weather deviations to determine how they affect buying patterns. Walmart's predictive data analytics software contains machine learning technologies that continuously improve the accuracy of analytics algorithms.

Walmart built the world's biggest private cloud to facilitate its data analytics processes. At its headquarters, Walmart also created a Data Café (Collaborative Analytics Facilities for Enterprise) to model, manipulate, and visualize data to create solutions. The Café uses Walmart's transaction data as well as data from 200 other data sources such as economic, gasoline, local events, social media, telecommunications, television, and weather data to predict outcomes and resolve issues to make Walmart stores more efficient, responsive, and profitable.

Employees are encouraged to submit their problems to Data Café experts for a solution usually produced in minutes rather than weeks and displayed on the Café's touchscreen smartboards. These real-time solutions help correct errors instantly, gain sales and marketing insights, and track customer trends and competitor strategies.

Here are two examples of Walmart's use of the Data Café. A grocery team could not figure out why sales in a product category had suddenly declined and used the Café to drill down into the data. They found that a pricing miscalculation resulted in the product being priced higher than it should have been in some stores. In a second example, Walmart data mining algorithms found that a specific cookie was popular at all Walmart stores except one. An investigation showed that a simple stocking oversight resulted in the cookies not being stocked on the store shelves. Ordering and stocking the cookies prevented the further loss of sales.

THE AIS AND BLOCKCHAIN

In 2008, Satoshi Nakamoto invented the blockchain to digitally record cryptocurrency transactions such as Bitcoin. Since then, blockchain technology has been adapted so that virtually everything of value can be recorded, and private blockchains have been developed for business use.

Just as people do not have to know exactly how the Internet or an automobile works, they do not need to know the technical details of how the blockchain works to use it. However, a basic knowledge of blockchain technology helps users make better use of the technology.

Blockchain got its name from its structure, which is individual digital records, called blocks, linked together using cryptography in a single list, called a chain. The blockchain isn't stored in a single location—it is a distributed ledger that functions as a decentralized database. Each computer in the distributed peer-to-peer network maintains a copy of the ledger to prevent a single point of failure. Since the blockchain is managed by a network that follows protocols for inter-node communication and validating new blocks, there is no need for a central authority that controls everything. The information recorded in the blockchain is made public, so everyone on the blockchain's peer-to-peer network has a copy of the blockchain and all transactions are accessible to everyone.

blockchain - Individual digital records, called blocks, linked together using cryptography in a single list, called a chain.

Here is a brief, high-level view of how the blockchain works; that is, how a transaction is added to a block and how a block is added to a chain. Blockchains are explained in more detail in Chapter 11.

1. **Initiate transaction.** Two parties, such as a buyer and a seller, decide to exchange something of value and request that a transaction be initiated. Instead of using actual buyer or seller names, a unique digital signature or identifier is used. This is analogous to using a part number for a product or a username for a person.
2. **Validate transaction.** The transaction is sent to the peer-to-peer network nodes who use algorithms to simultaneously validate transaction details, including its time, dollar amount, and participants. To achieve a consensus, a simple majority of 51% of the nodes must validate the block. The number of computers in the peer-to-peer networks can be as large as desired; the Bitcoin blockchain has millions, each with a copy of its blockchain ledger. In a public, permission-less blockchain platform like Bitcoin, every network node can record transactions and participate in the consensus process. In a private, permissioned chain, participation in the consensus process is restricted to approved nodes.
3. **Create a block.** Since each block in a chain can store up to 1 MB of data, the verified transactions are combined with hundreds or thousands of similar transactions to create a new block for the ledger. The transaction's dollar amount and the digital signatures of both parties are stored in the block.
4. **Calculate and insert a hash.** Each block is given two unique codes, or pieces, of identifying information called a hash, which distinguishes it from other blocks. Hash codes use a mathematical algorithm to turn digital information into a string of numbers and letters. One hash is that of the current block and the second is the hash of the block that precedes it in the chain. When a new block is added to the chain, it is linked to the previous block by storing a cryptographic hash generated from the contents of the previous block. The second hash ensures that the chain is never broken and that each block is recorded in a permanent and unalterable way. The second hash makes the block tamper resistant and secure; that is, it adds a high level of assurance that the prior block contents have not been changed. If the data on a block is edited in any way, that block's hash code changes, and the codes of all subsequent blocks change. This discrepancy makes it extremely difficult for information on the blockchain to be changed without notice. How a hash is created is discussed in Chapter 11.
5. **Complete transaction.** The block is added to the blockchain, and all the other computers storing the blockchain are updated automatically. This completes the transaction recording process, and the right of ownership of the item of value is passed from the seller to the buyer.

Blockchain has several significant advantages, including the following:

- **Accuracy.** Transactions are verified by many thousands of networked computers instead of error-prone humans. Even if a computer makes a computational mistake, the error would not spread to the rest of the blockchain unless at least 51% of the network's computers validated the mistake.

- **Transparency.** Blockchain data are transparent. That is, all transaction details, including participant user names, transaction amount, transaction date and time, and who entered the transaction, are open for everyone on the blockchain to see. This includes authorized regulators, auditors, etc.
- **Data consistency.** In older legacy systems, data are often located in multiple databases and finding data can be complex. The data can also be inconsistent among databases, with some of them updated and others not. With blockchain, data are stored in one location only.
- **Trust.** To ensure that blockchain networks can be trusted, computers that want to join the blockchain are tested. That is, new users are required to prove themselves before they can be a part of a blockchain network. For example, in Bitcoin's proof of work test, a system must expend significant computer power and energy to solve a complex math problem before they can add a block to the blockchain. While Bitcoin's proof of work does not make a hack impossible, the cost of organizing an attack would almost always outweigh the benefits that could be achieved from the attack.
- **No need for third parties.** The consensus process of all nodes in the network agreeing on the blockchain's content allows mutually distrustful parties to enter into transactions safely without trusted third parties.
- **Single set of books.** As both sides of a transaction are stored in a single source, that eliminates some of the need for a set of books for the buyer and for the seller. One set of books provides a trust level not present in current legacy systems.
- **Cost.** Blockchain eliminates the costs of human third-party verification and many transaction processing costs.
- **Decentralization.** By storing the blockchain on all network computers, the risks of data held centrally is eliminated. For example, if a copy of the blockchain is hacked or compromised, only that copy is affected. This reduces or eliminates the traditional requirement for file and database backups.
- **Efficiency.** Blockchain works all day, every day—and transactions can be finalized within minutes and considered secure in no more than a few hours. Contrast that with limited business hours and waiting days for transactions to clear and for money to be available.
- **Privacy.** Although many blockchains are public databases, where users can view transaction information, users are unable to access confidential data that identify those engaging in the transactions.
- **Security.** A blockchain is difficult to corrupt. There is no single point of failure; if one node goes down, there is a copy of the ledger on all the other nodes. Information is shared and continually reconciled by thousands of computers. New blocks are always added chronologically to the end of the blockchain. It is very difficult to go back and change a block's contents because each block contains its own hash and the hash of the previous block. If information is changed, the hashes for the previous and subsequent blocks also change and this disrupts the ledger's shared state. When other network computers become aware that the change has caused a problem, consensus is no longer possible. Until the problem is solved, no new blocks are added to the blockchain. In most cases, the block that caused the error is discarded and the nodes again attempt to achieve consensus. This process ensures that no single system or user can tamper with the transaction records or add invalid blocks to the blockchain.
- **Provenance.** Provenance is the history of ownership of something of value. The data collected by Blockchain shows who did what, when they did it, and the history of the item since it was entered in the blockchain. That history is transparent, verified by all network participants, and frequently reconciled.

While blockchain has many important advantages, there are significant challenges to its adoption, including political and regulatory issues. These challenges include the following:

- **Cost.** Cost is a blockchain advantage because transaction fees are less, but it is also a disadvantage because the technology needed to operate a blockchain is expensive. So are the thousands of hours expended to produce the custom software and back-end processes needed to insert blockchain technologies into current business systems. There are also the utility costs required to run the computers that process and store the blockchain.

- **Loss of privacy and confidentiality.** Since blockchain users are unable to identify those engaging in transactions, dishonest users can use blockchain networks like Bitcoin to make illegal purchases. To prevent this, some countries like the United States prohibit full anonymity by requiring online exchanges to collect customer information, verify their identity, and confirm that they are not on any list of known or suspected terrorists.
- **Susceptibility.** A 51% attack is difficult to execute due to the computational power required to gain majority control of a blockchain network. That might change as technology costs decrease and hackers are able to affordably rent computational power rather than buying it. In addition, these attacks are more difficult as the number of nodes in the blockchain network increases.

In summary, a blockchain is a public, global, cryptographically secure ledger that automatically records and verifies large volumes of digital transactions. The combination of blocks that cannot be changed, blocks linked together in a chain, and cryptography to secure everything creates a transaction recording system that can be trusted for transactions among untrusted partners.

Focus 1-3 briefly discusses some of the many blockchain applications in use today.

FOCUS 1-3 Current and Planned Uses of Blockchain

Blockchain was first used for digital currencies but has spread to many industries because it is a secure and cost-effective way to manage all types of digital transactions. Recent startups developed their business processes using newer technologies, so they are much more likely to use blockchain. As time passes, some of these blockchain-inspired startups become what some people call emerging disruptors as they begin displacing older and larger companies.

Established companies with older legacy information systems find it more challenging to use blockchain. They often discover that to achieve blockchain's advantages, they must change the way they do business.

Deloitte surveyed executives at 1,000 established companies about their blockchain experience and found 74% of respondents see compelling reasons to use it, though only 34% currently do. Some 41% expected to begin using blockchain, and almost 40% will invest at least $5 million in blockchain applications. Deloitte believes blockchain adoption is higher than their survey indicates because emerging disruptors were not included in the survey.

Here are just a few of the more prominent uses of blockchain:

- Banks only open during business hours and deposits take up to 3 days to clear. Blockchain is always open, and deposits can be seen in 10 minutes. It is estimated that blockchain could save banks $20 billion by eliminating money in-transit costs and consumers $16 billion in banking and insurance fees.
- Currently, healthcare data is stored by different institutions using different formats and standards, making it hard for doctors to understand a patient's medical history. Using blockchain technology, patient information can be signed, time-stamped, and stored securely on a distributed ledger. Doctors and patients can go to a single source to access a patient's health information, and patients have more control over their own health data. Blockchain could also help solve the problem of counterfeit drugs in the medical supply chain.
- Recording property rights occurs when a deed is delivered to the local recording office and manually entered in the county's database and public index. The process is costly, inefficient, time-consuming, error prone, and susceptible to fraud. Disputed property claims are difficult to reconcile. Blockchain can eliminate scanning documents and finding paper files in a recording office. Property owners can trust that their deed is accurate and permanent if its ownership is stored and verified on the blockchain.
- In 2016, Overstock.com was one of the first publicly traded company to use blockchain to sell and distribute company shares. Without blockchain, selling stock involves brokers, clearing houses, and custodians. The money and shares involved in the trade are frozen for up to 3 days. With blockchain peer-to-peer trading, there is no need for intermediaries, and the shares exchange hands within minutes. Companies are also developing a blockchain application for proxy voting.
- Manufacturing companies are developing applications to track the flow of materials, information, and payments as they move through their supply chains.

Source of Survey data: https://www2.deloitte.com/us/en/pages/consulting/articles/innovation-blockchain-survey.html

CLOUD COMPUTING, VIRTUALIZATION, AND THE INTERNET OF THINGS

virtualization - Running multiple systems simultaneously on one physical computer.

Recently, many organizations have embraced virtualization, cloud computing, and the Internet of things to enhance both efficiency and effectiveness. **Virtualization** takes advantage of the power and speed of modern computers to run multiple systems simultaneously on one physical computer. This cuts hardware costs because fewer computers need to be purchased. Fewer machines means lower maintenance costs. Data center costs also fall because less space needs to be rented, which also reduces utility costs.

cloud computing - Using a browser to remotely access software, data storage, hardware, and applications.

Cloud computing takes advantage of the high bandwidth of the modern global telecommunication network to enable employees to use a browser to remotely access software (software as a service), hardware (infrastructure as a service), and entire application environments (platform as a service). The arrangement is referred to as a "private," "public," or "hybrid" cloud, depending on whether the remotely accessed resources are entirely owned by the organization, a third party, or a mix of the two. Table 1-4 compares the different levels of service provided in the cloud to eating pizza. You can either make and bake a pizza in house, buy a frozen pizza and bake it, have a pizza delivered to your home, or go out to eat a pizza. As the table shows, you can do the same with computer services (the items in blue are done in house, and the items in red are done by a cloud provider).

Cloud computing can potentially generate significant cost savings. For example, instead of purchasing, installing, and maintaining separate copies of software for each end user, an organization can purchase one copy, install it on a central server, and pay for the right for a specified number of employees to simultaneously use a browser to remotely access and use that software. Public clouds eliminate the need for making major capital investments in IT, with organizations purchasing (and expensing) their use of computing resources on a pay-for-use or subscription basis. In addition to reducing costs, the centralization of computing resources with cloud computing (whether public, private, or hybrid) makes it easier to change software and hardware, thereby improving flexibility. The term **Internet of Things (IoT)** refers to the embedding of sensors in a multitude of devices (lights, heating and air conditioning, appliances, etc.) so that those devices can now connect to the Internet. The IoT has significant implications for information security.

Internet of Things (IoT) - Embedding sensors in devices so they can connect to the Internet.

THE AIS AND CORPORATE STRATEGY

Since most organizations have limited resources, it is important to identify the AIS improvements likely to yield the greatest return. Making a wise decision requires an understanding of the organization's overall business strategy. To illustrate, consider the results of a *CIO* magazine survey of 500 Chief Information Officers. Asked to identify the three most important skill sets for a CIO, more than 75% put strategic thinking and planning on their list.

Figure 1-5 shows three factors that influence the design of an AIS: developments in IT, business strategy, and organizational culture. It is also important to recognize that the design of the AIS can also influence the organization's culture by controlling the flow of information within the organization. For example, an AIS that makes information easily accessible and widely available is likely to increase pressures for more decentralization and autonomy.

TABLE 1-4 Comparing Cloud Services to Eating Pizza

Traditional (make pizza from scratch in house)	IaaS: Infrastructure as a Service (take and bake)	PaaS: Platform as a Service (pizza delivered)	SaaS: Software as a Service (dine out)
Dining table			
Soda			
Electricity and gas			
Oven			
Dough			
Toppings			

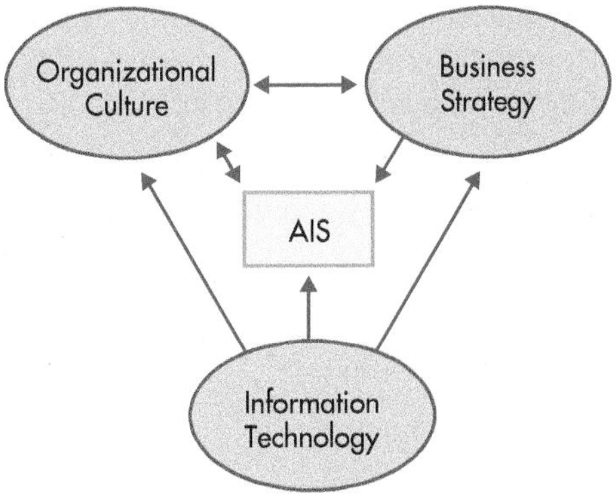

FIGURE 1-5
Factors Influencing Design of the AIS

IT developments can affect business strategy. For example, the Internet has profoundly affected the way many activities are performed, significantly affecting both strategy and strategic positioning. The Internet dramatically cuts costs, thereby helping companies to implement a low-cost strategy. If every company used the Internet to adopt a low-cost strategy, then the effects might be problematic. Indeed, one possible outcome may be intense price competition among firms, with the likely result that most of the cost savings provided by the Internet get passed on to the industry's customers, rather than being retained in the form of higher profits. Moreover, because every company can use the Internet to streamline its activities, a company is unlikely to gain a sustainable long-term competitive advantage.

An organization's AIS plays an important role in helping it adopt and maintain a strategic position. Achieving a close fit among activities requires that data are collected about each activity. It is also important that the information system collects and integrates both financial and nonfinancial data about the organization's activities.

THE ROLE OF THE AIS IN THE VALUE CHAIN

To provide value to their customers, most organizations perform a number of different activities. Figure 1-6 shows that those activities can be conceptualized as forming a **value chain** consisting of five **primary activities** that directly provide value to customers:

value chain - Linking all primary and support activities in a business. Value is added as a product passes through the chain.

primary activities - Value chain activities that produce, market, and deliver products and services to customers and provide post-delivery service and support.

1. ***Inbound logistics*** consists of receiving, storing, and distributing the materials an organization uses to create the services and products it sells. For example, an automobile manufacturer receives, handles, and stores steel, glass, and rubber.
2. ***Operations*** activities transform inputs into final products or services. For example, assembly line activities convert raw materials into a finished car and retailers remove goods from packing boxes and place the individual items on shelves for customers to purchase.
3. ***Outbound logistics*** activities distribute finished products or services to customers. An example is shipping automobiles to car dealers.

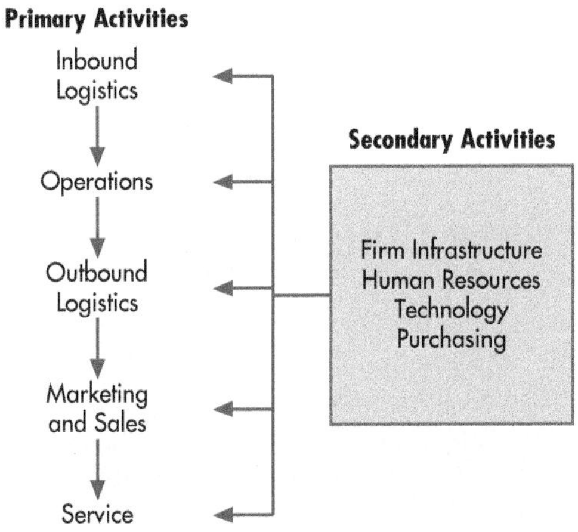

FIGURE 1-6
The Value Chain

4. ***Marketing and sales*** activities help customers buy the organization's products or services. Advertising is an example of a marketing and sales activity.
5. ***Service*** activities provide post-sale support to customers. Examples include repair and maintenance services.

support activities - Value chain activities such as firm infrastructure, technology, purchasing, and human resources that enable primary activities to be performed efficiently and effectively.

Support activities allow the five primary activities to be performed efficiently and effectively. They are grouped into four categories:

1. ***Firm infrastructure*** is the accounting, finance, legal, and general administration activities that allow an organization to function. The AIS is part of the firm infrastructure.
2. ***Human resources*** activities include recruiting, hiring, training, and compensating employees.
3. ***Technology*** activities improve a product or service. Examples include research and development, investments in IT, and product design.
4. ***Purchasing*** activities procure raw materials, supplies, machinery, and the buildings used to carry out the primary activities.

Using IT to redesign supply chain systems yields tremendous benefits and cost savings. For example, Tennessee Valley Authority, a power generator, reengineered its supply chain and created an enterprise-wide system that provides up-to-the-minute information, rather than the "current once a day" system that it replaced. The new system replaced 20 smaller and incompatible systems, reduced head count by 89 people, and saved $270 million in its first five years.

supply chain - An extended system that includes an organization's value chain as well as its suppliers, distributors, and customers.

An organization's value chain is a part of a larger system called a **supply chain**. As shown in Figure 1-7, a manufacturing organization interacts with its suppliers and distributors. By paying attention to its supply chain, a company can improve its performance by helping the others in the supply chain to improve their performance. For example, S&S can improve its purchasing and inbound logistics activities by implementing a more efficient just-in-time inventory management system that reduces its costs and minimizes the capital tied up in inventory. S&S can reap additional benefits if it links its new systems with its suppliers so they can perform their primary value chain activities more efficiently. For example, by providing more detailed and timely information about its inventory needs, S&S suppliers can more efficiently plan their production schedules. Part of the resultant cost reduction can be passed on to S&S in the form of lower product costs.

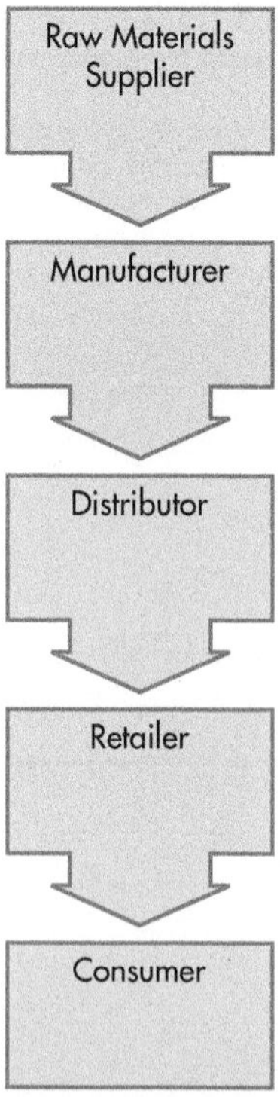

FIGURE 1-7
The Supply Chain

The problems created by an ineffective supply chain are illustrated by Limited Brands. Limited experienced explosive growth, including acquisitions of other retail companies such as Victoria's Secret and Abercrombie & Fitch. These acquisitions left Limited with a tangled web of more than 60 incompatible information systems. The problems came to a head one night when 400 trailers converged on a distribution center parking lot that could fit only 150 trailers. The trailers blocked traffic along all the highways around the distribution center and caused countless traffic and community problems. No one from Limited knew where all the trailers came from, what the merchandise was, or where it was to be sent. Chaos reigned until the merchandise could be routed to stores and other distribution centers. Limited solved many of its problems by installing a new, integrated system that greatly improved its supply chain processes and technologies. Developing the new system was not easy. Limited has more than 1,000 suppliers and sells its merchandise using various platforms, including retail stores, the Internet, catalogs, and third-party retailers.

Summary and Case Conclusion

Susan and Scott reflected on what they had done to try and understand what decisions S&S would need to make and the information needed to make them. They began by obtaining an understanding of S&S's basic business processes and key decisions that must be made to operate the business effectively. They followed that with an analysis of the internal and external parties that the AIS would have to interact with and the information the AIS would have to provide them.

Since S&S is a retail merchandising company, its business processes could be described in terms of four basic transaction cycles:

1. The *revenue cycle* encompasses all transactions involving sales to customers and the collection of cash receipts for those sales.
2. The *expenditure cycle* encompasses all transactions involving the purchase and payment of merchandise sold by S&S as well as other services it consumes such as rent and utilities.
3. The *human resources/payroll cycle* encompasses all the transactions involving the hiring, training, and payment of employees.
4. The *financing cycle* encompasses all transactions involving the investment of capital in the company, borrowing money, payment of interest, and loan repayments.

These four cycles interface with the *general ledger and reporting system,* which consists of all activities related to the preparation of financial statements and other managerial reports.

Scott and Susan will need a well-designed AIS to provide the information they need to effectively plan, manage, and control their business. Their AIS must be able to process data about sales and cash receipts, purchasing and paying for merchandise and services, payroll and tax-related transactions, and acquiring and paying for fixed assets. The company's AIS must also provide the information needed to prepare financial statements.

Fortunately, many computer-based accounting packages are available for the retail industry. As they begin looking at various software packages, however, Scott and Susan quickly learn that considerable accounting knowledge is required to choose the one that will best fit their business. Because neither has an accounting background, Scott and Susan decide that their next task will be to hire an accountant.

KEY TERMS

system 3
goal conflict 3
goal congruence 3
data 3
information 3
machine-readable 4
information overload 4
information technology (IT) 4
value of information 4
information system 5
business process 5
transaction 7
transaction processing 7
give-get exchange 7
business processes or transaction cycles 7
revenue cycle 7
expenditure cycle 8
production cycle or conversion cycle 8
human resources/payroll cycle 8
financing cycle 8
general ledger and reporting system 9
accounting information system (AIS) 10
accounting 10
artificial intelligence (AI) 12
data analytics 13
data dashboard 13
blockchain 15
virtualization 18
cloud computing 18
Internet of Things (IoT) 18
value chain 19
primary activities 19
support activities 20
supply chain 20

AIS in Action

CHAPTER QUIZ

1. Data differ from information in which way?
   a. Data are output, and information is input.
   b. Information is output, and data are input.
   c. Data are meaningful bits of information.
   d. There is no difference.
2. Which of the following is NOT a characteristic that makes information useful?
   a. It is accurate.
   b. It is timely.
   c. It is inexpensive.
   d. It is relevant.

3. Which of the following is a primary activity in the value chain?
   a. purchasing
   b. accounting
   c. post-sales service
   d. human resource management

4. Which transaction cycle includes interactions between an organization and its suppliers?
   a. revenue cycle
   b. expenditure cycle
   c. human resources/payroll cycle
   d. general ledger and reporting system

5. Which of the following is NOT a means by which information improves decision making?
   a. increases information overload
   b. reduces uncertainty
   c. provides feedback about the effectiveness of prior decisions
   d. identifies situations requiring management action

6. In the value chain concept, upgrading IT is considered what kind of activity?
   a. primary activity
   b. support activity
   c. service activity
   d. structured activity

7. In which cycle does a company ship goods to customers?
   a. production cycle
   b. financing cycle
   c. revenue cycle
   d. expenditure cycle

8. Which of the following is a function of an AIS?
   a. reducing the need to identify a strategy and strategic position
   b. transforming data into useful information
   c. allocating organizational resources
   d. automating all decision making

9. A firm, its suppliers, and its customers collectively form which of the following?
   a. supply chain
   b. value chain
   c. ERP system
   d. AIS

10. A performance report about all approved vendors during the previous 12 months is information MOST needed in which business process?
    a. paying vendors
    b. acquiring inventory
    c. selling merchandise
    d. paying employees

DISCUSSION QUESTIONS

1.1 The value of information is the difference between the benefits realized from using that information and the costs of producing it. Would you, or any organization, ever produce information if its expected costs exceeded its benefits? If so, provide some examples. If not, why?

1.2 Can the characteristics of useful information listed in Table 1-1 be met simultaneously? Or does achieving one mean sacrificing another?

1.3 You and a few of your classmates decided to become entrepreneurs. You came up with a great idea for a new mobile phone application that you think will make lots of money. Your business plan won second place in a local competition, and you are using the $10,000 prize to support yourselves as you start your company.
   a. Identify the key decisions you need to make to be successful entrepreneurs, the information you need to make them, and the business processes you will need to engage in.
   b. Your company will need to exchange information with various external parties. Identify the external parties, and specify the information received from and sent to each of them.

1.4 How do an organization's business processes and lines of business affect the design of its AIS? Give several examples of how differences among organizations are reflected in their AIS.

1.5 Figure 1-5 shows that organizational culture and the design of an AIS influence one another. What does this imply about the degree to which an innovative system developed by one company can be transferred to another company?

1.6 Figure 1-5 shows that developments in IT affect both an organization's strategy and the design of its AIS. How can a company determine whether it is spending too much, too little, or just enough on IT?

1.7 Apply the value chain concept to S&S. Explain how it would perform the various primary and support activities.

1.8 IT enables organizations to easily collect large amounts of information about employees. Discuss the following issues:

a. To what extent should management monitor employees' e-mail?
b. To what extent should management monitor which websites employees visit?
c. To what extent should management monitor employee performance by, for example, using software to track keystrokes per hour or some other unit of time? If such information is collected, how should it be used?
d. Should companies use software to electronically "shred" all traces of e-mail?
e. Under what circumstances and to whom is it appropriate for a company to distribute information it collects about the people who visit its website?

PROBLEMS

1.1 IT is continually changing the nature of accounting and the role of accountants. Write a two-page report describing what you think the nature of the accounting function and the AIS in a large company will be like in the year 2030.

1.2 The annual report is considered by some to be the single most important printed document that companies produce. In recent years, annual reports have become large documents. They now include such sections as letters to the stockholders, descriptions of the business, operating highlights, financial review, management discussion and analysis, a discussion of company internal controls, segment reporting, inflation data, and the basic financial statements. The expansion has been due in part to a general increase in the degree of sophistication and complexity in accounting standards and disclosure requirements for financial reporting.

The expansion also is reflective of the change in the composition and level of sophistication of users. Current users include not only stockholders but also financial and securities analysts, potential investors, lending institutions, stockbrokers, customers, employees, and—whether the reporting company likes it or not—competitors. Thus, a report originally designed as a device for communicating basic financial information now attempts to meet the diverse needs of an ever-expanding audience.

Users hold conflicting views on the value of annual reports. Some argue that they fail to provide enough information, whereas others believe disclosures in annual reports have expanded to the point where they create information overload. Others argue that the future of most companies depends on acceptance by the investing public and by its customers; therefore, companies should take this opportunity to communicate well-defined corporate strategies.

REQUIRED

a. Identify and discuss the basic factors of communication that must be considered in the presentation of the annual report.
b. Discuss the communication problems a corporation faces in preparing the annual report that result from the diversity of the users.

c. Select two types of information found in an annual report, other than the financial statements and accompanying footnotes, and describe how they are helpful to the users of annual reports.
d. Discuss at least two advantages and two disadvantages of stating well-defined corporate strategies in the annual report.
e. Evaluate the effectiveness of annual reports in fulfilling the information needs of the following current and potential users: shareholders, creditors, employees, customers, and financial analysts.
f. Annual reports are public and accessible to anyone, including competitors. Discuss how this affects decisions about what information should be provided in annual reports. (*CMA Examination, adapted*)

1.3 United Services Automotive Association (USAA) is one of the largest diversified financial services companies in the United States, with close to $75 billion in assets under management. One reason for its success is the use of IT to lower costs and improve customer service. USAA operates one of the most advanced and successful information systems in the world. Most of its communication with its widely scattered customers, mostly military officers and their families, is digital. It was the first U.S. bank to implement a remote deposit capture application for the iPhone.

Early on, USAA made a strategic choice to become one of the more technology-intensive companies in the world. It views IT as a strategic weapon and uses it in several ways, including the following:

- When customers call, USAA personnel greet them personally by name. Unlike many diversified companies, a customer representative can handle inquiries and transactions about all of USAA's products using a highly integrated database.
- USAA uses its extensive database to keep track of minute details, such as which auto parts are fixed most frequently. It also uses its database to find ways to reduce claims costs. For example, USAA discovered that repair shops would rather charge up to $300 to replace a windshield with punctures than to charge $40 to repair it. USAA began offering to waive the deductible if the owners would repair the windshield rather than replace it.
- USAA spent extensively to develop an image-processing system that digitizes all paper documents sent in by claimants. It takes only a few keystrokes for a policy service representative to retrieve pictures of all the documents in a customer's file. The system can sort and prioritize documents so that employees are always working on the most important and urgent tasks.
- USAA is a world leader in mobile banking. Customers can use their cell phones and other mobile devices to access and execute banking, investment, stock trading, and insurance applications such as filing claims. More than 70% of USAA's logins are from cell phone users.
- USAA was among the first financial institutions to use text and e-mail messaging and notification technologies, person-to-person payment applications, and social networking and personal financial management tools connected to bank accounts.

REQUIRED

a. Why should USAA collect data on which auto parts are fixed most frequently? What could it do with this data?
b. Even though USAA offered to waive the deductible, the repair shops still managed to convince 95% of the owners to replace rather than repair their damaged windshields. How could USAA use its AIS to persuade more shop owners to repair rather than replace their windshields?
c. How does the image-processing system at USAA add value to the organization?
d. How do the remote deposit capture and mobile banking system at USAA add value to the organization?
e. Do an Internet search and find out what other advancements USAA has introduced. For example, see if you can find out how USAA is using artificial intelligence, data analytics, blockchain, or some other emerging technology. Write a one-page report on each new application or other newsworthy item you find (maximum limit of three applications or items).

1.4. Match the description listed in the right column with the correct information characteristic listed in the left column.

___ **1.** Access restricted	a. A report was carefully designed so that its data was easily comprehended by the reader.
___ **2.** Accurate	b. A manager working on the weekend needed information about a customer's production requests and found it on the company's network.
___ **3.** Available	c. Before production reports are accepted, two clerks working independently must produce the same information.
___ **4.** Reputable	d. An accounts receivable aging report included all customer accounts.
___ **5.** Complete	e. A report was checked by three different people to make sure it was correct.
___ **6.** Concise	f. An accounts receivable aging report is used in credit-granting decisions.
___ **7.** Consistent	g. An accounts receivable aging report was received before the credit manager had to decide whether to extend credit to a customer.
___ **8.** Current	h. Needing help with a decision, a manager sought the opinion of a highly regarded expert.
___ **9.** Objective	i. To protect intellectual property, a company encrypted the data, stored it in a very secure facility, and limited its use to five people.
___ **10.** Relevant	j. Tired of keying supplier prices into a database, a purchasing manager insisted the data be sent in machine readable form.
___ **11.** Timely	k. After a lengthy, rambling presentation, a CEO insisted future presentations contain only pertinent facts and last no more than 30 minutes.
___ **12.** Useable	l. A new manager insisted that monthly reports look the same so she could compare a new month's results to previous months.
___ **13.** Understandable	m. After making a decision based on outdated data, a new CFO required all analysis to be conducted with up-to-date data.
___ **14.** Verifiable	n. Reluctant to rely on his personal feelings about a decision, a manager sought the opinion of an outside expert.

1.5. Classify each of the following items as belonging in the revenue, expenditure, human resources/payroll, production, or financing cycle.

a. Collect payment on customer accounts.
b. Complete a picking ticket for a customer order.
c. Decide how many units to make next month.
d. Disburse payroll checks to factory workers.
e. Draw upon line of credit.
f. Establish a $10,000 credit limit for a new customer.
g. Hire a new assistant controller.
h. Obtain a bank loan.
i. Pay federal payroll taxes.
j. Pay for raw materials.
k. Pay off mortgage on factory.
l. Pay property taxes on office building.

m. Pay sales commissions.
n. Pay utility bills.
o. Purchase raw materials.
p. Put purchased goods into the warehouse.
q. Record factory employee timecards.
r. Record goods received from vendor.
s. Sell concert tickets.
t. Sell DVD player.
u. Send an order to a vendor.
v. Send new employees to a business ethics course.
w. Update the allowance for uncollectible accounts.

1.6. This chapter discusses several new technologies that impact accounting information systems: XBRL, artificial intelligence, data analytics, and blockchain. Research and then write a three-page report on one of these four technologies. Be sure to describe the technology's current impact on the AIS and how it is used in actual businesses or how an attempt to implement it failed.

1.7. Match each of the following terms with its definition.

___	**1.**	Accounting information system	a. Exceeding the amount of information a human mind can absorb and process
___	**2.**	Artificial intelligence	b. Use of software and algorithms to find and solve problems and improve business performance
___	**3.**	Blockchain	c. The benefit provided by information minus the cost of producing it
___	**4.**	Business processes	d. A set of activities and tasks that help accomplish a specific organizational goal
___	**5.**	Data	e. An agreement to exchange goods or services in exchange for cash
___	**6.**	Data analytics	f. Process of capturing, processing, and storing transaction data for later use and for producing information output
___	**7.**	Data dashboard	g. Frequent exchanges such as surrendering cash for inventory and paying employees for labor
___	**8.**	Expenditure cycle	h. Activities associated with selling goods and services in exchange for cash or a future promise of cash
___	**9.**	General ledger and reporting system	i. Value chain activities that produce, market, and deliver products to customers and provide post-delivery support
___	**10.**	Give-get exchange	j. A system that collects, records, stores, and processes data to produce information for decision makers
___	**11.**	Goal congruence	k. Linking all the primary and support activities in a business
___	**12.**	Information	l. Activities such as firm infrastructure and technology that enable main activities to be performed efficiently and effectively
___	**13.**	Machine-readable	m. An organization's value chain as well as its vendors, distributors, and customers
___	**14.**	Primary activities	n. Activities associated with purchasing inventory for resale for cash or a promise to pay cash
___	**15.**	Production cycle	o. Data in a format that can be processed by a computer
___	**16.**	Revenue cycle	p. Computer systems that simulate human intelligence processes such as learning, reasoning, and self-improvement

___ 17.	Supply chain	q. Procedures and routines that carry out specific activities, achieve objectives, or solve problems
___ 18.	Support activities	r. Facts collected, recorded, stored, and processed by an information system
___ 19.	System	s. Activities associated with using labor, raw materials, and equipment to produce finished goods
___ 20.	Transaction	t. Organized and processed data that provide meaning and improve decision making
___ 21.	Value chain	u. Display of data points and performance indicators in easily understood charts, tables, or gauges
___ 22.	Value of information	v. Activities associated with hiring, compensating, promoting, and terminating employees
		w. Major give-get exchanges that occur frequently in most companies
		x. Information-processing operations involved in preparing reports for internal and external parties
		y. Individual digital records linked using cryptography in a single list called a chain
		z. A subsystem achieves its goals while contributing to the overall goal

AIS in Action Solutions

QUIZ KEY

1. Data differ from information in which way?
   a. Data are output, and information is input. [Incorrect. Data are facts and figures that, once organized, can become information. Therefore, data are inputs, and information is output.]
   ► **b.** Information is output, and data are input. [Correct.]
   c. Data are meaningful bits of information. [Incorrect. Information is organized and processed data that provide meaning.]
   d. There is no difference. [Incorrect. There is a difference. Data are unorganized facts and figures. Information is meaningful, organized, and processed data.]

2. Which of the following is NOT a characteristic that makes information useful?
   a. It is accurate. [Incorrect. This is one of the information characteristics listed in Table 1-1 on page 4.]
   b. It is timely. [Incorrect. This is one of the information characteristics listed in Table 1-1 on page 4.]
   ► **c.** It is inexpensive. [Correct. This is NOT one of the information characteristics listed in Table 1-1 on page 4.]
   d. It is relevant. [Incorrect. This is one of the information characteristics listed in Table 1-1 on page 4.]

3. Which of the following is a primary activity in the value chain?
   a. purchasing [Incorrect. This is a support activity.]
   b. accounting [Incorrect. This is a firm infrastructure support activity.]
   ► **c.** post-sales service [Correct. Service is a primary activity.]
   d. human resource management [Incorrect. This is a support activity.]

4. Which transaction cycle includes interactions between an organization and its suppliers?
  a. revenue cycle [Incorrect. The revenue cycle involves interactions between an organization and its customers.]
▶ **b.** expenditure [Correct.]
  c. human resources/payroll cycle [Incorrect. The human resources/payroll cycle involves interactions between an organization and its employees, government, and potential hires.]
  d. general ledger and reporting system [Incorrect. The general ledger and reporting system receives summary information from all cycles.]

5. Which of the following is NOT a means by which information improves decision making?
▶ **a.** increases information overload [Correct. Decision makers receiving too much information have difficulty incorporating all of the information into their decision framework, and, as a result, decision quality can be reduced rather than improved.]
  b. reduces uncertainty [Incorrect. More reliable information leads to less uncertainty and thus better decisions.]
  c. provides feedback about the effectiveness of prior decisions [Incorrect. Knowledge of effective and ineffective decisions can lead to better decisions in the future.]
  d. identifies situations requiring management action [Incorrect. Identifying the need for management action can lead to improved decision making.]

6. In the value chain concept, upgrading IT is considered what kind of activity?
  a. primary activity [Incorrect. Investing in IT is a support activity.]
▶ **b.** support activity [Correct. Technology activities, including investing in IT, are considered a support activity.]
  c. service activity [Incorrect. The value chain includes only primary and support activities. A service activity is a type of primary activity.]
  d. structured activity [Incorrect. The value chain includes only primary and support activities. A structured activity is neither a primary nor a secondary activity.]

7. In which cycle does a company ship goods to customers?
  a. production cycle [Incorrect. The production cycle involves the transformation of raw materials into finished goods.]
  b. financing cycle [Incorrect. The financing cycle deals with interactions between an organization and its lenders and owners.]
▶ **c.** revenue cycle [Correct. The revenue cycle involves interactions between an organization and its customers, such as shipping them goods.]
  d. expenditure cycle [Incorrect. The expenditure cycle involves interactions between an organization and its suppliers.]

8. Which of the following is a function of an AIS?
  a. reducing the need to identify a strategy and strategic position [Incorrect. An AIS does not reduce the need to identify a strategy. It provides information to executives for the purpose of making strategic decisions.]
▶ **b.** transforming data into useful information [Correct. This is one of the primary functions of an AIS.]
  c. allocating organizational resources [Incorrect. Decision makers allocate resources, and the purpose of the AIS is to provide information to the decision makers so that they can make the allocation.]
  d. automating all decision making [Incorrect. The AIS provides information to decision makers; it is not designed to automate all decision making.]

9. A firm, its suppliers, and its customers collectively form which of the following?

▶ **a.** supply chain [Correct. The supply chain is made up of the firm, its suppliers, and customers.]

b. value chain [Incorrect. The value chain is made up of primary and support activities within the firm.]

c. ERP system [Incorrect. An ERP system integrates all aspects of an organization's activities into one system.]

d. AIS [Incorrect. The AIS is made up of the human and capital resources within an organization that are responsible for collecting and processing transactions and preparing financial information.]

10. A performance report about all approved vendors during the previous 12 months is information MOST needed in which business process?

a. paying vendors [Incorrect. To pay a vendor, a company needs to know whether merchandise ordered was received in good condition. They do not need a 12-month history of vendor performance.]

▶ **b.** acquiring inventory [Correct. Companies want to acquire inventory from companies that have performed well in the past. A vendor performance report would disclose whether the vendor shipped inventory on time, whether the inventory was of the requested quality, whether the prices were as agreed upon, etc.]

c. selling merchandise [Incorrect. A 12-month history of vendor performance is usually not very helpful in trying to sell products to customers. More important would be customer tastes and preferences, customer credit status, etc.]

d. paying employees [Incorrect. It is very rare for an employee's pay to be based on a 12-month history of vendor performance. More important are hours worked, annual salary, sales figures to calculate commissions, etc.]

CHAPTER

2

Overview of Transaction Processing and Enterprise Resource Planning Systems

LEARNING OBJECTIVES

After studying this chapter, you should be able to:

1. Describe the data processing cycle used to process transactions, including how data is input, stored, and processed and how information is output.
2. Discuss how organizations use enterprise resource planning (ERP) systems to process transactions and provide information.

INTEGRATIVE CASE S&S

The grand opening of S&S is two weeks away. Scott Parry and Susan Gonzalez are working long hours to make the final arrangements for the store opening. Most of the employees have already been hired; training is scheduled for next week.

Susan has ordered inventory for the first month. The store is being remodeled and will have a bright, cheery decor. All seems to be in order—all, that is, except the accounting records.

Like many entrepreneurs, Scott and Susan have not given as much thought to their accounting records as they have to other parts of their business. Recognizing they need qualified accounting help, they hired a full-time accountant, Ashton Fleming. Scott and Susan think Ashton is perfect for the job because of his three years of experience with a national CPA (Certified Public Accountants) firm. Ashton is looking forward to working for S&S because he has always wanted to be involved in building a company from the ground up.

During Ashton's first day on the job, Susan gives him the invoices for the inventory she purchased and a folder with their bank loan documentation, with the first payment due after the grand opening. She also hands him a folder containing information on rental payments, utilities, and other expenses. Susan tells Ashton that she and Scott know little about accounting and he will run the accounting end of S&S. She adds that the only thing they have done so far is to open a checking account for S&S and that they have kept the check register updated to monitor their cash flow.

Designdepot_ltd/Shutterstock

Scott explains that the sales staff is paid a fixed salary and commissions and that all other employees are paid hourly rates. Employees are paid every two weeks, with their first paychecks due next week. Ashton asks Scott what accounting software the company is using. Scott replies that he and Susan have not had time to tackle that aspect yet. Scott and Susan looked at some of the popular packages but quickly realized that they did not know enough about accounting to make an intelligent choice. Scott then tells Ashton that his first task should be to purchase whatever accounting software he thinks will be best for S&S.

After Scott leaves, Ashton feels both excited and a little nervous about his responsibility for creating an accounting information system (AIS) for S&S. Although Ashton has audited many companies, he has never organized a company's books and is unsure how to go about it. A million questions run through his head. Here are just a few of them:

1. How should I organize the accounting records so that financial statements can be easily produced?
2. How am I going to collect and process data about all of S&S's transactions?
3. How do I organize all the data that will be collected?
4. How should I design the AIS so that the information provided is reliable and accurate?
5. How can I design procedures to ensure that they meet all government obligations, such as remitting sales, income, and payroll taxes?

Introduction

This chapter is divided into two major sections. The first section discusses the data processing cycle and its role in organizing business activities and providing information to users. It explains how organizations capture and enter data about business activities into their accounting information system (AIS) and how companies process data and transform it into useful information. It also discusses basic data storage concepts, showing how data are stored for further use. Finally, information output is discussed, including the different ways information is provided to users.

The second section discusses the role of the information system in modern organizations and introduces the concept of an enterprise resource planning (ERP) system. An ERP can help integrate all aspects of a company's operations with its traditional AIS. This section also describes the significant advantages of an ERP as well as significant challenges that must be overcome to implement an ERP system.

Transaction Processing: The Data Processing Cycle

Accountants and other system users play a significant role in the data processing cycle. For example, they interact with systems analysts to help answer questions such as these: What data should be entered and stored by the organization, and who should have access to them? How should data be organized, updated, stored, accessed, and retrieved? How can scheduled and unanticipated information needs be met? To answer these and related questions, the data processing concepts explained in this chapter must be understood.

data processing cycle - The four operations (data input, data storage, data processing, and information output) performed on data to generate meaningful and relevant information.

One important AIS function is to process company transactions efficiently and effectively. In manual (non-computer-based) systems, data are entered into journals and ledgers maintained on paper. In computer-based systems, data are entered into computers and stored in files and databases. The operations performed on data to generate meaningful and relevant information are referred to collectively as the **data processing cycle**. As shown in Figure 2-1, this process consists of four steps: data input, data storage, data processing, and information output.

DATA INPUT

The first step in processing input is to capture transaction data and enter them into the system. The data capture process is usually triggered by a business activity. Data must be collected about three facets of each business activity:

1. Each activity of interest
2. The resource(s) affected by each activity
3. The people who participate in each activity

For example, the most frequent revenue cycle transaction is a sale, either for cash or on credit. S&S may find it useful to collect the following data about a sales transaction:

- Date and time the sale occurred.
- Employee who made the sale and the checkout clerk who processed the sale.
- Checkout register where the sale was processed.
- Item(s) sold.
- Quantity of each item sold.
- List price and actual price of each item sold.
- Total amount of the sale.
- Delivery instructions.
- For credit sales: customer name, customer bill-to and ship-to addresses.

source documents - Documents used to capture transaction data at its source – when the transaction takes place. Examples include sales orders, purchase orders, and employee time cards.

Historically, most businesses used paper **source documents** to collect data about their business activities. They later transferred that data into the computer. When data are entered using computer screens, they often retain the same name and basic format as the paper source document. Table 2-1 lists some common transaction cycle activities and the source document or form used to capture data about that event. Examples of many of these documents can be found in Chapters 14 through 18. For example, a purchase order, used to request merchandise from suppliers, is shown in Chapter 15.

turnaround documents - Records of company data sent to an external party and then returned to the system as input. Turnaround documents are in machine-readable form to facilitate their subsequent processing as input records. An example is a utility bill.

Turnaround documents are company output sent to an external party, who often adds data to the document, and then are returned to the company as an input document. They are in machine-readable form to facilitate their subsequent processing as input records. An example is a utility bill sent to the customer, returned with the customer's payment, and read by a special scanning device when it is returned.

FIGURE 2-1
The Data Processing Cycle

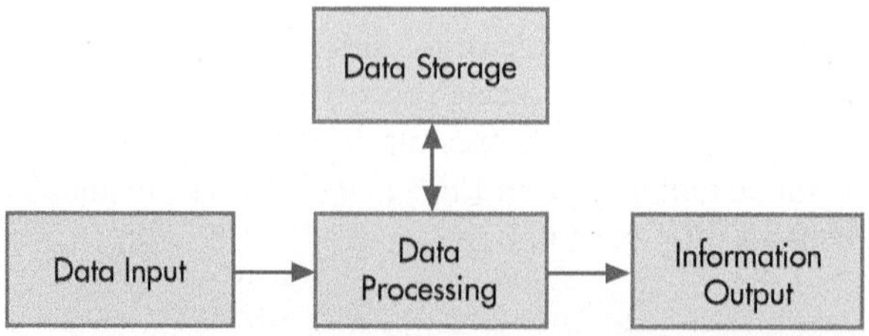

TABLE 2-1 Common Business Activities and Source Documents

Business Activity	Source Document
Revenue Cycle	
Take customer order	Sales order
Deliver or ship order	Delivery ticket or bill of lading
Receive cash	Remittance advice or remittance list
Deposit cash receipts	Deposit slip
Adjust customer account	Credit memo
Expenditure Cycle	
Request items	Purchase requisition
Order items	Purchase order
Receive items	Receiving report
Pay for items	Check or electronic funds transfer
Human Resources Cycle	
Collect employee withholding data	W-4 form
Record time worked by employees	Time cards
Record time spent on specific jobs	Job time tickets or time sheet

Source data automation devices capture transaction data in machine-readable form at the time and place of their origin. Examples include ATMs used by banks, point-of-sale (POS) scanners used in retail stores, and bar code scanners used in warehouses. Another good example of source data automation is the use of XBRL. Before XBRL, financial reports were submitted electronically to the SEC and others who wanted to use the information had to enter it into their system. With XBRL, financial data is encoded to make it machine readable, allowing other computers to use and analyze the information. This saves time, reduces errors, and makes much more information available for analytics. XBRL is discussed in more depth in Chapter 18.

source data automation - The collection of transaction data in machine-readable form at the time and place of origin. Examples are point-of-sale terminals and ATMs.

The second step in processing input is to make sure captured data are accurate and complete. One way to do this is to use source data automation or well-designed turnaround documents and data entry screens. Well-designed documents and screens improve accuracy and completeness by providing instructions or prompts about what data to collect, grouping logically related pieces of information close together, using checkoff boxes or pull-down menus to present the available options, and using appropriate shading and borders to clearly separate data items. Data input screens usually list all the data the user needs to enter. Sometimes these screens resemble source documents, and users fill out the screen the same way they would a paper source document.

Users can improve control either by using prenumbered source documents or by having the system automatically assign a sequential number to each new transaction. Prenumbering simplifies verifying that all transactions have been recorded and that none of the documents have been misplaced. (Imagine trying to balance a checkbook if the checks were not prenumbered.)

The third step in processing input is to make sure company policies are followed, such as approving or verifying a transaction. For example, S&S would not want to sell goods to a customer who was not paying his bills or to sell an item for immediate delivery that was out of stock. These problems are prevented by programming the system to check a customer's credit limit and payment history, as well as inventory status, before confirming a customer sale.

DATA STORAGE

A company's data are one of its most important resources. However, the mere existence of relevant data does not guarantee that they are useful. To function properly, an organization must have ready and easy access to its data. Therefore, accountants need to understand how data are organized and stored in an AIS and how they can be accessed. In essence, they need to know how to manage data for maximum corporate use.

Imagine how difficult it would be to read a textbook if it were not organized into chapters, sections, paragraphs, and sentences. Now imagine how hard it would be for S&S to find an invoice if all documents were randomly dumped into file cabinets. Fortunately, information general ledger - A ledger that contains summary-level data for every asset, liability, equity, revenue, and expense account of the organization.

subsidiary ledger - A ledger used to record detailed data for a general ledger account with many individual subaccounts, such as accounts receivable, inventory, and accounts payable.

control account - A title given to a general ledger account that summarizes the total amounts recorded in a subsidiary ledger. For example, the accounts receivable control account in the general ledger represents the total amount owed by all customers. The balances in the accounts receivable subsidiary ledger indicate the amount owed by each specific customer.

coding - The systematic assignment of numbers or letters to items to classify and organize them.

sequence codes - Items are numbered consecutively so that gaps in the sequence code indicate missing items that should be investigated. Examples include prenumbered checks, invoices, and purchase orders.

block code - Blocks of numbers reserved for specific categories of data, thereby helping to organize the data. An example is a chart of accounts.

group codes - Two or more subgroups of digits used to code an item. A group code is often used in conjunction with a block code.

mnemonic codes - Letters and numbers interspersed to identify an item. The mnemonic code is derived from the description of the item and is usually easy to memorize.

in an AIS is organized for easy and efficient access. This section explains basic data storage concepts and definitions.

LEDGERS Cumulative accounting information is stored in general and subsidiary ledgers. A **general ledger** contains summary-level data for every asset, liability, equity, revenue, and expense account. A **subsidiary ledger** contains detailed data for any general ledger account with many individual subaccounts. For example, the general ledger has an accounts receivable account that summarizes the total amount owed to the company by all customers. The subsidiary accounts receivable ledger has a separate record for each individual customer, with detailed information such as name, address, purchases, payments, account balance, and credit limit. Subsidiary ledgers are often used for accounts receivable, inventory, fixed assets, and accounts payable.

The general ledger account corresponding to a subsidiary ledger is called a **control account**. The relationship between the general ledger control account and the total of individual subsidiary ledger account balances helps maintain the accuracy of AIS data. Specifically, the sum of all subsidiary ledger account balances should equal the amount in the corresponding general ledger control account. Any discrepancy between them indicates that a recording error has occurred.

CODING TECHNIQUES Data in ledgers is organized logically using coding techniques. **Coding** is the systematic assignment of numbers or letters to items to classify and organize them.

- With **sequence codes**, items are numbered consecutively to account for all items. Any missing items cause a gap in the numerical sequence. Examples include prenumbered checks, invoices, and purchase orders.
- With a **block code**, blocks of numbers are reserved for specific categories of data. For example, S&S reserved the following numbers for major product categories:

Product Code	Product Type
1000000–1999999	Electric range
2000000–2999999	Refrigerator
3000000–3999999	Washer
4000000–4999999	Dryer

  Users can identify an item's type and model using the code numbers. Other examples include ledger account numbers (blocked by account type), employee numbers (blocked by department), and customer numbers (blocked by region).
- **Group codes**, which are two or more subgroups of digits used to code items, are often used in conjunction with block codes. If S&S uses a seven-digit product code number, the group coding technique might be applied as follows.

Digit Position	Meaning
1–2	Product line, size, style
3	Color
4–5	Year of manufacture
6–7	Optional features

  There are four subcodes in the product code, each with a different meaning. Users can sort, summarize, and retrieve information using one or more subcodes. This technique is often applied to general ledger account numbers.
- With **mnemonic codes**, letters and numbers are interspersed to identify an item. The mnemonic code is derived from the description of the item and is usually easy to memorize. For example, Dry300W05 could represent a low end (300), white (W) dryer (Dry) made by Sears (05).

The following guidelines result in a better coding system. The code should:

- Be consistent with its intended use, which requires that the code designer determine desired system outputs prior to selecting the code.
- Allow for growth. For example, don't use a three-digit employee code for a fast-growing company with 950 employees.

- Be as simple as possible to minimize costs, facilitate memorization and interpretation, and ensure employee acceptance.
- Be consistent with the company's organizational structure and across the company's divisions.

CHART OF ACCOUNTS A great example of coding is the **chart of accounts**, which is a list of the numbers assigned to each general ledger account. These account numbers allow transaction data to be coded, classified, and entered into the proper accounts. They also facilitate the preparation of financial statements and reports because data stored in individual accounts can easily be summed for presentation.

chart of accounts - A listing of all the numbers assigned to balance sheet and income statement accounts. The account numbers allow transaction data to be coded, classified, and entered into the proper accounts. They also facilitate financial statement and report preparation.

However, data stored in summary accounts cannot be easily analyzed and reported in more detail. Consequently, it is important that the chart of accounts contain sufficient detail to meet an organization's information needs. To illustrate, consider the consequences if S&S were to use only one general ledger account for all sales transactions. It would be easy to produce reports showing the total amount of sales for a given time period, but it would be very difficult to prepare reports separating cash and credit sales. Indeed, the only way to produce these latter reports would be to go back to original sales records to identify the nature of each sales transaction. If S&S used separate general ledger accounts for cash and credit sales, then reports showing both types of sales could be easily produced. Total sales could also be easily reported by summing each type of sale.

Table 2-2 shows the chart of accounts Ashton developed for S&S. Each account number is three digits long. The first digit represents the major account category and indicates where

TABLE 2-2 Sample Chart of Accounts for S&S

Account Code	Account Name	Account Code	Account Name
100–199	**Current Assets**	**400–499**	**Equity Accounts**
101	Checking Account	400	Common Stock
102	Savings Account	410	Retained Earnings
103	Petty Cash		
120	Accounts Receivable	**500–599**	**Revenues**
125	Allowance for Doubtful Accounts	501	Cash Sales
130	Notes Receivable	502	Credit Sales
150	Inventory	510	Sales Returns & Allowances
160	Supplies	511	Sales Discounts
170	Prepaid Rent	520	Interest Revenue
180	Prepaid Insurance	530	Miscellaneous Revenue
200–299	**Noncurrent Assets**	**600–799**	**Expenses**
200	Land	600	Cost of Goods Sold
210	Buildings	611	Wages Expense
215	Accumulated Depreciation—Buildings	612	Commissions Expense
230	Equipment	613	Payroll Tax Expense
235	Accumulated Depreciation—Equipment	620	Rent Expense
240	Furniture & Fixtures	630	Insurance Expense
245	Accumulated Depreciation—Furniture & Fixtures	640	Supplies Expense
250	Other Assets	650	Bad Debt Expense
		701	Depreciation Expense—Buildings
300–399	**Liabilities**	702	Depreciation Expense—Equipment
300	Accounts Payable	703	Depreciation Expense—Furniture & Fixtures
310	Wages Payable	710	Income Tax Expense
321	Employee Income Tax Payable		
322	FICA Tax Payable	**900–999**	**Summary Accounts**
323	Federal Unemployment Tax Payable	910	Income Summary
324	State Unemployment Tax Payable		
330	Accrued Interest Payable		
360	Other Liabilities		

it appears on S&S's financial statements. Thus, all current assets are numbered in the 100s, noncurrent assets are numbered in the 200s, and so on.

The second digit represents the primary financial subaccounts within each category. Again, the accounts are assigned numbers to match the order of their appearance in financial statements (in order of decreasing liquidity). Thus, account 120 represents accounts receivable, and account 150 represents inventory.

The third digit identifies the specific account to which the transaction data will be posted. For example, account 501 represents cash sales, and account 502 represents credit sales. Similarly, accounts 101 through 103 represent the various cash accounts used by S&S.

A chart of accounts is tailored to the nature and purpose of an organization. For example, the chart of accounts for S&S indicates that the company is a corporation. In contrast, a partnership would include separate capital and drawing accounts for each partner, instead of common stock and retained earnings. Likewise, because S&S is a retail organization, it has only one type of general ledger inventory account. A manufacturing company, in contrast, would have separate general ledger accounts for raw materials, work in process, and finished goods inventories.

Ashton left gaps in S&S's chart of accounts to allow for additional accounts. For example, when S&S has excess cash to invest in marketable securities, a new general ledger account can be created and assigned the number 110. When S&S opens stores in the future, he will add three digits to the chart of accounts to represent each store in the chain, so that S&S can track items in each store.

Subsidiary ledger accounts often have longer account codes than general ledger accounts. At S&S, each account receivable will have a seven-digit code. The first three digits are 120, the code for accounts receivable. The next four digits identify up to 10,000 individual customers.

general journal - A journal used to record infrequent or nonroutine transactions, such as loan payments and end-of-period adjusting and closing entries.

specialized journal - A journal used to record a large number of repetitive transactions such as credit sales, cash receipts, purchases, and cash disbursements.

JOURNALS Transaction data are often recorded in a journal before they are entered into a ledger. A journal entry shows the accounts and amounts to be debited and credited. A **general journal** is used to record infrequent or nonroutine transactions, such as loan payments and end-of-period adjusting and closing entries. A **specialized journal** records large numbers of repetitive transactions such as sales, cash receipts, and cash disbursements.

Table 2-3 is a sample sales journal. All transaction information is recorded in one line, with every entry a debit to accounts receivable and a credit to sales. There is no need to write an explanation of each entry, as is the case with general journal entries. Given the high number of daily sales transactions, the time saved by recording these transactions in a sales journal, rather than in the general journal, is considerable.

The Post Ref column indicates when transactions are posted to the appropriate ledger. In a manual system, ledgers are books; hence, the phrase "keeping the books" refers to the process of maintaining the ledgers.

Figure 2-2 shows how to journalize and post sales transactions. First, each credit sale is recorded in the sales journal. Then each sales journal entry is posted to the appropriate customer account in the accounts receivable subsidiary ledger (note the arrow linking the $1,876.50 sale to KDR Builders in the sales journal to the debit for $1,876.50 in the accounts

TABLE 2-3 Sample Sales Journal

		Sales Journal			Page 5
Date	**Invoice Number**	**Account Debited**	**Account Number**	**Post Ref**	**Amount**
Oct. 15	151	Brown Hospital Supply	120–035	✓	798.00
15	152	Greenshadows Hotel Suites	120–122	✓	1,267.00
15	153	Heathrow Apartments	120–057	✓	5,967.00
15	154	LMS Construction	120–173	✓	2,312.50
15	155	Gardenview Apartments	120–084	✓	3,290.00
15	156	KDR Builders	120–135	✓	1,876.50
		TOTAL	120/502		15,511.00

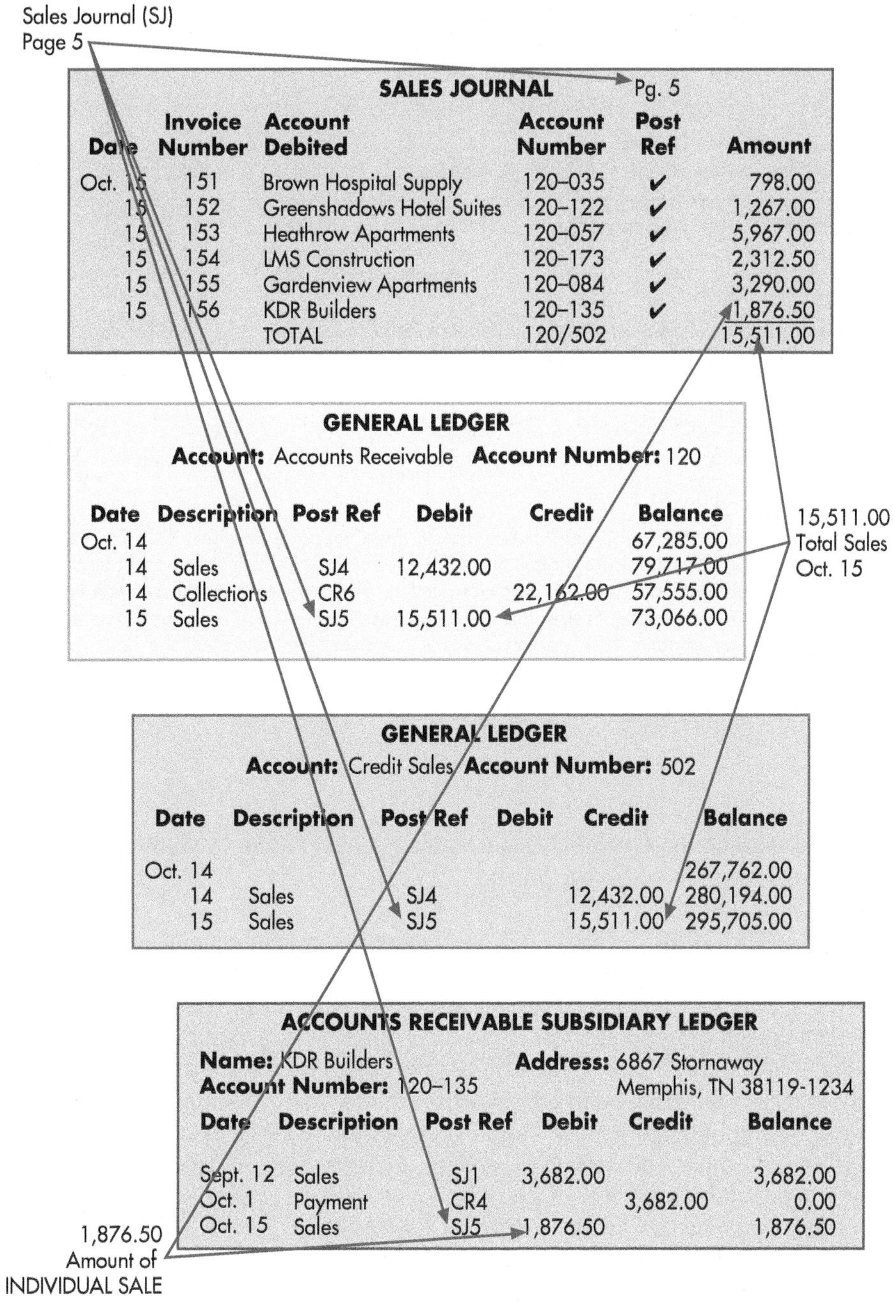

FIGURE 2-2
Recording and Posting a Credit Sale

receivable subsidiary ledger). Periodically, the total of all sales journal entries is posted to the general ledger (note the arrow showing the daily sales journal total of $15,511.00 posted to both the Accounts Receivable and the Credit Sales general ledger accounts).

AUDIT TRAIL Figure 2-2 shows how the posting references and document numbers provide an audit trail. An **audit trail** is a traceable path of a transaction through a data processing system from point of origin to final output, or backward from final output to point of origin. It is used to check the accuracy and validity of ledger postings. Observe that the SJ5 posting reference for the $15,511 credit to the sales account in the general ledger refers to page 5 of the sales journal. By checking page 5 of the sales journal, it is possible to verify that $15,511 represents the total credit sales recorded on October 15. Similarly, the posting reference for the $1,876.50 debit to the KDR Builders' account in the subsidiary accounts receivable ledger also refers to page 5 of the sales journal as the source of that entry. Furthermore, note that the sales journal lists the invoice numbers for each individual entry. This provides the means for

audit trail - A path that allows a transaction to be traced through a data processing system from point of origin to output or backwards from output to point of origin. It is used to check the accuracy and validity of ledger postings and to trace changes in general ledger accounts from their beginning balance to their ending balance.

FIGURE 2-3
Data Storage Elements

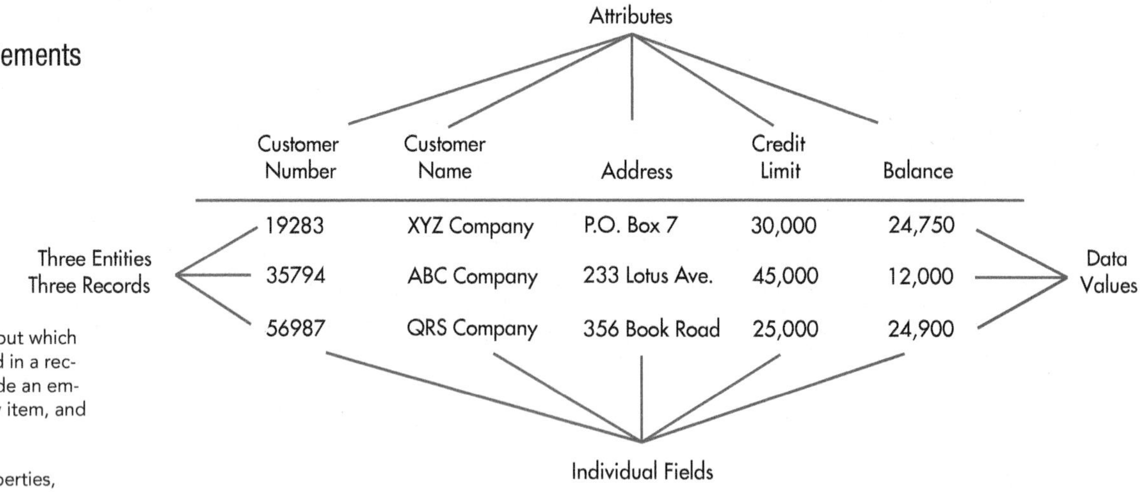

This accounts receivable file stores information about three separate entities: XYZ Company, ABC Company, and QRS Company. As a result, there are three records in the file. Five separate attributes are used to describe each customer: customer number, customer name, address, credit limit, and balance. There are, therefore, five separate fields in each record. Each field contains a data value that describes an attribute of a particular entity (customer). For example, the data value 19283 is the customer number for the XYZ Company.

entity - The item about which information is stored in a record. Examples include an employee, an inventory item, and a customer.

attributes - The properties, identifying numbers, and characteristics of interest of an entity stored in a database. Examples are employee number, pay rate, name, and address.

field - The portion of a data record where the data value for a particular attribute is stored. For example, in a spreadsheet, each row might represent a customer and each column an attribute of the customer. Each cell in a spreadsheet is a field.

record - A set of fields whose data values describe specific attributes of an entity, such as all payroll data relating to a single employee. An example is a row in a spreadsheet.

data value - The actual value stored in a field. It describes a particular attribute of an entity. For example, the customer name field would contain "ZYX Company" if that company were a customer.

file - A set of logically related records, such as the payroll records of all employees.

master file - A permanent file of records that stores cumulative data about an organization. As transactions take place, individual records within a master file are updated to keep them current.

transaction file - A file that contains the individual business transactions that occur during a specific fiscal period. A transaction file is conceptually similar to a journal in a manual AIS.

database - A set of interrelated, centrally controlled data files stored with as little data redundancy as possible. A database consolidates records previously stored in separate files into a common pool and serves a variety of users and data processing applications.

locating and examining the appropriate source documents in order to verify that the transaction occurred and it was recorded accurately.

COMPUTER-BASED STORAGE CONCEPTS An **entity** is something about which information is stored, such as employees, inventory items, and customers. Each entity has **attributes**, or characteristics of interest, that are stored, such as a pay rate and address. Each type of entity possesses the same set of attributes. For example, all employees possess an employee number, pay rate, and home address. The specific values for those attributes will differ. For example, one employee's pay rate might be $12.00 an hour, whereas another's might be $12.25.

Figure 2-3 shows that computers store data in a **field**. The fields containing data about entity attributes constitute a **record**. In Figure 2-3, each row represents a different record, and each column represents an attribute. Each intersecting row and column in Figure 2-3 is a field within a record, the contents of which are called a **data value**.

A **file** is a group of related records. A **master file**, like a ledger in a manual AIS, stores cumulative information about an organization. The inventory and equipment master files store information about important organizational resources. The customer, supplier, and employee master files store information about important agents with whom the organization interacts.

Master files are permanent; they exist across fiscal periods. However, individual master file records may change frequently. For example, individual customer accounts balances are updated to reflect new sales transactions and payments received. Periodically, new records are added to or removed from a master file, for example, when a new customer is added or a former customer deleted.

A **transaction file** contains records of individual business transactions that occur during a specific time. It is similar to a journal in a manual AIS. For example, S&S will have a daily sales transaction file and a cash receipts file. Both files will update individual customer account balances in the customer master file. Transaction files are not permanent and may not be needed beyond the current fiscal period. However, they are usually maintained for a specified period for backup purposes.

A set of interrelated, centrally coordinated files is referred to as a **database**. For example, the accounts receivable file might be combined with customer, sales analysis, and related files to form a customer database. Chapter 4 discusses database technology.

DATA PROCESSING

Once business activity data have been entered into the system, they must be processed to keep the databases current. The four different types of data processing activities, referred to as CRUD, are as follows:

1. ***Creating*** new data records, such as adding a newly hired employee to the payroll database.
2. ***Reading***, retrieving, or viewing existing data.
3. ***Updating*** previously stored data. Figure 2-4 depicts the steps required to update an accounts receivable record with a sales transaction. The two records are matched using the account number. The sale amount ($360) is added to the account balance ($1,500) to get a new current balance ($1,860).
4. ***Deleting*** data, such as purging the vendor master file of all vendors the company no longer does business with.

Updating done periodically, such as daily, is referred to as **batch processing**. Although batch processing is cheaper and more efficient, the data are current and accurate only immediately after processing. For that reason, batch processing is used only for applications, such as payroll, that do not need frequent updating and that naturally occur or are processed at fixed time periods.

batch processing - Accumulating transaction records into groups or batches for processing at a regular interval such as daily or weekly. The records are usually sorted into some sequence (such as numerically or alphabetically) before processing.

Most companies update each transaction as it occurs, referred to as **real-time processing** because it ensures that stored information is always current, thereby increasing its decision-making usefulness. It is also more accurate because data input errors can be corrected in real time or refused. It also provides significant competitive advantages. For example, FedEx updated its mission statement to include the phrase "Positive control of each package will be maintained by utilizing real-time electronic tracking and tracing systems." With FedEx's system, employees and customers can track the exact location of each package and estimate its arrival time.

real-time processing - The computer system processes data immediately after capture and provides updated information to users on a timely basis.

A combination of the two approaches is online batch processing, where transaction data are entered and edited as they occur and stored for later processing. Batch processing and real-time processing are summarized in Figure 2-5.

INFORMATION OUTPUT

The final step in the data processing cycle is information output. When displayed on a monitor, output is referred to as "soft copy." When printed on paper, it is referred to as "hard copy." Information is usually presented in one of three forms: a document, a report, or a query response.

Documents are records of transaction or other company data. Some, such as checks and invoices, are transmitted to external parties. Others, such as receiving reports and purchase

documents - Records of transaction or other company data. Examples include checks, invoices, receiving reports, and purchase requisitions.

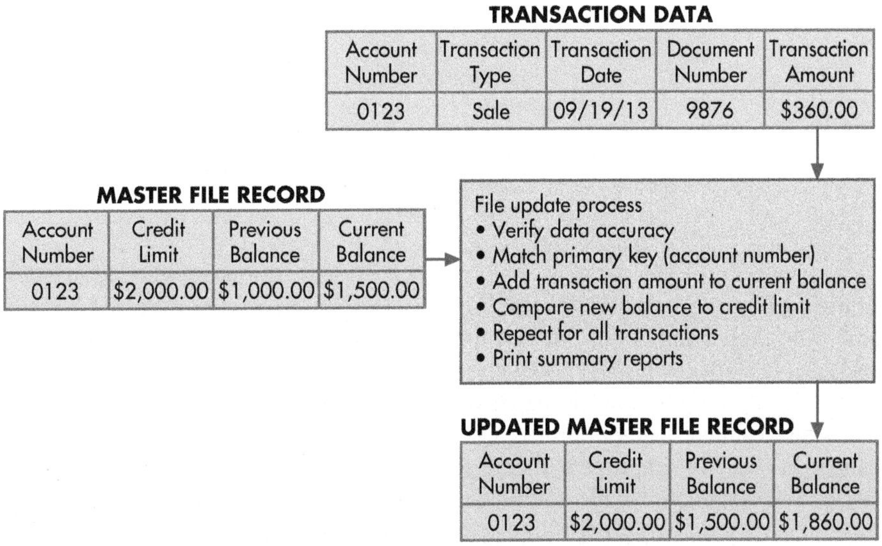

FIGURE 2-4
The Accounts Receivable File Update Process

FIGURE 2-5
Batch and Real-time Processing

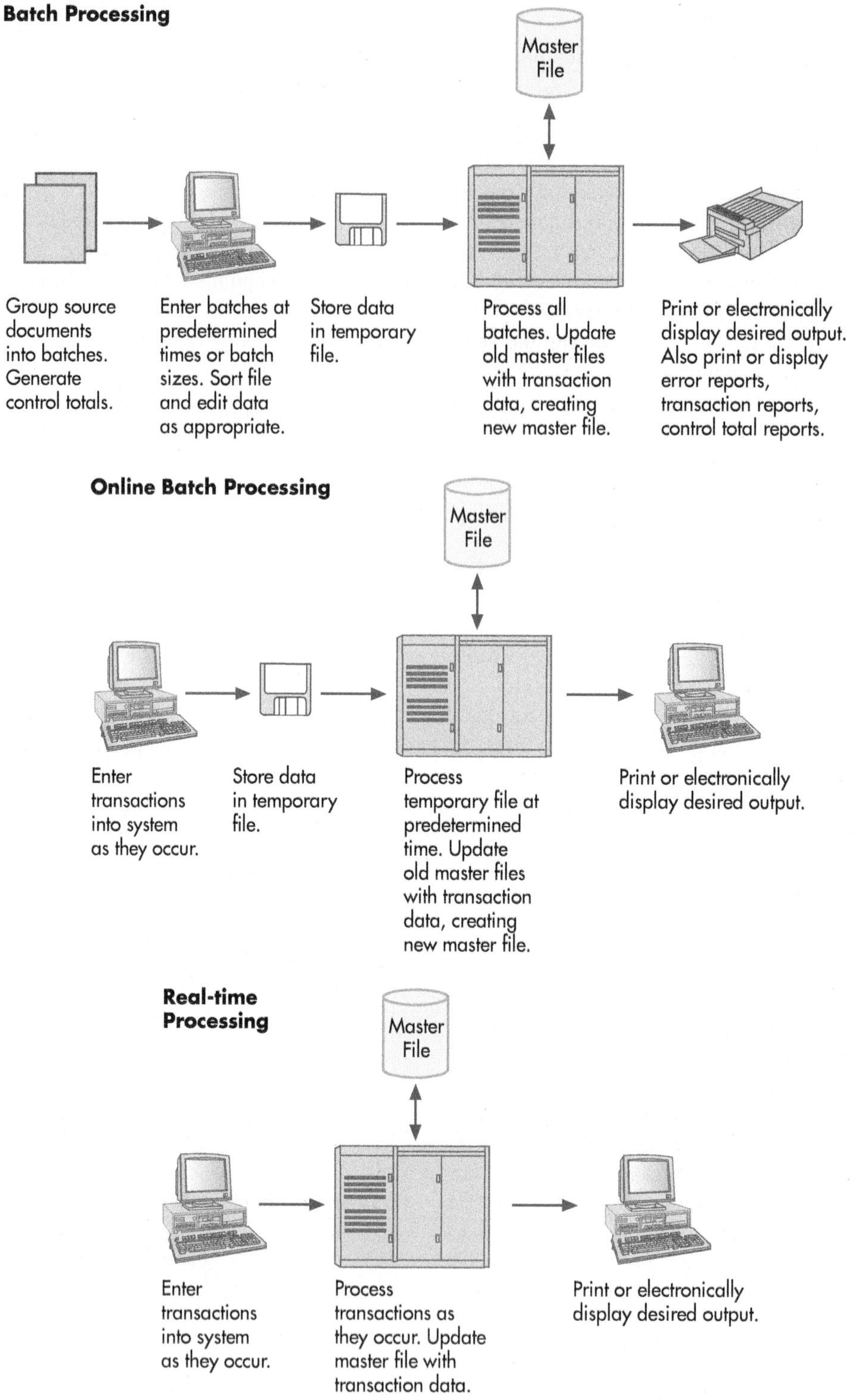
Batch Processing
Master File
Group source documents into batches. Generate control totals.
Enter batches at predetermined times or batch sizes. Sort file and edit data as appropriate.
Store data in temporary file.
Process all batches. Update old master files with transaction data, creating new master file.
Print or electronically display desired output. Also print or display error reports, transaction reports, control total reports.
Online Batch Processing
Master File
Enter transactions into system as they occur.
Store data in temporary file.
Process temporary file at predetermined time. Update old master files with transaction data, creating new master file.
Print or electronically display desired output.
Real-time Processing
Master File
Enter transactions into system as they occur.
Process transactions as they occur. Update master file with transaction data.
Print or electronically display desired output.

requisitions, are used internally. Documents can be printed out, or they can be stored as electronic images in a computer. For example, Toys 'R' Us uses electronic data interchange to communicate with its suppliers. Every year it processes over half a million invoices electronically, thereby eliminating paper documents and dramatically reducing costs and errors. This has resulted in higher profits and more accurate information.

reports - System output organized in a meaningful fashion used by employees to control operational activities, by managers to make decisions and design strategies, and by investors and creditors to understand a company's business activities.

Reports are used by employees to control operational activities and by managers to make decisions and to formulate business strategies. External users need reports to evaluate company profitability, judge creditworthiness, or comply with regulatory requirements. Some reports, such as financial statements and sales analyses, are produced on a regular basis. Others are produced on an exception basis to call attention to unusual conditions. For example, S&S could have its system produce a report to indicate when product returns exceed a certain percentage of sales. Reports can also be produced on demand. For example, Susan could produce a report to identify the salesperson who sold the most items during a specific promotional period.

The need for reports should be periodically assessed because they are often prepared long after they are needed, wasting time, money, and resources. For example, NCR Corporation reduced the number of reports from 1,200 to just over 100. Another company eliminated 6 million pages of reports, a stack four times higher than its 41-story headquarters building. One 25-page report took five days to prepare and sat unread.

A database **query** is used to provide the information needed to deal with problems and questions that need rapid action or answers. A user enters a request for a specific piece of information; it is retrieved, displayed, or analyzed as requested. Repetitive queries are often developed by information systems specialists. One-time queries are often developed by users. Some companies, such as Walmart, allow suppliers to access their databases to help them better serve Walmart's needs. Suppliers can gauge how well a product is selling in every Walmart store in the world and maximize sales by stocking and promoting items that are selling well.

query - A request for the database to provide the information needed to deal with a problem or answer a question. The information is retrieved, displayed or printed, and/or analyzed as requested.

Additional information about system output is contained in Chapters 14–18.

Transaction Processing: Blockchain

People have been engaging in business transactions for thousands of years. Originally, people kept track of, or accounted for, these transactions using a single-entry accounting system. We eventually graduated to the double entry bookkeeping system with the journals and ledgers and paper-based financial reports that have been used for hundreds of years. When computers were invented, we digitized the journals and ledgers and created transaction files and master files that did the job of paper-based journals and ledgers.

When the number of master files proliferated with its attendant data redundancies and inaccuracies, we combined multiple files into databases, which have grown larger and more complex over time. Each company involved in the transaction had its own way of capturing transaction data and storing transactions, often in centralized databases that provided better control and security. Customers and vendors must periodically reconcile its records to the other party in the transaction.

With computers also came a large variety of software programs to capture, store, process, and report accounting data. But these programs often did not capture non-financial data very well. Over time, accounting software has improved significantly. We now have intelligent or automated accounting products that provide automatic transaction recording, on demand accounting functions, and the automatic distribution of data, thereby doing away with many of the bookkeeping functions of old. These systems, which have machine learning and artificial intelligence embedded in them, store the data in the cloud. They also use smart portals for clients to transfer data and information back and forth.

When the parties to a transaction do not trust each other, a third-party steps in to hold the items of value being exchanged until both parties complete their side of the transaction. For example, when you buy a house, you use realtors and a title company to make sure a clear title is passed and to ensure the house conveys to the buyer and the money to pay for the house conveys to the seller. The titles are then recorded by county governments, creating a public record of what is owned by whom.

The advent of the Internet has had a tremendous impact on people and businesses. The Internet has many uses, including the ability to share information with large groups of people. There are many people-to-people interactions such as social media. There are also many business-to-consumer applications such as online shopping. Business-to-business transactions are also facilitated by the Internet. Many Internet transactions are processed and stored by older, traditional legacy systems.

With the advent of cryptocurrencies, a new technology called blockchain is changing the way financial transactions as well as many other types of transactions are recorded, processed, and stored. While the Internet is a network of information, a blockchain is a network of value and of trust. That is, items of value can be exchanged in a secure and trusted manner. Blockchain is more than a database; it is a new way to process, store, share, and search information. Blockchain, and how it works, is discussed in Chapters 1 and 11.

smart contract - A regular contract with the terms and agreed upon details built into the blockchain. Rules govern the blockchain's interaction with users. A smart contract can be automated and executed based on external triggers.

One use that was not profiled in Focus 1-3 is smart contracts. They are discussed briefly here as they are relevant to transaction processing. A **smart contract** is a regular contract with the terms and agreed upon details built into a blockchain. The organizations using the blockchain can establish the rules that govern the blockchain's interaction with its users. Among those rules would be who is authorized to review, mine, analyze, and audit the blockchain transaction details. These interactions can be automated and presented to users in data dashboards.

An organization can automate the execution of a smart contract based on external triggers. For example, sensors in a warehouse could recognize when ordered goods are delivered and the system could then trigger the payment of the agreed upon transaction amount. These transactions could also have the advantages described in Chapter 1 such as transparency, immutability, security, trust, and the elimination of third-party verification.

Enterprise Resource Planning (ERP) Systems

Traditionally, the AIS has been referred to as a transaction processing system because its only concern was financial data and accounting transactions. For example, when a sale took place, the AIS would record a journal entry showing only the date of the sale, a debit to either cash or accounts receivable, and a credit to sales. Other potentially useful nonfinancial information about the sale, such as the time of day that it occurred, would traditionally be collected and processed outside the AIS. Consequently, many organizations developed additional information systems to collect, process, store, and report information not contained in the AIS. Unfortunately, the existence of multiple systems creates numerous problems and inefficiencies. Often the same data must be captured and stored by more than one system, which not only results in redundancy across systems but also can lead to discrepancies if data are changed in one system but not in others. In addition, it is difficult to integrate data from the various systems.

enterprise resource planning (ERP) systems - Systems that integrate all aspects of an organization's activities—such as accounting, finance, marketing, human resources, manufacturing, inventory management—into one system. An ERP system is modularized; companies can purchase the individual modules that meet their specific needs. An ERP facilitates information flow among the company's various business functions and manages communications with outside stakeholders.

Enterprise resource planning (ERP) systems overcome these problems as they integrate all aspects of a company's operations with a traditional AIS. Most large and many medium-sized organizations use ERP systems to coordinate and manage their data, business processes, and resources. The ERP system collects, processes, and stores data and provides the information managers and external parties need to assess the company.

As shown in Figure 2-6, a properly configured ERP system uses a centralized database to share information across business processes and coordinate activities. This is important because an activity that is part of one business process often triggers a complex series of activities throughout many different parts of the organization. For example, a customer order may necessitate scheduling additional production to meet the increased demand. This may trigger an order to purchase more raw materials. It may also be necessary to schedule overtime or hire temporary help. Well-designed ERP systems provide management with easy access to up-to-date information about all of these activities in order to plan, control, and evaluate the organization's business processes more effectively.

ERP systems are modular, with each module using best business practices to automate a standard business process. This modular design allows businesses to add or delete modules as needed. Typical ERP modules include:

- Financial (general ledger and reporting system)—general ledger, accounts receivable, accounts payable, fixed assets, budgeting, cash management, and preparation of managerial reports and financial statements

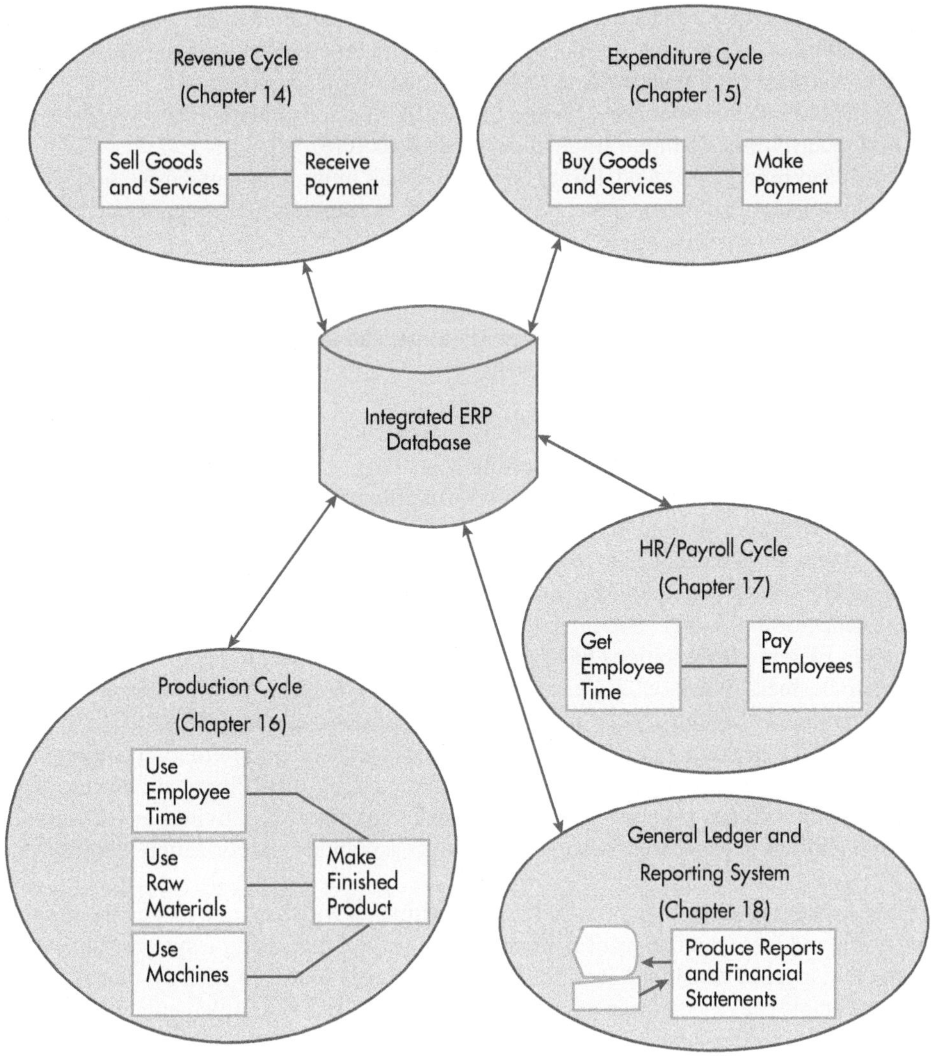

FIGURE 2-6
Integrated ERP System

- Human resources and payroll—human resources, payroll, employee benefits, training, time and attendance, benefits, and government reporting.
- Order to cash (revenue cycle)—sales order entry, shipping, inventory, cash receipts, commission calculation.
- Purchase to pay (disbursement cycle)—purchasing, receipt and inspection of inventory, inventory and warehouse management, and cash disbursements.
- Manufacturing (production cycle)—engineering, production scheduling, bill of materials, work-in-process, workflow management, quality control, cost management, and manufacturing processes and projects.
- Project management—costing, billing, time and expense, performance units, activity management.
- Customer relationship management—sales and marketing, commissions, service, customer contact, and call center support.
- System tools—tools for establishing master file data, specifying flow of information, access controls, and so on.

An ERP system, with its centralized database, provides significant advantages:

- An ERP provides an integrated, enterprise-wide, single view of the organization's data and financial situation. Storing all corporate information in a single database breaks down barriers between departments and streamlines the flow of information.
- Data input is captured or keyed once, rather than multiple times, as it is entered into different systems. Downloading data from one system to another is no longer needed.

- Management gains greater visibility into every area of the enterprise and greater monitoring capabilities. Employees are more productive and efficient because they can quickly gather data from both inside and outside their own department.
- The organization gains better access control. An ERP can consolidate multiple permissions and security models into a single data access structure.
- Procedures and reports are standardized across business units. This standardization can be especially valuable with mergers and acquisitions because an ERP system can replace the different systems with a single, unified system.
- Customer service improves because employees can quickly access orders, available inventory, shipping information, and past customer transaction details.
- Manufacturing plants receive new orders in real time, and the automation of manufacturing processes leads to increased productivity.

ERP systems also have significant disadvantages:

- Cost. ERP hardware, software, and consulting costs range from $50 to $500 million for a Fortune 500 company and upgrades can cost $50 million to $100 million. Midsized companies spend between $10 and $20 million.
- Amount of time required. It can take years to select and fully implement an ERP system, depending on business size, number of modules to be implemented, degree of customization, the scope of the change, and how well the customer takes ownership of the project. As a result, ERP implementations have a very high risk of project failure.
- Changes to business processes. Unless a company wants to spend time and money customizing modules, they must adapt to standardized business processes as opposed to adapting the ERP package to existing company processes. The failure to map current business processes to existing ERP software is a main cause of ERP project failures.
- Complexity. This comes from integrating many different business activities and systems, each having different processes, business rules, data semantics, authorization hierarchies, and decision centers.
- Resistance. Organizations that have multiple departments with separate resources, missions, profit and loss, and chains of command may believe that a single system has few benefits. It also takes considerable training and experience to use an ERP system effectively, and employee resistance is a major reason why many ERP implementations do not succeed. It is not easy to convince employees to change how they do their jobs, train them in new procedures, master the new system, and persuade them to share sensitive information. Resistance, and the blurring of company boundaries, can cause problems with employee morale, accountability, and lines of responsibility.

Reaping the potential benefits of ERP systems and mitigating their disadvantages requires conscious effort and involvement by top management. Top management's commitment to and support for the necessary changes greatly increase the chances of success.

Because ERP systems are complex and expensive, choosing one is not an easy task. In doing so, you must take great care to ensure that the ERP system has a module for every critical company process and that you are not paying for software modules that you do not need. One way to choose a suitable system is to select a package designed for your industry. Although cost is a huge concern, buying too cheaply can cost more in the long run if the system does not meet your needs because modification costs can be quite high. You can minimize the risk of buying the wrong package by researching the best ERP vendors. There are many ERP vendors, the two largest being SAP and Oracle. Other leading vendors are The Sage Group, Microsoft, and Infor.

Because it is too difficult for most companies to implement ERP software by themselves, they often hire an ERP vendor or a consulting company to do it for them. These firms usually provide three types of services: consulting, customization, and support. For most midsized companies, implementation costs range from the list price of the ERP user licenses to twice that amount. Large companies with multiple sites often spend three to five times the cost of the user license.

Because many processes automatically trigger additional actions in other modules, proper configuration is essential. This requires a sound understanding of all major business processes and their interactions so they can be defined. Examples include setting up cost/profit centers, credit approval policies, and purchase approval rules. In the configuration process, companies balance the way they want the system to operate with the way it lets them operate. If the way an ERP module operates is unacceptable, the company can modify the module. Alternatively, it can use an existing system and build interfaces between it and the ERP system. Both options are time consuming, costly, and result in fewer system integration benefits. In addition, the more customized a system becomes, the more difficult it is to communicate with suppliers and customers. To make configuration easier, ERP vendors are developing built-in "configuration" tools to address most customers' needs for system changes.

The importance of sound internal controls in an ERP cannot be overstated. The integrated nature of ERP systems means that unless every data item is validated and checked for accuracy at the time of initial entry, errors will automatically propagate throughout the system. Thus, data entry controls and access controls are essential. Most managers and employees see and have access to only a small portion of the system. This segregation of duties provides sound internal control. It is important to separate responsibility for custody of assets, authorization of activities that affect those assets, and recording information about activities and the status of organizational assets.

Summary and Case Conclusion

Ashton is aware that Scott and Susan plan to open additional stores in the near future and want to develop a website to conduct business over the Internet. Based on this information, Ashton will select an accounting package that will satisfy S&S's current and anticipated future needs. The software should be able to take care of all data processing and data storage tasks. Ashton will also make sure the software can interface with the source data automation devices he wants to use to capture most data input. The software must be capable of producing a full set of financial reports and be flexible enough to produce other useful information the company will need to be successful. Finally, Ashton realized his next step would be to select the software and produce some documentation of how the system worked.

KEY TERMS

data processing cycle 32
source documents 32
turnaround documents 32
source data automation 33
general ledger 34
subsidiary ledger 34
control account 34
coding 34
sequence codes 34
block code 34
group codes 34
mnemonic codes 34
chart of accounts 35
general journal 36
specialized journal 36
audit trail 37
entity 38
attributes 38
field 38
record 38
data value 38
file 38
master file 38
transaction file 38
database 38
batch processing 39
real-time processing 39
documents 39
reports 40
query 41
smart contract 42
enterprise resource planning (ERP) systems 42

AIS in Action

CHAPTER QUIZ

1. Which of the following is NOT a step in the data processing cycle?
   a. data collection
   b. data input
   c. data storage
   d. data processing

2. All of the information (name, GPA, major, etc.) about a particular student is stored in the same
   a. file
   b. record
   c. attribute
   d. field

3. Which of the following would contain the total value of all inventory owned by an organization?
   a. source document
   b. general ledger
   c. cash budget

4. Which of the following is most likely to be a general ledger control account?
   a. accounts receivable
   b. petty cash
   c. prepaid rent
   d. retained earnings

5. Which of the following documents is most likely to be used in the expenditure cycle?
   a. sales orders
   b. credit memo
   c. receiving report
   d. job time ticket

6. Which of the following is LEAST likely to be a specialized journal?
   a. sales journal
   b. cash receipts journal
   c. prepaid insurance journal
   d. cash disbursements journal

7. How does the chart of accounts list general ledger accounts?
   a. alphabetical order
   b. chronological order
   c. size order
   d. the order in which they appear in financial statements

8. Which of the following is NOT an advantage of an ERP system?
   a. better access control
   b. standardization of procedures and reports
   c. improved monitoring capabilities
   d. simplicity and reduced costs

9. Records of company data sent to an external party and then returned to the system as input are called
   a. turnaround documents
   b. source data automation documents
   c. source documents
   d. external input documents

10. Recording and processing information about a transaction at the time it takes place is referred to as which of the following?
    a. batch processing
    b. real-time processing
    c. captured transaction processing
    d. chart of accounts processing

DISCUSSION QUESTIONS

2.1 Table 2-1 lists some of the documents used in the revenue, expenditure, and human resources cycle. What kinds of input or output documents or forms would you find in the production (also referred to as the conversion) cycle?

2.2 With respect to the data processing cycle, explain the phrase "garbage in, garbage out." How can you prevent this from happening?

2.3 What kinds of documents are most likely to be turnaround documents? Do an Internet search to find the answer and example turnaround documents.

2.4 The data processing cycle in Figure 2-1 is an example of a basic process found throughout nature. Relate the basic input/process/store/output model to the functions of the human body.

2.5 Some individuals argue that accountants should focus on producing financial statements and leave the design and production of managerial reports to information systems specialists. What are the advantages and disadvantages of following this advice? To what extent should accountants be involved in producing reports that include more than just financial measures of performance? Why?

PROBLEMS

2.1 The chart of accounts must be tailored to an organization's specific needs. Discuss how the chart of accounts for the following organizations would differ from the one presented for S&S in Table 2-2.

a. university
b. bank
c. government unit (city or state)
d. manufacturing company
e. expansion of S&S to a chain of two stores

2.2 This chapter discusses the current and future uses of blockchain to process transactions and store data. Research the use of blockchain and find a non-cryptocurrency company that uses it. Also, research how people predict blockchain will be used to process transactions and store company data. Write a 3–4 page report about what you found about the current and future uses of blockchain.

2.3 An audit trail enables a person to trace a source document to its ultimate effect on the financial statements or work back from financial statement amounts to source documents. Describe in detail the audit trail for the following:

a. Purchases of inventory
b. Sales of inventory
c. Employee payroll

2.4 This chapter discusses the use of smart contracts. Research their use and write a 3–4 page report that describes one or more companies that use them. Include how the smart contract works as well as its advantages and disadvantages. Also, explain how people are predicting that smart contracts will evolve and how they will be used in the future.

2.5 Match the following terms with their definitions.

Term	Definition
___ 1. attribute	a. Contains summary-level data for every asset, liability, equity, revenue, and expense account
___ 2. audit trail	b. Items numbered consecutively to account for all items; missing items cause a gap in the numerical sequence
___ 3. batch processing	c. Path of a transaction through a data processing system from point of origin to final output, or backward from final output to point of origin
___ 4. block code	d. List of general ledger account numbers; allows transaction data to be coded, classified, and entered into proper accounts; facilitates preparation of financial statements and reports
___ 5. chart of accounts	e. Contents of a specific field, such as "George" in a name field
___ 6. coding	f. Portion of a data record that contains the data value for a particular attribute, like a cell in a spreadsheet
___ 7. control account	g. Company data sent to an external party and then returned to the system as input

____ 8. data processing cycle	h. Used to record infrequent or nonroutine transactions
____ 9. data value	i. Characteristics of interest that need to be stored
____ 10. database	j. Steps a company must follow to efficiently and effectively process data about its transactions
____ 11. entity	k. Something about which information is stored
____ 12. field	l. Stores cumulative information about an organization; like a ledger in a manual AIS
____ 13. general journal	m. Contains detailed data for any general ledger account with many individual subaccounts
____ 14. general ledger	n. Contains records of individual business transactions that occur during a specific time period
____ 15. group code	o. Updating each transaction as it occurs
____ 16. master file	p. Devices that capture transaction data in machine-readable form at the time and place of their origin
____ 17. mnemonic code	q. Used to record large numbers of repetitive transactions
____ 18. real-time processing	r. Set of interrelated, centrally coordinated files
____ 19. record	s. Two or more subgroups of digits used to code items
____ 20. sequence code	t. Updating done periodically, such as daily
____ 21. source data automation	u. Systematic assignment of numbers or letters to items to classify and organize them
____ 22. source documents	v. Letters and numbers, derived from the item description, interspersed to identify items; usually easy to memorize
____ 23. specialized journal	w. Initial record of a transaction that takes place; usually recorded on preprinted forms or formatted screens
____ 24. subsidiary ledger	x. Fields containing data about entity attributes, like a row in a spreadsheet
____ 25. transaction file	y. Sets of numbers reserved for specific categories of data
____ 26. turnaround documents	z. The general ledger account corresponding to a subsidiary ledger, where the sum of all subsidiary ledger entries should equal the amount in the general ledger account

2.6 For each of the following scenarios, identify which data processing method (batch or real-time) would be the most appropriate.

a. Query the database to accumulate the day's production costs for a single automobile part.
b. Identify and order a replacement drill bit broken during production.
c. Make an airline reservation.
d. Prepare a local utility's customer bills.

e. Prepare a bank deposit for customer checks received in the mail.
f. Process an order through an e-commerce website.
g. Process biweekly payroll checks.
h. Register for a university course.
i. Select and purchase tickets for a movie.
j. Take a customer order.
k. Make monthly customer payments.
l. Update inventory quantities for fast-moving inventory.

2.7 On their websites, you will find several online demonstrations for the SAP and Oracle ERP systems. Visit these websites and explore their content by doing the following:
a. Search the SAP site for corporate videos, and watch two of them. Explore the industries, services, solutions, and platforms that SAP offers. Read several of the articles, such as the ones about customer successes.
b. Explore the Oracle website just as you explored the SAP site.

REQUIRED

After viewing the websites, and based on your reading of the chapter, write a two-page paper that describes how an ERP can connect and integrate the revenue, expenditure, human resources/payroll, and financing cycles of a business.

2.8 Which of the following actions update a master file and which would be stored as a record in a transaction file?
a. Update customer address change
b. Update unit pricing information
c. Record daily sales
d. Record payroll checks
e. Change employee pay rates
f. Record production variances
g. Record sales commissions
h. Change employee office location
i. Update accounts payable balance
j. Change customer credit limit
k. Change vendor payment discount terms
l. Record purchases

2.9 You were hired to assist Ashton Fleming in designing an accounting system for S&S. Ashton has developed a list of the journals, ledgers, reports, and documents that he thinks S&S needs (see Table 2-4). He asks you to complete the following tasks:
a. Specify what data you think should be collected on each of the following four documents: sales invoice, purchase order, receiving report, employee time card.
b. Design a report to manage inventory.
c. Design a report to assist in managing credit sales and cash collections.
d. Visit a local office supply store and identify what types of journals, ledgers, and blank forms for various documents (sales invoices, purchase orders, etc.) are available. Describe how easily they could be adapted to meet S&S's needs.

2.10 Answer the following 10 multiple choice questions.

1. Which of the following statements is (are) true?
a. Well-designed documents and screens improve accuracy and completeness by providing instructions or prompts about what data to collect.
b. Online batch processing is where transaction data are entered, edited, and processed as they occur.
c. ERP implementation costs for large companies with multiple sites are usually about half the cost of the ERP user license.
d. In an ERP system, data entry controls such as validating data items and checking them for accuracy at the time of initial entry are not needed.
e. Data in ledgers is organized logically using coding techniques that assign numbers or letters to items to classify and organize them.

TABLE 2-4 Documents, Journals, and Ledgers for S&S

Title	Purpose
Documents	
Sales Invoice	Record cash and credit sales of merchandise
Service Invoice	Record sales of repair services
Delivery Ticket	Record delivery of merchandise to customers
Monthly Statement	Inform customers of outstanding account balances
Credit Memo	Support adjustments to customer accounts for sales returns and allowances and sales discounts; also support write-off of uncollectible accounts
Purchase Order	Order merchandise from vendors
Receiving Report	Record receipt of merchandise from vendors, indicating both quantity and condition of items received
Time Card	Record time worked by employees
Specialized Journals	
Sales	Record all credit sales
Cash Receipts	Record cash sales, payments from customers, and other cash receipts
Purchases	Record all purchases from vendors
Cash Disbursements	Record all cash disbursements
General Journal	Record infrequent, nonroutine transactions; also record adjusting and closing entries
Subsidiary Ledgers	
Accounts Receivable	Maintain details about amounts due from customers
Accounts Payable	Maintain details about amounts due to vendors
Inventory	Maintain details about each inventory item
Fixed Assets	Maintain details about each piece of equipment and other fixed assets
General Ledger	Maintain details about all major asset, liability, equity, revenue, and expense accounts

2. Which of the following statements is (are) true?
   a. With sequence codes, items are numbered consecutively to account for all items, and missing items cause a gap in the numerical sequence.
   b. The data capture or input process is usually triggered by a top management decision.
   c. Updating done periodically, such as daily or weekly, is referred to as batch processing.
   d. Cumulative accounting information is stored in general and subsidiary journals.
   e. Computers store data in a field; the fields containing data about entity attributes constitute a record.

3. Which of the following statements is (are) true?
   a. A chart of accounts facilitates preparing financial statements because data stored in individual accounts can easily be summed for presentation.
   b. Repetitive and frequently used database queries are usually developed by users; one-time queries are usually developed by information systems specialists.
   c. A database query can provide the information needed to deal with problems and questions that need rapid action or answers.
   d. A journal entry shows the accounts and amounts to be debited and credited.
   e. Transaction files are permanent and must be maintained for several years for backup purposes.

4. Which of the following statements is (are) true?
   a. A group code is derived from the description of the item and is usually easy to memorize.
   b. Using source data automation or well-designed turnaround documents and data entry screens helps ensure captured data are accurate and complete.

   c. It is usually best to let a user determine what data to input rather than have data input screens list the data the user needs to enter.
   d. If the sum of all subsidiary ledger account balances does not equal its general ledger control account balance, a recording error has occurred.
   e. Real-time processing updates transactions as they occur, helping ensure stored information is current and useful in making decisions.

5. Which of the following statements is (are) true?
   a. With mnemonic codes, blocks of numbers are reserved for specific categories of data.
   b. Input controls are improved by using pre-numbered source documents or by the system automatically assigning a sequential number to each transaction.
   c. In an integrated ERP system, undetected data entry errors can automatically propagate throughout the system.
   d. As ERP modules do not automatically trigger additional actions in other modules, it is less important to understand business processes and their interactions.
   e. A purchase to pay ERP module facilitates production scheduling, work-in-process, quality control, cost management, and manufacturing processes.

6. Which of the following statements is (are) true?
   a. Data is one of a company's most important resources but to function properly most organizations do not have to have the data readily and easily accessible.
   b. Turnaround documents are company output sent to an external party and returned as an input document.
   c. Each type of entity possesses the same set of attributes or characteristics of interest that are stored, but the specific data values for those attributes will differ depending on the entity.
   d. Reaping the potential benefits of ERP systems and mitigating their disadvantages requires conscious effort and involvement by top management.
   e. Real-time data processing is almost always cheaper and more efficient than batch processing.

7. Which of the following statements is (are) true?
   a. Source data automation devices capture transaction data in paper form at the time and place of their origin.
   b. Master files are permanent and exist across fiscal periods; individual master file records may change frequently.
   c. General ledgers are often used for accounts receivable, inventory, fixed assets, and accounts payable.
   d. If an ERP system does not meet your needs, it can almost always be inexpensively modified to meet your unique needs.
   e. When choosing an ERP system, make sure it has a module for every critical company process and you are not paying for modules you do not need.

8. Which of the following statements is (are) true?
   a. Documents are records of transaction or other company data that can be printed out or stored as electronic images in a computer.
   b. Transaction data are almost always recorded in a ledger before they are entered into a journal.
   c. Since batch processing data are current and accurate only immediately after processing, it is used for applications that do not need frequent updating.
   d. ERP systems are not effective in integrating non-financial company operations with a traditional accounting system.
   e. Well-designed screens improve accuracy and completeness by using checkoff boxes or pull-down menus to present the available options.

9. Which of the following statements is (are) true?
   a. A transaction file contains records of individual business transactions and is similar to a general ledger in a manual AIS.

b. To ensure credit sales policies are followed, the system can be programmed to check a customer's credit limit and payment history.
c. Use of pre-numbered documents makes it harder to verify that all transactions have been recorded and that none has been misplaced.
d. An ERP system uses a centralized database to share information across business processes and coordinate activities.
e. It is difficult for an ERP system to provide management with the up-to-date information needed to plan, control, and evaluate an organization's business.

10. Which of the following statements is (are) true?
a. The need for reports should be periodically assessed because they are often prepared long after they are needed—wasting time, money, and resources.
b. An audit trail is a transaction path through a data processing system from point of origin to final output, but not backward from final output to point of origin.
c. Accountants and systems developers do not need to understand how data are captured, organized, stored, processed, or accessed.
d. An AIS has traditionally been referred to as a transaction processing system because its only concern was financial data and accounting transactions.
e. A master file, like a ledger in a manual AIS, stores cumulative information about an organization.

CASE 2-1 Bar Harbor Blueberry Farm

The Bar Harbor Blueberry Farm is a family-owned, 200-acre farm that grows and sells blueberries to grocery stores, blueberry wholesalers, and small roadside stands. Bar Harbor has 25 full-time employees and hires 150 to 200 seasonal workers for the harvest.

For the past six summers, you have picked berries for Bar Harbor. When you graduated, you were hired as the full-time accountant/office manager. Until now, Bar Harbor kept most of its accounting records in a big file box. Jack Phillips, the owner, would like a more organized approach to the farm's accounting records. He has asked you to establish a proper set of books. You decide to start by establishing appropriate journals and ledgers for these transactions.

Presented below are a set of vendor invoices and a few partially completed journals and ledgers. Your job is to record these transactions and update the appropriate ledgers. Be sure to leave a proper audit trail. You may also use Excel, Great Plains, Peachtree, QuickBooks, or another accounting software package of your choosing to complete this problem.

VENDOR INVOICES

DATE	SUPPLIER INVOICE	SUPPLIER NAME	SUPPLIER ADDRESS	AMOUNT
March 7	AJ34	Bud's Soil Prep	PO Box 34	$2,067.85
March 11	14568	Osto Farmers Supply	45 Main	$ 67.50
March 14	893V	Whalers Fertilizer	Route 34	$5,000.00
March 21	14699	Osto Farmers Supply	45 Main	$3,450.37
March 21	10102	IFM Wholesale	587 Longview	$4,005.00
March 24	10145	IFM Wholesale	587 Longview	$ 267.88

PURCHASES JOURNAL

PAGE 1

DATE	SUPPLIER	SUPPLIER INVOICE	ACCOUNT NUMBER	POST REF	AMOUNT
March 7	Bud's Soil Prep	AJ34			$2,067.85

PAGE 1

DATE	SUPPLIER	SUPPLIER INVOICE	ACCOUNT NUMBER	POST REF	AMOUNT

GENERAL LEDGER

ACCOUNTS PAYABLE — **ACCOUNT NUMBER: 300**

DATE	DESCRIPTION	POST REF	DEBIT	CREDIT	BALANCE
March 1	Balance Forward				$18,735.55

GENERAL LEDGER

PURCHASES — **ACCOUNT NUMBER: 605**

DATE	DESCRIPTION	POST REF	DEBIT	CREDIT	BALANCE
March 1	Balance Forward				$54,688.49

ACCOUNTS PAYABLE SUBSIDIARY LEDGER

ACCOUNT NO: 23 — **BUD'S SOIL PREP** — **PO BOX 34** — **TERMS: 2/10, NET 30**

DATE	DESCRIPTION	DEBIT	CREDIT	BALANCE

ACCOUNT NO: 24 — **OSTO FARMERS SUPPLY** — **45 MAIN** — **TERMS: 2/10, NET 30**

DATE	DESCRIPTION	DEBIT	CREDIT	BALANCE

ACCOUNT NO: 36 — **WHALERS FERTILIZER** — **ROUTE 34** — **TERMS: 2/10, NET 30**

DATE	DESCRIPTION	DEBIT	CREDIT	BALANCE

ACCOUNT NO: 38 — **IFM WHOLESALE** — **587 LONGVIEW** — **TERMS: 2/10, NET 30**

DATE	DESCRIPTION	DEBIT	CREDIT	BALANCE

CASE 2-2 SDC

Ollie Mace is the controller of SDC, an automotive parts manufacturing firm. Its four major operating divisions are heat treating, extruding, small parts stamping, and machining. Last year's sales from each division ranged from $150,000 to $3 million. Each division is physically and managerially independent, except for the constant surveillance of Sam Dilley, the firm's founder.

The AIS for each division evolved according to the needs and abilities of its accounting staff. Mace is the first controller to have responsibility for overall financial management. Dilley wants Mace to improve the AIS before he retires in a few years so that it will be easier to monitor division performance. Mace decides to redesign the financial reporting system to include the following features:

- It should give managers uniform, timely, and accurate reports of business activity. Monthly reports should be uniform across divisions and be completed by the fifth day of the following month to provide enough time to take corrective actions to affect the next month's performance. Company-wide financial reports should be available at the same time.
- Reports should provide a basis for measuring the return on investment for each division. Thus, in addition to revenue and expense accounts, reports should show assets assigned to each division.
- The system should generate meaningful budget data for planning and decision-making purposes. Budgets should reflect managerial responsibility and show costs for major product groups.

Mace believes that a new chart of accounts is required to accomplish these goals. He wants to divide financial statement accounts into major categories, such as assets, liabilities, and equity. He does not foresee a need for more than 10 control accounts within each of these categories. From his observations to date, 100 subsidiary accounts are more than adequate for each control account.

No division has more than five major product groups. Mace foresees a maximum of six cost centers within any product group, including both the operating and nonoperating groups. He views general divisional costs as a non-revenue-producing product group. Mace estimates that 44 expense accounts plus 12 specific variance accounts would be adequate.

REQUIRED

Design a chart of accounts for SDC. Explain how you structured the chart of accounts to meet the company's needs and operating characteristics. Keep total account code length to a minimum, while still satisfying all of Mace's desires. *(CMA Examination, adapted)*

AIS in Action Solutions

QUIZ KEY

1. Which of the following is NOT a step in the data processing cycle?

▶ **a.** data collection [Correct. Data collection is a part of data input and is therefore not a step in the data processing cycle.]

b. data input [Incorrect. Data input is the first step in the data processing cycle. This is the step where data is captured, collected, and entered into the system.]

c. data storage [Incorrect. Data storage is the data processing cycle step where data is stored for future use by the company.]

d. data processing [Incorrect. Data processing is the data processing cycle step where stored data is updated with new input data.]

2. All of the information (name, GPA, major, etc.) about a particular student is stored in the same ________________.
- a. file [Incorrect. A file is designed to include information about many students.]
- ▶ **b.** record [Correct. A record should include all information maintained by the system about a particular entity, such as a student.]
- c. attribute [Incorrect. An attribute is a descriptor or a characteristic of an entity—in this example, the student's major is an attribute.]
- d. field [Incorrect. A field represents a data storage space—in this example, an accounting student would have "Accounting" stored in the major field.]

3. Which of the following would contain the total value of all inventory owned by an organization?
- a. source document [Incorrect. A source document contains data about a particular event or transaction.]
- ▶ **b.** general ledger [Correct. The general ledger maintains summary information on inventory and every other general ledger account.]
- c. cash budget [Incorrect. A cash budget provides information only on projected cash inflows and outflows.]

4. Which of the following is most likely to be a general ledger control account?
- ▶ **a.** accounts receivable [Correct. Accounts receivable is typically made up of many individual customer accounts maintained in a subsidiary ledger. The total of all individual customer accounts in the subsidiary ledger is maintained in the accounts receivable control account in the general ledger.]
- b. petty cash [Incorrect. Petty cash is made up of only one account.]
- c. prepaid rent [Incorrect. A subsidiary ledger containing multiple prepaid rent accounts is usually not necessary.]
- d. retained earnings [Incorrect. Retained earnings is typically comprised of only one account.]

5. Which of the following documents is most likely to be used in the expenditure cycle?
- a. sales order [Incorrect. The sales order is a revenue cycle document that captures the information about a customer's order.]
- b. credit memo [Incorrect. A credit memo is a revenue cycle document used to give a credit to a customer for damaged or returned goods.]
- ▶ **c.** receiving report [Correct. A receiving report is an expenditure cycle document used to record the receipt of goods from suppliers. Companies pay their suppliers based on the goods received and recorded on the receiving report.]
- d. job time ticket [Incorrect. A job time ticket is a production cycle document used to record time spent on specific jobs.]

6. Which of the following is LEAST likely to be a specialized journal?
- a. sales journal [Incorrect. A specialized journal is used to record large numbers of repetitive transactions. Most companies have a large number of sales.]
- b. cash receipts journal [Incorrect. A specialized journal is used to record large numbers of repetitive transactions. Most companies have a large number of cash receipts.]
- ▶ **c.** prepaid insurance journal [Correct. A specialized journal is used to record large numbers of repetitive transactions, and most companies have very few prepaid insurance transactions.]
- d. cash disbursements journal [Incorrect. A specialized journal is used to record large numbers of repetitive transactions. Most companies have a large number of cash disbursements.]

7. How does the chart of accounts list general ledger accounts?
   a. alphabetical order [Incorrect. General ledger accounts are listed in the order in which they appear in the financial statements, not in alphabetical order.]
   b. chronological order [Incorrect. General ledger accounts are listed in the order in which they appear in the financial statements, not according to the date they were created.]
   c. size order [Incorrect. General ledger accounts are listed in the order in which they appear in the financial statements, not according to their size.]
▶ **d.** the order in which they appear in financial statements [Correct.]

8. Which of the following is NOT an advantage of an ERP system?
   a. better access control [Incorrect. Better access control is an advantage because an ERP can consolidate multiple permissions and security models into a single data access structure.]
   b. standardization of procedures and reports [Incorrect. Standardization of procedures and reports is an advantage because procedures and reports can be standardized across business units, and in mergers and acquisitions they can replace the different systems with a single, unified system.]
   c. improved monitoring capabilities [Incorrect. Improved monitoring capabilities are an advantage because management gains greater visibility into every area of the enterprise that allows them to better monitor the organization.]
▶ **d.** simplicity and reduced costs [Correct. ERP systems are quite complex and costly; they do not offer the advantages of simplicity and reduced costs.]

9. Records of company data sent to an external party and then returned to the system as input are called ________________.

▶ **a.** turnaround documents [Correct. For example, a utility bill is sent to a customer, who then returns the bill with payment.]

b. source data automation documents [Incorrect. Source data automation is the capturing of input data in machine-readable form.]

c. source documents [Incorrect. Source documents collect data about business activities.]

d. external input documents [Incorrect. These documents originate from external sources.]

10. Recording and processing information about a transaction at the time it takes place is referred to as which of the following?

a. batch processing [Incorrect. Batch processing involves processing transactions in groups or batches all at the same time.]

▶ **b.** real-time processing [Correct. Real-time processing involves processing transactions as they occur.]

c. captured transaction processing [Incorrect. This is not a recognized transaction processing method.]

d. chart of accounts processing [Incorrect. The chart of accounts, although typically updated every so often, is not a transaction processing method.]

CHAPTER

3

Systems Documentation Techniques

LEARNING OBJECTIVES

After studying this chapter, you should be able to:

1. Prepare and use business process diagrams to understand, evaluate, and document information systems.
2. Prepare and use flowcharts to understand, evaluate, and document information systems.
3. Prepare and use data flow diagrams to understand, evaluate, and document information systems.

INTEGRATIVE CASE S&S

What a hectic few months it has been for Ashton Fleming! He helped S&S get started, helped get S&S through its weeklong grand opening, and was swamped with processing all the transactions from the highly successful grand opening. Because of its rapid growth, S&S has outgrown the initial rudimentary accounting information system (AIS) that Ashton selected. Lacking time and expertise, Ashton has engaged Computer Applications (CA), a systems consulting firm, to help S&S select and install a new and more powerful AIS.

During Ashton's first meeting with Kimberly Sierra, CA's manager, she asked about S&S's system requirements and management's expectations. Ashton had yet to think through these issues, so he could not answer her specifically. When she asked how S&S's system worked, Ashton plunged into a discussion about the use of various company documents, but Kimberly seemed unable to absorb his detailed explanations. Ashton thought that part of his discussion was helpful, but overall it was irrelevant to the issue at hand.

Ashton came away impressed by CA and Kimberly. He also realized the need to understand S&S's information requirements more clearly. From his days as an auditor, Ashton knew the value of good system documentation in helping unfamiliar users both understand and evaluate a system. Good system documentation would be a big help to him and Kimberly, as well as to Scott and Susan as they evaluate the current and proposed systems.

After sharing his conclusions with Susan and Scott, they enthusiastically approved Ashton's plan to document the current and proposed systems. They supported his taking a

Rawpixel/123RF

leadership role in moving toward a new system and were especially interested in diagrams or charts that would document their system and help them understand and evaluate it.

Introduction

documentation - Narratives, flowcharts, diagrams, and other written materials that explain how a system works.

narrative description - Written, step-by-step explanation of system components and how they interact.

Documentation explains how a system works, including the who, what, when, where, why, and how of data entry, data processing, data storage, information output, and system controls. Popular means of preparing human-readable documentation include diagrams, flowcharts, tables, and other graphical representations of data and information. These are supplemented by a **narrative description** of the system, a written step-by-step explanation of system components and interactions.

Documentation tools are important on the following levels:

1. At a minimum, you must be able to *read* documentation to determine how a system works.
2. You may need to *evaluate* documentation to identify internal control strengths and weaknesses and recommend improvements as well as to determine if a proposed system meets the company's needs.
3. More skill is needed to *prepare* documentation that shows how an existing or proposed system operates.

This chapter discusses the following human-readable documentation tools, which are used throughout this text:

1. ***Business process diagrams (BPD)***, which are graphical descriptions of the business processes used by a company.
2. ***Flowchart***, which is a graphical description of a system. There are several types of flow charts, including:
   a. ***Document flowchart***, which shows the flow of documents and information between departments or areas of responsibility.
   b. ***System flowchart***, which shows the relationship among the input, processing, and output in an information system.
   c. ***Program flowchart***, which shows the sequence of logical operations a computer performs as it executes a program.
3. ***Data flow diagram (DFD)***, a graphical description of data sources, data flows, transformation processes, data storage, and data destinations.

Accountants use documentation techniques extensively. Auditing standards require that independent auditors understand the automated and manual internal control procedures an entity uses. One good way to gain this understanding is to use business process models or flowcharts to document a system because such graphic portrayals more readily reveal internal control weaknesses and strengths.

The Sarbanes-Oxley Act (SOX) of 2002 requires an internal control report in public company annual reports that (1) states that management is responsible for establishing and maintaining an adequate internal control structure and (2) assesses the effectiveness of the company's internal controls. SOX also specifies that a company's auditor must evaluate management's assessment of the company's internal control structures and attest to its accuracy. The auditor's attestation should include a specific notation about significant defects or material noncompliance found during internal control tests. This means that both the company and its auditors have to document and test the company's internal controls. To do so, they must be able to prepare, evaluate, and read different types of documentation, such as business process models and flowcharts.

Documentation tools are also used extensively in the systems development process. In addition, the team members who develop information systems applications often change, and documentation tools help the new team members get up to speed quickly.

Documentation is easier to prepare and revise when a software package is used. Once a few basic commands are mastered, users can quickly and easily prepare, store, revise, and print presentation-quality documentation.

In addition to the human-readable documentation discussed above, there are different ways to prepare machine-readable system and process documentation. As explained in Chapters1 and 18, XBRL is a machine-readable documentation format that can be read and processed by a computer. XBRL helps the many different types of business information systems and stock exchanges around the world to communicate with each other.

XBRL data is machine readable and can be exchanged, validated, and analyzed automatically but is not human readable. The HTML language allows users to display data in Internet browsers, but it is not machine readable until someone retypes information, or copies and pastes it, into a computer system. A recent iteration of XBRL is Inline eXtensible Business Reporting Language (iXBRL), which reconciles HTML and XBRL data standards and makes traditional XBRL information readable from any web browser, just like an HTML document. In other words, iXBRL combines XBRL and HTML documents to create a single document that is both human readable and machine readable.

In the past, there were quality issues with XBRL corporate filings, resulting in the SEC and others not using XBRL data as much as anticipated. The SEC adopted iXBRL, which is an international standard, in 2018. Requiring the submission of financial statements of public companies and mutual funds in the iXBR format has produced higher quality data, which has resulted in the data gaining wider use by regulators, investors, and analysts. Chapter 18 discusses iXBRL in more depth.

Blockchain, discussed in Chapters 1, 2, and 11, is also a form of machine-readable documentation. Blockchain data is transparent in that transaction details can be seen by blockchain users. This includes names, amounts, date, time, who did what, when they did it, and the history of the item since it was entered in blockchain. Not only is that history transparent, it is stored and verified by all network participants and frequently reconciled, providing increased data accuracy and consistency. As both sides of a transaction are stored in single source, only one set of books is needed, providing an improved level of trust.

Business Process Diagrams

business process diagram (BPD) - A visual way to describe the different steps or activities in a business process.

A **business process diagram (BPD)** is a visual way to describe the different steps or activities in a business process. For example, there are many activities in the revenue cycle. Among them are receiving an order, checking customer credit, verifying inventory availability, and confirming customer order acceptance. Likewise, there are multiple activities involved in the expenditure cycle. Among them are shipping the goods ordered, billing the customer, and collecting customer payments. All of these activities can be shown on a BPD to give the reader an easily understood pictorial view of what takes place in a business process.

While BPDs can describe interactions within an entity as well as interactions between entities, the BPDs in the textbook do not document the activities performed by external parties. Thus, a BPD for the revenue cycle will only describe the functions performed by the selling company and a BPD for the expenditure cycle only depicts the activities performed by the purchasing company.

The Business Process Modeling Initiative Notation Working Group established standards for drawing BPDs. There are many different symbols that can be used in drawing a BPD. The text uses only a limited set of those symbols, as shown in Figure 3-1, to produce easy to create and understand BPDs.

General guidelines for preparing good business process guidelines are presented in Focus 3-1. In the text, the emphasis on BPDs is less on obeying the rules governing their

Symbol	Name	Explanation
◯	Start/Begin	The start or beginning of a process is represented by a small circle.
◯	End	The end of a process is represented by a small **bolded** circle.
▭	Activity in a process	An activity in a process is represented by a rounded-edge rectangle. An explanation of the activity is placed inside the rectangle.
◇	Decision	A decision made during the process is represented by a diamond. An explanation of the decision is placed inside the symbol.
→	Flow	The flow of data or information is indicated by an arrow.
┈┈▶	Annotation information	Information that helps explain a business process is entered in the BPD and, if needed, a bolded dashed arrow is drawn from the explanation to the symbol.

FIGURE 3-1

Business Process Diagram Symbols

FOCUS 3-1 Guidelines for Preparing Business Process Diagrams

1. *Identify and understand the business processes.* Develop this understanding by observing organization business processes and data flows, observing and interviewing those involved in the business process, reading a narrative description of the system, or walking through system transactions. Identify departments, job functions, and external parties. Identify business processes, documents, data flows, and data processing procedures.

2. *Ignore certain items.* Like DFDs, BPDs depict what happens, but do not specify how (i.e., by means of what technology) a process activity occurs. Therefore, BPDs do not need to be revised every time the technology used to accomplish the activity is changed. Unlike flowcharts, you do not need to show the documents as they flow through the system or show where they are stored.

3. *Decide how much detail to include.* Like a DFD, varying levels of detail can be shown. A BPD can show only higher-level activities or those higher-level activities can be broken up into subactivities that show more details. If the BPD is drawn in sufficient detail, it is easy to evaluate whether duties are properly segregated by examining the duties performed in every row.

4. *Organize diagram.* BPDs usually consist of two columns and as many rows as needed to explain the process. The first column shows the different employees or departments involved in the business process. The second column shows the activities performed by the employee shown in the first column. Each row, referred to as a "swim lane," contains the activities performed by the indicated employee or department. BPDs depict the major steps in a process sequentially, reading from left to right and top to bottom.

5. *Enter each business process on the diagram.* Show where each business process begins and ends. Show each activity in the business process in the order it takes place and in the appropriate row, using the appropriate symbols. Write an appropriate description inside each symbol; most activity descriptions will start with an action verb (take order, ship goods, etc.). Add annotation information as appropriate to make the diagram more understandable. Use arrowheads on all data flow lines to show the direction of the flow.

6. *Draw a rough sketch of the BPD.* Be more concerned with capturing content than with making a perfect drawing. Few systems can be diagramed in a single draft. Review it with the people familiar with the system. Refine the BPD as needed until the business process is depicted accurately and the diagram is easily understood.

7. *Draw a final copy of the BPD.* Place the BPD name, date, and preparer's name on each page.

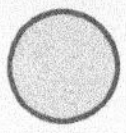

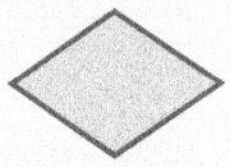

preparation and more on their clearly communicating the activities involved in the business process being depicted.

Ashton used the description of S&S's payroll processing procedure in Table 3-1 to identify five major data processing activities:

1. Updating the employee/payroll master file (first paragraph).
2. Handling employee compensation (second, fifth, and sixth paragraphs).
3. Generating management reports (third paragraph).
4. Paying taxes (fourth paragraph).
5. Posting entries to the general ledger (last paragraph).

The five activities and their data inflows and outflows are shown in Table 3-2.

Ashton prepared the BPD in Figure 3-2 to document payroll processing at S&S based on the narrative contained in Tables 3-1 and 3-2. You can practice creating a BPD by drawing one for the comprehensive problem, called Accuflow Cash Disbursements Process, at the end of the chapter quiz. You can then compare your diagram to the solution at the very end of the chapter. You can also read the detailed explanation of how the solution was prepared.

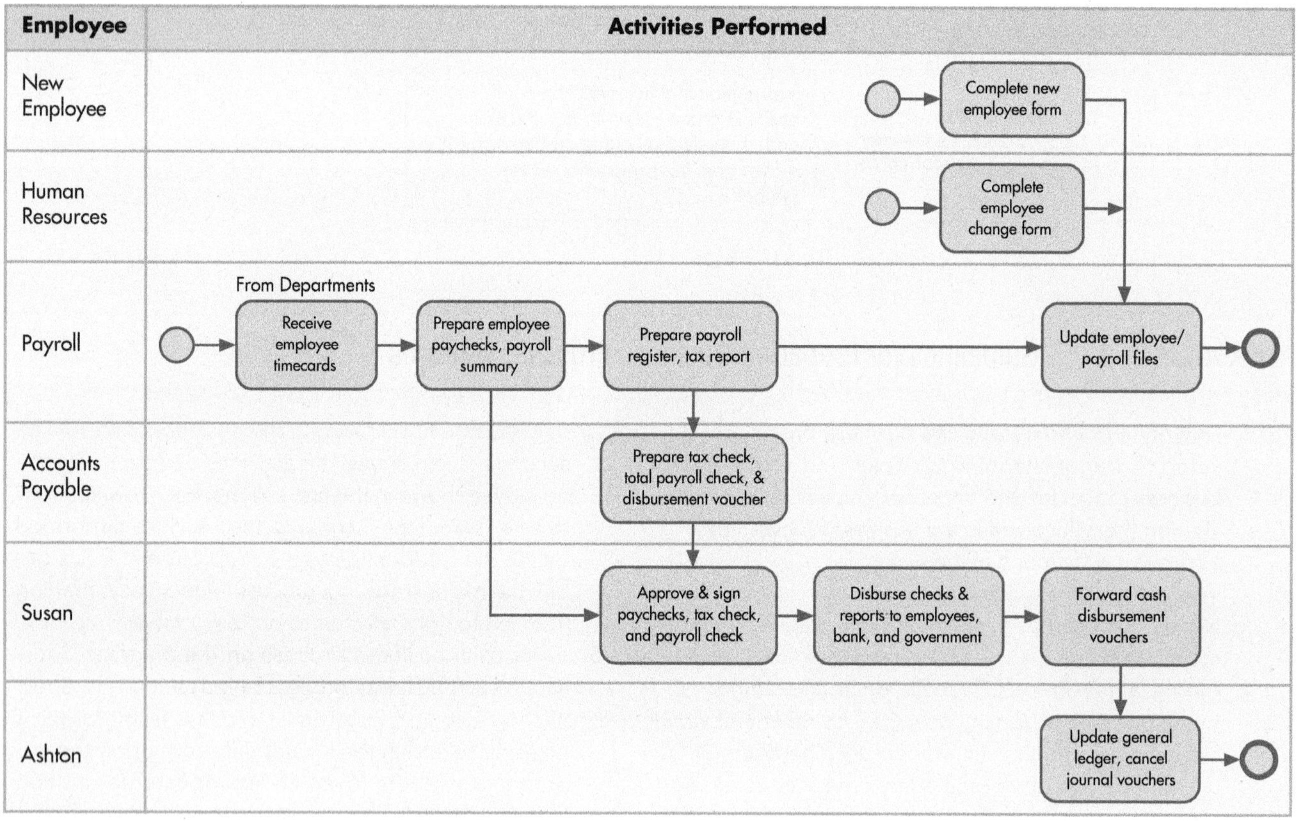

FIGURE 3-2
Business Process Diagram of Payroll Processing at S&S

TABLE 3-1 Narrative Description of Payroll Processing at S&S
When employees are hired, they complete a new-employee form. When a change to an employee's payroll status occurs, such as a raise or a change in the number of exemptions, the human resources department completes an employee change form. A copy of these forms is sent to payroll. These forms are used to create or update the records in the employee/payroll file and are then stored in the file. Employee records are stored alphabetically.

Some S&S employees are paid a salary, but most are hourly workers who record their time on time cards. At the end of each pay period, department managers send the time cards to the payroll department. The payroll clerk uses the time card data, data from the employee file (such as pay rate and annual salary), and the appropriate tax tables to prepare a two-part check for each employee. The clerk also prepares a two-part payroll register showing gross pay, deductions, and net pay for each employee. The clerk updates the employee file to reflect each employee's current earnings. The original copy of the employee paychecks is forwarded to Susan. The payroll register is forwarded to the accounts payable clerk. The time cards and the duplicate copies of the payroll register and paychecks are stored by date in the payroll file.

Every pay period, the payroll clerk uses the data in the employee/payroll file to prepare a payroll summary report for Susan so that she can control and monitor labor expenses. This report is forwarded to Susan, with the original copies of the employee paychecks.

Every month, the payroll clerk uses the data in the employee/payroll file to prepare a two-part tax report. The original is forwarded to the accounts payable clerk, and the duplicate is added to the tax records in the payroll file. The accounts payable clerk uses the tax report to prepare a two-part check for taxes and a two-part cash disbursements voucher. The tax report and the original copy of each document are forwarded to Susan. The duplicates are stored by date in the accounts payable file.

The accounts payable clerk uses the payroll register to prepare a two-part check for the total amount of the employee payroll and a two-part disbursements voucher. The original copy of each document is forwarded to Susan, and the payroll register and the duplicates are stored by date in the accounts payable file.

Susan reviews each packet of information she receives, approves it, and signs the checks. She forwards the cash disbursements vouchers to Ashton, the tax reports and payments to the appropriate governmental agency, the payroll check to the bank, and the employee checks to the employees. She files the payroll report chronologically.

Ashton uses the payroll tax and the payroll check cash disbursement vouchers to update the general ledger. He then cancels the journal voucher by marking it "posted" and files it numerically.

TABLE 3-2 Activities and Data Flows in Payroll Processing at S&S

Activities	Data Inputs	Data Outputs
Update employee/payroll file	New-employee form Employee change form	Updated employee/payroll file
Pay employees	Time cards Employee/payroll file Tax rates table	Employee checks Payroll register Updated employee/payroll file Payroll check Payroll cash disbursements voucher
Prepare reports	Employee/payroll file	Payroll report
Pay taxes	Employee/payroll file	Tax report Tax payment Payroll tax cash disbursements voucher Updated employee/payroll file
Update general ledger	Payroll tax cash disbursements voucher Payroll cash disbursements voucher	Updated general ledger

Flowcharts

A **flowchart** is a pictorial, analytical technique used to describe some aspect of an information system in a clear, concise, and logical manner. Flowcharts record how business processes are performed and how documents flow through the organization. They are also used to analyze how to improve business processes and document flows. Most flowcharts are drawn using a software program such as Visio, Word, Excel, or PowerPoint. Flowcharts use a standard set of symbols to describe pictorially the transaction processing procedures a company uses and the flow of data through a system. Flowcharting symbols are divided into four categories, as shown in Figure 3-3:

flowchart - An analytical technique that uses a standard set of symbols to describe pictorially some aspect of an IS in a clear, concise, and logical manner.

1. ***Input/output symbols*** show input to or output from a system.
2. ***Processing symbols*** show data processing, either electronically or by hand.
3. ***Storage symbols*** show where data is stored.
4. ***Flow and miscellaneous symbols*** indicate the flow of data, where flowcharts begin or end, where decisions are made, and how to add explanatory notes to flowcharts.

General guidelines for preparing good flowcharts are presented in Focus 3-2.

FIGURE 3-3
Common Flowcharting Symbols

Symbol	Name	Explanation
Input/OutputSymbols		
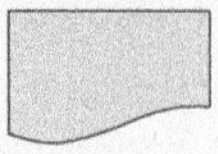	Document	An electronic or paper document or report
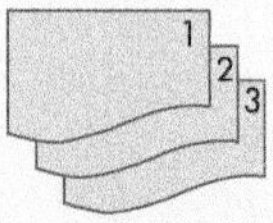	Multiple copies of one paper document	Illustrated by overlapping the document symbol and printing the document number on the face of the document in the upper right corner
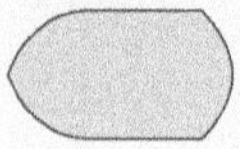	Electronic output	Information displayed by an electronic output device such as a terminal, monitor, or screen
	Electronic data entry	Electronic data entry device such as a computer, terminal, tablet, or phone
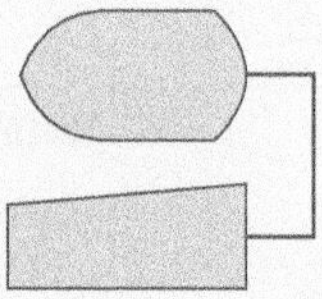	Electronic input and output device	The electronic data entry and output symbols are used together to show a device used for both
Processing Symbols		
	Computer processing	A computer-performed processing function; usually results in a change in data or information
	Manual operation	A processing operation performed manually
Storage Symbols		
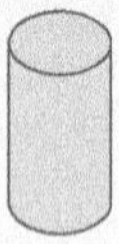	Database	Data stored electronically in a database
	Magnetic tape	Data stored on a magnetic tape; tapes are popular back-up storage mediums
	Paper document file	File of paper documents; letters indicate file-ordering sequence: N = numerically, A = alphabetically, D = by date
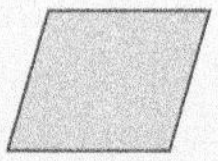	Journal/ledger	Paper-based accounting journals and ledgers

Symbol	Name	Explanation
Flow and Miscellaneous Symbols		
	Document or processing flow	Direction of processing or document flow; normal flow is down and to the right
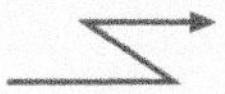	Communication link	Transmission of data from one geographic location to another via communication lines
	On-page connector	Connects the processing flow on the same page; its usage avoids lines crisscrossing a page
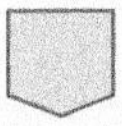	Off-page connector	An entry from, or an exit to, another page
	Terminal	A beginning, end, or point of interruption in a process; also used to indicate an external party
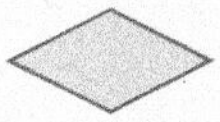	Decision	A decision-making step
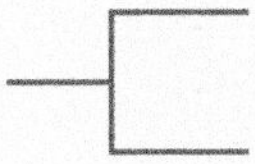	Annotation	Addition of descriptive comments or explanatory notes as clarification

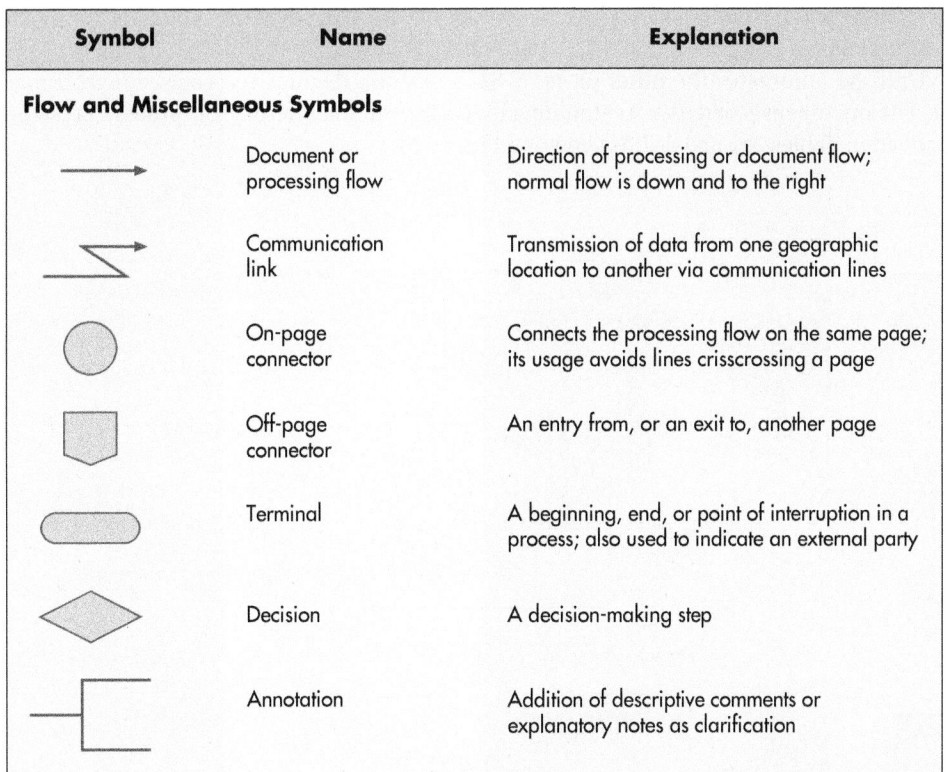

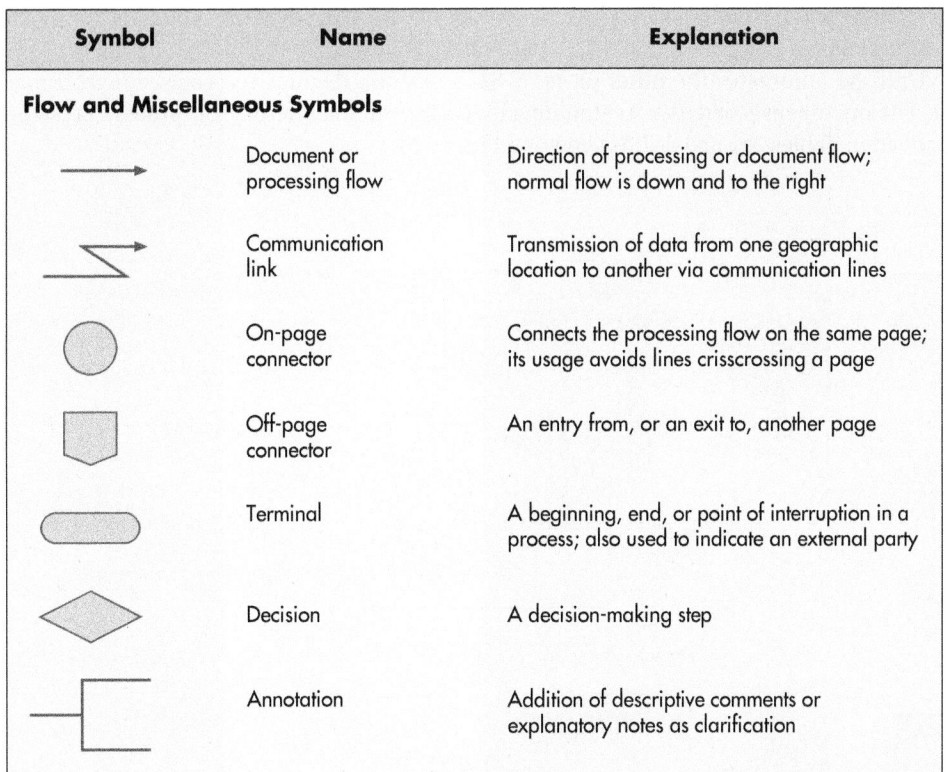

FIGURE 3-3
Continued

FOCUS 3-2 Guidelines for Preparing Flowcharts

1. *Understand the system.* Develop this understanding by interviewing users, developers, and management or having them complete a questionnaire; by reading a narrative description of the system; or by walking through system transactions.
2. *Identify the entities to be flowcharted.* Identify departments, job functions, and external parties. Identify business processes, documents, data flows, and data processing procedures.
3. *Organize flowchart.* Design the flowchart so that data flows from top to bottom and from left to right. Where appropriate, ensure that all procedures and processes are in proper order. Show where documents or processes originate, where data is processed, and where data is stored and sent. Show the final disposition of all documents to prevent loose ends that leave the reader dangling. Show data entered into or retrieved from a database as passing through a processing operation (a computer program) first. In document flowcharts, divide the flowchart into columns with labels.
4. *Clearly label all symbols.* Write a description of the source, input, process, output, or destination inside the symbol. Use arrowheads on all flow lines.
5. *Page connectors.* If a flowchart cannot fit on a single page, clearly number the pages and use off-page connectors to move from one page to another. Where desired, on-page connectors can be used to avoid excess flow lines and to produce a neat-looking page. Clearly label all connectors to avoid confusion.
6. *Draw a rough sketch of the flowchart.* Be more concerned with capturing content than with making a perfect drawing. Few systems can be flowcharted in a single draft. Review it with the people familiar with the system. Make sure all uses of flowcharting conventions are consistent.
7. *Draw a final copy of the flowchart.* Place the flowchart name, date, and preparer's name on each page.

TYPES OF FLOWCHARTS

Document flowcharts were developed to illustrate the flow of documents and data among areas of responsibility within an organization. They trace a document from its cradle to its grave, showing where each document originates, its distribution, its purpose, its disposition, and everything that happens as it flows through the system. A special type of flowchart, called an **internal control flowchart**, is used to describe, analyze, and evaluate internal controls. They are used to identify system weaknesses or inefficiencies, such as inadequate communication flows, insufficient segregation of

document flowcharts - Illustrate the flow of documents and data among areas of responsibility within an organization.

internal control flowchart - Used to describe, analyze, and evaluate internal controls, including identifying system strengths, weaknesses, and inefficiencies.

duties, unnecessary complexity in document flows, or procedures responsible for causing wasteful delays.

Until he automates the other parts of S&S, Ashton decides to process payroll manually. The document flowchart Ashton developed for the manual payroll process at S&S, as described in Tables 3-1 and 3-2, is shown in Figure 3-4.

FIGURE 3-4
Document Flowchart of Payroll Processing at S&S

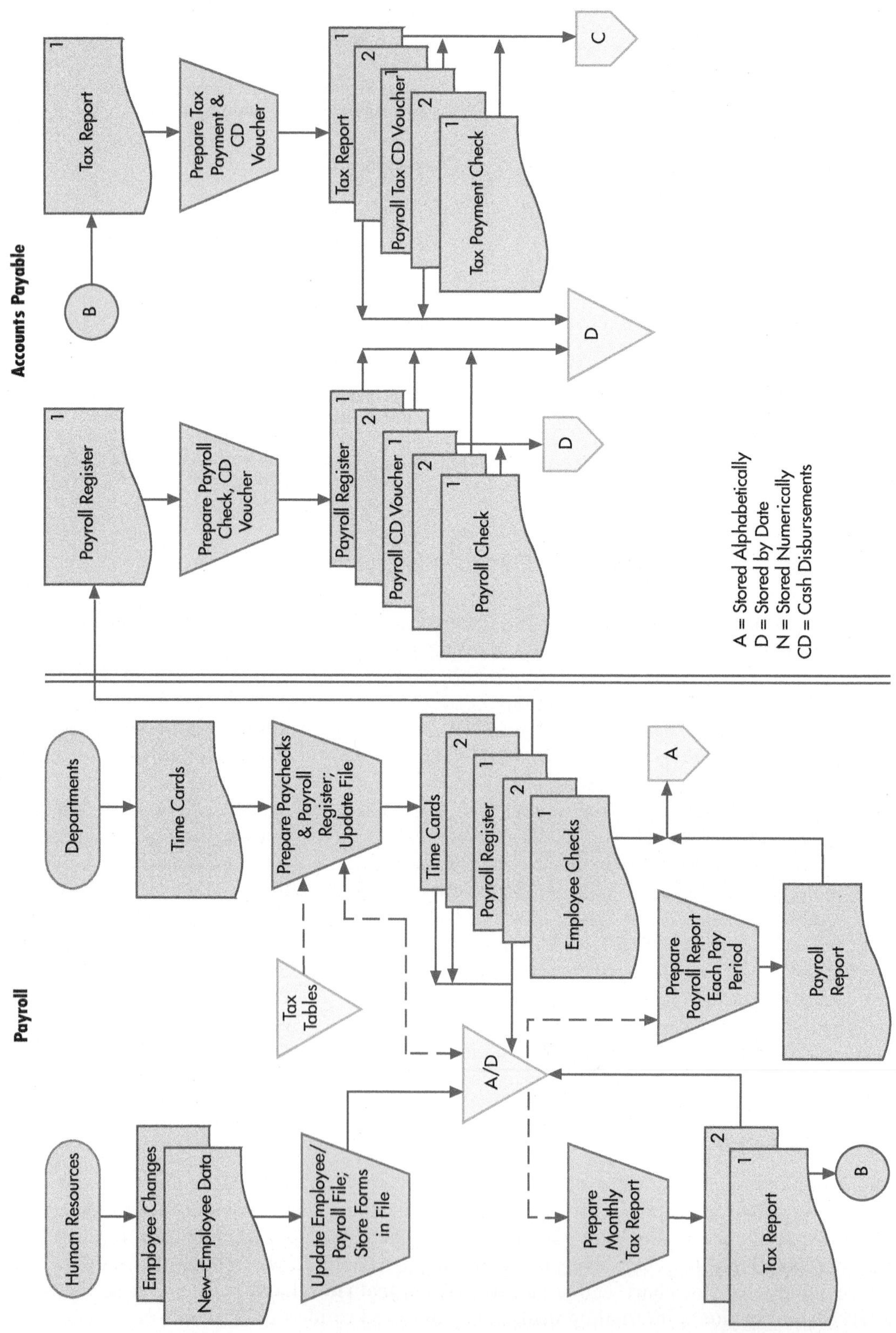

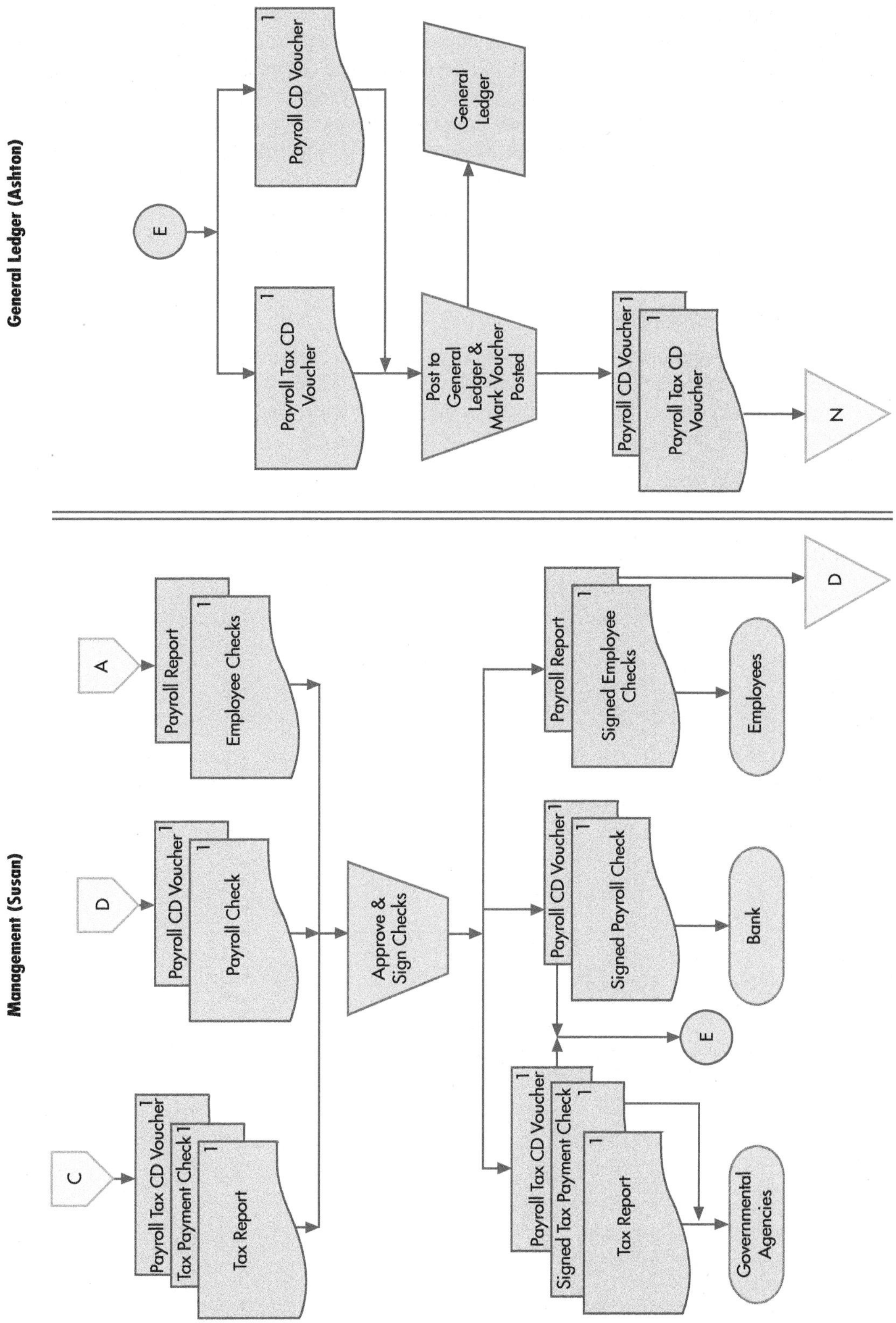

FIGURE 3-4
Continued

You can practice creating a document flowchart by drawing one for the comprehensive problem, called Accuflow Cash Disbursements Process, at the end of the chapter content. You can then compare your diagram to the solution at the very end of the chapter. You can also read the detailed explanation of how the solution was prepared.

system flowchart - Depicts the relationships among system input, processing, storage, and output.

A **system flowchart** depicts the relationships among system input, processing, storage, and output. The sales processing flowchart in Figure 3-5 represents Ashton's proposal to capture sales data using state-of-the-art sales terminals. The terminals will capture and edit the sales data and print a customer receipt. The terminals periodically send all sales data to corporate headquarters so that the accounts receivable, inventory, and sales/marketing databases and the general ledger can be updated. Management and other users can access the files at any time by using an inquiry processing system.

System flowcharts are used to describe data flows and procedures within an AIS. Each of the business process chapters (Chapters 14–18) uses a systems flowchart to provide an overview of how each business process works.

PROGRAM FLOWCHARTS

program flowchart - Illustrates the sequence of logical operations performed by a computer in executing a program.

A **program flowchart** illustrates the sequence of logical operations performed by a computer in executing a program. The relationship between system and program flowcharts is shown in Figure 3-6. A program flowchart describes the specific logic used to perform a process shown on a system flowchart.

FIGURE 3-5
System Flowchart of Sales Processing at S&S

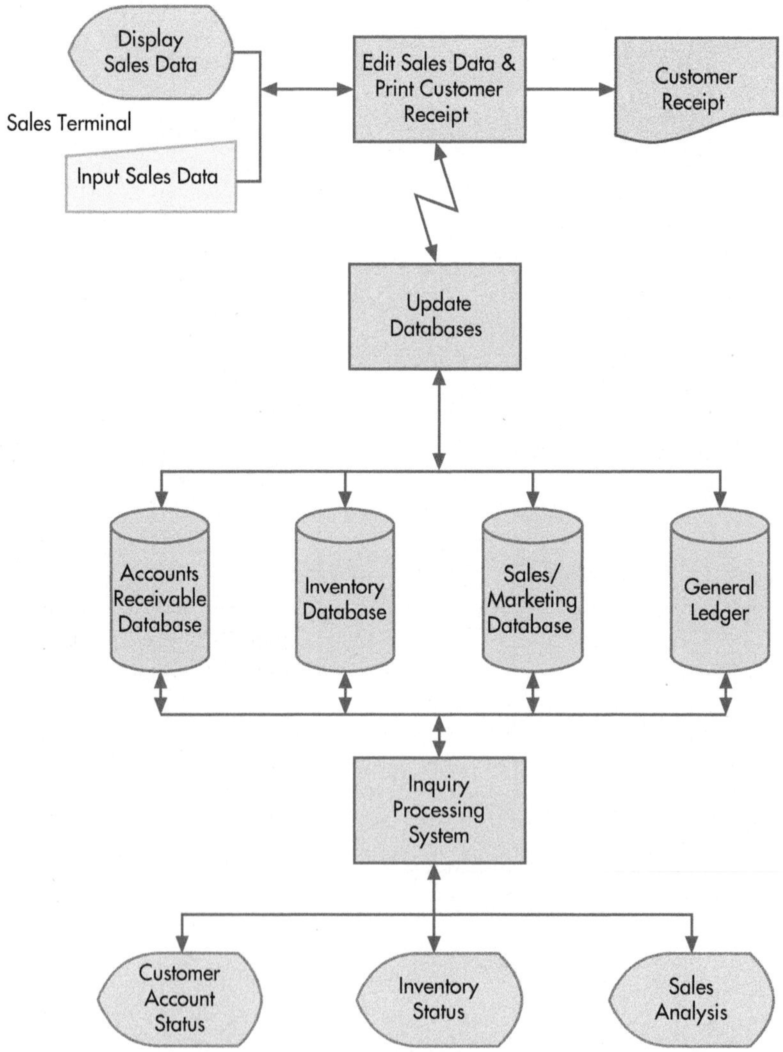

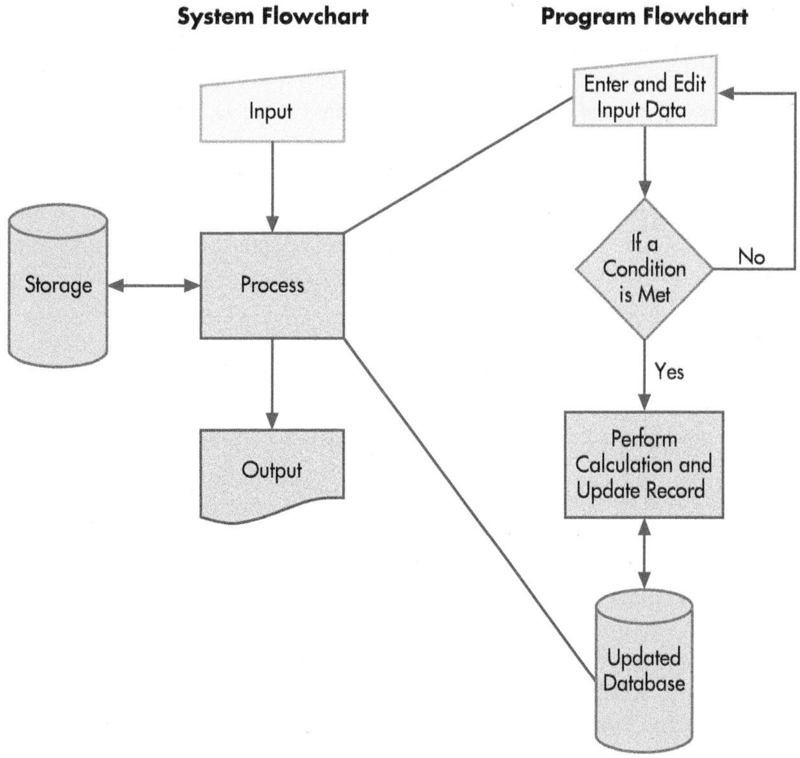

FIGURE 3-6

Relationship Between System and Program Flowcharts

Data Flow Diagrams

A **data flow diagram (DFD)** graphically describes the flow of data within an organization. It uses the first four symbols shown in Figure 3-7 to represent four basic elements: data sources and destinations, data flows, transformation processes, and data stores.

data flow diagram (DFD) - A graphical description of the flow of data within an organization, including data sources/destinations, data flows, transformation processes, and data storage.

Symbol	Name	Explanation
☐	Data sources and destinations	The people and organizations that send data to and receive data from the system are represented by square boxes. Data destinations are also referred to as data sinks.
⌒	Data flows	The flow of the data into or out of a process is represented by curved or straight lines with arrows.
◯	Transformation processes	The processes that transform data from inputs to outputs are represented by circles. They are often referred to as bubbles.
═	Data stores	The storage of data is represented by two horizontal lines.
△	Internal Control	An internal control. The internal controls are numbered and explained in an accompanying table. See Chapters 14–18.

FIGURE 3-7

Data Flow Diagram Symbols

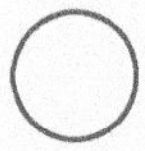

For example, Figure 3-8 shows that the input to process C is data flow B, which comes from data source A. The outputs of process C are data flows D and E. Data flow E is sent to data destination J. Process F uses data flows D and G as input and produces data flows I and G as output. Data flow G comes from and returns to data store H. Data flow I is sent to data destination K.

Figure 3-9 assigns specific titles to each of the processes depicted in Figure 3-8. Figures 3-8 and 3-9 will be used to examine the four basic elements of a DFD in more detail.

In Chapters 14 through 18, the basic DFD has been adapted so that it shows internal controls, using the triangle symbol (highway warning symbol) shown in Figure 3-7. The internal controls are numbered and an accompanying table explains the internal control. Users who do not wish to indicate internal controls simply ignore the triangle symbol.

data source - The entity that produces or sends the data entered into a system.

data destination - The entity that receives data produced by a system.

data flow - The movement of data among processes, stores, sources, and destinations.

A **data source** and a **data destination** are entities that send or receive data that the system uses or produces. An entity can be both a source and a destination. They are represented by squares, as illustrated by items A (customer), J (bank), and K (credit manager) in Figure 3-9.

A **data flow** is the movement of data among processes, stores, sources, and destinations. Data that pass between data stores and a source or destination go through a data transformation process. Data flows are labeled to show what data is flowing. The only exception is data flow between a process and a data store, such as data flow G in Figure 3-9, because the data flow is usually obvious. In data flow G, data from the accounts receivable file is retrieved, updated, and stored back in the file. Other data flows in Figure 3-9 are B (customer payment), D (remittance data), E (deposit), and I (receivables data).

If two or more data flows move together, a single line is used. For example, data flow B (customer payment) consists of a payment and remittance data. Process 1.0 (process payment) splits them and sends them in different directions. The remittance data (D) is used to update accounts receivable records, and the payment (E) is deposited in the bank. If the data flow separately, two lines are used. For example, Figure 3-10 shows two lines because customer inquiries (L) do not always accompany a payment (B). If represented by the same data flow, the separate elements and their different purposes are obscured, and the DFD is more difficult to interpret.

processes - Actions that transform data into other data or information.

Processes represent the transformation of data. Figure 3-9 shows that process payment (C) splits the customer payment into the remittance data and the check, which is deposited in the bank. The update receivables process (F) uses remittance (D) and accounts receivable (H) data to update receivable records and send receivables data to the credit manager.

data store - The place or medium where system data is stored.

A **data store** is a repository of data. DFDs do not show the physical storage medium (such as a server or paper) used to store the data. As shown in Figure 3-9, data stores (H) are represented by horizontal lines, with the name of the file written inside the lines.

FIGURE 3-8
Basic Data Flow Diagram Elements

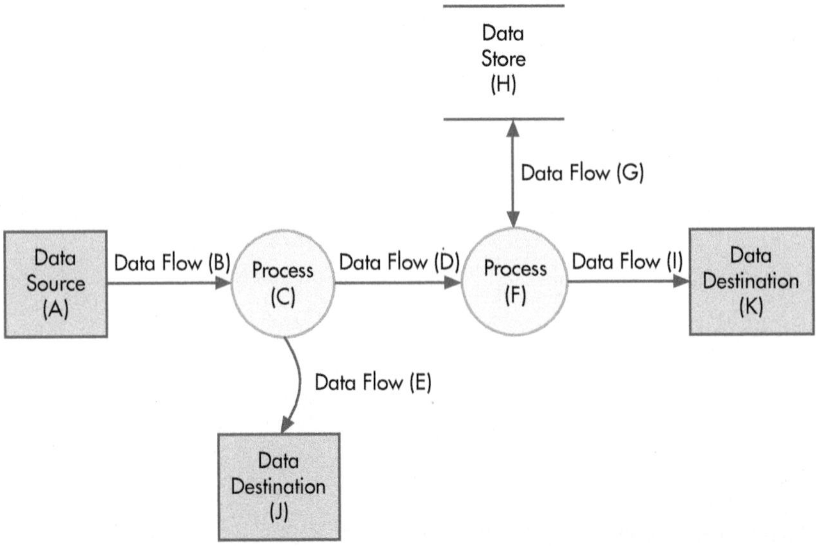

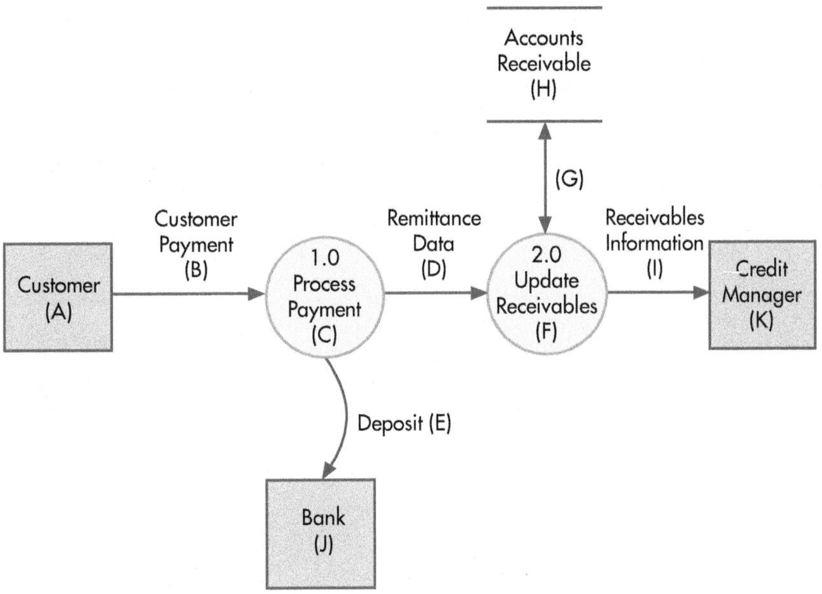

FIGURE 3-9
Data Flow Diagram of Customer Payment Process

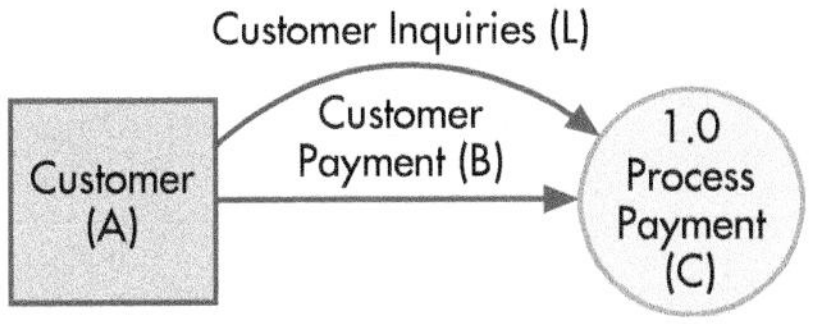

FIGURE 3-10
Splitting Customer Payments and Inquiries

SUBDIVIDING THE DFD

DFDs are subdivided into successively lower levels to provide ever-increasing amounts of detail because few systems can be fully diagrammed on one sheet of paper. Also, users have differing needs, and a variety of levels can better satisfy differing requirements.

The highest-level DFD is referred to as a **context diagram** because it provides the reader with a summary-level view of a system. It depicts a data processing system and the entities that are the sources and destinations of system inputs and outputs. For example, Ashton drew Figure 3-11 to document payroll processing procedures at S&S. The payroll processing system receives time card data from different departments and employee data from human resources. The system processes these data and produces (1) tax reports and payments for governmental agencies, (2) employee paychecks, (3) a payroll check deposited in the payroll account at the bank, and (4) payroll information for management.

context diagram - Highest-level DFD; a summary-level view of a system, showing the data processing system, its input(s) and output(s), and their sources and destinations.

Ashton used the description of S&S's payroll processing procedures in Table 3-1 to decompose the context diagram into successively lower levels, each with an increasing amount of detail. The five major payroll activities and their data inflows and outflows are shown in Table 3-2.

Ashton exploded his context diagram and created the Level 0 DFD (called Level 0 because there are zero meaningful decimal points—1.0, 2.0, etc.) shown in Figure 3-12. Notice that some data inputs and outputs have been excluded from this DFD. For example, in process 2.0, the data inflows and outflows not related to an external entity or to another process are not depicted (tax tables and payroll register). These data flows are internal to the "pay employees" activity and are shown on the next DFD level.

Ashton exploded process 2.0 (pay employees) to create a Level 1 DFD (it has one meaningful decimal place—2.1, 2.2, etc.). Figure 3-13 provides more detail about the data processes involved in paying employees, and it includes the tax rates table and the payroll register data flow omitted from Figure 3-12. In a similar fashion, each of the Figure 3-12 processes could be exploded, using a Level 1 DFD, to show a greater level of detail.

Some general guidelines for developing DFDs are shown in Focus 3-3.

You can practice creating the different levels of a DFD by drawing them for the comprehensive problem, called Accuflow Cash Disbursements Process, at the end of the chapter content. You can then compare your diagrams to the solution at the very end of the chapter. You can also read the detailed explanation of how the solution was prepared.

FIGURE 3-11
Context Diagram for S&S Payroll Processing

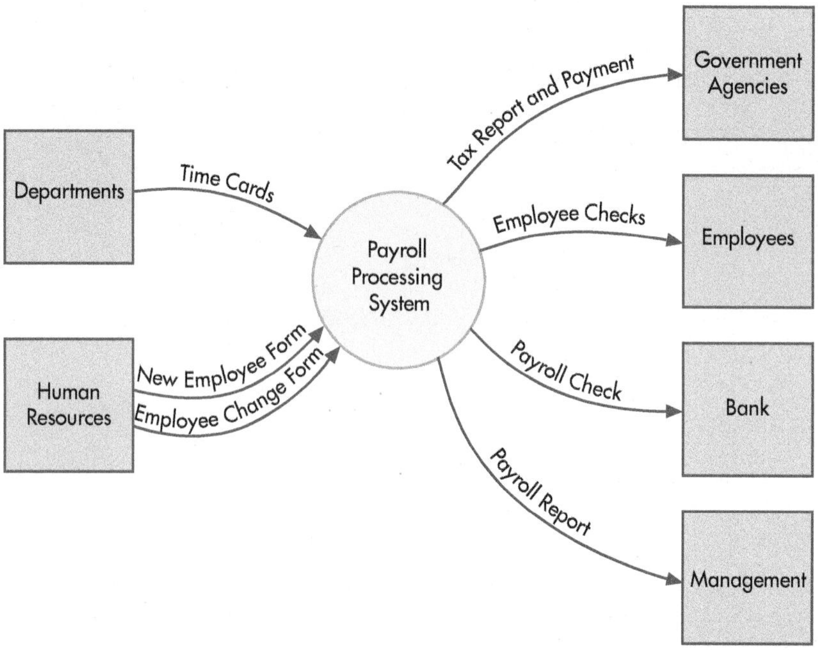

FIGURE 3-12
Level 0 DFD for S&S Payroll Processing

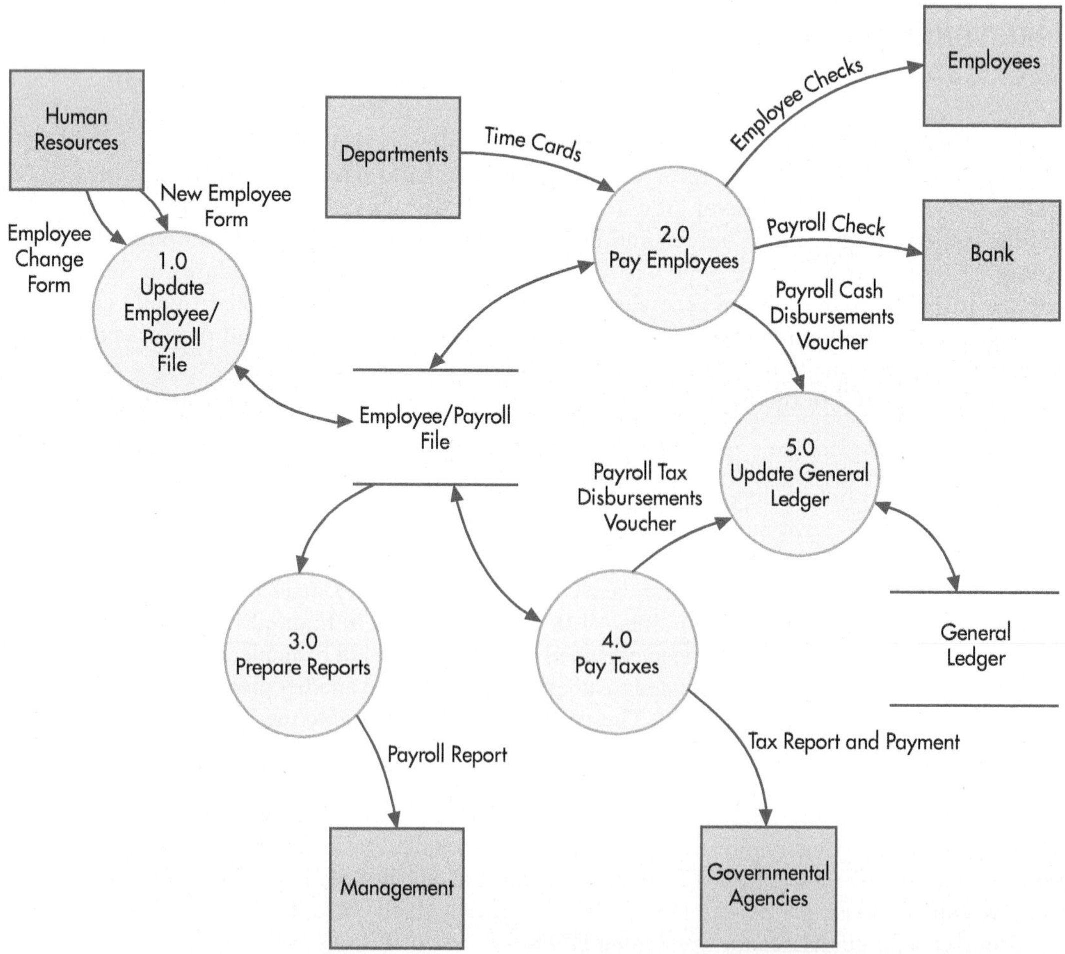

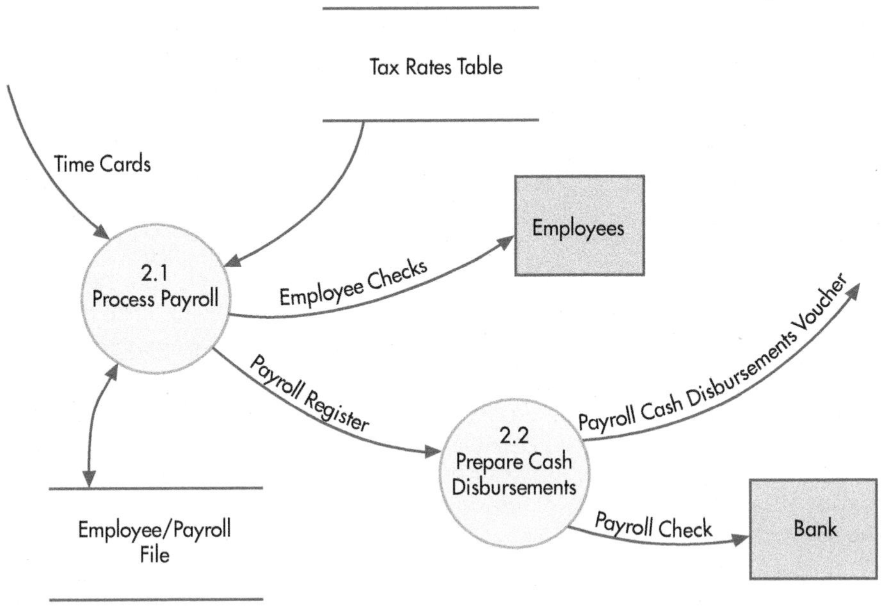

FIGURE 3-13
Level 1 DFD for Process 2.0 in S&S Payroll Processing

FOCUS 3-3 Guidelines for Drawing a DFD

1. *Understand the system.* Develop this understanding by observing organization data flows, observing and interviewing those who use and process the data or having them complete a questionnaire; by reading a narrative description of the system; or by walking through system transactions.
2. *Ignore certain aspects of the system.* A DFD is a diagram of the origins, flow, transformation, storage, and destinations of data. Only very important error paths are included; unimportant error paths are ignored. Determining how the system starts and stops is not shown.
3. *Determine system boundaries.* Determine what to include and exclude. Include all relevant data elements because excluded items will not be considered during system development.
4. *Develop a context diagram.* A context diagram depicts system boundaries. In the diagram's center is a circle with the name of the system. Outside entities the system interacts with directly are in boxes on either side, connected by data flows depicting the data passed between them. DFDs in successively more detail depict data flows inside the system.
5. *Identify data flows.* Identify all data flows (significant movement of data) entering or leaving the system, including where the data originate and their final destination. Data flows come from and go to a transformation process, a data store (file), or a source or destination. Data flows can move in two directions, shown as a line with arrows on both ends (see G in Figure 3-9).
6. *Group data flows.* A data flow can consist of one or more pieces of datum. Data elements that always flow together should be grouped together and shown as one data flow until they are separated. If the data do not always flow together, show them as separate data flows.
7. *Identify transformation processes.* Place a circle wherever work is required to transform one data flow into another. All transformation processes should have one or more incoming and outgoing data flows.
8. *Group transformation processes.* Transformation processes that are logically related or occur at the same time and place should be grouped together. Do not combine unrelated items into a single transformation process. If data are not processed together, or are sometimes processed differently, separate them.
9. *Identify all files or data stores.* Identify each temporary or permanent data repository, and identify each data flow into and out of it.
10. *Identify all data sources and destinations.* Include them on the DFD.
11. *Name all DFD elements.* Except for data flows into or out of data stores (the data store name is usually sufficient to identify the data flow), data elements should be given unique and descriptive names representing what is known about them. Naming data flows first forces you to concentrate on the all-important data

FOCUS 3-3 Continued

flows, rather than on the processes or stores. Processes and data stores typically take their names from the data inflows or outflows. Choose active and descriptive names, such as "update inventory" and "validate transaction," rather than "input data" or "update process." Process names should include action verbs such as *update, edit, prepare, reconcile*, and *record*.

12. ***Subdivide the DFD.*** A cluttered DFD is hard to read and understand. If you have more than five to seven processes on a page, decompose the context diagram into high-level processes. Explode these high-level processes into successively lower-level processes.
13. ***Give each process a sequential number.*** Giving each process a sequential number (lower to higher) helps readers navigate among the DFD levels.
14. ***Refine the DFD.*** Work through data flows several times. Each subsequent pass helps refine the diagram and identify the fine points. Organize the DFD to flow from top to bottom and from left to right.
15. ***Prepare a final copy.*** Do not allow data flow lines to cross each other; if necessary, repeat a data store or destination. Place the name of the DFD, the date prepared, and the preparer's name on each page.

Summary and Case Conclusion

Ashton prepared a BPD (Figure 3-2), a flowchart (Figure 3-4), and DFDs (Figures 3-12 and 3-13) of S&S's payroll processing system to document and explain the operation of the existing system. He was pleased to see that Scott and Susan were able to grasp the essence of the system from this documentation. The DFDs indicated the logical flow of data, the flowcharts illustrated the physical dimensions of the system, and the BPD showed the activities in each business process.

Susan and Scott agreed that Ashton should document the remainder of the system. The documentation would help all of them understand the current system. It would also help Ashton and the consultants design the new system. In fact, the payroll documentation had already helped them identify a few minor changes they wanted to make in their system. Using Figure 3-4, Susan now understands why the payroll clerk sometimes had to borrow the only copy of the payroll report that was prepared. She recommended that a second copy be made and kept in the payroll department. Susan also questioned the practice of keeping all the payroll records in one employee/payroll file. To keep the file from becoming unwieldy, she recommended that it be divided into three files: personal employee data, pay period documentation, and payroll tax data. A discussion with the payroll clerk verified that this approach would make payroll processing easier and more efficient.

Over the next few weeks, Ashton documented the remaining business processes. This process helped him identify inefficiencies and unneeded reports. He also found that some system documents were inadequately controlled. In addition, he got several ideas about how an automated system could help him reengineer the business processes at S&S. By substituting technology for human effort, outdated processes and procedures could be eliminated to make the system more effective.

When Ashton completed his analysis and documentation of the current system, Susan and Scott asked him to continue his work in designing a new system. To do that, Ashton must thoroughly understand the information needs of the various employees in the company. Then he can design a new system using the tools that were explained in this chapter. Systems development is discussed in Chapters 22 through 24.

KEY TERMS

documentation 59
narrative description 59
business process diagram (BPD) 60
flowchart 63
document flowcharts 65
internal control flowchart 65
system flowchart 68
program flowchart 68
data flow diagram (DFD) 69
data source 70
data destination 70
data flow 70
processes 70
data store 70
context diagram 71

AIS in Action

CHAPTER QUIZ

1. A DFD is a representation of which of the following?
   a. the logical operations performed by a computer program
   b. flow of data in an organization
   c. decision rules in a computer program
   d. computer hardware configuration

2. Documentation methods such as DFDs, BPDs, and flowcharts save both time and money, adding value to an organization.
   a. True
   b. False

3. Which of the following statements is FALSE?
   a. Flowcharts make use of many symbols.
   b. A document flowchart emphasizes the flow of documents or records containing data.
   c. DFDs help convey the timing of events.
   d. Both a and b are false.

4. A DFD consists of the following four basic elements: data sources and destinations, data flows, transformation processes, and data stores. Each is represented on a DFD by a different symbol.
   a. True
   b. False

5. All of the following are guidelines that should be followed in naming DFD data elements EXCEPT:
   a. Process names should include action verbs such as *update*, *edit*, *prepare*, and *record*.
   b. Make sure the names describe all the data or the entire process.
   c. Name only the most important DFD elements.
   d. Choose active and descriptive names.

6. The documentation skills that accountants require vary with their job function. However, they should at least be able to do which of the following?
   a. Read documentation to determine how the system works.
   b. Critique and correct documentation that others prepare.
   c. Prepare documentation for a newly developed information system.
   d. Teach others how to prepare documentation.

7. Which of the following statements is FALSE?
   a. A flowchart is an analytical technique used to describe some aspect of an information system in a clear, concise, and logical manner.
   b. Flowcharts use a standard set of symbols to describe pictorially the flow of documents and data through a system.
   c. Flowcharts are easy to prepare and revise when the designer utilizes a flowcharting software package.
   d. A system flowchart is a narrative representation of an information system.

8. Which of the following flowcharts illustrates the flow of data among areas of responsibility in an organization?
   a. program flowchart
   b. computer configuration chart
   c. system flowchart
   d. document flowchart

9. All of the following are recommended guidelines for making flowcharts more readable, clear, concise, consistent, and understandable EXCEPT:
   a. Divide a document flowchart into columns with labels.
   b. Flowchart all data flows, especially exception procedures and error routines.
   c. Design the flowchart so that flow proceeds from top to bottom and from left to right.
   d. Show the final disposition of all documents to prevent loose ends that leave the reader dangling.

10. How are data sources and destinations represented in a data flow diagram?
   a. as a square
   b. as a curved arrow
   c. as a circle
   d. as two parallel lines
   e. none of the above

COMPREHENSIVE PROBLEM

ACCUFLOW CASH DISBURSEMENTS PROCESS

SoftData, a vendor, sends an invoice to Accuflow for data warehousing support services. The invoice is sent directly to Megan Waters, the accounts payable clerk, who manually records the invoice in the accounts payable subsidiary ledger. Once the invoice is recorded, it is forwarded to Stan Phillips, the cash disbursements clerk, for processing. Stan prepares a check to pay the invoice and sends the check and invoice to John Sterling, the company treasurer. John approves and signs the check and cancels the invoice. John then mails the check to SoftData and returns the canceled invoice to Stan for recording in the cash disbursements journal and filing. Once a week, Megan manually posts disbursements from the cash disbursements journal to the accounts payable subsidiary ledger.

REQUIRED

Prepare a document flowchart, a BPD, a context diagram, a Level 0 data flow diagram, and a Level 1 DFD for the Accuflow cash disbursement process. To maximize learning from this problem, do your best to solve it before looking at the solution at the end of the chapter.

DISCUSSION QUESTIONS

3.1 Identify the DFD elements in the following narrative: A customer purchases a few items from a local grocery store. Jill, a salesclerk, enters the transaction in the cash register and takes the customer's money. At closing, Jill gives both the cash and the register tape to her manager.

3.2 Do you agree with the following statement: "Any one of the systems documentation procedures can be used to adequately document a given system"? Explain.

3.3 Compare the guidelines for preparing flowcharts, BPDs, and DFDs. What general design principles and limitations are common to all three documentation techniques?

3.4 Your classmate asks you to explain flowcharting conventions using real-world examples. Draw each of the major flowchart symbols from memory, placing them into one of four categories: input/output, processing, storage, and flow and miscellaneous. For each symbol, suggest several uses.

PROBLEMS

3.1 Prepare flowcharting segments for each of the following operations:
   a. Processing transactions stored on a sequential medium such as a magnetic tape to update a master file stored on magnetic tape
   b. Processing transactions stored on magnetic tape to update a database
   c. Querying a database and printing the query result
   d. Using a terminal to enter paper-based source document data and send it to a remote location where a corporate computer updates the company database
   e. Using a terminal to query your customer sales database
   f. A scheduled automatic backup of a database to an external hard drive
   g. Use a terminal to enter employee hours recorded on time cards to update both the payroll transaction file and the wage data in the payroll master file

h. Use a terminal to access a price list in the sales database to complete a purchase order. An electronic copy of the purchase order is sent to the vendor and a backup copy is printed and filed by vendor name
i. Make an airline reservation using your home computer

3.2 Employees at the Dewey Construction Company enter the work they perform on job-time tickets. Most construction sites have data input terminals that employees use to enter the time they start and stop work and the job code that represents the project they are working on. Every night the job-time ticket data for that day is sent electronically to company headquarters, where it is stored until payroll is processed.

A few construction sites are so remote that employees still fill out paper job-time tickets. These tickets are express mailed weekly to company headquarters, where they are scanned and processed.

Payroll is processed weekly. The job-time tickets are used to update the payroll database as well as the work-in-process database. Since all employees are paid electronically, no checks are printed; instead, the payroll system deposits an employee's net pay in the employee's bank account. Payments are made to government tax bodies and the company handling the employee's and the company's 401K plan contributions. All disbursements are accompanied by a report summarizing the disbursement. The system also produces pay stub data stored in a payroll transaction file and accessible to employees over the Internet. An electronic summary payroll report is created and sent to the payroll supervisor.

REQUIRED

a. Prepare a system flowchart for Dewey Construction Company's payroll processing.
b. Prepare a BPD for Dewey Construction Company's payroll processing.

3.3 ANGIC Insurance Company begins processing casualty claims when the claims department receives a notice of loss from a claimant. The claims department prepares and sends the claimant four copies of a proof-of-loss form on which the claimant must detail the cause, amount, and other aspects of the loss. The claims department also initiates a record of the claim, which is sent with the notice of loss to the data processing department, where it is filed by claim number.

The claimant must fill out the proof-of-loss forms with an adjuster's assistance. The adjuster must concur with the claimant on the estimated amount of loss. The claimant and adjuster each keep one copy of the proof-of-loss form. The adjustor files his copy numerically. The adjustor sends the first two copies to the claims department. Separately, the adjuster submits a report to the claims department, confirming the estimates on the claimant's proof-of-loss form.

The claims department authorizes a payment to the claimant, forwards a copy of the proof-of-loss form to data processing, and files the original proof-of-loss form and the adjuster's report alphabetically. The data processing department prepares payment checks and mails them to the customers, files the proof-of-loss form with the claim record, and prepares a list of cash disbursements, which it transmits to the accounting department, where it is reviewed.

REQUIRED

a. Prepare a document flowchart to reflect how ANGIC Insurance Company processes its casualty claims.
b. Prepare a BPD to reflect how ANGIC Insurance Company processes its casualty claims.

3.4 Beccan Company is a discount tire dealer operating 25 retail stores in a large metropolitan area. The company purchases all tires and related supplies using the company's central purchasing department to optimize quantity discounts. The tires and supplies are received at the central warehouse and distributed to the retail stores as needed. The perpetual inventory system at the central facility maintains current inventory records, designated reorder points, and optimum order quantities for each type and size of tire and other related supplies. Beccan has a state-of-the-art computer system and uses the following five documents in its inventory control system.

- **Retail stores requisition.** The retail stores electronically submit a retail store requisition to the central warehouse when they need tires or supplies. The warehouse shipping clerk fills the orders from inventory and authorizes store deliveries.
- **Purchase requisition.** The system notifies the inventory control clerk when the quantity on hand for an item stored in the central warehouse falls below the designated reorder point and prepares a purchase requisition. The inventory control clerk adjusts the purchase requisition as needed, approves it, and forwards it to the purchasing department.
- **Purchase order.** The system uses the data in the purchase requisition to prepare a purchase order and tentatively select a vendor based on selection criteria built into the system such as price and availability. The purchasing agent adjusts the order or vendor selection as needed, approves it, and e-mails it to the vendor. A copy of the purchase order is sent to accounts payable.
- **Receiving report.** For every purchase order, the system prepares a receiving report showing the goods ordered, but not the quantities ordered. When the goods arrive, the receiving clerk enters the date they arrived and the quantity of each item received. The completed receiving report is sent to accounts payable.
- **Invoice.** Vendors send Beccan an electronic invoice that shows the goods shipped, their prices, and the total amounts owed.

The following departments are involved in Beccan's inventory control system:

- **Retail stores.** Each store counts its inventory at the end of every quarter and reconciles it to the corporate database. On a weekly basis, each store reviews its inventory to determine what to requisition from the central warehouse. When a store runs out of inventory, or is dangerously low, it can send a rush order to the warehouse.
- **Inventory control department.** Responsible for the maintenance of all perpetual inventory records, including quantity on hand, reorder point, optimum order quantity, and quantity on order for each item carried.
- **Warehouse department.** Maintains the physical inventory of all items carried in stock. All orders from vendors are received (receiving clerk) and all distributions to retail stores are filled (shipping clerks) in this department.
- **Purchasing department.** Places all orders for items needed by the company.
- **Accounts payable department.** Maintains all open accounts with vendors and other creditors. Accounts payable reviews and reconciles the vendor invoice, purchase order, and receiving report. Any discrepancies are cleared up, and the vendor invoice is paid within 10 days of the receipt of goods by electronically transferring the amount due to the vendor's bank account.

REQUIRED

Prepare a BPD that documents Beccan's business processes. (*CMA Examination, adapted*)

3.5 As the internal auditor for No-Wear Products, you have been asked to document the company's payroll processing system. Based on your documentation, No-Wear hopes to develop a plan for revising the current system to eliminate unnecessary delays in paycheck processing. The head payroll clerk explained the system:

The payroll processing system at No-Wear Products is fairly simple. Time data are recorded in each department using time cards and clocks. It is annoying, however, when people forget to punch out at night, and we have to record their time by hand. At the end of the period, our payroll clerks enter the time card data into a payroll file for processing. Our clerks are pretty good—though I've had to make my share of corrections when they mess up the data entry.

Before the payroll file is processed for the current period, human resources sends us personnel changes, such as increases in pay rates and new employees. Our clerks enter this data into the payroll file. Usually, when mistakes get back to us, it's because human resources is recording the wrong pay rate or an employee has left and the department forgets to remove the record.

The data are processed and individual employee paychecks are generated. Several reports are generated for management—though I don't know what they do with them. In addition, the government requires regular federal and state withholding reports for tax purposes. Currently, the system generates these reports automatically, which is nice.

REQUIRED

a. Prepare a context diagram and Level 0 DFD to document the payroll processing system at No-Wear Products.
b. Prepare a document flowchart to document the payroll processing system at No-Wear Products.
c. Prepare a BPD to document the payroll processing system at No-Wear Products.

3.6 Ashton Fleming has decided to document and analyze the accounts payable process at S&S so the transition to a computerized system will be easier. He also hopes to improve any weaknesses he discovers in the system. In the following narrative, Ashton explains what happens at S&S:

Before S&S pays a vendor invoice, the invoice must be matched against the purchase order used to request the goods and the receiving report that the receiving department prepares. Because all three of these documents enter the accounts payable department at different times, a separate alphabetical file is kept for each type of document. The purchase orders forwarded from purchasing are stored in a purchase order file. The receiving reports are stored in a receiving report file. When vendor invoices are received, the accounts payable clerk records the amount due in the accounts payable file and files the invoices in the vendor invoice file.

S&S pays all accounts within 10 days to take advantage of early-payment discounts. When it is time to pay a bill, the accounts payable clerk retrieves the vendor invoice, attaches the purchase order and the receiving report, and forwards the matched documents to Ashton Fleming.

Ashton reviews the documents to ensure they are complete, prepares a two-part check, forwards all the documents to Susan, and records the check in the cash disbursements journal.

Susan reviews the documents to ensure that they are valid payables and signs the checks. She forwards the check to the vendor and returns the documents and the check copy to the accounts payable clerk. The clerk files the documents alphabetically in a paid invoice file. At the end of every month, the accounts payable clerk uses the accounts payable ledger to prepare an accounts payable report that is forwarded to Susan. After she is finished with the report, Susan files it chronologically.

REQUIRED

a. Prepare a context diagram and a Level 0 DFD to document accounts payable processing at S&S.
b. Prepare a document flowchart to document accounts payable processing at S&S.
c. Prepare a BPD to document accounts payable processing at S&S.

3.7 Ashton Fleming has asked you to document the cash receipts system at S&S. Ashton's narrative of the system follows:

Customer payments include cash received at the time of purchase and payments received in the mail. At day's end, the treasurer endorses all checks and prepares a deposit slip for the checks and the cash. A clerk deposits the checks, cash, and deposit slip at the local bank each day.

When checks are received as payment for accounts due, a remittance slip is included with the payment. The Treasurer sends this to accounts receivable. Data from the remittance slips are entered into the computer, and the accounts receivable database is updated. The remittance slips are stored in a file drawer by date.

Every week, accounts receivable generates a cash receipts report and an aged trial balance using the accounts receivable ledger. The cash receipts report is sent to Scott and Susan and one of them reviews it. A copy of the aged trial balance is sent to the credit and collections department, where it is reviewed.

REQUIRED

a. Develop a context diagram and a Level 0 DFD for the cash receipts system at S&S.
b. Prepare a document flowchart for the cash receipts system at S&S.
c. Prepare a BPD for the cash receipts system at S&S.

3.8 The local college requires that each student complete an online registration request form. The system checks the accounts receivable subsystem to ensure that no fees are owed. Next, for each course, the system checks the student transcript to ensure that he or she has completed the course prerequisites. Then the system checks class availability and, if there is room, adds the student's Social Security number to the class list.

The report back to the student shows the result of registration processing: If the student owes fees, a bill is sent and the registration is rejected. If prerequisites for a course are not fulfilled, the student is notified and that course is not registered. If the class is full, the student request is annotated with "course closed." If a student is accepted into a class, then the day, time, and room are shown next to the course number. Student fees and total tuition are computed and shown on the report. Student fee data is interfaced to the accounts receivable subsystem. When registration is complete, course enrollment reports are prepared for the instructors.

REQUIRED

a. Prepare a context diagram and at least two levels of DFDs for this process.
b. Prepare a flowchart to document this process.

3.9 Melanie is doing a study on various weight-loss plans and needs to determine an individual's weight status by calculating his or her body mass index. To calculate a person's body mass index, height must be measured in meters and weight measured in kilograms. The index is calculated by dividing a person's weight by the square of his height. The result is then compared to the following scale to determine the person's weight status: Below 18.5 = underweight; 18.5–24.5 = normal weight; over 25.0 = overweight. Five hundred people have agreed to participate in Melanie's study. With so many calculations to perform, she would like a computer program that will do this calculation for her. She decides to prepare a flowchart to help her properly design the computer program.

REQUIRED

Prepare a program flowchart to help Melanie program this process.

3.10 Match the flowchart or DFD segments in the right column to an appropriate description in the left column.

DFDS

1. Statements are prepared and sent to customers from data contained in the accounts receivable data store.

A.

2. A vendor sends a sales invoice to the accounts payable process.

B.

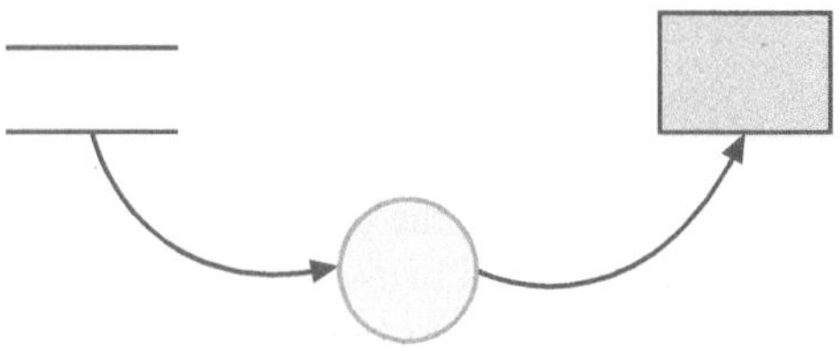

3. The cash receipt process updates the cash receipts data store.

C.

FLOWCHARTS

4. A two-part check is manually prepared from data on a vendor invoice.

D.

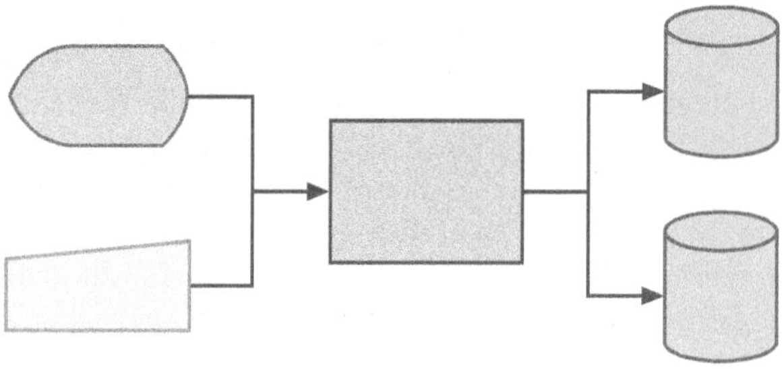

5. The system prepares a check that is mailed to the customer.

E.

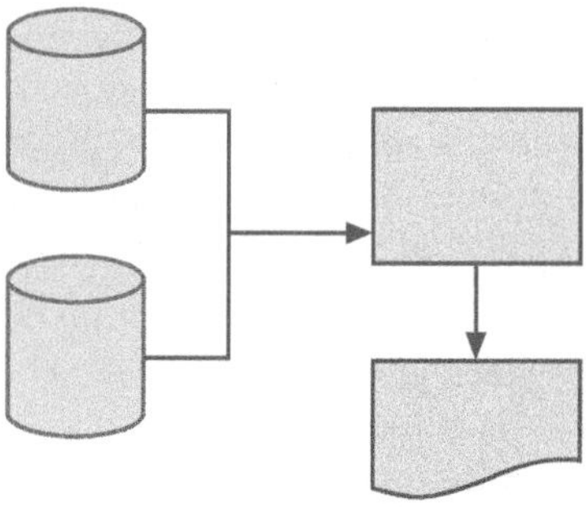

6. A report is prepared from data stored on magnetic tape.

F.

7. Billing data are entered into a system from a terminal and used to update both the sales order database and the customer database.

G.

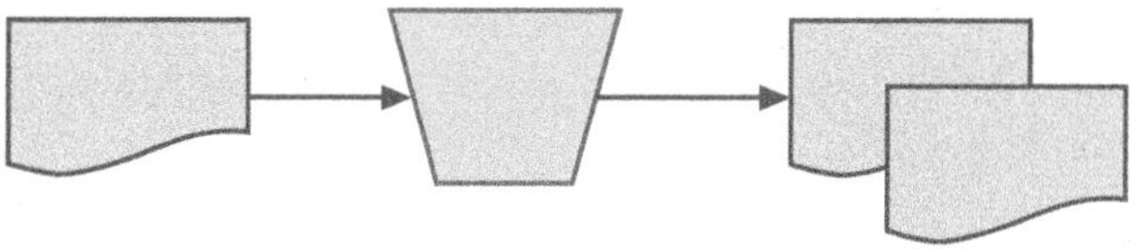

8. Data from a paper invoice are used to update the cash disbursements file.

H.

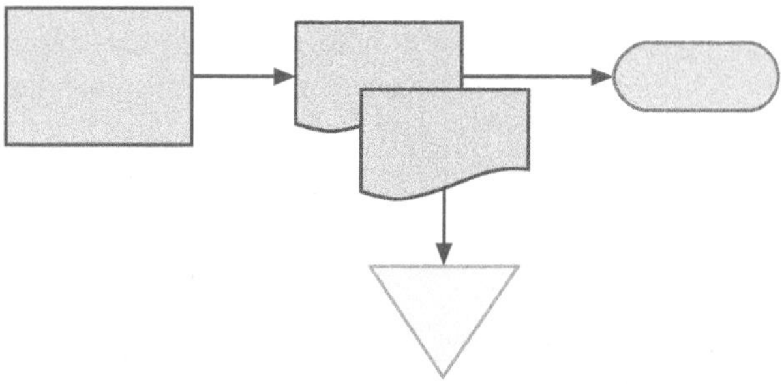

9. The system prepares two copies of a sales order; one copy is sent to the customer and the other is filed.

I.

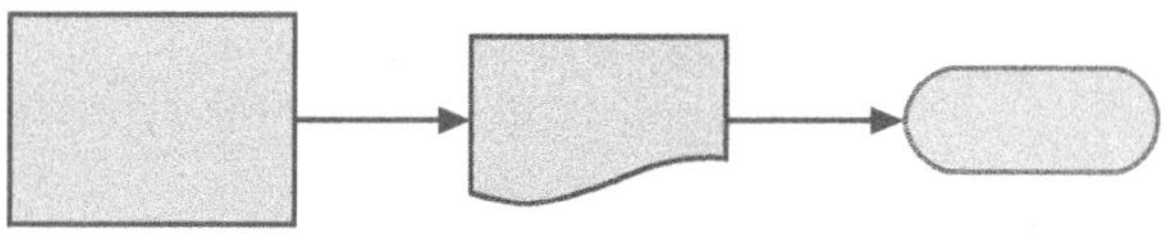

10. An accounts receivable aging report is prepared from the accounts receivable master file and the cash receipts master file.

J.

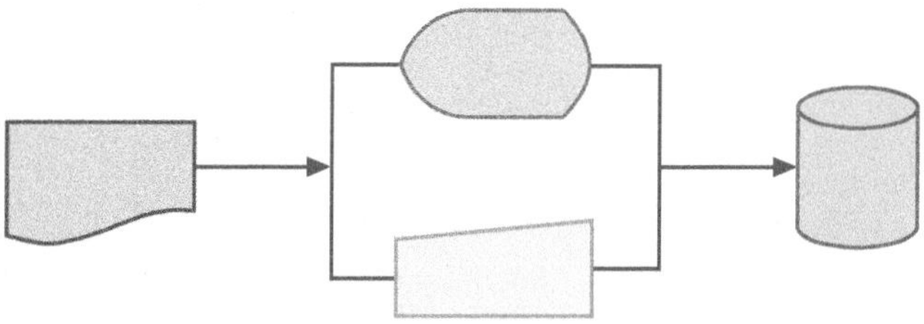

3.11 Replicate Figures 3.14, 3.15, and 3.17 found in the Comprehensive Problem Solution at the end of the chapter. Use Visio, Microsoft Word, Microsoft Excel, or some other documentation software package.

CASE 3-1 Dub 5

You are the systems analyst for the Wee Willie Williams Widget Works (also known as Dub 5). Dub 5 has been producing computer keyboard components for more than 20 years and has recently signed an exclusive 10-year contract to provide the keyboards for all Dell and HP personal computers. As the systems analyst, you have been assigned the task of documenting Dub 5's order-processing system.

Customer orders, which are all credit sales, arrive via e-mail and by phone. When an order is processed, a number of other documents are prepared. You have diagrammed the overall process and the documents produced, as shown in the context diagram shown below.

The following documents are created:

- Order processing creates a packing slip, which the warehouse uses to fill the order.
- A customer invoice is prepared and sent once the goods have been shipped.
- When orders are not accepted, an order rejection is sent to the customer, explaining why the order cannot be filled.
- A receivables notice, which is a copy of the customer invoice, is sent to the accounting department so accounts receivable records can be updated.

After reviewing your notes, you write the following narrative summary:

> When an order comes in, the order-processing clerk checks the customer's credit file to confirm credit approval and ensure that the amount falls within the credit limit. If either of these conditions is not met, the order is sent to the credit department. If an order meets both conditions, the order-processing clerk enters it into the system on a standard order form. The data on the form is used to update the company's customer file (in which the name, address, and other data are stored), and the form is placed in the company's open order file.
>
> When the credit department receives a rejected order, the credit clerk determines why the order has been rejected. If the credit limit has been exceeded, the customer is notified that the merchandise will be shipped as soon as Dub 5 receives payment. If the customer has not been approved for credit, a credit application is sent to the customer along with a notification that the order will be shipped as soon as credit approval is granted.
>
> Before preparing a packing slip, the system checks the inventory records to determine whether the company has the products ordered on hand. If the items are in stock, a packing slip is prepared and sent to the warehouse.
>
> Once notification of shipped goods has been received from the warehouse, a customer invoice is prepared. A copy is filed by the order-processing department, another is sent to the customer, and another is sent to the accounting department so that accounts receivables can be updated. A note is placed in the customer file indicating that the invoice has been sent.

From the information presented, complete a Level 0 DFD for order processing, a Level 1 DFD for the credit review process for Dub 5, and a BPD for order processing.

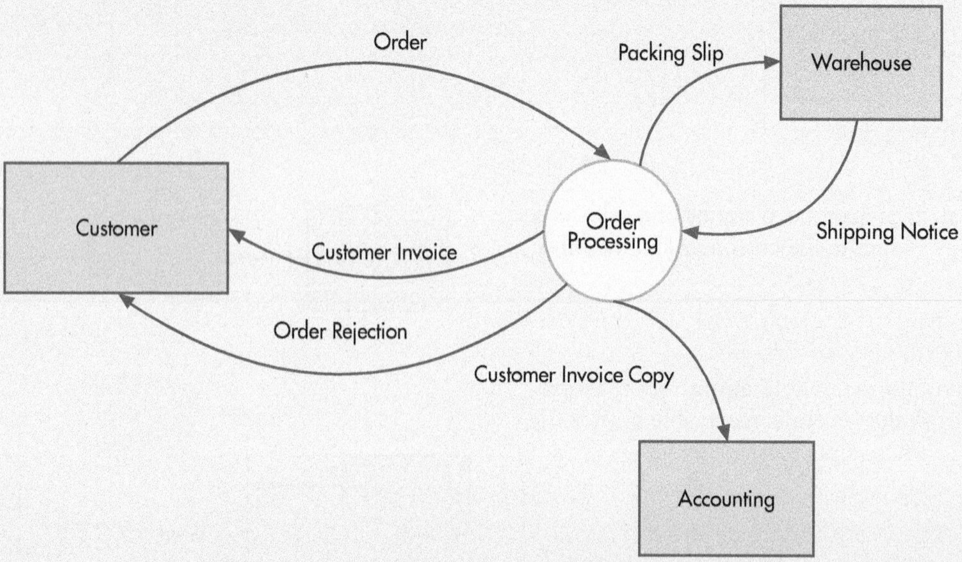

AIS in Action Solutions

QUIZ KEY

1. A DFD is a representation of which of the following?
   a. the logical operations performed by a computer program [Incorrect. This is a description of a program flowchart.]
   ► b. flow of data in an organization [Correct.]
   c. decision rules in a computer program [Incorrect. A DFD is a graphical representation of how data move through an organization. Decision rules are objective statements specific to computer programs.]
   d. computer hardware configuration [Incorrect. A computer hardware configuration shows how various parts of a computer fit together.]

2. Documentation methods such as DFDs, BPDs, and flowcharts save both time and money, adding value to an organization.
   ► a. True [Correct. A picture is worth a thousand words: Many people learn more and learn it more quickly by studying the DFD, BPD, or flowchart of a system than by reading a narrative description of the same system.]
   b. False [Incorrect]

3. Which of the following statements is FALSE?
   a. Flowcharts make use of many symbols. [Incorrect. The statement is true. See Figure 3-3 for an illustration of the many symbols used in flowcharts.]
   b. A document flowchart emphasizes the flow of documents or records containing data. [Incorrect. The statement is true. The reason it is called a document flowchart is that it shows the flow of documents or records containing data.]
   ► c. DFDs help convey the timing of events. [Correct. DFDs show data movement, but not necessarily the timing of the movement.]
   d. Both a and b are false. [Incorrect. As explained above, a and b are true statements.]

4. A DFD consists of the following four basic elements: data sources and destinations, data flows, transformation processes, and data stores. Each is represented on a DFD by a different symbol.
   ► a. True [Correct. The four elements of DFDs are illustrated in Figure 3-7.]
   b. False [Incorrect]

5. All of the following are guidelines that should be followed in naming DFD data elements EXCEPT:
   a. Process names should include action verbs such as *update*, *edit*, *prepare*, and *record*. [Incorrect. Action verbs should be used to name process data elements. See item 11 in Focus 3-3.]
   b. Make sure the names describe all the data or the entire process. [Incorrect. Data element names should reflect what is known about the element. See item 11 in Focus 3-3.]
   ► c. Name only the most important DFD elements. [Correct. All data elements should be named, with the exception of data flows into data stores, when the inflows and outflows make naming the data store redundant. See item 11 in Focus 3-3.]
   d. Choose active and descriptive names. [Incorrect. Active and descriptive names should be used in naming data elements. See item 11 in Focus 3-3.]

6. The documentation skills that accountants require vary with their job function. However, all accountants should at least be able to do which of the following?
   ► a. Read documentation to determine how the system works. [Correct. All accountants should at least be able to read and understand system documentation.]
   b. Critique and correct documentation that others prepare. [Incorrect. Although senior accountants may critique and correct documentation prepared by junior accountants, at a minimum all accountants need to be able to read and understand documentation.]

c. Prepare documentation for a newly developed information system. [Incorrect. Some accountants may need to develop internal control documentation, but system developers and analysts normally prepare systems documentation.]
d. Teach others how to prepare documentation. [Incorrect. Most accountants will not be asked to teach documentation skills.]

7. Which of the following statements is FALSE?
a. A flowchart is an analytical technique used to describe some aspect of an information system in a clear, concise, and logical manner. [Incorrect. This is the definition of a flowchart given previously in the text.]
b. Flowcharts use a standard set of symbols to describe pictorially the flow of documents and data through a system. [Incorrect. The symbols used for flowcharting are shown in Figure 3-3.]
c. Flowcharts are easy to prepare and revise when the designer utilizes a flowcharting software package. [Incorrect. There are a number of good flowcharting software packages that make it easy to draw and modify flowcharts.]
▶ **d.** A system flowchart is a narrative representation of an information system. [Correct. A flowchart is a graphical rather than a narrative representation of an information system.]

8. Which of the following flowcharts illustrates the flow of data among areas of responsibility in an organization?
a. program flowchart [Incorrect. A program flowchart documents a computer program.]
b. computer configuration chart [Incorrect. A computer configuration chart illustrates how computer hardware is arranged and implemented.]
c. system flowchart [Incorrect. A system flowchart illustrates the relationship among inputs, processes, and outputs of a system, but not areas of responsibility.]
▶ **d.** document flowchart [Correct. A document flowchart traces the life of a document from its cradle to its grave as it works its way through the areas of responsibility within an organization.]

9. All of the following are recommended guidelines for making flowcharts more readable, clear, concise, consistent, and understandable EXCEPT:
a. Divide a document flowchart into columns with labels. [Incorrect. Dividing the flowchart into columns helps make it more readable, clear, concise, consistent, and understandable.]
▶ **b.** Flowchart all data flows, especially exception procedures and error routines. [Correct. Including all exception procedures and error routines clutters the flowchart and makes it difficult to read and understand.]
c. Design the flowchart so that flow proceeds from top to bottom and from left to right. [Incorrect. Flowcharts should be prepared so that they are read like a book.]
d. Show the final disposition of all documents to prevent loose ends that leave the reader dangling. [Incorrect. All documents should be placed either in a file or sent to another entity.]

10. How are data sources and destinations represented in a data flow diagram?
▶ **a.** as a square [Correct. See Figure 3-7.]
b. as a curved arrow [Incorrect. A curved arrow represents a data flow. See Figure 3-7.]
c. as a circle [Incorrect. A circle represents a process. See Figure 3-7.]
d. as two parallel lines [Incorrect. Two parallel lines represent a data store. See Figure 3-7.]
e. as none of the above [Incorrect. Option a is correct.]

COMPREHENSIVE PROBLEM SOLUTION

BUSINESS PROCESS DIAGRAM

The first step in preparing a business process diagram is to identify and understand the business processes to be diagrammed. This includes identifying the primary players in Accuflow's cash disbursement process: Megan Waters (accounts payable clerk), Stan Phillips (cash disbursement clerk), and John Sterling (treasurer). Since we are documenting Accuflow's cash disbursement process, we do not include the vendor, SoftData, as one of our major players. Table 3-3 lists the functions performed by the three people involved in cash disbursements.

TABLE 3-3 Accuflow's Table of Functions

Accounts Payable Clerk (Megan Waters)	Cash Disbursements Clerk (Stan Phillips)	Treasurer (John Sterling)
Receives invoice	Prepares check	Approves and signs check
Records invoice	Records cash disbursement	Cancels invoice
Posts cash disbursement	Files cancelled invoice	Mails check

We will now explain each step in creating the BPD solution for Accuflow shown in Figure 3-14. The first step is to create two columns to show the employees involved and the activities they perform. Next, we create three rows, sometimes called "swim lanes" to show the three employees and the activities each of them performs in the cash disbursements process.

Because the process begins when Megan Waters receives an invoice from a vendor, a circle is placed in the upper left portion of the Accounts Payable Clerk column to show where the cash disbursement process begins (see Figure 3-1 for the BPD symbols).The first activity (shown by a rectangle in the BPD) is entering the vendor invoice in the accounts payable subsidiary ledger. An arrow representing the document's flow and the order of operations connects the beginning of the process (circle) and the first activity (rounded rectangle). Since we got the invoice from someone not represented in a swim lane, we write "From Vendor" above the rectangle.

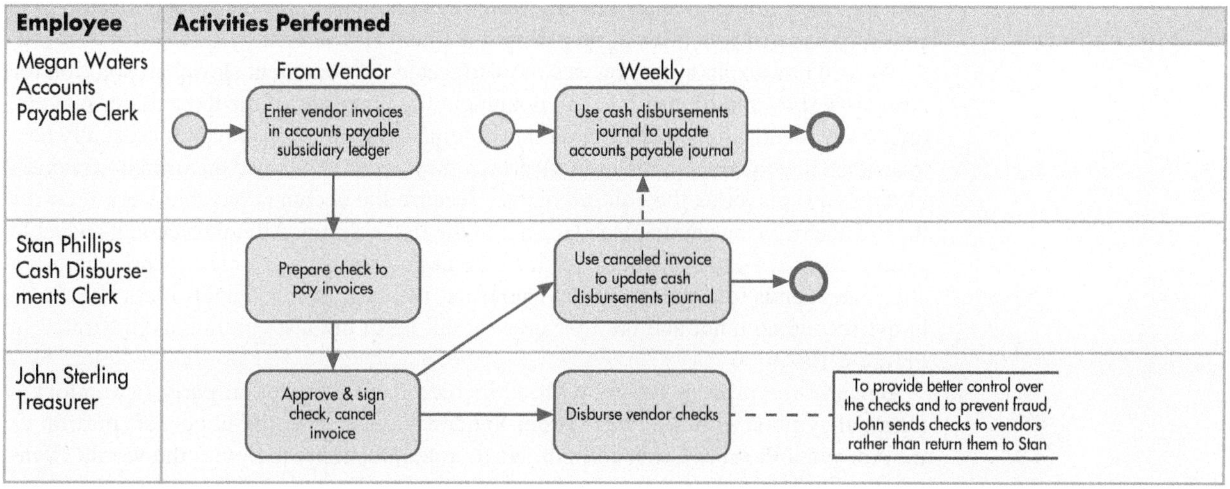

FIGURE 3-14
Accuflow's Business Process Diagram

The next activity is preparing checks to pay the invoices. Since that is done by Stan Phillips, the cash disbursements clerk, we draw the appropriate rectangle in his swim lane and connect the two rectangles with an arrow to indicate process flow. Note that, unlike a flowchart, in a BPD we do not show the documents created, their flow, or where they are stored. The emphasis is on the activities performed and the process flow.

The third activity in the cash disbursements process is John Sterling, the Treasurer, approving and signing the checks and canceling the invoice (marking it paid). That rectangle is drawn, the appropriate explanation placed inside it, and an arrow is drawn to show the process flow.

The fourth activity is the Treasurer sending the signed check to the vendor. There is no row or swim lane for the vendor; instead, the rectangle with "disburse vendor checks" communicates that the checks are sent to the external party. Internal controls can be highlighted on a BPD by explaining them and drawing a dotted arrow to the appropriate activity. In the Accuflow BPD, the annotation symbol (see Figure 3-3) is used, with the internal control description written inside the three-sided rectangle.

John sends the canceled invoice to Stan, who updates the cash disbursements journal, represented by another rectangle in Stan's swim lane and a connecting arrow between the two swim lanes. Accuflow receives and pays for invoices every day, and updating cash disbursements is the final daily activity in that business process; hence, the bolded circle to the right of the rectangle to indicate the end of that process.

There is one more activity in the process—Megan uses the cash disbursement journal to update the accounts payable journal. Since the timing of the activity is different (weekly rather than daily), it is shown as a separate activity with its own beginning and end. A dotted line connects the rectangles in Stan's and Megan's swim lanes to show that the flow is different than the other flows. The word "Weekly" is placed above the activity rectangle to indicate the different timing.

This completes the business process diagram for Accuflow's cash disbursements process.

FLOWCHART

The first step in preparing a document flowchart is to become familiar with the problem. The next step is to identify the primary actors or major players. In this problem there are three major players: Megan Waters (accounts payable clerk), Stan Phillips (cash disbursement clerk), and John Sterling (treasurer). Since we are documenting Accuflow's cash disbursement process, we are not interested in the internal workings of the vendor, SoftData. As a result, we do not include its activities on our flowchart. Note that forwarding to and receiving from the next major player (shown in Table 3-3) are not considered functions in preparing document flowcharts.

We will now explain, step by step, how to create the document flowchart solution for Accuflow shown in Figure 3-15. To document the functions of the three major players, divide the document flowchart into three columns, one for each player. It is usually best to arrange the columns in the order in which they occur and to use the primary function of the major player as the column name. Because the accounts payable clerk receives the invoice from the vendor, we place her in the first column. After the accounts payable clerk records the invoice, she sends it to the cash disbursements clerk, who prepares a check and sends it to the treasurer. Therefore, the cash disbursements clerk should be in the second column, and the treasurer should be in the last column, as illustrated in Figure 3-15.

Because the process begins with an invoice from an external party (a vendor), a terminal symbol with the term "From Vendor" is placed in the upper left portion of the Accounts Payable Clerk column. Next, a document symbol with the words "Vendor Invoice" printed inside it is placed below the terminal symbol. An arrow representing the document's flow and the order of operations connects the two symbols.

According to the narrative, Megan manually records the invoice in the accounts payable subsidiary ledger. Thus, a manual process symbol with the words "Record Invoice" is placed below the invoice document symbol, and the two symbols are connected with

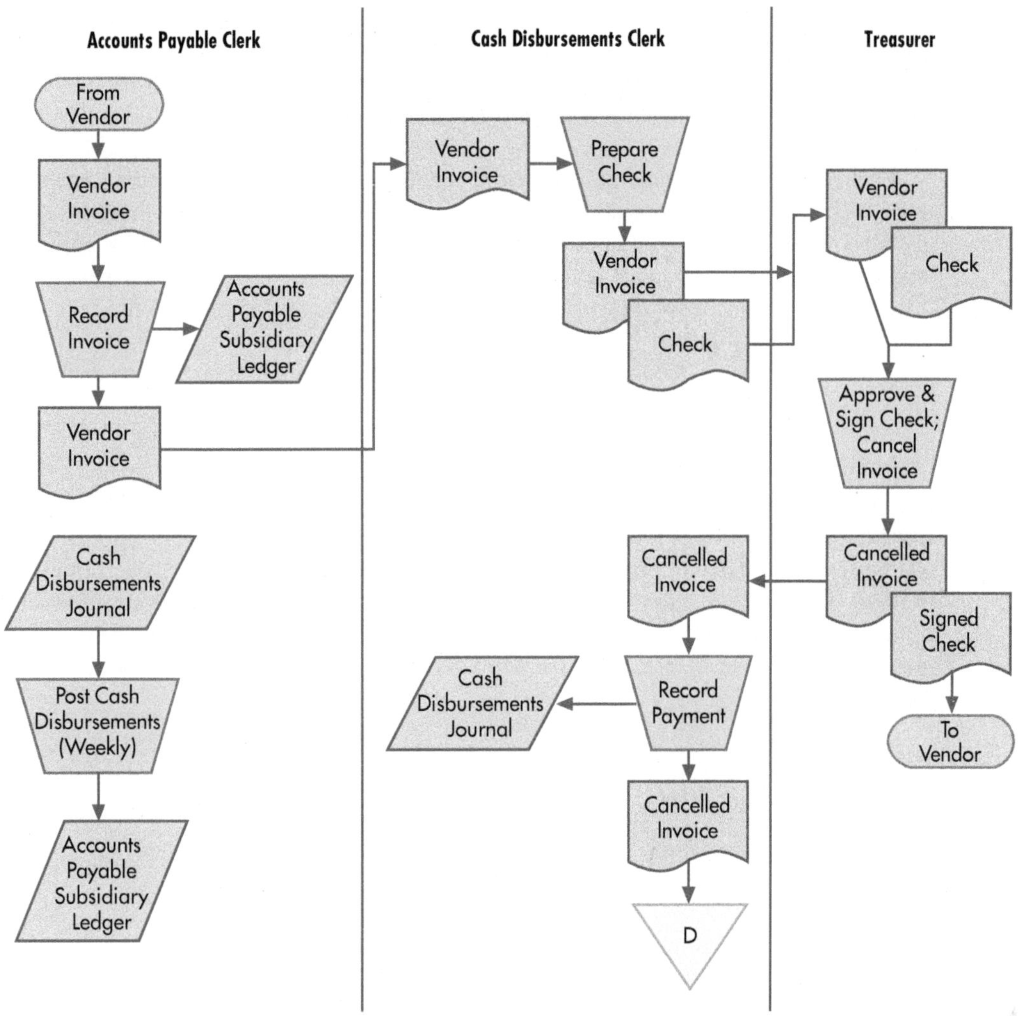

FIGURE 3-15
Accuflow's Document Flowchart

an arrow. Then, a journal/ ledger symbol is placed to the side of the manual process and an arrow is used to connect the two symbols. A new vendor invoice symbol is drawn below the record invoice symbol.

Because the vendor invoice moves from the accounts payable clerk to the cash disbursements clerk, the vendor invoice symbol is placed at the top of the cash disbursements column with an arrow connecting the two representations of the same document. We redraw the vendor invoice symbol in the cash disbursements clerk column to make the flowchart easier to read.

To show that the cash disbursement clerk prepares a check to pay the vendor invoice, a manual process symbol with "Prepare Check" inside it is placed next to the vendor invoice. We could have placed it below the invoice symbol but put it beside the symbol to save space. Two document symbols are placed below the manual process for the vendor invoice and the newly prepared check.

The cash disbursements clerk then sends the invoice and check to the treasurer. As a result, the vendor invoice and check appear in the Treasurer column. A manual symbol with "Approve & Sign Check; Cancel Invoice" inside is used to show that the check is signed and the invoice is cancelled. The documents are again shown in the flowchart, this time with new titles (Cancelled Invoice and Signed Check) to show the changed nature of the documents. The treasurer sends the signed check to the vendor, which is illustrated using a terminal symbol with words "To Vendor" written in it.

The cancelled invoice is used to record the cash disbursement in the cash disbursements journal, so it is sent back to the middle column (Cash Disbursements). A manual process symbol with "Record Payment" inside it and an arrow is used to show that the disbursement is recorded in the cash disbursements journal, represented by a journal/ledger symbol. To illustrate that the cancelled invoice is filed by date, it is shown, using appropriate arrows, as exiting the record payment manual process and entering a file. A "D" is placed in the file symbol to indicate that the documents are filed by date.

Each week, the accounts payable clerk manually posts entries from the cash disbursements journal to the accounts payable subsidiary ledger. To show this, the cash disbursements journal symbol is reproduced in the accounts payable clerk column, and a manual process symbol with the words "Post Cash Disbursements (Weekly)" is placed under it. An arrow shows data from this journal being entered into the accounts payable subsidiary ledger.

This completes the document flowchart for the Accuflow Company's cash disbursements process.

CONTEXT DIAGRAM

A context diagram is an overview of the data processing being documented. As such, a context diagram includes a single transformation process (circle or bubble) and the data sources and data destinations that send data to or receive data from the transformation process. Thus, the first step in preparing a context diagram is to draw a single circle or bubble and then label it with a name that best describes the process being documented. In this case, "Cash Disbursements System" effectively describes the process (see Figure 3-16).

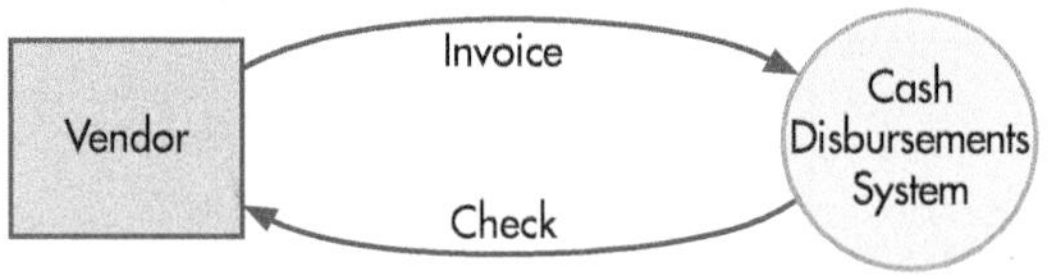

FIGURE 3-16 Accuflow's Context Diagram

The next step is to draw and label squares for the entities that either send data to the cash disbursements process or receive data from the cash disbursements process. In this example, there is a single entity—the vendor that acts as both a source and a destination of data to/from the cash disbursements process. In other processes, an outside entity could be just a source or a destination of data, and there could be more than one source or destination of data.

The last step is to connect the process (circle) with the source/destination (square) with arrows representing data flows. We have two arrows representing an invoice sent to Accuflow's cash disbursement process and a check sent to the vendor from Accuflow.

LEVEL 0 DATA FLOW DIAGRAM

In the context diagram, we saw the entire cash disbursements process in one bubble. In a Level 0 DFD, we break down the cash disbursements process into its major functions. In reading the narrative, we find the following five primary steps in the cash disbursements process:

1. Receive vendor invoice and record payable.
2. Prepare the check.
3. Sign and send the check and cancel the invoice.
4. Record the cash disbursement.
5. Post the cash disbursements to the accounts payable ledger.

Each of these processes is represented by a circle or bubble in Figure 3-17. Since this is the Level 0 DFD, we assign each of these processes a real number, with the first digit after the decimal point being a zero. We also place the circles in the order that the data should flow in the process. As a result, "Receive and Record Invoice" is assigned process 1.0, "Prepare Check" is assigned process 2.0, "Approve and Sign Check" is

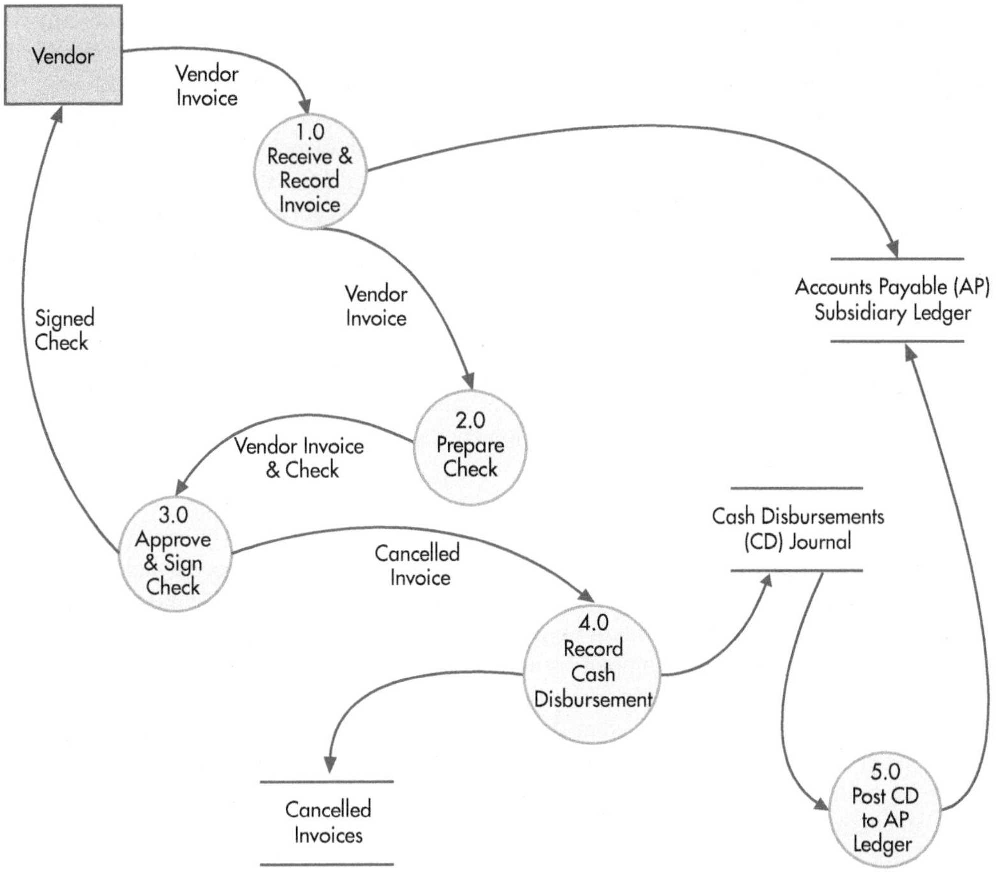

FIGURE 3-17
Accuflow's Level 0 Data Flow Diagram

3.0, "Record Cash Disbursement" is 4.0, and "Post Cash Disbursement to Accounts Payable Ledger" is 5.0. This numbering system allows us to decompose these processes into more detailed subprocesses and still keep a consistent numbering system. Thus, if we needed to decompose process 3.0 to a more detailed level, we could assign subprocess bubbles as 3.1, 3.2, 3.3, etc. We can even provide greater detail by decomposing process 3.1 into subprocesses 3.1.1, 3.1.2, 3.1.3, etc.

Next, we place the data sources and data destinations on the Level 0 DFD. Because we had only one data source and destination (i.e., the vendor), we draw a square and label it "Vendor." It is very important that we reconcile back to the context diagram when we prepare the different levels of DFDs. That is, the same data sources and destinations that appeared on the context diagram should appear on the Level 0 DFD. No new data sources and destinations should appear on the Level 0 DFD. If, when preparing the Level 0 DFD, you discover that a data source/destination is necessary to document the system properly, then you should revise the context diagram with the new data source/destination because the context diagram should represent the entire process.

Once the data source/destinations and processes are drawn, we then connect them by drawing the arrows between the appropriate symbols. These arrows represent the data moving or flowing from one process to another and from one source or destination to or from a particular process. Accordingly, we have a vendor invoice moving from the vendor to the "Receive and Record Invoice" process and from that process to the "Prepare Check" process. The vendor invoice and a check move from the "Prepare Check" process to the "Approve and Sign Check" process. We also have arrows leaving process 3.0 to represent the signed check being sent to the vendor and the cancelled invoice going to process 4.0, "Record Cash Disbursements."

Some processes require that data be stored. As a result, we also draw any necessary files or data stores. The Level 0 DFD is the first time data stores appear in a DFD set. (Note: Data stores should not be represented on a context diagram.) Data store labels should identify the data being sent to or from it. As a result, labeling the data flows to or from data stores is normally unnecessary. Data stores are prepared by drawing two parallel lines and inserting the name of the data store between the parallel lines.

In Figure 3-17, we have three data stores: the cash disbursements journal, accounts payable subsidiary ledger, and cancelled invoices data store. Because the cash disbursements journal is updated in process 4.0, a data flow is sent from the process 4.0 circle to the cash disbursements journal data store. To show that the accounts payable ledger is updated when invoices are received (process 1.0), an arrow is drawn from that process to the accounts payable ledger. To show that accounts payable is updated with data from the cash disbursements journal (process 5.0), a data flow arrow is drawn from the cash disbursements data store to process 5.0, and another data flow arrow is drawn from process 5.0 to the accounts payable subsidiary ledger data store. The update takes place weekly, but unlike document flowcharts, a DFD does not indicate the timing of data flows.

LEVEL 1 DATA FLOW DIAGRAM

When additional detail is needed to document data flows, a process bubble may be decomposed further. As indicated in Focus 3-3, to be clear, understandable, and easy to read, a DFD should contain no more than seven process bubbles. In the Accuflow example, we broke the company's data flows into five main processes. Each of these five processes can be further decomposed. To illustrate this, we will decompose process 3.0. The narrative indicates that the treasurer approves and signs the prepared check, sends it to the vendor, and cancels the invoice to prevent duplicate payments. Therefore, we will break down process 3.0 into process 3.1 (approve and sign check), 3.2 (send check to vendor), and 3.3 (cancel invoice). To display the three processes, we draw three circles and label them as shown on Figure 3-18. We also draw the data flows and label them. Notice that the vendor data source/destination is not needed on the Level 1 DFD since it is already shown on Level 0. Since it would clutter the DFD, and because we are showing greater detail on the Level 1 than on the Level 0 for one particular process, we do not replicate all of the processes and data stores in the Level 0 DFD.

FIGURE 3-18
Accuflow's Level 1 Data Flow Diagram

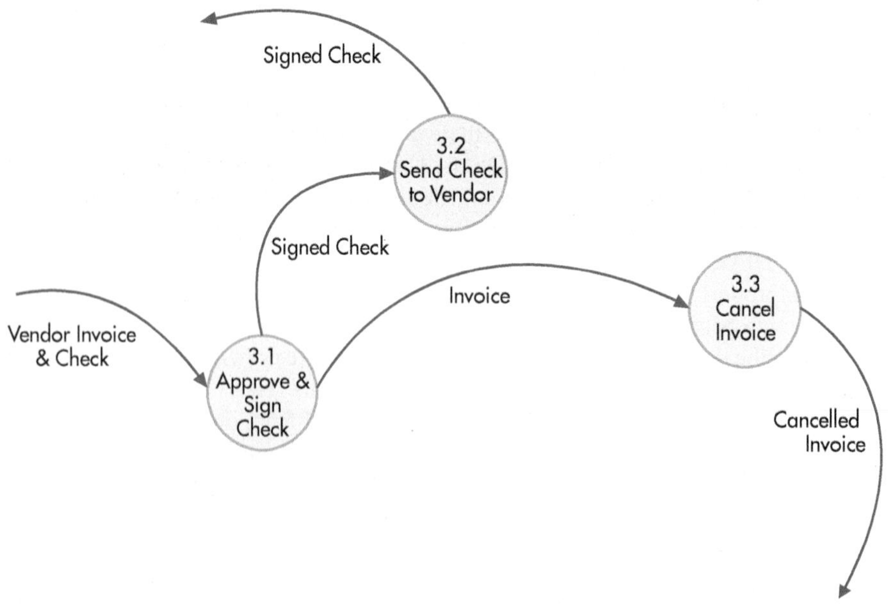

Data Analytics

PART

II

Rawpixel/123RF

CHAPTER **4**
Relational Databases

CHAPTER **5**
Introduction to Data Analytics in Accounting

CHAPTER **6**
Transforming Data

CHAPTER **7**
Data Analysis and Presentation

CHAPTER

4

Relational Databases

LEARNING OBJECTIVES

After studying this chapter, you should be able to:

1. Explain the importance and advantages of databases as well as the difference between database systems and file-based legacy systems.
2. Explain database systems, including logical and physical views, schemas, the data dictionary, and database management system (DBMS) languages.
3. Describe what a relational database is, how it organizes data, and how to create a set of well-structured relational database tables.
4. Query a relational database using visual methods as well as using structured query language.

INTEGRATIVE CASE S&S

S&S is very successful and operates five stores and a popular website. Ashton Fleming believes it is time to upgrade S&S's accounting information system (AIS) so that Susan and Scott can easily access the information they need to run their business. Most new AISs are based on a relational database. Since Ashton knows that Scott and Susan are likely to have questions, he prepared a brief report that explains why S&S's new AIS should be a relational database system. His report addresses the following questions:

1. What is a database system, and how does it differ from file-oriented systems?
2. What is a *relational* database system?
3. How do you design a well-structured set of tables in a relational database?
4. How do you query a relational database system?

Introduction

Relational databases underlie most modern integrated AISs. This chapter and Chapters 19 through 21 provide guidance in the design and implementation of a database. This chapter defines a database, with the emphasis on understanding the relational database structure and how to extract information from that structure. Chapter 19 introduces two tools used to design

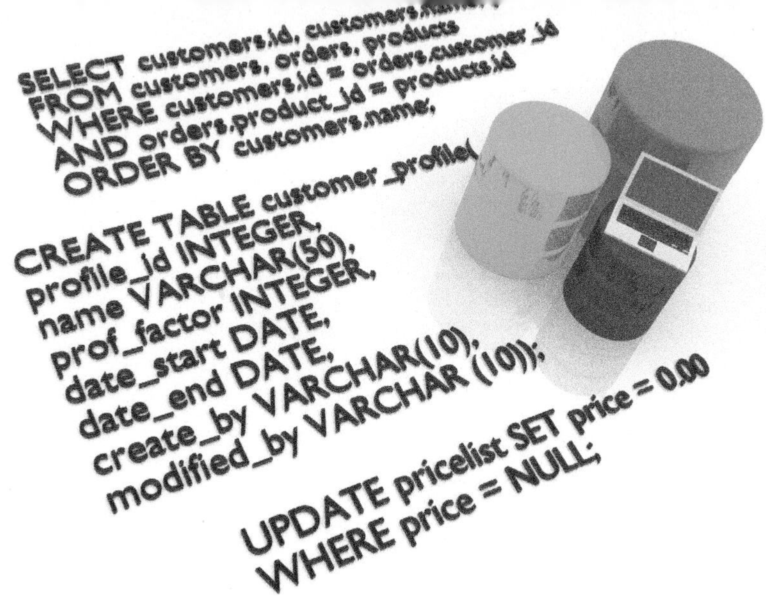

S.John/Shutterstock

databases—entity-relationship diagramming and REA data modeling—and demonstrates how to use them to build a data model. Chapter 20 explains how to implement an REA data model and how to produce the information needed to manage an organization. Chapter 21 discusses advanced data modeling and database design issues. Once stored in a relational database, the data are often combined with other sources of data to allow the business to analyze performance and make business decisions. These types of analysis are commonly referred to as data analytics. Chapters 5 through 7 discuss data analytics and how relational databases and other data are used to improve business decisions.

Databases and Files

To appreciate the power of databases, it is important to understand the nature of data stored in an accounting system. For financial reporting, an accounting system must necessarily store data about assets, liabilities, and equity. It must also store information about revenue and expense transactions. Accounting systems must also satisfy managerial, audit, tax, and control information needs. Thus, an accounting system must store information about budgets, transactions in progress, overhead, tax jurisdictions, access logs, etc. Historically separate systems were created for each information need as it arose. Each of these systems had its own programs and files. This led to a proliferation of redundant data in the files of the separate systems. This proliferation of silos of data created problems such as storing the same data in two or more overlapping files. The silos made it difficult to integrate the data to create an organization-wide view of the business' data. Updating redundant data in the various systems was problematic due to the differences in data structures and formats of each system. Extracting correct information (truth) from the systems was challenging because underlying data items might not agree. For example, a customer's address may be correctly updated in the shipping file but not the billing file. Note that Bank of America once had 36 million customer accounts in 23 separate systems. The data landscape of system-specific files is called the file approach as shown in Figure 4-1.

Databases were developed to address the proliferation of redundant data in the files of systems using the file approach. The goal of the database approach is to create an organization-wide database that stores all of the data needed to operate the business while linking data across various functions and eliminating redundancy. Figure 4-2 shows a data hierarchy representing a database in the database approach. The **database** is comprised of numerous entities about which the company wants to store data such as customers, sales, and inventory. Information about a single instance of an entity such as single customer is stored as a record. The attributes of that record are specified as fields. The attributes for a customer might include the name and address fields. At the entity level, it is common to think of records as rows and fields as columns. This structure allows databases to reduce the storage of redundant data. In summary, a database is an organized

database - A set of interrelated, centrally coordinated data tables stored electronically with as little data redundancy as possible.

FIGURE 4-1
File-Oriented Systems versus Database Systems

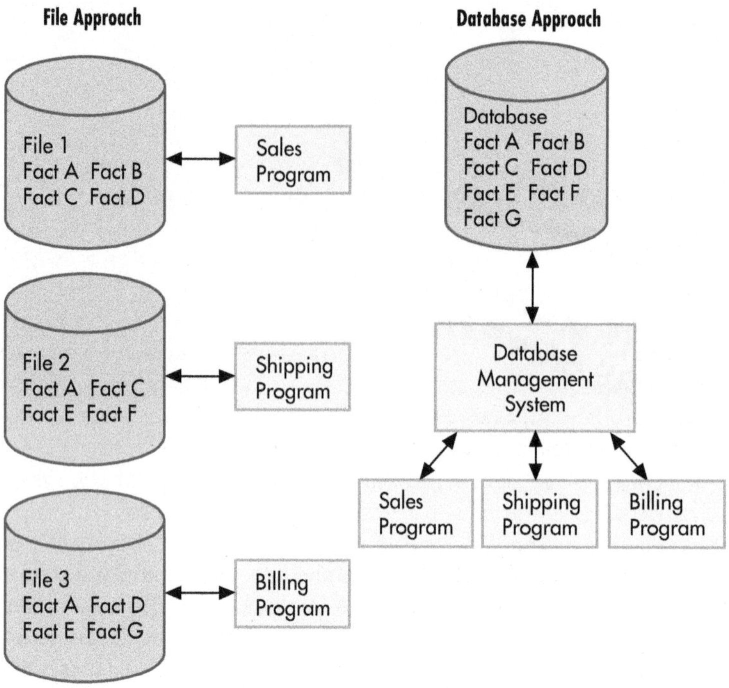

database management system (DBMS) - The program that manages and controls the data and the interfaces between the data and the application programs that use the data stored in the database.

database system - The database, the DBMS, and the application programs that access the database through the DBMS.

database administrator (DBA) - The person responsible for coordinating, controlling, and managing the database.

collection of data about a set of entities stored with as little data redundancy as possible. A database's value comes from the consolidation of data into a common pool that can serve a variety of users and data processing applications.

Figure 4-1 illustrates the differences between file-oriented systems and database systems. In the database approach, data is an organizational resource used by and managed for the entire organization, not just the originating department. A **database management system (DBMS)** is the program that manages and controls the data and the interfaces between the data and the application programs that use the data stored in the database. The database, the DBMS, and the application programs that access the database through the DBMS are referred to as the **database system**. The **database administrator (DBA)** is responsible for coordinating, controlling, and managing the database.

FIGURE 4-2
Basic Elements of Data Hierarchy

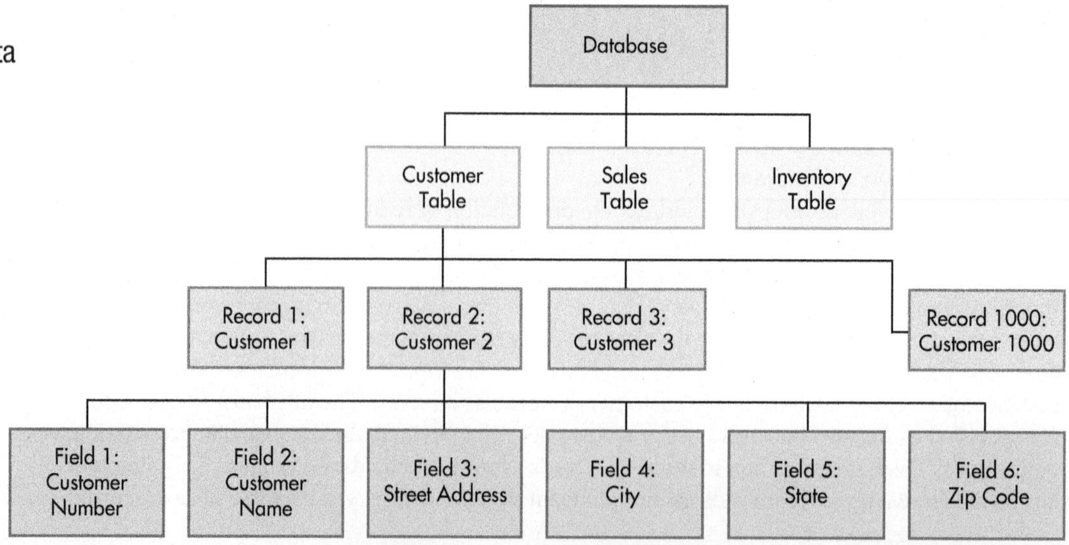

USING DATA WAREHOUSES FOR DATA ANALYTICS

The database noted previously is often called the **online transaction processing database (OLTP)** and is used to process normal business transactions. Many OLTP databases are able to process more than 1 million transactions a minute. While very important, the OLTP database is just one piece of the data infrastructure of the modern enterprise. To maintain the speed of the OLTP, older transaction data is often migrated from the transaction processing database to a data warehouse. A **data warehouse** is one or more very large databases containing both detailed and summarized data for a number of years and from numerous sources used for analysis rather than transaction processing. A data warehouse is one element of the enterprise data structure used for analytical processing. These enterprise data structures are discussed more fully in Chapter 5. For purposes of this chapter, we will use data warehouse generically to represent the enterprise data structure beyond the OLTP. It is not unusual for data warehouses to contain hundreds or thousands of terabytes of data. Some data warehouses are measured in petabytes (1,000 terabytes or 1 million gigabytes).

online transaction processing database (OLTP) - Database containing detailed current transaction data, usually in third normal form. Focuses on throughput, speed, availability, concurrency, and recoverability. Often used concurrently by hundreds of users.

data warehouse - Very large databases containing detailed and summarized data for a number of years used for analysis rather than transaction processing.

Data warehouses do not replace OLTP databases; they complement them by providing support for strategic decision making. Since data warehouses are not used for transaction processing, they are usually updated periodically rather than in real time. Whereas OLTP databases minimize redundancy and maximize the efficiency of updating them to reflect the results of current transactions, data warehouses allow redundancy to maximize query efficiency.

Analyzing large amounts of data for strategic decision making is referred to as data analytics. Chapter 7 provides guidance for descriptive, diagnostic, predictive, and prescriptive analytics. In data analytics, one can find a vast array of sophisticated tools that allow for multidimensional analysis, complex calculations, data projections, and simulations. These advanced tools often fall under the heading of **business intelligence**. Two main techniques are used in business intelligence: online analytical processing (OLAP) and data mining. **Online analytical processing (OLAP)** is using queries to investigate hypothesized relationships among data. For example, a manager may analyze supplier purchases for the last three years, followed by additional queries that "drill down" to lower levels by grouping purchases by item number and by fiscal period. **Data mining** is using sophisticated statistical analysis, including artificial intelligence techniques such as neural networks, to "discover" unhypothesized relationships in the data. For example, credit card companies use data mining to identify usage patterns indicative of fraud. Similarly, data mining techniques can identify previously unknown relationships in sales data that can be used in future promotions.

business intelligence - Analyzing large amounts of data for strategic decision making.

online analytical processing (OLAP) - Using queries to investigate hypothesized relationships among data.

data mining - Using sophisticated statistical analysis to "discover" unhypothesized relationships in the data.

Proper controls are needed to reap significant benefits from data warehousing. Data validation controls are needed to ensure that data warehouse input is accurate. Verifying the accuracy of data as it is placed in the warehouse is called cleaning data. It is one of the most expensive and time-consuming steps in maintaining a data warehouse. Data cleaning is addressed in Chapter 6. It is also important to control access to the data warehouse as well as to encrypt the stored data. Finally, it is important to regularly back up the data warehouse and store the backups securely.

Bank of America created a customer information database to provide customer service, marketing analysis, and managerial information. It was the largest in the banking industry, with more than 600 billion characters of data. It contained all bank data on checking and savings accounts; real estate, consumer, and commercial loans; ATMs; and bankcards. Although the bank spends $14 million a year to maintain the data warehouse, it is worth the cost. Queries that formerly averaged two hours took only five minutes. Minutes after Los Angeles suffered an earthquake, the bank sorted its $28 billion mortgage loan portfolio by zip code, identified loans in the earthquake area, and calculated its potential loan loss.

THE ADVANTAGES OF DATABASE SYSTEMS

Virtually all mainframes and servers use database technology, and database use in personal computers is growing rapidly. Most accountants are involved with databases through data entry, data processing, querying, or auditing. They also develop, manage, or evaluate the controls needed to ensure database integrity. Databases provide organizations with the following benefits:

- ***Data integration.*** Previously separate application files are combined into large "pools" of data that many application programs access. An example is an employee database that consolidates payroll, personnel, and job skills files.

- ***Data sharing***. Integrated data are more easily shared with authorized users from centralized data storage. Databases are easily browsed to research a problem or obtain detailed information underlying a report. The FBI, which does a good job of collecting data but a poor job of sharing it, is spending eight years and $400 million to integrate data from their different systems.
- ***Minimal data redundancy and data inconsistencies***. Because data items are usually stored only once, data redundancy and data inconsistencies are minimized.
- ***Data independence***. Because data and the programs that use them are independent of each other, each can be changed without changing the other. This facilitates programming and simplifies data management.
- ***Cross-functional analysis***. In a database system, relationships, such as the association between selling costs and promotional campaigns, can be explicitly defined and used in the preparation of management reports.

THE IMPORTANCE OF GOOD DATA

Incorrect database data can lead to bad decisions, embarrassment, and angry users. For example:

- A company sent half its mail-order catalogs to incorrect addresses. A manager finally investigated the large volume of returns and customer complaints. Correcting customer addresses in the database saved the company $12 million a year.
- Valparaiso, Indiana, used the county database to develop its tax rates. After the tax notices were mailed, a huge error was discovered: A $121,900 home was valued at $400 million and caused a $3.1 million property tax revenue shortfall. As a result, the city, the school district, and governmental agencies had to make severe budget cuts.

IBM estimates that poor quality data cost the U.S. economy more than $3.1 trillion a year. They found that one in three business leaders don't trust the information they use to make decisions, and 27% of respondents in one survey were unsure of how much of their data was inaccurate.

Managing data gets harder every year: The quantity of data generated and stored doubles every 18 months. To avoid outdated, incomplete, or erroneous data, management needs policies and procedures that ensure clean, or scrubbed, data. The Sarbanes-Oxley Act (SOX) states that top executives face prosecution and jail time if a company's financial data are not in order. Preventing and detecting bad data are discussed in more detail in Chapters 5 through 13.

Database Systems

LOGICAL AND PHYSICAL VIEWS OF DATA

In file-oriented systems, programmers must know the physical location and layout of records. Suppose a programmer wants a report showing customer number, credit limit, and current balance. To write the program, she must understand the location and length of the fields needed (i.e., record positions 1 through 10 for customer number) and the format of each field (alphanumeric or numeric). The report writing task becomes more complex if data from several files are used, as data linkages are not embedded in the files.

record layout - Document that shows the items stored in a file, including the order and length of the data fields and the type of data stored.

A **record layout** is a document that shows the items stored in a file, including the order and length of the data fields and the type of data stored in an accounts receivable file. Figure 4-3 shows a record layout of an accounts receivable file.

FIGURE 4-3
Accounts Receivable File Record Layout

Customer Number N	Customer Name A	Address A	Credit Limit N	Balance N
1 10	11 30	31 60	61 68	69 76

A = alphanumeric field
N = numeric field

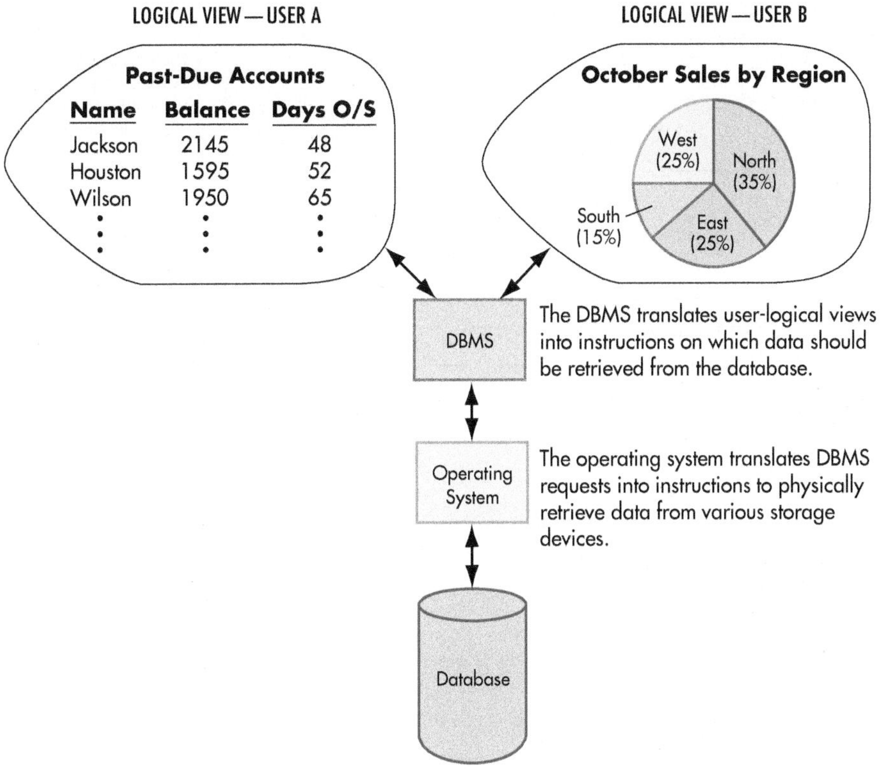

FIGURE 4-4
Function of the DBMS: To Support Multiple Logical Views of Data

Database systems overcome this problem by separating the storage of the data from the use of data elements. The database approach provides two separate views of the data: the physical view and the logical view. The **logical view** is how people conceptually organize and understand the relationships among data items. For example, a sales manager views all customer information as being stored in a table. The **physical view** refers to the way data are physically arranged and stored in the computer system.

logical view - How people conceptually organize, view, and understand the relationships among data items.

physical view - The way data are physically arranged and stored in the computer system.

As shown in Figure 4-4, database management (DBMS) software links the way data are physically stored with each user's logical view of the data. The DBMS allows users to access, query, or update the database without reference to how or where data are physically stored. Separating the logical and physical views of data also means that users can change their logical view of data without changing the way data are physically stored. Likewise, the DBA can change physical storage to improve system performance without affecting users or application programs.

SCHEMAS

A **schema** is a description of the data elements in a database, the relationships among them, and the logical model used to organize and describe the data. There are three levels of schemas: the external, the conceptual, and the internal. Figure 4-5 shows the relationships among these three levels. The **external-level schema** is a user's logical view of their portion of a database, each of which is referred to as a **subschema**. The elements used in these subschemas are drawn from the conceptual schema. The **conceptual-level schema**, the organization-wide view of the *entire* database, lists all data elements and the relationships among them. This is the DBA's view of the entire database. The **internal-level schema**, a low-level view of the database, describes how the data are stored and accessed, including record layouts, definitions, addresses, and indexes. Figure 4-5 connects each of the levels with bidirectional arrows to represent schema mappings. The DBMS uses the mappings to translate a user's or a program's request for data (expressed in terms of logical names and relationships) into the indexes and addresses needed to physically access the data.

At S&S, the conceptual schema for the revenue cycle database contains data about customers, sales, cash receipts, sales personnel, cash, and inventory. External subschemas are derived from this schema, each tailored to the needs of different users or programs. Each subschema

schema - A description of the data elements in a database, the relationships among them, and the logical model used to organize and describe the data.

external-level schema - An individual user's view of portions of a database; also called a subschema.

subschema - A subset of the schema; the way the user defines the data and the data relationships.

conceptual-level schema - The organization-wide view of the entire database that lists all data elements and the relationships between them.

internal-level schema - A low-level view of the entire database describing how the data are actually stored and accessed.

FIGURE 4-5
Three Levels of Schemas

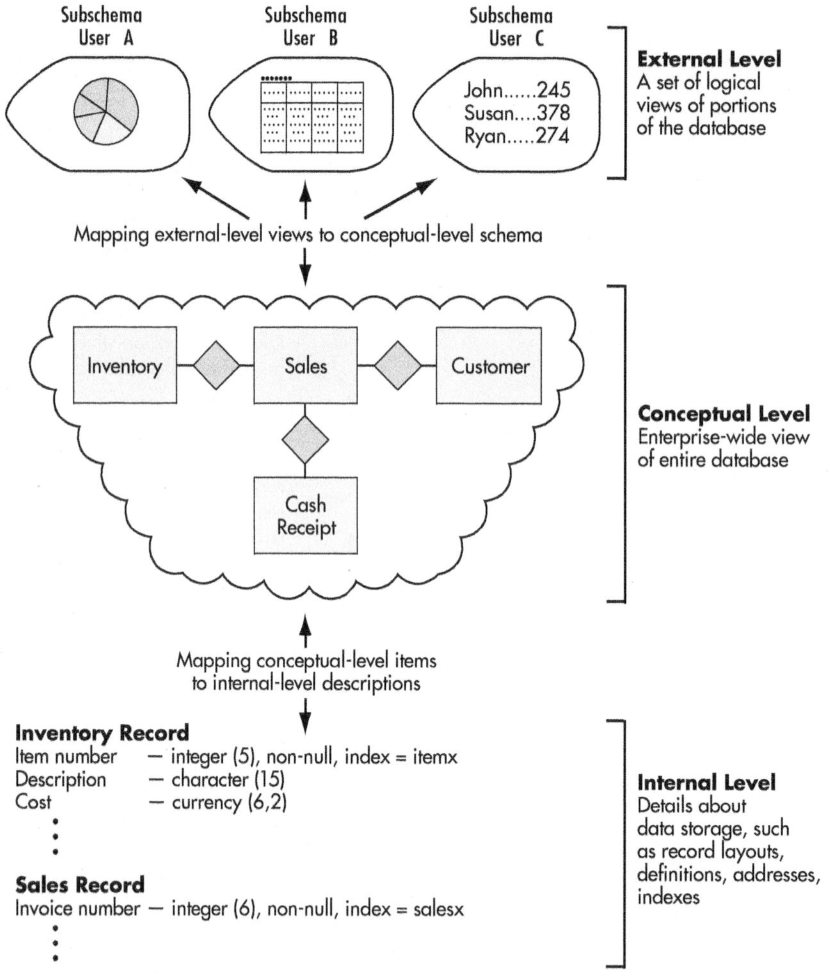

access rights - Permissions granted to create, read, update, and delete data, database records, or data files.

grants specific types of **access rights** to those portions of the database the user needs to perform their duties. Likewise, it prevents access to other portions of the database. Four basic access rights can be granted in a subschema: Create (C), Read (R), Update (U), and Delete (D) (CRUD). You may remember these four as data processing activities in Chapter 2. We are now tying those activities to the subschemas of those users permitted to perform the activities for each data element in the data dictionary. Access rights can be defined at the table level as well as the attribute level. For our examples, we will set access rights at the attribute level. For example, the sales order entry subschema would include R access to customer credit limits, R access to customer balances, and C and R access to all attributes of data entered on a sales order. U and D rights would not be given. D rights are rarely given to anyone for transaction data in an accounting system because the ability to delete transaction information challenges the data integrity of the entire system. Reversing entries are used to back out errors in transactions. The sales order entry schema would not be given access to cost of inventory or bank account balances. Keep in mind that these access rights are imposed at the database level, not at the application level. Consider a clerk entering a sales order transaction. The clerk may be able to update or delete mistakes in the form as the data is being entered. However, once the transaction is posted to the database, they will not be able to update or delete data in that transaction.

THE DATA DICTIONARY

data dictionary - Information about the structure of the database, including a description of each data element.

A **data dictionary** contains information about the structure of the database. As shown in Table 4-1, for each data element stored in the database, there is a record in the dictionary describing it. The DBMS maintains the data dictionary, whose inputs include new or deleted data elements and changes in data element names, descriptions, or uses. Relations, subschemas, access rights, and indexes are also defined in the data dictionary. Outputs include reports for programmers, designers, and users, such as (1) programs or reports using a data item, (2) synonyms for the

TABLE 4-1 Example of a Data Dictionary

Data Element Name	Description	Records in Which Contained	Source	Field Length	Field Type	Programs in Which Used	Outputs in Which Contained	Authorized Users	Other Data Names
Customer-ID	Unique identifier of each customer	A/R record, customer record, sales analysis record	Customer number listing	10	Numeric	A/R update, customer file update, sales analysis update, credit analysis	A/R aging report, customer status report, sales analysis report, credit report	No restrictions	None
Customer-Name	Complete name of customer	Customer record	Initial customer order	20	Alphanumeric	Customer file update, statement processing	Customer status report, monthly statement	No restrictions	None
Address	Street, city, state, and zip code	Customer record	Credit application	30	Alphanumeric	Customer file update, statement processing	Customer status report, monthly statement	No restrictions	None
CreditLimit	Maximum credit that can be extended to customer	Customer record, A/R record	Credit application	8	Numeric	Customer file update, A/R update, credit analysis	Customer status report, A/R aging report, credit report	D. Dean G. Allen H. Heaton	CR_limit
Balance	Balance due from customer on credit purchases	A/R record, sales analysis record	Various sales and payment transactions	8	Numeric	A/R update, sales analysis update, statement processing, credit analysis	A/R aging report, sales analysis report, monthly statement, credit report	G. Burton B. Heninger S. Summers	Cust_bal

data elements in a file, and (3) data elements used by a user. These reports are used for system documentation, for database design and implementation, and as part of the audit trail.

DBMS LANGUAGES

data definition language (DDL) - DBMS language that builds the data dictionary, creates the database, describes logical views, and specifies record or field security constraints.

structured query language (SQL) - Standardized commercial programming language designed for managing data in relational database systems. Even though it is standardized, variations exist among different database systems.

data manipulation language (DML) - DBMS language that changes database content, including data element creations, updates, insertions, and deletions.

data query language (DQL) - High-level, English-like, DBMS language that contains powerful, easy-to-use commands that enable users to retrieve, sort, order, and display data.

report writer - DBMS language that simplifies report creation.

data model - An abstract representation of database contents.

relational data model - A two-dimensional table representation of data; each row represents a unique entity (record) and each column is a field where record attributes are stored.

tuple - A row in a table that contains data about a specific item in a database table.

A DBMS has several languages. The **data definition language (DDL)** builds the data dictionary, creates the database, describes logical views for each user, and specifies record or field security constraints. Examples of DDL commands in **structured query language (SQL)** would be the CREATE, DROP, and ALTER statements. The **data manipulation language (DML)** changes database content, including data, updates, insertions, and deletions. SQL examples would include INSERT, UPDATE, TRUNCATE, and DROP statements. The **data query language (DQL)** is a high-level, English-like language that contains powerful, easy-to-use commands that enable users to retrieve, sort, order, and display data. An example of a DQL statement is the SELECT statement in the SQL language. A **report writer** simplifies report creation. Users specify the data elements they want printed, and the report writer searches the database, extracts the data elements, and prints them in the user-specified format. The DQL and report writer are available to users to interrogate the database. The DML is only given to those who maintain data in the database. The DDl should be restricted to authorized administrators and programmers.

Relational Databases

A DBMS is characterized by the logical **data model**, or abstract representation of database contents like the conceptual view noted in Figure 4-5. As most new DBMSs are relational databases, this chapter focuses primarily on them. The **relational data model** represents conceptual- and external-level schemas as if data are stored in two-dimensional tables like the one shown in Table 4-2. The data are actually stored not in tables, but in the manner described in the internal-level schema.

A relational database is a collection of two-dimensional tables with each table representing an object about which we wish to collect and store information. Each row in a table, called a **tuple**, contains data about a specific occurrence of an entity. Each column contains data about an attribute of that entity. For example, the table represented in Table 4-2 represents data about the inventory of the business. Each row contains data about a particular inventory item that S&S carries, and each column contains data about specific inventory attributes, such as description, color, and price. Similarly, each row in a Customer table contains data about a specific customer, and each column contains data about customer attributes, such as name and address.

TABLE 4-2 Sample Inventory Table for S&S

Inventory

ItemID	Description	Color	VendorID	QuantityOnHand	ListPrice
1036	Refrigerator	White	30023	12	1199
1038	Refrigerator	Black	30023	7	1299
1039	Refrigerator	Stainless	30023	5	1499
2061	Range	White	30011	6	799
2063	Range	Stainless	30011	5	999
3541	Washer	White	30008	15	499
3544	Washer	Black	30008	10	699
3785	Dryer	White	30019	12	399
3787	Dryer	Black	30019	8	499

TYPES OF ATTRIBUTES

A **primary key** is the database attribute, or combination of attributes, that uniquely identifies a specific row in a table. The primary key in Table 4-2 is ItemID, as it uniquely identifies each merchandise item that S&S sells. Usually, the primary key is a single attribute. In some tables, two or more attributes must work together to uniquely identify a specific row in a table. The primary key of the Sales_Inventory table in Table 4-5 is the combination of SalesInvoiceID and ItemID.

primary key - Database attribute, or combination of attributes, that uniquely identifies each row in a table.

A **foreign key** is an attribute in one table that is also a primary key in another table and is used to link the two tables. CustomerID in Table 4-5 is the primary key in the Customer table and a foreign key in the Sales table. In the Sales table, CustomerID links a sale to data about the customer who made the purchase, as contained in the Customer table (see arrows connecting tables).

foreign key - An attribute in a table that is also a primary key in another table; used to link the two tables.

Other nonkey attributes in a table store important information about that entity. The inventory table in Table 4-2 contains information about the description, color, vendor number, quantity on hand, and price of each item S&S carries.

DESIGNING A RELATIONAL DATABASE FOR S&S, INC.

In a manual accounting system, S&S would capture sales information on a preprinted sales invoice that provides both a logical and physical view of the data collected. Physical storage of sales invoice data is simple; a copy of the invoice is stored in a file cabinet.

Storing the same data in a computer is more complex. Suppose S&S wanted to store five sales invoices (numbered 11101 to 11105) electronically. On several invoices, a customer buys more than one item. Let us look at the effects of several ways of storing this information.

1: Store All Data in One Table with Each Data Element Represented as a Column. S&S could store sales data in one table, as illustrated in Table 4-3. This approach has two disadvantages. First, it stores lots of redundant data. Examine invoice 11102 in Table 4-3. Because three inventory items are sold, three rows are needed to adequately capture information about each of the items sold. Yet, invoice and customer data (columns 1 to 9) are recorded three times. Likewise, inventory descriptions and unit prices are repeated each time an item is sold. Because sales volumes are high in a retail store (remember, Table 4-3 represents only five invoices), such redundancy makes tables unnecessarily large and error-prone.

Second, problems occur when invoice data are stored in these types of tables. The first is called an **update anomaly**. Changing a customer's address involves searching the entire table and changing every occurrence of that customer's address. Overlooking the update of even one row creates an inconsistency because multiple addresses would exist for the same customer. The business would not know the "true" customer address. This could result in mailings to old addresses and other errors.

update anomaly - Improper database organization where a non-primary key item is stored multiple times; updating the item in one location and not the others causes data inconsistencies.

An **insert anomaly** would occur in our example with regard to recording new inventory items for sale. We would not be able to store information about a new inventory item in the Sales table until that item is sold. If we did attempt to store information about the new inventory item before it sold, the Sale and Customer information would be blank. The SalesInvoiceID is part of the primary key and cannot be blank as it helps uniquely identify the record.

insert anomaly - Improper database organization that results in the inability to add records to a database.

A **delete anomaly** occurs when deleting a row has unintended consequences. If customer information is stored in the sales table as represented in Table 4-3 and a particular customer only made one purchase, then deleting the row of that purchase results in the loss of all information for that customer. For example, deleting SalesInvoice 11104 would delete all information about customer Rodney Wern.

delete anomaly - Improper organization of a database that results in the loss of all information about an entity when a row is deleted.

2: Vary the Number of Columns for Repeating Items. An alternative to Table 4-3 is to record sales invoice and customer data once and add additional columns to record each item sold. Table 4-4 illustrates this approach. Although this reduces data redundancy and eliminates some anomalies associated with Table 4-3, it has drawbacks. S&S would have to decide in advance how many item items could be sold in a transaction (i.e., how many columns to put in the table; note in Table 4-4 that to store each additional item requires six additional columns—Item, Quantity, Description, Color, Unit Price, and Extended Amount). If columns are created

TABLE 4-3 Example of Storing All Sales Data for S&S in One Table

Sales

SalesInvoiceID	SaleDate	CustomerID	CustomerName	Street	City	State	Description	Color	ItemID	Quantity	SoldPrice	ExtendedAmount
11101	10/15/2021	151	Vivian Rodgers	204 NoContent Street	Phoenix	AZ	Refrigerator	Stainless	1039	2	1450	2900
11101	10/15/2021	151	Vivian Rodgers	204 NoContent Street	Phoenix	AZ	Range	Stainless	2063	1	950	950
11102	10/15/2021	152	Lola Doyle	504 Gateway Place	Mesa	AZ	Refrigerator	White	1036	1	1199	1199
11102	10/15/2021	152	Lola Doyle	504 Gateway Place	Mesa	AZ	Range	White	2061	1	799	799
11102	10/15/2021	152	Lola Doyle	504 Gateway Place	Mesa	AZ	Washer	White	3541	2	499	998
11103	10/28/2021	151	Vivian Rodgers	204 NoContent Street	Phoenix	AZ	Refrigerator	Black	1038	2	1201	2402
11104	10/31/2021	153	Rodney Wern	500 Serverr Place	Chandler	AZ	Refrigerator	Stainless	1039	1	1499	1499
11105	11/14/2021	152	Lola Doyle	504 Gateway Place	Mesa	AZ	Range	Stainless	2063	1	999	999
11105	11/14/2021	152	Lola Doyle	504 Gateway Place	Mesa	AZ	Washer	Black	3544	2	650	1300
11105	11/14/2021	152	Lola Doyle	504 Gateway Place	Mesa	AZ	Dryer	Black	3787	2	450	900

TABLE 4-4 Example of Storing S&S Sales Data by Adding Columns for Each Additional Item Sold

SalesAlt

SalesInvoiceID	Columns 2-9	ItemID_1	Quantity_1	SoldPrice_1	ExtendedAmt_1	ItemID_2	Quantity_2	SoldPrice_2	Extend
11101	Same 8	1039	2	1450	2900	2063	1	950	
11102	columns as	1036	1	1199	1199	2061	1	799	
11103	in	1038	2	1201	2402				
11104	Table 4-3	1039	1	1499	1499				
11105	above	2063	1	999	999	3544	2	650	

to store a sale of four items (24 columns), how would data about a sale involving eight items (48 columns) be stored? If columns are created for the sale of eight items, however, there will be a great deal of wasted space, as is the case for sales invoices 11103 and 11104.

3: The Solution: A Set of Related Tables. The data redundancies and storage problems in Tables 4-3 and 4-4 are solved using a **relational database**. The set of tables in Table 4-5 represent a well-structured relational database.

relational database - A database built using the relational data model.

BASIC REQUIREMENTS OF A RELATIONAL DATABASE

We now turn to the guidelines used to develop a properly structured relational database.

1. ***Every column in a row must be single valued.*** In a relational database, there can only be one value per cell. At S&S, each sale can involve more than one item. On invoice 11102, the customer bought a refrigerator, a range, and a washer. If ItemID were an attribute in the Sales table, it would have to take on three values (item numbers 1036, 2061, and 3541). To solve this problem, a Sales_Inventory table was created that lists each item sold on an invoice. The third line in the Sales_Inventory table in Table 4-5 shows invoice 11102 and item number 1036 (refrigerator). The fourth line shows invoice 11102 and item 2061 (range). The fifth line shows invoice 11102 and item 3542 (washer). This table repeats the invoice number as often as needed to show all the items purchased on a sales invoice.
2. ***Primary keys cannot be null.*** A primary key cannot uniquely identify a row in a table if it is null (blank). A nonnull primary key ensures that every row in a table represents something and that it can be identified. This is referred to as the **entity integrity rule**. In the Sales_Inventory table in Table 4-5, no single field uniquely identifies each row. However, the first two columns, taken together, do uniquely identify each row and constitute the primary key.
3. ***Foreign keys, if not null, must have values that correspond to the value of a primary key in another table.*** Foreign keys link rows in one table to rows in another table. In Table 4-5, CustomerID can link each sales transaction with the customer who participated in that event only if the Sales table CustomerID value corresponds to an actual customer number in the Customer table. This constraint, called the **referential integrity rule**, ensures database consistency. Foreign keys can contain null values. For example, when customers pay cash, CustomerID in the sales table can be blank.
4. ***All nonkey attributes in a table must describe a characteristic of the object identified by the primary key.*** Most tables contain other attributes in addition to the primary and foreign keys. In the Customer table in Table 4-5, CustomerID is the primary key, and customer name, street, city, and state are important facts that describe the customer.

entity integrity rule - A nonnull primary key ensures that every row in a table represents something and that it can be identified.

referential integrity rule - Foreign keys which link rows in one table to rows in another table must have values that correspond to the value of a primary key in another table.

These four constraints produce a well-structured (normalized) database in which data are consistent and data redundancy is minimized and controlled. In Table 4-5, having a table for each entity of interest avoids the anomaly problems discussed previously and minimizes redundancy. Redundancy is not eliminated, as certain items, such as SalesInvoiceID, appear in more than one table when they are foreign keys. The referential integrity rule ensures that there are no update anomaly problems with the foreign keys.

TABLE 4-5 Set of Relational Tables for Storing S&S Sales Data

Customer

CustomerID	CustomerName	Street	City	State
151	Vivian Rodgers	204 NoContent Street	Phoenix	AZ
152	Lola Doyle	504 Gateway Place	Mesa	AZ
153	Rodney Wern	500 Serverr Place	Chandler	AZ
154	John Clark	200 OK Ave	Snowflake	AZ
155	Shona Ojeda	404 NoFound Lane	Winslow	AZ

Sales

SalesInvoiceID	SaleDate	SalesPerson	CustomerID
11101	10/15/2021	C. Sanchez	151
11102	10/15/2021	B. Green	152
11103	10/28/2021	B. Green	151
11104	10/31/2021	C. Sanchez	153
11105	11/14/2021	C. Sanchez	152

Sales_Inventory

SalesInvoiceID	ItemID	Quantity	SoldPrice
11101	1039	2	1450
11101	2063	1	950
11102	1036	1	1199
11102	2061	1	799
11102	3541	2	499
11103	1038	2	1201
11104	1039	1	1499
11105	2063	1	999
11105	3544	2	650
11105	3787	2	450

Inventory

ItemID	Description	Color	VendorID	QuantityOnHand	ListPrice
1036	Refrigerator	White	30023	12	1199
1038	Refrigerator	Black	30023	7	1299
1039	Refrigerator	Stainless	30023	5	1499
2061	Range	White	30011	6	799
2063	Range	Stainless	30011	5	999
3541	Washer	White	30008	15	499
3544	Washer	Black	30008	10	699
3785	Dryer	White	30019	12	399
3787	Dryer	Black	30019	8	499

When data about objects of interest are stored in separate database tables, it is easy to add new data by adding another row to the table. For example, adding a new customer is as simple as adding a new row to the Customer table. Thus, the tables depicted in Table 4-5 are free from insert anomalies.

Relational databases also simplify data deletion. Deleting sales invoice 11104, the only sale to customer 153, does not erase all data about that customer because it is stored in the Customer table. This avoids delete anomalies.

Another benefit of the schema shown in Table 4-5 is that space is used efficiently. The Sales_ Inventory table contains a row for each item sold on each invoice. There are no blank rows, yet all sales data are recorded. In contrast, the schema in Table 4-4 results in much wasted space.

TWO APPROACHES TO DATABASE DESIGN

One way to design a relational database, called **normalization**, begins by assuming that everything is initially stored in one large table. Rules are then followed to decompose that initial table into a set of tables that are called *third normal form (3NF)* because they are free of update, insert, and delete anomalies. The details of the normalization process are found in the Appendix to this chapter.

normalization - Following relational database creation rules to design a relational database that is free from delete, insert, and update anomalies.

In an alternative design approach, called **semantic data modeling**, the designer uses knowledge of business processes and information needs to create a diagram that shows what to include in the database. This diagram is used to create a set of relational tables that are already in 3NF.

semantic data modeling - Using knowledge of business processes and information needs to create a diagram that shows what to include in a fully normalized database (in 3NF).

Semantic data modeling has significant advantages. First, using a system designer's knowledge of business processes facilitates the efficient design of transaction processing databases. Second, the graphical model explicitly represents the organization's business processes and policies and, by facilitating communication with system users, helps ensure that the new system meets users' actual needs. Semantic data modeling is discussed in Chapters 19 through 21. Chapter 19 introduces two semantic data modeling tools, entity-relationship diagramming and REA modeling, used to design transaction processing databases. Chapter 20 discusses how to implement an REA data model in a relational database. Chapter 21 discusses special topics in REA modeling.

CREATING RELATIONAL DATABASE QUERIES

To retrieve stored data, users query databases. A query is a structured request for information from the database. This section of the chapter shows you how to query databases in Microsoft Access using both the query design grid and the SQL view. The query design grid of Access is Microsoft's implementation of a query-by-example (QBE) query interface, which is designed to make querying easy. However, QBE interfaces are not standardized among database products. Therefore, we will also demonstrate writing queries in SQL in the SQL view of Access. A primer of the SQL language can be found in Focus 4-1. Learning SQL is valuable because most conventions of the SQL language are standardized across database products. Thus, learning to write queries in SQL allows you to apply your query skill to database products beyond Access.

Download the S&S In-Chapter Database from http://www.pearsonhighered.com/romney to follow along in creating the queries illustrated in this section. Open the database and select the Create ribbon to see the ribbon in the top half of Table 4-6. Create a query window by pressing the Query Design button. This option is outlined in blue in Table 4-6. Clicking on the Query Design button produces the Show Table window shown in the middle portion of Table 4-6. By adding a table and closing the Show Table window, the menu option of choosing between the Design view and the SQL view appears. These options are shown in the lower portion of Table 4-6. Once a query is defined, these view options are used to switch between managing queries through QBE or the SQL language.

We will use the tables in Table 4-5 to walk through the steps needed to create and run five queries.

QUERY 1

Query 1 responds to the following data request: List the invoice numbers, dates, and salesperson for sales made to Lola Doyle.

The Sales and Customer tables contain the four items needed to respond to this query: SalesInvoiceID, SaleDate, SalesPerson, and CustomerName. To create the query using the QBE approach, click the "Query Design" button (see Table 4-6), and select the Sales and Customer tables by double-clicking on their names or by single-clicking on the name and clicking the "Add" button. (Caution: If more tables than necessary are selected or the linkages between tables are not properly specified, the query may not produce correct information). Click on Close to make the Show Table window disappear. As shown in the Design View of Table 4-7, a line between the two tables connects the CustomerID fields (the Customer table primary key and the Sales table foreign key). This connection appears because the database creator established the primary key – foreign key link in the Relationships menu of Access.

To choose the fields presented in the output, double-click on SalesInvoiceID, SaleDate, SalesPerson, and CustomerName or drag and drop them into the Field row. Access automatically checks the box in the Show line, so the field will be shown in the output when the query is run.

FOCUS 4-1 SQL Query Basics

Structured Query Language (SQL) is used in all relational DBMSs. Although there are differences in language parameters for several database vendors, the majority of commands are interchangeable among DBMSs. We present a primer on the SELECT statement in the SQL language as implemented in Access. The purpose of the SELECT statement is to extract data from a database.

The SELECT, FROM, and WHERE clauses are our starting point. In this primer, we will use ALLCAPS to indicate SQL statement syntax, although SQL isn't case sensitive. Consider the following SQL statement:

```
SELECT Table1.Field1, Table2.Field4, Table1.Field2
FROM Table1 INNER JOIN Table2 ON Table1.Field1
= Table2.Field3
WHERE Table2.Field5 = 4;
```

The SELECT clause lists fields to be displayed from both Table1 and Table2. Syntax for selecting a field is the table name, a period, then the field name. At times, you will see both table names and field names enclosed in square brackets such as [Table1].[Field1]. This enclosure is only necessary if Tables or Fields are poorly named. If you use spaces, special characters, or reserved words (such as "select" or "order") in your names, you will need to use square brackets. You may also see fields presented without the table name present. This is permitted as long as the field name is unambiguous, meaning that it is uniquely named in the database.

The FROM clause chooses the tables from which the data is queried. In this case, it indicates that data comes from Table1 and Table2. It also provides the linkage between those tables. The JOIN linkage indicates that only the rows satisfying the ON criteria are available in the output set. INNER JOIN is the most commonly used join operator and indicates that only matching rows should be included in the output set. If you see a JOIN without INNER, LEFT, or RIGHT, you may assume it is an INNER JOIN. A LEFT JOIN indicates that all rows from the table listed on the left side of the JOIN operator would be included in the output set, along with data from the right table that satisfies the ON criteria. The opposite would be true for a RIGHT JOIN. If more than two tables are queried in a FROM clause, parentheses must be used to specify the order in which sets of tables are joined.

The WHERE clause filters rows from the joined dataset created in the FROM clause. The criteria typically compares a field to a specified value using operators such as >, >=, =, <=, <, and <>. Wildcards such as * are used in comparisons to text values. Also available are criteria operators such as LIKE, IN, and BETWEEN. If multiple criteria are used, the additional criteria are combined using AND or OR operators between each criteria. A criteria can also be negated with a NOT operator.

Presenting the output of a query in sorted order is accomplished with the ORDER BY clause. Adding the clause ORDER BY Table1.Field1 ASC, Table2.Field4 DESC after the WHERE clause would sort the output first by Field1 in ascending order, then by Field4 in descending order.

```
SELECT Table1.Field1, Table2.Field4, Table1.Field2
FROM Table1 INNER JOIN Table2 ON Table1.Field1
= Table2.Field3
WHERE Table2.Field5 = 4
ORDER BY Table1.Field1 ASC, Table2.Field4 DESC;
```

Now, with the basics out of the way, we return to the SELECT clause to mention its flexibility beyond just selecting columns for display. You can also perform mathematical operations, data formatting, and other functions within the SELECT clause. For example, you could present the result of dividing Field3 by Field4 as SELECT Field3/Field4 AS Ratio. In this example, the value of Field3 is divided by Field4 within each row. The result is presented in the output set as a column named Ratio which was specified by the alias operator AS. You might choose to round that calculation to two decimal places by changing the clause to SELECT ROUND(Field3/Field4,2) AS Ratio. Two other SELECT parameters we will note are DISTINCT and TOP. SELECT DISTINCT Field1 would present only distinct or unique rows in the output set. SELECT TOP 5 Field1 would limit the display to the first 5 rows of the output set.

All of the commands above act on one row of data at a time. SQL is also capable of summarizing data across rows through the use of aggregate functions like COUNT, SUM, MIN, MAX, and AVG. When aggregate functions are used, the rows of the output dataset are reduced or summarized through aggregation. To sum all rows of Field1 in a dataset, the SQL statement would be SELECT SUM(Table1.Field1) AS SumField1 FROM Table1. The output set would have one row regardless of the number of rows in Table1. The output would be the sum of all values in Field1.

Creating a SUM for subsets of data requires the use of a new clause, the GROUP BY clause. The purpose of the GROUP BY is to define the subsets for the aggregate function. Thus, if we want a sum of Field1 for each distinct value of Field2, the SQL statement would be:

```
SELECT Table1.Field2, SUM(Table1.Field1) AS
SumField1
FROM Table1
GROUP BY Table1.Field2
```

The output set would contain as many rows as there are unique values for Field2. The columns presented would be the value of Field2 in the first column accompanied by the sum of the values in Field1 that match the value in Field2. In practice, each non-aggregated field in the SELECT statement must also be in the GROUP BY clause.

FOCUS 4-1 Continued

The HAVING clause is the final piece of an aggregate function. The function of the HAVING clause is to filter rows produced by the aggregate function. For example, if we wanted to present only those rows of Field2 for which the sum of Field1 was greater than 1,000, the SQL would read:

SELECT Table1.Field2, SUM(Table1.Field1) as SumField1
FROM Table1
GROUP BY Table1.Field2
HAVING SUM(Table1.Field1)>1000.

At first, the HAVING clause appears to operate the same as the WHERE clause. The chief difference is that the WHERE clause cannot filter based on the values produced by the aggregate operator since the WHERE clause is executed before the aggregate function. The HAVING clause can filter rows like the WHERE clause, and it can filter rows based on the computation of the aggregate function.

The SQL language is very flexible. Nesting of SQL statements within other SQL statements is common. For example, a data request for Field1 and Field2 from Table1 where the value of Field2 is greater than the overall average of Field4 in Table2 may seem quite complex. We can break the data request into multiple simple requests. In this case, the first part of the request would be written in SQL as SELECT Table1.Field1, Table1.Field2 FROM Table1 WHERE Table1.Field2 >?, where the ? is the value needed from the second part of the request. The SQL for the second part of the request can be written as SELECT AVG(Table2.Field4) FROM Table2. Putting the two pieces together would generate the final SQL of:

SELECT Table1.Field1, Table1.Field2
FROM Table1
WHERE Table1.Field2 >
(SELECT AVG(Table2.Field4)
FROM Table2);

Note that the second query is included in parentheses as a subquery. The subquery will execute first and return a single value. The main query can then execute utilizing that value.

TABLE 4-6 Creating Queries in the Microsoft Access Database

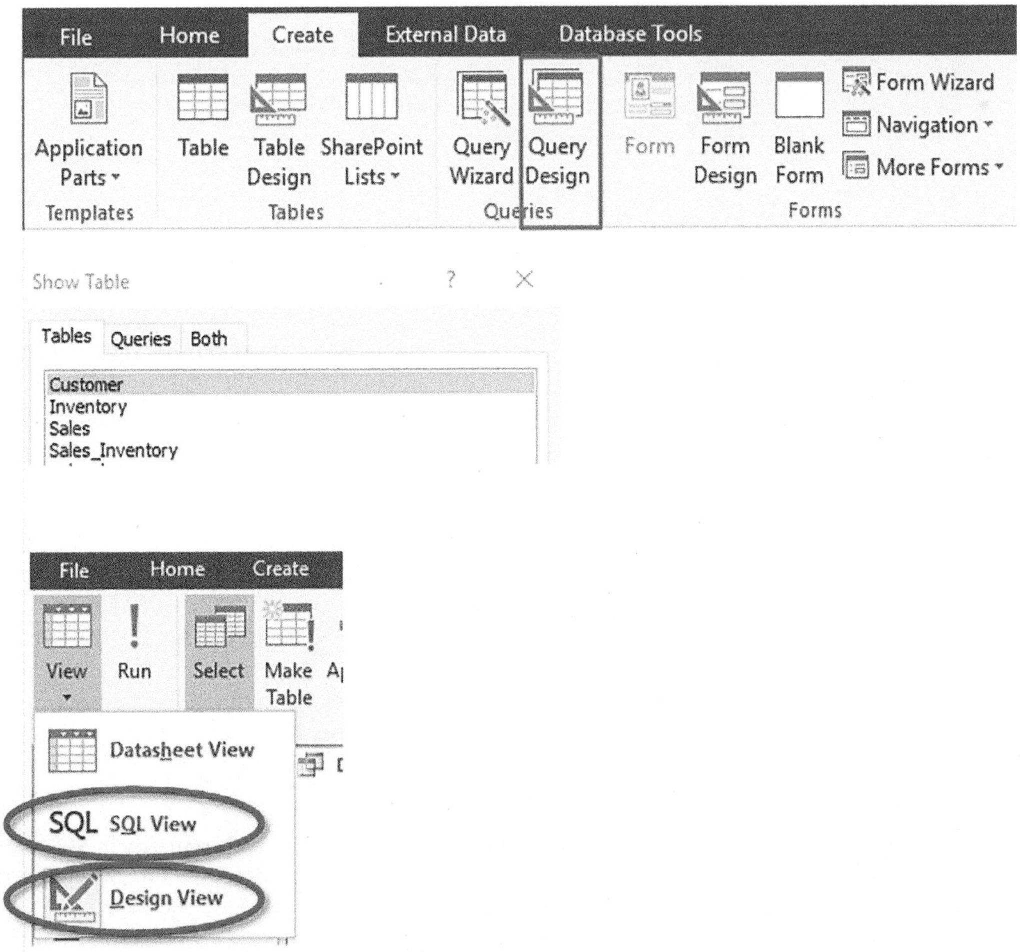

TABLE 4-7 Completed Query 1

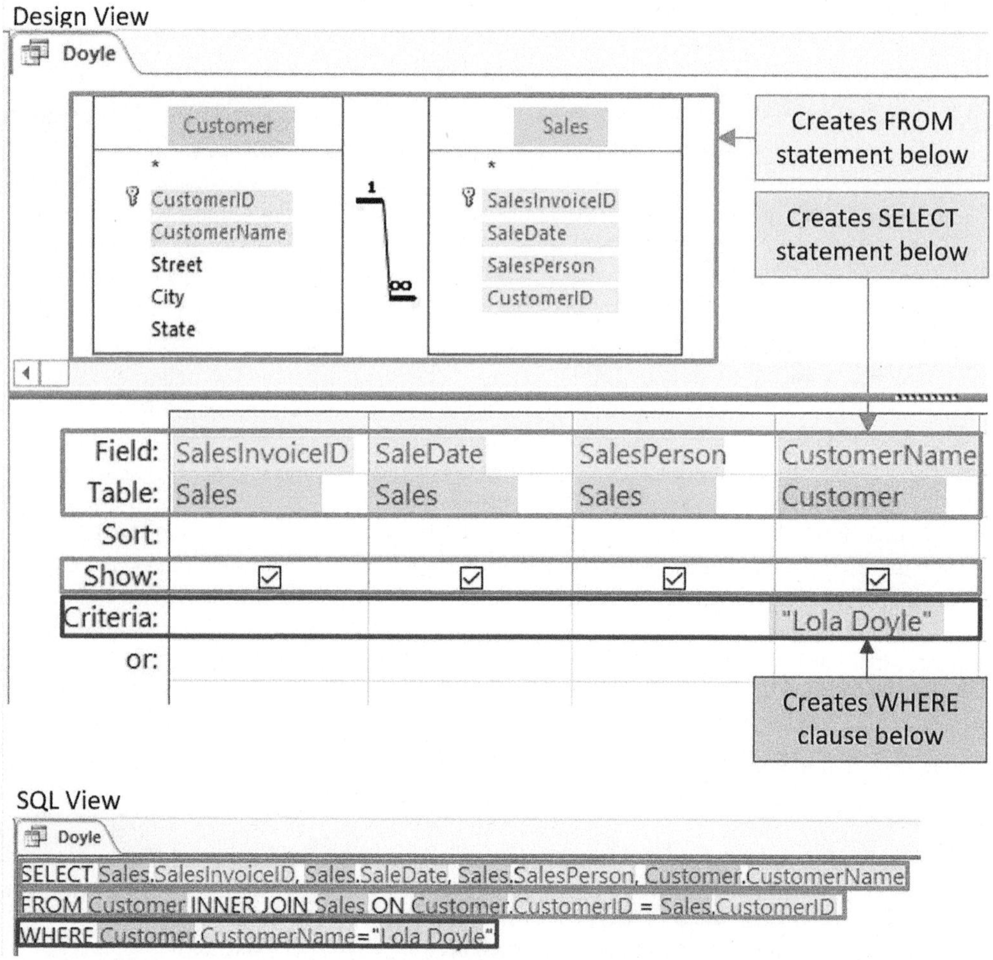

Since only sales to Lola Doyle are to be presented, enter her name in the Criteria line of the CustomerName column. Access will automatically put quote marks around the criteria. The completed QBE version (Design View) of the query is shown in the first panel of Table 4-7.

By pressing SQL View in the View dropdown menu in the upper left-hand corner of the Design ribbon as shown in the bottom of Table 4-6, Access presents the SQL statement generated by the QBE interface. A color map overlays Table 4-7 to illustrate how each panel in the Design View maps to the SQL statements in the SQL view. Note that the first action of choosing the tables created the FROM statement. Dragging fields to the Field row created the SELECT statement. Finally, entering a criterion on the Criteria row created the WHERE clause.

Run the query by clicking on the red ! (exclamation) mark on the Query Tools Design ribbon. Table 4-8 shows the tables used, the relationship of the primary and foreign keys between tables, and the query output dataset. The query can now be saved with the title "Doyle." Save it by pressing "Ctrl s", and then enter "Doyle" in the Query Name box. Clicking OK finishes the task. When the query is rerun, the saved name of "Doyle" will appear as the tab name as shown in the bottom portion of Table 4-8. This saved query not only provides the information requested, it is also useable as an input to future queries.

QUERY 2

As Query 1 was created primarily in Design view, we will create Query 2 primarily in SQL view.

Query 2 responds to a data request: List the SaleDate, Description, and Quantity for each transaction in which refrigerators were sold in October.

TABLE 4-8 Query 1 Relationships and Query Answer

Sales

SalesInvoiceID	SaleDate	SalesPerson	CustomerID
11101	10/15/2021	C. Sanchez	151
11102	10/15/2021	B. Green	152
11103	10/28/2021	B. Green	151
11104	10/31/2021	C. Sanchez	153
11105	11/14/2021	C. Sanchez	152
0			0

Customer

CustomerID	CustomerName	Street	City	State
151	Vivian Rodgers	204 NoContent Street	Phoenix	AZ
152	Lola Doyle	504 Gateway Place	Mesa	AZ
153	Rodney Wern	500 Serverr Place	Chandler	AZ
154	John Clark	200 OK Ave	Snowflake	AZ
155	Shona Ojeda	404 NoFound Lane	Winslow	AZ
0				

Doyle

SalesInvoiceID	SaleDate	SalesPerson	CustomerName
11102	10/15/2021	B. Green	Lola Doyle
11105	11/14/2021	C. Sanchez	Lola Doyle

The Sales, Inventory, and Sales_Inventory tables contain the three items needed to respond to the query request: SaleDate, Description, and Quantity. To create this query, click on the Query Design button in the Create ribbon as shown in Table 4-6 for Query 1. Immediately click on Close in the Show Table window without adding any tables. Now click on SQL View in the upper left-hand corner as shown in the bottom portion of Table 4-6. The word SELECT will be visible as in Table 4-9. The SQL view allows the SQL statement to be written from scratch. The pattern of writing SQL implied in QBE will be followed. QBE starts by selecting the tables to be used. In SQL, write the FROM clause to choose the tables that will be used in the statement. Write the name of each table, along with the key-pair relationship noted in Table 4-5. Starting with Sales and Sales_Inventory, write FROM Sales INNER JOIN Sales_Inventory ON Sales.SalesInvoiceID = Sales_Inventory.SalesInvoiceID. So far, this FROM statement will join records from the two tables where SalesInvoiceIDs match. To designate that the join of Sales and Sales_Inventory is completed before we join the third table (Inventory), we must put parentheses around this join. Place the parentheses, then add the second join to the completed first join. The FROM statement continues as FROM (Sales INNER JOIN Sales_Inventory ON Sales.SalesInvoiceID = Sales_Inventory.SalesInvoiceID) INNER JOIN Inventory ON Sales_Inventory.ItemID = Inventory.ItemID. The FROM statement is now complete.

TABLE 4-9 SQL View

Query1

```
SELECT;
```

Next, complete the SELECT statement by writing the names of the fields to be presented. SELECT Sales.SaleDate, Inventory.Description, Sales_Inventory.Quantity. Now the query can be completed by writing the WHERE clause; WHERE Inventory.Description = "Refrigerator" AND Sales.SaleDate BETWEEN #10/1/2021# AND #10/31/2021#. (Access interprets elements surrounded by the # as date/time elements in the same way that it treats elements surrounded by quotes as text.) The completed query, along with the Design View and Datasheet View, are shown in Table 4-10. In the SQL View, line feeds and extra spaces were added to better present the SQL statement. Line feeds and extra spaces are ignored by the SQL interpreter when running the query. Use "Cntl s" to save the query as "RefrigeratorsOctober."

TABLE 4-10 Completed Query 2 and Answer

SQL View

RefrigeratorsOctober

```
SELECT Sales.SaleDate, Inventory.Description, Sales_Inventory.Quantity
FROM (Sales INNER JOIN Sales_Inventory ON Sales.SalesInvoiceID = Sales_Inventory.SalesInvoiceID)
     INNER JOIN Inventory ON Inventory.ItemID = Sales_Inventory.ItemID
WHERE Inventory.Description="Refrigerator" AND Sales.SaleDate BETWEEN #10/1/2021# AND #10/31/2021#;
```

Design View

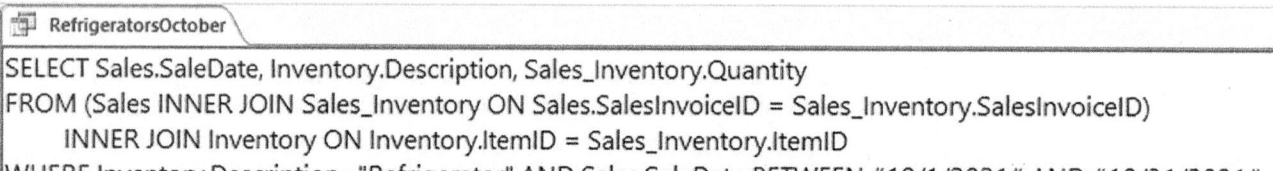

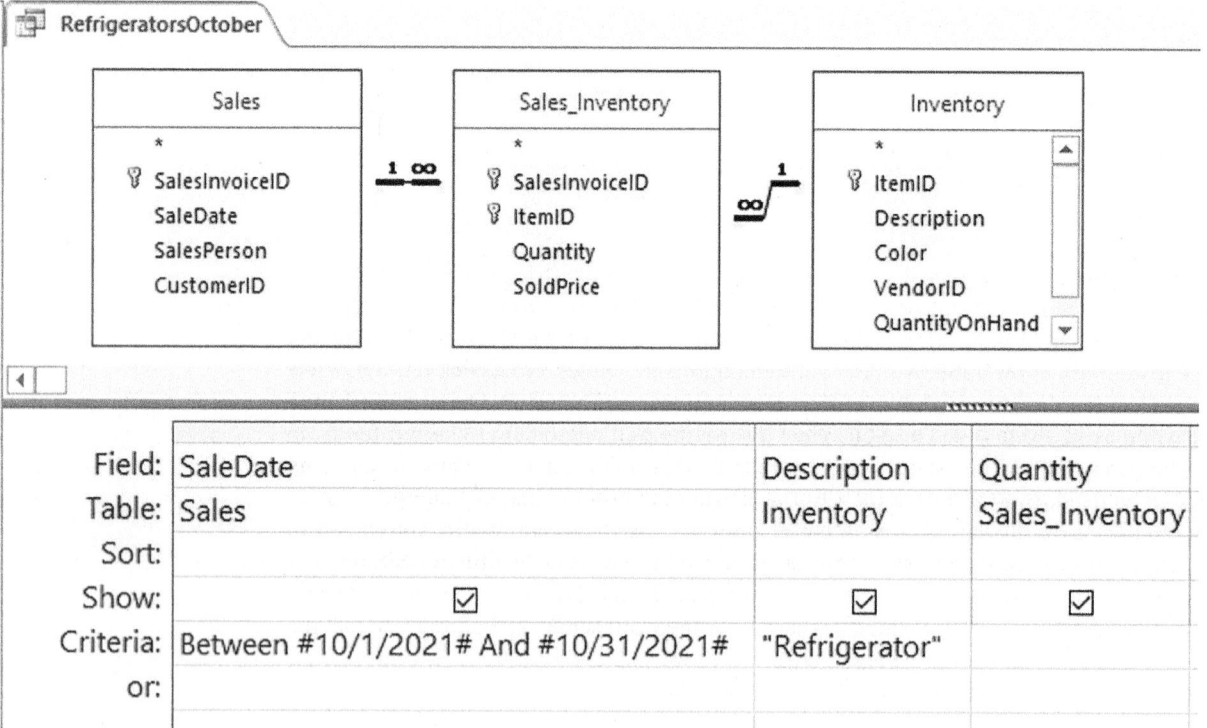

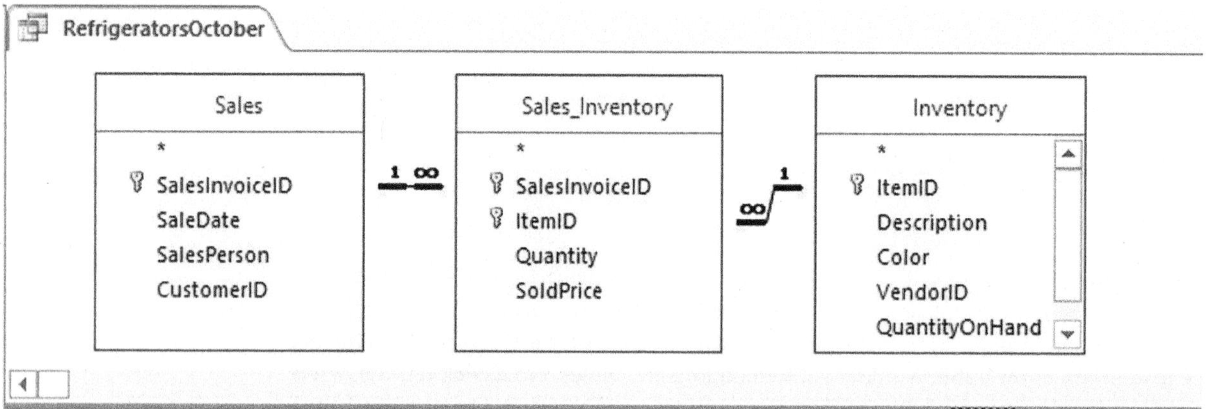

Field:	SaleDate	Description	Quantity
Table:	Sales	Inventory	Sales_Inventory
Sort:			
Show:	☑	☑	☑
Criteria:	Between #10/1/2021# And #10/31/2021#	"Refrigerator"	
or:			

Datasheet View

RefrigeratorsOctober

SaleDate	Description	Quantity
10/15/2021	Refrigerator	1
10/28/2021	Refrigerator	2
10/15/2021	Refrigerator	2
10/31/2021	Refrigerator	1
*		

QUERY 3

Query 3 builds on Query 2. The sales manager wants to know how many refrigerators were sold in October:

Build this query in Design view by opening the Design view of Query 2 and then adding the summation. With Design view of Query 2 open, notice the Totals button in the Show/Hide portion of the Query Tools Design ribbon highlighted in Table 4-11. When clicked, a new row labeled Total appears (compare Tables 4-10 and 4-12). Click the down-arrow symbol in the Quantity column of the Totals line and select Sum from the dropdown menu. The remaining two fields in the Total line will show Group By; change these to Where. Uncheck the Show box in the SaleDate and Description columns. Running the query in Table 4-12 produces the answer shown.

A careful examination of the SQL view may be unsettling. When Access generates the SQL View of a query, it often presents the tables in the FROM statement in haphazard order. It then adds parentheses to get the interpreter to execute the joins in proper order. In addition, Access adds parentheses in many locations that are not needed for proper execution. The SQL generator is simply not concerned with readability of the SQL and errs on the side of adding parentheses when in doubt. The SQL in Table 4-12 has been rearranged for readability. The key points are that the selection of Sum in the Total row in Design view created the aggregate function of SUM in the SELECT statement along with the use of AS to create an alias for the summed total. Notice that the Description and SaleDate fields are not in the SELECT statement anymore because you unchecked the Show box for each column.

QUERY 4

Query 4 responds to the data request: List Description and SumOfQuantity of inventory types that sold 2 or more units in the month of October.

The first step in solving this query is to understand what is meant by "inventory type" in the request. Close inspection of Inventory shows that the values in the Description field are identical for all Refrigerators. They are also identical for all Ranges and so forth. The Color field is used to distinguish between the various Refrigerators carried by the business. Thus, we may infer that the Description field represents an inventory type in this limited dataset. (A deeper discussion of database design would include a discussion of whether this field should be moved to a separate table and linked back to this table. For now, let us query the database as it is.)

With this understanding of inventory type, consider where the criteria of >=2 should go. The challenge is that the criteria must be evaluated against the sum of each inventory type for all transactions in the month. That sum will need to be computed before the criteria can be applied. In SQL, the HAVING clause is designed for this exact purpose. The WHERE clause is used for filtering rows prior to the execution of aggregate functions, while the HAVING clause is used for filtering rows after the execution of aggregate functions. Write this query in SQL.

Table 4-13 shows the difference between Query 3, which summed Refrigerators and Query 4, which shows all inventory types that sold 2 or more units. While the data request is very different, the SQL statements are quite similar. From Query 3, we simply remove the filter of Refrigerator from the WHERE clause, add the Inventory.Description in the SELECT and GROUP BY statements, and finally add the HAVING clause which repeats the Sum(Sales_Inventory.Quantity) in the SELECT statement with the criteria >=2.

Table 4-14 shows the complete Query for Query 4 in both Design View and SQL View, along with the response data. Inspection of the Design View shows four changes from the Design View of Query 3: removing Refrigerator from the Criteria row of Description, ticking the Show box of Description, changing the Total row of Description to Group By, and placing the >=2 criteria in the Quantity field.

TABLE 4-11 Design Ribbon

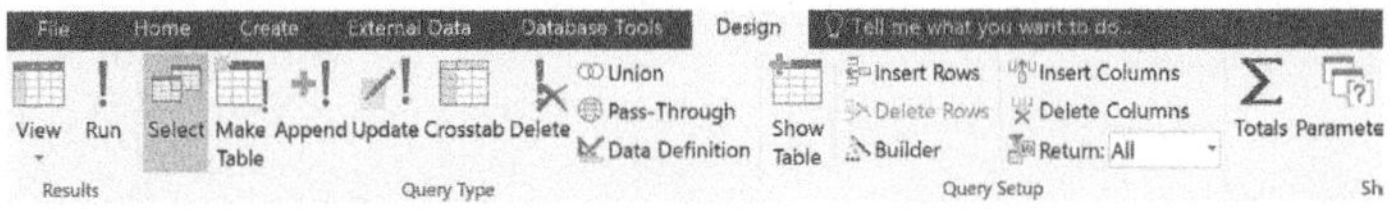

TABLE 4-12 Completed Query 3 and Answer

Design View

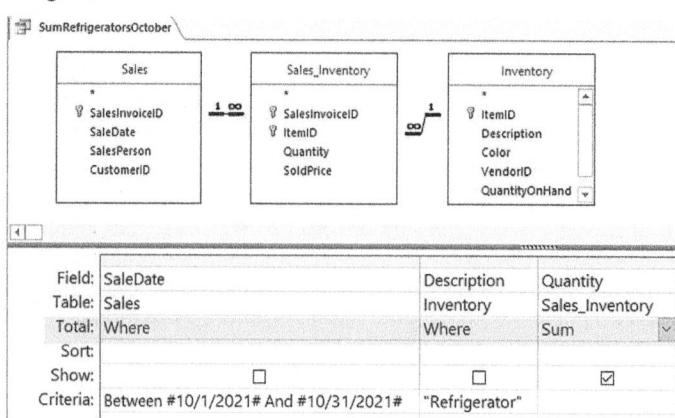

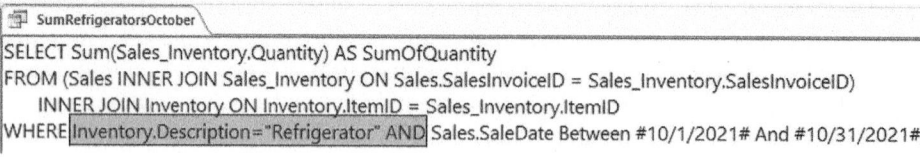

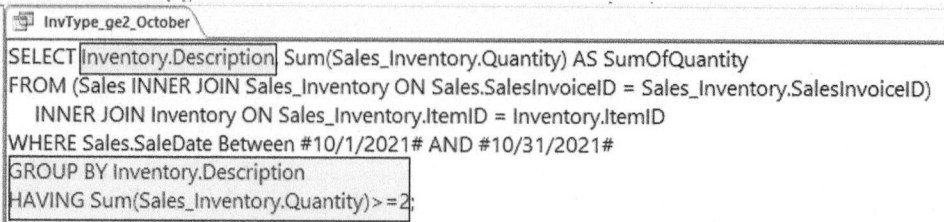

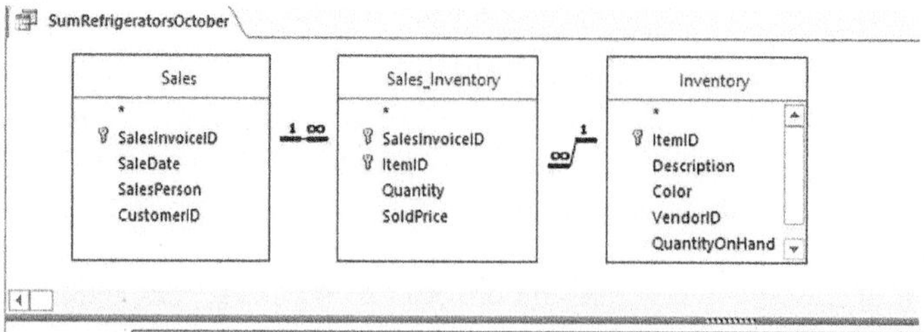

Field:	SaleDate	Description	Quantity
Table:	Sales	Inventory	Sales_Inventory
Total:	Where	Where	Sum
Sort:			
Show:	☐	☐	☑
Criteria:	Between #10/1/2021# And #10/31/2021#	"Refrigerator"	

SQL View

SumRefrigeratorsOctober

```
SELECT Sum(Sales_Inventory.Quantity) AS SumOfQuantity
FROM (Sales INNER JOIN Sales_Inventory ON Sales.SalesInvoiceID = Sales_Inventory.SalesInvoiceID)
    INNER JOIN Inventory ON Inventory.ItemID = Sales_Inventory.ItemID
WHERE Inventory.Description="Refrigerator" AND Sales.SaleDate Between #10/1/2021# And #10/31/2021#;
```

Datasheet View

SumRefrigeratorsOctober

SumOfQuantity
6

TABLE 4-13 SQL View of Query 3 and Query 4

SQL View Query 3

SumRefrigeratorsOctober

```
SELECT Sum(Sales_Inventory.Quantity) AS SumOfQuantity
FROM (Sales INNER JOIN Sales_Inventory ON Sales.SalesInvoiceID = Sales_Inventory.SalesInvoiceID)
    INNER JOIN Inventory ON Inventory.ItemID = Sales_Inventory.ItemID
WHERE Inventory.Description="Refrigerator" AND Sales.SaleDate Between #10/1/2021# And #10/31/2021#;
```

SQL View Query 4

InvType_ge2_October

```
SELECT Inventory.Description, Sum(Sales_Inventory.Quantity) AS SumOfQuantity
FROM (Sales INNER JOIN Sales_Inventory ON Sales.SalesInvoiceID = Sales_Inventory.SalesInvoiceID)
   INNER JOIN Inventory ON Sales_Inventory.ItemID = Inventory.ItemID
WHERE Sales.SaleDate Between #10/1/2021# AND #10/31/2021#
GROUP BY Inventory.Description
HAVING Sum(Sales_Inventory.Quantity)>=2;
```

TABLE 4-14 Completed Query 4 and Answer

SQL View

InvType_ge2_October

```
SELECT Inventory.Description, Sum(Sales_Inventory.Quantity) AS SumOfQuantity
FROM (Sales INNER JOIN Sales_Inventory ON Sales.SalesInvoiceID = Sales_Inventory.SalesInvoiceID)
   INNER JOIN Inventory ON Sales_Inventory.ItemID = Inventory.ItemID
WHERE Sales.SaleDate Between #10/1/2021# AND #10/31/2021#
GROUP BY Inventory.Description
HAVING Sum(Sales_Inventory.Quantity)>=2;
```

Design View

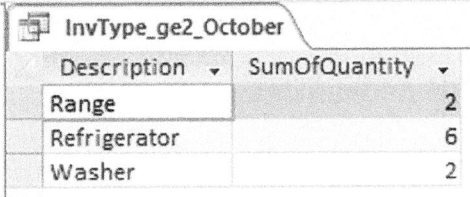

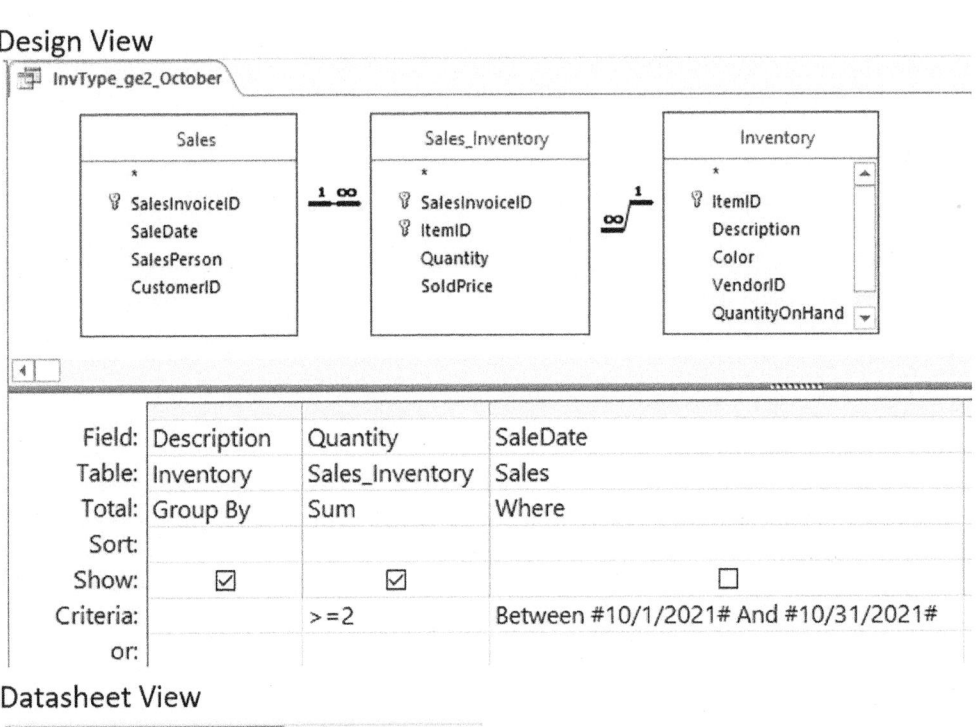

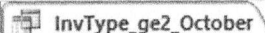

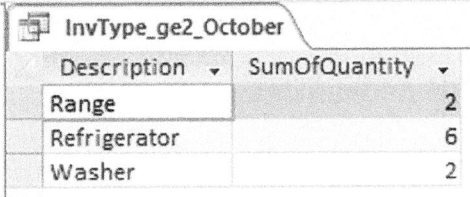

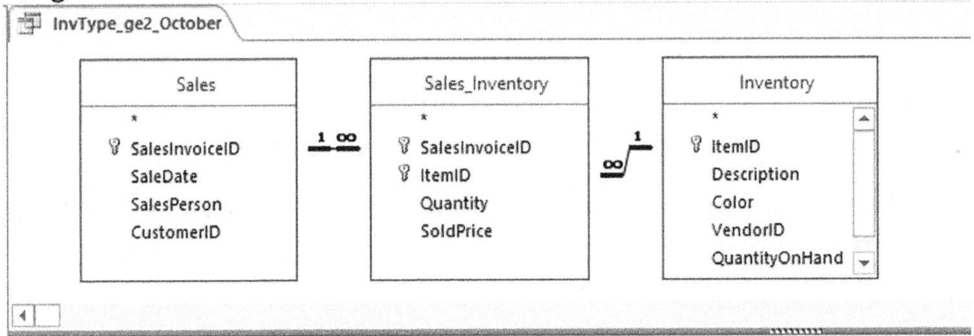

Field:	Description	Quantity	SaleDate
Table:	Inventory	Sales_Inventory	Sales
Total:	Group By	Sum	Where
Sort:			
Show:	☑	☑	☐
Criteria:		>=2	Between #10/1/2021# And #10/31/2021#
or:			

Datasheet View

InvType_ge2_October

Description	SumOfQuantity
Range	2
Refrigerator	6
Washer	2

QUERY 5

Query 5 responds to a data request: List SaleDate and InvoiceTotal for each invoice in October.

The InvoiceTotal field does not exist in the database. It will need to be created from the Quantity and SoldPrice fields. Thus, the fields needed for this query are SalesInvoiceID and SaleDate from Sales and Quantity and SoldPrice from Sales_Inventory. Build the FROM statement for those two tables. The FROM statement will be: FROM Sales INNER JOIN Sales_Inventory ON Sales.SalesInvoiceID = Sales_Inventory.SalesInvoiceID. The frequent repeating of table names can become tiresome. In this FROM statement, we will introduce the concept of aliasing table names, which is the use of an alternate name for a table or set within the query statement. Table aliasing happens in the FROM statement by declaring a new name immediately after entering the actual table name. An AS operator is optional in creating the alias of a table. Aliaising can improve the readability of your SQL. The FROM statement with aliases reads: FROM Sales AS s INNER JOIN Sales_Inventory AS si ON s.SalesInvoiceID = si.SalesInvoiceID. Notice that once the two aliases are created, they are used in place of the table name in all other parts of the query.

The SELECT statement displays three pieces of information: SalesInvoiceID, SaleDate, and the invoice total. At present, invoice total doesn't exist in the database. Generally, calculable data is not stored in databases since storing calculated data would result in an update anomaly if any value used in the calculation is changed. To calculate the total, start by multipling Quantity by SoldPrice within each row of the invoice. Label this LineTotal. Now sum LineTotal for each invoice. The first step demonstrates the use of mathematical operators within a row as contrasted with mathematical operations between rows. Operations within a row are not aggregate functions. They are presented as operations between field names using typical math operators such as *, /, +, –. Functions are also available for use within a row such as ABS() for absolute value. The second step of summing across rows will be the aggregate function SUM as seen earlier. The aggregations created by aggregate functions depend on applying the appropriate GROUP BY and HAVING clauses that act on the aggregate function.

The first step, the mathematical operation within a row, is shown in the SELECT statement. At this point, the SELECT statement will read: SELECT s.SalesInvoiceID, s.SaleDate, (si.Quantity * si.SoldPrice) AS LineTotal. Note both the alias table names as well as the alias of LineTotal that has been given as the name of the calculated field. Now we can proceed to the second step of summing the rows of an invoice. This is done by placing the SUM aggregate operator in front of the calculation of LineTotal. The query is actually calculating LineTotal on the fly and summing as it goes through the rows of the data. The SELECT statement now reads: SELECT s.SalesInvoiceID, s.SaleDate, SUM(si.Quantity * si.SoldPrice) AS InvoiceTotal. We updated the alias of this calculated column to reflect its current output.

Before specifying the GROUP BY, note that the WHERE clause will not change from prior queries in filtering for transactions in October. WHERE s.SaleDate BETWEEN #10/1/2021# AND #10/31/2021#.

Now add the appropriate GROUP BY and HAVING clauses. Every other field in the SELECT that is not an aggregate function should be included in the GROUP BY. The GROUP BY will read: GROUP BY s.SalesInvoiceID, s.SaleDate. The HAVING statement is used to filter rows based on aggregated values. This is in contrast to filtering for non-aggregate criteria which is typically done in the WHERE clause. Filtering for invoices totaling less than 1,000 is done by writing: HAVING SUM(si.Quantity * si.SoldPrice) <1000. Notice the replication of the SUM formula from the SELECT without the alias. In this data request, filtering based on aggregated values is not needed, thus no HAVING clause will be used. The completed query is shown in Table 4-15.

DATABASE SYSTEMS AND THE FUTURE OF ACCOUNTING

Database systems expand accounting's ability to produce real-time dynamic reports of all aspects of the accounting equation. Databases are capturing increasing amounts of transaction data beyond what was captured through accounting journals and ledgers in double entry accounting. Presently, data about even the smallest movements of materials in production, inventory defects, machine operations, and employee effort can be captured in real time. Management can access the information they need whenever they want it. For example, tables storing information about assets can include historical costs as well as current replacement costs, market values, and real-time utilization. Thus, managers may look at data in many ways beyond those predefined by accounting standards. They may create metrics and dashboards that provide insight beyond traditional accounting measures. Further, DBMSs are capable of integrating financial, operational, and external data. For example, customer satisfaction data can be stored in the database, giving managers a richer set of data for analysis and decision making. The new challenge is not whether data can be captured about all phases of business transactions, but how to harness the value of that information.

TABLE 4-15 Completed Query 5 and Answer

SQL View

InvoiceTotal

```
SELECT s.SalesInvoiceID, s.SaleDate, Sum([si].[Quantity]*[si].[SoldPrice]) AS InvoiceTotal
FROM Sales AS s INNER JOIN Sales_Inventory AS si ON s.SalesInvoiceID = si.SalesInvoiceID
WHERE s.SaleDate Between #10/1/2021# And #10/31/2021#
GROUP BY s.SalesInvoiceID, s.SaleDate;
```

Design View

InvoiceTotal

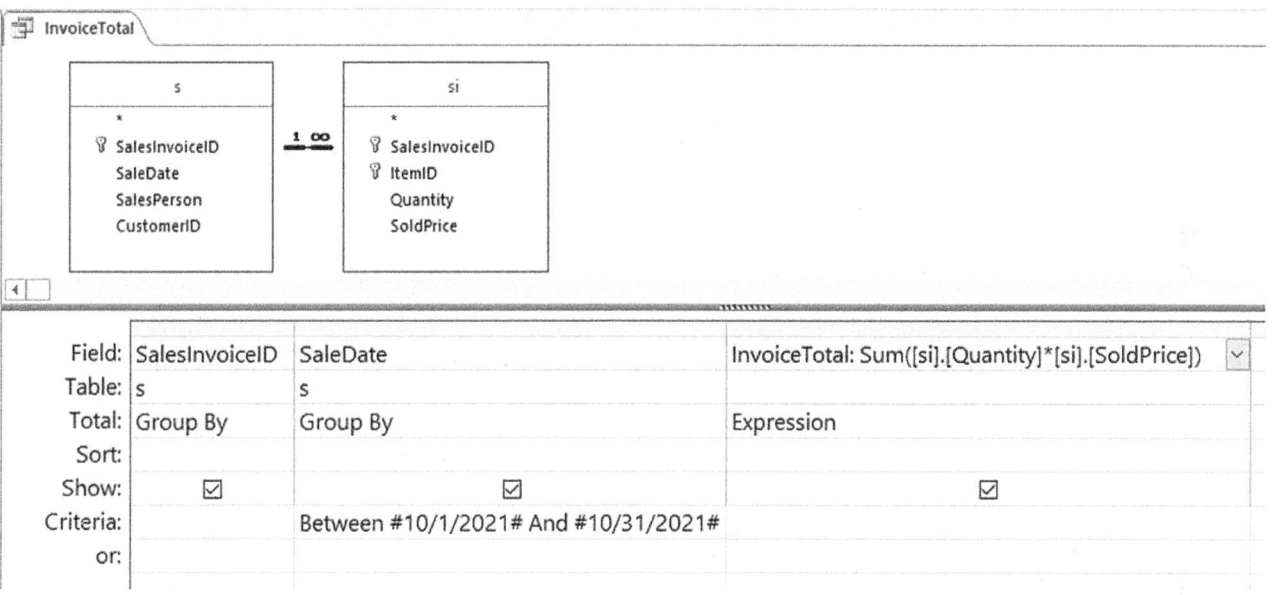

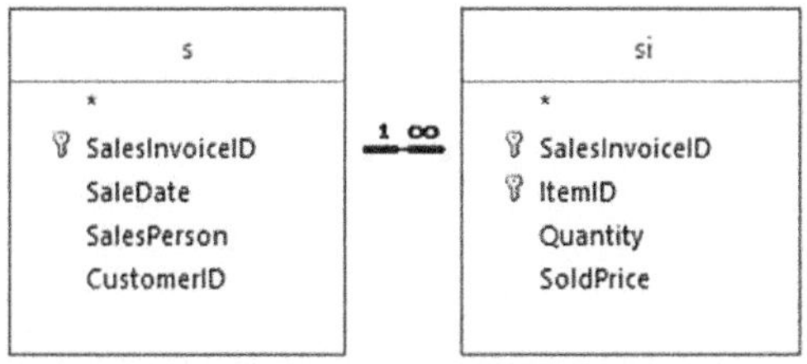

Field:	SalesInvoiceID	SaleDate	InvoiceTotal: Sum([si].[Quantity]*[si].[SoldPrice])
Table:	s	s	
Total:	Group By	Group By	Expression
Sort:			
Show:	☑	☑	☑
Criteria:		Between #10/1/2021# And #10/31/2021#	
or:			

Datasheet View

InvoiceTotal

SalesInvoiceID	SaleDate	InvoiceTotal
11101	10/15/2021	3850
11102	10/15/2021	2996
11103	10/28/2021	2402
11104	10/31/2021	1499

Chapters 5 through 7 highlight the skills that accountants and managers need to be able to extract value from data captured in databases and other data sources.

Accountants must understand database systems so they can help design and use the databases of the future. Such participation is important for ensuring that adequate controls are included in those systems to safeguard the data and ensure the reliability of the information produced.

Summary and Case Conclusion

Ashton prepared a report for Scott and Susan summarizing what he knew about databases. He explained that a database management system (DBMS), the software that makes a database system work, is based on a logical data model that shows how users perceive the way the data is stored. Many DBMSs are based on the relational data model that represents data as being stored in tables. Every row in a relational table has only one data value in each column. Neither row nor column position is significant. These properties support the use of simple, yet powerful, query languages for interacting with the database. Users only need to interact with their logical view to query the data they want and do not need to be concerned with how the data are physically stored or retrieved. The DBMS functions as an intermediary between the user and the database, thereby hiding the complex addressing schemes actually used to retrieve and update the information stored in the database.

After reading Ashton's report, Scott and Susan agreed that it was time to upgrade S&S's database and to hire a consulting firm to help select and install the new system. They asked Ashton to oversee the design process to ensure that the new system meets their needs Scott and Susan recognize the need to train all employees to be able to interact with the database and query for the information they need.

KEY TERMS

database 93
database management system (DBMS) 94
database system 94
database administrator (DBA) 94
online transaction processing database (OLTP) 95
data warehouse 95
business intelligence 95
online analytical processing (OLAP) 95
data mining 95
record layout 96
logical view 97
physical view 97
schema 97
external-level schema 97
subschema 97
conceptual-level schema 97
internal-level schema 97
access rights 98
data dictionary 98
data definition language (DDL) 100
structured query languange (SQL) 100
data manipulation language (DML) 100
data query language (DQL) 100
report writer 100
data model 100
relational data model 100
tuple 100
primary key 101
foreign key 101
update anomaly 101
insert anomaly 101
delete anomaly 101
relational database 103
entity integrity rule 103
referential integrity rule 103
normalization 105
semantic data modeling 105

AIS in Action

CHAPTER QUIZ

1. What is each row in a relational database table called?
   a. tuple
   b. relation
   c. attribute
   d. anomaly

2. The relational data model portrays data as being stored in ________.
   a. objects
   b. hierarchies
   c. tables
   d. files

3. How a user conceptually organizes and understands data is referred to as the ______.
   a. logical view
   b. physical view
   c. data model view
   d. data organization view

4. Which of the following attributes would most likely be a primary key?
   a. supplier name
   b. supplier number
   c. supplier zip code
   d. supplier account balance

5. Which of the following is an individual user's view of the database?
   a. internal-level schema
   b. conceptual-level schema
   c. external-level schema
   d. logical-level schema

6. Which of the following would managers most likely use to retrieve information about sales during the month of October?
   a. DQL
   b. DML
   c. DSL
   d. DDL

7. How many columns of output would be returned by the following SQL query?

```
SELECT Table1.Field2, Table1.Field3, Table2.Field3, Table2.Field5
FROM Table1 INNER JOIN Table2 ON Table1.Field1 = Table2.Field4
WHERE Table2.Field5 = 3;
```

   a. 1
   b. 2
   c. 3
   d. 4

8. The constraint that all foreign keys must have either null values or the value of a primary key in another table is referred to as which of the following?
   a. referential integrity rule
   b. entity integrity rule
   c. foreign key value rule
   d. null value rule

9. The constraint that all primary keys must have non-null data values is referred to as which of the following?
   a. referential integrity rule
   b. entity integrity rule
   c. normalization rule
   d. relational data model rule

10. Which of the following clauses properly filters the rows in an SQL query to values greater than 3 in Field4 from Table3?
   a. SELECT Table3.Field4 > 3
   b. WHERE Table3.Field4 > 3
   c. WHERE Field4.Table3 > 3
   d. FROM Table3.Field4 > 3

COMPREHENSIVE PROBLEM

The Butler Financing Company runs a mortgage brokerage business that matches lenders and borrowers. Table 4-16 lists some of the data that Butler maintains on its borrowers and lenders. The data are stored in a spreadsheet that must be manually updated for each new borrower, lender, or mortgage. This updating is error-prone, which has harmed the business. In addition, the spreadsheet has to be sorted in many different ways to retrieve the necessary data.

Create a database from Butler's spreadsheet that does not have any of the data anomalies explained in this chapter. To test the database, prepare a query to show which borrowers and appraisers are associated with loans from Excel Mortgage.

TABLE 4-16 Butler Financing Company Spreadsheet

Borrower ID	Last-Name	First-Name	Current-Address	ReqMort-Amount (Requested Mortgage Amount)	LenderID	Lender-Name	Lender-Address	Appraiser ID	Appraiser-Name
450	Adams	Jennifer	450 Peachtree Rd.	$245,000	13	Excel Mortgage	6890 Sheridan Dr.	8	Advent Appraisers
451	Adamson	David	500 Loop Highway	$124,688	13	Excel Mortgage	6890 Sheridan Dr.	9	Independent Appraisal Service
452	Bronson	Paul	312 Mountain Dr.	$345,000	14	CCY	28 Buckhead Way	10	Jones Property Appraisers
453	Brown	Marietta	310 Loop Highway	$57,090	15	Advantage Lenders	3345 Lake Shore Dr.	10	Jones Property Appraisers
454	Charles	Kenneth	3 Commons Blvd.	$34,000	16	Capital Savings	8890 Coral Blvd.	8	Advent Appraisers
455	Coulter	Tracey	1367 Peachtree Rd.	$216,505	13	Excel Mortgage	6890 Sheridan Dr.	8	Advent Appraisers
456	Foster	Harold	678 Loop Highway	$117,090	12	National Mortgage	750 16 St.	9	Independent Appraisal Service
457	Frank	Vernon	210 Bicayne Blvd.	$89,000	12	National Mortgage	750 16 St.	10	Jones Property Appraisers
458	Holmes	Heather	1121 Bicayne Blvd.	$459,010	16	Capital Savings	8890 Coral Blvd.	10	Jones Property Appraisers
459	Johanson	Sandy	817 Mountain Dr.	$67,900	15	Advantage Lenders	3345 Lake Shore Dr.	9	Independent Appraisal Service
460	Johnson	James	985 Loop Highway	$12,000	12	National Mortgage	750 16 St.	10	Jones Property Appraisers
461	Jones	Holly	1650 Washington Blvd.	$67,890	15	Advantage Lenders	3345 Lake Shore Dr.	9	Independent Appraisal Service

DISCUSSION QUESTIONS

4.1 Contrast the logical and the physical views of data, and discuss why separate views are necessary in database applications. Describe which perspective is most useful for each of the following employees: a programmer, a manager, and an internal auditor. How will understanding logical data structures assist you when designing and using database systems?

4.2 The relational data model represents data as being stored in tables. Spreadsheets are another tool that accountants use to employ a tabular representation of data. What are some similarities and differences in the way these tools use tables? How might an accountant's familiarity with the tabular representation of spreadsheets facilitate or hinder learning how to use a relational DBMS?

4.3 Some people believe database technology may eliminate the need for double-entry accounting. This creates three possibilities: (1) the double-entry model will be abandoned; (2) the double-entry model will not be used directly, but an external-level schema based on the double-entry model will be defined for accountants' use; or (3) the double-entry model will be retained in database systems. Which alternative do you think is most likely to occur? Why?

4.4 Relational DBMS query languages provide easy access to information about the organization's activities. Does this mean that online, real-time processing should be used for all transactions? Does an organization need real-time financial reports? Why, or why not?

4.5 Why is it so important to have good data?

4.6 What is a data dictionary, what does it contain, and how is it used?

4.7 Compare and contrast the file-oriented approach and the database approach. Explain the main advantages of database systems.

PROBLEMS

4.1 The following data elements comprise the conceptual-level schema for a database:

billing address
cost
credit limit
customer name
customer number
description
invoice number
item number
price
quantity on hand
quantity sold
shipping address
terms

REQUIRED

a. Identify three potential users and design a subschema for each. Justify your design by explaining why each user needs access to the subschema data elements. Specify the type of rights you would give to your potential user for each data element in their subschema. Address the rights of Create, Read, Update, and Delete.
b. Use Microsoft Access or some other relational database product to create the schema tables. Specify the primary key(s), foreign key(s), and other data for each table. Test your model by entering sample data in each table.

4.2 Most DBMS packages contain data definition, data manipulation, and data query languages.

REQUIRED

For each of the following, indicate which language would be used and why.

a. The inventory serial number field is extended in the inventory records to allow for recognition of additional inventory items with serial numbers containing more than 10 digits.
b. A database administrator defines the logical structure of the database.

c. The manager of inventory control requests a report of all inventory items whose QuantityOnHand is below the ReorderPoint.
d. An accountant uses RPA to write a bot to update the fixed-assets records stored in the database.
e. The human resources manager requests a report noting all employees who are retiring within five years.
f. A user develops a program to print out all purchases made during the past two weeks.
g. An additional field is added to the fixed-asset records to record the estimated salvage value of each asset.

4.3 Ashton wants to store the following data about S&S's purchases of inventory:

item number
date of purchase
vendor number
vendor address
vendor name
purchase price
quantity purchased
employee number
employee name
purchase order number
description
quantity on hand
extended amount
total amount of purchase

REQUIRED

a. Design a set of relational tables to store this data. Name each table and field in accordance with good database design. Do all the data items need to be stored in a table? If not, which ones do not need to be stored, and why do they not need to be stored?
b. Identify the primary key for each table.
c. Identify the foreign keys needed in the tables to implement referential integrity.
d. Implement your tables using any relational database product to which you have access.
e. Test your specification by entering sample data in each table.
f. Create a few queries to retrieve or analyze the data you stored.

4.4 Retrieve the Chapter 4 Relational Database (in Microsoft Access format) from http://www.pearsonhighered.com/romney or create the tables in Table 4-5 in a relational DBMS product.

REQUIRED

Write queries to answer the following questions. Your instructor may specify the method of acquiring the database noted above and whether to use Design view or SQL view.

a. List Customers that live in the city of Winslow. Provide CustomerID, CustomerName, and Street.
b. List all sales for which SalesPerson "B. Green" was responsible. Provide SalesInvoiceID, SaleDate, CustomerID, and CustomerName.
c. List all inventory items sold to "Lola Doyle." Provide SaleDate, ItemID, Description, and Quantity.

Queries with aggregate functions

d. How many different kinds of inventory items does S&S sell? Use NumOfItems as the name of the output column.
e. How many sales were made during October? Use NumOfSales as the name of your output column.

f. How many sales were made to each customer? List CustomerID, CustomerName, and NumOfSales. Sort the list by NumOfSales in descending order.
g. How many units of each product were sold? Provide ItemID, Description, Color, and SumOfQuantity. Sort the list by ItemID in ascending order.
h. List the total of each invoice. Compute this by summing Quantity times SoldPrice for all the items on each invoice. Name the total InvoiceTotal. Provide SalesInvoiceID, SaleDate, SalesPerson, and InvoiceTotal. Sort the list by InvoiceTotal in descending order.

*Advanced queries that may require nesting or reference to earlier queries.

i. What were total sales in October? Provide TotalSales. You may reuse your query from question h.
j. What was the average amount of a sales transaction? Provide AvgSales. You may reuse your query from question h.
k. Which product sold the most units? Provide ItemID, Description, Color, and SumOfQuantity. You may reuse your query from question g.
l. Which salesperson made the largest sale? Provide the SalesPersons name and the amount of the sale. You may reuse your query from question h.

4.5 The tables in Table 4-17 reveal the structure of a database for the following queries. Build the database and enter data from these tables in a relational DBMS package, build the database and import an expanded dataset formatted in Excel available at http://www.pearsonhighered.com/romney, or retrieve the database from http://www.pearsonhighered.com/romney (in Microsoft Access format).

TABLE 4-17 Problem 4.5 Tables

Customer

CustomerID	CustomerName	City	State	CreditLimit
1000	Smith	Phoenix	AZ	2500
1001	Jones	St. Louis	MO	1500
1002	Jeffries	Atlanta	GA	4000
1003	Gilkey	Phoenix	AZ	5000
1004	Lankford	Phoenix	AZ	2000
1005	Zeile	Chicago	IL	2000
1006	Pagnozzi	Salt Lake City	UT	5000
1007	Arocha	Chicago	IL	1000

Inventory

ItemID	Description	StdCost	ListPrice	QuantityOnHand
1010	Blender	14	29.95	200
1015	Toaster	12	19.95	300
1020	Mixer	23	33.95	250
1025	Television	499	699.95	74
1030	Freezer	799	999.95	32
1035	Refrigerator	699	849.95	25
1040	Radio	45	79.97	100
1045	Clock	79	99.95	300

Sales

Invoice	SaleDate	SalesPerson	CustomerID	Amount
101	10/3/2018	Wilson	1000	1,549.90
102	10/5/2018	Mahomet	1003	299.95
103	10/5/2018	Jackson	1002	1,449.80
104	10/15/2018	Drezen	1000	799.90
105	10/15/2018	Martinez	1005	849.95
106	10/16/2018	Martinez	1007	99.95
107	10/29/2018	Mahomet	1002	2,209.70
108	11/3/2018	Martinez	1000	779.90

Sales_Inventory

Invoice	ItemID	Quantity	SellPrice
101	1025	1	699.95
101	1035	1	849.95
102	1045	3	99.95
103	1010	1	29.95
103	1015	1	19.95
103	1025	2	699.95
104	1025	1	699.95
104	1045	1	99.95
105	1035	1	849.95
106	1045	1	99.95
107	1030	1	999.95
107	1035	1	849.95
107	1040	2	79.97
107	1045	2	99.95
108	1025	1	689.95
108	1045	1	89.95

*Life-long learning opportunity: see pp. xxiii–xxiv in preface.

REQUIRED

Write queries to answer the following questions. Your instructor may specify the method of acquiring the database noted above and whether to use Design view or SQL view.

a. For which items are there at least 100 units in QuantityOnHand?
b. What were the item numbers, price, and quantity of each item sold on invoice number 103?
c. Which customers made purchases from Martinez? Provide CustomerName and SalesPerson. (Show customer names only once, even if they purchased from Martinez multiple times.)
d. List Invoice, SaleDate, SalesPerson, CustomerName, and Amount for Invoices whose Amount is more than $1,500. Sort the Amount from largest to smallest.
e. List Invoice, ItemID, Description, SellPrice, ListPrice, Quantity, and compute the Extension (SellPrice * Quantity) for all items sold where the SellPrice is different than the ListPrice. Sort by ItemID in descending order.
f. Compute the profit margin for each item sold. Calculate the profit margin as (SellPrice – StdCost)/SellPrice. List Invoice, SaleDate, ItemID, SellPrice, Quantity, and computed ProfitMargin. Sort by ProfitMargin in descending order.
g. Compute the profit for each line of the invoices. Calculate the profit as (SellPrice – StdCost) * Quantity. List Invoice, SaleDate, ItemID, SellPrice, Quantity, and computed Profit. Sort by Invoice in ascending, then Profit in descending order.

Queries with aggregate functions

h. How many sales transactions were made in October? Name your output column Num_Of_Sales
i. How many customers live in Arizona? List the State and CountOfCustomers.
j. How many customers live in each state? List the State and CountOfCustomers. Sort the list alphabetically by State.
k. How much did each salesperson sell based on Sales.Amount? List SalesPerson and TotalAmount. Sort from largest TotalAmount to smallest.
l. How many units of each item were sold? List ItemID, Description, and TotalSold. Sort on TotalSold in ascending order.
m. Compute a total for each invoice based on Quantity times SellPrice. Name your total InvoiceTotal. Display Invoices where InvoiceTotal does not equal Amount. List Invoice, SaleDate, SalesPerson, Amount, and InvoiceTotal. If no rows meet your criteria, consider changing the value of Amount for Invoice 101 to a different value to test your query.

Advanced queries that may require nesting or reference to earlier queries.

n. Show invoices for the customer(s) with the largest credit limit. List CreditLimit, CustomerName, Invoice, SaleDate, and Amount.
o. Show invoices that are two times larger than the average invoice based on Amount. List Invoice, SaleDate, and Amount.

4.6 The BusyB Company wants to store data about its employee skills. Each employee may possess one or more specific skills, and several employees may have the same skill. Include the following facts in the database:

date hired
date of birth
date skill acquired
employee name
employee number
pay rate
skill name
skill number
supervisor

REQUIRED

a. Design a set of relational tables to store these data. Name each table and field in accordance with good database design.
b. Identify the primary key for each table, and identify any needed foreign keys.
c. Implement your schema using any relational DBMS. Specify primary and foreign keys, and enforce referential integrity. Demonstrate the soundness of your design by entering sample data in each table.

4.7 You want to extend the schema shown in Table 4-18 to include information about customer payments. Some customers make installment payments on each invoice. Others write a check to pay for several different invoices. You want to store the following information:

amount applied to a specific invoice
cash receipt number
customer name
customer number
date of the payment
employee who processed the payment
invoice to which payment applies
total amount received

TABLE 4-18 Database That Needs to Be Extended

Inventory

ItemID	Description	QuantityOnHand	ListPrice
10573	24" Monitor	13	$295.00
10574	27" Monitor	8	$395.00
10622	Laser Printer	22	$355.00
10623	Color Laser Print	5	$545.00
10624	Mult-function Pr	12	$495.00

Customer

CustomerID	CustName	Street	City	State	ZipCode	CreditLimit	AccountBalance
11255	G. Hwang	2993 Main	Mesa	AZ	85281	$4,000.00	$875.00
12971	J. Jackson	466 W. Oak	Tempe	AZ	85281	$5,000.00	$2,588.00
13629	P. Szabo	246 E. Palm	Mesa	AZ	85281	$6,000.00	$3,955.00
15635	S. Martinez	2866 Spring	Tempe	AZ	85287	$5,000.00	$250.00
18229	B. Sosnik	1733 Apache	Tempe	AZ	85287	$3,000.00	$1,675.00

Sales

InvoiceID	SaleDate	EmployeeID	CustomerID	TotalAmount
10001	9/8/2021	25	15637	$285.00
10002	9/10/2021	22	12971	$890.00
10003	9/24/2021	24	13629	$1,065.00
10004	10/1/2021	25	11255	$295.00
10005	10/11/2021	22	15637	$820.00
10006	10/25/2021	25	18229	$590.00

Sales_Inventory

InvoiceID	ItemID	Quantity	SellPrice
10001	10573	1	$285.00
10002	10574	1	$395.00
10002	10624	1	$495.00
10003	10622	3	$355.00
10004	10573	1	$295.00
10005	10573	1	$285.00
10005	10623	1	$535.00
10006	10573	2	$295.00

REQUIRED

a. Modify the set of tables in Table 4-18 to store this additional data. Name each table and field in accordance with good database design.
b. Identify the primary key for each new table you create.
c. Implement your schema using any relational DBMS package. Indicate which attributes are primary and foreign keys, and enter sample data in each table you create.

4.8 Create relational tables that solve the update, insert, and delete anomalies in Table 4-19. Name each table and field in accordance with good database design.

4.9 Create relational tables that solve the update, insert, and delete anomalies in Table 4-20. Name each table and field in accordance with good database design.

4.10 From the database created in the comprehensive problem (also available at http://www.pearsonhighered.com/romney), perform queries based on the tables and query grid shown in Table 4-21. Your instructor may specify whether you are to use Design view or SQL view.

a. Which borrowers use Advent Appraisers? List BorrowerID, LastName, and AppraiserName.
b. List all of the property appraisers with the letter "d" in their name, sorted by name. List AppriaiserID and AppraiserName.
c. List all of the lenders who have participated in a transaction that used AppraiserID 8. Provide LenderName, BorrowerID, and ReqMortAmount.
d. List the lenders that lent more than $100,000. Provide LenderName and AppraiserName. Only list each combination of LenderName and AppraiserName once.

Queries that use aggregate functions

e. What is the average amount borrowed from each lender? Provide LenderID, LenderName, and AvgMortAmt. Sort by AvgMortAmt in descending order. Consider using ROUND() to present at two decimal places.

TABLE 4-19 Invoice Table

InvoiceID	ShipDate	Order Date	CustomerID	Customer-Name	ItemID	Description	Quantity
52	6-19-21	5-25-21	201	Johnson	103	Trek 9000	5
52	6-19-21	5-25-21	201	Johnson	122	Nimbus 4000	8
52	6-19-21	5-25-21	201	Johnson	10	Izzod 3000	11
52	6-19-21	5-25-21	201	Johnson	71	LD Trainer	12
57	6-20-21	6-01-21	305	Henry	535	TR Standard	18
57	6-20-21	6-01-21	305	Henry	115	NT 2000	15
57	6-20-21	6-01-21	305	Henry	122	Nimbus 4000	5

TABLE 4-20 Purchase Order (PO) Table

Purchase-OrderID	Purchase-OrderDate	PartID	Description	UnitPrice	Quantity-Ordered	VendorID	VendorName	Vendor-Address
2	3/9/21	334	XYZ	$30	3	504	KL Supply	75 Stevens Dr.
2	3/9/21	231	PDQ	$50	5	504	KL Supply	75 Stevens Dr.
2	3/9/21	444	YYM	$80	6	504	KL Supply	75 Stevens Dr.
3	4/5/21	231	PDQ	$45	2	889	Oscan Inc	55 Cougar Cir.

TABLE 4-21 Selected Query Screen for Chapter Comprehensive Problem

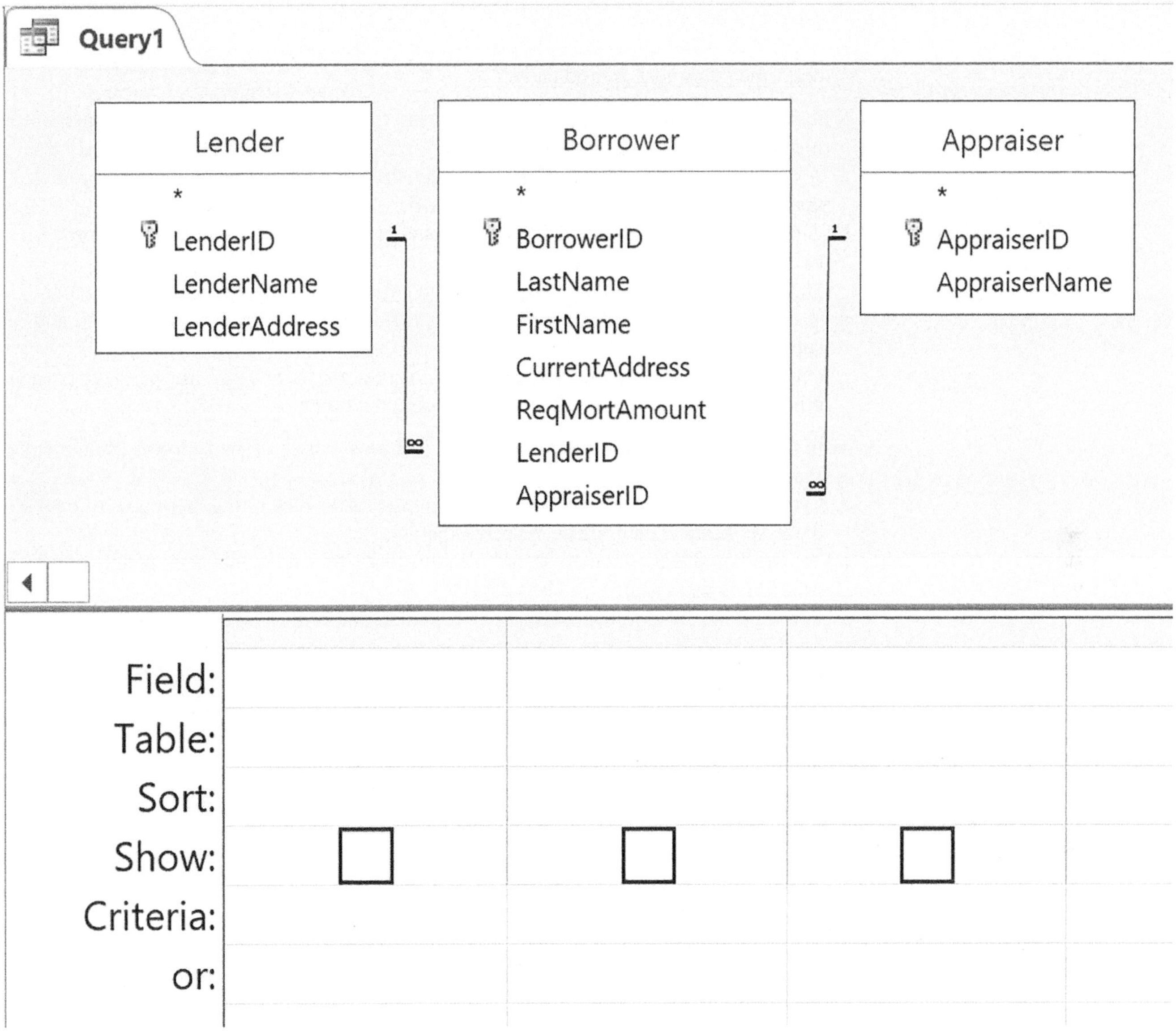

f. How many appraisals did each appraiser perform? Provide AppraiserName and CountOfAppraisals.

Advanced queries that may require nesting or reference to earlier queries.

g. Which borrower requested the largest mortgage? Provide BorrowerID, LastName, and ReqMortAmount.
h. Which borrower requested the smallest mortgage? Provide BorrowerID, LastName, and ReqMortAmount.

4.11 Answer the following multiple-choice questions.

1. With respect to data warehouses, databases, and files, which of the following statement(s) is (are) true?

a. Few mainframes and servers use database technology, and database use in personal computers is growing slowly.
b. Analyzing large amounts of data for strategic decision making is often referred to as strategic processing.

c. Databases were developed to address the proliferation of master files, which were created each time a need for information arose.
d. A DBMS manages and controls the interface between stored data and the application programs that use the data.
e. Since data warehouses are only used for transaction processing, they are updated in real time rather than periodically.

2. With respect to data warehouses, databases, and files, which of the following statement(s) is (are) true?
a. A database system consists of the database, the DBMS, and the application programs that access the database through the DBMS.
b. A problem with databases is data inconsistencies because the same data is stored in two or more master files.
c. Data mining is using queries to investigate hypothesized relationships among data.
d. A data warehouse is one or more very large databases containing both detailed and summarized data for a number of years.
e. Data sharing refers to data and the programs that use them being independent of each other; each can be changed without changing the other.

3. With respect to data warehouses, databases, and files, which of the following statement(s) is (are) true?
a. Cross-functional analysis refers to combining master files into larger pools of data so more application programs can access the data.
b. To avoid outdated, incomplete, or erroneous data, management needs policies and procedures that ensure scrubbed data.
c. In the master file approach, data is an organizational resource used by and managed for the entire organization, not just the originating department.
d. Data warehouses complement transaction processing databases by providing support for strategic decision making.
e. OLAP is using sophisticated statistical analysis to find unhypothesized relationships in data.

4. With respect to data warehouses, databases, and files, which of the following statement(s) is (are) true?
a. While it is important to regularly back up transaction processing databases, that is not the case with data warehouses.
b. The database controller (DBC) is responsible for coordinating, controlling, and managing the database.
c. Since strategic decision making requires access to large amounts of historical data, organizations are building separate databases called data warehouses.
d. Data warehouses minimize redundancy, while transaction processing databases are purposely redundant to maximize query efficiency.
e. Data validation controls that ensure input accuracy are one of the most time-consuming and expensive steps in creating a data warehouse.

5. With respect to databases and files, which of the following statement(s) is (are) true?
a. A DBA can change physical storage to improve system performance without affecting users or application programs.
b. There is a record in the data dictionary that describes each file in the database.
c. The DQL is used to change the database, such as creating, deleting, and updating records.
d. A schema describes data elements and the relationships among them in a user's logical view of the data.
e. In file-based systems, programmers do not need to know the physical location and layout of records like they do in databases.

6. With respect to database systems, which of the following statement(s) is (are) true?
   a. The physical view of data is how people conceptually organize and understand the relationships among data items.
   b. The DML builds the data dictionary, creates the database, describes logical views for each user, and specifies security constraints.
   c. A record layout shows the items stored in a file, including the type of data stored and both the order and length of the data fields.
   d. A DBMS allows users to query or update a database without knowing where data are actually stored.
   e. The external-level schema is the organization-wide view of a database and lists all data elements and the relationships among them.

7. With respect to database systems, which of the following statement(s) is (are) true?
   a. The DDL and DML should be restricted to authorized administrators and programmers; the DQL is available to users.
   b. A report writer is a high-level, English-like language with powerful, easy-to-use commands to help sort, order, and update data.
   c. DBMS software links the way data are physically stored with each user's logical view of the data.
   d. A subschema can prevent access to those portions of the database that do not apply to it.
   e. An individual user's view of portions of a database is referred to as an internal-level schema.

8. With respect to relational databases, which of the following statement(s) is (are) true?
   a. The referential integrity rule ensures that there are no update anomaly problems with the foreign keys.
   b. A delete anomaly occurs when deleting a row has unintended consequences.
   c. Each relational table row is called a couple and contains data about a specific item in the table; each column contains data about an attribute of that item.
   d. The normalization process is used to create a set of relational tables in 3NF.
   e. In a relational database, there can be no more than two values per cell.

9. With respect to relational databases, which of the following statement(s) is (are) true?
   a. A foreign key is only found in one table; it is not allowed to be in another table.
   b. When data about objects of interest are stored in separate database tables, it is easier to avoid insert anomalies.
   c. Semantic data modeling uses a system designer's knowledge of business processes to create tables in 3NF.
   d. According to the entity integrity rule, a primary key can uniquely identify a table row if it is blank.
   e. An insert anomaly occurs when there is no way to update records to a database.

CASE 4-1 Research Project

As in all areas of IT, DBMSs are constantly changing and improving. Research how businesses are using DBMSs, and write a report of your findings. Address the following issues:

1. Which popular DBMS products are based on the relational data model?
2. Which DBMS products are based on a logical model other than the relational data model?
3. What are the relative strengths and weaknesses of the different types (relational versus other logical models) of DBMSs?

AIS in Action Solutions

QUIZ KEY

1. What is each row in a relational database table called?
   - ▶ a. tuple [Correct. A tuple is also called a row in a relational database.]
   - b. relation [Incorrect. A relation is a table in a relational database.]
   - c. attribute [Incorrect. Each column in a relational database is an attribute that describes some characteristic of the entity about which data are stored.]
   - d. anomaly [Incorrect. An anomaly is a problem in a database, such as an insert anomaly or a delete anomaly.]

2. The relational data model portrays data as being stored in ________.
   - a. objects [Incorrect. An object-oriented database portrays data as being stored as objects.]
   - b. hierarchies [Incorrect. A hierarchical database portrays data as being stored in hierarchies.]
   - ▶ c. tables [Correct. The relational data model portrays data as being stored in a table or relation format.]
   - d. files [Incorrect. The file-based data model portrays data as being stored in files.]

3. How a user conceptually organizes and understands data is referred to as the ________.
   - ▶ a. logical view [Correct. The logical view shows how a user conceptually organizes and understands data.]
   - b. physical view [Incorrect. The physical view shows how and where data are physically stored.]
   - c. data model view [Incorrect. This is not a typical database view.]
   - d. data organization view [Incorrect. This is not a typical database view.]

4. Which of the following attributes would most likely be a primary key?
   - a. supplier name [Incorrect. The primary key must be unique. The same name could be used by multiple entities.]
   - ▶ b. supplier number [Correct. A unique number can be assigned as a primary key for each entity.]
   - c. supplier zip code [Incorrect. The primary key must be unique. More than one supplier could reside in the same zip code.]
   - d. supplier account balance [Incorrect. The primary key must be unique. The same account balance, such as a $0.00 balance, could be maintained by multiple entities.]

5. Which of the following is an individual user's view of the database?
   - a. internal-level schema [Incorrect. The internal-level schema represents how the data are actually stored and accessed.]
   - b. conceptual-level schema [Incorrect. A conceptual-level schema is the organization-wide view of the entire database.]
   - ▶ c. external-level schema [Correct. The external-level schema represents an individual user's view of the database.]
   - d. logical-level schema [Incorrect. This is not a schema mentioned in the text.]

6. Which of the following would managers most likely use to retrieve information about sales during the month of October?
   - ▶ a. DQL [Correct. DQL—data query language—is used to retrieve information from a database.]
   - b. DML [Incorrect. DML—data manipulation language—is used for data maintenance.]
   - c. DSL [Incorrect. DSL is not a DBMS language.]
   - d. DDL [Incorrect. DDL—data definition language—is used to build the data dictionary, create a database, describe logical views, and specify any limitations or constraints on security.]

7. How many columns of output would be returned by the following SQL query?

   SELECT Table1.Field2, Table1.Field3, Table2.Field3, Table2.Field5

FROM Table1 INNER JOIN Table2 ON Table1.Field1 = Table2.Field4
WHERE Table2.Field5 = 3;

a. 1 [Incorrect. This response may indicate a misunderstanding of the WHERE clause.]
b. 2 [Incorrect. This response may indicate confusion with the number of tables.]
c. 3 [incorrect. This response may be a misunderstanding of the WHERE clause criteria.]
▶ **d.** 4 [Correct. The number of output columns is determined by the number of columns listed in the SELECT clause. There are four columns listed. Table1.Field2, Table1.Field3, Table2.Field3, Table2.Field5]

8. The constraint that all foreign keys must have either null values or the value of a primary key in another table is referred to as which of the following?
▶ **a.** referential integrity rule [Correct. The referential integrity rule stipulates that foreign keys must have values that correspond to the value of a primary key in another table or be empty.]
b. entity integrity rule [Incorrect. This rule states that every primary key in a relational table must have a non-null value.]
c. foreign key value rule [Incorrect. The text does not discuss a foreign key value rule.]
d. null value rule [Incorrect. The text does not discuss a null value rule.]

9. The constraint that all primary keys must have non-null data values is referred to as which of the following?
a. referential integrity rule [Incorrect. The referential integrity rule stipulates that foreign keys must have values that correspond to the value of a primary key in another table or be empty.]
▶ **b.** entity integrity rule [Correct. Every primary key in a relational table must have a non-null value.]
c. normalization rule [Incorrect. The text does not discuss a normalization rule.]
d. relational data model rule [Incorrect. The text does not discuss a relational data mode rule.]

10. Which of the following clauses properly filters the rows in an SQL query to values greater than 3 in Field Field4 from Table3?
a. SELECT Table3.Field4 > 3 [Incorrect. The SELECT clause indicates which columns are in the output set.]
▶ **b.** WHERE Table3.Field4 > 3 [Correct. The WHERE clause filters rows. This criterion indicates the value in Table 3. Field 4 has to be greater than 3]
c. WHERE Field4.Table3 > 3 [Incorrect. In this WHERE clause the table and field notation is backwards.]
d. FROM Table3.Field4 > 3 [Incorrect. The FROM clause indicates which tables are used in the query.]

COMPREHENSIVE PROBLEM SOLUTION

Since Lender and Appraiser data are repeated throughout Table 4-16, the spreadsheet contains update, insert, and delete anomalies. To eliminate anomaly problems and reduce redundancy, we break the spreadsheet into three smaller tables: Borrowers (Table 4-22), Lenders (Table 4-23), and Appraisers (Table 4-24). We also rename data attributes to follow principles of database design.

BorrowerID, LenderID, and AppraiserID are the primary keys because each uniquely identifies the rows in their respective tables. The primary keys from the Lender and Appraiser tables are added to the Borrower table as foreign keys so that the Lender and Appraiser tables will have a direct link to the Borrower table.

Creating smaller tables with primary and foreign keys solves the three anomaly problems:

- The insert anomaly is solved because a new lender and appraiser can be added without requiring a borrower.
- The delete anomaly is solved because deleting a borrower that decides not to pursue a mortgage does not delete information about the lender and appraiser.

- The update anomaly is solved because there is only one row in one table to update when a lender moves and changes its address, instead of changing all spreadsheet rows that store the lender address.

After the data are entered into the Microsoft Access tables, we can query the database. The query in Table 4-25 finds the borrowers and appraisers associated with loans from Excel Mortgage. This query is created as follows using Design View:

- From the Query menu option, select Create Query in Design View.
- Add all three tables to your Query Design. Access automatically links the primary and foreign keys.

TABLE 4-22 Borrower Table

BorrowerID (Primary Key)	LastName	FirstName	CurrentAddress	ReqMort-Amount	LenderID (Foreign Key to Lender Table)	AppraiserID (Foreign Key to Appraiser Table)
450	Adams	Jennifer	450 Peachtree Rd.	$245,000	13	8
451	Adamson	David	500 Loop Highway	$124,688	13	9
452	Bronson	Paul	312 Mountain Dr.	$345,000	14	10
453	Brown	Marietta	310 Loop Highway	$57,090	15	10
454	Charles	Kenneth	3 Commons Blvd.	$34,000	16	8
455	Coulter	Tracey	1367 Peachtree Rd.	$216,505	13	8
456	Foster	Harold	678 Loop Highway	$117,090	12	9
457	Frank	Vernon	210 Bicayne Blvd.	$89,000	12	10
458	Holmes	Heather	1121 Bicayne Blvd.	$459,010	16	10
459	Johanson	Sandy	817 Mountain Dr.	$67,900	15	9
460	Johnson	James	985 Loop Highway	$12,000	12	10
461	Jones	Holly	1650 Washington Blvd.	$67,890	15	9

TABLE 4-23 Lender Table

LenderID (Primary Key)	LenderName	LenderAddress
12	National Mortgage	750 16 St.
13	Excel Mortgage	6890 Sheridan Dr.
14	CCY	28 Buckhead Way
15	Advantage Lenders	3345 Lake Shore Dr.
16	Capital Savings	8890 Coral Blvd.

TABLE 4-24 Appraiser Table

AppraiserID (Primary Key)	AppraiserName
8	Advent Appraisers
9	Independent Appraisal Service
10	Jones Property Appraisers

TABLE 4-25 Borrowers with Loans from Excel Mortgage

Query Design

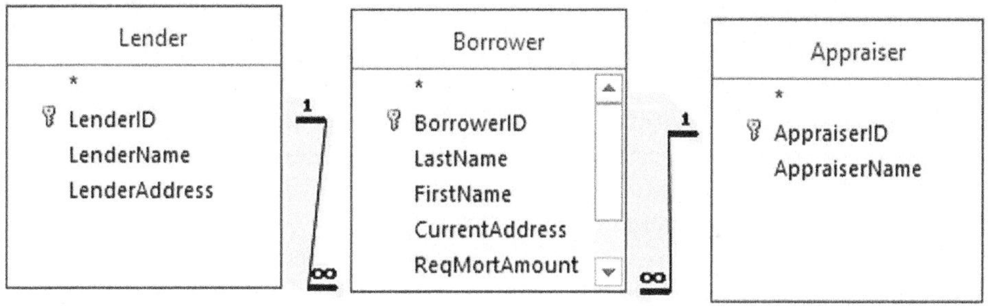

Field:	BorrowerID	LastName	FirstName	LenderName	AppraiserName
Table:	Borrower	Borrower	Borrower	Lender	Appraiser
Sort:					
Show:	☑	☑	☑	☑	☑
Criteria:				"Excel Mortgage"	
or:					

SQL View

```
SELECT Borrower.BorrowerID, Borrower.LastName, Borrower.FirstName, Lender.LenderName, Appraiser.AppraiserName
FROM (Lender INNER JOIN Borrower ON Lender.LenderID = Borrower.LenderID )
INNER JOIN Appraiser ON Appraiser.AppraiserID = Borrower.AppraiserID
WHERE Lender.LenderName = "Excel Mortgage";
```

Query Results

BorrowerID	LastName	FirstName	LenderName	AppraiserName
450	Adams	Jennifer	Excel Mortgage	Advent Appraisers
451	Adamson	David	Excel Mortgage	Independent Appraisal Service
455	Coulter	Tracey	Excel Mortgage	Advent Appraisers

- Select the following fields: Borrower Number, Last Name, First Name, Lender Name, and Property Appraiser Name.
- Specify Excel Mortgage as the criteria in the Lender Name column.
- Run the query.

Or in SQL View:

- Specify the columns to be presented.
  SELECT Borrower.BorrowerID, Borrower.LastName, Borrower.FirstName, Lender.LenderName, Appraiser.AppraiserName
- Using the FROM statement, select the tables needed and define their key linkages.
  FROM (Lender INNER JOIN Borrower ON Lender.LenderID = Borrower.LenderID)
  INNER JOIN Appraiser ON Appraiser.AppraiserID = Borrower.AppraiserID
- Apply the filtering criteria in the WHERE clause.
  WHERE Lender.LenderName = "Excel Mortgage";

Appendix: Data Normalization

As indicated in the accompanying chapter, if data is not normalized, three anomalies (update, insert, and delete) may be present and, if so, will cause data errors. In this appendix, we demonstrate the first three iterative steps in transforming unnormalized data to relational tables. The steps are called "normal forms." Thus, we will demonstrate how to create first normal form (1NF), second normal form (2NF), and third normal form (3NF). The flowchart in Figure A4-1 graphically describes the normalization process.

Suppose all the fields of information desired for an invoicing system are represented on the sheet of paper as shown in Figure A4-2.

Additional normal forms exist and theoretical work continues in this area. The first three normal forms are sufficient for this text and most database implementations.

Table A4-1 illustrates what a table containing data from all the fields for three invoices might look like. There are data fields for each of the following: invoice number, sale date, customer number, customer name, product code, product description, quantity sold, and sales price. This is an unnormalized table, the starting point for the normalization process.

A table is in 1NF when the following is true:

- Repeating groups have been removed.
- A unique primary key exists for each record.

We first notice multiple values in the Product Code, Description, Quantity, and Price cells for each invoice. We must reduce each cell to one value per cell. We remove these repeating groups by creating new rows for each of the product values for each invoice. In these new rows, we replicate the invoice information to complete each new row. Now each cell is single valued. We can verify that we haven't lost any information as we still know the products, prices, and quantities for each invoice and its associated customer.

Next, we look for a primary key. A primary key is a data field or a combination of data fields that uniquely identifies each row in the table. If a record cannot be uniquely identified using a

FIGURE A4-1
A Graphical Representation of the Normalization Process

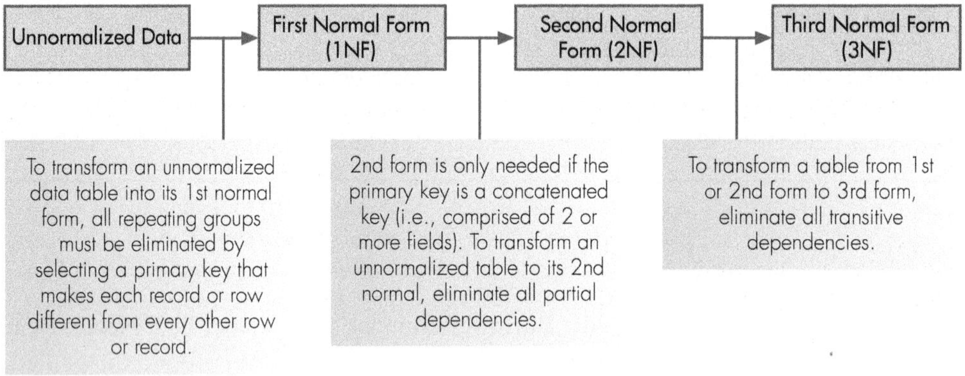
Unnormalized Data
First Normal Form (1NF)
Second Normal Form (2NF)
Third Normal Form (3NF)
To transform an unnormalized data table into its 1st normal form, all repeating groups must be eliminated by selecting a primary key that makes each record or row different from every other row or record.
2nd form is only needed if the primary key is a concatenated key (i.e., comprised of 2 or more fields). To transform an unnormalized table to its 2nd normal, eliminate all partial dependencies.
To transform a table from 1st or 2nd form to 3rd form, eliminate all transitive dependencies.

FIGURE A4-2
Invoice Record

Invoice

100101 11/2/2021 345 Smith

Product	Description	Quantity	Price
R2345	Blister Blocker	1	15.01
R254	Flip Belt	1	7.99
R521	LED band	2	12.25
R152	KT Tape	3	6.65

TABLE A4-1 Invoice Table (Unnormalized Form)

Invoice	Sale Date	Cust ID	Cust Name	Product Code	Description	Quantity	Price
100101	11/2/21	345	Smith	R152	KT Tape	3	6.65
				R2345	Blister Blocker	1	15.01
				R254	Flip Belt	1	7.99
				R521	LED band	2	12.25
100102	11/4/21	346	Huang	R254	Flip Belt	1	7.29
				R435	Slider Disks	2	5.54
100103	11/5/21	345	Smith	R2345	Blister Blocker	1	15.01
				R435	Slider Disks	2	5.99

single data field, a concatenated key (two or more data fields which, when combined, uniquely identify each record) is used. Alternatively, a new column with unique values is created.

Table A4-2 shows the data in 1NF. We chose to use the combination of Invoice Number and Product Code as our primary key (denoted PK). By knowing an Invoice Number and Product Code, we can navigate to the unique instance of that product on that invoice. The choice of this combined key demands that a product cannot be listed twice on an invoice since doing so would cause that combination of a Product Code and Invoice Number to be duplicated. They would no longer uniquely identify a row.

A table is in 2NF when the following is true:

- Already in 1NF form (each record is uniquely identified and therefore unique).
- No attribute depends on only a portion of the primary key (partial dependency).

The process of iterating through second normal form is only needed when the primary key identified in 1NF is concatenated (made up of more than one data field). If there is no concatenated key, you can skip 2NF and go directly to 3NF.

In Table A4-2, the primary key of our 1NF is the combination of Invoice Number and Product Code. Thus, we must examine each non-key element to see if the values of that element depend on (or are defined by) one part of the primary key. Since Sale Date, Customer Number, and Customer Name depend on the Invoice Number, and not the Product Code, we have a "partial dependency." Said another way, by knowing invoice number, we can find the sale date and customer regardless of the product code. This partial dependency is eliminated by moving fields dependent on that portion of the key to another table while establishing and maintaining a link to the original table. The link is established by also copying the appropriate portion of the primary key to the new table while eliminating duplicate rows. Table A4-3 shows the newly created table, which by examining its content can be identified as the Invoice Table. Table A4-4 shows the fields remaining in the original table.

TABLE A4-2 Invoice Table (1NF)

Invoice (PK)	Sale Date	Cust ID	Cust Name	Product Code (PK)	Description	Quantity	Price
100101	11/2/21	345	Smith	R152	KT Tape	3	6.65
100101	11/2/21	345	Smith	R2345	Blister Blocker	1	15.01
100101	11/2/21	345	Smith	R254	Flip Belt	1	7.99
100101	11/2/21	345	Smith	R521	LED band	2	12.25
100102	11/4/21	346	Huang	R254	Flip Belt	1	7.29
100102	11/4/21	346	Huang	R435	Slider Disks	2	5.54
100103	11/5/21	345	Smith	R2345	Blister Blocker	1	15.01
100103	11/5/21	345	Smith	R435	Slider Disks	2	5.99

TABLE A4-3 Invoice Table (2NF)

Invoice (PK)	Sale Date	Cust ID	Cust Name
100101	11/2/21	345	Smith
100102	11/4/21	346	Huang
100103	11/5/21	345	Smith

We continue to examine the remaining non-key elements for partial dependencies in Table A4-4. We see that Description is dependent on Product Code. Quantity is dependent on the combination of Invoice and Product Code in that we must know both to know the quantity sold. Price is less obvious. One might suppose that price depends solely on Product Code. This may be true if Price represented List Price or the price at which goods are held for sale. A careful examination reveals that some products have been sold at different prices. For example, product R254 sold for 7.99 on invoice 100101 but sold for 7.29 on invoice 100102. This indicates that the Price field in this dataset represents the actual selling price in the transaction and therefore depends on both Invoice and Product Code. In other words, if we consider Price as solely dependent on Product Code, which value for price would we keep for R245? By keeping only one, we would be losing information. Let's rename Price to SoldPrice based on this new understanding.

We will transfer Description and a copy of Product Code to a new table (Table A4-5). We identify Product Code as a Primary Key in this table. The remaining fields are shown in Table A4-6, with the additional notation of Product Code as a Foreign Key. With all partial dependencies removed, we are now in 2NF.

A table is in 3NF when the following is done:

- Already in 2NF.
- No transitive dependencies exist. That is, all data fields functionally depend on the primary key and only the primary key.

A transitive dependency occurs when a data field can be identified or determined by a field other than the primary key. In other words, a transitive dependency exists when one data field is functionally dependent on another data field. In our example, we need to look at Tables A4-3, A4-5, and A4-6 for transitive dependencies. In Table A4-3, we find that Customer Name depends on the field of Customer ID. By knowing Customer ID, we know Customer Name. We need to remove Customer name to another table while carrying a linking key to that table. Table A4-7 is created with this information. We identify Customer ID as the primary key in this table. The remaining fields are shown in Table A4-8 with the added notation of Foreign Key for the Customer ID. There are no further transitive dependencies in these tables. Neither Table A4-5 nor Table A4-6 have transitive dependencies. Table A4-5 cannot have a transitive dependency because there is only one non-key field. Table A4-6 does not have transitive dependencies because Price does not determine Quantity and Quantity does not determine Price.

TABLE A4-4 Invoice_Products Table (1NF)

Invoice (PK)(FK)	Product Code (PK)	Description	Quantity	Price
100101	R152	KT Tape	3	6.65
100101	R2345	Blister Blocker	1	15.01
100101	R254	Flip Belt	1	7.99
100101	R521	LED band	2	12.25
100102	R254	Flip Belt	1	7.29
100102	R435	Slider Disks	2	5.54
100103	R2345	Blister Blocker	1	15.01
100103	R435	Slider Disks	2	5.99

TABLE A4-5 Products Table (2NF & 3NF)

Product Code (PK)	Description
R152	KT Tape
R2345	Blister Blocker
R254	Flip Belt
R435	Slider Disks
R521	LED band

TABLE A4-6 Invoice_Products Table (2NF & 3NF)

Invoice (PK)(FK)	Product Code (PK)(FK)	Quantity	SoldPrice
100101	R152	3	6.65
100101	R2345	1	15.01
100101	R254	1	7.99
100101	R521	2	12.25
100102	R254	1	7.29
100102	R435	2	5.54
100103	R2345	1	15.01
100103	R435	2	5.99

Our final set of tables are:

1. Table A4-5: Products table (3NF)
2. Table A4-6: Invoice_Products table (3NF)
3. Table A4-7: Customer table (3NF)
4. Table A4-8: Invoice table (3NF).

One way to remember the three normal forms is to think of Perry Mason. When Perry Mason called someone to testify in court, the witness always had to swear to "tell the truth, the whole truth, and nothing but the truth." Each row in a 1NF table has a uniquely identified truth (a primary key). A 2NF table is like the "whole truth" part of the oath (each attribute or data field depends on the whole primary key, not just part of the primary key). The 3NF table is like the "nothing but the truth" part of the oath (each attribute depends on nothing but the primary key (on the primary key and on no other attribute or data field).

If data tables are not broken down to 3NF, problems will occur. These problems are called the update, insert, and delete anomalies and are explained in the chapter. If an unnormalized table is refined to a set of 3NF tables, the update, insert, and delete anomalies are far less likely to occur.

Summary

The normalization process starts with all relevant data items in an unnormalized table. The normalization process then begins by:

1. Removing all repeating groups of data to create the 1NF with an identified primary key.
2. Removing partial dependencies (attributes dependent on part of the primary key) to create the 2NF. This applies only when the 1NF table has a concatenated key.
3. Removing all transitive dependencies (nonprimary key attributes, or data fields, dependent on other nonprimary key attributes, or data fields) to create the 3NF.

TABLE A4-7 Customer Table (3NF)

Cust ID (PK)	Cust Name
345	Smith
346	Huang

TABLE A4-8 Invoice Table (3NF)

Invoice (PK)	Sale Date	Cust ID (FK)
100101	11/2/21	345
100102	11/4/21	346
100103	11/5/21	345

CHAPTER

5

Introduction to Data Analytics in Accounting

LEARNING OBJECTIVES

After studying this chapter, you should be able to:

1. Explain what makes a good question and evaluate questions relative to the SMART framework.
2. Describe the extract, transform, and load (ETL) process and key components of each step of the process.
3. Explain the differences between descriptive, diagnostic, predictive, and prescriptive analytics. Understand the situations for which each type of analytic is appropriate.
4. List the principles that lead to high-quality data visualizations.
5. Describe how automation interacts with the analytics mindset and when data analytics is not the right tool for making a decision.

INTEGRATIVE CASE S&S

S&S implemented a new AIS built on a relational database system. They collect and store all of the data for the accounting system in one integrated system. However, as S&S continues to grow, Ashton realizes they are creating data at an increasing rate. In addition to the accounting system data, they have implemented other systems that track such things as social media, Internet traffic, and many other things.

Working with all of the different systems has become cumbersome. Ashton and his team are increasingly receiving requests for different data analyses, and often these requests require the team to join the disparate data together. For example, to help them run the business, management wants reports that integrate social media, physical store information, past performance, vendor and customer information, and predicted trends for the future. The external and internal auditors want reports related to following financial reporting rules and other compliance requirements, often in real-time. It seems that everyone wants Ashton to provide data, and they want it immediately.

At the same time data demands are increasing, other employees refuse to use the data analyses that Ashton and his team currently prepare for them. These employees ignore these

Ppbig/123RF

analyses, saying they are hard to understand and they wish they could just do the analysis themselves. Ashton's team spends a great deal of time preparing these reports, so he is uncertain why they are not having more impact and how he can allow employees to conduct their own analyses.

Ashton realizes the company's data needs are expanding rapidly and that he needs to come up with a plan to deal with this challenge or the company will face serious growth and compliance problems. He also realizes he needs to better understand how to produce useful data analyses to help S&S succeed. Ashton has blocked out the next week to develop a plan to deal with data at S&S. He plans to present to the owners a data plan that addresses the following issues:

1. Developing a framework to help guide S&S's use of data.
2. Developing a structure for data that integrates all of S&S's data and allows more users to access the data.
3. Creating employee training that shows the value of data analyses and teaches them what makes it useful.

Introduction

Data is proliferating at an exponential rate. This data proliferation is caused by increasing computer processing power, increasing storage capacity, and increasing bandwidth. At present, there is no sign of slowing for any of the accelerators. In the Internet of Things (IoT) world, coupled with 5G bandwidth, more and more data will come from more and more sources. What good is all this data? Can businesses leverage this plethora of data to exact insights and competitive advantage? This chapter explores data analytics and accompanying toolsets needed to turn this mountain of data into useful information.

Using data appropriately has become especially important for accountants. Accountants in all different practice areas are using data in exciting ways. As a few examples:

- Auditors, both internal auditors and external auditors, can test full populations of transactions rather than a small sample by using data analytics and automation. They are also able to provide greater evidence the company is complying with accounting rules by examining a greater variety of data.
- Corporate accountants use data to make better decisions such as how to accurately cost products and services. Increased data allows them to make more accurate assessments of risks and to identify opportunities to preserve and enhance value.
- Tax professionals face regulators who use analytics to identify tax returns that are likely too aggressive. Data analytics also allow tax professionals to provide more real-time estimates of tax consequences of business decisions. This increases the ability of tax professionals to influence top management business decisions.

- Investment advisors use data to identify more favorable investment opportunities to recommend to their clients.

big data - Data sets characterized by huge amounts (volume) of frequently updated data (velocity) in various formats (variety), for which the quality may be suspect (veracity).

data volume - The amount of data created and stored by an organization.

data velocity - The pace at which data is created and stored.

data variety - The different forms data can take.

data veracity - The quality or trustworthiness of data.

As shown in these examples, accountants need to understand data and how it is changing business. To understand the scope of the data revolution, it is important to consider the four V's of big data: volume, velocity, variety, and veracity. **Big data** is the term companies use to describe the massive amounts of data they now capture, store, and analyze. **Data volume** refers to the amount of data created and stored by an organization. **Data velocity** refers to the pace at which data is created and stored. **Data variety** refers to the different forms data can take. **Data veracity** refers to the quality or trustworthiness of data.

The airline industry provides an example of how the 4 V's of big data impact business. One critical factor for airline success is accurately estimating flight arrival and departure times. Arrival and departure times are critical to not only coordinate passenger schedules and on-time arrival metrics but also for ground support of restocking and cleaning planes. Before big data, airline industries relied on pilots to predict their arrival times. Pilots typically made their final prediction during the final approach to the airport—a stressful time where pilot attention is better spent focusing on landing the aircraft.

To improve arrival time predictions, airlines turned to the company PASSUR Aerospace. Rather than rely on pilot estimates, PASSUR Aerospace uses a variety of data to better predict arrival times by combining publicly available information such as flight schedules and weather data with data they collect from passive radar stations they installed near airports. These radar stations have high data velocity, passing information to PASSUR Aerospace every 4.6 seconds. Collecting all this data has resulted in PASSUR Aerospace having significant data volume because it keeps a historical record of data to better inform future predictions. The proof of the veracity of the data is that PASSUR Aerospace has virtually eliminated the gap between actual and estimated plane arrival times.

Airline companies also use big data to improve customer relations, to improve maintenance schedules, to plan better airplane routes, to improve employee scheduling, and to solve a host of other business challenges. Indeed, big data combined with data analytics is transforming the airline industry. Note that big data alone does not lead to these improvements; rather, business professionals must analyze the big data to reveal insights that lead to these improvements. To be successful in the future with big data, it is important to understand more than tools and techniques; it is critical to develop an appropriate mindset that allows you to think about data holistically.

FOCUS 5-1 Knowledge Needed by Future Accountants

"The skill sets required for the auditor of the future are always evolving. To help you stay ahead of the curve, the Center for Audit Quality, in collaboration with the leading public company accounting firms and the American Institute of CPAs, developed this roadmap to help students understand what they will need to become successful auditors." So begins the document titled "Mindset, Behaviors, Knowledge & Skills Building a Roadmap for the Auditor of the Future," a thought paper meant to guide students and educators on what skill sets students who enter the auditing profession will need in the future. Although directed to future auditors, this list mirrors advice given to other professional accounting groups. The document lists the following key mindsets, behaviors, and knowledge that future auditors should possess:

- Mindsets: analytics mindset, global mindset, growth mindset, innovative mindset.
- Behaviors: professional skepticism, critical thinking, logic, lifelong learning, embraces challenges, adaptability to new situations, adaptability when interacting with others, cultural awareness, curiosity, and leadership.
- Knowledge: proficiency in accounting and auditing, technology, psychology, and communication.

The past reputation of accountants being "just bean counters" no longer applies in the digital age. The business world expects accountants to do and to be more than they ever have been in the past. To read the full document produced by the CAQ, go to https://www.thecaq.org/mindset-behaviors-knowledge-skills-building-roadmap-auditor-future.

A **mindset** is a mental attitude, a way of thinking, or frame of mind. Mindsets are powerful collections of beliefs and thoughts that shape how you think and feel and what you do. In the accounting domain, the Center for Audit Quality (or CAQ)—a nonpartisan nonprofit public policy organization focused on improving external audit quality—suggests one critical mindset for future accountants to develop is the **analytics mindset**. The CAQ defines an analytics mindset as the "ability to visualize, articulate, conceptualize, or solve both complex and simple problems by making decisions that are sensible given the available information [and] ability to identify trends through analysis of data/information." The Big 4 accounting firm EY provides a more tractable definition of the analytics mindset used as a framework in this chapter. According to EY, an analytics mindset is the ability to

mindset - A mental attitude, a way of thinking, or a frame of mind.

analytics mindset - A way of thinking that centers on the correct use of data and analysis for decision making.

- Ask the right questions.
- Extract, transform, and load relevant data.
- Apply appropriate data analytic techniques.
- Interpret and share the results with stakeholders.

This analytics mindset definition closely resembles the scientific method of asking a question, gathering data, testing the data, and reporting the results of testing. This time-honored method of knowledge acquisition has produced many of the technological advancements enjoyed in modern society. This chapter guides you to develop an analytics mindset in an accounting context.

Ask the Right Questions

Chapter 1 defined data as facts that are collected, recorded, stored, and processed by a system. As such, data by themselves offer little value. Only when data is transformed into information does it provide value. To start the process of transforming data into information, one must have a question or desired outcome. Asking the right question is the first step of the analytics mindset.

To define "right" or "good" questions in the context of data analytics, start by establishing objectives that are SMART: **s**pecific, **m**easurable, **a**chievable, **r**elevant, and **t**imely. A good data analytic question is

- *Specific:* needs to be direct and focused to produce a meaningful answer.
- *Measurable:* must be amenable to data analysis and thus the inputs to answering the question must be measurable with data.
- *Achievable:* should be able to be answered and the answer should cause a decision maker to take an action.
- *Relevant:* should relate to the objectives of the organization or the situation under consideration.
- *Timely:* must have a defined time horizon for answering.

These principles help guide asking good data analytic questions. One important point discussed at the end of the chapter is the need to realize that not all questions can or even should be answered with data.

Extract, Transform, and Load Relevant Data

The process of extracting, transforming, and loading data is often abbreviated as the **ETL process**. The ETL process is often the most time-consuming part of the analytics mindset process. One of the reasons the ETL process can be so time-consuming is that the process typically differs for every different program, database, or system that stores or uses data. This results in numerous instances of exporting data from one program or system, transforming the data into a format another program or system can use, and then loading the transformed data into the second program or system.

ETL process - A set of procedures for blending data. The acronym stands for extract, transform, and load data.

Given the challenges of the ETL process, the American Institute of Certified Public Accountants (AICPA) developed a set of Audit Data Standards for guidance in this process. These standards are voluntary, recommended ways companies can deal with the ETL process for accounting data. The standards are designed so that a base standard provides guidance for all types of accounting data and then specific standards deal with the general ledger and subledgers. Best practices from these standards will be referenced throughout this text.

This chapter discusses each component of the ETL process separately. Before studying each of these components, realize that in practice these components often are mixed together. For example, a data analyst might transform data while extracting it from a system. Repetitive ETL processes can be fully automated so the extracting, transforming, and loading data is done entirely by a computer program in what appears to be a single, unified step. Learning about each component is valuable, but as you gain experience, the separate components will blend together when you work with data.

EXTRACTING DATA

Extracting data is the first step in the ETL process. This section presents the extraction process as three steps: (1) understand data needs and the data available, (2) perform the data extraction, and (3) verify the data extraction quality and document what you have done.

UNDERSTAND DATA NEEDS AND THE DATA AVAILABLE Before extracting data, data needs should be carefully defined. This relates to the first step of the analytics mindset of asking the right question. Defining the question well makes it easier to define what data is needed to address the question. Without defining the data well early in the process, it is more likely that the wrong data or incomplete data will be extracted. If this happens, the entire ETL process may have to be repeated, wasting significant time and effort.

After defining the needed data, the next step is to understand the data itself, which entails understanding things like location, accessibility, and structure of the data. Organizations have many different approaches to storing data based on currency and frequency of access to the data and the type and intended use of the data. Companies often organize their data by creating data warehouses, data marts, and/or data lakes. While several slightly different definitions of these storage concepts are in practice, a data warehouse generally describes the storage of structured data from many different sources in an organization.

structured data - Data that is highly organized and fits into fixed fields.

unstructured data - Data that has no uniform structure.

semi-structured data - Data that has some organization but is not fully organized to be inserted into a relational database.

Structured data refers to data that is highly organized and fits into fixed fields. Examples include accounting data like a general ledger, data in a relational database, and most types of spreadsheet data. In contrast, **unstructured data** is data that has no uniform structure. Examples include images, audio files, documents, social media, tweets, emails, videos, and presentations. In between these two, **semi-structured data** is organized in some ways but is not fully organized to be inserted into a relational database. Examples include data stored in csv, xml, or JSON formats and various forms of streamed data (such as logs or machine-generated operation data). Data warehouses typically store only structured data or data that has been transformed into structured data.

Data warehouses can be massive as they collect data from multiple sources across the organization. As of 2014, Facebook had a data warehouse with 300 petabytes of data in 800,000 tables. To put that in perspective, 1 petabyte is the equivalent of 500 *billion* pages of standard typed text. Biologists estimate that the human brain can hold a maximum of 2.5 petabytes of data.

data marts - Data repositories that hold structured data for a subset of an organization.

Given the immense size of data warehouses, it is often more efficient to process data in smaller data repositories holding structured data, called **data marts**. For example, a company may design a separate data mart for all data in geographic regions like North America, South America, and Europe; or companies can create data marts by function such as a sales and a marketing data mart. The smaller size of the data mart makes it faster to access the data. It also provides tighter internal control by making it easier to restrict user access to only data relevant to their position.

data lake - Collection of structured, semi-structured, and unstructured data stored in a single location.

Finally, a **data lake** is a collection of structured, semi-structured, and unstructured data stored in a single location. When companies create data lakes, they typically attempt to add all data in the organization to the data lake as well as relevant data from outside the organization. For a car manufacturing company, a data lake may contain structured data like financial information but also unstructured data such as pictures of vehicles, movies of crash testing, performance logs from their cars, and social media data about the company.

The size of data lakes can cause problems if they become so large that it allows important data to become dark data. **Dark data** is information the organization has collected and stored that would be useful for analysis but is not analyzed and is thus generally ignored. Data lakes can also become **data swamps**, which are data repositories that are not accurately documented so that the stored data cannot be properly identified and analyzed. Data goes dark or turns into a data swamp for many reasons, including the organization not understanding the value of data analysis or not devoting sufficient resources to maintaining and analyzing the data. When top company officials have an analytics mindset, they are more likely to understand the value of data analysis and devote sufficient resources so that less data goes dark and data lakes do not become data swamps.

dark data - Information the organization has collected and stored that would be useful for analysis but is not analyzed and is thus generally ignored.

data swamps - Data repositories that are not accurately documented so that the stored data cannot be properly identified and analyzed.

Companies design their data warehouses, data marts, and data lakes in many ways. For example, a company can design a data warehouse to connect to all sources of transaction or structured data and then create a data mart using the data from the data warehouse. Alternatively, a company may design data marts to connect to all sources of transaction data and then choose to aggregate all of the data mart data into a data warehouse. Typically, data warehouses are of primary importance and thus are used to build data lakes. However, companies can also create their data warehouses, data marts, and data lakes to all independently access sources of data. A visual depiction of some of these alternative structures is show in Figure 5-1.

To properly extract data from various data repositories, it is important to understand the design of the organization's data lake, data warehouse, and data mart(s). Knowing the structure helps a user identify where the needed data resides and how to properly access it.

Typically, the best way to understand the structure of data is to consult the data dictionary. The data dictionary should contain **metadata**, which is data that describes other data. Examples of data dictionary metadata is the number of characters allowed in different fields, the type of

metadata - Data that describes other data.

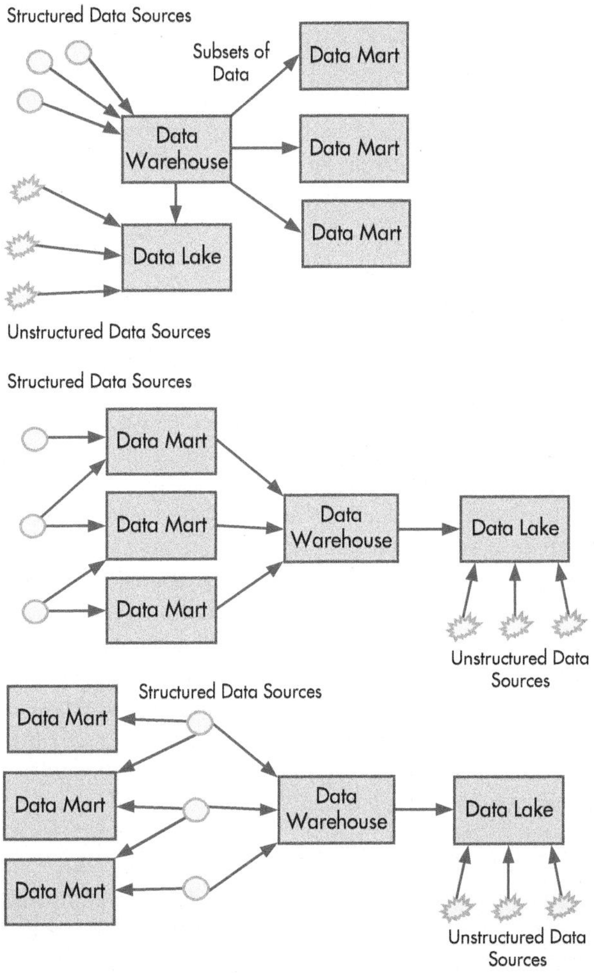

FIGURE 5-1
Three Alternative Structures: Data Warehouse, Data Mart, and Data Lake

characters allowed in fields (e.g., integer, text, date/time), and the format of data in a particular field. Maintaining up-to-date and correct metadata in a data dictionary can help prevent data from going dark and data lakes from turning into data swamps. Carefully examining the data dictionary to gather an understanding of the data and the underlying objects represents an important part of the ETL process.

The previous discussion assumes the data for analysis resides within the organization. An analysis sometimes requires data from outside of the organization. For example, comparing prices with a competitor requires the collection of the competitor prices, which may be obtained by scraping price data from the Internet and adding it to the data environment. Before extracting information from other sources, consider the moral, ethical, and legal (privacy and ownership) ramifications whenever data is gathered external to the organization.

EXTRACT THE DATA With a firm understanding of data needs and the location and properties of the data, you are prepared to extract the needed data. Organizations often have internal controls that restrict access to different types of data. Data extraction may require receiving permission from the data owner. The **data owner** is the person or function in the organization who is accountable for the data and can give permission to access and analyze the data.

data owner - The person or function in the organization who is accountable for the data and can give permission to access and analyze the data.

flat file - Text file that contains data from multiple tables or sources and merges that data into a single row.

delimiter - Character, or series of characters, that marks the end of one field and the beginning of the next field.

text qualifier - Two characters that indicate the beginning and ending of a field and tell the program to ignore any delimiters contained between the characters.

With permission from the data owner, the data will then need to be extracted into separate files or into a flat file. A **flat file** is a text file that contains data from multiple tables or sources and merges that data into a single row. Flat files are often preferable to separate files because it can make it easier and faster to analyze the data.

When including data in a flat file, a delimiter (also called a field separator) needs to be used to distinguish fields on a single line. A **delimiter** is a character, or series of characters, that marks the end of one field and the beginning of the next field. The Audit Data Standards recommends using a pipe delimiter, which is the vertical line between quotes "|". Pipes make useful delimiters because they are rarely used in other contexts. Two common, but less effective delimiters are commas and tabs. Commas and tabs are less effective because they are used frequently in standard writing and thus can confuse a computer program. The program may not know if the comma or tab is meant to be a delimiter or part of the information contained in a field.

A **text qualifier** is two characters that indicate the beginning and ending of a field and tell the program to ignore any delimiters contained between the characters. For example, Microsoft Excel and Microsoft Access use a quote at the beginning and the end of a field to indicate that any delimiters contained in that field should be ignored.

Table 5-1 provides three examples of delimiters and text qualifiers. The first example shows a flat file that uses a pipe delimiter and quotes for text delimiters. When the file is imported, the program can parse the data easily into the correct cells. In contrast, the second example uses a comma delimiter and no text qualifiers. In this case, the extra commas contained in the PerformanceReview field cause a problem when parsing the data into columns. The computer program would try to create two extra columns, causing an error because there are no column names for these erroneous columns. The third example fixes this problem by using text qualifiers with the comma delimiter. In this case, the program can easily understand how the data is to be parsed and placed in the appropriate column.

Two additional items to note in Table 5-1. First, often a program will only include text qualifiers when they are necessary to aid in parsing. Note how text qualifiers are not included in the header row. Many programs would not include text qualifiers for performance reviews if no delimiters (i.e., commas) were contained in the field. Second, the use of a high-quality delimiter, such as the pipe symbol, makes it less important to use text qualifiers.

It is also important to consider how or if each row will be uniquely identified. As explained in Chapter 4, primary keys are used to uniquely identify a row of data in a relational database table. Recall that a primary key is an attribute or combination of attributes that uniquely identifies each row in a table. Including primary keys in a data extraction can be valuable if you need to extract more data and merge it with a previous extraction.

VERIFY THE DATA EXTRACTION QUALITY AND DOCUMENT WHAT WAS DONE Once the data has been extracted, it is best practice to verify that the extraction was complete, accurate, and approved. Batch processing controls studied in Chapter 13 can be useful to verify the quality of the data. For example, counting the number of records in the extracted data set and

TABLE 5-1 Examples of Delimiters and Text Qualifiers

Pipe Delimited, Text Qualifiers						
Flat File, Header Row	Fname|Lname|PerformanceScore|"PerformanceReview"					
Flat File, Data Row	Renee|Armstrong|99|"Smiles a lot, Enthusiastic, could improve technique"					
Separated Data, Header Row	FName	LName	PerformanceScore	PerformanceReview		
Separated Data, Data Row	Renee	Armstrong	99	Smiles a lot, Enthusiastic, could improve technique		
Comma Delimited, No Text Qualifiers						
Flat File, Header Row	Fname,Lname,PerformanceScore,PerformanceReview					
Flat File, Data Row	Renee,Armstrong,99,Smiles a lot, Enthusiastic, could improve technique					
Separated Data, Header Row	FName	LName	PerformanceScore	PerformanceReview	**ERROR**	**ERROR**
Separated Data, Data Row	Renee	Armstrong	99	Smiles a lot	Enthusiastic	could improve technique
Comma Delimited, Text Qualifiers						
Flat File, Header Row	Fname,Lname,PerformanceScore,PerformanceReview					
Flat File, Data Row	Renee,Armstrong,99,"Smiles a lot, Enthusiastic, could improve technique"					
Separated Data, Header Row	FName	LName	PerformanceScore	PerformanceReview		
Separated Data, Data Row	Renee	Armstrong	99	Smiles a lot, Enthusiastic, could improve technique		

comparing the count with a count of records in the source data provides some evidence that the extraction is complete.

An additional verification step used by auditors is to reperform the data extraction for a sample of records and compare the smaller data extract with the full data extract. If the data is the same in both the sample and the full data extract, it provides evidence that the extraction process was done correctly.

The final data extraction best practice is to create a new data dictionary containing all of the information about the fields in the data extraction. Often this new data dictionary can be created by copying items from the source file data dictionary and updating those fields based on any changes made in the extraction process. It is good practice to include metadata that lists where the data came from in this new data dictionary. When data added to the extraction are external to the organization or were not previously defined in a data dictionary, it is important to accurately define the data in the new data dictionary. This allows everyone who uses the data extraction to correctly understand the data before they analyze it and helps avoid creating a data swamp.

TRANSFORMING DATA

Standardizing, structuring, and cleaning the data so that it is in the format needed for data analysis is called the data transformation process. Given the amount of time spent on and complexity of transforming data, Chapter 6 discusses this topic in detail. In this section, an overview of the four step transformation process is provided. The four steps are:

1. Understand the data and the desired outcome.
2. Standardize, structure, and clean the data.

3. Validate data quality and verify data meets data requirements.
4. Document the transformation process.

UNDERSTAND THE DATA AND THE DESIRED OUTCOME The first step in transforming data is to understand the extracted data and the desired data outcome when the transformation process is finished. If a data dictionary is not provided with the extracted data, the individual transforming the data should create a data dictionary and make sure they understand the data they obtained from the extraction process.

It is also important to understand the specifications for the transformed data, including which file format the data should be in when transformed, which delimiters should be used, what level of detail should be provided, how the data should be filtered, how the data should be structured for analysis, and any other specifications needed for the loading process.

STANDARDIZE, STRUCTURE, AND CLEAN THE DATA This is generally the most time-consuming part of the transformation process. Consider a small business that needs to perform a relatively straightforward analysis comparing employee payroll expense from one year to the next after implementing a new AIS. Each system outputs the data differently, aggregates the data files at different levels, uses different delimiters, and uses different primary keys. The bulk of time needed to perform the task is spent transforming the data to the point that the two years of data can be properly joined for analysis.

Transforming data can involve a virtually endless combination of techniques to insure the data is of high quality and is accurate and complete. Transforming data requires being resourceful and creative in understanding and fixing all the issues that exist in the data.

VALIDATE DATA QUALITY AND ACHIEVEMENT OF DATA REQUIREMENTS Data can have errors from when it is originally recorded. Given the complexity of the transformation process, it is also easy to introduce errors during this process. Therefore, it is critical to validate the data after it has been transformed to make sure the data is free from errors. The validation process can be simple like performing a visual scan of the data or more complex such as performing an audit of the data. Chapter 6 describes how to validate data quality.

Data may be of high quality, meaning all the errors are corrected, and still be useless if it does not meet the requirements for the ETL process. A laboriously transformed data file about customers is worthless if the intended analysis was supposed to be about vendors. Making sure the data meets the data requirements is critical to a successful transformation process.

DOCUMENT THE TRANSFORMATION PROCESS The last step of the transformation process is to once again update the data dictionary. Often different individuals extract, transform, and load the data. Thus, documenting changes made between each step in the process is vital for the next person in the process. Also, once data is transformed, it is often accessed by many different people. Without high-quality documentation of the transformation process, these individuals may use the data inappropriately in their analysis.

LOADING DATA

Once the data has been structured and cleaned, it is ready to be imported into whatever tool is used for analysis. If the data has been properly transformed, this process usually is relatively quick and easy. However, there are a few important considerations when loading data.

First, the transformed data must be stored in a format and structure acceptable to the receiving software. Some data may need to be saved as a text file using delimiters. Alternatively, the data may be placed into a schema such as XBRL or JSON or into a relational set of tables. If the data is imported into a database that enforces referential integrity, for example, then it is important to make sure the data is loaded in the correct sequence, so the referential integrity rule is not violated.

Second, programs may treat some data formats differently than expected. It is important to understand how the new program will interpret data formats. Because some data formatting is treated differently than expected, the Audit Data Standards recommend stripping out or standardizing most formatting, such as removing commas used as thousands separators, always using the minus sign to indicate negative numbers (instead of using parentheses), and using standard date formats.

Once the data is successfully loaded into the new program, it is important to update or create a new data dictionary, as the person who loaded the data often is not available to answer questions when the data is used. Appropriate documentation can aid in future understanding and prevent the need to reperform the entire ETL process.

Apply Appropriate Data Analytic Techniques

Data analytics fall into four categories: descriptive analytics, diagnostic analytics, predictive analytics, and prescriptive analytics. **Descriptive analytics** are information that results from the examination of data to understand the past. That is, descriptive analytics answer the question, "what happened?" or "what is happening?" The computation of accounting ratios, such as return on investment or gross margin, is an example of descriptive analytics. **Diagnostic analytics** build on descriptive analytics and try to answer the question "why did this happen?" These types of analytics attempt to determine causal relationships—for example, does increasing the IT budget in an organization increase employee efficiency and effectiveness?

descriptive analytics - Information that results from the examination of data to understand the past, answers the question "what happened?"

diagnostic analytics - Information that attempts to determine causal relationships, answers the question "why did this happen?"

Predictive and prescriptive analytics are both forward looking. **Predictive analytics** are information that results from analyses that focus on predicting the future—they address the question "what might happen in the future?" An example of predictive analytics is forecasting future events like stock prices or currency exchange rates. **Prescriptive analytics** are information that provide a recommendation of what *should* happen; they answer the question "what should be done?" An example of prescriptive analytics is the creation of algorithms that predict whether an individual or company will pay back their loan and then make a recommendation about whether a loan should be extended or not. Prescriptive analytics can also be programmed to take action—in the case of a loan, the loan may be granted without the need of a human to review the application.

predictive analytics - Information that results from analyses that focus on predicting the future, answers the question, "what might happen in the future?"

prescriptive analytics - Information that results from analyses to provide a recommendation of what should happen, answers the question "what should be done?"

Within these three categories of data analytics are numerous data analytic techniques that range from very basic and simple, like computing an average or a ratio, to very complex, like using neural nets or machine learning. To be expert in all areas of data analytics would require advanced training in statistics, computer science, and mathematics as well as domain knowledge in an area like accounting, economics, finance, or marketing. Because of the interdisciplinary breadth required in data analytics, typically individuals master a particular area and then have a more general understanding of other areas so they can search out experts when needed.

Two of the Big 4 accounting firms have followed this approach of recommending mastery in some areas and exposure to other ideas for what the average accountant should know about data analytics. Specifically, they highlight techniques and tools for which a new hire should have an awareness, working knowledge, and mastery. Having an awareness means that you know what a tool or technique is and can do, but you could not perform the action on your own. Typically, you would direct the task to someone else who has mastered the tool or technique to perform the task. Having a working knowledge of techniques and tools means that when the supervisor asks you to do a task, you have experience performing similar tasks, but you likely would need to review how to do something. With some effort, however, you would be able to complete the task with little to no help from others. Mastery of a content means that if your supervisor comes to you with a project, you could immediately work on that project and have a deep understanding of the techniques and tools necessary to complete the project.

The list of skills released by the Ernst & Young Foundation can be seen in Figure 5-2. These recommendations should be seen as examples of each category rather than an exhaustive, complete list of skills that should be in each category. As data analytics evolves, the techniques and tools that will help achieve success will also evolve. PricewaterhouseCoopers (PwC) encourages the following for accounting students:

- Basic computing courses that cover a contemporary coding language such as Python or Java. It should cover "core skills in legacy technologies (Microsoft Excel and Access),

Apply appropriate data analytics techniques			
Understand the purpose of different types of data analytics techniques and how to determine which techinques are most appropriate for the objectives of your analysis (objectives might include a need to prove or disprove an expectation, if one was developed)	► Master • Ratio • Sorting • Aggregation • Trends • Comparison • Forecasting • Basic descriptive statistics (mean,standard deviation, maximum and minimum, quartile) • Querying	► Working Knowledge • Cluster analysis • Inferential statistics (T-statistics, P-values) • Correlation analysis • Regression	► Awareness • Artificial intelligence • Machine learning • Cognitive computing • Neural networks • Data mining • Other emerging technologies
Gain familiarity with analytics tools	► Master • Excel • Basic database (Access) • Visualization (Tableau, Spotfire, Qlik, Microsoft BI)	► Working Knowledge • Query languages (SQL) • Career-path specific ► Audit – ACL, IDEA TeamMate ► Tax ► Managerial ► Forensic	► Awareness • Programming languages (VBA, Python, Pearl, Java, PHP) • Statistics (R, SAS, SPSS) • Database tools (SAP, Oracle, Microsoft) • SSIS packages

FIGURE 5-2
Ernst & Young Foundation Recommended Data Analytics Skills

especially in teaching the complex power of spreadsheet software" and "core skills with both structured and unstructured databases (SQL, MongoDB, Hadoop, etc.)."

- A first statistics course that covers programming with a statistics program like R, cleaning data, data visualization tools like Tableau SpotFire or Qlikview, and skills related to exploratory data analysis (descriptive statistics, basic exploratory multivariate statistics).
- A second statistics course that expands coverage of the statistics software and deals with advanced topics like statistical inference, dealing with missing data or design issues, univariate and multivariate regression, logistic regression, machine learning, and predictive tools.

Both firms agree that a critical skill required of all new hires is the ability to self-teach new concepts, a desire to learn, and a desire to stay up on what is the "latest and greatest" in the fast-changing world of technology. In addition, although there are lots of new and exciting technologies like blockchain and artificial intelligence, the basics of working with a spreadsheet program, understanding databases, and how to visualize data are of preeminent importance. Similarly, mastery of basic techniques like understanding ratio analysis, querying databases, and understanding basic statistics should not be overlooked before mastering more advanced techniques.

Interpret and Share the Results with Stakeholders

The final step of the analytics mindset is to interpret the data analysis and share the results with appropriate stakeholders. This section separately describes interpreting the results and sharing the results with others.

INTERPRETING RESULTS

In theory, interpretation of the output of your analytic tool is straightforward—describe what the analytics or visualizations are saying. However, in practice, interpreting results can be much more complicated. Interpreting results requires human judgment. Often, humans make mistakes or interpret results in erroneous ways.

One common way people interpret results incorrectly relates to correlation and causation. Correlation tells if two things happen at the same time. Causation tells that the occurrence of one thing will cause the occurrence of a second thing. Consider a company in Idaho selling winter snow gear. In the hot month of June, they decide to launch a large marketing campaign for the next six months to advertise a new line of snow gear, spending more money each month to advertise. At the end of the year in the middle of the winter, the company compares the advertising dollars and sales revenue for snow gear and finds a positive correlation—meaning as more money is spent on advertising, more snow gear is sold. One might be tempted to suggest that the marketing campaign caused snow gear sales. This may or may not be the case. This data cannot determine whether snow gear sales were caused by or only correlated with the marketing campaign. A competing explanation is that the increase in sales from June to December was caused by the changing of seasons in Idaho from summer to winter. The coming of winter may have caused more people to buy snow gear even without advertising.

A second common misinterpretation of results is noted in psychology research. Psychology research provides evidence of systematic biases in the way people interpret results. One example of a bias that influences interpretation of results is called confirmation bias—the tendency of individuals to interpret evidence to support their desired belief or position. You might see this in the context of a manager evaluating an employee's performance. Suppose the manager has a pre-existing desire to give the employee a positive rating because they are friends. The manager is likely to interpret any information about the employee more positively than an independent evaluator because of their pre-existing desire to rate their friend well. Thus, the employee may receive an evaluation higher than merited because the information was not interpreted correctly.

You should strive to interpret results objectively, making sure you fully understand what the results of analyses mean. This takes training and practice to do effectively.

SHARING RESULTS

Sharing data analytics results with others is often called data storytelling, or storytelling. **Data storytelling** is the process of translating often complex data analyses into more easy to understand terms to enable better decision making. Storytelling can help simplify all of the complexities that go into the process of gathering data, analyzing data, and interpreting data.

data storytelling - The process of translating often complex data analyses into more easy to understand terms to enable better decision making.

To tell a successful data story, first remember the question that initiated the analytics process. As part of generating an appropriate question, the story designer considers the objectives of the stakeholder. The story should answer the questions and achieve the objectives of the stakeholder. That does not mean the designer has to agree with or even support the objective, but the designer should design the story to discuss and to address the objective.

A second component of effective storytelling is to consider the audience. Examples of some things to consider about the audience include their experience with the particular data and data analytics in general; how much detail they will desire to answer the question; will the story be presented in person or via a report/email; how important is the question (i.e., how much time will they devote to this question); and whether the stakeholder needs a "quick" answer or an in-depth, detailed answer. Based on understanding what the audience wants, the story designer can design a story to meet the stakeholder's needs.

A third component is the use of data visualizations. **Data visualization** is the use of a graphical representation of data to convey meaning. A shorthand name for data visualizations used in practice is "viz" or "vizs." A common way to display data vizs is with a data dashboard, or dashboard for short. A **data dashboard** is a display of important data points, metrics, and key performance indicators in easily understood data visualizations.

data visualization - Use of a graphical representation of data to convey meaning.

data dashboard - Display of important data points, metrics, and key performance indicators in easily understood data visualizations.

Data visualization is a powerful way to communicate quickly and effectively. For example, a CIO might be concerned that costs for new computer technology are skyrocketing. One less effective presentation technique might be to report to the CIO that computer technology costs have increased 47% while all other expenses have increased 35% and sales have only increased 14%. The same information can be included in a dashboard and more vividly displayed in a line chart that shows computer technology costs, other expenses, and revenues changing over time. This chart quickly highlights what the CIO cares about and is easier to digest and remember than a wordy sentence.

Successful data visualization is both an art and a science. The art portion of visualization relates to understanding how others will interpret the visualization, using creativity to convey the message, and making a viz beautiful. The science portion of visualization relates to understanding basic principles of sound design. Good principles of visualization design include:

- Choosing the right type of visualization.
- Simplifying the presentation of data.

- Emphasizing what is important.
- Representing the data ethically.

Vizs that follow these basic principles will be more effective in communicating the story. Chapter 7 provides more discussion and examples of each of these principles.

Additional Data Analytics Considerations

To understand data analytics, it is important to cover two additional topics that span multiple parts of the analytics mindset: (1) automating steps within the analytics process and (2) understanding when analyzing data is not sufficient to produce high-quality judgments and decisions.

AUTOMATION

automation - The application of machines to automatically perform a task once performed by humans.

Automation is the application of machines to automatically perform a task once performed by humans. For example, instead of manually copying and pasting data from a computer database into another program, a computer program can be written that automatically performs this task. Automation is often thought about in the context of manufacturing. Many automotive companies now use robots to perform welding on an assembly line rather than have a human perform this task. However, automation is not limited to manufacturing; it has been an important part of accounting, and business more generally, for a long time. The first computer systems that collected accounting data were programmed to automatically add up the credit amounts and debit amounts of journal entries to make sure they balanced. This replaced humans who previously performed this task.

robotic process automation (RPA) - Computer software that can be programmed to automatically perform tasks across applications just as human workers do.

bot - Autonomous computer program designed to perform a specific task.

Business automation ranges on a spectrum from very basic to very complex. Very basic automation requires a very defined process so that a programmer can design all of the logic needed to perform every step of the task. Often, this type of automation is carried out with **robotic process automation (RPA)** software, which is computer software that can be programmed to automatically perform tasks across applications just as human workers do. A person using RPA designs an RPA **bot**, which is an autonomous computer program designed to perform a specific task. Rather than creating the bot using a scripted computer programming language, many of the leading providers of RPA software, such as Automation Anywhere, BluePrism, and UIPath, allow users to build bots with a simple click-and-drop interface. At the other end of the automation spectrum is automation that can recognize patterns, learn over time, and perform much more complex tasks. This type of automation is performed using tools like machine learning, artificial intelligence, and cognitive computing.

While some companies are working to create advanced automation solutions, most companies are still working to automate tasks on the basic automation side of the spectrum. For example, recent research finds that one of the Big 4 accounting firms automated 1 million human hours of tasks in 2017 and that the accounting firm planned to increase this amount 10 times in the next three years. These automated tasks will never again be performed by humans, but rather only by the "digital employees"—the bots. Indeed, a vice president of the RPA company UIPath said their goal "is to have a bot on every desktop" expressing the desire that RPA should be used by every employee to free the employee from doing mundane, routine work.

Companies are using RPA and other automation software to automate tasks within their analytics processes. For example, in relation to asking the right question, the company Aera Technology has developed technology to create a "self-driving enterprise." That is, the technology tries to "make real-time recommendations, predict outcomes, and take action autonomously" or said differently, it tries to develop questions the business should be asking, answer them without requiring human interaction, and perform the appropriate response. As an example, the technology might examine past sales and predict that a particular store may have a shortage of an item and then automatically ship the item from whichever storehouse would be least expensive.

Professionals actively look for ways to automate the ETL process. RPA is one tool that can be used to automate ETL tasks. For example, a student intern working for a small accounting firm was tasked with consolidating tax data for 420 C-corporation tax returns. The task normally took previous interns a total of 430 hours to complete, with 80 of those hours checking for human data entry errors. The intern spent 35 hours designing a bot to perform the consolidation task. When finished, the bot ran overnight and completed the entire task with no errors. Moving forward, the annual task can be completed in one night with the click of a few buttons and require virtually no human hours of work.

Related to automating the data analysis portion of an analytics mindset, as of 2019, Tableau, the software visualization company, built a new "Ask Data" feature that allows the user to type in a question and the computer automatically analyzes the data and produces a visualization that tries to answer the question. The user does not need to know how to use the program to build a visualization—the program automates the analysis and production of results.

Finally, the automation of sharing results with others is often performed with the creation and continual update of data dashboards. The process of producing the data dashboard is typically automated so a user can review real-time data at any time.

Although automating activities can often improve efficiency and effectiveness, not all activities are candidates for successful automation. Activities that are best for basic automation are those that are frequently performed, time-consuming, repetitive, rules based, and stable. Automating frequent, time-consuming, repetitive tasks frees workers to focus on more value-adding tasks.

Be aware that there are risks and concerns related to automation. If a task is automated incorrectly, the automation will efficiently enter incorrect data or alter data to be incorrect. It is critical to make sure automation works exactly as desired on training data before activating it on live data. Similarly, the automation needs to be periodically reviewed. If the task changes and the automation is not updated, the automation can again cause problems.

FOCUS 5-2 Automation

In February 1996, "the match that changed [chess] history" was held between reigning world chess champion Garry Kasparov and Deep Blue, an IBM supercomputer. Kasparov came into the match as the heavy favorite—some claim he is the greatest chess grandmaster of all time. He also had history on his side: A chess-playing computer had never beat a reigning world champion under normal chess tournament conditions. In the first game, the unthinkable happened, Deep Blue beat Kasparaov. Kasparov went on to beat Deep Blue 4 games to 2, but the initial loss set in motion the end of human dominance in chess. In a rematch the following year, Deep Blue beat Kasparov 3-½ games to 2-½ games.

Since the Kasparov vs. Deep Blue chess game, automated computer programs have beat human experts in other tasks, including IBM's Watson beating the all-time winningest Jeopardy contestant Ken Jennings and Google's AlphaGo beating one of the world's most dominant players, Lee Sedol, in the game Go. This last feat is especially impressive as Go has so many possible different moves that it is not possible to program a computer to try every combination to win the game, like programmers often program the computers to do when playing a human in chess.

What is the common thread among these different games pitting human vs. machine? In these cases, computers are programmed to better analyze and use data to make decisions than humans. However, the story suggesting computer domination of humans does not end there. After losing to Deep Blue, Kasparov started a chess tournament where "anything goes," meaning you could enter the competition as an individual human, automated computer program, or teams that combine any combination of humans and computers. The fascinating outcome of these tournaments was that a human or a computer did not strictly dominate, rather the winners of these tournaments were usually the combination of a human and a computer program. In describing this winning combination, Kasparov introduced the idea of digital/human centaurs (a centaur is a half-human and half-horse mythical creature). Kasparov found that half-human and half-computer "centaurs" were the best combination for winning chess competitions.

The business world readily embraces this "centaur" approach. Accounting firms are beginning to refer to their human employees and their digital employees. Digital employees are computer programs that complete a task, which was often previously performed by a human. Business teams are often made up of different experts, with a technology and data expert included to harness the power of technology. All trends point to a future where humans and computers will interact to perform business tasks better than either can do alone.

Finally, the human element of automation should be considered. Many employees are concerned when a company implements automation because they worry they will lose their jobs. Automation can be used to reduce headcount, but it also can be used to reduce boring, repetitive work so that employees are freed to do more interesting, value-added tasks. An organization needs to consider the human response to automation before beginning the automation process.

DATA ANALYTICS IS NOT ALWAYS THE RIGHT TOOL

While this chapter focuses on data analytics, it is important to note that data analytics is not always the correct tool to reach the best outcome. Reliable data does not exist for aspects of many questions. For example, human judgment or intuition may be able to account for sentiment factors that cannot be reliably measured. That is, just because a data analysis (from data that is collectible) suggests to take one course of action does not always mean that this is the best decision for an individual or organization.

As an example of when data analytics might fall short, consider a scenario where a data analyst analyzes how much money her company could make from committing a fraud and the likelihood of getting caught. Although this type of data analysis might show that the company would benefit from committing a fraud because the payoff would be large and the chance of getting caught is low, an ethical CEO would realize that the potential choice is wrong and should not be chosen, no matter what the data analysis reported.

Data analysis has both strengths and weaknesses, both should be understood and respected. As you move forward as a business professional, use data to make better decisions, but also remember the importance of intuition, expertise, ethics, and other sources of knowledge that are not easy to quantify but that can have a significant impact on performance.

Summary and Case Conclusion

At the end of the week, Ashton is pleased with his plan for dealing with data at S&S. He has decided that all employees at S&S need to be trained on the value of having an analytics mindset—a mindset of how to approach and use data. He specifically recommends that employees are taught how to extract, transform, and load their own data; analyze it; and then present it in a convincing manner.

To provide employees the ability to access S&S's data, Ashton has designed a new structure for all of the data at S&S. He proposes that S&S create a data lake, a data warehouse, and data marts. In this way, he can create and manage appropriate access of the data to each stakeholder. He is sure the auditors will appreciate the internal controls he plans to implement around the data while employees will be able to better solve their own data needs.

After reviewing the current analyses that Ashton and his team provides, he realizes the reports are often dated and not well designed. Ashton recommends working with employees to better design reports for their intended purpose and then automating the creation of these reports so the users can access real-time reports when they need them. The new data lake, data warehouse, and data mart structure will allow S&S to more easily automate the production of these reports.

Ashton is confident that his plans will help S&S to make better decisions based on data. He is eager to implement these changes and help S&S be proactive rather than reactive with their data.

KEY TERMS

big data 138
data volume 138
data velocity 138
data variety 138
data veracity 138
mindset 139
analytics mindset 139
ETL process 139
structured data 140
unstructured data 140
semi-structured data 140
data marts 140
data lake 140
dark data 141
data swamps 141

metadata 141
data owner 142
flat file 142
delimiter 142
text qualifier 142
descriptive analytics 145
diagnostic analytics 145
predictive analytics 145
prescriptive analytics 145
data storytelling 147
data visualization 147
data dashboard 147
automation 148
robotic process automation (RPA) 148
bot 148

AIS in Action

CHAPTER QUIZ

1. Unstructured data internal or external to the organization is usually gathered and stored in which of the following?
   a. data dictionary
   b. data lake
   c. data mart
   d. data warehouse

2. Which one of the following items would be the best primary key for a table containing information about customers?
   a. customer ID
   b. customer full name
   c. customer phone number
   d. customer email address

3. Which one of the following characters would be the best delimiter (the delimiter is listed between the quotes)?
   a. ","
   b. "@"
   c. "|"
   d. All of the above

4. An online sales company designed a program to evaluate customer purchases. After each purchase, the program analyzes which product the customer is most likely to buy next and e-mails the customer a coupon for a discount on this new product. What type of analytics is this an example of?
   a. descriptive analytics
   b. diagnostic analytics
   c. predictive analytics
   d. prescriptive analytics

5. When sharing the results of an analysis, which of the following is NOT a key principle to follow?
   a. Simplify the presentation of data.
   b. Present the visualization in a timely manner.
   c. Ethically represent the data.
   d. Emphasize what is important.

6. Which of the steps of an analytics mindset is the most difficult to automate?
   a. Ask the right questions.
   b. Extract, transform, and load relevant data.
   c. Apply appropriate data analytics techniques.
   d. Interpret and share the results with stakeholders.

7. All of the following characteristics of data are important in distinguishing big data from regular data EXCEPT:
   a. velocity
   b. variety
   c. visualization
   d. volume

8. You are given an extract of one field from a database. The field has the value "11815 N. Diamond Dr." Which type of data is contained in this field?
   a. structured data
   b. unstructured data
   c. semi-structured data
   d. None of the above

9. Programming a computer program to automatically perform a task previously performed by a human is an example of which of the following?
   a. warehousing data
   b. the ETL process
   c. establishing SMART objectives
   d. robotic process automation (RPA)

10. Good questions for data adhere to all of the following principles EXCEPT:
   a. accurate
   b. timely
   c. measurable
   d. specific

DISCUSSION QUESTIONS

5.1 The first step of an analytics mindset is to ask the right questions. How do you learn how to ask the right questions? How would you teach someone else how to ask the right questions?

5.2 This chapter discusses several different ways to structure data warehouses, data marts, and data lakes. Discuss the diagrams listed in the book or diagram your own structures for data warehouses, data marts, and data lakes, and discuss the pros and cons of each structure.

5.3 Companies are automating many accounting tasks. Is automation good or bad? Consider this question from the view of accounting students, accounting practitioners, other business professionals, and society as a whole. What should be done to achieve the good aspects of automating accounting tasks while minimizing the poor aspects?

5.4 The end of this chapter suggests that data analytics are not always appropriate for a decision context. Identify three unique business situations for which data analytics may not be appropriate. Identify why data analytics are not appropriate in these situations and how a decision maker should make their decision without using data.

PROBLEMS

5.1 Match the following terms with their definitions or examples.

___	**1.** analytics mindset	a.	Information that results from the examination of data to understand the past, answer the question "what happened?"
___	**2.** automation	b.	Application of machines to automatically perform a task once performed by humans
___	**3.** bot	c.	Amount of data created and stored by an organization
___	**4.** dark data	d.	Collection of structured, semi-structured, and unstructured data stored in a single location
___	**5.** data lake	e.	Autonomous computer program designed to perform a specific task
___	**6.** data mart	f.	Different forms data can take
___	**7.** data storytelling	g.	Computer software that can be programmed to automatically perform tasks across applications just as human workers do
___	**8.** data swamps	h.	Information that results from analyses that focus on predicting the future, answer the question "what might happen in the future?"
___	**9.** data variety	i.	A character, or series of characters, that mark the end of one field and the beginning of the next field
___	**10.** data velocity	j.	Data that describes other data
___	**11.** data veracity	k.	Use of a graphical representation of data to convey meaning

___ **12.** data visualization	l.	Quality or trustworthiness of data
___ **13.** data volume	m.	Data repositories that are not accurately documented so that the stored data cannot be properly identified and analyzed
___ **14.** delimiter	n.	Way of thinking that centers on the correct use of data and analysis for decision making
___ **15.** descriptive analytics	o.	Process of translating often complex data analyses into more easy to understand terms to enable better decision making
___ **16.** diagnostic analytics	p.	Data that has no uniform structure
___ **17.** ETL process	q.	Two characters that indicate the beginning and ending of a field and tell the program to ignore any delimiters contained between the characters
___ **18.** flat file	r.	Set of procedures for blending data; the acronym stands for extract, transform, and load data
___ **19.** metadata	s.	Information that attempts to determine causal relationships, answers the question "why did this happen?"
___ **20.** predictive analytics	t.	Information that results from analyses to provide a recommendation of what should happen, answers the question "what should be done?"
___ **21.** prescriptive analytics	u.	Text file that contains data from multiple tables or sources and merges that data into a single row
___ **22.** robotic process automation (RPA)	v.	Data repositories that hold structured data for a subset of an organization
___ **23.** structured data	w.	Pace at which data is created and stored
___ **24.** text qualifier	x.	Data that is highly organized and fits into fixed fields
___ **25.** unstructured data	y.	Storage of structured data from many different sources in an organization
	z.	Information the organization has collected and stored that would be useful for analysis but is not analyzed and is thus generally ignored

5.2 For each of the following examples, indicate whether the data is structured, semi-structured, unstructured, or a mix of each. Explain your answer.

1. A company runs many social media campaigns to increase sales. The company collects data about the amount spent on each ad campaign, the number of people who click on each ad, whether each person clicking on an ad completed a purchase, and the location (city and country) of each person who clicked on an ad.
2. A company performs performance evaluations of all its employees each quarter. The evaluations include comments made by peers of each employee, a supervisor's write-up of performance during the quarter with a rating on a 5-point scale, and performance metrics relative to their job title (e.g., sales completed for sales people, units repaired for repair people, etc.).
3. A call center records all phone calls between employees and customers. The company stores the data for review if any allegations are made of inappropriate employee behavior.
4. A company scrapes data from a review website where customers can write in about products they have purchased. The company analyzes each of the reviews but only records the number of words in the review, a rating of the tone of the review (scores from −3 to +3), and the number of stars given (1 to 4).
5. A university tracks student's course registrations each semester. The university records the course number, course description, and course credit hours for each student.
6. A mechanic keeps a digital catalog of all part numbers and part descriptions for each type of vehicle the company services.
7. A non-profit organization keeps a record of all past donors. The organization tracks names, dates of donations, amount donated, and additional comments about the donor and their donation.

8. An online retailer tracks IP addresses from each web visit. The retailer monitors IP addresses to see if visits are coming from IP addresses known to hack company websites.
9. A company scrapes data from a review website where customers can write in about products they have purchased. The company stores each of the written reviews.
10. A company owns a football stadium. During games, the company takes high-definition photos of all fans. The company stores these images and plans eventually to use advanced technologies to see which fans wear the team's colors so they can market clothing to them.

5.3 Consider the following scenario. You are a tax professional meeting with a new client to help them make strategic tax planning decisions. You know that clients can choose from a variety of tax positions that vary in aggressiveness. A very conservative tax position will result in paying higher taxes but reduce the likelihood of an IRS audit and fine. In contrast, an aggressive tax position will result in lower taxes but increase the likelihood of an IRS audit and fine. As this is a new client, you want to assess their appetite for taking aggressive versus conservative tax positions. An intern prepared a list of questions to ask the client. Review the list of questions below.

REQUIRED

For each question, decide whether it is a SMART question or not. If not a SMART question, then rewrite the question and explain why you changed the question. Consider each question independent of the others, meaning redundancy between questions is okay, as you would not likely ask all of these questions. This exercise helps you practice developing SMART questions.

1. You want to take an aggressive tax position, right?
2. Why do you pay taxes?
3. What do you think Congress should do to reform personal income taxes in this country?
4. How much money do you want to save on taxes?

5.4 Consider the following scenario. You are a new staff internal auditor for a national restaurant chain. Your manager assigns you to visit a new restaurant location that is performing poorly. In preparing for your visit, you search customer review websites and find that many customers are complaining about the cleanliness of the restaurant. When you alert your manager to this, she is concerned about potential health code violations. She asks you to prepare a list of questions that you will ask the employees related to the cleanliness of the restaurant. Your manager wants to assess the risk of health code violation and understand why it is offending customers.

REQUIRED

Prepare a series of questions to ask the employees. Remember the SMART principles as you design your questions. For each question, list to whom you plan to ask the question, and discuss how the question applies one or more of the SMART principles. Each question does not need to apply all of the SMART principles, but your combination of questions should address all of the SMART principles.

5.5 For each of the following situations, indicate whether the analysis is an example of a descriptive analytic, diagnostic analytic, predictive analytic, or prescriptive analytic.

1. An accounting firm is trying to understand if its external audit fees are appropriate. They compute a regression using public data from all companies in their industry to understand the factors associated with higher audit.
2. A self-driving car company uses artificial intelligence to help clean its historic social media data so they can analyze trends.
3. An airline downloads weather data for the past 10 years to help build a model that will estimate future fuel usage for flights.
4. A shipyard company runs a computer simulation of how a tsunami would damage its shipyards, computing damages in terms of destruction and lost production time.
5. An online retail company tracks past customer purchases. Based on the amount customers previously spent, the program automatically computes purchase discounts for current customer purchases to build loyalty.

6. An all-you-can-eat restaurant uses automated conveyer belts to bring cold food to the chefs for preparation. The conveyer belts bring the food to the chefs based on algorithms that monitor the number of people entering and leaving the restaurant.
7. A large manufacturer of farm equipment continuously analyzes data sent from engine sensors to understand how load, temperature, and other factors influence engine failure.
8. A small tax services business provides its financial statements to a bank to get a loan so it can buy a new building to grow its business.

5.6 The same data can be provided to you in many different ways. Below are four extracts of the same data. The first extract is properly formatted for import into the company database. Notice, that this extract uses a pipe delimiter, puts each unique record on a different row, and uses text qualifiers of a single quote when commas are present. Your task is to discuss how to transform the other extracts so they can be imported into the company database.

REQUIRED

For each of the other three data extracts, do the following:

- Describe if delimiters are present, and if so, what they are.
- Describe if text qualifiers are present, and if so, what they are.
- Describe the steps you would take to prepare each extract for importing into the company's database.

Correct Format for Import

```
PrimaryKey|CustomerName|CustomerAddress|Description|CreditLimit
1001|Camp-a-lot Corporation|'2103 County Rd W #VV, Seymour, WI, 54165'|Buys mostly in summer|10000
1002|Outdoors Forever Inc.|'3145, Lake Geneva, WI, 53147'|New customer|5000
1003|AllPro Camping|'12303 233rd Ave, Trevor, WI, 53179'|Wants confirmations by telephone, email, and mail|'15,000'
1004|Camping Extreme LLC|'8153 W Holly Rd, Mequon, WI, 53097'||7000
1005|JD Camping Company|'9624 N Lamplighter Ln, Thiensville, WI, 53092'|Sells goods on consignment|'10,000'
```

1. Extract 1

```
PrimaryKey,CustomerName,CustomerAddress,Description,CreditLimit
1001,Camp-a-lot Corporation,2103 County Rd W #VV, Seymour, WI, 54165,Buys mostly in summer,10000
1002,Outdoors Forever Inc.,3145, Lake Geneva, WI, 53147,New customer,5000
1003,AllPro Camping,'12303 233rd Ave, Trevor, WI, 53179,Wants confirmations by telephone, email, and mail,15,000
1004,Camping Extreme LLC,8153 W Holly Rd, Mequon, WI, 53097,,7000
1005,JD Camping Company,9624 N Lamplighter Ln, Thiensville, WI, 53092,Sells goods on consignment,10,000
```

2. Extract 2

```
PrimaryKeyCustomerName  CustomerAddress Description      CreditLimit
1001Camp-a-lot Corporation       "2103 County Rd W #VV, Seymour, WI, 54165"      Buys mostly in summer    10000
1002Outdoors Forever Inc.        "3145, Lake Geneva, WI, 53147"  New customer    5000
1003AllPro Camping       "12303 233rd Ave, Trevor, WI, 53179"    Wants confirmations by telephone, email, and mail          15,000
1004Camping Extreme LLC "8153 W Holly Rd, Mequon, WI, 53097"            7000
1005JD Camping Company  "9624 N Lamplighter Ln, Thiensville, WI, 53092" Sells goods on consignment       10,000
```

3. Extract 3

```
PrimaryKey       CustomerName     CustomerAddress|Description|CreditLimit\r\n1001 Camp-a-lot Corporation     '2103 County
Rd W #VV, Seymour, WI, 54165'|Buys mostly in summer|10000\r\n1002       Outdoors Forever Inc.     '3145, Lake Geneva,
WI, 53147'|New customer|5000\r\n1003     AllPro Camping    '12303 233rd Ave, Trevor, WI, 53179'|Wants confirmations by
telephone, email, and mail|'15,000'\r\n1004      Camping Extreme LLC      '8153 W Holly Rd, Mequon, WI, 53097'||
7000\r\n1005     JD Camping Company       '9624 N Lamplighter Ln, Thiensville, WI, 53092'|Sells goods on
consignment|'10,000'\r\n
```

5.7 Excel Project: ETL in Excel

You are to analyze production patterns for a company producing lawn equipment. The company wants to understand which regions and which managers produce the most units. They also want to know if they are producing more units than the minimum run requirement for each production run. The minimum run requirement is the number of units that must be produced to be profitable for each type of inventory item. Go to the student download page at http://www.pearsonhighered.com/romney and download the files labeled "P5-7tbl_Batch.csv", "P5-7tbl_Products.csv", "P5-7tbl_ProductsBatch .txt", and "P5-7.xlsx". The first three files are exported from systems that produce different output formats.

REQUIRED

Import each of the csv and txt files into the Excel file. Import each file into the sheet with the same name as the file. Pay attention to the delimiters in each file and whether the file uses text qualifiers or not. Combine the data from the three sheets to the tab labeled "P5-7tbl_AllData". Once you have all the data gathered correctly into the "P5-7tbl_AllData" tab, answer the following questions, listing each answer on the appropriate sheet (e.g., Solution1 sheet, Solution2 sheet, and Solution3 sheet):

1. How many units did each location produce?
2. How many units did each manager produce?
3. How many product batch runs produced fewer units than the minimum run size?

5.8 Excel Project: Well-Designed Visualizations
The following visualization (viz) shows all state taxes and fees collected for the state of New York from 2014 to 2018, inclusive.

REQUIRED

For this viz, do the following:

1. Describe ways you would change the viz to (a) simplify the data presentation and (b) properly emphasize the objective of the stakeholder. Assume the objective of the stakeholder of this viz is to compare how each type of tax collections changes over time.

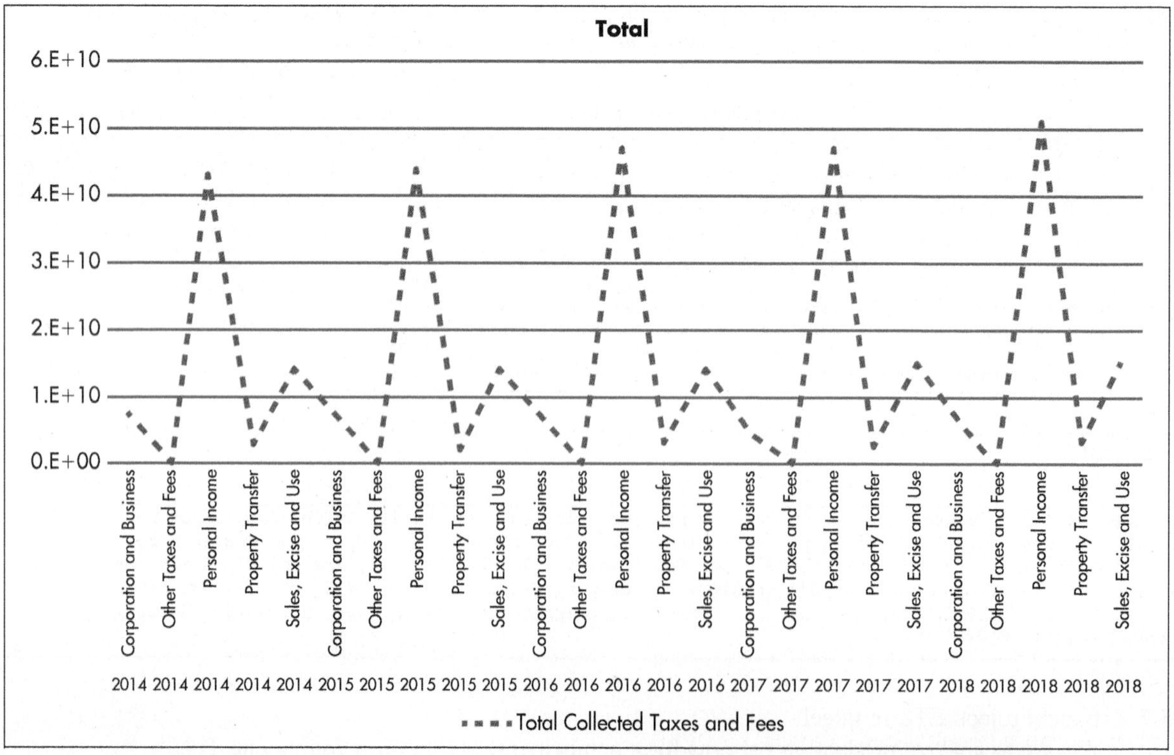

2. Go to the student download page at http://www.pearsonhighered.com/romney and download the files labeled "P5-8NewYorkTaxes.xlsx". Implement some of the ideas you suggested for part 1 to simplify the viz and emphasize importance.

5.9 For the viz listed in problem 5.8, describe ways you could change the viz to present the data in unethical ways. How could using one of these unethical viz presentation techniques hurt the institution using this data and damage your career?

5.10 Automation is significantly changing the accounting profession. Search to find an example of how a company has automated an accounting task during the last year. Prepare a memo that summarizes the following:
- Describe how the accountant(s) performed the task before and after the automation.
- Describe the benefits the company realized because of the automation.
- Describe any drawbacks to using automation.
- Based on your learning, suggest one additional area in accounting that is likely to be automated in the future. Justify why you believe this area will be automated.

*The following case was developed by the Ernst & Young Academic Resource Center, which is sponsored by the Ernst & Young Foundation. Robotic process automation is growing in importance in the accounting profession. Several RPA vendors provide free trial software, including Automation Anywhere (*https://www.automationanywhere.com/lp/community-edition*) and UIPath (*https://www.uipath.com/freetrial-or-community*). Download one of these software packages and complete the following case.**

CASE 5-1 Robotic Process Automation—Wood's Amazing Woods Inc.

OVERVIEW

Wood's Amazing Woods Inc. (Wood's), a small company in Idaho, sells wood products. Founder Jason Woodworth has focused most of his attention on providing excellent service and products but not on keeping his accounting system updated. Wood's currently has a manual billing process to bill customers for the wood products sold. That work is performed by a billing specialist, Emily Young, a recent accounting graduate. Jason would like to completely automate his currently manual billing process to drive productivity and cost savings. Jason also wants to provide Emily with the opportunity to do some data analytics on their financial information and reduce her overtime during the end of the month for better work–life balance.

You will build a bot for each case part starting with a simple billing scenario in part I. The bot you will build in each subsequent case builds on the first bot and is more complex than the previous bot as more complexity will be added to the billing process. Recall that the basic function of a bot is to recreate the steps a human would do in a process.

This case uses a simplified automation process that is modified from what would happen in an actual accounting firm or business in several ways. For example, companies typically would use more sophisticated software than the Excel files used in this case; however, the process of creating bots is the same for simple and more sophisticated software. In addition, companies typically have solutions to provide automated billings. This case uses this simplified scenario to teach the introductory principles of building bots and does not necessarily demonstrate a typical process that would be automated in practice. Although the case simplifies the software and the process, the basic skills of building an RPA are applicable to all automation settings.

BEFORE YOU BEGIN

- Save all of the provided Excel files for the case (go to the student download page at http://www.pearsonhighered.com/romney and download the files) into the same folder on your hard drive. You should build the bot so that the first sequence allows the user to input the file path for the folder where the files are located. Choose a file path that does not have too long of a name. Store this file path as a variable and then use this variable as a reference to load/save/move/etc. any files. This way, the bot can be moved to other computers and still function (i.e., be graded by your professor).
  - Innovation_mindset_case_studies_RPA_Billing_MasterInvoice.xlsx
  - Innovation_mindset_case_studies_RPA_Billing_InvoiceData1.xlsx

* Life-long learning opportunity: see pp. xxiii–xxiv in preface.

CASE 5-1 Continued

- Innovation_mindset_case_studies_RPA_Billing_InvoiceData2.xlsx
- Innovation_mindset_case_studies_RPA_Billing_InvoiceData3.xlsx
- Organize your thinking in a flowchart before you begin programming your bot. This makes it more likely that you will not forget key parts of the process. It also allows you the ability to develop your bot in segments or sections, which can make troubleshooting much easier.

OBJECTIVE

Your task is to build a bot that automates the billing process. Ultimately, a billing specialist should be able to open the RPA software and run the bot, which should perform all the steps described in the manual process (following) without any human interaction, with one exception. When the bot is run, it should require the user to enter a file folder location where the files are currently and will be saved when done. This allows the bot to be transferable to other computers and still run successfully.

PART I

Wood's Amazing Woods Inc. currently uses the following manual process to bill its customers:

- The billing specialist, Emily Young, opens the Excel file with the invoice data, Innovation_mindset_case_studies_RPA_Billing_InvoiceData1.xlsx.
- She reviews the data and opens the Excel invoice template, Innovation_mindset_case_studies_RPA_Billing_MasterInvoice.xlsx.
- Emily creates a unique invoice for each record in the invoice data.
- She saves the updated invoice template file for each customer as "Innovation_mindset_case_studies_RPA_Billing_MasterInvoice_*InvoiceNumber*.xlsx" (where *InvoiceNumber* is replaced by the invoice number being billed).

  In the invoice data file, there is only a single record.

REQUIRED

- Your bot is required to create an invoice for the one invoice.

PART II

Wood's Amazing Woods Inc. currently uses the same billing process as in Part I but uses the invoice data Excel file, Innovation_mindset_case_studies_RPA_Billing_InvoiceData2.xlsx. In this invoice data, there are multiple records for billing.

REQUIRED

- Your bot is required to create an invoice for each customer who should be billed. The bot should be programmed so it can complete the task for any number of records included in the invoice data. In other words, you should not hard code all the values—instead, you should use programming to loop through all of the rows and create invoices accordingly.

PART III

Wood's Amazing Woods Inc. currently uses the following manual process to bill its customers.

- The billing specialist, Emily Young, opens the Excel file with the invoice data, Innovation_mindset_case_studies_RPA_Billing_InvoiceData3.xlsx. There are multiple records in this data.
- She then reviews the data and opens the Excel invoice template, Innovation_mindset_case_studies_RPA_Billing_MasterInvoice.xlsx.
- Emily creates a unique invoice for each record in the invoice data if the customer has not already been billed.
  - Customers who have been billed have dates in the column labeled "Billed." If the field is empty, then the customer needs to be billed.
  - If a customer has already been billed, Emily skips this customer and goes on to the next customer.
- She then saves the updated invoice template file for each customer as "Innovation_mindset_case_studies_RPA_Billing_MasterInvoice_*InvoiceNumber*.xlsx" (where *InvoiceNumber* is replaced by the invoice number being billed).
- Once she is finished creating the invoices for each customer, she opens the invoice data Excel file, Innovation_mindset_case_studies_RPA_Billing_InvoiceData3.xlsx. and updates the "Billed" column with the current billing date.
- Finally, she saves the file as Innovation_mindset_case_studies_RPA_Billing_InvoiceData3_Complete.xlsx.

REQUIRED

- Your bot is required to create an invoice for each customer who has not been previously billed. The bot should be programmed so it can complete the task for any number of records included in invoice data. In other words, you should not hard code all the values—instead, you should use programming to loop through all of the files and create invoices accordingly.

AIS in Action Solutions

QUIZ KEY

1. Unstructured data internal or external to the organization is usually gathered and stored in which of the following?
   a. data dictionary [Incorrect. A data dictionary contains information, like metadata, defining information stored in a data lake, mart, or warehouse.]
   ▶ b. data lake [Correct. Data lakes store unstructured data.]
   c. data mart [Incorrect. Data marts typically store only structured data.]
   d. data warehouse [Incorrect. Data warehouses typically store only structured data.]

2. Which one of the following items would be the best primary key for a table containing information about customers?
   ▶ a. customer ID [Correct. This is a unique field assigned by the company.]
   b. customer full name [Incorrect. There are people with the same name, so this would not necessarily be unique.]
   c. customer phone number [Incorrect. Phone numbers can get reassigned, so this is not always unique.]
   d. customer email address [Incorrect. Email addresses can get reassigned, so this is not always unique.]

3. Which one of the following characters would be the best delimiter (the delimiter is listed between the quotes)?
   a. "," [Incorrect. Commas are often used as regular parts of speech and so are not ideal for delimiters.]
   b. "@" [Incorrect. Ampersands are often used as part of emails and thus are not ideal for a delimiter.]
   ▶ c. "|" [Correct. Pipe characters are rarely used in writing and thus make for a good delimiter.]
   d. All of the above [Incorrect. Although all of these are commonly used, the pipe character is superior to the comma and tab because it is rarely used in everyday writing.]

4. An online sales company designed a program to evaluate customer purchases. After each purchase, the program analyzes which product the customer is most likely to buy next and e-mails the customer a coupon for a discount on this new product. What type of analytic is this an example of?
   a. descriptive analytics [Incorrect. This analytic does more than summarize something that has already happened.]
   b. diagnostic analytics [Incorrect. This analytic does not explain what happened in the past.]
   c. predictive analytics [Incorrect. This analytic does predict the future, but it goes one step further to say what should happen.]
   ▶ d. prescriptive analytics [Correct. This analytic predicts what happens and then does it.]

5. When sharing the results of an analysis, which of the following is NOT a key principle to follow?
   a. Simplify the presentation of data. [Incorrect. Simplification makes it easier to understand the purpose of the visualization.]
   ▶ b. Present the visualization in a timely manner. [Correct. While timeliness may be important in many settings, it is not a key component of how to share data analytics results.]
   c. Ethically represent the data. [Incorrect. Reporting the data honestly is critical when sharing results.]
   d. Emphasize what is important. [Incorrect. Emphasis makes it easier to understand the most important aspects of a visualization.]

6. Which of the steps of an analytics mindset is the most difficult to automate?

► a. Ask the right questions. [Correct. This step involves using creativity, understanding context, and other attributes that are difficult to automate.]

b. Extract, transform, and load relevant data. [Incorrect. Computers are often programmed to reduce the tedium of the ETL process.]

c. Apply appropriate data analytics techniques. [Incorrect. Computers are often programmed to automatically perform analyses.]

d. Interpret and share the results with stakeholders. [Incorrect. Computers are often programmed to automatically generate results, such as dashboards and distribute results; for example, sending an email.]

7. All of the following characteristics of data are important in distinguishing big data from regular data EXCEPT:

a. velocity [Incorrect. Big data is generated at a faster rate than regular data.]

b. variety [Incorrect. Big data encompasses more forms than regular data.]

► c. visualization [Correct. Visualizing data is important for sharing both big data and regular data.]

d. volume [Incorrect. Big data has much higher volumes of data than regular data.]

8. You are given an extract of one field from a database. The field has the value "11815 N. Diamond Dr." Which type of data is contained in this field?

► a. structured data [Correct. The data has a defined structure that can be easily fit into a database field.]

b. unstructured data [Incorrect. The data has the traditional structure of an address in the United States.]

c. semi-structured data [Incorrect. The data has structure and can easily be inserted into a database field.]

d. None of the above [Incorrect. The value "11815 N. Diamond Dr." has a defined structure that can be easily fit into a database field.]

9. Programming a computer program to automatically perform a task previously performed by a human is an example of which of the following?

a. warehousing data [Incorrect. Warehousing data relates to how data is structured in an organization.]

b. the ETL process [Incorrect. ETL relates to how data is extracted, transformed, and loaded for analysis. It can be performed by automation but does not have to be automated.]

c. establishing SMART objectives [Incorrect. This relates to asking good questions and not computers performing tasks]

▶ d. robotic process automation [Correct. The question contains the definition of RPA.]

10. Good questions for data adhere to all of the following principles EXCEPT:

▶ a. accurate [Correct. Accuracy is a principle related to high-quality data but not necessarily good questions.]

b. timely [Incorrect. Good questions have well-defined time horizons for answering.]

c. measurable [Incorrect. Good questions must be measurable to be answered.]

d. specific [Incorrect. Good questions need to be direct and focused to produce a meaningful answer.]

CHAPTER

6

Transforming Data

LEARNING OBJECTIVES

After studying this chapter, you should be able to:

1. Describe the principles of data structuring related to aggregating data, data joining, and data pivoting.
2. Describe data parsing, data concatenation, cryptic data values, misfielded data values, data formatting, and data consistency and how they relate to data standardization.
3. Describe how to diagnose and fix the data cleaning errors related to data duplication, data filtering, data contradiction errors, data threshold violations, violated attribute dependencies, and data entry errors.
4. List and describe four different techniques to perform data validation.

INTEGRATIVE CASE S&S

Ashton successfully helped the organization transform its culture and adopt an analytics mindset for dealing with data. The company successfully built a data structure that consists of a data lake, a data warehouse, and data marts. With the new structure, employees are able to fulfill many of their data needs, allowing data analysts more time to analyze data and not just locate and clean data for others.

Although data handling at S&S has improved, Ashton still receives requests for extracting, transforming, and loading data into other applications that either have not been added to the current data architecture or require other special processing. Such is the current case with which Ashton is dealing.

S&S purchased another company that used a different enterprise resource planning (ERP) system. The two systems don't work well together—storing data in different formats, with different field names, and a host of other challenges. Although S&S plans to better integrate these two systems, until then Ashton has become frustrated trying to make business decisions because he cannot seem to get a clear picture of what is happening due to incompatible data. Ashton has been trying to figure out how to merge and clean the data to be able to improve S&S's decision making.

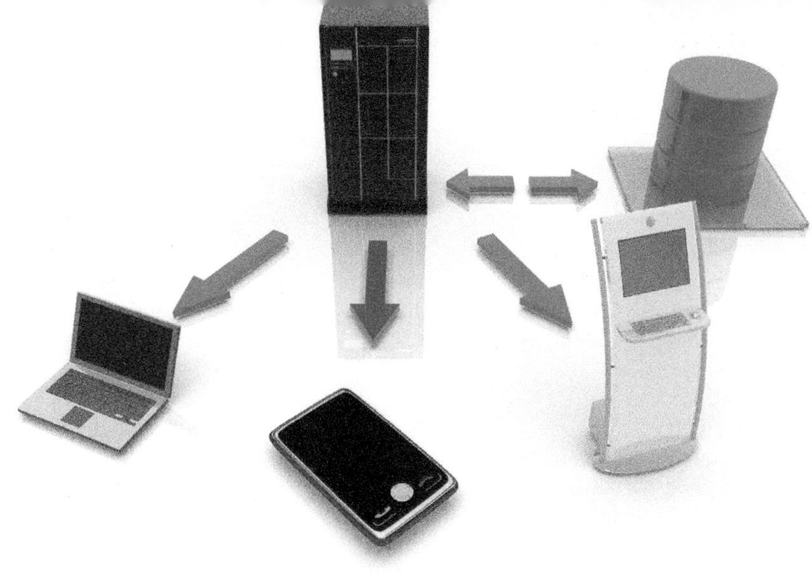

S.John/Shutterstock

To figure this problem out, Ashton decided to study a subset of S&S's data that contains information about its vendors. He had an IT specialist export data from the two systems into a combined flat file for his review. He hopes to be able to understand all of the differences that exist in the data so he can recommend ways to clean the data going forward.

The data extract Ashton is analyzing is shown in Figure 6-1, and an extract of the data dictionary describing the merged data is shown in Figure 6-2. This data dictionary provides abbreviated metadata of the data extract. Figure 6-3 contains additional information about Product ID, one of the fields in Figure 6-1. This chapter will use this data to teach principles related to transforming data.

Introduction

IBM estimates that poor quality data costs the United States economy $3.1 trillion per year and that 1 in 3 business decision makers don't trust the information they use to make decisions. A worldwide survey conducted by Experian shows that business executives believe that 26% of their total data may be inaccurate, and it is getting worse over time. While some of the errors are complex, many are simple, including incomplete data, outdated data, duplicate information, or simple errors in the data (e.g., spelling mistakes, typos, etc.).

So what is to be done? The ideal is to capture and store clean data. The internal controls presented in Chapters 10–13 address methods of capturing accurate data. Even with strong internal controls, data can still become "dirty" or need to be transformed for alternate uses. Data can become dirty by such things as changing events in the world (e.g, customer changes a phone number), merging various data sources that store the same type of data differently, or making mistakes in dealing with data. When this happens, the data needs to be transformed in

FIGURE 6-1
Extract of Vendor Data

	A	B	C	D	E	F	G	H	I	J	K	L	M	N	O
1	**RowNumber**	**VendorName**	**FName**	**LName**	**PhoneNumber**	**Address**	**City**	**State**	**ZipCode**	**EarlyPayDiscount**	**ProdCat**	**ProdID**	**UnitsPurch**	**TotalCosts**	**AvgCostPerUnit**
2	1	Oster	DeShawn	Williams	907961-4917	1535 N Hickory St	MI	Owosso	48867	2/10 N30	1	3	186	2068.32	€ 0.0899
3	2	Black and Decker	Milton	Armstrong	(844) 986-0858	1000 Stanley Dr	NC	Concord	94519	2/10 N30	1	3	227	2220.06	€ 0.1022
4	3	KitchenAid	Chiyo	Tanaka	3605659487	1701 Kitchen Aid Way	Ohio	Greenville	45331		1	2	210	$ 40,849.20	€ 0.0051
5	4	Black and Decker	M.	Armstrong	(844) 986-0858	1000 Stanley Dr	NC	Concord	94519	2/10 N30	3	1	273	$ 10,851.75	€ 0.0252
6	5	Black and Decker	Milton	Armstrong	(844) 986-0858	1000 Stanley Dr	NC	Concord	94519	2/10 N30	2.00	2	80	$ 568.00	€ 0.1408
7	6	Panasonic	Maryam	Ahmad	(551) 7779393	7625 Panasonic Way	CA	SanDgieo	92154	2/10 N15	1	2	51	7882.56	€ 0.0065
8	7	B&D	Milton G.	Armstrong	(844) 986-0858	1000 Stanley Dr	NC	Concord	94519	2/10 N30	2.00	1	281	2529	€ 0.1111
9	8	Panasonic	Maryam	Ahmad	(551) 7779393	7625 Panasonic Way	CA	SanDgieo	92154	2/10 N15	2.00	2	386	5693.5	€ 0.0678
10	9	KitchenAid	Chiyo	Tanaka	3605659487	1701 Kitchen Aid Way	Ohio	Greenville	45331		1	3	171	2433.33	€ 0.0703
11	10	Oster	DeShawn	Williams	907961-4917	1535 N Hickory St	MI	Owosso	48867	2/10 N30	1	1	263	5062.75	€ 0.0519
12	11	Oster	DeShawn	Williams	907961-4917	1535 N Hickory St	MI	Owosso	48867	2/10 N30	1	2	248	$ 20,889.04	€ 0.0119
13	12	Honeywell	Larsena	Hansen	(790)447-1783	10640 Freeport Dr	KY	Louisville	40258-1893	1/10 N30	2.00	2	54	$ 621.00	€ 0.0870
14	13	Calphalon	Jacobsen	Sofia	(933) 937-5654 (208)	20750 Midstar Dr	Ohio	Bowling Green	43402-9215		1	1	261	$ 19,509.75	€ 0.0134
15	14	B&D	Milton	Armstrong	(844) 986-0858	1000 Stanley Dr	NC	Concord	94519	2/10 N30	1	2	262	$ 15,982.00	€ 0.0164
16	15	Honeywell	Larsena	Hansen	(790)447-1783	10640 Freeport Dr	KY	Louisville	40258-1893	1/10 N30	2.00	1	346	$ 4,895.90	€ 0.0707
17	16	Black and Decker	Milton	Armstrong	(801) 473-5329	1000 Stanley Dr	NC	Concord	94519	2/10 N30	3	2	122	$ 2,172.82	€ 0.0561
18	17	Panasonic	Maryam	Ahmad	(551) 7779393	7625 Panasonic Way	CA	SanDgieo	92154	2/10 N15	1	2	51	$ 7,882.56	€ 0.0065

FIGURE 6-2
Abbreviated Data Dictionary for Vendor Data Extract

Data Element Name	Description	Field Length	Field Type
VendorName	Vendor complete company name	50	Alphanumeric
FName	Vendor customer representative first name	50	Alphanumeric
LName	Vendor customer representative last name	50	Alphanumeric
PhoneNumber	Saved as 10-digit number, formatted as (###) ###-####	10	Numeric (integer)
Address	Vendor street address	100	Alphanumeric
City	Vendor city	50	Alphanumeric
State	Vendor state in 2-digit abbreviated form	2	Alphanumeric
ZipCode	Vendor 5-digit zip code	5	Numeric (integer)
EarlyPayDiscount	Terms for early payment discount	25	Alphanumeric
ProdCat	Unique identifier for each product category: 1=kitchen appliances; 2=fans; 3=hand tools	6	Numeric (integer)
ProdID	Unique identifier for each product in a product category. Figure 6-3 contains full categorization	6	Numeric (integer)
UnitsPurch	Total number of units purchased	15	Numeric (integer)
TotalCosts	Total costs listed in USD	15	Numeric (double)
AvgCostPerUnit	TotalCosts divided by UnitsPurch listed in USD	15	Numeric (double)

a way that restores its quality. This chapter presents a four-step process for transforming data that will maintain or improve data quality: (1) structure the data, (2) standardize the data, (3) clean the data, and (4) validate the data.

The data transformation process spans the life of data. That is, while data transformation is specifically a step of the extract, transform, and load (ETL) process, it also occurs when data is gathered, stored, and analyzed. Understanding the transformation process is valuable for all data stages. Before discussing the steps of the transformation process, we review the attributes of high-quality data. These attributes form the objectives of the data transformation process.

ATTRIBUTES OF HIGH-QUALITY DATA

Chapter 1 discusses how information must have multiple attributes—such as being accurate, available, concise, relevant, etc.—to be valuable for decision making. To create information that has these attributes, the underlying data must also have certain attributes. While data scientists debate about the various attributes of high-quality data, there is general agreement that at a minimum, data must be accurate, complete, consistent, timely, and valid in order to create useful information. Table 6-1 repeats the definitions for accurate, complete, consistent, and timely from Chapter 1 and adds valid to the list. The table also gives an example of a violation of each attribute.

These attributes are critical to business success, as the following historical example demonstrates: NASA lost a $125 million Mars orbiter because of inconsistent data. It took NASA 10 months to fly the orbiter to Mars. Once the orbiter approached Mars, it was designed to orbit the planet and make scientific measurements. The orbiter was unable to enter its designed orbiting pattern. The problem? Two different engineering teams in the company had inappropriately designed systems to control the orbiter. One team used the imperial measurement

FIGURE 6-3
Product ID (ProdID) Table

ProdCat	ProdID	ProdDesc
1	1	Blender
1	2	Microwave
1	3	Toaster
2	1	Box Fan
2	2	Desk Fan
3	1	Hand Drill
3	2	Jigsaw

TABLE 6-1 Attributes of High-Quality Data

Attribute	Definition	Example of Violation of Attribute
Accurate	Correct; free of error; accurately represents events and activities	A sale occurred on December 27 but is recorded as occurring the following year on January 4.
Complete	Does not omit aspects of events or activities; of enough breadth and depth	An annual evaluation of vendor performance only contains 7 months of data.
Consistent	Presented in same format over time	A company switches the denomination of amounts (e.g., thousands, millions, etc.) irregularly.
Timely	Provided in time for decision makers to make decisions	Customer purchasing metrics are 2 years old.
Valid	Data measures what it is intended to measure; conforms to syntax rules and to requirements	There are only 7 unique job positions at a company but 9 different positions are attributed to employees—2 answers are not valid.

system (i.e., feet, miles), while the other team used the metric system (e.g., meters, kilometers). This inconsistency in the data resulted in a software failure and the loss of a very expensive Mars orbiter.

In every interaction with data, it is critical to make sure the data has the attributes of high-quality data. If any of these attributes are missing, the data will need to be remedied. While not all data problems can be remedied by data transformation, the four-step process introduced in this chapter will help improve data quality.

Data Structuring

Data structure describes the way data are stored, including the relationships between different fields. **Data structuring** is the process of changing the organization and relationships among data fields to prepare the data for analysis. Extracted data often needs to be structured in a manner that will enable analysis. This can entail aggregating the data at different levels of detail, joining different data together, and/or pivoting the data.

data structuring - The process of changing the organization and relationships among data fields to prepare the data for analysis.

AGGREGATE DATA

Aggregate data is the presentation of data in a summarized form. Aggregate data has fewer details than disaggregated data. As an example, consider the typical sales process and reporting of data. When a business makes a sale, it records a credit to sales revenue in a database. This is fully disaggregated sales data. In aggregation, the company might sum sales data around a corresponding attribute. For example, summing sales by sales manager removes the detail of each sale but allows the business to evaluate manager performance. Similarly, a company may fully aggregate sales data by summing all sales to create the sales revenue line item on the income statement.

aggregate data - The presentation of data in a summarized form.

When transforming data, it is critical to understand the level of aggregation for each data source because combining data aggregated at different levels can create problems. For example, S&S could analyze the vendor purchases shown in Figure 6-1 by aggregating, or summing, all individual purchases to produce the total units purchased from each vendor and the total expenditures for each vendor. Figure 6-4 shows this higher level aggregation as well as aggregating across all vendors.

When data is aggregated, information is lost. That is, with the data aggregated in Figure 6-4 at the individual vendor level, it is no longer possible to know to which products the UnitsPurch and TotalCosts fields relate. The only way to analyze data at the product level

FIGURE 6-4
Examples of Different Levels of Aggregating Data

Aggegated at the Vendor Level			*Aggregated for All Vendors*	
VendorName	**UnitsPurch**	**TotalCosts**	**UnitsPurch**	**TotalCosts**
B&D	543	$ 18,511.00	3,472	$ 152,111.54
Black and Decker	702	$ 15,812.63		
Calphalon	261	$ 19,509.75		
Honeywell	400	$ 5,516.90		
KitchenAid	381	$ 43,282.53		
Oster	697	$ 28,020.11		
Panasonic	488	$ 21,458.62		

would be to go back to the original disaggregated data because it cannot be extracted from the aggregated data. Best practice for storing data is to store the information in as disaggregated form as possible and then aggregate the data through querying for other uses.

DATA JOINING

As discussed in Chapter 4, a key part in querying databases is joining information from different tables into a single table so that the joined data can be analyzed.[1] Frequently in the ETL process, data is queried from the database into a single flat file, as seen in the S&S dataset. The table created in the S&S example required joining data that was likely contained in different database tables such as the vendor table (e.g., all fields from VendorName to EarlyPayDiscount), from the product table (e.g., fields ProdCat and ProdID), and from a transaction table that recorded purchases (e.g., fields UnitsPurch and TotalCosts).

DATA PIVOTING

data pivoting - A technique that rotates data from rows to columns.

Data pivoting is rotating data from rows to columns. Some software programs are designed to use pivoted data rather than unpivoted data. Understanding the design of the program into which the data will be loaded will help you determine if data needs to be pivoted or not.

The S&S data in Figure 6-1 could be pivoted in a variety of ways to make it easier to interpret the data. Figure 6-5 shows a pivot of the data so that the vendor names are listed in each row and the columns show the different product categories. Note that when data is pivoted, the data often will be aggregated in some way. For example, in the pivoted data the total product costs are summed for each vendor and product category.

Figure 6-6 shows the data in Figure 6-5 pivoted back into a different form. The Figure 6-6 form is much closer to the original but aggregated at a higher level. Since the information

FIGURE 6-5
Pivoting S&S Data

	ProdCat		
VendorName	**1**	**2**	**3**
B&D	$ 15,982.00	$ 2,529.00	
Black and Decker	$ 2,220.06	$ 568.00	$ 13,024.57
Calphalon	$ 19,509.75		
Honeywell		$ 5,516.90	
KitchenAid	$ 43,282.53		
Oster	$ 28,020.11		
Panasonic	$ 15,765.12	$ 5,693.50	

[1]Data joining is also referred to as data merging and data aggregation. The last term, data aggregation, can be confusing, given the previous discussion of aggregate data. Aggregating data is the process of summarizing data at different levels of detail, while data aggregation is the process of combining different data sources. To avoid confusion, we will use the term data joining to refer to data aggregation throughout the text.

VendorName	ProdCat	TotalCosts
B&D	1	$15,982.00
B&D	2	$ 2,529.00
Black and Decker	1	$ 2,220.06
Black and Decker	2	$ 568.00
Black and Decker	3	$13,024.57
Calphalon	1	$19,509.75
Honeywell	2	$ 5,516.90
KitchenAid	1	$43,282.53
Oster	1	$28,020.11
Panasonic	1	$15,765.12
Panasonic	2	$ 5,693.50

FIGURE 6-6
Pivoting Figure 6-5 Data

about individual products was lost in pivoting the data to Figure 6-5, individual products cannot be displayed in the pivot from Figure 6-5 to Figure 6-6. This is another example of how aggregating data results in a loss of detail that cannot be recaptured unless the original data is analyzed.

Data Standardization

Data standardization is the process of standardizing the structure and meaning of each data element so it can be analyzed and used in decision making. Data standardization is particularly important when merging data from several sources. Achieving standardized data may involve changing data to a common format, data type, or coding scheme. Data standardization also encompasses ensuring the information is contained in the correct field and the fields are organized in a useful manner. When dealing with a database file or a flat file format, think of data standardization as making sure the columns of information are correct. In doing so, several important things should be considered, including data parsing and data concatenation, cryptic data values, misfielded data values, and data formatting and data consistency. Focus 6-1 shows the importance of data standardization in practice.

data standardization - The process of standardizing the structure and meaning of each data element so it can be analyzed and used in decision making.

DATA PARSING AND DATA CONCATENATION

Separating data from a single field into multiple fields is called **data parsing**. For example, an employee code might be saved in a single field as "N-0504-2002". As discussed in Chapter 2, this employee code is a combination of a mnemonic code, a sequence code, and a group code. The first element is a mnemonic code which indicates that the employee works at the North Office (the "N"). The second is a sequence code (employee number 0504). The last element is a group code representing the year of hire (2002). Data parsing separates this information, contained in a single field, into three different fields so that the different items can be separately analyzed.

data parsing - Separating data from a single field into multiple fields.

In the S&S data, the column labeled EarlyPayDiscount contains information about the terms for early payment. For row 1, the entry "2/10 N30" signifies that S&S receives a 2% discount if they pay in 10 days; otherwise, the full amount is due in 30 days. To be more useful, the information should be parsed into three columns as shown in Figure 6-7. With the data parsed into three columns, it is easier to use the data for decision making.

Data parsing is often an iterative process that relies heavily on pattern recognition. Since data often follow multiple patterns, parsing can usually be performed in several ways, any of

FOCUS 6-1 Data Standardization Success Story

In the mid-2000s, cellphones began to be successfully used for navigating not only streets but also public transportation. Prior to that time, you had to look up public transportation schedules, often still in paper form, for each different transit authority. Bibiana McHugh, an IT manager at a transportation company in Portland, Oregon, was fed up with this difficulty. Recognizing that the general public already used Google web apps for transportation needs, she contacted Google and partnered with them to create Google Transit. Using the data at her company, they were able to build an app for helping people find public transit information. Upon launch, the interest was so high across the world that they decided to scale the app they had built for the city of Portland across the globe. To make scaling possible, they generated open data standards for all public transportation agencies to use. Transit agencies voluntarily adopted these data standards. The standards continued to evolve so that now, thanks to standardized data, the general public can quickly and easily find public transportation options in most places in the world.

Data standards make it possible for different parties to use and share data. This makes it easier to build apps for analyzing and displaying data from different sources. In auditing, the American Institute of Certified Public Accountants (AICPA) has established audit data standards so that external auditors can more easily use the data produced by different clients. When the data standards are followed, the standardization of data saves auditors time so they are able to charge lower fees and conduct a more thorough audit.

which can yield a valid output. For the S&S example, the EarlyPayDiscount field could be parsed in the following alternative ways:

- Select the first digit to put in the DiscountRate Column. Select the third and fourth digits to put in the DiscountDays column, and then select the seventh and eighth digits for the BalanceDueDays column.
- Select all data before the forward slash to put in the DiscountRate column. Select the data between the forward slash and first space and put it in the DiscountDays column. Select all the data after the N to put into the BalanceDueDays column.
- Split the data into columns based on the space. From the new first column (that contains the DiscountRate and DiscountDays information), take all numerical digits before the slash and put them in the DiscountRate column and, reading from right to left, take all digits until it comes to the forward slash and put them in the DiscountDays column. With the new second column from the original split (i.e., the "N30" information), remove all alpha characters and place any numerical characters in the BalanceDueDays column.

FIGURE 6-7
Data Parsing Example

	Original Column	*New Columns*		
RowNumber	**EarlyPayDiscount**	**DiscountRate**	**DiscountDays**	**BalanceDueDays**
1	2/10 N30	2	10	30
2	2/10 N30	2	10	30
3				
4	2/10 N30	2	10	30
5	2/10 N30	2	10	30
6	2/10 N15	2	10	15
7	2/10 N30	2	10	30
8	2/10 N15	2	10	15
9				
10	2/10 N30	2	10	30
11	2/10 N30	2	10	30
12	1/10 N30	1	10	30
13				
14	2/10 N30	2	10	30
15	1/10 N30	1	10	30
16	2/10 N30	2	10	30
17	2/10 N15	2	10	15

Notice that each of these approaches make different assumptions about the structure of the data contained in the original EarlyPayDiscount field. In the S&S example, all of these patterns hold for the 17 rows displayed. However, when datasets contain millions of rows, identifying a pattern that applies to all, or even a subset of rows, is much more challenging. When one pattern cannot be identified for all rows, often patterns can be identified for sets of rows. These patterns can be used to iteratively parse the appropriate sets of rows. The challenge of parsing data correctly is one reason why the ETL process can be so challenging.

Data concatenation is combining data from two or more fields into a single field. In the S&S data, Ashton would like to have one field that lists the full name of each vendor representative as shown in Figure 6-8. To do this, the original columns of FName and LName need to be combined, or concatenated, into a single field. Notice that when FName and LName are concatenated there is also a space added between the first and last name. Without the space, the new column would list names like "DeShawnWilliams" and "MiltonArmstrong"—which makes the data messy and would require later cleaning.

data concatenation - The combining of data from two or more fields into a single field.

Data concatenation is often used to create a unique identifier for a row. Notice in Figure 6-1 that ProductID has some of the same values as ProductCategory. That is, ProductCategory 1 has ProductID's of 1, 2, and 3 and ProductCategory 2 also has ProductID's of 1 and 2. Thus, the ProductID does not uniquely identify each product; rather, the combination of ProductID and ProductCategory identifies each product at S&S. In this case, it would be useful to concatenate ProductID and ProductCategory so that each product can be uniquely identified. This could be done by creating a new column labeled ProductCatID that adds a dash character, so the final result is "1-1" and "1-2" where the first number shows the product category number and the second number shows the product ID.

CRYPTIC DATA VALUES

Cryptic data values are data items that have no apparent meaning without understanding the underlying coding scheme. For example, a consulting firm may keep track of positions in the organization such as partner, senior consultant, and research analyst by entering into the database the number 1 for partner, 2 for senior consultant, and 3 for research analyst. Without understanding the code, the numbers in the column for employee position have no meaning.

cryptic data values - Data items that have no meaning without understanding a coding scheme.

In the S&S data, Ashton notices that he is unable to tell what the values in ProdCat and ProdID mean. Referring to the data dictionary, he learns that a ProdCat of 1 is for kitchen appliances, 2 for fans, and 3 for hand tools. Similarly, ProdID is defined in the data dictionary by referring to another table displayed in Figure 6-3.

	Original Columns			*New Column*
RowNumber	**FName**	**LName**		**FullName**
1	DeShawn	Williams		DeShawn Williams
2	Milton	Armstrong		Milton Armstrong
3	Chiyo	Tanaka		Chiyo Tanaka
4	M.	Armstrong		M. Armstrong
5	Milton	Armstrong		Milton Armstrong
6	Maryam	Ahmad		Maryam Ahmad
7	Milton G.	Armstrong		Milton G. Armstrong
8	Maryam	Ahmad		Maryam Ahmad
9	Chiyo	Tanaka		Chiyo Tanaka
10	DeShawn	Williams		DeShawn Williams
11	DeShawn	Williams		DeShawn Williams
12	Larsena	Hansen		Larsena Hansen
13	Jacobsen	Sofia		Jacobsen Sofia
14	Milton	Armstrong		Milton Armstrong
15	Larsena	Hansen		Larsena Hansen
16	Milton	Armstrong		Milton Armstrong
17	Maryam	Ahmad		Maryam Ahmad

FIGURE 6-8
Data Concatenation Example

Ashton considers two possible solutions for this problem: (1) to replace the values in the ProdID and ProdCat columns with the words rather than the numbers or (2) to add new columns to the flat file that identify what the ProdID and the ProdCat values mean. Ashton decides on the second option because keeping the original IDs will allow him to later merge additional data into his file if he needs it. Typically, the cryptic data values problem is handled through joining additional data into the file or by replacing the values. If storage space is not an issue and there is no concern over the complexity of the working file, it is generally advisable to join data rather than replace values.

dummy variable or dichotomous variable - A data field that contains only two responses, typically 0 or 1.

For some fields, there is a general understanding of what cryptic values mean. When a field contains only two different responses, typically 0 or 1, this field is called a **dummy variable or dichotomous variable**. In this case, standard practice is to use a 1 to signify the presence and 0 the absence of the attribute. For example, if the field captures data about whether a vendor is a preferred vendor or not, the value of 1 would suggest they are a preferred vendor and 0 that they are not. With dummy variables, best practice is to give them a meaningful name rather than a generic name. So, for the previous example, rather than naming the field VendorStatus, naming the field PreferredVendor is superior because the user knows the meaning of values 0 and 1 in this field without referring to the data dictionary.

MISFIELDED DATA VALUES

misfielded data values - Data values that are correctly formatted but not listed in the correct field.

Misfielded data values are data values that are correctly formatted but do not belong in the field. As an example, if a data field for city contains the country name Germany, the data values are misfielded. The value Germany should be entered in a data field for country.

Misfielded data values can be a problem with an entire field (i.e., the entire column) or with individual values (i.e., entries in a row). Correcting this problem can be considered either a data standardization or a data cleaning step. How this problem is categorized is less important than recognizing and fixing the problem in the dataset.

For S&S, notice that the entries in the City and State columns are backwards. That is, the City field holds a state value and the State field holds city values. The data should be corrected so that each field holds the appropriate information.

DATA FORMATTING AND DATA CONSISTENCY

MI5, the United Kingdom's domestic counter-intelligence and security agency, learned the importance of data formatting and data consistency when they "bugged" 134 incorrect phone numbers. The cause of the mistake was a spreadsheet formatting error that altered the last three digits of each telephone number to be "000" instead of the true last three digits. Data values should have the same format as all other data values in the same field and match the data type specified in the data dictionary. Similarly, every value in a field should be stored in the same way, which is referred to as **data consistency**.

data consistency - The principle that every value in a field should be stored in the same way.

One of the best examples showing the similarities and differences in data formatting and data consistency relates to how calendar dates are displayed and stored in databases and spreadsheets. Dates can be displayed in many different formats. For example, each of these date formats represents the same date: April 3, 1982; 3 April 1982; 03/04/82; and 04/03/82. Dates are formatted differently because of differences in preference, display space, or geographic location—different countries choose to arrange days, months, and years differently. A single format should be chosen and used for all dates in a field and typically all dates contained in a file. The chosen format should be documented in the data dictionary using a mnemonic representation like dd/mm/yyyy to represents days, months, and year.

Although dates are often formatted differently for display, they typically are stored in a consistent manner in the underlying systems. There are several common ways to store dates digitally. Most typical is to store dates as the amount of time since a specific calendar date. For example, Microsoft Excel stores dates as serial dates meaning the number of days since January 1, 1900, plus a fractional portion to represent the hour of the 24-hour day. The date 1:00 a.m. on November 11, 1979 is actually stored in Excel as the number "29170.041$\bar{6}$". Other programs store dates using Unix epoch time (sometimes called Unix epoch or epoch time), which is the number of seconds that have elapsed since January 1,

1970, not counting leap seconds. In Unix epoch time, 1:00 a.m. on November 11, 1979 is stored as "311130000". Data consistency within time data is particularly problematic when it comes from different time zones. Thus, time data in most enterprise systems is stored according to Coordinated Universal Time (UTC). When local time is needed, it is computed based on the stored UTC value and the local time zone. Data consistency requires that the information stored for each field be stored the same way. When storing a date value, one field should not switch between the serial date and the epoch time storage designs. Rather, it should use only one of these two designs.

This textbook categorizes data formatting and data consistency issues together because it is often hard to determine from viewing data whether a problem is a formatting or a consistency issue. Furthermore, when given a flat file or an extraction of data, fixing formatting and consistency issues likely uses the same techniques. Distinguishing between formatting and consistency issues is more important when trying to fix the original source data.

The S&S data has both data formatting and data consistency errors—and some errors that could be caused by either or both issues. For example, the PhoneNumber field shows phone numbers formatted in six different ways. Notice how sometimes the formats have parentheses around the area code, sometimes there are spaces in different places, and the dashes are not always included. An example of each of the different formats are listed in Figure 6-9.

FIGURE 6-9
Examples of Different Data Formats

PhoneNumber
907961-4917
(844) 986-0858
3605659487
(551) 7779393
(790)447-1783
(551) 7779393

From the S&S data extract, it is not clear whether the data is stored in the database in different ways (data consistency) or just displayed in different formats. The data dictionary says that the data are intended to be stored in the same way (as a 10-digit number), so it is likely that the problem was a formatting problem that occurred when creating the data extract. Regardless of the underlying problem, the solution is that the PhoneNumber field needs to be manipulated to be consistent in appearance, as inconsistent formatting of the data can make it more difficult to analyze the data. In the phone number example, if someone wanted to extract the area code for all of the phone numbers, he would need to perform a much more complex parsing and extraction exercise because of the poor formatting. If the data always contained the area code between the parentheses, it would make the extraction of the area code a relatively straightforward exercise.

The S&S data in Figure 6-1 contain additional data consistency and data formatting problems in the following fields: VendorName, FName, ZipCode, EarlyPayDiscount, ProdCat, TotalCosts, and AvgCostPerUnit. Take a minute to see if you can find the errors in each of these fields before reviewing the bullet points below.

- VendorName: The Black and Decker vendor name is sometimes written in its entirety and sometimes abbreviated B&D. This is likely the same company and not two different companies with similar initials because the address is the same for both types of entries. The same company name should be listed for every instance of Black and Decker.
- FName: There are two problems in this field. The same person's name is sometimes listed in different ways; that is, Milton Armstrong is listed as Milton Armstrong, M. Armstrong, and Milton G. Armstrong. This is likely the same person because all the different name iterations have the same address. The second problem is that the data is aligned in different ways: lines 9, 14, and 16 are right justified and all the other entries are left justified.
- ZipCode: Sometimes the zip code contains the 5-digit zip code and other times it contains a 9-digit zip code.
- EarlyPayDiscount: The data in the field has inconsistent alignment (left, center, and right). While alignment is unlikely to influence data analysis, good practice is to use consistent alignment for a field.
- ProdCat: The field does not consistently show the same number of decimal places for numbers. For this field, the decimals are meaningless, and the data should only show whole numbers.
- TotalCosts: The field sometimes shows dollar signs and a different number of decimal places for different values. Since total cost data is collected at the penny level, these should all be formatted to that level.
- AvgCostPerUnit: The error is that the euro currency marker is used even though this company is in the United States and the total cost information is denominated in the U.S. dollar (see the data dictionary description).

Data Cleaning

dirty data - Data that is inconsistent, inaccurate, or incomplete.

data cleaning - The process of updating data to be consistent, accurate, and complete.

A survey of 16,000 users on Kaggle, a popular website for data scientists owned by Google, reveals that the biggest problem data scientists face is dirty data. **Dirty data** is data that is inconsistent, inaccurate, or incomplete. To be useful, dirty data must be cleaned. **Data cleaning** is the process of updating data to be consistent, accurate, and complete.

Costs of dirty data can be exceptionally high, both in terms of dollars and reputation. Fidelity's Magellan fund learned this when they reported to shareholders that they expected to pay a $4.32 per share dividend at the end of the year. However, no year-end dividend was issued. Fidelity later reported to shareholders that they wouldn't be receiving the predicted dividend because a tax accountant missed inputting a minus sign on a $1.3 billion net capital loss. Thus, the system treated it as a gain—a total error of $2.6 billion dollars. Below are some of the common errors to look for in cleaning data.

DATA DE-DUPLICATION

data de-duplication - The process of analyzing data and removing two or more records that contain identical information.

Data de-duplication is the process of analyzing the data and removing two or more records that contain identical information. In the S&S data, one might be concerned there is significant duplicate data in the columns related to vendor attributes (e.g., names, phone numbers, addresses) because they show a lot of repeated data. Although these items repeat, it does not mean that a row is a duplicate of another row. That is, each row represents a unique product within a product category, and since some vendors sell multiple products to S&S, some of their information is repeated. In contrast, row 17 appears to be an exact duplicate of row 6—as the information on the rows are identical. Note that the formatting of the rows sometimes differs, but formatting is not considered for data de-duplication, rather only the values of the fields are compared. Row 17 should be examined in more detail to see if it occurred on the exact same day at the same time and does not represent two similar orders. If found to be an exact duplicate, in most circumstances, row 17 should be deleted.

Duplicate data means that all information for a record is exactly the same as another record when, in reality, there were not two identical occurrences of whatever is measured. Note there is one exception to this general rule. As seen in the S&S data, the value in the RowNumber field is different for the two records. Often row identifiers are added to a file without considering if there are duplicate rows. In this case, the identifier may not exactly match between records even though all the rest of the information is duplicative. The second record is still a duplicate even though the row identifiers don't match, as is the case in the S&S example where the field RowNumber has different values for row 6 and row 17. When looking for duplicate values, be aware of how the data is constructed to decide whether the row identifiers are likely to indicate a duplicate or not.

DATA FILTERING

data filtering - The process of removing records or fields of information from a data source.

The process of removing records or fields of information from a data source is called **data filtering**. Companies often collect information about many vendors, even if they have not purchased from all of them. In the transformation of data, a data analyst might filter out inactive vendors (no purchases in the last year) to analyze active vendors. This is an example of filtering information. Typically, columns are filtered out of the data during the extraction process; however, when extra columns are included in the data extraction, removing unnecessary columns of data can be performed in the transformation process. In the example of vendors, the data analyst may receive an extraction of vendor information that contains the vendor representative. If this field is not necessary for the analysis, it can be filtered out of the dataset.

The S&S data has several irrelevant records included in the file. Ashton intended to analyze products in the kitchen appliances and fans product category—product category 1 and 2—but his file also contains information about product category 3, hand tools. Ashton can filter the data to delete the two ProdCat 3 records.

Another important filtering question is what to do with missing or empty values (referred to as null values). Notice in the S&S data that the EarlyPayDiscount field contains null values for several rows. There is no hard rule for what to do with null values. The first step to take when a null value is encountered is to go back to the original source data and verify that the information was not lost in extracting the data. If the original source data contains the missing information, the missing data should be added to the file.

Once the missing values are verified as validly missing or empty, there are generally three approaches to take. The first approach retains the null values and continues with the transformation process. When the data is analyzed, the analyst will decide how to manage the null values. The second approach is to delete the record with null values and document the deletion in the analysis log because it may change inferences made when analyzing the data. The third approach is to perform a **data imputation**, which is the process of replacing a null or missing value with a substituted value. Data imputation only works with numeric data (so it is not possible for the missing payment terms in the S&S data).

data imputation - The process of replacing a null or missing value with a substituted value.

There are many different types of data imputation, each with strengths and weaknesses. One approach is to replace all null values with the mean of the column of the non-null values in the data. Other imputations replace the value with a random value from the dataset or use statistical models, like regression, to compute a replacement value. Regardless of the method chosen, it is critical to document in the analysis log when values have been imputed and the method used. The analyst often adds an additional column that uses a dichotomous value to indicate which values have been imputed.

DATA CONTRADICTION ERRORS

Data contradiction errors exist when the same entity is described in two conflicting ways. For example, a data file contains information about a manufacturing plant in two different records; however, the physical address of the manufacturing plant is different in each record even though each record is meant to reference the same physical location.

data contradiction errors - An error that exists when the same entity is described in two conflicting ways.

In the S&S dataset, Milton Armstrong's telephone number on line 16 is different than his phone number on all other lines. Due to the contradiction error in Milton's phone number, we do not know the true value. The phone number should be corrected so that Milton's phone number is the same throughout the dataset. This contradiction error may have been caused by incomplete updates between the two separate systems from which the data came. Milton updated his phone number, but it was only recorded in one system. The reason this is most likely a data contradiction error is that Milton's address is the exact same in all the other records. If there were two different people named Milton Armstrong that lived at the exact same house and each had a different phone number, this would not be considered a data contradiction error. Contradiction errors need to be investigated and resolved appropriately. In this case, one might query the updated logs of each system to determine which phone number was most recently updated. One could call each number and resolve the issue directly with the vendor.

DATA THRESHOLD VIOLATIONS

Data threshold violations are data errors that occur when a data value falls outside an allowable level. An example would be a field capturing the number of children a taxpayer claims as dependents in which the taxpayer lists the value of "300." Acceptable thresholds for a field can be found in the data dictionary. In this case, let us assume that the field attributes indicate that the field is numeric with a length of 2. The "300" value would violate this threshold. Additionally, the data dictionary may establish a range of acceptable values for this field as between 0 and 15. The "300" value would also violate this threshold. Alternatively, a value of "65" would not violate the field attribute but would still be in violation of acceptable values.

data threshold violations - Data errors that occur when a data value falls outside an allowable level.

In the S&S data, the PhoneNumber field always displays 10 numeric characters, except for line 13. On line 13, the phone number contains 13 numeric characters because of the extra "(208)". Notice this example only considered numeric characters as the data dictionary defined this field using numeric characters and not formatting. This threshold violation will need to be investigated and resolved. Both errors in the value of the data and in the attributes of the data can cause data threshold violations.

VIOLATED ATTRIBUTE DEPENDENCIES

violated attribute dependencies - Errors that occur when a secondary attribute in a row of data does not match the primary attribute.

Violated attribute dependencies are errors that occur when a secondary attribute does not match the primary attribute. For example, if a record accurately indicates a person lives in Nauvoo, Illinois but mistakenly lists the zip code as 26354, there is a violated attribute dependency because the zip code for Nauvoo, Illinois is 62354. A transposition of the first two digits of the zip code has created an attribute dependency violation. The data in the secondary attribute, in this example zip code, needs to be corrected to match the primary attribute, in this example city.

In the S&S data, there is a violated attribute dependency in the field ZipCode. The zip code for Concord, North Carolina is not 94519 (which is the zip code for Concord, California), but rather 28027. All instances where the zip code is wrong for Concord, North Carolina should be replaced with the correct values.

DATA ENTRY ERRORS

data entry errors - All types of errors that come from inputting data incorrectly.

Data entry errors are all types of errors that come from inputting data incorrectly. Data entry errors often occur in human data entry, such as misspelling words, transposing digits in numeric strings, and failing to enter data. Data entry errors can also be introduced by the computer system. For example, a system may fail to record the first two digits of a year, and so it is not clear if the date is meant to be 1910 or 2010. Controls around prevention and detection of data entry errors are discussed extensively in Chapter 13.

Data entry errors may be indistinguishable from data formatting and data consistency errors in an output data file. For example, the previous error of the inconsistent names of Milton Armstrong, M. Armstrong, and Milton G. Armstrong may have been caused by data input errors, formatting differences between systems, or data consistency errors in how the data was structured. When correcting the problem in source data, it will be important to understand which type of error is occurring so the appropriate fix can be administered; however, in data cleaning, it is less important to distinguish between these three types of errors and more important to correct them.

A data entry error in the S&S data not likely caused by data formatting or data consistency problems is the misspelling of San Diego as "SanDgieo" for rows 6, 8, and 17. Likely, someone simply input the data incorrectly.

Data Validation

data validation - The process of analyzing data to make certain the data has the properties of high-quality data: accuracy, completeness, consistency, timeliness, and validity.

Before, during, and while finalizing the data transformation process, one should analyze whether the data has the properties of high-quality data. Analyzing data to make sure it has these properties is called **data validation**.

Data validation is both a formal and informal process. Often companies have a formal data validation process that follows the transformation process. Informally, data validation is performed in parallel with each transformation. For example, if a column of information listing customer names shows that all names were recorded fully capitalized, one might want to change the formatting such that only the first letter of the first and last name are capitalized. After performing this operation, it is important to check to see if it was done correctly and completely—which is an example of informal data validation.

Data validation is an important precursor to data cleaning. The techniques used to validate data once cleaned are also useful for discovering problems in the data that need to be fixed. Thus, data validation is an iterative process that both helps identify what needs to be transformed in the data as well as verify that the data has been transformed correctly.

The techniques used to validate data can be thought of as a continuum from simple to complex. As there is rarely a clear stopping point for data validation, the importance of the data analysis and the availability of resources (both time and money) will guide the decision on deciding which of these techniques to use. These techniques include visual inspection, basic statistical tests, auditing a sample of data, and advanced testing techniques.

VISUAL INSPECTION

visual inspection - Examining data using human vision to see if there are problems.

Visual inspection is exactly what it sounds like—examining data using human vision to see if there are problems. When examining data, one should look for each of the different problems listed above. Visual inspection is particularly helpful in finding data standardization issues because it is easy to quickly scan an entire column. Visual scanning also is useful in identifying if data parsing or concatenation is necessary, finding if data is misfielded, and identifying data formatting and data consistency problems.

Visual inspection is easy to accomplish when the dataset is small, but even when large, visually inspecting the data can be done efficiently. Consider the following two techniques. First, sort the data in each column in ascending and then descending order. The sorting of data can reveal missing values and the wrong type of data in a column. For example, if a column should have numeric values, sorting will show if there are also characters contained in some entries in the column.

Second, copy a column of data to a new environment and then remove all duplicate values in the data copied. The reduced list, especially coupled with sorting, can be reviewed more quickly and may show data consistency errors like the "Milton Armstrong" naming problems discussed above. It can also help show if there are inappropriate values in the data. For example, if the data should only contain whole numbers between 1 and 5, examining a list of unique values will reveal if some entries contain decimals or are outside the acceptable range.

BASIC STATISTICAL TESTS

Several basic statistical tests can be performed to validate the data. The types of tests that can be conducted differ for numeric fields and text fields.

For numeric fields, compute basic descriptive statistics for each field such as the minimum, maximum, mean, median, and sum (or total). Examine these descriptive statistics for unreasonable values such as negative amounts for product prices or large outliers. Comparing totals from the transformed data with totals from the original data sources will show if the transformation process inappropriately changed values. This will allow testing to see if the dataset contains a complete set of all the original transactions. Consider computing descriptive statistics before and after complex transformations to determine if the transformation was successful or created unintended errors.

For text fields, a similar comparison can be made by counting the number of total records or the number of distinct records present before and after a data transformation. For text fields, it is also possible to compute the length of each value and compare this amount to pre-transformation lengths to see if there are changes.

AUDIT A SAMPLE

One of the best techniques for assuring data quality is to audit a sample of the data. Select a sample of rows, columns, or both and analyze each value to make sure it is valid. One can trace the transformed values back to the original data sources to make sure they accurately reflect what was originally captured. To ensure completeness, select a sample of data items from the original data sources and make sure all those items are listed in the final dataset.

There are many ways to choose a sample of data to audit. If there is a particular data item that is very important, select all records that have that data item present. In contrast, if understanding the cleanliness of the overall dataset is desired, selecting a random sample will allow for the computation of an overall error rate in the population. As an example, imagine the dataset Ashton selects has 100,000 records. Ashton chooses to audit 1,000 records, or 1% of the total number of records. If in those 1,000 records Ashton finds 70 errors, Ashton can compute a 7% error rate for his sample. Because Ashton randomly selected the 1,000 records, Ashton can assume the 7% error rate is the same across the entire set of 100,000 transactions—meaning there are likely 7,000 errors in the entire dataset. If Ashton tracks each type of error, he can estimate the quantity of each type in the transformed dataset. If the error rate exceeds an acceptable level, Ashton should continue the standardization and cleaning process.

ADVANCED TESTING TECHNIQUES

A deeper understanding of the content of data can allow for more sophisticated data validation tests. As an example, accountants know that every journal entry should have a balanced set of debit and credit entries. If an accountant has extracted journal entries, she can analyze the extracted data to make sure the balance of credits equals the balance of debits. She can also test the relationship between sub-ledgers and the general ledger in extracted data; namely, that the sum of the balances in all of the sub-ledgers should equal the total in the general ledger. Testing within a transaction could be done by comparing the sum of quantities times prices of items in a transaction with the total of that transaction. With an understanding of the data, one can leverage that knowledge to check if the transformed data conforms to accounting rules, thus providing evidence of the quality of your data.

Summary and Case Conclusion

Ashton carefully reviewed the data extract he was given by the IT department. He noticed many problems in the data and was able to correct them before analyzing the vendor information.

Ashton was also able to document the errors he found and send that list back to the data owners. With the list of errors, the data owners corrected the source data in their systems (see corrected extract of data in Figure 6-10). In this way, all future users of the vendor data will not have to repair the same data errors again. The list of errors will also be useful as S&S incorporates the new system into their existing data architecture.

FIGURE 6-10
Transformed Extract of S&S Vendor Data

	A	B	C	D	E	F	G	H	I	J	K	L	M	N	O	P	Q	R	S
1	RowNumber	VendorName	FName	LName	PhoneNumber	Address	City	State	ZipCode	DiscountRate	DiscountDays	BalanceDueDays	ProdCat	CatDesc	ProdID	ProdDesc	UnitsPurch	TotalCosts	AvgCostPerUnit
2	1	Oster	DeShawn	Williams	(907) 961-4917	1535 N Hickory St	Owosso	MI	48867	2	10	30	1	Kitchen Appliances	3	Toaster	186	$ 2,068.32	$ 11.12
3	2	Black and Decker	Milton	Armstrong	(844) 986-0858	1000 Stanley Dr	Concord	NC	28027	2	10	30	1	Kitchen Appliances	3	Toaster	227	$ 2,220.06	$ 9.78
4	3	KitchenAid	Chiyo	Tanaka	(360) 565-9487	1701 Kitchen Aid Way	Greenville	OH	45331				1	Kitchen Appliances	2	Microwave	210	$40,849.20	$ 194.52
5	4	Black and Decker	Milton	Armstrong	(844) 986-0858	1000 Stanley Dr	Concord	NC	28027	2	10	30	3	Hand tools	1	Hand Drill	273	$10,851.75	$ 39.75
6	5	Black and Decker	Milton	Armstrong	(844) 986-0858	1000 Stanley Dr	Concord	NC	28027	2	10	30	2	Fans	2	Desk Fan	80	$ 568.00	$ 7.10
7	6	Panasonic	Maryam	Ahmad	(551) 777-9393	7625 Panasonic Way	San Diego	CA	92154	2	10	15	1	Kitchen Appliances	2	Microwave	51	$ 7,882.56	$ 154.56
8	7	Black and Decker	Milton	Armstrong	(844) 986-0858	1000 Stanley Dr	Concord	NC	28027	2	10	30	2	Fans	1	Box Fan	281	$ 2,529.00	$ 9.00
9	8	Panasonic	Maryam	Ahmad	(551) 777-9393	7625 Panasonic Way	San Diego	CA	92154	2	10	15	2	Fans	2	Desk Fan	386	$ 5,693.50	$ 14.75
10	9	KitchenAid	Chiyo	Tanaka	(360) 565-9487	1701 Kitchen Aid Way	Greenville	OH	45331				1	Kitchen Appliances	3	Toaster	171	$ 2,433.33	$ 14.23
11	10	Oster	DeShawn	Williams	(907) 961-4917	1535 N Hickory St	Owosso	MI	48867	2	10	30	1	Kitchen Appliances	1	Blender	263	$ 5,062.75	$ 19.25
12	11	Oster	DeShawn	Williams	(907) 961-4917	1535 N Hickory St	Owosso	MI	48867	2	10	30	1	Kitchen Appliances	2	Microwave	248	$20,889.04	$ 84.23
13	12	Honeywell	Larsena	Hansen	(790) 447-1783	10640 Freeport Dr	Louisville	KY	40258	1	10	30	2	Fans	2	Desk Fan	54	$ 621.00	$ 11.50
14	13	Calphalon	Sofia	Bruner	(933) 937-5654	20750 Midstar Dr	Bowling Green	OH	43402				1	Kitchen Appliances	1	Blender	261	$19,509.75	$ 74.75
15	14	Black and Decker	Milton	Armstrong	(844) 986-0858	1000 Stanley Dr	Concord	NC	28027	2	10	30	1	Kitchen Appliances	2	Microwave	262	$15,982.00	$ 61.00
16	15	Honeywell	Larsena	Hansen	(790) 447-1783	10640 Freeport Dr	Louisville	KY	40258	1	10	30	2	Fans	1	Box Fan	346	$ 4,895.90	$ 14.15
17	16	Black and Decker	Milton	Armstrong	(844) 986-0858	1000 Stanley Dr	Concord	NC	28027	2	10	30	3	Hand tools	2	Jigsaw	122	$ 2,172.82	$ 17.81

KEY TERMS

data structuring 165
aggregate data 165
data pivoting 166
data standardization 167
data parsing 167
data concatenation 169
cryptic data values 169
dummy variable or dichotomous variable 170
misfielded data values 170
data consistency 170
dirty data 172
data cleaning 172
data de-duplication 172
data filtering 172
data imputation 173
data contradiction errors 173
data threshold violations 173
violated attribute dependencies 174
data entry errors 174
data validation 174
visual inspection 175

AIS in Action

CHAPTER QUIZ

1. In which step of the data transformation process would you analyze whether the data has the properties of high-quality data?
   a. data structuring
   b. data standardization
   c. data cleaning
   d. data validation

2. As part of the data standardization process, often items contained in different fields for the same record need to be combined into a single field. This process is called:
   a. aggregating data
   b. data aggregation
   c. data concatenation
   d. data parsing

3. Which of the following reasons describes why transforming data is necessary?
   a. Data aggregated at different levels needs to be joined.
   b. Data within a field has various formats.
   c. Multiple data values are contained in the same field and need to be separated.
   d. All of the above

Use the following image to answer questions 4 through 10.

	Column 1	Column 2	Column 3	Column 4	Column 5	Column 6	Column 7
Row Number	EmpName	EmpNumb	DOB	Date of Hire	Department	Position	Pay Rate
1	Hudson, Wallace	1302053	4/3/1986	9/18/2013	101	Accountant I	$ 1,329.50
2	Salah, Modeste	1103024	7/28/1986	7/29/2006	101	Accountant I	$ 28.81
4	Shakeel, Randolf	7110077	8/29/1989	4/24/2012	101	Admin Assistant	$ 19.88
5	Janine, Manish	1307059	8/24/1990	1/18/2015	101	Admin Assistant	$ 16.86
6	Marshall, Marylou	1192991	4/19/1979	12/18/2013	250	IT Director	$ 64.11
7	Clemence, Suzanne	100AFB	11/22/1962	11/7/2012	250	IT Manager	$ 20.07
8	Melissa, Herbert	1101023	5/23/1968	6/19/2013	250	IT Manager	$ 64.60
9	Melissa, Herbert	1101023	5/23/1968	6/19/2013	250	IT Manager	$ 64.60
10	Hilda, Elwood	1501072	10/19/1968	10/18/2012	250	IT Support	$ 31.68
11	Lowell, Candice	1307060	7/3/1985	8/3/2012	101	Sr. Accountant	$ 35.22
12	Nikolas, Lesley	1001495	25-Jan-50	41977	50	President & CEO	$ 79.10

4. In column 3, which of the following problems do you find?
   a. data consistency error
   b. data imputation error
   c. data contradiction error
   d. violated attribute dependencies

5. In column 5, which of the following problems do you find?
   a. data pivoting error
   b. violated attribute dependencies
   c. data consistency error
   d. cryptic values

6. In column 7, row 1, which of the following problems do you find?
   a. data consistency error
   b. data parsing error
   c. data threshold violation
   d. misfielded data value

7. In row 8 and row 9, which of the following problems do you find?
   a. data contradiction error
   b. data concatenation error
   c. data aggregation error
   d. duplicate values

8. In column 2, row 7, which of the following problems do you find?
   a. data threshold violation
   b. data entry error
   c. violated attribute dependencies
   d. dichotomous variable problem

9. Column 4, row 12, is most likely an example of which of the following?
a. data imputation
b. cryptic data value
c. violated attribute dependencies
d. listing the date in serial date format

10. Which of the following could be used to catch the problems listed in the figure?
a. visual inspection
b. basic statistical tests
c. auditing a sample
d. All of the above

DISCUSSION QUESTIONS

6.1 Why is transforming data necessary, and why does it take so much time? What ways can you think of to reduce the time needed to transform data?

6.2 For each of the data quality attributes listed in Table 6-1, discuss a business scenario that would be harmed if data did not have the data attribute. As you prepare these scenarios, are there other attributes of data that should be added to Table 6-1? If so, why?

6.3 Companies are increasingly operating throughout the entire world. As such, the data companies collect can differ based on the country where the data is captured. This chapter identified two problems that can exist in data based on operating throughout the world: different formats for dates and capturing time stamps in different locations. What are other possible challenges you would observe in data captured throughout the world?

6.4 What are the strengths and weaknesses of each of the four data validation procedures discussed in this chapter? What are other possible ways to validate data?

PROBLEMS

6.1 Match the following terms with their definitions or examples:

Term		Definition or example
___ **1.** aggregate data	a.	Process of analyzing data to make certain the data has the properties of high-quality data: accuracy, completeness, consistency, timeliness, and validity
___ **2.** cryptic data values	b.	Data values that are correctly formatted but not listed in the correct field
___ **3.** data cleaning	c.	All types of errors that come from inputting data incorrectly
___ **4.** data concatenation	d.	Examining data using human vision to see if there are problems
___ **5.** data consistency	e.	Process of tracing extracted or transformed values back to their original source
___ **6.** data contradiction errors	f.	Data items that have no meaning without understanding a coding scheme
___ **7.** data de-duplication	g.	The process of standardizing the structure and meaning of each data element so it can be analyzed and used in decision making
___ **8.** data entry errors	h.	Technique that rotates data from a state of rows to a state of columns
___ **9.** data filtering	i.	Errors that occur when a secondary attribute in a row of data does not match the primary attribute
___ **10.** data imputation	j.	Data field that contains only two responses, typically a 0 or 1; also called a dichotomous variable
___ **11.** data parsing	k.	Principle that every value in a field should be stored in the same way

___ 12.	data pivoting	l.	Process of changing the organization and relationships among data fields to prepare the data for analysis
___ 13.	data standardization	m.	Data errors that occur when a data value falls outside an allowable level
___ 14.	data structuring	n.	Data field that contains only two responses, typically a 0 or 1; also called a dummy variable
___ 15.	data threshold violations	o.	Process of updating data to be consistent, accurate, and complete
___ 16.	data validation	p.	Data that is inconsistent, inaccurate, or incomplete
___ 17.	dichotomous variable	q.	Separating data from a single field into multiple fields
___ 18.	dirty data	r.	Combining data from two or more fields into a single field
___ 19.	dummy variable	s.	Process of replacing a null or missing value with a substituted value
___ 20.	misfielded data values	t.	Process of removing records or fields of information from a data source
___ 21.	violated attribute dependencies	u.	Process of analyzing data and removing two or more records that contain identical information
___ 22.	visual inspection	v.	Presentation of data in a summarized form
		w.	Error that occurs when the same entity is described in two conflicting ways
		x.	Pocess of ordering data to reveal unexpected values

6.2 Excel Project: Data Pivoting
You are a data analyst for the city of Burlington, Vermont. Download the data file "P6-2BurlingtonVermontData.xlsx" from the student download page at http://www.pearsonhighered.com/romney, which contains the annual account balance information for city departments for six fiscal years. For this problem, use the sheet titled "Annual Data"—it contains data aggregated to the annual level for the city departments.

REQUIRED

Using this data, prepare a PivotTable in a new sheet to answer each of the following questions:

a. Have total department budgets changed each year? To answer the question, create a PivotTable that shows the budgeted amount of expenditures for each fiscal year. Do not include grand totals. Add conditional formatting data bars to show which amounts are the greatest.
b. Which funds have the largest expense budgets for fiscal year 6? Create a PivotTable that shows fund names and budgeted amounts for fiscal year 6. Sort the data so the greatest budget amounts are listed at the top.
c. Regardless of department, organization, or fund, which type of activities were most costly during the entire time period (hint: view the "Detail_Description" field)? How much did they pay for this activity?

6.3 Excel Project: Aggregating Data at Different Levels
You are an internal auditor for the city of Burlington, Vermont. Download the data file "P6-3BurlingtonVermontData.xlsx" from the student download page at http://www.pearsonhighered.com/romney, which contains the annual account balance information for city departments for six fiscal years. There are two sheets in this workbook. The "Annual Data" sheet contains data aggregated to the annual level for the city departments. The "Monthly Data" sheet contains data aggregated to the monthly level for the city departments. You are planning to perform audit procedures on the "Monthly Data." Before you do, verify that the data in this sheet matches the data in the "Annual Data" worksheet, which you already verified as correct.

REQUIRED

Analyze the two sheets. Based on your analysis, answer the following questions:

a. Under what circumstances can you NOT use the "Annual Data" sheet for your audit? Said differently, why might you need the data in the "Monthly Data" sheet for your audit?

b. On a separate worksheet in Excel, create a summary of the data that shows the total dollar amount of transactions for the two different sheets. Are these the same for both datasets?

c. Does the total amount for transactions differ for the different departments and years? Create two sheets: the first sheet should compare departments and the second sheet should compare years. What do you learn from these analyses?

d. Based on your analysis in the previous questions, suggest the areas you believe are most important to investigate further. Why do you believe these areas are the most important to investigate further?

6.4 Excel Project: Parsing Data

Go to the student download page at http://www.pearsonhighered.com/romney and download the file labeled "P6-4CustomerData.xlsx". For this problem, assume your supervisor gave you this file and said it contains information about customers. The file has several fields merged together, and your supervisor wants you to parse them into separate fields.

REQUIRED

Separate the fields as instructed in parts a and b below.

a. Parse the data on the "Data – Simplified" sheet. Put your solution on the "Simplified Solution" sheet. The image below shows the solution for the first three rows. Your solution should separate the information using only formulas. Leave the formulas in your solution file for evaluation. As a hint, this problem can be solved using a combination of the LEFT, RIGHT, MID, FIND, and VALUE formulas.

CustomerID	Name	Address	CityStateZip	CustomerNumber	SalesRegion	City	State	ZipCode
7562-Region 1	Kirk Barrett	7890 E. Branch Street	Janesville, WI 53546	7562	Region 1	Janesville	WI	53546
8073-Region 1	Debbie Banks	383 Fulton Ave.	Zeeland, MI 49464	8073	Region 1	Zeeland	MI	49464
7575-Region 4	Natalie Harper	8741 Princeton Road	Newington, CT 6111	7575	Region 4	Newington	CT	6111

b. Parse the data on the "Data – Advanced" sheet. Put your solution on the "Advanced Solution" sheet. The image below shows the solution for the first three rows. Your solution should separate the information using only formulas. Leave the formulas in your solution file for evaluation. As a hint, this problem can be solved using a combination of the LEFT, RIGHT, MID, FIND, TRIM, SUBSTITUTE, REPT, LEN, and VALUE formulas.*

CustomerID	Name	Address	CustomerNumber	SalesRegion	StreetAddress	City	State	ZipCode
7562-Region 1	Kirk Barrett	7890 E. Branch Street Janesville, WI 53546	7562	Region 1	7890 E. Branch Street	Janesville	WI	53546
8073-Region 1	Debbie Banks	383 Fulton Ave. Zeeland, MI 49464	8073	Region 1	383 Fulton Ave.	Zeeland	MI	49464
7575-Region 4	Natalie Harper	8741 Princeton Road Newington, CT 06111	7575	Region 4	8741 Princeton Road	Newington	CT	6111

6.5 Excel Project: Fixing Cryptic Data Using Data Concatenation

You work at a non-profit that seeks to help people start businesses in third world countries so those people can lift themselves out of poverty. Your organization has found more success working in countries that have policies that make it easier to start a business. You have been asked to explore which countries your organization should consider entering. To do this, go to the student download page at http://www.pearsonhighered.com/romney

* Life-long learning opportunity: see pp. xxiii–xxiv in preface.

and download the file labeled "P6-5StartingABusiness.xlsx". This dataset provides information about the relative ease of starting a business and doing business in countries around the world. The Excel spreadsheet contains three years of data in multiple sheets. The data is not easy to understand as it is spread across multiple sheets and the "Final Report" sheet currently only shows cryptic data values for the Country and Year. The data for this problem comes from The World Bank: Doing Business dataset: see http://www.doingbusiness.org/en/data for more information.

REQUIRED

Do the following

a. Fill out the "Final Report" sheet so that it looks like the image below. You should use formulas to prepare the final report. Leave the formulas in your solution file for evaluation. As a hint, this problem can be solved using a combination of the VLOOKUP and CONCATENATE functions. Add columns to the sheets to complete the task with these formulas as needed.

CountryCode	YearCode	CountryName	Year	CountryNameYear	Ease of doing business score global (DB17-19 methodology)	Score-Starting a business
1	8	Afghanistan	2017	Afghanistan2017	38.94	90.35
1	9	Afghanistan	2018	Afghanistan2018	37.13	82.55
1	10	Afghanistan	2019	Afghanistan2019	47.77	92.04

b. Fill out the "Final Report – Advanced" sheet so that it looks like the image below. You should use formulas to prepare the final report. Leave the formulas in your solution file for evaluation. For this problem, you are only allowed to use combinations of the following functions: INDEX, MATCH, and CONCATENATE. You will NOT need to add columns to complete the task.

CountryCode	YearCode	CountryName	Year	Ease of doing business score global (DB17-19 methodology)	Score-Starting a business
1	8	Afghanistan	2017	38.94	90.35
1	9	Afghanistan	2018	37.13	82.55
1	10	Afghanistan	2019	47.77	92.04

c. Compare and contrast the formulas you used to answer part a and part b. Research both types of formulas and discuss which formulas are better for use in practice.*

6.6 Excel Project: Formatting Data Consistently

You are preparing to analyze data about the Washington, DC Public Schools from January 2009 to February 2019. Go to the student download page at http://www.pearsonhighered.com/romney and download the file labeled "P6-6WashingtonDCData.xlsx". Notice that the formatting of the data in the fields "Transaction_Date" and "Transaction_Amount" has become corrupt and each entry can be formatted in many ways. Note, all of the data in the "Transaction_Date" field contains a date (so any numbers are stored date values). All of the data listed in the "Transaction_Amount" column refer to dollar amounts.

REQUIRED

For the two fields, format the data in each field to be consistent within each column. Justify the choice you made for the data format you chose to use for each column. Describe the process you went through to make sure you formatted all the data correctly. The data in the "Transaction_Date" column only needs to be accurate at the day, month, and year level (so do not worry about time information in the column if it is present). The data in the "Transaction_Amount" column needs to be accurate at the penny level.*

* Life-long learning opportunity: see pp. xxiii–xxiv in preface.

6.7 Excel Project: Auditing a Data Extract
You work as an auditor for the city of Washington, DC and have been asked to audit employee purchasing card (p-cards) expenses. You have been asked to validate that the cleaned data for a sample of the p-card transactions match original records from before the transformation process. Go to the student download page at http://www.pearsonhighered.com/romney and download the file labeled "P6-7WashingtonDCDataAudit.xlsx". The file contains two sheets. The sheet labeled "Population" includes all p-card transactions from January 2009 to February 2019. The sheet labeled "Sample" contains the 20 transactions from 2019 you have selected for examination.

REQUIRED

a. Determine whether all the data in the sample transactions matches records in the original data. If there are errors, document any you find.
b. Once you are finished, estimate how many errors are likely for each field in the 2019 data.

6.8 For the S&S case discussed in this chapter, you receive the following output containing basic descriptive statistics for some of the columns in the full dataset (the chapter example problem contained a small excerpt of data; this problem uses more data). S&S has a total of 60 products that customers purchase across 3 categories.

REQUIRED

List the concerns you have with the data and discuss what steps you would take for each concern identified.

	RowNumber	VendorName	DiscountRate	ProdCat	ProdID	UnitsPurch	TotalCosts
Count of non-null values	453	443	453	453	453	453	452
Count of null values	0	10	0	0	0	0	5
Mean	227.00	NA	1.79	2.05	10.31	231.19	$ 6,315
Median	227.00	NA	1.50	2.00	9.00	228.00	$ 4,671
Max	453	NA	100.0	3.0	25.0	449.0	$ 21,550
Min	1	NA	0	1	1	-150	$ 18
Number of Unique Values	451	27	8	8	25	298	438

6.9 Excel Project: Creating Data Errors
This problem asks you to create a dataset with specified errors.

REQUIRED

a. Create a fake dataset that has at least 20 rows and 6 columns. The dataset can relate to any setting in accounting or business. In the dataset, include at least one of each of the following types of errors: cryptic data values, data contradiction errors, data entry errors, data threshold violations, misfielded data values, and violated attribute dependencies.
b. Prepare a memo to go with your dataset that describes the nature of the data. Then define each error and describe the example error you included in your dataset.

6.10 Search the Internet for an example of a business project failure caused by a failure in some part of the ETL process. Based on the example you find, discuss the principles from this chapter that the company failed to follow. In addition, discuss the reasons why you think the company failed to follow these principles.

The following case was developed by the Ernst & Young Academic Resource Center, which is sponsored by the Ernst & Young Foundation.

CASE 6-1 Hotel Data Cleaning Case

For this case, you received a data file, **Analytics_mindset_case_studies_ETL_Case4.xlsx** (go to the student download page at http://www.pearsonhighered.com/romney to download this file). It includes 789 lines of journal entries for 11 days from a hotel and conference center (on the tab labeled JELineItems) as well as other important accounting-relevant datasets on these other tabs: BusinessUnits, ChartOfAccounts, PreparerInfo, and Source. The following is a select list of data fields from this file noting the field name and field description tabs on which the data field is located.

Field Name	Field Description	Tab
JENumber	Unique identifier for each journal entry	JELineItems
GLAccountNumber	GL account number from chart of accounts; tab labeled GLAccounts contains the full information about the GL accounts	JELineItems and ChartOfAccounts
BusinessUnitID	Business unit number (1–8) of the journal entry	JELineItems, BusinessUnits, and PreparerInfo
PreparerID	Employee ID for employee who initiated the transaction; for transactions recorded initially in a subsystem (e.g., GuestSYS or POS), the PreparerID is listed as the system and not the employee • *Note that the PreparerID is not unique. The company starts all ID numbering over for each business unit. Thus, the combination of the PreparerID and BusinessUnit number is unique for each employee.*	JELineItems and PreparerInfo
SourceID	Unique identifier for each source	JELineItems and Source
EffectiveDate	Date entry was posted to the GL as occurring; the *EffectiveDate* is the date that the transaction is posted in the GL and recognized as revenue. The corporate office, therefore, is recognizing revenue throughout the year based on this date, rather than the date it is meeting its performance obligations, which you would consider the "right" effective date for proper accounting treatment. However, the corporate office performs year-end cutoff procedures to account for this at a level of materiality that, year over year, would suit corporate and ensure that amounts are properly stated.	JELineItems
JEDescription	Description of transaction; may include vendor or guest name, etc.	JELineItems
Debit	Debit amount of entry (positive)	JELineItems
Credit	Credit amount of entry (negative)	JELineItems
Amount	Total amount of journal entry line item (may be positive or negative)	JELineItems
BusinessUnit	Business unit name (e.g., hotel, food and beverage) of journal entry	BusinessUnits
BUDescription	Description of each business unit	BusinessUnits
AccountType	For each account, a high-level description of which type of general ledger account it is (e.g., asset, liability, equity, expense, revenue)	ChartOfAccounts

Field Name	Field Description	Tab
AccountClass	For each account, a more detailed description of which type of general ledger account it is (e.g., accounts receivable, cash, payroll expense)	ChartOfAccounts
GLAccountName	Name of general ledger account from chart of accounts	ChartOfAccounts
PreparerName	Name of employee	PreparerInfo
Source	Describes payment type or other source type of transaction (CASH RECEIPT, CHECK, CREDIT CARD RECEIPT, CREDIT MEMO, PAYROLL JV, PAYROLL MANUAL JV, PAYROLL S/B JV, PURCHASE CARD, REGULAR JV)	Source

REQUIRED

- You have been asked to prepare a single, flat file (i.e., spreadsheet) with all of the data fields from each tab within the data file combined in a single sheet labeled Case 6-1 solution. This sheet is already provided in the workbook. The journal entry line item data and the required column headers (attributes) have already been copied into this new spreadsheet. You are required to populate the remaining fields with accurate data.
- Management wants to create a repeatable ETL data process for this scenario. This requires a template that uses a consistently formatted dataset. Therefore, you should retain formulas in your final sheet for columns K through Q, and you should not add, delete, or move any data in any of the other sheets.
- Your final sheet should look like the following screenshot. (The first three rows are provided, showing the correct answer. Make sure your rows have the formula entered in them).

	A	B	C	D	E	F	G	H	I	J	K	L	M	N	O	P	Q
1	JENumber	GLAccountNumber	BusinessUnit	PreparerID	SourceID	EffectiveDate	JEDescription	Debit	Credit	Amount	BusinessUnit	BUDescription	GLAccountName	AccountType	AccountClass	PreparerName	Source
2	2033520	76930	1	101	1002	6/20/2020	TELECOM GTA JUN 2016	36.90		36.90	FOOD SERVICE	Transactions related to food and beverage service. Includes all guest transactions in the hotel restaurants, catering-related transactions and food service payroll.	Telecommunications - Other	Expenses	SG&A	Carolyn Slater|Food Operations Manager	CHECK
3	2033520	11845	1	101	1002	6/20/2020	TELECOM GTA JUN 2016		-36.90	-36.90	FOOD SERVICE	Transactions related to food and beverage service. Includes all guest transactions in the hotel restaurants, catering-related transactions and food service payroll.	Operating Bank Account	Assets	Cash	Carolyn Slater|Food Operations Manager	CHECK

AIS in Action Solutions

QUIZ KEY

1. In which step of the data transformation process would you analyze whether the data has the properties of high-quality data?
   a. data structuring [Incorrect. Data structuring relates to changing the organization and relationships among data fields and not verifying the data quality.]
   b. data standardization [Incorrect. Data standardization relates to changing the formatting of the data and not verifying data quality.]
   c. data cleaning [Incorrect. Data cleaning occurs once you assess data to not be of high quality.]
   ▶ d. data validation [Correct. Data validation happens throughout the ETL process to make sure data is high quality.]

2. As part of the data standardization process, often items contained in different fields for the same record need to be combined into a single field. This process is called:
   a. aggregating data [Incorrect. Aggregating data is the process of combining data in the same field for different records.]
   b. data aggregation [Incorrect. Data aggregation is the process of combining different data sources.]
   ▶ c. data concatenation [Correct. Data concatenation is the process of combining data in two fields into a single cell.]
   d. data parsing [Incorrect. Data parsing is the separation of data in the same field into two separate fields]

3. Which of the following reasons describes why transforming data is necessary?
   a. Data aggregated at different levels needs to be joined. [Part of Correct Answer. All the answers are an example of why transforming data is necessary.]
   b. Data within a field has various formats. [Part of Correct Answer. All the answers are an example of why transforming data is necessary.]
   c. Multiple data values are contained in the same field and need to be separated. [Part of Correct Answer. All the answers are an example of why transforming data is necessary.]
   ▶ d. All of the above [Correct. All of the above are examples of why transforming data is necessary.]

Use the following image to answer questions 4 through 10.

	Column 1	Column 2	Column 3	Column 4	Column 5	Column 6	Column 7
Row Number	**EmpName**	**EmpNumb**	**DOB**	**Date of Hire**	**Department**	**Position**	**Pay Rate**
1	Hudson, Wallace	1302053	4/3/1986	9/18/2013	101	Accountant I	$ 1,329.50
2	Salah, Modeste	1103024	7/28/1986	7/29/2006	101	Accountant I	$ 28.81
4	Shakeel, Randolf	7110077	8/29/1989	4/24/2012	101	Admin Assistant	$ 19.88
5	Janine, Manish	1307059	8/24/1990	1/18/2015	101	Admin Assistant	$ 16.86
6	Marshall, Marylou	1192991	4/19/1979	12/18/2013	250	IT Director	$ 64.11
7	Clemence, Suzanne	100AFB	11/22/1962	11/7/2012	250	IT Manager	$ 20.07
8	Melissa, Herbert	1101023	5/23/1968	6/19/2013	250	IT Manager	$ 64.60
9	Melissa, Herbert	1101023	5/23/1968	6/19/2013	250	IT Manager	$ 64.60
10	Hilda, Elwood	1501072	10/19/1968	10/18/2012	250	IT Support	$ 31.68
11	Lowell, Candice	1307060	7/3/1985	8/3/2012	101	Sr. Accountant	$ 35.22
12	Nikolas, Lesley	1001495	25-Jan-50	41977	50	President & CEO	$ 79.10

4. In column 3, which of the following problems do you find?
   ▶ a. data consistency error [Correct. The dates are not formatted consistently.]
   b. data imputation error [Incorrect. Data imputation is a way of filling in null values.]
   c. data contradiction error [Incorrect. Data contradiction errors are when the same entity is described in two different ways.]
   d. violated attribute dependencies [Incorrect. Violated attributed dependencies occur when a secondary attribute does not match the primary attribute.]

5. In column 5, which of the following problems do you find?
   a. data pivoting error [Incorrect. Data pivoting is not an error but rather a way of rotating data.]
   b. violated attribute dependencies [Incorrect. Violated attribute dependencies occur when a secondary attribute does not match the primary attribute.]
   c. data consistency error [Incorrect. Data consistency refers to storing values in the same way; all of the values appear to be stored the same as all the other values in the column.]
   ▶ d. cryptic values [Correct. Cryptic values is correct because the numbers have no meaning without referring to the another data table.]

6. In column 7, row 1, which of the following problems do you find?

a. data consistency error [Incorrect. The value appears to be stored the same as all the other values in the column.]

b. data parsing error [Incorrect. Data parsing is a way of splitting data into two fields and is not a problem.]

▶ c. data threshold violation [Correct. The amount listed is so far above everyone else, including the President and CEO, that it likely falls outside the allowable level.]

d. misfielded data value [Incorrect. Misfielded data values are correctly formatted values but put in the wrong field.]

7. In row 8 and row 9, which of the following problems do you find?

a. data contradiction error [Incorrect. Data contradiction errors occur when the same entity is described in two different ways.]

b. data concatenation error [Incorrect. Data concatenation refers to the combining of values in two fields into a single field.]

c. data aggregation error [Incorrect. Data aggregation errors is a made up error.]

▶ d. duplicate values [Correct. All of the information on row 9 matches the information on row 8.]

8. In column 2, row 7, which of the following problems do you find?

a. data threshold violation [Incorrect. A data threshold violation is an error when the data falls outside an allowable level.]

▶ b. data entry error [Correct. The employee number includes letters instead of numbers, likely because the data was entered incorrectly.]

c. violated attribute dependencies [Incorrect. Violated attributed dependencies occur when a secondary attribute does not match the primary attribute.]
d. dichotomous variable problem [Incorrect. A dichotomous variable is a data field that only allows two values.]

9. Column 4, row 12, is most likely an example of which of the following?
a. data imputation [Incorrect. Data imputation is a way of filling in null values.]
b. cryptic data value [Incorrect. The number has meaning, and you do not need to refer to the data dictionary or another data table to understand it.]
c. violated attribute dependencies [Incorrect. Violated attributed dependencies occur when a secondary attribute does not match the primary attribute.]
▶ d. listing the date in serial date format [Correct. This is the value that Excel would store when a date is listed in a cell. The number corresponds to the date 12/4/2014.]

10. Which of the following could be used to catch the problems listed in the figure?
a. visual inspection [Part of Correct Answer. While visual inspection would be helpful, using multiple methods is a better answer.]
b. basic statistical tests [Part of Correct Answer. While basic statistical tests would be helpful, using multiple methods is a better answer.]
c. auditing a sample [Part of Correct Answer. While auditing a sample would be helpful, using multiple methods is a better answer.]
▶ d. All of the above [Correct. All of the above are steps to validate the data and would be useful in finding the problems listed in the figure.]

CHAPTER

7 Data Analysis and Presentation

LEARNING OBJECTIVES

After studying this chapter, you should be able to:

1. Define and give examples of descriptive, diagnostic, predictive, and prescriptive analytics.
2. Describe when each type of analytic is most appropriately used in a business context.
3. Select the correct type of visualization format for visualizing data.
4. Understand design principles of simplification, emphasis, and ethical data presentation to design high-quality data visualizations.

INTEGRATIVE CASE

S&S is planning to offer their stock to the public to fund its planned growth. As part of the initial public offering, executive leadership at S&S will go on a "roadshow." A roadshow is a marketing pitch to potential investors designed to increase demand for shares in the company. Executive management has asked Ashton to prepare a series of data analyses that highlight how S&S has performed in the past, how it currently is performing, and project how it will perform in the future. Management wants Ashton to automate the production of these reports, so at a moment's notice the management team can provide up-to-date visualizations about the company.

Ashton knows these analyses are very important to the success of the public offering. He also knows that deciding how to present the data will influence how investors understand, interpret, and remember the information about S&S. Ashton returns to his team to discuss what data they should analyze and how they should present the results.

Dusit/Shutterstock

Introduction

TD Bank Group is a leading Canadian bank and one of the largest banks in North America. They spent five years constructing a data lake so more employees could access bank data without depending on a small data science team to access and analyze data for them. The bank also invested heavily in tools and training that made it easier for all employees to perform their own analysis and visualization of the data. TD Bank reports that these changes resulted in 90% productivity improvements for analytics projects, 60% reduction in data management costs, and 30% reduction in repeat customer complaints.

The TD Bank Group experience highlights the importance of the analytics mindset process. Asking the right questions and gathering the data through the extract, transform, and load (ETL) process is not sufficient. The data must be properly analyzed and shared in a meaningful way. Said differently, all the work of generating high-quality questions and extracting and transforming data is of little value if useful insight cannot be gathered from the data and shared with others in a meaningful way. The TD Bank Group was able to provide the tools and training so that employees could successfully analyze data and share results with others, which lead to better decisions.

This chapter focuses on the last two parts of an analytics mindset: (1) applying appropriate data analytic techniques and (2) interpreting and sharing the results with stakeholders.

Data Analysis

There are four categories of data analytics: descriptive, diagnostic, predictive, and prescriptive. As shown in Figure 7-1, these four categories of analytics differ in terms of their complexity and the value they add to the organization. To become an expert in these analytic categories requires significant training. This chapter provides an overview of each type of analytic. A deep understanding of each area requires additional advanced courses in data analytics.

DESCRIPTIVE ANALYTICS

Descriptive analytics are computations that address the basic question of "what happened?" External auditors use many descriptive analytics, including computing profit margins and leverage ratios to examine if business risk changed significantly during a period and to identify possible fraud. Corporate accountants compute descriptive analytics to understand how the business is performing. Metrics such as cost-per-unit, inventory turnover ratios, customer acquisition costs, and variance of budgets-to-actual expenses and revenues are examples of descriptive analytics.

FIGURE 7-1
Importance and Contribution of Different Analytics

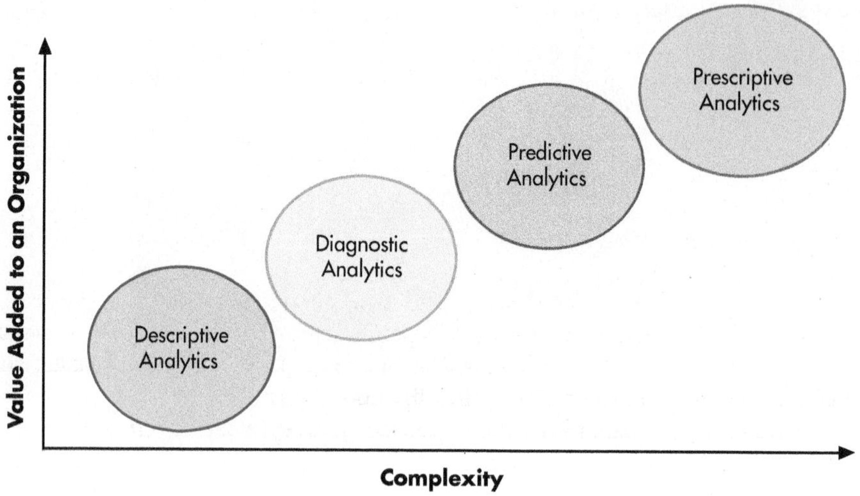

exploratory data analysis - An approach to examining data that seeks to explore the data without testing formal models or hypotheses.

Descriptive analytics use **exploratory data analysis** techniques. Exploratory data analysis is an approach that explores data without testing formal models or hypotheses. This type of analysis is often used for the following:

- To find mistakes in the data.
- To understand the structure of data.
- To check assumptions required by more formal statistical modeling techniques.
- To determine the size, direction, and strength of relationships between variables.

When examining new data, seek to understand the central tendency of the data, the spread of the data, the distribution of the data, and correlations in the data. Central tendency of the data refers to determining a value that reflects the center of the data distribution. The most common measures of central tendency are the mean and median. The mean is the average amount—that is, the sum of all the values divided by the number of observations in the dataset. The median is the value that separates the higher half of the values from the lower half of the values.

outlier - A data point, or a few data points, that lie an abnormal distance from other values in the data.

Comparing mean and median values can provide insight to the central tendency as means can be highly influenced by outliers whereas medians are influenced significantly less by outliers. An **outlier** is a data point, or a few data points, that lie an abnormal distance from other values in the data. Identifying outliers is important because they can exert undue influence on the computation of many analytics—which may lead to erroneous interpretations of the data.

The spread of the data refers to the dispersion of data around the central value. The most common measures of spread are the range of the data and the standard deviation of the data. The range of the data is the difference between the lowest and highest values. The standard deviation is a statistical computation that measures the dispersion of data around the mean.

Sometimes people also talk about spread by referring to quartiles. Three quartile points create the four ranges: starting from the lowest point, the first quartile cutoff is the point between the lowest 25% of the data and the highest 75% of the data, the second quartile cutoff is the same as the median, and the third quartile cutoff is the point between the lowest 75% of the data and the highest 25% of the data.

The distribution of the data is a statistical term that refers to how often values in the data occur or repeat. Distributions are important to understand the shape of the data and for determining which statistical tests may be properly applied to analyze data. The validity of each statistical test is dependent on the data meeting the test's assumed distribution. The most common distribution is the normal distribution, which looks like the famous bell-shaped curve. Understanding the distribution of data is also helpful in identifying outliers.

Finally, correlations in data refer to how closely two items fluctuate together in a dataset. The most common measure of correlation is a correlation coefficient measured as a value from −1 to 1. A value of −1 means the two variables are negatively correlated—as one variable goes up, the other goes down by the same relative amount. A value of 1 means the two variables are positively correlated—as one variable goes up, the other goes up by the same relative amount. A correlation of 0 means there is no relation in the movement of the variables. As an example of correlation, if a company increases fees for customers paying bills late, there will likely be an increase in the number of bills paid on time (positive correlation) as customers try to avoid late fees. Increasing late fees will likely be related to a decrease in customer satisfaction (negative correlation) as customers are upset when they are assessed a late fee. Note that correlation is distinct from causation. Correlation versus causation was addressed in Chapter 5.

Central tendency, spread, distributions, and correlations are often depicted visually because the visual representations of these concepts are quick to interpret, easy to understand, and indicate areas that need further exploration. Any visual representation of data, such as a graph, diagram, or animation, is called a **visualization**, or viz for short.

visualization - Any visual representation of data, such as a graph, diagram, or animation; called a viz for short.

Descriptive analytics can also be performed on qualitative data by first transforming the qualitative data into numbers. For example, a company may want to examine social media data to see if people are saying positive or negative things about their company. Tweets and Facebook posts are qualitative data, but they can be transformed into quantitative data by doing such things as counting positive and negative social media mentions or using text analysis software to give a numerical score of the tone of the tweet. This qualitative data transformed into quantitative data can then be analyzed as discussed previously.

DIAGNOSTIC ANALYTICS

Diagnostic analysis goes beyond examining what happened to try to answer the question, "why did this happen?" Within diagnostic analysis, both informal and formal analyses can be conducted. Informal diagnostic analysis builds on descriptive analytics. It includes using logic and basic tests to try to reveal relationships in the data that explain why something happened. For example, if a company observes that the overall gross margin fell in the last quarter (a descriptive analytic), they might examine the mix of products sold. The analysis can be as simple as creating a table that shows all products sold in the last quarter versus the previous quarter, then computing the difference to see if more or fewer products with high/low gross margin sold. Analysts often must ask follow-up questions and perform analyses related to these questions to uncover the true underlying cause. For example, if a large quantity of low gross margin products were sold, the data analyst could again investigate why this was the case and may find that the marketing department advertised these products heavily in the last quarter. In turn, that might lead the analyst to ask why the marketing department focused on those products. The process continues until the analyst has discovered the root cause. A general rule of thumb is the "5 Why's" principle, which states that it often requires asking "Why?" five times in order to uncover the true reason why something happened.

In the preceding example, the analysis is informal in the sense that logic guided the investigation and simple descriptive statistics and inquiry were used to answer the question of why gross margin decreased. Diagnostic analytics can also be much more formal and employ confirmatory data analysis techniques. **Confirmatory data analysis** tests a hypothesis and provides statistical measures of the likelihood that the evidence (data) refutes or supports a hypothesis. While a full consideration of statistical testing is beyond the scope of this text, we cover several basic principles that are important for understanding hypothesis testing. The basic process of testing a hypothesis involves the following steps:

confirmatory data analysis - Testing a hypothesis and providing statistical evidence of the likelihood that the evidence refutes or supports a hypothesis.

1. State a null and alternative hypothesis.
2. Select a level of significance for refuting the null hypothesis.
3. Collect a sample of data and compute the probability value.
4. Compare the computed probability against the level of significance and determine if the evidence refutes the null hypothesis. Failing to refute the hypothesis is seen as support of the alternative hypothesis.

A hypothesis should be worded as a testable statement, not a question, about a general relationship between two ideas, groups, or concepts. As an example, the statement, "if we pay employees more, they will be less likely to leave our company" is a testable statement that relates two ideas (paying employees more and employees leaving). In contrast, the statements "we should pay our employees more" and "should we pay our employees more?" are not hypotheses.

null hypothesis - A proposed explanation worded in the form of an equality, meaning that one of the two concepts, ideas, or groups will be no different than the other concept, idea, or group.

alternative hypothesis - A proposed explanation worded in the form of an inequality, meaning that one of the two concepts, ideas, or groups will be greater or less than the other concept, idea, or group.

type I error - The incorrect rejection of a true null hypothesis.

type II error - The failure to reject a false null hypothesis.

Generally, a hypothesis should be thought of as two statements, a **null hypothesis** and an **alternative hypothesis**, although sometimes both are not explicitly stated. A null hypothesis is a statement of equality, suggesting there is no relationship between concepts or ideas in the hypothesis. An alternative hypothesis is a statement of inequality, suggesting that one concept, idea, or group is related to another concept, idea, or group. In the example used above, a null hypothesis would be "paying employees more will have no effect on their likelihood of leaving the company." The alternative form would express our tentative belief about the relationship between pay and retention (i.e., "paying employees more decreases the likelihood of employees leaving the company").

With the null and alternative hypotheses specified, two errors are possible. A **type I error** is the incorrect rejection of a true null hypothesis. A **type II error** is the failure to reject a false null hypothesis.

Continuing with the example of employee pay and leaving the company, assume the null hypothesis is true: There is no relation between pay and leaving the company. A type I error would be analyzing data and concluding there is a relation, either positive or negative, between paying employees more and them leaving the company. In contrast, a type II error would be finding no relation between pay and leaving the company if the true relation is that paying more does decrease the rate employees leave the company. As a second more concise example, consider a fire alarm. If an alarm goes off while there is no fire, this is a type I error. If an alarm does not go off while there is a fire, this is a type II error.

In statistics, the criteria for choosing between the null and alternative hypothesis is called the level of significance. The level of significance is the probability of accepting a type I error. General scientific rules of thumb use probability levels of 0.05, or sometimes a more lenient 0.10. This means that if the data you analyze return a probability level of 0.04, you would conclude that you should reject the null hypothesis and the evidence supports the alternative hypothesis. Still, be aware that the 0.04 means there is a 4% chance you are committing a type I error—it may in fact be that the null hypothesis is true. Thus, based on using statistics in science you never can "prove" the null or alternative hypothesis are true. Rather, you can provide evidence favoring one or the other hypothesis, but there is always the possibility—even if it is remote—that the opposite hypothesis is true.

Once a level of significance is decided on, one must collect and analyze data. The ideal way to collect data is to collect a random sample of data. The analysis of data can take many forms, including t-tests, regressions, analysis of variance (ANOVA), etc. If one is unable to collect a random sample of data, then more advanced statistical techniques must be used to try to control for the possibility that something other than what is being studied is causing the results. These various statistical techniques allow for the computation of the relevant probability. In the final step, one computes the relevant probability and evaluates whether it is greater than or less than the pre-decided level of significance in order to reach the appropriate conclusion.

effect size - A quantitative measure of the magnitude of the effect.

Note that hypothesis testing only reveals whether there is a relation (or not) between the two variables measured—it does not indicate the importance of the relation. That is, by using the steps above, one might find paying employees more is related to them leaving less, meaning the computed probability is below the pre-determined level of significance threshold. The **effect size**, which is a quantitative measure of the magnitude of the effect, reveals the importance of the relation. If turnover is reduced by 1% for every additional $100,000 increase in an employee's salary, we may conclude that pay is not a practically important factor in turnover. Other things, like culture, vacation policy, or healthcare benefits may be more important in determining why employees leave for another organization. There are statistical computations for estimating if an effect size is meaningful. Alternatively, one can decide the cutoff for level of effect size as part of step 2, setting the effect level and then comparing whether the observed effect size is larger than the criterion.

The purpose of performing the steps of hypothesis testing is to help understand why a phenomenon happened. The challenges with this method are that it requires careful design to get proper inference. Even in the era of big data, one often finds that the needed data has not been collected or is not available. For example, a company may wish to analyze if customers would respond to a discount offer. Given that the company has data about its customer's buying habits, they may do hypothesis testing based on this data. However, after proceeding with this analysis, they may find their inferences are incorrect because they didn't consider they only used data from existing customers. Data from potential customers was missing.

It can be very expensive and time-consuming to collect the data to perform these analyses properly. For this reason, many business decisions are made without formal hypothesis testing. However, for important decisions, it is critical to perform more formal hypothesis testing to increase the likelihood of making a better decision.

PREDICTIVE ANALYTICS

Predictive analytics go a step further than diagnostic analytics to answer the question "what is likely to happen in the future?" Successful predictive analytics can be transformative in an organization. Amazon.com uses customer purchasing and search patterns to predict (and then display) other products the customer might be interested in purchasing. Match.com uses sophisticated prediction algorithms that consider users' stated preferences and their browsing and searching activities in order to match each client with potentially successful future love interests. Boston Medical Center created Hospital IQ, an analytics solution that helps health-care centers predict demand patterns for health services—allowing health centers to improve staffing and health outcomes.

Predictive analytics use historical data to find patterns likely to manifest themselves in the future—the more data, the better chance of finding patterns. The dramatic increases in computing power and in available historical data allow computers to find relations that humans cannot. However, to be successful, predictive analytics require that future events are predictable based on past data and that the organization has collected the necessary data for prediction. To help understand predictive analytics better, consider the following steps:

1. Select the target outcome.
2. Find and prepare the appropriate data.
3. Create and validate a model.

The first step to creating a predictive analytic model is to decide what outcome is to be predicted. This outcome is called a target variable, an outcome variable, or a dependent variable. The target variable could be either a categorical value or a numeric value. **Categorical data** take on a limited number of assigned values to represent different groups while numeric values are continuous. A categorical value answers the question "which one?" A numeric value answers a question such as "how much?" For example, a prediction of whether men or women are more likely to purchase a product would be a categorical value (i.e., male/female), whereas a prediction of how much a customer is likely to spend would be a numeric value.

categorical data - Data items that take on a limited number of assigned values to represent different groups.

The second step is to find and prepare the appropriate data. This entails the ETL process discussed in Chapter 6. Predictive analytics perform better when they are developed with a variety of data about many potential causes of the outcome. Collecting data that may only be tangentially related to the outcome often can be valuable because data scientists are finding that such data can be predictive of outcomes.

The third step is the creation of the model. Variable selection is important in the creation of a model. For predictive analytics, models can be generated and tested with all possible combinations of input data. Models are evaluated according to their overall fit to the data and their ability to predict future outcomes. To test a model, the data should be split into a training dataset and a test dataset. The **training dataset** is used to create the model for future prediction, whereas the **test dataset** is used to assess how well the model predicts the target outcome. If one tests their model on the same data used to train it, there is a danger of **data overfitting**. Data overfitting occurs when a model fits training data very well but does not predict well when applied to other datasets. Thus, using separate training and test datasets is a valuable guard against overfitting.

training dataset - A subset of data used to train a model for future prediction.

test dataset - A subset of data not used for the development of a model but used to test how well the model predicts the target outcome.

data overfitting - When a model is designed to fit training data very well but does not predict well when applied to other datasets.

Once the training set is created, different models can be developed from the data. When the target outcome is a numeric value, use one of the many forms of a regression for prediction (e.g., multivariate linear regression, regression trees, and polynomial regression are a few possibilities). When the target outcome is a categorical value, use **classification analysis**. Classification analyses are various techniques that identify characteristics of groups (or populations) and then tries to use those characteristics to classify new observations into one of those groups. For example, predicting whether or not a customer will be a repeat customer would use classification analysis techniques. Popular predictive analytic classification techniques include logistic regression, random forests, decision trees, k-nearest neighbors, and support vector machines. Each of these techniques create a model from training data. Once a model has been created, it must be validated. Validation tests balance the accuracy of predicting the target outcome correctly with overfitting the data by examining the performance of the model on the test dataset. Once the model has been validated, it can be used in business decision making.

classification analyses - Techniques that identify various groups and then try to classify new observations into one of those groups.

Models rarely stay the same over time as the relationships between variables change. For example, think how much models predicting customer purchasing habits have changed because the Internet facilitates online shopping rather than going to a physical store. As the relationship between variables change, models need to be updated. This can be done by creating new models following the same process outlined above, or it can be automated using learning models such as machine learning.

Machine learning is an application of artificial intelligence that allows computer systems to improve and update prediction models on their own. That is, machine learning allows computers to learn and to improve over time without human intervention. Machine learning and predictive analytics are closely related as machine learning algorithms are often used in predictive analytics. For example, a regression model may be designed to predict customer credit ratings. The model continues to learn and adapt as it makes predictions, learns outcomes, and uses all of that data to improve the prediction model.

machine learning - An application of artificial intelligence that allows computer systems to improve and update prediction models without explicit programming.

PRESCRIPTIVE ANALYTICS

Prescriptive analytics answers the question "what should be done?" Prescriptive analytics can be either recommendations to take or programmed actions a system can take based on predictive analytics results. While only a small percentage of companies are using prescriptive analytics, many are working toward this goal.

As an example, consider United Parcel Services (UPS), which delivers more than 20 million packages and documents worldwide each day. The success of UPS is driven by how its drivers deliver packages. While managers initially designed routes based on their experience, the company decided to design a real-time prescriptive analytic solution. The program and subsequent updates optimize driver's delivery routes to save time, minimize driving distance, reduce emissions, increase safety, and ultimately boost the bottom line. UPS estimates that in one year, they eliminated 13,000 metric tons of carbon emissions and 206 million minutes of truck idling time (saving 1.5 million gallons of fuel), which added up to saving $300 million to $400 million in costs by replacing managerial intuitions with prescriptive models to design driver routes.

Prescriptive analytics use techniques such as artificial intelligence, machine learning, and other statistics to generate predictions. The key to being successful is the development of initial predictive models and then applying appropriate learning algorithms so those models continue to improve their recommendations over time. This is still an emerging area expected to grow and mature over the coming years.

COMMON PROBLEMS WITH DATA ANALYTICS

Proper data analysis can produce tremendous outcomes for organizations; however, there are concerns related to all analyses that must be carefully considered as they can render poor or even erroneous results.

The acronym GIGO stands for "garbage in, garbage out" and refers to the concept that data analysis is of no value if the underlying data is not of high quality. Analyses based on poor data are common when the data architecture is not properly designed, maintained, and documented.

Even if the data is of high quality, the modeling involved in creating an analytic can be problematic. As previously mentioned, data overfitting is producing an analysis that corresponds too exactly to a set of data such that when additional data is used with the model, it does not predict future observations reliably. Determining the correct model requires testing and evaluation using a test dataset.

Two other common problems are interrelated and both relate to the misuse of a well-designed model. **Extrapolation beyond the range** of data is a process of estimating a value that is beyond the data used to create the model. Assume you are predicting how the square footage of a home influences the sales price of the home. If all the data for creating a model is for homes from 2,000 square feet to 3,000 square feet, extrapolating beyond the range of data would be using this model to predict the price of a home with 7,000 square feet. Since the model was not created for homes this large, the model may not accurately predict prices for homes that large. Thus, it is important to use models created using data as similar as possible to what is being predicted. If this is violated, it can result in disastrous consequences like the failures described in Focus 7-1.

extrapolation beyond the range - A process of estimating a value beyond the range of the data used to create the model.

A related issue is failing to consider the variation inherent in a model. Variation refers to the spread of the data about a prediction. No model completely eliminates variation. Often, individuals will misuse data analyses to report a single number as a prediction and believe that the outcome will be that number. For example, in using data to predict the weather, a weatherperson might say the temperature will be 80 degrees tomorrow. However, the chance of the temperature being exactly 80 degrees is quite low because of the variation that remains in the model. It would be better for the weatherperson to predict that the temperature tomorrow is likely in a specified range and provide their confidence level—for example, the weatherperson could report that she is 95% confident the temperature will be between 75 degrees and 85 degrees. This means that 95 times out of 100, the temperature will fall between those two amounts.

Variation and extrapolation go together because as one extrapolates a greater distance from the data values used to create the model and the point of prediction, the variation increases. Thus, predicting outcomes from new data outside of the range of data on which the prediction model was built will result in a greater likelihood of prediction error. Being aware of these concerns with data analytics can help you avoid making mistakes with data analyses.

FOCUS 7-1 Dangers from the Misuse of Data Analytics

On January 28, 1986, the Space Shuttle Challenger exploded 73 seconds into flight, killing all seven passengers on board. The explosion was caused by a failure of the O-rings surrounding the gas used to propel the shuttle. Before the crash, NASA knew that O-ring failures were a possibility and had tested to see how robust the O-rings were to different launch time temperatures. The problem is that most of the testing was done at temperatures ranging from about 50 to 80 degrees Fahrenheit, whereas the temperature the morning of the launch was 28 degrees Fahrenheit. Mission control did not fully appreciate the large variance surrounding possible failures of the O-rings at the low temperature. The failure to extrapolate correctly, in this case, caused seven people to lose their lives.

On March 11, 2011, Japan was rocked by a 6.6 magnitude earthquake. The earthquake damaged the Fukushima Daiichi nuclear reactor causing three nuclear meltdowns that released radioactive materials into the environment. Although the designers of the nuclear power plant designed the plant to withstand an earthquake and tsunami, they did not design it to withstand an earthquake and tsunami of the magnitude experienced in 2011. Some analysts believe the plant was not correctly designed because engineers overfit data predicting the likelihood of the magnitude of earthquake in that part of Japan. The overfitting of the data resulted in a prediction of a lower magnitude earthquake and thus the plant was not built to high enough standards.

These examples clearly illustrate the importance of proper data analysis.

Data Presentation

The common expression, "a picture is worth a thousand words" accurately conveys what researchers have found about the human brain being programmed to process visual information better than written information. Indeed, researchers have identified several benefits of visualizing data relative to reading, including:

- Visualized data is processed faster than written or tabular information.
- Visualizations are easier to use. Users need less guidance to find information with visualized data.
- Visualization supports the dominant learning style of the population because most learners are visual learners.

Consider the benefits of data visualization from the experiences of a direct sales company. The company invested heavily in analytics to create models that predicted in which neighborhoods potential customers were most likely to purchase the company's products. However, the analysis did not help salespeople until the company realized they had to use a better medium than sending a long report to the salespeople. The company simplified the data presentation by providing each salesperson with a map that had a colored layer showing the likelihood of finding new customers in different areas. Armed with this visualization, the salespeople were more motivated and immediately able to see where to focus their work to yield the highest returns.

To be helpful, data needs to be presented using the right visualization, and the visualization needs to be designed correctly. The next sections consider these two vital choices.

CHOOSING THE RIGHT VISUALIZATION

Different visualizations are designed to convey different messages. Choosing the right type of visualization strengthens the ability of the viz to communicate effectively. Data can be presented in many different forms, including static graphics, tables, videos, static and dynamic models, etc. This chapter focuses on static graphics because they are the most prevalent type of visualization in business and the only ones that can be used in print.

In deciding which type of visualization to use, this section highlights the five main purposes for visualizing data in business and then discusses which type of visualization graphic is most commonly used for each purpose. The five main purposes for visualization are: comparison, correlation, distribution, trend evaluation, and part-to-whole. Figure 7-2 provides a thumbnail example of the types of charts used for each category.

COMPARISON Comparing data across categories or groups represents the most common reason to create a visualization in business. Comparison visualizations require both numeric and categorical data values. As shown in Figure 7-2, the most common type of visualization used in making comparisons is a bar chart (also called a bar graph, bar plot, or, if rotated, a column chart or rotated bar chart). A bar chart puts the categorical data variable on the x-axis (or on the y-axis if the chart is rotated) and then plots the numerical value on the other axis.

A variation of the bar chart that is also useful for comparison is the bullet graph. The bullet graph adds a "bullet" or a small line by each bar that indicates an important benchmark. Benchmarks include things like budgeted amounts, goals, expected progress, etc. Using the bullet allows the graph to present more information, usually of secondary importance, without adding an extra bar or other clutter. Examples of charts related to the comparison principle that can be computed from the S&S data include:

- A bar chart comparing pay differences between men and women.
- A bar chart that shows a comparison of job satisfaction and performance by college degree.
- A bullet chart that compares current year performance ratings for each employee to their previous year's performance ratings (using a bullet to show prior year performance).

CORRELATION Another common visualization is comparing how two numeric variables fluctuate with each. As shown in Figure 7-2, the most common correlation viz is a scatterplot,

FIGURE 7-2
Visualization Purposes and Types

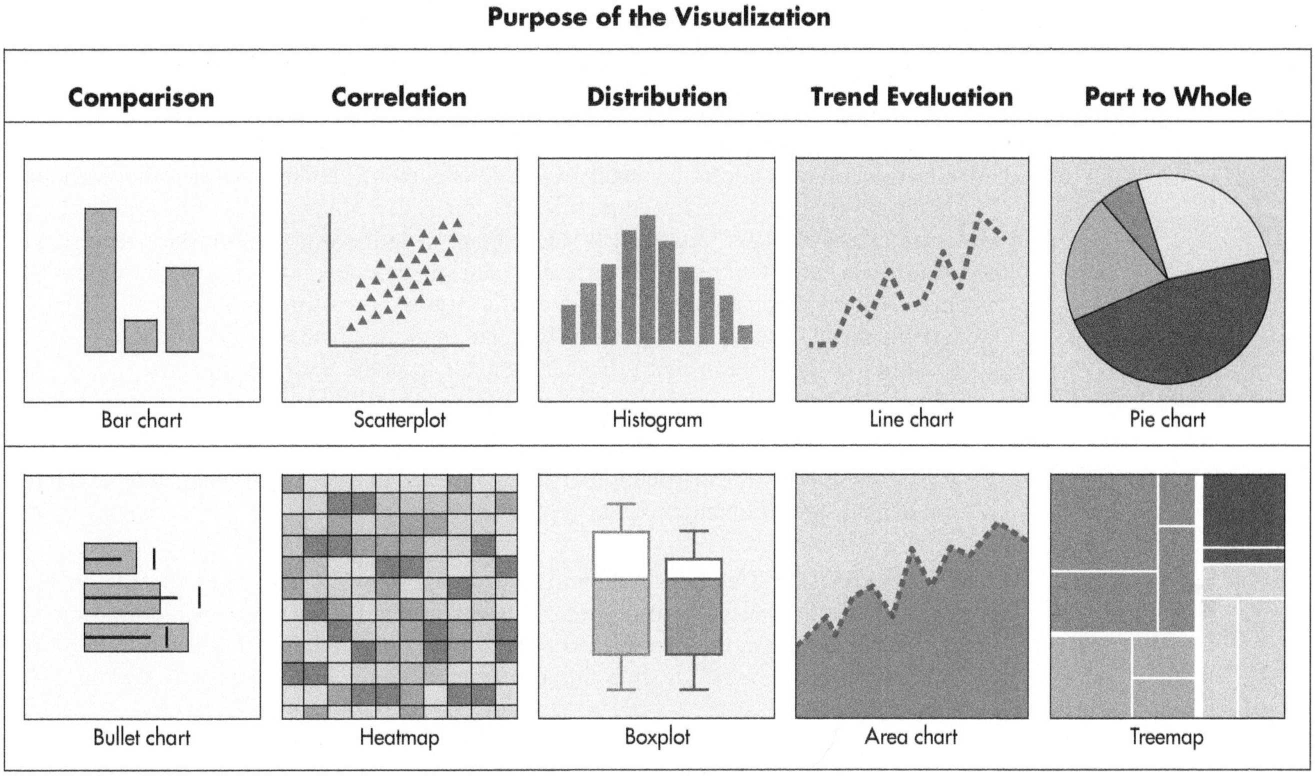

where a numeric variable is listed on the x-axis, a different numeric variable is listed on the y-axis, and the values of each are plotted in the data area. Often, a regression line and a regression equation are superimposed on a viz to show the overall statistical relation between the two variables.

The second most frequent correlation visualization is a heatmap. A heatmap looks like a data table, but instead of showing data values it shows colors that relate to the magnitude of the different entries. Heat maps allow a representation of correlation between a numeric and non-numeric field if the non-numeric field can be ordered in a meaningful way. In the S&S dataset, a heatmap might be used to display the relation between income and college education where the college education categories are ordered from the least amount of education to the most amount of education. Other examples of charts related to the correlation principle that can be made from the S&S data include:

- A scatterplot showing the relation between job performance and income.
- A scatterplot showing the relation between job satisfaction and job performance.
- A heatmap that shows the relation between training and job performance. In this case, you might use a heatmap instead of a scatterplot if you think the relationship is not linear but rather depends on "levels" of training; for example, creating groups for every 10 hours of completed training.

DISTRIBUTION Distribution visualizations show the spread of numeric data values. Showing distribution can help develop a deeper understanding of data than by just examining simple descriptive statistics like the minimum, maximum, and average. For example, two stocks may have the same average return on investment of 10% over the last 6 years. However, knowing that one stock returned a negative 10% return for 3 of those years and a positive 30% return for the other 3 years versus the other stock that returned 10% every year is important information if an investor wants to invest his or her money for just 1 year. Although distribution information can be presented numerically in various statistical terms such as variance and skewness, most people find it easier to grasp when it is displayed visually.

The two most common distribution visualizations are histograms and boxplots (also called box-and-whisker plots). For a histogram, a single numeric value is divided into equal-sized bins, and the bin sizes are listed on the x-axis. Then, a bar is used to show the count of each value that falls into the bins.

A boxplot draws a line at the median value for a numeric variable and then shows another line for the upper quartile and lower quartile (the connection of these lines forms the box). The box usually has "whiskers" attached. It is important to define what the whiskers represent in the viz because they often represent different values in practice, including the minimum and maximum, a certain percentile of the response, a standard deviation, or some multiple of the interquartile range—which is the distance from the first quartile to the third quartile.

Examples of distribution charts that can be made from the S&S data include:

- A histogram showing salary by bins of $10,000.
- A boxplot showing the distribution of employee performance ratings.
- A boxplot showing the distribution of salary for each of three departments (the boxplot would have three different boxplots represented).

TREND EVALUATION Trend evaluation visualizations show changes over an ordered variable, most often a measurement of time. The difference between visualizations showing trends and correlation is that the axis in a trend viz is ordered. The line chart is the most typical viz used to show trends. In a line chart, the x-axis is an ordered unit such as days, months, or years.

A second chart type used to show trends is the area chart. An area chart is the same as a line chart except the area between the line(s) and the x-axis is filled in. Compared to line charts, area charts help focus on a trend rather than individual values, and so area charts are useful when trying to show a progression over time. Examples from the S&S data related to the evaluate trends purpose include:

- A line chart showing how compensation has changed each year for each employee.
- An area chart showing how total compensation for each year differs by department.

PART-TO-WHOLE Part-to-whole visualizations, such as pie charts, show which items make up the parts of a total. Be careful with pie charts—they are the most overused and misused visualization type in practice. Pie charts are often misused to communicate comparisons or trends where bar chart or line graphs are better charts. Pie charts are most appropriate when showing percentages that sum up to 100% and the data only has a few categories.

Treemaps use nested rectangles to show the amount that each group or category contributes. Examples from the S&S data related to the part-to-whole purpose include:

- A pie chart showing the percentage of total employee pay for each department.
- A treemap showing how different academic degrees make up the total amount of pay.

OTHER VISUALIZATION PURPOSES There are visualization types and purposes other than the five most common discussed above. Examples include spatial data such as maps with data overlays and network diagrams or Sankey diagrams that show the flow of data. Visualization types can also be combined to fulfill multiple purposes. For example, combo charts that show both bars and lines can be useful for communicating comparison and trends. Sometimes, the most appropriate data visualization medium is to present numbers in a table (e.g., a spreadsheet). A few examples of when tables are more appropriate than charts is when listing precise numbers is important, looking up individual values is important, and showing both detailed and summary data. Designers must consider the purpose of the visualization and then choose or even create a visualization that fulfills that purpose. When using more complex visualization types, it is especially important to consider the design principles presented next.

DESIGNING HIGH-QUALITY VISUALIZATIONS

High-quality visualizations follow three important design principles: simplification, emphasis, and ethical presentation. **Simplification** refers to making a visualization easy to interpret and understand. **Emphasis** in design is assuring the most important message is easily identifiable. **Ethical data presentation** refers to avoiding the intentional or unintentional use of deceptive practices that can alter the user's understanding of the data being presented.

simplification - In design, making a visualization easy to interpret and understand.

emphasis - In design, assuring the most important message is easily identifiable.

ethical data presentation - Avoiding the intentional or unintentional use of deceptive practices that can alter the user's understanding of the data being presented.

Within each of these different design principles are different techniques and options to improve the ability of the viz to communicate effectively. The principles and techniques can be applied to the four main parts of a viz: the title, axes (including labels, tick marks, and lines), legend, and data area. The data area in a visualization is the area where the lines/bar/slices/etc. are displayed. Simplification, emphasis, and ethical presentation can enhance the ability of each of these parts of a viz to individually and in combination effectively communicate a message.

PRINCIPLE: SIMPLIFICATION Visualizations are more effective when they simplify the presentation of data to clearly and concisely communicate the objective of the visualization. Standard visualization tools often include far more information than is necessary, so care is needed to "prune back" the visualization. As an example, see Figure 7-3, which contains a visualization with far too much information in each of the four areas of the viz.

FIGURE 7-3

Example of an Overly Complicated Visualization

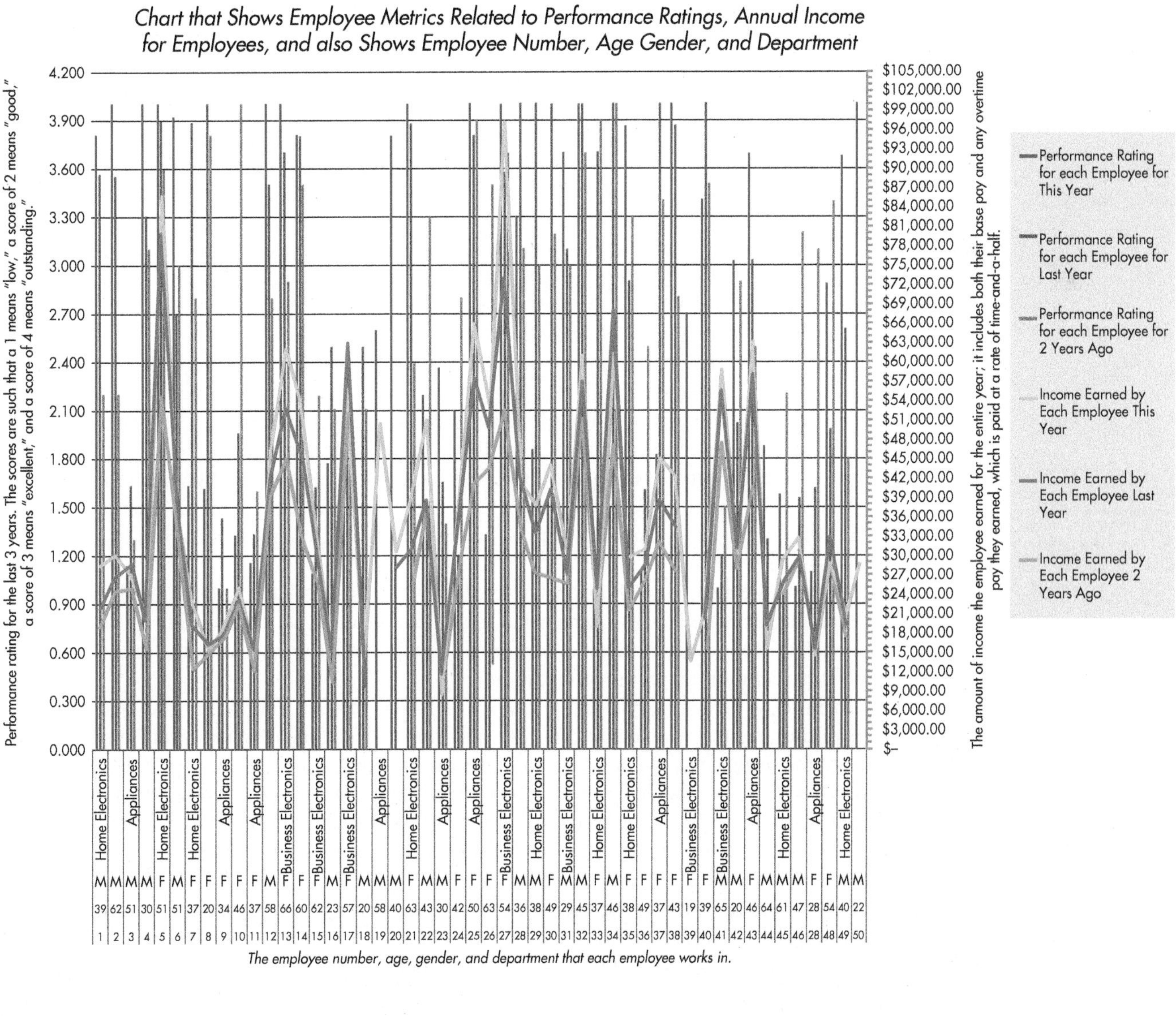

Figure 7-3 shows a poor visualization that is overly complicated in several ways. The descriptions in the title and labels are too long. Too much information is crammed into the data area. The axes are difficult to interpret and provide too much information. The legend contains too much writing and is not placed near the data.

A visualization can be simplified by considering three important techniques that will enhance the design of all visualizations: quantity, distance, and orientation.

Quantity. Visualizations are most impactful when they follow the Goldilocks principle of containing not too much and not too little, but just the right amount of data. When examining the quantity of information, examine each of the separate elements of a viz and then consider how the elements work together.

For the areas that contain text, such as the titles, labels, and legend, a poorly designed viz typically contains too little information in the title and too much information in labels and the legend. Titles serve as an important way to orient readers. The title in Figure 7-3 is too long. Labeling it something like "Employee Metrics" is too short and could relate to virtually anything. A title such as "HR Metrics for Employee Performance and Income over the Last 3 Years" allows a user to fully understand the data depicted. In contrast, the labels and legend in Figure 7-3 are too long and contain unnecessary information. A change on the left axis to "Performance Rating from 1 (low) to 5 (high)" is succinct but provides sufficient information to interpret the data.

The axes contain too much data. The performance rating axis (on the left of the viz) ranges from 1 to 5 and yet the axis increments in 0.3 steps and only goes up to 4.2. In addition, each number lists 3 decimal places, which is too much detail relative to the data presented. Similarly, the income axis (on the right of the viz) is too finely measured and includes too many decimal places. Both axes could be simplified using less wordy information. The x-axis could be improved by deciding which, if any, of the data related to age, employee number, and department are necessary.

In addition to the wordiness of the viz, it also suffers from information overload. It is simply trying to present too much information. There are too many lines, bars, and colors in the data area. One way to overcome the problem of overcrowding information is to put information in multiple vizs. For example, Figure 7-3 could be divided into a separate viz for performance and another for income. Alternatively, if it is important to consider income and performance together, the viz could be simplified by how many years of information are presented or by not presenting the information for all employees. Reducing the quantity of information displayed in the data section will improve the ability of users to interpret the viz and more clearly communicate a message.

A viz can also use too many formats. In Figure 7-3, the lines marking the different units in the background are too complicated and "busy." Similarly, the different coloring of the legend and the apparently random use of different types of fonts, bolding, and italics all create a complicated, hard-to-understand viz. Additional features not present in Figure 7-3 that should be avoided are the unnecessary use of 3-D designs, colors that have no meaning (e.g., making each bar a different color for each employee), and using too many colors. A general rule of thumb is to use no more than 3–5 groups, and associated different colors, lines, or bars.

Distance. The technique of distance refers to how far apart related information is presented. For example, in Figure 7-3, to learn what the colors mean in the data section of the viz, you must refer to the legend, which requires moving your eyes from the data area of the viz. This makes it harder to interpret the information.

To improve distance, consider Figure 7-4. In the top viz, the y-axis shows how many hours of training are completed, and colors are defined in a legend to the right. The lower viz removes the distance in the numbers for each bar by using a label at the top of each bar. The lower viz also moves the department labels directly over each relevant color rather than using a legend. Notice how in the lower viz it is much faster to understand the differences in training hours in the different departments because the information is presented closer together. Removing distance aids in understanding.

A side benefit of removing distance is that often you remove other unnecessary information. In Figure 7-4, removing distance also removed the axis label, and the label in the legend allows the viz to be spread out using the same amount of space.

FIGURE 7-4
Example of Simplifying a Visualization Using Distance

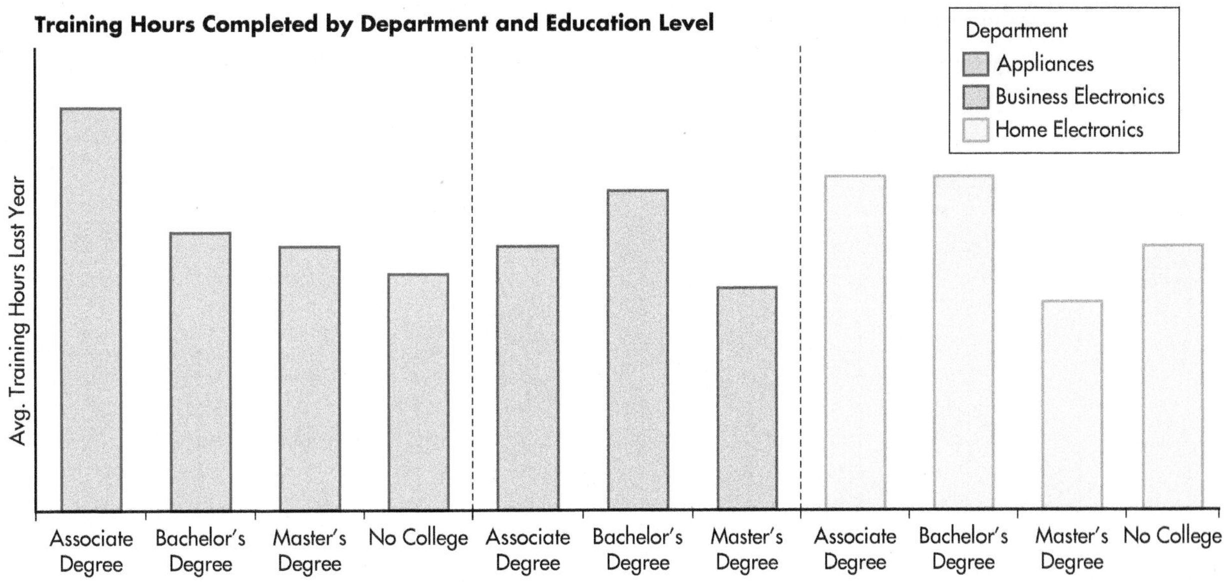

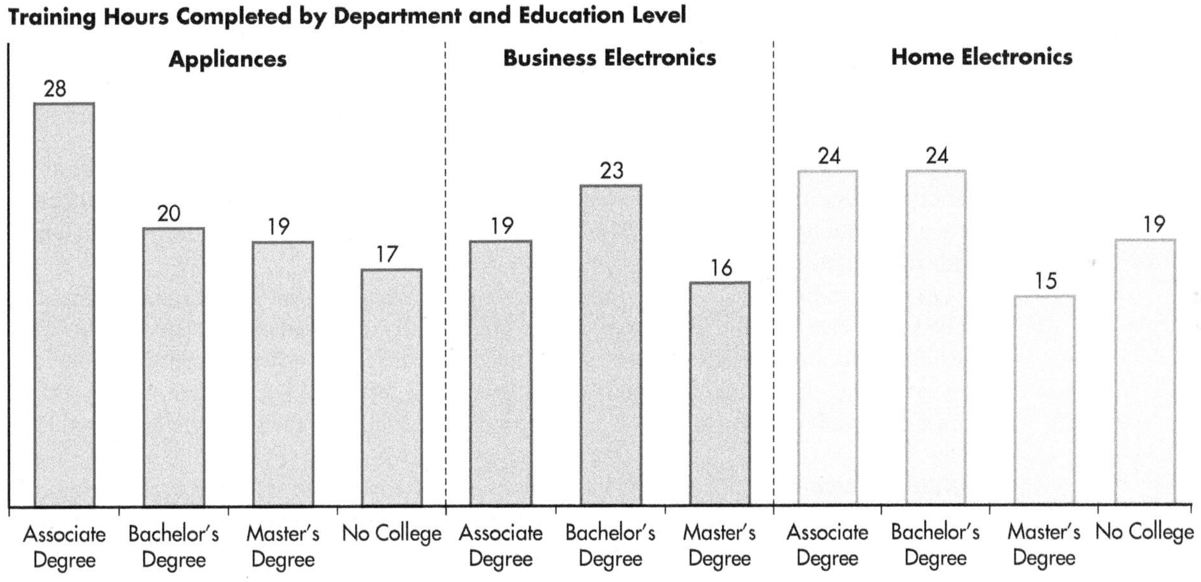

A second use of distance to simplify a visualization is the distance between relevant comparison groups. In Figure 7-4, the data is designed so that is easier to compare the number of training hours across degree within a department because all of the degree information is grouped together. If the purpose of the viz is rather to focus on comparisons across departments for each education level, it would make more sense to group the results by degree, as shown in Figure 7-5. In Figure 7-5, it is much easier to make comparisons across departments within an education level because the information is presented close together.

Orientation. Data is easier to understand if it is oriented in the correct fashion. If you return to Figure 7-3, notice how on the x-axis the department information is written in a vertical fashion. This requires someone to turn their head to read the information easily. It is easier to read text if the text is rotated to appear in a horizontal fashion.

FIGURE 7-5
Example of Grouping Data Differently to Reduce Distance

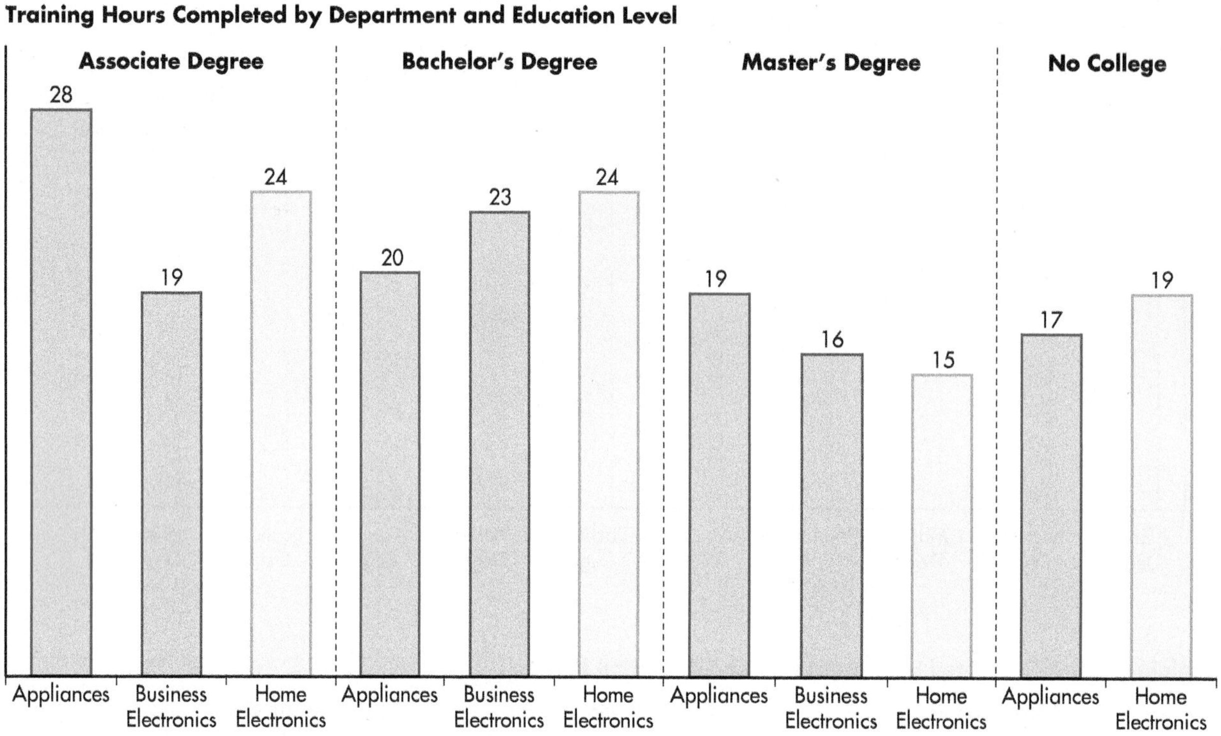

One way to improve orientation is to change the direction of an entire chart. Bar charts are most often printed with the bars in a vertical format. However, the same chart can be turned so that the bars are presented in a horizontal fashion and make it much easier to read the labels, as shown in Figure 7-6.

Orientation also applies to how the data is sorted. When presenting data, the information can be sorted based on the labels, typically alphabetically, or based on the values of the data, typically in ascending or descending order. The choice of sorting order or sorting attribute can simplify finding the correct information and processing what the information means relative to other groups. It can also serve as a tool to emphasize, which is the principle discussed next.

PRINCIPLE: EMPHASIS Most visualizations are created to help decision makers improve their decision-making quality. Thus, high-quality vizs should emphasize the data that is most relevant, important, or timely, for the decision maker. Understanding what to emphasize depends on the objective of the situation. It also means that the data analyst needs to understand the decision context—not just data analytics techniques.

Once an objective has been decided, three different techniques can be used to more effectively emphasize data: highlighting, weighting, and ordering.

Highlighting. The technique of highlighting includes using colors, contrasts, call-outs, labeling, fonts, arrows, and any other technique that brings attention to an item. While highlighting can be applied to all areas of a viz, most often highlighting is applied to the data area of the viz.

Colors are a particularly valuable highlighting tool. Figure 7-7 shows three different ways to color information about departments. The left panel uses highlighting to call attention to the home electronics department. With this color highlighting, it is very easy for the user to quickly locate the information for home electronics. If the purpose is to draw attention to the home electronic department relative to the other departments, this color highlighting scheme is the most effective. The middle panel with all grey highlighting does not help the user understand what is important. The user must interpret the data and may not pay attention to the message the viz is trying to communicate. The right panel highlights each different department. This coloring

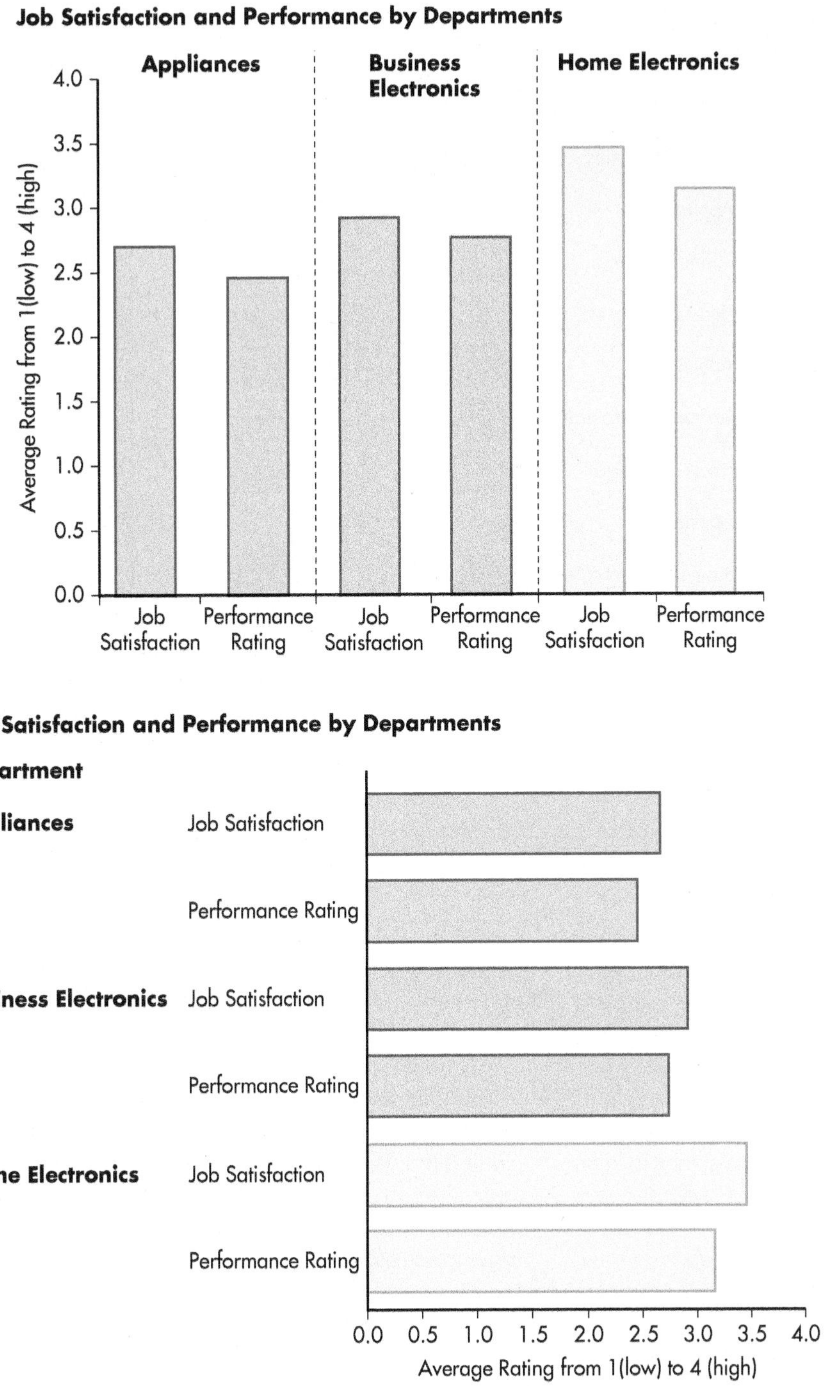

FIGURE 7-6
Example of Improving Orientation to Simplify a Viz

scheme aids in highlighting departments, but it is not helpful to call attention to any details. If understanding different departments is not important, then removing the department coloring can simplify the visualization. As seen in this viz, depending on the purpose of the visualization, different color schemes can help highlight, and thus emphasize, what is most important.

When visualizations do not use different colors, using different shading as a contrast is highly effective. In the visualization in Figure 7-7, the orange color in the first panel could be replaced with black or a different texture and it would serve the same highlighting role. When using colors and contrasts, be aware of the meanings of colors and common problems that can occur when using colors, as explained in Focus 7-2.

Other ways to highlight information are to use labels, arrows, and graphics. When deciding on what to highlight, remember the principle of simplification and do not use so many highlights that the viz becomes cluttered.

FIGURE 7-7
Use of Color to Improve Highlighting

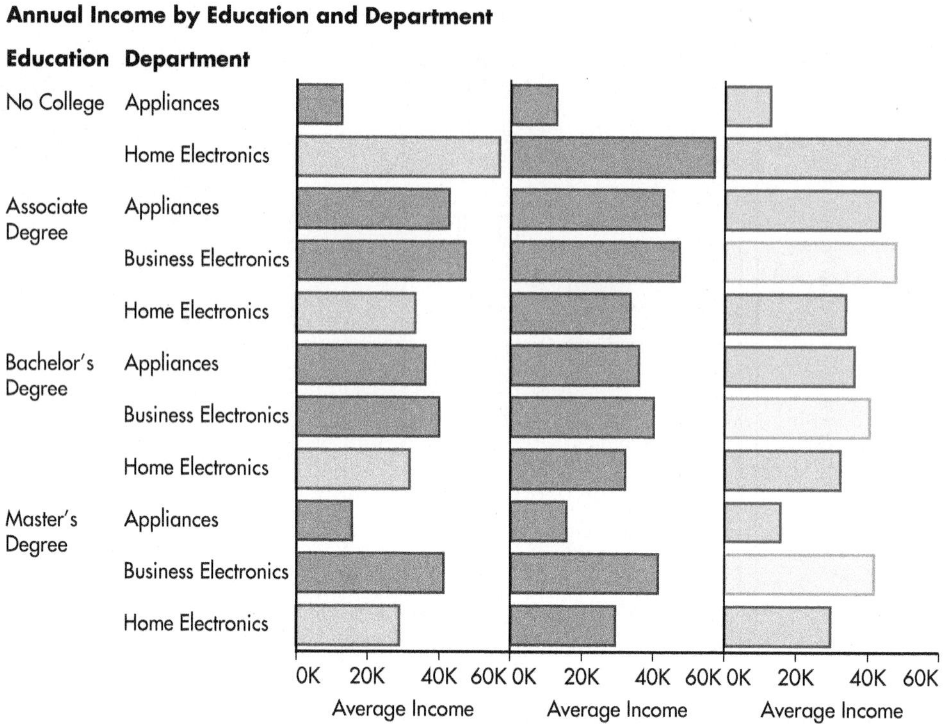

FOCUS 7-2 The Power of Color

Color is a very powerful tool that can be used to emphasize and simplify a visualization. For example, using the same colors across visualizations, especially on a dashboard, can simplify the dashboard. Using the color grey typically says that this data item is less important, so using other colors with grey can easily emphasize what is important.

Although color is useful, there are several things to keep in mind when dealing with color. Within a culture, colors often have natural meanings—for example, in Western culture, green means go and red means stop and blue often represents male and pink represents female. If colors are used contrary to their natural meaning, people may misunderstand the viz. Be aware that natural meanings can differ across cultures. For example, in the United States, stock price increases are shown in green and decreases in red. In China, it is the opposite—red means increases and green means decreases in value. Also note that in western culture, yellow signifies happiness, warmth, and joy. In contrast, in Chinese culture, yellow is associated with vulgarity. So using yellow for a viz in China to depict something pure or holy would be at odds with how the culture uses the color.

Be sensitive in using colors. Choose contrasting colors that will be easily recognized by someone who is color blind. Particularly challenging for the color blind are green/red, green/brown, and blue/purple combinations. It is better to use monochrome, patterns, or color-blind sensitive color pallettes.

Colors can be represented as gradients (e.g., various shades of blue) or as distinct colors (e.g., blue, red, green). Gradients are typically used to indicate progressions from low to high, whereas distinct colors represent categories. Thus, to represent various levels of income, use a color gradient; to indicate differences in categories (e.g., different store locations), use distinct colors.

visual weight - In design, the amount of attention an element attracts.

Weighting. **Visual weight** refers to the amount of attention an element attracts. There are various techniques to increase visual weight, including color, complexity, contrast, density, and size. Figure 7-8 shows examples of each of these techniques and discusses how each technique can be used to increase or decrease visual weight. These techniques can be used in combination to create even greater emphasis than using them separately. As with highlighting, be careful that the use of visual weighting to create emphasis does not create an overly complex visualization that reduces simplicity.

Technique	Increases Visual Heaviness	Decreases Visual Heaviness
Color: The color properties of saturation and darkness/lightness can be used to increase visual weight. More saturated and darker colors are heavier. Also, the heaviest to lightest colors are red, blue, green, orange, and yellow.		
Contrast: The greater the contrast in shades or colors of an object relative to its background the heavier the visual object will appear.	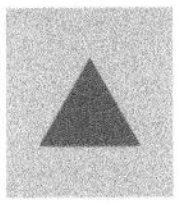	
Complexity: As objects have more shapes or patterns they are perceived as heavier.	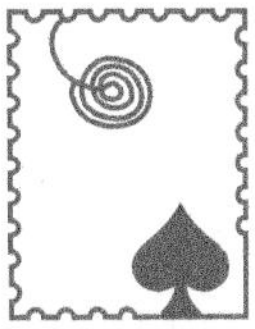	
Density: Objects that are presented closer together are heavier than objects that are dispersed.		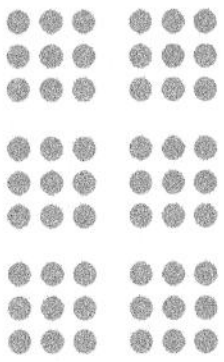
Size: The larger the size of an object, the greater its visual weight.		

FIGURE 7-8
Depictions of Techniques to Increase Visual Weight

Ordering. **Data ordering** is the intentional arranging of visualization items to produce emphasis. The two most common ways of ordering data are (1) by using categories on the axes and (2) by the values of the data. These methods are almost always superior to just ordering the data in a random form.

data ordering - The intentional arranging of visualization items in a way to produce emphasis.

Figure 7-9 presents three bar graphs for the income of employees in the business electronics division using each of the standard ordering techniques. Notice how ordering the data by the data element of salary emphasizes the top and the bottom positions; that is, who is making the most and the least income. In contrast, the alphabetical ordering makes it easier to locate a name—which can be valuable to simplify a visualization in some contexts. The random ordering does not help to simplify or emphasize the data and should therefore be avoided.

Data ordering can be combined with other techniques to enhance emphasis. For example, using coloring or size changes with ordering can produce greater emphasis. In Figure 7-9, adding a contrasting color to one of the employees would help emphasize that employee's income relative to all other employees.

PRINCIPLES: ETHICAL DATA PRESENTATION The final visualization presentation principle is to be ethical. As defined by the School of Law at New York University, **data deception** is "a graphical depiction of information, designed with or without an intent to deceive, that may create a belief about the message and/or its components, which varies from the actual message." To avoid data deception, consider the following principles:

data deception - A graphical depiction of information, designed with or without an intent to deceive, that may create a belief about the message and/or its components, which varies from the actual message.

1. Show representations of numbers proportional to the reported number (starting the y-axis at zero helps ensure this).
2. In vizs designed to depict trends, show time progressing from left to right on the x-axis.
3. Present complete data given the context.

FIGURE 7-9
Use of Ordering to Emphasize Data

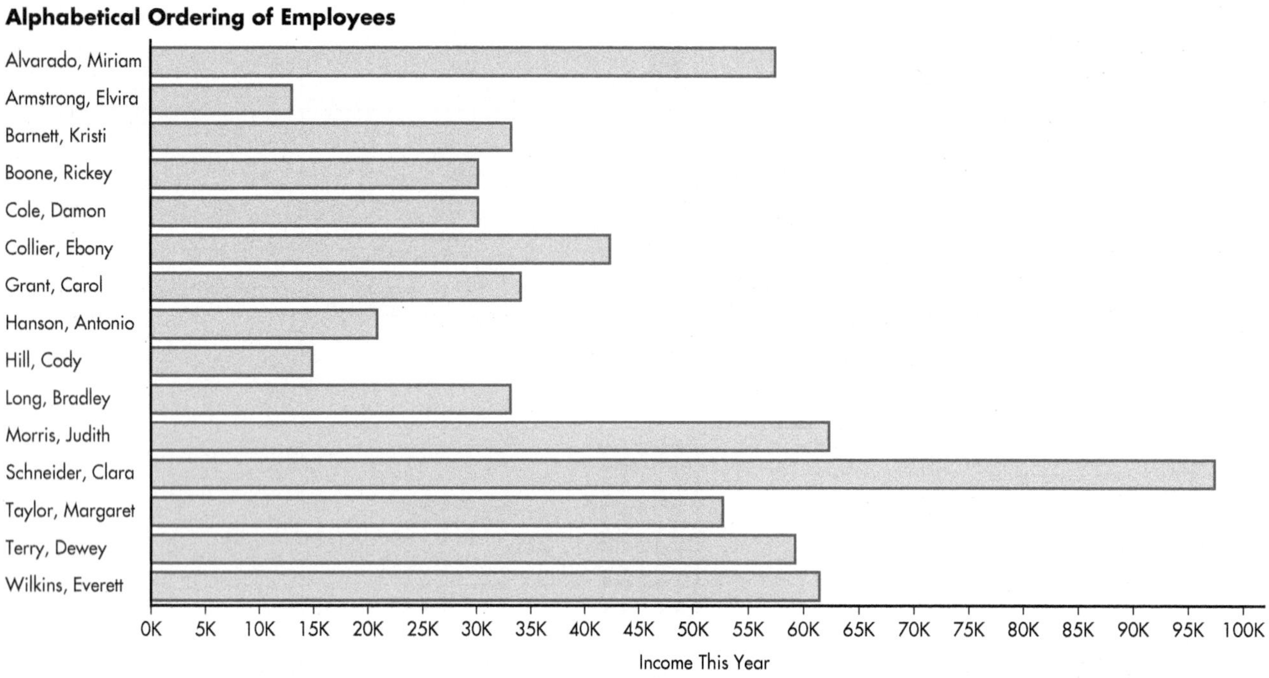

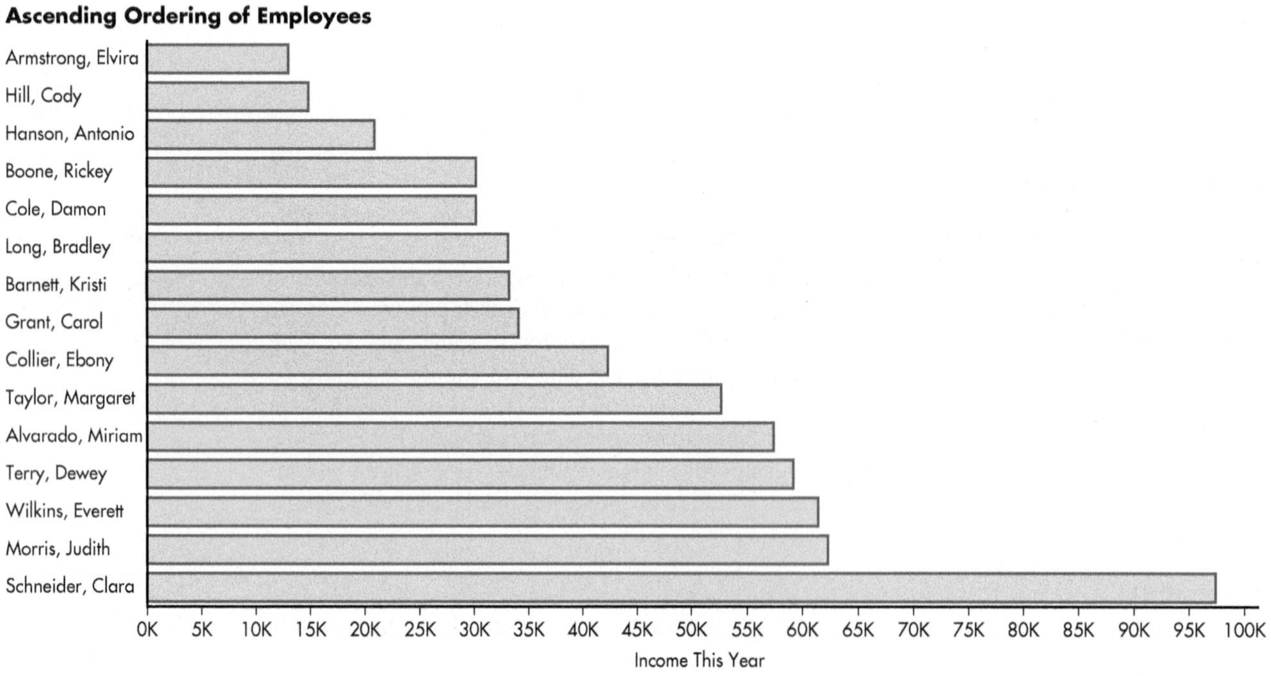

FIGURE 7-9 (Continued)
Use of Ordering to Emphasize Data

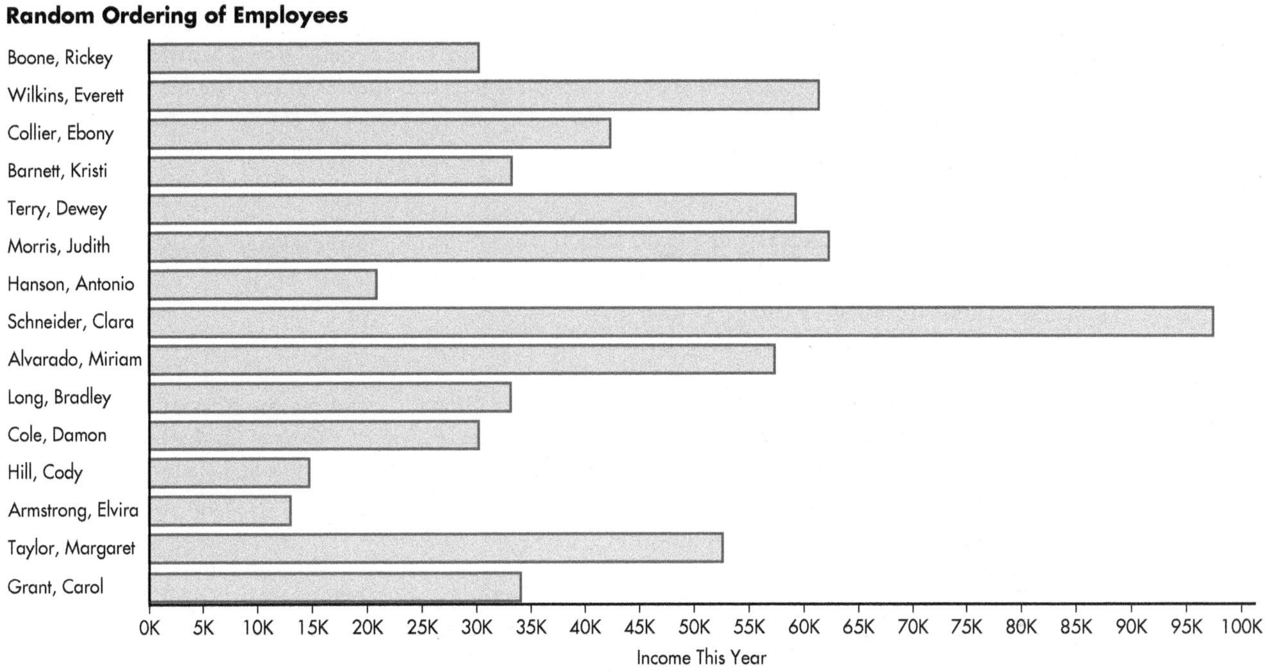

The viz on the left of Figure 7-10 shows a common violation of the first ethical principle. At first glance, it appears that Jason Young is twice as satisfied with his job as Annette Weaver. However, the labels (which are often omitted when being unethical with data presentation) show that Jason is only 0.1 points higher than Annette. The problem is a truncated y-axis that makes the difference look a lot larger than it really is. When the y-axis starts at zero, as is the

FIGURE 7-10
Example of Non-proportional Display of Data

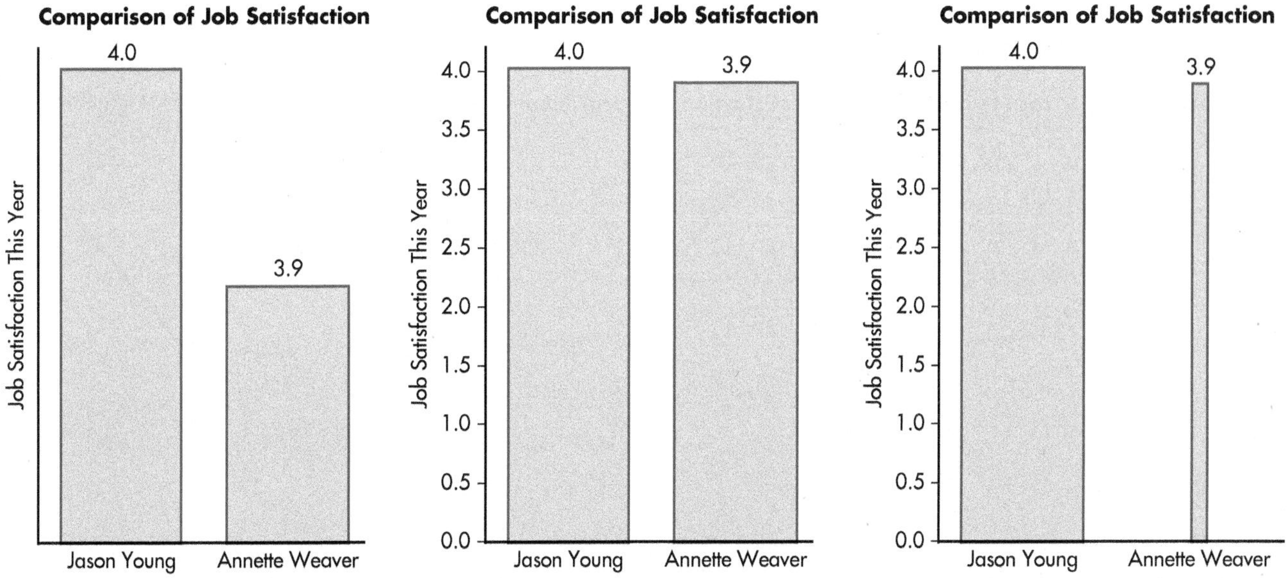

case in the center of Figure 7-10, the difference between Jason and Annette is more correctly displayed as a very small difference. Axes should almost always start at zero to avoid visual distortion in differences. Note that many software packages can create misleading graphics if the default choices are used.

Other ways to visually distort information are to use visual weight inappropriately. For example, in a bar chart if one of the bars is displayed as much thicker than the other, it makes the thicker bar appear to be much more important because of increased visual weight—as is the case in the viz on the right of Figure 7-10. If the size of the bar is supposed to convey meaning, using different sizes will distort the interpretation. Bar widths, or anything else used to represent a bar such as a logo, should be of the same width.

The viz on the left of Figure 7-11 shows a violation of the second ethical principle. The viz appears to show Lucas Median becoming less satisfied with his job over time. This is incorrect for two reasons. As seen in the center of Figure 7-11, the axis is clearly labeled with the most recent time on the left and gets older as it moves to the right. Nonetheless, many would argue that even the viz in the center still violates ethical principles. The problem with this viz is that most people expect time to be shown so that the progression is from oldest on the left to most recent on the right. Reverse scaling of the axes confuses the user. The viz on the right of Figure 7-11 presents time ordered as expected and thereby reduces any misunderstanding.

To illustrate a violation of the third ethical principle, consider the closing price of the Dow Jones Industrial Average for a one-year time period, as show in Figure 7-12. The chart is simplified by truncating the y-axis and removing all labels. Below the full year chart are three separate "cuts" of the data. Each of these cuts suggest a very different pattern for the market—it's doing great, doing horrible, or not doing much at all. The different presentation of the data can have significant impact on attitudes related to economics or politics; yet, each is incomplete and does not present "the entire story." Ethical design requires the presentation of the complete story so that the user can make their own inferences about the data.

Ethical data presentation is closely related to the attributes of high-quality data studied in Chapter 1 and Chapter 6. That is, ethical data presentation shows complete, accurate, consistent, timely, and valid data. As you design data visualizations, make sure to be ethical in your presentation choices.

FIGURE 7-11
Example of Visualization Poor Labeling

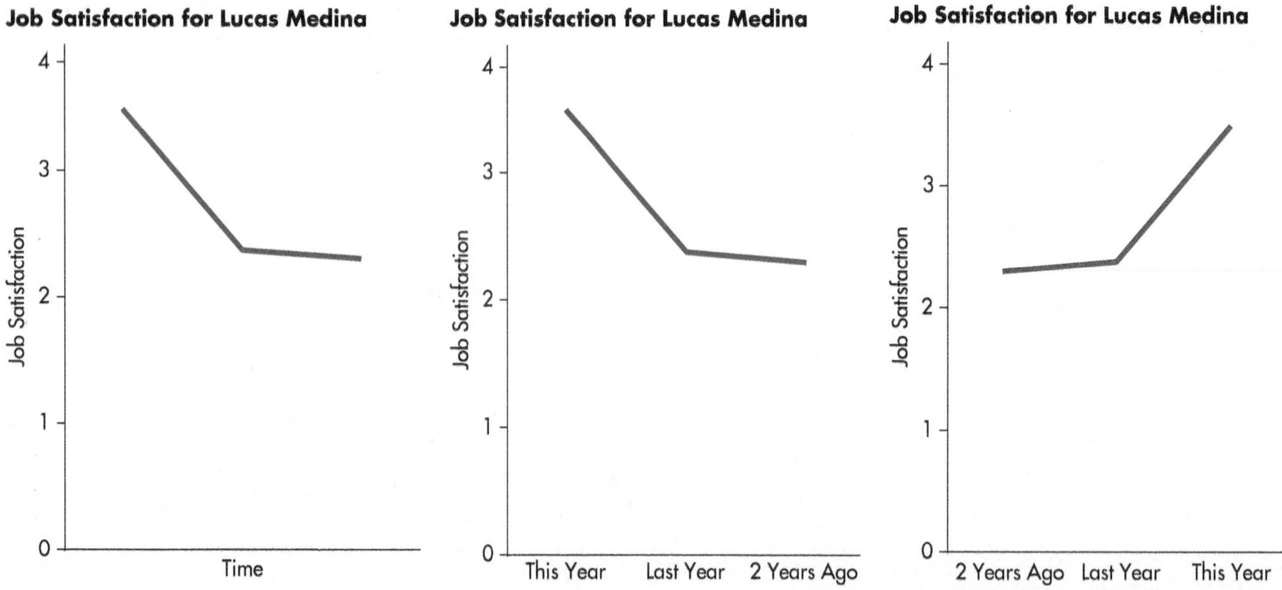

FIGURE 7-12
Example of Incomplete Visualization Presentation

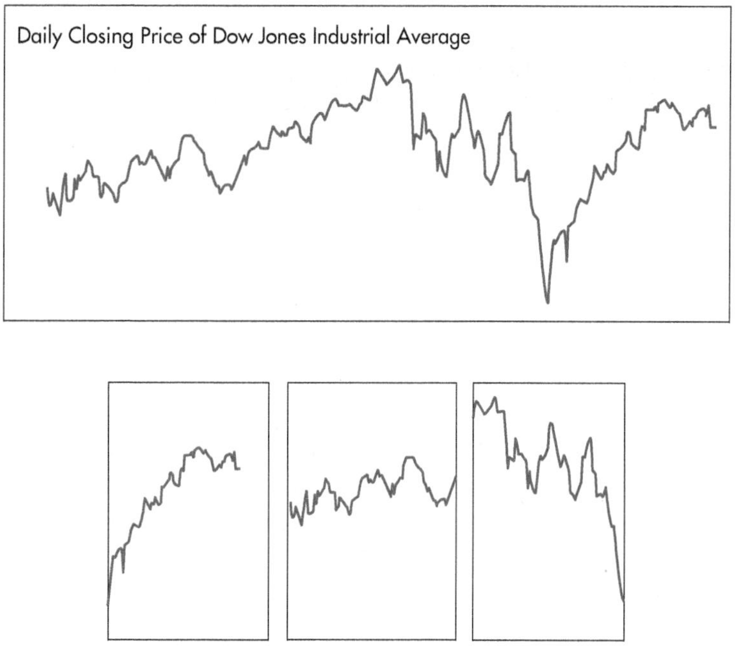

Summary and Case Conclusion

Ashton and his team carefully reviewed the data at S&S and designed a dynamic presentation. The presentation integrated descriptive, diagnostic, and predictive statistics. Furthermore, in automating the creation of the data analyses, Ashton designed predictive and prescriptive analytics into a forward-looking management tool. Specifically, the computer system simulated likely future business outcomes and produced a report of how the company will likely perform over the next 6 months, 1 year, and 5 years on key investing ratios. The system also produced recommendations of changes the company could make to improve each of the investing ratios.

Ashton and his team carefully scrutinized each report and designed them to be simple and to emphasize why S&S would make a great investment. The analyses were instrumental in S&S having a very successful initial public stock offering (IPO). With the additional capital and the new data analysis tools, S&S is primed for continued success.

KEY TERMS

exploratory data analysis 190
outlier 190
visualization 191
confirmatory data analysis 191
null hypothesis 192
alternative hypothesis 192
type I error 192
type II error 192
effect size 192
categorical data 193
training dataset 193
test dataset 193
data overfitting 193
classification analyses 194
machine learning 194
extrapolation beyond the range 195
simplification 199
emphasis 199
ethical data presentation 199
visual weight 204
data ordering 205
data deception 205

AIS in Action

CHAPTER QUIZ

1. A company wants to determine how to decrease employee turnover. In order to do this, they test whether paying off an employee's student debt will cause fewer employees to leave. The analytic test of whether paying off an employee's student debt causes lower turnover is an example of which type of analytic?
   a. descriptive
   b. diagnostic
   c. predictive
   d. prescriptive

2. You co-own a theme park. You believe that the longer customers stay in the park, the hungrier they will be which would increase the amount they spend on food. Your co-owner believes that the longer customers stay in the park, the more likely they are to feel nauseated which would decrease the amount they spend on food. Both of you gather data and find analytic evidence supporting your belief. If the true relation is that there is no relation between time in the park and food sales, what type of error did your co-owner make?
   a. type I error
   b. type II error
   c. GIGO error
   d. data overfitting error

3. A data analyst develops a classification model to predict whether a customer will be unsatisfied, neither satisfied nor unsatisfied, or satisfied with their online purchasing experience. The data item of customer satisfaction is an example of what type of data?
   a. training data
   b. model testing data
   c. categorical data
   d. None of the above

4. A company uses a boxplot in a visualization. What is likely the purpose of the visualization?
   a. comparison
   b. correlation
   c. distribution
   d. part to whole

5. Which chart type is best for depicting trends over time?
   a. area chart
   b. bar chart
   c. pie chart
   d. histogram

6. Which of the following is NOT a good reason to visualize data?
   a. Users can find information more quickly with visualized data.
   b. Visualized data is processed faster than written information.
   c. Visualizations help the majority of people to learn better.
   d. Building visualizations does not take as much time as writing a report.

7. Which of the following is a technique to simplify data presentations?
   a. highlighting
   b. weighting
   c. ordering
   d. distance

8. A general rule of thumb is that a visualization should only have 3–5 groups in the data area. Putting in more or less than this amount violates which principle?
   a. ethical data presentation principle
   b. Goldilocks principle
   c. emphasis principle
   d. color contrast principle

9. Making an item in the data area of a viz larger to increase emphasis is an example of using which principle?
   a. highlighting
   b. weighting
   c. ordering
   d. It's a poor design choice; items should all be the same size.

10. Which of the following can be used to present data unethically?
a. selectively presenting only part of a viz
b. with an axis, showing the most recent time closest to the origin
c. truncating or stretching the axes
d. All of the above

DISCUSSION QUESTIONS

7.1 Fill in the chart below by describing one analytic for each analytic type that the business function could perform.

	Descriptive	Diagnostic	Predictive	Prescriptive
Accounting and finance				
Information technology				
Human resources				
Marketing				
Production				

7.2 The chapter discusses common data problems related to GIGO, overfitting, extrapolation, and not respecting variation inherent in model predictions. Describe a situation different from the ones listed in the textbook demonstrating why each of these is problematic in an accounting or business setting. What other data problems can you identify?

7.3 In what circumstances is data visualization better than using text explanations and tables of numeric data? In what situations is it worse? Justify your reasoning.

7.4 Figure 7.2 lists the best chart type for each visualization purpose. Select a chart type and describe why it is less than ideal for the other purposes listed in Figure 7.2.

PROBLEMS

7.1 Match each term with its definition.

1. alternative hypothesis	a. In design, making a visualization easy to interpret and understand
2. categorical data	b. Approach to examining data that seeks to explore the data says without testing formal models or hypotheses
3. classification analyses	c. Design rule suggesting that a viz should not contain too much or too little, but just the right amount of data
4. confirmatory data analysis	d. Avoiding the intentional or unintentional use of deceptive practices that can alter the user's understanding of the data being presented
5. data deception	e. Intentional arranging of visualization items in a way to produce emphasis
6. data ordering	f. Proposed explanation worded in the form of an inequality, meaning that one of the two concepts, ideas, or groups will be greater or less than the other concept, idea, or group

7. data overfitting	g. Any visual representation of data, for example graphs, diagrams, or animations
8. effect size	h. Subset of data used to train a model for future prediction
9. emphasis	i. Quantitative measure of the magnitude of the effect
10. ethical presentation	j. Graphical depiction of information, designed with or without an intent to deceive, that may create a belief about the message and/or its components, which varies from the actual message
11. exploratory data analysis	k. Data items that take on a limited number of assigned values to represent different groups
12. extrapolation beyond the range	l. Subset of data not used for the development of a model but used to test how well the model predicts the target outcome
13. machine learning	m. Process of estimating a value beyond the range of data used to create the model
14. null hypothesis	n. When a model is designed to fit training data very well but does not predict well when applied to other datasets
15. outlier	o. In design, the amount of attention that an element attracts
16. simplification	p. Testing a hypothesis and providing statistical evidence of the likelihood that the evidence refutes or supports a hypothesis
17. test dataset	q. In design, making it easy to know what is most important
18. training dataset	r. Data point, or a few data points, that lie an abnormal distance from other values in the data
19. type I error	s. Incorrect rejection of a true null hypothesis
20. type II error	t. Techniques that identify various groups and then try to classify a new observation into one of those groups
21. visual weight	u. Application of artificial intelligence that allows computer systems to improve and to update prediction models without explicit programming
22. visualization	v. Proposed explanation worded in the form of an equality, meaning that one of the two concepts, ideas, or groups will be no different than the other concept, idea, or group
	w. Failure to reject a false null hypothesis
	x. Concept that data analysis is of no value if the underlying data is not of high quality
	y. Data dispersion around the central value

7.2 Excel Problem

Walmart Inc. has made historical sales data available for 45 stores located in different regions throughout the United States. Go to the student download page at http://www.pearsonhighered.com/romney and download the files labeled "WalmartSales.csv" and "WalmartFeatures.csv".

REQUIRED

Using this data, compute the following descriptive statistics:

a. Central tendency: Regardless of store, compute the mean and the median weekly sales for all departments and for each department individually. Choose one department that has a large difference between the median and the mean and discuss why they are so different and how using only one of the metrics could lead to a poor business decision.

b. Data spread: Compute the minimum, maximum, and standard deviation for weekly sales for each department. Which department number has the greatest spread? Why might it be important for a store manager to understand the different spreads of weekly sales for each department?
c. Data distribution: Create a histogram for the weekly sales of departments 12 and 16. What are the implications of the different distribution of sales for these two departments? Create one hypothesis for why you think these departments may have a different distribution.
d. Correlations: Compute two correlations: (1) the correlation of weekly sales with temperature and (2) the correlation of weekly sales with fuel prices. Interpret what the correlation coefficient means for each correlation. Which variable, temperature or fuel prices, is more highly correlated with sales? Create a hypothesis of why you think one of these variables has a higher correlation with sales.*

7.3 Excel Problem
Walmart Inc. has made historical sales data available for 45 stores located in different regions throughout the United States. Go to the student download page at http://www.pearsonhighered.com/romney and download the files labeled "WalmartSales.csv" and "WalmartFeatures.csv".

REQUIRED

Using this data, answer the question "which elements best explain why department sales differ?" To do this, compute the following regression models. For each model, interpret the output for each variable and discuss the important business insights you can derive from the model results (Hint: be careful in setting up the data that you transform it correctly).
a. Regress total sales for each department on unemployment.
b. Regress weekly sales data on temperature, fuel prices, CPI, unemployment, and IsHoliday.*

7.4 For each of the following scenarios, list the purpose(s) of the visualization and the type(s) of visualization that would best fulfill the purpose(s). Justify your choice.
a. A stock analyst is showing a potential customer how projected returns from various mutual funds will affect the size of retirement savings over time.
b. A tax accountant is showing the CFO how the accumulated effect of asset depreciation differs using Modified Accelerated Cost Recovery System (MACRS) depreciation, straight-line depreciation, accelerated depreciation, and units of production depreciation.
c. A marketing analyst prepares a viz to show which countries present the best opportunity for expansion to increase profits.
d. A corporate accountant is examining how much variability there is in individual customer spending in response to a social media campaign about company advances in social responsibility.
e. A large conglomerate corporation operates businesses in several different industries. The CEO wants to see how much each industry contributes to the overall profits of the corporation.
f. The manager of a movie theater wants to understand how attendance at his movie theater is affected by prices.

7.5 Excel Problem
Walmart Inc. has made historical sales data available for 45 stores located in different regions throughout the United States. Go to the student download page at http://www.pearsonhighered.com/romney and download the files labeled "WalmartSales.csv" and "WalmartFeatures.csv". Using this data, a data analyst produced a viz to try to explain how temperature and fuel prices relate to average weekly sales. The visualization has the following elements: the black line represents weekly sales, the bars represent average weekly temperatures, the blue coloring on the bars shows median weekly fuel prices, and the red line is a regression trend line that corresponds to the equation shown on the chart.

---

* Life-long learning opportunity: see pp. xxiii–xxiv in preface.

REQUIRED

For this chart, do the following:

a. Discuss how you would simplify the chart to show how temperature and fuel prices relate to average weekly sales.
b. Download the data and make a new visualization (or visualizations) that presents the information in a simplified form.

7.6 The Maryland Transit Administration publishes the cost per passenger for citizens using local bus, light rail, metro rail, mobility paratransit, MARC (Maryland Area Regional Commuter) train, contracted commuter bus, and taxi. The cost per passenger is calculated by taking the total operating costs of each respective mode of transportation and dividing it by the total number of annual trips. They produced the following generic viz to show their data.

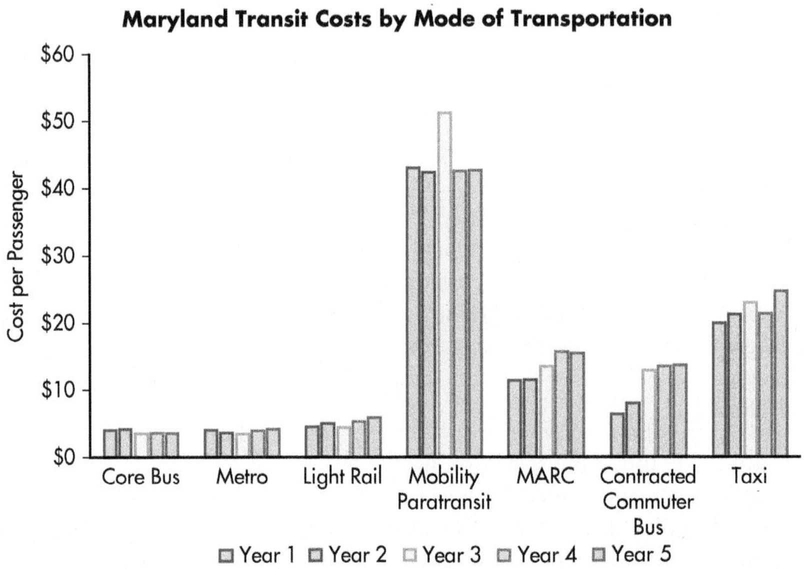

REQUIRED

Do the following:

a. Discuss how this chart fails to use emphasis appropriately.
b. Generate two scenarios where emphasis would be important. Write a short summary of the scenario.
c. Go to the student download page at http://www.pearsonhighered.com/romney and download the file labeled "P7-6MarylandTransitCosts.xlsx". For each scenario, create a visualization that emphasizes what is important relative to the scenario you designed for part b. Describe the design element(s) you chose to emphasize what is important.

7.7 In the state of Maryland, Montgomery County passed a law that requires all retail establishments to charge a five-cent tax on each paper or plastic carryout bag. Retailers retain 1 cent of the 5 cents for the bags they sell to a customer. The other 4 cents must be remitted to the county. Go to the student download page at http://www.pearsonhighered.com/romney and download the file labeled "P7-7MarylandBagTax.xlsx". This file provides the actual amount companies collected, the amount they paid to the city each month (labeled "Amount Due"), and the amount they retained from the tax.

REQUIRED

Using this data, create a separate visualization to accomplish each of the following objectives.

a. Create a visualization that emphasizes the vendors who contributed the most to the bag taxes collected by the county. Provide a brief explanation of which emphasis technique(s) you used.
b. Create a visualization that emphasizes which cities paid the most bag taxes to the county. Provide a brief explanation of which emphasis technique(s) you used. Exclude all items that have a null value in the City field.
c. Create a visualization that examines the annual trend in amounts collected for each city over time. Exclude all items that have a null value in the City field. Emphasize the city of Germantown in the visualization. Provide a brief explanation of which emphasis technique(s) you used.

7.8 Walmart Inc. has made historical sales data available for 45 stores located in different regions throughout the United States. Go to the student download page at http://www.pearsonhighered.com/romney and download the files labeled "WalmartSales.csv" and "WalmartFeatures.csv". For this problem, assume you are the manager of department 92 at store 23.

REQUIRED

Using this data, make two visualizations. One visualization should make your department appear to be the most profitable of all other department 92s by using unethical data presentation techniques. You can use any techniques other than changing the data. The second visualization should ethically present the performance of your department. Discuss how you manipulated the data in the unethical visualization to make your store appear better than it actually is performing.

7.9 Search the Internet and find two visualizations. One visualization should be an example of a poorly designed visualization but that is not misleading or unethical. The other visualization should be a visualization you believe is misleading or unethical. Paste each visualization in your answer document and then, using principles discussed in the chapter, describe why the first chart is poorly designed and why the second chart is unethical. Discuss why there is a difference between poor design and unethical design.

The following case was developed by the Ernst & Young Academic Resource Center, which is sponsored by the Ernst & Young Foundation.

CASE 7-1 Analyzing Gamified Training

PART 1: BACKGROUND

You are the chief technology officer (CTO) of an international bank. A key component of your job is to manage risk within the bank related to information technology (IT). Banks face significant regulatory oversight and must have well-functioning internal controls to prevent and detect any problems related to IT. Within the IT area, data security and privacy are high-risk areas. As such, you must design and implement internal controls to reduce risk. One key preventive internal control that your bank has implemented is employee training.

As part of this control, all bank employees must complete regular IT trainings. The feedback you have received about past trainings is that they are tedious and boring. You are concerned that employees may not engage fully in the trainings and, thus, the control is not helping reduce the risk of an IT security incident. If there is a significant IT security incident on your watch, you are likely to lose your job.

At a recent conference, you heard of a new way to increase interest in and learning from training: gamification of training. Gamification is the application of gaming techniques—like using points, badges, leaderboards, stories, etc.—to non-game scenarios. As one gamified vendor representative explained, "We take traditional training courses and make them more fun by making them a game. Your employees will engage at a deeper level, learning significantly more than in any traditional training session, and have fun while doing it!"

The possibility of making IT security training more interesting has piqued your interest. You need to make a recommendation to the rest of the executive team about whether you will purchase and implement gamified training for your next wave of IT security training or go with a traditional training module. To help you make an informed decision, you reach out to a friend at another bank who recently implemented a gamified IT security training module at her bank. She sends you a data file and memo for you to analyze to help inform your decision.

Before you go any further, you remember your training about the importance of using an analytics mindset. You decide to review the training material before continuing.

IMPLEMENTING AN ANALYTICS MINDSET

Having and using an analytics mindset are critical in accounting and business. An analytics mindset is the ability to:

- Ask the right questions.
- Extract, transform, and load relevant data.
- Apply appropriate data analytics techniques.
- Interpret and share the results with stakeholders.

In this setting, using an analytics mindset means using data to inform your decision, rather than going with your "gut feeling," another person's recommendation, or using another way of deciding. Given that you have data from a similar bank, it makes sense to see what you can learn (and recognize what you cannot learn) by using their data.

REQUIRED

1. As a CTO, there are many things you need to consider when choosing the best IT security training program for your employees. Develop a list of questions (at least five) for which you want answers to make the best decision about whether you should implement a gamified training model.
2. Review the memo and descriptions of the data sent from your friend in the appendix. Also, review the data and consider the following (go to the student download page at http://www.pearsonhighered.com/romney and download the file labeled "Analytics_mindset_case_studies_Gamification_P1.xlsx"):
    - Which questions that you generated in the first requirement can you answer or not answer by using the data?
    - What additional data would you need to answer the questions you developed?
    - What are the limitations of the data provided by your friend?
3. Prepare a recommendation for the rest of your organization's executives about whether your organization should use gamified training.
    - Use a visualization software package to create visualizations that can be sent to everyone before the meeting. Give thought to how you will display your analyses so that it is understandable and convincing.
    - Make sure your deliverable clearly states the problem, your recommendation, the reasons supporting your recommendation, and any key questions and issues you were not able to address (and what you would need to address them).

CASE 7-1 Appendix

MEMO FROM FRIEND

Our bank recently decided to try a gamified IT training model. Before providing the training, we sent a survey to a number of our employees to test their IT security knowledge (this group has not done any recent IT training). We received 325 usable responses from this group (Group 1). We then had all employees of the bank complete the gamified training. Afterward, we asked all employees to fill out a survey. We received 531 usable responses from this group (Group 2). For Group 2, we asked the same questions we used to measure IT security knowledge as we did with Group 1. We also asked Group 2 numerous questions about how much these employees enjoyed the training, how they rated it, etc. A full description of the questions and data fields in the Excel file is included below.

A few notes about the data file:

- Any time a field is blank, it means there is no response for that question from the employee. Be careful as you import data to make certain that the values reflect that they are missing rather than showing the value as zero.
- It may be obvious, but there is no data about Group 1's satisfaction with the training because they had not yet completed the training.

- The data does not include personally identifiable information, like an email address, so the data between the two groups cannot be linked for an employee who participated in both surveys. You might consider how this could influence the interpretation of your results.

Here's a description of the data in the Excel file.

- ID—a randomly generated unique identifier for each employee response in the dataset.
- ReceivedTraining—a dummy variable that equals "Yes" if the employee filled out the survey after completing the gamified training and "No" if the employee did not participate in the gamified training.
- TotalKnowledge—the percentage score of the employee on the IT security knowledge test. Scores can range from 0.00000 (missed every question) to 1.00000 (answered every question correctly).

The next data fields measure how employees who completed the gamified training scored on the bank's learning objectives. Each question was measured on a 7-point scale with 1 = strongly disagree, 2 = disagree, 3 = somewhat disagree, 4 = neither agree nor disagree, 5 = somewhat agree, 6 = agree, and 7 = strongly agree.

- BetterPerform—the answer to "I can better perform my job because of this training."
- ContentNeeded—the answer to "This program provided the training content that I needed for my job."
- UnderstandResponsibilities—the answer to "After the training, I feel proficient in the following areas: I understand my responsibilities for protecting information."
- ApplyTechniques—the answer to "After the training, I feel proficient in the following areas: I can apply the risk management techniques used in protecting information."
- KnowImportance—the answer to "After the training, I feel proficient in the following areas: I know the reputational importance of effective information security and the consequences of information being lost or stolen."

All of the next data fields used the same basic question: "Please compare the most recently completed gamified training that used an interactive, game-style approach with your last training experience that did not use this approach. Please rate which was better using the following dimensions. . . ."

Employees could select any number on a 7-point scale with responses anchored at 1 = gamified training, 4 = they were the same, and 7 = traditional training. Employees rated their satisfaction with the training based on the following words:

- Enjoyable
- Interesting
- Fun
- Informative
- Boring
- Waste of time

The next data fields contain rankings of different types of training. Employees were asked to "Please provide a rank ordering of what you would prefer for future training." A ranking of 1 was the most preferred, followed by 2, 3, 4, and 5 being the least preferred. The types of training that were ranked include the following (with description):

- RankGamified—online training using an interactive, game-style approach
- RankOnlineVoice—online training using mostly written materials with voiceover (e.g., PowerPoint presentation with a narrator)
- RankWritten—online training containing only written material
- RankLecture—in-person training with a traditional approach
- RankOther—other; please describe

Analytics Mindset Gamification

PART 2

To provide additional evidence about how a gamified training approach compares with more traditional training approaches, you conduct an experiment. Experiments have several advantages over surveys (like the data you analyzed in Part 1). In a true experiment, you can randomly assign participants to do different things (called conditions in experimental talk). Randomly assigning participants creates equal comparisons because any unique factors should be represented equally in each group. For example, assume in Part 1 that the group that did not receive gamified training included the least intelligent and least motivated people in the company. When comparing the responses, you wouldn't know whether differences in the performance of the gamified training were caused by the training or the differences in motivation and intelligence of the groups. If you can randomly assign participants to either complete the training or not complete the training, then there should be an approximately equal number of intelligent and motivated people in each group (especially as you have larger groups participate), so any differences should be caused by the training and not other factors.

In the experiment, there are three different groups:

- Group 1 received no training at all.
- Group 2 received a traditional training course that did not use gamification.
- Group 3 received a gamified training course.

Participants in all three groups answered the same knowledge questions as in Part 1. Participants in Groups 2 and 3 also answered the satisfaction questions related to enjoyable, interesting, fun, informative, boring, and waste of time. In the experiment, these questions were measured on a 7-point scale with 1 = strongly disagree, 2 = disagree, 3 = somewhat disagree, 4 = neither agree nor disagree, 5 = somewhat agree, 6 = agree, and 7 = strongly agree.

In the experiment, there is one additional field labeled TypeOfTraining, which lists whether they received "No training," "Non-gamified training," or "Gamified training."

REQUIRED

1. Brainstorm the advantages and disadvantages for using an experiment versus a survey. What are the strengths and weaknesses of each approach?
2. Prepare a recommendation for the rest of your organization's executives about whether you should use gamified training based on the experimental data (go to the student download page at http://www.pearsonhighered.com/romney and download the file labeled "Analytics_mindset_case_studies_Gamification_P2.xlsx").
   - Use a visualization software package to create a story that can be sent to everyone before the meeting. Give thought to how you will display your analysis so that it is understandable and convincing.
   - Make sure your deliverable clearly states the problem, your recommendation, the reasons supporting your recommendation, and any key questions and issues you were not able to address (and what you would need to address them). Also, consider the following questions:
     - Do you reach a different conclusion based on the experimental data versus the survey data?
     - Which data do you think is more convincing?

What evidence supports your recommendation and does not support your recommendation? Why do you believe the evidence supporting your recommendation is more convincing than the evidence that does not support your recommendation?

AIS in Action Solutions

QUIZ KEY

1. A company wants to determine how to decrease employee turnover. In order to do this, they test whether paying off an employee's student debt will cause fewer employees to leave. The analytic testing whether paying off an employee's student debt causes lower turnover is an example of which type of analytic?
   a. descriptive [Incorrect. The analytic does not explain what happened but rather why something happened.]
   ▶ **b.** diagnostic [Correct. The analytic is explaining why there is a relationship between two variables.]
   c. predictive [Incorrect. Although the company wants to determine how to reduce employee turnover, which would suggest a predictive analytic, they are computing an analytic that tests if turnover is caused by paying off student debt.]
   d. prescriptive [Incorrect. The analytic does not try to determine what should be done but explains why something happened.]

2. You co-own a theme park. You believe that the longer customers stay in the park, the hungrier they will be which would increase the amount they spend on food. Your co-owner believes that the longer customers stay in the park, the more likely they are to feel nauseated which would decrease the amount they spend on food. Both of you gather data and

find some evidence supporting your belief. If the true relation is that there is no relation between time in the park and food sales, what type of error did your co-owner make?

- ▶ a. type I error [Correct. Both you and your co-owner incorrectly rejected the null hypothesis in favor of an alternative hypothesis.]
- b. type II error [Incorrect. The null hypothesis was rejected in this setting, whereas a type II error is the failure to reject a null hypothesis.]
- c. GIGO error [Incorrect. GIGO relates to data quality, not inferences made from the data.]
- d. data overfitting error [Incorrect. While data overfitting may have contributed to the type I error, there is not enough information to know if this is the case or not.]

3. A data analyst develops a classification model to predict whether a customer will be unsatisfied, neither satisfied nor unsatisfied, or satisfied with their online purchasing experience. The data item of customer satisfaction is an example of what type of data?

- a. training data [Incorrect. The dataset used to generate the model would be the training data, but the individual data item is just one part of the dataset.]
- b. model testing data [Incorrect. The dataset used to test the model would be the model testing data, but the individual data item is just one part of the dataset.]
- ▶ c. categorical data [Correct. The customer satisfaction data item can only be one of three values.]
- d. None of the above [Incorrect. Categorical data is the correct answer.]

4. A company uses a boxplot in a visualization. What is likely the purpose of the visualization?

- a. comparison [Incorrect. Comparisons are usually shown with bar charts or bullet charts.]
- b. correlation [Incorrect. Correlations are usually shown with scatterplots or heatmaps.]
- ▶ c. distribution [Correct. Boxplots show the distribution of data]
- d. part to whole [Incorrect. Part to whole are usually shown with pie charts or treemaps.]

5. Which chart type is best for depicting trends over time?

- ▶ a. area chart [Correct. An area chart shows trends and is particularly useful to emphasize trends over time.]
- b. bar chart [Incorrect. Bar charts are useful for showing comparisons.]
- c. pie chart [Incorrect. Pie charts are useful for showing part to whole.]
- d. histogram [Incorrect. Histograms are useful for showing distribution.]

6. Which of the following is NOT a good reason to visualize data?

- a. Users can find information more quickly with visualized data. [Incorrect. Research has found this a benefit of visualizing data.]
- b. Visualized data is processed faster than written information. [Incorrect. Research has found this a benefit of visualizing data.]
- c. Visualizations help the majority of people to learn better. [Incorrect. Research has found this a benefit of visualizing data.]
- ▶ d. Building visualizations does not take as much time as writing a report. [Correct. While this may be true in some cases, building a good visualization may take more time than writing a report in other cases.]

7. Which of the following is a technique to simplify data presentations?

- a. highlighting [Incorrect. Highlighting is used to emphasize, not simplify.]
- b. weighting [Incorrect. Weighting is used to emphasize, not simplify.]
- c. ordering [Incorrect. Ordering is used to emphasize, not simplify.]
- ▶ d. distance [Correct. Reducing distance between visual element and description simplifies a presentation. The other answers are all techniques to emphasize data presentations, not to simplify them.]

8. A general rule of thumb is that a visualization should only have 3–5 groups in the data area. Putting in more or less than this amount violates which principle?

- a. ethical data presentation principle [Incorrect. It is bad form, but not unethical, to make a poorly designed viz.]

► **b.** Goldilocks principle [Correct. The Goldilocks principle says that a viz should not contain too much or too little data.]
c. emphasis principle [Incorrect. The quantity of information in a viz relates to simplification not emphasis.]
d. color contrast principle [Incorrect. Color contrast relates to weighting, which is an emphasis technique.]

9. Making an item in the data area of a viz larger to increase emphasis is an example of using which principle?
a. highlighting [Incorrect. Highlighting does not change the size of a data item.]
► **b.** weighting [Correct. Size is an important way to increase visual heaviness, which emphasizes the item.]
c. ordering [Incorrect. Ordering does not change the size of a data item.]
d. It's a poor design choice; items should all be the same size. [Incorrect. Using different sizes is an appropriate design choice in many situations to emphasize something that is important.]

10. Which of the following can be used to present data unethically?
a. selectively presenting only part of a viz [Part of Correct Answer. This technique can deceive the user by hiding useful information.]
b. with an axis, showing the most recent time closest to the origin [Part of Correct Answer. Most people expect the oldest date to be closest to the origin.]
c. truncating or stretching the axes [Part of Correct Answer. Axes should be clearly labeled and generally start at 0.]
► **d.** All the above [Correct. All of the above can be used to unethically present data.]

Control of Accounting Information Systems

PART III

Dboystudio/Shutterstock

CHAPTER 8
Fraud and Errors

CHAPTER 9
Computer Fraud and Abuse Techniques

CHAPTER 10
Control and Accounting Information Systems

CHAPTER 11
Controls for Information Security

CHAPTER 12
Confidentiality and Privacy Controls

CHAPTER 13
Processing Integrity and Availability Controls

CHAPTER

8

Fraud and Errors

LEARNING OBJECTIVES

After studying this chapter, you should be able to:

1. Explain the threats faced by modern information systems.
2. Define *fraud* and describe both the different types of fraud and the auditor's responsibility to detect fraud.
3. Discuss who perpetrates fraud and why it occurs, including the pressures, opportunities, and rationalizations that are present in most frauds.
4. Define *computer fraud* and discuss the different computer fraud classifications.
5. Explain how to prevent and detect computer fraud and abuse.

INTEGRATIVE CASE Northwest Industries

Jason Scott is an internal auditor for Northwest Industries, a forest products company. On March 31, he reviewed his completed tax return and noticed that the federal income tax withholding on his final paycheck was $5 more than the amount indicated on his W-2 form. He used the W-2 amount to complete his tax return and made a note to ask the payroll department what happened to the other $5. The next day, Jason was swamped, and he dismissed the $5 difference as immaterial.

On April 16, a coworker grumbled that the company had taken $5 more from his check than he was given credit for on his W-2. When Jason realized he was not the only one with the $5 discrepancy, he investigated and found that all 1,500 employees had the same $5 discrepancy. He also discovered that the W-2 of Don Hawkins, the payroll programmer, had thousands of dollars more in withholdings reported to the Internal Revenue Service (IRS) than had been withheld from his paycheck.

Jason knew that when he reported the situation, management was going to ask questions, such as:

1. What constitutes a fraud, and is the withholding problem a fraud?
2. How was the fraud perpetrated? What motivated Don to commit it?

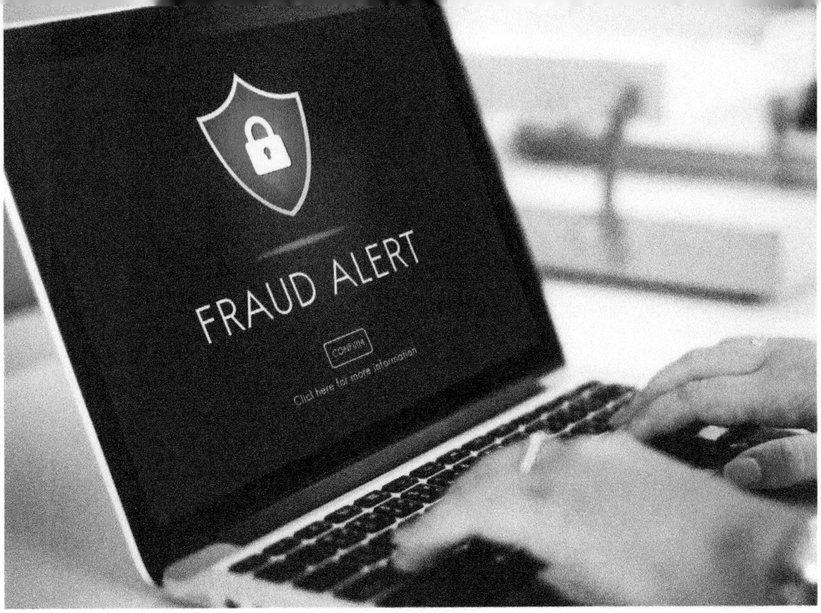

Rawpixel.com/Shutterstock

3. Why did the company not catch these mistakes? Was there a breakdown in controls?
4. How can the company detect and prevent fraud?
5. How vulnerable is the company's computer system to fraud?

Introduction

As accounting information systems (AIS) grow more complex to meet our escalating needs for information, companies face the growing risk that their systems may be compromised. For example, recent surveys show that 49% of companies have experienced fraud, 67% have had a security breach, more than 45% were targeted by organized crime, and 60% reported financial losses. In 2018, U.S. companies experienced 12,449 data breaches—a 424% increase over 2017.

The six chapters in Part III focus on control concepts. Fraud and errors are the topic of this chapter. Computer fraud and abuse techniques are the topic of Chapter 9. Chapter 10 explains general principles of control in business organizations and describes a comprehensive business risk and control framework. Chapter 11 introduces five basic principles that contribute to systems reliability and then focuses on security—the foundation on which the other four principles rest. Chapter 12 discusses two of the other four principles of systems reliability: confidentiality and privacy. Chapter 13 discusses the last two principles: processing integrity and availability.

This chapter discusses fraud and errors in five main sections: AIS threats, introduction to fraud, who perpetrates fraud and why, computer fraud, and preventing and detecting fraud and abuse.

AIS Threats

The four types of AIS threats a company faces are summarized in Table 8-1 and are now discussed.

NATURAL AND POLITICAL DISASTERS

Natural and political disasters—such as fires, floods, earthquakes, hurricanes, tornadoes, blizzards, wars, and attacks by terrorists—can destroy an information system and cause many companies to fail. For example:

- Terrorist attacks on the World Trade Center in New York City and on the Federal Building in Oklahoma City destroyed or disrupted all the systems in those buildings.
- A flood in Chicago destroyed or damaged 400 data processing centers. A flood in Des Moines, Iowa, buried the city's computer systems under eight feet of water. Hurricanes and earthquakes have destroyed numerous computer systems and severed communication lines. Other systems were damaged by falling debris, water from ruptured sprinkler systems, and dust.
- A very valid concern for everyone is what is going to happen when cyber-attacks are militarized; that is, the transition from disruptive to destructive attacks. For more on this, see Focus 8-1.

TABLE 8-1 Threats to Accounting Information Systems

Threats	Examples
Natural and political disasters	Fire or excessive heat
	Floods, earthquakes, landslides, hurricanes, tornadoes, blizzards, snowstorms, and freezing rain
	War and attacks by terrorists
Software errors and equipment malfunctions	Hardware or software failure
	Software errors or bugs
	Operating system crashes
	Power outages and fluctuations
	Undetected data transmission errors
Unintentional acts	Accidents caused by human carelessness, failure to follow established procedures, and poorly trained or supervised personnel
	Innocent errors or omissions
	Lost, erroneous, destroyed, or misplaced data
	Logic errors
	Systems that do not meet company needs or cannot handle intended tasks
Intentional acts	Sabotage
	Misrepresentation, false use, or unauthorized disclosure of data
	Misappropriation of assets
	Financial statement fraud
	Corruption
	Computer fraud—attacks, social engineering, malware, etc.

FOCUS 8-1 Electronic Warfare

Shortly after Obama was elected President, he authorized cyber-attacks on computer systems that run Iran's main nuclear enrichment plants. The intent was to delay or destroy Iran's nuclear-weapons program. The attacks were based on the Stuxnet virus, which was developed with help from a secret Israeli intelligence unit. The attack damaged 20% of the centrifuges at the Natanz uranium enrichment facility (Iran denied its existence) by spinning them too fast. This was the first known cyber-attack intended to harm a real-world physical target.

A hacker group that is a front for Iran retaliated using distributed denial of service attacks (DDoS) to bring online systems at major American banks to their knees. Most denial of service attacks use botnets, which are networks of computers that the bot-herder infected with malware. However, the Iranians remotely hijacked and used "clouds" of thousands of networked servers located in cloud computing data centers around the world. The attack inundated bank computers with encryption requests (they consume more system resources), allowing the hackers to cripple sites with fewer requests. The cloud services were infected with a sophisticated malware, which evaded detection by antivirus programs and made it very difficult to trace the malware back to its user. The scale and scope of these attacks and their effectiveness is unprecedented, as there have never been that many financial institutions under simultaneous attack.

Defense Secretary Leon E. Panetta claimed that the United States faces the possibility of a "cyber-Pearl Harbor" because it is increasingly vulnerable to hackers who could shut down power grids, derail trains, crash airplanes, spill oil and gas, contaminate water supplies, and blow up buildings containing combustible materials. They can disrupt financial and government networks, destroy critical data, and illegally transfer money. They can also cripple a nation's armed forces, as they rely on vulnerable computer networks. All of these attacks are especially scary because they can be done remotely, in a matter of seconds, and done either immediately or at any predetermined date and time. A large-scale attack could create an unimaginable degree of chaos in the United States. The most destructive attacks would combine a cyber-attack with a physical attack.

Both to be better able to use cyber weapons and to defend against them, the United States has created a new U.S. Cyber Command that will have equal footing with other commands in the nation's military structure. In addition, intelligence agencies will search computer networks worldwide

FOCUS 8-1 Continued

looking for signs of potential attacks on the United States. Cyber weapons have been approved for preemptive attacks, even if there is no declared war, if authorized by the president—and if an imminent attack on the United States warrants it. The implications are clear: The United States realizes that cyber weapons are going to be used and needs to be better at using them than its adversaries.

Unfortunately, bolstering cyber security and safeguarding systems is significantly lagging the advancement of technology and the constant development of new cyber-attack tools. Making it ever harder, advancements such as cloud computing and the use of mobile devices emphasize access and usability rather than security. Most companies and government agencies need to increase their security budgets significantly to develop ways to combat the attacks. It is estimated that the market demand for cyber security experts is more than 100,000 people per year and the median pay is close to six figures.

SOFTWARE ERRORS AND EQUIPMENT MALFUNCTIONS

Software errors, operating system crashes, hardware failures, power outages and fluctuations, and undetected data transmission errors constitute a second type of threat. A federal study estimated yearly economic losses due to software bugs at almost $60 billion. More than 60% of companies studied had significant software errors. Examples of errors include:

- More than 50 million people in the Northeast were left without power when an industrial control system in part of the grid failed. Some areas were powerless for four days, and damages from the outage ran close to $10 billion.
- At Facebook, an automated system for verifying configuration value errors backfired, causing every single client to try to fix accurate data it perceived as invalid. Since the fix involved querying a cluster of databases, that cluster was quickly overwhelmed by hundreds of thousands of queries a second. The resultant crash took the Facebook system offline for two-and-a-half hours.
- As a result of tax system bugs, California failed to collect $635 million in business taxes.
- A bug in Burger King's software resulted in a $4,334.33 debit card charge for four hamburgers. The cashier accidentally keyed in the $4.33 charge twice, resulting in the overcharge.

UNINTENTIONAL ERRORS

A third type of threat, unintentional acts such as accidents or innocent errors and omissions, is the greatest risk to information systems and causes the greatest dollar losses. The Computing Technology Industry Association estimates that human errors cause 80% of security problems. Forrester Research estimates that employees unintentionally create legal, regulatory, or financial risks in 25% of their outbound e-mails. Chapter 10 discusses many of the controls and procedures used to eliminate or minimize both human errors and fraud. In addition, Chapters 14 through 18 discuss how to minimize human errors and fraud in the main business processes in organizations.

Unintentional acts are caused by human carelessness, failure to follow established procedures, and poorly trained or supervised personnel. Users lose or misplace data and accidentally erase or alter files, data, and programs. Computer operators and users enter the wrong input or erroneous input, use the wrong version of a program or the wrong data files, or misplace data files. Systems analysts develop systems that do not meet company needs, that leave them vulnerable to attack, or that are incapable of handling their intended tasks. Programmers make logic errors. Examples of unintentional acts include the following:

- A data entry clerk at Mizuho Securities mistakenly keyed in a sale for 610,000 shares of J-Com for 1 yen instead of the sale of 1 share for 610,000 yen. The error cost the company $250 million.

- A programmer made a one-line-of-code error that priced all goods at Zappos, an online retailer, at $49.95—even though some of the items it sells are worth thousands of dollars. The change went into effect at midnight, and by the time it was detected at 6:00 A.M., the company had lost $1.6 million on goods sold far below cost.
- A bank programmer mistakenly calculated interest for each month using 31 days. Before the mistake was discovered, more than $100,000 in excess interest was paid.
- When employees at the University of Washington Medicine moved data from one server to another, human error exposed the personal information of nearly 1 million patients. The error was discovered when a patient found his data after googling himself.
- UPS lost a box of computer tapes containing sensitive information on 3.9 million Citigroup customers.
- Jefferson County, West Virginia, released a new online search tool that exposed the personal information of 1.6 million people.
- McAfee, the antivirus software vendor, mistakenly identified svchost.exe, a crucial part of the Windows operating system, as a malicious program in one of its updates. Hundreds of thousands of PCs worldwide had to be manually rebooted—a process that took 30 minutes per machine. A third of the hospitals in Rhode Island were shut down by the error. One company reported that the error cost them $2.5 million.

INTENTIONAL ACTS

sabotage - An intentional act where the intent is to destroy a system or some of its components.

A fourth threat is an intentional act such as a computer crime, a fraud, or **sabotage**, which is deliberate destruction or harm to a system. Information systems are increasingly vulnerable to attacks. Examples of intentional acts include the following:

- In a recent three-year period, the number of networks that were compromised rose 700%. Experts believe the actual number of incidents is six times higher than reported because companies tend not to report security breaches. Symantec estimates that hackers attack computers more than 8.6 million times per day. One computer-security company reported that in the cases they handled that were perpetrated by Chinese hackers, 94% of the targeted companies didn't realize that their systems had been compromised until someone else told them. The median number of days between when an intrusion started and when it was detected was 416.
- The Sobig virus wreaked havoc on millions of computers, including shutting down train systems for up to six hours.
- In Australia, a disgruntled employee hacked into a sewage system 46 times over two months. Pumps failed, and a quarter of a million gallons of raw sewage poured into nearby streams, flooding a hotel and park.
- A programmer was able to download OpenTable's database due to an improperly designed **cookie** (data a website stores on your computer to identify the site so you do not have to log on each time you visit the site).
- A hacker stole 1.5 million credit and debit card numbers from Global Payments, resulting in an $84 million loss and a 90% drop in profits in the quarter following disclosure.
- The activist hacker group called Anonymous played Santa Claus one Christmas, indicating they were "granting wishes to people who are less fortunate than most." They were inundated with requests for iPads, iPhones, pizzas, and hundreds of other things. They hacked into banks and sent more than $1 million worth of virtual credit cards to people.

cookie - A text file created by a website and stored on a visitor's hard drive. Cookies store information about who the user is and what the user has done on the site.

Cyber thieves have stolen more than $1 trillion worth of intellectual property from businesses worldwide. General Alexander, former director of the National Security Agency, called cyber theft "the greatest transfer of wealth in history." When the top cyber cop at the FBI was asked how the United States was doing in its attempt to keep computer hackers from stealing data from corporate networks, he said, "We're not winning."

Chapters 10 through 13 discuss the controls necessary to prevent or at least minimize the four types of threats just discussed. The remainder of this chapter discusses a very important type of intentional act: fraud.

Introduction to Fraud

Fraud is gaining an unfair advantage over another person. Legally, for an act to be fraudulent there must be:

fraud - Any and all means a person uses to gain an unfair advantage over another person.

1. A *false statement, representation, or disclosure.*
2. A *material fact*, which is something that induces a person to act.
3. An *intent to deceive.*
4. A *justifiable reliance*; that is, the person relies on the misrepresentation to take an action.
5. An *injury or loss* suffered by the victim.

Annual economic losses resulting from fraudulent activity each year are staggering. It is rare for a week to go by without the national or local press reporting another fraud of some kind. These frauds range from a multimillion-dollar fraud that captures the attention of the nation to an employee defrauding a local company out of a small sum of money.

The Association of Certified Fraud Examiners (ACFE) conducts periodic comprehensive fraud studies and releases its findings. *Report to the Nation on Occupational Fraud and Abuse 2016 Global Fraud Study* indicates that:

- A typical organization loses 5% of its annual revenue to fraud, with yearly global fraud losses of more than $3.7 trillion.
- The median loss for all 2,410 cases in the ACFE study was $150,000, with 23.2% having losses of $1 million or more.
- More than 83% were asset misappropriation frauds with a median loss of $125,000. The most frequent misappropriation schemes were billing and check tampering.
- Less than 10% were financial statement fraud, with a much higher $975,000 median loss.
- More than 35% were corruption frauds, with a median loss of $200,000. Corruption was much more frequent in larger organizations than in smaller ones.
- A fraudster's level of authority was strongly correlated with the size of the fraud. Owner/executive frauds took longer to detect and were more than four times as costly as manager-perpetrated frauds and more than 11 times as costly as employee frauds.
- Small businesses, with fewer and less effective internal controls, were more vulnerable to fraud than large ones. In addition, they were impacted much more by the fraud losses due to their limited resources.
- Frauds are more likely to be detected by an anonymous tip than by audits or any other means. The most common ways to receive tips are by phone hotlines, email, or an online form.
- More than 75% of the frauds occurred in accounting, operations, sales, upper management, customer service, purchasing, and finance.
- In almost 41% of the frauds studied, the company did not report fraud to the police, most frequently because they feared bad publicity.
- The most prominent organizational weakness in the cases studied was a lack of internal controls, followed by overriding internal controls.
- The implementation of controls to prevent fraud resulted in lower fraud losses and quicker fraud detection. The most frequently implemented anti-fraud controls were external financial statement audits, a written code of conduct, and financial statement certification by management.
- The perpetrator tried to conceal the fraud in 94.5% of the cases, most frequently by creating or altering physical documents.
- In 79% of the fraud cases studied, perpetrators displayed behavioral warning signs, or red flags, such as living beyond their means, financial difficulties, unusually close association with a vendor or customer, and recent divorce or family problems that created a perceived financial need in the perpetrator's mind.
- Most occupational fraudsters are first-time offenders; they had never been charged or convicted of fraud.
- The more individuals involved in a fraud, the higher the losses.

Most fraud perpetrators are knowledgeable insiders with the requisite access, skills, and resources. Because employees understand a company's system and its weaknesses, they are white-collar criminals - Typically, businesspeople who commit fraud. White-collar criminals usually resort to trickery or cunning, and their crimes usually involve a violation of trust or confidence.

corruption - Dishonest conduct by those in power which often involves actions that are illegitimate, immoral, or incompatible with ethical standards. Examples include bribery and bid rigging.

investment fraud - Misrepresenting or leaving out facts in order to promote an investment that promises fantastic profits with little or no risk. Examples include Ponzi schemes and securities fraud.

better able to commit and conceal a fraud. The controls used to protect corporate assets make it more difficult for an outsider to steal from a company. Fraud perpetrators are often referred to as **white-collar criminals**.

There are a great many different types of frauds. We briefly define and give examples of some of those and then provide a more extended discussion of some of the most important ones to businesses.

Corruption is dishonest conduct by those in power and it often involves actions that are illegitimate, immoral, or incompatible with ethical standards. There are many types of corruption; examples include bribery and bid rigging.

Investment fraud is misrepresenting or leaving out facts in order to promote an investment that promises fantastic profits with little or no risk. There are many types of investment fraud; examples include Ponzi schemes and securities fraud.

Two types of frauds that are important to businesses are misappropriation of assets (sometimes called employee fraud) and fraudulent financial reporting (sometimes called management fraud). These two types of fraud are now discussed in greater depth.

MISAPPROPRIATION OF ASSETS

misappropriation of assets - Theft of company assets by employees.

Misappropriation of assets is the theft of company assets by employees. Examples include the following:

- Albert Milano, a manager at *Reader's Digest* responsible for processing bills, embezzled $1 million over a five-year period. He forged a superior's signature on invoices for services never performed, submitted them to accounts payable, forged the endorsement on the check, and deposited it in his account. Milano used the stolen funds to buy an expensive home, five cars, and a boat.
- A bank vice president approved $1 billion in bad loans in exchange for $585,000 in kickbacks. The loans cost the bank $800 million and helped trigger its collapse.
- A manager at a Florida newspaper went to work for a competitor after he was fired. The first employer soon realized its reporters were being scooped. An investigation revealed the manager still had an active account and password and regularly browsed its computer files for information on exclusive stories.
- In a recent survey of 3,500 adults, half said they would take company property when they left and were more likely to steal e-data than assets. More than 25% said they would take customer data, including contact information. Many employees did not believe taking company data is equivalent to stealing.

The most significant contributing factor in most misappropriations is the absence of internal controls and/or the failure to enforce existing internal controls. A typical misappropriation has the following important elements or characteristics. The perpetrator:

- Gains the trust or confidence of the entity being defrauded.
- Uses trickery, cunning, or false or misleading information to commit fraud.
- Conceals the fraud by falsifying records or other information.
- Rarely terminates the fraud voluntarily.
- Sees how easy it is to get extra money; need or greed impels the person to continue. Some frauds are self-perpetuating; if perpetrators stop, their actions are discovered.
- Spends the ill-gotten gains. Rarely does the perpetrator save or invest the money. Some perpetrators come to depend on the "extra" income, and others adopt a lifestyle that requires even greater amounts of money. For these reasons, there are no small frauds—only large ones that are detected early.
- Gets greedy and takes ever-larger amounts of money at intervals that are more frequent, exposing the perpetrator to greater scrutiny and increasing the chances the fraud is discovered. The sheer magnitude of some frauds leads to their detection. For example, the accountant at an auto repair shop, a lifelong friend of the shop's owner, embezzled ever-larger sums of money over a seven-year period. In the last year of the fraud, the embezzler took more than $200,000. Facing bankruptcy, the owner eventually laid off the accountant and had his wife take over the bookkeeping. When the company immediately began doing better, the wife hired a fraud expert who investigated and uncovered the fraud.

- Grows careless or overconfident as time passes. If the size of the fraud does not lead to its discovery, the perpetrator eventually makes a mistake that does lead to the discovery.

FRAUDULENT FINANCIAL REPORTING

The National Commission on Fraudulent Financial Reporting (the Treadway Commission) defined **fraudulent financial reporting** as intentional or reckless conduct, whether by act or omission, that results in materially misleading financial statements. Management falsifies financial statements to deceive investors and creditors, increase a company's stock price, meet cash flow needs, or hide company losses and problems. The Treadway Commission studied 450 lawsuits against auditors and found undetected fraud to be a factor in half of them.

fraudulent financial reporting - Intentional or reckless conduct, whether by act or omission, that results in materially misleading financial statements.

Through the years, many highly publicized financial statement frauds have occurred. In each case, misrepresented financial statements led to huge financial losses and a number of bankruptcies. The most frequent "cook the books" schemes involve fictitiously inflating revenues, holding the books open (recognizing revenues before they are earned), closing the books early (delaying current expenses to a later period), overstating inventories or fixed assets, and concealing losses and liabilities.

The Treadway Commission recommended four actions to reduce fraudulent financial reporting:

1. Establish an organizational environment that contributes to the integrity of the financial reporting process.
2. Identify and understand the factors that lead to fraudulent financial reporting.
3. Assess the risk of fraudulent financial reporting within the company.
4. Design and implement internal controls to provide reasonable assurance of preventing fraudulent financial reporting.[1]

The ACFE found that an asset misappropriation is 17 times more likely than fraudulent financial reporting but that the amounts involved are much smaller. As a result, auditors and management are more concerned with fraudulent financial reporting even though they are more likely to encounter misappropriations. The following section discusses an auditors' responsibility for detecting material fraud.

SAS NO. 99 (AU-C SECTION 240): THE AUDITOR'S RESPONSIBILITY TO DETECT FRAUD

Statement on Auditing Standards (SAS) No. 99, *Consideration of Fraud in a Financial Statement Audit*, became effective in December 2002. SAS No. 99 requires auditors to:

- ***Understand fraud.*** Because auditors cannot effectively audit something they do not understand, they must understand fraud and how and why it is committed.
- ***Discuss the risks of material fraudulent misstatements.*** While planning the audit, team members discuss among themselves how and where the company's financial statements are susceptible to fraud.
- ***Obtain information.*** The audit team gathers evidence by looking for fraud risk factors; testing company records; and asking management, the audit committee of the board of directors, and others whether they know of past or current fraud. Because many frauds involve revenue recognition, special care is exercised in examining revenue accounts.
- ***Identify, assess, and respond to risks.*** The evidence is used to identify, assess, and respond to fraud risks by varying the nature, timing, and extent of audit procedures and by evaluating carefully the risk of management overriding internal controls.
- ***Evaluate the results of their audit tests.*** Auditors must evaluate whether identified misstatements indicate the presence of fraud and determine its impact on the financial statements and the audit.

[1]Copyright ©1987 by the National Commission on Fraudulent Financial Reporting.

- ***Document and communicate findings.*** Auditors must document and communicate their findings to management and the audit committee.
- ***Incorporate a technology focus.*** SAS No. 99 recognizes the impact technology has on fraud risks and provides commentary and examples recognizing this impact. It also notes the opportunities auditors have to use technology to design fraud-auditing procedures.

Through the years there have been improvements to and reorganizations of auditing standards. The fraud standards are now referred to as AU-C Section 240.

Who Perpetrates Fraud and Why

When researchers compared the psychological and demographic characteristics of white-collar criminals, violent criminals, and the public, they found significant differences between violent and white-collar criminals. They found few differences between white-collar criminals and the public. Their conclusion: Many fraud perpetrators look just like you and me.

Some fraud perpetrators are disgruntled and unhappy with their jobs and seek revenge against employers. Others are dedicated, hard-working, and trusted employees. Most have no previous criminal record; they were honest, valued, and respected members of their community. In other words, they were good people who did bad things.

Computer fraud perpetrators are typically younger and possess more computer experience and skills. Some are motivated by curiosity, a quest for knowledge, the desire to learn how things work, and the challenge of beating the system. Some view their actions as a game rather than as dishonest behavior. Others commit computer fraud to gain stature in the hacking community.

A large and growing number of computer fraud perpetrators are more predatory in nature and seek to turn their actions into money. These fraud perpetrators are more like the blue-collar criminals that look to prey on others by robbing them. The difference is that they use a computer instead of a gun.

Many first-time fraud perpetrators that are not caught, or that are caught but not prosecuted, move from being "unintentional" fraudsters to "serial" fraudsters.

Malicious software is a big business and a huge profit engine for the criminal underground, especially for digitally savvy hackers in Eastern Europe. They break into financial accounts and steal money. They sell data to spammers, organized crime, hackers, and the intelligence community. They market malware, such as virus-producing software, to others. Some work with organized crime. A recently convicted hacker was paid $150 for every 1,000 computers he infected with his adware and earned hundreds of thousands of dollars a year.

Cyber-criminals are a top FBI priority because they have moved from isolated and uncoordinated attacks to organized fraud schemes targeted at specific individuals and businesses. They use online payment companies to launder their ill-gotten gains. To hide their money, they take advantage of the lack of coordination between international law enforcement organizations.

THE FRAUD TRIANGLE

For most predatory fraud perpetrators, all the fraudster needs is an opportunity and the criminal mind-set that allows him/her to commit the fraud. For most first-time fraud perpetrators, three conditions are present when fraud occurs: a pressure, an opportunity, and a rationalization. This is referred to as the fraud triangle, and is the middle triangle in Figure 8-1.

pressure - A person's incentive or motivation for committing fraud.

PRESSURES A **pressure** is a person's incentive or motivation for committing fraud. Three types of pressures that lead to misappropriations are shown in the Employee Pressure Triangle in Figure 8-1 and are summarized in Table 8-2.

Financial pressures often motivate misappropriation frauds by employees. Examples of such pressures include living beyond one's means, heavy financial losses, or high personal debt. Often, the perpetrator feels the pressure cannot be shared and believes fraud is the best way out of a difficult situation. For example, Raymond Keller owned a grain elevator where he stored grain for local farmers. He made money by trading in commodities and built a lavish house overlooking the Des Moines River. Heavy financial losses created a severe cash

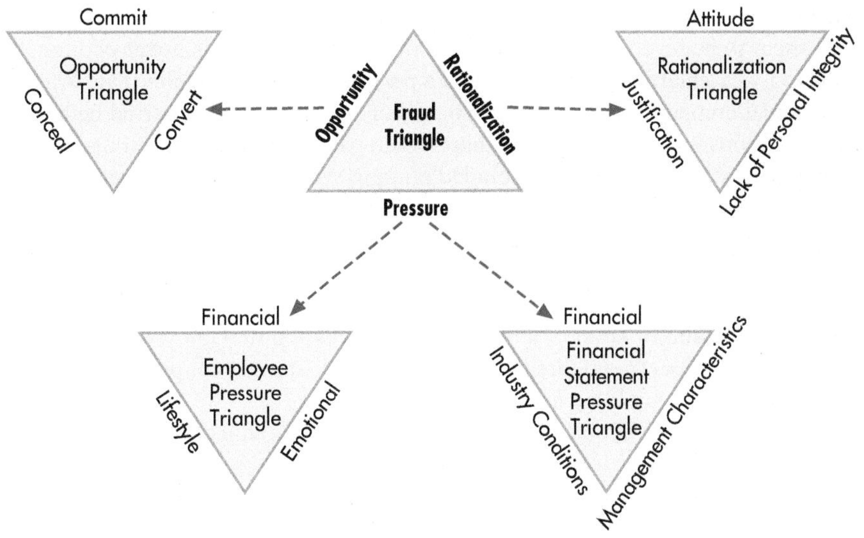

FIGURE 8-1
Fraud Triangle

shortage and high debt. He asked some farmers to wait for their money, gave others bad checks, and sold grain that did not belong to him. Finally, the seven banks to which he owed more than $3 million began to call their loans. When a state auditor showed up unexpectedly, Raymond took his life rather than face the consequences of his fraud.

A second type of pressure is emotional. Many employee frauds are motivated by greed. Some employees turn to fraud because they have strong feelings of resentment or believe they have been treated unfairly. They may feel their pay is too low, their contributions are not appreciated, or the company is taking advantage of them. A California accountant, passed over for a raise, increased his salary by 10%, the amount of the average raise. He defended his actions by saying he was only taking what was rightfully his. When asked why he did not increase his salary by 11%, he responded that he would have been stealing 1%.

Other people are motivated by the challenge of "beating the system" or subverting system controls and breaking into a system. When a company boasted that its new system was impenetrable, a team of individuals took less than 24 hours to break into the system and leave a message that the system had been compromised.

Some people commit fraud to keep pace with other family members or win a "who has the most or best" competition. A plastic surgeon, making $800,000 a year, defrauded his clinic of $200,000 to compete in the family "game" of financial one-upmanship.

TABLE 8-2 Pressures That Can Lead to Employee Fraud

Financial	Emotional	Lifestyle
Living beyond one's means	Excessive greed, ego, pride, ambition	Gambling habit
High personal debt/expenses	Performance not recognized	Drug or alcohol addiction
"Inadequate" salary/income	Job dissatisfaction	Sexual relationships
Poor credit ratings	Fear of losing job	Family/peer pressure
Heavy financial losses	Need for power or control	
Bad investments	Overt, deliberate nonconformity	
Tax avoidance	Inability to abide by or respect rules	
Unreasonable quotas/goals	Challenge of beating the system	
	Envy or resentment against others	
	Need to win financial one-upmanship competition	
	Coercion by bosses/top management	

Other people commit fraud due to some combination of greed, ego, pride, or ambition that causes them to believe that no matter how much they have, it is never enough. Thomas Coughlin was a vice-chairman of Walmart and a personal friend of founder Sam Walton. Even though his annual compensation exceeded $6 million, over a five-year period he had subordinates create fictitious invoices so that Walmart would pay for hundreds of thousands of dollars of personal expenses. These expenses included hunting vacations, a $2,590 pen for Coughlin's dog, and a $1,400 pair of alligator boots. Dennis Kozlowski and Mark Swartz, the CEO and CFO of Tyco International, were convicted of stealing $170 million from Tyco by abusing the company's loan program and by granting themselves unauthorized bonuses.

A third type of employee pressure is a person's lifestyle. The person may need funds to support a gambling habit or support a drug or alcohol addiction. One young woman embezzled funds because her boyfriend threatened to leave her if she did not provide him the money he needed to support his gambling and drug addictions.

Three types of organizational pressures that motivate management to misrepresent financial statements are shown in the Financial Statement Pressure triangle in Figure 8-1 and summarized in Table 8-3. A prevalent financial pressure is a need to meet or exceed earnings expectations to keep a stock price from falling. Managers create significant pressure with unduly aggressive earnings forecasts or unrealistic performance standards or with incentive programs that motivate employees to falsify financial results to keep their jobs or to receive stock options and other incentive payments. Industry conditions such as new regulatory requirements or significant market saturation with declining margins can motivate fraud.

opportunity - The condition or situation that allows a person or organization to commit and conceal a dishonest act and convert it to personal gain.

OPPORTUNITIES As shown in the Opportunity Triangle in Figure 8-1, **opportunity** is the condition or situation, including one's personal abilities, that allows a perpetrator to do three things:

1. ***Commit the fraud.*** The theft of assets is the most common type of misappropriation. Most instances of fraudulent financial reporting involve overstatements of assets or revenues, understatements of liabilities, or failures to disclose information.
2. ***Conceal the fraud.*** To prevent detection when assets are stolen or financial statements are overstated, perpetrators must keep the accounting equation in balance by inflating

TABLE 8-3 Pressures That Can Lead to Financial Statement Fraud

Management Characteristics	Industry Conditions	Financial
Questionable management ethics, management style, and track record	Declining industry	Intense pressure to meet or exceed earnings expectations
Unduly aggressive earnings forecasts, performance standards, accounting methods, or incentive programs	Industry or technology changes leading to declining demand or product obsolescence	Significant cash flow problems; unusual difficulty collecting receivables, paying payables
Significant incentive compensation based on achieving unduly aggressive goals	New regulatory requirements that impair financial stability or profitability	Heavy losses, high or undiversified risk, high dependence on debt, or unduly restrictive debt covenants
Management actions or transactions with no clear business justification	Significant competition or market saturation, with declining margins	Heavy dependence on new or unproven product lines
Oversensitivity to the effects of alternative accounting treatments on earnings per share	Significant tax changes or adjustments	Severe inventory obsolescence or excessive inventory buildup
Strained relationship with past auditors		Economic conditions (inflation, recession)
Failure to correct errors on a timely basis, leading to even greater problems		Litigation, especially management vs. shareholders
High management/employee turnover		Impending business failure or bankruptcy
Unusual/odd related-party relationships		Problems with regulatory agencies
		High vulnerability to rise in interest rates
		Poor or deteriorating financial position
		Unusually rapid growth or profitability compared to companies in same industry
		Significant estimates involving highly subjective judgments or uncertainties

other assets or decreasing liabilities or equity. Concealment often takes more effort and time and leaves behind more evidence than the theft or misrepresentation. Taking cash requires only a few seconds; altering records to hide the theft is more challenging and time-consuming.

One way for an employee to hide a theft of company assets is to charge the stolen item to an expense account. The perpetrator's exposure is limited to a year or less, because expense accounts are zeroed out at the end of each year. Perpetrators who hide a theft in a balance sheet account must continue the concealment.

Another way to hide a theft of company assets is to use a lapping scheme. In a **lapping** scheme, an employee of Company Z steals the cash or checks customer A mails in to pay the money it owes to Company Z. Later, the employee uses funds from customer B to pay off customer A's balance. Funds from customer C are used to pay off customer B's balance, and so forth. Because the theft involves two asset accounts (cash and accounts receivable), the cover-up must continue indefinitely unless the money is replaced or the debt is written off the books.

lapping - Concealing the theft of cash by means of a series of delays in posting collections to accounts receivable.

An individual, for his own personal gain or on behalf of a company, can hide the theft of cash using a check-kiting scheme. In **check kiting**, cash is created using the lag between the time a check is deposited and the time it clears the bank. Suppose an individual or a company opens accounts in banks A, B, and C. The perpetrator "creates" cash by depositing a $1,000 check from bank B in bank C and withdrawing the funds. If it takes two days for the check to clear bank B, he has created $1,000 for two days. After two days, the perpetrator deposits a $1,000 check from bank A in bank B to cover the created $1,000 for two more days. At the appropriate time, $1,000 is deposited from bank C in bank A. The scheme continues—writing checks and making deposits as needed to keep the checks from bouncing—until the person is caught or he deposits money to cover the created and stolen cash. Electronic banking systems make kiting harder because the time between a fraudster depositing the check in one bank and the check being presented to the other bank for payment is shortened.

check kiting - Creating cash using the lag between the time a check is deposited and the time it clears the bank.

3. ***Convert the theft or misrepresentation to personal gain***. In a misappropriation, fraud perpetrators who do not steal cash or use the stolen assets personally must convert them to a spendable form. For example, employees who steal inventory or equipment sell the items or otherwise convert them to cash. In cases of falsified financial statements, perpetrators convert their actions to personal gain through indirect benefits; that is, they keep their jobs, their stock rises, they receive pay raises and promotions, or they gain more power and influence.

Table 8-4 lists frequently mentioned opportunities. Many opportunities are the result of a deficient system of internal controls, such as deficiencies in proper segregation of duties, authorization procedures, clear lines of authority, proper supervision, adequate documents and records, safeguarding assets, or independent checks on performance. Management permits fraud by inattention or carelessness. Management commits fraud by overriding internal controls or using a position of power to compel subordinates to perpetrate it. The most prevalent opportunity for fraud results from a company's failure to design and *enforce* its internal control system.

Companies who do not perform a background check on potential employees risk hiring a "phantom controller." In one case, a company president stopped by the office one night, saw a light on in the controller's office, and went to see why he was working late. The president was surprised to find a complete stranger at work. An investigation showed that the controller was not an accountant and had been fired from three jobs over the prior eight years. Unable to do the accounting work, he hired someone to do his work for him at night. What he was good at was stealing money—he had embezzled several million dollars.

Other factors provide an opportunity to commit and conceal fraud when the company has unclear policies and procedures, fails to teach and stress corporate honesty, and fails to prosecute those who perpetrate fraud. Examples include large, unusual, or complex transactions; numerous adjusting entries at year-end; questionable accounting practices; pushing accounting principles to the limit; related-party transactions; incompetent personnel, inadequate staffing, rapid turnover of key employees, lengthy tenure in a key job, and lack of training.

TABLE 8-4 Opportunities Permitting Employee and Financial Statement Fraud

Internal Control Factors	Other Factors
Failure to enforce/monitor internal controls	Large, unusual, or complex transactions
Management's failure to be involved in the internal control system	Numerous adjusting entries at year-end
Management override of controls	Related-party transactions
Managerial carelessness, inattention to details	Accounting department that is understaffed, overworked
Dominant and unchallenged management	Incompetent personnel
Ineffective oversight by board of directors	Rapid turnover of key employees
No effective internal auditing staff	Lengthy tenure in a key job
Infrequent third-party reviews	Overly complex organizational structure
Insufficient separation of authorization, custody, and record-keeping duties	No code of conduct, conflict-of-interest statement, or definition of unacceptable behavior
Too much trust in key employees	Frequent changes in auditors, legal counsel
Inadequate supervision	Operating on a crisis basis
Unclear lines of authority	Close association with suppliers/customers
Lack of proper authorization procedures	Assets highly susceptible to misappropriation
No independent checks on performance	Questionable accounting practices
Inadequate documents and records	Pushing accounting principles to the limit
Inadequate system for safeguarding assets	Unclear company policies and procedures
No physical or logical security system	Failing to teach and stress corporate honesty
No audit trails	Failure to prosecute dishonest employees
Failure to conduct background checks	Low employee morale and loyalty
No policy of annual vacations, rotation of duties	

Frauds occur when employees build mutually beneficial personal relationships with customers or suppliers, such as a purchasing agent buying goods at an inflated price in exchange for a vendor kickback. Fraud can also occur when a crisis arises and normal control procedures are ignored. A Fortune 500 company had three multimillion-dollar frauds the year it disregarded standard internal control procedures while trying to resolve a series of crises.

rationalization - The excuse that fraud perpetrators use to justify their illegal behavior.

RATIONALIZATIONS A **rationalization** allows perpetrators to justify their illegal behavior. As shown in the Rationalization Triangle in Figure 8-1, this can take the form of a justification ("I only took what they owed me"), an attitude ("The rules do not apply to me"), or a lack of personal integrity ("Getting what I want is more important than being honest"). In other words, perpetrators rationalize that they are not being dishonest, that honesty is not required of them, or that they value what they take more than honesty and integrity. Some perpetrators rationalize that they are not hurting a real person, but a faceless and nameless computer system or an impersonal company that will not miss the money. One such perpetrator stole no more than $20,000, the maximum loss the insurance company would reimburse.

The most frequent rationalizations include the following:

- I am only "borrowing" it, and I will repay my "loan."
- You would understand if you knew how badly I needed it.
- What I did was not that serious.
- It was for a good cause (the Robin Hood syndrome: robbing the rich to give to the poor).
- In my very important position of trust, I am above the rules.
- Everyone else is doing it.
- No one will ever know.
- The company owes it to me; I am taking no more than is rightfully mine.

Fraud occurs when people have high pressures; an opportunity to commit, conceal, and convert; and the ability to rationalize away their personal integrity. Fraud is less likely to occur when people have few pressures, little opportunity, and high personal integrity. Usually all three elements of the fraud triangle must be present to some degree before a person commits fraud.

Likewise, fraud can be prevented by eliminating or minimizing one or more fraud triangle elements. Although companies can reduce or minimize some pressures and rationalizations, their greatest opportunity to prevent fraud lies in reducing or minimizing opportunity by implementing a good system of internal controls. Controls are discussed in Chapters 10 through 13.

Computer Fraud

Computer fraud is any fraud that requires computer technology to perpetrate it. Examples include:

computer fraud - Any type of fraud that requires computer technology to perpetrate.

- Unauthorized theft, use, access, modification, copying, or destruction of software, hardware, or data.
- Theft of assets covered up by altering computer records.
- Obtaining information or tangible property illegally using computers.

THE RISE IN COMPUTER FRAUD

It is estimated that computer fraud costs the United States somewhere between $70 billion and $125 billion a year and that the costs increase significantly each year. Computer systems are particularly vulnerable for the following reasons:

- People who break into corporate databases can steal, destroy, or alter massive amounts of data in very little time, often leaving little evidence. One bank lost $10 million in just a few minutes.
- Computer fraud can be much more difficult to detect than other types of fraud.
- Some organizations grant employees, customers, and suppliers access to their system. The number and variety of these access points significantly increase the risks.
- Computer programs need to be modified illegally only once for them to operate improperly for as long as they are in use.
- Personal computers (PCs) are vulnerable. It is difficult to control physical access to each PC that accesses a network, and PCs and their data can be lost, stolen, or misplaced. Also, PC users are generally less aware of the importance of security and control. The more legitimate users there are, the greater the risk of an attack on the network.
- Computer systems face a number of unique challenges: reliability, equipment failure, dependency on power, damage from water or fire, vulnerability to electromagnetic interference and interruption, and eavesdropping.

As early as 1979, *Time* magazine labeled computer fraud a "growth industry." Most businesses have been victimized by computer fraud. Recently, a spy network in China hacked into 1,300 government and corporate computers in 103 countries. The number of incidents, the total dollar losses, and the sophistication of the perpetrators and the schemes used to commit computer fraud are increasing rapidly for several reasons:

1. ***Not everyone agrees on what constitutes computer fraud.*** Many people do not believe that copying software constitutes computer fraud. Software publishers think otherwise and prosecute those who make illegal copies. Some people do not think it is a crime to browse someone else's computer files if they do no harm, whereas companies whose data are browsed feel much differently.
2. ***Many instances of computer fraud go undetected.*** A few years ago, it was estimated that U.S. Defense Department computers were attacked more than a half million times per year, with the number of incidents increasing 50% to 100% per year. Defense Department staffers and outside consultants made 38,000 "friendly hacks" on their networks to evaluate security. Almost 70% were successful, and the Defense Department detected only 4% of the attacks. The Pentagon, which has the U.S. government's most advanced hacker-awareness program, detected and reported only 1 in 500 break-ins. The Defense Department estimates that more than 100 foreign spy agencies are working to gain access to U.S. government computers as well as an unknown number of criminal organizations.

3. ***A high percentage of frauds is not reported*.** Many companies believe the adverse publicity would result in copycat fraud and a loss of customer confidence, which could cost more than the fraud itself.
4. ***Many networks are not secure*.** Dan Farmer, who wrote SATAN (a network security testing tool), tested 2,200 high-profile websites at government institutions, banks, and newspapers. Only three sites detected and contacted him.
5. ***Internet sites offer step-by-step instructions on how to perpetrate computer fraud and abuse*.** For instance, an Internet search found thousands of sites telling how to conduct a "denial of service" attack, a common form of computer abuse.
6. ***Law enforcement cannot keep up with the growth of computer fraud*.** Because of lack of funding and skilled staff, the FBI investigates only 1 in 15 computer crimes.
7. ***Calculating losses is difficult*.** It is difficult to calculate total losses when information is stolen, websites are defaced, and viruses shut down entire computer systems.

This increase in computer fraud created the need for the cyber sleuths discussed in Focus 8-2.

COMPUTER FRAUD CLASSIFICATIONS

As shown in Figure 8-2, computer fraud can be categorized using the data processing model.

INPUT FRAUD The simplest and most common way to commit a computer fraud is to alter or falsify computer input. It requires little skill; perpetrators need only understand how the system operates so they can cover their tracks. For example:

FOCUS 8-2 Cyber Sleuths

Two forensic experts, disguised as repair people, entered an office after hours. They took a digital photograph of three employee desks, made a copy of each employee's hard drive, and used the photo to leave everything as they found it. When the hard drive copy was analyzed, they found evidence of a fraud and notified the company who had hired them. The company turned the case over to law enforcement for investigation and prosecution.

The forensic experts breaking into the company and copying the data worked for a Big Four accounting firm. The accountants, turned cyber sleuths, specialize in catching fraud perpetrators. Cyber sleuths come from a variety of backgrounds, including accounting, information systems, government, law enforcement, military, and banking.

Cyber sleuths need the following skills:

- *Ability to follow a trail, think analytically, and be thorough.* Fraud perpetrators leave tracks, and a cyber sleuth must think analytically to follow paper and electronic trails and uncover fraud. They must be thorough so they do not miss or fail to follow up on clues.
- *Good understanding of information technology (IT).* Cyber sleuths need to understand data storage, data communications, and how to retrieve hidden or deleted files and e-mails.
- *Ability to think like a fraud perpetrator.* Cyber sleuths must understand what motivates perpetrators, how they think, and the schemes they use to commit and conceal fraud.
- *Ability to use hacking tools and techniques.* Cyber sleuths need to understand the tools computer criminals use to perpetrate fraud and abuse.

Another way to fight crime is to develop software to examine bank or accounting records for suspicious transactions. Pattern recognition software searches millions of bank, brokerage, and insurance accounts and reviews trillions of dollars worth of transactions each day. Some companies, such as PayPal, use the software to lower their fraud rates significantly.

This software is based on a mathematical principle known as Benford's Law. In 1938, Frank Benford discovered that one can predict the first or second digit in a set of naturally occurring numerical data with surprising accuracy. Benford found that the number 1 is the first digit 31% of the time, compared to only 5% for the number 9. Pattern recognition software uses Benford's Law to examine company databases and transaction records to root out accounting fraud.

Students seeking to find their niche in life should be aware that if playing James Bond sounds appealing, then a career as a computer forensics expert might be the way to go.

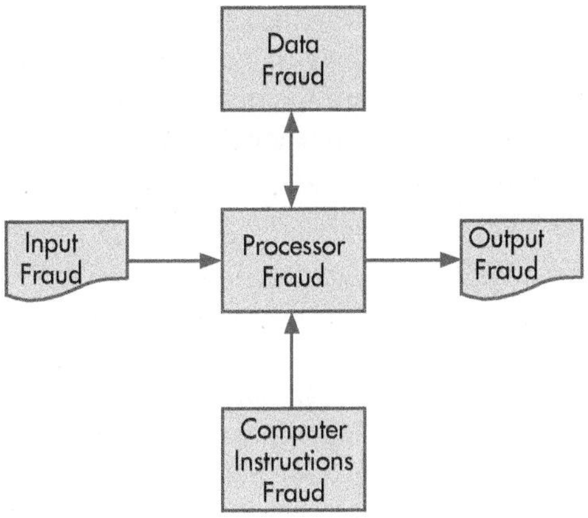

FIGURE 8-2
Computer Fraud Classifications

- A man opened a bank account in New York and had blank bank deposit slips printed that were similar to those available in bank lobbies, except that his account number was encoded on them. He replaced the deposit slips in the bank lobby with his forged ones. For three days, bank deposits using the forged slips went into his account. The perpetrator withdrew the money and disappeared. He was never found.
- A man used desktop publishing to prepare bills for office supplies that were never ordered or delivered and mailed them to local companies. The invoices were for less than $300, an amount that often does not require purchase orders or approvals. A high percentage of the companies paid the bills.
- An employee at the Veteran's Memorial Coliseum sold customers full-price tickets, entered them as half-price tickets, and pocketed the difference.
- Railroad employees entered data to scrap more than 200 railroad cars. They removed the cars from the railway system, repainted them, and sold them.
- A company providing on-site technical support created exact duplicates of the checks used to pay them, using off-the-shelf scanners, graphics software, and printers. If the double payments were caught, the bank checked their microfiche copies of the two identical checks, assumed a clerical error had occurred, and wrote off the loss as a gesture of maintaining good customer relations.

PROCESSOR FRAUD Processor fraud includes unauthorized system use, including the theft of computer time and services. For example:

- An insurance company installed software to detect abnormal system activity and found that employees were using company computers to run an illegal gambling website.
- Two accountants without the appropriate access rights hacked into Cisco's stock option system, transferred more than $6.3 million of Cisco stock to their brokerage accounts, and sold the stock. They used part of the funds to support an extravagant lifestyle, including a $52,000 Mercedes-Benz, a $44,000 diamond ring, and a $20,000 Rolex watch.

COMPUTER INSTRUCTIONS FRAUD Computer instructions fraud includes tampering with company software, copying software illegally, using software in an unauthorized manner, and developing software to carry out an unauthorized activity. This approach used to be uncommon because it required specialized programming knowledge. Today, it is more frequent because of the many web pages that tell users how to create them.

DATA FRAUD Illegally using, copying, browsing, searching, or harming company data constitutes data fraud. The biggest cause of data breaches is employee negligence.

Companies now report that their losses are greater from the electronic theft of data than from stealing physical assets. It is estimated that, on average, it costs a company $6.6 million, including lost business, to recover from a data breach.

Company employees are much more likely to perpetrate data fraud than outsiders are. A recent study shows that 59% of employees who lost or left a job admitted to stealing confidential company information. Almost 25% of them had access to their former employer's computer system. In addition, more cases are beginning to surface of employees stealing their employer's intellectual properties and selling them to foreign companies or governments.

In the absence of controls, it is not hard for an employee to steal data. For example, an employee using a small flash drive can steal large amounts of data and remove it without being detected. In today's world, you can even buy wristwatches with a USB port and internal memory.

The following are some recent examples of stolen data:

- The office manager of a Wall Street law firm sold information to friends and relatives about prospective mergers and acquisitions found in Word files. They made several million dollars trading the securities.
- A 22-year-old Kazakh man broke into Bloomberg's network and stole account information, including that of Michael Bloomberg, the mayor of New York and the founder of the financial news company. He demanded $200,000 in exchange for not using or selling the information. He was arrested in London when accepting the ransom.
- A software engineer tried to steal Intel's new microprocessor plans. Because he could view but not copy or print the plans, he photographed them screen by screen late at night in his office. Unbeknownst to him, one of Intel's controls was to notify security when the plans were viewed after business hours. He was caught red-handed and arrested.
- Cyber-criminals used sophisticated hacking and identity theft techniques to hack into seven accounts at a major online brokerage firm. They sold the securities in those accounts and used the cash to pump up the price of low-priced, thinly traded companies they already owned. Then they sold the stocks in their personal accounts for huge gains. E-trade lost $18 million and Ameritrade $4 million in similar pump-and-dump schemes.
- The U.S. Department of Veterans Affairs was sued because an employee laptop containing the records of 26.5 million veterans was stolen, exposing them to identity theft. Soon thereafter, a laptop with the records of 38,000 people disappeared from a subcontractor's office.

Data can also be changed, damaged, destroyed, or defaced, especially by disgruntled employees and hackers. Vandals broke into the NCAA's website before basketball tournament pairings were announced and posted swastikas, racial slurs, and a white-power logo. The Air Force, CIA, and NASA have also been the victims of high-profile website attacks. A Computer Security Institute analyst described the problem as "cyberspace vandals with digital spray cans."

Data can be lost as a result of negligence or carelessness. Particularly good sources of confidential data are the hard drives of used computers donated to charity or resold. A professor at a major university bought 10 used computers for his computer forensics class. Using commercially available software, his students found highly confidential data on 8 of the 10 hard drives.

Deleting files does not erase them. Even reformatting a hard drive may not wipe it clean. To erase a hard drive completely, special software must be used. When used computers are to be disposed of, the best way to protect data is to destroy the hard drive.

OUTPUT FRAUD Unless properly safeguarded, displayed or printed output can be stolen, copied, or misused. A Dutch engineer showed that some monitors emit television-like signals that, with the help of some inexpensive electronic gear, can be displayed on a television screen. Under ideal conditions, the signals can be picked up from monitors two miles away. One engineer set up equipment in the basement of an apartment building and read a monitor on the eighth floor.

Fraud perpetrators use computers to forge authentic-looking outputs, such as a paycheck. A fraud perpetrator can scan a company paycheck, use desktop publishing software to erase the payee and amount, and print fictitious paychecks. Losses to check fraud in the United States total more than $20 billion a year.

Preventing and Detecting Fraud and Abuse

To prevent fraud, organizations must create a climate that makes fraud less likely, increases the difficulty of committing it, improves detection methods, and reduces the amount lost if a fraud occurs. These measures are summarized in Table 8-5 and discussed in Chapters 10 through 13.

TABLE 8-5 Summary of Ways to Prevent and Detect Fraud and Errors

Make Fraud and Errors Less Likely to Occur

- Create an organizational culture that stresses integrity and commitment to ethical values and competence.
- Adopt an organizational structure, management philosophy, operating style, and risk appetite that minimizes the likelihood of fraud.
- Obtain Board of Director and C-level buy-in and support for the corporate application of security standards and require oversight from an active, involved, and independent audit committee of the board of directors.
- Assign authority and responsibility for business objectives to specific departments and individuals, encourage them to use initiative to solve problems, and hold them accountable for achieving those objectives.
- Identify the events that lead to increased fraud and error risk, and take steps to prevent, avoid, share, or accept that risk.
- Develop a comprehensive set of security policies to guide the design and implementation of specific control procedures, and communicate them effectively to company employees.
- Ensure that corporate security standards are applied to all new technologies before they are implemented.
- Continuously improve security policies and procedures as threats change and evolve.
- Automate security processes where it is possible to do so.
- Implement human resource policies for hiring, compensating, evaluating, promoting, and discharging employees that send messages about the required level of ethical behavior and integrity.
- Develop a comprehensive set of anti-fraud policies that clearly set forth the expectation for honest and ethical behavior and explain the consequences of dishonest and fraudulent acts.
- Effectively supervise employees, including monitoring their performance and correcting their errors.
- Provide employee support programs; this provides a place for employees to turn to when they face pressures they might be inclined to resolve by perpetrating a fraud.
- Maintain open communication lines with employees, customers, suppliers, and relevant external parties (banks, regulators, tax authorities, etc.).
- Create and implement a company code of conduct to put in writing what the company expects of its employees.
- Train employees in integrity and ethical considerations, as well as security and fraud prevention measures.
- Require annual employee vacations and signed confidentiality agreements; periodically rotate duties of key employees.
- Implement formal and rigorous project development and acquisition controls, as well as change management controls.
- Increase the penalty for committing fraud by prosecuting fraud perpetrators more vigorously.

Increase the Difficulty of Committing Fraud

- Develop and implement a strong system of internal controls.
- Segregate the accounting functions of authorization, recording, and custody.
- Implement a proper segregation of duties between systems functions.
- Restrict physical and remote access to system resources to authorized personnel.
- Require transactions and activities to be authorized by appropriate supervisory personnel. Have the system authenticate the person, and their right to perform the transaction, before allowing the transaction to take place.
- Use properly designed documents and records to capture and process transactions.
- Safeguard all assets, records, and data.
- Require independent checks on performance, such as reconciliation of two independent sets of records, where practical.
- Implement computer-based controls over data input, computer processing, data storage, data transmission, and information output.
- Encrypt stored and transmitted data and programs to protect them from unauthorized access and use.
- When disposing of used computers, destroy the hard drive to keep criminals from mining recycled hard drives.
- Fix software vulnerabilities by installing operating system updates, as well as security and application programs.

Improve Detection Methods

- Develop and implement a fraud risk assessment program that evaluates both the likelihood and the magnitude of fraudulent activity and assesses the processes and controls that can deter and detect the potential fraud.
- Create an audit trail so individual transactions can be traced through the system to the financial statements and financial statement data can be traced back to individual transactions.
- Conduct periodic external and internal audits, as well as special network security audits; these can be especially helpful if sometimes performed on a surprise basis.
- Install fraud detection software.
- Implement a fraud hotline.
- Motivate employees to report fraud by implementing whistleblower rewards and protections for those who come forward.
- Employ a computer security officer, computer consultants, and forensic specialists as needed.
- Monitor system activities, including computer and network security efforts, usage and error logs, and all malicious actions. Use intrusion detection systems to help automate the monitoring process.

TABLE 8-5 Continued

Reduce Losses from Fraud and Errors
- Maintain adequate insurance.
- Develop comprehensive contingency, disaster recovery, and business continuity plans.
- Store backup copies of program and data files in a secure off-site location.
- Use software to monitor system activity and recover from the different types of threats.

USING DATA ANALYTICS TO PREVENT AND DETECT FRAUD

In addition to the items in Table 8-5, data analytics can be used to help prevent and detect fraud and errors. The fundamentals of data analytics were discussed in Chapters 5 through 7. Here, we give a brief overview of how data analytics can be used for fraud prevention and detection.

Fraud is often detected by identifying trends, patterns, anomalies, and exceptions in data that are often referred to as red flags of fraud. Auditors often test accounts and data by taking a sample of a population and then projecting this sample result onto the entire population. This is not very effective when trying to detect fraud. Fraud detection is much more effective when data analytics software tools are used to examine an entire data population, especially when the fraud is hidden in a very large amount of data. Using data analytics software, every transaction or item in the data can be compared against selected criteria and any items identified as anomalies, unusual, or unexpected could be tagged for human examination. Thus, data analytics don't directly detect fraud; instead, experienced humans are needed to examine and understand any suspicious activities identified and to determine if fraud is involved. For example, fraud analytics software at an insurance company could compare each new claim to a fraud model that predicts the likelihood that the claim is bogus. If the fraud probability is high enough, it is routed to a fraud investigator for further investigation. Otherwise, the claim is forwarded to the claim processing department.

To use data analytics to effectively detect and deter fraud, investigators must have a thorough understanding of the fraud analytics tool used and understand the organization, its business, its practices and procedures, and its data. They must be able to recognize and correct any errors in the data examined by the analytics tool and be aware of common fraud indicators related to the data examined. Then they use their knowledge and understanding to create effective data analytics tests, with an understanding that it is more important to find higher risk anomalies than lower risk ones. They use their understanding of the business and their fraud investigation skills to examine the data analysis results to determine if an anomaly has a reasonable explanation, is the result of an unintentional error, or constitutes fraud. This often requires the investigator to examine company and transaction documentation, interview people, and evaluate a company's policies and procedures.

Not only is detecting and preventing fraud a difficult task, fraud is an adaptive crime as new technologies and new information systems provide perpetrators with new ways to commit fraud. For example, recent research shows that Internet-based transactions are 10 times more likely to be fraudulent than in-store transactions. Accordingly, investigators need to continuously improve their analytics tests. The first time an analytics test is used, there are often many anomalies; few of them are errors and even fewer are fraudulent transactions. An analysis of the anomalies and the tests used can help refine the analytics and result in fewer non-error and non-fraud anomalies in the future.

There are several important benefits to using data analytics to prevent and detect fraud. They can be used to:

- Test for the most frequent types of fraud schemes: financial statement, asset misappropriation, and corruption.
- Examine data reactively or proactively; that is, they can be used to detect fraud that has occurred and test transactions as they occur to prevent fraud from occurring.

- Identify fraud before it becomes material; that is, there are no small frauds, only frauds detected before they grow very large.
- Help investigators focus detection efforts on suspicious and high-risk transactions.
- Analyze numeric and non-numeric data and compare data from internal and diverse, external sources.
- Test internal controls to determine how well they are working, thereby allowing investigators to fix internal control weaknesses.

Likewise, there are some challenges to overcome in order to use data analytics to prevent and detect fraud. They include:

- Properly scoping out what data or account is to be tested.
- Obtaining the proper data in a clean (minimal errors) and electronic format.
- Large numbers of false positives (anomalies that are neither errors or frauds).
- Dealing with various and complex software systems, data storage systems, and business processes.
- Dealing with data security, processing integrity, availability, privacy, and confidentiality concerns.
- Cost of acquiring data analytics software and training employees to use it effectively.
- Fraud perpetrators do not want to be caught so they try to conceal their fraudulent activities; the better they conceal them, the harder the fraud is to detect.

Data analytics can be used to test for all kinds of data, including accounting, financial, internal communications and documents, and external benchmarking data. Data analytics can be used to test documents and processes for sales and cash collections (see Chapter 14), purchasing and cash disbursement (see Chapter 15), manufacturing and inventory (see Chapter 16), human resources and payroll (see Chapter 17), and financial reports (see Chapter 18). It can also be used to test unstructured data such as social media activity, news releases, emails, and texts.

Data analytics is an excellent tool to use to examine big data, which are data repositories characterized by some combination of very large data quantity, volume, velocity, diversity, or variety. Systems that use these repositories are often complex and contain data that may require data analytics software to help connect dots between data from within and without the data repositories in order to explain relationships, discover insights, and improve business processes and decision-making.

Many data analytics techniques are used to detect fraud. Here are a few of the more frequently used:

- Outlier detection. Items outside the range of similar data can indicate fraud, such as a purchase or sales order number out of sequence. To combat fraud, some banks will notify users of a check number significantly out of order.
- Anomaly detection using trends and patterns. Anything unexpected, out of the ordinary, or not in line with expected trends or patterns can indicate fraud. One way to perpetrate cash disbursements fraud is to begin making payments to an inactive vendor. Examining this new activity might uncover a fraud.
- Regression analysis. This statistical method helps evaluate how strong the connection is between two or more data items. For example, there may be a historical relationship between shipping costs and sales. If sales were to increase dramatically without a corresponding increase in shipping costs, that might indicate fictitious sales.
- Semantic modeling. Using semantic analysis, investigators can analyze both structured and unstructured text for hidden clues to fraudulent activity. For example, computers can analyze reports written by those involved in an automobile insurance claim (policy holders, claims adjusters, insurance agents, and police) to see if there are inconsistencies that might indicate a fraudulent claim.

Another popular data analytics technique to detect fraud is called Benford's Law. It is explained in Focus 8-3.

FOCUS 8-3 Using Benford's Law to Detect Fraud

Benford's Law is a probability distribution for the likelihood of a digit in a large set of naturally occurring numbers. It states that in certain large sets of numbers, the number 1 will be the first digit 30.1% of the time. The number 2 is the first digit 17.61% of the time. Likewise, probability distribution percentages can also be calculated for digits 0 and 3 through 9. The following table shows what percent of the time a specific number between 0 and 9 (see first column) will appear as the first through fourth digit (shown in the next four columns). Note in each column the decreasing frequency with which larger numbers are used.

Number	1st Digit	2nd Digit	3nd Digit	4th Digit
0		11.968%	10.178%	10.018%
1	30.103%	11.389%	10.138%	10.014%
2	17.609%	10.882%	10.097%	10.010%
3	12.494%	10.433%	10.057%	10.006%
4	9.691%	10.031%	10.018%	10.002%
5	7.918%	9.668%	9.979%	9.998%
6	6.695%	9.337%	9.940%	9.994%
7	5.799%	9.035%	9.902%	9.990%
8	5.115%	8.757%	9.864%	9.986%
9	4.576%	8.500%	9.827%	9.982%

This makes sense logically. In most naturally occurring numbering and counting systems, the numerical sequence begins with a 1 and then increases, making lower numbers more frequent than larger ones.

The law is usually not applicable when numbers are assigned, such as telephone numbers and Social Security numbers. Nor are they applicable to small data sets or those with a stated minimum and maximum, like ATM fees or limits on withdrawal amounts. However, the law does apply to many types of accounting data such as cash receipts and disbursements, credit card transactions, purchase orders, inventory quantities, and customer balances and refunds.

When a large set of numbers is expected to follow Benford's Law, fraud investigators can use the law to help detect fraud and errors. The investigator can create a distribution of the first few digits of the numbers and compare it to the Benford's Law tables. Any anomalies can be investigated to see if they indicate fraud. Here are a few brief examples of how Benford's Law was or could have been used to test data for fraud:

- Benford's Law is used to test for fabricated tax returns since valid tax data usually follows Benford's Law, whereas fraudulent returns do not.
- A research study showed that Greece may have manipulated economic data to qualify to join the European Union
- The unrealistic returns paid in the Bernie Madoff Ponzi schemes were significantly different than what would have been expected using the Benford probability distribution. Applying the Benford probabilities to the scam would likely have uncovered anomalies leading to the detecting of the fraud.

Problem 8.10 refers you to a *Journal of Accountancy* article where Benford's Law is explained in greater detail and where you are shown how use Excel to perform a Benford's Law test.

Summary and Case Conclusion

Needing evidence to support his belief that Don Hawkins had committed a fraud, Jason Scott expanded the scope of his investigation. A week later, Jason presented his findings to the president of Northwest. To make his case hit close to home, Jason presented her with a copy of her IRS withholding report and pointed out her withholdings. Then he showed her a printout of payroll withholdings and pointed out the $5 difference, as well as the difference of several thousand dollars in Don Hawkins's withholdings. This got her attention, and Jason explained how he believed a fraud had been perpetrated.

During the latter part of the previous year, Don had been in charge of a payroll program update. Because of problems with other projects, other systems personnel had not reviewed the update. Jason asked a former programmer to review the code changes. She found program code that subtracted $5 from each employee's withholdings and added it to Don's withholdings. Don got his hands on the money when the IRS sent him a huge refund check.

Don apparently intended to use the scheme every year, as he had not removed the incriminating code. He must have known there was no reconciliation of payroll withholdings with the IRS report. His simple plan could have gone undetected for years if Jason had not overheard someone in the cafeteria talk about a $5 difference.

Jason learned that Don had become disgruntled when he was passed over the previous year for a managerial position. He made comments to coworkers about favoritism and unfair treatment and mentioned getting even with the company somehow. No one knew where he got the money, but Don purchased an expensive sports car in April, boasting that he had made a sizable down payment.

When the president asked how the company could prevent this fraud from happening again, Jason suggested the following guidelines:

1. Review internal controls to determine their effectiveness in preventing fraud. An existing control—reviewing program changes—could have prevented Don's scheme had it been followed. As a result, Jason suggested a stricter enforcement of the existing controls.
2. Put new controls into place to detect fraud. For example, Jason suggested a reconciliation of the IRS report and payroll record withholdings.
3. Train employees in fraud awareness, security measures, and ethical issues.

Jason urged the president to prosecute the case. She was reluctant to do so because of the adverse publicity and the problems it would cause Don's wife and children. Jason's supervisor tactfully suggested that if other employees found out that Don was not prosecuted, it would send the wrong message to the rest of the company. The president finally conceded to prosecute if the company could prove that Don was guilty. The president agreed to hire a forensic accountant to build a stronger case against Don and try to get him to confess.

KEY TERMS

sabotage 226
cookie 226
fraud 227
white-collar criminals 228
corruption 228
investment fraud 228
misappropriation of assets 228
fraudulent financial reporting 229
pressure 230
opportunity 232
lapping 233
check kiting 233
rationalization 234
computer fraud 235

AIS in Action

CHAPTER QUIZ

1. Which of the following is a fraud in which later payments on account are used to pay off earlier payments that were stolen?
   a. lapping
   b. kiting
   c. Ponzi scheme
   d. salami technique
2. Which type of fraud is associated with 50% of all auditor lawsuits?
   a. kiting
   b. fraudulent financial reporting
   c. Ponzi schemes
   d. lapping
3. Which of the following statements is false?
   a. The psychological profiles of white-collar criminals differ from those of violent criminals.
   b. The psychological profiles of white-collar criminals are significantly different from those of the general public.
   c. There is little difference between computer fraud perpetrators and other types of white-collar criminals.
   d. Some computer fraud perpetrators do not view themselves as criminals.

4. Which of the following conditions is/are usually necessary for a fraud to occur? (Select all correct answers.)
   a. pressure
   b. opportunity
   c. explanation
   d. rationalization

5. Which of the following is not an example of computer fraud?
   a. theft of money by altering computer records
   b. obtaining information illegally using a computer
   c. failure to perform preventive maintenance on a computer
   d. unauthorized modification of a software program

6. Which of the following causes the majority of computer security problems?
   a. human errors
   b. software errors
   c. natural disasters
   d. power outages

7. Which of the following is not one of the responsibilities of auditors in detecting fraud according to SAS No. 99?
   a. evaluating the results of their audit tests
   b. incorporating a technology focus
   c. discussing the risks of material fraudulent misstatements
   d. catching the perpetrators in the act of committing the fraud

8. Which of the following control procedures is most likely to deter lapping?
   a. encryption
   b. continual update of the access control matrix
   c. background check on employees
   d. periodic rotation of duties

9. Which of the following is the most important, basic, and effective control to deter fraud?
   a. enforced vacations
   b. logical access control
   c. segregation of duties
   d. virus protection controls

10. Once fraud has occurred, which of the following will reduce fraud losses? (Select all correct answers.)
   a. insurance
   b. regular backup of data and programs
   c. contingency plan
   d. segregation of duties

DISCUSSION QUESTIONS

8.1 Do you agree that the most effective way to obtain adequate system security is to rely on the integrity of company employees? Why, or why not? Does this seem ironic? What should a company do to ensure the integrity of its employees?

8.2 You are the president of a multinational company in which an executive confessed to kiting $100,000. What is kiting, and what can your company do to prevent it? How would you respond to the confession? What issues must you consider before pressing charges?

8.3 Discuss the following statement by Roswell Steffen, a convicted embezzler: "For every foolproof system, there is a method for beating it." Do you believe a completely secure computer system is possible? Explain. If internal controls are less than 100% effective, why should they be employed at all?

8.4 Revlon hired Logisticon to install a real-time invoice and inventory processing system. Seven months later, when the system crashed, Revlon blamed the Logisticon programming bugs they discovered and withheld payment on the contract. Logisticon contended that the software was fine and that it was the hardware that was faulty. When Revlon again refused payment, Logisticon repossessed the software by disabling the software and rendering the system unusable. After a three-day standoff, Logisticon reactivated the system. Revlon sued Logisticon, charging them with trespassing, breach of contract, and misappropriation of trade secrets (Revlon passwords). Logisticon countersued for breach of contract. The companies settled out of court.

Would Logisticon's actions be classified as sabotage or repossession? Why? Would you find the company guilty of committing a computer crime? Be prepared to defend your position to the class.

8.5 Because improved computer security measures sometimes create a new set of problems—user antagonism, sluggish response time, and hampered performance—some people believe the most effective computer security is educating users about good moral conduct. Richard Stallman, a computer activist, believes software licensing is antisocial because it prohibits the growth of technology by keeping information away from potential users. He believes high school and college students should have unlimited access to computers without security measures so that they can learn constructive and civilized behavior. He states that a protected system is a puzzle and, because it is human nature to solve puzzles, eliminating computer security so that there is no temptation to break in would reduce hacking.

Do you agree that software licensing is antisocial? Is ethical teaching the solution to computer security problems? Would the removal of computer security measures reduce the incidence of computer fraud? Why, or why not?

PROBLEMS

8.1 Match the terms with their definitions:

___ 1. corruption	a. Intentional act with the intent to destroy a system or its components
___ 2. fraud	b. Text file created by a website and stored on a visitor's computer that tells who the user is and what they have done
___ 3. rationalization	c. Any means a person uses to gain an unfair advantage over another person
___ 4. sabotage	d. Business people who commit fraud by resorting to trickery; their crimes usually involve a violation of trust or confidence
___ 5. cookie	e. Dishonest conduct by those in power; involves illegitimate, immoral, or unethical actions
___ 6. lapping	f. Software used to do harm
___ 7. opportunity	g. Theft of company assets by employees
___ 8. investment fraud	h. Intentional or reckless conduct that results in materially misleading financial statements
___ 9. computer fraud	i. Person's incentive or motivation for committing fraud
___ 10. check kiting	j. Resistance to change intended to destroy, cripple, or weaken system effectiveness
___ 11. white-collar criminals	k. Concealing theft of cash by delaying the posting of accounts receivable collections
___ 12. fraudulent financial reporting	l. Creating cash using the lag between the time a check is deposited and the time it clears the bank
___ 13. misappropriation of assets	m. Excuse fraud perpetrators use to justify their illegal behavior

____ **14.** pressure

n. Any type of fraud that requires computer technology to perpetrate

o. Condition that allows a person to commit and conceal a fraud and convert it to personal gain

p. Techniques or psychological tricks used to allow perpetrators to gain access to a building, computer, or network

q. Misrepresenting or omitting facts to promote an investment that promises fantastic profits with little or no risk

8.2 Select the correct answer(s) for the following multiple-choice questions. Note that there may be more than one correct answer.

1. Which of the following statements is (are) true?
   a. The type of computer fraud that is the most difficult because it requires the most skill is computer instructions fraud.
   b. Losses from the theft of physical assets are much greater than those from the electronic theft of data.
   c. In the absence of controls, it is not hard for a dishonest employee to steal data.
   d. The biggest cause of data breaches is organized hacker groups.
   e. The type of computer fraud that is simplest and most common and that requires the least amount of skill is data fraud.
2. Which of the following statements is (are) true?
   a. Strong, mutually beneficial personal relationships with suppliers is unlikely to result in fraud.
   b. Fraud is highly unlikely to occur when a crisis arises, and normal controls are suspended.
   c. Perpetrators who do not steal cash or use the stolen assets usually convert the assets to a spendable form.
   d. A huge fraud opportunity arises when a company has clear policies and procedures and teaches and stresses honesty.
   e. The biggest fraud opportunity arises from a company's failure to design and enforce its internal control system.
3. The number of incidents and the total dollar losses from computer fraud are increasing rapidly for which of the following reasons?
   a. Many companies are moving to cloud services where there are few data security controls.
   b. Internet sites offer step-by-step instructions on how to perpetrate computer fraud and abuse.
   c. Law enforcement is not interested in preventing or prosecuting computer fraud.
   d. There are no laws against computer fraud, so prosecution is difficult.
   e. Many instances of computer fraud go undetected, and many computer frauds are not reported.
4. SAS No. 99 requires auditors to ________________________.
   a. limit discussion among audit team members of how and where the company's financial statements have been susceptible to fraud in prior years due to confidentiality concerns
   b. understand fraud and why it is committed
   c. limit the use of technology in the audit due to management's ability to change or manipulate electronic records
   d. document and communicate findings to the general public
   e. identify, assess, and respond to risks by varying the nature, timing, and extent of audit procedures
   f. evaluate the results of their audit tests to determine whether misstatements indicate the presence of fraud

5. Which of the following actions did the Treadway Commission recommended to reduce fraudulent financial reporting?
   a. Design and implement internal controls to provide reasonable assurance of preventing fraudulent financial reporting.
   b. Establish financial incentives that promote integrity in the financial reporting process.
   c. Identify and understand the factors that lead to fraudulent financial reporting.
   d. Assess the risk of corruption and misappropriation of assets within the company.
6. Which of the following statements is (are) true?
   a. Perpetrators can hide an asset theft by charging the stolen item to an expense account.
   b. To prevent detection when an asset is stolen, the perpetrator must inflate liabilities or decrease assets.
   c. Committing a fraud almost always takes more effort and time than concealing it.
   d. An individual can hide the theft of cash using a check-kiting scheme.
   e. A lapping scheme is used to commit a fraud but not to conceal it.
7. A group of people perpetuating paycheck fraud moved from town to town in the Pacific Northwest. A member of that group obtained a paycheck from the largest employer in the town by paying a premium to the check's value. They then scanned the check and used a variety of software packages to prepare fictitious paychecks from the employer. The group arrived on the next payday, cashed the checks at local establishments, and moved to another town before the checks were presented for payment at the local bank. This is an example of what type of fraud?
   a. input
   b. processor
   c. output
   d. computer instruction
   e. data
8. In a typical asset misappropriation, the perpetrator ____________.
   a. does not attempt to conceal the fraud
   b. terminates the fraud as soon as the desired amount of money is taken to avoid detection
   c. gains the trust or confidence of the entity being defrauded
   d. saves a large portion of the stolen money
   e. uses trickery, cunning, or false or misleading information to commit fraud
   f. gets greedy and takes ever-larger amounts of money or grows careless or overconfident, leading to a mistake that leads to the fraud's detection
9. Cyber sleuths need which of the following skills?
   a. ability to follow a trail, think analytically, and be thorough
   b. ability to use their computer engineering experience to evaluate the hardware used by the company
   c. ability to think like a fraud perpetrator and use hacking tools and techniques
   d. ability to use their legal training to properly prepare the evidence needed to prosecute perpetrators
   e. ability to do complex programming so they can develop their own software to examine corporate data and records
10. Which of the following statements is (are) true about computer fraud perpetrators?
   a. They are typically younger and are motivated by curiosity, the challenge of beating the system, and gaining stature in the hacking community.
   b. They write and sell malicious software that infect computers with viruses or can be used to steal money or data that can be sold.
   c. They do not see themselves as criminals and rarely, if ever, seek to turn their actions into money.
   d. They are a top FBI priority because they organize fraud schemes targeted at specific individuals and businesses.

8.3 The computer frauds that are publicly revealed represent only the tip of the iceberg. Although many people perceive that the major threat to computer security is external, the more dangerous threats come from insiders. Management must recognize these problems and develop and enforce security programs to deal with the many types of computer fraud.

REQUIRED

Explain how each of the following six types of fraud is committed. Using the format provided, identify a different method of protection for each, and describe how it works. *(CMA Examination, adapted)*

Type of Fraud	Explanation	Identification and Description of Protection Methods
a. Input manipulation		
b. Program alteration		
c. File alteration		
d. Data theft		
e. Sabotage		
f. Theft of computer time		

8.4 You were asked to investigate extremely high, unexplained merchandise shortages at a department store chain. You found the following:

a. The receiving department supervisor owns and operates a boutique carrying many of the same labels as the chain store. The general manager is unaware of the ownership interest.
b. The receiving supervisor signs receiving reports showing that the total quantity shipped by a supplier was received and then diverts 5% to 10% of each shipment to the boutique.
c. The store is unaware of the short shipments because the receiving report accompanying the merchandise to the sales areas shows that everything was received.
d. Accounts Payable paid vendors for the total quantity shown on the receiving report.
e. Based on the receiving department supervisor's instructions, quantities on the receiving reports were not counted by sales personnel.

REQUIRED

Classify each of the five situations as a fraudulent act, a red flag or symptom of fraud, an internal control weakness, or an event unrelated to the investigation. Justify your answers. *(CIA Examination, adapted)*

8.5 For each of the following independent cases of employee fraud, recommend how to prevent similar problems in the future.

a. Abnormal inventory shrinkage in the audiovisual department at a retail chain store led internal auditors to conduct an in-depth audit of the department. They learned that one customer frequently bought large numbers of small electronic components from a certain cashier. The auditors discovered that they had colluded to steal electronic components by not recording the sale of items the customer took from the store.
b. During an unannounced audit, auditors discovered a payroll fraud when they, instead of department supervisors, distributed paychecks. When the auditors investigated an unclaimed paycheck, they discovered that the employee quit four months previously after arguing with the supervisor. The supervisor continued to turn in a time card for the employee and pocketed his check.
c. Auditors discovered an accounts payable clerk who made copies of supporting documents and used them to support duplicate supplier payments. The clerk deposited the duplicate checks in a bank account she had opened using a name similar to that of the supplier. *(CMA Examination, adapted)*

8.6 An auditor found that Rent-A-Wreck management does not always comply with its stated policy that sealed bids be used to sell obsolete cars. Records indicated that several vehicles with recent major repairs were sold at negotiated prices. Management vigorously assured the auditor that performing limited repairs and negotiating with knowledgeable buyers resulted in better sales prices than the sealed-bid procedures. Further investigation revealed that the vehicles were sold to employees at prices well below market value. Three managers and five other employees pleaded guilty to criminal charges and made restitution.

REQUIRED

a. List the fraud symptoms that should have aroused the auditor's suspicion.
b. What audit procedures would show that fraud had in fact occurred? *(Adapted from CIA Examination)*

8.7 A bank auditor met with the senior operations manager to discuss a customer's complaint that an auto loan payment was not credited on time. The customer said the payment was made on May 5, its due date, at a teller's window using a check drawn on an account in the bank. On May 10, when the customer called for a loan pay-off balance so he could sell the car, he learned that the payment had not been credited to the loan. On May 12, the customer went to the bank to inquire about the payment and meet with the manager. The manager said the payment had been made on May 11. The customer was satisfied because no late charge would have been assessed until May 15. The manager asked whether the auditor was comfortable with this situation.

The auditor located the customer's paid check and found that it had cleared on May 5. The auditor traced the item back through the computer records and found that the teller had processed the check as being cashed. The auditor traced the payment through the entry records of May 11 and found that the payment had been made with cash instead of a check.

REQUIRED

What type of embezzlement scheme is this, and how does it work?
(CIA Examination, adapted)

8.8 An accountant with the Atlanta Olympic Games was charged with embezzling more than $60,000 to purchase a Mercedes-Benz and to invest in a certificate of deposit. Police alleged that he created fictitious invoices from two companies that had contracts with the Olympic Committee: International Protection Consulting and Languages Services. He then wrote checks to pay the fictitious invoices and deposited them into a bank account he had opened under the name of one of the companies. When he was apprehended, he cooperated with police to the extent of telling them of the bogus bank account and the purchase of the Mercedes-Benz and the CD. The accountant was a recent honors graduate from a respected university who, supervisors stated, was a very trusted and loyal employee.

a. How does the accountant fit the profile of a fraudster? How does he not fit the profile?
b. What fraud scheme did he use to perpetrate his fraud?
c. What controls could have prevented his fraud?
d. What controls could have detected his fraud?

8.9 The *Journal of Accountancy* periodically publishes an article called "What Is Your Fraud IQ?" It consists of 10 or more multiple-choice questions dealing with various aspects of fraud. The answers, as well as an explanation of each answer, are provided at the end of the article. Visit the *Journal of Accountancy* site (http://www.journalofaccountancy.com) and search for the articles. Read and answer the questions in three of these articles, and then check your answers.

8.10 To learn more about Benford's Law (discussed in Focus 8-3), do the following:

a. Read the article "Using Excel and Benford's Law to Detect Fraud" by J. Carlton Collins in the April 2017 issue of *Journal of Accountancy*. Then watch the almost 7-minute instructional video at the end of the article.

b. Replicate what the author does in the video. Use Excel to download a population of data, select the first digit, count how many incidents of each digit from 1–9 occur in the data, and then chart the occurrences to see that the data conforms to Benford's Law.
c. Find another population of data on the Internet and repeat the process. Did your data conform to Benford's Law? Why or why not?
d. Write a 3-page paper discussing what you found as you completed parts a through c of the problem. Also discuss how you could use Benford's Law at work or in some other capacity of your life. You may want to investigate Benford's Law more and include what you found in your report.

8.11 Research the following two topics and write a 3-page paper discussing what you found.
a. There are several fraud analytics software packages on the market. Investigate them and try to determine what software is used most frequently, which ones are the least and most expensive, and what the major features of the software are.
b. The chapter discussed just a few of the many data analytics techniques used to detect fraud. Research data analytics techniques and include in your report how the techniques are used, which companies have used them, and what the companies found when using the technique.

CASE 8-1 David L. Miller: Portrait of a White-Collar Criminal

There is an old saying: Crime doesn't pay. However, for David Miller crime paid for two Mercedes-Benz sedans; a lavish suburban home; a condominium at Myrtle Beach; expensive suits; tailored and monogrammed shirts; diamond, sapphire, ruby, and emerald rings for his wife; and a new car for his father-in-law. Though Miller confessed to embezzling funds from six different employers over a 20-year period, he has never been prosecuted or incarcerated—in large part because his employers never turned him in.

Miller was fired from his first employer for stealing $200. After an assortment of odd jobs, he worked as an accountant for a local baker. Miller was caught embezzling funds and paid back the $1,000 he stole. Again, law enforcement was not notified, and he was quietly dismissed.

Several months after Miller started work at Wheeling Bronze, his third victim, the president discovered a $30,000 cash shortfall and several missing returned checks. An extensive search found the canceled checks, with forged signatures, in an outdoor sand pile. Miller confessed to the scheme and was given the choice of repaying the stolen funds or being prosecuted. When Miller's parents mortgaged their home and repaid the stolen money, he escaped prosecution.

Miller's fourth victim was Robinson Pipe Cleaning. When Miller was caught embezzling funds, he again avoided prosecution by promising to repay the $20,000 he stole.

Miller's fifth victim was Crest Industries, where he worked as accountant. He was an ideal employee—dedicated and hard working, doing outstanding work. He was quickly promoted to office manager and soon purchased a new home, car, and wardrobe. Two years later, Crest auditors discovered that $31,000 was missing. Miller had written several checks to himself, recorded them as payments to suppliers, and intercepted and altered the monthly bank statements. With the stolen money, he financed his lifestyle and repaid Wheeling Bronze and Robinson Pipe Cleaning. Once again, Miller tearfully confessed, claiming he had never embezzled funds previously. Miller showed so much remorse that Crest hired a lawyer for him. He promised to repay the stolen money, gave Crest a lien on his house, and was quietly dismissed. Because Crest management did not want to harm Miller's wife and three children, Crest never pressed charges.

Miller's sixth victim was Rustcraft Broadcasting Company. When Rustcraft was acquired by Associated Communications, Miller moved to Pittsburgh to become Associated's new controller. Miller immediately began dipping into Associated's accounts. Over a six-year period, Miller embezzled $1.36 million, $450,000 of that after he was promoted to CFO. Miller circumvented the need for two signatures on checks by asking executives leaving on vacation to sign several checks "just in case" the company needed to disburse funds while he was gone. Miller used the checks to siphon funds to his personal account. To cover the theft,

CASE 8-1 Continued

Miller removed the canceled check from the bank reconciliation and destroyed it. The stolen amount was charged to a unit's expense account to balance the company's books.

While working at Associated, Miller bought a new house, new cars, a vacation home, and an extravagant wardrobe. He was generous with tips and gifts. His $130,000 salary could not have supported this lifestyle, yet no one at Associated questioned the source of his conspicuous consumption. Miller's lifestyle came crashing down while he was on vacation and the bank called to inquire about a check written to Miller. Miller confessed and, as part of his out-of-court settlement, Associated received most of Miller's personal property.

Miller cannot explain why he was never prosecuted. His insistence that he was going to pay his victims back usually satisfied his employers and got him off the hook. He believes these agreements actually contributed to his subsequent thefts; one rationalization for stealing from a new employer was to pay back the former one. Miller believes his theft problem is an illness, like alcoholism or compulsive gambling, that is driven by a subconscious need to be admired and liked by others. He thought that by spending money, others would like him. Ironically, he was universally well liked and admired at each job, for reasons that had nothing to do with money. In fact, one Associated coworker was so surprised by the thefts that he said it was like finding out that your brother was an ax murderer. Miller claims he is not a bad person; he never intended to hurt anyone, but once he got started, he could not stop.

After leaving Associated, Miller was hired by a former colleague, underwent therapy, and now believes he has resolved his problem with compulsive embezzlement.

1. How does Miller fit the profile of the average fraud perpetrator? How does he differ? How did these characteristics make him difficult to detect?
2. Explain the three elements of the Opportunity Triangle (commit, conceal, convert), and discuss how Miller accomplished each when embezzling funds from Associated Communications. What specific concealment techniques did Miller use?
3. What pressures motivated Miller to embezzle? How did Miller rationalize his actions?
4. Miller had a framed T-shirt in his office that said, "He who dies with the most toys wins." What does this tell you about Miller? What lifestyle red flags could have tipped off the company to the possibility of fraud?
5. Why do companies hesitate to prosecute white-collar criminals? What are the consequences of not prosecuting? How could law enforcement officials encourage more prosecution?
6. What could the victimized companies have done to prevent Miller's embezzlement?

Source: Based on Bryan Burrough, "David L. Miller Stole from His Employer and Isn't in Prison," *The Wall Street Journal*, September 19, 1986, 1.

CASE 8-2 Heirloom Photo Plans

Heirloom Photos sells a $900 photography plan to rural customers using a commissioned sales force. Rather than pay the price up front, most customers pay $250 down and make 36 monthly payments of $25 each. The $900 plan includes the following:

1. A coupon book good for one free sitting every six months for the next five years (10 sittings) at any Heirloom-approved photo studio. The customer receives one free 11-by-14-inch black-and-white print. Additional photos or color upgrades can be purchased at the photographer's retail prices.
2. To preserve the 11-by-14-inch photos, the family name is embossed in 24-carat gold on a leather-bound photo album.

The embossed leather album, with a retail value of $300, costs Heirloom $75. Each sitting and free 11-by-14-inch print, with a retail value of $150, costs Heirloom only $50 because photographers are given exclusive rights to all Heirloom customers in a geographic region and have the opportunity to offer customers upgrades to color and/or more pictures.

CASE 8-2 Continued

The commissioned sales staff is paid on the 10th of each month, based upon the prior month's sales. The commission rates are as follows:

Number of Plans Sold	Commission	Quantity Bonus
Fewer than 100	$100 per plan	
101 to 200	$125 per plan	On sale of plan #101, $2,500 is paid to cover the extra $25 on the first 100 sales
More than 200	$150 per plan	On sale of plan #201, $5,000 is paid to cover the extra $25 on the first 200 sales

More than 70% of all agents sell at least 101 plans per year; 40% sell more than 200. There is a strong sales surge before year-end as customers purchase plans to give as holiday gifts. About 67% of all agents reach their highest incentive level in late November or December. Heirloom treats the sales staff and the photographers as independent contractors and does not withhold any income or payroll taxes on amounts paid to them.

Salespeople send Heirloom's accounting department the order form, the total payment or the down payment, and the signed note for $650 if the customer finances the transaction. Often, the payment is a handwritten money order. Because many customers live in rural areas, the return address is often a Post Office box, and some customers do not have phones. Heirloom does not perform any credit checks of customers.

Heirloom makes the following entries at the time a new contract is recorded:

To Record Sale of the Contract (Assumes Contract Financed)		
Cash	250	
Note Receivable	650	
Sales of photo plans		900
To Record Expenses Related to the Sale		
Album expense	65	
Embossing/shipping	10	
Sales expense	130	
Album inventory		65
Accounts Payable		10
Commissions Payable		130
(Sales expense is estimated using the average cost paid to salespersons in the prior year.)		
To Record the Liability for Photographer Sittings Expense		
Photographer expense	500	
Accrued liabilities		500

Because the entire cost of the photographer is accrued, the company points to the last entry to show how conservative its accounting is.

After waiting 10 days for the check or money order to clear, Heirloom embosses and ships the album, the photo coupon book, and a payment coupon book with 36 payments of $25. Customers mail a payment coupon and a check or money order to a three-person Receivables Department at headquarters. The Receivables employees open the envelopes, post the payments to the receivables records, and prepare the bank deposit.

The photo coupon book has 10 coupons for photographer sessions, each good for a specific six-month period. If not used within the six-month period, the coupon expires.

Each month, the credit manager sends letters and makes phone calls to collect on delinquent accounts. Between 35% and 40% of all customers eventually stop paying on their notes, usually either early in the contract (months 4 to 8) or at the two-year point (months 22 to 26).

Notes are written off when they are 180 days delinquent. Heirloom's CFO and credit manager use their judgment to adjust the Allowance for Bad Debts monthly. They are confident they can accurately predict the Allowance balance needed at any time, which historically has been about 5% of outstanding receivables.

Agricultural product prices in the area where Heirloom sells its plans have been severely depressed for the second straight year.

Heirloom has been growing quickly and finds that it is continually running short of cash, partly because of the large salaries paid to the two equal owners and their wives. (The wives each receive $100,000 to serve as the treasurer and the secretary; very little, if any, time is required in these duties.) In addition, Heirloom spent large amounts of cash to buy its headquarters, equipment and furnishings, and expensive automobiles for the two owners, their wives, and the four vice presidents.

Heirloom needs to borrow from a local bank for corporate short-term operating purposes. It is willing to pledge unpaid contracts as collateral for a loan. A local bank president is willing to lend Heirloom up to 70% of the value of notes receivable that are not more than 60 days overdue. Heirloom must also provide, by the fifth day of each month, a note receivable aging list for the preceding month and a calculation showing the maximum amount Heirloom may borrow under the agreement.

1. Figure 8-3 shows the employees and external parties that deal with Heirloom. Explain how Heirloom could defraud the bank and how each

CASE 8-2 Continued

internal and external party, except the bank, could defraud Heirloom.

2. What risk factor, unusual item, or abnormality would alert you to each fraud?
3. What control weaknesses make each fraud possible?
4. Recommend one or more controls to prevent or detect each means of committing fraud.

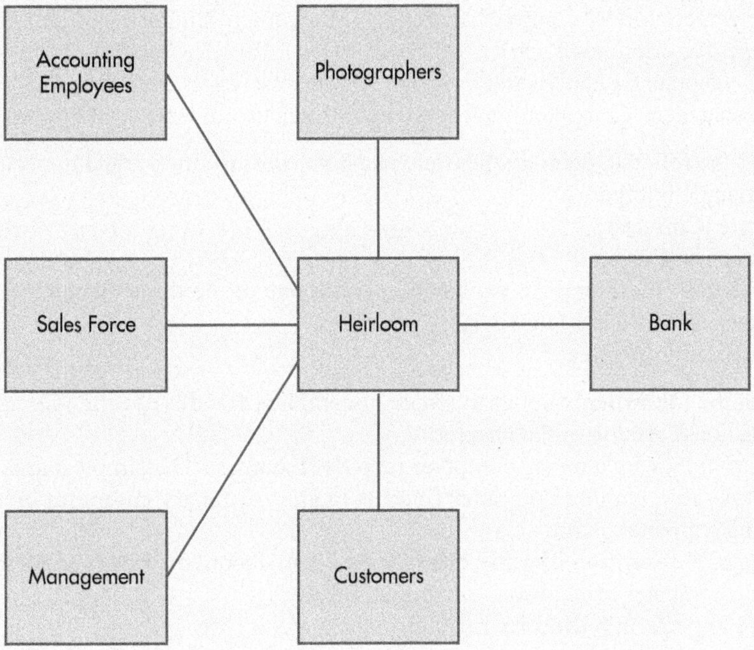

FIGURE 8-3
Internal and External Relationships at Heirloom Photos

AIS in Action Solutions

QUIZ KEY

1. Which of the following is a fraud in which later payments on account are used to pay off earlier payments that were stolen?
   ▶ a. lapping [Correct.]
   b. kiting [Incorrect. In a kiting scheme, the perpetrator creates cash by transferring money between banks.]
   c. Ponzi scheme [Incorrect. In a Ponzi scheme, money from new investors is used to pay off earlier investors.]
   d. salami technique [Incorrect. The salami technique involves stealing tiny slices of money over a period of time.]

2. Which type of fraud is associated with 50% of all auditor lawsuits?
   a. kiting [Incorrect. Losses from kiting, a scheme involving bank transfers, are not large enough to be associated with 50% of auditor lawsuits.]
   ▶ b. fraudulent financial reporting [Correct. Attesting to fraudulent financial statements is the basis of a large percentage of lawsuits against auditors.]
   c. Ponzi schemes [Incorrect. Ponzi schemes, in which money from new investors is used to pay off earlier investors, are investment frauds that often do not involve auditors.]
   d. lapping [Incorrect. Losses from lapping, in which later payments on account are used to pay off earlier payments that were stolen, are not large enough to be associated with 50% of auditor lawsuits.]

3. Which of the following statements is false?
   a. The psychological profiles of white-collar criminals differ from those of violent criminals. [Incorrect. This is a true statement. Psychologically, white-collar criminals are very different than violent criminals.]
   ▶ **b.** The psychological profiles of white-collar criminals are significantly different from those of the general public. [Correct. This is false; the psychological profile of white-collar criminals is similar to that of the general public.]
   c. There is little difference between computer fraud perpetrators and other types of white-collar criminals. [Incorrect. This is a true statement. Although different things can motivate perpetrators of computer fraud, they share many similarities with other types of white-collar criminals.]
   d. Some computer fraud perpetrators do not view themselves as criminals. [Incorrect. This is a true statement. Computer fraud perpetrators often do not view what they do as wrong.]

4. Which of the following conditions is/are usually necessary for a fraud to occur? (See the Fraud Triangle in Figure 8-1.)
   ▶ **a.** pressure [Correct.]
   ▶ **b.** opportunity [Correct.]
   c. explanation [Incorrect. An explanation is not one of the three elements of the fraud triangle, as shown in Figure 8-1.]
   ▶ **d.** rationalization [Correct.]

5. Which of the following is not an example of computer fraud? (See the "Computer Fraud Classifications" section of the chapter.)
   a. theft of money by altering computer records [Incorrect. The simplest and most common way to commit a computer fraud is to alter or falsify computer input, such as altering computer records.]
   b. obtaining information illegally using a computer [Incorrect. One type of data fraud is using a computer to acquire information illegally.]
   ▶ **c.** failure to perform preventive maintenance on a computer [Correct. This is poor management of computer resources, but it is not computer fraud.]
   d. unauthorized modification of a software program [Incorrect. Tampering with company software is a type of computer instructions fraud.]

6. Which of the following causes the majority of computer security problems?
   ▶ **a.** human errors [Correct. The Computing Technology Industry Association estimates that human errors cause 80% of security problems. These unintentional acts usually are caused by human carelessness, failure to follow established procedures, and poorly trained or supervised personnel.]
   b. software errors [Incorrect. Although a federal study estimated yearly economic losses due to software bugs at almost $60 billion a year and revealed that more than 60% of companies studied had significant software errors in the previous year, it is not the main cause of computer security issues.]
   c. natural disasters [Incorrect. Natural disasters—such as fires, floods, earthquakes, hurricanes, tornadoes, and blizzards—can destroy an information system and cause a company to fail. When a disaster strikes, many companies are affected at the same time. However, this is not a frequent occurrence and is not the main cause of computer security problems.]
   d. power outages [Incorrect. Massive power failures caused by defective software occasionally occur and leave hundreds of thousands of people and businesses without power, but this is not the main cause of computer security issues.]

7. Which of the following is not one of the responsibilities of auditors in detecting fraud according to SAS No. 99?
   a. evaluating the results of their audit tests. [Incorrect. When an audit is completed, auditors must evaluate whether any identified misstatements indicate the presence of fraud. If they do, the auditor must determine the impact of this on the financial statements and the audit.]

b. incorporating a technology focus. [Incorrect. SAS No. 99 recognizes the impact technology has on fraud risks and provides commentary and examples specifically recognizing this impact. It also notes the opportunities the auditor has to use technology to design fraud-auditing procedures.]
c. discussing the risks of material fraudulent misstatements. [Incorrect.While planning the audit, team members should discuss among themselves how and where the company's financial statements might be susceptible to fraud.]
▶ **d.** catching the perpetrators in the act of committing the fraud. [Correct. SAS No. 99 does not require auditors to witness the perpetrators committing fraud.]

8. Which of the following control procedures is most likely to deter lapping?
a. encryption [Incorrect. Encryption is used to code data in transit so it cannot be read unless it is decoded. It does not stop employees from lapping accounts receivable payments.]
b. continual update of the access control matrix [Incorrect. The access control matrix specifies what computer functions employees can perform and what data they can access with a computer. It does not stop employees from lapping accounts receivable payments.]
c. background check on employees [Incorrect. A background check can help screen out dishonest job applicants, but it does not stop employees from lapping accounts receivable payments.]
▶ **d.** periodic rotation of duties [Correct. Lapping requires a constant and ongoing cover-up to hide the stolen funds. Rotating duties such that the perpetrator does not have access to the necessary accounting records will most likely result in the fraud's discovery.]

9. Which of the following is the most important, basic, and effective control to deter fraud?
a. enforced vacations [Incorrect. Enforced vacations will prevent or deter some, but not all, fraud schemes.]
b. logical access control [Incorrect. Logical access controls will prevent or deter some, but not all, fraud schemes.]
▶ **c.** segregation of duties [Correct. Segregating duties among different employees is the most effective control for the largest number of fraud schemes because it makes it difficult for any single employee to both commit and conceal a fraud.]
d. virus protection controls [Incorrect. Virus protection controls will help prevent some computer-related abuses, but they are unlikely to deter much fraud.]

10. Once fraud has occurred, which of the following will reduce fraud losses? (Select all correct answers.)
▶ **a.** insurance [Correct. The right insurance will pay for all or a portion of fraud losses.]
▶ **b.** regular backup of data and programs [Correct. Regular backup helps the injured party recover lost or damaged data and programs.]
▶ **c.** contingency plan [Correct. A contingency plan helps the injured party restart operations on a timely basis.]
d. segregation of duties [Incorrect. Segregation of duties is an effective method of deterring fraud but does not help a company recover from fraud once it occurs.]

CHAPTER 9

Computer Fraud and Abuse Techniques

LEARNING OBJECTIVES

After studying this chapter, you should be able to:

1. Compare and contrast computer attack and abuse tactics.
2. Explain how social engineering techniques are used to gain physical or logical access to computer resources.
3. Describe the different types of malware used to harm computers.

INTEGRATIVE CASE | **Northwest Industries**

Northwest Industries wants to expand its service area and has been negotiating to buy Remodeling Products Centers (RPC), a competitor that operates in an area contiguous to Northwest. Jason Scott was part of a team sent to look over RPC's books before the deal was finalized. At the end of their first day, RPC's computer system crashed. The team decided to finish up what work they could and to let RPC's information technology (IT) people get the system up that night.

The next day, RPC's system was still down, so Jason tried to log into Northwest's computer system. It seemed to take forever to access, and then Jason found that system response was rather slow. His manager called the corporate office and found that there was something wrong with Northwest's system. It was assumed that the problem had something to do with communications with RPC's computers.

Jason's team was assigned to do a computer fraud and abuse evaluation of RPC's system while they waited. Since Jason had never participated in such a review, he was told to go back to the hotel where he could get on the Internet and spend the day researching the different ways computer systems could be attacked.

Introduction

Cybercriminals and cybersecurity personnel are involved in an ongoing war. Cybercriminals have devised an ever-increasing number of ways to commit computer fraud and abuse. And for every innovation cybersecurity professionals develop to minimize computer security risks

Borislav Marinic/123RF

and reduce the costs of cybercrime, the increasing number of cybercriminals find a way to breach the security measures, attack organizations, steal information and monetary assets, or destroy or damage computer systems. Some cybercriminals are well funded by high-level officials in foreign governments and are developing state-of-the-art attack approaches that are stealthy, clever, and precise. They are also capable of identifying information assets of significant value.

Online crime is now bigger and more costly than the global illegal drugs trade. The costs to find, investigate, contain, and recover from cybercrimes is estimated to exceed $1 trillion a year. And that does not include the significant costs incurred due to business disruption, lost productivity, and reputational damage. One survey found that over a one-year period, the average number of cyberattacks per organization increased by more than 10%, from 130 to 145 attacks per year. Most security experts expect the costs of data breaches and cyberattacks, as well as their frequency and their severity, to get worse rather than better as time passes.

This chapter discusses some of the more common computer fraud and abuse techniques in three sections: computer attacks and abuse, social engineering, and malware. These classifications are not distinct; there is a lot of overlap among the categories. For example, social engineering methods are often used to launch computer attacks.

Computer Attacks and Abuse

All computers connected to the Internet, especially those with important trade secrets or valuable IT assets, are under constant attack from hackers, foreign governments, terrorist groups, disaffected employees, industrial spies, and competitors. These people attack computers looking for valuable data or trying to harm the computer system. This means that preventing attacks is a constant battle. On a busy day, large web hosting farms suffer millions of attack attempts. This section describes some of the more common attack techniques.

It is helpful to understand the following six steps that many criminals use to attack information systems:

1. ***Conduct reconnaissance.*** Bank robbers usually do not just drive up to a bank and attempt to rob it. Instead, they first study their target's physical layout to learn about the controls the bank has in place (alarms, number of guards, placement of cameras, etc.). Similarly, computer attackers begin by collecting information about their target. Perusing an organization's financial statements, SEC filings, website, and press releases can yield much valuable information. The objective of this initial reconnaissance is to learn as much as possible about the target and to identify potential vulnerabilities.
2. ***Attempt social engineering.*** Why go through all the trouble of trying to break into a system if you can get someone to let you in? Attackers will often try to use information obtained during their initial reconnaissance to "trick" an unsuspecting employee into granting them access. The use of deception to obtain unauthorized access to information

resources is referred to as social engineering and can take place in countless ways, limited only by the creativity and imagination of the attacker. Social engineering attacks often take place over the telephone, via email, or by leaving USB drives in the targeted organization's parking lot or restrooms. An unsuspecting employee who plugs the USB drive into a computer will load a program that gives the attacker access to the system. Social engineering is the topic of the next major section of this chapter.

3. ***Scan and map the target.*** If social engineering is not possible or is unsuccessful, more detailed reconnaissance can be conducted to identify potential points of remote entry. This often involves the use of a variety of automated tools that identify computers that can be remotely accessed as well as the types of software they are running.
4. ***Research.*** After identifying specific targets and learning which versions of software are running on them, an attacker can research known vulnerabilities for those programs and learn how to take advantage of them.
5. ***Execute the attack.*** The criminal takes advantage of a vulnerability to obtain unauthorized access to the information system.
6. ***Cover tracks.*** After penetrating the victim's information system, most attackers attempt to cover their tracks and create "back doors" they can use to obtain access if their initial attack is discovered and controls are implemented to block that method of entry.

hacking - Unauthorized access, modification, or use of an electronic device or some element of a computer system.

The different techniques used to attack computer information systems are now discussed. **Hacking** is the unauthorized access, modification, or use of an electronic device or some element of a computer system. Most hackers break into systems using known flaws in operating systems or application programs, or as a result of poor access controls. One software-monitoring company estimates there are more than 7,000 known flaws in software released in any given year. The following examples illustrate hacking attacks and the damage they cause:

- Russian hackers broke into Citibank's system and stole $10 million from customer accounts.
- A hacker penetrated a software supplier's computer and used its "open pipe" to a bank customer to install a powerful Trojan horse in the bank's computer.
- In the worst security breach in gaming history, 101 million Sony PlayStation accounts were hacked, crashing the network for more than a month. More than 12 million credit card numbers, e-mail addresses, passwords, home addresses, and other data were stolen.
- Unknown hackers penetrated Bangladesh's central bank and entered a series of fraudulent money transfers. Four requests totaling $81 million went through but in the fifth, to the Shalika Foundation, the hackers misspelled foundation as "fandation." Deutsche Bank, the routing bank, stopped the transaction to seek clarification. Shalika did not exist and the Bangledesh bank found an additional $870 million in fraudulent transfers waiting to be sent. If the perpetrators had bothered to use a spell checker, they might have gotten away with almost $1 billion.

hijacking - Gaining control of someone else's computer to carry out illicit activities, such as sending spam without the computer user's knowledge.

botnet - A network of powerful and dangerous hijacked computers that are used to attack systems or spread malware.

zombies - Hijacked computers, typically part of a botnet, that are used to launch a variety of Internet attacks.

bot herder - The person who creates a botnet by installing software on PCs that responds to the bot herder's electronic instructions.

Focus 9-1 discusses how a professor and his students track down computer criminals.

Hijacking is gaining control of a computer to carry out illicit activities without the user's knowledge. A **botnet**, short for robot network, is a powerful network of hijacked computers, called **zombies**, that are used to attack systems or spread malware. A **bot herder** installs software that responds to the hacker's electronic instructions on unwitting PCs. Bot software is delivered in a variety of ways, including Trojans, e-mails, instant messages, Tweets, or an infected website. Bot herders use the combined power of the hijacked computers to mount a variety of Internet attacks. Worldwide, there are more than 2,000 botnets containing more than 10 million computers (10% of online computers), many of them for rent. In one study, the United States led the world in the number of PCs in botnets, with more than 2.2 million. And that was after Microsoft, in a single three-month period, cleaned up more than 6.5 million infected computers.

Botnets send out more than 90 billion unsolicited e-mails per day, about one-third of all e-mails sent. The botnet Grum, one of the largest-ever shut down, generated 18% of the world's spam. The owner of the Bredolab botnet was reportedly taking in more than 80,000 British pounds a month.

Bot toolkits and easy-to-use software are available on the Internet showing hackers how to create their own botnets; hacking is now almost as simple as picking and choosing features and clicking on a checkbox. The Mariposa botnet, containing almost 13 million computers in 190 countries, was created by three men without any advanced hacker skills.

FOCUS 9-1 Professor and Students Help Track Down Computer Criminals

A group of criminals, from the safety of their own homes, stole $70 million from the payroll accounts of 400 American companies using computer malware named Zeus. Zeus is a Trojan horse that infects computers when their users click on certain attachments and e-mail links, such as fake ads on reputable websites, Facebook links that are phishing scams, or counterfeit e-mails from a bank. After the computer is compromised, Zeus targets the user's banking information by recording keystrokes when a username and password is entered. This information is sent by e-mail or text message to the malware's creators. The hackers make large, unauthorized transfers to accounts run by a network of money mules.

In the Trident Breach case, 90 hackers created a complex criminal network involving 3,000 money mules that spanned two continents. At first, the hackers recruited unwitting Americans to be their mules with e-mails promising work-at-home jobs that required the "employees" to open bank accounts. After the banks caught on to this tactic, the hackers recruited students from southern Russia. The students were sent to America with fake passports and work/study visas and told to open multiple bank accounts to receive stolen cash. The students wired the money back to Russia after subtracting an 8% to 10% commission. The hackers and mules managed to avoid detection until Gary Warner got involved.

Dr. Warner is a professor of computer forensics and justice studies and a member of InfraGard, a 50,000-person watchdog group that keeps an eye on U.S. infrastructure and the Internet. Using complex data-mining techniques, Warner was able to trace the origins of the Zeus infection, and many of the hackers and all but 18 of the mules were caught. After the FBI posted wanted posters of the mules, Warner's students used what they learned in class to track the mules. By searching Facebook and VKontakte (a Russian equivalent of Facebook) they were able to identify at-large mules. Many of the mules had posted pictures of themselves with wads of cash and new cars. All but one was arrested.

Zeus can be fine-tuned by its user to record account information for social networking sites, e-mail accounts, or other online financial services. With its versatility and stealth, Zeus is difficult to detect even with up-to-date antivirus software. A Zeus package can be purchased for anywhere from $3,000 to $10,000. An estimated 3.6 million computers in the United States are infected with Zeus. Hopefully, with the help of better antiviral software and people like Gary Warner, Zeus will soon be a thing of the past.

Botnets are used to perform a **denial-of-service (DoS) attack**, which is designed to make a resource unavailable to its users. In an e-mail DoS attack, so many e-mails (thousands per second) are received, often from randomly generated false addresses, that the Internet service provider's e-mail server is overloaded and shuts down. Another attack involves sending so many web page requests that the web server crashes. An estimated 5,000 DoS attacks occur per week. The websites of online merchants, banks, governmental agencies, and news agencies are frequent victims. The following examples illustrate DoS attacks and the damage they cause:

denial-of-service (DoS) attack - A computer attack in which the attacker sends so many e-mail bombs or web page requests, often from randomly generated false addresses, that the Internet service provider's e-mail server or the web server is overloaded and shuts down.

- A DoS attack shut down 3,000 websites for 40 hours on one of the busiest shopping weekends of the year.
- CloudNine, an Internet service provider, went out of business after DoS attacks prevented its subscribers and their customers from communicating.
- An estimated 1 in 12 e-mails carried the MyDoom virus at its peak. The virus turned its host into a zombie that attacked Microsoft. Other companies, such as Amazon, Yahoo, CNN, and eBay, have all suffered similar DoS attacks.

A **brute force attack** is a trial-and-error method that uses software to guess information, such as the user ID and the password, needed to gain access to a system. It is the electronic equivalent of trying every key on a very large key ring to find the one that opens a locked door. The success of a brute force attack is a factor of two things: (1) the computing power used and (2) enough time to generate the number of combinations needed. Brute force attacks are used by criminals as well as security personnel to test an organization's network security.

brute force attack - Trial-and-error method that uses software to guess information, such as the user ID and the password, needed to gain access to a system.

Using brute-force attack software, two Ukrainian hackers cracked the passwords of news wire companies. When they found news releases that would move a stock's price, they sold the information to seven traders who bought the stock before the news was released and sold it after the news came out. The traders netted $30 million, including a $1 million profit from owning Caterpillar for less than one day.

password cracking - Recovering passwords by trying every possible combination of upper- and lower-case letters, numbers, and special characters and comparing them to a cryptographic hash of the password.

There are different types and variations of brute force attacks. In brute force **password cracking**, passwords stored in or transmitted by a computer system are recovered by trying every possible combination of upper- and lower-case letters, numbers, and special characters and comparing them to a cryptographic hash of the password. Newer computers can brute force crack an 8-character alphanumeric password in less than two hours. Password cracking is used to help users recover forgotten passwords but can also be used to gain unauthorized system access.

dictionary attack - Software that generates user ID and password guesses using a dictionary of possible user IDs and passwords to reduce the number of guesses required.

In a **dictionary attack**, software generates user IDs and password guesses using a dictionary of possible user IDs and passwords to reduce the number of guesses required. Spammers use dictionary attacks (also called directory harvest attacks) to guess e-mail addresses at a company and send blank e-mail messages. Messages not returned usually have valid e-mail addresses and are added to spammer e-mail lists. These attacks are a major burden to corporate e-mail systems and Internet service providers. Some companies receive more dictionary attack e-mail than valid e-mail messages. One day, 74% of the e-mail messages Lewis University received were for nonexistent addresses. Companies use e-mail filtering software to detect these attacks; unfortunately, spammers continue to find ways around the rules used in e-mail filtering software.

Credential recycling is another type of brute force attack that reuses usernames and passwords from other data breaches to try to break into other systems. A reverse brute-force attack uses a common password (the most common one is "password)" to use brute force to find a username to go with that password. Brute force attacks are also used to look for hidden web pages. The attack tests different addresses to see if they return a valid webpage that has vulnerabilities, can be otherwise exploited, or contains sensitive or confidential information.

The best defenses against brute force attacks are monitoring system activity, longer and more complex passwords, limiting the number of login attempts, and using multifactor authentication.

spamming - Simultaneously sending the same unsolicited message to many people, often in an attempt to sell them something.

Spamming is simultaneously sending the same unsolicited message to many people at the same time, often in an attempt to sell something. Spam not only reduces the efficiency benefits of e-mail but also is a source of many viruses, worms, spyware programs, and other types of malware discussed later in the chapter. The volume of spam is overwhelming many e-mail systems. An estimated 250 billion e-mails are sent every day (2.8 million per second); 80% are spam and viruses. The Federal Trade Commission estimates that 80% of spam is sent from botnets. Spams are annoying and costly, and 10% to 15% offer products or services that are fraudulent. In retaliation, some spammers are spammed in return with thousands of messages, causing their e-mail service to fail. Such retaliation affects innocent users and can result in the closure of an e-mail account. Spammers scan the Internet for addresses posted online, hack into company databases, and steal or buy mailing lists. An AOL employee stole the names and e-mail addresses of 92 million people and sold them to spammers.

spoofing - Altering some part of an electronic communication to make it look as if someone else sent the communication in order to gain the trust of the recipient.

Spoofing is making an electronic communication look as if someone else sent it to gain the trust of the recipient. Spoofing can take various forms, including the following:

e-mail spoofing - Making a sender address and other parts of an e-mail header appear as though the e-mail originated from a different source.

- **E-mail spoofing** is making an e-mail appear as though it originated from a different source. Many spam and phishing attacks use special software to create random sender addresses. A former Oracle employee was charged with breaking into the company's computer network, falsifying evidence, and committing perjury for forging an e-mail message to support her charge that she was fired for ending a relationship with the company CEO. Using cell phone records, Oracle lawyers proved that the supervisor who had supposedly fired her and written the e-mail was out of town when the e-mail was written and could not have sent it. The employee was found guilty of forging the e-mail message and faced up to six years in jail.

caller ID spoofing - Displaying an incorrect number on the recipient's caller ID display to hide the caller's identity.

- **Caller ID spoofing** is displaying an incorrect number on a caller ID display to hide the caller's identity. Caller ID spoof attacks on cell phones have increased dramatically because many people use them for online banking. The spoofers trick cellphone users into divulging account information by sending an automated call or text message that appears to come from their bank. Using the divulged information, the fraudsters call the bank, spoofing the victim's phone number, and answer the security questions. They then instruct the bank to transfer cash and/or issue credit cards to addresses the fraudster controls.

- **IP address spoofing** is creating Internet Protocol (IP) packets with a forged source IP address to conceal the identity of the sender or to impersonate another computer system. IP spoofing is most frequently used in DoS attacks.
- **SMS spoofing** is using the short message service (SMS) to change the name or number a text message appears to come from. In Australia, a woman got a call asking why she had sent the caller multiple adult message texts every day for the past few months. Neither she nor her mobile company could explain the texts, as her account showed that they were not coming from her phone. When she realized there was no way of blocking the messages, she changed her mobile number to avoid any further embarrassment by association.
- **Web-page spoofing**, also called phishing, is discussed later in the chapter.

IP address spoofing - Creating Internet Protocol packets with a forged IP address to hide the sender's identity or to impersonate another computer system.

SMS spoofing - Using short message service (SMS) to change the name or number a text message appears to come from.

web-page spoofing - See *phishing*.

Every computer software program represents a potential point of attack because it probably contains flaws, called **vulnerabilities**, that can be exploited to either crash the system or take control of it. A **zero-day attack** (or *zero-hour attack*) is an attack between the time a new software vulnerability is discovered and the time a software developer releases a **patch** that fixes the problem. When hackers detect a new vulnerability, they "release it into the wild" by posting it on underground hacker sites. Word spreads quickly, and the attacks begin. It takes companies time to discover the attacks, study them, develop an antidote, release the patch to fix the problem, install the patch on user systems, and update antivirus software. One way software developers minimize the vulnerability window is to monitor known hacker sites so they know about the vulnerability when the hacker community does.

vulnerabilities - Software program flaws that a hacker can exploit to either crash a system or take control of it.

zero-day attack - An attack between the time a new software vulnerability is discovered and "released into the wild" and the time a software developer releases a patch to fix the problem.

patch - Code released by software developers that fixes a particular software vulnerability.

Vulnerability windows last anywhere from hours to forever if users do not patch their system. A national retailing firm employee used the server that clears credit card transactions to download music from an infected website. The music contained Trojan horse software that allowed Russian hackers to take advantage of an unpatched, known vulnerability to install software that collected and sent credit card data to 16 different computers in Russia every hour for four months until it was detected.

Researchers used a zero-day exploit to remotely hack into the Uconnect infotainment system in a Jeep and gain control of the vehicle. From a laptop located miles away, they changed the temperature settings and the radio station, turned on the wiper fluids and windshield wipers, and disabled the accelerator so the car slowly came to a stop. While no harm came to the car or driver, imagine what could have happened had a hacker had malicious intentions. Fiat Chrysler had to recall 1.4 million vehicles to fix the vulnerability in the world's first automotive cybersecurity recall.

Cybercrooks take advantage of Microsoft's security update cycle by timing new attacks right before or just after "Patch Tuesday"—the second Tuesday of each month, when the software maker releases its fixes. The term "zero-day Wednesday" describes this strategy.

Cross-site scripting (XSS) is a vulnerability in dynamic web pages that allows an attacker to bypass a browser's security mechanisms and instruct the victim's browser to execute code, thinking it came from the desired website. Most attacks use executable JavaScript, although HTML, Flash, or other code the browser can execute are also used. XSS flaws are the most prevalent flaws in web applications today and occur anywhere a web application uses input from a user in the output it generates without validating or encoding it. The likelihood that a site contains XSS vulnerabilities is extremely high. Finding these flaws is not difficult for attackers; there are many free tools available that help hackers find them, create the malicious code, and inject it into a target site. Many prominent sites have had XSS attacks, including Google, Yahoo, Facebook, MySpace, and MediaWiki. In fact, MediaWiki has had to fix more than 30 XSS weaknesses to protect Wikipedia.

cross-site scripting (XSS) - A vulnerability in dynamic web pages that allows an attacker to bypass a browser's security mechanisms and instruct the victim's browser to execute code, thinking it came from the desired website.

An example of how XSS works follows. Luana hosts a website that Christy frequently uses to store all her financial data. To use the website, Christy logs on using her username and password. While searching for vulnerable websites, Miles finds that Luana's website has an

XSS vulnerability. Miles creates a URL to exploit it and sends it to Christy in an e-mail that motivates Christy to click on it while logged into Luana's website. The XSS vulnerability is exploited when the malicious script embedded in Miles's URL executes in Christy's browser, as if it came directly from Luana's server. The script sends Christy's session cookie to Miles, who hijacks Christy's session. Miles can now do anything Christy can do. Miles can also send the victim's cookie to another server, inject forms that steal Christy's confidential data, disclose her files, or install a Trojan horse program on her computer. Miles can also use XSS to send a malicious script to her husband Jeremy's computer. Jeremy's browser has no way of knowing that the script should not be trusted; it thinks it came from a trusted source and executes the script.

Miles could also execute XSS by posting a message with the malicious code to a social network. When Brian reads the message, Miles's XSS will steal his cookie, allowing Miles to hijack Brian's session and impersonate him.

Attempting to filter out malicious scripts is unlikely to succeed, as attackers encode the malicious script in hundreds of ways so it looks less suspicious to the user. The best way to protect against XSS is HTML sanitization, which is a process of validating input and only allowing users to input predetermined characters. Companies also try to identify and remove XSS flaws from a web application. To find flaws, companies review their code, searching for all the locations where input from an HTTP request could enter the HTML output.

buffer overflow attack - When the amount of data entered into a program is greater than the amount of the input buffer. The input overflow overwrites the next computer instruction, causing the system to crash. Hackers exploit this by crafting the input so that the overflow contains code that tells the computer what to do next. This code could open a back door into the system.

A **buffer overflow attack** happens when the amount of data entered into a program is greater than the amount of the memory (the input buffer) set aside to receive it. The input overflow usually overwrites the next computer instruction, causing the system to crash. Hackers exploit this buffer overflow by carefully crafting the input so that the overflow contains code that tells the computer what to do next. This code could open a back door into the system, provide the attacker with full control of the system, access confidential data, destroy or harm system components, slow system operations, and carry out any number of other inappropriate acts. Buffer overflow exploits can occur with any form of input, including mail servers, databases, web servers, and FTPs. Many exploits have been written to cause buffer overflows. The Code Red worm used a buffer overflow to exploit a hole in Microsoft's Internet Information Services.

SQL injection (insertion) attack - Inserting a malicious SQL query in input such that it is passed to and executed by an application program. This allows a hacker to convince the application to run SQL code that it was not intended to execute.

In an **SQL injection (insertion) attack**, malicious code in the form of an SQL query is inserted into input so it can be passed to and executed by an application program. The idea is to convince the application to run SQL code that it was not intended to execute by exploiting a database vulnerability. It is one of several vulnerabilities that can occur when one programming language is embedded inside another. A successful SQL injection can read sensitive data from the database; modify, disclose, destroy, or limit the availability of the data; allow the attacker to become a database administrator; spoof identity; and issue operating system commands. An SQL injection attack can have a significant impact that is limited only by the attacker's skill and imagination and system controls.

Albert Gonzalez used SQL injection techniques to create a back door to corporate systems and stole data on more than 170 million credit cards. At the time, his $200 million fraud was the largest such fraud to ever be reported. He was sentenced to 20 years in prison, the harshest computer crime sentence in American history up to that point in time. Like most fraud perpetrators, he spent his ill-gotten gains, including buying a Miami condominium, an expensive car, Rolex watches, and a Tiffany ring for his girlfriend. He threw himself a $75,000 birthday party and stayed in lavish hotels and resorts. He even complained about having to count $340,000 by hand after his currency-counting machine broke.

man-in-the-middle (MITM) attack - A hacker placing himself between a client and a host to intercept communications between them.

As shown in Figure 9-1, a **man-in-the-middle (MITM) attack** places a hacker between a client and a host and intercepts network traffic between them. An MITM attack is often called a session hijacking attack. MITM attacks are used to attack public-key encryption systems where sensitive and valuable information is passed back and forth. For example, Linda sniffs and eavesdrops on a network communication and finds David sending his public key to Teressa so that they can communicate securely. Linda substitutes her forged public key for David's key and steps in the middle of their communications. If Linda can successfully impersonate both David and Teressa by intercepting and relaying the messages to each other, they believe they are communicating securely. Once an MITM presence is established, the hacker

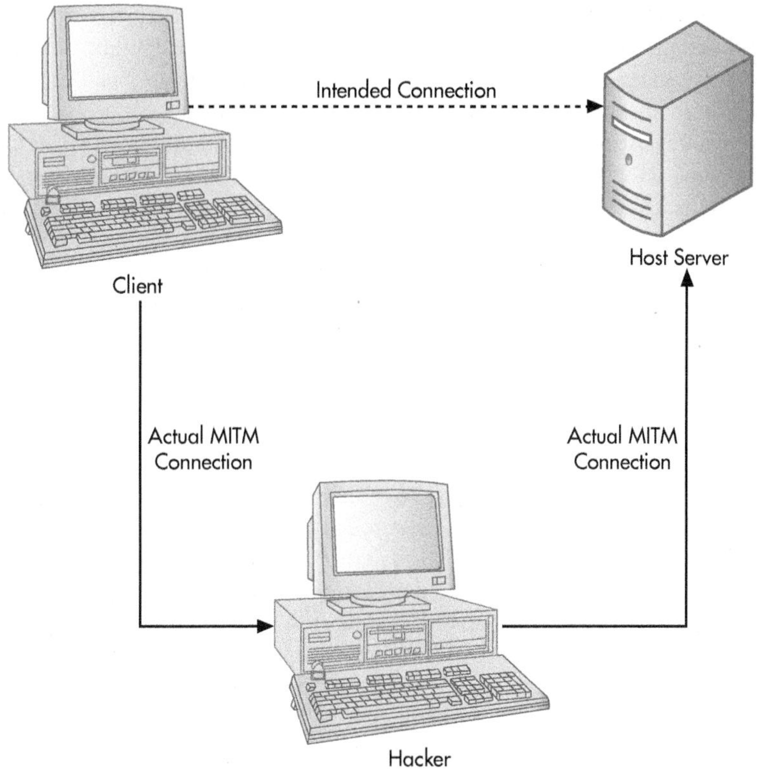

FIGURE 9-1
Man-in-the-Middle Cyber-Attack

can read and modify client messages, mislead the two parties, manipulate transactions, and steal confidential data. To prevent MITM attacks, most cryptographic protocols authenticate each communication endpoint. Many of the spoofing techniques discussed in the chapter are used in MITM attacks.

Masquerading/impersonation is pretending to be an authorized user to access a system. This is possible when the perpetrator knows the user's ID number and password or uses her computer after she has logged in (while the user is in a meeting or at lunch).

Cybercriminals impersonated a high level corporate executive and tricked an employee in Ubiquity Networks' Hong Kong subsidiary into wiring $47 million into a fraudulent bank account. According to the FBI, hundreds of companies in 64 countries around the globe have lost more than $1 billion as a result of schemes that use publicly available information to exploit weaknesses in corporate email systems.

Piggybacking has several meanings:

1. The clandestine use of a neighbor's Wi-Fi network; this can be prevented by enabling the security features in the wireless network.
2. Tapping into a communications line and electronically latching onto a legitimate user before the user enters a secure system; the legitimate user unknowingly carries the perpetrator into the system.
3. An unauthorized person following an authorized person through a secure door, bypassing physical security controls such as keypads, ID cards, or biometric identification scanners.

War dialing is programming a computer to dial thousands of phone lines searching for dial-up modem lines. Hackers break into the PC attached to the modem and access the network to which it is connected. This approach got its name from the movie *War Games*. Much more problematic in today's world is **war driving**, which is driving around looking for unprotected wireless networks.

Phreaking is attacking phone systems. The most common reason for the attack is to obtain free phone line access, transmit malware, and steal and destroy data. One telephone company lost $4.5 million in 3 days when details on how to use its phone lines for free were published on the Internet. Phreakers also break into voice mail systems, as the New York Police Department

masquerading/impersonation - Gaining access to a system by pretending to be an authorized user. This requires that the perpetrator know the legitimate user's ID and passwords.

piggybacking - (1) Tapping into a communications line and electronically latching onto a legitimate user who unknowingly carries the perpetrator into the system. (2) The clandestine use of a neighbor's Wi-Fi network. (3) An unauthorized person following an authorized person through a secure door, bypassing physical security controls.

war dialing - Programming a computer to dial thousands of phone lines searching for dial-up modem lines. Hackers hack into the PC attached to the modem and access the network to which it is connected.

war driving - Driving around looking for unprotected home or corporate wireless networks.

phreaking - Attacking phone systems to obtain free phone line access; use phone lines to transmit malware; and to access, steal, and destroy data.

learned. The hackers changed the voice mail greeting to say that officers were too busy drinking coffee and eating doughnuts to answer the phone and to call 119 (not 911) in case of an emergency. Other hackers have hijacked calls, rerouted them to their own call centers, and asked callers to identify themselves by divulging confidential information. To protect a system from phreakers, companies use a voice firewall that scans inbound and outbound voice traffic, terminates any suspicious activity, and provides real-time alerts.

podslurping - Using a small device with storage capacity (iPod, flash drive) to download unauthorized data from a computer.

Podslurping is using a small device with storage capacity, such as an iPod or Flash drive, to download unauthorized data. Security expert Abe Usher created slurp.exe and copied all document files from his computer in 65 seconds. Usher now makes a version of his program for security audits that does not copy files but generates a report of the information that could have been stolen in a real attack.

salami technique - Stealing tiny slices of money from many different accounts.

The **salami technique** is used to embezzle money a "salami slice" at a time from many different accounts. A disgruntled employee programmed the company computer to increase all production costs by a fraction of a percent and place the excess in the account of a dummy vendor he controlled. Every few months, the fraudulent costs were raised another fraction of a percent. Because all expenses were rising together, no single account would call attention to the fraud. The perpetrator was caught when a teller failed to recognize the payee name on a check the perpetrator was trying to cash. The salami scheme was part of the plot line in several films, including *Superman III*, *Hackers*, and *Office Space*.

round-down fraud - Instructing the computer to round down all interest calculations to two decimal places. The fraction of a cent rounded down on each calculation is put into the programmer's account.

One salami technique has been given a name. In a **round-down fraud**, all interest calculations are truncated at two decimal places and the excess decimals put into an account the perpetrator controls. No one is the wiser, since all the books balance. Over time, these fractions of a cent add up to a significant amount, especially when interest is calculated daily.

economic espionage - Theft of information, trade secrets, and intellectual property.

Economic espionage is the theft of information, trade secrets, and intellectual property. Losses are estimated to be $450 billion a year, with losses increasing by 323% during one five-year period. Almost 75% of losses are to an employee, former employee, contractor, or supplier. The FBI is investigating about 800 separate incidents of economic espionage at any point in time. Toshiba paid $465 million to Lexar Media as compensation for trade secrets provided by a member of Lexar's board of directors.

cyber-bullying - Using computer technology to support deliberate, repeated, and hostile behavior that torments, threatens, harasses, humiliates, embarrasses, or otherwise harms another person.

Cyber-bullying is using the Internet, cell phones, or other communication technologies to support deliberate, repeated, and hostile behavior that torments, threatens, harasses, humiliates, embarrasses, or otherwise harms another person. Cyber-bullying is especially prevalent among young people; almost half of all teens and preteens report some form of cyber-bullying. Legislation penalizing cyber-bullying has been passed in many states.

sexting - Exchanging sexually explicit text messages and revealing pictures with other people, usually by means of a phone.

Sexting is exchanging sexually explicit text messages and revealing pictures, usually by means of a phone. One particularly degrading form of cyber-bullying is posting or sharing these pictures and messages with people who were never intended to see or read them. An estimated 88% of all self-made sexual images and videos sent by young people to friends are uploaded to other websites. Parasite porn sites constantly comb the Internet and social media sites for such materials, as their business is displaying sexually explicit images and videos of young people. Anyone involved in transmitting nude pictures of someone under the age of 18 can be charged with dealing in child pornography.

Internet misinformation - Using the Internet to spread false or misleading information.

Internet misinformation is using the Internet to spread false or misleading information. McDonald's spent seven years fighting false accusations on websites. After 313 days of testimony and a cost of $16 million, McDonald's won and was awarded $94,000. A website mocked the verdict, called its campaign "unstoppable," and set up shop under a new name. Another form of Internet misinformation is pretending to be someone else and posting web-based messages that damage the reputation of the impersonated person. Even subtler is entering bogus information in legitimate news stories. One young man broke into Yahoo's news pages and replaced the name of an arrested hacker with that of Bill Gates.

e-mail threats - Threats sent to victims by e-mail. The threats usually require some follow-up action, often at great expense to the victim.

Perpetrators also send unsolicited **e-mail threats**. Global Communications sent messages threatening legal action if an overdue amount was not paid within 24 hours. The court action could be avoided by calling an 809 area code (the Caribbean). Callers got a clever recording that responded to the caller's voice. The responses were designed to keep callers on the phone as long as possible because they were being billed at $25 per minute.

Internet auction fraud - Using an Internet auction site to defraud another person.

Internet auction fraud is using an Internet auction site to defraud another person. According to the FBI, 45% of the complaints they receive are about Internet auction fraud. Internet auction fraud can take several forms. For example, a seller can use a false identity or partner with someone to drive up the bid price. A person can enter a very high bid to win the auction and then cancel his bid, allowing his partner, who has the next highest, and much lower, bid to win. The seller can fail to deliver the merchandise, or the buyer can fail to make the agreed-upon payment. The seller can deliver an inferior product or a product other than the one sold. In a recent case, three art dealers were convicted of casting bids in more than 1,100 of each other's eBay auctions to drive up the price of their merchandise over a five-year period. Many of the 120 defrauded consumers paid thousands of dollars more than they would have without the fake bids.

Internet pump-and-dump fraud is using the Internet to pump up the price of a stock and then selling it. Pump-and-dump fraudsters do three things. First, they buy a significant number of shares in small, low-priced, thinly traded penny stocks without driving up their price. Second, they use spam e-mails, texts, Tweets, and Internet postings to disseminate overly optimistic or false information about the company to create a buying frenzy that drives up the stock price. Third, they sell their shares to unsuspecting investors at inflated prices and pocket a handsome profit. Once they stop touting the stock, its price crumbles, and investors lose their money. In a recent fraud, fraudsters quietly acquired shares in 15 thinly traded public companies. They used sophisticated hacking and identity fraud techniques, such as installing keystroke-logging software on computers in hotel business centers and Internet cafes, to gain access to online brokerage accounts. The hackers sold the securities in those accounts, used the money to purchase large quantities of the 15 companies' stock to pump up their share prices, and sold their stock for a $732,941 profit. The pump-and-dump operation, which was perpetrated in a few hours, cost U.S. brokerage firms an estimated $2 million.

Internet pump-and-dump fraud - Using the Internet to pump up the price of a stock and then sell it.

As the popularity of cryptocurrency has risen, so has **cryptocurrency fraud** where investors are defrauded in a variety of cryptocurrency-related fraud schemes. Some cryptocurrencies are not intended to defraud but fail, leaving investors with huge losses. Other cryptocurrencies are created with the intent to commit fraud, with annual losses in the billions of dollars. For example, some crypto criminals create fake initial coin offerings, create enough media attention to attract gullible investors, and then disappear—leaving their investors with coins that have little or no value. To increase the amount they steal, some fraudsters pump up the price of their coins before they dump them and disappear. Another popular scheme is setting up fake cryptocurrency exchanges or wallets and accepting crypto-coin deposits that are never returned. Some cryptocurrencies are designed to be Ponzi schemes (or turn into them when the currency begins to lose value), where the money from later investors is used to pay off earlier investors. Ponzi schemes eventually collapse when insufficient new investors can be found. Crypto criminals often use software to interact with Internet-based instant messaging systems frequented by cryptocurrency investors. The interaction is designed to drive traffic to their fraudulent cryptocurrency offering.

cryptocurrency fraud - Defrauding investors in a variety of cryptocurrency-related fraud schemes, such as fake initial coin offerings and fake exchanges and wallets.

Companies advertising online pay from a few cents to more than $10 for each click on their ads. **Click fraud** is manipulating click numbers to inflate advertising bills. As many as 30% of all clicks are not legitimate. That is no small sum, given that total revenues from online advertising exceed $15 billion a year. Examples of how click fraud is perpetrated include (1) companies clicking on a competitor's ad to drive up their advertising costs, (2) web page owners who get a commission to host a pay-per-click ad clicking to boost commissions, and (3) ad agencies inflating the number of clicks to make an ad campaign appear more effective. Most click fraudsters are cyber criminals who create websites with nothing on them but ads and use their botnets to repeatedly click on the ads. Some porn sites increase their revenues by perpetrating click fraud. When a person clicks on the site, software causes (1) dozens of hidden-to-the-user pages to appear that are filled with links to sites that pay a referral commission and (2) the user's computer to click on the links. The porn operator later receives payment for sending their users to the sites.

click fraud - Manipulating the number of times an ad is clicked on to inflate advertising bills.

Software piracy is the unauthorized copying or distribution of copyrighted software. Three frequent forms of software piracy include: (1) selling a computer with preloaded illegal software, (2) installing a single-license copy on multiple machines, and (3) loading software on a network server and allowing unrestricted access to it in violation of the software license agreement.

software piracy - The unauthorized copying or distribution of copyrighted software.

It is estimated that for every legal software sale, between seven and eight illegal copies are made. Within days of being released, most new software is on the Internet and available free to those who want to download it illegally. An estimated 43% of software is pirated;

in some countries, more than 90% is pirated. The software industry estimates the economic losses due to software piracy exceed $50 billion a year.

The Business Software Alliance, which files lawsuits against software pirates, found 1,400 copies of unlicensed software at an adult vocational school in Los Angeles and claimed $5 million in damages. Individuals convicted of software piracy are subject to fines of up to $250,000 and jail terms of up to five years. However, they are often given more creative punishments. A Puget Sound student was required to write a 20-page paper on the evils of software piracy and copyright infringement and perform 50 hours of community service wiring schools for Internet usage. Failure to comply would subject him to a $10,000 fine and a copyright infringement lawsuit.

Social Engineering

social engineering - The techniques or psychological tricks used to get people to comply with the perpetrator's wishes in order to gain physical or logical access to a building, computer, server, or network. It is usually to get the information needed to obtain confidential data.

Hackers are increasing their attacks on a key company weakness—the careless or unsuspecting employee who is often the means of facilitating successful cyberattacks. **Social engineering** refers to techniques or psychological tricks used to get people to comply with the perpetrator's wishes in order to gain physical or logical access to a building, computer, server, or network—usually to get the information needed to access a system and obtain confidential data. Often, the perpetrator has a conversation with someone to trick, lie to, or otherwise deceive the victim. Often the perpetrator has information, knowledge, authority, or confidence that makes it appear that he or she belongs or knows what they are doing.

Fraudsters take advantage of the following seven human traits to entice a person to reveal information or take a specific action:

1. Compassion—The desire to help others who present themselves as needing help.
2. Greed—People are more likely to cooperate if they get something free or think they are getting a once-in-a-lifetime deal.
3. Sex Appeal—People are more likely to cooperate with someone who is flirtatious or viewed as "hot."
4. Sloth—Few people want to do things the hard way, waste time, or do something unpleasant; fraudsters take advantage of our lazy habits and tendencies.
5. Trust—People are more likely to cooperate with people who gain their trust.
6. Urgency—An immediate need that must be met leads people to be more cooperative and accommodating.
7. Vanity—People are more likely to cooperate if they are told they are going to be more popular or successful.

Establishing the following policies and procedures—and training people to follow them—can help minimize social engineering:

1. Never let people follow you into a restricted building.
2. Never log in for someone else on a computer, especially if you have administrative access.
3. Never give sensitive information over the phone or through e-mail.
4. Never share passwords or user IDs.
5. Be cautious of anyone you do not know who is trying to gain access through you.

Focus 9-2 discusses how social engineering is used on Facebook to perpetrate fraud. The remainder of this section discusses various social engineering issues and techniques.

identity theft - Assuming someone's identity, usually for economic gain, by illegally obtaining confidential information such as a Social Security number or a bank account or credit card number.

Identity theft is assuming someone's identity, usually for economic gain, by illegally obtaining and using confidential information, such as a Social Security number or a bank account or credit card number. A recent report showed that more than 12 million victims had more than $21 billion stolen in a recent calendar year. The report also said that there is a new victim of identity fraud once every three seconds and that one in four consumers who received a data breach notice from a company also became a victim of identity theft.

Identity thieves empty bank accounts, apply for credit cards, run up large debts, and take out mortgages and loans. By carefully covering his tracks and having all bills sent to an address he controls, the identity thief can prolong the scheme because the victim will not know

FOCUS 9-2 Facebook: The New Fraud Frontier

The websites that are the most dangerous fraud and security risks are porn sites and software-sharing sites. Close behind are social networks such as Facebook, making social media the new fraud frontier for the following reasons. First, people are more likely to disclose personal information to "friends" on social networks. Second, many people do not properly protect the information they post on social network sites. Third, people use the same password since remembering separate passwords for every site is too much hassle. Because of the first two items, it is easier for fraudsters to get access to your personal information than through other means. And when they have it, they have the information needed to defraud you.

Facebook fraudsters also use a variety of phishing attempts disguised as Facebook games or widgets that require personal information to be disclosed. For example, suppose someone challenged you to find out who knows you best by posting:

I want to know which one of you knows me best. What is my middle name; birthday; favorite food, soda, and color; pet's name; eye and hair color, Mom's maiden name; and grandma's and grandpa's names. What was my first car? Who is my best friend? Who is the love of my life?

As your friends answer, they disclose many of the facts your financial institutions ask when they verify your identity. This allows your "friends" to try to access your accounts and credit cards.

Another approach is to send a message that says, "Look at the funny video I found of you." When the link is clicked, a message tells you to update your video player. Without adequate security software, clicking on the update installs malware that captures data on the websites you visit and your sign-in and password information. Again, the fraudster has the information needed to defraud you.

The "we are stuck" e-mail used to perpetrate identity theft has migrated to instant messaging on Facebook. It is so effective because it preys on people's desires to help a friend in need. Instead of helping, you lose money or give away the information needed to defraud you.

Facebook is aware of these and other schemes to defraud you. You can learn how Facebook is combatting them by visiting Facebook's security page.

what is happening until considerable damage has been caused. Victims can usually prove they are not responsible for the debts or missing funds, but it takes significant time to clean up credit records and restore reputations. Until the identity theft is cleared up, victims often are denied loans and credit cards, refused phone contracts, and chased by debt collectors for money they do not owe.

A convicted felon incurred $100,000 of credit card debt, took out a home loan, purchased homes and consumer goods, and filed for bankruptcy in the victim's name. He phoned and mocked his victim because the victim could not do anything because identity theft was not a crime at the time. The victim spent four years and $15,000 to restore his credit and reputation. The identity thief served a brief sentence for lying while buying a gun and did not have to make restitution. This and similar cases resulted in Congress making identity theft a federal offense in 1998.

Pretexting is using an invented scenario (the pretext) to increase the likelihood that a victim will divulge information or do something. The pretext is more than just a simple lie; it usually involves creating legitimacy in the target's mind that makes impersonation possible. One approach pretexters use is to pretend to conduct a security survey and lull the victim into disclosing confidential information by asking 10 innocent questions before asking the confidential ones. They also call help desks and claim to be an employee who has forgotten a password. They call users and say they are testing the system and need a password. They pose as buyers, prospective employees, or salespeople to get plant tours. They use voice-changing devices to make a male voice sound like a female voice or use spoofing devices to make it appear they are phoning from the intended victim's phone.

pretexting - Using an invented scenario (the pretext) that creates legitimacy in the target's mind in order to increase the likelihood that a victim will divulge information or do something.

The chairwoman of Hewlett-Packard (H-P) was forced to resign after H-P hired a private investigator to catch H-P directors who had leaked confidential information to reporters. The private investigator pretended to be someone he was not to get private phone records and other confidential information of directors and journalists. As a result, Congress passed a bill making the use of pretexting to obtain a person's phone records illegal.

posing - Creating a seemingly legitimate business, collecting personal information while making a sale, and never delivering the product.

phishing - Sending an electronic message pretending to be a legitimate company, usually a financial institution, and requesting information or verification of information and often warning of a consequence if it is not provided. The request is bogus, and the information gathered is used to commit identity theft or to steal funds from the victim's account.

Posing is creating a seemingly legitimate business (often selling new and exciting products), collecting personal information while making a sale, and never delivering the product. Fraudsters also create Internet job listing sites to collect confidential information.

Phishing is sending an electronic message pretending to be a legitimate company, usually a financial institution, and requesting information or verification of information and often warning of some negative consequence if it is not provided. The recipient is asked to either respond to the bogus request or visit a web page and submit data. The message often contains a link to a web page that appears legitimate. The web page has company logos, familiar graphics, phone numbers, and Internet links that appear to be those of the victimized company. It also has a form requesting everything from a home address to an ATM card's PIN.

In the early days, each phishing e-mail resulted in tens of thousands of calls to bank call centers, disrupted business, and cost hundreds of thousands of dollars to handle the deluge of calls. An estimated 2 million Americans have been fooled by phishing scams, with yearly losses exceeding $3.2 billion. It is easy to launch a phishing attack because hackers sell inexpensive kits that lead people through the process.

Phishers are becoming more sophisticated. Early phishing scams sent messages to everyone. Targeted versions of phishing, called spear phishing, have emerged. For example, they may target known customers of a specific company, as they are more likely to open an e-mail from a company they know than from a stranger. These spear phishing messages often look identical to authentic e-mails, including the use of company e-mail addresses, logos, and electronic watermarks. Furthermore, they usually do not include typos and poor English, which were trademarks of earlier phishing e-mails.

Phishers are also using additional tactics, such as advertisements that link to a malicious site, an e-mail that pretends to be an important work file, a job posting on a legitimate job board, a fake LinkedIn request, a fake auction, and a fake IRS request for information. Some phishing e-mails secretly install software that spies on or hijacks the user's computer. The software captures log-on names or takes pictures of the user's screen when he logs into his financial institution.

The IRS has set up a website and an e-mail address (phishing@irs.gov) where people can forward suspicious e-mails that purport to be from the IRS. In a recent IRS phishing attack, e-mail recipients were told that they were due a refund and were directed to a website that looked just like the IRS website and contained forms that looked just like IRS forms. To claim the refund, the taxpayer had to enter confidential information that facilitated identity theft.

A group of international hackers stole an estimated $1 billion from more than 100 banks in 30 countries in one of the biggest and most sophisticated banking hacks in history. The perpetrators used phishing schemes to access bank systems and insert malware that covertly gathered information about bank operations. When they had the information they needed, they stole funds by transferring money to fake accounts in other banks and withdrew it using ATMs and online banking transfers. The hackers often limited their thefts to avoid detection and return later to victimize the bank again.

vishing - Voice phishing; it is like phishing except the victim enters confidential data by phone.

Voice phishing, or **vishing**, is like phishing except that the victim enters confidential data by phone. Among other things, perpetrators use caller ID spoofing to fool the victim into thinking they are talking to their financial institution.

To avoid being phished or vished, be highly skeptical of any message that suggests you are the target of illegal activity. Ignore e-mails that request confidential information. Do not call a number given in an unsolicited message. If you are concerned, call the institution using a number you know is valid to ensure that account information has not been tampered with.

carding - Activities performed on stolen credit cards, including making a small online purchase to determine whether the card is still valid and buying and selling stolen credit card numbers.

Carding refers to activities performed on stolen credit cards, including making a small online purchase to determine whether the card is still valid and buying and selling stolen credit card numbers. Scores of underground websites facilitate carding, with some rating the reliability of sellers the same way eBay does. Cyber-criminal gangs run many of the carding sites.

pharming - Redirecting website traffic to a spoofed website.

Pharming is redirecting website traffic to a spoofed website. If you could change XYZ Company's number in the phone book to your phone number, people using the phone book to call XYZ Company would reach you instead. Similarly, each website has a unique IP (Internet) address (four groupings of numbers separated by three periods). There is a DNS (think phone book) that converts a domain (website) name to an IP address. Pharmers change the IP address in the DNS to an IP address they control. Compromised DNS servers are referred to as "poisoned." Once these files are poisoned, all subsequent requests to visit that website are directed to the spoofed site.

Pharming is a very popular social engineering tool for two reasons. First, it is difficult to detect because the user's browser shows the correct website. Antivirus and spyware removal software are currently ineffective protections against pharming. Instead, complicated antipharming techniques are required. Second is the ability to target many people at a time through domain spoofing rather than one at a time with phishing e-mails.

One pharming attack targeted 65 financial firms, including PayPal, eBay, Discover Card, and American Express. The sophisticated and multipronged attack involved thousands of computers, multiple IP addresses in multiple countries, and a flood of fraudulent spam. The two-and-a-half-day pharming attack was so successful, resilient, and hard to correct that it was evident that a professional team planned it. The first e-mail spam contained bogus news that the Australian Prime Minister was struggling for his life after a heart attack. The e-mail contained a link to a newspaper story from *The Australian*. The second e-mail lure had a link to news of a cricket match in Australia. When people clicked on the links, they were redirected to one of five malicious websites that infected their computers with pharming malware.

An **evil twin** is a wireless network with the same name (called *Service Set Identifier*, or *SSID*) as a legitimate wireless access point. The hacker either uses a wireless signal that is stronger than the legitimate signal or disrupts or disables the legitimate access point by disconnecting it, directing a DoS against it, or creating radio frequency interference around it. Users are unaware that they connect to the evil twin. The perpetrator monitors the traffic looking for confidential information. Hackers also use evil twins to unleash a wide variety of malware and to install software to attack other computers. After a small coffee shop advertised free wireless Internet, there was an increase in identity thefts. The police discovered that a man living next to the coffee shop had set up an evil twin and was stealing confidential information.

evil twin - A wireless network with the same name (*Service Set Identifier*) as a legitimate wireless access point. Users are connected to the twin because it has a stronger wireless signal or the twin disrupts or disables the legitimate access point. Users are unaware that they connect to the evil twin and the perpetrator monitors the traffic looking for confidential information.

Typosquatting/URL hijacking is setting up similarly named websites so that users making typographical errors when entering a website name are sent to an invalid site. For example, typing goggle.com instead of google.com might lead to a cyber-squatter site that:

- Tricks the user into thinking she is at the real site because of a copied or a similar logo, website layout, or content. These sites often contain advertising that appeals to the person looking for the real domain name. The typosquatter might also be a competitor.
- Is very different from what was wanted. One typosquatter sent people looking for a children's site to a pornographic website.
- Distributes malware such as viruses, spyware, and adware.

typosquatting/URL hijacking - Setting up similarly named websites so that users making typographical errors when entering a website name are sent to an invalid site.

To stop typosquatting, companies send a cease-and-desist letter to the offender, purchase the website address, or file a lawsuit. Google won a case against a Russian typosquatter who registered domain names such as googkle.com and gooigle.com. The lawsuit was decided on three criteria: The domain names were obvious misspellings of google.com, the Russian had no independent claims or interest in the names, and he used the websites to infect computers with malware. Google was given possession of the domain names.

To prevent typosquatting, a company (1) tries to obtain all the web names similar to theirs to redirect people to the correct site, or (2) uses software to scan the Internet and find domains that appear to be typosquatting. Parents can use the same software to restrict access to sites that squat on typos of children's websites.

Scavenging/dumpster diving is searching documents and records to gain access to confidential information. Some identity thieves search garbage cans, communal trash bins, and city dumps to find information. Oracle Corporation was embarrassed a few years ago when investigators it hired were caught going through the trash of companies that supported its rival, Microsoft. The investigators had paid building janitors $1,200 for the trash. In another instance, Jerry Schneider discovered Pacific Telephone computer operating guides in a trash bin on his way home from high school. Over time, his scavenging activities resulted in a technical library that allowed him to steal $1 million worth of electronic equipment.

scavenging/dumpster diving - Searching documents and records to gain access to confidential information. Scavenging methods include searching garbage cans, communal trash bins, and city dumps.

In **shoulder surfing**, as its name suggests, perpetrators look over a person's shoulders in a public place to get information such as ATM PIN numbers or user IDs and passwords. Fraudsters also use sophisticated skimming devices placed right over a card-reader slot to capture data stored on a card's magnetic strip. Fraudsters have even placed Bluetooth-enabled

shoulder surfing - When perpetrators look over a person's shoulders in a public place to get information such as ATM PIN numbers or user IDs and passwords.

devices inside locked gasoline pump handles to capture card data. Other fraudsters shoulder surf from a distance using binoculars or cameras. In South America, a man hid a video camera in some bushes and pointed it at a company president's computer, which was visible through a first-floor window. A significant business acquisition almost fell through because of the information on the recording. Shoulder surfers can be foiled by blocking the surfer's view of the input device.

Lebanese looping - Inserting a sleeve into an ATM that prevents it from ejecting the card. The perpetrator pretends to help the victim, tricking the person into entering the PIN again. Once the victim gives up, the thief removes the card and uses it and the PIN to withdraw money.

In **Lebanese looping**, the perpetrator inserts a sleeve into an ATM that prevents the ATM from ejecting the card. When it is obvious that the card is trapped, the perpetrator approaches the victim and pretends to help, tricking the person into entering her PIN again. Once the victim gives up, the thief removes the card and uses the card and PIN to withdraw as much money as the ATM allows. All forms of ATM fraud result in estimated annual losses of $1 billion.

skimming - Double-swiping a credit card in a legitimate terminal or covertly swiping a credit card in a small, hidden, handheld card reader that records credit card data for later use.

Skimming is double-swiping a credit card in a legitimate terminal or covertly swiping a credit card in a small, hidden, handheld card reader that records credit card data for later use. Commonly committed in retail outlets such as restaurants and carried out by employees with a legitimate reason to possess the victim's cards, annual skimming losses exceed $1 billion. A part-time employee at a gas station skimmed the cards of 80 customers, including the owner, who was a relative, and stole more than $200,000.

chipping - Planting a small chip that records transaction data in a legitimate credit card reader. The chip is later removed or electronically accessed to retrieve the data recorded on it.

Chipping is planting a small chip that records transaction data in a legitimate credit card reader. The chip is later removed or electronically accessed to retrieve the data recorded on it.

eavesdropping - Listening to private communications or tapping into data transmissions intended for someone else. One way to intercept signals is by setting up a wiretap.

Eavesdropping is listening to private communications or tapping into data transmissions. The equipment needed to set up a wiretap on an unprotected communications line is readily available at local electronics stores. One alleged wiretapping fraud involved Mark Koenig, a 28-year-old telecommunications consultant, and four associates. Federal agents say the team pulled crucial data about Bank of America customers from telephone lines and used it to make 5,500 fake ATM cards. Koenig and his friends allegedly intended to use the cards over a long weekend to withdraw money from banks across the country. Authorities were tipped off, and they were apprehended before they could use the cards.

Malware

malware - Any software that is used to do harm.

This section describes **malware**, which is any software used to do harm. Malware is a constant and fast-growing concern, as well as an expensive one, with the average attack costing $2.6 million. Heartland Payment Systems was the victim of one of the largest-ever security breaches in U.S. history. More than 130 million credit card numbers were stolen, and Heartland spent more than $12.6 million in legal costs and fines associated with the security breach.

There are a billion unique pieces of malware in the database of McAfee, a leading cyber security company. It is estimated that more than 200 million new malware samples are created each calendar year. One reason for this is the elaborate and extensive online underground fraud discussed in Focus 9-3.

Malware is not restricted to computers. As many as 2 million new pieces of mobile device malware are discovered each year. This malware ranges from fake versions of legitimate apps to banking apps that generate unwanted advertisements. One attack targeted Israel Defense Force soldiers who downloaded a fake dating app that infected their phones. It captured location and contact data, listened to their phone calls, and used the camera on their phones. Many free phone apps are a form of adware, which is discussed later in the chapter.

Most malware is the result of installation or injection by a remote attacker. It is spread using several approaches, including shared access to files, e-mail attachments, and remote access vulnerabilities.

The U.S. Navy Warfare Center created a visual malware app that uses a person's phone to secretly record his environment and then reconstructs it as a 3D virtual model. The user is tricked into downloading and running the PlaceRaider app, which gives the malware permission to embed itself in the camera app. The app mutes the phone's shutter sound; takes photos and records the time, location, and orientation of the phone; filters out photos with blurred or dark images; and sends everything to a central server where a 3D model of the location is

FOCUS 9-3 The Online Underground Fraud Community

Tens of thousands of people are involved in the online underground fraud community. They perform one or more of the following functions:

Malware writers create new viruses, spyware, and Trojan horses that are used to infect computers. Most do not use their product. Instead, they sell it, usually for "educational purposes" to try to avoid prosecution. Many malware writers rigorously test their malware so they can guarantee it will not be discovered by current antivirus programs. When antivirus software is updated, the author will supply a new version that again avoids detection.

Malware owners buy the malware (often custom written) for as little as $250. For an additional fee (often $25 a month), the malware user can receive updates that keep the malware from being detected.

Botnet owners control an army of malware-infected zombie computers. Malware owners hire the botnet owners to send millions of spam e-mails or to initiate hundreds of thousands of Trojan attacks to capture data they can sell.

Identity fraudsters buy the malware-captured information and identities. A complete identity (name, address, ID, credit card numbers, and bank account details) can sell for as much as $6 and a credit card number for as much as 5% of the unused credit limit. Identity fraudsters use the stolen identities or package them (country of origin, remaining balance, etc.) and sell them.

Identity intermediaries buy stolen credit card identities, buy goods online, and have the goods sent to a drop service. To make sure they are paid by the drop service, identity intermediaries often use guarantors.

Drop services employ **drops** (criminal fences or unsuspecting individuals) to sell the goods online or to people or stores looking for cheap goods. The drop services keep an agreed-upon commission, pay their drops, and send the remainder to the identity intermediary.

Guarantors guarantee that the various people who deal with each other make the agreed-upon exchanges. For example, they make sure that an identity intermediary is paid their cut of the sale of any goods, even if individual drops don't pay up. They also provide an escrow service; a buyer will transfer payment to the guarantor and the seller will transmit the virus code or the credit card numbers. If the goods check out and the funds are good, they are both distributed. Guarantors receive up to 3% of the transaction amount for their services.

On the other side are people trying to protect systems and people.

Antivirus software vendors produce software that combats malware. Most antivirus programs detect malware by electronically scanning communications and files for software signatures (code fragments, akin to DNA fragments). Antivirus software is reactive; it does not detect a new signature until a virus is "in the wild" and attacking systems. When a new virus is found, the antivirus software is updated to prevent further problems. Unfortunately, malware authors download the new signatures and modify their malware so it is no longer recognized by the antivirus programs.

As in most industries, each of the above groups have competitors and compete based on price, service, and product quality. This competition results in increasing innovation in the online fraud community. This does not bode well for companies and individuals. As the fraudsters get better, our data will become much less secure unless those fighting online fraud match or exceed the innovation produced by the online underground fraud community.

created. In the wrong hands, the app could be used to steal identity-related information, credit card details, financial information, and data on computer screens. The app could also be used to identify items worth stealing and to determine when the user will be away.

Spyware software secretly monitors and collects personal information about users and sends it to someone else. The information is gathered by logging keystrokes, monitoring websites visited, and scanning documents on the computer's hard drive. Spyware can also hijack a browser, replacing a computer's home page with a page the spyware creator wants you to visit. Unless the spyware is removed, resetting a browser home page lasts only until the computer is rebooted. Spyware can also hijack search requests, returning results chosen by the spyware rather than the results desired. Spyware infections, of which users are usually unaware, come from the following:

spyware - Software that secretly monitors computer usage, collects personal information about users, and sends it to someone else, often without the computer user's permission.

- Downloads such as file-sharing programs, system utilities, games, wallpaper, screen savers, music, and videos.
- Websites that secretly download spyware. This is called *drive-by downloading*.
- A hacker using security holes in web browsers and other software.
- Malware masquerading as antispyware security software.

- A worm or virus.
- Public wireless networks. At Kinko's in Manhattan, an employee gathered the data needed to open bank accounts and apply for credit cards in the names of the people using Kinko's wireless network.

Spyware is especially problematic for companies with employees who telecommute or remotely access the network. Spyware on these computers record the user's network interactions, copy corporate data, and introduce spyware to the entire organization. A main source of spyware is adult-oriented sites. The computers of people who visit those sites are infected, and when they log onto their corporate systems those infections are passed to their employer's internal network.

adware - Spyware that causes banner ads to pop up on a monitor, collects information about the user's web-surfing and spending habits, and forwards it to the adware creator, often an advertising or media organization. Adware usually comes bundled with freeware and shareware downloaded from the Internet.

Adware is spyware that can pop banner ads on a monitor, collect information about the user's web-surfing and spending habits, and forward it to the adware creator. Adware companies charge for each computer showing its ads. They increase the number of computers with adware by paying shareware developers to bundle the adware with their software. This allows shareware developers to make money without charging for their software. One company that engages in digital media content sharing offers users a $30 version or a free version. The license agreement for the free software discloses the adware (hence making it "legal" spyware), but most users do not read the agreement and are not aware it is installed. Reputable adware companies claim sensitive or identifying data are not collected. However, there is no way for users to effectively control or limit the data collected and transmitted.

One study found that 80% of inspected computers were infected with spyware, each machine containing on average 93 spyware or adware components. Another study estimated that 90% of computers connected to the Internet had spyware, with 90% of the owners unaware of the infection. The best protection against spyware and adware is a good antispyware software package that neutralizes or eliminates it and prevents its installation. One downside is that after the spyware or adware is erased, the free software that was its host may not work. To protect yourself, use multiple antispyware programs; unlike antivirus software and firewalls, they don't conflict with each other.

Some malware developers intentionally make their software difficult to uninstall. Malware companies sometimes battle each other over whose software will infect a computer. Some of them have developed **torpedo software** that destroys competing malware, resulting in "malware warfare" between competing developers.

torpedo software - Software that destroys competing malware. This sometimes results in "malware warfare" between competing malware developers.

scareware - Malicious software of no benefit that is sold using scare tactics.

Scareware is software that is often malicious, is of little or no benefit, and is sold using scare tactics. That is, it uses fear to motivate some sort of user action. The most common scare tactic is a dire warning that a computer is infected with a virus, spyware, or some other catastrophic problem. Some scareware even warns that a user's job, career, or marriage is at risk. The scareware creators offer a solution—a free computer scan using their fake antivirus software. Accepting the free scan does several things. First, it does not perform a scan. Second, it claims to find dozens of problems and again warns of dire consequences if the computer is not cleaned up. Third, it often introduces the very problems that scared the consumer into trying the software. Fourth, it encourages the consumer to buy the fake antivirus software to clean the computer and keep it clean.

Consumers are infected with scareware by means of online advertisements, Internet search results, and social networks such as Facebook, YouTube, and Twitter. Because some scareware is so realistic, it has succeeded in fooling large segments of the population. To deceive consumers, the software looks and feels like legitimate security software, the e-mails look like they come from legitimate security software companies, and the pop-ups look like they come from the user's operating system. Scareware scammers also create web pages about celebrity news and other hot topics that appear at the top of Google search results; clicking on any of the many links on the web page launches the scareware. Scammers also steal Facebook and Twitter account log-ons, send messages carrying a tainted web link to the victim's contacts, and rely on the high trust common to social networks to trick users into launching scareware.

There are tens of thousands of different scareware packages, with the number rising almost 600% in a recent six-month period. In another growth comparison, Microsoft reported that its free Malicious Software Removal Tool cleaned scareware off 7.8 million PCs in one six-month period, compared to 5.3 million in the prior six months.

Scareware can be spotted several ways. First, the scare tactics are a big giveaway; legitimate companies will not try to scare you into using their products. A second giveaway is poor English; most scareware comes from countries where English is not the creator's first language.

The Federal Trade Commission sued the perpetrators of a massive scareware scheme that offered fake computer scans that falsely claimed to detect viruses, spyware, system errors, and illegal pornography. They tricked more than a million people into spending $1.9 million to buy fake computer security products, including DriveCleaner, XP Antivirus, WinAntivirus, ErrorSafe, and WinFixer.

Cyber-extortion is threatening to harm a company or a person if a specified amount of money is not paid. The owner of a credit card processor received an e-mail listing his clients as well as their credit card numbers. The e-mail told him to pay $50,000 in six payments, or the data would be sent to his clients. An investigation showed that his system had been successfully penetrated and that customer data had been copied. Not believing the attacker, the owner did nothing. The extortionists released the data, and he spent weeks trying to reassure his irate customers. His efforts were futile; his customers abandoned him, and within six months, he shut down his business.

cyber-extortion - Threatening to harm a company or a person if a specified amount of money is not paid.

One type of cyber-extortion is **ransomware**, which locks you out of all your programs and data by encrypting them. That means you can't run your installed security programs and, if it disables your USB ports and DVD drives, you can't load new security programs to combat it. It directs your browser to the perpetrator's website, where the victim is informed that a monetary payment made directly to a bank must be made to have the software removed. Most ransomware is delivered via websites or a spam e-mail that motivates the recipient to open an infected file. Staying current with new software releases and updates is crucial to blocking these downloads. Frequent data backups to external storage devices are a great way to not have to pay the ransom.

ransomware - Software that encrypts programs and data until a ransom is paid to remove it.

Hackers perpetrated a ransomware attack on Hollywood Presbyterian Medical Center and demanded $3.6 million for a decryption key that would restore their data. The hospital tried to solve the problem for more than a week while they used pen and paper for record-keeping and transported some patients to nearby hospitals for tests and treatment. The hospital finally decided that the best way to restore its systems and data was to pay the ransom. They negotiated the fee down to $17,000, paid in bitcoin.

Keylogger software records computer activity, such as a user's keystrokes, e-mails sent and received, websites visited, and chat session participation. Parents use the software to monitor their children's computer usage, and businesses use it to monitor employee activity. Law enforcement uses it to detect or prevent crime. A Drug Enforcement Administration agent persuaded a federal judge to authorize him to sneak into an Escondido, California, office believed to be a front for manufacturing the drug Ecstasy. Copying the contents of all hard drives and installing keystroke loggers successfully thwarted their plans to distribute Ecstasy.

keylogger - Software that records computer activity, such as a user's keystrokes, e-mails sent and received, websites visited, and chat session participation.

Fraud perpetrators use key loggers to capture and send confidential information. More than 10,000 unique key logging software programs are available in underground chat rooms; most are free or inexpensive. Computers are infected with key logging software when they visit corrupt websites or download free software. One enterprising student installed key logging software on his teacher's computer, recorded her typed exam answers, and decoded the keystrokes. He was caught trying to sell exam answers to other students.

A **Trojan horse** is a set of malicious computer instructions in an authorized and otherwise properly functioning program. In one study, Trojans were the malware of choice, as they were used in more than 66% of all infections. Unlike viruses and worms, the code does not try to replicate itself. Some Trojans give the creator the power to control the victim's computer remotely. Most Trojan infections occur when a user runs an infected program received in an e-mail, visits a malicious website, or downloads software billed as helpful add-ons to popular software programs.

Trojan horse - A set of unauthorized computer instructions in an authorized and otherwise properly functioning program.

In Israel, companies were sent business proposals on a disk that contained the Trojan. In another case, visitors to an adult site were told to download a special program to see the pictures. This program disconnected them from their Internet service providers and connected them to a service that billed them $2 a minute until they turned off their computers. More than 800,000 minutes were billed, with some phone bills as high as $3,000, before the scam was detected. The HotLan Trojan caused infected computers to sign up for Microsoft Hotmail and Google Gmail accounts and used them for spamming. More than 514,000 Hotmail accounts and 49,000 Gmail accounts were created in a single day.

One type of Trojan horse relies on the curiosity of the victim. The attacker creates a malware-infected CD ROM or USB flash drive, gives it a legitimate looking and curiosity piquing label (company logo, accompanied by 4Q Evaluation and Salary Data), leaves it where it can be found (bathroom, desktop, hallway), and waits for a curious employee to try to read the file. The file installs the Trojan on the employee's computer, likely giving the attacker access to the company's internal computer network.

time bomb/logic bomb - A program that lies idle until some specified circumstance or a particular time triggers it. Once triggered, the program sabotages the system by destroying programs or data.

A **time bomb/logic bomb** is a Trojan horse that lies idle until triggered by a specified date or time, by a change in the system, by a message sent to the system, or by an event that does not occur. Once triggered, the bomb goes off, destroying programs, data, or both. Disgruntled company insiders who want to get even with their company write time or logic bombs. Anticipating that he would not receive a bonus or new contract, Roger Duronio planted a Trojan horse time bomb at USB PaineWebber. Several weeks after he left the firm, the trigger date of March 4 arrived. His 60 lines of malicious code attacked the company's 2,000 servers and deleted company files just as the stock market opened. The effects were catastrophic. Broker computers were out of commission for days or weeks, depending on how badly the machines were damaged and the existence of branch backup tapes. Some 20% of the computers had no backup tapes, and some servers were never fully restored. More than 400 employees and 200 IBM consultants worked feverishly, at a cost of $3.1 million, to restore the system. Duronio cashed out his IRA and sold USB stock short, figuring to make a killing when the stock plunged. It never did, and he lost money on his short sale. Duronio was sentenced to eight years in prison.

There are legal uses of time and logic bombs, such as in trial versions of software. The software becomes unusable after a certain amount of time passes or after the software has been used a certain number of times.

trap door/back door - A set of computer instructions that allows a user to bypass the system's normal controls.

A **trap door/back door** is a set of computer instructions that allows a user to bypass the system's normal controls. Programmers create trap doors so they can modify programs during systems development and then remove them before the system is put into operation. The back door can also be created by a virus or worm or by a disgruntled programmer. Anyone who discovers a trap door can enter the program. Security consultants claim that back doors are frequently discovered in organizations. BackOrifice, Netbus, and SubSeven are tools intruders use to gain remote, back door access to systems with Windows software. Jonathan James, the first juvenile sent to prison for hacking, installed a back door into a Department of Defense server, accessed sensitive e-mails, and captured employee user names and passwords.

packet sniffers - Programs that capture data from information packets as they travel over the Internet or company networks. Captured data is sifted to find confidential or proprietary information.

Packet sniffers capture data from information packets as they travel over networks. Captured data are examined to find confidential or proprietary information. In Sweden, Dan Egerstad's packet sniffer looked for key words such as *government*, *military*, *war*, *passport*, and *visa*. He intercepted e-mails from embassies and governments, many with visa and passport data.

steganography program - A program that can merge confidential information with a seemingly harmless file, password protect the file, and send it anywhere in the world, where the file is unlocked and the confidential information is reassembled. The host file can still be heard or viewed because humans are not sensitive enough to pick up the slight decrease in image or sound quality.

Steganography is writing hidden messages in such a way that no one, apart from the sender and intended recipient, suspects their existence. Steganography messages do not attract attention to themselves, whereas an encrypted message arouses suspicion. A **steganography program** hides data files inside a host file, such as a large image or sound file. The software merges the two files by removing scattered bytes from the host file and replacing them with data from the hidden file. The steganography program password protects the merged file, and the only way to reassemble the hidden file is to key the password into the same steganography program. The host file can still be heard or viewed because human visual and auditory senses are not sensitive enough to pick up the slight decrease in image or sound quality that the hidden file causes. Company employees can merge confidential information with a seemingly harmless file and send it anywhere in the world, where the confidential information is reassembled.

Steganography is used by terrorists, as it is an effective way for a spy to transmit information and receive orders. Some experts believe steganography was one way terrorists communicated in planning the September 11, 2001 terrorist attacks on the United States. A *USA Today* article alleged that Al-Qaeda operatives sent hundreds of messages hidden in digital photographs sold on eBay.

rootkit - A means of concealing system components and malware from the operating system and other programs; can also modify the operating system.

A **rootkit** conceals processes, files, network connections, memory addresses, systems utility programs, and system data from the operating system and other programs. Rootkits often modify the operating system or install themselves as drivers. A rootkit is used to hide the presence of trap doors, sniffers, and key loggers; conceal software that originates a DoS or an e-mail spam attack; and access user names and log-in information. Unlike viruses and worms, rootkits do not spread to other systems. Rootkit software is readily available on the Internet. Several vendors sell programs that detect rootkits, and security vendors include rootkit detection in their antivirus products. When a rootkit is detected, it is better to reinstall the operating system from scratch rather than spend the time and effort to delete it from the system. In a famous instance of rootkit use, Sony music CDs secretly placed a copy-protection rootkit on Windows computers. The software inadvertently opened security holes that allowed viruses to break in. Sony had to recall all CDs that included the software.

A computer **virus** is a segment of self-replicating, executable code that attaches itself to a file or program. During its replication phase, the virus spreads to other systems when the infected file or program is downloaded or opened by the recipient. Newer viruses can mutate each time they infect a computer, making them more difficult to detect and destroy. Many viruses lie dormant for extended periods without causing damage, except to propagate themselves. In one survey, 90% of respondents said their company was infected with a virus during the prior 12 months.

virus - A segment of executable code that attaches itself to a file, program, or some other executable system component. When the hidden program is triggered, it makes unauthorized alterations to the way a system operates.

During the attack phase, usually triggered by some predefined event, viruses destroy or alter data or programs, take control of the computer, destroy the hard drive's file allocation table, delete or rename files or directories, reformat the hard drive, change the content of files, or keep users from booting the system or accessing data on the hard drive. A virus can intercept and change transmissions, display disruptive images or messages, or cause the screen image to change color or disappear. Many viruses automatically send e-mails, faxes, or text messages with the victim's name as the source. As the virus spreads, it takes up space, clogs communications, and hinders system performance. Computer virus symptoms include computers that will not start or execute; unexpected read or write operations; an inability to save files; long program load times; abnormally large file sizes; slow systems operation; incessant pop-ups; and unusual screen activity, error messages, or file names.

A bad virus attack shut down a bank with 200 servers and 10,000 desktop computers for four days. During the downtime, the bank was locked out of its system, and customer accounts could not be accessed. A firm that specializes in fixing virus attacks eventually restored the system. The Sobig virus, written by Russian hackers, infected an estimated 1 of every 17 e-mails several years ago. The virus took months to write and was released in ever-improving versions. A year later, the MyDoom virus infected 1 in 12 e-mails and did $4.75 billion in damages.

Every day, virus creators send an estimated 1 billion virus-infected e-mail messages. The creators are getting good at making them look authentic. One recent virus came in an e-mail that appeared to come from Microsoft—the Microsoft logo and copyright were included in the message window launched by the virus. The e-mail told the recipient to use the attached patch to fix a security flaw in either Microsoft Internet Explorer or Outlook. Instead, opening the attachment downloaded malicious software that installed a back door allowing the perpetrator to control the computer.

It is estimated that viruses and worms cost businesses more than $55 billion a year. A computer system can be protected from viruses by following the guidelines listed in Focus 9-4.

A computer **worm** is a self-replicating computer program similar to a virus, with some exceptions:

worm - Similar to a virus, except that it is a program rather than a code segment hidden in a host program. A worm also copies itself automatically and actively transmits itself directly to other systems.

1. A virus is a segment of code hidden in or attached to a host program or executable file, whereas a worm is a stand-alone program.
2. A virus requires a human to do something (run a program, open a file, etc.) to replicate itself, whereas a worm does not and actively seeks to send copies of itself to other network devices.
3. Worms harm networks (if only by consuming bandwidth), whereas viruses infect or corrupt files or data on a targeted computer.

Worms often reside in e-mail attachments and reproduce by mailing themselves to the recipient's mailing list, resulting in an electronic chain letter. Some recent worms have completely shut down e-mail systems. Worms are not confined to personal computers; thousands of worms infect cell phones each year by jumping from phone to phone over wireless networks.

FOCUS 9-4 Keeping Your Computers Virus-Free

Here are some practical suggestions for protecting computers from viruses:

- Install reputable and reliable antivirus software that scans for, identifies, and destroys viruses. Use only one antivirus program; multiple programs conflict with each other.
- Do not fall for ads touting free antivirus software; much of it is fake and contains malware.
- Do not fall for pop-up notices that warn of horrible threats and offer a free scan of your computer. Although no scan actually takes place, the program reports dozens of dangerous infections and tells you to purchase and download their fake antivirus program to clean it up.
- Make sure that the latest versions of the antivirus programs are used. National City Bank in Cleveland installed some new laptops. The manufacturer and the bank checked the laptops for viruses but did not use the latest antivirus software. A virus spread from the laptop hard drives to 300 network servers and 12,000 workstations. It took more than two days to eradicate the virus from all bank systems.
- Scan all incoming e-mail for viruses at the server level as well as at users' desktops.
- Do not download anything from an e-mail that uses noticeably bad English, such as terrible grammar and misspelled words. Many viruses come from overseas perpetrators whose first language is not English.
- All software should be certified as virus-free before you load it into the system. Be wary of software from unknown sources: They may be virus bait—especially if their prices or functionality sound too good to be true.
- Deal only with trusted software retailers.
- Some software suppliers use electronic techniques to make tampering evident. Ask whether the software you are purchasing has such protection.
- Check new software on an isolated machine with virus-detection software. Software direct from the publisher has been known to have viruses.
- Have two backups of all files. Data files should be backed up separately from programs to avoid contaminating backup data.
- If you use flash drives or CDs, do not put them in strange machines; they may become infected. Do not let others use those storage devices on your machine. Scan all new files with antiviral software before data or programs are copied to your machine.

A worm usually does not live very long, but it is quite destructive while alive. It takes little technical knowledge to create a worm or virus. Many websites provide applications that enable unsophisticated users to create worms.

An early and destructive worm, perpetrated by Robert T. Morris, affected 6,000 computers in a very short time. More recently, MySpace had to go offline to disable a worm that added more than 1 million friends to the hacker's site in less than a day. MySpace profiles were infected by a worm after viewing a QuickTime video containing malicious software that replaced the links in the user's page with links to a phishing site. The devastating Conficker worm infected 25% of enterprise Window PCs.

Many viruses and worms exploit known software vulnerabilities than can be corrected with a software patch. Therefore, a good defense against them is making sure that all software patches are installed as soon as they are available.

bluesnarfing - Stealing (snarfing) contact lists, images, and other data using flaws in Bluetooth applications.

bluebugging - Taking control of someone else's phone to make or listen to calls, send or read text messages, connect to the Internet, forward the victim's calls, and call numbers that charge fees.

Recent viruses and worms have attacked cell phones and personal electronic devices using text messages, Internet page downloads, and Bluetooth wireless technology. Flaws in Bluetooth applications open the system to attack. **Bluesnarfing** is stealing (snarfing) contact lists, images, and other data using Bluetooth. A reporter for TimesOnline accompanied Adam Laurie, a security expert, around London scanning for Bluetooth-compatible phones. Before a Bluetooth connection can be made, the person contacted must agree to accept the link. However, Laurie has written software to bypass this control and identified vulnerable handsets at an average rate of one per minute. He downloaded entire phonebooks, calendars, diary contents, and stored pictures. Phones up to 90 meters away were vulnerable.

Bluebugging is taking control of someone else's phone to make or listen to calls, send or read text messages, connect to the Internet, forward the victim's calls, and call numbers that charge fees. These attacks will become more popular as phones are used to pay for items purchased. When a hacker wants something, all he will have to do is bluebug a nearby phone and make a purchase. To prevent these attacks, a Bluetooth device can be set to make it hard for other devices to recognize it. Antivirus software for phones helps deal with such problems.

Many other devices—such as home security systems, home appliances, automobiles, and elevators—are beginning to be targeted by viruses and worms.

Table 9-1 summarizes, in alphabetical order, the computer fraud and abuse techniques discussed in the chapter.

TABLE 9-1 Computer Fraud and Abuse Techniques

Technique	Description
Adware	Spyware that collects and forwards data to advertising companies or causes banner ads to pop up as the Internet is surfed.
Bluebugging	Taking control of a phone to make calls, send text messages, listen to calls, or read text messages.
Bluesnarfing	Stealing contact lists, images, and other data using Bluetooth.
Botnet, bot herders	A network of hijacked computers. Bot herders use the hijacked computers, called zombies, in a variety of attacks.
Buffer overflow attack	Inputting so much data that the input buffer overflows. The overflow contains code that takes control of the computer.
Brute force attack	Trial-and-error method that uses software to guess information, such as the user ID and the password, needed to gain access to a system.
Caller ID spoofing	Displaying an incorrect number on the recipient's caller ID display to hide the identity of the caller.
Carding	Verifying credit card validity; buying and selling stolen credit cards.
Chipping	Planting a chip that records transaction data in a legitimate credit card reader.
Click fraud	Manipulating the number of times an ad is clicked on to inflate advertising bills.
Cross-site scripting (XSS) attack	Exploits web page security vulnerabilities to bypass browser security mechanisms and create a malicious link that injects unwanted code into a website.
Cyber-bullying	Using computer technology to harm another person.
Cyber-extortion	Requiring a company to pay money to keep an extortionist from harming a computer or a person.
Cryptocurrency fraud	Defrauding investors in a variety of cryptocurrency-related fraud schemes, such as fake initial coin offerings and fake exchanges and wallets.
Denial-of-service attack	An attack designed to make computer resources unavailable to its users. For example, so many e-mail messages that the Internet service provider's e-mail server is overloaded and shuts down.
Dictionary attack	Software that guesses user IDs and passwords using a dictionary of user IDs and passwords to reduce the number of guesses required.
Eavesdropping	Listening to private voice or data transmissions.
Economic espionage	The theft of information, trade secrets, and intellectual property.
E-mail spoofing	Making a sender address and other parts of an e-mail header appear as though the e-mail originated from a different source.
E-mail threats	Sending a threatening message asking recipients to do something that makes it possible to defraud them.
Evil twin	A wireless network with the same name as another wireless access point. Users unknowingly connect to the evil twin; hackers monitor the traffic looking for useful information.
Hacking	Unauthorized access, modification, or use of an electronic device or some element of a computer system.
Hijacking	Gaining control of someone else's computer for illicit activities.
Identity theft	Assuming someone's identity by illegally obtaining confidential information such as a Social Security number.
Internet auction fraud	Using an Internet auction site to commit fraud.
Internet misinformation	Using the Internet to spread false or misleading information.
Internet pump-and-dump fraud	Using the Internet to pump up the price of a stock and then sell it.
IP address spoofing	Creating IP packets with a forged IP address to hide the sender's identity or to impersonate another computer system.
Keylogger	Using spyware to record a user's keystrokes.
Lebanese looping	Inserting a sleeve into an ATM so that it will not eject the victim's card, pretending to help the victim as a means of obtaining his PIN, and using the card and PIN to drain the account.
Malware	Software that is used to do harm.
Man-in-the-middle (MITM) attack	A hacker placing himself between a client and a host to intercept network traffic; also called *session hijacking*.

continued

TABLE 9-1 Continued

Masquerading/impersonation	Gaining access to a system by pretending to be an authorized user. The impersonator enjoys the same privileges as the legitimate user.
Packet sniffers	Inspecting information packets as they travel across computer networks.
Password cracking	Recovering passwords by trying every possible combination of upper and lower case letters, numbers, and special characters and comparing them to a cryptographic hash of the password.
Pharming	Redirecting traffic to a spoofed website to obtain confidential information.
Phishing	Communications that request recipients to disclose confidential information by responding to an e-mail or visiting a website.
Phreaking	Attacking phone systems to get free phone access; using phone lines to transmit viruses and to access, steal, and destroy data.
Piggybacking	1. Clandestine use of someone's Wi-Fi network. 2. Tapping into a communications line and entering a system by latching onto a legitimate user. 3. Bypassing physical security controls by entering a secure door when an authorized person opens it.
Podslurping	Using a small device with storage capacity (iPod, Flash drive) to download unauthorized data from a computer.
Posing	Creating a seemingly legitimate business, collecting personal data while making a sale, and never delivering items sold.
Pretexting	Acting under false pretenses to gain confidential information.
Ransomware	Software that encrypts programs and data until a ransom is paid to remove it.
Rootkit	Software that conceals processes, files, network connections, and system data from the operating system and other programs; can also change the operating system.
Round-down fraud	Truncating interest calculations at two decimal places and placing truncated amounts in the perpetrator's account.
Salami technique	Stealing tiny slices of money over time.
Scareware	Malicious software of no benefit that is sold using scare tactics.
Scavenging/dumpster diving	Searching for documents and records in garbage cans, communal trash bins, and city dumps to obtain confidential information.
Sexting	Exchanging sexually explicit text messages and pictures, usually by phone.
Shoulder surfing	Watching or listening to people enter or disclose confidential data.
Skimming	Double-swiping a credit card or covertly swiping it in a card reader to record the data for later use.
SMS spoofing	Using short message service (SMS) to change the name or number a text message appears to come from.
Social engineering	Techniques that trick a person into disclosing confidential information.
Software piracy	Unauthorized copying or distribution of copyrighted software.
Spamming	Sending an unsolicited message to many people at the same time.
Spoofing	Making an electronic communication look like someone else sent it.
Spyware	Software that monitors computing habits and sends that data to someone else, often without the user's permission.
SQL injection attack	Inserting a malicious SQL query in input such that it is passed to and executed by an application program.
Steganography	Hiding data inside a host file, such as a large image or sound file.
Time bomb/logic bomb	Software that sits idle until a specified circumstance or time triggers it, destroying programs, data, or both.
Torpedo software	Software that destroys competing malware.
Trap door/back door	A back door into a system that bypasses normal system controls.
Trojan horse	Unauthorized code in an authorized and properly functioning program.
Typosquatting/URL hijacking	Websites with names similar to real websites; users making typographical errors are sent to a site filled with malware.
Virus	Executable code that attaches itself to software, replicates itself, and spreads to other systems or files. When triggered, it makes unauthorized alterations to the way a system operates.
Vishing	Voice phishing, in which e-mail recipients are asked to call a phone number that asks them to divulge confidential data.
War dialing	Dialing phone lines to find idle modems to use to enter a system, capture the attached computer, and gain access to its network(s).
War driving	Looking for unprotected wireless networks using a car.
Web-page spoofing	Also called *phishing*.

TABLE 9-1 Continued

Worm	Similar to a virus; a program rather than a code segment hidden in a host program. Actively transmits itself to other systems. It usually does not live long but is quite destructive while alive.
Zero-day attack	Attack between the time a software vulnerability is discovered and a patch to fix the problem is released.
Zombie	A hijacked computer, typically part of a botnet, that is used to launch a variety of Internet attacks.

Summary and Case Conclusion

It took RPC two days to get its system back up to the point that the audit team could continue their work. RPC had been hit with multiple problems at the same time. Hackers had used packet sniffers and eavesdropping to intercept a public key RPC had sent to Northwest. That led to an MITM attack, which allowed the hacker to intercept all communications about the pending merger. It also opened the door to other attacks on both systems.

Law enforcement was called in to investigate the problem, and they were following up on three possibilities. The first was that hackers had used the intercepted information to purchase stock in both companies, leak news of the purchase to others via Internet chat rooms, and, once the stock price had been pumped up, to dump the stock of both companies. There did seem to be significant, unusual trading in the two companies' stock in the last few months. The second possibility was hackers exploiting system weaknesses they had found, stealing confidential data on RPC's customers, and causing considerable harm when they were done to cover their tracks. The third possibility was economic espionage and Internet terrorism. They received an anonymous tip that one of Northwest's competitors was behind the attack. It would take weeks or even months to track down all the leads and determine who had caused the problem and why.

Jason's research helped him understand the many ways outside hackers and employees attack systems. He never knew there were so many different things that could be spoofed in systems. He was also intrigued by some of the more technical attacks, such as XSS, buffer overflow attacks, MITM attacks, and SQL injection. He also found it interesting to learn how people use computers to defraud or harm other individuals and companies, such as Internet terrorism, misinformation, auction fraud, cyber-bullying, and cyber-extortion.

Jason was familiar with some of the social engineering techniques he read about, such as pretexting, posing, pharming, and phishing. However, he was unfamiliar with many of the techniques such as Lebanese looping, evil twin, chipping, and typosquatting. He had a similar experience when learning about malware. He was familiar with spyware, adware, Trojan horses, viruses, and key loggers. He learned many new things when he read about scareware, ransomware, steganography, rootkits, and bluebugging.

Jason's research also gave him a perspective on past and future uses of computer fraud and abuse techniques. He learned that many hacker attacks use more than one technique. For example, hackers often send spam e-mails that lure the victim to a website that downloads either a keylogger software or code that either hijacks the computer and turns it into a botnet zombie or tries to trick the user into disclosing confidential information. He also learned that hackers take advantage of people who share personal information on social networking sites.

With the harvested personal information that makes it easier to target specific people, cyber-attacks are increasingly successful in tricking even savvy users into making a mistake. For example, past phishing attacks used a generic spam e-mail message that was obviously bogus. Newer attacks use current-events issues or hot-button topics. Attacks that are even more sophisticated use information about the intended target to make them look legitimate. For example, the e-mail may use stolen information, such as the victim's employer or a friend or family member, to induce them to open an attachment or visit a website.

Lastly, Jason learned there is a plethora of fraud software on the market and that hackers compete to make the most easy-to-use tools. As a result, hackers do not need to be programmers; they just need to know whom they want to target and check a few boxes. For example, with Zeus, one of the most popular and successful data-stealing toolkits, cyber criminals can generate detailed reports on each website visited. They can also use the program's powerful search engine to browse through their victims' machines and find detailed information, such as which banks they use. Conversely, the best hackers are more knowledgeable than in the past and use sophisticated technologies. For example, zombies on a botnet used an automated SQL injection attack to compromise more than 500,000 websites last year, stealing sensitive information and injecting malware into the site.

KEY TERMS

hacking 258
hijacking 258
botnet 258
zombies 258
bot herder 258
denial-of-service (DoS) attack 259
brute force attack 259
password cracking 260
dictionary attack 260
spamming 260
spoofing 260
e-mail spoofing 260
caller ID spoofing 260
IP address spoofing 261
SMS spoofing 261
web-page spoofing 261
vulnerabilities 261
zero-day attack 261
patch 261
cross-site scripting (XSS) 261
buffer overflow attack 262
SQL injection (insertion) attack 262
man-in-the-middle (MITM) attack 262
masquerading/impersonation 263
piggybacking 263
war dialing 263
war driving 263
phreaking 263
podslurping 264
salami technique 264
round-down fraud 264
economic espionage 264
cyber-bullying 264
sexting 264
Internet misinformation 264
e-mail threats 264
Internet auction fraud 264
Internet pump-and-dump fraud 265
cryptocurrency fraud 265
click fraud 265
software piracy 265
social engineering 266
identity theft 266
pretexting 267
posing 268
phishing 268
vishing 268
carding 268
pharming 268
evil twin 269
typosquatting/URL hijacking 269
scavenging/dumpster diving 269
shoulder surfing 269
Lebanese looping 270
skimming 270
chipping 270
eavesdropping 270
malware 270
spyware 271
adware 272
torpedo software 272
scareware 272
cyber-extortion 273
ransomware 273
keylogger 273
Trojan horse 273
time bomb/logic bomb 274
trap door/back door 274
packet sniffers 274
steganography program 274
rootkit 274
virus 275
worm 275
bluesnarfing 276
bluebugging 276

AIS in Action

CHAPTER QUIZ

1. A set of instructions to increase a programmer's pay rate by 10% is hidden inside an authorized program. It changes and updates the payroll file. What is this computer fraud technique called?
   a. virus
   b. worm
   c. trap door
   d. Trojan horse

2. Which computer fraud technique involves a set of instructions hidden inside a calendar utility that copies itself each time the utility is enabled until memory is filled and the system crashes?
   a. logic bomb
   b. trap door
   c. virus
   d. Trojan horse

3. Interest calculations are truncated at two decimal places, and the excess decimals are put into an account the perpetrator controls. What is this fraud called?
   a. typosquatting
   b. URL hijacking
   c. chipping
   d. round-down fraud

4. A perpetrator attacks phone systems to obtain free phone line access or uses telephone lines to transmit viruses and to access, steal, and destroy data. What is this computer fraud technique called?
   a. phishing
   b. phreaking
   c. pharming
   d. vishing

5. Fraud perpetrators threaten to harm a company if it does not pay a specified amount of money. What is this computer fraud technique called?
   a. cyber-terrorism
   b. blackmailing
   c. cyber-extortion
   d. scareware

6. Techniques used to obtain confidential information, often by tricking people, are referred to as what?
   a. pretexting
   b. posing
   c. social engineering
   d. identity theft

7. What type of software secretly collects personal information about users and sends it to someone else without the user's permission?
   a. rootkit
   b. torpedo software
   c. spyware
   d. malware

8. What type of software conceals processes, files, network connections, memory addresses, systems utility programs, and system data from the operating system and other programs?
   a. rootkit
   b. spyware
   c. malware
   d. adware

9. Which type of computer attack takes place between the time a software vulnerability is discovered and the time software developers release a software patch that fixes the problem?
   a. posing
   b. zero-day attack
   c. evil twin
   d. software piracy

10. Someone redirects a website's traffic to a bogus website, usually to gain access to personal and confidential information. What is this computer fraud technique called?
    a. vishing
    b. phishing
    c. pharming
    d. phreaking

DISCUSSION QUESTIONS

9.1 When U.S. Leasing (USL) computers began acting sluggishly, computer operators were relieved when a software troubleshooter from IBM called. When he offered to correct the problem they were having, he was given a log-on ID and password. The next morning, the computers were worse. A call to IBM confirmed USL's suspicion: Someone had impersonated an IBM repairman to gain unauthorized access to the system and destroy the database. USL was also concerned that the intruder had devised a program that would let him get back into the system even after all the passwords were changed. What techniques might the impostor have employed to breach USL's internal security? What could USL do to avoid these types of incidents in the future?

9.2 What motives do people have for hacking? Why has hacking become so popular in recent years? Do you regard it as a crime? Explain your position.

9.3 The UCLA computer lab was filled to capacity when the system slowed and crashed, disrupting the lives of students who could no longer log into the system or access data to prepare for finals. IT initially suspected a cable break or an operating system failure, but diagnostics revealed nothing. After several frustrating hours, a staff member ran a virus detection program and uncovered a virus on the lab's main server. The virus was eventually traced to the computers of unsuspecting UCLA students. Later that evening, the system was brought back online after infected files were replaced with backup copies. What conditions made the UCLA system a potential breeding ground for the virus? What symptoms indicated that a virus was present?

PROBLEMS

9.1 A few years ago, news began circulating about a computer virus named Michelangelo that was set to "ignite" on March 6, the birthday of the famous Italian artist. The virus attached itself to the computer's operating system boot sector. On the magical date, the virus would release itself, destroying all of the computer's data. When March 6 arrived, the virus did minimal damage. Preventive techniques limited the damage to isolated personal and business computers. Though the excitement surrounding the virus was largely illusory, Michelangelo helped the computer-using public realize its systems' vulnerability to outside attack.

REQUIRED

a. What is a computer virus? Cite at least three reasons why no system is completely safe from a computer virus.
b. Why do viruses represent a serious threat to information systems? What damage can a virus do to a computer system?
c. How does a virus resemble a Trojan horse?
d. What steps can be taken to prevent the spread of a computer virus?

9.2 The controller of a small business received the following e-mail with an authentic-looking e-mail address and logo:

From: *Big Bank [antifraud@bigbank.com]*
To: *Justin Lewis, Controller, Small Business USA*
Subject: *Official Notice for all users of Big Bank!*

Due to the increased incidence of fraud and identity theft, we are asking all bank customers to verify their account information on the following web page: www.antifraudbigbank.com

Please confirm your account information as soon as possible. Failure to confirm your account information will require us to suspend your account until confirmation is made.

A week later, the following e-mail was delivered to the controller:

From: *Big Bank [antifraud@bigbank.com]*
To: *Justin Lewis, Controller, Small Business USA*
Subject: *Official Notice for all users of Big Bank!*

Dear Client of Big Bank,
Technical services at Big Bank is currently updating our software. Therefore, we kindly ask that you access the website shown below to confirm your data. Otherwise, your access to the system may be blocked.web.da-us.bigbank.com/signin/scripts/login2/user_setup.jsp

We are grateful for your cooperation.

REQUIRED

a. What should Justin do about these e-mails?
b. What should Big Bank do about these e-mails?
c. Identify the computer fraud and abuse technique illustrated.

9.3 A purchasing department received the following e-mail.

Dear Accounts Payable Clerk,
You can purchase everything you need online—including peace of mind—when you shop using Random Account Numbers (RAN). RAN is a free service for Big Credit Card customers that substitutes a random credit card number in place of your normal credit card number when you make online purchases and payments. This random number provides you with additional security. Before every online purchase, simply get a new number from RAN to use at each new vendor. Sign up for an account at www.bigcreditcard.com. Also, take advantage of the following features:

- *Automatic Form automatically completes a vendor's order form with the RAN, its expiration date, and your shipping and billing addresses.*
- *Set the spending limit and expiration date for each new RAN.*
- *Use RAN once or use it for recurring payments for up to one year.*

REQUIRED

Explain which computer fraud and abuse techniques could be prevented using a random account number that links to your corporate credit card.

9.4 Computer Fraud and Abuse Techniques.

Match the Internet-related computer fraud and abuse technique in the left column with the scenario in the right column. The scenarios on the right may be used once, more than once, or not at all.

____ 1. adware	a. Software that monitors and reports a user's computing habits
____ 2. botnet	b. A program stored in a web page and executed by a web browser
____ 3. bot herder	c. Sending an e-mail instructing the recipient to do something or else suffer adverse consequences
____ 4. click fraud	d. Using the Internet to pass off the work of another as your own
____ 5. DoS	e. E-mailing an unsolicited message to many people at the same time
____ 6. e-mail threats	f. Creating websites with names similar to real websites so users making errors while entering a website name are sent to a hacker's site
____ 7. hijacking	g. An e-mail warning regarding a virus that, in reality, does not exist
____ 8. Internet misinformation	h. A spam blog that promotes affiliated websites to increase their Google PageRank
____ 9. key logger	i. Software that collects consumer surfing and purchasing data
____ 10. pharming	j. E-mails that look like they came from a legitimate source but are actually from a hacker who is trying to get the user to divulge personal information

____ 11. phishing	k. Making an e-mail look like it came from someone else
____ 12. spamming	l. Gaining control of a computer to carry out unauthorized illicit activities
____ 13. spyware	m. Using the Internet to disrupt communications and e-commerce
____ 14. spoofing	n. Diverting traffic from a legitimate website to a hacker's website to gain access to personal and confidential information
____ 15. typosquatting	o. A network of hijacked computers
	p. Using a legion of compromised computers to launch a coordinated attack on an Internet site
	q. Use of spyware to record a user's keystrokes
	r. Hackers that control hijacked computers
	s. Circulating lies or misleading information using the world's largest network
	t. Overloading an Internet service provider's e-mail server by sending hundreds of e-mail messages per second from randomly generated false addresses
	u. Inflating advertising revenue by clicking online ads numerous times

9.5 Match the computer fraud and abuse technique in the left column with the definition in the right column. The definition on the right may be used once, more than once, or not at all.

____ 1. packet sniffing	a. Intercepting Internet and other network transmissions
____ 2. round-down fraud	b. E-mails instructing a user to call a phone number where they are asked to divulge personal information
____ 3. bluebugging	c. Deep packet filtering
____ 4. scavenging	d. Illegally obtaining confidential information, such as Social Security number, about another person so that it can be used for financial gain
____ 5. chipping	e. Placing truncated decimal places in an account controlled by the perpetrator
____ 6. eavesdropping	f. Copying company data, such as computer files, without permission
____ 7. salami technique	g. Searching for unprotected wireless networks in a vehicle
____ 8. evil twin	h. Searching for modems on unprotected phone lines in order to access the attached computer and gain access to the network(s) to which it is attached
____ 9. war dialing	i. Making phone calls and sending text messages using another user's phone without physically holding that phone
____ 10. vishing	j. Concealing data within a large MP3 file
____ 11. phreaking	k. Capturing data from devices that use Bluetooth technology

____ 12. piggybacking	l. Embezzling small fractions of funds over time
____ 13. war driving	m. Covertly swiping a credit card in a card reader that records the data for later use
____ 14. bluesnarfing	n. Gaining access to a protected system by latching onto a legitimate user
____ 15. identity theft	o. Searching through garbage for confidential data
	p. A rogue wireless access point masquerading as a legitimate access point
	q. Devices that hide IP addresses
	r. Use of spyware to record a user's keystrokes
	s. Intercepting and/or listening in on private voice and data transmissions
	t. Using telephone lines to transmit viruses and to access, steal, and destroy data
	u. Inserting a chip that captures financial data in a legitimate credit card reader
	v. Altering data before or during entry into a computer system
	w. Decoding and organizing captured network data

9.6 Computer Fraud and Abuse Techniques.

Match the computer fraud and abuse technique in the left column with the scenario in the right column. The scenarios on the right may be used once, more than once, or not at all.

____ 1. dictionary attack	a. Guessing user IDs and passwords using a dictionary of user IDs and passwords
____ 2. hacking	b. Segment of executable code that attaches itself to software
____ 3. logic bomb	c. Recovering passwords by trying every possible combination of characters and comparing them to a cryptographic hash of the password
____ 4. malware	d. Malicious computer code that specifically targets a computer's start-up instructions
____ 5. masquerading	e. Using a wireless network without permission
____ 6. password cracking	f. Covertly swiping a credit card in a card reader that records the data for later use
____ 7. piggybacking	g. Concealing data within a large MP3 file
____ 8. posing	h. Attack occurring between the discovery of a software vulnerability and the release of a patch to fix the problem
____ 9. pretexting	i. Entering a system using a back door that bypasses normal system controls
____ 10. rootkit	j. Using software to guess company addresses, send employees blank e-mails, and add unreturned messages to spammer e-mail lists
____ 11. shoulder surfing	k. Unauthorized code in an authorized and properly functioning program
____ 12. skimming	l. Software used to do harm
____ 13. social engineering	m. Program that can replicate itself and travel over networks

____ 14. software piracy	n. Pretending to be a legitimate user, thereby gaining access to a system and all the rights and privileges of the legitimate user
____ 15. steganography	o. Special code or password that bypasses security features
____ 16. trap door	p. Unauthorized copying or distribution of copyrighted software
____ 17. Trojan horse	q. Software that conceals processes, files, network connections, and system data from the operating system and other programs
____ 18. virus	r. Methods used to trick someone into divulging personal information
____ 19. worm	s. Software that sits idle until a specified circumstance or time triggers it
____ 20. zero-day attack	t. Duplicating software, music, or movies
	u. Acting under false pretenses to gain confidential information
	v. Observing or listening to users as they divulge personal information
	w. Gaining access to a computer system without permission
	x. Creating a seemingly legitimate business, collecting personal information while making a sale, and never delivering the item sold

9.7 Computer Fraud and Abuse Techniques.

Match the computer fraud and abuse technique in the left column with the scenario in the right column. The scenarios on the right may be used once, more than once, or not at all.

____ 1. buffer overflow attack	a. Inserting a sleeve to trap a card in an ATM, pretending to help the owner to obtain his PIN, and using the card and PIN to drain the account
____ 2. carding	b. Segment of executable code that attaches itself to software
____ 3. caller ID spoofing	c. Using a small storage device to download unauthorized data from a computer
____ 4. cyber-extortion	d. Malicious computer code that specifically targets a computer's start-up instructions
____ 5. cyber-bullying	e. Malicious software that people are frightened into buying
____ 6. economic espionage	f. Covertly swiping a credit card in a card reader that records the data for later use
____ 7. e-mail spoofing	g. Using the Internet to inflate a stock price so it can be sold for a profit
____ 8. IP address spoofing	h. Exchanging explicit messages and pictures by telephone
____ 9. Internet auction fraud	i. Inserting a malicious database query in input in a way that it can be executed by an application program
____ 10. Internet pump-and-dump fraud	j. So much input data that storage is exceeded; excess input contains code that takes control of the computer

____ **11.** Lebanese looping	k. Making an electronic communication appear as though it originated from a different source
____ **12.** man-in-the-middle (MITM) attack	l. Creating packets with a forged address to impersonate another computing system
____ **13.** podslurping	m. Fake computer networking protocol messages sent to an Ethernet LAN to determine a network host's hardware address when only its IP address is known
____ **14.** ransomware	n. Changing the name or number a text message appears to come from
____ **15.** scareware	o. Special code or password that bypasses security features
____ **16.** sexting	p. Link containing malicious code that takes a victim to a vulnerable website where the victim's browser executes the malicious code embedded in the link
____ **17.** SQL injection	q. Using social networking to harass another person
____ **18.** SMS spoofing	r. Displaying an incorrect phone number to hide the caller's identity
____ **19.** XSS attack	s. Software that encrypts programs and data until a payment is made to remove it
	t. A hacker placing himself between a client and a host to intercept network traffic
	u. Demand for payment to ensure a hacker does not harm a computer
	v. Theft of trade secrets and intellectual property
	w. Using a site that sells to the highest bidder to defraud another person
	x. Verifying credit card validity
	y. Secretly changing an already open browser tab

9.8 You have learned about many computer fraud and abuse techniques used to harm people and computer systems. This is a self-directed assignment to learn more about some of the techniques discussed in the book and techniques not covered in the text.

a. Go online and research four computer fraud or abuse techniques. Two of the techniques already discussed in the text can be researched, but look for at least two additional techniques.
b. Write a four-page report (one page for each of the four techniques) on your findings. For each technique, the write-up should include items such as the following:
   1. An explanation of the technique, what it is used for, how it works, etc. For a technique covered in the text, your write-up must go beyond what is discussed there. Simply repeating what is in the text is not acceptable.
   2. Any available estimates illustrating how extensively the technique is used or the losses caused by its use.
   3. Examples illustrating how companies or individuals have been victimized by the techniques.
   4. What is being done, if anything, to prevent or minimize the impact of the technique.
   5. Print media or URL references showing where you got your information.
c. If instructed by your professor, come prepared to present your findings to the class.

9.9 Identify the computer fraud and abuse technique used in each of the following actual examples of computer wrongdoing.

a. A teenage gang known as the "414s" broke into the Los Alamos National Laboratory, Sloan-Kettering Cancer Center, and Security Pacific Bank. One gang member appeared in *Newsweek* with the caption "Beware: Hackers at play."

b. Daniel Baas was the systems administrator for a company that did business with Acxiom, who manages customer information for companies. Baas exceeded his authorized access and downloaded a file with 300 encrypted passwords, decrypted the password file, and downloaded Acxiom customer files containing personal information. The intrusion cost Acxiom more than $5.8 million.
c. Cyber-attacks left high-profile sites such as Amazon.com, eBay, Buy.com, and CNN Interactive staggering under the weight of tens of thousands of bogus messages that tied up the retail sites' computers and slowed the news site's operations for hours.
d. Susan Gilmour-Latham got a call asking why she was sending the caller multiple adult text messages per day. Her account records proved the calls were not coming from her phone. Neither she nor her mobile company could explain how the messages were sent. After finding no way to block the unsavory messages, she changed her mobile number to avoid further embarrassment by association.
e. A federal grand jury in Fort Lauderdale claimed that four executives of a rental-car franchise modified a computer-billing program to add five gallons to the actual gas tank capacity of their vehicles. Over three years, 47,000 customers who returned a car without topping it off ended up paying an extra $2 to $15 for gasoline.
f. A mail-order company programmer truncated odd cents in sales-commission accounts and placed them in the last record in the commission file. Accounts were processed alphabetically, and he created a dummy sales-commission account using the name of Zwana. Three years later, the holders of the first and last sales-commission accounts were honored. Zwana was unmasked and his creator fired.
g. MicroPatent, an intellectual property firm, was notified that their proprietary information would be broadcast on the Internet if they did not pay a $17 million fee. The hacker was caught by the FBI before any damage was done.
h. When Estonia removed a Russian World War II war memorial, Estonian government and bank networks were knocked offline in a distributed DoS attack by Russian hackers. A counterfeit letter of apology for removing the memorial statue was placed on the website of Estonia's prime minister.
i. eBay customers were notified by e-mail that their accounts had been compromised and were being restricted unless they re-registered using an accompanying hyperlink to a web page that had eBay's logo, home page design, and internal links. The form had a place for them to enter their credit card data, ATM PINs, Social Security number, date of birth, and their mother's maiden name. Unfortunately, eBay hadn't sent the e-mail.
j. A teenager hijacked the eBay.de domain name and several months later the domain name for a large New York ISP. Both hijacked websites pointed to a site in Australia.
k. Travelers who logged into the Alpharetta, Georgia, airport's Internet service had personal information stolen and picked up as many as 45 viruses. A hacker had set up a rogue wireless network with the same name as the airport's wireless access network.
l. Criminals in Russia used a vulnerability in Microsoft's server software to add a few lines of Java code to users' copies of Internet Explorer. The code recorded the users' keyboard activities, giving the criminals access to usernames and passwords at many banking websites. The attacks caused $420 million in damage.
m. America Online subscribers received a message offering free software. Users who opened the attachments unknowingly unleashed a program hidden inside another program that secretly copied the subscriber's account name and password and forwarded them to the sender.
n. Rajendrasinh Makwana, an Indian citizen and IT contractor who worked at Fannie Mae's Maryland facility, was terminated at 1:00 P.M. on October 24. Before his network access was revoked, he created a program to wipe out all 4,000 of Fannie Mae's servers on the following January 31.
o. A man accessed millions of ChoicePoint files by claiming in writing and on the phone to be someone he was not.
p. A 31-year-old programmer unleashed a Visual Basic program by deliberately posting an infected document to an alt.sex Usenet newsgroup using a stolen AOL account. The program evaded security software and infected computers using the Windows operating system and Microsoft Word. On March 26, the Melissa program appeared on thousands of e-mail systems disguised as an important message from a colleague or

friend. The program sent an infected e-mail to the first 50 e-mail addresses on the users' Outlook address book. Each infected computer would infect 50 additional computers, which in turn would infect another 50 computers. The program spread rapidly and exponentially, causing considerable damage. Many companies had to disconnect from the Internet or shut down their e-mail gateways because of the vast amount of e-mail the program was generating. The program caused more than $400 million in damages.

q. Microsoft filed a lawsuit against two Texas firms that produced software that sent incessant pop-ups resembling system warnings. The messages stated "CRITICAL ERROR MESSAGE! REGISTRY DAMAGED AND CORRUPTED" and instructed users to visit a website to download Registry Cleaner XP at a cost of $39.95.
r. As many as 114,000 websites were tricked into running database commands that installed malicious HTML code redirecting victims to a malicious web server that tried to install software to remotely control the web visitors' computers.
s. Zeus records log-in information when the user of the infected computer logs into a list of target websites, mostly banks and other financial institutions. The user's data is sent to a remote server where it is used and sold by cyber criminals. The new version of Zeus will significantly increase fraud losses, given that 30% of Internet users bank online.
t. It took Facebook 15 hours to kill a Facebook application that infected millions of PCs with software that displays a constant stream of pop-up ads. The program posted a "Sexiest Video Ever" message on Facebook walls that looked like it came from a friend. Clicking the link led to a Facebook installation screen, where users allowed the software to access their profiles and walls. Once approved, the application told users to download an updated, free version of a popular Windows video player. Instead, it inserted a program that displayed pop-up ads and links. A week later a "Distracting Beach Babes" message did the same thing.
u. Robert Thousand, Jr. discovered he lost $400,000 from his Ameritrade retirement account shortly after he began receiving a flood of phone calls with a 30-second recording for a sex hotline. An FBI investigation revealed that the perpetrator obtained his Ameritrade account information, called Ameritrade to change his phone number, created several VoIP accounts, and used automated dialing tools to flood the dentist's phones in case Ameritrade called his real number. The perpetrator requested multiple monetary transfers, but Ameritrade would not process them until they reached Thousand to verify them. When the transfers did not go through, the attacker called Ameritrade, gave information to verify that he was Thousand, claimed he had been having phone troubles, and told Ameritrade he was not happy that the transfers had not gone through. Ameritrade processed the transfers, and Thousand lost $400,000.
v. The Internet Crime Complaint Center reports a "hit man" scam. The scammer claims that he has been ordered to assassinate the victim and an associate has been ordered to kill a family member. The only way to prevent the killings is to send $800 so an Islamic expatriate can leave the United States.
w. In an economic stimulus scam, individuals receive a phone call from President Obama telling them to go to a website to apply for the funds. To receive the stimulus money, victims have to enter personal identification information, complete an online application, and pay a $28 fee.

9.10 On a Sunday afternoon at a hospital in the Pacific Northwest, computers became sluggish, and documents would not print. Monday morning, the situation became worse when employees logged on to their computers. Even stranger things happened— operating-room doors would not open, pagers would not work, and computers in the intensive care unit shut down. By 10:00 A.M., all 50 IT employees were summoned. They discovered that the hospital was under attack by a botnet that exploited a Microsoft operating system flaw and installed pop-up ads on hospital computers. They got access to the first computer on Sunday and used the hospital's network to spread the infection to other computers. Each infected computer became a zombie that scanned the network looking for new victims. With the network clogged with zombie traffic, hospital communications began to break down. The IT staff tried to halt the attack by shutting off the hospital's Internet connection, but it was too late. The bots were inside the hospital's computer system and infecting other computers faster than they could be cleaned. Monday afternoon IT figured out which malware the bots were installing and wrote a script, which was pushed out hourly, directing computers to remove the bad code. The script helped to slow the bots down a bit. (*Source:* D. Gage, *Baseline Security*, February 6, 2007.)

REQUIRED

a. What could the hospital do to stop the attack and contain the damage?
b. Which computer fraud and abuse technique did the hackers use in their attack on the hospital?
c. What steps should the hospital have taken to prevent the damage caused by the attack?

9.11 Answer the following multiple-choice questions.

1. A hacker from Croatia inserted a malicious string of code in a popular news website's database. When a researcher from a financial institution requested a page from the website, it was sent along with the malicious string. The researcher's browser executed the string inside the response and sent the researcher's cookies to the hacker. The hacker used the cookies to impersonate the researcher. What computer fraud approach did the hacker use to obtain the cookies?
a. man-in-the middle attack
b. cross-site scripting attack
c. hijacking attack
d. buffer overflow attack
e. impersonation

2. When your cell phone dies, a nodding acquaintance gives you a USB wall charger. Unbeknownst to you, this device can eavesdrop on most wireless Microsoft keyboards. To which computer fraud and abuse technique could this device expose you to?
a. packet sniffer
b. Trojan horse
c. keylogger
d. back door
e. ransomware

3. Sanford Wallace sent phishing messages to Facebook users that tricked 500,000 of them into providing their passwords and user account information. He accessed their accounts and over a three-month period posted more than 27 million messages on their friends' timelines. Since he violated a court order to not access Facebook, he was sentenced to 30 months in jail. Wallace went to jail for which kind of attack?
a. SQL injection
b. buffer overflow
c. podslurping
d. phreaking
e. spamming

4. After experiencing a larger than usual number of credit card frauds, the bank issuing the cards was able to determine that most of the credit cards had been used in only one location—a restaurant in New York City. An investigation uncovered a waiter who was double swiping credit cards and using the captured data to make online purchases where a physical card was not required. This is an example of ______________.
a. skimming
b. chipping
c. piggybacking
d. eavesdropping
e. QR barcode replacement

5. You find a web application that uses the following query structure to authenticate users: "SELECT * FROM userstable WHERE username = 'userinput1' and password ='userinput2';" You replace userinput1 with 'OR 1=1'; which gives you access to the database without having to enter a user name or password as "1=1" is always true and the rest of the query is ignored. What computer fraud and abuse technique is this?

a. zero-day attack
b. URL hijacking attack
c. SQL injection
d. buffer overflow attack
e. web page spoofing

6. A man used false names, addresses, and social security numbers to create 58,000 banking and brokerage accounts. To verify that the accounts were set up properly, the institutions would make deposits of less than a dollar into the account. He kept the funds instead of letting the institutions take them back out of the account. This is an example of which computer fraud technique?
a. Internet misinformation
b. money leakage
c. salami technique
d. dollar diddling
e. round-down fraud

7. You visited Moviepass.tv, a movie download service, and browsed the movie selections at the site. Three days later, oversized pop-up ads began to appear claiming you signed up for a three-day free trial but had not cancelled before the trial period had ended. The pop-ups demanded payment of $29.95; if it was not paid within 48 hours, the site would initiate legal proceedings against you. You have most likely become a victim of what type of malware?
a. worm
b. keylogger
c. rootkit
d. Trojan horse
e. scareware

8. After a Windows vulnerability was discovered, the point-of-sale payment card system of more than 100 companies was attacked by crooks. Microsoft released a patch to fix the vulnerability a few weeks later. This is which of the following types of computer fraud and abuse?
a. zero-day attack
b. cross-site scripting attack
c. SQL injection attack
d. man-in-the middle attack
e. password cracking attack

9. A few years ago, the Japanese government announced that computers in the country's parliament suffered a cyberattack originating in China. The Japanese computers were infected when a politician opened an e-mail attachment containing malicious computer instructions. The code spread to other computers in parliament. The Japanese government was most likely a victim of what type of malware?
a. scareware
b. Trojan horse virus
c. superzapping
d. torpedo software
e. trap door

10. You receive an email that says: "We are offering you a special $50 coupon for being such a good customer. This offer is limited to the first 100 people, so click here immediately to claim your reward." You click on the embedded link and are taken to a website that asks you to enter your bank account ID and password. This is an example of which computer fraud and abuse technique?
a. Lebanese looping
b. evil twin
c. phishing
d. URL hijacking
e. phreaking

CASE 9-1 Shadowcrew

At 9:00 P.M., Andrew Mantovani, cofounder of the group Shadowcrew, received a knock at his door while chatting on his computer. For Mantovani and 27 others, that knock marked the end of Shadowcrew, which provided online marketplaces and discussion forums for identity thieves. Shadowcrew members used the organization's website to traffic in stolen Social Security numbers, names, e-mail addresses, counterfeit driver's licenses, birth certificates, and foreign and domestic passports. It also shared best practices for carrying out fraudulent activity. By the time it was shut down, Shadowcrew had trafficked in at least 1.7 million credit cards and was responsible for more than $4.3 million in fraud losses.

Considered the online equivalent of the Russian Mafia, Shadowcrew operated as a highly sophisticated and hierarchical organization. All users operated under aliases, never revealing their true names or other personal information. Operations and communications were conducted using proxy servers that hid the location and identity of the users. Shadowcrew users were divided into five different roles: administrators, moderators, reviewers, vendors, and members.

Administrators Shadowcrew administrators were the heads of the organization.

Moderators A dozen moderators, chosen from the general membership based on proven skill in fraudulent activity, controlled the flow of information.

Reviewers Reviewers tested the quality of illicit goods (credit cards, passports, etc.) trafficked on the Shadowcrew site. For example, reviewers would run a test called a "dump check" on credit card numbers by hacking into a retailer's cash register system. The fraudster accessed the system through back doors used by technical support personnel to remotely perform maintenance or repairs. The reviewer would then enter a trivial charge of $1 or $2 to see whether the charge was approved. Reviewers would then write up and post detailed descriptions of the credit cards or other merchandise tested.

Vendors Vendors managed the sale of stolen data. Prices were posted and products were sold using an auction forum much like eBay. Payments were processed via Western Union money transfers or an electronic currency and were made using a fraud victim's stolen data.

Members Thousands of people used the Shadowcrew website to gather and share information on committing identity fraud. Shadowcrew practiced open registration, but more sensitive discussion areas were password protected, and members needed another trusted member to vouch for them in order to join the forum.

Members could be promoted up the organization by providing quality products or by sharing new or unique tips or techniques for committing fraud. Shadowcrew punished acts of disloyalty. For instance, one disloyal group member had his actual name, address, and phone number posted on the website for all to see.

Shadowcrew's demise began when MasterCard informed the United States government that a hundred websites promoted and supported identity fraud. The United States Secret Service covertly infiltrated Shadowcrew. Acting as trusted members, agents set up a Virtual Private Network (VPN) over which Shadowcrew leaders could conduct illicit business. The VPN allowed the Secret Service to track the organization's doings and discover the real identities and locations of Shadowcrew users.

It was vital that all arrests occur simultaneously because any one of the targets could instantly warn the others via Shadowcrew's discussion forum. With the help of the Justice Department, Homeland Security, the Royal Canadian Mounted Police, Europol, and local police departments, authorities simultaneously knocked on the suspects' doors at precisely 9:00 P.M. The operation led to 28 arrests, 21 in the United States. Rather than immediately deactivating the website, investigators replaced the home page with the following warning: "Activities by Shadowcrew members are being investigated by the United States Secret Service." Under a picture of hands clutching bars of a jail cell, agents listed the criminal charges that Shadowcrew members faced and called on visitors to turn themselves in: "Contact your local United States Secret Service field office before we contact you!"

(*Source:* J. McCormick and D. Gage, *Baseline Security,* March 7, 2005.)

1. How did Shadowcrew members conceal their identities? How can average citizens protect their identities while interacting online?
2. How has the Internet made detecting and identifying identity fraudsters difficult?
3. What are some of the most common electronic means of stealing personal information?
4. What is the most common way that fraudsters use personal data?
5. What measures can consumers take to protect against the online brokering of their personal data?
6. What are the most effective means of detecting identity theft?
7. What pieces of personal information are most valuable to identity fraudsters?

AIS in Action Solutions

QUIZ KEY

1. A set of instructions to increase a programmer's pay rate by 10% is hidden inside an authorized program. It changes and updates the payroll file. What is this computer fraud technique called?
   a. virus [Incorrect. A virus damages a system using a segment of executable code that attaches itself to software, replicates itself, and spreads to other systems or files.]
   b. worm [Incorrect. A worm is a program that hides in a host program and copies and actively transmits itself directly to other systems.]
   c. trap door [Incorrect. A trap door is entering a system using a back door that bypasses normal system controls.]
   ▶ d. Trojan horse [Correct. Placing unauthorized computer instructions, such as fraudulently increasing an employee's pay, in an authorized and properly functioning program is an example of a Trojan horse.]

2. Which computer fraud technique involves a set of instructions hidden inside a calendar utility that copies itself each time the utility is enabled until memory is filled and the system crashes?
   a. logic bomb [Incorrect. A logic bomb sabotages a system using a program that lies idle until some specified circumstance or a particular time triggers it.]
   b. trap door [Incorrect. A trap door is a means of bypassing normal system controls to enter a system.]
   ▶ c. virus [Correct. A virus damages a system using a segment of executable code that attaches itself to software, replicates itself, and spreads to other systems or files.]
   d. Trojan horse [Incorrect. Placing unauthorized computer instructions, such as fraudulently increasing an employee's pay, in an authorized and properly functioning program is an example of a Trojan horse.]

3. Interest calculations are truncated at two decimal places, and the excess decimals are put into an account the perpetrator controls. What is this fraud called?
   a. typosquatting [Incorrect. Typosquatting is the practice of setting up websites with names similar to real websites so that users who make typographical errors when typing website names are sent to a site filled with malware.]
   b. URL hijacking [Incorrect. URL hijacking is another name for typosquatting, which is explained above.]
   c. chipping [Incorrect. Chipping is planting a chip that records transaction data in a legitimate credit card reader.]
   ▶ d. round-down fraud [Correct.]

4. A perpetrator attacks phone systems to obtain free phone line access or uses telephone lines to transmit viruses and to access, steal, and destroy data. What is this computer fraud technique called?
   a. phishing [Incorrect. Phishing is the practice of sending e-mails requesting recipients to visit a web page and verify data or fill in missing data. The e-mails and websites look like legitimate companies, primarily financial institutions.]
   ▶ b. phreaking [Correct.]
   c. pharming [Incorrect. Pharming is redirecting traffic to a spoofed website to gain access to personal and confidential information.]
   d. vishing [Incorrect. Vishing is voice phishing, in which e-mail recipients are asked to call a phone number where they are asked to divulge confidential data.]

5. Fraud perpetrators threaten to harm a company if it does not pay a specified amount of money. What is this fraud technique called?
   a. cyber-terrorism [Incorrect. Cyber-terrorism, or Internet terrorism, is using the Internet to disrupt communications and e-commerce.]

b. blackmailing [Incorrect. Blackmailing is the extortion of money or something else of value from a person by the threat of exposing a criminal act or discreditable information.]
▶ c. cyber-extortion [Correct.]
d. scareware [Incorrect. Scareware is software of limited or no benefit, often malicious in nature, that is sold using scare tactics. The most common scare tactic is a dire warning that the person's computer is infected with viruses, spyware, or some other catastrophic problem.]

6. Techniques used to obtain confidential information, often by tricking people, are referred to as what?
a. pretexting [Incorrect. Pretexting is one specific type of social engineering. It involves acting under false pretenses to gain confidential information.]
b. posing [Incorrect. Posing is one specific type of social engineering in which someone creates a seemingly legitimate business, collects personal information while making a sale, and never delivers the item sold.]
▶ c. social engineering [Correct.]
d. identity theft [Incorrect. Identity theft is a type of social engineering in which one person assumes another's identity, usually for economic gain, by illegally obtaining confidential information, such as a Social Security number.]

7. What type of software secretly collects personal information about users and sends it to someone else without the user's permission?
a. rootkit [Incorrect. A rootkit is software that conceals processes, files, network connections, and system data from the operating system and other programs.]
b. torpedo software [Incorrect. Torpedo software is software that destroys competing malware, resulting in "malware warfare" between competing developers.]
▶ c. spyware [Correct.]
d. malware [Incorrect. *Malware* is a general term that applies to any software used to do harm. There is a more specific correct answer to this question.]

8. What type of software conceals processes, files, network connections, memory addresses, systems utility programs, and system data from the operating system and other programs?
▶ a. rootkit [Correct.]
b. spyware [Incorrect. Spyware is software that is used to monitor computing habits and send that data to someone else, often without the computer user's permission.]
c. malware [Incorrect. Malware is any software that is used to do harm.]
d. adware [Incorrect. Adware is software used to collect web-surfing and spending data and forward it to advertising or media organizations. It also causes banner ads to pop up on computer monitors as the Internet is surfed.]

9. Which type of computer attack takes place between the time a software vulnerability is discovered and the time software developers release a software patch that fixes the problem?
a. posing [Incorrect. Posing is creating a seemingly legitimate business, collecting personal information while making a sale, and never delivering the item sold.]
▶ b. zero-day attack [Correct.]
c. evil twin [Incorrect. An evil twin is a wireless network with the same name as a local wireless access point that unsuspecting people use, allowing hackers to monitor the network's traffic looking for useful information.]
d. software piracy [Incorrect. Software piracy is the illegal copying of computer software.]

10. Someone redirects a website's traffic to a bogus website, usually to gain access to personal and confidential information. What is this computer fraud technique called?

a. vishing [Incorrect. Vishing is voice phishing, in which e-mail recipients are asked to call a phone number where they are asked to divulge confidential data.]

b. phishing [Incorrect. Phishing is sending e-mails requesting recipients to visit a web page and verify data or fill in missing data. The e-mails and websites look like those of legitimate companies, primarily financial institutions.]

► c. pharming [Correct.]

d. phreaking [Incorrect. Phreaking is attacking phone systems and using telephone lines to transmit viruses and to access, steal, and destroy data.

CHAPTER

10

Control and Accounting Information Systems

LEARNING OBJECTIVES

After studying this chapter, you should be able to:

1. Explain basic control concepts and explain why computer control and security are important.
2. Compare and contrast the COBIT, COSO, and ERM control frameworks.
3. Describe the major elements in the control environment of a company.
4. Describe the control objectives companies need to set and how to identify threats that affect organizational uncertainty.
5. Explain how to assess and respond to risk using the Enterprise Risk Management (ERM) model.
6. Describe control activities commonly used in companies.
7. Describe how to communicate information and monitor control processes in organizations.

INTEGRATIVE CASE Springer's Lumber & Supply

Jason Scott, an internal auditor for Northwest Industries, is auditing Springer's Lumber & Supply, Northwest's building materials outlet in Bozeman, Montana. His supervisor, Maria Pilier, asked him to trace a sample of purchase transactions from purchase requisition to cash disbursement to verify that proper control procedures were followed. Jason is frustrated with this task, and for good reasons:

- The purchasing system is poorly documented.
- He keeps finding transactions that have not been processed as Ed Yates, the accounts payable manager, said they should be.
- Purchase requisitions are missing for several items personally authorized by Bill Springer, the purchasing vice president.
- Some vendor invoices have been paid without supporting documents, such as purchase orders and receiving reports.

Petr Vaclavek/Shutterstock

- Prices for some items seem unusually high, and there are a few discrepancies in item prices between the vendor invoice and the corresponding purchase order.

Yates had a logical answer for every question Jason raised and advised Jason that the real world is not as tidy as the world portrayed in college textbooks. Maria also has some concerns:

- Springer's is the largest supplier in the area and has a near monopoly.
- Management authority is held by the company president, Joe Springer, and his two sons, Bill (the purchasing vice president) and Ted (the controller). Several relatives and friends are on the payroll. Together, the Springers own 10% of the company.
- Lines of authority and responsibility within the company are loosely defined and confusing.
- Maria believes that Ted Springer may have engaged in "creative accounting" to make Springer's one of Northwest's best-performing retail outlets.

After talking to Maria, Jason ponders the following issues:

1. Because Ed Yates had a logical explanation for every unusual transaction, should Jason describe these transactions in his report?
2. Is a violation of control procedures acceptable if management has authorized it?
3. Maria's concerns about Springer's loosely defined lines of authority and possible use of "creative accounting" are matters of management policy. With respect to Jason's control procedures assignment, does he have a professional or an ethical responsibility to get involved?

Introduction

WHY THREATS TO ACCOUNTING INFORMATION SYSTEMS ARE INCREASING

In most years, more than 60% of organizations experience a major failure in controlling the security and integrity of their computer systems. Reasons for the failures include the following:

- Information is available to an unprecedented number of workers. Chevron, for example, has more than 35,000 PCs.
- Information on distributed computer networks is hard to control. At Chevron, information is distributed among many systems and thousands of employees worldwide. Each system and each employee represent a potential control vulnerability point.
- Customers and suppliers have access to each other's systems and data. For example, Walmart allows vendors to access their databases. Imagine the confidentiality problems as these vendors form alliances with Walmart competitors.

Organizations have not adequately protected data for several reasons:

- Some companies view the loss of crucial information as a distant, unlikely threat.
- The control implications of moving from centralized computer systems to Internet-based systems are not fully understood.
- Many companies do not realize that information is a strategic resource and that protecting it must be a strategic requirement. For example, one company lost millions of dollars because it did not protect data transmissions. A competitor tapped into its phone lines and obtained faxes of new product designs.
- Productivity and cost pressures motivate management to forgo time-consuming control measures.

threat - Any potential adverse occurrence or unwanted event that could injure the AIS or the organization.

exposure/impact - The potential dollar loss if a particular threat becomes a reality.

likelihood/risk - The probability that a threat will come to pass.

Any potential adverse occurrence is called a **threat**. The potential dollar loss from a threat is called the **exposure/impact**. The probability that it will happen is called the **likelihood/risk** of the threat.

Overview of Control Concepts

internal controls - The processes and procedures implemented to provide reasonable assurance that control objectives are met.

Internal controls are the processes implemented to provide reasonable assurance that the following control objectives are achieved:

- Safeguard assets—prevent or detect their unauthorized acquisition, use, or disposition.
- Maintain records in sufficient detail to report company assets accurately and fairly.
- Provide accurate and reliable information.
- Prepare financial reports in accordance with established criteria.
- Promote and improve operational efficiency.
- Encourage adherence to prescribed managerial policies.
- Comply with applicable laws and regulations.

Internal control is a process because it permeates an organization's operating activities and is an integral part of management activities. Internal control provides reasonable assurance—complete assurance is difficult to achieve and prohibitively expensive. In addition, internal control systems have inherent limitations, such as susceptibility to simple errors and mistakes, faulty judgments and decision making, management overrides, and collusion.

Developing an internal control system requires a thorough understanding of information technology (IT) capabilities and risks, as well as how to use IT to achieve an organization's control objectives. Accountants and systems developers help management achieve their control objectives by (1) designing effective control systems that take a proactive approach to eliminating system threats and that detect, correct, and recover from threats when they occur; and (2) making it easier to build controls into a system at the initial design stage than to add them after the fact.

Internal controls perform three important functions:

preventive controls - Controls that deter problems before they arise.

detective controls - Controls designed to discover control problems that were not prevented.

corrective controls - Controls that identify and correct problems as well as correct and recover from the resulting errors.

1. **Preventive controls** deter problems before they arise. Examples include hiring qualified personnel, segregating employee duties, and controlling physical access to assets and information.
2. **Detective controls** discover problems that are not prevented. Examples include duplicate checking of calculations and preparing bank reconciliations and monthly trial balances.
3. **Corrective controls** identify and correct problems as well as correct and recover from the resulting errors. Examples include maintaining backup copies of files, correcting data entry errors, and resubmitting transactions for subsequent processing.

general controls - Controls designed to make sure an organization's information system and control environment is stable and well managed.

application controls - Controls that prevent, detect, and correct transaction errors and fraud in application programs.

Internal controls are often segregated into two categories:

1. **General controls** make sure an organization's control environment is stable and well managed. Examples include security; IT infrastructure; and software acquisition, development, and maintenance controls.
2. **Application controls** prevent, detect, and correct transaction errors and fraud in application programs. They are concerned with the accuracy, completeness, validity, and authorization of the data captured, entered, processed, stored, transmitted to other systems, and reported.

Robert Simons, a Harvard business professor, has espoused four levers of control to help management reconcile the conflict between creativity and controls.

1. A **belief system** describes how a company creates value, helps employees understand management's vision, communicates company core values, and inspires employees to live by those values.
2. A **boundary system** helps employees act ethically by setting boundaries on employee behavior. Instead of telling employees exactly what to do, they are encouraged to creatively solve problems and meet customer needs while meeting minimum performance standards, shunning off-limit activities, and avoiding actions that might damage their reputation.
3. A **diagnostic control system** measures, monitors, and compares actual company progress to budgets and performance goals. Feedback helps management adjust and fine-tune inputs and processes so future outputs more closely match goals.
4. An **interactive control system** helps managers to focus subordinates' attention on key strategic issues and to be more involved in their decisions. Interactive system data are interpreted and discussed in face-to-face meetings of superiors, subordinates, and peers.

belief system - System that describes how a company creates value, helps employees understand management's vision, communicates company core values, and inspires employees to live by those values.

boundary system - System that helps employees act ethically by setting boundaries on employee behavior.

diagnostic control system - System that measures, monitors, and compares actual company progress to budgets and performance goals.

interactive control system - System that helps managers to focus subordinates' attention on key strategic issues and to be more involved in their decisions.

Regrettably, not all organizations have an effective internal control system. For instance, one report indicated that the FBI is plagued by IT infrastructure vulnerabilities and security problems, some of which were identified in an audit 16 years previously. Specific areas of concern were security standards, guidelines, and procedures; segregation of duties; access controls, including password management and usage; backup and recovery controls; and software development and change controls.

THE FOREIGN CORRUPT PRACTICES AND SARBANES–OXLEY ACTS

In 1977, the **Foreign Corrupt Practices Act (FCPA)** was passed to prevent companies from bribing foreign officials to obtain business. Congress incorporated language from an American Institute of Certified Public Accountants (AICPA) pronouncement into the FCPA that required corporations to maintain good systems of internal control. Unfortunately, these requirements were not sufficient to prevent further problems.

Foreign Corrupt Practices Act (FCPA) - Legislation passed to prevent companies from bribing foreign officials to obtain business; also requires all publicly owned corporations maintain a system of internal accounting controls.

Companies who violate the FCPA are subject to fines. Recently, a large multinational U.S. bank agreed to pay a $264 million fine for allegedly hiring the children of Chinese rulers, who were not qualified for the jobs they were given, to win business from the Chinese government. Another example is Odebrecht, a Brazilian conglomerate, who was required to pay a record $2.6 billion fine to Brazil, the United States, and Switzerland for paying kickbacks to government officials and Petrobras management in return for oil and gas contracts. The corruption was so bad that authorities set the fine amount as high as they thought it was possible for Odebrecht to pay without having to declare bankruptcy. In the aftermath of the Petrobras corruption scandal, Odebrecht's CEO was sentenced to 19 years in jail and Brazil's president was impeached.

In the late 1990s and early 2000s, news stories were reporting accounting frauds at Enron, WorldCom, Xerox, Tyco, Global Crossing, Adelphia, and other companies. When Enron, with $62 billion in assets, declared bankruptcy in December 2001, it was the largest bankruptcy in U.S. history. In June 2002, Arthur Andersen, once the largest CPA firm, collapsed. The Enron bankruptcy was dwarfed when WorldCom, with more than $100 billion in assets, filed for bankruptcy in July 2002. In response to these frauds, Congress passed the **Sarbanes–Oxley Act (SOX)** of 2002. SOX applies to publicly held companies and their auditors and was designed to prevent financial statement fraud, make financial reports more transparent, protect investors, strengthen internal controls, and punish executives who perpetrate fraud.

Sarbanes–Oxley Act (SOX) - Legislation intended to prevent financial statement fraud, make financial reports more transparent, provide protection to investors, strengthen internal controls at public companies, and punish executives who perpetrate fraud.

SOX is the most important business-oriented legislation in the last 80 years. It changed the way boards of directors and management operate and had a dramatic impact on CPAs who audit them. The following are some of the most important aspects of SOX:

- **Public Company Accounting Oversight Board (PCAOB).** SOX created the **Public Company Accounting Oversight Board (PCAOB)** to control the auditing profession. The PCAOB sets and enforces auditing, quality control, ethics, independence, and other auditing standards. It consists of five people who are appointed by the Securities and Exchange Commission (SEC).

Public Company Accounting Oversight Board (PCAOB) - A board created by SOX that regulates the auditing profession; created as part of SOX.

- **New rules for auditors.** Auditors must report specific information to the company's audit committee, such as critical accounting policies and practices. SOX prohibits auditors from performing certain nonaudit services, such as information systems design and implementation. Audit firms cannot provide services to companies if top management was employed by the auditing firm and worked on the company's audit in the preceding 12 months.
- **New roles for audit committees.** Audit committee members must be on the company's board of directors and be independent of the company. One member of the audit committee must be a financial expert. The audit committee hires, compensates, and oversees the auditors, who report directly to them.
- **New rules for management.** SOX requires the CEO and CFO to certify that (1) financial statements and disclosures are fairly presented, were reviewed by management, and are not misleading; and that (2) the auditors were told about all material internal control weaknesses and fraud. If management knowingly violates these rules, they can be prosecuted and fined. Companies must disclose, in plain English, material changes to their financial condition on a timely basis.
- **New internal control requirements.** Section 404 requires companies to issue a report accompanying the financial statements stating that management is responsible for establishing and maintaining an adequate internal control system. The report must contain management's assessment of the company's internal controls, attest to their accuracy, and report significant weaknesses or material noncompliance.

After SOX was passed, the SEC mandated that management must:

- Base its evaluation on a recognized control framework. The most likely frameworks, formulated by the Committee of Sponsoring Organizations (COSO), are discussed in this chapter.
- Disclose all material internal control weaknesses.
- Conclude that a company does not have effective financial reporting internal controls if there are material weaknesses.

Control Frameworks

This section discusses three frameworks used to develop internal control systems.

COBIT FRAMEWORK

Control Objectives for Information and Related Technology (COBIT) - A security and control framework that allows (1) management to benchmark the security and control practices of IT environments, (2) users of IT services to be assured that adequate security and control exist, and (3) auditors to substantiate their internal control opinions and advise on IT security and control matters.

The Information Systems Audit and Control Association (ISACA) developed the **Control Objectives for Information and Related Technology (COBIT)** framework. COBIT consolidates control standards from many different sources into a single framework that allows (1) management to benchmark security and control practices of IT environments, (2) users to be assured that adequate IT security and controls exist, and (3) auditors to substantiate their internal control opinions and to advise on IT security and control matters.

The COBIT 2019 framework describes best practices for the effective governance and management of IT. COBIT 2019 is based on the following five key principles of IT governance and management. These principles help organizations build an effective governance and management framework that protects stakeholders' investments and produces the best possible information system.

1. **Meeting stakeholder needs.** This helps users customize business processes and procedures to create an information system that adds value to its stakeholders. It also allows the company to create the proper balance between risk and reward.
2. **Covering the enterprise end-to-end.** This does not just focus on the IT operation, it integrates all IT functions and processes into companywide functions and processes.

3. **Applying a single, integrated framework.** This can be aligned at a high level with other standards and frameworks so that an overarching framework for IT governance and management is created.
4. **Enabling a holistic approach.** This provides a holistic approach that results in effective governance and management of all IT functions in the company.
5. **Separating governance from management.** This distinguishes between governance and management.

As shown in Figure 10-1, there are five governance and management objectives in COBIT 2019. The objective of governance is to create value by optimizing the use of organizational resources to produce desired benefits in a manner that effectively addresses risk. Governance is the responsibility of the board of directors who (1) evaluate stakeholder needs to identify objectives, (2) provide management with direction by prioritizing objectives, and (3) monitor management's performance.

Management is responsible for planning, building, running, and monitoring the activities and processes used by the organization to pursue the objectives established by the board of directors. Management also periodically provides the board of directors with feedback that can be used to monitor achievement of the organization's objectives and, if necessary, to re-evaluate and perhaps modify those objectives.

The governance and management of IT are ongoing processes. The board of directors and management monitor the organization's activities and use that feedback to modify existing plans and procedures or develop new strategies to respond to changes in business objectives and new developments in IT.

COBIT 2019 is a comprehensive framework that helps enterprises achieve their IT governance and management objectives. This comprehensiveness is one of the strengths of COBIT 2019 and underlies its growing international acceptance as a framework for managing and controlling information systems.

Figure 10-2 is the COBIT 2019 process reference model. The model identifies the five governance processes (referred to as evaluate, direct and monitor—or EDM) and 35 management processes. The 35 management processes are broken down into the following four domains:

1. Align, plan, and organize (APO).
2. Build, acquire, and implement (BAI).
3. Deliver, service, and support (DSS).
4. Monitor, evaluate, and assess (MEA).

It is not possible to cover all of COBIT 2019 in this text. Instead, in Chapters 11 through 13 we focus on the portions of COBIT 2019 most directly relevant to accountants, auditors, and accounting information systems. This includes the business processes and control activities that affect the accuracy of an organization's financial statements and its compliance with external regulations such as SOX, the Health Insurance Portability and Accountability Act (HIPAA), and the security standards mandated by the credit card industry.

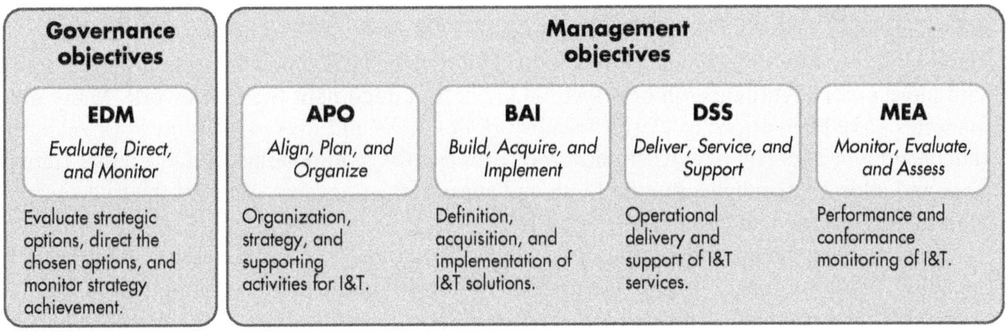

FIGURE 10-1
COBIT 2019 Governance and Management Objectives

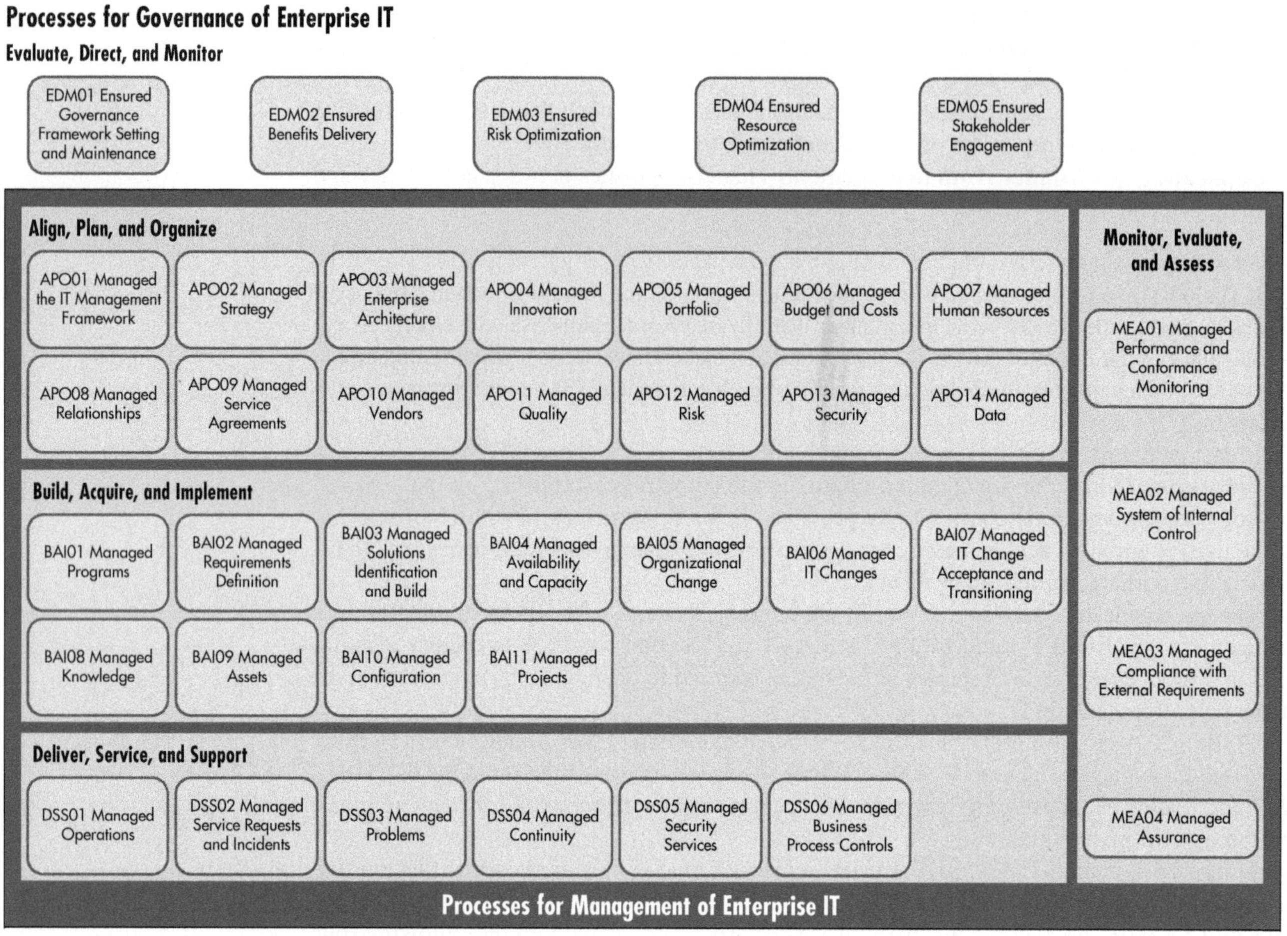

FIGURE 10-2

COBIT 2019 Process Reference Model

COSO'S INTERNAL CONTROL FRAMEWORK

Committee of Sponsoring Organizations (COSO) - A private-sector group consisting of the American Accounting Association, the AICPA, the Institute of Internal Auditors, the Institute of Management Accountants, and the Financial Executives Institute.

Internal Control—Integrated Framework (IC) - A COSO framework that defines internal controls and provides guidance for evaluating and enhancing internal control systems.

The **Committee of Sponsoring Organizations (COSO)** consists of the American Accounting Association, the AICPA, the Institute of Internal Auditors, the Institute of Management Accountants, and the Financial Executives Institute. In 1992, COSO issued **Internal Control—Integrated Framework (IC)**, which is widely accepted as the authority on internal controls and is incorporated into policies, rules, and regulations used to control business activities.

In 2013, the IC framework was updated to better deal with current business processes and technological advancements. For example, in 1992, very few businesses used the Internet, sent e-mail, or stored their data in the cloud. The revised IC framework also provides users with more precise guidance on how to implement and document the framework. Many new examples have been added to clarify framework concepts and make the framework easier to understand and use. The new IC framework keeps the five components of the original framework and adds 17 principles that build on and support the concepts. Each of the five components has at least two and up to five principles.

The five components and 17 principles of the IC framework are summarized in Table 10-1. Because COSO Internal Control—Integrated Framework is the most commonly used control framework, the text uses it to explain internal controls. Focus 10-1 explains other COSO control frameworks.

FOCUS 10-1 COSO's Enterprise Risk Management Frameworks

Enterprise Risk Management—Integrated Framework (ERM)

To improve the risk management process, in 2004 COSO developed a second control framework called Enterprise Risk Management—Integrated Framework (ERM). ERM is the process the board of directors and management use to set strategy, identify events that may affect the entity, assess and manage risk, and provide reasonable assurance that the company achieves its objectives and goals. The basic principles behind ERM are as follows:

- Companies are formed to create value for their owners.
- Management must decide how much uncertainty it will accept as it creates value.
- Uncertainty results in risk, which is the possibility that something negatively affects the company's ability to create or preserve value.
- Uncertainty results in opportunity, which is the possibility that something positively affects the company's ability to create or preserve value.
- The ERM framework can manage uncertainty as well as create and preserve value.

Enterprise Risk Management—Integrating with Strategy and Performance

After ERM was published, new risks emerged and the complexity of existing risk changed. To address this, the ERM framework was updated in 2017 and retitled Enterprise Risk Management—Integrating with Strategy and Performance. The new title recognizes and highlights how important it is to consider risk in setting company strategy and in helping companies improve their performance. The new framework contains 20 control principles that are divided into the following five interrelated components:

1. **Governance and Culture:** Governance sets the organization's tone, including oversight responsibilities for enterprise risk management. Culture relates to a company's ethical values, desired behaviors, and understanding of risk.
2. **Strategy and Objective Setting:** Strategic planning should include corporate strategy, objective setting, and enterprise risk management. A company's appetite for risk should be aligned with strategy. Business objectives should be created to put strategy into practice. Strategies and business objectives should consider the need to identify, assess, and respond to risk.
3. **Performance:** Entities should identify and assess the risks that affect its strategy and business objectives, prioritize them based on their risk appetite, and determine how to respond to each risk. The risk response process should include an assessment of the total amount of risk the entity assumes. Key risk stakeholders should be informed of the risk assessment and response process and its findings.
4. **Review and Revision:** The entity should review the performance of ERM components to determine how well they are functioning over time, and determine what revisions are needed.
5. **Information, Communication, and Reporting:** It is essential to continuously obtain and share information from internal and external sources with all necessary levels of the organization.

The control principles in the five components cover all aspects of enterprise risk that can accommodate different viewpoints and operating structures. Adhering to them provides stakeholders, management, and the board with a reasonable expectation that the entity understands and is managing strategy and business objective risks.

Improving Organizational Resiliency: New Guidance Addresses Environmental, Social, and Governance-related Risks (ESG)

In 2018, COSO released new ERM guidance: Improving Organizational Resiliency: New Guidance Addresses Environmental, Social, and Governance-Related Risks (ESG). ESG-related risks are increasing in number and severity world-wide, raising demand for ESG-related insight. The ESG guidance was designed to be easily integrated with COSO's Enterprise Risk Management—Integrating with Strategy and Performance guidance. The ESG documentation includes:

- Methods for overcoming ESG risks related to all five of ERM's components.
- Ways to manage ESG risks.
- Methods for managing ESG risks by developing and maintaining a continuous improvement culture.

The ERM Framework versus the Internal Control Framework

The IC framework has been widely adopted as the way to evaluate internal controls, as required by SOX. The more comprehensive ERM frameworks take a risk-based approach rather than a controls-based approach. ERM controls are flexible and relevant because they are linked to current organizational objectives. The ERM model also recognizes that risk, in addition to being controlled, can be accepted, avoided, diversified, shared, or transferred.

TABLE 10-1 Five Components and 17 Principles of COSO's Internal Control Model

Component	Description
Control environment	This is the foundation for all other components of internal control. The core of any business is its people—their individual attributes, including integrity, discipline, ethical values, and competence—and the environment in which they operate. They are the engine that drives the organization and the foundation on which everything rests. 1. Commitment to integrity and ethics 2. Internal control oversight by the board of directors, independent of management 3. Structures, reporting lines, and appropriate responsibilities in the pursuit of objectives established by management and overseen by the board 4. A commitment to attract, develop, and retain competent individuals in alignment with objectives 5. Holding individuals accountable for their internal control responsibilities in pursuit of objectives
Risk assessment	The organization must identify, analyze, and manage its risks. Managing risk is a dynamic process. Management must consider changes in the external environment and within the business that may be obstacles to its objectives. 6. Specifying objectives clearly enough for risks to be identified and assessed 7. Identifying and analyzing risks to determine how they should be managed 8. Considering the potential of fraud 9. Identifying and assessing changes that could significantly impact the system of internal control
Control activities	Control policies and procedures help ensure that the actions identified by management to address risks and achieve the organization's objectives are effectively carried out. Control activities are performed at all levels and at various stages within the business process and over technology. 10. Selecting and developing controls that might help mitigate risks to an acceptable level 11. Selecting and developing general control activities over technology 12. Deploying control activities as specified in policies and relevant procedures
Information and communication	Information and communication systems capture and exchange the information needed to conduct, manage, and control the organization's operations. Communication must occur internally and externally to provide information needed to carry out day-to-day internal control activities. All personnel must understand their responsibilities. 13. Obtaining or generating relevant, high-quality information to support internal control 14. Internally communicating information, including objectives and responsibilities, necessary to support the other components of internal control 15. Communicating relevant internal control matters to external parties
Monitoring	The entire process must be monitored, and modifications made as necessary so the system can change as conditions warrant. Evaluations ascertain whether each component of internal control is present and functioning. Deficiencies are communicated in a timely manner, with serious matters reported to senior management and the board. 16. Selecting, developing, and performing ongoing or separate evaluations of the components of internal control 17. Evaluating and communicating deficiencies to those responsible for corrective action, including senior management and the board of directors, where appropriate

The Control Environment

control environment - The company culture that is the foundation for all other internal control components, as it influences how organizations establish strategies and objectives; structure business activities; and identify, assess, and respond to risk.

The **control environment**, or company culture, influences how organizations establish strategies and objectives; structure business activities; and identify, assess, and respond to risk. It is the foundation for all other ERM components. A weak or deficient control environment often results in breakdowns in risk management and control. It is essentially the same thing as the control environment in the IC framework.

A control environment consists of the following:

1. Management's philosophy, operating style, and risk appetite.
2. Commitment to integrity, ethical values, and competence.
3. Internal control oversight by the board of directors.
4. Organizational structure.

5. Methods of assigning authority and responsibility.
6. Human resource standards that attract, develop, and retain competent individuals.
7. External influences.

Enron is an example of an ineffective control environment that resulted in financial failure. Although Enron appeared to have an effective ERM system, its control environment was defective. Management engaged in risky and dubious business practices, which the board of directors never questioned. Management misrepresented the company's financial condition, lost the confidence of shareholders, and finally filed for bankruptcy.

MANAGEMENT'S PHILOSOPHY, OPERATING STYLE, AND RISK APPETITE

Collectively, an organization has a philosophy, or shared beliefs and attitudes, about risk that affects policies, procedures, oral and written communications, and decisions. Companies also have a **risk appetite**, which is the amount of risk they are willing to accept to achieve their goals. To avoid undue risk, risk appetite must be in alignment with company strategy.

risk appetite - The amount of risk a company is willing to accept to achieve its goals and objectives. To avoid undue risk, risk appetite must be in alignment with company strategy.

The board of directors and top management must set the proper tone at the top; that is, they need to demonstrate through their actions that they support integrity and the necessity for a strong internal control system. The more responsible management's philosophy and operating style, and the more clearly they are communicated, the more likely employees will behave responsibly. If management has little concern for internal controls and risk management, then employees are less diligent in achieving control objectives. The culture at Springer's Lumber & Supply provides an example. Maria Pilier found that lines of authority and responsibility were loosely defined and suspected management might have used "creative accounting" to improve company performance. Jason Scott found evidence of poor internal control practices in the purchasing and accounts payable functions. These two conditions may be related; management's loose attitude may have contributed to the purchasing department's inattentiveness to good internal control practices.

Management's philosophy, operating style, and risk appetite can be assessed by answering questions such as these:

- Does management take undue business risks to achieve its objectives, or does it assess potential risks and rewards prior to acting?
- Does management manipulate performance measures, such as net income, so they are seen in a more favorable light?
- Does management pressure employees to achieve results regardless of the methods, or does it demand ethical behavior? In other words, do the ends justify the means?

COMMITMENT TO INTEGRITY, ETHICAL VALUES, AND COMPETENCE

Organizations need a culture that stresses integrity and commitment to ethical values and competence. Ethics pays—ethical standards are good business. Integrity starts at the top, as company employees adopt top management attitudes about risks and controls. A powerful message is sent when the CEO, confronted with a difficult decision, makes the ethically correct choice.

Companies endorse integrity by:

- Developing a written code of conduct that explicitly describes honest and dishonest behaviors. For example, most purchasing agents agree that accepting $5,000 from a supplier is dishonest, but a weekend vacation is not as clear-cut. A major cause of dishonesty comes from rationalizing unclear situations and allowing the criterion of expediency to replace the criterion of right versus wrong. Companies should document that employees have read and understand the code of conduct.
- Put processes in place to use the company's code of conduct to evaluate individual and team performance and to address any deviations in a timely and consistent manner.
- Actively teaching and requiring the code of conduct—for example, making it clear that honest reports are more important than favorable ones.
- Avoiding unrealistic expectations or incentives that motivate dishonest or illegal acts, such as overly aggressive sales practices, unfair or unethical negotiation tactics, and bonuses excessively based on reported financial results.

- Consistently rewarding honesty and giving verbal labels to honest and dishonest behavior. If companies punish or reward honesty without labeling it as such, or if the standard of honesty is inconsistent, then employees will display inconsistent moral behavior.
- Requiring employees to report dishonest or illegal acts and disciplining employees who knowingly fail to report them. All dishonest acts should be investigated, and dishonest employees should be dismissed and prosecuted to show that such behavior is not allowed.
- Making a commitment to competence. Companies should hire competent employees with the necessary knowledge, experience, training, and skills.

INTERNAL CONTROL OVERSIGHT BY THE BOARD OF DIRECTORS

An involved board of directors represents shareholders and provides an independent review of management that acts as a check and balance on its actions. It is important that the board approve company strategy and review security policies. The board should also evaluate management and management decision making. To do so, the board needs members with the skills and expertise necessary to ask senior management probing questions. They also need enough members who are independent of management so the board can objectively evaluate them. If needed, the board should supplement their expertise by hiring outside consultants. For example, they may need help evaluating the security, processing integrity, availability, confidentiality, and privacy of the company's information systems. The board must also be willing and able to take any needed actions to protect the company's shareholders.

audit committee - The outside, independent board of director members responsible for financial reporting, regulatory compliance, internal control, and hiring and overseeing internal and external auditors.

SOX requires public companies to have an **audit committee** of outside, independent directors. The audit committee is responsible for financial reporting, regulatory compliance, internal control, and hiring and overseeing internal and external auditors, who report all critical accounting policies and practices to them.

ORGANIZATIONAL STRUCTURE

A company's organizational structure provides a framework for planning, executing, controlling, and monitoring operations. Important aspects of the organizational structure include the following:

- Centralization or decentralization of authority.
- A direct or matrix reporting relationship.
- Organization by industry, product line, location, or marketing network.
- How allocation of responsibility affects information requirements.
- Organization of and lines of authority for accounting, auditing, and information system functions.
- Size and nature of company activities.

A complex or unclear organizational structure may indicate serious problems. For example, ESM, a brokerage company, used a multilayered organizational structure to hide a $300 million fraud. Management hid stolen cash in their financial statements using a fictitious receivable from a related company.

In today's business world, hierarchical structures, with layers of management who supervise others, are being replaced with flat organizations of self-directed work teams that make decisions without needing multiple layers of approval. The emphasis is on continuous improvement rather than periodic reviews and appraisals. These organizational structure changes impact the nature and type of controls used.

METHODS OF ASSIGNING AUTHORITY AND RESPONSIBILITY

Management should make sure employees understand entity goals and objectives, assign authority and responsibility for goals and objectives to departments and individuals, hold the individuals accountable for achieving them, and encourage the use of initiative to solve problems. It is especially important to identify who is responsible for the company's information security policy.

policy and procedures manual - A document that explains proper business practices, describes needed knowledge and experience, explains document procedures, explains how to handle transactions, and lists the resources provided to carry out specific duties.

Authority and responsibility are assigned and communicated using formal job descriptions, employee training, operating schedules, budgets, a code of conduct, and written policies and procedures. The **policy and procedures manual** explains proper business practices, describes needed knowledge and experience, explains document procedures, explains how to handle transactions, and lists the resources provided to carry out specific duties. The manual includes the chart of accounts and copies of forms and documents. It is a helpful on-the-job reference for current employees and a useful tool for training new employees.

HUMAN RESOURCES STANDARDS THAT ATTRACT, DEVELOP, AND RETAIN COMPETENT INDIVIDUALS

One of the greatest control strengths is the honesty of employees; one of the greatest control weaknesses is the dishonesty of employees. Human resource (HR) policies and practices governing working conditions, job incentives, and career advancement can be a powerful force in encouraging honesty, efficiency, and loyal service. HR policies should convey the required level of expertise, competence, ethical behavior, and integrity required. The following HR policies and procedures are important.

PLAN AND PREPARE FOR SUCCESSION The Board of Directors and management must make plans and prepare for management succession. Top management may need to be replaced at any time for any number of reasons, and an entity should develop a deep management bench—the deeper, the better. While this is most important at the company's highest levels, the company should also plan and prepare for successions in all levels of management as that leads to the desired deep bench of qualified candidates for important management positions.

HIRING Employees should be hired based on educational background, experience, achievements, honesty and integrity, and meeting written job requirements. All company personnel, including cleaning crews and temporary employees, should be subject to hiring policies. Some fraudsters pose as janitors or temporary employees to gain physical access to company computers.

Applicant qualifications can be evaluated using resumes, reference letters, interviews, and background checks. A thorough **background check** includes talking to references, checking for a criminal record, examining credit records, and verifying education and work experience. Many applicants include false information in their applications or resumes. Philip Crosby Associates (PCA) hired John Nelson, MBA, CPA, without conducting a background check. In reality, his CPA designation and glowing references were phony. Nelson was actually Robert W. Liszewski, who had served 18 months in jail for embezzling $400,000. By the time PCA discovered this, Liszewski had embezzled $960,000 using wire transfers to a dummy corporation, supported by forged signatures on contracts and authorization documents.

background check - An investigation of a prospective or current employee that involves verifying their educational and work experience, talking to references, checking for a criminal record or credit problems, and examining other publicly available information.

Many firms hire background check specialists because some applicants buy phony degrees from website operators who "validate" the bogus education when employers call. Some applicants even pay hackers to break into university databases and enter fake graduation or grade data.

COMPENSATING, EVALUATING, AND PROMOTING Poorly compensated employees are more likely to feel resentment and financial pressures that can motivate fraud. Fair pay and appropriate bonus incentives help motivate and reinforce outstanding employee performance. Employees should be given periodic performance appraisals to help them understand their strengths and weaknesses. Promotions should be based on performance and qualifications.

TRAINING Training programs should teach new employees their responsibilities; expected levels of performance and behavior; and the company's policies and procedures, culture, and operating style. Employees can be trained by conducting informal discussions and formal meetings, issuing periodic memos, distributing written guidelines and codes of professional ethics, circulating reports of unethical behavior and its consequences, and promoting security and fraud training programs. Ongoing training helps employees tackle new challenges, stay ahead of the competition, adapt to changing technologies, and deal effectively with the evolving environment.

Fraud is less likely to occur when employees believe security is everyone's business, are proud of their company and protective of its assets, and recognize the need to report fraud. Such a culture has to be created, taught, and practiced. Acceptable and unacceptable behavior should be defined. Many computer professionals see nothing wrong with using corporate computer resources to gain unauthorized access to databases and browse them. The consequences of unethical behavior (reprimands, dismissal, and prosecution) should also be taught and reinforced.

MANAGING DISGRUNTLED EMPLOYEES Some disgruntled employees, seeking revenge for a perceived wrong, perpetrate fraud or sabotage systems. Companies need procedures to identify disgruntled employees and either help them resolve their feelings or remove them from sensitive jobs. For example, a company may choose to establish grievance channels and provide employee counseling. Helping employees resolve their problems is not easy to do, however, because most employees fear that airing their feelings could have negative consequences.

DISCHARGING Dismissed employees should be removed from sensitive jobs immediately and denied access to the information system. One terminated employee lit a butane lighter under a smoke detector located just outside the computer room. It set off a sprinkler system that ruined most of the computer hardware.

VACATIONS AND ROTATION OF DUTIES Fraud schemes that require ongoing perpetrator attention are uncovered when the perpetrator takes time off. Periodically rotating employee duties and making employees take vacations can achieve the same results. For example, the FBI raided a gambling establishment and discovered that Roswell Steffen, who earned $11,000 a year, was betting $30,000 a day at the racetrack. The bank where he worked discovered that he embezzled and gambled away $1.5 million over a three-year period. A compulsive gambler, Steffen borrowed $5,000 to bet on a "sure thing" that did not pan out. He embezzled ever-increasing amounts in an effort to win back the money he had "borrowed." Steffen's scheme was simple: He transferred money from inactive accounts to his own account. If anyone complained, Steffen, the chief teller with the power to resolve these types of problems, replaced the money by taking it from another inactive account. When asked, after his arrest, how the fraud could have been prevented, Steffen said the bank could have coupled a two-week vacation with several weeks of rotation to another job function. Had the bank taken these measures, Steffen's embezzlement, which required his physical presence at the bank, would have been almost impossible to cover up.

CONFIDENTIALITY AGREEMENTS AND FIDELITY BOND INSURANCE All employees, suppliers, and contractors should sign and abide by a confidentiality agreement. Fidelity bond insurance coverage of key employees protects companies against losses arising from deliberate acts of fraud.

PROSECUTE AND INCARCERATE PERPETRATORS Most fraud is not reported or prosecuted for several reasons:

1. Companies are reluctant to report fraud because it can be a public relations disaster. The disclosure can reveal system vulnerabilities and attract more fraud or hacker attacks.
2. Law enforcement and the courts are busy with violent crimes and have less time and interest for computer crimes in which no physical harm occurs.
3. Fraud is difficult, costly, and time-consuming to investigate and prosecute.
4. Many law enforcement officials, lawyers, and judges lack the computer skills needed to investigate and prosecute computer crimes.
5. Fraud sentences are often light. A famous example involved C. Arnold Smith, former owner of the San Diego Padres, who was named Mr. San Diego of the Century. Smith was involved in the community and made large political contributions. When investigators discovered he had stolen $200 million from his bank, he pleaded no contest. His sentence was four years of probation. He was fined $30,000, to be paid at the rate of $100 a month for 25 years with no interest. Mr. Smith was 71 at the time. The embezzled money was never recovered.

EXTERNAL INFLUENCES

External influences include requirements imposed by stock exchanges, the Financial Accounting Standards Board (FASB), the PCAOB, and the SEC. They also include requirements imposed by regulatory agencies, such as those for banks, utilities, and insurance companies.

Risk Assessment and Risk Response

Management is responsible for identifying and assessing the threats the company faces. As discussed in Chapter 8, this should include an assessment of all threats, including natural and political disasters, software errors and equipment failures, unintentional acts, and the possibility of intentional acts such as fraud. Considering the risk of fraud is especially important, as it is one of the 17 principles included in the IC framework. Management must identify and analyze risks to determine how they should be managed. They must also identify and assess changes that could significantly impact the system of internal control.

The risks of an identified threat are assessed in several different ways: likelihood, positive and negative impacts, individually and by category, their effect on other organizational units, and on an inherent and a residual basis. **Inherent risk** is the susceptibility of a set of accounts or transactions to significant control problems in the absence of internal control. **Residual risk** is the risk that remains after management implements internal controls or some other response to risk. Companies should assess inherent risk, develop a response, and then assess residual risk.

inherent risk - The susceptibility of a set of accounts or transactions to significant control problems in the absence of internal control.

residual risk - The risk that remains after management implements internal controls or some other response to risk.

To align identified risks with the company's tolerance for risk, management must take an entity-wide view of risk. They must assess a risk's likelihood and impact, as well as the costs and benefits of the alternative responses. Management can respond to risk in one of four ways:

- **Reduce.** Reduce the likelihood and impact of risk by implementing an effective system of internal controls.
- **Accept.** Accept the likelihood and impact of the risk.
- **Share.** Share risk or transfer it to someone else by buying insurance, outsourcing an activity, or entering into hedging transactions.
- **Avoid.** Avoid risk by not engaging in the activity that produces the risk. This may require the company to sell a division, exit a product line, or not expand as anticipated.

Accountants and systems designers help management design effective control systems to reduce inherent risk. They also evaluate internal control systems to ensure that they are operating effectively. They assess and reduce risk using the risk assessment and response strategy shown in Figure 10-3. The first step, threat identification, has already been discussed.

ESTIMATE LIKELIHOOD AND IMPACT

Some threats pose a greater risk because they are more likely to occur. Employees are more likely to make a mistake than to commit fraud, and a company is more likely to be the victim of a fraud than an earthquake. The likelihood of an earthquake may be small, but its impact could destroy a company. The impact of fraud is usually not as great because most instances of fraud do not threaten a company's existence. Likelihood and impact must be considered together. As either increases, both the materiality of the threat and the need to protect against it rise.

Software tools help automate risk assessment and response. Blue Cross Blue Shield of Florida uses ERM software that lets managers enter perceived risks; assess their nature, likelihood, and impact; and assign them a numerical rating. An overall corporate assessment of risk is developed by aggregating all the rankings.

IDENTIFY CONTROLS

Management should identify controls that protect the company from each threat. Preventive controls are usually superior to detective controls. When preventive controls fail, detective controls are essential for discovering the problem. Corrective controls help recover from any problems. A good internal control system should employ all three.

ESTIMATE COSTS AND BENEFITS

The objective in designing an internal control system is to provide reasonable assurance that threats do not take place. No internal control system provides foolproof protection against all threats because having too many controls is cost-prohibitive and negatively affects operational efficiency. Conversely, having too few controls will not provide the needed reasonable assurance.

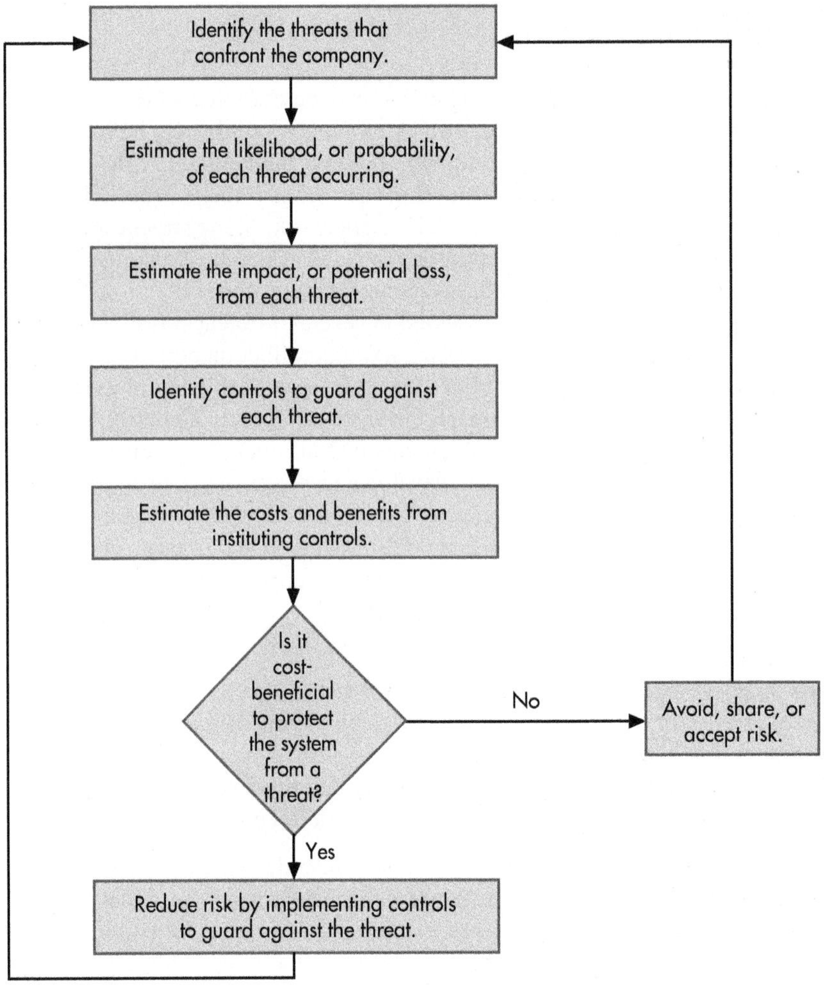

FIGURE 10-3
Risk Assessment Approach to Designing Internal Controls

The benefits of an internal control procedure must exceed its costs. Benefits, which can be hard to quantify accurately, include increased sales and productivity, reduced losses, better integration with customers and suppliers, increased customer loyalty, competitive advantages, and lower insurance premiums. Costs are usually easier to measure than benefits. A primary cost element is personnel, including the time to perform control procedures, the costs of hiring additional employees to achieve effective segregation of duties, and the costs of programming controls into a computer system.

expected loss - The mathematical product of the potential dollar loss that would occur should a threat become a reality (called *impact* or *exposure*) and the risk or probability that the threat will occur (called *likelihood*).

One way to estimate the value of internal controls involves **expected loss**, the mathematical product of impact and likelihood:

$$\text{Expected loss} = \text{Impact} \times \text{Likelihood}$$

The value of a control procedure is the difference between the expected loss with the control procedure(s) and the expected loss without it.

DETERMINE COST/BENEFIT EFFECTIVENESS

Management should determine whether a control is cost beneficial. For example, at Atlantic Richfield data errors occasionally required an entire payroll to be reprocessed, at a cost of \$10,000. A data validation step would reduce the threat likelihood from 15% to 1%, at a cost of \$600 per pay period. The cost/benefit analysis that determined that the validation step should be employed is shown in Table 10-2.

In evaluating internal controls, management must consider factors other than those in the expected cost/benefit calculation. For example, if something threatens an organization's existence, its extra cost can be viewed as a catastrophic loss insurance premium.

TABLE 10-2 Cost/Benefit Analysis of Payroll Validation Procedure

	Without Validation Procedure	With Validation Procedure	Net Expected Difference
Cost to reprocess entire payroll	$10,000	$10,000	
Likelihood of payroll data errors	15%	1%	
Expected reprocessing cost ($10,000 × likelihood)	$1,500	$100	$1,400
Cost of validation procedure	$0	$600	$(600)
Net expected benefit of validation procedure			$800

IMPLEMENT CONTROL OR ACCEPT, SHARE, OR AVOID THE RISK

Cost-effective controls should be implemented to reduce risk. Risks not reduced must be accepted, shared, or avoided. Risk can be accepted if it is within the company's risk tolerance range. An example is a risk with a small likelihood and a small impact. A response to reduce or share risk helps bring residual risk into an acceptable risk tolerance range. A company may choose to avoid the risk when there is no cost-effective way to bring risk into an acceptable risk tolerance range.

Control Activities

Control activities are policies, procedures, and rules that provide reasonable assurance that control objectives are met and risk responses are carried out. It is management's responsibility to develop a secure and adequately controlled system. Management must make sure that:

control activities - Policies, procedures, and rules that provide reasonable assurance that control objectives are met and risk responses are carried out.

1. Controls are selected and developed to help reduce risks to an acceptable level.
2. Appropriate general controls are selected and developed over technology.
3. Control activities are implemented and followed as specified in company policies and procedures.

The information security officer and the operations staff are responsible for ensuring that control procedures are followed.

Controls are much more effective when placed in the system as it is built, rather than as an afterthought. As a result, managers need to involve systems analysts, designers, and end users when designing computer-based control systems. It is important that control activities are in place during the end-of-the-year holiday season because a disproportionate amount of computer fraud and security break-ins takes place during this time. Some reasons for this are (1) extended employee vacations mean that there are fewer people to "mind the store"; (2) students are out of school and have more time on their hands; and (3) lonely counterculture hackers increase their attacks.

Control procedures fall into the following categories:

1. Proper authorization of transactions and activities.
2. Segregation of duties.
3. Project development and acquisition controls.
4. Change management controls.
5. Design and use of documents and records.
6. Safeguarding assets, records, and data.
7. Independent checks on performance.

Focus 10-2 discusses how a violation of specific control activities, combined with control environment factors, resulted in a fraud.

PROPER AUTHORIZATION OF TRANSACTIONS AND ACTIVITIES

authorization - Establishing policies for employees to follow and then empowering them to perform certain organizational functions. Authorizations are often documented by signing, initializing, or entering an authorization code on a document or record.

Because management lacks the time and resources to supervise each company activity and decision, it establishes policies for employees to follow and then empowers them. This empowerment, called **authorization**, is an important control procedure. Authorizations are

FOCUS 10-2 Control Problems in a School District

The audit report for a school district disclosed serious internal control deficiencies. To improve controls, the district (1) selected a new software package, (2) standardized accounting procedures, (3) instituted purchase order procedures, (4) implemented a separation of duties, and (5) created a control system for vending machine cash and inventory.

After the changes, the director noted that middle school fee balances were low and asked the auditors to investigate. The secretary, responsible for depositing student fees daily and sending them to the central office, said the low amount was due to the principal's waiver of fees for students who qualified for free or reduced-cost lunches. The principal denied having waived the fees.

The auditor examined fee cards for each child and found that the daily deposits did not agree with the dates on student fee cards. They also discovered that the secretary was in charge of a faculty welfare fund that was never audited or examined, nor was it subject to the newly implemented internal controls. Deposits to the fund were checks from the faculty and cash from the vending machines. To perpetrate her $20,000 fraud, the secretary had stolen all the cash from the vending machines, replaced the payee name on vendor checks with her name, and deposited student fees into the faculty welfare fund to cover up the stolen money.

The secretary was immediately discharged. Because the secretary was bonded, the district was able to recover all of its missing funds.

The school district strengthened controls. Internal auditors examine all funds at the schools. Control of faculty welfare funds was transferred to a faculty member. Because the investigation revealed the secretary's prior criminal record, a background check was required for all future hires.

often documented by signing, initializing, or entering an authorization code on a document or record. Computer systems can record a **digital signature**, a means of electronically signing a document with data that cannot be forged. Digital signatures are discussed in Chapter 12.

digital signature - A means of electronically signing a document with data that cannot be forged.

Certain activities or transactions may be of such consequence that management grants **specific authorization** for them to occur. For example, management review and approval may be required for sales in excess of $50,000. In contrast, management can authorize employees to handle routine transactions without special approval, a procedure known as **general authorization**. Management should have written policies on both specific and general authorization for all types of transactions.

specific authorization - Special approval an employee needs in order to be allowed to handle a transaction.

general authorization - The authorization given employees to handle routine transactions without special approval.

Employees who process transactions should verify the presence of appropriate authorizations. Auditors review transactions to verify proper authorization, as their absence indicates a possible control problem. For example, Jason Scott discovered that some purchases did not have a purchase requisition. Instead, they had been "personally authorized" by Bill Springer, the purchasing vice president. Jason also found that some payments had been authorized without proper supporting documents, such as purchase orders and receiving reports. These findings raise questions about the adequacy of Springer's internal control procedures.

SEGREGATION OF DUTIES

Good internal control requires that no single employee be given too much responsibility over business transactions or processes. An employee should not be in a position to commit *and* conceal fraud. Segregation of duties is discussed in two separate sections: segregation of accounting duties and segregation of systems duties.

segregation of accounting duties - Separating the accounting functions of authorization, custody, and recording to minimize an employee's ability to commit fraud.

SEGREGATION OF ACCOUNTING DUTIES As shown in Figure 10-4, effective **segregation of accounting duties** is achieved when the following functions are separated:

- ***Authorization***—approving transactions and decisions.
- ***Recording***—preparing source documents; entering data into computer systems; and maintaining journals, ledgers, files, or databases.
- ***Custody***—handling cash, tools, inventory, or fixed assets; receiving incoming customer checks; writing checks.

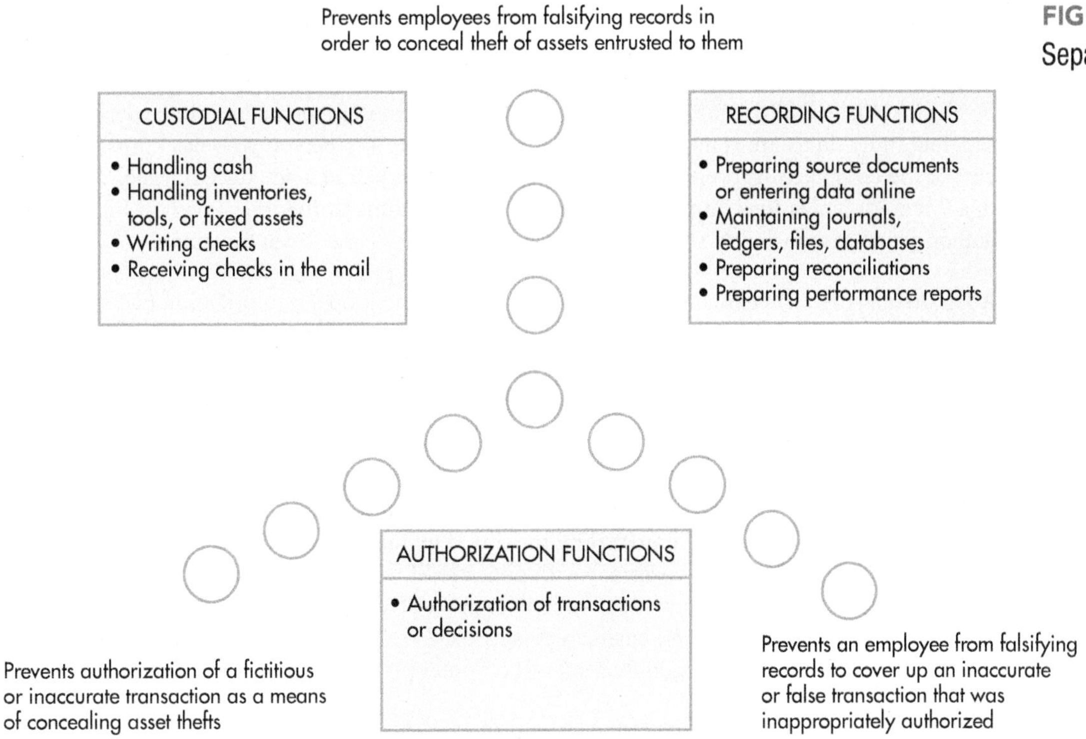
Prevents employees from falsifying records in order to conceal theft of assets entrusted to them
CUSTODIAL FUNCTIONS
• Handling cash
• Handling inventories, tools, or fixed assets
• Writing checks
• Receiving checks in the mail
RECORDING FUNCTIONS
• Preparing source documents or entering data online
• Maintaining journals, ledgers, files, databases
• Preparing reconciliations
• Preparing performance reports
AUTHORIZATION FUNCTIONS
• Authorization of transactions or decisions
Prevents authorization of a fictitious or inaccurate transaction as a means of concealing asset thefts
Prevents an employee from falsifying records to cover up an inaccurate or false transaction that was inappropriately authorized

FIGURE 10-4
Separation of Duties

If one person performs two of these functions, problems can arise. For example, the city treasurer of Fairfax, Virginia, embezzled $600,000. When residents used cash to pay their taxes, she kept the currency and entered the payments on property tax records, but did not report them to the controller. Periodically, she made an adjusting journal entry to bring her records into agreement with those of the controller. When she received checks in the mail that would not be missed if not recorded, she put them in the cash register and stole that amount of cash. Because the treasurer was responsible for both the *custody* of cash receipts and the *recording* of those receipts, she was able to steal cash receipts and falsify the accounts to conceal the theft.

The utilities director of Newport Beach, California, embezzled $1.2 million. Responsible for authorizing transactions, he forged invoices for easement documents authorizing payments to real or fictitious property owners. Finance department officials gave him the checks to deliver to the property owners. He forged signatures and deposited the checks in his own account. Because he was given *custody* of the checks, he could *authorize* fictitious transactions and steal the payments.

The payroll director of the Los Angeles Dodgers embezzled $330,000. He credited employees for hours not worked and received a kickback of 50% of the extra compensation. He added fictitious names to the Dodgers payroll and cashed the paychecks. The fraud was discovered while he was ill and another employee performed his duties. Because the perpetrator was responsible for *authorizing* the hiring of employees and for *recording* employee hours, he did not need to prepare or handle the paychecks. The company mailed the checks to the address he specified.

In a system with effective separation of duties, it is difficult for any single employee to embezzle successfully. Detecting fraud where two or more people are in **collusion** to override controls is more difficult because it is much easier to commit and conceal the fraud. For example, two women at a credit card company colluded. One woman authorized new credit card accounts, and the other wrote off unpaid accounts of less than $1,000. The first woman created a new account for each of them using fictitious data. When the amounts outstanding neared the $1,000 limit, the woman in collections wrote them off. The process would then be repeated. They were caught when a jilted boyfriend seeking revenge reported the scheme to the credit card company.

collusion - Cooperation between two or more people in an effort to thwart internal controls.

Employees can collude with other employees, customers, or vendors. The most frequent employee/vendor collusion includes billing at inflated prices, performing substandard work and receiving full payment, payment for nonperformance, duplicate billings, and improperly purchasing more goods from a colluding company. The most frequent employee/customer collusion includes unauthorized loans or insurance payments, receipt of assets or services at unauthorized discount prices, forgiveness of amounts owed, and unauthorized extension of due dates.

SEGREGATION OF SYSTEMS DUTIES In an information system, procedures once performed by separate individuals are sometimes combined. Therefore, any person who has unrestricted access to the computer, its programs, and live data could perpetrate and conceal fraud. To combat this threat, organizations implement **segregation of systems duties**. As shown in Figure 10-5, authority and responsibility should be divided clearly among the seven functions.

segregation of systems duties - Implementing control procedures to clearly divide authority and responsibility within the information system function.

AUTHORIZATION. As explained earlier in the chapter, the proper authorization of transactions and activities is an important control activity. For example, management should:

- Give general authorization to process transactions, such as paying vendors when the goods ordered are received. However, a payment over a certain sum could require specific authorization.
- Approve new business relationships such as a new customer or vendor. If an unapproved vendor was added to the company's database, an employee might be able to make a payment to them as a way of embezzling money. If an unapproved customer was added, sales could be made to a customer with poor credit who is unable to pay.
- Approve all new user account activations to prevent an unauthorized person from having access to company data and business processes.
- Approve the creation or modification of computer programs to prevent unauthorized programs and code.
- Approve the final versions of all new programs and program modifications to ensure they are efficient and do not contain code that harms the organization or that otherwise facilitates unapproved actions.

DATA ENTRY. The data entry function is responsible for entering or capturing the data for all business transactions. They are also responsible for the creation of all new user accounts and all new business relationships after their creation has been authorized. Likewise, when authorized to do so, they are responsible for the deletion of no longer needed user accounts and business relationships.

systems analysts - People who help users determine their information needs and design systems to meet those needs.

programmers - People who use the analysts' design to create and test computer programs.

PROGRAMMING. **Systems analysts** help users determine their information needs and design systems to meet those needs. Computer **programmers**, using the system analyst's design, are responsible for developing, coding, and testing all new software applications. They are also responsible for the modification of all existing applications. As explained, they need approval to start the program development or modification activities, and their final products should also be approved.

FIGURE 10-5
Segregation of System Duties

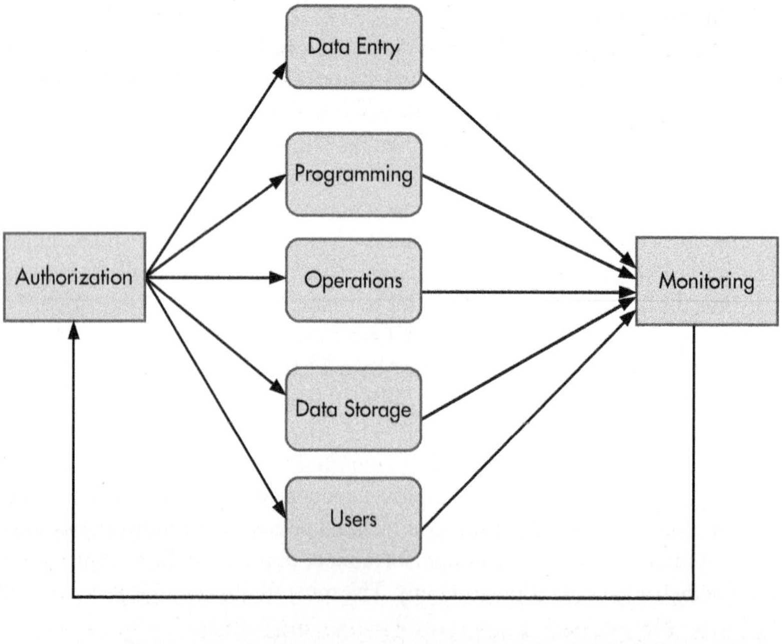

OPERATIONS. **Computer operators** run the software on the company's computers and ensure that data are properly entered, processed correctly, properly stored, and that the needed output is produced. As explained in Chapter 2, transactions can be processed in batch mode (such as periodic payroll) or real time mode (such as airline reservations). Operations may also be responsible for processing approved updates to master accounts such as address changes for customers and vendors).

computer operators - People who operate the company's computers.

DATA STORAGE. The data storage function is responsible for physically storing and maintaining custody of corporate databases, files, and computer programs. They are also responsible for maintaining backup copies of essential company data offsite in a secure location. They maintain physical custody of the IT hardware elements needed for computer operations and processing. Along with users, they are also responsible for safekeeping computer outputs.

USERS. **Users** record transactions, authorize data to be processed, have logical access to company data, and produce system output. They are responsible for safekeeping any data they may access or distribute as system output.

users - People who record transactions, authorize data processing, and use system output.

MANAGEMENT. Top management is responsible for all aspects of a company, including its information system. Since top management have many responsibilities and may not be information system experts, they can employ several different people to help them manage and monitor the AIS. The larger the organization, the more likely top management is to use these people. Some examples of the personnel management teams can use include:

- **Systems administrators** make sure all information system components operate smoothly and efficiently.
- **Network managers** ensure that devices are linked to the organization's internal and external networks and that those networks operate properly.
- **Security management** make sure that systems are secure and protected from internal and external threats.
- **Change management** makes sure changes are made smoothly and efficiently and do not negatively affect systems reliability, security, confidentiality, integrity, and availability.
- **Data control** ensures that source data have been properly approved, monitors the flow of work through the computer, reconciles input and output, maintains a record of input errors to ensure their correction and resubmission, and distributes systems output.
- Database administrators, as described in Chapter 4, are responsible for coordinating, controlling, and managing the database.

systems administrators - People responsible for making sure a system operates smoothly and efficiently.

network managers - People who ensure that the organization's networks operate properly.

security management - People who make sure systems are secure and protected from internal and external threats.

change management - Process of making sure changes are made smoothly and efficiently and do not negatively affect the system.

data control - People who ensure that source data is approved, monitor the flow of work, reconcile input and output, handle input errors, and distribute systems output.

The monitoring function shown in Figure 10-5 is discussed later in the chapter. Allowing a person to perform two or more of the seven functions shown in Figure 10-5 exposes the company to fraud. For example, if a credit union programmer uses actual data to test her program, she could erase her car loan balance during the test. Likewise, if a computer operator has access to programming logic and documentation, he might be able to increase his salary while processing payroll. The key to preventing fraud is to restrict the ability of employees to commit a fraud, conceal it, and convert the fraudulent action into personal gain.

PROJECT DEVELOPMENT AND ACQUISITION CONTROLS

It is important to have a proven methodology to govern the development, acquisition, implementation, and maintenance of information systems. It should contain appropriate controls for management approval, user involvement, analysis, design, testing, implementation, and conversion. These methodologies are discussed in Chapters 22 through 24.

Important systems development controls include the following:

1. A **steering committee** guides and oversees systems development and acquisition.
2. A **strategic master plan** is developed and updated yearly to align an organization's information system with its business strategies. It shows the projects that must be completed, and it addresses the company's hardware, software, personnel, and infrastructure requirements.
3. A **project development plan** shows the tasks to be performed, who will perform them, project costs, completion dates, and **project milestones**—significant points when

steering committee - An executive-level committee to plan and oversee the information systems function.

strategic master plan - A multiple-year plan of the projects the company must complete to achieve its long-range goals.

project development plan - A document that shows how a project will be completed.

project milestones - Points where progress is reviewed and actual and estimated completion times are compared.

data processing schedule - A schedule that shows when each data processing task should be performed.

system performance measurements - Ways to evaluate and assess a system.

throughput - The amount of work performed by a system during a given period of time.

utilization - The percentage of time a system is used.

response time - How long it takes for a system to respond.

postimplementation review - Review, performed after a new system has been operating for a brief period, to ensure that it meets its planned objectives.

systems integrator - An outside party hired to manage a company's systems development effort.

progress is reviewed and actual and estimated completion times are compared. Each project is assigned to a manager and team who are responsible for its success or failure.

4. A **data processing schedule** shows when each task should be performed.
5. **System performance measurements** are established to evaluate the system. Common measurements include **throughput** (output per unit of time), **utilization** (percentage of time the system is used), and **response time** (how long it takes for the system to respond).
6. A **postimplementation review** is performed after a development project is completed to determine whether the anticipated benefits were achieved.

Some companies hire a **systems integrator** to manage a systems development effort involving its own personnel, its client, and other vendors. These development projects are subject to the same cost overruns and missed deadlines as systems developed internally. For example, Westpac Banking began a five-year, $85 million systems development project to decentralize its systems, create new financial products, and downsize its systems department. Three years and $150 million later, no usable results had been attained, and it was clear the scheduled completion date would not be met. With a runaway on its hands, Westpac fired IBM, the primary software developer, and brought in Accenture to review the project and develop recommendations for salvaging it.

Companies using systems integrators should use the same project management processes and controls as internal projects. In addition, they should:

- **Develop clear specifications.** This includes exact descriptions and system definitions, explicit deadlines, and precise acceptance criteria. Suffolk County, New York, spent 12 months and $500,000 preparing detailed specifications for a $16 million criminal justice system before accepting bids. Only 6 of 22 invited integrators bid on the project because of the county's rigorous cost and quality standards. County officials believe their diligent up-front efforts helped ensure their new system's success and saved the county $3 million.
- **Monitor the project.** Companies should establish formal procedures for measuring and reporting a project's status. The best approach is to divide the project into manageable tasks, assign responsibility for each task, and meet at least monthly to review progress and assess quality.

CHANGE MANAGEMENT CONTROLS

Organizations modify existing systems to reflect new business practices and to take advantage of IT advancements. Those in charge of changes should make sure they do not introduce errors and facilitate fraud. Behavioral aspects of change are discussed in Chapter 22 and change management controls are discussed in Chapter 13.

DESIGN AND USE OF DOCUMENTS AND RECORDS

The proper design and use of electronic and paper documents and records help ensure the accurate and complete recording of all relevant transaction data. Their form and content should be as simple as possible, minimize errors, and facilitate review and verification. Documents that initiate a transaction should contain a space for authorizations. Those that transfer assets need a space for the receiving party's signature. Documents should be sequentially prenumbered so each can be accounted for. An audit trail facilitates tracing individual transactions through the system, correcting errors, and verifying system output. Document, form, and screen design are discussed in Chapter 24.

SAFEGUARD ASSETS, RECORDS, AND DATA

A company must protect its cash and physical assets as well as its information. A reporter for Reuters noticed that Intentia, a Swedish software developer, released its first- and second-quarter earnings reports on websites with nearly identical web addresses. He guessed the third-quarter web address, found their unreleased numbers, and ran a story on the disappointing results. Intentia filed criminal hacking charges, but they were dismissed. The Swedish Stock Exchange censured Intentia for not protecting its financial information.

Employees are a much greater security risk than outsiders are. They are better able to hide their illegal acts because they know system weakness better. Almost 50% of companies report that insiders access data without the proper authorization. A software engineer at America Online was charged with selling 92 million e-mail addresses he illegally obtained using another employee's identity (ID) and password. An Internet gambling business bought the names and used them to increase company earnings by $10,000 to $20,000 a day. The data theft was not uncovered for a year, until an anonymous tipster informed authorities that the gambling business was reselling the names to spammers selling herbal male enhancement products.

Employees also cause unintentional threats, such as accidentally deleting company data, opening virus-laden e-mail attachments, or trying to fix hardware or software without the appropriate expertise. These can result in crashed networks and hardware and software malfunctions as well as corrupt data.

Blockchain can protect data and records as it is tamper-resistant, though not tamper-proof. There are many reasons why it results in a much higher level of transaction integrity. Processed transactions are verified by thousands of networked computers instead of error-prone humans. Duplicate copies of the blockchain are stored on all network computers, eliminating the risks that come with data held centrally. This means there is no single point of failure; if one node goes down, there is a copy of the ledger on the other nodes. Blockchain data is transparent; that is, all transaction details are open for all authorized users to see. Both sides of a transaction are stored in a single source, which can eliminate the need for two sets of books (for the buyer and the seller). One set of books provides a trust level not present in current legacy systems. New blocks are added chronologically to the chain, and blocks are referenced in subsequent blocks. That makes it very difficult to go back and change block contents or add invalid blocks inside the chain because each block contains its own hash and the hash of the previous block. If data is changed or added, the hashes for the previous and subsequent blocks also change, and this disrupts the ledger's shared state. When other network computers become aware that the change has caused a problem, consensus is no longer possible, and future blocks cannot be added until the problem is resolved. Blockchain was introduced in Chapters 1 and 2 and is discussed in more detail in Chapter 12.

Chapters 11 through 13 discuss computer-based controls that help safeguard assets. In addition, it is important to:

- **Create and enforce appropriate policies and procedures.** All too often, policies and procedures are created but not enforced. A laptop with the names, Social Security numbers, and birthdates of 26.5 million people was stolen from the home of a Veteran Affairs (VA) Department analyst. The VA did not enforce its policies that sensitive data be encrypted and not leave VA offices. Notifying all 26.5 million people and buying them a credit-checking service cost taxpayers $100 million. Two years prior to the theft, an inspector general report identified the inadequate control of sensitive data as a weakness, but it had never been addressed.
- **Maintain accurate records of all assets.** Periodically reconcile the recorded amounts of company assets to physical counts of those assets.
- **Restrict access to assets.** Restricting access to storage areas protects inventories and equipment. Cash registers, safes, lockboxes, and safety deposit boxes limit access to cash and paper assets. More than $1 million was embezzled from Perini Corp. because blank checks were kept in an unlocked storeroom. An employee made out checks to fictitious vendors, ran them through an unlocked check-signing machine, and cashed the checks.
- **Protect records and documents.** Fireproof storage areas, locked filing cabinets, backup files, and off-site storage protect records and documents. Access to blank checks and documents should be limited to authorized personnel. In Inglewood, California, a janitor stole 34 blank checks, wrote checks from $50,000 to $470,000, forged the names of city officials, and cashed them.

INDEPENDENT CHECKS ON PERFORMANCE

Independent checks on performance, done by someone other than the person who performs the original operation, help ensure that transactions are processed accurately. They include the following:

- **Top-level reviews.** Management should monitor company results and periodically compare actual company performance to (1) planned performance, as shown in budgets, targets, and forecasts; (2) prior period performance; and (3) competitors' performance.

analytical review - The examination of the relationships between different sets of data.

- **Analytical reviews.** An **analytical review** is an examination of the relationships between different sets of data. For example, as credit sales increase, so should accounts receivable. In addition, there are relationships between sales and accounts such as cost of goods sold, inventory, and freight out.
- **Reconciliation of independently maintained records.** Records should be reconciled to documents or records with the same balance. For example, a bank reconciliation verifies that company checking account balances agree with bank statement balances. Another example is comparing subsidiary ledger totals with general ledger totals.
- **Comparison of actual quantities with recorded amounts.** Significant assets are periodically counted and reconciled to company records. At the end of each clerk's shift, cash in a cash register drawer should match the amount on the cash register tape. Inventory should be periodically counted and reconciled to inventory records.
- **Double-entry accounting.** The maxim that debits equal credits provides numerous opportunities for independent checks. Debits in a payroll entry may be allocated to numerous inventory and/or expense accounts; credits are allocated to liability accounts for wages payable, taxes withheld, employee insurance, and union dues. After the payroll entries, comparing total debits and credits is a powerful check on the accuracy of both processes. Any discrepancy indicates the presence of an error.
- **Independent review.** After a transaction is processed, a second person reviews the work of the first, checking for proper authorization, reviewing supporting documents, and checking the accuracy of prices, quantities, and extensions.

Communicate Information and Monitor Control Processes

The seventh component in the ERM model is information and communication. The last component is monitoring. Both are discussed in this section of the chapter.

INFORMATION AND COMMUNICATION

Information and communication systems should capture and exchange the information needed to conduct, manage, and control the organization's operations. The primary purpose of an accounting information system (AIS) is to gather, record, process, store, summarize, and communicate information about an organization. This includes understanding how transactions are initiated, data are captured, files are accessed and updated, data are processed, and information is reported. It includes understanding accounting records and procedures, supporting documents, and financial statements. These items provide an **audit trail**, which allows transactions to be traced back and forth between their origination and the financial statements.

audit trail - A path that allows a transaction to be traced through a data processing system from point of origin to output or backward from output to point of origin.

In addition to identifying and recording all valid transactions, an AIS should properly classify transactions, record transactions at their proper monetary value, record transactions in the proper accounting period, and properly present transactions and related disclosures in the financial statements.

Communication must occur internally and externally to provide information needed to carry out day-to-day internal control activities. All personnel must understand their responsibilities.

The updated IC framework specifies that the following three principles apply to the information and communication process:

1. Obtain or generate relevant, high-quality information to support internal control.
2. Internally communicate the information, including objectives and responsibilities, necessary to support the other components of internal control.
3. Communicate relevant internal control matters to external parties.

Accounting systems generally consist of several subsystems, each designed to process a particular type of transaction using the same sequence of procedures, called accounting cycles. The major accounting cycles and their related control objectives and procedures are detailed in Chapters 14 through 18.

MONITORING

The internal control system that is selected or developed must be continuously monitored, evaluated, and modified as needed. Any deficiencies must be reported to senior management and the board of directors. Key methods of monitoring performance are discussed in this section.

PERFORM INTERNAL CONTROL EVALUATIONS Internal control effectiveness is measured using a formal or a self-assessment evaluation. A team can be formed to conduct the evaluation, or it can be done by internal auditing.

IMPLEMENT EFFECTIVE SUPERVISION Effective supervision involves training and assisting employees, monitoring their performance, correcting errors, and overseeing employees who have access to assets. Supervision is especially important in organizations without responsibility reporting or an adequate segregation of duties.

USE RESPONSIBILITY ACCOUNTING SYSTEMS Responsibility accounting systems include budgets, quotas, schedules, standard costs, and quality standards; reports comparing actual and planned performance; and procedures for investigating and correcting significant variances.

MONITOR SYSTEM ACTIVITIES Risk analysis and management software packages review computer and network security measures, detect illegal access, test for weaknesses and vulnerabilities, report weaknesses found, and suggest improvements. Cost parameters can be entered to balance acceptable levels of risk tolerance and cost-effectiveness. Software also monitors and combats viruses, spyware, adware, spam, phishing, and inappropriate e-mails. It blocks pop-up ads, prevents browsers from being hijacked, and validates a phone caller's ID by comparing the caller's voice to a previously recorded voiceprint. Software can help companies recover from malicious actions. One risk management package helped a company recover from a disgruntled employee's rampage. After a negative performance evaluation, the perpetrator ripped cables out of PCs, changed the inventory control files, and edited the password file to stop people from logging on to the network. The software quickly identified the corrupted files and alerted company headquarters. The damage was undone by utility software, which restored the corrupted file to its original status.

All system transactions and activities should be recorded in a log that indicates who accessed what data, when, and from which online device. These logs should be reviewed frequently and used to monitor system activity, trace problems to their source, evaluate employee productivity, control company costs, fight espionage and hacking attacks, and comply with legal requirements. One company used these logs to analyze why an employee had almost zero productivity and found that he spent six hours a day on porn sites.

The Privacy Foundation estimated that one-third of all American workers with computers are monitored, and that number is expected to increase. Companies who monitor system activities should not violate employee privacy. One way to do that is to have employees agree in writing to written policies that include the following:

- The technology an employee uses on the job belongs to the company.
- E-mails received on company computers are not private and can be read by supervisory personnel. This policy allowed a large pharmaceutical company to identify and terminate an employee who was e-mailing confidential drug-manufacturing data to an external party.
- Employees should not use technology to contribute to a hostile work environment.

TRACK PURCHASED SOFTWARE AND MOBILE DEVICES The Business Software Alliance (BSA) tracks down and fines companies that violate software license agreements. To comply with copyrights and protect themselves from software piracy lawsuits, companies should periodically conduct software audits. There should be enough licenses for all users, and the company should not pay for more licenses than needed. Employees should be informed of the consequences of using unlicensed software.

The increasing number of mobile devices should be tracked and monitored because their loss could represent a substantial exposure. Items to track are the devices, who has them, what tasks they perform, the security features installed, and what software the company needs to maintain adequate system and network security.

CONDUCT PERIODIC AUDITS External, internal, and network security audits can assess and monitor risk as well as detect fraud and errors. Informing employees of audits helps resolve privacy issues, deters fraud, and reduces errors. Auditors should regularly test system controls and periodically browse system usage files looking for suspicious activities. During the security audit of a health care company, auditors pretending to be computer support staff persuaded 16 of 22 employees to reveal their user IDs and passwords. They also found that employees testing a new system left the company's network exposed to outside attacks.

Internal audits assess the reliability and integrity of financial and operating information, evaluate internal control effectiveness, and assess employee compliance with management policies and procedures as well as applicable laws and regulations. The internal audit function should be organizationally independent of accounting and operating functions. Internal audit should report to the audit committee, not the controller or chief financial officer.

One internal auditor noted that a department supervisor took the office staff to lunch in a limousine on her birthday. Wondering whether her salary could support her lifestyle, he investigated and found she set up several fictitious vendors, sent the company invoices from these vendors, and cashed the checks mailed to her. Over a period of several years, she embezzled more than $12 million.

computer security officer (CSO) - An employee independent of the information system function who monitors the system, disseminates information about improper system uses and their consequences, and reports to top management.

EMPLOY A COMPUTER SECURITY OFFICER AND A CHIEF COMPLIANCE OFFICER A **computer security officer (CSO)** is in charge of system security, independent of the information system function, and reports to the chief operating officer (COO) or the CEO. The overwhelming tasks related to SOX and other forms of compliance have led many companies to delegate all compliance issues to a **chief compliance officer (CCO)**. Many companies use outside computer consultants or in-house teams to test and evaluate security procedures and computer systems.

chief compliance officer (CCO) - An employee responsible for all the compliance tasks associated with SOX and other laws and regulatory rulings.

forensic investigators - Individuals who specialize in fraud, most of whom have specialized training with law enforcement agencies such as the FBI or IRS or have professional certifications such as Certified Fraud Examiner (CFE).

ENGAGE FORENSIC SPECIALISTS **Forensic investigators** who specialize in fraud are a fast-growing group in the accounting profession. Their increasing presence is due to several factors, most notably SOX, new accounting rules, and demands by boards of directors that forensic investigations be an ongoing part of the financial reporting and corporate governance process. Most forensic investigators received specialized training with the FBI, IRS, or other law enforcement agencies. Investigators with the computer skills to ferret out fraud perpetrators are in great demand. The Association of Certified Fraud Examiners sponsors a Certified Fraud Examiner (CFE) professional certification program. To become a CFE, candidates must pass a two-day exam. Currently there are about 35,000 CFEs worldwide.

computer forensics specialists - Computer experts who discover, extract, safeguard, and document computer evidence such that its authenticity, accuracy, and integrity will not succumb to legal challenges.

Computer forensics specialists discover, extract, safeguard, and document computer evidence such that its authenticity, accuracy, and integrity will not succumb to legal challenges. Computer forensics can be compared to performing an "autopsy" on a computer system to determine whether a crime was committed as well as who committed it, and then marshalling the evidence lawyers need to prove the charges in court. Some of the more common matters investigated are improper Internet usage; fraud; sabotage; the loss, theft, or corruption of data; retrieving "erased" information from e-mails and databases; and figuring out who performed certain computer activities. A Deloitte & Touche forensics team uncovered evidence that helped convict a Giant Supermarket purchasing manager who had accepted more than $600,000 in supplier kickbacks.

INSTALL FRAUD DETECTION SOFTWARE Fraudsters follow distinct patterns and leave clues behind that can be discovered by fraud detection software. ReliaStar Financial used software from IBM to detect the following:

- A Los Angeles chiropractor submitted hundreds of thousands of dollars in fraudulent claims. The software identified an unusual number of patients who lived more than 50 miles away from the doctor's office and flagged these bills for investigation.
- A Long Island doctor submitted weekly bills for a rare and expensive procedure normally done only once or twice in a lifetime.
- A podiatrist saw four patients and billed for 500 separate procedures.

neural networks - Computing systems that imitate the brain's learning process by using a network of interconnected processors that perform multiple operations simultaneously and interact dynamically.

Neural networks (programs with learning capabilities) can accurately identify fraud. The Visa and MasterCard operation at Mellon Bank uses a neural network to track 1.2 million accounts. It can spot illegal credit card use and notify the owner shortly after the card is stolen. It can also spot trends before bank investigators do. For example, an investigator learned about a new fraud from another bank. When he went to check for the fraud, the neural network had already identified it and had printed out transactions that fit its pattern. The software cost the bank less than $1 million and paid for itself in six months.

IMPLEMENT A FRAUD HOTLINE People witnessing fraudulent behavior are often torn between two conflicting feelings. Although they want to protect company assets and report fraud perpetrators, they are uncomfortable blowing the whistle, so all too often they remain silent. This reluctance is stronger if they are aware of whistle-blowers who have been ostracized, been persecuted, or suffered damage to their careers.

SOX mandates a mechanism for employees to report fraud and abuse. A **fraud hotline** is an effective way to comply with the law and resolve whistle-blower conflict. In one study, researchers found that 33% of 212 frauds were detected through anonymous tips. The insurance industry set up a hotline to control $17 billion a year in fraudulent claims. In the first month, more than 2,250 calls were received; 15% resulted in investigative action. The downside of hotlines is that many calls are not worthy of investigation; some are motivated by a desire for revenge, some are vague reports of wrongdoing, and others have no merit.

fraud hotline - A phone number employees can call to anonymously report fraud and abuse.

Summary and Case Conclusion

One week after Jason and Maria filed their audit report, they were summoned to the office of Northwest's director of internal auditing to explain their findings. Shortly thereafter, a fraud investigation team was dispatched to Bozeman to take a closer look at the situation. Six months later, a company newsletter indicated that the Springer family sold its 10% interest in the business and resigned from all management positions. Two Northwest executives were transferred in to replace them. There was no other word on the audit findings.

Two years later, Jason and Maria worked with Frank Ratliff, a member of the high-level audit team. After hours, Frank told them the investigation team examined a large sample of purchasing transactions and all employee timekeeping and payroll records for a 12-month period. The team also took a detailed physical inventory. They discovered that the problems Jason identified—including missing purchase requisitions, purchase orders, and receiving reports, as well as excessive prices—were widespread. These problems occurred in transactions with three large vendors from whom Springer's had purchased several million dollars of inventory. The investigators discussed the unusually high prices with the vendors but did not receive a satisfactory explanation. The county business-licensing bureau revealed that Bill Springer held a majority ownership interest in each of these companies. By authorizing excessive prices to companies he owned, Springer earned a significant share of several hundred thousand dollars of excessive profits, all at the expense of Northwest Industries.

Several Springer employees were paid for more hours than they worked. Inventory was materially overstated; a physical inventory revealed that a significant portion of recorded inventory did not exist and that some items were obsolete. The adjusting journal entry reflecting Springer's real inventory wiped out much of their profits over the past three years.

When confronted, the Springers vehemently denied breaking any laws. Northwest considered going to the authorities but was concerned that the case was not strong enough to prove in court. Northwest also worried that adverse publicity might damage the company's position in Bozeman. After months of negotiation, the Springers agreed to the settlement reported in the newsletter. Part of the settlement was that no public statement would be made about any alleged fraud or embezzlement involving the Springers. According to Frank, this policy was normal. In many fraud cases, settlements are reached quietly, with no legal action taken, so that the company can avoid adverse publicity.

KEY TERMS

threat 298
exposure/impact 298
likelihood/risk 298
internal controls 298
preventive controls 298
detective controls 298
corrective controls 298
general controls 298
application controls 298
belief system 299
boundary system 299
diagnostic control system 299
interactive control system 299
Foreign Corrupt Practices Act (FCPA) 299
Sarbanes–Oxley Act (SOX) 299
Public Company Accounting Oversight Board (PCAOB) 299
Control Objectives for Information and Related Technology (COBIT) 300
Committee of Sponsoring Organizations (COSO) 302
Internal Control—Integrated Framework (IC) 302
control environment 304
risk appetite 305
audit committee 306
policy and procedures manual 306
background check 307
inherent risk 309
residual risk 309
expected loss 310
control activities 311
authorization 311
digital signature 312
specific authorization 312
general authorization 312
segregation of accounting duties 312
collusion 313
segregation of systems duties 314
systems analysts 314
programmers 314
computer operators 315
users 315
systems administrators 315
network managers 315
security management 315
change management 315
data control 315
steering committee 315
strategic master plan 315
project development plan 315
project milestones 315
data processing schedule 316
system performance measurements 316
throughput 316
utilization 316
response time 316
postimplementation review 316
systems integrator 316
analytical review 318
audit trail 318
computer security officer (CSO) 320
chief compliance officer (CCO) 320
forensic investigators 320
computer forensics specialists 320
neural networks 320
fraud hotline 321

AIS in Action

CHAPTER QUIZ

1. COSO identified five interrelated components of internal control. Which of the following is not one of those five?
   a. risk assessment
   b. internal control policies
   c. monitoring
   d. information and communication

2. To achieve effective segregation of duties, certain functions must be separated. Which of the following is not a correct listing of systems duties that must be segregated?
   a. data entry, users, operations
   b. authorization, data storage, data output
   c. programming, authorization, data storage
   d. monitoring, data entry, operations

3. Which of the following statements is true?
   a. COSO's enterprise risk management framework is narrow in scope and is limited to financial controls.
   b. COSO's internal control integrated framework has been widely accepted as the authority on internal controls.
   c. The Foreign Corrupt Practices Act had no impact on internal accounting control systems.
   d. It is easier to add controls to an already designed system than to include them during the initial design stage.

4. All other things being equal, which of the following is true?
a. Detective controls are superior to preventive controls.
b. Corrective controls are superior to preventive controls.
c. Preventive controls are equivalent to detective controls.
d. Preventive controls are superior to detective controls.

5. Which of the following statements about the control environment is false?
a. Management's attitudes toward internal control and ethical behavior have little impact on employee beliefs or actions.
b. An overly complex or unclear organizational structure may be indicative of problems that are more serious.
c. A written policy and procedures manual is an important tool for assigning authority and responsibility.
d. Supervision is especially important in organizations that cannot afford elaborate responsibility reporting or are too small to have an adequate separation of duties.

6. To achieve effective segregation of duties, certain functions must be separated. Which of the following is the correct listing of the accounting-related functions that must be segregated?
a. control, recording, and monitoring
b. authorization, recording, and custody
c. control, custody, and authorization
d. monitoring, recording, and planning

7. Which of the following is not an independent check?
a. bank reconciliation
b. periodic comparison of subsidiary ledger totals to control accounts
c. trial balance
d. re-adding the total of a batch of invoices and comparing it with your first total

8. Which of the following is a control procedure relating to both the design and the use of documents and records?
a. locking blank checks in a drawer
b. reconciling the bank account
c. sequentially prenumbering sales invoices
d. comparing actual physical quantities with recorded amounts

9. Which of the following is the correct order of the risk assessment steps discussed in this chapter?
a. identify threats, estimate risk and exposure, identify controls, estimate costs and benefits
b. identify controls, estimate risk and exposure, identify threats, estimate costs and benefits
c. estimate risk and exposure, identify controls, identify threats, estimate costs and benefits
d. estimate costs and benefits, identify threats, identify controls, estimate risk and exposure

10. Your current system is deemed 90% reliable. A major threat has been identified with an impact of $3 million. Two control procedures exist to deal with the threat. Implementation of control A would cost $100,000 and reduce the likelihood to 6%. Implementation of control B would cost $140,000 and reduce the likelihood to 4%. Implementation of both controls would cost $220,000 and reduce the likelihood to 2%. Given the data, and based solely on an economic analysis of costs and benefits, what should you do?
a. Implement control A only.
b. Implement control B only.
c. Implement both controls A and B.
d. Implement neither control.

DISCUSSION QUESTIONS

10.1 Answer the following questions about the audit of Springer's Lumber & Supply.
a. What deficiencies existed in the control environment at Springer's?
b. Do you agree with the decision to settle with the Springers rather than to prosecute them for fraud and embezzlement? Why, or why not?
c. Should the company have told Jason and Maria the results of the high-level audit? Why, or why not?

10.2 Effective segregation of duties is sometimes not economically feasible in a small business. What internal control elements do you think can help compensate for this threat?

10.3 One function of the AIS is to provide adequate controls to ensure the safety of organizational assets, including data. However, many people view control procedures as "red tape." They also believe that instead of producing tangible benefits, business controls create resentment and loss of company morale. Discuss this position.

10.4 In recent years, Supersmurf's external auditors have given clean opinions on its financial statements and favorable evaluations of its internal control systems. Discuss whether it is necessary for this corporation to take any further action to comply with the Sarbanes–Oxley Act.

10.5 When you go to a movie theater, you buy a prenumbered ticket from the cashier. This ticket is handed to another person at the entrance to the movie. What kinds of irregularities is the theater trying to prevent? What controls is it using to prevent these irregularities? What remaining risks or exposures can you identify?

10.6 Some restaurants use customer checks with prenumbered sequence codes. Each food server uses these checks to write up customer orders. Food servers are told not to destroy any customer checks; if a mistake is made, they are to void that check and write a new one. All voided checks are to be turned in to the manager daily. How does this policy help the restaurant control cash receipts?

10.7 Compare and contrast the following three frameworks: COBIT, COSO Integrated Control, and ERM.

PROBLEMS

10.1 You are an audit supervisor assigned to a new client, Go-Go Corporation, which is listed on the New York Stock Exchange. You visited Go-Go's corporate headquarters to become acquainted with key personnel and to conduct a preliminary review of the company's accounting policies, controls, and systems. During this visit, the following events occurred:

a. You met with Go-Go's audit committee, which consists of the corporate controller, treasurer, financial vice president, and budget director.
b. You recognized the treasurer as a former aide to Ernie Eggers, who was convicted of fraud several years ago.
c. Management explained its plans to change accounting methods for depreciation from the accelerated to the straight-line method. Management implied that if your firm does not concur with this change, Go-Go will employ other auditors.
d. You learned that the financial vice president manages a staff of five internal auditors.
e. You noted that all management authority seems to reside with three brothers, who serve as chief executive officer, president, and financial vice president.
f. You were told that the performance of division and department managers is evaluated on a subjective basis because Go-Go's management believes that formal performance evaluation procedures are counterproductive.
g. You learned that the company has reported increases in earnings per share for each of the past 25 quarters; however, earnings during the current quarter have leveled off and may decline.
h. You reviewed the company's policy and procedures manual, which listed policies for dealing with customers, vendors, and employees.
i. Your preliminary assessment is that the accounting systems are well designed and that they employ effective internal control procedures.
j. Some employees complained that some managers occasionally contradict the instructions of other managers regarding proper data security procedures.

k. After a careful review of the budget for data security enhancement projects, you feel the budget appears to be adequate.
l. The enhanced network firewall project appeared to be on a very aggressive implementation schedule. The IT manager mentioned that even if he put all of his personnel on the project for the next five weeks, he still would not complete the project in time. The manager has mentioned this to company management, which seems unwilling to modify the schedule.
m. Several new employees have had trouble completing some of their duties, and they do not appear to know who to ask for help.
n. Go-Go's strategy is to achieve consistent growth for its shareholders. However, its policy is not to invest in any project unless its payback period is no more than 48 months and yields an internal rate of return that exceeds its cost of capital by 3%.
o. You observe that company purchasing agents wear clothing and exhibit other paraphernalia from major vendors. The purchasing department manager proudly displays a picture of himself holding a big fish on the deck of a luxury fishing boat that has the logo of a major Go-Go vendor painted on its wheelhouse.

REQUIRED

The information you have obtained suggests potential problems relating to Go-Go's control environment. Identify the problems, and explain them in relation to the control environment concepts discussed in this chapter.

10.2 Explain how the principle of separation of duties is violated in each of the following situations. Also, suggest one or more procedures to reduce the risk and exposure highlighted in each example.

a. A payroll clerk recorded a 40-hour work-week for an employee who had quit the previous week. He then prepared a paycheck for this employee, forged her signature, and cashed the check.
b. While opening the mail, a cashier set aside, and subsequently cashed, two checks payable to the company on account.
c. A cashier prepared a fictitious invoice from a company using his brother-in-law's name. He wrote a check in payment of the invoice, which the brother-in-law later cashed.
d. An employee of the finishing department walked off with several parts from the storeroom and recorded the items in the inventory ledger as having been issued to the assembly department.
e. A cashier cashed a check from a customer in payment of an account receivable, pocketed the cash, and concealed the theft by properly posting the receipt to the customer's account in the accounts receivable ledger.
f. Several customers returned clothing purchases. Instead of putting the clothes into a return bin to be put back on the rack, a clerk put the clothing in a separate bin under some cleaning rags. After her shift, she transferred the clothes to a gym bag and took them home.
g. A receiving clerk noticed that four cases of MP3 players were included in a shipment when only three were ordered. The clerk put the extra case aside and took it home after his shift ended.
h. An insurance claims adjuster had check-signing authority of up to $6,000. The adjuster created three businesses that billed the insurance company for work not performed on valid claims. The adjuster wrote and signed checks to pay for the invoices, none of which exceeded $6,000.
i. An accounts payable clerk recorded invoices received from a company that he and his wife owned and authorized their payment.
j. A cashier created false purchase return vouchers to hide his theft of several thousand dollars from his cash register.
k. A purchasing agent received a 10% kickback of the invoice amount for all purchases made from a specific vendor.

10.3 Match the terms with their definitions:

____ 1. inherent risk	a.	Outside party hired to manage systems development effort
____ 2. general authorization	b.	Probability that a threat will come to pass
____ 3. control environment	c.	Risk that remains after management implements internal controls or some other response to risk
____ 4. corrective controls	d.	Cooperation between two or more people to thwart internal controls
____ 5. risk appetite	e.	Special approval needed to handle a transaction.
____ 6. application controls	f.	Company culture that is the foundation for all other internal control components
____ 7. systems integrator	g.	Person who ensures an organization's networks operate properly
____ 8. utilization	h.	Ensures source data is approved, monitors work flow, and handles input errors
____ 9. security management	i.	Susceptibility of accounts or transactions to control problems in absence of internal control
____ 10. strategic master plan	j.	Path used to trace a transaction from origin to output or from output to origin
____ 11. specific authorization	k.	Amount of work performed during a given time period
____ 12. collusion	l.	Electronically signing a document with data that cannot be forged
____ 13. throughput	m.	Controls that prevent, detect, and correct transaction errors and fraud in transaction processing programs
____ 14. systems administrator	n.	Given to employees to handle routine transactions without special approval
____ 15. residual risk	o.	Controls that identify and correct problems and recover from resulting errors
____ 16. data control	p.	Responsible for making sure a system operates smoothly and efficiently
____ 17. likelihood	q.	Document that shows how a project will be completed
____ 18. analytical review	r.	Amount of risk company is willing to accept to achieve its goals and objectives
____ 19. exposure	s.	Makes sure systems are secure and protected from internal and external threats
____ 20. systems analysts	t.	Percentage of time a system is used
____ 21. audit trail	u.	Examining relationships between different sets of data
____ 22. audit committee	v.	Potential dollar loss if a threat becomes a reality
____ 23. digital signature	w.	Outside, independent directors responsible for financial reporting, regulatory compliance, and internal control
	x.	Controls designed to discover control problems not prevented
	y.	Multiple year plan of projects company must complete to achieve long-range goals
	z.	Help users determine their information needs and design systems to meet those needs

10.4 The Gardner Company, a client of your firm, has come to you with the following problem. It has three clerical employees who must perform the following functions:

a. Maintain the general ledger (G/L) master file
b. Maintain the accounts payable ledger (A/P) master file
c. Maintain the accounts receivable ledger (A/R) master file
d. Handle and send disbursements (vendor payments)
e. Issue credits on returns and allowances
f. Reconcile the bank account
g. Handle and deposit receipts (customer payments)

Assuming equal abilities among the three employees, the company asks you to assign the seven functions to them to maximize internal control and minimize the possibility of fraud. Assume that these employees will perform no accounting functions other than the ones listed.

REQUIRED

a. What is the key to preventing fraud when assigning duties to employees?
b. Decide whether each of the above seven jobs is a custody, recording, or authorization function.
c. List unsatisfactory pairings of the seven functions listed.
d. Explain how you would distribute the seven functions among the three employees. Assume that except for the nominal jobs of the bank reconciliation and the issuance of credits on returns and allowances, all functions require an equal amount of time.
e. Thinking beyond this problem, why should the IT staff not have custody of physical assets? What IT functions need to be segregated?

10.5 During a recent review, ABC Corporation discovered that it has a serious internal control problem. It is estimated that the impact associated with this problem is $1 million and that the likelihood is currently 5%. Two internal control procedures have been proposed to deal with this problem. Procedure A would cost $25,000 and reduce likelihood to 2%; procedure B would cost $30,000 and reduce likelihood to 1%. If both procedures were implemented, likelihood would be reduced to 0.1%.

REQUIRED

a. What is the estimated expected loss associated with ABC Corporation's internal control problem before any new internal control procedures are implemented?
b. Compute the revised estimate of expected loss if procedure A were implemented, if procedure B were implemented, and if both procedures were implemented.
c. Compare the estimated costs and benefits of procedure A, procedure B, and both procedures combined. If you consider only the estimates of cost and benefit, which procedure(s) should be implemented?
d. What other factors might be relevant to the decision?
e. Use the Goal Seek function in Microsoft Excel to determine the likelihood of occurrence without the control and the reduction in expected loss if the net benefit/cost is 0. Do this for procedure A, procedure B, and both procedures together.

10.6 The management at Covington, Inc., recognizes that a well-designed internal control system provides many benefits. Among the benefits are reliable financial records that facilitate decision making and a greater probability of preventing or detecting errors and fraud. Covington's internal auditing department periodically reviews the company's accounting records to determine the effectiveness of internal controls. In its latest review, the internal audit staff found the following eight conditions:

1. Daily bank deposits do not always correspond with cash receipts.
2. Bad debt write-offs are prepared and approved by the same employee.
3. There are occasional discrepancies between physical inventory counts and perpetual inventory records.
4. Alterations have been made to physical inventory counts and to perpetual inventory records.

5. There are many customer refunds and credits.
6. Many original documents are missing or lost. However, there are substitute copies of all missing originals.
7. An unexplained decrease in the gross profit percentage has occurred.
8. Many documents are not approved.

REQUIRED

For each of the eight conditions detected by the Covington internal audit staff:

a. Describe a possible cause of the condition.
b. Recommend actions to be taken and/or controls to be implemented that would correct the condition. (*CMA, adapted*)

10.7 Consider the following two situations:

1. Many employees of a firm that manufactures small tools pocket some of the tools for their personal use. Because the quantities taken by any one employee are immaterial, the individual employees do not consider the act as fraudulent or detrimental to the company. The company is now large enough to hire an internal auditor. One of the first things she did was to compare the gross profit rates for industrial tools to the gross profit for personal tools. Noting a significant difference, she investigated and uncovered the employee theft.
2. A manufacturing firm's controller created a fake subsidiary. He then ordered goods from the firm's suppliers, told them to ship the goods to a warehouse he rented, and approved the vendor invoices for payment when they arrived. The controller later sold the diverted inventory items, and the proceeds were deposited to the controller's personal bank account. Auditors suspected something was wrong when they could not find any entries regarding this fake subsidiary office in the property, plant, and equipment ledgers or a title or lease for the office in the real-estate records.

REQUIRED

For the situations presented, describe the recommendations the internal auditors should make to prevent similar problems in the future. (*CMA, adapted*)

10.8 Tralor Corporation manufactures and sells several different lines of small electric components. Its internal audit department completed an audit of its expenditure processes. Part of the audit involved a review of the internal accounting controls for payables, including the controls over the authorization of transactions, accounting for transactions, and the protection of assets. The auditors noted the following items:

1. Routine purchases are initiated by inventory control notifying the purchasing department of the need to buy goods. The purchasing department fills out a prenumbered purchase order and gets it approved by the purchasing manager. The original of the five-part purchase order goes to the vendor. The other four copies are for purchasing, the user department, receiving for use as a receiving report, and accounts payable.
2. For efficiency and effectiveness, purchases of specialized goods and services are negotiated directly between the user department and the vendor. Company procedures require that the user department and the purchasing department approve invoices for any specialized goods and services before making payment.
3. Accounts payable maintains a list of employees who have purchase order approval authority. The list was updated two years ago and is seldom used by accounts payable clerks.
4. Prenumbered vendor invoices are recorded in an invoice register that indicates the receipt date, whether it is a special order, when a special order is sent to the requesting department for approval, and when it is returned. A review of the register indicated that there were seven open invoices for special purchases, which had been forwarded to operating departments for approval over 30 days previously and had not yet been returned.
5. Prior to making entries in accounting records, the accounts payable clerk checks the mathematical accuracy of the transaction, makes sure all transactions are properly documented (the purchase order matches the signed receiving report and the vendor's invoice), and obtains departmental approval for special purchase invoices.

6. All approved invoices are filed alphabetically. Invoices are paid on the 5th and 20th of each month, and all cash discounts are taken regardless of the terms.
7. The treasurer signs the checks and cancels the supporting documents. An original document is required for a payment to be processed.
8. Prenumbered blank checks are kept in a locked safe accessible only to the cash disbursements department. Other documents and records maintained by the accounts payable section are readily accessible to all persons assigned to the section and to others in the accounting function.

REQUIRED

Review the eight items listed, and decide whether they represent an internal control strength or weakness.

a. For each internal control strength you identified, explain how the procedure helps achieve good authorization, accounting, or asset protection control.
b. For each internal control weakness you identified, explain why it is a weakness and recommend a way to correct the weakness. (*CMA, adapted*)

10.9 Lancaster Company makes electrical parts for contractors and home improvement retail stores. After their annual audit, Lancaster's auditors commented on the following items regarding internal controls over equipment:

1. The operations department that needs the equipment normally initiates a purchase requisition for equipment. The operations department supervisor discusses the proposed purchase with the plant manager. If there are sufficient funds in the requesting department's equipment budget, a purchase requisition is submitted to the purchasing department once the plant manager is satisfied that the request is reasonable.
2. When the purchasing department receives either an inventory or an equipment purchase requisition, the purchasing agent selects an appropriate supplier and sends them a purchase order.
3. When equipment arrives, the user department installs it. The property, plant, and equipment control accounts are supported by schedules organized by year of acquisition. The schedules are used to record depreciation using standard rates, depreciation methods, and salvage values for each type of fixed asset. These rates, methods, and salvage values were set 10 years ago during the company's initial year of operation.
4. When equipment is retired, the plant manager notifies the accounting department so the appropriate accounting entries can be made.
5. There has been no reconciliation since the company began operations between the accounting records and the equipment on hand.

REQUIRED

Identify the internal control weaknesses in Lancaster's system, and recommend ways to correct them. (*CMA, adapted*)

10.10 The Langston Recreational Company (LRC) manufactures ice skates for racing, figure skating, and hockey. The company is in Kearns, Utah, so it can be close to the Olympic Ice Shield, where many Olympic speed skaters train.

Given the precision required to make skates, tracking manufacturing costs is very important to management so it can price the skates appropriately. To capture and collect manufacturing costs, the company acquired an automated cost accounting system from a national vendor. The vendor provides support, maintenance, and data and program backup service for LRC's system.

LRC operates one shift, five days a week. All manufacturing data are collected and recorded by Saturday evening so that the prior week's production data can be processed. One of management's primary concerns is how the actual manufacturing process costs compare with planned or standard manufacturing process costs. As a result, the cost accounting system produces a report that compares actual costs with standard costs and provides the difference, or variance. Management focuses on significant variances as one means of controlling the manufacturing processes and calculating bonuses.

Occasionally, errors occur in processing a week's production cost data, which requires the entire week's cost data to be reprocessed at a cost of $34,500. The current risk of error without any control procedures is 8%. LRC's management is currently considering a set of cost accounting control procedures that is estimated to reduce the risk of the data errors from 8% to 3%. This data validation control procedure is projected to cost $1,000 per week.

REQUIRED

a. Perform a cost/benefit analysis of the data validation control procedures.
b. Based on your analysis, make a recommendation to management regarding the control procedure.
c. The current risk of data errors without any control procedures is estimated to be 8%. The data control validation procedure costs $1,000 and reduces the risk to 3%. At some point between 8% and 3% is a point of indifference—that is, Cost of reprocessing the data without controls = Cost of processing the data with the controls + Cost of controls. Use a spreadsheet application such as Excel Goal Seek to find the solution.

CASE 10-1 The Greater Providence Deposit & Trust Embezzlement

Nino Moscardi, president of Greater Providence Deposit & Trust (GPD&T), received an anonymous note in his mail stating that a bank employee was making bogus loans. Moscardi asked the bank's internal auditors to investigate the transactions detailed in the note. The investigation led to James Guisti, manager of a North Providence branch office and a trusted 14-year employee who had once worked as one of the bank's internal auditors. Guisti was charged with embezzling $1.83 million from the bank using 67 phony loans taken out over a three-year period.

Court documents revealed that the bogus loans were 90-day notes requiring no collateral and ranging in amount from $10,000 to $63,500. Guisti originated the loans; when each one matured, he would take out a new loan, or rewrite the old one, to pay the principal and interest due. Some loans had been rewritten five or six times.

The 67 loans were taken out by Guisti in five names, including his wife's maiden name, his father's name, and the names of two friends. These people denied receiving stolen funds or knowing anything about the embezzlement. The fifth name was James Vanesse, who police said did not exist. The Social Security number on Vanesse's loan application was issued to a female, and the phone number belonged to a North Providence auto dealer.

Lucy Fraioli, a customer service representative who cosigned the checks, said Guisti was her supervisor and she thought nothing was wrong with the checks, though she did not know any of the people. Marcia Perfetto, head teller, told police she cashed checks for Guisti made out to four of the five persons. Asked whether she gave the money to Guisti when he gave her checks to cash, she answered, "Not all of the time," though she could not recall ever having given the money directly to any of the four, whom she did not know.

Guisti was authorized to make consumer loans up to a certain dollar limit without loan committee approvals, which is a standard industry practice. Guisti's original lending limit was $10,000, the amount of his first fraudulent loan. The dollar limit was later increased to $15,000 and then increased again to $25,000. Some of the loans, including the one for $63,500, far exceeded his lending limit. In addition, all loan applications should have been accompanied by the applicant's credit history report, purchased from an independent credit rating firm. The loan taken out in the fictitious name would not have had a credit report and should have been flagged by a loan review clerk at the bank's headquarters.

News reports raised questions about why the fraud was not detected earlier. State regulators and the bank's internal auditors failed to detect the fraud. Several reasons were given for the failure to find the fraud earlier. First, in checking for bad loans, bank auditors do not examine all loans and generally focus on loans much larger than the ones in question. Second, Greater Providence had recently dropped its computer services arrangement with a local bank in favor of an out-of-state bank. This changeover may have reduced the effectiveness of the bank's control procedures. Third, the bank's loan review clerks were rotated frequently, making follow-up on questionable loans more difficult.

Guisti was a frequent gambler and used the embezzled money to pay gambling debts. The bank's losses totaled $624,000, which was less than the $1.83 million in bogus loans because Guisti used a portion of the borrowed money to repay loans as they came due. The bank's bonding company covered the loss.

The bank experienced other adverse publicity prior to the fraud's discovery. First, the bank was fined $50,000 after pleading guilty to failure to report cash transactions exceeding $10,000, which is a felony. Second, bank owners took the bank private after a lengthy public battle with the State Attorney General, who alleged that the bank inflated its assets and overestimated its capital surplus to make its balance sheet look stronger. The bank denied this charge.

1. How did Guisti commit the fraud, conceal it, and convert the fraudulent actions to personal gain?
2. Good internal controls require that the custody, recording, and authorization functions be separated. Explain which of those functions Guisti had and how the failure to segregate them facilitated the fraud.
3. Identify the preventive, detective, and corrective controls at GPD&T, and discuss whether they were effective.
4. Explain the pressures, opportunities, and rationalizations that were present in the Guisti fraud.
5. Discuss how Greater Providence Deposit & Trust might improve its control procedures over the disbursement of loan funds to minimize the risk of this type of fraud. In what way does this case indicate a lack of proper segregation of duties?
6. Discuss how Greater Providence might improve its loan review procedures at bank headquarters to minimize its fraud risk. Was it a good idea to rotate the assignments of loan review clerks? Why, or why not?
7. Discuss whether Greater Providence's auditors should have been able to detect this fraud.
8. Are there any indications that the control environment at Greater Providence may have been deficient? If so, how could it have contributed to this embezzlement?

Source: John Kostrezewa, "Charge: Embezzlement," *Providence Journal-Bulletin* (July 31, 1988): F-1.

AIS in Action Solutions

QUIZ KEY

1. COSO identified five interrelated components of internal control. Which of the following is not one of those five?
   a. risk assessment [Incorrect. The organization must be aware of and deal with the risks it faces.]
   ▶ b. internal control policies [Correct. Internal control policies are not one of COSO's five components of internal control. However, control environment and control activities are two of the five internal control framework components.]
   c. monitoring [Incorrect. The entire internal control process must be monitored, and modifications made as necessary.]
   d. information and communication [Incorrect. The primary purpose of an AIS is to process and communicate information about an organization, and these activities are an essential part of an internal control system.]

2. To achieve effective segregation of duties, certain functions must be separated. Which of the following is not a correct listing of systems duties that must be segregated?
   a. data entry, users, operations [Correct. See Figure 10-5.]
   ▶ b. authorization, data storage, data output [Incorrect. See Figure 10-5. Data output is not one of the functions that must be segregated. Both the data storage function and users must be responsible for controlling output.]
   c. programming, authorization, data storage [Correct. See Figure 10-5.]
   d. monitoring, data entry, operations [Correct. See Figure 10-5.]

3. Which of the following statements is true?
   a. COSO's enterprise risk management framework is narrow in scope and is limited to financial controls. [Incorrect. The ERM framework incorporates all kinds of internal controls, not just financial controls, and provides an all-encompassing focus on the broader subject of enterprise risk management.]
   ▶ b. COSO's internal control integrated framework has been widely accepted as the authority on internal controls. [Correct. The internal control integrated framework is the accepted authority on internal controls and is incorporated into policies, rules, and regulations that are used to control business activities.]

c. The Foreign Corrupt Practices Act had no impact on internal accounting control systems. [Incorrect. The Foreign Corrupt Practices Act specifically requires corporations to maintain good systems of internal accounting control.]
d. It is easier to add controls to an already designed system than to include them during the initial design stage. [Incorrect. The opposite is true—it is easier to include internal controls at the initial design stage than after the system is already designed.]

4. All other things being equal, which of the following is true?
a. Detective controls are superior to preventive controls. [Incorrect. The reverse is true—preventive controls are superior to detective controls. Preventive controls keep an error or irregularity from occurring. Detective controls uncover an error or irregularity after the fact.]
b. Corrective controls are superior to preventive controls. [Incorrect. The reverse is true—preventive controls are superior to corrective controls. Preventive controls keep an error or irregularity from occurring. Corrective controls fix an error after the fact.]
c. Preventive controls are equivalent to detective controls. [Incorrect. Preventive controls keep an error or irregularity from occurring. Detective controls uncover an error or irregularity after the fact.]
▶ **d.** Preventive controls are superior to detective controls. [Correct. With respect to controls, it is always of utmost importance to prevent errors from occurring.]

5. Which of the following statements about the control environment is false?
▶ **a.** Management's attitudes toward internal control and ethical behavior have little impact on employee beliefs or actions. [Correct. This statement is false. Management's attitude toward internal control is critical to the organization's effectiveness and success. They set the "tone at the top" that other employees follow.]
b. An overly complex or unclear organizational structure may be indicative of problems that are more serious. [Incorrect. This is a true statement. Management may intentionally build overly complex or unclear organizational structures to hide fraud or errors.]
c. A written policy and procedures manual is an important tool for assigning authority and responsibility. [Incorrect. This is a true statement. A written policy and procedures manual explains proper business practices, describes the knowledge and experience needed by key personnel, and lists the resources provided to carry out specific duties.]
d. Supervision is especially important in organizations that cannot afford elaborate responsibility reporting or are too small to have an adequate separation of duties. [Incorrect. This is a true statement. In many organizations, effective supervision takes the place of more expensive controls. Effective supervision involves training and assisting employees, monitoring their performance, correcting errors, and safeguarding assets by overseeing employees who have access to them.]

6. To achieve effective segregation of duties, certain functions must be separated. Which of the following is the correct listing of the accounting-related functions that must be segregated?
a. control, recording, and monitoring [Incorrect. See Figure 10-4.]
▶ **b.** authorization, recording, and custody [Correct. See Figure 10-4.]
c. control, custody, and authorization [Incorrect. See Figure 10-4.]
d. monitoring, recording, and planning [Incorrect. See Figure 10-4.]

7. Which of the following is not an independent check?
a. bank reconciliation [Incorrect. A bank reconciliation is an independent check, as are top-level reviews, analytical reviews, reconciling two independently maintained sets of records, comparisons of actual quantities with recorded amounts, double-entry accounting, and independent reviews.]
b. periodic comparison of subsidiary ledger totals to control accounts [Incorrect. A periodic comparison of subsidiary ledger totals to control accounts is an independent check, as are top-level reviews, analytical reviews, reconciling two independently maintained sets of records, comparisons of actual quantities with recorded amounts, double-entry accounting, and independent reviews.]

c. trial balance [Incorrect. A trial balance is an independent check, as are top-level reviews, analytical reviews, reconciling two independently maintained sets of records, comparisons of actual quantities with recorded amounts, double-entry accounting, and independent reviews.]

▶ **d.** re-adding the total of a batch of invoices and comparing it with your first total [Correct. One person performing the same procedure twice using the same documents, such as re-adding invoice batch totals, is not an independent check because it does not involve a second person, a second set of documents or records, or a second process.]

8. Which of the following is a control procedure relating to both the design and the use of documents and records?

a. locking blank checks in a drawer [Incorrect. Locking blank checks in a drawer is not a control procedure related to the design of documents.]

b. reconciling the bank account [Incorrect. Reconciling the bank account is not a control procedure related to the design of documents.]

▶ **c.** sequentially prenumbering sales invoices [Correct. Designing documents so that they are sequentially prenumbered and then using them in order is a control procedure relating to both the design and the use of documents.]

d. comparing actual physical quantities with recorded amounts [Incorrect. Comparing actual quantities to recorded amounts is not a control procedure related to the design of documents.]

9. Which of the following is the correct order of the risk assessment steps discussed in this chapter?

▶ **a.** identify threats, estimate risk and exposure, identify controls, estimate costs and benefits [Correct. See Figure 10-3.]

b. identify controls, estimate risk and exposure, identify threats, estimate costs and benefits [Incorrect. See Figure 10-3.]

c. estimate risk and exposure, identify controls, identify threats, estimate costs and benefits [Incorrect. See Figure 10-3.]

d. estimate costs benefits, identify threats, identify controls, estimate risk and exposure [Incorrect. See Figure 10-3.]

10. Your current system is deemed to be 90% reliable. A major threat has been identified with an impact of $3,000,000. Two control procedures exist to deal with the threat. Implementation of control A would cost $100,000 and reduce the likelihood to 6%. Implementation of control B would cost $140,000 and reduce the likelihood to 4%. Implementation of both controls would cost $220,000 and reduce the likelihood to 2%. Given the data, and based solely on an economic analysis of costs and benefits, what should you do?

a. Implement control A only. [Incorrect. Control procedure A provides a net benefit of only $20,000, whereas control procedure B provides a net benefit of $40,000.]

▶ **b.** Implement control B only. [Correct. Control procedure B provides a net benefit of $40,000. Procedure A and the combination of A and B provide a benefit of only $20,000.]

c. Implement both controls A and B. [Incorrect. The combination of procedures A and B provides a net benefit of only $20,000, whereas control procedure B provides a net benefit of $40,000.]

d. Implement neither control. [Incorrect. Both controls provide a net benefit. Control procedure B provides a net benefit of $40,000. Procedure A and the combination of A and B each provide a net benefit of $20,000.]

Expected Loss = Impact × Likelihood ($300,000 = $3,000,000 × 10%)

Control Procedure	Likelihood	Impact	Revised Expected Loss	Reduction in Expected Loss	Cost of Control(s)	Net Benefit (Cost)
A	0.06	$3,000,000	$180,000	$120,000	$100,000	$20,000
B	0.04	$3,000,000	$120,000	$180,000	$140,000	$40,000
Both	0.02	$3,000,000	$ 60,000	$240,000	$220,000	$20,000

CHAPTER

11 Controls for Information Security

LEARNING OBJECTIVES

After studying this chapter, you should be able to:

1. Explain how security and the other four principles in the Trust Services Framework affect systems reliability.
2. Explain three fundamental concepts: why information security is a management issue, how people's behavior impacts security, and the time-based model of information security.
3. Describe the controls that can be used to protect an organization's information.
4. Describe the controls that can be used to timely detect that an organization's information system is under attack.
5. Discuss how organizations can timely respond to attacks against their information system.
6. Explain how virtualization, cloud computing, and the Internet of Things affect information security.

INTEGRATIVE CASE Northwest Industries

Jason Scott's next assignment is to review the internal controls over Northwest Industries' information systems. Jason obtains a copy of COBIT 2019 and is impressed by its thoroughness. However, he tells his friend that he feels overwhelmed in trying to use COBIT 2019 to plan his audit of Northwest Industries. His friend suggests that he examine the Trust Services Framework developed jointly by the American Institute of Certified Public Accountants (AICPA) and the Canadian Institute of Chartered Accountants (CICA) to guide auditors in assessing the reliability of an organization's information system and to perform attestation services related to cybersecurity. After reviewing the framework, Jason concludes that he can use it to guide his audit effort. He decides that he will begin by focusing on the controls designed to provide

FuzzBones/Shutterstock

reasonable assurance about information security. He writes down the following questions that will guide his investigation:

1. What controls does Northwest Industries employ to prevent unauthorized access to its accounting system?
2. How can successful and unsuccessful attempts to compromise the company's accounting system be detected in a timely manner?
3. What procedures are in place to respond to security incidents?

Introduction

Management wants assurance that the information produced by the organization's own accounting system is reliable. Management also wants assurance about the reliability of the cloud service providers with whom it contracts. Finally, management wants assurance that the organization is compliant with an ever-increasing array of regulatory and industry requirements, including Sarbanes–Oxley (SOX), the Health Insurance Portability and Accountability Act (HIPAA) and updates to it in the Health Information Technology for Economic and Clinical Health Act (HITECH), the EU's General Data Privacy Regulation (GDPR), and the Payment Card Industry Data Security Standards (PCI-DSS).

As noted in Chapter 10, COBIT 2019 is a comprehensive framework of best practices relating to all aspects of the governance and management of IT. However, in this book we focus on only those portions of COBIT 2019 that most directly pertain to the reliability of an information system and compliance with regulatory standards. Consequently, we organize this chapter and the next two around the principles in the Trust Services Framework, which was developed jointly by the AICPA and the CICA to provide guidance for assessing the reliability of information systems. Nevertheless, because COBIT 2019 is an internationally recognized framework used by many organizations, auditors and accountants need to be familiar with it. Therefore, throughout our discussion we reference the relevant sections of COBIT 2019 that relate to each topic so that you can understand how the principles that contribute to systems reliability are also essential to effectively managing an organization's investment in IT.

The Trust Services Framework organizes IT-related controls into five principles that jointly contribute to systems reliability:

1. ***Security***—access (both physical and logical) to the system and its data is controlled and restricted to legitimate users.
2. ***Confidentiality***—sensitive organizational information (e.g., marketing plans, trade secrets) is protected from unauthorized disclosure.

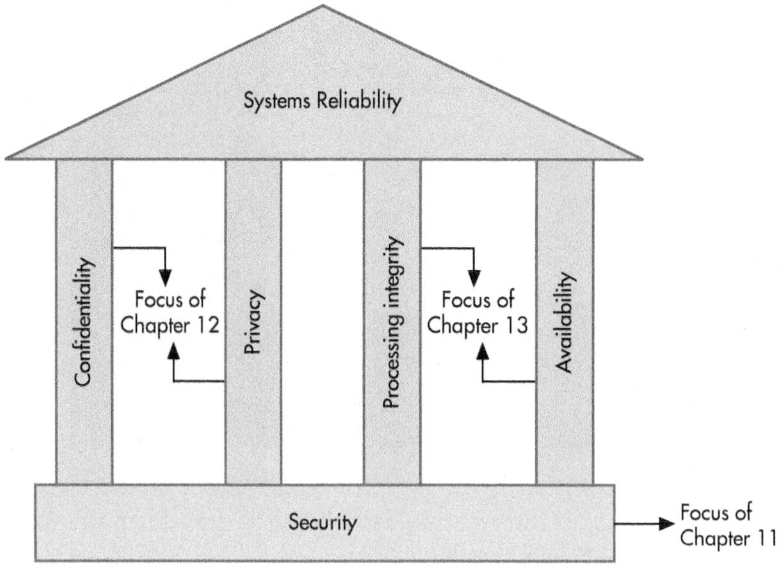

FIGURE 11-1
Relationships Among the Five Trust Services Principles for Systems Reliability

3. ***Privacy***—personal information about customers, employees, suppliers, or business partners is collected, used, disclosed, and maintained only in compliance with internal policies and external regulatory requirements and is protected from unauthorized disclosure.
4. ***Processing Integrity***—data are processed accurately, completely, in a timely manner, and only with proper authorization.
5. ***Availability***—the system and its information are available to meet operational and contractual obligations.

As Figure 11-1 shows, information security is the foundation of systems reliability and is necessary for achieving each of the other four principles. Information security procedures restrict system access to authorized users only, thereby protecting the confidentiality of sensitive organizational data and the privacy of personal information collected from customers. Information security procedures protect information integrity by preventing submission of unauthorized or fictitious transactions and preventing unauthorized changes to stored data or programs. Finally, information security procedures provide protection against a variety of attacks, including viruses and worms, thereby ensuring that the system is available when needed. This chapter focuses on information security. Chapter 12 discusses the IT controls relevant to protecting the confidentiality of an organization's intellectual property and the privacy of information it collects about its customers and business partners. Chapter 13 then covers the IT controls designed to ensure the integrity and availability of the information produced by an organization's accounting system.

Three Fundamental Information Security Concepts

1. SECURITY IS A MANAGEMENT ISSUE, NOT JUST A TECHNOLOGY ISSUE

Although effective information security requires the deployment of technological tools such as firewalls, antivirus, and encryption, senior management involvement and support throughout all phases of the security life cycle (see Figure 11-2) is absolutely essential for success. The first step in the security life cycle is to assess the information security-related threats that the organization faces and select an appropriate response. Information security professionals possess the expertise to identify potential threats and to estimate their likelihood and impact. However, senior management must choose which of the four risk responses described in Chapter 10 (reduce, accept, share, or avoid) is appropriate to adopt so that the resources invested in information security reflect the organization's risk appetite.

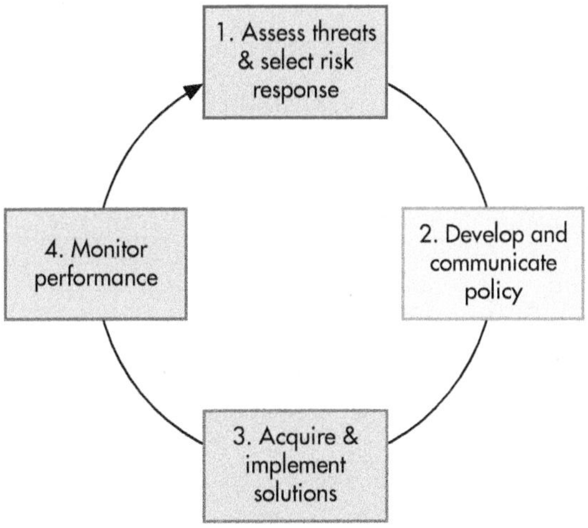

FIGURE 11-2
The Security Life Cycle

Step 2 involves developing information security policies and communicating them to all employees. Senior management must participate in developing policies because they must decide the sanctions they are willing to impose for noncompliance. In addition, the active support and involvement of top management is necessary to ensure that information security training and communication are taken seriously. To be effective, this communication must involve more than just handing people a written document or sending them an e-mail and asking them to sign an acknowledgment that they received and read the notice. Instead, employees must receive regular, periodic reminders about security policies and training on how to comply with them.

Step 3 of the security life cycle involves the acquisition or building of specific technological tools. Senior management must authorize investing the necessary resources to mitigate the threats identified and achieve the desired level of security. Finally, step 4 in the security life cycle entails regular monitoring of performance to evaluate the effectiveness of the organization's information security program. Advances in IT create new threats and alter the risks associated with old threats. Therefore, management must periodically reassess the organization's risk response and, when necessary, make changes to information security policies and invest in new solutions to ensure that the organization's information security efforts support its business strategy in a manner consistent with management's risk appetite.

Many functions play a role in implementing an organization's information security program. The information technology function is responsible for installing and maintaining the various technological solutions. The risk and compliance group must work with management to design policies to ensure compliance with various regulations about security and privacy. All employees with access to the system need to understand and comply with security policies. Information security professionals have expertise in information security and regularly monitor those solutions to be sure they function effectively as well as monitor compliance with policies. The internal audit function periodically performs an independent review of the efficiency and effectiveness of the organization's information security program.

The fact that multiple functions are involved in information security is another reason why security is an important issue for senior management. First, whenever multiple organizational functions or groups deal with a common issue, there is the possibility that a lack of effective communication will result in separate "silos" so that each function approaches their task without coordinating with the work of the other groups. A second and even more dysfunctional potential problem whenever multiple organizational functions share responsibility for a task is a lack of cooperation and "turf" battles. Only senior management's involvement can overcome these two potential problems. Focus 11-1 summarizes recent research that finds that not only does senior management involvement in and support for information security mitigate those potential problems, but it actually improves the overall effectiveness of the organization's information security program.

FOCUS 11-1 How Senior Management Can Improve the Organization's Information Security

Research indicates that top management needs to demonstrate their support for information security by exhibiting the following behaviors:

- Provide adequate resources for information security.
- Regularly communicate the importance of information security.
- Demonstrate, by their actions, that they believe information security is important.
- Adopting a proactive approach to potential security threats, instead of reacting to problems after they happen.
- Including information security issues whenever assessing the risk of any new initiative.

Doing so creates a "security-aware" organizational culture in which all employees believe information security is important. As a result, employee compliance with security policies increases. Visible top management support for information security also improves the design of internal controls, reducing the number of security-related weaknesses.

But perhaps the most important result of top management support for information security is that it improves the relationship between the information security and internal audit functions, reducing "turf" battles between the functions and increasing the sharing of information between them. This is important because a better relationship between those two functions improves security in a number of ways, including:

1. Increased detection of attacks *before* they cause material harm to the organization. This is the ultimate objective of security.
2. More timely detection of attacks after they have caused harm. This is important because you cannot "stop the bleeding" until you know you have a cut. The magnitude of the damage caused by many of the major security breaches in recent years is partly because the affected organizations did not even know they had been attacked for months or even years.
3. Improved ability to detect serious issues involving employee noncompliance with security policies. Security policies are designed to reduce risk; conversely, noncompliance with those policies increases the risk that employee action (or inaction) will result in a security incident. More timely detection of noncompliance enables managers to take countermeasures and better enforce compliance with policies.
4. Improved ability to detect security-related material internal control weaknesses. Such weaknesses represent vulnerabilities that attackers can exploit. More timely detection enables organizations to remedy those vulnerabilities.

Source: Steinbart, P. J., R. L. Raschke, G. Gal, & W. N. Dilla. 2018. "The Influence of a good relationship between the internal audit and information security functions on information security outcomes," *Accounting, Organizations and Society* 71: pp. 15–29.

2. PEOPLE: THE CRITICAL FACTOR

People can either be the "weakest link" in security or an important asset. To make employees a positive part of the organization's security efforts, management must create a "security-conscious" culture and provide continuous security awareness training. The discussion of the COSO framework in Chapter 10 stressed how top management's risk attitudes and behaviors create either an internal environment that supports and reinforces sound internal control or one that effectively negates written control policies. The same principle holds regarding information security. Indeed, both COBIT 2019 and the Trust Services Framework specifically identify an organization's culture and ethics as one of the critical enablers for effective information security. To create a security-conscious culture in which employees comply with organizational policies, top management must not only communicate the organization's security policies, but must also lead by example. Employees are more likely to comply with information security policies when they see their managers do so. Conversely, if employees observe managers violating an information security policy, for example by writing down a password and affixing it to a monitor, they are likely to imitate that behavior.

Employee skills and competencies are another critical enabler for effective information security. Employees must understand how to follow the organization's security policies. The importance of training is reflected in the fact that security awareness training is discussed as a key practice to support several of COBIT 2019's 35 management processes. It is especially important to train new employees because criminals often target newly hired employees with sophisticated phishing emails.

All employees should be taught *why* security measures are important to the organization's long-run survival. They also need to be trained to follow safe computing practices, such as never opening unsolicited e-mail attachments, using only approved software, not sharing passwords, and taking steps to physically protect laptops. Training is especially needed to educate employees about social engineering attacks. For example, employees should be taught never to divulge passwords or other information about their accounts or their workstation configurations to anyone who contacts them by telephone, e-mail, or instant messaging and claims to be part of the organization's information systems security function. Employees also need to be trained not to allow other people to follow them through restricted access entrances. This social engineering attack, called *piggybacking*, can take place not only at the main entrance to the building but also at any internal locked doors, especially to rooms that contain computer equipment. Piggybacking may be attempted not only by outsiders but also by other employees who are not authorized to enter a particular area. Piggybacking often succeeds because many people feel it is rude to not let another person come through the door with them or because they want to avoid confrontations. Role-playing exercises are particularly effective for increasing sensitivity to and skills for dealing with social engineering attacks.

Security awareness training is also important for senior management because in recent years many social engineering attacks, such as spear phishing, have been targeted at them. Thus far, the discussion of training has focused on the protection component of the time-based model of security by teaching employees and managers how to prevent problems. But training can also improve both timely detection and response if both employees and managers are trained not only to avoid certain behaviors, but also to promptly notify information security whenever they receive suspicious emails or other forms of social engineering.

However, an organization's investment in security training will be effective only if management clearly demonstrates that it supports employees who follow prescribed security policies. This is especially important for combating social engineering attacks because countermeasures may sometimes create embarrassing confrontations with other employees. For example, one of the authors heard an anecdote about a systems professional at a major bank who refused to allow a person who was not on the list of authorized employees to enter the room housing the servers that contained the bank's key financial information. The person denied entry happened to be a new executive who was just hired. Instead of reprimanding the employee, the executive demonstrated the bank's commitment to and support for strong security by writing a formal letter of commendation for meritorious performance to be placed in the employee's performance file. It is this type of visible top management support for security that enhances the effectiveness of all security policies. Top management also needs to support the enforcement of penalties, up to and including dismissal, against employees who willfully violate security policies. Doing so not only sends a strong message to other employees but also may sometimes lessen the consequences to the organization if an employee engages in illegal behavior. Training of information security professionals is also important. New developments in technology continuously create new security threats and make old solutions obsolete. Therefore, it is important for organizations to support continuing professional education for their security specialists.

3. THE TIME-BASED MODEL OF INFORMATION SECURITY

The goal of the **time-based model of information security** is to employ a combination of preventive, detective, and corrective controls to protect information assets long enough for an organization to detect that an attack is occurring and to take timely steps to thwart the attack before any information is lost or compromised. The time-based model of information security can be expressed in the following formula:

time-based model of information security - Implementing a combination of preventive, detective, and corrective controls that protect information assets long enough to enable an organization to recognize that an attack is occurring and take steps to thwart it before any information is lost or compromised.

$$P > D + R, \text{ where}$$

P = the time it takes an attacker to break through the various controls that protect the organization's information assets.
D = the time it takes for the organization to detect that an attack is in progress.
R = the time it takes to respond to and stop the attack.

If the equation is satisfied (i.e., if $P > D + R$ is true), then the organization's information security procedures are effective. Otherwise, security is ineffective.

defense-in-depth - Employing multiple layers of controls to avoid a single point-of-failure.

Organizations attempt to satisfy the objective of the time-based model of security by employing the strategy of **defense-in-depth**, which entails using multiple layers of controls in order to avoid having a single point of failure. Defense-in-depth recognizes that although no control can be 100% effective, the use of overlapping, complementary, and redundant controls increases overall effectiveness because if one control fails or gets circumvented, another may succeed.

The time-based model of security provides a means for management to identify the most cost-effective approach to improving security by comparing the effects of additional investments in preventive, detective, or corrective controls. For example, management may be considering the investment of an additional $100,000 to enhance security. One option might be the purchase of a new firewall that would increase the value of P by 10 minutes. A second option might be to upgrade the organization's intrusion detection system in a manner that would decrease the value of D by 12 minutes. A third option might be to invest in new methods for responding to information security incidents so as to decrease the value of R by 30 minutes. In this example, the most cost-effective choice would be to invest in additional corrective controls that enable the organization to respond to attacks more quickly.

Although the time-based model of security provides a sound theoretical basis for evaluating and managing an organization's information security practices, it should not be viewed as a precise mathematical formula. One problem is that it is hard, if not impossible, to derive accurate, reliable measures of the parameters P, D, and R. In addition, even when those parameter values can be reliably calculated, new IT developments can quickly diminish their validity. For example, discovery of a major new vulnerability can effectively reduce the value of P to zero. Consequently, the time-based model of security is best used as a high-level framework for strategic analysis, to clearly illustrate the principle of defense-in-depth and the need to employ multiple preventive, detective, and corrective controls.

Table 11-1 lists the various preventive, detective, and corrective controls organizations can use to satisfy the time-based model of security. As Figure 11-3 shows, the various controls fit together like pieces in a puzzle to collectively provide defense-in-depth. Notice that each piece of the puzzle is held by a person, reflecting the fact that the overall effectiveness of an organization's security program depends on its employees and management.

TABLE 11-1 Preventive, Detective, and Corrective Controls Used to Satisfy the Time-Based Model of Security

Time-Based Model Component	Examples
Protection	• Physical security: access controls (locks, guards, etc.) • Process: User access controls (authentication and authorization) • IT solutions ○ Anti-malware ○ Network access controls (firewalls, intrusion prevention systems, etc.) ○ Device and software hardening (configuration controls) ○ Encryption
Detection	• Log analysis • Intrusion detection systems • Honeypots • Continuous monitoring
Response	• Computer incident response teams (CIRT) • Chief information security officer (CISO)

FIGURE 11-3
Pieces of the Security Puzzle

Protecting Information Resources

PHYSICAL SECURITY: ACCESS CONTROLS

It is absolutely essential to control physical access to information resources. A skilled attacker needs only a few minutes of unsupervised direct physical access in order to bypass existing information security controls. For example, an attacker with unsupervised direct physical access can install a keystroke logging device that captures a user's authentication credentials, thereby enabling the attacker to subsequently obtain unauthorized access to the system by impersonating a legitimate user. Someone with unsupervised physical access could also insert special "boot" disks that provide direct access to every file on the computer and then copy sensitive files to a portable device such as a USB drive or an iPod. Alternatively, an attacker with unsupervised physical access could simply remove the hard drive or even steal the entire computer. We now describe several of the most important physical access controls discussed in COBIT 2019 management practice DSS05.05.

Physical access control begins with entry points to the building itself. Ideally, there should only be one regular entry point that remains unlocked during normal office hours. Fire codes usually require additional emergency exits, but these should not permit entry from the outside and should be connected to an alarm system that is automatically triggered whenever the fire exit is opened. In addition, either a receptionist or a security guard should be stationed at the main entrance to verify the identity of employees. Visitors should be required to sign in and be escorted by an employee wherever they go in the building.

Once inside the building, physical access to rooms housing computer equipment must also be restricted. These rooms should be securely locked and all entry/exit monitored by closed-circuit television systems. Multiple failed access attempts should trigger an alarm. Rooms housing servers that contain especially sensitive data should supplement regular locks with stronger technologies—card readers, numeric keypads, or various biometric devices, such as iris or retina scanners, fingerprint readers, or voice recognition. Focus 11-2 describes an especially elaborate set of physical access controls referred to as a *man-trap*.

Access to the wiring used in the organization's LANs also needs to be restricted in order to prevent wiretapping. That means that cables and wiring should not be exposed in areas accessible to casual visitors. Wiring closets containing telecommunications equipment need to be securely locked. If wiring closets are shared with other tenants of an office building, the organization should place its telecommunications equipment inside locked steel cages to prevent unauthorized physical access by anyone else with access to that wiring closet. Wall jacks not in current use should be physically disconnected from the network to prevent someone from just plugging in their laptop and attempting to access the network.

FOCUS 11-2 Controlling Physical Access with Man-Traps

Financial institutions, defense contractors, and various intelligence agencies store especially valuable data. Therefore, they often need to employ much more elaborate physical access control measures to their data centers than those used by most other organizations. One such technique involves the use of specially designed rooms called man-traps. These rooms typically contain two doors, each of which uses multiple authentication methods to control access. For example, entry to the first door may require that the person both insert an ID card or smart card into a reader and enter an identification code into a keypad. Successful authentication opens the first door and provides access to the entrance room. Once inside the room, the first door automatically closes behind the person, locks, and cannot be opened from inside the room. The other door, which opens into the data center, is also locked. Thus, the person is now trapped in this small room (hence the name *man-trap*). The only way out is to successfully pass a second set of authentication controls that restrict access through the door leading to the data center. Typically, this involves multifactor authentication that includes a biometric credential. Failure to pass this second set of tests leaves the person in the room until members of the security staff arrive.

Laptops, cell phones, and tablets require special attention to their physical security because they frequently store sensitive information and are so easily lost or stolen. The major cost is not the price of replacing the device, but rather the loss of the confidential information it contains and the costs of notifying those affected. Often, companies also have to pay for credit-monitoring services for customers whose personal information was lost or stolen. There may even be class action lawsuits and fines by regulatory agencies.

Ideally, employees should not store any sensitive information on laptops or other personal devices. If sensitive organizational information must be stored on a laptop or other portable device, it should be encrypted so that if the device is lost or stolen the information will be inaccessible. To deal with the threat of laptop theft, employees should be trained to always lock their laptops to an immovable object. This is necessary even when in the office, as there have been cases where thieves disguised as cleaning crews have stolen laptops and other equipment during working hours. Some organizations also install special software on laptops and other mobile devices that sends a message to a security server whenever the device connects to the Internet. Then, if the device is lost or stolen, its location can be identified the next time it is connected to the Internet. The security server can also send a reply message that permanently erases all information stored on the device.

It is also important to restrict physical access to network printers because they often store document images on their hard drives. There have been cases where intruders have stolen the hard drives in those printers, thereby gaining access to sensitive information.

Finally, an especially promising way to achieve defense-in-depth is to integrate physical and remote access control systems. For example, if an organization uses keypads, card or badge readers, or biometric identifiers to control and log physical access to the office, that data should be used when applying remote access controls. This would identify situations likely to represent security breaches, such as when an employee who supposedly is inside the office is simultaneously trying to log into the system remotely from another geographically distant location.

PROCESS: USER ACCESS CONTROLS

It is important to understand that "outsiders" are not the only threat source. An employee may become disgruntled for any number of reasons (e.g., being passed over for a promotion) and seek revenge, or may be vulnerable to being corrupted because of financial difficulties, or may be blackmailed into providing sensitive information. Therefore, organizations need to implement a set of controls designed to protect their information assets from unauthorized use and access by employees. To accomplish that objective, COBIT 2019 management practice DSS05.04 stresses the need for controls to manage user identity and logical access so that it is possible to uniquely identify everyone who accesses the organization's information system and track the actions that they perform. Implementing DSS05.04 involves the use of two related but distinct types of user access controls: authentication controls and authorization controls.

AUTHENTICATION CONTROLS **Authentication** is the process of verifying the identity of the person or device attempting to access the system. The objective is to ensure that only legitimate users can access the system.

authentication - Verifying the identity of the person or device attempting to access the system.

Three types of credentials can be used to verify a person's identity:

1. Something the person knows, such as passwords or personal identification numbers (PINs).
2. Something the person has, such as smart cards or ID badges.
3. Some physical or behavioral characteristic (referred to as a **biometric identifier**) of the person, such as fingerprints or typing patterns.

biometric identifier - A physical or behavioral characteristic used as an authentication credential.

Individually, each authentication method has its limitations. Passwords can be guessed, lost, written down, or given away. Physical identification techniques (cards, badges, USB devices, etc.) can be lost, stolen, or duplicated. Biometric techniques are not 100% accurate, sometimes rejecting legitimate users (called the false rejection rate) and sometimes allowing access to unauthorized people (called the false acceptance rate). These problems occur because biometric authentication systems use only a sample of data points from the characteristic. For example, instead of storing a complete fingerprint, the system merely records the presence or absence of a feature at a number of data points, resulting in a string of binary digits where a 1 indicates that a feature exists and a 0 indicates that it does not. It then compares that string of binary digits to the sample stored when the person enrolled in the system and created their biometric credential. Because the system uses a sample, acceptance or rejection is based on whether the biometric data collected when attempting to log in exceeds the threshold percentage match set by the organization. Consequently, if the person does not use the same amount of pressure when attempting to use a fingerprint scanner to log in or has changed their hairstyle or has a cold, the resulting biometric sample may not sufficiently match what was stored and the person will be falsely rejected. That is why many devices use a PIN as an alternative way to authenticate in case the biometric fails. Conversely, someone with sufficiently similar characteristics (e.g., an identical twin) might "fool" the system and be improperly granted access (a false acceptance).

There are also security concerns about storage of the biometric information itself. Biometric templates, such as the digital representation of an individual's fingerprints or voice, must be stored somewhere. The compromising of those templates would create serious, life-long problems for the donor because biometric characteristics, unlike passwords or physical tokens, cannot be replaced or changed. In addition, many biometric credentials cannot be used by everybody. For example, people with cerebral palsy or multiple sclerosis cannot use fingerprint scanners, and some religions may not agree to the use of facial identification systems. Consequently, to avoid potential legal issues arising from discrimination against specific groups, organizations that wish to use biometrics must employ multiple alternative biometrics, which adds cost and the complexity associated with integrating and managing multiple systems.

Although none of the three basic authentication credentials, by itself, is foolproof, the use of two or all three types in conjunction, a process referred to as **multifactor authentication**, is quite effective. For example, requiring a user both to insert a smart card in a card reader and enter a password provides much stronger authentication than using either method alone. In some situations, using multiple credentials of the same type, a process referred to as **multimodal authentication**, can also improve security. For example, many online banking sites use several things that a person knows (password, user ID, and recognition of a graphic image) for authentication. Similarly, because most laptops now are equipped with a camera and a microphone, plus a fingerprint reader, it is possible to employ multimodal biometric authentication involving a combination of face, voice, and fingerprint recognition to verify identity.

multifactor authentication - The use of two or more *types* of authentication credentials in conjunction to achieve a greater level of security.

multimodal authentication - The use of multiple authentication credentials of the *same type* to achieve a greater level of security.

Both multifactor authentication and multimodal authentication are examples of applying the principle of defense-in-depth. However, multifactor authentication is better than multimodal because the credentials are independent of one another. Therefore, compromising one credential does not affect the probability of successfully compromising another. For example, compromising someone's password does not affect the likelihood of stealing their smart card. In contrast, compromising someone's password may make it easier to obtain the answers to any security questions because the person may have used the same password for their social media accounts.

Passwords are likely to continue to be used as part of the authentication process because they can be entered on any type of device. Indeed, in some situations, such as public kiosks, they may be the only type of credential that can be easily used. Therefore, Focus 11-3 discusses the principles that determine the strength of passwords as an authentication credential.

FOCUS 11-3 Effectiveness of Passwords as Authentication Credentials

The effectiveness of using passwords as authentication credentials depends upon several factors:

- **Length.** The single most important factor affecting the strength of a password is its length. The longer, the better. The reason length is so important is that the number of possibilities that must be "guessed" by an attacker equals c^L, where c = the number of possible characters (digits, letters, etc.) that can be used in each position in the password and L = the length of the password. To understand the effect of doubling the number of character types versus doubling its length, consider the PIN used for an ATM. Typically, the PIN is 4 digits long, which means that there are 10^4 (10,000) possible PINs. If instead of numbers, each character was a letter, thereby more than doubling the number of choices for each position (26 versus 10), there would be 26^4 (456,976) possible PINs. In contrast, continuing to use only digits but doubling the length of the PIN to 8 digits results in 10^8 (100,000,000) possible PINs.
- **Multiple character types.** Using a mixture of upper- and lowercase alphabetic, numeric, and special characters increases the strength of the password.
- **Randomness.** Passwords should not be easily guessed. Therefore, they should not be words found in dictionaries. Nor should they be words with either a preceding or following numeric character (such as 3Diamond or Diamond3). They must also not be related to the employee's personal interests or hobbies; special-purpose password-cracking dictionaries that contain the most common passwords related to various topics are available on the Internet. For example, the password Ncc1701 appears, at first glance, to fit the requirements of a strong password because it contains a mixture of upper- and lowercase characters and numbers. But *Star Trek* fans will instantly recognize it as the designation of the starship *Enterprise*. Consequently, Ncc1701 and many variations on it (changing which letters are capitalized, replacing the number 1 with the ! symbol, etc.) are included in most password-cracking dictionaries and, therefore, are quickly compromised.
- **Kept secret.** Passwords must be kept secret to be effective. However, a problem with strong passwords, such as dX%m8K#2, is that they are not easy to remember. Consequently, when following the requirements for creating strong passwords, people tend to write those passwords down. This weakens the value of the password by changing it from something they know to something they have—which can then be stolen and used by anyone.

Finally, organizations should consider the "usability" of their password policies and login software. For example, requiring long passwords or passphrases may increase the rate of login failures due to "typos," which may tempt employees to adopt undesirable solutions like having their browser "remember" their credentials. However, most people are reasonably accurate typists when using word processing applications. The problem with long passphrases arises because people are not used to typing 15- or 20-character phrases that do not permit punctuation. Therefore, permitting the use of spaces between words may be a way to increase the strength of login credentials by encouraging the use of long passphrases, without the frustration of increasing the rate of login failures.

Similarly, it is difficult to create strong credentials that are easy to remember. Consequently, requiring people to frequently change their passwords or passphrases means that people often adopt undesirable behaviors like adding a number at the beginning or end of a strong password and then only changing that number each time they have to change their credential, or using the same password on multiple systems. In recognition of this problem, more recent guidance suggests that organizations should only require employees to change passwords after a breach, instead of on a fixed schedule (e.g., every 6 months).

One promising way to improve the usability of passwords is through a process called single sign on, whereby a person enters their credential only once and the system automatically remembers and reuses it to access different subsystems and programs. However, this ease of use also creates a single point of failure and makes the creation of strong (i.e., long) passwords or passphrases even more important.

It is important to authenticate not only people but also every device attempting to connect to the network. Every workstation, printer, or other computing device needs a network interface card (NIC) to connect to the organization's internal network. Each NIC has a unique identifier, referred to as its media access control (MAC) address. Therefore, an organization can restrict network access to only corporate-owned devices by comparing the device's MAC to a list of recognized MAC addresses. However, software can be used to change a device's MAC address, thereby enabling malicious users to "spoof" their device's identity. A stronger way to authenticate devices involves the use of digital certificates that employ encryption techniques to assign unique identifiers to each device. Digital certificates and encryption are discussed in Chapter 12.

AUTHORIZATION CONTROLS **Authorization** is the process of restricting access of authenticated users to specific portions of the system and limiting what actions they are permitted to perform. As COBIT 2019 management practice DSS06.03 explains, the objective is to structure an individual employee's rights and privileges in a manner that establishes and maintains adequate segregation of duties. For example, a customer service representative should not be authorized to access the payroll system. In addition, customer service representatives should be permitted only to read, but not to change, the prices of inventory items.

authorization - The process of restricting access of authenticated users to specific portions of the system and limiting what actions they are permitted to perform.

Authorization controls are often implemented by creating an **access control matrix** (Figure 11-4). When an authenticated employee attempts to access a particular information systems resource, the system performs a **compatibility test** that matches the user's authentication credentials against the access control matrix to determine whether that employee should be allowed to access that resource and perform the requested action. It is important to regularly update the access control matrix to reflect changes in job duties due to promotions or transfers. Otherwise, over time an employee may accumulate a set of rights and privileges incompatible with proper segregation of duties.

access control matrix - A table used to implement authorization controls (see Figure 11-4).

compatibility test - Matching the user's authentication credentials against the access control matrix to determine whether that employee should be allowed to access that resource and perform the requested action.

Figure 11-5 shows how the information contained in an access control matrix is used to implement authorization controls in an ERP system. The upper portion of the screenshot shows that for each employee role, the system provides a number of predefined combinations of permissions to enforce common access restrictions. For example, the first entry (Employee Restrictions) opens a dialog box asking whether employees in this role can view records for other employees (appropriate for managers) or only their own. The lower portion of the screenshot shows that controls can be designed for each specific activity performed by this employee role. Clicking on the word "Edit" to the right of a specific activity brings up another screen where specific permissions (read, edit, create, delete) can be assigned to specific subsets of records and even to fields within those records.

It is possible to achieve even greater control and segregation of duties by using business process management systems to embed authorization into automated business processes, rather than relying on a static access control matrix. For example, authorization can be granted only to perform a specific task for a specific transaction. Thus, a particular employee may be permitted to access credit information about the customer who is currently requesting service, but simultaneously prevented from "browsing" through the rest of the customer

User	Files			Programs			
User ID	A	B	C	1	2	3	4
NHale	0	0	1	0	0	0	0
JPJones	0	2	0	0	0	0	1
BArnold	1	1	0	1	1	0	0
....	....	....	....	....	....	....	....

Codes for File Access:
0 = No access
1 = Read/display only
2 = Read/display and update
3 = Read/display, update, create, and delete

Codes for Program Access:
0 = No access
1 = Execute

FIGURE 11-4
Example of an Access Control Matrix

FIGURE 11-5
Implementing Authorization Controls in an ERP System

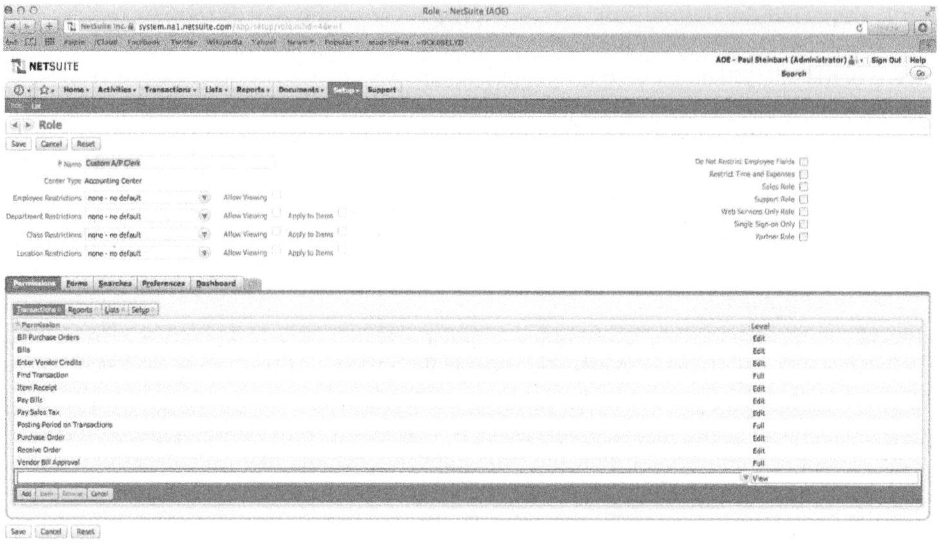

Source: 2010 © NetSuite Inc.

file. In addition, business process management systems enforce segregation of duties because employees can perform only the specific tasks that the system has assigned them. Employees cannot delete tasks from their assigned task list, and the system sends reminder messages until the task is completed—two more measures that further enhance control. Business process management software also can instantly route transactions that require specific authorization (such as a credit sale above a certain amount) electronically to a manager for approval. The transaction cannot continue until authorization is granted, but because the need for such approval is indicated and granted or denied electronically, this important control is enforced without sacrificing efficiency.

Like authentication controls, authorization controls can and should be applied not only to people but also to devices. For example, including MAC addresses or digital certificates in the access control matrix makes it possible to restrict access to the payroll system and payroll master files to only payroll department employees and only when they log in from their desktop or assigned laptop computer. After all, why would a payroll clerk need to log in from a workstation located in the warehouse or attempt to establish dial-in access from another country? Applying authentication and authorization controls to both humans and devices is another way in which defense-in-depth increases security.

IT SOLUTIONS: ANTIMALWARE CONTROLS

Malware (e.g., viruses, worms, keystroke logging software, etc.) is a major threat. Malware can damage or destroy information or provide a means for unauthorized access. Therefore, COBIT 2019 section DSS05.01 lists malware protection as one of the keys to effective security, specifically recommending the following:

1. Malicious software awareness education.
2. Installation of antimalware protection tools on all devices.
3. Centralized management of patches and updates to antimalware software.
4. Regular review of new malware threats.
5. Filtering of incoming traffic to block potential sources of malware.
6. Training employees not to install unapproved software.

IT SOLUTIONS: NETWORK ACCESS CONTROLS

Most organizations provide employees, customers, and suppliers with remote access to their information systems. Usually this access occurs via the Internet, but some organizations still maintain their own proprietary networks or provide direct dial-up access by modem. Many organizations also provide wireless access to their systems. We now discuss the various methods that can be used to satisfy COBIT 2019 management practice DSS05.02, which addresses security of the organization's network and all means of connecting to it.

PERIMETER DEFENSE: ROUTERS, FIREWALLS, AND INTRUSION PREVENTION SYSTEMS Figure 11-6 shows the relationship between an organization's information system and the Internet. A device called a **border router** connects an organization's information system to the Internet. Behind the border router is the main **firewall**, which can be either a special-purpose hardware device or software running on a general-purpose computer, that controls both inbound and outbound communication between the system behind the firewall and other networks. The **demilitarized zone (DMZ)** is a separate network located outside the organization's internal information system that permits controlled access from the Internet to selected resources, such as the organization's e-commerce web server. Together, the border router and firewall act as filters to control which information is allowed to enter and leave the organization's information system. To understand how they function, it is first necessary to briefly discuss how information is transmitted on the Internet.

border router - A device that connects an organization's information system to the Internet.

firewall - A special-purpose hardware device or software running a general-purpose computer that controls both inbound and outbound communication between the system behind the firewall and other networks.

demilitarized zone (DMZ) - A separate network located outside the organization's internal information system that permits controlled access from the Internet.

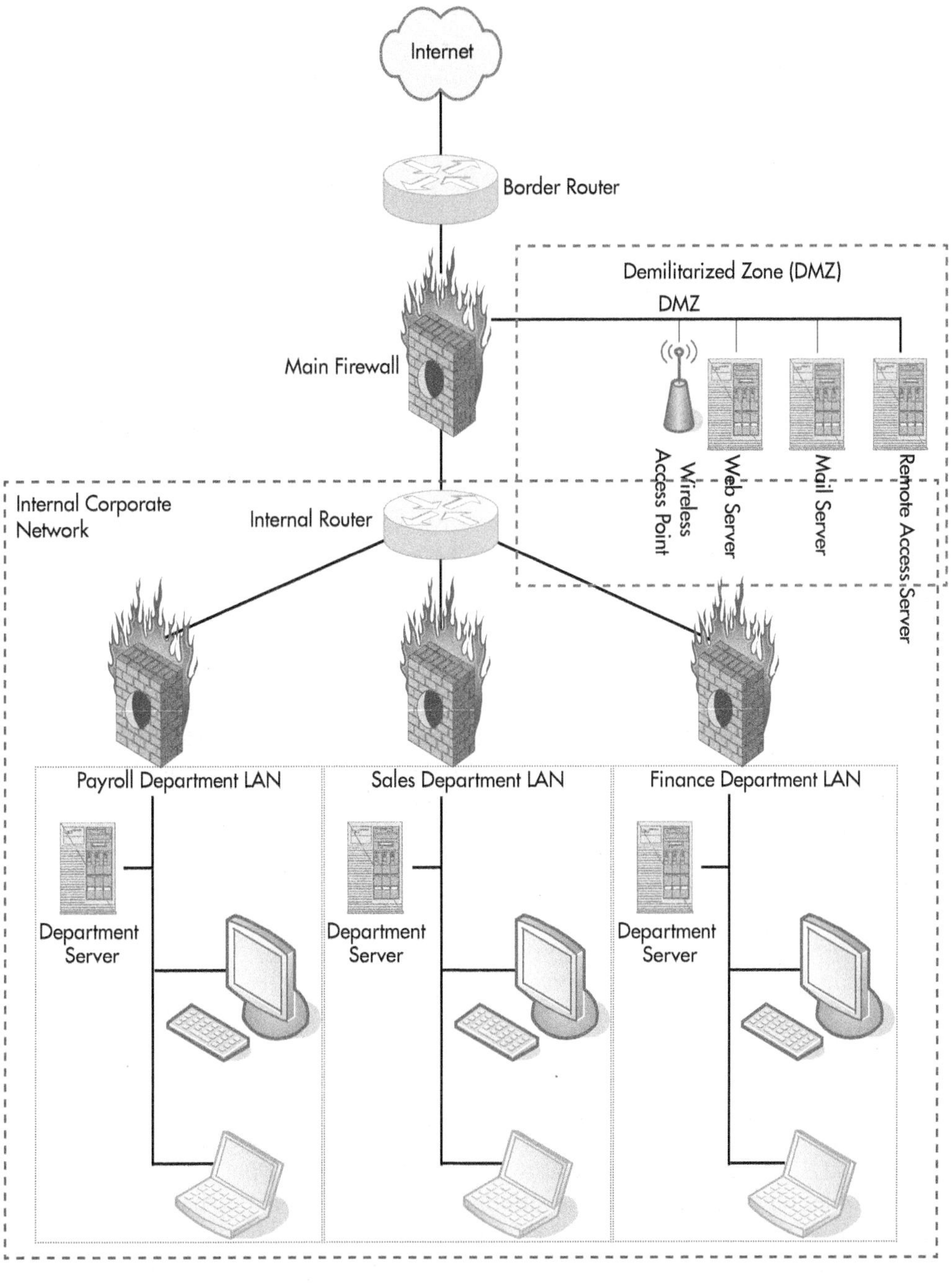

FIGURE 11-6
Example Organizational Network Architecture

FIGURE 11-7
How Files Are Broken into Packets to Be Sent over Networks and then Reassembled by the Receiving Device

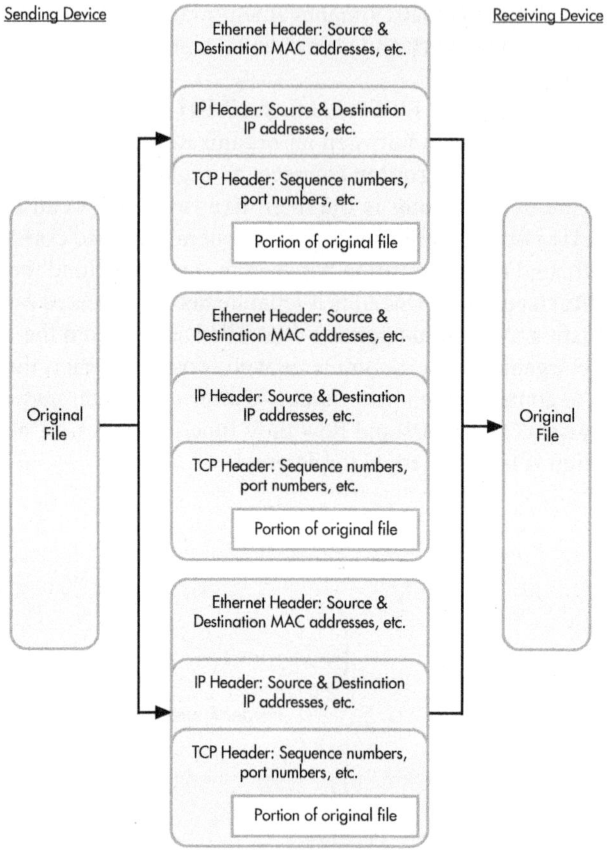

Figure 11-7 shows that when you send a file (document, spreadsheet, database, etc.) to another person or to a printer, the entire file seldom is transmitted intact. In most cases, it is broken up into a series of small pieces that are individually sent and reassembled upon delivery. The reason this happens is that almost every local area network uses the Ethernet protocol, which is designed to transmit information in packets with a maximum size of about 1,440 bytes (1.4 kB). Most files, however, are much larger and therefore are divided into thousands of packets. Each packet must be properly labeled so that the entire file can be correctly reassembled at the destination. The information to accomplish that is contained in the Transmission Control Protocol (TCP), Internet Protocol (IP), and Ethernet headers. The TCP header contains fields that specify the sequential position of that packet in relation to the entire file and the port numbers (addresses) on the sending and receiving devices from which the file originates and where it is to be reassembled. The IP header contains fields that specify the network address (IP address) of the sending and receiving devices. **Routers** are special-purpose devices designed to read the source and destination address fields in IP packet headers to decide where to send (route) the packet next. The Ethernet header contains the MAC addresses of the sending and receiving device, which is used to control the flow of traffic on the local area network (LAN).

routers - Special purpose devices designed to read the source and destination address fields in IP packet headers to decide where to send (route) the packet next.

Controlling Access by Filtering Packets. Routers and firewalls control access by filtering individual packets. Organizations own one or more border routers that connect their internal networks to the Internet Service Provider. Those border routers and the organization's main firewall use sets of IF-THEN rules, called **access control lists (ACLs)**, to determine what to do with arriving packets.

access control lists (ACLs) - Sets of IF-THEN rules used to determine what to do with arriving packets.

Figure 11-8 is a screenshot from a tool called Wireshark and shows what packets look like. The IF-THEN rules in an ACL refer to the contents of specific fields in the packet headers. The border router must examine the destination IP address field in the IP packet header to determine whether the packet is intended for the organization or should be forwarded back out onto the Internet. If the packet's destination IP address is the organization, the rules in the border router's ACL examine the source address field in the IP packet header to block packets from specific undesirable sources (e.g., known gambling or porn sites). All other packets with the organization's IP address in the destination field are passed to the main firewall for further screening. The rules in the organization's main firewall's ACL look at other fields in the IP and TCP packet headers to determine whether to block the incoming packet or permit it to enter. Note, however, that firewalls do not block *all* traffic, but only filter it. That is why all the firewalls in Figure 11-6 have holes in them—to show that certain kinds of traffic can pass through.

The process described in the previous paragraph of examining various fields in a packet's IP and TCP headers to decide what to do with the packet is referred to as **packet filtering**. Packet filtering is fast and can catch patently undesirable traffic, but its effectiveness is limited. Undesirable traffic can get through if the source IP address is not on the list of unacceptable sources or if the sender purposely disguises the true source address. Thus, just as censorship of physical mail is more effective if each envelope or package is opened and inspected, control over network traffic is more effective if firewalls examine the actual data (i.e., the portion of the file contained in the TCP packet), a process referred to as **deep packet inspection**. For example, web application firewalls use deep packet inspection to better protect an organization's e-commerce web server by examining the contents of incoming packets to permit requests for data using the HTML "get" command, but block attempts to use the HTML "put" command

packet filtering - A process that uses various fields in a packet's IP and TCP headers to decide what to do with the packet.

deep packet inspection - A process that examines the data in the body of a TCP packet to control traffic, rather than looking only at the information in the IP and TCP headers.

FIGURE 11-8

Screenshot from Wireshark Depicting Packet Structure

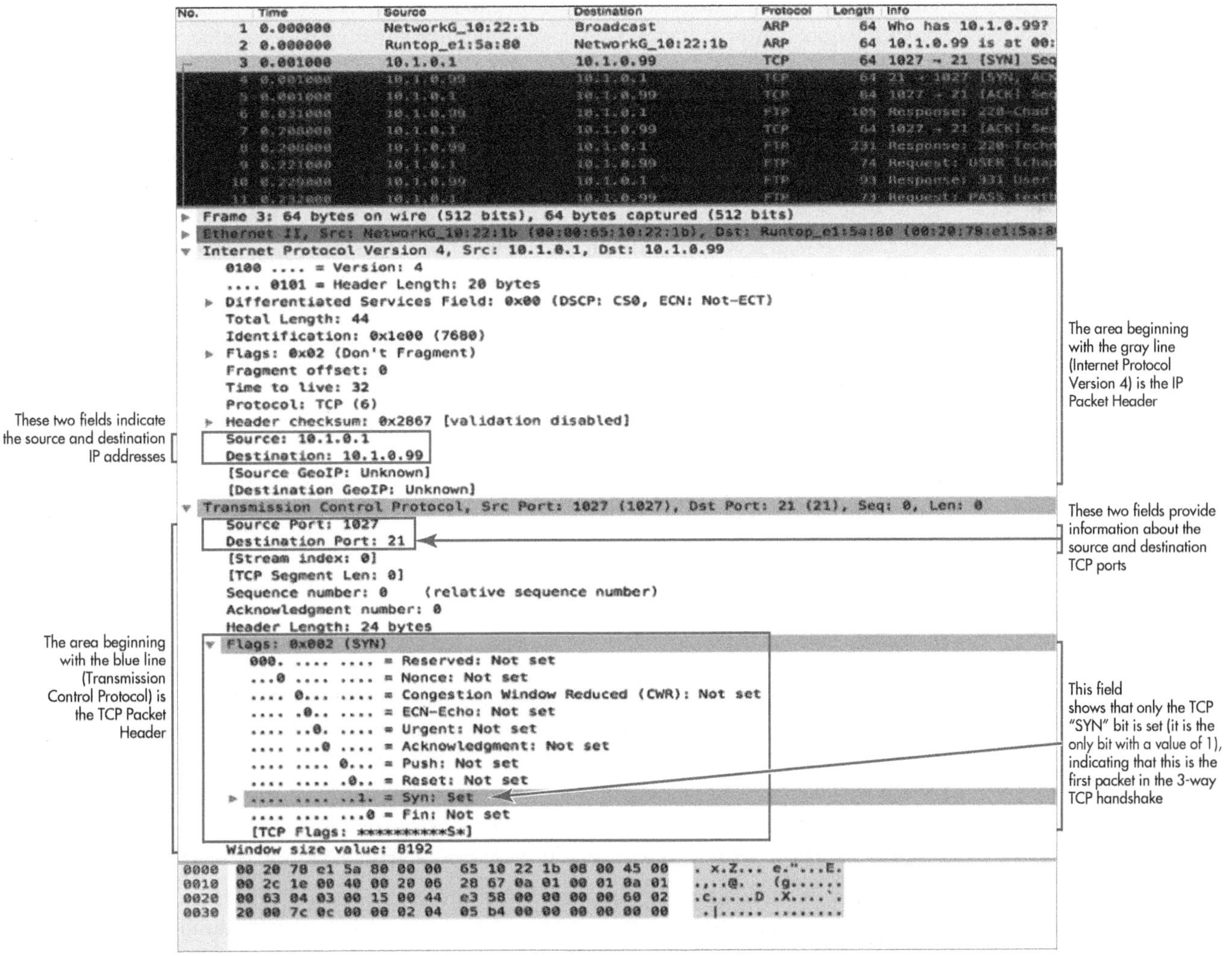

that could be used to deface the website. The added control provided by deep packet inspection, however, comes at the cost of speed: It takes more time to examine the up to 1.4 kB of data in a packet than just the 40 or so bytes in the IP and TCP headers. Therefore, only firewalls perform deep packet inspection; routers do not.

intrusion prevention systems (IPS) - Software or hardware that monitors patterns in the traffic flow to identify and automatically block attacks.

Whereas routers and firewalls examine individual packets, network **intrusion prevention systems (IPS)** monitor *patterns* in the traffic flow to identify and automatically block attacks. This is important because examining a pattern of traffic is often the only way to identify undesirable activity. For example, a web application firewall performing deep packet inspection would permit incoming packets that contained allowable HTML commands to connect to TCP ports 80 and 443 on the organization's e-commerce web server, but would block all incoming packets to other TCP ports on the web server. The firewall's actions are limited to protecting the web server. A network IPS, in contrast, could identify that a sequence of packets attempting to connect to various TCP ports on the e-commerce web server is an indicator of an attempt to scan and map the web server (step 3 in the process of a targeted attack as discussed in Chapter 6). The IPS would not only block the offending packets, but also would block all subsequent traffic coming from that source and notify a security administrator that an attempted scan was in progress. Thus, IPSs provide the opportunity for real-time response to attacks.

A network IPS consists of a set of sensors and a central monitor unit that analyzes the data collected. Sensors must be installed on each network segment over which real-time monitoring is desired. For example, given the network architecture depicted in Figure 11-6, the organization might place IPS sensors on the DMZ, behind the main firewall, and behind each of the firewalls used to segment portions of the internal network.

IPSs use two primary techniques to identify undesirable traffic patterns. The simplest approach is to compare traffic patterns to a database of signatures of known attacks. A more sophisticated approach involves developing a profile of "normal" traffic and using statistical analysis to identify packets that do not fit that profile. The beauty of this approach is that it blocks not only known attacks, for which signatures already exist, but also new attacks.

Using Defense-in-Depth to Restrict Network Access. The use of multiple perimeter filtering devices is more efficient and effective than relying on only one device. Thus, most organizations use border routers to quickly filter out obviously bad packets and pass the rest to the main firewall. The main firewall does more detailed checking, and then other firewalls perform deep packet inspection to more fully protect specific devices such as the organization's web server and e-mail server. In addition, an IPS monitors the traffic passed by the firewalls to identify and block suspicious network traffic patterns that may indicate that an attack is in progress.

Figure 11-6 illustrates one other dimension of the concept of defense-in-depth: the use of multiple internal firewalls to segment different departments within the organization. Recall that many security incidents involve employees, not outsiders. Internal firewalls help to restrict what data and portions of the organization's information system particular employees can access. This not only increases security but also strengthens internal control by providing a means for enforcing segregation of duties.

SECURING WIRELESS ACCESS Wireless access is convenient and easy, but it also provides another venue for attack and extends the perimeter that must be protected. For example, a number of companies have experienced security incidents in which intruders obtained unauthorized wireless access to the organization's corporate network from a laptop while sitting in a car parked outside the building.

It is not enough to monitor the parking lot because wireless signals can often be picked up miles away. Figure 11-6 shows that an important part of securing wireless access is to place all wireless access points (the devices that accept incoming wireless communications and permit the sending device to connect to the organization's network) in the DMZ. This treats all wireless access as though it were coming in from the Internet and forces all wireless traffic to go through the main firewall and any IPSs used to protect the perimeter of the internal network. In addition, the following procedures need to be followed to adequately secure wireless access:

- Turn on available security features. Most wireless equipment is sold and installed with these features disabled. For example, the default installation configuration for most wireless routers does not turn on encryption.

- Authenticate all devices attempting to establish wireless access to the network *before* assigning them an IP address. This can be done by treating incoming wireless connections as attempts to access the network from the Internet and routing them first through a remote access server or other authentication device.
- Configure all authorized wireless devices to operate only in infrastructure mode, which forces the device to connect only to wireless access points. (Wireless devices can also be set to operate in ad hoc mode, which enables them to communicate directly with any other wireless device. This is a security threat because it creates peer-to-peer networks with little or no authentication controls.) In addition, predefine a list of authorized MAC addresses, and configure wireless access points to accept connections only if the device's MAC address is on the authorized list.
- Use noninformative names for the access point's address, which is called a service set identifier (SSID). SSIDs such as "payroll," "finance," or "R&D" are more obvious targets to attack than devices with generic SSIDs such as "A1" or "X2."
- Reduce the broadcast strength of wireless access points, locate them in the interior of the building, and use directional antennas to make unauthorized reception off-premises more difficult. Special paint and window films can also be used to contain wireless signals within a building.
- **Encrypt all wireless traffic.** This is absolutely essential to protect the confidentiality and privacy of wireless communications because they are transmitted "over the air" and are therefore inherently susceptible to unauthorized interception.

Finally, it is easy and inexpensive for employees to set up unauthorized wireless access points in their offices. Therefore, information security or internal audit staff must periodically test for the existence of such rogue access points, disable any that are discovered, and appropriately discipline the employees responsible for installing them.

IT SOLUTIONS: DEVICE AND SOFTWARE HARDENING CONTROLS

Firewalls and IPSs are designed to protect the network perimeter. However, just as many homes and businesses supplement exterior door locks and alarm systems with locked cabinets and safes to store valuables, an organization should enhance information system security by supplementing preventive controls on the network perimeter with additional preventive controls on the workstations, servers, printers, and other devices (collectively referred to as **endpoints**) that comprise the organization's network. COBIT 2019 management practice DSS05.03 describes the activities involved in managing endpoint security. Three areas deserve special attention: (1) endpoint configuration, (2) user account management, and (3) software design.

endpoints - Collective term for the workstations, servers, printers, and other devices that comprise an organization's network.

ENDPOINT CONFIGURATION Endpoints can be made more secure by modifying their configurations. Default configurations of most devices typically turn on a large number of optional settings that are seldom, if ever, used. Similarly, default installations of many operating systems turn on many special-purpose programs, called *services*, that are not essential. Turning on unnecessary features and extra services makes it more likely that installation will be successful without the need for customer support. This convenience, however, comes at the cost of creating security weaknesses. Every program running represents a potential point of attack because it probably contains flaws, called vulnerabilities, that can be exploited to either crash the system or take control of it. Therefore, any optional programs and features not used should be disabled. Tools called **vulnerability scanners** can be used to identify unused and, therefore, unnecessary programs that represent potential security threats.

vulnerability scanners - Automated tools designed to identify whether a given system possesses any unused and unnecessary programs that represent potential security threats.

The ever-increasing size and complexity of software programs almost guarantees that they contain numerous vulnerabilities. To understand why, consider that many programs contain millions of lines of code. Even if that code is 99.99% free of "bugs," that means that for every million lines of code there are likely 100 possible problems that could represent a vulnerability. That is why both attackers and security consulting firms are constantly testing for vulnerabilities in widely used software. Once a vulnerability has been identified, it is important to take timely steps to remediate it because it will not be long before an **exploit**, which is a program

exploit - A program designed to take advantage of a known vulnerability.

designed to take advantage of a known vulnerability, is created. Although it takes considerable skill to create an exploit, once it is published on the Internet it can be easily used by anyone.

patch - Code released by software developers that fixes a particular vulnerability.

patch management - The process of regularly applying patches and updates to software.

The widespread availability of many exploits and their ease of use make it important for organizations to take steps to quickly correct known vulnerabilities in software they use. A **patch** is code released by software developers that fixes a particular vulnerability. **Patch management** is the process for regularly applying patches and updates to all software used by the organization. Many security incidents occur because organizations fail to timely install patches, enabling criminals to exploit well-known vulnerabilities. However, patch management is not as straightforward as it sounds. Patches represent modifications to already complex software. Consequently, patches sometimes create new problems because of unanticipated side effects. Therefore, organizations need to carefully test the effect of patches prior to deploying them; otherwise, they run the risk of crashing important applications. Further complicating matters is the fact that there are likely to be multiple patches released each year for each software program used by an organization. Thus, organizations may face the task of applying hundreds of patches to thousands of machines every year. This is one area where IPSs hold great promise. If an IPS can be quickly updated with the information needed to respond to new vulnerabilities and block new exploits, the organization can use the IPS to buy the time needed to thoroughly test patches before applying them.

hardening - The process of modifying the default configuration of endpoints to eliminate unnecessary settings and services.

This process of modifying the default configuration of endpoints to eliminate unnecessary settings and services is called **hardening**. In addition to hardening, every endpoint needs to be running antivirus and firewall software that is regularly updated. It may also be desirable to install intrusion prevention software directly on the endpoint to prevent unauthorized attempts to change the device's hardened configuration.

USER ACCOUNT MANAGEMENT COBIT 2019 management practice DSS05.04 stresses the need to carefully manage all user accounts, especially those accounts that have unlimited (administrative) rights on that computer. Administrative rights are needed in order to install software and alter most configuration settings. These powerful capabilities make accounts with administrative rights prime targets for attackers. Therefore, employees who need administrative powers on a particular computer should be assigned two accounts: one with administrative rights and another that has only limited privileges. These employees should be trained to log in under their limited account to perform routine daily duties and to log in to their administrative account only when they need to perform some action, such as installing new software, which requires administrative rights. It is especially important that the employee use a limited regular user account when browsing the web or reading e-mail. This way, if the employee visits a compromised website or opens an infected e-mail, the attacker will acquire only limited rights on the machine. Although the attacker can use other tools to eventually obtain administrative rights on that machine, other security controls might detect and thwart such attempts to escalate privileges before they can be completed. In contrast, if the employee was using an account with administrative rights, the malware would totally compromise the device before any other controls could detect that there was a problem. Finally, it is important to change the default passwords on all administrative accounts created during initial installation of any software or hardware because those account names and their default passwords are publicly available on the Internet and thus provide attackers with an easy way to compromise a system.

SOFTWARE DESIGN As organizations have increased the effectiveness of their perimeter security controls, attackers have increasingly targeted vulnerabilities in application programs. Buffer overflows, SQL injection, and cross-site scripting are common examples of attacks against the software running on websites. These attacks all exploit poorly written software that does not thoroughly check user-supplied input prior to further processing. Consider the common task of soliciting user input such as name and address. Most programs set aside a fixed amount of memory, referred to as a buffer, to hold user input. However, if the program does not carefully check the size of data being input, an attacker may enter many times the amount of data that was anticipated and overflow the buffer. The excess data may be written to an area of memory normally used to store and execute commands. In such cases, an attacker may be able to take control of the machine by sending carefully crafted commands in the excess data. Similarly, SQL injection attacks occur whenever web application software that interfaces with a database server does not filter user input, thereby permitting an attacker to embed SQL commands within a data entry request and have those commands executed on the database server. Cross-site scripting attacks occur when web application software does not carefully filter user input before returning any of that data to the browser, in which case the victim's browser will execute any embedded malicious script.

The common theme in all of these attacks is the failure to "scrub" user input to remove potentially malicious code. The solution is to train programmers to treat all input from external users as untrustworthy and to carefully check it before performing further actions. In order to prevent cross-site scripting attacks, programmers also need to filter all output returned to a browser to remove any embedded script. Poor programming techniques affect not only internally created code but also software purchased from third parties. Consequently, section BAI03 of the COBIT 2019 framework specifies the need to carefully design security into all new applications and section APO10 prescribes best practices for managing the risks associated with purchasing software.

IT SOLUTIONS: ENCRYPTION

Encryption provides a final layer of defense to prevent unauthorized access to sensitive information. We discuss encryption in more detail in Chapter 12 because of its importance to achieving the security principles of protecting confidentiality of organizational information and the privacy of personal information collected from customers, employees, and business partners.

Detecting Attacks

As noted earlier, preventive controls are never 100% effective in blocking all attacks. Therefore, COBIT 2019 management practices DSS02 and DSS03 describe the activities organizations also need to enable timely detection of intrusions and problems. This section discusses the four types of detective controls listed in Table 11-1: log analysis, intrusion detection systems, honeypots, and continuous monitoring. All four can help satisfy the goal of the time-based model of security by reducing the value of D (the time it takes to detect a problem).

LOG ANALYSIS

Most systems come with extensive capabilities for logging who accesses the system and what specific actions each user performed. These logs form an audit trail of system access. Like any other audit trail, logs are of value only if they are routinely examined. **Log analysis** is the process of examining logs to identify evidence of possible attacks.

log analysis - The process of examining logs to identify evidence of possible attacks.

It is especially important to analyze logs of failed attempts to log on to a system and failed attempts to obtain access to specific information resources. For example, Figure 11-9 presents a portion of security log from a computer running the Windows operating system that shows that a user named "rjones" unsuccessfully tried to log onto a computer named "payroll server." The goal of log analysis is to determine the reason for this failed log-on attempt. One possible explanation is that rjones is a legitimate user who forgot his or her password. Another possibility is that rjones is a legitimate user but is not authorized to access the payroll server. Yet another possibility is that this may represent an attempted attack by an unauthorized user.

It is also important to analyze changes to the logs themselves (i.e., "to audit the audit trail"). Log records are routinely created whenever the appropriate event occurs. However, log records are not normally deleted or updated. Therefore, finding such changes to a log file indicates that the system has likely been compromised.

Logs need to be analyzed regularly to detect problems in a timely manner. This is not easy because logs can quickly grow in size. Another problem is that many devices produce logs with proprietary formats, making it hard to correlate and summarize logs from different devices. Software tools such as security information and event management (SIEM) systems attempt to address these issues by converting vendor-specific log formats into common representations and producing reports that correlate and summarize information from multiple sources.

FIGURE 11-9
Example of a System Log

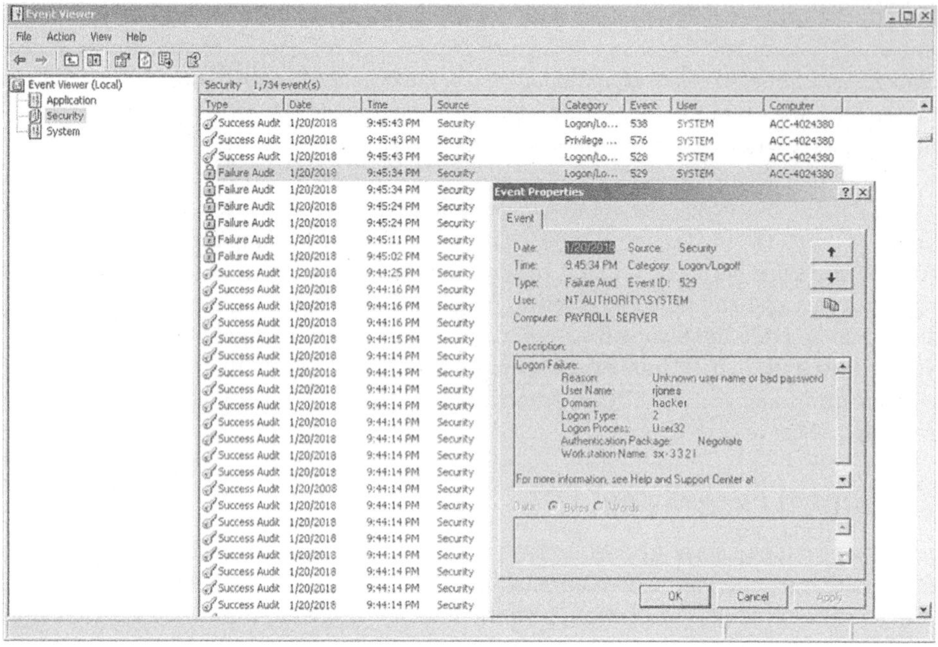

The information security function can then use advanced analytics techniques to analyze this voluminous log data to identify situations that need further investigation.

INTRUSION DETECTION SYSTEMS

intrusion detection systems (IDSs) - Systems that create logs of all network traffic that was permitted to pass the firewall and then analyze those logs for signs of attempted or successful intrusions.

Network **intrusion detection systems (IDSs)** consist of a set of sensors and a central monitoring unit that create logs of network traffic that was permitted to pass the firewall and then analyze those logs for signs of attempted or successful intrusions. Like a network IPS, a network IDS functions by comparing observed traffic to its rulebase. In addition, an IDS can be installed on a specific device to monitor unauthorized attempts to change that device's configuration. The main difference between an IDS and an IPS is that an IDS only produces a warning alert when it detects a suspicious pattern of network traffic; it is then up to the human responsible for monitoring the IDS to decide what course of action to take. In contrast, an IPS not only issues an alert but also automatically takes steps to stop a suspected attack.

HONEYPOTS

honeypot - A decoy system used to provide early warning that an insider or outsider is attempting to search for confidential information.

An important defensive tool that many organizations use is called a **honeypot**. A honeypot is a system that looks like a legitimate part of the organization's internal network but is just a decoy system. For example, a honeypot may be configured to emulate a research and development server or some other potentially attractive target. Because it is a decoy system, attempts to access the honeypot provide early warning that someone, either an employee or an outsider, is searching for confidential information. The information security team can then monitor the attempted intrusion and intervene when appropriate.

CONTINUOUS MONITORING

COBIT 2019 management practices MEA01, MEA02, and MEA03 stress the importance of continuously monitoring both employee compliance with the organization's information security policies and overall performance of business processes. Such monitoring is an important detective control that can timely identify potential problems and identify opportunities to improve existing controls. Measuring compliance with policies is straightforward, but effectively monitoring performance requires judgment and skill. Accountants can provide value by drawing on COBIT 2019's discussion of possible metrics for evaluating information security to help management design effective reports that highlight areas most in need of attention.

Responding to Attacks

Timely detection of problems, although important, is not enough. As COBIT 2019 management practice MEA01.05 explains, organizations also need procedures to undertake timely corrective actions. Many corrective controls, however, rely on human judgment. Consequently, their effectiveness depends to a great extent on proper planning and preparation. We now discuss two particularly important controls listed in Table 11-1: (1) establishment of a computer incident response team (CIRT) and (2) designation of a specific individual, typically referred to as the Chief Information Security Officer (CISO), with organization-wide responsibility for information security. Both of these can help satisfy the time-based model of security by reducing the value of R, the time it takes to respond to a problem.

COMPUTER INCIDENT RESPONSE TEAM (CIRT)

A key component to being able to respond to security incidents promptly and effectively is the establishment of a **computer incident response team (CIRT)**. The CIRT should include not only technical specialists but also senior operations management because some potential responses to security incidents have significant economic consequences. For example, it may be necessary to temporarily shut down an e-commerce server. The decision to do so is too important to leave to the discretion of IT security staff; only management possesses the breadth of knowledge to properly evaluate the costs and benefits of such an action, and only it should have the authority to make that decision.

computer incident response team (CIRT) - A team responsible for dealing with major security incidents.

The CIRT should lead the organization's incident response process through the following four steps:

1. *Recognition* that a problem exists. Typically, this occurs when an IPS or IDS signals an alert, but it can also be the result of log analysis by a systems administrator.
2. *Containment* of the problem. Once an intrusion is detected, prompt action is needed to stop it and to contain the damage.
3. *Recovery*. Damage caused by the attack must be repaired. This may involve eradicating any malware and restoring data from backup and reinstalling corrupted programs. We will discuss backup and disaster recovery procedures in more detail in Chapter 13.
4. *Follow-up*. Once recovery is in process, the CIRT should lead the analysis of how the incident occurred. Steps may need to be taken to modify existing security policy and procedures to minimize the likelihood of a similar incident occurring in the future. An important decision that needs to be made is whether to attempt to catch and punish the perpetrator. If the organization decides to prosecute the attacker(s), it needs to immediately involve forensic experts to ensure that all possible evidence is collected and maintained in a manner that makes it admissible for use in court.

Communication is vital throughout all four steps in the incident response process. Therefore, multiple methods of notifying members of the CIRT are necessary. For example, IPSs and IDSs might be configured to send e-mail alerts. However, if the system goes down or is compromised, the e-mail alerts may not work. Traditional telephones and cell phones provide good alternative channels for sending the initial alerts and subsequent communications.

It is also important to regularly practice the incident response plan, including the alert process. It is much better to discover a gap in the plan during a practice run than when a real incident occurs. Regular practice helps identify the need for change in response to technological changes. For example, many organizations are switching from a traditional telephone system to one based on voice-over IP (VoIP). This can save considerable money, but it also means that if the computer network goes down, so, too, does the phone system. This side effect may not be noticed until the incident response plan is practiced.

CHIEF INFORMATION SECURITY OFFICER (CISO)

COBIT 2019 identifies organizational structure as a critical enabler to achieve effective controls and security. It is especially important that organizations assign responsibility for information security to someone at an appropriate senior level of management because organizations that do so are more likely to have a well-trained incident response team than do organizations that do not make someone accountable for information security. One way to satisfy this objective is to create the position of CISO, who should be independent of other information systems functions and should report to either the chief operating officer (COO) or the chief executive officer (CEO). The CISO must understand the company's technology environment and work with the chief information officer (CIO) to design, implement, and promote sound security policies and procedures. The CISO should also be an impartial assessor and evaluator of the IT environment. Accordingly, the CISO should have responsibility for ensuring that vulnerability and risk assessments are performed regularly and that security audits are carried out periodically. The CISO also needs to work closely with the person in charge of physical security because unauthorized physical access can allow an intruder to bypass the most elaborate logical access controls.

Monitor and Revise Security Solutions

The fourth stage in the security life cycle (refer back to Figure 11-2) involves monitoring performance and remedying any identified deficiencies, which corresponds to the final component in the COSO-ERM framework: Monitor Control Processes. This section discusses two key processes in such monitoring: penetration testing and change management.

PENETRATION TESTING

penetration test - An *authorized* attempt to break into the organization's information system.

COBIT 2019 control processes MEA01 and MEA02 state the need to periodically test the effectiveness of business processes and internal controls (including security procedures). Penetration testing provides a rigorous way to test the effectiveness of an organization's information security. A **penetration test** is an *authorized* attempt by either an internal audit team or an external security consulting firm to break into the organization's information system. These teams try everything possible to compromise a company's system. Because there are numerous potential attack vectors, penetration tests almost always succeed. Thus, their value is not so much in demonstrating that a system *can* be broken into, but in identifying where additional protections are most needed to increase the time and effort required to compromise the system. Penetration testing also provides data about the effectiveness of the organization's ability to timely detect and respond to an attack.

CHANGE CONTROLS AND CHANGE MANAGEMENT

Organizations constantly modify their information systems to reflect new business practices and to take advantage of advances in IT. Change control and change management refer to the formal process used to ensure that modifications to hardware, software, or processes do not reduce systems reliability. Good change control often results in *better* operating performance because there are fewer problems to fix. Companies with good change management and change control processes also experience lower costs when security incidents do happen. Indeed, the ability to quickly identify unauthorized changes and sanction those responsible for intentionally circumventing the change control and change management process is one of the most important characteristics that distinguishes top-performing organizations from all others. Therefore, it is not surprising that two of COBIT 2019's key processes deal with managing change (BAI06) and the procedures for testing and transitioning to new solutions (BAI07). Characteristics of a well-designed change control and change management process include:

- Documentation of all change requests, identifying the nature of the change, its rationale, date of the request, and outcome of the request.
- Documented approval of all change requests by appropriate levels of management. It is especially important that senior management review and approve major changes to processes and systems in order to ensure that the proposed change is consistent with the organization's long-term strategic plans.
- Testing of all changes in a separate system, not the one used for daily business processes. This reduces the risk that "bugs" in modifications disrupt normal business.
- Conversion controls to ensure that data is accurately and completely transferred from the old to the new system. Internal auditors should review the conversion process to verify that the change was properly authorized and tested.
- Updating of all documentation (program instructions, system descriptions, procedures manuals, etc.) to reflect the newly implemented changes.

- A special process for timely review, approval, and documentation of "emergency changes" as soon after the crisis as is practical. All emergency changes need to be logged to provide an audit trail. A large number or marked increase in the number of emergency changes is a potential red flag of other problems (poor configuration management procedures, lack of preventive maintenance, or political "game-playing" to avoid the normal change control process).
- Development and documentation of "backout" plans to facilitate reverting to previous configurations if the new change creates unexpected problems.
- Careful monitoring and review of user rights and privileges *during* the change process to ensure that proper segregation of duties is maintained.

Security Implications of Virtualization, Cloud Computing, and the Internet of Things

Virtualization and cloud computing alter the risk of some information security threats. For example, unsupervised physical access in a virtualization environment exposes not just one device but also the entire virtual network to the risk of theft or destruction and compromise. Similarly, compromising a cloud provider's system may provide unauthorized access to multiple systems. Moreover, because public clouds are, by definition, accessible via the Internet, configuration errors may expose sensitive data to unauthorized access. Cloud file-sharing services can also be used to distribute malware. Public clouds also raise concerns about the other aspects of systems reliability (confidentiality, privacy, processing integrity, and availability) because the organization is outsourcing control of its data and computing resources to a third party. Management can obtain information about the security of services outsourced to third party cloud providers by obtaining a copy of the cloud provider's Type 2 System and Organization Controls (SOC) 2 report. A Type 2 SOC 2 report describes the controls used by a service provider (e.g., a cloud provider, payroll service, etc.) and a CPA's opinion about the operating effectiveness of those controls.

Although virtualization and cloud computing can increase the risk of some threats, both developments also offer the opportunity to significantly improve overall security. For example, implementing strong access controls in the cloud or over the server that hosts a virtual network provides good security over all the systems contained therein. The important point is that all of the controls discussed previously in this chapter remain relevant in the context of virtualization and cloud computing. Strong user access controls, ideally involving the use of multifactor authentication, and physical access controls are essential. Virtual firewalls, IPS, and IDS need to be deployed both by cloud providers to isolate virtual machines and cloud customers from one another, and by organizations to properly restrict employee access to only those portions of the system necessary to perform their assigned jobs. Files need to be scanned for malware before being downloaded from the cloud; conversely, files need to be scanned before being uploaded to prevent the exfiltration of sensitive information. The need for timely detection of problems continues to exist, as does the need for corrective controls such as patch management. Thus, virtualization and cloud computing can have either positive or negative effects on the overall level of information security, depending upon how well the organization or the cloud provider implements the various layers of preventive, detective, and corrective controls.

The Internet of Things (IoT) also has significant implications for information security. On the one hand, it makes the design of an effective set of controls much more complex. Traditionally, information security focused on controlling access to a limited number of endpoints: laptops, desktop computers, servers, printers, and mobile devices. The move to the IoT means that many other devices found in work settings now provide a potential means of accessing the corporate network and, therefore, must be secured. On the other hand, the IoT provides an opportunity to enhance physical access control. For example, myriads of tiny sensors can be deployed throughout the office, warehouse, and production areas to provide real-time information about movements into and out of those areas. In addition, organizations can use the sensors in wearable devices to track the location of employees and visitors. Thus, the net effect of the IoT on an organization's ability to satisfy the time-based model of security depends upon how well it addresses and uses this new development.

Summary and Case Conclusion

Jason Scott finished his review of Northwest Industries' information systems security procedures and prepared an interim report for his supervisor. The report began by explaining that security was one of five principles of systems reliability. Because absolute security is not practical, the report noted that Northwest Industries' goal should be to adopt the time-based model of security and employ a combination of detective and corrective controls that would allow the company to detect and respond to attacks in less time than it would take an intruder to break through its preventive controls and successfully attack the system. In addition, the report pointed out the value of deploying redundant, overlapping controls to provide layers of defense-in-depth.

Jason's report then described and evaluated the various security procedures in place at Northwest Industries. Physical access to the company's office is limited to one main entrance, which is staffed at all times by a security guard. All visitors have to sign in at the security desk and are escorted at all times by an employee. Access to rooms with computing equipment requires insertion of an employee badge in a card reader plus entry of a PIN in a keypad lock on the door. Remote access controls include a main firewall that performs packet filtering and a web application firewall that uses deep packet inspection to filter all traffic going to the web server. There are additional internal firewalls that segregate different business functions from one another. The information security staff regularly scans all equipment for vulnerabilities and makes sure that every employee's workstation is running a current version of the company's antivirus software as well as a firewall. To improve security awareness, all employees attend monthly hour-long workshops that cover a different current security issue each month. The company uses intrusion detection systems, and top management receives monthly reports on the effectiveness of system security. Corrective controls include a computer incident response team and quarterly practice of an incident response plan. Jason concluded that because senior management of Northwest Industries considers information security to be an integral part of the organization's processes, similar to quality, it has taken steps to implement proactive and effective information security practices.

However, Jason identified two weaknesses related to change control. One point of concern was that several "emergency changes" made during the past year were not documented. The second issue was that in order to save money, Northwest Industries did not have a separate test environment, but gave its programmers direct access to the transaction processing system to make changes. To rectify the first issue, Jason recommended that the CIO should assign someone the responsibility for ensuring that all changes were properly documented. To address the second issue, Jason recommended that Northwest Industries invest in virtualization technology to create a separate testing and development environment and that it remove programmers' access to the transaction processing system.

Jason's supervisor was pleased with his interim report. She asked Jason to continue his review of the Northwest Industries' information systems by examining two of the other principles of systems reliability in the AICPA's Trust Services Framework: confidentiality and privacy.

KEY TERMS

time-based model of information security 339
defense-in-depth 340
authentication 343
biometric identifier 343
multifactor authentication 343
multimodal authentication 343
authorization 345
access control matrix 345
compatibility test 345
border router 347
firewall 347
demilitarized zone (DMZ) 347
routers 348
access control lists (ACLs) 348
packet filtering 349
deep packet inspection 349
intrusion prevention systems (IPS) 350
endpoints 351
vulnerability scanners 351
exploit 351
patch 352
patch management 352
hardening 352
log analysis 353
intrusion detection systems (IDSs) 354
honeypot 354
computer incident response team (CIRT) 355
penetration test 356

AIS in Action

CHAPTER QUIZ

1. Which of the following statements is true?
   a. The concept of defense-in-depth reflects the fact that security involves the use of a few sophisticated technical controls.
   b. Information security is necessary for protecting confidentiality, privacy, integrity of processing, and availability of information resources.
   c. The time-based model of security can be expressed in the following formula: $P < D + R$.
   d. Information security is primarily an IT issue, not a managerial concern.

2. Which of the following is a preventive control?
   a. training
   b. log analysis
   c. CIRT
   d. virtualization

3. The control procedure designed to restrict what portions of an information system an employee can access and what actions he or she can perform is called ____________.
   a. authentication
   b. authorization
   c. intrusion prevention
   d. intrusion detection

4. A weakness an attacker can take advantage of to either disable or take control of a system is called a(n) ____________.
   a. exploit
   b. patch
   c. vulnerability
   d. attack

5. Which of the following is a corrective control designed to fix vulnerabilities?
   a. virtualization
   b. patch management
   c. penetration testing
   d. authorization

6. Which of the following is a detective control?
   a. hardening endpoints
   b. physical access controls
   c. penetration testing
   d. patch management

7. Which of the following statements is true?
   a. "Emergency" changes need to be documented once the problem is resolved.
   b. Changes should be tested in a system separate from the one used to process transactions.
   c. Change controls are necessary to maintain adequate segregation of duties.
   d. All of the above are true.

8. Which of the following techniques is the most effective way for a firewall to protect the perimeter?
   a. deep packet inspection
   b. packet filtering
   c. access control list
   d. All of the above are equally effective.

9. Which of the following combinations of credentials is an example of multifactor authentication?
   a. voice recognition and a fingerprint reader
   b. PIN and ATM cards
   c. a password and a user ID
   d. All of the above

10. Modifying default configurations to turn off unnecessary programs and features to improve security is called ____________.
    a. user account management
    b. defense-in-depth
    c. vulnerability scanning
    d. hardening

DISCUSSION QUESTIONS

11.1 Explain why an organization would want to use all of the following information security controls: firewalls, intrusion prevention systems, intrusion detection systems, honeypots, and a CIRT.

11.2 Your school is thinking about requiring the use of a biometric, in addition to a password, to access resources such as e-mail and the learning management system. The administration has asked for student input. Which biometric, if any, would you be willing to have your school use? Why?

11.3 Reliability is often included in service level agreements (SLAs) when an organization is outsourcing. The toughest thing is to decide how much reliability is enough. Consider the objective of availability or uptime. What is the difference between 95%, 99%, 99.99%, and 99.9999% availability? Hint: Think in terms of what those levels of availability mean in terms of annual downtime.

11.4 How might security affect an organization's merger and acquisitions process?

11.5 Some people object to the use of honeypots, viewing them as a form of entrapment. What do you think?

11.6 Should section 404 of Sarbanes–Oxley be extended to include cybersecurity?

11.7 Security experts now encourage the use of long passphrases such as "I like to eat chocolate covered espresso beans when I watch a movie." Would you be willing to use such a passphrase to log in to your school's e-mail every day? Why? Would your answer differ if you could use that same passphrase for the entire time you were a student and would only have to change your passphrase if the school's e-mail had been breached?

PROBLEMS

11.1 Match the following terms with their definitions:

___ 1. vulnerability	a. Code that corrects a flaw in a program
___ 2. exploit	b. Verification of claimed identity
___ 3. authentication	c. Firewall technique that filters traffic by examining only the information in packet headers to the rules in an ACL
___ 4. authorization	d. Flaw or weakness in a program
___ 5. demilitarized zone (DMZ)	e. Test that determines the time it takes to detect and respond to an attack
___ 6. deep packet inspection	f. Subnetwork accessible from the Internet but separate from the organization's internal network
___ 7. router	g. Device that connects an organization to the Internet
___ 8. honeypot	h. Device that has no real function, but merely serves as a decoy
___ 9. firewall	i. Device that provides perimeter security by filtering packets
___ 10. hardening	j. Set of employees assigned responsibility for resolving problems and incidents
___ 11. CIRT	k. Restricting the actions a user is permitted to perform
___ 12. patch	l. Improving security by removing or disabling unnecessary programs and features

____ 13. change control and change management	m. Device that uses the Internet Protocol (IP) to send packets across networks
____ 14. packet filtering	n. Detective control that identifies weaknesses in devices or software
____ 15. border router	o. Plan that ensures modifications to an information system do not reduce its security
____ 16. vulnerability scan	p. Process of applying code supplied by a vendor to fix a problem in that vendor's software
____ 17. penetration test	q. Software code that can be used to take advantage of a flaw and compromise a system
____ 18. patch management	r. Firewall technique that filters traffic by examining not just packet header information but also the contents of a packet

11.2 (Excel problem) The CISO of the ABC company is considering how to increase the strength of employee passwords. Currently, passwords must be 10 characters, they must be case-sensitive (i.e., include both lower- and upper-case alphabetic characters), and they must contain at least two numbers.

a. Calculate the size of the search space of possible passwords given the current password requirements.
b. Calculate the size of the search space of possible passwords if the current password requirements were changed so that they must contain at least two special characters (e.g., $, #, @, etc.) from a list of 66 commonly available symbols.
c. Calculate the size of the search space of possible passwords if the current password requirements were changed so that passwords must be 20 characters long.
d. Which modification to the current password requirements (adding the requirement to include special symbols or increasing the length from 10 to 20) increases the strength of the password the most?
e. Which modification do you recommend? Why?

11.3 Refer to Figure 11-6 to answer the following questions:

a. Where would you locate a honeypot to detect new attack methods by outsiders? Why?
b. Where would you locate a honeypot to detect insider attacks? Why?
c. Where would you locate IPS and/or IDS sensors? Why?
d. What kinds of filtering would you expect to see done by the firewall that protects the payroll department that would not be done by the main firewall? Why?
e. Should another wireless access point be located on the finance department LAN? Why?
f. What kinds of filtering should be done by the border router? Why?
g. Why do the firewall symbols all have a hole in them?

11.4 Which preventive, detective, and/or corrective controls would best mitigate the following threats?

a. An employee's laptop was stolen at the airport. The laptop contained personal information about the company's customers that could potentially be used to commit identity theft.
b. A salesperson successfully logged into the payroll system by guessing the payroll supervisor's password.
c. A criminal remotely accessed a sensitive database using the authentication credentials (user ID and strong password) of an IT manager. At the time the attack occurred, the IT manager was logged into the system at his workstation at company headquarters.
d. An employee received an e-mail purporting to be from her boss informing her of an important new attendance policy. When she clicked on a link embedded in the e-mail to view the new policy, she infected her laptop with a keystroke logger.

e. A company's programming staff wrote custom code for the shopping cart feature on its website. The code contained a buffer overflow vulnerability that could be exploited when the customer typed in the ship-to address.
f. A company purchased the leading "off-the-shelf" e-commerce software for linking its electronic storefront to its inventory database. A customer discovered a way to directly access the back-end database by entering appropriate SQL code.
g. Attackers broke into the company's information system through a wireless access point located in one of its retail stores. The wireless access point had been purchased and installed by the store manager without informing central IT or security.
h. An employee picked up a USB drive in the parking lot and plugged it into his laptop to "see what was on it." As a result, a keystroke logger was installed on that laptop.
i. Once an attack on the company's website was discovered, it took more than 30 minutes to determine who to contact to initiate response actions.
j. To facilitate working from home, an employee installed a modem on his office workstation. An attacker successfully penetrated the company's system by dialing into that modem.
k. An attacker gained access to the company's internal network by installing a wireless access point in a wiring closet located next to the elevators on the fourth floor of a high-rise office building that the company shared with seven other companies.

11.5 What are the advantages and disadvantages of the three types of authentication credentials (something you know, something you have, and something you are)? Specifically address the following points:
a. Ease of use
b. Universality (can it be used on all kinds of devices: desktops, laptops, tablets, phones, public kiosks with touch screen interfaces?)
c. Revocability
d. Strength of proof of identity if used as the only authentication credential
e. Ease of losing or having stolen/compromised
f. Timeliness of noticing it is lost or stolen/compromised
g. Cost
h. User acceptance

11.6 a. Use the following facts to assess the time-based model of security for the ABC Company; how well does the existing system protect ABC? Assume the best-, average-, and worst-case estimates are independent for each component of the model.
- Estimated time that existing controls will protect the system from attack = 14 minutes (worst case), 18 minutes (average case), and 22 minutes (best case)
- Estimated time to detect that an attack is happening = 6 minutes (best case), 9 minutes (average case) and 12 minutes (worst case)
- Estimated time to respond to an attack once it has been detected = 5 minutes (best case), 10 minutes (average case), and 15 minutes (worst case)

b. The company is considering investing an additional $100,000 to improve its security. Given the following possibilities, which single investment would you recommend? Explain your answer.
- An investment of $100,000 in better perimeter defenses would change the estimates for protection time to 20 minutes (worst case), 24 minutes (average case), and 30 minutes (best case).
- An investment of $100,000 in better detection systems would change the estimates for detection time to 3 minutes (best case), 5 minutes (average case), and 8 minutes (worst case).
- An investment of $100,000 in training would change the estimates for response time to 1 minute (best case), 2 minutes (average case), and 4 minutes (worst case).

11.7 Explain how the following items individually and collectively affect the overall level of security provided by using a password as an authentication credential.

a. Length
b. Complexity requirements (which types of characters are required to be used: numbers, alphabetic, case-sensitivity of alphabetic, special symbols such as $ or !)
c. Maximum password age (how often password must be changed)
d. Minimum password age (how long a password must be used before it can be changed)
e. Maintenance of password history (how many prior passwords the system remembers to prevent reselection of the same password when the user is required to change passwords)
f. Account lockout threshold (how many failed log-in attempts are allowed before the account is locked)
g. Time frame during which account lockout threshold is applied (i.e., if lockout threshold is five failed log-in attempts, the time frame is the period during which those five failures must occur: within 15 minutes, 1 hour, 1 day, etc.)
h. Account lockout duration (how long the account remains locked after the user exceeds the maximum allowable number of failed log-in attempts)

11.8 Secure configuration of endpoints includes properly configuring your browser and your smartphone. Visit the Center for Internet Security's website (www.cisecurity.org). Navigate to the "Configuration Benchmarks" and download the benchmark for either your favorite browser or your smartphone. Adjust the settings for java, javascript, and plugins to the recommended settings. Then test the properly configured device on the following tasks:

a. Access your university e-mail account
b. Access your personal e-mail account
c. Use your favorite search engine to find information about travel tours to Easter Island
d. Attempt to book a flight
e. Play an online game (Sudoku, Kenken, etc.)

REQUIRED

Write a brief report that explains the effects, if any, of the more secure device configuration when you attempted each task.

11.9 Given the following list of potential authentication credentials, identify as many combinations as possible that can be used to implement (a) a multimodal authentication process and (b) a multifactor authentication process. Consider both combinations of two and of three credentials. List of possible credentials:

- Passphrase
- Smartphone that displays text to enter
- Security question
- Voice recognition
- USB flash drive that displays a different code every 60 seconds
- Picture to be identified from a set of pictures

11.10 Answer the following nine multiple-choice questions.

1. The system employs a compatibility test to decide whether to let a particular employee update records in a particular file. The compatibility test is a part of the aspect of access control referred to as ________.
   a. authentication
   b. authorization
   c. accountability

2. The set of instructions for taking advantage of a flaw in a program is called a(n) ________.
   a. vulnerability
   b. patch
   c. update
   d. exploit

3. Firewalls are most effective in reducing the ability of an attacker to ________.
   a. conduct initial reconnaissance
   b. research vulnerabilities and exploits
   c. scan and map the target
   d. All of the above are prevented by firewalls.
   e. None of the above are prevented by firewalls.

4. A company's current password policy requires that passwords be alphanumeric, case-sensitive, and 10 characters long. Which one of the following changes to a company's password policy will increase password strength the **most**?
   a. Require passwords to also include special characters (such as $, &, etc.).
   b. Require passwords to be 15 characters long.
   c. Both of the above changes would have the same effect on password strength.

5. Which of the following set of authentication credentials provides the strongest access control?
   a. A password and a security question
   b. A PIN and a smart card
   c. Voice recognition and a fingerprint
   d. All of the combinations of credentials are equally strong.

6. A firewall that uses ________ would be most effective in detecting and stopping an attempt to deface the organization's website by sending an HTML "PUT" command to its web server.
   a. static packet filtering
   b. stateful packet filtering
   c. deep packet inspection

7. In addition to encryption, organizations should ________ to effectively secure wireless communications.
   a. place all wireless access points in the DMZ
   b. configure all wireless clients to operate in ad hoc mode
   c. Do both of the above.
   d. Do none of the above.

8. Which of the following statements are true?
   a. IT developments such as virtualization, cloud computing, and the Internet of Things weaken information security.
   b. A large number of emergency changes is a potential red flag of other problems.
   c. Information security is improved when the CISO reports to the CIO.
   d. All of the statements are true.
   e. None of the statements are true.

9. ABC bank wants to strengthen the security of its online bill pay features. Therefore, it decides that in addition to a password, users must also correctly enter a 6-digit number sent to their smartphone. This is an example of a process referred to as ________.
   a. multifactor authentication
   b. multimodal authentication
   c. Neither of the other statements are true.

CASE 11-1 Assessing Change Control and Change Management

Read the article "Security Controls that Work" by Dwayne Melancon in the *Information Systems Control Journal*, 2007, volume 4 (available http://www.isaca.org/Journal/Past-Issues/2007/Volume-4/Pages/Security-Controls-That-Work1.aspx). Write a report that answers the following questions:

1. What are the differences between high-performing organizations and medium- and low-performing organizations in terms of normal operating performance? Detection of security breaches? Percentage of budget devoted to IT?
2. Which controls were used by almost all high-performing organizations but not used by any low- or medium-performers?
3. What three things do high-performing organizations never do?
4. What metrics can an IT auditor use to assess how an organization is performing in terms of change controls and change management? Why are those metrics particularly useful?

CASE 11-2 Research Project

Research a security incident selected by your instructor and answer the following questions:

a. When the breach occurred
b. When the breach was discovered
c. How and by whom the breach was discovered
d. Consequences of the breach to the organization

1. Effect on stock prices
2. Effect on future sales
3. Cost of remuneration (e.g., credit monitoring) offered to customers
4. Regulatory fines

e. Effect on the CISO and CIO (did either or both resign or get fired?)
f. Nature of any disclosures by the company (attach the statements); in your opinion, did the company accept responsibility for the problem or try to excuse it? Defend your answer.
g. The company's plans/response to the incident: What does it plan to do differently in the future?
h. Lessons learned: In your opinion, what could the company have done differently to either reduce the likelihood of the incident happening, mitigate the consequences of the breach, or both?

Deliverable:
Your instructor will choose whether you are to submit a written report, make an oral presentation to the class, or both.

AIS in Action Solutions

QUIZ KEY

1. Which of the following statements is true?

a. The concept of defense-in-depth reflects the fact that security involves the use of a few sophisticated technical controls. [Incorrect. The concept of defense-in-depth is based on the idea that, given enough time and resources, any single control, no matter how sophisticated, can be overcome—therefore, the use of redundant, overlapping controls maximizes security.]

▶ b. Information security is necessary for protecting confidentiality, privacy, integrity of processing, and availability of information resources. [Correct. As Figure 11-1 shows, security is the foundation for achieving the other four components of system reliability.]

c. The time-based model of security can be expressed in the following formula: $P < D + R$. [Incorrect. The formula is $P > D + R$.]

d. Information security is primarily an IT issue, not a managerial concern. [Incorrect. Security is primarily a managerial issue because only management can choose the most appropriate risk response to protect the organization's information resources.]

2. Which of the following is a preventive control?
- ▶ **a.** training [Correct. Training is designed to prevent employees from falling victim to social engineering attacks and unsafe practices such as clicking on links embedded in e-mail from unknown sources.]
- b. log analysis [Incorrect. Log analysis involves examining a record of events to discover anomalies. Thus, it is a detective control.]
- c. CIRT [Incorrect. The purpose of a computer incident response team is to respond to and remediate problems and incidents. Thus, it is a corrective control.]
- d. virtualization [Incorrect. Virtualization involves using one physical computer to run multiple virtual machines. It is primarily a cost-control measure, not an information security control procedure.]

3. The control procedure designed to restrict what portions of an information system an employee can access and what actions he or she can perform is called ________.
- a. authentication [Incorrect. Authentication is the process of verifying a user's identity to decide whether or not to grant that person access.]
- ▶ **b.** authorization [Correct. Authorization is the process of controlling what actions—read, write, delete, etc.—a user is permitted to perform.]
- c. intrusion prevention [Incorrect. Intrusion prevention systems monitor patterns in network traffic to identify and stop attacks.]
- d. intrusion detection [Incorrect. Intrusion detection is a detective control that identifies when an attack has occurred.]

4. A weakness an attacker can take advantage of to either disable or take control of a system is called a[n] ________.
- a. exploit [Incorrect. An exploit is the software code used to take advantage of a weakness.]
- b. patch [Incorrect. A patch is code designed to fix a weakness.]
- ▶ **c.** vulnerability [Correct. A vulnerability is any weakness that can disable or take control of a system.]
- d. attack [Incorrect. An attack is the action taken against a system. To succeed, it exploits a vulnerability.]

5. Which of the following is a corrective control designed to fix vulnerabilities?
- a. virtualization [Incorrect. Virtualization involves using one physical computer to run multiple virtual machines. It is primarily a cost-control measure, not an information security control procedure.]
- ▶ **b.** patch management [Correct. Patch management involves replacing flawed code that represents a vulnerability with corrected code, called a patch.]
- c. penetration testing [Incorrect. Penetration testing is detective control.]
- d. authorization [Incorrect. Authorization is a preventive control used to restrict what users can do.]

6. Which of the following is a detective control?
- a. endpoint hardening [Incorrect. Hardening is a preventive control that seeks to eliminate vulnerabilities by reconfiguring devices and software.]
- b. physical access controls [Incorrect. Physical access controls are a preventive control designed to restrict access to a system.]
- ▶ **c.** penetration testing [Correct. Penetration testing is a detective control designed to identify how long it takes to detect and respond to an attack.]
- d. patch management [Incorrect. Patch management is a corrective control that fixes vulnerabilities.]

7. Which of the following statements is true?
   a. "Emergency" changes need to be documented once the problem is resolved. [Incorrect. This statement is true, but so are b and c.]
   b. Changes should be tested in a system separate from the one used to process transactions. [Incorrect. This statement is true, but so are a and c.]
   c. Change controls are necessary to maintain adequate segregation of duties. [Incorrect. This statement is true, but so are a and b.]
▶ **d.** All of the above are true. [Correct.]

8. Which of the following techniques is the most effective way for a firewall to protect the perimeter?
▶ **a.** deep packet inspection [Correct. Deep packet inspection examines the contents of the data in the body of the IP packet, not just the information in the packet header. This is the best way to catch malicious code.]
   b. packet filtering [Incorrect. Packet filtering examines the headers of IP packets. It can be fooled by attacks that spoof source or destination addresses or which hide malicious code inside the packet.]
   c. access control lists [Incorrect. Access control lists are a set of rules that can be used to perform either packet filtering or deep packet inspection.]
   d. All of the above are equally effective. [Incorrect. Choice b is less effective than choice a, and choice c is part of both packet filtering and deep packet inspection.]

9. Which of the following combinations of credentials is an example of multifactor authentication?
   a. voice recognition and a fingerprint reader [Incorrect. This is a combination of two biometric credentials and is an example of multimodal authentication.]
▶ **b.** PIN and ATM cards [Correct. The PIN is something a person knows; the ATM card is something a person has.]
   c. password and a user ID [Incorrect. These are both things a person knows and thus represent an example of multimodal authentication.]
   d. All of the above [Incorrect. Only choice b is correct.]

10. Modifying default configurations to turn off unnecessary programs and features to improve security is called ________.
   a. user account management [Incorrect. User account management is a preventive control that limits what a user can do.]
   b. defense-in-depth [Incorrect. Defense-in-depth is the general security principle of using multiple overlapping controls to protect a system.]
   c. vulnerability scanning [Incorrect. Vulnerability scanning is a detective control designed to identify weaknesses.]
▶ **d.** hardening [Correct. This is the definition of hardening.]

CHAPTER 12

Confidentiality and Privacy Controls

LEARNING OBJECTIVES

After studying this chapter, you should be able to:

1. Describe the controls that can be used to protect the confidentiality of an organization's information and the privacy of personal information collected from customers, suppliers, and employees.
2. Discuss how the Generally Accepted Privacy Principles (GAPP) framework provides guidance in developing a comprehensive approach to protecting privacy that satisfies the requirements of privacy regulations such as the EU's General Data Privacy Regulation.
3. Discuss how different types of encryption systems work, and explain the difference between encryption and hashing.
4. Explain how to create a digital signature and how it provides a means to create legally enforceable contracts.
5. Discuss how blockchain works.

INTEGRATIVE CASE Northwest Industries

Jason Scott was preparing for his meeting with the Northwest Industries' chief information security officer (CISO). Although Jason was satisfied that Northwest Industries' computer security policies and procedures provided the company with adequate protection against intrusions, he was concerned about other aspects of systems reliability. In particular, he wanted to learn what Northwest Industries was doing to address the following issues:

1. Protecting the confidentiality of sensitive corporate information, such as marketing plans and trade secrets.
2. Protecting the privacy of personal information it collected from customers, employees, suppliers, and business partners.

Jason planned to use his interview with the CISO to obtain a general understanding of the company's information systems controls to protect confidentiality and privacy. He then planned to follow up by collecting evidence about the effectiveness of those controls and whether Northwest's policies and procedures were compliant with new privacy regulations.

LHF Graphics/Shutterstock; Vector Plus Image/Shutterstock

Introduction

Chapter 11 discussed information security, which is the fundamental principle of systems reliability. This chapter covers two other important principles of reliable systems in the Trust Services Framework: (1) preserving the confidentiality of an organization's intellectual property and (2) protecting the privacy of personal information it collects from customers, employees, suppliers, and business partners. We discuss the topic of encryption in detail because it is a critical tool for protecting both confidentiality and privacy. We also discuss hashing because it plays an important role in creating both digital signatures and blockchains.

Protecting Confidentiality and Privacy

Organizations possess a myriad of sensitive information, including strategic plans, trade secrets, cost information, legal documents, and process improvements. This intellectual property often is crucial to the organization's long-run competitive advantage and success. Consequently, preserving the confidentiality of the organization's intellectual property, and similar information shared with it by its business partners, has long been recognized as a basic objective of information security. Organizations also need to protect the privacy of personal information they collect from suppliers, customers, and employees. The objectives for confidentiality and privacy are the same: protect sensitive information from unauthorized access and disclosure. Consequently, as Figure 12-1 shows, the same four basic actions must be taken to protect both confidentiality and privacy: (1) identify and classify the information to be protected, (2) encrypt the information, (3) control access to the information, and (4) train employees to properly handle the information.

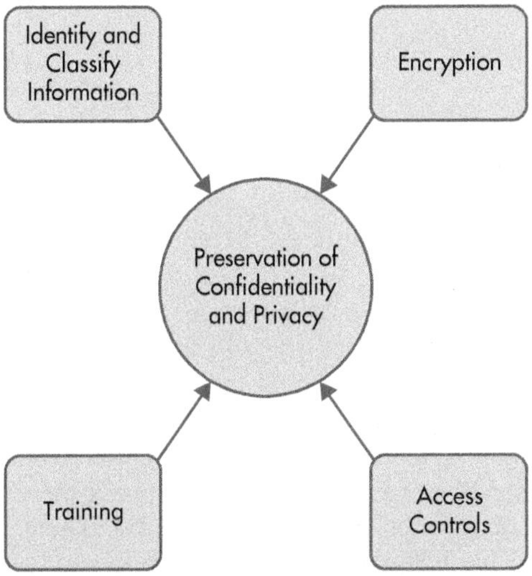

FIGURE 12-1 Components of Protecting Confidentiality and Privacy

IDENTIFY AND CLASSIFY INFORMATION TO BE PROTECTED

The first step to protect confidentiality and privacy is to identify where such information resides and who has access to it. This sounds easy, but undertaking a thorough inventory of every digital and paper store of information is both time-consuming and costly because it involves examining more than just the contents of the organization's financial systems. For example, manufacturing firms typically employ large-scale factory automation. Those systems contain instructions that may provide significant cost advantages or product quality enhancements over those of competitors and therefore must be protected from unauthorized disclosure or tampering.

After the information that needs to be protected has been identified, the next step is to classify the information in terms of its value to the organization. Control Objectives for Information and Related Technology (COBIT) 2019 management practice APO01.07 points out that classification is the responsibility of information owners, not information security professionals, because only the former understand how the information is used. This classification process is critical because you must know the value of information in order to assess the relative costs and benefits of alternative solutions to protecting it.

PROTECTING SENSITIVE INFORMATION WITH ENCRYPTION

Encryption (to be discussed later in this chapter) is an extremely important and effective tool to protect confidentiality and privacy. It is the only way to protect information in transit over the Internet. It is also a necessary part of defense-in-depth to protect information stored on websites or in a public cloud. For example, many accounting firms have created secure portals that they use to share sensitive audit, tax, or consulting information with clients. Encrypting the client's data that is stored on the portal provides an additional layer of protection in the event of unauthorized access to the portal. Similarly, encrypting information stored in a public cloud protects it from unauthorized access by employees of the cloud service provider or by anyone else who is using that same cloud. Encrypting customers' personal information not only protects it from unauthorized disclosure but also can save organizations money. Many states have passed data breach notification laws that require organizations to notify customers after any event, such as the loss or theft of a laptop or portable media device, that may have resulted in the unauthorized disclosure of customer personal information. This can be expensive for businesses that have hundreds of thousands or millions of customers. The costly notification requirement is usually waived, however, if the lost or stolen customer information was encrypted.

Encryption, however, is not a panacea. Encryption only protects information while it is stored or being transmitted, not during processing, because information must be decrypted in order to be processed. Thus, the employees (such as the Database Administrator and data analysts) who run the programs that use sensitive information can potentially view confidential information. Similarly, full disk encryption of laptops only protects the information until someone successfully authenticates and logs onto the laptop. Encryption also does not protect information when it is displayed on a monitor or printed in a report. Consequently, protecting confidentiality and privacy requires application of the principle of defense-in-depth, supplementing encryption with the other two components in Figure 12-1: access controls and training.

CONTROLLING ACCESS TO SENSITIVE INFORMATION

Chapter 11 discussed how organizations use authentication and authorization controls to restrict access to information systems that contain sensitive information. Authentication and authorization controls, however, are not sufficient to protect confidentiality and privacy because they only control initial access to sensitive information that is stored digitally. Organizations need to protect sensitive information throughout its entire life cycle, including distribution and disposal, regardless of whether it is stored digitally or physically. Thus, the basic authentication and authorization controls discussed in Chapter 11 need to be supplemented with additional digital and physical access controls.

information rights management (IRM) - Software that offers the capability not only to limit access to specific files or documents but also to specify the actions (read, copy, print, download, etc.) that individuals granted access to that resource can perform. Some IRM software even has the capability to limit access privileges to a specific period of time and to remotely erase protected files.

Information rights management (IRM) software provides an additional layer of protection to sensitive information stored in digital format, offering the capability not only to limit access to specific files or documents but also to specify the actions (read, copy, print, download to USB devices, etc.) that individuals granted access to that resource can perform. Some IRM software even has the capability to limit those privileges to a specific period of time and to remotely erase protected files. Either the creator of the information or the person responsible for managing it must assign the access rights. To access an IRM-protected resource, a person must first authenticate to the IRM server, which then downloads code to that person's computer that enables access to the information.

Today, organizations constantly exchange information with their business partners and customers. Therefore, protecting confidentiality also requires controls over outbound communications. One tool for accomplishing that is **data loss prevention (DLP)** software, which works like antivirus programs in reverse, blocking outgoing messages (whether e-mail, IM, or other means) that contain key words or phrases associated with the intellectual property or other sensitive data the organization wants to protect. DLP software is a preventive control. It can and should be supplemented by embedding code called a **digital watermark** in documents. The digital watermark is a detective control that enables an organization to identify confidential information that has been disclosed. When an organization discovers documents containing its digital watermark on the Internet, it has evidence that the preventive controls designed to protect its sensitive information have failed. It should then investigate how the compromise occurred and take appropriate corrective action.

data loss prevention (DLP) - Software that works like antivirus programs in reverse, blocking outgoing messages (e-mail, instant messages, etc.) that contain key words or phrases associated with intellectual property or other sensitive data the organization wants to protect.

digital watermark - Code embedded in documents that enables an organization to identify confidential information that has been disclosed.

It is especially important to prevent programmers from having access to personal information such as credit card numbers, telephone numbers, and social security numbers. In developing new applications, programmers often have to use "realistic" data to test the new system. It is tempting, and easy, to provide them with a copy of the data in the organization's transaction processing system. Doing so, however, gives programmers access to customers' personal information. To protect privacy, organizations should run **data masking** programs that replace such personal information with fake values (e.g., replace a real social security number with a different set of numbers that have the same characteristics, such as 123-45-6789) before sending that data to the program development and testing system. The fake data are called tokens; hence, data masking is often referred to as **tokenization.**

data masking - Protecting privacy by replacing sensitive personal information with fake data. Also called tokenization.

tokenization - Another word for data masking.

Organizations also need to train employees on how to manage and protect personal information collected from customers. This is especially important for medical and financial information. Obviously, intentional misuse of such information can have serious negative economic consequences, including significant declines in stock prices. Unintentional disclosure of such personal information can also create costly problems, however. For example, someone denied health or life insurance because of improper disclosure of personal information is likely to sue the organization that was supposed to restrict access to that data.

The basic physical access controls discussed in Chapter 11 are designed to prevent someone with unsupervised access from quickly downloading and copying gigabytes of confidential information onto a USB drive, an iPod, a cell phone, or other portable device. It is especially important to restrict access to rooms that contain printers, digital copiers, and fax machines because such devices typically possess large amounts of RAM, which may store any confidential information that was printed. In addition, laptops and workstations should run password-protected screen savers automatically after a few minutes of inactivity to prevent unauthorized viewing of sensitive information. Screen protection devices that limit the distance and angle from which information on a laptop or workstation monitor can be seen provide additional means to safeguard sensitive information, particularly in areas to which visitors have access.

COBIT 2019 management practice DSS05.06 discusses the need to also control physical access to sensitive information stored in physical documents. It also stresses the importance of proper *disposal* of sensitive information. Printed reports and microfilm containing sensitive information should be shredded before being thrown out. Proper disposal of computer media requires use of special software designed to "wipe" the media clean by repeatedly overwriting the disk or drive with random patterns of data. Using built-in operating system commands to delete that information is insufficient because many utility programs exist that can recover such deleted files. Indeed, there are numerous stories about people who have purchased used computers, cell phones, digital copy machines, and other devices and discover sensitive information on those devices the previous owner thought had been deleted. Probably the safest alternative is to physically destroy (e.g., by incineration) magnetic and optical media that have been used to store extremely sensitive data.

Access controls designed to protect confidentiality and privacy must be continuously reviewed and modified to respond to new threats created by technological advances. For example, until recently wiretaps were the only serious threat to the confidentiality of telephone conversations, and the difficulty of setting them up meant the risk of that threat was relatively low. Voice over Internet Protocol (VoIP) technology, however, routes telephone conversations as packets over the Internet. This means VoIP telephone conversations are as vulnerable to interception as any other information sent over the Internet. Therefore, VoIP conversations about sensitive topics should be encrypted.

Virtualization and cloud computing also affect the risk of unauthorized access to sensitive information. An important control in virtual environments, including internally managed "private" clouds, is to use virtual firewalls to restrict access between different virtual machines that coexist on the same physical server. In addition, virtual machines that store highly sensitive data should not be hosted on the same physical server with virtual machines accessible via the Internet because of the risk that a skilled attacker might be able to break out of the latter and compromise the former. With public clouds, the data is stored elsewhere, and access occurs over the Internet via browsers. Therefore, all communication between users and the cloud must be encrypted. Browser software, however, often contains numerous vulnerabilities. Consequently, highly sensitive data probably should not be stored in a public cloud because of lack of control over where that information is actually stored and because of the risk of unauthorized access by other cloud customers, who may include competitors, or even by employees of the cloud provider.

TRAINING

Training is arguably the most important control for protecting confidentiality and privacy. Employees need to know what information they can share with outsiders and what information needs to be protected. For example, employees often do not realize the importance of information they possess, such as time-saving steps or undocumented features they have discovered when using a particular software program. Therefore, it is important for management to inform employees who will attend external training courses, trade shows, or conferences whether they can discuss such information or whether it should be protected because it provides the company a cost savings or quality improvement advantage over its competitors.

Employees also need to be taught *how* to protect sensitive data. Training should cover such topics as how to use encryption software and the importance of always logging out of applications and using a password-protected screen saver before leaving their laptop or workstation unattended to prevent other employees from obtaining unauthorized access to that information. Employees also need to know how to code reports they create to reflect the importance of the information contained therein so that other employees will know how to handle those reports. They also need to be taught not to leave reports containing sensitive information in plain view on their desks. Training is particularly important concerning the proper use of e-mail, instant messaging (chat), and blogs because it is impossible to control the subsequent distribution of information once it has been sent or posted through any of those methods. For example, it is important to teach employees not to routinely use the "reply all" option with e-mail because doing so may disclose sensitive information to people who should not see it.

With proper training, employees can play an important role in protecting the confidentiality of an organization's information and the privacy of sensitive personal information about suppliers, customers, and employees. For example, if employees understand their organization's data classification scheme, they may recognize situations in which sensitive information has not been properly protected and proactively take appropriate corrective actions.

Privacy Regulations and Generally Accepted Privacy Principles

Concerns about protecting individual privacy have resulted in numerous government regulations.

THE EU'S GDPR AND U.S. LAWS

One of the strictest and most far-reaching privacy regulations is the European Union's General Data Privacy Regulation (GDPR). The GDPR imposes huge fines (up to 4% of global revenues) for issues such as not properly obtaining consent to collect and use personal information or not being able to document that the organization has taken a proactive approach to protecting privacy (referred to as "privacy by design"). The GDPR affects an organization's security measures, particularly its incident response process, because it requires organizations to notify regulators within 72 hours of discovering a breach. The GDPR also grants people a number of new rights, including access to the data that organizations have about them, correction of errors in that stored data, deletion of personal information stored about them (referred to as the "right to be forgotten"), and revocation of consent to sell or share their information with other organizations. Although it is an EU regulation, the GDPR affects any organization that collects and stores information about European residents, which means, given that most companies do business globally, that it applies to virtually every organization. Likewise, the California Consumer Privacy Act (CCPA) of 2018, which contains provisions similar to the GDPR and applies to California residents, affects most organizations because almost every company has customers in California. In addition to the CCPA and other state disclosure laws, a number of federal regulations, including the Health Insurance Portability and Accountability Act (HIPAA), the Health Information Technology for Economic and Clinical Health Act (HITECH), and the Financial Services Modernization Act (commonly referred to as the Gramm–Leach–Bliley Act, representing the names of its three Congressional sponsors), impose specific requirements on organizations to protect the privacy of their customers' personal information.

GENERALLY ACCEPTED PRIVACY PRINCIPLES

To help organizations cost-effectively comply with these myriad requirements, the American Institute of Certified Public Accountants (AICPA) and the Canadian Institute of Chartered Accountants (CICA) jointly developed a framework called *Generally Accepted Privacy Principles (GAPP)*. GAPP identifies and defines the following 10 internationally recognized best practices for protecting the privacy of customers' personal information:

1. ***Management.*** Organizations need to establish a set of procedures and policies for protecting the privacy of personal information they collect from customers as well as information about their customers obtained from third parties such as credit bureaus. They should assign responsibility and accountability for implementing those policies and procedures to a specific person or group of employees. Indeed, the GDPR requires that certain kinds of organizations must create the position of a Data Privacy Officer.
2. ***Notice.*** An organization should provide notice about its privacy policies and practices at or before the time it collects personal information from customers, or as soon as practicable thereafter. The notice should clearly explain what information is being collected, the reasons for its collection, and how the information will be used. The principle of notice should also apply to any monitoring and logging for security purposes.
3. ***Choice and consent.*** Organizations should explain the choices available to individuals and obtain their consent prior to the collection and use of their personal information. The nature of the choices offered differs across countries. In the United States, the default policy is called **opt-out**, which allows organizations to collect personal information about customers unless the customer explicitly objects. In contrast, the default policy in Europe is **opt-in**, meaning that organizations cannot collect personally identifying information unless customers explicitly give them permission to do so. The GDPR further requires that consent must be demonstrated by a clear affirmative act (i.e., websites cannot use "pre-ticked boxes") and that people must truly have a "free choice" such that they can continue to interact with the organization or website, albeit in a more restricted manner, even when they withhold their consent. However, even in the United States, GAPP recommends that organizations follow the opt-in approach and obtain explicit positive consent prior to collecting and storing sensitive personal information, such as financial or health records, political opinions, religious beliefs, and prior criminal history.
4. ***Collection.*** An organization should collect only the information needed to fulfill the purposes stated in its privacy policies. One particular issue of concern is the use of cookies on websites. A **cookie** is a text file created by a website and stored on a visitor's hard disk. Cookies store information about what the user has done on the site. Most websites create multiple cookies per visit to make it easier for visitors to navigate to relevant portions of the website. It is important to note that cookies are text files, which means they

opt-out - Referred to as *implicit consent* because companies can assume it is okay to collect and use customers' personal information unless they explicitly object.

opt-in - Referred to as *explicit consent* because organizations cannot collect and use customers' personal information unless they explicitly agree to allow such actions.

cookie - A text file created by a website and stored on a visitor's hard drive. Cookies store information about who the user is and what the user has done on the site.

cannot "do" anything besides store information. They do, however, contain personal information that may increase the risk of identity theft and other privacy threats. Browsers can be configured to not accept cookies, and GAPP recommends that organizations employ procedures to accede to such requests and not surreptitiously use cookies.

5. ***Use, retention, and disposal.*** Organizations should use customers' personal information only in the manner described in their stated privacy policies and retain that information only as long as it is needed to fulfill a legitimate business purpose. When the information is no longer useful, it should be disposed of in a secure manner. This means that organizations need to create policies to ensure that *all* devices (desktops, laptops, tablets, copiers, etc.) that have been used to store personal information are properly "sanitized" by securely wiping all information stored in the device before disposing of it. Organizations also need to assign someone responsibility for ensuring compliance with those policies. The need to focus on the final stage of the information life cycle (deletion) has become more important now that both the GDPR and the CCPA establish a right for customers to request that an organization securely delete information about them (referred to as a "right to be forgotten"). Note that deletion of data no longer used not only complies with regulations but also provides an economic benefit by reducing the potential costs from a data breach because the organization will need to notify and provide compensation, such as free credit monitoring, to fewer people affected by the incident.
6. ***Access.*** An organization should provide individuals with the ability to access, review, and correct the personal information stored about them.
7. ***Disclosure to third parties.*** Organizations should disclose their customers' personal information to third parties only in the situations and manners described in the organization's privacy policies and only to third parties who provide the same level of privacy protection as the organization that initially collected the information. This principle has implications for using cloud computing because storing customers' personal information in the cloud may make it accessible to the cloud provider's employees; hence, such information should be encrypted at all times.
8. ***Security.*** An organization must take reasonable steps to protect its customers' personal information from loss or unauthorized disclosure. Indeed, it is not possible to protect privacy without adequate information security. Therefore, organizations must use the various preventive, detective, and corrective controls discussed in Chapter 11 to restrict access to their customers' personal information. However, achieving an acceptable level of information security is not sufficient to protect privacy because security only protects against unauthorized access to the data but does not control what authorized users do with that data. It is also necessary to train employees to avoid practices that can result in the unintentional or inadvertent breach of privacy. E-mail presents a threat vector to consider. For example, several years ago drug manufacturer Eli Lilly sent an e-mail about its antidepressant drug Prozac to 669 patients. However, because it used the cc: function to send the message to all patients, the e-mails revealed the identities of other patients. Another often-overlooked area concerns the release of electronic documents. Just as special procedures are used to black out (redact) personal information on paper documents, organizations should train employees to use procedures to remove such information on electronic documents in a manner that prevents the recipient of the document from recovering the redacted information.
9. ***Quality.*** Organizations should maintain the integrity of their customers' personal information and employ procedures to ensure it is reasonably accurate. Providing customers with a way to review the personal information stored by the organization (as required by the GDPR and discussed in GAPP principle 6) can be a cost-effective way to achieve this objective.
10. ***Monitoring and enforcement.*** Organizations must periodically verify that their employees are complying with stated privacy policies. In addition, organizations should establish procedures for responding to customer complaints, including the use of a third-party dispute resolution process.

In summary, GAPP shows that protecting the privacy of customers' personal information requires first implementing a combination of policies, procedures, and technology, then training everyone in the organization to act in accordance with those plans, and subsequently monitoring compliance. Only senior management possesses the authority and the resources to accomplish this, which reinforces that all aspects of systems reliability are, at bottom, a managerial issue and not just an IT issue. Because accountants and auditors serve as trusted advisors to senior management, they too need to be knowledgeable about these issues.

IDENTITY THEFT One privacy-related issue of growing concern is identity theft. **Identity theft** is the unauthorized use of someone's personal information for the perpetrator's benefit. Often, identity theft is a financial crime, in which the perpetrator obtains loans or opens new credit cards in the victim's name and sometimes loots the victim's bank accounts. However, a growing proportion of identity theft cases involve fraudulently obtaining medical care and services. Medical identity theft can have life-threatening consequences because of errors it may create in the victim's medical records, such as changing information about drug allergies or prescriptions. It may even cause victims to lose their insurance coverage if the thief has used up their annual or lifetime cap for coverage of a specific illness. Tax identity theft is another growing problem. Perpetrators typically use the victim's social security number to file a fraudulent claim for a refund early in the tax-filing season. Victims only learn of the crime after filing their tax return and then receiving a letter from the IRS informing them that more than one return was filed using their social security number. It can take months for victims to resolve the problem and obtain any legitimate refund they are due.

identity theft - Assuming someone's identity, usually for economic gain.

Focus 12-1 discusses the steps that individuals should take to minimize the risk of becoming a victim of any of these forms of identity theft. Organizations, however, also have a role to play in preventing identity theft. Customers, employees, suppliers, and business partners entrust organizations with their personal information. Organizations economically benefit from having access to that information. Therefore, in addition to regulatory requirements, organizations have an ethical and moral obligation to implement controls to protect the personal information that they collect.

FOCUS 12-1 Protecting Yourself from Identity Theft

Victims of identity theft often spend much time and money to recover from it. Fortunately, there are a number of simple steps you can take to minimize your risk of becoming a victim of identity theft.

- Contact all major credit bureaus and put a credit freeze in place.
- Shred all documents that contain personal information, especially unsolicited credit card offers, before discarding them. Crosscut shredders are much more effective than strip-cut shredders.
- Securely store documents that contain sensitive personal and financial information (e.g., tax returns and financial statements). Paper documents should be kept in a locked file cabinet and digital files should be encrypted.
- Never send personal information (social security number, passport number, etc.) in unencrypted e-mail.
- Beware of e-mail, telephone, and print requests to "verify" personal information that the requesting party should already possess. For example, credit card companies will never need to ask you for the three- or four-digit security code on your card. Similarly, the IRS will never e-mail you asking you to send personally identifying information in response to an audit or in order to obtain your refund.
- Do not carry your social security card with you.
- Resist requests to provide your social security number to businesses that ask for it, as it is seldom needed for most transactions.
- Print only your initials and last name, rather than your full name, on checks. This prevents a thief from knowing how you sign your name.
- Limit the amount of other information (address and phone number) preprinted on checks, and consider totally eliminating such information.
- Do not place outgoing mail containing checks or personal information in your mailbox for pickup.
- Do not carry more than a few blank checks with you.
- Use special software to thoroughly clean any digital media prior to disposal, or physically destroy the media. It is especially important to thoroughly erase or destroy hard drives (for computers, printers, *and* copy machines) prior to donating or disposing of obsolete equipment because they likely contain information about financial transactions.
- Monitor your credit reports regularly.
- File a police report as soon as you discover that your purse or wallet was lost or stolen.
- Make photocopies of driver's licenses, passports, and credit cards. Store this information, along with the telephone numbers of all your credit cards, in a safe location to facilitate notifying appropriate authorities in the case that those documents are lost or stolen.
- Immediately cancel any stolen or lost credit cards.

Encryption

Encryption is a preventive control that can be used to protect both confidentiality and privacy. Encryption protects data while it is in transit over the Internet and provides one last barrier that must be overcome by an intruder who has obtained unauthorized access to stored information. As we will see later, encryption also strengthens authentication procedures and plays an essential role in ensuring and verifying the validity of e-business transactions. Therefore, it is important for accountants, auditors, and systems professionals to understand encryption.

encryption - The process of transforming normal text, called *plaintext*, into unreadable gibberish, called *ciphertext*.

plaintext - Normal text that has not been encrypted.

ciphertext - Plaintext transformed into unreadable gibberish using encryption.

decryption - Transforming ciphertext back into plaintext.

As shown in Figure 12-2, **encryption** is the process of transforming normal content, called **plaintext**, into unreadable gibberish, called **ciphertext**. **Decryption** reverses this process, transforming ciphertext back into plaintext. Figure 12-2 shows that both encryption and decryption involve use of a key and an algorithm. Computers represent both plaintext and ciphertext as a series of binary digits (0s and 1s). Encryption and decryption keys are also strings of binary digits; for example, a 256-bit key consists of a string of 256 0s and 1s. The algorithm is a formula for using the key to transform the plaintext into ciphertext (encryption) or the ciphertext back into plaintext (decryption). Most documents are longer than the key, so the encryption process begins by dividing the plaintext into blocks, with each block equal in length to the key. Then the algorithm is applied to the key and each block of plaintext. For example, if a 512-bit key is used, the computer first divides the document or file into 512-bit-long blocks and then combines each block with the key in the manner specified by the algorithm. The result is a ciphertext version of the document or file, equal in size to the original. To reproduce the original document, the computer first divides the ciphertext into 512-bit blocks and then applies the decryption key to each block.

FIGURE 12-2
Steps in the Encryption and Decryption Process

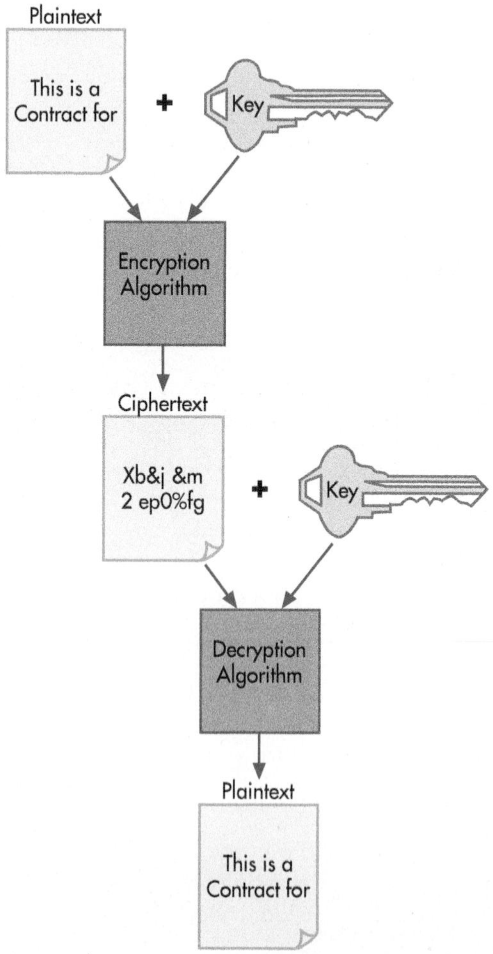

FACTORS THAT INFLUENCE ENCRYPTION STRENGTH

Three important factors determine the strength of any encryption system: (1) key length, (2) encryption algorithm, and (3) policies for managing the cryptographic keys.

KEY LENGTH Longer keys provide stronger encryption by reducing the number of repeating blocks in the ciphertext. This makes it harder to spot patterns in the ciphertext that reflect patterns in the original plaintext. For example, a 24-bit key encrypts plaintext in blocks of 24 bits. It takes 8 bits to represent each letter in the English language. Thus, a 24-bit key encrypts English plaintext in chunks of three letters. This makes it easy to use information about relative word frequencies, such as the fact that *the* is one of the most common three-letter words in English, to "guess" that the most commonly recurring pattern of 24 bits in the ciphertext probably represents the word *the* and proceed to "break" the encryption. That's why most encryption keys are at least 256 bits long (corresponding to 32 English letters) and often 1,024 bits or longer.

ENCRYPTION ALGORITHM The nature of the algorithm used to combine the key and the plaintext is important. A strong algorithm is difficult, if not impossible, to break by using brute-force guessing techniques. Secrecy is not necessary for strength. Indeed, the procedures used by the most accepted and widely used encryption algorithms are publicly available. Their strength is due not to the secrecy of their procedures but to the fact that they have been rigorously tested and demonstrated to resist brute-force guessing attacks. Therefore, organizations should not attempt to create their own "secret" encryption algorithm but instead should purchase products that use widely accepted standard algorithms whose strength has been proven.

POLICIES FOR MANAGING CRYPTOGRAPHIC KEYS The management of cryptographic keys is often the most vulnerable aspect of encryption systems. No matter how long the keys are, or how strong an encryption algorithm is, if the keys have been stolen, the encryption can be easily broken. Therefore, cryptographic keys must be stored securely and protected with strong access controls. Best practices include (1) not storing cryptographic keys in a browser or any other file that other users of that system can readily access and (2) using a strong (and long) passphrase to protect the keys.

Organizations also need sound policies and procedures for issuing and revoking keys. Keys should be issued only to employees who handle sensitive data and need the ability to encrypt it. It is also important to promptly revoke (cancel) keys when an employee leaves or when there is reason to believe the key has been compromised and to notify everyone who has relied upon those keys that they are no longer valid.

TYPES OF ENCRYPTION SYSTEMS

Table 12-1 compares the two basic types of encryption systems. **Symmetric encryption systems** use the same key both to encrypt and to decrypt. AES is an example of a symmetric encryption system. It is commonly included in most operating systems. **Asymmetric encryption systems** use two keys that are created as a matched pair. One key, called the **public key**, is widely distributed and made available to everyone; the other, called the **private key**, is kept secret and known only to the owner of that pair of keys. RSA and elliptic curve cryptography are examples of asymmetric encryption systems.

Either the public or the private asymmetric key can be used to encrypt, but only the other matching key in that pair can decrypt. Thus, anyone can use the public key to encrypt a file and securely send it to the owner of that key because only the owner possesses the corresponding private key and therefore is the only person who can decrypt that file. Conversely, encrypting something with your private key makes it possible for anyone to verify that you sent that file: If the recipient can successfully decrypt the file using your public key, it proves that the file must have been encrypted by you because you are (or should be) the only person with access to your private key.

For both types of encryption systems, loss or theft of the encryption keys are major threats. Should the keys be lost, the encrypted information cannot be recovered. One solution to this is to use encryption software that creates a built-in master key that can be used to

symmetric encryption systems - Encryption systems that use the same key both to encrypt and to decrypt.

asymmetric encryption systems - Encryption systems that use two keys (one public, the other private); either key can encrypt, but only the other matching key can decrypt.

public key - One of the keys used in asymmetric encryption systems. It is widely distributed and available to everyone.

private key - One of the keys used in asymmetric encryption systems. It is kept secret and known only to the owner of that pair of public and private keys.

TABLE 12-1 Comparison of Symmetric and Asymmetric Encryption Systems

	Symmetric Encryption	Asymmetric Encryption
Number of keys	One key. Same secret key used both to encrypt and decrypt.	Two keys. One key is made public, the other kept private. Either key can encrypt, but only the other matching key can decrypt.
Advantages	• Speed—much faster.	• Everyone can use your public key to communicate with you. • No need to store keys for each party with whom you wish to communicate. • Can be used to create legally binding digital signatures.
Disadvantages	• Requires separate key for everyone who wishes to communicate. • Must find secure way to share the secret key with other party.	• Speed—much slower. • Requires PKI to validate ownership of public keys.
Risk issues	• Protecting shared secret key from loss or theft.	• Protecting private key from loss or theft.
Primary use	• Encryption of large amounts of information.	• Creation of digital signatures. • Secure exchange of symmetric keys via e-mail.

key escrow - The process of storing a copy of an encryption key in a secure location.

decrypt anything encrypted by that software. An alternative is a process called **key escrow**, which involves making copies of all encryption keys used by employees and storing those copies securely. Theft of the encryption keys eliminates the value of encryption. In symmetric systems, if the shared secret key is stolen, the attacker can access any information encrypted with it. In asymmetric systems, the public key is intended to be widely distributed, but the private key must be stored securely. If your private key is compromised, the attacker will not only be able to decrypt all information sent to you by other people who encrypted that information with your public key, but can also use your private key to impersonate you and even create legally binding digital signatures (which we will explain later) in your name.

Symmetric encryption is much faster than asymmetric encryption, but it has two major problems. First, both parties (sender and receiver) need to know the shared secret key. This means that the two parties need to have some method for securely exchanging the key that will be used to both encrypt and decrypt. E-mail is not a solution because anyone who can intercept the e-mail would know the secret key. Thus, some other method of exchanging keys is needed. Although this could be done by telephone, postal mail, or private delivery services, such techniques quickly become cost-prohibitive, particularly for global communications. The second problem is that a separate secret key needs to be created for use by each party with whom the use of encryption is desired. For example, if Company A wants to encrypt information it shares with companies B and C, but prevent B and C from having access to the other's information, it needs to create two encryption keys, one for use with Company B and the other for use with Company C. Otherwise, if Company A shared only one common secret key with both B and C, either company could decrypt any information to which it obtained access, even if intended for the other company. Thus, secure management of keys quickly becomes more complex as the number of participants in a symmetric encryption system increases.

Asymmetric encryption systems solve both of these problems. It does not matter who knows the public key because any text encrypted with the public key can only be decrypted by using the corresponding private key. Therefore, the public key can be distributed by e-mail or even be posted on a website so that anyone who wants to can send encrypted information to the owner of that public key. Also, any number of parties can use the same public key to send encrypted messages because only the owner of the corresponding private key can decrypt the messages. Returning to our earlier example, both companies B and C can use Company A's public key to communicate securely with A. Company B need not fear that Company C could intercept that communication because the information can only be decrypted by using Company A's private key, which Company C does not have. Asymmetric encryption systems also greatly simplify the process of managing cryptographic keys. Company A does not need to create and manage separate keys for each company from which it wants to receive information over the Internet securely; instead, it needs to create just one pair of public and private keys. Company A also does not need to store the public keys of other companies to which it wishes to send information securely because it can always obtain the other company's public key from that company's website or via e-mail.

The main drawback to asymmetric encryption systems is speed. Asymmetric encryption is much (thousands of times) slower than symmetric encryption, making it impractical for use to exchange large amounts of data over the Internet. Consequently, e-business uses both types of encryption systems. Symmetric encryption is used to encode most of the data being exchanged, and asymmetric encryption is used to safely send via e-mail the symmetric key to the recipient for use in decrypting the ciphertext. The shared secret key is secure even though it is sent via e-mail because if the sender uses the recipient's public key to encrypt it, only the intended recipient, who is the only person possessing the corresponding private key, can decrypt that shared secret symmetric key. As will be discussed later, asymmetric encryption is also used in combination with a process called hashing to create legally binding digital signatures.

VIRTUAL PRIVATE NETWORKS (VPNs)

To protect confidentiality and privacy, information must be encrypted not only within a system, but also when it is in transit over the Internet. As Figure 12-3 shows, encrypting information while it traverses the Internet creates a **virtual private network (VPN)**, so named because it provides the functionality of a privately owned secure network without the associated costs of leased telephone lines, satellites, and other communication equipment. Using VPN software to encrypt information while it is in transit over the Internet in effect creates private communication channels, often referred to as *tunnels*, which are accessible only to those parties possessing the appropriate encryption and decryption keys. VPNs also include controls to authenticate the parties exchanging information and to create an audit trail of the exchange. Thus, VPNs ensure that sensitive information is exchanged securely and in a manner that can provide proof of its authenticity.

virtual private network (VPN) - Using encryption and authentication to securely transfer information over the Internet, thereby creating a "virtual" private network.

There are two basic types of VPNs. One type uses a browser, encrypting the traffic with SSL or TLS, (the same protocols that produce the familiar "lock" symbol whenever you engage in online shopping or banking); the other type uses IPSec, a version of the IP protocol that incorporates encryption as part of the process of creating IP packets. Both types of VPNs provide a secure means of exchanging sensitive information over the Internet but create problems for other components of information security. For example, recall from Chapter 11 that firewalls function by inspecting the contents of packets. Firewalls, however, cannot examine packets that are encrypted. There are three commonly used approaches to dealing with this problem. One is to configure the firewall to send encrypted packets to a computer in the demilitarized zone (DMZ) that decrypts them; that computer then sends the decrypted packets back through the firewall for filtering before being allowed into the internal network. Although this approach allows the firewall to screen all incoming packets, it means that sensitive

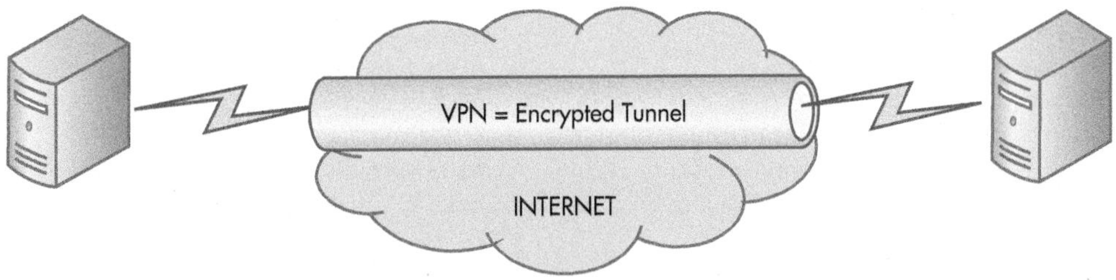

FIGURE 12-3
Virtual Private Networks [VPNs]

information is unencrypted both in the DMZ and within the internal network. A second approach is to configure the main firewall to allow encrypted packets to enter the internal network and decrypt them only at their final destination. Although this approach protects the confidentiality of sensitive information until it reaches the appropriate destination, it creates potential holes in access controls because not all incoming packets are filtered by the firewall. The third approach is to have the firewall also function as the VPN termination point, decrypting all incoming traffic and then inspecting the content. This approach is costly, creates a single point of failure (if the firewall goes down, so too does the VPN), and means that sensitive information is not encrypted while traveling on the internal corporate network. Thus, organizations must choose which systems reliability objective is more important: confidentiality (privacy) or security. Unfortunately, this type of dilemma is not limited to firewalls; antivirus programs, intrusion prevention systems, and intrusion detection systems also have difficulty in dealing with encrypted packets. This necessity of making trade-offs among different components of systems reliability is another reason that information security and controls is a managerial concern, and not just an IT issue.

Hashing

hashing - Transforming plaintext of any length into a short code called a hash.

hash - Plaintext transformed into short code.

Hashing is a process that takes plaintext of any length and creates a short code called a message digest, popularly referred to as a **hash**. For example, the SHA-256 algorithm creates a 256-bit hash, regardless of the size of the original plaintext. Table 12-2 shows that hashing differs from encryption in two important aspects. First, encryption always produces ciphertext similar in size to the original plaintext, but hashing always produces a hash that is of a fixed short length, regardless of the size of the original plaintext. The second difference is that encrypted text can be decrypted, thereby recovering the original plaintext, but it is not possible to transform a hash back into the original plaintext. Thus, sending someone a hash is *not* a way to protect confidentiality or privacy because the recipient can never recover any information from the hash. There is, however, an important property of hashing algorithms that makes it useful to send a hash of a document to another party, along with that original document. Hashing algorithms use every bit in the original plaintext to calculate the hash value. Changing *any* character in the document being hashed, such as replacing a 1 with a 7, adding or removing a single space, or even switching from upper- to lowercase, produces a different hash value. This property of hashing algorithms provides a means to test the integrity of a document, to verify whether two copies of a document, each stored on a different device, are identical. If each copy is run through the same hashing algorithm and the resulting hashes are the same, then the two copies are identical; if the two hashes are different, then one of the copies has been altered. This ability to verify integrity plays an important role in creating legally binding digital signatures and is an essential component underlying blockchains.

TABLE 12-2 Comparison of Hashing and Encryption

Hashing	Encryption
1. Any size input yields same fixed-size output. For example, SHA-256 hashing algorithm produces a 256-bit hash for each of the following: • a one-sentence document • a one-page document • a 10-page document 2. One-way function [cannot reverse, or "unhash" to recover original document].	1. Output size approximately the same as input size. For example: • a one-sentence document becomes a one-sentence encrypted document • a one-page document becomes a one-page encrypted document • a 10-page document becomes a 10-page encrypted document 2. Reversible [can decrypt ciphertext back to plaintext].

DIGITAL SIGNATURES

An important issue for business transactions has always been **nonrepudiation**, or how to create legally binding agreements that cannot be unilaterally repudiated by either party. Traditionally, this has been accomplished by physically signing contracts and other documents. In event of a dispute, experts can examine the signature to ascertain its genuineness. Today, however, many business transactions occur digitally using the Internet. How can businesses obtain the same level of assurance about the enforceability of a digital transaction that a signed document provides for a paper-based transaction? The answer is to use both hashing and asymmetric encryption to create a legally binding digital signature.

nonrepudiation - Creating legally binding agreements that cannot be unilaterally repudiated by either party.

As Figure 12-4 shows, creating a **digital signature** is a two-step process. The document creator first generates a hash of the document (or file) and then encrypts that hash using his or her private key. The resulting encrypted hash is a digital signature that provides assurance about two important issues: (1) that a copy of a document or file has not been altered, and (2) who created the original version of a digital document or file. Thus, digital signatures provide assurance that someone cannot enter into a digital transaction and then subsequently deny they had done so and refuse to fulfill their side of the contract.

digital signature - A hash encrypted with the hash creator's private key.

How do digital signatures provide this assurance? First, remember that an important property of a hash is that it reflects every bit in a document. Therefore, if two hashes are identical, it means two documents or files are identical. Consequently, just as a photocopy can be compared to an original to verify that it has not been altered, comparing a hash of a document on one computer to a hash of a document on another computer provides a way to determine whether two documents are identical. Second, remember that in asymmetric encryption systems, something encrypted with a private key can only be decrypted with the corresponding public key. Therefore, if something can be decrypted with an entity's public key, it must have been encrypted with that entity's corresponding private key, which proves that the information had to have been encrypted by the owner of that pair of public and private keys.

Figure 12-5 shows how both of these facts work together to provide nonrepudiation. A customer creates a purchase order and a digital signature for that order. The customer sends both the purchase order and the digital signature to the supplier, along with information about which hashing algorithm was used to create the digital signature. The supplier uses the stated hashing algorithm to generate a hash from its copy of the purchase order. The supplier also uses the customer's public key to decrypt the customer's digital signature. The result of decrypting the digital signature is a hash. If the supplier successfully uses the customer's public key to decrypt the customer's digital signature, it proves that the customer did indeed create and send that digital signature. It also proves that the customer must have possessed some file or document that was first hashed and then encrypted using the customer's private key to create that digital signature. If the hash obtained by decrypting the customer's digital signature matches the hash created by running the supplier's copy of the purchase order through the same hashing algorithm, it proves that the document used by the customer to create its digital signature was the purchase order now possessed by the supplier.

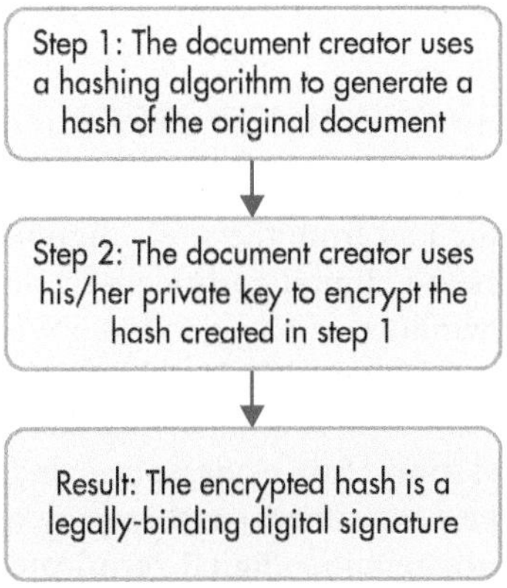

FIGURE 12-4
Creating a Digital Signature

FIGURE 12-5
Example of Digital Signature Usage

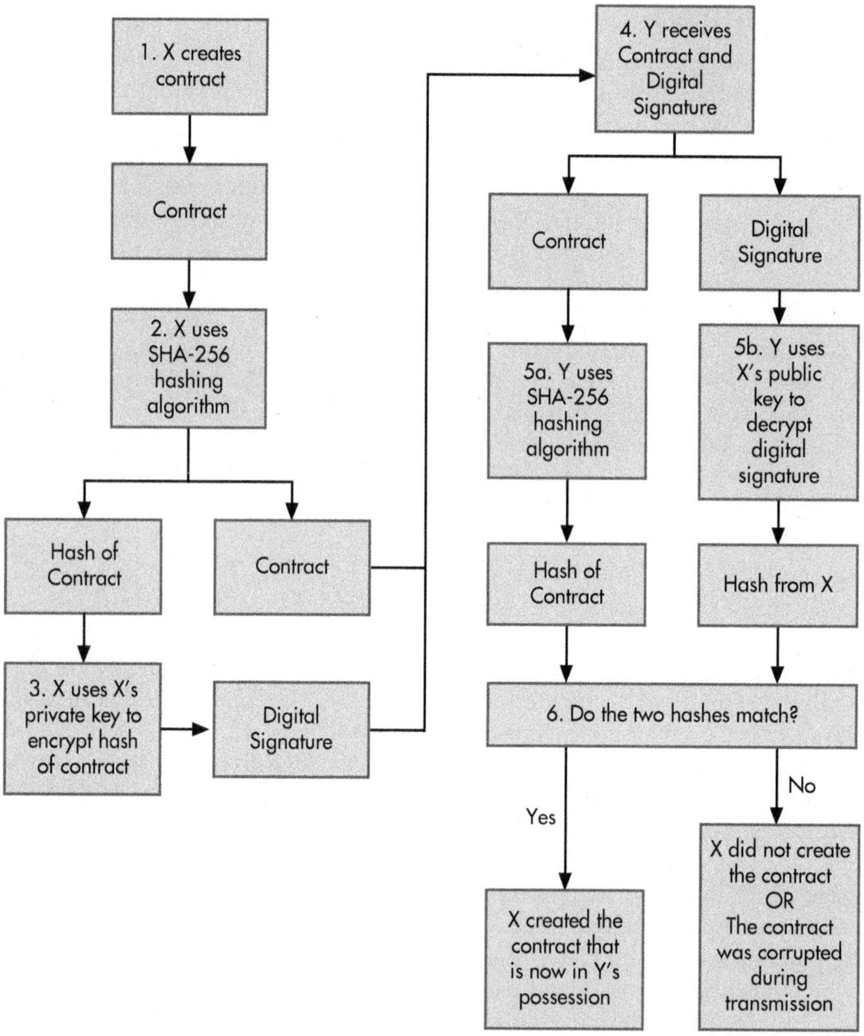

Thus, the customer cannot unilaterally repudiate (deny making) the order in the event of a dispute because the supplier can follow the steps just described to prove that the customer did indeed create and send that purchase order.

One question still remains, however. Successfully using a public key to decrypt a document or file proves that the party possessing the corresponding private key created it. But how can the recipient be sure of the other party's identity? Returning to our prior example, how can a supplier know that the public key purportedly belonging to a customer really belongs to a legitimate customer and not to a criminal who created that pair of public and private keys? For that matter, how does the supplier obtain the customer's public key? The answers to these questions involve the use of digital certificates and a public key infrastructure.

DIGITAL CERTIFICATES AND PUBLIC KEY INFRASTRUCTURE

digital certificate - An electronic document that certifies the identity of the owner of a particular public key and contains that party's public key.

Usually, you obtain another party's public key by going to their website, where your browser automatically extracts the public key from the site's digital certificate. (You can manually examine the contents of a website's digital certificate by double-clicking on the lock icon that appears in your browser window when you visit a website.) A **digital certificate** is an electronic document that contains an entity's public key and certifies the identity of the owner of that particular public key. Thus, digital certificates function like the digital equivalent of a driver's license or passport. Just as passports and drivers licenses are issued by a trusted independent party (the government) and employ mechanisms such as holograms and watermarks to prove they are genuine, digital certificates are issued by an organization called a **certificate authority** and contain the certificate authority's digital signature to prove they are genuine. Commercial certificate authorities, such as Digicert and Symantec, typically issue digital certificates intended for e-business use. These certificate authorities charge a fee to issue a pair of public and private keys and collect evidence to verify the claimed identity of the person or organization purchasing those keys and the corresponding digital certificate.

certificate authority - An organization that issues public and private keys and records the public key in a digital certificate.

This system for issuing pairs of public and private keys and corresponding digital certificates is called a **public key infrastructure (PKI)**. The entire PKI system hinges on trusting the certificate authorities that issue the keys and certificates. One important factor concerns the procedures the certificate authority uses to verify the identity of an applicant for a digital certificate. Several classes of digital certificates exist. The cheapest, and least trustworthy, may involve nothing more than verifying the applicant's e-mail address. The most expensive certificates may require verification of the applicant's identity through use of credit reports and tax returns. Digital certificates are valid for only a specified period of time. Thus, a second important criterion for assessing the reliability of a certificate authority is the procedures it uses to update certificates and revoke expired digital certificates.

public key infrastructure (PKI) - The system for issuing pairs of public and private keys and corresponding digital certificates.

Browsers are designed to automatically check the validity of a website's digital certificate. The issuing certificate authority signs digital certificates and browsers come preloaded with the public keys of widely recognized certificate authorities. The browser uses that stored public key to decrypt the certificate authority's digital signature, which yields a hash of the digital certificate. The browser then creates its own hash of the digital certificate; if the two hashes match, the certificate is valid. If not, the browser displays a warning that site's certificate is invalid and asks you whether you want to proceed. Browsers also check the expiration date of a digital certificate and warn you if it has expired. Note that browsers play a critical role in PKI. If a criminal can compromise your browser and store the criminal's public key, your browser can be tricked into accepting a fake digital certificate created and signed by the criminal. The best way to prevent this threat is to always be sure your browser is fully patched and up to date.

BLOCKCHAIN

Hashing also plays an integral role in blockchains. Blockchain technology was originally developed to support the crypto-currency Bitcoin to prevent "double-spending" the same coin, but it has since been adopted for use in a variety of industries to create reliable audit trails for any business process. A **blockchain** is a distributed ledger of hashed documents with copies stored on multiple computers. An important characteristic of a blockchain is that it cannot be unilaterally altered by any one entity. (However, a majority of participants, or a centralized authority running a non-public blockchain, can agree to alter the blockchain. For example, after a theft of a large amount of the crypto-currency Ethereum, participants agreed to alter the blockchain to prevent the stolen "coins" from being used.)

blockchain - A distributed ledger of hashed documents.

Figure 12-6 shows the role of hashing in the three-step process that creates a blockchain. In this example, a blockchain is created to serve as an audit trail for a business process. Step 1 begins by collecting a batch of documents and calculating hash values for each document. Pairs of those hashes are then concatenated together, and that result is in turn hashed. This is repeated until just one root hash for the entire block has been created. Step 2 then validates the new block by a process called *mining*, which uses three inputs (a random number, called a **nonce**; the root hash just calculated in step 1; and the root hash of the most recently validated block in the chain) to generate a header hash value that begins with a prescribed number of leading zeroes. The number of leading zeroes is arbitrary and agreed on by all participants in a specific blockchain network. For example, a blockchain network consisting of all the members in a manufacturer's supply chain might be designed to require that a block-validating header hash must begin with six leading zeroes. In that case, mining would involve repeatedly generating a nonce and then hashing the combination of (1) that nonce, (2) the root hash of the newest block, and (3) the root hash of the last validated block in the chain until a nonce is found that generates a header hash with six leading zeroes. Once such a header hash value is generated, it becomes the block-validating hash value that will be stored in the header of this new block of transactions. Finally, the newly validated block is appended to the end of

nonce - A random number; used in the mining process to validate a new block in a blockchain.

FIGURE 12-6
How Hashing Updates a Blockchain

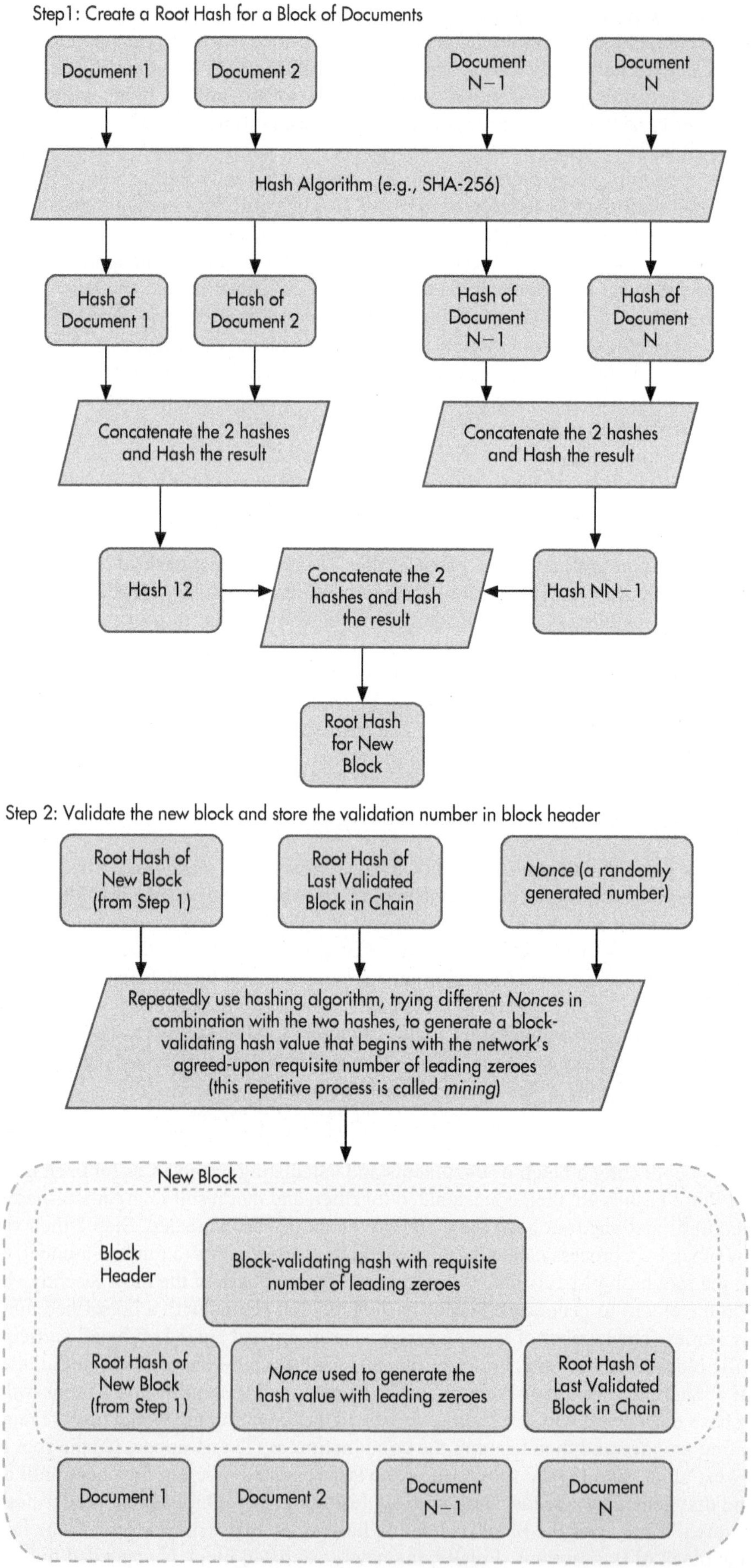

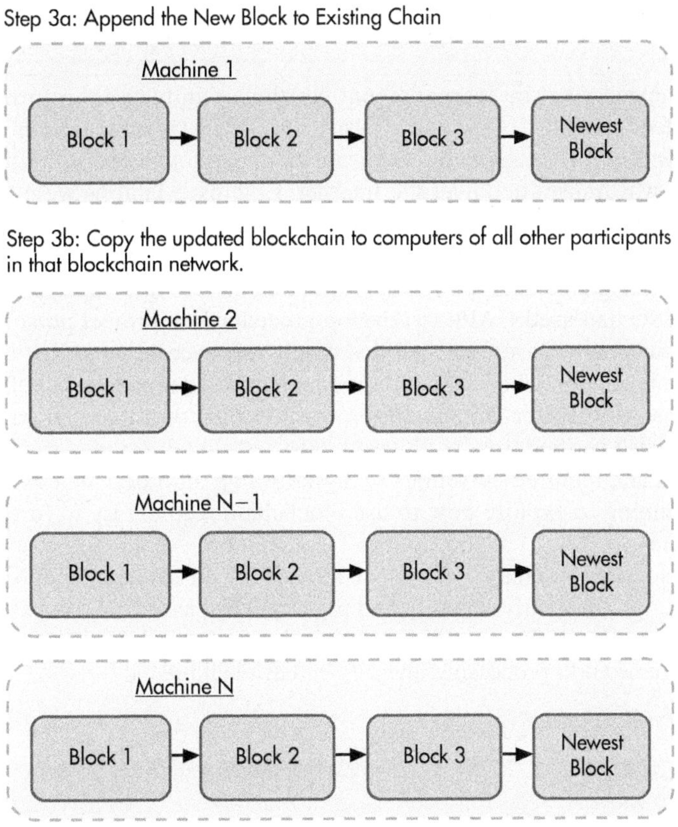

the existing chain (step 3a in Figure 12-6), and then the updated chain is copied to all other participants in the blockchain network (step 3b in Figure 12-6). The process then repeats for each new block of documents.

Let's examine why this three-step blockchain procedure creates a reliable audit trail. Recall that hashing produces a unique value for the data being hashed. Therefore, any change in the underlying data results in a different hash value. Consequently, if someone edits one of the underlying documents, such as changing the terms in a particular sales invoice, the altered document would have a different hash value than the original. Now refer back to step 1 in Figure 12-6. If the hash of one of the documents in a block changes, so too would all subsequent hashes generated from pairs of documents. Ultimately, the root hash for the entire batch would be different than what it was originally. Consequently, step 2 in the process would not work because the combination of the new root hash, the root hash of the previously validated block, and the nonce would no longer generate a header hash with the required number of leading zeroes. Now, it is theoretically possible for the person who altered the original document to simply redo the mining process in step 2 to find a new nonce that generates a header hash with the requisite number of leading zeroes for the altered batch of transactions. The person could then repeat that process for each subsequent block in the chain and eventually create a new blockchain. However, all that effort would only change the copy of the blockchain stored on that one computer. But the altered blockchain would not match the copies distributed on the computers of all the other participants in the blockchain network. Thus, the distributed nature of the blockchain provides a means to identify any attempts to unilaterally alter any of the original documents, which is why the blockchain process creates a reliable audit trail.

Nevertheless, a blockchain will only produce a reliable audit trail if it has been properly implemented. Just as errors in implementing encryption can introduce vulnerabilities that negate the value of encryption, errors in implementing blockchain can result in unreliable records. Thus, auditors will need to be able to examine a blockchain to verify that it is working correctly.

Summary and Case Conclusion

Jason Scott reviewed what he learned about Northwest Industries' information systems controls to protect confidentiality and privacy. Confidential information about business plans and personal information collected from customers was encrypted both in storage and whenever it was transmitted over the Internet. Employee laptops were configured with VPN software so they could securely access the company's information systems when they worked at home or while traveling on business. Northwest Industries employed a key escrow system to manage the encryption keys; Jason had tested and verified that it worked as planned. The CISO had used GAPP to develop procedures to protect personal information collected from customers. Jason verified that employees received detailed training on how to handle such information when initially hired and attended mandatory "refresher" courses every six months. Multifactor authentication was used to control access to the company's databases. Jason also verified that Northwest Industries digitally signed transactions with its business partners and required customers to digitally sign all orders that exceeded $10,000. It was also beginning to explore how to use blockchain technology to further improve its business processes.

Based on his report, Jason's supervisor and the CIO were satisfied with Northwest Industries' measures to protect confidentiality and privacy. They asked Jason next to examine the controls in place to achieve the remaining two principles of systems reliability in the AICPA's Trust Services Framework: processing integrity and availability.

KEY TERMS

information rights management (IRM) 370
data loss prevention (DLP) 371
digital watermark 371
data masking 371
tokenization 371
opt-out 373
opt-in 373
cookie 373
identity theft 375
encryption 376
plaintext 376
ciphertext 376
decryption 376
symmetric encryption systems 377
asymmetric encryption systems 377
public key 377
private key 377
key escrow 378
virtual private network (VPN) 379
hashing 380
hash 380
nonrepudiation 381
digital signature 381
digital certificate 382
certificate authority 383
public key infrastructure (PKI) 383
blockchain 383
nonce 383

AIS in Action

CHAPTER QUIZ

1. Which of the following statements is true?

a. Encryption is sufficient to protect confidentiality and privacy.

b. Cookies are text files that only store information. They cannot perform any actions.

c. The controls for protecting confidentiality are not effective for protecting privacy.

d. All of the above are true.

2. A digital signature is created by hashing a document and then encrypting the hash with the signer's ___________.

a. private key

b. public key

c. symmetric key

d. None of the above

3. Able wants to send a file to Baker over the Internet and protect the file so that only Baker can read it and verify that it came from Able. What should Able do?
   a. Encrypt the file using Able's public key, and then encrypt it again using Baker's private key.
   b. Encrypt the file using Able's private key, and then encrypt it again using Baker's private key.
   c. Encrypt the file using Able's public key, and then encrypt it again using Baker's public key.
   d. Encrypt the file using Able's private key, and then encrypt it again using Baker's public key.

4. Which of the following statements is true?
   a. Encryption and hashing are both reversible (can be decoded).
   b. Encryption is reversible, but hashing is not.
   c. Hashing is reversible, but encryption is not.
   d. Neither hashing nor encryption is reversible.

5. Confidentiality focuses on protecting ____________.
   a. personal information collected from customers
   b. a company's annual report stored on its website
   c. merger and acquisition plans
   d. All of the above

6. Which of the following statements about obtaining consent to collect and use a customer's personal information is true?
   a. The default policy in Europe is opt-out, but in the United States the default is opt-in.
   b. The default policy in Europe is opt-in, but in the United States the default is opt-out.
   c. The default policy in both Europe and the United States is opt-in.
   d. The default policy in both Europe and the United States is opt-out.

7. One of the 10 Generally Accepted Privacy Principles concerns security. According to GAPP, what is the nature of the relationship between security and privacy?
   a. Privacy is a necessary, but not sufficient, precondition to effective security.
   b. Privacy is both necessary and sufficient to effective security.
   c. Security is a necessary, but not sufficient, precondition to protect privacy.
   d. Security is both necessary and sufficient to protect privacy.

8. Which of the following statements is true?
   a. Symmetric encryption is faster than asymmetric encryption and can be used to provide nonrepudiation of contracts.
   b. Symmetric encryption is faster than asymmetric encryption but cannot be used to provide nonrepudiation of contracts.
   c. Asymmetric encryption is faster than symmetric encryption and can be used to provide nonrepudiation of contracts.
   d. Asymmetric encryption is faster than symmetric encryption but cannot be used to provide nonrepudiation of contracts.

9. Which of the following statements is true?
   a. VPNs protect the confidentiality of information while it is in transit over the Internet.
   b. Encryption limits firewalls' ability to filter traffic.
   c. A digital certificate contains that entity's public key.
   d. All of the above are true.

10. Which of the following can organizations use to protect the privacy of a customer's personal information when giving programmers a realistic data set with which to test a new application?
    a. digital signature
    b. digital watermark
    c. data loss prevention
    d. data masking

DISCUSSION QUESTIONS

12.1 From the viewpoint of the customer, what are the advantages and disadvantages to the opt-in versus the opt-out approaches to collecting personal information? From the viewpoint of the organization desiring to collect such information?

12.2 How does the development of the Intenet of Things affect privacy?

12.3 The GDPR gives people the right to request that organizations delete their personal data. What are some of the technical issues that make this difficult to do?

12.4 What privacy concerns might arise from the use of biometric authentication techniques? What about the embedding of radio frequency identification (RFID) tags in products such as clothing? What other technologies might create privacy concerns?

12.5 What do you think an organization's duty or responsibility to protect the privacy of its customers' personal information should be? Why?

12.6 Assume you have interviewed for a job online and now receive an offer of employment. The job requires you to move across the country. The company sends you a digital signature along with the contract. How does this provide you with enough assurance to trust the offer so that you are willing to make the move?

PROBLEMS

12.1 Match the terms with their definitions:

____ 1. virtual private network (VPN)	a. Random number used to validate a new block in a blockchain
____ 2. data loss prevention (DLP)	b. A hash encrypted with the creator's private key
____ 3. digital signature	c. Company that issues pairs of public and private keys and verifies the identity of the owner of those keys
____ 4. digital certificate	d. Secret mark used to identify proprietary information
____ 5. data masking	e. Encrypted tunnel used to transmit information securely across the Internet
____ 6. symmetric encryption	f. Replacing real data with fake data
____ 7. blockchain	g. Unauthorized use of facts about another person to commit fraud or other crimes
____ 8. plaintext	h. Distributed ledger of hashed documents
____ 9. hashing	i. Process of turning ciphertext into plaintext
____ 10. ciphertext	j. Document or file that can be read by anyone who accesses it
____ 11. information rights management (IRM)	k. Used to store an entity's public key, often found on websites
____ 12. certificate authority	l. Procedure to filter outgoing traffic to prevent confidential information from leaving
____ 13. nonrepudiation	m. Process that transforms a document or file into a fixed-length string of data
____ 14. digital watermark	n. Document or file that must be decrypted to be read

____ **15.** asymmetric encryption	o. Copy of an encryption key stored securely to enable decryption if the original encryption key becomes unavailable
____ **16.** key escrow	p. Encryption process that uses a pair of matched keys, one public and the other private; either key can encrypt something, but only the other key in that pair can decrypt
____ **17.** nonce	q. Encryption process that uses the same key to both encrypt and decrypt
	r. Inability to unilaterally deny having created a document or file or having agreed to perform a transaction
	s. Software that limits what actions (read, copy, print, etc.) can be performed by users granted access to a file or document

12.2 Cost-effective controls to provide confidentiality require valuing the information to be protected. This involves classifying information into discrete categories. Propose a minimal classification scheme that could be used by any business, and provide examples of the type of information that would fall into each of those categories.

12.3 Download a hash calculator from the course website (or use one provided by your instructor) or use an online hash calculator for this exercise. Use it to create SHA-256 (or any other hash algorithm your instructor assigns) hashes for the following:

a. A document that contains this text: "I will pay you $10.39 to walk the dog."
b. A document that contains this text: "I will pay you $1039 to walk the dog."
c. A document that contains this text: "I will pay you $10.39 to walk the Dog."
d. A document that contains this text: "I will pay you $10.39 to walk the dog." (Note: this message contains two spaces between the words "to" and "walk").
e. Make a copy of the document used in step a, and calculate its hash value.
f. What do the results of steps a–d show?
g. What does comparing the hash from step a to the hash from step e tell you?

12.4 Accountants often need to print financial statements with the words "DO NOT COPY" appearing in light type in the background.

a. Create a watermark with the phrase "DO NOT COPY" in a Word document. Print out a document that displays that watermark.
b. Create the same watermark in Excel, and print out a spreadsheet page that displays that watermark.
c. Can you make your watermark "invisible" so that it can be used to detect whether a document containing sensitive information has been copied to an unauthorized location? How? How could you use that "invisible" watermark to detect violation of copying policy?

12.5 Create a spreadsheet to compare current monthly mortgage payments versus the new monthly payments if the loan were refinanced, as shown:

REFINANCING CALCULATOR

Instructions: Only enter data into highlighted cells; do not enter data into cells without highlighting

Current loan amount	$500,000
Current term (years)	30
Current interest rate	5%
Current monthly payment	$2,684.11
New loan amount	$400,000
New loan term (years)	25
New interest rate	4.50%
New monthly payment	$2,223.33

REQUIRED

a. Restrict access to the spreadsheet by encrypting it.
b. Further protect the spreadsheet by limiting users to the ability to select and enter data only in the six highlighted cells.

Hint: The article "Keeping Secrets: How to Protect Your Computer from Snoops and Spies," by Theo Callahan in the July 2007 issue of the *Journal of Accountancy*, explains how to do this using Excel 2003. Review the article, and then use Excel's built-in help function to learn how to do this with later versions of Excel.*

12.6 Visit Symantec.com or any other security software vendor assigned by your instructor and download a trial version of encryption software.

a. Use the software to encrypt a file.
b. Send the encrypted file to your instructor and to a friend.
c. Try to open an encrypted file you receive from your friend or from your instructor. Print a screenshot to show what happens.
d. List all the options for importing the key needed to decrypt an encrypted file you receive from your friend or instructor. Which do you think is most secure? Easiest? Explain why.
e. Import (or install) the key needed to decrypt an encrypted file you receive from your friend or instructor. E-mail the decrypted file to whomever sent it to you and obtain verification that it is the plaintext version of the encrypted file they sent you.

12.7 Blockchain is used by many companies, including accounting firms. Select a company (or choose one identified by your professor), and research how it uses blockchain. Write a brief report summarizing how that company is using blockchain, and explain the benefits it provides.

12.8 Practice encryption using any encryption capabilities provided by your computer's operating system and third-party encryption software.

REQUIRED

a. Use your computer operating system's built-in encryption capability to encrypt a file. Create another user account on your computer, and log in as that user. Which of the following actions can you perform?
   1. Open the file.
   2. Copy the file to a USB drive.
   3. Move the file to a USB drive.
   4. Rename the file.
   5. Delete the file.
b. Download and install a copy of another encryption software program recommended by your instructor. Use the software to encrypt some files on a USB drive and then try to perform the same five actions listed in requirement a.
c. Write a brief report that compares the third-party encryption software's functionality to that of the built-in encryption functionality provided by your computer's operating system. Which is easier to use? Why? What are the limits (in terms of performing the five tasks) of each?

12.9 Explore and test various browser privacy settings.

a. Open your favorite browser and print a screenshot of your current settings.
b. Go to www.cisecurity.org and obtain the recommended best practices for privacy settings for your browser. Change your existing settings to those best practices. Use your browser to perform these tasks: (1) search for information about identity theft protection products, (2) open and read your personal e-mail account, (3) open and read your university or work-related e-mail account, (4) attempt to purchase something from amazon.com or any other site (you need not actually make the purchase, just try to at least get to the point in the shopping cart where

---

* Life-long learning opportunity: see pp. xxiii–xxiv in preface.

you are asked to enter your credit card number), and (5) log in to your favorite social networking site. What was the effect, if any, of changing your privacy settings?

c. Repeat step b above for another browser. Which browser makes it easier to configure privacy settings? Are there any differences between the browsers in terms of using them after you have changed the privacy settings to those recommended by the cisecurity.org benchmark documents?

12.10 Explore the power of the :bcc feature to protect privacy.

a. Write a message and send it to yourself plus use the :cc feature to send it to a set of people, including one of your other e-mail accounts in the :cc list.
b. Repeat step a, but this time send the e-mail only to yourself and then list everyone in the :bcc field.
c. Use your other e-mail account (the one you included in the :cc and :bcc fields) to open the two e-mail messages. Use all available options (e.g., view full header, etc.) to see what you can learn about the recipient lists for both e-mails. What is the power of the :bcc field?

12.11 Answer all of the following multiple-choice questions:

1. Websites often provide a link to the organization's privacy policy. Doing so most directly satisfies the requirements of the section of GAPP referred to as ________.
a. management
b. notice
c. quality
d. collection

2. Which of the following factors increase the strength of an encryption solution?
a. Securely storing encryption keys somewhere other than in the browser
b. Keeping the encryption algorithm secret
c. Using a 24-bit encryption key
d. All three options increase the strength of an encryption solution.
e. None of the three factors increase the strength of an encryption solution.

3. Able wants to send an encrypted document to Baker as an email attachment. If Able wants to securely send Baker the key to decrypt the document, Able should encrypt the key using ________.
a. Able's public asymmetric key
b. Able's private asymmetric key
c. Baker's public asymmetric key
d. Baker's private asymmetric key

4. Which of the following is the **most important** reason why it is virtually impossible for one entity in a blockchain network to unilaterally alter a document after it has been recorded and validated in a new block of transactions?
a. The use of a nonce to validate each block
b. The existence of multiple copies of the blockchain on many different computers
c. Digital signatures
d. Digital certificate

5. GAPP stresses the importance of obtaining consent when collecting, using, and sharing information about customers. If a company's policy is to ask customers for permission to collect sensitive personal information and then only asks questions about sensitive matters (such as political beliefs or sexual orientation) after the customer agrees to answer such questions, it is following the process referred to as ________.
a. explicit consent (opt-out)
b. explicit consent (opt-in)
c. implicit consent (opt-out)
d. implicit consent (opt-in)

6. Which of the following statements is true?
   a. A file encrypted with X's private key can only be decrypted by using X's private key.
   b. A file encrypted with X's private key can only be decrypted using X's public key.
   c. A file encrypted with X's private key can only be decrypted by using Y's private key.
   d. A file encrypted with X's private key can only be decrypted using Y's public key.

7. To decrypt a digital signature, the recipient uses the ________.
   a. sender's private key
   b. sender's public key
   c. recipient's private key
   d. recipient's public key

8. When is encryption **least** effective in protecting the confidentiality of sensitive data?
   a. At rest
   b. While it is being processed
   c. While it is transmitted over the Internet
   d. Encryption is equally effective in protecting confidentiality at all stages of the data processing cycle.

9. Which of the following is the most reliable way to acquire a company's public asymmetric key to be confident it really is owned by that company?
   a. Obtain it from a digital signature posted on that company's website.
   b. Obtain it directly from the company by means of an encrypted email.
   c. Obtain it from a valid digital certificate issued by a trusted certificate authority and posted on the company's website.
   d. Obtain it directly from the company via a USB delivered by a trusted delivery service (e.g., FedEx, UPS, or DHL).

10. The system used to issue pairs of asymmetric encryption keys and digital certificates is called a ________.
    a. VPN
    b. key escrow
    c. PKI
    d. tokenization or data masking

CASE 12-1 Protecting Privacy of Tax Returns

The department of taxation in your state is developing a new computer system for processing individual and corporate income-tax returns. The new system features direct data input and inquiry capabilities. Taxpayers are identified by social security number (for individuals) and federal tax identification number (for corporations). The new system should be fully implemented in time for the next tax season.

The new system will serve three primary purposes:

1. Tax return data will automatically input into the system either directly (if the taxpayer files electronically) or by a clerk at central headquarters scanning a paper return received in the mail.
2. The returns will be processed using the main computer facilities at central headquarters. Processing will include four steps:
   a. Verifying mathematical accuracy
   b. Auditing the reasonableness of deductions, tax due, and so on, through the use of edit routines, which also include a comparison of current and prior years' data
   c. Identifying returns that should be considered for audit by department revenue agents
   d. Issuing refund checks to taxpayers
3. Inquiry services. A taxpayer will be allowed to determine the status of his or her return or get

information from the last 3 years' returns by calling or visiting one of the department's regional offices or by accessing the department's website and entering his or her social security number.

The state commissioner of taxation and the state attorney general are concerned about protecting the privacy of personal information submitted by taxpayers. They want to have potential problems identified before the system is fully developed and implemented so that the proper controls can be incorporated into the new system.

REQUIRED

Describe the potential privacy problems that could arise in each of the following three areas of processing, and recommend the corrective action(s) to solve each problem identified:

a. data input
b. processing of returns
c. data inquiry (CMA examination, adapted)

CASE 12-2 Generally Accepted Privacy Principles

Obtain a copy of Generally Accepted Privacy Principles from the AICPA's website (www.aicpa.org). Use it to answer the following questions:

1. What is the difference between confidentiality and privacy?
2. How many categories of personal information exist? Why?
3. In terms of the principle of choice and consent, what does GAPP recommend concerning opt-in versus opt-out?
4. Can organizations outsource their responsibility for privacy?
5. What does principle 1 state concerning top management's and the board of directors' responsibility for privacy?
6. What does principle 1 state concerning the use of customers' personal information when organizations test new applications?
7. Obtain a copy of your university's privacy policy statement. Does it satisfy GAPP criterion 2.2.3? Why?
8. What does GAPP principle 3 say about the use of cookies?
9. What are some examples of practices that violate management criterion 4.2.2?
10. What does management criterion 5.2.2 state concerning retention of customers' personal information? How can organizations satisfy this criterion?
11. What does management criterion 5.2.3 state concerning the disposal of personal information? How can organizations satisfy this criterion?
12. What does management criterion 6.2.2 state concerning access? What controls should organizations use to achieve this objective?
13. According to GAPP principle 7, what should organizations do if they wish to share personal information they collect with a third party?
14. What does GAPP principle 8 state concerning the use of encryption?
15. What is the relationship between GAPP principles 9 and 10?

AIS in Action Solutions

QUIZ KEY

1. Which of the following statements is true?
   a. Encryption is sufficient to protect confidentiality and privacy. [Incorrect. Encryption is not sufficient because sensitive information cannot be encrypted at all times—it must be decrypted during processing, when displayed on a monitor, or included in a printed report.]
   ▶ b. Cookies are text files that only store information. They cannot perform any actions. [Correct. Cookies are text files, not executable programs. They can, however, store sensitive information, so they should be protected.]

c. The controls for protecting confidentiality are not effective for protecting privacy. [Incorrect. The same set of controls—encryption, access controls, and training—can be used to protect both confidentiality and privacy.]
d. All of the above are true. [Incorrect. Statements a and c are false.]

2. A digital signature is ________.
► **a.** created by hashing a document and then encrypting the hash with the signer's private key [Correct. Creating a hash provides a way to verify the integrity of a document, and encrypting it with the signer's private key provides a way to prove that the sender created the document.]
b. created by hashing a document and then encrypting the hash with the signer's public key [Incorrect. Anyone could encrypt something with the signer's public key. Therefore, this process cannot be used to prove who created a document.]
c. created by hashing a document and then encrypting the hash with the signer's symmetric key [Incorrect. A symmetric key is possessed by more than one party, so encrypting something with it does not provide a means to prove who created a document.]
d. none of the above [Incorrect. Only choices b and c are incorrect; choice a is correct.]

3. Able wants to send a file to Baker over the Internet and protect the file so that only Baker can read it and verify that it came from Able. What should Able do?
a. Encrypt the file using Able's public key, and then encrypt it again using Baker's private key. [Incorrect. Able does not know Baker's private key.]
b. Encrypt the file using Able's private key, and then encrypt it again using Baker's private key. [Incorrect. Able does not know Baker's private key.]
c. Encrypt the file using Able's public key, and then encrypt it again using Baker's public key. [Incorrect. Baker does not know Able's private key and therefore cannot decrypt the file encrypted with Able's public key.]
► **d.** Encrypt the file using Able's private key, and then encrypt it again using Baker's public key. [Correct. Encrypting it with Baker's public key means that only Baker can decrypt it. Then, Baker can use Able's public key to decrypt the file—if the result is understandable, it had to have been created by Able and encrypted with Able's private key.]

4. Which of the following statements is true?
a. Encryption and hashing are both reversible (can be decoded). [Incorrect. Hashing is irreversible.]
► **b.** Encryption is reversible, but hashing is not. [Correct. Encryption can be reversed to decrypt the ciphertext, but hashing cannot be reversed.]
c. Hashing is reversible, but encryption is not. [Incorrect. Hashing is irreversible, but encryption is reversible.]
d. Neither hashing nor encryption is reversible. [Incorrect. Encryption is reversible, a process called decryption.]

5. Confidentiality focuses on protecting ________.
a. personal information collected from customers [Incorrect. Protecting customers' personal information relates to the principle of privacy.]
b. a company's annual report stored on its website [Incorrect. A company's annual report is meant to be available to the public.]
► **c.** merger and acquisition plans [Correct. Merger and acquisition plans are sensitive information that should not be made public until the deal is consummated.]
d. all of the above [Incorrect. Statements a and b are false.]

6. Which of the following statements about obtaining consent to collect and use a customer's personal information is true?
a. The default policy in Europe is opt-out, but in the United States the default is opt-in. [Incorrect. The default policy in Europe is opt-in, and in the United States it is opt-out.]
► **b.** The default policy in Europe is opt-in, but in the United States the default is opt-out. [Correct.]

c. The default policy in both Europe and the United States is opt-in. [Incorrect. The default policy in Europe is opt-in, and in the United States it is opt-out.]
d. The default policy in both Europe and the United States is opt-out. [Incorrect. The default policy in Europe is opt-in, and in the United States it is opt-out.]

7. One of the 10 Generally Accepted Privacy Principles concerns security. According to GAPP, what is the nature of the relationship between security and privacy?
a. Privacy is a necessary, but not sufficient, precondition to effective security. [Incorrect. Security is one of the 10 criteria in GAPP because you need security in order to have privacy. Security alone, however, is not enough—that is why there are nine other criteria in GAPP.]
b. Privacy is both necessary and sufficient to effective security. [Incorrect. Security is one of the 10 criteria in GAPP because you need security in order to have privacy. Security alone, however, is not enough—that is why there are nine other criteria in GAPP.]
▶ c. Security is a necessary, but not sufficient, precondition to protect privacy. [Correct.]
d. Security is both necessary and sufficient to protect privacy. [Incorrect. Security is one of the 10 criteria in GAPP because you need security in order to have privacy. Security alone, however, is not enough—that is why there are nine other criteria in GAPP.]

8. Which of the following statements is true?
a. Symmetric encryption is faster than asymmetric encryption and can be used to provide nonrepudiation of contracts. [Incorrect. Symmetric encryption cannot be used for nonrepudiation because both parties share the key, so there is no way to prove who created and encrypted a document.]
▶ b. Symmetric encryption is faster than asymmetric encryption but cannot be used to provide nonrepudiation of contracts. [Correct. Symmetric encryption is faster than asymmetric encryption, but it cannot be used for nonrepudiation; the key is shared by both parties, so there is no way to prove who created and encrypted a document.]
c. Asymmetric encryption is faster than symmetric encryption and can be used to provide nonrepudiation of contracts. [Incorrect. Symmetric encryption is faster than asymmetric encryption.]
d. Asymmetric encryption is faster than symmetric encryption but cannot be used to provide nonrepudiation of contracts. [Incorrect. Symmetric encryption is faster than asymmetric encryption. Also, asymmetric encryption can be used to provide nonrepudiation because encrypting a contract with the creator's private key proves that the encrypter did indeed create the contract.]

9. Which of the following statements is true?
a. VPNs protect the confidentiality of information while it is in transit over the Internet. [Incorrect. This statement is true, but so are the others.]
b. Encryption limits firewalls' ability to filter traffic. [Incorrect. This statement is true—firewalls cannot apply their rules to encrypted packets—but so are the others.]
c. A digital certificate contains that entity's public key. [Incorrect. This statement is true, but so are the others.]
▶ d. All of the above are true. [Correct. All three statements are true.]

10. Which of the following can organizations use to protect the privacy of a customer's personal information when giving programmers a realistic data set with which to test a new application?
a. digital signature [Incorrect. A digital signature is used for nonrepudiation. However, because it is an encrypted hash, it cannot be used to test programming logic.]
b. digital watermark [Incorrect. A digital watermark is used to identify proprietary data, but it does not protect privacy.]
c. data loss prevention [Incorrect. Data loss prevention is designed to protect confidentiality by filtering outgoing messages to prevent sensitive data from leaving the company.]
▶ d. data masking [Correct. Masking replaces actual values with fake ones, but the result is still the same type of data, which can then be used to test program logic.]

CHAPTER

13

Processing Integrity and Availability Controls

LEARNING OBJECTIVES

After studying this chapter, you should be able to:

1. Identify and explain the input, processing, and output controls designed to ensure processing integrity.
2. Identify and explain controls designed to ensure systems availability by minimizing the risk of system downtime and enabling efficient recovery and resumption of operations.

INTEGRATIVE CASE Northwest Industries

Jason Scott began his review of Northwest Industries' processing integrity and availability controls by meeting with the chief financial officer (CFO) and the chief information officer (CIO). The CFO mentioned that she had just read an article about how spreadsheet errors had caused several companies to make poor decisions that cost them millions of dollars. She wanted to be sure that such problems did not happen to Northwest Industries. She also stressed the need to continue to improve the monthly closing process so that management would have more timely information. The CIO expressed concern about the company's lack of planning for how to continue business operations in the event of a major natural disaster, such as Hurricane Sandy, which had forced several small businesses to close. Jason thanked them for their input and set about collecting evidence about the effectiveness of Northwest Industries' procedures for ensuring processing integrity and availability.

Introduction

The previous two chapters discussed the first three principles of systems reliability identified in the Trust Services Framework: security, confidentiality, and privacy. This chapter addresses the remaining two Trust Services Framework principles: processing integrity and availability.

Alexskopje/Shutterstock; Stuart Miles/Shutterstock

Processing Integrity

The processing integrity principle of the Trust Services Framework states that a reliable system produces information that is accurate, complete, timely, and valid. Table 13-1 lists the basic controls over the input, processing, and output of data that COBIT 2019 process DSS06 identifies as essential for processing integrity.

INPUT CONTROLS

The phrase "garbage in, garbage out" highlights the importance of input controls. If the data entered into a system are inaccurate, incomplete, or invalid, the output will be too. Consequently, only authorized personnel acting within their authority should prepare source documents. In addition, forms design, cancellation and storage of source documents, and automated data entry controls are needed to verify the validity of input data.

FORMS DESIGN Source documents and other forms should be designed to minimize the chances for errors and omissions. Two particularly important forms design controls involve sequentially prenumbering source documents and using turnaround documents.

1. All source documents should be sequentially prenumbered. Prenumbering improves control by making it possible to verify that no documents are missing. (To understand this, consider the difficulty you would have in balancing your checking account if none of your checks were numbered.) When sequentially prenumbered source data documents are used, the system should be programmed to identify and report missing or duplicate source documents.
2. As explained in Chapter 2, companies use turnaround documents to eliminate the need for an external party to submit information that the organization already possesses, such as the customer's account number. Instead, that data is preprinted in machine-readable format on the turnaround document. An example is a utility bill that a special scanning device reads when the bill is returned with a payment. Turnaround documents improve accuracy by eliminating the potential for input errors when entering data manually.

CANCELLATION AND STORAGE OF SOURCE DOCUMENTS Source documents that have been entered into the system should be canceled so they cannot be inadvertently or fraudulently reentered into the system. Paper documents should be defaced, for example, by stamping them "paid." Electronic documents can be similarly "canceled" by setting a flag field to indicate that the document has already been processed. *Note:* Cancellation does *not* mean disposal. Original source documents (or their electronic images) should be retained for as long as needed to satisfy legal and regulatory requirements and provide an audit trail.

TABLE 13-1 Application Controls for Processing Integrity

Process Stage	Threats/Risks	Controls
Input	Data that is: • Invalid • Unauthorized • Incomplete • Inaccurate	Forms design, cancellation and storage of documents, authorization and segregation of duties controls, visual scanning, data entry controls
Processing	Errors in output and stored data	Data matching, file labels, batch totals, cross-footing and zero-balance tests, write-protection mechanisms, database processing integrity controls
Output	• Use of inaccurate or incomplete reports • Unauthorized disclosure of sensitive information • Loss, alteration, or disclosure of information in transit	Reviews and reconciliations, encryption and access controls, parity checks, message acknowledgment techniques, blockchain

field check - An edit check that tests whether the characters in a field are of the correct field type (e.g., numeric data in numeric fields).

sign check - An edit check that verifies that the data in a field have the appropriate arithmetic sign.

limit check - An edit check that tests a numerical amount against a fixed value.

range check - An edit check that tests whether a data item falls within predetermined upper and lower limits.

size check - An edit check that ensures the input data will fit into the assigned field.

completeness check (or test) - An edit check that verifies that all data required have been entered.

validity check - An edit test that compares the ID code or account number in transaction data with similar data in the master file to verify that the account exists.

reasonableness test - An edit check of the logical correctness of relationships among data items.

check digit - ID numbers (such as inventory item number) can contain a check digit computed from the other digits.

check digit verification - Recalculating a check digit to verify that a data entry error has not been made.

DATA ENTRY CONTROLS Source documents should be scanned for reasonableness and propriety before being entered into the system. However, this manual control must be supplemented with automated data entry controls, such as the following:

- A **field check** determines whether the characters in a field are of the proper type. For example, a check on a field that is supposed to contain only numeric values, such as a U.S. zip code, would indicate an error if it contained alphabetic characters.
- A **sign check** determines whether the data in a field have the appropriate arithmetic sign. For example, the quantity-ordered field should never be negative.
- A **limit check** tests a numerical amount against a fixed value. For example, the regular hours-worked field in weekly payroll input must be less than or equal to 40 hours. Similarly, the hourly wage field should be greater than or equal to the minimum wage.
- A **range check** tests whether a numerical amount falls between predetermined lower and upper limits. For example, a marketing promotion might be directed only to prospects with incomes between $50,000 and $99,999.
- A **size check** ensures that the input data will fit into the assigned field. For example, the value 458,976,253 will not fit in an eight-digit field. As discussed in Chapter 11, size checks are especially important for applications that directly accept end-user input, providing a way to prevent buffer overflow vulnerabilities.
- A **completeness check (or test)** verifies that all required data items have been entered. For example, sales transaction records should not be accepted for processing unless they include the customer's shipping and billing addresses.
- A **validity check** compares the ID code or account number in transaction data with similar data in the master file to verify that the account exists. For example, if product number 65432 is entered on a sales order, the computer must verify that there is indeed a product 65432 in the inventory database.
- A **reasonableness test** determines the correctness of the logical relationship between two data items. For example, overtime hours should be zero for someone who has not worked the maximum number of regular hours in a pay period.
- ID codes (such as part numbers) can contain a **check digit** that is computed from the other digits. For example, the system could assign each new inventory item a nine-digit number, then calculate a tenth digit from the original nine and append that calculated number to the original nine to form a 10-digit part number. Data entry devices can then be programmed to perform **check digit verification**, which involves recalculating the check digit to identify data entry errors. Continuing our example, check digit verification could be used to

verify accuracy of an inventory item number by using the first nine digits to calculate what the tenth digit should be. If an error is made in entering any of the ten digits, the calculation made on the first nine digits will not match the tenth, or check digit. Note that check digit verification only tests whether an ID code in a transaction record *could* exist and is designed to catch transposition errors (e.g., entering 35689 instead of 35869 as a part number). A validity check is the only way to verify that the ID code really does exist.

The preceding data entry tests are used for both batch processing and online real-time processing. Additional data input controls differ for the two processing methods.

ADDITIONAL BATCH PROCESSING DATA ENTRY CONTROLS

- Batch processing works more efficiently if the transactions are sorted so that the accounts affected are in the same sequence as records are stored in the master file. For example, accurate batch processing of sales transactions to update customer account balances requires that the sales transactions file first be sorted by customer account number. A **sequence check** tests whether a transaction file is in the proper numerical or alphabetical sequence.
- An error log that identifies data input errors (date, cause, problem) facilitates timely review and resubmission of transactions that cannot be processed.
- **Batch totals** calculate numeric values for a batch of input records. Batch totals are used to ensure that all records in a batch are processed correctly. The following are three commonly used batch totals:

  1. A **financial total** sums a field that contains monetary values, such as the total dollar amount of all sales for a batch of sales transactions.
  2. A **hash total** sums a nonfinancial numeric field, such as the total of the quantity-ordered field in a batch of sales transactions. Unlike financial totals, hash totals have no inherent meaning. For example, it is possible to sum up the invoice numbers in a batch of sales transactions but the result is meaningless; its only purpose is to serve as an input control.
  3. A **record count** is the number of records in a batch.

ADDITIONAL ONLINE DATA ENTRY CONTROLS

- **Prompting**, in which the system requests each input data item and waits for an acceptable response, ensures that all necessary data are entered (i.e., prompting is an online completeness check).
- **Closed-loop verification** checks the accuracy of input data by using it to retrieve and display other related information. For example, if a clerk enters an account number, the system could retrieve and display the account name so that the clerk could verify that the correct account number had been entered.
- A transaction log includes a detailed record of all transactions, including a unique transaction identifier, the date and time of entry, and who entered the transaction. If an online file is damaged, the transaction log can be used to reconstruct the file. If a malfunction temporarily shuts down the system, the transaction log can be used to ensure that transactions are not lost or entered twice.

PROCESSING CONTROLS

Controls are also needed to ensure data is processed correctly. Important processing controls include the following:

- ***Data matching.*** In certain cases, two or more items of data must be matched before an action can take place. For example, before paying a vendor, the system should verify that information on the vendor invoice matches information on both the purchase order and the receiving report.
- ***File labels.*** File labels need to be checked to ensure that the correct and most current files are being updated. Both external labels that are readable by humans and internal labels that are written in machine-readable form on the data recording media should be

sequence check - An edit check that determines if a transaction file is in the proper numerical or alphabetical sequence.

batch totals - The sum of a numerical item for a batch of documents, calculated prior to processing the batch, when the data are entered, and subsequently compared with computer-generated totals after each processing step to verify that the data was processed correctly.

financial total - A type of batch total that equals the sum of a field that contains monetary values.

hash total - A type of batch total generated by summing values for a field that would not usually be totaled.

record count - A type of batch total that equals the number of records processed at a given time.

prompting - An online data entry completeness check that requests each required item of input data and then waits for an acceptable response before requesting the next required item.

closed-loop verification - An input validation method that uses data entered into the system to retrieve and display other related information so that the data entry person can verify the accuracy of the input data.

header record - Type of internal label that appears at the beginning of each file and contains the file name, expiration date, and other file identification information.

trailer record - Type of internal label that appears at the end of a file; in transaction files, the trailer record contains the batch totals calculated during input.

used. Two important types of internal labels are header and trailer records. The **header record** is located at the beginning of each file and contains the file name, expiration date, and other identification data. The **trailer record** is located at the end of the file; in transaction files it contains the batch totals calculated during input. Programs should be designed to read the header record *prior* to processing, to ensure that the correct file is being updated. Programs should also be designed to read the information in the trailer record *after* processing, to verify that all input records have been correctly processed.

- ***Recalculation of batch totals.*** Batch totals should be recomputed as each transaction record is processed, by comparing a running total calculated during processing to the corresponding batch total calculated during input and stored in the trailer record. Any discrepancies indicate a processing error. Often, the nature of the discrepancy provides a clue about the type of error that occurred. For example, if the recomputed record count is smaller than the original, one or more transaction records were not processed. Conversely, if the recomputed record count is larger than the original, either additional unauthorized transactions were processed, or some transaction records were processed twice. If a financial or hash total discrepancy is evenly divisible by 9, the likely cause is a **transposition error**, in which two adjacent digits were inadvertently reversed (e.g., 46 instead of 64). Transposition errors may appear to be trivial but can have enormous financial consequences. For example, consider the effect of misrecording the interest rate on a loan as 6.4% instead of 4.6%.

transposition error - An error that results when numbers in two adjacent columns are inadvertently exchanged (for example, 64 is written as 46).

cross-footing balance test - A processing control that verifies accuracy by comparing two alternative ways of calculating the same total.

zero-balance test - A processing control that verifies that the balance of a control account equals zero after all entries to it have been made.

- ***Cross-footing and zero-balance tests.*** Often totals can be calculated in multiple ways. For example, in spreadsheets a grand total can be computed either by summing a column of row totals or by summing a row of column totals. These two methods should produce the same result. A **cross-footing balance test** compares the results produced by each method to verify accuracy. A **zero-balance test** applies this same logic to verify the accuracy of processing that involves control accounts. For example, the payroll clearing account is debited for the total gross pay of all employees in a particular time period. It is then credited for the amount of all labor costs allocated to various expense categories. The payroll clearing account should have a zero balance after both sets of entries have been made; a nonzero balance indicates a processing error.
- ***Write-protection mechanisms.*** These protect against overwriting or erasing of data files stored on magnetic media. Write-protection mechanisms have long been used to protect master files from accidentally being damaged. Technological innovations also necessitate the use of write-protection mechanisms to protect the integrity of transaction data. For example, radio frequency identification (RFID) tags used to track inventory need to be write-protected so that unscrupulous customers cannot change the price of merchandise.
- ***Concurrent update controls.*** Errors can occur when two or more users attempt to update the same record simultaneously. **Concurrent update controls** prevent such errors by locking out one user until the system has finished processing the transaction entered by the other.

concurrent update controls - Controls that lock out users to protect individual records from errors that could occur if multiple users attempted to update the same record simultaneously.

OUTPUT CONTROLS

Careful checking of system output provides additional control over processing integrity. Important output controls include the following:

- ***User review of output.*** Users should carefully examine system output to verify that it is reasonable and complete, and that they are the intended recipients.
- ***Reconciliation procedures.*** Periodically, all transactions and other system updates should be reconciled to control reports, file status/update reports, or other control mechanisms. In addition, general ledger accounts should be reconciled to subsidiary account totals on a regular basis. For example, the balance of the inventory control account in the general ledger should equal the sum of the item balances in the inventory database. The same is true for the accounts receivable, capital assets, and accounts payable control accounts.
- ***External data reconciliation.*** Database totals should periodically be reconciled with data maintained outside the system. For example, the number of employee records in the

payroll file can be compared with the total number of employees in the human resources database to detect attempts to add fictitious employees to the payroll database. Similarly, inventory on hand should be physically counted and compared to the quantity on hand recorded in the database. The results of the physical count should be used to update the recorded amounts and significant discrepancies should be investigated.

- ***Data transmission controls.*** Organizations also need to implement controls designed to minimize the risk of data transmission errors. Whenever the receiving device detects a data transmission error, it requests the sending device to retransmit that data. Generally, this happens automatically, and the user is unaware that it has occurred. For example, the Transmission Control Protocol (TCP) discussed in Chapter 11 assigns a sequence number to each packet and uses that information to verify that all packets have been received and to reassemble them in the correct order. Two other common data transmission controls are checksums and parity bits.

  1. ***Checksums.*** When data are transmitted, the sending device can calculate a hash of the file, called a **checksum**. The receiving device performs the same calculation and sends the result to the sending device. If the two hashes agree, the transmission is presumed to be accurate. Otherwise, the file is resent.
  2. ***Parity bits.*** Computers represent characters as a set of binary digits called bits. Each bit has two possible values: 0 or 1. Many computers use a seven-bit coding scheme, which is more than enough to represent the 26 letters in the English alphabet (both upper- and lowercase), the numbers 0 through 9, and a variety of special symbols ($, %, &, etc.). A **parity bit** is an extra digit added to the beginning of every character that can be used to check transmission accuracy. Two basic schemes are referred to as *even parity* and *odd parity*. In even parity, the parity bit is set so that each character has an even number of bits with the value 1; in odd parity, the parity bit is set so that an odd number of bits in the character have the value 1. For example, the digits 5 and 7 can be represented by the seven-bit patterns 0000101 and 0000111, respectively. An even parity system would set the parity bit for 5 to 0, so that it would be transmitted as 00000101 (because the binary code for 5 already has two bits with the value 1). The parity bit for 7 would be set to 1 so that it would be transmitted as 10000111 (because the binary code for 7 has 3 bits with the value 1). The receiving device performs **parity checking**, which entails verifying that the proper number of bits are set to the value 1 in each character received.
  3. ***Blockchain.*** As explained in Chapter 12, blockchains provide a way to ensure that validated transactions and documents are not altered. Integrity is assured by hashing the contents of each block and then storing multiple copies of the entire chain on different devices.

checksum - A data transmission control that uses a hash of a file to verify accuracy.

parity bit - An extra bit added to every character; used to check transmission accuracy.

parity checking - A data transmission control in which the receiving device recalculates the parity bit to verify accuracy of transmitted data.

ILLUSTRATIVE EXAMPLE: CREDIT SALES PROCESSING

We now use the processing of credit sales to illustrate how many of the application controls that have been discussed actually function. Each transaction record includes the following data: sales invoice number, customer account number, inventory item number, quantity sold, sale price, and delivery date. If the customer purchases more than one product, there will be multiple inventory item numbers, quantities sold, and prices associated with each sales transaction. Processing these transactions includes the following steps: (1) entering and editing the transaction data; (2) updating the customer and inventory records (the amount of the credit purchase is added to the customer's balance; for each inventory item, the quantity sold is subtracted from the quantity on hand); and (3) preparing and distributing shipping and/or billing documents.

INPUT CONTROLS As sales transactions are entered, the system performs several preliminary validation tests. Validity checks identify transactions with invalid account numbers or invalid inventory item numbers. Field checks verify that the quantity-ordered and price fields contain only numbers and that the date field follows the correct MM/DD/YYYY format. Sign checks verify that the quantity sold and sale price fields contain positive numbers. A range check verifies that the delivery date is not earlier than the current date nor later than the company's advertised delivery policies. A completeness check tests whether any necessary fields (e.g., delivery address) are blank. If batch processing is being used, the sales are grouped into batches (typical size = 50) and one of the following batch totals is calculated and stored with the batch: a financial total of the total sales amount, a hash total of invoice numbers, or a record count.

PROCESSING CONTROLS The system reads the header records for the customer and inventory master files and verifies that the most current version is being used. As each sales invoice is processed, limit checks are used to verify that the new sale does not increase that customer's account balance beyond the pre-established credit limit. If it does, the transaction is temporarily set aside and a notification sent to the credit manager. If the sale is processed, a sign check verifies that the new quantity on hand for each inventory item is greater than or equal to zero. A range check verifies that each item's sales price falls within preset limits. A reasonableness check compares the quantity sold to the item number and compares both to historical averages. If batch processing is being used, the system calculates the appropriate batch total and compares it to the batch total created during input; if the two batch totals do not agree, an error report is generated and someone investigates the cause of the discrepancy.

OUTPUT CONTROLS Billing and shipping documents are routed to only authorized employees in the accounting and shipping departments, who visually inspect them for obvious errors. A control report that summarizes the transactions that were processed is sent to the sales, accounting, and inventory control managers for review. Each quarter inventory in the warehouse is physically counted and the results compared to recorded quantities on hand for each item. The cause of discrepancies is investigated and adjusting entries are made to correct recorded quantities.

The preceding example illustrated the use of application controls to ensure the integrity of processing business transactions. Focus 13-1 explains the importance of processing integrity controls in nonbusiness settings, too.

FOCUS 13-1 Ensuring the Processing Integrity of Electronic Voting

Electronic voting may eliminate some of the types of problems that occur with manual or mechanical voting. For example, electronic voting software could use limit checks to prevent voters from attempting to select more candidates than permitted in a particular race. A completeness check would identify a voter's failure to make a choice in every race, and closed-loop verification could then be used to verify whether that was intentional. (This would eliminate the "hanging chad" problem created when voters fail to punch out the hole completely on a paper ballot.)

Nevertheless, there are concerns about electronic voting, particularly its audit trail capabilities. At issue is the ability to verify that only properly registered voters did indeed vote and that they voted only once. Although no one disagrees with the need for such authentication, there is debate over whether electronic voting machines can create adequate audit trails without risking the loss of voters' anonymity.

There is also debate about the overall security and reliability of electronic voting. Some security experts suggest that election officials should adopt the methods used by the state of Nevada to ensure that electronic gambling machines operate honestly and accurately, which include the following:

- ***Access to the source code.*** The Nevada Gaming Control Board keeps copies of all software. It is illegal for casinos to use any unregistered software. Similarly, security experts recommend that the government should keep copies of the source code of electronic voting software.
- ***Hardware checks.*** Frequent on-site spot checks of the computer chips in gambling machines are made to verify compliance with the Nevada Gaming Control Board's records. Similar tests should be done to voting machines.
- ***Tests of physical security.*** The Nevada Gaming Control Board extensively tests how machines react to stun guns and large electric shocks. Voting machines should be similarly tested.
- ***Background checks.*** All gambling machine manufacturers are carefully scrutinized and registered. Similar checks should be performed on voting machine manufacturers, as well as election software developers.

PROCESSING INTEGRITY CONTROLS IN SPREADSHEETS

Most organizations have thousands of spreadsheets that are used to support decision-making. Yet, because end users almost always develop spreadsheets, they seldom contain adequate application controls. Therefore, it is not surprising that many organizations have experienced serious problems caused by spreadsheet errors. For example, an August 17, 2007, article in *CIO Magazine*[1] describes how spreadsheet errors caused companies to lose money, issue erroneous dividend payout announcements, and misreport financial results.

Careful testing of spreadsheets before use could have prevented these kinds of costly mistakes. Although most spreadsheet software contains built-in "audit" features that can easily detect common errors, spreadsheets intended to support important decisions need more thorough testing to detect subtle errors. It is especially important to check for *hardwiring*, where formulas contain specific numeric values (e.g., sales tax = 8.5% × A33). Best practice is to use reference cells (e.g., store the sales tax rate in cell A8) and then write formulas that include the reference cell (e.g., change the previous example to sales tax = A8 × A33). The problem with hardwiring is that the spreadsheet initially produces correct answers, but when the hardwired variable (e.g., the sales tax rate in the preceding example) changes, the formula may not be corrected in every cell that includes that hardwired value. In contrast, following the recommended best practice and storing the sales tax value in a clearly labeled cell means that when the sales tax rate changes, only that one cell needs to be updated. This best practice also ensures that the updated sales tax rate is used in every formula that involves calculating sales taxes.

Availability

Interruptions to business processes due to the unavailability of systems or information can cause significant financial losses. Consequently, COBIT 2019 control processes DSS01 and DSS04 address the importance of ensuring that systems and information are available for use whenever needed. The primary objective is to minimize the risk of system downtime. It is impossible, however, to completely eliminate the risk of downtime. Therefore, organizations also need controls designed to enable quick resumption of normal operations after an event disrupts system availability. Table 13-2 summarizes the key controls related to these two objectives.

MINIMIZING RISK OF SYSTEM DOWNTIME

Organizations can undertake a variety of actions to minimize the risk of system downtime. COBIT 2019 management practice DSS01.05 identifies the need for preventive maintenance, such as cleaning disk drives and properly storing magnetic and optical media, to reduce the

TABLE 13-2 Availability: Objectives and Key Controls

Objective	Key Controls
1. To minimize risk of system downtime	• Preventive maintenance • Fault tolerance • Data center location and design • Training • Patch management and antivirus software
2. Quick and complete recovery and resumption of normal operations	• Backup procedures • Disaster recovery plan (DRP) • Business continuity plan (BCP)

[1]Thomas Wailgum, "Eight of the Worst Spreadsheet Blunders," *CIO Magazine* (August 2007), available at http://www.cio.com/article/2438188/enterprise-software/eight-of-the-worst-spreadsheet-blunders.html.

fault tolerance - The capability of a system to continue performing when there is a hardware failure.

redundant arrays of independent drives (RAID) - A fault tolerance technique that records data on multiple disk drives instead of just one to reduce the risk of data loss.

risk of hardware and software failure. The use of redundant components provides **fault tolerance**, which is the ability of a system to continue functioning in the event that a particular component fails. For example, many organizations use **redundant arrays of independent drives (RAID)** instead of just one disk drive. With RAID, data is written to multiple disk drives simultaneously. Thus, if one disk drive fails, the data can be readily accessed from another.

COBIT 2019 management practices DSS01.04 and DSS01.05 address the importance of locating and designing the data centers housing mission-critical servers and databases so as to minimize the risks associated with natural and human-caused disasters. Common design features include the following:

- Raised floors provide protection from damage caused by flooding.
- Fire detection and suppression devices reduce the likelihood of fire damage.
- Adequate air-conditioning systems reduce the likelihood of damage to computer equipment due to overheating or humidity.
- Cables with special plugs that cannot be easily removed reduce the risk of system damage due to accidental unplugging of the device.
- Surge-protection devices provide protection against temporary power fluctuations that might otherwise cause computers and other network equipment to crash.
- An **uninterruptible power supply (UPS)** system provides protection in the event of a prolonged power outage, using battery power to enable the system to operate long enough to back up critical data and safely shut down. (However, it is important to regularly inspect and test the batteries in a UPS to ensure that it will function when needed.)
- Physical access controls reduce the risk of theft or damage.

uninterruptible power supply (UPS) - An alternative power supply device that protects against the loss of power and fluctuations in the power level by using battery power to enable the system to operate long enough to back up critical data and safely shut down.

Training can also reduce the risk of system downtime. Well-trained operators are less likely to make mistakes and will know how to recover, with minimal damage, from errors they do commit. That is why COBIT 2019 management practice DSS01 stresses the importance of defining and documenting operational procedures and ensuring that IT staff understand their responsibilities.

System downtime can also occur because of computer malware (e.g., ransomware can make applications and data inaccessible). Therefore, it is important to install, run, and keep current antivirus and anti-spyware programs. These programs should be automatically invoked not only to scan e-mail, but also any removable computer media (CDs, DVDs, USB drives, etc.) that are brought into the organization. A patch management system provides additional protection by ensuring that vulnerabilities that can be exploited by malware are fixed in a timely manner.

RECOVERY AND RESUMPTION OF NORMAL OPERATIONS

The preventive controls discussed in the preceding section can minimize, but not entirely eliminate, the risk of system downtime. Hardware malfunctions, software problems, or human error can cause data to become inaccessible. For example, RAID devices can experience catastrophic failures, rendering all the drives useless. That's why senior management needs to answer two fundamental questions:

1. How much data are we willing to recreate from source documents (if they exist) or potentially lose (if no source documents exist)?
2. How long can we function without our information system?

recovery point objective (RPO) - The amount of data the organization is willing to reenter or potentially lose.

recovery time objective (RTO) - The maximum tolerable time to restore an organization's information system following a disaster, representing the length of time that the organization is willing to attempt to function without its information system.

Figure 13-1 shows the relationship between these two questions. When a problem occurs, data about everything that has happened since the last backup is lost unless it can be reentered into the system. Thus, management's answer to the first question determines the organization's **recovery point objective (RPO)**, which represents the maximum amount of data that the organization is willing to have to reenter or potentially lose. The RPO is inversely related to the frequency of backups: the smaller the desired RPO, the more frequently backups need to be made. The answer to the second question determines the organization's **recovery time objective (RTO)**, which is the maximum tolerable time to restore an information system after a disaster. Thus, the RTO represents the length of time that the organization is willing to attempt to function without its information system.

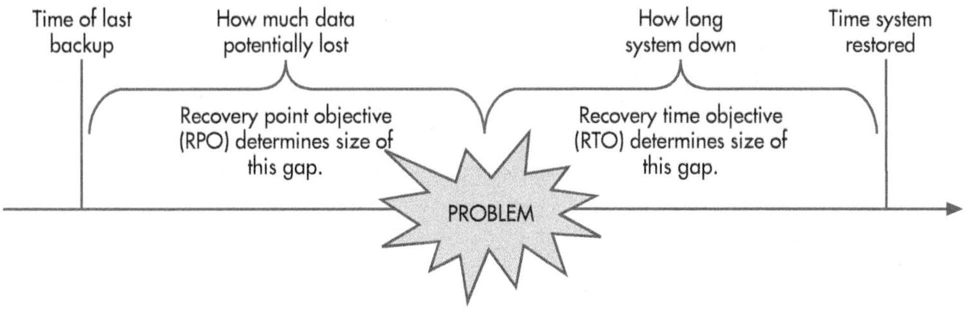

FIGURE 13-1
Relationship of Recovery Point Objective and Recovery Time Objective

DATA BACKUP PROCEDURES Data backup procedures are designed to deal with situations where information is not accessible because the relevant files or databases have become corrupted as a result of hardware failure, software problems, or human error, but the information system itself is still functioning. Several different backup procedures exist. A **full backup** is an exact copy of the entire database. Full backups are time-consuming, so most organizations only do full backups weekly and supplement them with daily partial backups. Figure 13-2 compares the two types of daily partial backups:

1. An **incremental backup** involves copying only the data items that have changed since the last *partial* backup. This produces a set of incremental backup files, each containing the results of one day's transactions. Restoration involves first loading the last full backup and then installing each subsequent incremental backup in the proper sequence.
2. A **differential backup** copies all changes made since the last *full* backup. Thus, each new differential backup file contains the cumulative effects of all activity since the last full backup. Consequently, except for the first day following a full backup, daily differential backups take longer than incremental backups. Restoration is simpler, however, because the last full backup needs to be supplemented with only the most recent differential backup, instead of a set of daily incremental backup files.

Deduplication is causing many organizations to eliminate making full backups and to continuously make incremental partial backups instead. **Deduplication** uses hashing to identify

full backup - Exact copy of an entire database.

incremental backup - A type of partial backup that involves copying only the data items that have changed since the last *partial* backup. This produces a set of incremental backup files, each containing the results of one day's transactions.

differential backup - A type of partial backup that involves copying all changes made since the last full backup. Thus, each new differential backup file contains the cumulative effects of all activity since the last full backup.

deduplication - A process that uses hashing to identify and backup only those portions of a file or database that have been updated since the last backup.

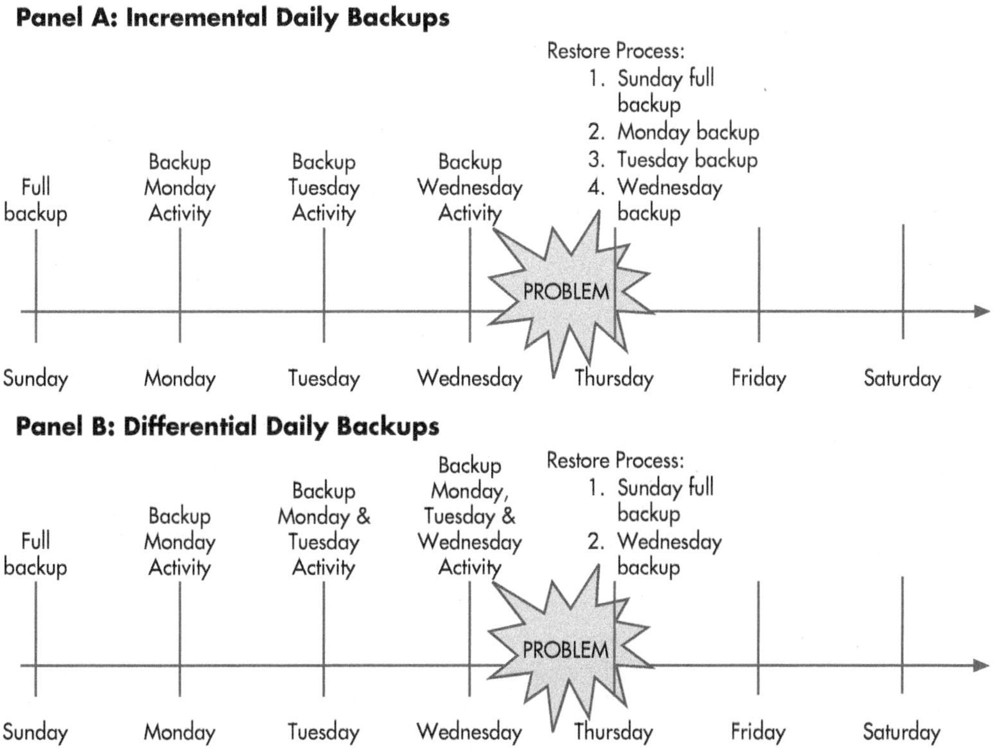

FIGURE 13-2
Comparison of Incremental and Differential Daily Backups

and backup only those portions of a file or database that have been updated since the last backup. The deduplication process works by dividing a file or database into uniform-sized chunks. Each chunk is hashed, and the chunk's hash value is compared to the hash values of all chunks in the hash file from the previous backup. Recall that identical hash values mean that two data sets are bit-for-bit identical. Thus, any data chunk with a hash file that matches a value in the hash file from the previous backup has not been changed. Consequently, it does not need to be backed up again. Instead, only those data chunks whose current hash values do not match any values in the hash file from the previous backup need to be backed up this time. Typically, only a small percentage of a database or file has been changed since the last backup; therefore, deduplication results in fast backups. The restore process then involves using the most current file of chunk hashes to identify the appropriate incremental backup files that need to be combined to recreate the complete file or database.

No matter which backup procedure is used, multiple backup copies should be created. One copy can be stored on-site, for use in the event of relatively minor problems, such as failure of a hard drive. In the event of a more serious problem, such as a fire or flood, any backup copies stored on-site will likely be destroyed or inaccessible. Therefore, a second backup copy needs to be stored off-site. These backup files can be transported to the remote storage site either physically (e.g., by courier) or electronically. In either case, the same security controls need to be applied to backup files as are used to protect the original copy of the information. This means that backup copies of sensitive data should be encrypted both in storage and during electronic transmission. Access to backup files also needs to be carefully controlled and monitored.

It is also important to periodically practice restoring a system from its backups. This verifies that the backup procedure is working correctly and that the backup media (tape or disk) can be successfully read by the hardware in use.

The purpose of backups is to enable restoration of data in the event that the original copy becomes inaccessbile. Consequently, backups are retained for only a relatively short period of time. For example, many organizations maintain only several months of backups. Some information, however, must be stored much longer. An **archive** is a copy of a database, master file, or software retained indefinitely as a historical record, usually to satisfy legal and regulatory requirements. Archives are used to retrieve selected data, not to restore entire files or databases. Consequently, archive software includes indexing features to facilitate quick retrieval, but backup software does not. Therefore, retaining backups for years is not a viable alternative to creating true archives. As with backups, multiple copies of archives should be made and stored in different locations. Unlike backups, archives are seldom encrypted because their long retention times increase the risk of losing the decryption key. Consequently, physical and logical access controls are the primary means of protecting archive files.

archive - A copy of a database, master file, or software retained indefinitely as a historical record, usually to satisfy legal and regulatory requirements.

What media should be used for backups and archives, tape or disk? Disk backup is faster, and so is the time required to retrieve the data. Tape, however, is cheaper, easier to transport, and more durable. In addition, because tapes are typically stored offline, they are less likely to be infected by ransomware. Consequently, many organizations use both media. Data are first backed up to disk, for speed, and then transferred to tape.

Special attention needs to be paid to backing up and archiving e-mail because it has become an important repository of organizational behavior and information. Indeed, e-mail often contains solutions to specific problems. E-mail also frequently contains information relevant to lawsuits. It may be tempting for an organization to consider a policy of periodically deleting all e-mail, to prevent a plaintiff's attorney from finding a "smoking gun" and to avoid the costs of finding the e-mail requested by the other party. Most experts, however, advise against such policies because other parties are likely to possess copies of the e-mail. Therefore, a policy of regularly deleting all e-mail means that the organization will not be able to tell its side of the story; instead, the court (and jury) will only read the e-mail presented by the other party to the dispute. There have also been cases where the courts have fined organizations millions of dollars for failing to produce requested e-mail in a timely manner. Therefore, organizations need to back up and archive important e-mail while also periodically purging the large volume of routine, trivial e-mail.

DISASTER RECOVERY AND BUSINESS CONTINUITY PLANNING Backups are designed to mitigate problems when one or more files or databases become corrupted because of hardware, software, or human error. Disaster recovery plans and business continuity plans are designed to mitigate more serious problems.

A **disaster recovery plan (DRP)** outlines the procedures to restore an organization's IT function in the event that its data center is destroyed. Organizations have three basic options for replacing their IT infrastructure, which includes not just computers, but also network components such as routers and switches, software, data, Internet access, printers, and supplies. The first option is to contract for use of a **cold site**, which is an empty building prewired for necessary telephone and Internet access. However, a cold site does not contain any computing equipment; instead, the organization has a contract with one or more vendors to provide all necessary equipment within a specified period of time.

disaster recovery plan (DRP) - A plan to restore an organization's IT capability in the event its data center is destroyed.

cold site - A disaster recovery option that relies on access to an alternative facility prewired for necessary telephone and Internet access, but does not contain any computing equipment.

A second option is to contract for use of a **hot site**, which is a facility not only prewired for telephone and Internet access but also contains all the computing and office equipment the organization needs to perform its essential business activities. The third option is **real-time mirroring**, which involves maintaining two copies of the database at two separate data centers at all times and updating both databases in real-time as each transaction occurs.

hot site - A disaster recovery option that relies on access to a completely operational alternative data center not only prewired but also contains all necessary hardware and software.

real-time mirroring - Maintaining complete copies of a database at two separate data centers and updating both copies in real time as each transaction occurs.

The different DRP options (cold site, hot site, or real-time mirroring) vary in cost, with cold sites being least expensive and real-time mirroring most expensive. However, the choice should not be driven by cost but should reflect management's decisions about tolerable RPO and RTO. For some organizations, both RPO and RTO must be as close to zero as possible. Airlines and financial institutions, for example, cannot operate without their information systems, nor can they afford to lose data about transactions because they have so many every minute. For such organizations, the goal is not recovery but resiliency (i.e., they must be able to continue functioning no matter what happens). Real-time mirroring provides maximum resiliency because both RPO and RTO are close to zero. Transactions are backed up in real time, and if something happens to one data center, the organization can immediately shift all processing to the other. Thus, real-time mirroring is the appropriate DRP choice when RPO, RTO, or both must be close to zero.

Some organizations can tolerate the potential loss of some data and have the ability to operate for a period of time without their AIS. If management has decided that it can tolerate RTO and RPO ranging from hours up to a full day, the choice of a hot site as a DRP strategy is warranted. Using a cold site for DRP is appropriate only if management can tolerate having both RTO and RPO greater than one day.

Organizations can choose to build their own hot site or cold site, or they can contract with a third party for the use of such facilities. Using a third-party site is less expensive, but it does carry the risk of not being available when needed. Most providers of hot and cold sites "oversell" their capacity under the assumption that at any one time only a few clients will need to use the facilities. Normally, that is a safe assumption. However, in the event of a major calamity, such as Hurricanes Katrina and Sandy, that affects every organization in a geographic area, it means that some organizations may not be able to use the services for which they contracted. (The ability to sue for failure to provide the services is not a compensating control because the organization may be out of business by the time the lawsuit is settled.)

Whereas a DRP focuses on how to resume IT operations in the event that an organization's main data center becomes unavailable, a **business continuity plan (BCP)** specifies how to resume all business processes, including relocating to new offices and hiring temporary replacements, in the event of a major calamity. Such planning is important because more than half of the organizations without a DRP and a BCP never reopen after being forced to close down for more than a few days because of a disaster. Thus, having both a DRP and a BCP can mean the difference between surviving a major catastrophe such as a hurricane or terrorist attack and going out of business. Focus 13-2 describes how planning helped NASDAQ survive the complete destruction of its offices in the World Trade Center on September 11, 2001.

business continuity plan (BCP) - A plan that specifies how to resume all business processes in the event of a major calamity.

Simply having a DRP and a BCP, however, is not enough. Both plans must be well documented. The documentation should include not only instructions for notifying appropriate staff and the steps to take to resume operations, but also vendor documentation of all hardware and software. It is especially important to document the numerous modifications made to default

FOCUS 13-2 How NASDAQ Recovered from September 11

Thanks to its effective disaster recovery and BCPs, NASDAQ was up and running six days after the September 11, 2001, terrorist attack that destroyed the twin towers of the World Trade Center. NASDAQ's headquarters were located on the 49th and 50th floors of One Liberty Plaza, just across the street from the World Trade Center. When the first plane hit, NASDAQ's security guards immediately evacuated personnel from the building. Most of the employees were out of the building by the time the second plane crashed into the other tower. Although employees were evacuated from the headquarters and the office in Times Square had temporarily lost telephone service, NASDAQ was able to relocate to a backup center at the nearby Marriott Marquis hotel. Once there, NASDAQ executives went through their list of priorities: first, their employees; next, the physical damage; and last, the trading industry situation.

Effective communication became essential in determining the condition of these priorities. NASDAQ attributes much of its success in communicating and coordinating with the rest of the industry to its dress rehearsals for Y2K. While preparing for the changeover, NASDAQ had regular nationwide teleconferences with all the exchanges. This helped it organize similar conferences after the 9/11 attack. NASDAQ had already planned for one potential crisis, and this proved helpful in recovering from a different, unexpected, crisis. By prioritizing and teleconferencing, the company was able to quickly identify problems and the traders who would need extra help before NASDAQ could open the market again.

NASDAQ's extremely redundant and dispersed systems also helped it quickly reopen the market. Executives carried more than one mobile phone so that they could continue to communicate in the event one carrier lost service. Every trader was linked to two of NASDAQ's 20 connection centers located throughout the United States. The centers are connected to each other using two separate paths and sometimes two distinct vendors. Servers are kept in different buildings and have two network topologies. In addition to Manhattan and Times Square, NASDAQ had offices in Maryland and Connecticut. This decentralization allowed it to monitor the regulatory processes throughout the days following the attack. It also lessened the risk of losing all NASDAQ's senior management.

NASDAQ also invested in interruption insurance to help defer the costs of closing the market. All of this planning and foresight saved NASDAQ from losing what could have been tens of millions of dollars.

configurations, so that the replacement system has the same functionality as the original. Failure to do so can create substantial costs and delays in implementing the recovery process. Detailed operating instructions are also needed, especially if temporary replacements have to be hired. Finally, copies of all documentation need to be stored both on-site and off-site so that it is available when needed.

Periodic testing and revision are probably the most important components of effective DRPs and BCPs. Most plans fail their initial test because it is impossible to fully anticipate everything that could go wrong. Testing can also reveal details that were overlooked. For example, Hurricane Sandy forced many businesses to close their headquarters for a few days. Unfortunately, some companies discovered that although they could resume IT operations at a backup site located in another geographic region, they could not immediately resume normal customer service because they had not duplicated their headquarters' phone system's ability to automatically reroute and forward incoming calls to employees' mobile and home phones. The time to discover such problems is not during an actual emergency, but rather in a setting in which weaknesses can be carefully and thoroughly analyzed and appropriate changes in procedures made. Therefore, DRPs and BCPs need to be tested on at least an annual basis to ensure that they accurately reflect recent changes in equipment and procedures. It is especially important to test the procedures involved in the transfer of actual operations to cold or hot sites. Finally, DRP and BCP documentation needs to be updated to reflect any changes in procedures made in response to problems identified during tests of those plans.

EFFECTS OF VIRTUALIZATION AND CLOUD COMPUTING Virtualization can significantly improve the efficiency and effectiveness of disaster recovery and resumption of normal operations. A virtual machine is just a collection of software files. Therefore, if the physical server hosting that machine fails, the files can be installed on another host machine within minutes. Thus, virtualization significantly reduces the time needed to recover (RTO) from hardware problems. Note that virtualization does not eliminate the need for backups; organizations still need to create periodic "snapshots" of desktop and server virtual machines and then replicate those snapshots on a network drive so that the machines can be recreated. A second copy of the snapshot should also be replicated to the cloud (or stored in a separate data center) in case the primary data center hosting the virtual machines gets destroyed. Virtualization can also be used to support real-time mirroring in which two copies of each virtual machine are run in tandem on two separate physical hosts. Every transaction is processed on both virtual machines. If one fails, the other picks up without any break in service.

Cloud computing has both positive and negative effects on availability. Cloud computing providers typically utilize banks of redundant servers in multiple locations, thereby reducing the risk that a single catastrophe could result in system downtime and the loss of all data. However, if a public cloud provider goes out of business, it may be difficult, if not impossible, to retrieve any data stored in the cloud. Therefore, a policy of making regular backups and storing those backups somewhere other than with the primary cloud provider is critical.

As discussed in the chapter on security, organizations should examine the SOC-2 Type 2 report on the cloud provider's IT controls. In addition, accountants need to assess the long-run financial viability of a cloud provider before their organization commits to outsource any of its data or applications to a public cloud. Use of the cloud also does not eliminate the need to consider RTO and RPO because not everything can be timely backed up to or restored from the cloud. For example, it is not practical to transfer databases that run into the hundreds of terabytes via the Internet; instead, such large data stores must be recorded on disk or tape and physically transported. Furthermore, although some cloud solutions do include backup, some do not and specifically state in the contract that backup is the customer's responsibility. Finally, use of the cloud does not eliminate the need for both DRPs and BCPs because organizations need to plan for how their employees will access the resources stored in the cloud in the event that the home office is destroyed.

Summary and Case Conclusion

Jason's report assessed the effectiveness of Northwest Industries' controls designed to ensure processing integrity. To minimize data entry, and the opportunity for mistakes, Northwest Industries mailed turnaround documents to customers, which were returned with their payments. All data entry was done online, with extensive use of input validation routines to ensure the accuracy of the information entering the system. Managers reviewed output for reasonableness, and the accuracy of key components of financial reports was regularly cross-validated with independent sources. For example, inventory was counted quarterly, and the results of the physical counts were reconciled to the quantities stored in the system.

Jason was concerned about the effectiveness of controls designed to ensure systems availability, however. He noted that although Northwest Industries had developed a disaster recovery and business continuity plan, those plans had not been reviewed or updated for three years. Of even greater concern was the fact that many portions of the plan had never been tested. Jason's biggest concern, however, related to backup procedures. All files were backed up weekly, on Saturdays, onto DVDs, and incremental backups were made each night, but no one had ever practiced restoring the data. In addition, the backups were not encrypted, and the only copy was stored on-site in the main server room on a shelf by the door.

Jason concluded his report with specific recommendations to address the weaknesses he had found. He recommended that Northwest Industries immediately test its backup restoration procedures, encrypt its backup files, and store a second copy of all backups offsite. Jason also recommended testing the DRP and BCP plans. Jason felt confident that once those recommendations were implemented, management could be reasonably assured that Northwest Industries' information systems had satisfied the AICPA's Trust Services framework criteria and principles for systems reliability.

KEY TERMS

field check 398
sign check 398
limit check 398
range check 398
size check 398
completeness check (or test) 398
validity check 398
reasonableness test 398
check digit 398
check digit verification 398
sequence check 399
batch totals 399
financial total 399
hash total 399
record count 399
prompting 399
closed-loop verification 399
header record 400
trailer record 400
transposition error 400
cross-footing balance test 400
zero-balance test 400
concurrent update controls 400
checksum 401
parity bit 401
parity checking 401
fault tolerance 404
redundant arrays of independent drives (RAID) 404
uninterruptible power supply (UPS) 404
recovery point objective (RPO) 404
recovery time objective (RTO) 404
full backup 405
incremental backup 405
differential backup 405
deduplication 405
archive 406
disaster recovery plan (DRP) 407
cold site 407
hot site 407
real-time mirroring 407
business continuity plan (BCP) 407

AIS in Action

CHAPTER QUIZ

1. Which of the following measures the amount of data that might be potentially lost as a result of a system failure?
   a. recovery time objective (RTO)
   b. recovery point objective (RPO)
   c. disaster recovery plan (DRP)
   d. business continuity plan (BCP)
2. Which data entry application control would detect and prevent entry of alphabetic characters as the price of an inventory item?
   a. field check
   b. limit check
   c. reasonableness check
   d. sign check
3. Which of the following controls would prevent entry of a nonexistent customer number in a sales transaction?
   a. field check
   b. completeness check
   c. validity check
   d. batch total
4. Which disaster recovery strategy involves contracting for use of a physical site to which all necessary computing equipment will be delivered within 24 to 36 hours?
   a. virtualization
   b. cold site
   c. hot site
   d. data mirroring
5. Which of the following statements is true?
   a. Incremental daily backups are faster to perform than differential daily backups, but restoration is slower and more complex.
   b. Incremental daily backups are faster to perform than differential daily backups, and restoration is faster and simpler.
   c. Differential daily backups are faster to perform than incremental daily backups, but restoration is slower and more complex.
   d. Differential daily backups are faster to perform than incremental daily backups, and restoration is faster and simpler.

6. Information that needs to be stored securely for 10 years or more would most likely be stored in which type of file?
   a. backup
   b. archive
   c. encrypted
   d. log

7. Which of the following is an example of the kind of batch total called a hash total?
   a. the sum of the purchase amount field in a set of purchase orders
   b. the sum of the purchase order number field in a set of purchase orders
   c. the number of completed documents in a set of purchase orders
   d. All of the above

8. Which of the following statements is true?
   a. Virtualization significantly reduces RTO for hardware problems.
   b. Cloud computing reduces the risk that a single catastrophe from either a natural disaster or terrorist attack would result in significant downtime and loss of availability.
   c. Backups still need to be made when using either virtualization or cloud computing.
   d. All of the above are true.

9. Which of the following provides detailed procedures to resolve the problems resulting from a flash flood that completely destroys a company's data center?
   a. backup plan
   b. disaster recovery plan (DRP)
   c. business continuity plan (BCP)
   d. archive plan

10. Which of the following is a control that can be used to verify the accuracy of information transmitted over a network?
    a. completeness check
    b. check digit
    c. parity bit
    d. size check

DISCUSSION QUESTIONS

13.1 Two ways to create processing integrity controls in Excel spreadsheets are to use the built-in Data Validation tool or to write custom code with IF statements. What are the relative advantages and disadvantages of these two approaches?

13.2 Do you think the problem of hard-wiring in formulas in spreadsheets is still an issue? Why? In your formal instruction on Excel, were you taught not to hard-wire formulas?

13.3 For each of the three basic options for replacing IT infrastructure (cold sites, hot sites, and real-time mirroring), give an example of an organization that could use that approach as part of its DRP. Be prepared to defend your answer.

13.4 Use the numbers 10 to 19 to show why transposition errors are always divisible by 9.

13.5 Some data entry controls not only prevent errors, but also prevent security attacks (e.g., size checks on input fields in web forms not only ensure the correct amount of data is entered, but also prevent buffer overflows). Nevertheless, because many applications do not follow those best practices, buffer overflows continue to happen. Do you think code developers should be held legally liable for not following secure coding practices?

13.6 Why do you think surveys continue to find that a sizable percentage of organizations either do not have formal disaster recovery and business continuity plans or have not tested and revised those plans for more than a year?

PROBLEMS

13.1 Match the terms with their definitions:

Term	Definition
___ **1.** business continuity plan (BCP)	a. File used to store information for long periods of time
___ **2.** completeness check	b. Plan that describes how to resume IT functionality after a disaster
___ **3.** hash total	c. Application control that verifies that the quantity ordered is greater than 0
___ **4.** incremental daily backup	d. Control that counts the number of odd or even bits in order to verify that all data were transmitted correctly
___ **5.** archive	e. Application control that tests whether a customer is 18 or older
___ **6.** field check	f. Daily backup plan that copies all changes since the last full backup
___ **7.** sign check	g. Plan that, in the event the organization's data center is unavailable, contracts for use of an alternate site that has all necessary computing and network equipment, plus Internet connectivity
___ **8.** cold site	h. Plan that, in the event the organization's data center is unavailable, contracts for use of an alternate site prewired for Internet connectivity but has no computing or network equipment
___ **9.** limit check	i. Application control that ensures a customer's ship-to address is entered in a sales order
___ **10.** zero-balance test	j. Application control that involves use of an account that should not have a balance after processing
___ **11.** recovery point objective (RPO)	k. Application control that involves comparing the sum of a set of columns to the sum of a set of rows
___ **12.** recovery time objective (RTO)	l. Measure of the length of time an organization is willing to function without its information system
___ **13.** record count	m. Measure of the amount of data an organization is willing to reenter or possibly lose in the event of a disaster
___ **14.** validity check	n. Batch total that does not have any intrinsic meaning
___ **15.** check digit verification	o. Batch total that represents the number of transactions processed
___ **16.** closed-loop verification	p. Application control that validates the correctness of one data item in a transaction record by comparing it to the value of another data item in that transaction record
___ **17.** parity checking	q. Application control that verifies an account number entered in a transaction record matches an account number in the related master file

_____ **18.** reasonableness test

_____ **19.** financial total

r. Plan that describes how to resume business operations after a major calamity, such as Hurricane Katrina, that destroys not only an organization's data center but also its headquarters

s. Data entry application control that verifies the accuracy of an account number by recalculating the last number as a function of the preceding numbers

t. Daily backup procedure that copies only the activity that occurred on that particular day

u. Data entry application control that could be used to verify that only numeric data are entered into a field

v. Data entry application control in which the system displays the value of a data item and asks the user to verify that the system has accessed the correct record

w. Batch total that represents the total dollar value of a set of transactions

13.2 Excel Problem
Enter the following data into a spreadsheet, and then perform the following tasks:

Employee Number	Pay Rate	Hours Worked	Gross Pay	Deductions	Net Pay
468921	15.00	28	420.00	325.00	95.00
357942	16.50	50	825.00	205.00	620.00
816543	5.00	40	200.00	45.00	245.00
963248	57.60	40	2304.00	10.00	2294.00

REQUIRED

a. Calculate examples of these batch totals:
   - hash total
   - financial total
   - record count

b. Assume the following rules govern normal data:
   - Employee numbers are five digits in length and range from 10000 through 99999.
   - Maximum pay rate is \$35, and minimum is \$15.
   - Hours worked should never exceed 40.
   - Deductions should be between 10% and 35% of gross pay.

   Give a specific example of an error or probable error in the data set that each of the following controls would detect:
   - field check
   - limit check
   - range check
   - reasonableness test
   - cross-footing balance test

c. Create a control procedure that would prevent, or at least detect, each of the errors in the data set.

13.3 Excel Problem

The Scorpion Railroad provides rides on diesel and steam trains through the scenic Arizona desert. It owns 32 engines, each with a unique serial number consisting of 6 digits. Printed below are data for trips on September 10. Each trip lasts a minimum of 1.5 hours.

Serial #	Trip Date	Engine Type	Departure Time	Return Time
173954	09/10	D	09:15	11:46
624974	09/01	S	10:25	10:23
130856	09/10	E	12:30	16:42
442751	09/11	D	13:45	17:43
820451	09/10	DD	15:00	18:32
003876	09/10	S	15:30	15:45

Valid train codes (engine type column): D = Diesel, S = Steam

REQUIRED

a. Identify and describe any errors in the data.
b. For each of the five data fields, suggest one or more input edit controls that could be used to detect input errors.
c. Enter the data in a spreadsheet, and create appropriate controls to prevent or at least detect the input errors.
d. Suggest other controls to minimize the risk of input errors.

13.4 **REQUIRED**

Retrieve the spreadsheet from Blackboard and edit it to include the following controls:

1. Annual fee cannot exceed 8% of purchase cost.
2. Training costs cannot exceed $12,000 in year 0 and $3,000 thereafter.
3. Annual savings due to efficiency cannot exceed $5,000, but must be zero in year 0.
4. Cell C2 (highlighted in yellow to the right of the word "Answer") must force entry of either "YES" or "NO"—no other values can be accepted.
5. Your name must appear in cell C3, and the cell must ensure that any name entered cannot exceed 30 characters total.
6. Cell B8 (annual fee) must NOT permit any alphabetic text.
7. The reduction in risk due to the security investment (cell B18) must range between 2% and 8%, inclusive.
8. Lock the spreadsheet so that data can only be entered in these cells (all highlighted in yellow in the spreadsheet):
   a. C2
   b. C3
   c. B8
   d. B10
   e. B12
   f. B18

Request: Should we invest $100,000 in the proposed security solution to reduce the risk of an issue below 10%?

Answer:
Your name:

			Year						
			0	1	2	3	4	5	Total
Purchase cost (initial)			$100,000						$100,000
Annual fee	$0			$0	$0	$0	$0	$0	$0
Training costs	$0		$0	$0	$0	$0	$0	$0	$0
Savings due to efficiency	$0		$0	$0	$0	$0	$0	$0	$0
Reduction in threat:									
Impact	$500,000								
Current risk	10%								
Expected loss	$50,000								
New risk	4.0%								
New expected loss	$20,000								
Benefit	$30,000	annually	$0	$30,000	$30,000	$30,000	$30,000	$30,000	$150,000
Total cash outflows			$100,000	$0	$0	$0	$0	$0	$100,000
Total benefits			$0	$30,000	$30,000	$30,000	$30,000	$30,000	$150,000
Net benefits			-$100,000	$30,000	$30,000	$30,000	$30,000	$30,000	$50,000
Discount rate	10%								
Discounted value			-$100,000	$27,273	$24,793	$22,539	$20,490	$18,628	$13,724
NPV	$13,723.60								
IRR	15%								

13.5 Answer all of the following multiple-choice questions.

1. An employee who is paid a salary of $50,000 submitted a request to withhold $50 per paycheck in voluntary deductions to a 401(K) plan. The next weekly paycheck was for a net amount of $50. The employee was furious. Which of the following controls would be most effective in detecting this problem prior to distributing the paychecks?
   a. financial total
   b. size check
   c. limit check
   d. reasonableness test
   e. record count

2. A control that checks whether a date is entered in the date ordered field is called a ________.
   a. date check
   b. compatibility test
   c. field check
   d. validity check
   e. range check

3. A sales representative mistakenly entered a nonexistent account number into the customer number field on a sales form. As a result, the goods were shipped, but the customer was never billed. Which type of control would be most effective in preventing this type of problem?
   a. turnaround document
   b. reasonableness test
   c. prompting
   d. range check
   e. check digit verification

4. Which type of batch total would detect the fact that exactly three time cards got lost during processing, which meant that three employees did not receive a paycheck?
   a. financial total
   b. record count
   c. hash total
   d. None of the three would detect the problem.
   e. All three choices would detect the problem.

5. Testing whether or not all employees are less than 65 years old would be an example of a ________.
   a. reasonableness test
   b. sign check
   c. check digit verification
   d. limit check
   e. validity check

6. An employee entered the wrong account number on the memo line of the check mailed to a supplier. Consequently, another customer's account was credited for that payment. The most effective way to prevent such problems would be to use ________.
   a. turnaround documents
   b. a validity check of customer account numbers
   c. closed loop verification
   d. check digit verification of customer account numbers

7. Which input control is designed to prevent a buffer overflow attack?
   a. size check
   b. reasonableness test
   c. range check
   d. field check

8. A data entry application control that ensures data entered into the quantity ordered field is greater than zero is called a ________.
   a. sign check
   b. validity check
   c. reasonableness check
   d. zero-balance check
   e. size check

9. An application control that compares the amount of an employee's raise to that employee's existing salary is called a ________.
   a. limit check
   b. range test
   c. reasonableness test
   d. check digit verification
   e. size check

10. An organization uses batch processing to update customer accounts. During the process, the computer first sorts all sales transactions by customer number. That process is done so that during batch processing the system can perform a ________.
   a. reasonableness test
   b. completeness check
   c. sequence check
   d. cross-footing balance test
   e. record count

13.6 The ABC Company is considering the following options for its backup plan:

1. Daily full backups:
   - Time to perform backup = 60 minutes
   - Size of backup = 200 GB
   - Time to restore from backup = 45 minutes

2. Weekly full backups on Saturdays, plus daily incremental backups:
   - Same requirements as option 1 to make and restore the full backup on Saturday, plus
   - Time to perform daily backup = 10 minutes
   - Size of daily backup = 40 GB
   - Time to restore each daily backup file = 10 minutes plus 5 minutes to find and load each incremental file after the first one

3. Weekly full backups plus daily differential backup:
   - Same requirements as option 1 to make and restore the full backup on Saturday, plus
   - Time to perform daily backup = 20 minutes first day, growing by 20 minutes each day thereafter
   - Size of daily backup = 40 GB first day, growing by 20 GB each day
   - Time to restore differential backup file = 10 minutes first day, increasing by 10 minutes each subsequent day

All backups (whether partial or full) must be retained for a full week. Which approach would you recommend? Why?

13.7 Which control(s) would best mitigate the following threats?

a. The hours-worked field in a payroll transaction record contained the value 400 instead of 40. As a result, the employee received a paycheck for $6,257.24 instead of $654.32.

b. The accounts receivable file was destroyed because it was accidentally used to update accounts payable.

c. During processing of customer payments, the digit 0 in a payment of $204 was mistakenly typed as the letter "O." As a result, the transaction was not processed correctly, and the customer erroneously received a letter that the account was delinquent.

d. A salesperson mistakenly entered an online order for 50 laser printers instead of 50 laser printer toner cartridges.

e. A 20-minute power brownout caused a mission-critical database server to crash, shutting down operations temporarily.

f. A fire destroyed the data center, including all backup copies of the accounts receivable files.

g. After processing sales transactions, the inventory report showed a negative quantity on hand for several items.

h. A customer order for an important part did not include the customer's address. Consequently, the order was not shipped on time, and the customer called to complain.

i. When entering a large credit sale, the clerk typed in the customer's account number as 45982 instead of 45892. That account number did not exist. The mistake was not caught until later in the week, when the weekly billing process was run. Consequently, the customer was not billed for another week, delaying receipt of payment.

j. A visitor to the company's website entered 400 characters into the five-digit Zip code field, causing the server to crash.

k. Two traveling sales representatives accessed the parts database at the same time. Salesperson A noted that there were still 55 units of part 723 available and entered an order for 45 of them. While salesperson A was keying in the order, salesperson B, in another state, also noted the availability of 55 units for part 723 and entered an order for 33 of them. Both sales reps promised their customer next-day delivery. Salesperson A's customer, however, learned the next day that the part would have to be back-ordered. The customer canceled the sale and vowed to never again do business with the company.

l. The warranty department manager was upset because special discount coupons were mailed to every customer who had purchased the product within the past three years, instead of to only those customers who had purchased the product within the past three months.

m. The clerk entering details about a large credit sale mistakenly typed in a nonexistent account number. Consequently, the company never received payment for the items.

n. A customer filled in the wrong account number on the portion of the invoice being returned with payment. Consequently, the payment was credited to another customer's account.

o. A batch of 73 time sheets was sent to the payroll department for weekly processing. Somehow, one of the time sheets did not get processed. The mistake was not caught until payday, when one employee complained about not receiving a paycheck.

p. Sunspot activity resulted in the loss of some data being sent to the regional office. The problem was not discovered until several days later, when managers attempted to query the database for that information.

13.8 MonsterMed Inc. (MMI) is an online pharmaceutical firm. MMI has a small systems staff that designs and writes MMI's customized software. The data center is installed in the basement of its two-story headquarters building. The data center is equipped with fire suppression equipment and an uninterruptible power supply system.

Because the programming staff is small and the work demands have increased, backups are only made when time permits. The backup files are stored in a locked cabinet in the data center. Recently, due to several days of heavy rains, MMI's building recently experienced serious flooding that destroyed not only the computer hardware but also all the data and program files that were on-site.

REQUIRED

Identify at least five weaknesses in MonsterMed Inc.'s backup and DRP procedures. *(CPA Examination, adapted)*

13.9 Excel Problem

1. Create data validation rules in a spreadsheet to perform each of the following controls:
   a. Limit check—that values in the cell are greater than 30
   b. Range check—that values in the cell are between 15 and 65
   c. Sign check—that values in the cell are negative
   d. Field check—that values in the cell are only numeric
   e. Size check—that the cell accepts no more than 9 characters of text
   f. Reasonableness check—that the cell's value at more than twice the value of the cell to its left
   g. Validity check—that a value exists in a list of allowable values

2. Enter the following values into cells in your spreadsheet in a row below the last row used for the data validation rules in step 1:
   a. 75
   b. happy
   Now create the following data validation rules for those two cells:
      i. for the cell containing the value "75" create a data validation rule that all values must be less than 50
      ii. for the cell containing the word "happy" create a data validation rule that requires text to have a maximum length of 4 characters

   Do the validation rules work? What does that reveal about the ability to use data validation rules after data has already been entered? What happens if you apply the "Circle Invalid Data" tool to those cells?

13.10 The ABC Company runs its e-commerce website 24/7. Backups and system maintenance are performed between midnight and 8:00 AM. For each of the following scenarios, determine whether the company's current backup procedures enable it to meet its recovery objectives, and explain why:

a. Scenario 1:
   - Recovery point objective = 36 hours
   - Daily backups at 1:00 A.M., process takes 3 hours; e-commerce transactions that occur during that time are stored in a new file, not part of that backup
   - One copy of backup tapes picked up daily at 4:00 A.M. for storage off-site

b. Scenario 2: Company makes daily incremental backups Monday through Saturday at 3:00 A.M. each night and full backups weekly, on Sundays at 1:00 P.M.
   - Recovery time objective = 5 hours
   - Time to do full backup = 3 hours
   - Time to restore from full backup = 1 hour
   - Time to make incremental daily backup = 1 hour
   - Time to restore each incremental daily backup = 40 minutes

c. Scenario 3: Company makes daily differential backups Monday through Saturday at 3:00 A.M. each night and full backups weekly, on Sundays at 1:00 P.M.

- Recovery time objective = 6 hours
- Time to do full backup = 4 hours
- Time to restore from full backup = 3 hours
- Time to do differential daily backups = 1 hour on Monday, increasing by 45 minutes each successive day
- Time to restore differential daily backup = 45 minutes for Monday's backup, increasing by 30 minutes each successive day

13.11 Answer all of the following multiple-choice questions.

1. A tsunami destroys an organization's headquarters and its main warehouse. Which of the following documents would contain instructions on how to respond to that problem?
   a. DRP
   b. BCP

2. A company makes full backups every Friday night and partial backups on Mondays, Tuesdays, Wednesdays, and Thursdays. Which of the following is true?
   a. On Wednesday, it would take less time to do an incremental backup than a differential backup, but it would take more time to restore the system from incremental backups than from differential backups.
   b. On Wednesday, it would take less time to do an incremental backup than a differential backup, and it would also take less time to restore the system from incremental backups than from differential backups.
   c. On Wednesday, it would take more time to do an incremental backup than a differential backup, but it would take less time to restore the system from incremental backups than from differential backups.
   d. On Wednesday, it would take more time to do an incremental backup than a differential backup, and it would also take more time to restore the system from incremental backups than from differential backups.

3. Which of the following statements is true?
   a. If a company needs to keep a copy of tax-related data about the costs of its manufacturing facility indefinitely, it should archive that information.
   b. Archives should be encrypted, but backups should not be encrypted.
   c. The way to recover after a hard drive fails is to restore the most recent archive of the database.
   d. Best practice for backup and recovery is to have two copies of an archive: one on-site and the other off-site.
   e. None of the statements above are true.

4. Fault tolerance procedures/devices/controls contribute to achieving the system reliability objective referred to as ________.
   a. confidentiality
   b. privacy
   c. processing integrity
   d. availability
   e. security

5. An organization leases a building prewired for both telephone and Internet access. It installs 30 servers and 25 desktop machines to be used as a test environment. However, in the event that disaster destroys the company's data center, the test environment can be converted for use as a backup data center within 3–5 hours. The organization has adopted the approach to disaster recovery planning referred to as ________.
   a. a hot site
   b. a cold site
   c. real-time mirroring

6. Which of the following disaster recovery options is most appropriate when the values for both RTO and RPO are 2 days or longer?
   a. hot site
   b. cold site
   c. real-time mirroring

7. Which measure is primarily designed to determine the frequency of making backups?
   a. RPO
   b. RTO

8. Which of the following approaches to the issue of availability produces the smallest RTO and RPO?
   a. hot site
   b. cold site
   c. real-time mirroring
   d. All of the above result in the same RTO and RPO.

9. Which of the following statements is true?
   a. Deduplication encourages organizations to switch to making differential instead of incremental partial backups.
   b. Deduplication encourages organizations to switch to making incremental instead of differential partial backups.
   c. Deduplication encourages organizations to switch to making incremental partial backups instead of full backups.
   d. Deduplication encourages organizations to switch to making differential partial backups instead of full backups.

CASE 13-1 Ensuring Systems Availability

The *Journal of Accountancy* (available at www.aicpa.org) published a series of articles that address different aspects of disaster recovery and business continuity planning:

1. Gerber and E. R. Feldman, "Is Your Business Prepared for the Worst?" *Journal of Accountancy* (April 2002): 61–64.
2. McCarthy, "The Best-Laid Plans," *Journal of Accountancy* (May 2004): 46–54.
3. Myers, "Katrina's Harsh Lessons," *Journal of Accountancy* (June 2006): 54–63.
4. Phelan and M. Hayes, "Before the Deluge—and After," *Journal of Accountancy* (April 2003): 57–66.
5. Drew and K. Tysiac, "Preparing for Disaster," *Journal of Accountancy* (May 2013): 26–31.

REQUIRED

a. Read one or more of these articles that your professor assigns. For each article assigned by your professor, complete the following table, summarizing what each article said about a specific COBIT 2019 management practice (a particular article may not address all the listed management practices):

Cobit 2019 Control Objective	Points Discussed in Article
1. Define the business continuity policy, objectives, and scope.	
2. Choose a cost-effective continuity strategy that will ensure timely and effective recovery from a disaster.	
3. Document the procedures for disaster recovery and resumption of business operations.	
4. Test the DRP and BCP.	
5. Periodically review the DRP and BCP. Update as required.	
6. Train employees on DRP and BCP procedures.	
7. Establish and document backup procedures.	
8. Conduct a post resumption review and assess the adequacy of the DRP and BCP.	

b. What point(s) did the article(s) raise that were surprising to you? Why?

CASE 13-2 Ensuring Process Integrity in Spreadsheets

Obtain a copy of the article "How to Debug Excel Spreadsheets" by Rayman Meservy and Marshall Romney published in the *Journal of Accountancy* (November 2015, pp. 46–52) from either your school library or from the website www.aicpa.org. The spreadsheet referenced in the article is available for download from the course website. Download the spreadsheet and follow along with the steps in the article. Write a report that answers the following questions (these are not completely answered in the article). Include screenshots to support your answers. Hint: The questions below are listed in the sequence in which you will encounter them when working through the steps described in the article.

1. How do you know when the "Trace Precedents" rule has located the cell that contains the source of a chain of errors?
2. Which cells are affected by the error in cell AL4?
3. Explain the nature of the circular reference in the original formula in cell AB6.
4. When you used the "Error Checking" tool, which cells did Excel find? For which of those cells did Excel suggest the correct solution? For which cells did you decide to ignore Excel's error message? Why?
5. In the section "Other Error-Checking Tips," the article points out that the formula for dropping the lowest score ignores blanks. Instead of doing the nonpermanent solution described in the article, create a permanent solution that will successfully handle any future missing quizzes or assignments (i.e., fix the formula so that it will correctly drop a blank cell instead of the lowest non-blank cell).
6. Write a data validation rule that would prevent the kind of error that exists in cell U53, so that you do not have to rely on manually identifying such an error and manually correcting it.
7. The final paragraph of the section "Other Error-Checking Tips" asks whether there remain any other cells that have values amid a column of formulas. Did you find any?
8. The final section of the article asks you to examine the formulas to see if they are correct. Did you find any logic errors? Explain.

AIS in Action Solutions

QUIZ KEY

1. Which of the following measures the amount of data that might be potentially lost as a result of a system failure?
   a. recovery time objective (RTO) [Incorrect. The RTO measures the time that an organization may have to function without its information system.]
   ▶ b. recovery point objective (RPO) [Correct. The RPO measures the time between the last data backup and the occurrence of a problem.]
   c. disaster recovery plan (DRP) [Incorrect. A DRP specifies the procedures to restore IT operations.]
   d. business continuity plan (BCP) [Incorrect. A BCP specifies the procedures to resume business processes.]

2. Which data entry application control would detect and prevent entry of alphabetic characters as the price of an inventory item?
   ▶ a. field check [Correct. Field checks test whether data are numeric or alphabetic.]
   b. limit check [Incorrect. A limit check compares an input value against a fixed number.]
   c. reasonableness check [Incorrect. A reasonableness check compares two data items to determine whether the values of both are reasonable.]
   d. sign check [Incorrect. A sign check determines whether a numeric field is positive or negative.]

3. Which of the following controls would prevent entry of a nonexistent customer number in a sales transaction?
   a. field check [Incorrect. A field check tests only whether data are numeric or alphabetic.]
   b. completeness check [Incorrect. A completeness check would ensure that a customer number was entered, but it does not test whether the customer number exists.]
   ▶ c. validity check [Correct. A validity check compares a customer number entered into a transaction record against the customer numbers that exist in the master file or database.]
   d. batch total [Incorrect. A batch total is used to verify completeness of data entry.]

4. Which disaster recovery strategy involves contracting for use of a physical site to which all necessary computing equipment will be delivered within 24 to 36 hours?
   a. virtualization [Incorrect. Virtualization is a strategy to make better use of resources by running multiple virtual machines on one physical host. It is not a disaster recovery strategy.]
   ▶ b. cold site [Correct.]
   c. hot site [Incorrect. A hot site is an infrastructure replacement strategy which contracts for use of a physical site that contains all necessary computer and network equipment.]
   d. data mirroring [Incorrect. Data mirroring is a fault-tolerant backup strategy in which the organization maintains a second data center and all transactions are processed on both systems as they occur.]

5. Which of the following statements is true?
   ▶ a. Incremental daily backups are faster to perform than differential daily backups, but restoration is slower and more complex. [Correct.]
   b. Incremental daily backups are faster to perform than differential daily backups, and restoration is faster and simpler. [Incorrect. Incremental daily backups produce separate backup files for each day since the last full backup, making restoration more complex.]
   c. Differential daily backups are faster to perform than incremental daily backups, but restoration is slower and more complex. [Incorrect. Differential daily backups are slower than incremental daily backups, but restoration is faster and simpler because only the most recent differential daily backup and the last full backup files are required.]
   d. Differential daily backups are faster to perform than incremental daily backups, and restoration is faster and simpler. [Incorrect. Differential daily backups are slower to perform than incremental daily backups.]

6. Information that needs to be stored securely for 10 years or more would most likely be stored in which type of file?
   a. backup [Incorrect. Backups are for short-term storage; archives are for long-term storage.]
   ► b. archive [Correct.]
   c. encrypted [Incorrect. Long-term retention uses archives, which are usually not encrypted.]
   d. log [Incorrect. A log is part of an audit trail.]

7. Which of the following is an example of the kind of batch total called a hash total?
   a. the sum of the purchase amount field in a set of purchase orders [Incorrect. This is an example of a financial total.]
   ► b. the sum of the purchase order number field in a set of purchase orders [Correct. The sum of purchase order numbers has no intrinsic meaning.]
   c. the number of completed documents in a set of purchase orders [Incorrect. This is an example of a record count.]
   d. All of the above [Incorrect. Choices a and c are incorrect.]

8. Which of the following statements is true?
   a. Virtualization significantly reduces RTO for hardware problems. [Incorrect. This statement is true, but so are b and c.]
   b. Cloud computing reduces the risk that a single catastrophe from either a natural disaster or terrorist attack would result in significant downtime and loss of availability. [Incorrect. This statement is true, but so are a and c.]
   c. Backups still need to be made when using either virtualization or cloud computing. [Incorrect. This statement is true, but so are a and b.]
   ► d. All of the above are true. [Correct.]

9. Which of the following provides detailed procedures to resolve the problems resulting from a flash flood that completely destroys a company's data center?
   a. backup plan [Incorrect. Backup plans focus solely on making a duplicate copy of files in the event that the original becomes corrupted because of hardware malfunctions, software problems, or human error.]
   ► b. disaster recovery plan (DRP) [Correct. A DRP focuses on restoring an organization's IT functionality.]
   c. business continuity plan (BCP) [Incorrect. A BCP focuses on restoring not only IT, but also all business processes.]
   d. archive plan [Incorrect. An archive plan deals with long-term retention of data.]

10. Which of the following is a control that can be used to verify the accuracy of information transmitted over a network?
   a. completeness check [Incorrect. A completeness check is a data input control to ensure that all necessary data are entered.]
   b. check digit [Incorrect. A check digit is a data input control designed to detect miskeying of account numbers.]
   ► c. parity bit [Correct. A parity bit is a communications control that counts the number of bits in order to verify the integrity of data sent and received.]
   d. size check [Incorrect. A size check is a data input control to ensure that the amount of data entered does not exceed the space set aside for it. Size checks are especially important for programs that accept input from users because they can prevent buffer overflow attacks.]

Accounting Information Systems Applications

PART IV

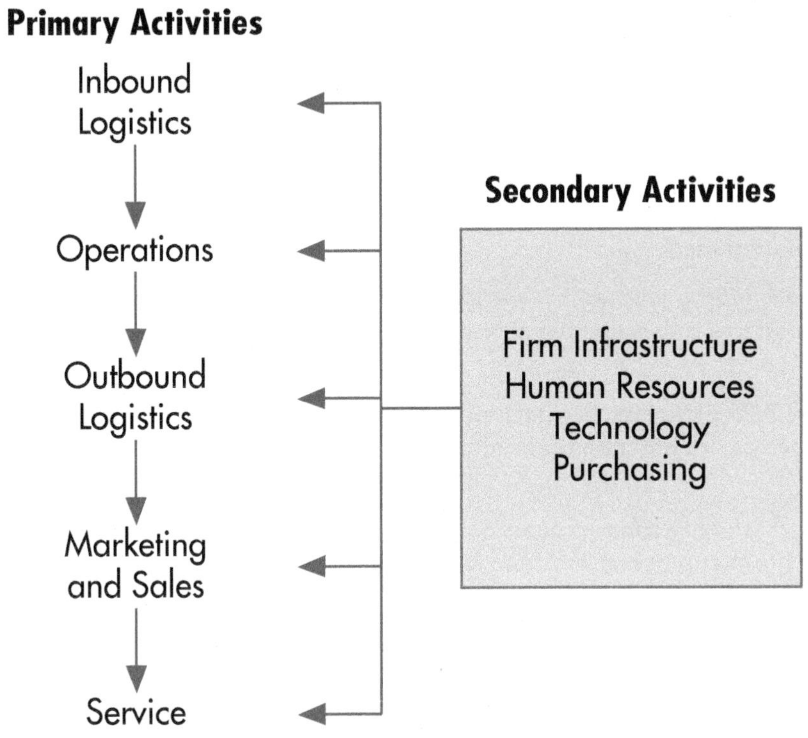

CHAPTER **14**
The Revenue Cycle: Sales to Cash Collections

CHAPTER **15**
The Expenditure Cycle: Purchasing to Cash Disbursements

CHAPTER **16**
The Production Cycle

CHAPTER **17**
The Human Resources Management and Payroll Cycle

CHAPTER **18**
General Ledger and Reporting System

CHAPTER

14 The Revenue Cycle: Sales to Cash Collections

LEARNING OBJECTIVES

1. Describe the basic business activities in the revenue cycle and discuss the general threats to that process and the controls that can be used to mitigate those threats.
2. Explain the ***sales order entry*** process, key decisions that need to be made and threats to that process, and describe the controls that can be used to mitigate those threats.
3. Explain the ***shipping*** process, key decisions that need to be made and threats to that process, and describe the controls that can be used to mitigate those threats.
4. Explain the ***billing*** process, key decisions that need to be made and threats to that process, and describe the controls that can be used to mitigate those threats.
5. Explain the ***cash collections*** process, key decisions that need to be made and threats to that process, and describe the controls that can be used to mitigate those threats.

INTEGRATIVE CASE Alpha Omega Electronics

Alpha Omega Electronics (AOE) manufactures a variety of inexpensive consumer electronic products, including calculators, digital clocks, radios, pagers, toys, games, and small kitchen appliances. Like most manufacturers, AOE does not sell its products directly to individual consumers, but only to retailers. Figure 14-1 shows a partial organization chart for AOE.

Linda Spurgeon, president of AOE, called an executive meeting to discuss two pressing issues. First, AOE has been steadily losing market share for the past three years. Second, cash flow problems have necessitated increased short-term borrowing. At the executive meeting, Trevor Whitman, vice president of marketing, explained that one reason for AOE's declining market share is that competitors are apparently providing better customer service. When Linda asked for specifics, however, Trevor admitted that his opinion was based on recent conversations with two major customers. He also admitted that he could not

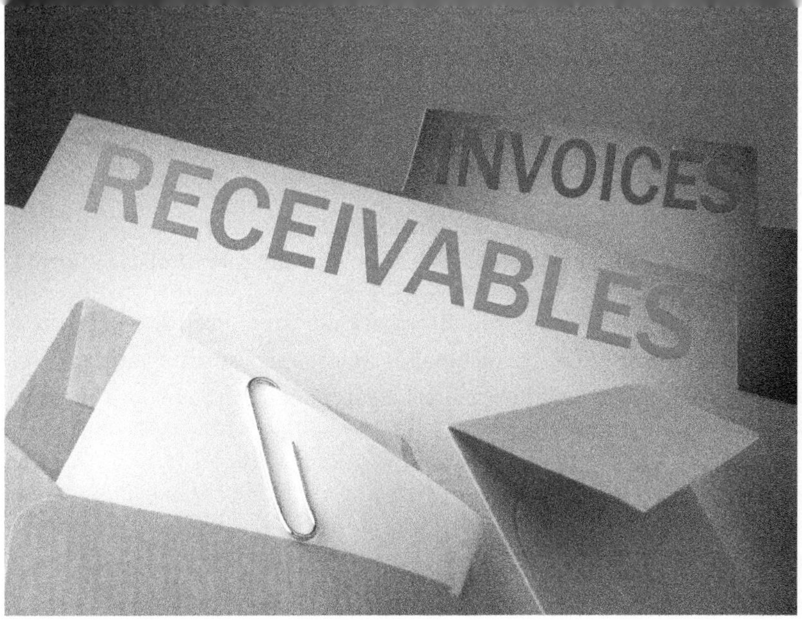

Alejandro Dans Neergaard/Shutterstock

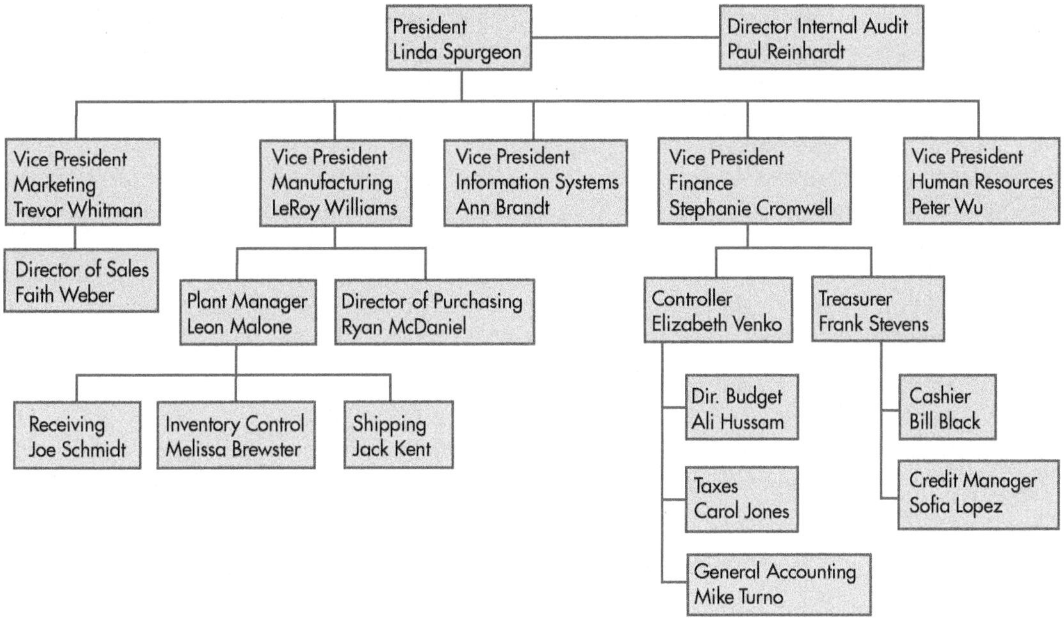

FIGURE 14-1
Partial Organization Chart for Alpha Omega Electronics

readily identify AOE's 10 most profitable customers. Linda then asked Elizabeth Venko, the controller, about AOE's cash flow problems. Elizabeth explained that the most recent accounts receivable aging schedule indicated a significant increase in the number of past-due customer accounts. Consequently, AOE has had to increase its short-term borrowing because of delays in collecting customer payments. In addition, the Best Value Company, a retail chain that has been one of AOE's major customers, recently went bankrupt. Elizabeth admitted that she is unsure whether AOE will be able to collect the large balance due from Best Value.

Linda was frustrated with the lack of detailed information regarding both issues. She ended the meeting by asking Elizabeth and Trevor to work with Ann Brandt, vice president of information systems, to develop improved reporting systems so that AOE could more closely monitor and take steps to improve both customer service and cash flow management. Specifically, Linda asked Elizabeth, Trevor, and Ann to address the following issues:

1. How could AOE improve customer service? What information does marketing need to perform its tasks better?
2. How could AOE identify its most profitable customers and markets?

3. How can AOE improve its monitoring of credit accounts? How would any changes in credit policy affect both sales and uncollectible accounts?
4. How could AOE improve its cash collection procedures to better control cash flow?

The AOE case shows how deficiencies in the information system used to support revenue cycle activities can create significant problems for an organization. As you read this chapter, think about how a well-designed information system can improve both the efficiency and effectiveness of an organization's revenue cycle activities.

Introduction

revenue cycle - The recurring set of business activities and data processing operations associated with providing goods and services to customers and collecting cash in payment for those sales.

The **revenue cycle** is a recurring set of business activities and related information processing operations associated with providing goods and services to customers and collecting cash in payment for those sales (Figure 14-2). The primary external exchange of information is with customers. Information about revenue cycle activities also flows to the other accounting cycles. For example, the expenditure and production cycles use information about sales transactions to initiate the purchase or production of additional inventory to meet demand. The human resources management/payroll cycle uses information about sales to calculate sales commissions and bonuses. The general ledger and reporting function uses information produced by the revenue cycle to prepare financial statements and performance reports.

The revenue cycle's primary objective is to provide the right product in the right place at the right time for the right price. To accomplish that objective, management must make the following key decisions:

- To what extent can and should products be customized to individual customers' needs and desires?
- How much inventory should be carried, and where should that inventory be located?
- How should merchandise be delivered to customers? Should the company perform the shipping function itself or outsource it to a third party that specializes in logistics?

FIGURE 14-2
The Context Diagram of the Revenue Cycle

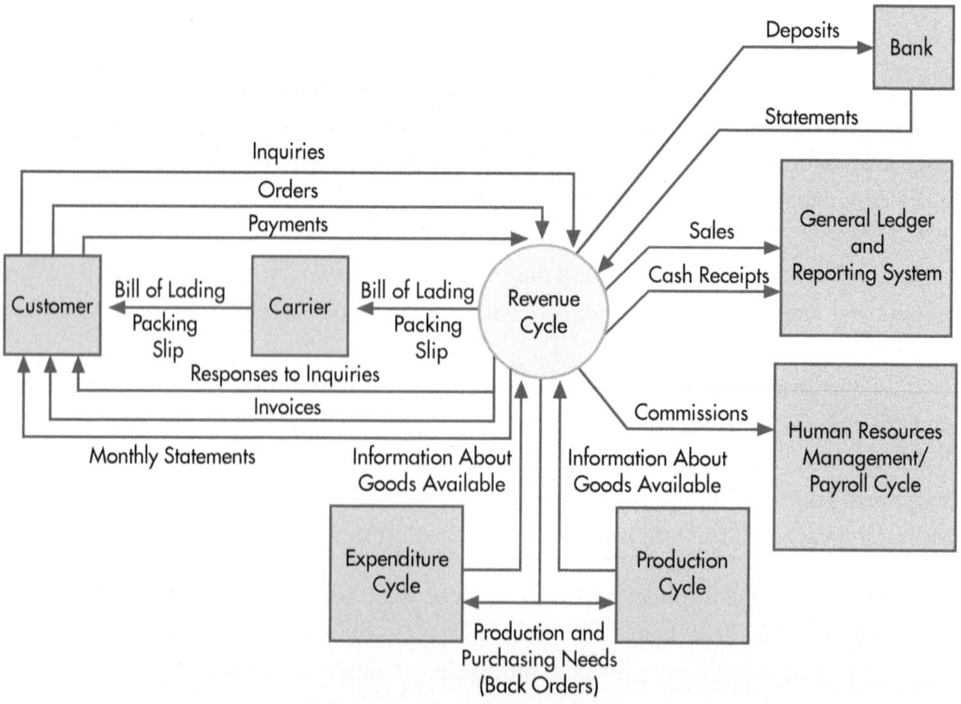

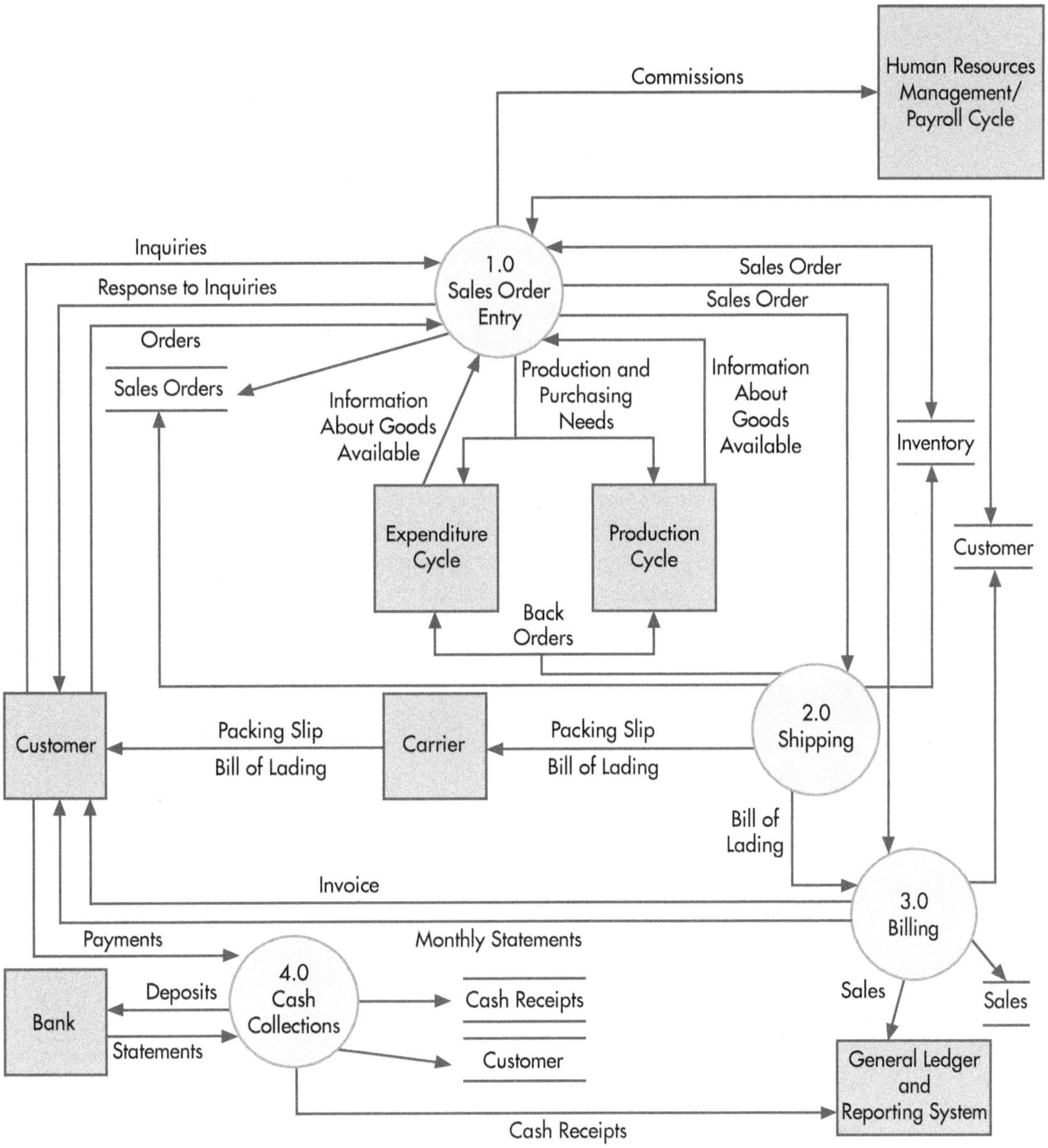

FIGURE 14-3
Level 0 Data Flow Diagram: Revenue Cycle

- What are the optimal prices for each product or service?
- Should credit be extended to customers? If so, what credit terms should be offered? How much credit should be extended to individual customers?
- How can customer payments be processed to optimize cash flow?

The answers to those questions guide how an organization performs the four basic revenue cycle activities depicted in Figure 14-3:

1. Sales order entry.
2. Shipping.
3. Billing.
4. Cash collections.

This chapter explains how an organization's information system supports each of those activities. We begin by describing the design of the revenue cycle information system and the basic controls necessary to ensure that it provides management with reliable information. We then discuss in detail each of the four basic revenue cycle activities. For each activity, we describe how the information needed to perform and manage those activities is collected, processed, and stored. We also explain the controls necessary to ensure not only the reliability of that information but also the safeguarding of the organization's resources.

Revenue Cycle Information System

Like most large organizations, AOE uses an enterprise resource planning (ERP) system. Figure 14-4 shows the portion of the ERP system that supports AOE's revenue cycle business activities.

PROCESS

AOE's customers can place orders directly via the Internet. In addition, salespeople use portable laptops to enter orders when calling on customers. The sales department enters customer orders received over the telephone, by fax, or by mail. Regardless of how an order is initially received, the system quickly verifies customer creditworthiness, checks inventory availability, and notifies the warehouse and shipping departments about the approved sale. Warehouse and shipping employees enter data about their activities as soon as they are performed, thereby updating information about inventory status in real time. Nightly, the invoice program runs in batch mode, generating paper or electronic invoices for customers who require invoices. Some of AOE's customers still send checks to one of the regional banks with which AOE has established electronic lockboxes, but an increasing number remit their payments electronically. Each day, the banks send AOE a file containing remittance data, which the system uses to update the company's cash account balances and customer accounts.

THREATS AND CONTROLS

Table 14-1 lists the threats that occur throughout the various stages of the revenue cycle and the controls that can be used to mitigate those threats. Figure 14-4 shows that all revenue cycle

FIGURE 14-4
Overview of ERP System Design to Support the Revenue Cycle

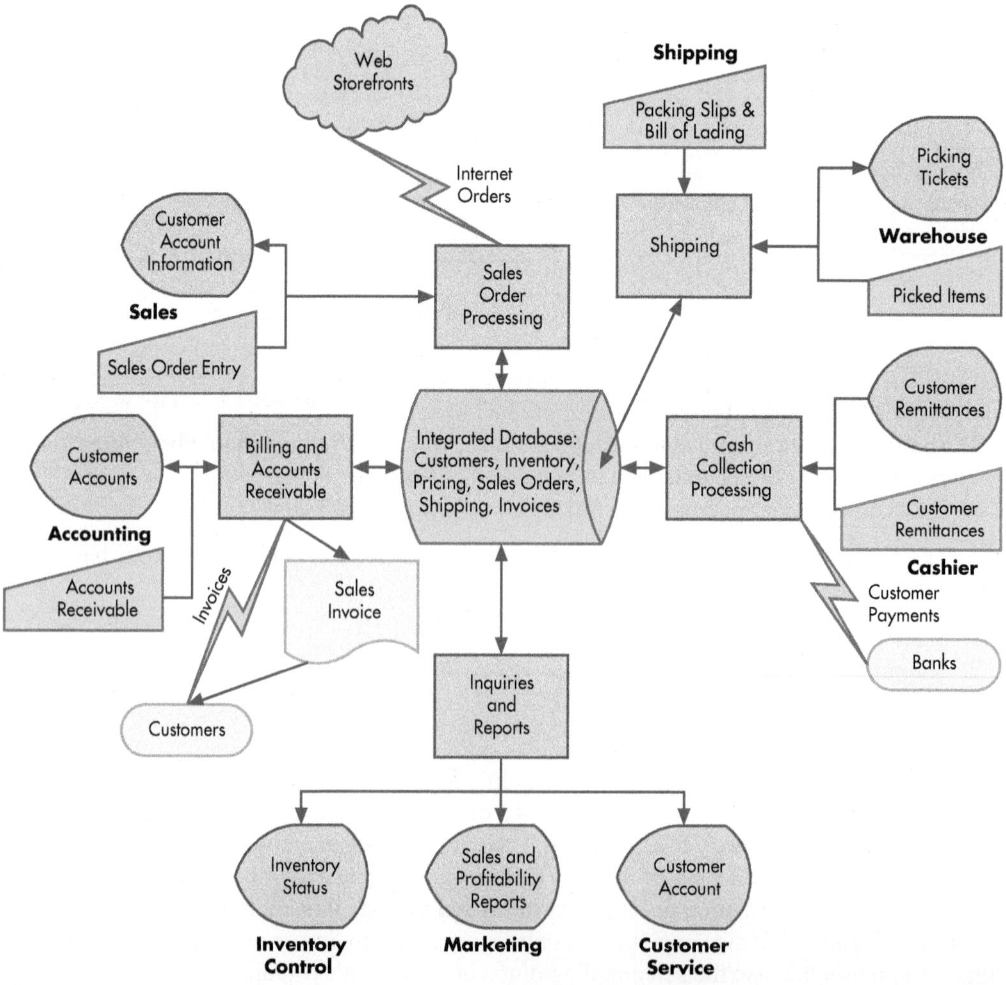

TABLE 14-1 Threats and Controls in the Revenue Cycle

Activity	Threat	Controls (First Number Refers to the Corresponding Threat)
General issues throughout entire revenue cycle	1. Inaccurate or invalid master data 2. Unauthorized disclosure of sensitive information 3. Loss or destruction of data 4. Poor performance	1.1 Data processing integrity controls 1.2 Restriction of access to master data 1.3 Review of all changes to master data 2.1 Access controls 2.2 Encryption 2.3 Tokenization of customer personal information 3.1 Backup and disaster recovery procedures 4.1 Managerial reports
Sales order entry	5. Incomplete/inaccurate orders 6. Invalid orders 7. Uncollectible accounts 8. Stockouts or excess inventory 9. Loss of customers	5.1 Data entry edit controls (see Chapter 13) 5.2 Restriction of access to master data 6.1 Digital signatures or written signatures 7.1 Credit limits 7.2 Specific authorization to approve sales to new customers or sales that exceed a customer's credit limit 7.3 Aging of accounts receivable 8.1 Perpetual inventory control system 8.2 Use of bar codes or RFID 8.3 Training 8.4 Periodic physical counts of inventory 8.5 Sales forecasts and activity reports 9.1 CRM systems, self-help websites, and proper evaluation of customer service ratings
Shipping	10. Picking the wrong items or the wrong quantity 11. Theft of inventory 12. Shipping errors (delay or failure to ship, wrong quantities, wrong items, wrong addresses, duplication)	10.1 Bar-code and RFID technology 10.2 Reconciliation of picking lists to sales order details 11.1 Restriction of physical access to inventory 11.2 Documentation of all inventory transfers 11.3 RFID and bar-code technology 11.4 Restrict ability to cancel sales 11.5 Control creation of and shipments to "one-time" customers 11.6 Periodic physical counts of inventory and reconciliation to recorded quantities 12.1 Reconciliation of shipping documents with sales orders, picking lists, and packing slips 12.2 Use RFID systems to identify delays 12.3 Data entry via bar-code scanners and RFID 12.4 Data entry edit controls (if shipping data entered on terminals) 12.5 Configuration of ERP system to prevent duplicate shipments
Billing	13. Failure to bill 14. Billing errors 15. Posting errors in accounts receivable 16. Inaccurate or invalid credit memos	13.1 Separation of billing and shipping functions 13.2 Periodic reconciliation of invoices with sales orders, picking tickets, and shipping documents 14.1 Configuration of system to automatically enter pricing data 14.2 Restriction of access to pricing master data 14.3 Data entry edit controls 14.4 Reconciliation of shipping documents (picking tickets, bills of lading, and packing list) to sales orders 15.1 Data entry controls 15.2 Reconciliation of batch totals 15.3 Mailing of monthly statements to customers 15.4 Reconciliation of subsidiary accounts to general ledger 16.1 Segregation of duties of credit memo authorization from both sales order entry and customer account maintenance 16.2 Configuration of system to block credit memos unless there is either corresponding documentation of return of damaged goods or specific authorization by management

(continued)

TABLE 14-1 Continued

Activity	Threat	Controls (First Number Refers to the Corresponding Threat)
Cash collections	17. Theft of cash 18. Cash flow problems	17.1 Segregation of duties—the person who handles (deposits) payments from customers should not also: a. Post remittances to customer accounts b. Create or authorize credit memos c. Reconcile the bank account 17.2 Use of EFT, FEDI, and lockboxes to minimize handling of customer payments by employees 17.3 Obtain and use a UPIC to receive EFT and FEDI payments from customers 17.4 Immediately upon opening mail, create list of all customer payments received 17.5 Prompt, restrictive endorsement of all customer checks 17.6 Having two people open all mail likely to contain customer payments 17.7 Use of cash registers 17.8 Daily deposit of all cash receipts 18.1 Lockbox arrangements, EFT, or credit cards 18.2 Discounts for prompt payment by customers 18.3 Cash flow budgets

activities depend on the integrated database that contains information about customers, inventory, and pricing. Therefore, the first general threat listed in Table 14-1 is inaccurate or invalid master data. Errors in customer master data could result in shipping merchandise to the wrong location, delays in collecting payments because of sending invoices to the wrong address, or making sales to customers that exceed their credit limits. Errors in inventory master data can result in failure to timely fulfill customer orders due to unanticipated shortages of inventory, which may lead to loss of future sales. Errors in pricing master data can result in customer dissatisfaction due to overbilling or lost revenues due to underbilling.

Control 1.1 in Table 14-1 shows that one way to mitigate the threat of inaccurate or invalid master data is to use the various processing integrity controls discussed in Chapter 13 to minimize the risk of data input errors. It is also important to use the authentication and authorization controls discussed in Chapter 11 to restrict access to that data and configure the system so that only authorized employees can make changes to master data (control 1.2 in Table 14-1). This requires changing the default configurations of employee roles in ERP systems to appropriately segregate incompatible duties. However, because such preventive controls can never be 100% effective, Table 14-1 (control 1.3) also indicates that an important detective control is to regularly produce a report of all changes to master data and review them to verify that the database remains accurate.

A second general threat in the revenue cycle is unauthorized disclosure of sensitive information, such as pricing policies or personal information about customers. Table 14-1 (control 2.1) shows that one way to mitigate the risk of this threat is to configure the system to employ strong access controls that limit who can view such information. It is also important to configure the system to limit employees' ability to use the system's built-in query capabilities to access only those specific tables and fields relevant to performing their assigned duties. In addition, sensitive data should be encrypted (control 2.2) in storage to prevent IT employees who do not have access to the ERP system from using operating system utilities to view sensitive information. The organization should also design its websites to encrypt information requested from customers while that information is in transit over the Internet. However, because encryption does not protect information during processing, organizations should also tokenize customer personal information (control 2.3) to protect it from being viewed by employees who have authority to perform various revenue cycle activities.

A third general threat in the revenue cycle concerns the loss or destruction of master data. The best way to mitigate the risk of this threat is to employ the backup and disaster recovery procedures (control 3.1) that were discussed in Chapter 13. A best practice is to implement

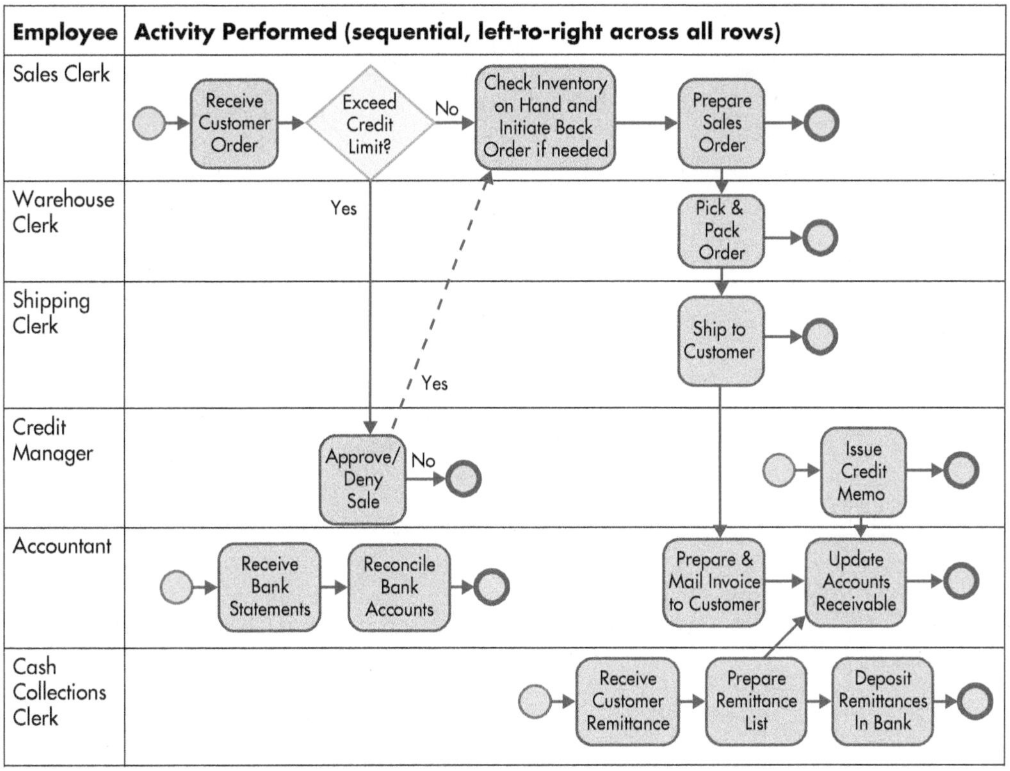

FIGURE 14.5
Business Process Diagram of Revenue Cycle Activities Depicting Segregation of Duties

the ERP system as three separate instances. One instance, referred to as production, is used to process daily activity. A second is used for testing and development. A third instance should be maintained as an online backup to the production system to provide near real-time recovery.

Accurate master data enables management to better use an ERP system's extensive reporting capabilities to monitor performance (see threat 4 in Table 14-1). Accountants should use their knowledge about the underlying business processes to design innovative reports (control 4.1) that provide management with insights beyond those provided by traditional financial statements. For example, companies have always closely monitored sales trends. Additional information is needed, however, to identify the causes of changes in that measure. Metrics such as sales per customer, customer satisfaction ratings, and number of repeat customers can provide such information. Tracking trends in sales returns and allowances is also useful both for identifying signs of increasing customer dissatisfaction as well as potential theft by employees. Accountants can also use their data analytic skills to help identify potential frauds. For example, as companies increasingly shift advertising spend to digital ads, accountants should request detailed data supporting digital advertising charges to verify that those costs reflect actual ad views by humans and not non-human traffic by bots.

The remainder of this chapter discusses each of the steps in the revenue cycle, describing the process, threats, and mitigating controls. As you read each section, refer to Figure 14-5 to see how proper segregation of duties minimizes the risk of fraud.

Sales Order Entry

The revenue cycle begins with the receipt of orders from customers. The sales department, which reports to the vice president of marketing (refer to Figure 14-1), typically performs the sales order entry process, but increasingly customers are themselves entering much of this data through forms on a company's website storefront.

Figure 14-6 shows that the sales order entry process entails three steps: taking the customer's order, checking and approving customer credit, and checking inventory availability. Figure 14-6 also includes an important related event that may be handled either by the sales order department or by a separate customer service department (which typically also reports to the vice president of marketing): responding to customer inquiries.

FIGURE 14-6
Level 1 Data Flow Diagram: Sales Order Entry (annotated to identify threats)

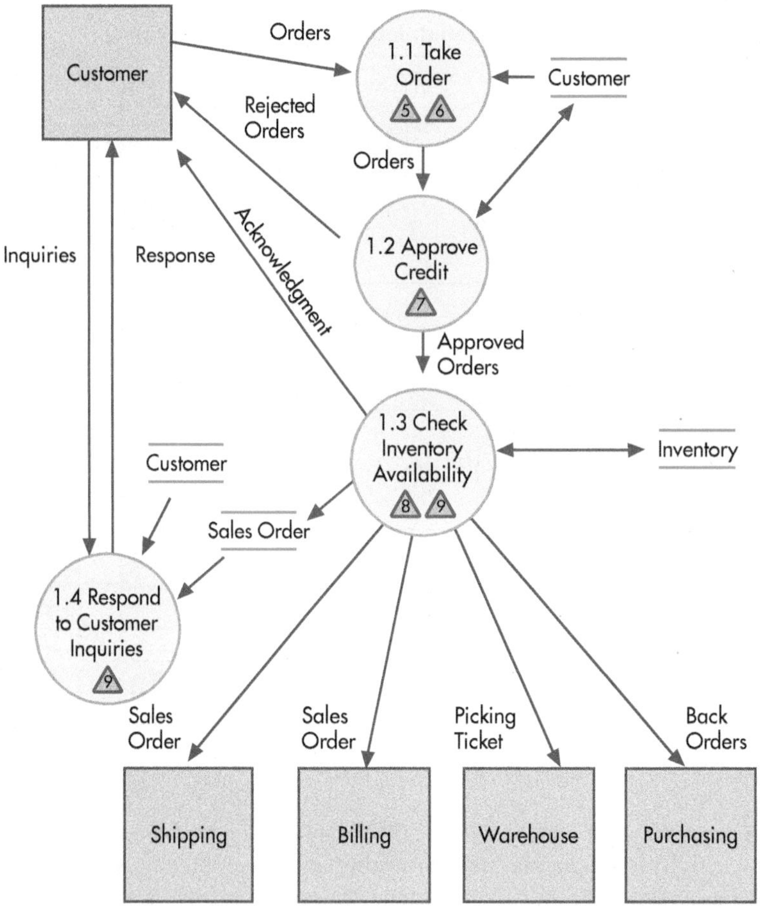

TAKING CUSTOMER ORDERS

sales order - The document created during sales order entry listing the item numbers, quantities, prices, and terms of the sale.

Customer order data are recorded on a sales order document. In the past, organizations used paper documents; today, as Figure 14-7 shows, the **sales order** document is usually an electronic form displayed on a computer monitor screen (interestingly, many ERP systems continue to refer to these data entry screens as documents). Examination of Figure 14-7 reveals that the sales order contains information about item numbers, quantities, prices, and other terms of the sale.

FIGURE 14-7
Example of a Sales Order Document (Order Entry Screen)

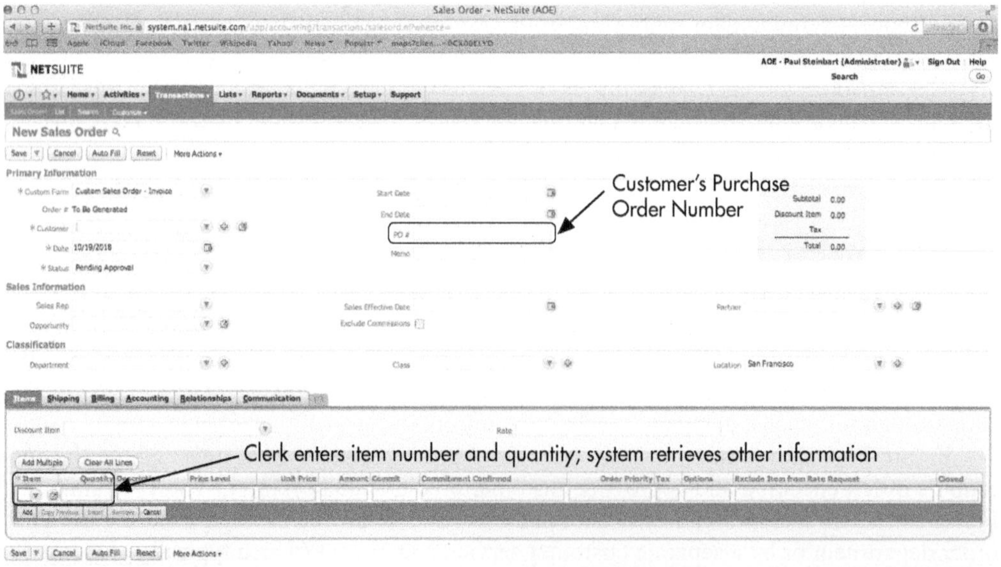

Source: 2010 © NetSuite Inc.

PROCESS Traditionally, customer orders were entered into the system by employees. Increasingly, organizations seek to leverage IT to have customers do more of the data entry themselves. One way to accomplish this is to have customers complete a form on the company's website. Another is for customers to use **electronic data interchange (EDI)** to submit the order electronically in a format compatible with the company's sales order processing system. Both techniques improve efficiency and cut costs. Focus 14-1 describes how another recent IT development, QR codes, can further improve the efficiency and effectiveness of interacting with customers.

electronic data interchange (EDI) - The use of computerized communications and a standard coding scheme to submit business documents electronically in a format that can be automatically processed by the recipient's information system.

Besides cutting costs, IT also provides opportunities to increase sales. One technique, used by many Internet retailers, is to use sales history information to create marketing messages tailored to the individual customer. For example, once an Amazon.com customer selects a book, the website suggests related books that other customers have purchased when they bought the one the customer has already selected. Amazon.com and other Internet retailers also use sales history data to create customized electronic coupons that they periodically send to customers to encourage additional purchases. Another technique involves the use of interactive sales order entry systems that allow customers to customize products to meet their exact needs. Such interactive sales order entry systems not only increase sales but also help improve cash flow in two ways. First, because many sales are built to order, less capital needs to be tied up in carrying a large inventory of finished goods. Second, the build to order model allows companies to collect all or part of the payment in advance, possibly even before they have to pay for the raw materials.

The effectiveness of a website depends largely on its design, however. Therefore, companies should regularly review records of customer interaction on their websites to quickly identify potential problems. A hard-to-use website may actually hurt sales by frustrating customers and creating ill will. Conversely, a well-designed website can provide useful insights. For example, when managers at National Semiconductor noticed a marked increase in customer interest in the company's new heat sensors, they ramped up production so that the company was able to satisfy increased demand for those products.

Like AOE, many companies continue to employ a sales staff in addition to using a website storefront because of the benefits associated with face-to-face contact with existing and prospective business customers. Information technology provides many opportunities to improve sales force efficiency and effectiveness, a process referred to as sales force automation. Storing promotional information online is cheaper than printing and mailing those materials to sales representatives. E-mail and instant messaging (IM) reduce the costs and time it takes to inform sales staff of pricing changes and sales promotions. Both techniques also can be used to provide sales staff with last-minute reminders about a particular customer's special needs and interests and to enable management to quickly approve special deals. E-mail and IM also reduce the need for salespeople to return to the home office, thereby increasing the proportion of time they can spend with customers. Technology also enhances the quality of sales presentations. Laptop computers and tablets enable salespeople to make multimedia presentations, which improves their ability to demonstrate and explain the capabilities and features of complex technical products.

FOCUS 14-1 Using QR Codes to Improve Interactions with Customers

QR codes are two-dimensional bar codes that can be scanned with a smartphone. They provide potential customers with access to multimedia anywhere at anytime. For example, consider a charity fund-raising event such as an outdoor concert. QR codes can be printed on posters, displayed on video screens, and included in the program. When attendees scan the code, they are directed to a mobile website where they can make a donation via their smartphone. Such a process is likely to result in a higher percentage of attendees actually donating because they can act immediately upon their impulse. QR codes can also increase sales by enhancing customer service. For example, in South Korea, the grocery chain Tesco places display cases stocked with commonly purchased items at subway stops. Consumers can scan the QR codes next to the items they want, then enter their account number, and the groceries are delivered to their home within an hour. QR codes also facilitate real-time changes to advertising: The seller need only log in to that account, change the content at that one central location, and every subsequent time that a potential customer scans a QR code in a magazine, transportation stop, or other location, he or she will see the new updated information.

THREATS AND CONTROLS A basic threat during sales order entry is that important data about the order will be either missing or inaccurate (threat 5 in Table 14-1). This not only creates inefficiencies (someone will have to call the customer back and reenter the order in the system), but also may negatively affect customer perceptions and, thereby, adversely affect future sales. ERP systems use a variety of data entry edit controls (control 5.1) that were discussed in Chapter 13 to mitigate this threat. For example, completeness checks can ensure that all required data, such as both shipping and billing addresses, are entered. Automatic lookup of reference data already stored in the customer master file, such as customer addresses, prevents errors by eliminating data entry. To illustrate, examine the sales order entry screen depicted in Figure 14-7. In the header section (the top portion of the screen), the salesperson need only enter the name of the customer in the sold-to and ship-to fields, and the system pulls the rest of the information from the customer master file. In the detail section (the lower portion of the figure), the salesperson needs to enter only the item number and quantity ordered, and the rest of the information is pulled from the inventory and pricing master files. Note that by looking up the reference data, the ERP system is necessarily performing a validity check of the customer name and inventory item number entered by the salesperson. It also enforces proper segregation of duties by preventing the salesperson from altering prices for friends. ERP systems should also be configured to perform reasonableness tests to compare the quantity ordered with item numbers and past sales history.

Data entry controls also need to be incorporated in website forms and EDI systems used to accept customer orders. Of course, all of these data entry controls presuppose that the master data is accurate, which is why Table 14-1 also indicates the need to restrict access to the integrated database (control 5.2) to prevent unauthorized changes that could destroy the integrity of the data.

A second threat associated with the sales order entry activity concerns the legitimacy of orders (threat 6 in Table 14-1). If a company ships merchandise to a customer and the customer later denies having placed the order, there is a potential loss of assets. Even if the goods are returned, the company wasted time and money to both ship them and to receive them back. For paper-based transactions, the legitimacy of customer orders is established by the customer's signature. As explained in Chapter 12, digital signatures (control 6.1) provide similar assurance of legitimacy and the evidence to support nonrepudiation for electronic transactions.

Finally, accountants can help managers to better monitor sales activity by using their knowledge about business processes to design reports that focus on key performance drivers. For example, reports that break down sales by salesperson, region, or product provide a means to evaluate sales order entry efficiency and effectiveness. Reports that show marginal profit contribution by product, distribution channel, region, salesperson, or customer can provide additional insights about the need to change current practices.

CREDIT APPROVAL

Most business-to-business sales are made on credit. Therefore, another revenue cycle threat listed in Table 14-1 (threat 7) is the possibility of making sales that later turn out to be uncollectible. Requiring proper authorization for each credit sale diminishes this threat.

For existing customers with well-established payment histories, a formal credit check for each sale is usually unnecessary. Instead, management gives sales staff general authorization to approve orders from customers in good standing, meaning those without past-due balances, provided that such sales do not increase the customer's total account balance beyond their credit limit (control 7.1). A **credit limit** is the maximum allowable account balance that management wishes to allow for a customer based on that customer's past credit history and ability to pay. Thus, for existing customers, credit approval simply involves checking the customer master file to verify the account exists, identifying the customer's credit limit, and verifying that the amount of the order plus any current account balance does not exceed this limit. This can be done automatically by the system.

credit limit - The maximum allowable credit account balance for each customer, based on past credit history and ability to pay.

The system can also automatically flag orders that require specific authorization because they exceed a customer's preapproved credit limit. For such cases, and for sales to new customers, Table 14-1 shows that someone *other than the sales representative* should specifically approve extension of credit (control 7.2). This is especially important if the sales staff is paid on commission because their motivation is to make sales, not focus on collectability. The organization chart for AOE (see Figure 14-1) shows how most companies segregate these duties. The credit manager, who sets credit policies and approves the extension of credit to

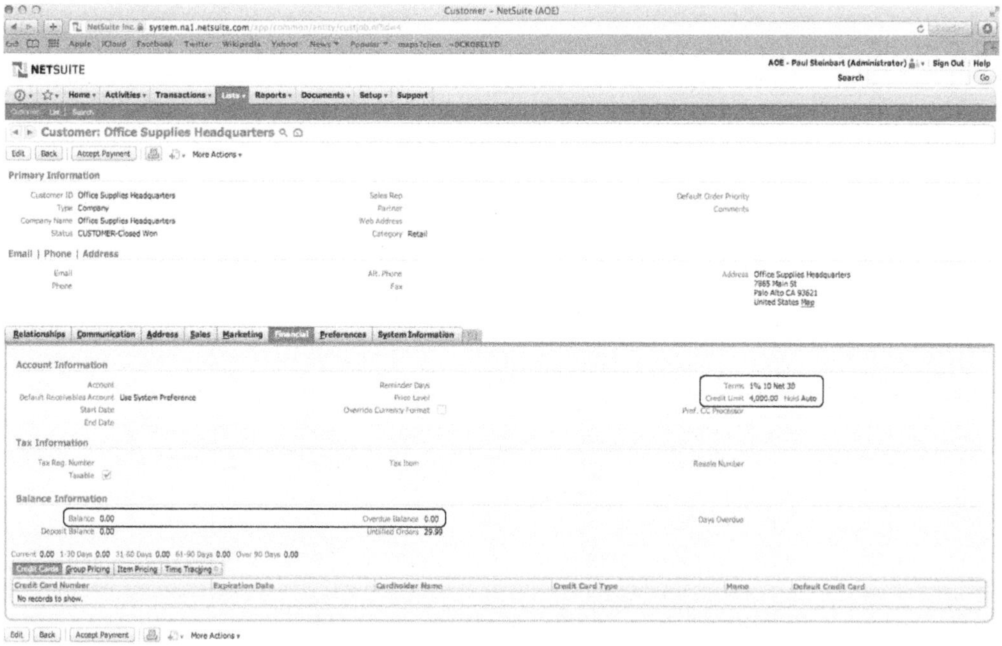

Source: 2010 © NetSuite Inc.

FIGURE 14-8
Sample Inquiry Screen for Checking Customer Credit

new customers and the raising of credit limits for existing customers, is independent of the marketing function. To enforce this segregation of duties in ERP systems, sales order entry clerks should be granted read-only access to information about individual customer credit limits; the ability to actually change credit limits should be granted only to the credit manager. Figure 14-8 shows some of the information (e.g., current balance, current status of account, etc.) the system makes available to help the credit manager decide whether to adjust a customer's credit limit. The quality of those decisions depends upon maintaining accurate and current information about account balances, sales, and customer remittances.

To be effective, credit approval must occur *before* the goods are released from inventory and shipped to the customer. Nevertheless, problems will occur, and some customers will end up not paying off their accounts. Therefore, careful monitoring of accounts receivable (control 7.3) is extremely important. A useful report for doing this is an **accounts receivable aging report**, which lists customer account balances by length of time outstanding (Figure 14-9). The information provided by such reports is useful for projecting the timing of future cash inflows related to sales, deciding whether to increase the credit limit for specific customers, and for estimating bad debts. Management needs to regularly review the accounts receivable aging report because prompt attention to customers who fall behind in

accounts receivable aging report - A report listing customer account balances by length of time outstanding.

Customer	Amount	Current	1–30 Days Past Due	31–60 Days Past Due	61–90 Days Past Due	Over 90 Days Past Due
Able						
Invoice 221	$3,450	$3,450				
Invoice 278	2,955	2,955				
Total	$6,405	$6,405				
Baker						
Invoice 178	$4,500			$4,500		
Invoice 245	2,560	2,560				
Total	$7,060	$2,560		$4,500		
Other Accounts	$185,435	$137,935	$28,500	$5,500	$2,500	$11,000
Totals	$198,900	$146,900	$28,500	$10,000	$2,500	$11,000

FIGURE 14-9
Example of an Accounts Receivable Aging Report

FIGURE 14-10
Sample Inquiry Screen for Checking Inventory Availability

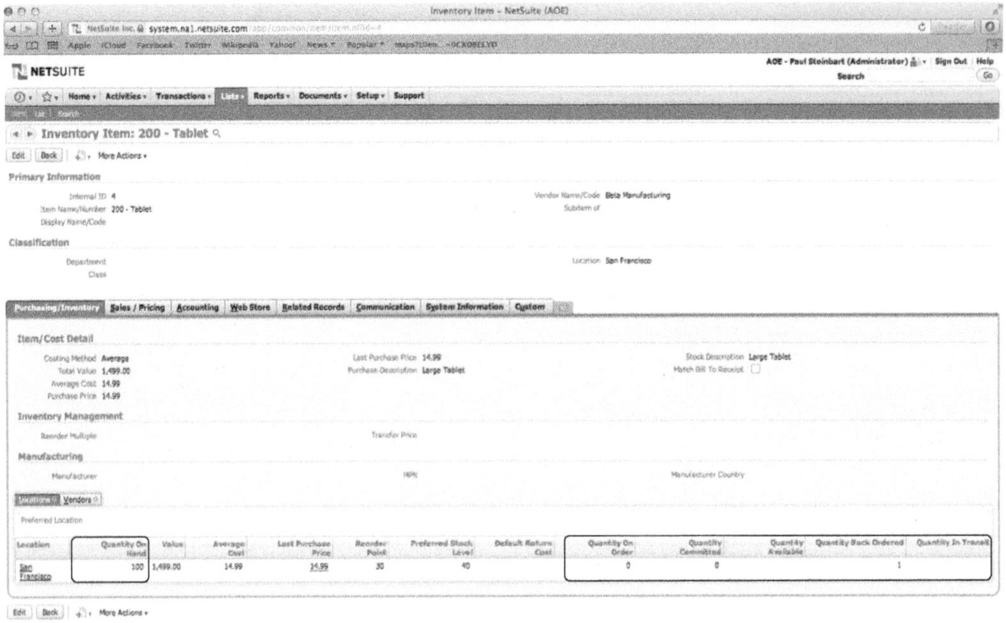

Source: 2010 © NetSuite Inc.

their payments can minimize losses. Such a report could have enabled AOE to spot problems with the Best Value Company earlier, so that it could have stopped making additional credit sales. In addition, reports that show trends in bad-debt expense can help management decide whether changes are needed in credit policies.

CHECKING INVENTORY AVAILABILITY

In addition to checking a customer's credit, salespeople also need to determine whether sufficient inventory is available to fill the order, so that customers can be informed of the expected delivery date.

PROCESS Figure 14-10 shows an example of the information typically available to the sales order staff: quantity on hand, quantity already committed to other customers, and quantity available. If sufficient inventory is available to fill the order, the sales order is completed, and the quantity-available field in the inventory file for each item ordered is reduced by the amount ordered. The shipping, inventory control, and billing departments are then notified of the sale, and an acknowledgment may be sent to the customer. If there is not sufficient inventory on hand to fill the order, a **back order** authorizing the purchase or production of those items must be created. In manufacturing companies, creating a back order involves notifying the production department to initiate the production of the requested items. In retail companies, the purchasing department would be notified about the need to order the required items.

back order - A document authorizing the purchase or production of items that is created when there is insufficient inventory to meet customer orders.

Once inventory availability has been determined, the system then generates a **picking ticket** that lists the items and quantities of each item that the customer ordered. The picking ticket authorizes the inventory control function to release merchandise to the shipping department. Although traditionally a paper document, picking tickets today are often electronic forms that may be displayed on portable handheld devices or on monitors built into forklifts. To improve efficiency, the picking ticket often lists the items by the sequence in which they are stored in the warehouse, rather than in the order listed on the sales order.

picking ticket - A document that lists the items and quantities ordered and authorizes the inventory control function to release that merchandise to the shipping department.

THREATS AND CONTROLS Accurate inventory records are important to prevent both stockouts and excess inventory (threat 8 in Table 14-1). Stockouts may result in lost sales if customers are not willing to wait and instead purchase from another source. Conversely, excess inventory increases carrying costs and may even require significant markdowns that reduce profitability. Frequent markdowns can change a company's image to that of a discount retailer, thereby conditioning customers to expect price cuts.

Integrated ERP systems, like the one depicted in Figure 14-4, facilitate the use of the perpetual inventory method (control 8.1), which reduces the risk of unexpected stockouts or excessive inventories. However, the accuracy of the perpetual inventory records requires careful data entry during performance of revenue cycle activities. In particular, shipping and sales clerks must correctly record the quantity of items removed from inventory and delivered to customers. This task is particularly error-prone in retail establishments. For example, when customers purchase multiple items with the same price, the checkout clerks may scan only one item and then enter the total quantity purchased. Although this will generate the correct total sales amount, it will introduce errors into the inventory records. The recorded quantity-on-hand for the one item that was physically scanned will be too low, and the recorded quantity-on-hand for the other varieties of that item will be too high. Proper handling of sales returns is another task that contributes to inaccurate inventory records, particularly in retail establishments. In clothing stores, for example, when a customer returns a wrong-sized item and exchanges it for another, the clerks should enter the exchange into the system. Often, especially during extremely busy sales periods, the clerks simply make the exchange and put the returned item back on the shelf but fail to make the proper entry in the system. Consequently, the system's records for both items are inaccurate.

Replacing bar codes with radio-frequency identification (RFID) tags (control 8.2 in Table 14-1) can eliminate many of these problems because the data entry occurs automatically. For situations where use of bar codes or RFID tags is uneconomical or not practical, training and regular reminders from management can reduce the frequency of the undesired behavior (control 8.3). Nevertheless, because the behaviors described above are likely to occur during particularly busy times, periodic physical counts of inventory (control 8.4) are necessary to verify the accuracy of recorded amounts. Figure 14-11 shows an example of a physical inventory worksheet report. Notice that it lists each inventory item and the quantity that should be on hand, according to system records and the results of the physical count.

Sales forecasts (control 8.5 in Table 14-1) are another tool to help companies better predict inventory needs and thereby reduce the risk of stockouts or carrying excess inventory. Accountants can also prepare reports that enable sales managers to identify the need to adjust those forecasts. For example, reports about the frequency and size of back orders can identify items for which forecasts need to be adjusted to better avoid stockouts. Conversely, reports that break down sales by item can identify slow-moving products in time to prevent excessive stockpiling.

RESPONDING TO CUSTOMER INQUIRIES

Besides processing customer orders, as Figure 14-6 shows, the sales order entry process also includes responding to customer inquiries. Sometimes these inquiries precede an order, and often they occur after orders have been placed. In either case, responding to customer inquiries promptly and accurately is extremely important to a company's long-run success. The objective is to retain customers (threat 9 in Table 14-1). This is important because a general marketing rule of thumb is that it costs at least five times as much to attract and make a sale to a new customer as it does to make a repeat sale to an existing customer. One way to monitor

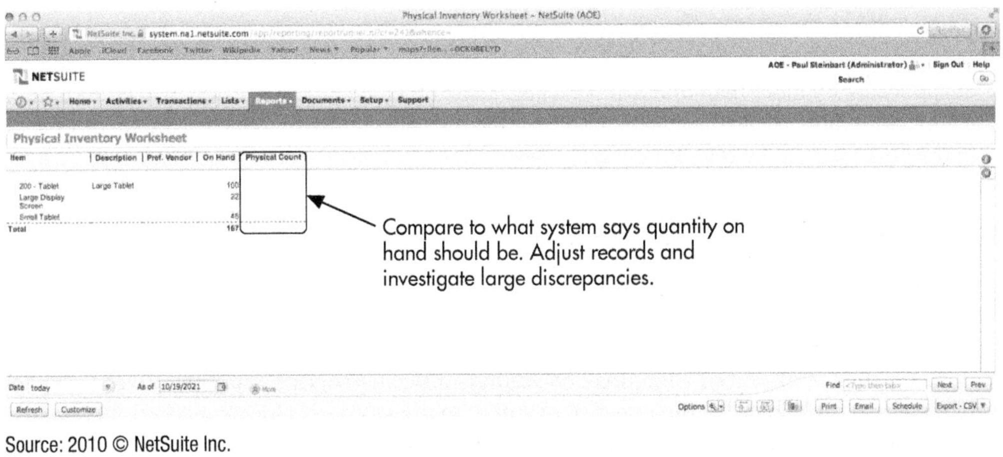
NETSUITE
Physical Inventory Worksheet
Compare to what system says quantity on hand should be. Adjust records and investigate large discrepancies.

Source: 2010 © NetSuite Inc.

FIGURE 14-11
Example of Physical Inventory Worksheet Report

retention performance is to periodically produce a report that "ages" customers by the number of years they have made purchases. However, retention requires more than merely satisfying customers. It requires creating loyalty. Research indicates that if customer satisfaction is rated on a 1-to-5 scale, with 5 representing completely satisfied and 1 representing completely dissatisfied, customers who rated their satisfaction level at 5 were many times more likely to make repeat purchases than were customers who rated their satisfaction level only at 4. Moreover, that same research indicates that the key to generating total satisfaction, and thereby retaining customers, is the quality and nature of the post-sale customer contacts.

customer relationship management (CRM) systems - Software that organizes information about customers in a manner that facilitates efficient and personalized service.

Customer service is so important that many companies use special software packages, called **customer relationship management (CRM) systems**, to support this vital process (control 9.1). CRM systems help organize detailed information about customers to facilitate more efficient and more personalized service. Customer service can be further improved by using data such as cumulative sales over multiple time periods to identify "preferred" customers. CRM systems also help generate additional sales. For example, after responding to a customer inquiry, a customer service representative can use information about customer preferences and transaction history to suggest other products that may be of interest to the customer. Detailed data about customer requirements and business practices can also be used to proactively contact customers about the need to reorder.

Many customer inquiries are routine, however. Consequently, companies can and should use IT to automate the response to common requests, such as questions about account balances and order status, so that sales order and customer service representatives can concentrate their time and effort on handling the more complex, nonroutine inquiries. For example, websites provide a cost-effective alternative to traditional toll-free telephone customer support, automating that process with a list of frequently asked questions (FAQs). Advances in artificial intelligence techniques also make it possible to create automated advice-giving tools (called "chat bots") that parse customer input to provide canned responses to common questions when ordering. Additional social media tools such as blogs and discussion boards can also be used to create virtual communities where customers can share information and useful tips with one another. Websites also enable customers to use PINs to directly access their account information and to check on the status of orders. All of these techniques can significantly reduce customer service costs. Wells Fargo, for example, found that customers with online access to their accounts made 40% fewer calls to the customer service department than did customers without such access.

It is impossible, however, to anticipate every question customers may ask. Therefore, websites designed to provide customer service should include an IM or chat feature to enable customers to obtain real-time expert assistance and advice for dealing with special issues the FAQ list does not satisfactorily address. Image processing technology can further improve the efficiency and effectiveness of managing customer accounts. The digital images of customer remittances and invoices can be stored electronically and then be easily retrieved, manipulated, and integrated with other images and data to produce various types of output. Doing so provides employees fast access to all documents relating to a customer and eliminates the time wasted searching through file cabinets for lost paperwork. If a customer needs a duplicate copy of a monthly statement or an invoice to replace a lost original, it can be retrieved, printed, and faxed while the employee is talking to the customer on the phone. Image processing also can facilitate resolving customer complaints because the same image can be viewed simultaneously by more than one person. Thus, a customer account representative and a credit manager could both review an image of a document in question while discussing the problem with the customer on the telephone. Image processing also reduces the space and cost associated with storing paper documents. The savings in this area can be substantial: One optical disk can store thousands of documents, in a fraction of the space.

It is important for accountants to design reports that will assist managers in *properly* evaluating the performance of customer service representatives by incorporating both internal and external measures. Failure to include both types of data can result in reports that cause dysfunctional behavior. For example, reports that use only internal data, such as number of inquiries handled per unit of time, may encourage customer service representatives to try to maximize their efficiency at the expense of satisfying customers. Conversely, relying solely on customer satisfaction ratings removes incentives to be efficient.

Finally, recall that post-sales service is an important primary activity in the value chain. This activity is also usually handled by customer service representatives. One especially important action involves proactively contacting customers about product recalls or the need for warranty repairs. Blockchain technology streamlines the process of identifying which customers purchased the affected products.

Shipping

The second basic activity in the revenue cycle (circle 2.0 in Figure 14-3) is filling customer orders and shipping the desired merchandise. As Figure 14-12 shows, this process consists of two steps: (1) picking and packing the order and (2) shipping the order. The warehouse and shipping departments perform these activities, respectively. Both functions include custody of inventory and, as shown in Figure 14-1, report ultimately to the vice president of manufacturing.

PICK AND PACK THE ORDER

The first step in filling a customer order involves removing the correct items from inventory and packaging them for delivery.

PROCESS The picking ticket generated by the sales order entry process triggers the pick and pack process. Warehouse workers use the picking ticket to identify which products, and the quantity of each product, to remove from inventory and then record the quantities of each item actually picked. The inventory is then transferred to the shipping department.

AOE, like many companies, has made significant investments in automated warehouse systems consisting of computers, bar-code scanners, conveyer belts, and communications technology. The goal of such investments is to reduce the time and cost of moving inventory into and out of the warehouse while also improving the accuracy of perpetual inventory systems. Wireless technology, in particular, increases warehouse productivity by eliminating the need for workers to repeatedly return to a centralized dispatch center to receive printed instructions. Instead, forklifts with radio-frequency data communication (RFDC) terminals provide employees with information about which items to pick next and where they are located. Equipping warehouse workers with headsets to listen to computer-synthesized voice instructions about what items to pick and package for delivery results in fewer mistakes than occur when employees try to read a small terminal screen in dim light. Focus 14-2 explains how some companies use robots to totally automate order picking.

RFID tags improve the efficiency and accuracy of tracking inventory movement. With bar codes, the item or box must be positioned properly so that the bar code can be read by the

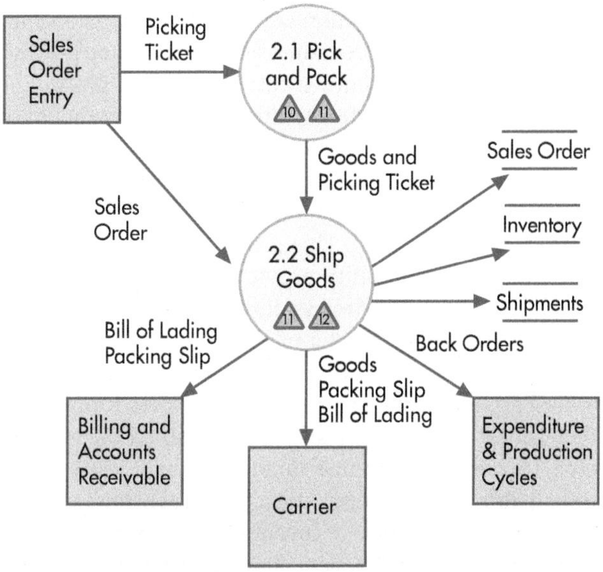

FIGURE 14-12
Level 1 Data Flow Diagram: Shipping (annotated to include threats)

FOCUS 14-2 Using Robots to Increase Efficiency and Effectiveness in the Warehouse

Companies such as Amazon.com, Crate & Barrel, Dillard's, the Gap, and Walgreens are using robots to dramatically improve the efficiency and effectiveness of their warehouse operations. Whereas in most warehouses workers must roam the warehouse (either on foot or on fork lifts) to pick inventory ordered by customers, workers in warehouses that use Kiva Systems' battery-powered robots remain at stations around the perimeter of the room. The orange-colored robots use a combination of optical scanning technology, bar codes, and wireless communications to locate items. Inventory is stored on movable shelving units, called pods, which the robots can go under and "lift." The robots then bring the pods to the worker, who removes the desired quantity of items from the shelves and then packs the items in boxes to be shipped to customers. Eliminating the need for workers to travel around the warehouse often results in one worker being able to pack up to three times as many orders in a given time period. By having the same worker fill an entire order, the system also reduces the opportunity for errors that can occur when several different workers sequentially fill portions of an order.

scanner. Switching to an RFID tag eliminates this need to align items with scanners; instead, the tags can be read as the inventory moves throughout the warehouse. In addition, each RFID tag can store detailed information to facilitate proper storage and routing of the inventory item. For companies that handle large volumes of merchandise, such as Federal Express and UPS, RFID's ability to reduce by even a few seconds the time it takes to process each package can yield enormous cost savings.

Automated warehouse systems not only cut costs and improve efficiency in handling inventory but also can allow for more customer-responsive shipments. For example, manufacturers can use bar-code and RFID systems in their warehouses to facilitate packing and shipping related items (e.g., matching shirts and ties) together. The cartons can then be either bar-coded or RFID-tagged so that retailers can quickly check in the merchandise and move it to the selling floor. These services not only save retailers time and money but also help improve turnover, thereby increasing the manufacturer's sales.

THREATS AND CONTROLS One potential problem is the risk of picking the wrong items or in the wrong quantity (threat 10 in Table 14-1). The automated warehousing technologies described earlier can minimize the chance of such errors. Bar-code and RFID scanners (control 10.1), in particular, virtually eliminate errors when they are used by the system to automatically compare the items and quantities picked by warehouse workers with the information on sales orders (control 10.2).

Another threat involves the theft of inventory (threat 11). In addition to a loss of assets, theft also makes inventory records inaccurate, which can lead to problems in filling customer orders. Table 14-1 lists several control procedures that can reduce the risk of inventory theft. First, inventory should be kept in a secure location to which physical access is restricted (control 11.1). Second, all inventory transfers within the company should be documented (control 11.2). Inventory should be released to shipping employees based only on approved sales orders. Both warehouse and shipping employees should sign the document accompanying the goods (or make the appropriate acknowledgment of the transfer online) at the time the goods are transferred from inventory to shipping. This procedure facilitates tracking the cause of any inventory shortages, and the accountability provided encourages employees to prepare and maintain accurate records. The use of wireless communications technologies and RFID tags (control 11.3) can provide real-time tracking of inventory in transit, which may help reduce theft. It is also important to restrict the ability to cancel sales (control 11.4) to someone other than sales staff. This segregation of duties prevents employees from authorizing the shipment of merchandise to themselves or to a friend and then canceling the sale to avoid having to pay for the stolen inventory. Similarly, it is important to configure the system to restrict the ability to create, delete, and ship to "one-time" customers (control 11.5) to prevent employees from using that technique to conceal theft of inventory. Finally, recorded amounts of inventory should be periodically reconciled with physical counts of inventory on hand (control 11.6), and the employees responsible for inventory custody should be held accountable for any shortages.

As with the other steps in the revenue cycle, accountants can help managers better monitor performance by designing useful reports. Note that the order-picking process does not involve any direct interaction with customers. Therefore, reports using only internally generated measures such as orders filled per unit of time are sufficient.

SHIP THE ORDER

After the merchandise has been removed from the warehouse, it is shipped to the customer.

PROCESS The shipping department should compare the physical count of inventory with the quantities indicated on the picking ticket and with the quantities indicated on the sales order. Discrepancies can arise either because the items were not stored in the location indicated on the picking ticket or because the perpetual inventory records were inaccurate. In such cases, the shipping department needs to initiate the back ordering of the missing items and enter the correct quantities shipped on the packing slip.

After counting the goods delivered from the warehouse, the shipping clerk enters the sales order number, item number(s), and quantities in the system. This process updates the quantity-on-hand field in the inventory master file. It also produces a packing slip and multiple copies of the bill of lading. The **packing slip** (see Figure 14-13) lists the quantity and

packing slip - A document listing the quantity and description of each item included in a shipment.

AOE
2431 Bradford Lane
San Francisco CA 94403
US

Packing Slip

Order Date	Order #
9/13/2021	458

Ship To
Hardware City 4742 Mesa Drive Mesa AZ 85284 United States

Ship Date	Ship Via	Tracking #
9/15/2021	UPS Ground	

Item	Description	Order	Back Ordered	Shipped
Nikon Pix 5000	Mega Zoom for those close up shots	4		4
Warranty 1 yr $100–500	1 yr parts and labor warranty on any hardware priced between $100–500	4		4

AOE

Customer Return Form

Ship Returns To
2431 Bradford Lane San Francisco CA 94493 US

R.A. #	Customer	Order #
	Hardware City	458

Item	Quantity	Reason for Returning

FIGURE 14-13
Example of a Packing Slip

bill of lading - A legal contract that defines responsibility for goods while they are in transit.

description of each item included in the shipment. The **bill of lading** is a legal contract that defines responsibility for the goods in transit. It identifies the carrier, source, destination, and any special shipping instructions, and it indicates who (customer or vendor) must pay the carrier (see Figure 14-14). A copy of the bill of lading and the packing slip accompany the shipment. If the customer is to pay the shipping charges, this copy of the bill of lading may serve as a *freight bill*, to indicate the amount the customer should pay to the carrier. In other cases, the freight bill is a separate document.

One important decision that needs to be made when filling and shipping customer orders concerns the choice of delivery method. Traditionally, many companies have maintained their own truck fleets for deliveries. Increasingly, however, manufacturers are outsourcing this function to commercial carriers such as DHL, Federal Express, Ryder System, Inc., Schneider

FIGURE 14-14
Sample Bill of Lading

STRAIGHT BILL OF LADING —SHORT FORM **Not Negotiable.**

Shipper's No.

Carrier **Carrier's No.**

RECEIVED, subject to the classifications and tariffs in effect on the date of the issue of this Bill of Lading.

at ______ **20** ______ **from** ______

the property described below, in apparent good order, except as noted (contents and condition of contents of packages unknown), marked, consigned, and destined as indicated below, which said carrier (the word carrier being understood throughout this contract as meaning any person or corporation in possession of the property under the contract) agrees to carry to its usual place of delivery at said destination, if on its route, otherwise to deliver to another carrier on the route to said destination. It is mutually agreed, as to each carrier of all or any of said property over all or any portion of said route to destination, and as to each party at any time interested in any or all of said property, that every service to be performed hereunder shall be subject to all terms and conditions of the Uniform Domestic Straight Bill of Lading set forth (1) in Uniform Freight Classification in effect on the date hereof, if this is a rail or a rail-water shipment, or (2) in the applicable motor carrier classification or tariff if this is a motor carrier shipment.

Shipper hereby certifies that he is familiar with all the terms and conditions of the said bill of lading, including those on the back thereof, set forth in the classification or tariff which governs the transportation of this shipment, and the said terms and conditions are hereby agreed to by the shipper and accepted for himself and his assigns.

Consigned to ______

(Mail or street address of consignee — For purposes of notification only.)

Destination ______ State ______ Zip Code ______ County ______

Delivery Address ★ ______

(★ To be filled in only when shipper desires and governing tariffs provide for delivery thereat.)

Route ______

Delivering Carrier Car or Vehicle Initials No.

No. Packages	Kind of Package, Description of Articles, Special Marks, and Exceptions	*Weight (Sub. to Cor.)	Class or Rate	Check Column

Subject to Section 7 of Conditions of applicable bill of lading, if this shipment is to be delivered to the consignee without recourse on the consignor, the consignor shall sign the following statement.

The carrier shall not make delivery of this shipment without payment of freight and all other lawful charges.

(Signature of Consignor.)

If charges are to be prepaid, write or stamp here, "To Be Prepaid."

*If the shipment moves between two ports by a carrier by water, the law requires that the bill of lading shall state whether it is "carrier's or shipper's weight."

NOTE—Where the rate is dependent on value, shippers are required to state specifically in writing the agreed or declared value of the property.

The agreed or declared value of the property is hereby specifically stated by the shipper to be not exceeding

per

†"The fiber boxes used for this shipment conform to the specifications set forth in the box maker's certificate thereon, and all other requirements of Uniform Freight Classification."

†Shipper's imprint in lieu of stamp; not a part of bill of lading approved by the Interstate Commerce Commission.

Received $ ______ to apply in prepayment of the charges on the property described hereon.

Agent or Cashier

Per ______

amount prepaid

Charges advanced:
$

______ Shipper, per ______ Agent, Per ______

Permanent post office address of shipper, ______

Logistics, UPS, and YRC. Outsourcing deliveries reduces costs and allows manufacturers to concentrate on their core business activity (the production of goods). Selecting the proper carrier, however, requires collecting and monitoring information about carrier performance (e.g., percentage of on-time deliveries and damage claims) because customers will blame the company, not the carrier, for delivery problems.

Another important decision concerns the location of distribution centers. Increasingly, many customers are asking suppliers and manufacturers to deliver products only when needed. Consequently, suppliers and manufacturers must use logistics software tools to identify the optimal locations to store inventory in order to minimize the total amount of inventory carried and to meet each customer's delivery requirements. Logistics software also helps optimize daily activities, such as how to most efficiently use 17 available trucks to make 300 deliveries to various locations in one metropolitan area.

Globalization adds further complexity to outbound logistics. The efficiency and effectiveness of different distribution methods, such as trucking or rail, differ around the world. Taxes and regulations in various countries can also affect distribution choices. Therefore, an organization's information system must include logistics software that can maximize the efficiency and effectiveness of its shipping function.

THREATS AND CONTROLS Table 14-1 indicates that two potential problems are theft (threat 11) and shipping errors (threat 12). We discussed the various controls to reduce the threat of theft in the prior section. Regular reconciliation of information about shipments with sales orders (control 12.1) enables timely detection of delay or failure to ship goods to customers. In addition, RFID systems (control 12.2) can provide real-time information on shipping status and thus provide additional information about possible delays. If the seller learns that a shipment is going to be late, prompt notification can help the customer revise its plans accordingly. The cost of providing such notifications is minimal, especially if done via e-mail or IM, but the effort is likely to significantly improve customer satisfaction and loyalty.

Shipping the wrong items or quantities of merchandise and shipping to the wrong location can cause customer dissatisfaction, resulting in the loss of future sales. Shipping errors may also result in the loss of assets if customers do not pay for goods erroneously shipped. To minimize the risk of shipping errors, ERP systems like the one depicted in Figure 14-4 should be configured to compare the quantities and item numbers entered by shipping employees to the information on the sales order and to display a warning about any discrepancies so that the problem can be corrected prior to shipment. Of course, the effectiveness of this control depends upon the accuracy of the information collected about outgoing shipments. To reduce data entry errors by shipping employees, bar codes and RFID tags should be used whenever possible (control 12.3). If shipping data must be entered manually at a terminal, data entry controls such as field checks, limit or range checks, and completeness tests are necessary (control 12.4).

Duplicate shipments result in increased costs associated with shipping and then processing the return of merchandise. To mitigate this threat, ERP systems should be configured to "block" the line items on sales orders once shipping documents are printed (control 12.5) to prevent using that same sales order to authorize another shipment of the same goods to the same customer. Companies that still use paper documents can reduce the risk of duplicate shipments by sequentially prenumbering all shipping documents, requiring that they be matched with the supporting sales order and picking ticket, and then marking those documents in a manner that prevents their reuse.

Billing

The third basic activity in the revenue cycle (circle 3.0 in Figure 14-3) involves billing customers. Figure 14-15 shows that this involves two separate, but closely related, tasks: invoicing and updating accounts receivable, which are performed by two separate units within the accounting department.

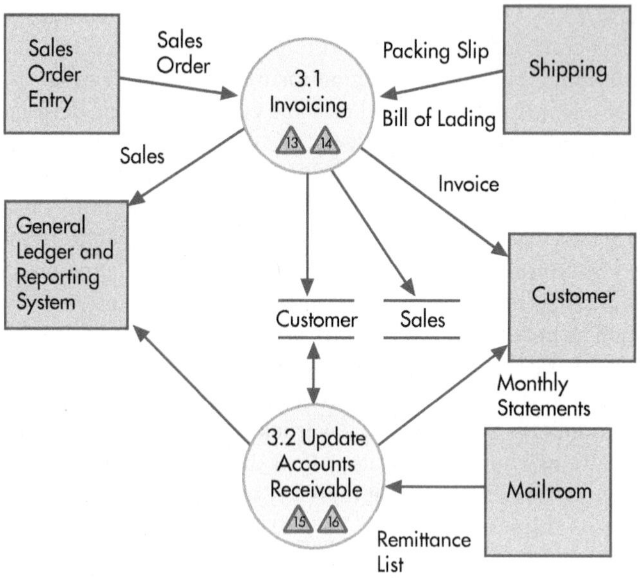

FIGURE 14-15
Level 1 Data Flow Diagram: Billing Process (annotated to include threats)

INVOICING

Accurate and timely billing for shipped merchandise is crucial. The invoicing activity is just an information processing activity that repackages and summarizes information from the sales order entry and shipping activities. It requires information from the shipping department identifying the items and quantities shipped and information about prices and any special sales terms from the sales department.

sales invoice - A document notifying customers of the amount of a sale and where to send payment.

PROCESS The basic document created in the billing process is the **sales invoice** (Figure 14-16), which notifies customers of the amount to be paid and where to send payment. Like many companies, AOE still prints paper invoices that it mails to many of its smaller customers. Larger customers, however, receive invoices via EDI. EDI not only eliminates printing and postage costs, but also the labor involved in performing those tasks. For companies that generate hundreds of thousands of sales invoices annually, saving even a few seconds, and pennies, per invoice can yield significant cost reductions. EDI invoices and online bill payment also benefit customers by reducing their time and costs, which should increase both satisfaction and loyalty.

In fact, a well-designed accounting system can entirely eliminate the need to create and store invoices, at least with customers that have sophisticated systems of their own. To understand this concept, reexamine the information included in a typical sales invoice (see Figure 14-16). The invoice indicates the quantity of each item sold and the price charged for that item; but the price is usually set at the time the order is placed, and the actual quantity sold is known at the time the merchandise is shipped to the customer. Thus, the selling company's accounting system already contains all the information needed to calculate the amount of the sale at the time the goods are shipped. That is why invoices are often printed in a batch process without any manual data entry. Conversely, the buyer knows the price at the time the order is placed and knows the quantity purchased when the goods are received. Consequently, if both companies have accurate transaction processing systems, it may be possible to establish an agreement in which the buyer will automatically remit payments within a specified number of days after receiving the merchandise. The seller sends an electronic notification, usually via e-mail, when the goods are shipped and the customer sends an electronic acknowledgment when the goods are received. Most auto manufacturers have established such relationships with their major suppliers. Note that the seller can still monitor and determine accounts receivable by reconciling shipments to customer remittances because accounts receivable represents all shipments for which the seller has not yet been paid. The attraction of such invoiceless billing is that it saves both the seller and buyer considerable amounts of time and money by eliminating the need to perform a traditional business process (invoicing) that does not provide any new information.

AOE
2431 Bradford Lane
San Francisco, CA
99403

Invoice

Date	Invoice #
9/16/2021	3091380

Bill To	Ship To
Hardware City 35 Appliance Way Phoenix AZ 85201 United States	Hardware City 4742 Mesa Drive Mesa AZ 85284 United States

Terms	Due Date	PO #	Sales Rep	Ship Via	Tracking Numbers
Net 30	10/16/2021		JKL	UPS Ground	

Item	Qty	Description	Price	Amount
Nikon Pix 5000	4	Mega Zoom for those close up shots	200.00	800.00
Warranty 1 yr $100–500	4	1 yr parts and labor warranty on any hardware priced between $100–500	19.95	79.80

Subtotal	879.80
Shipping Cost (UPS Ground)	30.04
Total	$909.84

FIGURE 14-16
Example of a Sales Invoice

An integrated ERP system also provides the opportunity to merge the billing process with the sales and marketing function by using data about a customer's past purchase history to send information about related products and services. Such customized advertising may generate additional sales with little if any incremental costs.

THREATS AND CONTROLS One threat associated with the invoicing process is a failure to bill customers (threat 13 in Table 14-1), which results in the loss of assets and erroneous data about sales, inventory, and accounts receivable. Segregating the shipping and billing functions (control 13.1) reduces the risk that this occurs intentionally. Otherwise, an employee performing both functions could ship merchandise to friends without billing them. To reduce the risk of *unintentional* failure to bill, ERP systems need to be configured to regularly compare sales orders, picking tickets, and shipping documents with sales invoices to produce reports of shipments for which an invoice has not been created (control 13.2). (For invoiceless systems, this control involves matching sales orders to shipping documents.) Management needs to regularly review such reports and take corrective action. In paper-based systems, prenumbering all documents and periodically accounting for them identifies shipments that have not been invoiced.

Billing errors (threat 14 in Table 14-1), such as pricing mistakes and billing customers for items not shipped or on back order, represent another potential threat. Overbilling can result in customer dissatisfaction, and underbilling results in the loss of assets. Incorrect calculation of sales taxes, or, due to the Supreme Court's 2018 decision in *South Dakota v. Wayfair*, failure to collect sales taxes on sales made across state lines can result in fines and penalties. Pricing mistakes can be avoided by having the system retrieve the appropriate data from the pricing master file (control 14.1) and by restricting the ability of employees to make changes to that data (control 14.2). If employees must enter billing data manually, the use of the data entry edit controls discussed in Chapter 13 can minimize errors (control 14.3). Mistakes involving quantities shipped can be caught by reconciling the quantities listed on the packing slips with those on the sales order (control 14.4).

open-invoice method - Method for maintaining accounts receivable in which customers typically pay according to each invoice.

remittance advice - A copy of the sales invoice returned with a customer's payment that indicates the invoices, statements, or other items being paid.

balance-forward method - Method of maintaining accounts receivable in which customers typically pay according to the amount shown on a monthly statement, rather than by individual invoices. Remittances are applied against the total account balance, rather than specific invoices.

monthly statement - A document listing all transactions that occurred during the past month and informing customers of their current account balance.

MAINTAIN ACCOUNTS RECEIVABLE

The accounts receivable function, which reports to the controller, performs two basic tasks: It uses the information on the sales invoice to debit customer accounts and subsequently credits those accounts when payments are received.

PROCESS The two basic ways to maintain accounts receivable are the open-invoice and the balance-forward methods. The two methods differ in terms of when customers remit payments, how those payments are applied to update the accounts receivable master file, and the format of the monthly statement sent to customers. Under the **open-invoice method**, customers typically pay according to each invoice. Usually, two copies of the invoice are mailed to the customer, who is requested to return one copy with the payment. This copy is a turnaround document called a **remittance advice**. Customer payments are then applied against specific invoices. In contrast, under the **balance-forward method**, customers typically pay according to the amount shown on a monthly statement, rather than by individual invoices. The **monthly statement** lists all transactions, including both sales and payments, that occurred during the past month and informs customers of their current account balances (Figure 14-17). The monthly statement often has a tear-off portion

FIGURE 14-17
Example of a Monthly Statement

MONTHLY STATEMENT
Alpha Omega Electronics
2431 Bradford Lane
San Francisco, CA 99403

March 2021

Hardware City
35 Appliance Way
Phoenix, AZ 85201

Invoice Number	Date	Current	Past Due 1–30	Past Due 31–60	Past Due 61–90	Past Due Over 90
34567	3/20/2021	4292.50				
34591	3/27/2021	2346.50				
	Totals	6639.00				
				Total Amount Due	6639.00	

Please detach here and return with remittance

Bill date 03/31/2021
Account number 73256
Payment due 04/10/2021
Total amount due 6639.00
Amount enclosed

Pay To: AOE
PO Box 7341
San Francisco, CA 99403-7341

containing preprinted information, including the customer's name, account number, and balance. Customers are asked to return this stub, which serves as a remittance advice, with payment. Remittances are applied against the total account balance, rather than against specific invoices.

One advantage of the open-invoice method is that it is conducive to offering discounts for prompt payment, as invoices are individually tracked and aged. It also results in a more uniform flow of cash collections throughout the month. A disadvantage of the open-invoice method is the added complexity required to maintain information about the status of each individual invoice for each customer. Consequently, the open-invoice method is typically used by business whose customers are primarily other businesses because the number of individual transactions is relatively small and the dollar value of those transactions is high. Companies with large numbers of customers who make many small purchases each month, such as utility companies and credit card issuers (e.g., Citibank) typically use the balance-forward method. For them, this method is more efficient and reduces costs by avoiding the need to process cash collections for each individual sale. It is also more convenient for the customer to make one monthly remittance.

Many companies that use the balance-forward method use a process called cycle billing to prepare and mail monthly statements to their customers. Under **cycle billing**, monthly statements are prepared for subsets of customers at different times. For example, the customer master file might be divided into four parts, and each week monthly statements would be prepared for one-fourth of the customers. Cycle billing produces a more uniform flow of cash collections throughout the month and reduces the time that the computer system is dedicated to printing monthly statements. Cycle billing can significantly affect processing requirements. Consider the case of a utility company serving several million customers in a large metropolitan area. If it prepared monthly statements for all its customers at the same time, even if it took only 1 second to print out each one, its printers would be tied up for several days.

cycle billing - Producing monthly statements for subsets of customers at different times.

Adjustments to a customer's account are sometimes necessary. For example, customer accounts may be credited to reflect either the return of items or allowances granted for damaged goods. To credit a customer's account for returned goods, the credit manager must obtain information from the receiving dock that the goods were actually returned and placed back in inventory. Upon notification from the receiving department that the goods have been returned, the credit manager issues a **credit memo** (Figure 14-18), which authorizes the crediting of the customer's account. If the damage to the goods is minimal, the customer may agree to keep them for a price reduction. In such cases, the credit manager issues a credit memo to reflect the amount that should be credited to the customer's account. A copy of the credit memo is sent to accounts receivable to authorize an adjustment to the customer's account balance; another copy is sent to the customer.

credit memo - A document, approved by the credit manager, authorizing the billing department to credit a customer's account.

After repeated attempts to collect payment have failed, it may be necessary to write off a customer's account. In such cases, the credit manager issues a credit memo to authorize the write-off. Unlike the cases involving damaged or returned goods, however, a copy of the credit memo used to authorize the write-off of an account is not sent to the customer.

THREATS AND CONTROLS Errors in maintaining customer accounts (threat 15 in Table 14-1) can lead to the loss of future sales and also may indicate possible theft of cash. The data entry edit checks discussed in Chapter 13 can minimize the risk of errors in maintaining customer accounts (control 15.1). For example, validity checks and closed-loop verification can ensure that the correct customer account is being updated, and field checks can ensure that only numeric data is entered for sales and payments. Customer payments are often processed in batches, so batch totals (control 15.2) can provide an additional means to detect posting errors. Specifically, the sum of all customer payments processed should equal the change to the total of all customer account balances. To ensure that all remittances were processed, the number of customer accounts updated should be compared with the number of checks received. These reconciliations should be performed by someone other than the individual involved in processing the original transactions because (1) it is easier to catch someone else's mistakes than one's own, and (2) it provides a means to identify possible cases of fraud. Mailing monthly account statements to every customer (control 15.3) provides an additional independent

FIGURE 14-18
Example of a Credit Memo

11121

CREDIT MEMORANDUM

Alpha Omega Electronics
2431 Bradford Lane
San Francisco, CA 99403

Credit To: Hardware City
35 Appliance Way
Phoenix, AZ 85201

Date April 7, 2021
Salesperson FRM

Apply To Invoice Number	Date	Customer's Order No.
34603	April 1, 2021	7413

Quantity	Item Number	Description	Unit Price	Amount
3	4120	PCS	85.00	255 00

Reason Credit Issued: Units damaged during shipment.
Returned on April 6, 2021

Received By: ALZ   Authorized By: PJS

We Credit Your Account For This Amount 255 00

review of posting accuracy because customers will complain if their accounts have not been properly credited for payments they remitted. In legacy systems, another important control to verify the accuracy of updates to accounts receivable involved reconciling the subsidiary accounts receivable records with the general ledger (control 15.4). After customer payments are processed, the sum of all individual customer account balances (the accounts receivable subsidiary file) should equal the total balance of the accounts receivable control account in the general ledger. If the two are not equal, an error in posting has probably occurred, and all transactions just entered should be reexamined. In ERP systems, however, postings to general ledger control accounts can occur only through the subsidiary ledger and are only made by the system itself. Although this eliminates the possibility of discrepancies between the subsidiary and general ledger arising from data entry errors, configuration errors may sometimes allow errors to occur.

Threat 16 listed in Table 14-1 is that an employee may issue credit memos to write-off account balances for friends or to cover up the theft of cash or inventory. Proper segregation of duties (control 16.1) can reduce the risk of this threat. To prevent employees from stealing inventory by making sales to friends who are then written off, the ERP system should be configured so that the person who can issue credit memos does not also have rights to enter sales orders or to maintain customer accounts. To prevent theft of cash, the person who handles cash should not be able to issue credit memos. The system should also be configured to match all credit memos to sales invoices. In addition, the system should be configured to block credit memos for which there does not exist validated documentation that the goods have been returned by the customer (control 16.2). Blocking forces specific managerial review and approval of cases where the company agrees to let the customer both keep the merchandise and receive credit.

Cash Collections

The final step in the revenue cycle is collecting and processing payments from customers (circle 4.0 in Figure 14-3).

PROCESS

Because cash and customer checks can be stolen so easily, it is important to take appropriate measures to reduce the risk of theft. As discussed more fully in the section on controls, this means that the accounts receivable function, which is responsible for recording customer remittances, should not have physical access to cash or checks. Instead, the cashier, who reports to the treasurer (see Figure 14-1), handles customer remittances and deposits them in the bank.

How then, does the accounts receivable function identify the source of any remittances and the applicable invoices that should be credited? One method involves mailing the customer two copies of the invoice and requesting that one be returned with the payment. This remittance advice is then routed to accounts receivable, and the actual customer payment is sent to the cashier. An alternative solution is to have mailroom personnel prepare a **remittance list**, which is a document identifying the names and amounts of all customer remittances, and send it to accounts receivable. Yet another alternative is to photocopy all customer remittances and send the copies to accounts receivable while forwarding the actual remittances to the cashier for deposit.

remittance list - A document listing names and amounts of all customer payments received in the mail.

Managing cash flow is important to overall profitability, as the AOE case showed. Therefore, companies are continually seeking ways to speed up the receipt of payments from customers. One way to do this when customers send payments directly to the company is to use Remote Deposit Capture software to scan customer checks and then transmit an encrypted digital file to the bank. Doing so eliminates the time and cost associated with going to the bank to make a physical deposit.

Another way to speed up the processing of customer payments involves the use of a lockbox arrangement with a bank. A **lockbox** is a postal address to which customers send their remittances. The participating bank picks up the checks from the Post Office box and deposits them in the company's account. The bank then sends the remittance advices, an electronic list of all remittances, and photocopies of all checks to the company. Having customers send payments to a lockbox eliminates the delay associated with processing customer remittances before depositing them. Cash flow can be further improved by selecting several banks around the country to maintain lockboxes, with the locations chosen to minimize the time customer checks are in the mail. Similarly, establishing lockbox arrangements with foreign banks reduces the time it takes to collect payments from sales to international customers.

lockbox - A postal address to which customers send their remittances.

Information technology can provide additional efficiencies in the use of lockboxes. In an **electronic lockbox** arrangement, the bank electronically sends the company information about the customer account number and the amount remitted as soon as it receives and scans those checks. This method enables the company to begin applying remittances to customer accounts before the photocopies of the checks arrive.

electronic lockbox - A lockbox arrangement (see *lockbox*) in which the bank electronically sends the company information about the customer account number and the amount remitted as soon as it receives payments.

Lockbox arrangements, however, eliminate only those delays associated with internal processing of remittances mailed directly to the company. With **electronic funds transfer (EFT)**, customers send their remittances electronically to the company's bank and thus eliminate the delay associated with the time the payment is in the mail system. EFT also reduces the time lag before the bank makes the deposited funds available to the company. EFT is usually accomplished through the banking system's Automated Clearing House (ACH) network.

electronic funds transfer (EFT) - The transfer of funds through use of online banking software.

EFT, however, involves only the transfer of funds. To properly credit customer accounts, companies also need additional data about each remittance, such as invoice numbers and discounts taken. Although every bank can do EFT through the ACH system, not every bank possesses the EDI capabilities necessary to process the related remittance data. Consequently, many companies have had to separate the EFT and EDI components of processing customer payments, as shown in the top panel of Figure 14-19. This complicates the selling company's task of properly crediting customer accounts for payments because information about the total amount of funds received arrives separately from information about the invoices that payment

FIGURE 14-19
EFT and FEDI

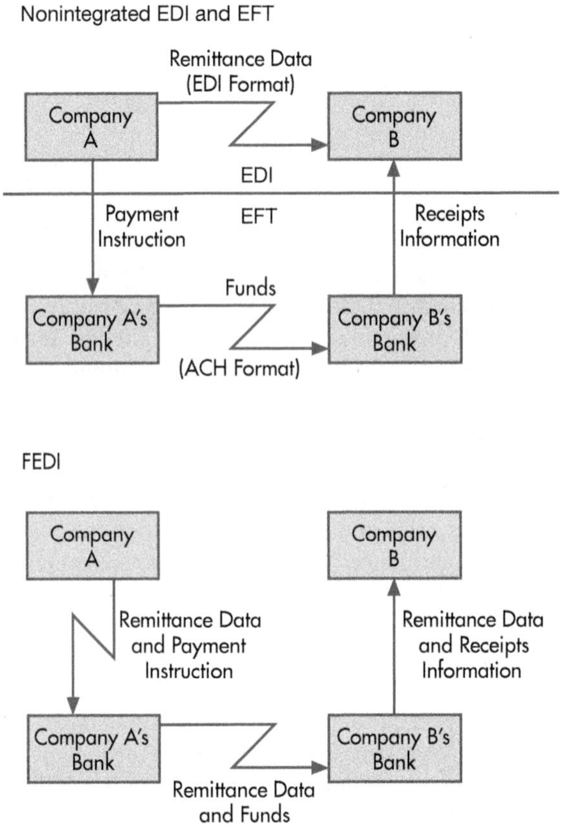

should be applied against. Similarly, the customer's task is complicated by the need to send information about the payment to two different parties.

financial electronic data interchange (FEDI) - The combination of EFT and EDI that enables both remittance data and funds transfer instructions to be included in one electronic package.

Financial electronic data interchange (FEDI) solves these problems by integrating the exchange of funds (EFT) with the exchange of the remittance data (EDI). As shown in the lower panel of Figure 14-19, the customer sends both remittance data and funds transfer instructions together. Similarly, the seller receives both pieces of information simultaneously. Thus, FEDI completes the automation of both the billing and cash collections processes. To fully reap the benefits of FEDI, however, requires that both the selling company and its customers use banks capable of providing EDI services.

Companies can also speed the collection process by accepting credit cards or debit cards. The benefits are that the card issuer usually transfers the funds within two days of the sale and the selling company avoids the risk of uncollectible accounts. These benefits must be weighed against the costs of accepting such cards, which typically range from 2% to 4% of the gross sales price. Companies can also sell past-due customer accounts receivable, a process referred to as **factoring**, to a firm that specializes in such collections. Typically, the cost of factoring is 1% to 2% of the account balances, which may be cheaper than drawing on a line of credit.

factoring - Selling accounts receivable at a discount to a firm that specializes in collections of past-due accounts.

THREATS AND CONTROLS

The primary objective of the cash collections function is to safeguard customer remittances. Special control procedures must be utilized because cash is so easy to steal (threat 17 in Table 14-1). Segregation of duties is the most effective control procedure for reducing the risk of such theft (control 17.1). Employees who have physical access to cash should not have responsibility for recording or authorizing any transactions involving its receipt. Specifically, the following pairs of duties should be segregated:

1. ***Handling cash or checks and posting remittances to customer accounts.*** A person performing both of these duties could commit the special type of embezzlement called *lapping* that was discussed in Chapter 8. Therefore, only the remittance data should be sent to the accounts receivable department, with customer payments being sent to the cashier.

Such an arrangement establishes two mutually independent control checks. First, the total credits to accounts receivable recorded by the accounting department should equal the total debit to cash representing the amount deposited by the cashier. Second, the copy of the remittance list sent to the internal audit department can be compared with the validated deposit slips and bank statements to verify that all checks the organization received were deposited. Finally, the monthly statements mailed to customers provide another layer of control because customers would notice the failure to properly credit their accounts for payments remitted.

2. ***Handling cash or checks and authorizing credit memos.*** A person performing both of these duties could conceal theft of customer payments by creating a credit memo equal to the amount stolen. The theft is concealed because the credit memo reduces the customer's balance by the amount stolen, so the customer is unlikely to notice and complain.
3. ***Handling cash or checks and reconciling the bank statement.*** An important detective control is reconciliation of the bank account statement with the balance of cash recorded in the company's information system. Having this reconciliation performed by someone who does not have access to cash or customer remittances provides an independent check on the cashier and prevents manipulation of the bank statement to conceal the theft of cash. Otherwise, the employee performing the bank reconciliation could record miscellaneous bank fees equal to the amount of cash stolen.

In ERP systems, employee roles must be properly configured to segregate these combinations of incompatible duties. In addition, the system should be configured to require specific approval by an appropriate manager of high-risk transactions, such as issuing credit memos without requiring the customer to return the merchandise.

In general, the handling of money and checks within the organization should be minimized. The optimal methods are a bank lockbox arrangement or the use of EFT, FEDI, or credit cards for customer payments (control 17.2), which totally eliminates employee access to customer payments. When customers pay via EFT or FEDI, sellers should obtain a **universal payment identification code (UPIC)** from their bank (control 17.3). The UPIC is a number that enables customers to remit payments via an ACH credit without requiring the seller to divulge detailed information about its bank account. The costs of these arrangements must be weighed against the benefits of reduced internal processing costs and faster access to customer payments. If customer payments must be processed internally, prompt documentation of remittances is crucial because the risk of loss is greatest at the time of first receipt. Therefore, a list of all checks received should be prepared *immediately* after opening the mail (control 17.4). The checks should also be restrictively endorsed at that time (control 17.5). To further minimize the risk of misappropriating any cash or checks received, two people should open all incoming mail (control 17.6).

universal payment identification code (UPIC) - A number that enables customers to remit payments via an ACH credit without requiring the seller to divulge detailed information about its bank account.

Retail stores and organizations that receive cash directly from customers should use cash registers that automatically produce a written record of all cash received (control 17.7). In these situations, customers also can play a role in controlling cash collections. For example, many stores use signs to inform customers that their purchase is free if they fail to get a receipt or that receipts marked with a red star entitle them to a discount. Such policies encourage customers to watch that employees actually ring up the cash sale and do so correctly. Accepting mobile payments by customers is another way that retail stores can reduce the risk of employees stealing customer payments.

All customer remittances should be deposited, intact, in the bank each day (control 17.8). Daily deposits reduce the amount of cash and checks at risk of theft. Depositing all remittances intact, and not using any of them for miscellaneous expenditures, facilitates reconciliation of the bank statement with the records of sales, accounts receivable, and cash collections. ERP systems should be configured to require that all cash collections transactions be processed through an approved list of bank accounts.

Finally, as the AOE case illustrated, cash flow problems are a serious concern (threat 18 in Table 14-1). The use of lockbox arrangements, EFT, credit cards, and offering discounts for early payment can speed up cash collections (controls 18.1 and 18.2). However, the best control procedure to reduce the risk of unanticipated cash shortfalls is to use a **cash flow budget** (control 18.3). As Figure 14-20 shows, a cash flow budget presents estimates of cash inflows (projected collections from sales) and outflows (outstanding payables). A cash flow budget can alert an organization to a pending short-term cash shortage, thereby enabling it to plan

cash flow budget - A budget that shows projected cash inflows and outflows for a specified period.

FIGURE 14-20
Sample Cash Flow Budget

	January	February	March	April
Beginning Balance	10,000	11,000	8,000	8,000
Projected Cash Receipts:				
Cash Sales	7,000	8,500	8,000	9,000
Collections on Account	26,000	29,000	28,000	30,000
Total Cash Available (A)	43,000	48,500	44,000	47,000
Projected Cash Disbursements (B)	(32,000)	(41,000)	(39,000)	(36,000)
Projected Ending Cash Balance (C = A – B)	11,000	7,500	5,000	11,000
Desired Minimum Balance (D)	8,000	8,000	8,000	8,000
Amount Needed to Borrow	0	500	3,000	0
Ending Balance	11,000	8,000	8,000	11,000

ahead to secure short-term loans or factor some of its accounts receivable at the best possible rates. Conversely, an organization that knows a surplus of cash is pending can take steps to invest those excess funds to earn the best possible returns. Regular monitoring of a cash flow budget would have helped AOE avoid the need for short-term borrowing at unfavorable rates.

Summary and Case Conclusion

An organization's accounting system should be designed to maximize the efficiency and effectiveness with which the four basic revenue cycle activities (sales order entry, shipping, billing, and cash collections) are performed. It must also incorporate adequate internal control procedures to mitigate such threats as uncollectible sales, billing errors, and lost or misappropriated inventory and cash. Control procedures also are needed to ensure that the information provided for decision making is both accurate and complete. Finally, to facilitate strategic decision making, the accounting system should be designed to accommodate the integration of internally generated data with data from external sources.

At the next executive meeting, Elizabeth summarized the proposals that she, Trevor, and Ann developed to provide the information needed to better manage customer relationships and cash flows. Among the recommendations were the following:

1. Equip the sales force with wireless-enabled pen-based tablets. Trevor Whitman, vice president of marketing, believes that AOE will still need its sales staff to visit existing customers to identify which additional products can be profitably carried. Sales staff also will continue to make cold calls on prospective customers to try to convince them to carry AOE's products. As they walk down store aisles, sales representatives can check off the items that need to be restocked and then write in the appropriate quantities. When the order is complete, they can transmit the order back to headquarters. The system can check the customer's credit status and inventory availability and confirm orders within minutes, including an estimated delivery date. After the customer approves the order, the system will immediately update all affected files so that current information about inventory status is available to other sales representatives.
2. Improve warehouse and shipping efficiency by replacing bar codes with RFID tags.
3. Improve billing process efficiency by increasing the number of customers who agree to participate in invoiceless sales relationships and, when possible, by using EDI to transmit invoices to those customers who still require them.
4. In an effort to improve customer service, periodically survey and monitor customer satisfaction with AOE's products and performance.
5. Improve efficiency of cash collections by encouraging customers to use EFT and, preferably, FEDI to remit payments. Obtain a UPIC from their bank to avoid having to share detailed bank account information with customers. Develop and monitor cash flow budgets monthly to anticipate short-term borrowing needs.
6. Improve efficiency of accounts receivable by automating as much of the process as possible.

Linda Spurgeon approved these proposals. She then asked Elizabeth and Ann to turn their attention to solving several problems related to AOE's expenditure cycle business activities.

KEY TERMS

revenue cycle 428
sales order 434
electronic data interchange (EDI) 435
credit limit 436
accounts receivable aging report 437
back order 438
picking ticket 438
customer relationship management (CRM) systems 440
packing slip 443
bill of lading 444
sales invoice 446
open-invoice method 448
remittance advice 448
balance-forward method 448
monthly statement 448
cycle billing 449
credit memo 449
remittance list 451
lockbox 451
electronic lockbox 451
electronic funds transfer (EFT) 451
financial electronic data interchange (FEDI) 452
factoring 452
universal payment identification code (UPIC) 453
cash flow budget 453

AIS in Action

CHAPTER QUIZ

1. Which activity is part of the sales order entry process?
a. setting customer credit limits
b. preparing a bill of lading
c. checking customer credit
d. approving sales returns

2. Which document often accompanies merchandise shipped to a customer?
a. picking ticket
b. packing slip
c. credit memo
d. sales order

3. Which method is most likely used when a company offers customers discounts for prompt payment?
a. open-invoice method
b. balance-forward method
c. accounts receivable aging method
d. cycle billing method

4. Which of the following techniques is the most efficient way to process customer payments and update accounts receivable?
a. EFT
b. UPIC
c. FEDI
d. ACH

5. Which of the following revenue cycle activities can potentially be eliminated by technology?
a. sales order entry
b. shipping
c. billing
d. cash collections

6. The integrated database underlying an ERP system results in which of the following general threats to the revenue cycle?
a. inaccurate or invalid master data
b. unauthorized disclosure of sensitive information
c. loss or destruction of data
d. all of the above

7. Which document is used to authorize the release of merchandise from inventory control (warehouse) to shipping?
a. picking ticket
b. packing slip
c. shipping order
d. sales invoice

8. Which of the following provides a means both to improve the efficiency of processing customer payments and also to enhance control over those payments?
a. CRM
b. lockboxes
c. aging accounts receivable
d. EDI

9. For good internal control, who should approve credit memos?
a. credit manager
b. sales manager
c. billing manager
d. controller

10. For good internal control over customer remittances, the mailroom clerk should separate the checks from the remittance advices and send the customer payments to which department?
a. billing
b. accounts receivable
c. cashier
d. sales

DISCUSSION QUESTIONS

14.1 Customer relationship management systems hold great promise, but their usefulness is determined by the amount of personal data customers are willing to divulge. How can companies encourage customers to share useful personal information? How might changes in privacy regulations, such as the EU's GDPR, affect this?

14.2 Some products, such as music and software, can be digitized. How does this affect each of the four main activities in the revenue cycle?

14.3 Many companies use accounts receivable aging schedules to project future cash inflows and bad-debt expense. Review the information typically presented in such a report (see Figure 14-8). Which specific metrics can be calculated from those data that might be especially useful in providing early warning about looming cash flow or bad-debt problems?

14.4 Table 14-1 suggests that restricting physical access to inventory is one way to reduce the threat of theft. How can information technology help accomplish that objective?

14.5 Invoiceless billing has been adopted by many large businesses for business-to-business transactions. What are the barriers, if any, to its use in sales to consumers?

14.6 If AOE decides to begin selling directly to individual consumers, what changes will it need to make in its business processes?

PROBLEMS

14.1 Match the terms with their definitions:

____	**1.** CRM system	a. Document used to authorize reducing the balance in a customer account
____	**2.** open-invoice method	b. Process of dividing customer account master file into subsets and preparing invoices for one subset at a time
____	**3.** credit memo	c. System that integrates EFT and EDI information
____	**4.** credit limit	d. System that contains customer-related data organized in a manner to facilitate customer service, sales, and retention
____	**5.** cycle billing	e. Electronic transfer of funds
____	**6.** FEDI	f. Method of maintaining accounts receivable that generates one payment for all sales made the previous month

____ 7. remittance advice	g. Method of maintaining customer accounts that generates payments for each individual sales transaction
____ 8. lockbox	h. Maximum possible account balance for a customer
____ 9. back order	i. Electronic invoicing
____ 10. picking ticket	j. Post Office box to which customers send payments
____ 11. bill of lading	k. Document used to indicate stockouts exist
____ 12. factoring	l. Document used to establish responsibility for shipping goods via a third party
____ 13. accounts receivable aging report	m. Document that authorizes removal of merchandise from inventory
____ 14. EFT	n. Turnaround document returned by customers with payments
____ 15. UPIC	o. Number other than the company's real bank account number that customers can use to remit payments to a company's bank account
	p. Selling accounts receivable to a firm that specializes in collecting past due accounts
	q. Document that shows the amounts of accounts receivable that are current and past due

14.2 What internal control procedure(s) would provide protection against the following threats?

a. Workers on the shipping dock steal goods, claiming that the inventory shortages reflect errors in the inventory records.
b. An employee posts the sales amount to the wrong customer account because he incorrectly keys the customer account number into the system.
c. An employee makes a credit sale to a customer who is already four months behind in making payments on his account.
d. An employee authorizes a credit memo for a sales return when the goods were never actually returned.
e. An employee writes off a customer's accounts receivable balance as uncollectible to conceal the theft of subsequent cash payments from that customer.
f. Customers are billed for the quantity ordered, but the quantity shipped is actually less because some items have been back ordered.
g. The mailroom clerk steals checks and then endorses them for deposit into the clerk's personal bank account.
h. The cashier steals funds by cashing several checks from customers.
i. A waiter steals cash by destroying the customer sales ticket for customers who paid cash.
j. Goods are shipped to a customer, but that customer is not billed.
k. A business loses sales because of stockouts of several products for which the computer records indicated there was adequate quantity on hand.
l. A business experiences unauthorized disclosure of the buying habits of several well-known customers.
m. A business loses all information about amounts owed by customers in New York City because the master database for that office was destroyed in a fire.
n. The company's website is unavailable for seven hours because of a power outage.
o. Customers' credit card numbers are intercepted and stolen while being sent to the company's website.
p. A sales clerk sells a $7,000 wide-screen TV to a friend and alters the price to $700.

q. A shipping clerk who is quitting to start a competing business copies the names of the company's 500 largest customers and offers them lower prices and better terms if they purchase the same product from the clerk's new company.
r. A fire in the office next door damages the company's servers and all optical and magnetic media in the server room. The company immediately implements its disaster recovery procedures and shifts to a backup center several miles away. The company has made full daily backups of all files and has stored a copy at the backup center. However, none of the backup copies are readable.
s. A clerk in a retail clothing store accepts returns from customers but, instead of putting the clothes back on the rack, hides them under the counter and then puts them into his gym bag and takes them home.

14.3 For good internal control, which of the following duties can be performed by the same individual? Explain your answer.
1. Approving changes to customer credit limits
2. Sales order entry
3. Shipping merchandise
4. Billing customers
5. Depositing customer payments
6. Maintaining accounts receivable
7. Issuing credit memos
8. Reconciling the organization's bank accounts
9. Checking inventory availability

14.4 Download the spreadsheet from the course website and perform the following tasks.

REQUIRED

a. Create a formula in column F to calculate how many days a particular invoice has been outstanding.
b. Create a formula in column G that attaches the correct label to each invoice (e.g., if the invoice is 0–30 days old, the label should be "0–30"; if it is 31–60 days old, the label should be "31–60", etc.) according to the table in the upper right corner of the spreadsheet.
c. Create a pivot table that shows the sum, count, and average values for each of the four categories of accounts receivable.
d. Create a pivot table that shows total amounts and count of invoices by both category (e.g., 0–30, 31–60, etc.) and region (East, West, North, South).
e. Modify the pivot table in step d to be able to filter the results by salesperson.

14.5 Create a questionnaire checklist that can be used to evaluate controls for each of the four basic activities in the revenue cycle (sales order entry, shipping, billing, and cash collections).

REQUIRED

a. For each control issue, write a Yes/No question such that a "No" answer represents a control weakness. For example, one question might be, "Are customer credit limits set and modified by a credit manager with no sales responsibility?"
b. For each Yes/No question, write a brief explanation of why a "No" answer represents a control weakness.

14.6 Excel Project. Accountants should help managers understand trends in revenue cycle activities. One important issue concerns granting credit to customers. Trends in bad debt expense (BDE) to write-offs (WO) provide insights into the accuracy of credit granting policies. It is also important to monitor how long it will take to write off the current balance in the allowance for doubtful accounts (BADA Exhaustion Rate).

---

* Life-long learning opportunity: see pp. xxiii–xxiv in preface.

REQUIRED

a. Create a spreadsheet that contains the following data:

Year	Year 1	Year 2	Year 3	Year 4	Year 5
BDE/WO	1.81	0.98	1.08	1.27	0.94
BADA/WO	1.42	1.73	1.89	1.48	1.26
BADA Exhaustion Rate (years)	1.33	1.81	1.67	1.35	1.20

b. Create a two-dimensional columnar chart that displays the data values for each variable for the five years.

c. Create a new chart that will display a two-dimensional columnar chart that shows a rolling five-year window of the variables. Add the following data for Year 6 and Year 7 to your spreadsheet to demonstrate that the new chart shows only Years 1–5 values:

Year	Year 6	Year 7
BDE/WO	1.1	1.3
BADA/WO	1.3	1.1
BADA Exhaustion Rate (years)	1.5	1.6

(*Hint:* Read the article "Simplify Your Future with Rolling Charts," by James A. Weisel in the July 2012 issue of the *Journal of Accountancy* for an explanation of how to create a rolling chart (requirement c for this problem)—and take care to follow Excel's rules for naming ranges. Read the article "Assessing the Allowance for Doubtful Accounts: Using historical data to evaluate the estimation process," by Mark E. Riley and William R. Pasewark in the September 2009 issue of the *Journal of Accountancy* for an explanation of how the variables used in this problem can help you evaluate a company's process for estimating the allowance for doubtful accounts. The *Journal of Accountancy* is available either in print or online at www.aicpa.org.)*

14.7 O'Brien Corporation is a midsized, privately owned industrial instrument manufacturer supplying precision equipment to manufacturers in the Midwest. The corporation is 10 years old and uses an integrated ERP system. The administrative offices are located in a downtown building, and the production, shipping, and receiving departments are housed in a renovated warehouse a few blocks away.

Customers place orders on the company's website, by fax, or by telephone. All sales are on credit, FOB destination. During the past year, sales have increased dramatically, but 15% of credit sales have had to written off as uncollectible, including several large online orders to first-time customers who denied ordering or receiving the merchandise.

Customer orders are picked and sent to the warehouse, where they are placed near the loading dock in alphabetical sequence by customer name. The loading dock is used both for outgoing shipments to customers and for receipt of incoming deliveries. There are 10 to 20 incoming deliveries every day, from a variety of sources.

The increased volume of sales has resulted in a number of errors in which customers were sent the wrong items. There have also been some delays in shipping because items that supposedly were in stock could not be found in the warehouse. Although a perpetual inventory is maintained, there has been no physical count of inventory for two years. When an item is missing, the warehouse staff writes the information down in a log book. Once a week, the warehouse staff uses the log book to update the inventory records.

The system is configured to prepare the sales invoice only after shipping employees enter the actual quantities sent to a customer, thereby ensuring that customers are billed only for items actually sent and not for anything on back order.

REQUIRED

a. Identify at least three weaknesses in O'Brien Corporation's revenue cycle procedures, explain the associated problem, and propose a solution. Present your answer in a three-column table with these headings: Weakness, Problem, Solution.

b. Draw a BPMN diagram to depict O'Brien Corporation's revenue cycle revised to incorporate your solutions to step a. (*CPA Examination, adapted*)

---

* Life-long learning opportunity: see pp. xxiii–xxiv in preface.

14.8 Parktown Medical Center, Inc., is a small health care provider owned by a publicly held corporation. It employs 7 salaried physicians, 10 nurses, 3 support staff, and 3 clerical workers. The clerical workers perform such tasks as reception, correspondence, cash receipts, billing, and appointment scheduling. All are adequately bonded.

Most patients pay for services rendered by cash or check on the day of their visit. Sometimes, however, the physician who is to perform the respective services approves credit based on an interview. When credit is approved, the physician files a memo with one of the clerks to set up the receivable using data the physician generates.

The servicing physician prepares a charge slip that is given to one of the clerks for pricing and preparation of the patient's bill. At the end of the day, one of the clerks uses the bills to prepare a revenue summary and, in cases of credit sales, to update the accounts receivable subsidiary ledger.

The front office clerks receive cash and checks directly from patients and give each patient a prenumbered receipt. The clerks take turns opening the mail. The clerk who opens that day's mail immediately stamps all checks "for deposit only." Each day, just before lunch, one of the clerks prepares a list of all cash and checks to be deposited in Parktown's bank account. The office is closed from 12 noon until 2:00 P.M. for lunch. During that time, the office manager takes the daily deposit to the bank. During the lunch break the clerk who opened the mail that day uses the list of cash receipts and checks to update patient accounts.

The clerks take turns preparing and mailing monthly statements to patients with unpaid balances. One of the clerks writes off uncollectible accounts only after the physician who performed the respective services believes the account will not pay and communicates that belief to the office manager. The office manager then issues a credit memo to write off the account, which the clerk processes.

The office manager supervises the clerks, issues write-off memos, schedules appointments for the doctors, makes bank deposits, reconciles bank statements, and performs general correspondence duties.

Additional services are performed monthly by a local accountant who posts summaries prepared by the clerks to the general ledger, prepares income statements, and files the appropriate payroll forms and tax returns.

REQUIRED

a. Identify at least three weaknesses in Parktown's revenue cycle procedures, explain the associated problem, and propose a solution. Present your answer in a three-column table with these headings: Weakness, Problem, Solution.
b. Draw a BPMN diagram to depict Parktown's revenue cycle revised to incorporate your solutions to step a. (*CPA Examination, adapted*)

14.9 The Family Support Center is a small charitable organization. It has only four full-time employees: two staff, an accountant, and an office manager. The majority of its funding comes from two campaign drives, one in the spring and one in the fall. Donors make pledges over the telephone. Some donors pay their pledge by credit card during the telephone campaign, but many prefer to pay in monthly installments by check. In such cases, the donor pledges are recorded during the telephone campaign, and the donors are then mailed pledge cards. Donors mail their contributions directly to the charity. Most donors send a check, but occasionally some send cash. Most donors return their pledge card with their check or cash donation, but occasionally the Family Support Center receives anonymous cash donations. The procedures used to process donations are as follows:

Sarah, a staff member who has worked for the Family Support Center for 12 years, opens all mail. She sorts the donations from the other mail and prepares a list of all donations, indicating the name of the donor (or anonymous), amount of the donation, and the pledge number (if the donor returned the pledge card). Sarah then sends the list, cash, and checks to the accountant.

The accountant enters the information from the list into the computer to update the Family Support Center's files. The accountant then prepares a deposit slip (in duplicate) and deposits all cash and checks into the charity's bank account at the end of each day. No funds are left on the premises overnight. The validated deposit slip is then filed by date. The accountant also mails an acknowledgment letter thanking each donor. Monthly, the accountant retrieves all deposit slips and uses them to reconcile the Family Support Center's bank statement. At this time, the accountant also reviews the pledge files and sends a follow-up letter to those people who have not yet fulfilled their pledges.

Each employee has a computer workstation connected to the internal network. Employees are permitted to surf the web during lunch hours. Each employee has full access to the charity's accounting system, so that anyone can fill in for someone else who is out sick or on vacation. Each Friday, the accountant makes a backup copy of all computer files. The backup copy is stored in the office manager's office.

REQUIRED

a. Identify two major control weaknesses in the Family Support Center's cash receipts procedures. For each weakness you identify, suggest a method to correct that weakness. Your solution must be specific—*identify which specific employees should do what. Assume that no new employees can be hired.*
b. Describe the IT control procedures that should exist in order to protect the Family Support Center from loss, alteration, or unauthorized disclosure of data.

14.10 Figure 14-21 depicts the activities performed in the revenue cycle by the Newton Hardware Company.

REQUIRED

a. Identify at least three weaknesses in Newton Hardware's revenue cycle. Explain the resulting threat, and suggest methods to correct the weakness.
b. Identify ways to use IT to streamline Newton's revenue cycle activities. Describe the control procedures required in the new system. (*CPA Examination, adapted*)

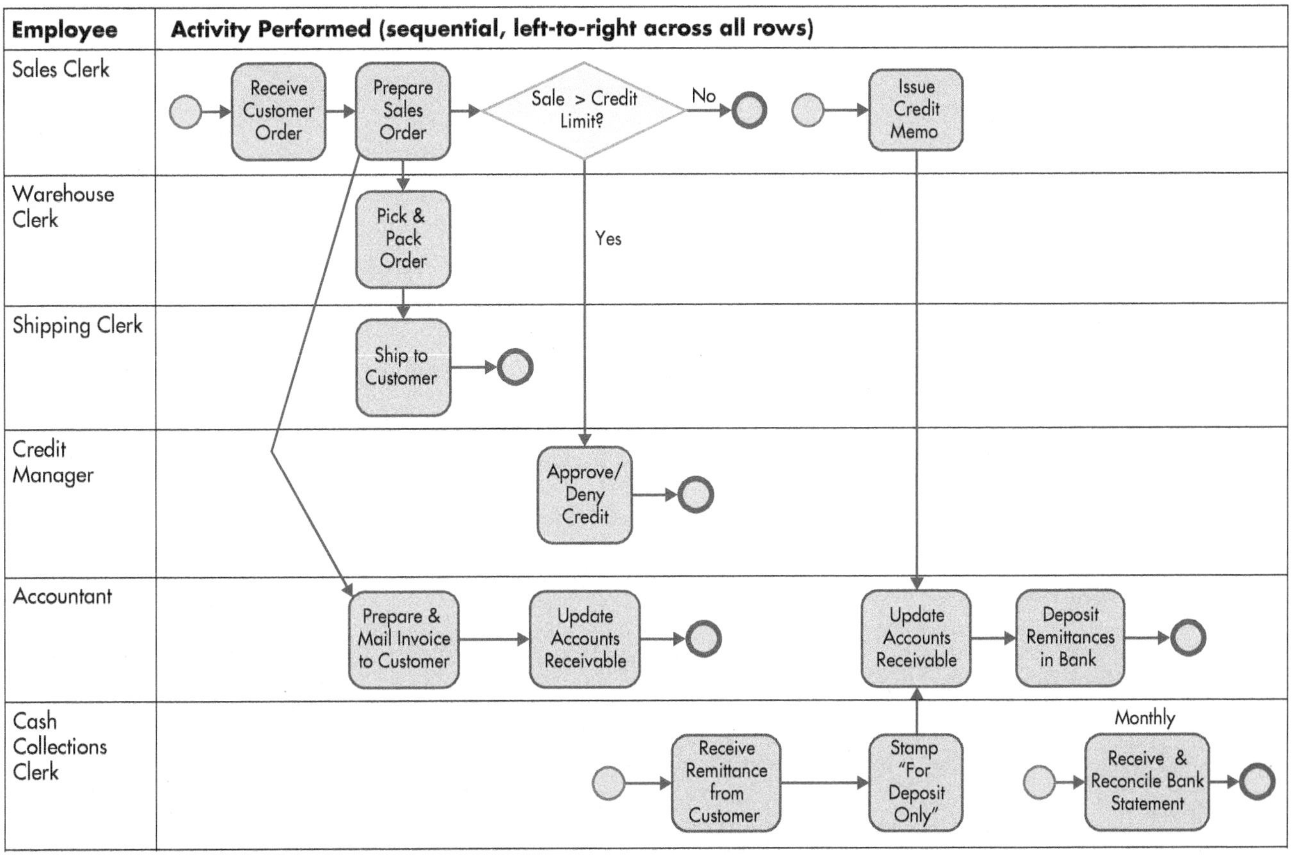

FIGURE 14-21
Newton Hardware Company Revenue Cycle Procedures

14.11 Match the threats in the first column to the appropriate control procedures in the second column (more than one control may address the same threat).

Threat	Applicable Control Procedures
____ 1. Uncollectible sales	a. Restricted access to master data
____ 2. Mistakes in shipping orders to customers	b. Encryption of customer information while in storage
____ 3. Crediting customer payments to the wrong account	c. Backup and disaster recovery procedures
____ 4. Theft of customer payments	d. Digital signatures
____ 5. Theft of inventory by employees	e. Physical access controls on inventory
____ 6. Excess inventory	f. Segregation of duties of handling cash and maintaining accounts receivable
____ 7. Reduced prices for sales to friends	g. Reconciliation of packing lists with sales orders
____ 8. Orders later repudiated by customers who deny placing them	h. Reconciliation of invoices with packing lists and sales orders
____ 9. Failure to bill customers	i. Use of bar codes or RFID tags
____ 10. Errors in customer invoices	j. Periodic physical counts of inventory
____ 11. Cash flow problems	k. Perpetual inventory system
____ 12. Loss of accounts receivable data	l. Use of either EOQ, MRP, or JIT inventory control system
____ 13. Unauthorized disclosure of customer personal information	m. Lockboxes or electronic lockboxes
____ 14. Failure to ship orders to customers	n. Cash flow budget
	o. Mailing of monthly statements to customers
	p. Credit approval by someone not involved in sales
	q. Segregation of duties of shipping and billing
	r. Periodic reconciliation of prenumbered sales orders with prenumbered shipping documents

14.12 Answer all of the following multiple-choice questions.

1. Which of the following pairs of duties combines the functions of *custody* and *authorization* in a manner that would allow an employee to conceal the theft of a customer's payment?
   a. Handling cash receipts plus maintaining accounts receivable
   b. Writing checks plus reconciling the bank statement
   c. Handling cash receipts plus issuing credit memos
   d. All of the above
   e. None of the above

2. Which of the following violates proper segregation of duties?
   a. The same person maintains both accounts receivable and accounts payable.
   b. The same person approves sales orders that exceed a customer's credit limit and processes and reconciles the bank account.
   c. The same person handles customer payments and has access to blank checks.
   d. All of the above
   e. None of the above

3. Which of the following types of fraud requires access to the accounts receivable master file?
   a. lapping
   b. kiting
   c. theft of inventory
   d. None of the above

4. The CEO is concerned about the possibility of employees stealing inventory. In the formal language used for risk analysis, theft of inventory is referred to as a(n) ________.
   a. risk
   b. exposure
   c. expected loss
   d. threat
   e. none of the above

5. For good internal control in an ERP system, sales staff should be permitted to ________.
   a. adjust customer credit limits
   b. issue credit memos
   c. both of the above
   d. neither of the above

6. Which of the following procedures, **by itself**, is **most effective** at preventing employees from stealing cash?
   a. restrictively endorsing all checks from customers upon receipt
   b. having someone who has no access to cash reconcile the bank accounts
   c. sending monthly statements to customers
   d. using lockboxes for customer remittances
   e. creating invoices so the bottom portion is to be returned as a remittance advice

7. Which of the following combinations of duties can the same employee perform without violating the principle of segregation of duties?
   a. shipping inventory and billing customers
   b. issuing credit memos and maintaining accounts receivable
   c. taking customer orders and checking inventory availability
   d. All of the above
   e. None of the above

8. Which of the following is an example of the type of fraud referred to as misappropriation of assets?
   a. embezzlement
   b. lapping
   c. inventory theft
   d. All of the above
   e. None of the above

9. Which of the following controls would be most effective in mitigating the risk of inventory theft?
   a. reconciling shipping documents to sales orders, picking lists, and packing slips
   b. separating the functions of shipping and billing
   c. documentation of all transfers of inventory between employees
   d. use of lockboxes

10. For effective internal control, which of the following duties can the person who handles customer payments also perform?
   a. issue credit memos
   b. reconcile the bank account
   c. maintain accounts receivable
   d. All of the above
   e. None of the above

14.13 Excel Project.

REQUIRED

a. Create a spreadsheet that contains the following data:

Salesperson	Date	Calls Made
Smith	07/05	75
Barnes	07/11	133
Martinez	07/13	95
Jackson	08/02	125
Hsu	08/04	102
Smith	08/04	152
Barnes	08/15	151
Hsu	08/16	101
Barnes	08/17	100
Martinez	08/19	153
Jackson	08/20	151
Smith	08/22	190
Barnes	08/23	158
Martinez	08/28	100
Jackson	09/03	109
Hsu	09/06	159
Jackson	09/10	104
Hsu	09/11	105
Smith	09/14	101
Barnes	09/19	102
Martinez	09/22	106
Jackson	09/29	190
Hsu	09/30	160

b. On the same worksheet, but to the right of the data above, create the following table to show calls made by each salesperson this quarter. Use the sumproduct function to create a formula that automatically calculates the total calls handled.

Calls Made by Salesperson this Quarter

	July	August	September
Barnes			
Hsu			
Jackson			
Martinez			
Smith			

(*Hint:* Read the article "Supercharge Your Excel Sum Operations: Add data by up to 30 criteria," by J. D. Kern in the July 2009 issue of the *Journal of Accountancy* for an explanation of the sumproduct function and the use of double dashes. The *Journal of Accountancy* is available either in print or online at www.aicpa.org.)*

* Life-long learning opportunity: see pp. xxiii–xxiv in preface.

14.14 The following table presents the results of using a CAAT tool to interrogate the XYZ Company's ERP system for revenue cycle activities. It shows the number of times each employee performed a specific task.

	Take Order	Approve Credit	Ship Inventory	Maintain A/R	Issue Credit Memo	Bill Customer	Deposit Customer Remittances	Reconcile Bank Account
Employee A	250					15		
Employee B	305							
Employee C	275	5		10				
Employee D					10		5	
Employee E			400					
Employee F			430			25		
Employee G						600		
Employee H				400			20	1
Employee I				430	25			
Employee J							650	

REQUIRED

Identify five examples of improper segregation of duties and explain the nature of each problem you find.

CASE 14-1 Research Project: How CPA Firms Are Leveraging New Developments in IT

Find articles from the past year in the *Journal of Accountancy*, the *New Accountant*, and any other magazine suggested by your instructor that explain how CPA firms are using IT developments (e.g., the cloud, BYOD, mobile, etc.). Write a report that explains the benefits of the new technology (cost reduction, revenue increases, customer attraction and retention, etc.) and how the firm mitigates any new threats associated with that technology.

AIS in Action Solutions

QUIZ KEY

1. Which activity is part of the sales order entry process?
   a. setting customer credit limits [Incorrect. The credit department, not the sales department, sets credit limits.]
   b. preparing a bill of lading [Incorrect. This occurs as part of the shipping process.]
   ► c. checking customer credit [Correct. Checking customer credit and inventory availability are two key parts of the sales order entry process.]
   d. approving sales returns [Incorrect. Someone outside the sales department should approve all returns.]

2. Which document often accompanies merchandise shipped to a customer?
   a. picking ticket [Incorrect. The picking ticket is used by warehouse workers to fill the order. If a copy of the picking ticket is used as a packing slip, it is referred to as a packing slip.]
   ► b. packing slip [Correct. This document specifies what is being shipped.]
   c. credit memo [Incorrect. A credit memo is used to adjust a customer's account balance for sales returns, allowances, or write-offs.]
   d. sales order [Incorrect. This is a source document created during sales order entry.]

3. Which method is most likely used when a company offers customers discounts for prompt payment?
   ▶ a. open-invoice method [Correct. The open-invoice method provides a means to offer discounts because it facilitates aging each invoice to verify whether a discount should be granted.]
   b. balance-forward method [Incorrect. The balance-forward method does not facilitate tracking the age of individual invoices and thus is difficult to use to offer discounts for early payment of individual invoices.]
   c. accounts receivable aging method [Incorrect. Aging of accounts receivable is a control measure designed to timely detect potential uncollectible accounts.]
   d. cycle billing method [Incorrect. Cycle billing is a method of smoothing the timing of cash receipts by billing different subsets of the customer file each week.]

4. Which of the following techniques is the most efficient way to process customer payments and update accounts receivable?
   a. EFT [Incorrect. EFT deals only with the transfer of funds. It does not include remittance information necessary to update accounts receivable.]
   b. UPIC [Incorrect. UPIC stands for Uniform Payment Identification Code and is used to enable customers to remit EFT payments without divulging the receiving company's bank account information.]
   ▶ c. FEDI [Correct. FEDI integrates EFT, for processing customer payments, with EDI, for processing related remittance data to update accounts receivable.]
   d. ACH [Incorrect. ACH stands for "Automated Clearing House," the private communications network used by financial institutions to transfer funds.]

5. Which of the following revenue cycle activities can potentially be eliminated by technology?
   a. sales order entry [Incorrect. IT may change how sales orders are entered, but the sales process must always begin with taking the customer's order.]
   b. shipping [Incorrect. The product must always be shipped to the customer. The manner may change, particularly for products that can be digitized, but there is still a shipping process.]
   ▶ c. billing [Correct. The use of integrated ERP systems makes printing invoices superfluous because both the seller and customer already know all the information included in the invoice. Some large manufacturers have already moved to invoiceless systems with their major suppliers.]
   d. cash collections [Incorrect. IT may change how the funds are received, but sellers will always need to collect payments from customers.]

6. The integrated database underlying an ERP system results in which of the following general threats to the revenue cycle?
   a. inaccurate or invalid master data [Incorrect. Table 14-1 shows that this is not the only general threat to the revenue cycle.]
   b. unauthorized disclosure of sensitive information [Incorrect. Table 14-1 shows that this is not the only general threat to the revenue cycle.]
   c. loss or destruction of data [Incorrect. Table 14-1 shows that this is not the only general threat to the revenue cycle.]
   ▶ d. all of the above [Correct.]

7. Which document is used to authorize the release of merchandise from the inventory control [warehouse] to shipping?
   ▶ a. picking ticket [Correct. A picking ticket is generated by sales order entry to authorize removal of inventory to be shipped to the customer.]
   b. packing slip [Incorrect. The packing slip accompanies the shipment and lists the contents of the shipment.]
   c. shipping order [Incorrect. A shipping order is an internal document used to record what was shipped when the shipping function is performed in-house; a bill of lading serves the same purpose when a third-party common carrier is used to deliver merchandise.]
   d. sales invoice [Incorrect. A sales invoice documents the terms of the sale and requests payment.]

8. Which of the following provides a means to both improve the efficiency of processing customer payments and also enhance control over those payments?

a. CRM [Incorrect. CRM stands for "customer relationship management" and is a process used to improve customer satisfaction and retention.]

▶ b. lockboxes [Correct. The use of lockboxes eliminates the delays involved in processing customer payments and then depositing them. It also improves control because customer payments are not directly handled by any employees.]

c. aging accounts receivable [Incorrect. Aging accounts receivable is an important control for managing customer accounts, but not for processing payments.]

d. EDI [Incorrect. EDI stands for "electronic data interchange." It is used to exchange documents, but not to process customer payments.]

9. For good internal control, who should approve credit memos?

▶ a. credit manager [Correct. This is the credit manager's function.]

b. sales manager [Incorrect. The same person who authorizes sales should not also authorize credit memos to adjust customer accounts for those sales.]

c. billing manager [Incorrect. The billing manager is in charge of invoicing customers and should not have authority to reduce accounts receivable by issuing credit memos.]

d. controller [Incorrect. The controller is responsible for the recording function and should not also be able to authorize changes to accounts via credit memos.]

10. For good internal control over customer remittances, the mailroom clerk should separate the checks from the remittance advices and send the customer payments to which department?

a. billing [Incorrect. Billing creates invoices but should not be involved in processing payments from customers.]

b. accounts receivable [Incorrect. Accounts receivable performs the recording function and should not also have physical custody of assets.]

▶ c. cashier [Correct. This is the cashier's job. The cashier function has custody of cash accounts.]

d. sales [Incorrect. The sales department authorizes release of merchandise and should not also have custody of assets.]

CHAPTER 15

The Expenditure Cycle: Purchasing to Cash Disbursements

LEARNING OBJECTIVES

1. Discuss the basic business activities and related information processing operations in the expenditure cycle, explain the general threats to those activities, and describe the controls that can mitigate those threats.
2. Explain the process and key decisions involved in ***ordering goods and services***, identify the threats to those activities, and describe the controls that can mitigate those threats.
3. Explain the process and key decisions involved in ***receiving goods and services***, identify the threats to those activities, and describe the controls that can mitigate those threats.
4. Explain the process and key decisions involved in ***approving supplier invoices*** for goods and services, identify the threats to those activities, and describe the controls that can mitigate those threats.
5. Explain the process and key decisions involved in making ***cash disbursements*** to suppliers, identify the threats to those activities, and describe the controls that can mitigate those threats.

INTEGRATIVE CASE Alpha Omega Electronics

Although the new enterprise resource planning (ERP) system at Alpha Omega Electronics (AOE) has enabled the company to slash its costs associated with purchasing and accounts payable, Linda Spurgeon, AOE's president, is convinced that additional improvements are needed. She is particularly concerned about issues recently raised by LeRoy Williams, vice president of manufacturing for AOE. LeRoy is upset because several production runs were delayed at the Wichita plant because components that AOE's inventory records indicated as being in stock actually were not on hand. There were also delays at the Dayton plant because suppliers either did not deliver components on time or delivered substandard products. Furthermore, Linda is concerned because AOE was defrauded of $8 million it sent via wire transfer in response to an e-mail, purportedly from one of its suppliers, stating the supplier had changed bank accounts and requesting that AOE remit its next payment to the new bank.

Linda asked Elizabeth Venko, the controller, and Ann Brandt, AOE's vice president of information systems, for some recommendations on how AOE's new ERP system could help solve these problems. Specifically, she asked Elizabeth and Ann to address the following issues:

1. What must be done to ensure that AOE's inventory records are current and accurate to avoid unexpected components shortages like those experienced at the Wichita plant?
2. How could the problems at the Dayton plant be avoided in the future? What can be done to ensure timely delivery of quality components?
3. Is it possible to reduce AOE's investment in materials inventories?
4. How could the information system provide better information to guide planning and production?
5. How could IT be used to further reengineer expenditure cycle activities?
6. How can AOE protect itself from additional fraudulent wire transfers?

As this case reveals, deficiencies in the information system used to support expenditure cycle activities can create significant financial problems for an organization. Current and accurate information about inventories, suppliers, and the status of outstanding purchase orders is crucial for managing the expenditure cycle effectively. As you read this chapter, think about how to solve AOE's problems with its expenditure cycle activities.

Introduction

expenditure cycle - A recurring set of business activities and related data processing operations associated with the purchase of and payment for goods and services.

The **expenditure cycle** is a recurring set of business activities and related information processing operations associated with the purchase of and payment for goods and services (Figure 15-1). This chapter focuses on the acquisition of raw materials, finished goods,

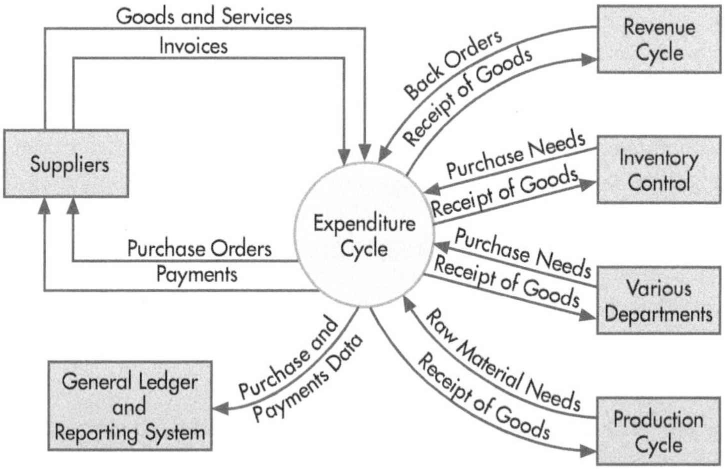

FIGURE 15-1
Context Diagram of the Expenditure Cycle

supplies, and services. Chapters 16 and 17 address two other special types of expenditures: the acquisition of fixed assets and labor services, respectively.

In the expenditure cycle, the primary external exchange of information is with suppliers (vendors). Within the organization, information about the need to purchase goods and materials flows to the expenditure cycle from the revenue and production cycles, inventory control, and various departments. Once the goods and materials arrive, notification of their receipt flows back to those sources from the expenditure cycle. Expense data also flow from the expenditure cycle to the general ledger and reporting function for inclusion in financial statements and various management reports.

The primary objective in the expenditure cycle is to minimize the total cost of acquiring and maintaining inventories, supplies, and the various services the organization needs to function. To accomplish this objective, management must make the following key decisions:

- What is the optimal level of inventory and supplies to carry?
- Which suppliers provide the best quality and service at the best prices?
- How can the organization consolidate purchases across units to obtain optimal prices?
- How can information technology (IT) be used to improve both the efficiency and accuracy of the inbound logistics function?
- How can the organization maintain sufficient cash to take advantage of any discounts suppliers offer?
- How can payments to vendors be managed to maximize cash flow?

The answers to those questions guide how an organization performs the four basic expenditure cycle activities depicted in Figure 15-2:

1. Ordering materials, supplies, and services.
2. Receiving materials, supplies, and services.
3. Approving supplier invoices.
4. Cash disbursements.

This chapter explains how an organization's information system supports each of those activities. We begin by describing the design of the expenditure cycle information system and the basic controls necessary to ensure that it provides management with reliable information to assess operational efficiency and effectiveness. We then discuss in detail each of the four basic expenditure cycle activities. For each activity, we describe how the information needed to perform and manage those activities is collected, processed, and stored. We also explain the controls necessary to ensure not only the reliability of that information but also the safeguarding of the organization's resources.

Expenditure Cycle Information System

As Table 15-1 shows, the activities in the expenditure cycle are mirror images of the basic activities performed in the revenue cycle. These close linkages between the buyer's expenditure cycle activities and the seller's revenue cycle activities have important implications for the design of both parties' accounting information systems. Specifically, by applying new IT developments to reengineer expenditure cycle activities, companies create opportunities for suppliers to reengineer their revenue cycle activities. Conversely, using IT to redesign a company's revenue cycle can create opportunities for customers to modify their own expenditure cycles. In fact, the changes in one company's operations may *necessitate* corresponding changes in the operations of other companies with which it does business. For example, the major automobile manufacturers and many large retailers, such as Walmart, require their suppliers to transmit invoices via electronic data interchange (EDI), or they will not do business with them. Consequently, those suppliers must modify their revenue cycle process to incorporate the use of EDI.

PROCESS

Like most large organizations, AOE uses an ERP system. Figure 15-3 shows the portion of the ERP system that supports AOE's expenditure cycle business activities.

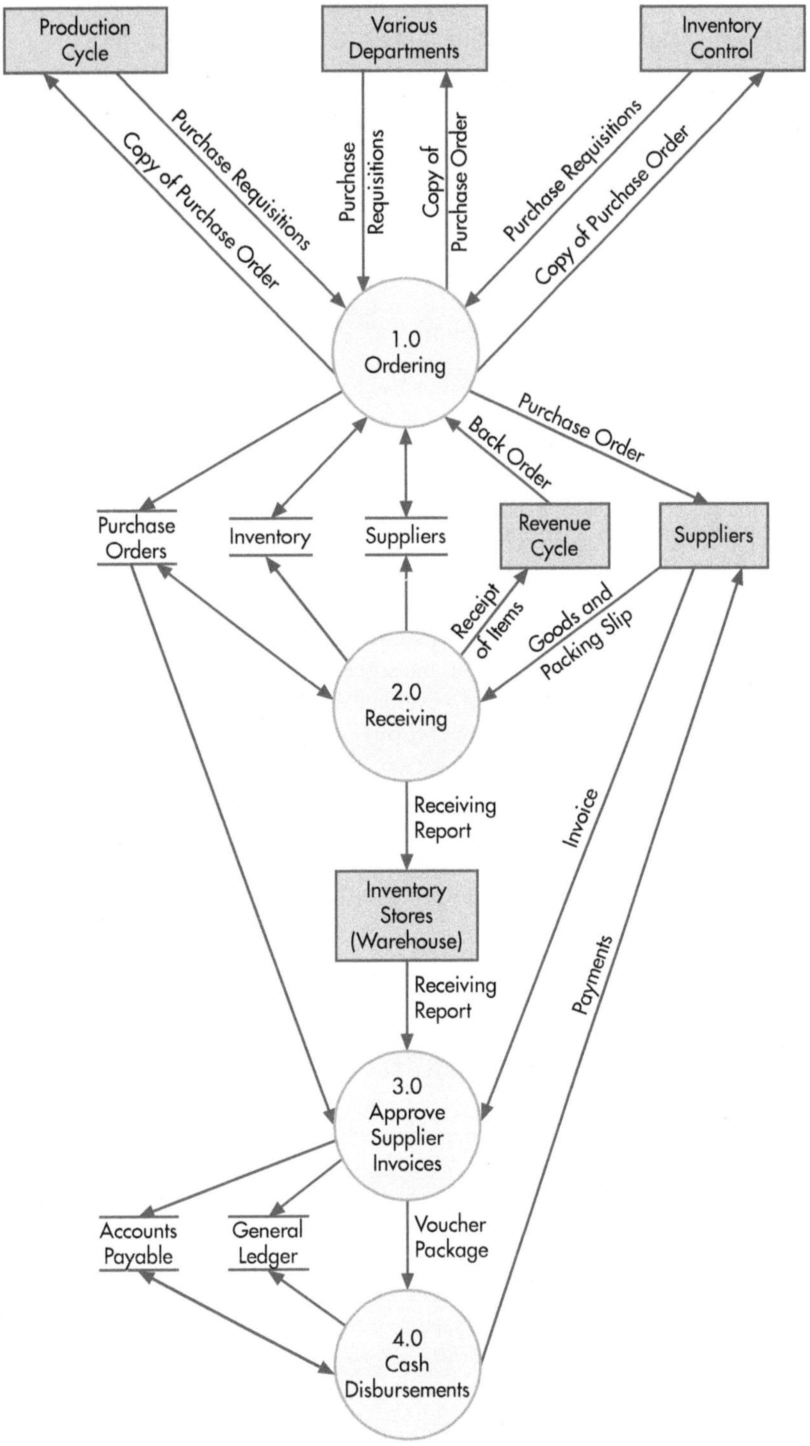

FIGURE 15-2
Level 0 Data Flow Diagram for the Expenditure Cycle

Although Figure 15-3 shows that AOE's inventory control department has primary responsibility for ensuring an adequate quantity of materials and supplies, any department can submit a request to purchase items. Once a purchase request has been approved, the system searches the inventory master file to identify the preferred supplier for that item. The system then creates a purchase order that is sent to the supplier via EDI. (If necessary, paper copies are printed and mailed.) The receiving department has access to the open purchase order file so that it can plan for and verify the validity of deliveries. Accounts payable is notified of orders so that it can plan for pending financial commitments. The department that generated the purchase requisition is also notified that its request has been approved.

TABLE 15-1 Comparison of Revenue and Expenditure Cycle Activities

Revenue Cycle Activity	Expenditure Cycle Activity
Sales order entry—process orders from customers	Ordering of materials, supplies, and services—send orders to suppliers
Shipping—deliver merchandise or services to customers (outbound logistics)	Receiving—receive merchandise or services from suppliers (inbound logistics)
Billing—send invoices to customers	Processing invoices—review and approve invoices from suppliers
Cash collections—process payments from customers	Cash disbursements—process payments to suppliers

Major suppliers send electronic notification of coming deliveries, which enables AOE to plan to have adequate staffing to process incoming shipments at its warehouses. When a shipment arrives, the receiving-dock workers use the inquiry processing system to verify that an order is expected from that supplier. Most suppliers bar-code or RFID (radio frequency identification) tag their products to facilitate the counting of the goods. Receiving-dock workers inspect the goods and use an online terminal to enter information about the quantity and condition of items received. The system checks that data against the open purchase order, and any discrepancies are immediately displayed on the screen so that they can be resolved. The exact time of the delivery also is recorded to help evaluate supplier performance.

Upon transfer of the goods to the warehouse, the inventory clerk verifies the count of the items and enters that data in the system. For suppliers who do not send invoices, the system uses information from the inventory clerk acknowledging the transfer of items from the receiving department to automatically schedule a payment according to the terms agreed on when the order was placed. EDI invoices automatically update accounts payable. Accounts payable clerks manually enter information from suppliers who send paper invoices.

FIGURE 15-3
Overview of ERP System Design to Support the Expenditure Cycle

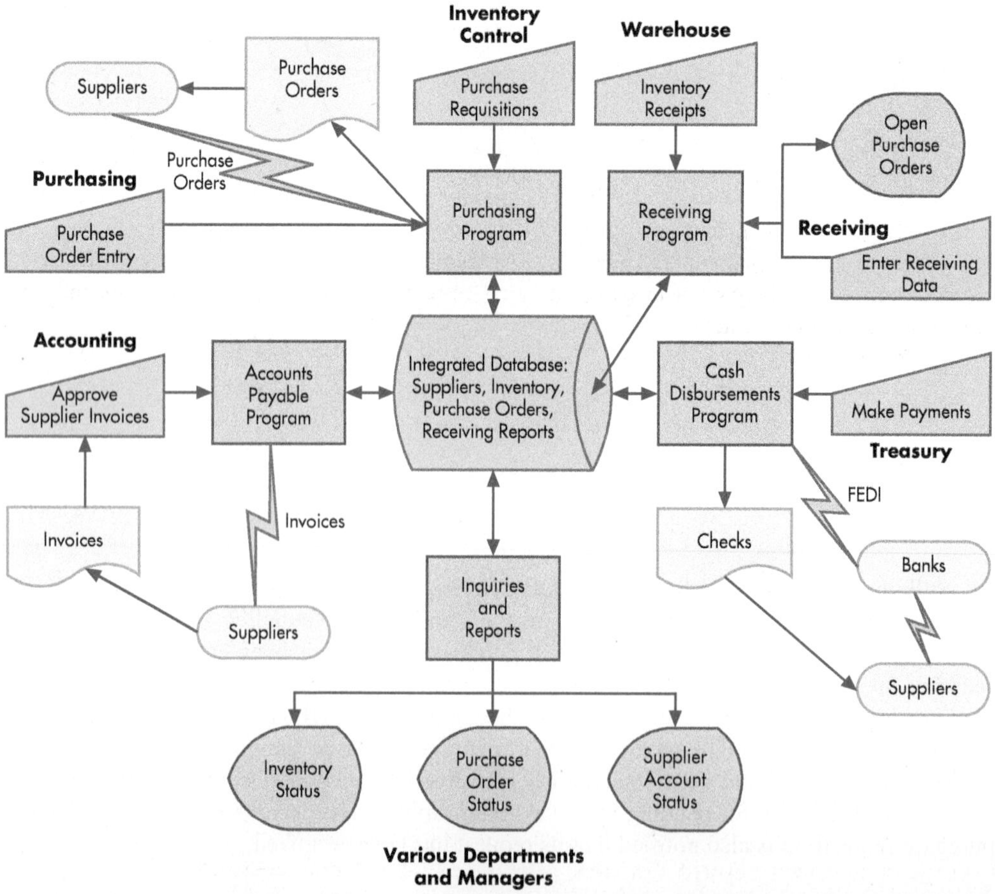

The system then compares the supplier invoice with the information contained in the purchase order and receiving report to ensure accuracy and validity. For purchases of supplies or services that do not usually involve purchase orders and receiving reports, the invoice is sent to the appropriate supervisor for approval. The supplier invoice itself is also checked for mathematical accuracy. The system automatically schedules invoices for payment by due date.

AOE, like most companies, uses batch processing to pay its suppliers. Each day, the treasurer uses the inquiry processing system to review the invoices that are due and approves them for payment. AOE makes payments to some of its larger suppliers using financial electronic data interchange (FEDI) but still prints paper checks for many of its smaller suppliers. When an electronic funds transfer (EFT) payment is authorized or a check is printed, the system updates the accounts payable, open-invoice, and general ledger files. For each supplier, the totals of all vouchers are summed, and that amount is subtracted from the balance field in that supplier's master file record. The relevant purchase orders and receiving reports are flagged to mark that those transactions have been paid. The invoices that are paid are then deleted from the open-invoice file. A remittance advice is prepared for each supplier, which lists each invoice being paid and the amounts of any discounts or allowances taken. For payments made by EFT, the remittance data accompany the EFT payment as part of the FEDI package. For payments made by check, the printed remittance advice accompanies the signed check. After all disbursement transactions have been processed, the system generates a summary journal entry, debiting accounts payable and crediting cash, and posts that entry to the general ledger.

The cashier reviews checks against the supporting documents and then signs them. Checks above a specified amount also require a second signature by the treasurer or another authorized manager. The cashier then mails the signed checks and remittance advices to the suppliers. EFT transactions are also performed by the cashier and reviewed by the treasurer.

The easy access to up-to-date, accurate information enables managers to closely monitor performance. However, the quality of decisions depends upon the accuracy of the information in the database. It is also important to properly segregate duties in order to prevent fraudulent cash disbursements. We now discuss the general threats associated with the expenditure cycle activities and explain the controls that can mitigate them.

THREATS AND CONTROLS

Figure 15-3 shows that all expenditure cycle activities depend on the integrated database that contains information about suppliers, inventory, and purchasing activities. Therefore, the first general threat listed in Table 15-2 is inaccurate or invalid master data. Errors in the supplier master data could result in ordering from unapproved suppliers, purchasing materials of inferior quality, untimely deliveries, sending payments to the wrong address, and fraudulent disbursements to fictitious suppliers. Errors in the inventory master data can result in production delays due to unanticipated shortages of key materials or unnecessary purchases and excess inventory. Errors in the purchasing master data can result in unauthorized purchases and failure to take advantage of negotiated discounts.

Table 15-2 shows that one way to mitigate the threat of inaccurate or invalid master data is to employ the data processing integrity controls (control 1.1) described in Chapter 13. It is also important to restrict access to expenditure cycle master data and configure the system so that only authorized employees can make changes to master data (control 1.2). This requires changing the default configurations of employee roles in ERP systems to appropriately segregate incompatible duties. For example, consider the situation where an accounts payable clerk enters the name of a supplier who is not currently on the list of approved suppliers. The default configuration of many ERP systems would result in a prompt asking whether the clerk wants to create a new supplier record. This violates proper segregation of duties by permitting the person responsible for recording payments to suppliers to also authorize the creation of new accounts. Similarly, the default configurations of many ERP systems permit accounts payable staff not only to read the prices of various products and the current balances owed to suppliers but also to change the values of those data items. These examples are just some of the many configuration settings that need to be reviewed to ensure proper segregation of duties. However, because such preventive controls can never be 100% effective, Table 15-2 also indicates that an important detective control is to regularly produce a report of all changes to master data and review them to verify that the database remains accurate (control 1.3).

TABLE 15-2 Threats and Controls in the Expenditure Cycle

Activity	Threat	Controls (First Number Refers to the Corresponding Threat)
General issues throughout entire expenditure cycle	1. Inaccurate or invalid master data 2. Unauthorized disclosure of sensitive information 3. Loss or destruction of data 4. Poor performance	1.1 Data processing integrity controls 1.2 Restriction of access to master data 1.3 Review of all changes to master data 2.1 Access controls 2.2 Encryption 3.1 Backup and disaster recovery procedures 4.1 Managerial reports
Ordering	5. Stockouts and excess inventory 6. Purchasing items not needed 7. Purchasing at inflated prices 8. Purchasing goods of inferior quality 9. Unreliable suppliers 10. Purchasing from unauthorized suppliers 11. Kickbacks	5.1 Perpetual inventory system 5.2 Bar coding or RFID tags 5.3 Periodic physical counts of inventory 6.1 Perpetual inventory system 6.2 Review and approval of purchase requisitions 6.3 Centralized purchasing function 7.1 Price lists 7.2 Competitive bidding 7.3 Review of purchase orders 7.4 Budgets 8.1 Purchasing only from approved suppliers 8.2 Review and approval of purchases from new suppliers 8.3 Tracking and monitoring product quality by supplier 8.4 Holding purchasing managers responsible for rework and scrap costs 9.1 Requiring suppliers to possess quality certification (e.g., ISO 9000) 9.2 Collecting and monitoring supplier delivery performance data 10.1 Maintaining a list of approved suppliers and configuring the system to permit purchase orders only to approved suppliers 10.2 Review and approval of purchases from new suppliers 10.3 EDI-specific controls (access, review of orders, encryption, policy) 11.1 Prohibit acceptance of gifts from suppliers 11.2 Job rotation and mandatory vacations 11.3 Requiring purchasing agents to disclose financial and personal interests in suppliers 11.4 Supplier audits
Receiving	12. Accepting unordered items 13. Mistakes in counting 14. Not verifying receipt of services 15. Theft of inventory	12.1 Requiring existence of approved purchase order prior to accepting any delivery 13.1 Do not inform receiving employees about quantity ordered 13.2 Require receiving employees to sign receiving report 13.3 Incentives 13.4 Use of bar codes and RFID tags 13.5 Configuration of the ERP system to flag discrepancies between received and ordered quantities that exceed tolerance threshold for investigation 14.1 Budgetary controls 14.2 Audits 15.1 Restriction of physical access to inventory 15.2 Documentation of all transfers of inventory between receiving and inventory employees 15.3 Periodic physical counts of inventory and reconciliation to recorded quantities 15.4 Segregation of duties: custody of inventory versus receiving
Approving supplier invoices	16. Errors in supplier invoices 17. Mistakes in posting to accounts payable	16.1 Verification of invoice accuracy 16.2 Requiring detailed receipts for procurement card purchases 16.3 ERS 16.4 Verification of freight bill and use of approved delivery channels 17.1 Data entry edit controls 17.2 Reconciliation of detailed accounts payable records with the general ledger control account

TABLE 15-2 Continued

Activity	Threat	Controls (First Number Refers to the Corresponding Threat)
Cash disbursements	18. Failure to take advantage of discounts for prompt payment 19. Paying for items not received 20. Duplicate payments 21. Theft of cash 22. Check alteration 23. Cash flow problems	18.1 Filing of invoices by due date for discounts 18.2 Cash flow budgets 19.1 Requiring that all supplier invoices be matched to supporting documents acknowledged by both receiving and inventory control 19.2 Budgets (for services) 19.3 Verification of all receipts for travel expenses 19.4 Use of corporate credit cards for travel expenses 20.1 Requiring a complete voucher package for all payments 20.2 Policy to pay only from original copies of supplier invoices 20.3 Cancelling all supporting documents when payment is made 21.1 Physical security of blank checks and check-signing machine 21.2 Periodic accounting of all sequentially numbered checks by cashier 21.3 Access controls to EFT terminals 21.4 Use of dedicated computer and browser for online banking 21.5 ACH blocks on accounts not used for payments 21.6 Separation of check-writing function from accounts payable 21.7 Requiring dual signatures on checks greater than a specific amount 21.8 Regular reconciliation of bank account with recorded amounts by someone independent of cash disbursements procedures 21.9 Restriction of access to supplier master file 21.10 Limiting the number of employees with ability to create one-time suppliers and to process invoices from one-time suppliers 21.11 Running petty cash as an imprest fund 21.12 Surprise audits of petty cash fund 22.1 Check-protection machines 22.2 Use of special inks and papers 22.3 "Positive Pay" arrangements with banks 23.1 Cash flow budget

A second general threat in the expenditure cycle is unauthorized disclosure of sensitive information, such as banking information about suppliers and special pricing discounts offered by preferred suppliers. Table 15-2 shows that one way to mitigate the risk of this threat is to configure the system to employ strong access controls that limit who can view such information (control 2.1). It is also important to configure the system to limit employees' ability to use the system's built-in query capabilities to specific tables and fields. In addition, sensitive data should be encrypted (control 2.2) in storage to prevent IT employees who do not have access to the ERP system from using operating system utilities to view sensitive information. Information exchanged with suppliers over the Internet should also be encrypted during transmission.

As Table 15-2 shows, a third general threat in the expenditure cycle concerns the loss or destruction of master data. The best way to mitigate the risk of this threat is to employ the backup and disaster recovery procedures (control 3.1) that were discussed in Chapter 13. A best practice is to implement the ERP system as three separate instances. One instance, referred to as *production*, is used to process daily activity. A second is used for testing and development. A third instance should be maintained as an online backup to the production system to provide near real-time recovery.

An ERP system's extensive reporting capabilities (control 4.1) can be used to monitor the threat of poor performance. Because inventory represents a sizable investment of working capital, reports that help manage inventory are especially valuable. A key measure to evaluate inventory management is inventory turnover, which is the ratio of cost of goods sold divided by inventory on hand. Consider the following example: annual sales are $500 million, and annual cost of goods sold total $360 million. An inventory turnover ratio of 1 means that the company is effectively carrying a year's supply of inventory, tying up $360 million. Improving the inventory turnover ratio to 3 would reduce that unprofitable investment to $120 million, thereby freeing up $240 million that could be used for other purposes.

Accountants need to understand how business activities are performed in order to design other reports that can help management better manage inventory. For example, it is useful to monitor the percentage of requisitions filled from inventory on hand. For critical items, this should be close to 100% to avoid stockouts and delays in filling customer orders. For most items, however, such a high fill rate is undesirable because it requires carrying too much inventory. Other reports can help management identify the relative importance of various inventory items. For example, it may be useful to classify items along several dimensions, such as frequency of purchase, frequency of use or resale, and contribution to profitability. Items frequently purchased and used and that make a significant contribution to profitability are of high importance and should be managed so as to maintain high fill rates. In contrast, management may wish to consider eliminating items seldom purchased, infrequently used, and that do not contribute much to profitability. As we will see in the following sections, accountants can help managers by designing a variety of detailed reports and metrics relevant to evaluating each business activity in the expenditure cycle.

Accountants also need to ensure that proper segregation of duties exists to minimize the risk of fraud. Figure 15-4 depicts how to properly segregate the various activities in the expenditure cycle. Refer to it as we discuss the appropriate internal controls for each step in the expenditure cycle.

FIGURE 15-4

BPM Diagram Showing Segregation of Duties across Expenditure Cycle Activities

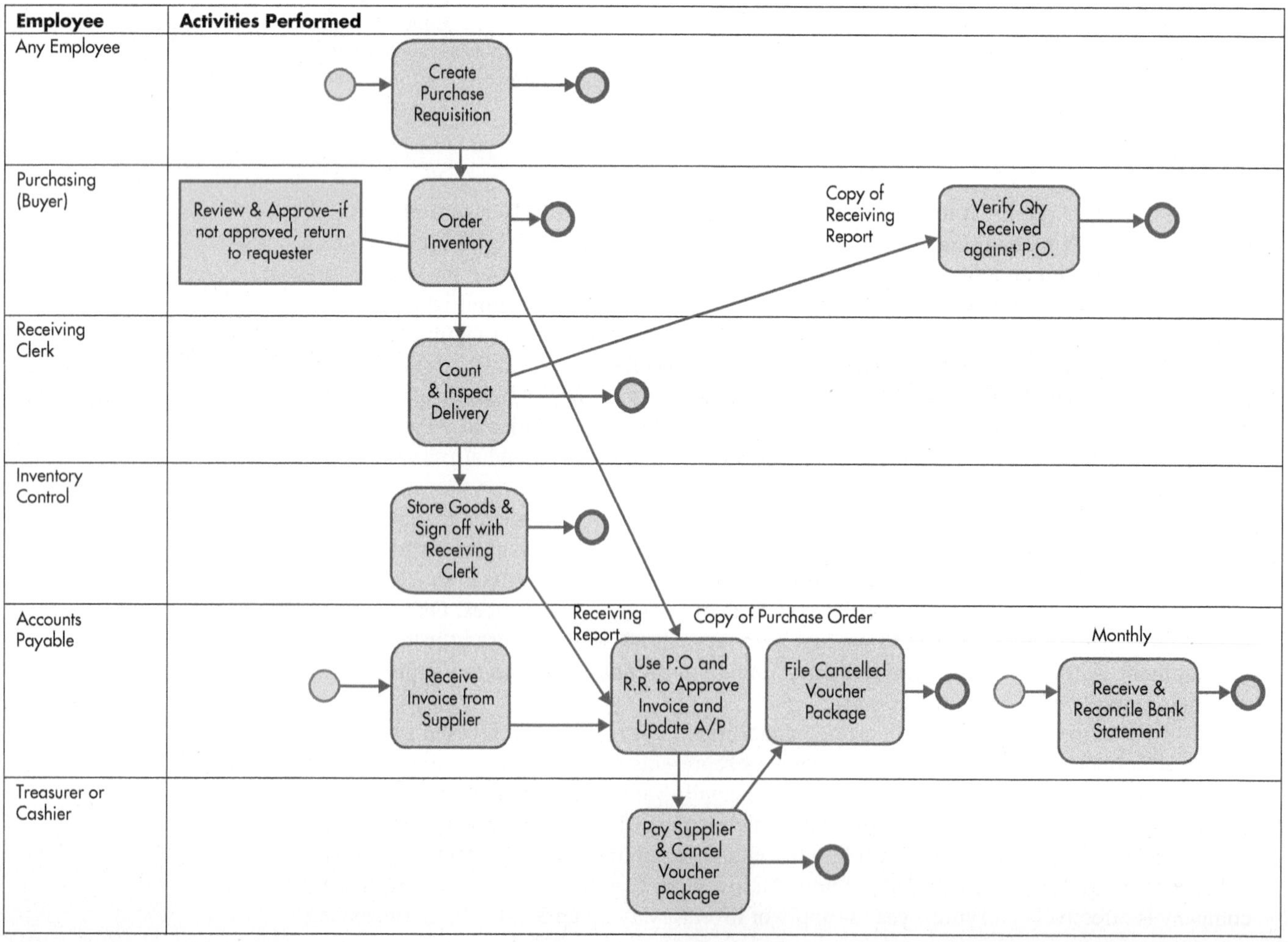

Ordering Materials, Supplies, and Services

The first major business activity in the expenditure cycle (circle 1.0 in Figure 15-2) is ordering inventory, supplies, or services. Figure 15-5 shows that this involves first identifying what, when, and how much to purchase, and then choosing from which supplier to purchase.

IDENTIFYING WHAT, WHEN, AND HOW MUCH TO PURCHASE

As the introductory case showed, inaccurate inventory records can create significant problems for organizations. Therefore, accountants and systems professionals need to understand best practices for managing inventory.

PROCESS The traditional approach to managing inventory is to maintain sufficient stock so that production can continue without interruption even if inventory use is greater than expected or if suppliers are late in making deliveries. This traditional approach is often called the **economic order quantity (EOQ)** approach because it is based on calculating an optimal order size to minimize the sum of ordering, carrying, and stockout costs. *Ordering costs* include all expenses associated with processing purchase transactions. *Carrying costs* are those associated with holding inventory. *Stockout costs* are those that result from inventory shortages, such as lost sales or production delays.

economic order quantity (EOQ) - The optimal order size to minimize the sum of ordering, carrying, and stockout costs.

Actual application of the EOQ approach varies depending on the type of item. For high-cost or high-use items, such as the computer chips and displays AOE uses, all three types of costs are included in the formula. For low-cost or low-usage items, such as the screws and springs AOE uses to assemble its products, ordering and carrying costs are usually ignored, and the sole objective is to maintain sufficient inventory levels. The EOQ formula is used to calculate *how much* to order. The **reorder point** specifies *when* to order. Companies typically set the reorder point based on delivery time and desired levels of safety stock to handle unexpected fluctuations in demand.

reorder point - Specifies the level to which the inventory balance of an item must fall before an order to replenish stock is initiated.

The traditional EOQ approach to inventory control often results in carrying significant amounts of inventory. The money invested in carrying inventory earns nothing. Consequently, in recent years many large U.S. manufacturing companies have minimized or even eliminated the amount of inventory on hand by adopting either materials requirements planning or just-in-time inventory management systems.

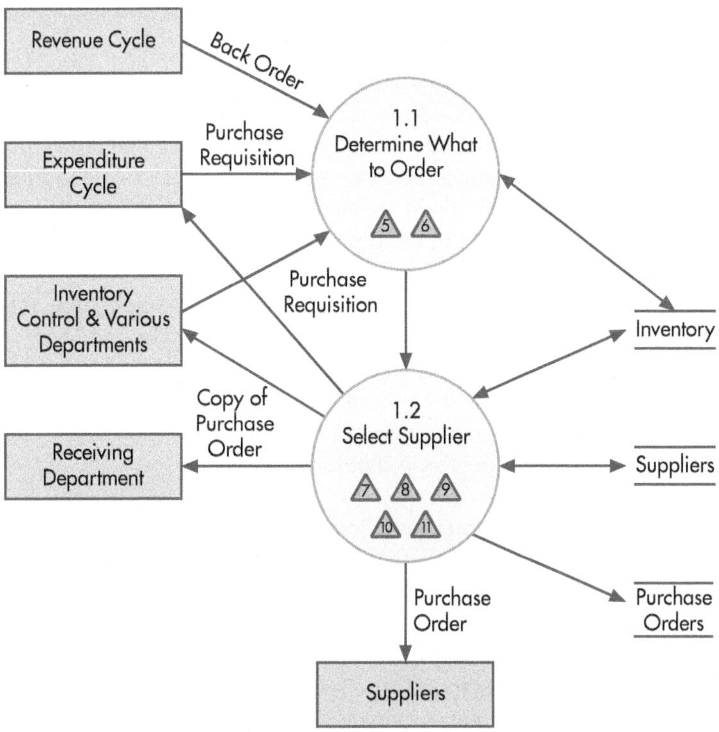

FIGURE 15-5
Level 1 Data Flow Diagram: Ordering Materials, Supplies, and Services (annotated to include threats)

materials requirements planning (MRP) - An approach to inventory management that seeks to reduce required inventory levels by improving the accuracy of forecasting techniques to better schedule purchases to satisfy production needs.

Materials requirements planning (MRP) seeks to reduce required inventory levels by improving the accuracy of forecasting techniques to better schedule purchases to satisfy production plans. For example, the production planning department of a company using MRP would use sales forecasts to prepare a detailed schedule specifying the quantities of each finished product to manufacture in a specified time period, such as the next three months. This schedule and the engineering specifications for each product identify the quantities of raw materials, parts, and supplies needed in production and the point in time when they will be needed. Thus, MRP systems reduce uncertainties about when raw materials are needed and therefore enable companies to carry less inventory.

just-in-time (JIT) inventory system - A system that minimizes or virtually eliminates inventories by purchasing and producing goods only in response to actual, rather than forecasted, sales.

A **just-in-time (JIT) inventory system** attempts to minimize, if not totally eliminate, finished goods inventory by purchasing and producing goods only in response to actual, rather than forecasted, sales. Consequently, JIT systems are characterized by frequent deliveries of small amounts of materials, parts, and supplies directly to the specific locations that require them when they are needed, rather than by infrequent bulk deliveries to a central receiving and storage facility. Therefore, a factory using a JIT system will have multiple receiving docks, each assigned to accept deliveries of items needed at nearby work centers.

A major difference between MRP and JIT systems is production scheduling. MRP systems schedule production to meet forecasted sales, thereby creating an "optimal" quantity of finished goods inventory. JIT systems schedule production in response to customer demands, thereby virtually eliminating finished goods inventory, but they require carrying sufficient quantities of raw materials in order to quickly adjust production in response to consumer demand. Both MRP and JIT systems can reduce costs and improve efficiency. Choosing between them depends, in part, on the types of products a company sells. MRP systems are more effectively used with products that have predictable patterns of demand, such as consumer staples. For such items, companies can plan purchases to minimize stockouts (with the resultant lost sales) while simultaneously minimizing the risk of overstocking and the subsequent costs of marking down or scrapping the excess inventory. In contrast, JIT inventory systems are especially useful for products that have relatively short life cycles and for which demand cannot be accurately predicted, such as toys associated with specific movies. In such cases, it is important that the business be able to quickly speed up production to meet unanticipated demand as well as to quickly stop production to avoid accumulating large inventories that must be marked down for clearance because the product is no longer in demand.

purchase requisition - A document or electronic form that identifies the requisitioner; specifies the delivery location and date needed; identifies the item numbers, descriptions, quantity, and price of each item requested; and may suggest a supplier.

A request to purchase goods or supplies is triggered either by the inventory control function or when employees notice a shortage of materials. Regardless of its source, the need to purchase goods or supplies often results in the creation of a **purchase requisition** that identifies the requisitioner; specifies the delivery location and date needed; identifies the item numbers, descriptions, quantity, and price of each item requested; and may suggest a supplier. Figure 15-6 shows a typical purchase requisition data entry screen used in ERP systems for all employee-initiated purchase requests. Minimizing the amount of data that must be manually entered improves both efficiency and accuracy. Thus, in Figure 15-6, the employee initiating the purchase request needs to complete only the supplier (vendor), date required, and location (where to ship the merchandise) fields in the header section (the top of the screen) and the item number and quantity requested in the details section. The system then pulls up all the other relevant information from the related master files.

You probably noticed the similarity in design to the sales order data entry screen (see Figure 14-7). This is intentional; it makes it easier for employees to learn how to perform new job duties arising from promotions or transfers. Notice that in Figure 15-6 the "Supervisor Approval" box is checked. This ensures proper review of all employee-initiated purchase requests. The person approving the purchase requisition would enter the department number and account number to which the purchase should be charged.

THREATS AND CONTROLS Inaccurate inventory records can result in stockouts that lead to lost sales or to carrying excess inventory that increases costs (threat 5). To reduce the risk of these problems, the perpetual inventory method should be used to ensure that information about inventory stocks is always current (control 5.1). However, data entry errors can result in inaccurate perpetual inventory records because even expert typists do make mistakes. Therefore, using information technology (control 5.2) to eliminate the need for manual data entry can improve the accuracy of perpetual inventory records.

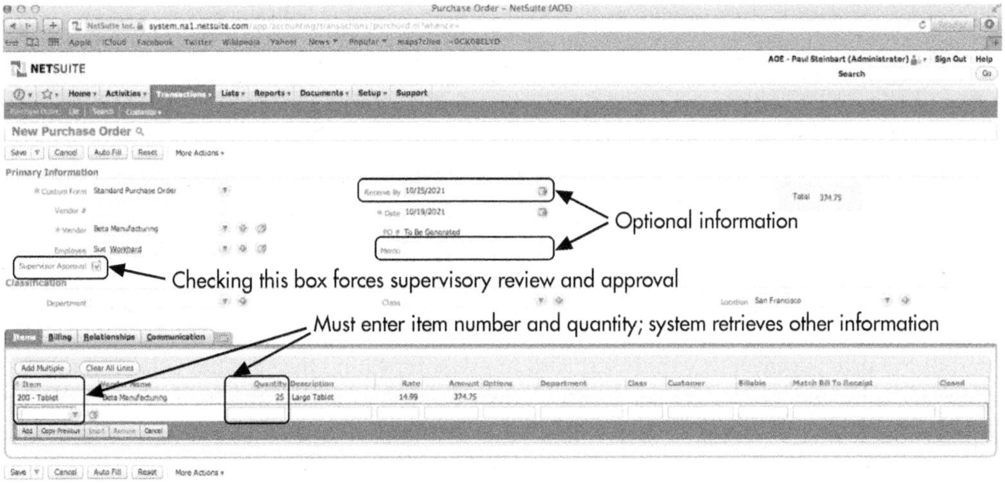

FIGURE 15-6
Purchase Requisition Data Entry Screen

Source: 2010 © NetSuite Inc.

Bar-coding is one option, but it is not a panacea. Errors can still occur if employees attempt to save time by scanning one item and then manually entering the quantity. For example, a grocery store orders 12 varieties of a private-brand soda, but the receiving clerk may scan only one can and then manually enter the number purchased. Since the flavors are all priced the same, the amount of the purchase is correctly calculated. The perpetual inventory records will be incorrect, however, because the exact count of the flavors purchased is not correctly recorded.

Affixing RFID tags to individual products eliminates the problems just discussed because the reader automatically records each item. RFID technology is also more efficient than bar codes because there is no need for a human to align the bar code on the product with the reader. However, RFID technology is more expensive than bar-coding and cannot be used for every type of product.

It is also important to periodically count inventory on hand and investigate any discrepancies between those counts and the perpetual inventory records (control 5.3 in Table 15-2). One annual physical inventory count will generally not be sufficient to maintain accurate inventory records, especially for MRP and JIT systems. Instead, an *ABC cost analysis* should be used to classify items according to their importance: The most critical items (A items) should be counted most frequently, and the least critical items (C items) can be counted less often. If such interim counts reveal significant discrepancies with inventory records, a comprehensive count of all inventory should be immediately undertaken. This approach might have alerted management at AOE's Wichita plant in the chapter introductory case about shortages of key components early enough to avoid production delays.

Another threat is purchasing items not currently needed. Accurate perpetual inventory records (control 6.1) ensure the validity of purchase requisitions that the inventory control system automatically generates. Supervisors need to review and approve purchase requisitions (control 6.2) that individual employees initiate. A related problem is multiple purchases of the same item by different subunits of the organization. As a result, the organization may be carrying a larger inventory than desired and may fail to take advantage of volume discounts that might be available. A centralized purchasing function (control 6.3) mitigates this threat.

CHOOSING SUPPLIERS

Once the need to purchase has been identified, the next step is to select a supplier. Purchasing agents (sometimes called buyers) usually perform this task. In manufacturing companies such as AOE, the purchasing function is closely related to the production cycle. Thus, as Figure 14-1 shows, Ryan McDaniel, the head of the purchasing department at AOE, reports directly to LeRoy Williams, the vice president of manufacturing.

PROCESS Several factors should be considered when selecting suppliers:

- Price.
- Quality of materials.
- Dependability in making deliveries.

Note that properly evaluating suppliers involves more than just comparing prices. Companies also incur costs, such as rework and scrap, related to the quality of the products purchased. There are also costs associated with supplier delivery performance (such as the problems described in the introductory case at AOE's Dayton plant). Supplier dependability is especially important for companies that use JIT systems because late deliveries can bring the entire system to a halt.

Once a supplier has been selected for a product, the supplier's identity should become part of the product inventory master record to avoid repeating the supplier selection process for every subsequent order. (In some cases, however, such as for the purchase of high-cost and low-usage items, management may explicitly want to reevaluate all potential suppliers each time that product is ordered.) A list of potential alternative suppliers for each item should also be maintained, in case the primary supplier is out of stock of a needed item.

purchase order - A document that formally requests a supplier to sell and deliver specified products at designated prices. It is also a promise to pay and becomes a contract once the supplier accepts it.

A **purchase order** (Figure 15-7) is a document or electronic form that formally requests a supplier to sell and deliver specified products at designated prices. It is also a promise to pay and becomes a contract once the supplier accepts it. The purchase order includes the names of the supplier and purchasing agent, the order and requested delivery dates, the delivery location and shipping method, and information about the items ordered. Frequently, several purchase orders are generated to fill one purchase requisition because different vendors may be the preferred suppliers for the various items requested. The quantity ordered may also differ from that requested to allow the purchaser to take advantage of quantity discounts.

blanket purchase order or blanket order - A commitment to purchase specified items at designated prices from a particular supplier for a set time period, often one year.

Many companies maintain special purchasing arrangements with important suppliers. A **blanket purchase order or blanket order** is a commitment to purchase specified items at designated prices from a particular supplier for a set time period, often one year. Blanket purchase orders reduce the buyer's uncertainty about reliable sources of raw materials and help the supplier plan its capacity and operations more effectively.

FIGURE 15-7
Example of a Purchase Order (items in bold are pre-printed)

Alpha Omega Electronics **No. 2463**

Billing Address: **2431 Bradford Lane**
San Francisco, CA 94403
(314) 467-2341

Reference the above number on all invoices and shipping documents

PURCHASE ORDER

To: Best Office Supply
4567 Olive Blvd.
Dayton, OH 33422-1234

Ship To: AOE, Inc.
1735 Sandy Dr.
Dayton, OH 33421–2243

Vendor Number:	**Order Date:**	**Requisition Number:**	**Buyer:**	**Terms:**
121	07/03/2021	89010	Fred Mozart	1/10, n/30

F.O.B.	**Ship Via:**	**Delivery Date:**	**Remarks:**
Destination	Your choice	07/15/2021	

Item	**Item Number**	**Quantity**	**Description**	**Unit Price**
1	32047	15 boxes	Xerox 4200 paper, 20 wt., 10 ream box	$33.99
2	80170	5 boxes	Moore 2600 continuous form, 20 lb.	$31.99
3	81756	20 boxes	CD cases, box of 10	$ 6.49
4	10407	100	700 MB CDs, 1 box	$19.99

Approved by: Susan Beethoven

The major cost driver in the purchasing function is the number of purchase orders processed. Thus, finding ways to reduce the number of orders processed and to streamline the steps involved can yield significant savings. Using EDI is one way to improve the purchasing process. EDI reduces costs by eliminating the clerical work associated with printing and mailing paper documents. EDI also reduces the time between recognizing the need to reorder an item and subsequently receiving it also is reduced. Consequently, the risk of running out of stock is diminished, which can significantly increase profitability. In the past, EDI was expensive because it required the use of proprietary third-party networks and software. However, the development of standards for EDI over the Internet (EDINT), such as the AS2 protocol for secure electronic exchange of documents, has drastically cut the costs of EDI.

Vendor-managed inventory programs provide another means of reducing purchase and inventory costs. A **vendor-managed inventory (VMI)** program essentially outsources much of the inventory control and purchasing function: Suppliers are given access to sales and inventory data and are authorized to automatically replenish inventory when stocks fall to predetermined reorder points. This arrangement cuts carrying costs by reducing the amount of inventory on hand and lowers processing costs by eliminating the need to generate and exchange formal purchase orders.

vendor-managed inventory (VMI) - Practice in which manufacturers and distributors manage a retail customer's inventory using EDI. The supplier accesses its customer's point-of-sale system in order to monitor inventory and automatically replenish products when they fall to agreed-upon levels.

Reverse auctions provide yet another technique to reduce purchasing-related expenses. In reverse auctions, suppliers compete with one another to meet demand at the lowest price. Although reverse auctions can yield significant cost savings, because the primary focus is on price, they are probably best suited to the purchase of commodity items rather than critical components for which quality, vendor reliability, and delivery performance are important.

One other way to reduce purchasing-related costs is to conduct a pre-award audit. Pre-award audits are typically used for large purchases that involve formal bids by suppliers. The internal auditor visits each potential supplier who has made the final cut in the contracting process to verify the accuracy of its bid. Pre-award audits often identify simple mathematical errors in complex pricing formulas and other discrepancies that, when corrected, can provide considerable savings.

EDI, vendor-managed inventory, reverse auctions, and pre-award audits are techniques for reducing the purchasing-related costs of raw materials and finished goods inventory. New IT developments can also change how companies account for their inventory. Traditionally, most companies have used the LIFO, FIFO, or weighted-average approaches to allocate costs to inventory and cost of goods sold. RFID, however, provides the capability to track individual inventory items. Thus, RFID makes it possible for companies to more accurately account for actual inventory-related costs by switching to the specific identification method for accounting for inventories.

THREATS AND CONTROLS Table 15-2 lists five threats to placing orders with suppliers. One (threat 7) involves purchasing items at inflated prices. The cost of purchased components represents a substantial portion of the total cost of many manufactured products. Therefore, companies strive to secure the best prices for the items they purchase. Several procedures can help ensure that companies do not pay too much for specific products. Price lists for frequently purchased items should be stored in the computer and consulted when orders are made (control 7.1). The prices of many low-cost items can be readily determined from catalogs. Competitive, written bids should be solicited for high-cost and specialized products (control 7.2). Purchase orders should be reviewed (control 7.3) to ensure that these policies have been followed.

Budgets (control 7.4) are also helpful in controlling purchasing expenses. Purchases should be charged to an account that is the responsibility of the person or department approving the requisition. Actual costs should be compared periodically with budget allowances. To facilitate control, these reports should highlight any significant deviations from budgeted amounts for further investigation (the principle of management by exception).

In attempting to obtain the lowest possible prices, another threat is purchasing inferior-quality products. Substandard products can result in costly production delays. Moreover, the costs of scrap and rework often result in higher total production costs than if higher-quality, more expensive materials had been initially purchased. Through experience, buyers often learn which suppliers provide the best-quality goods at competitive prices. Such informal knowledge should be incorporated into formal control procedures so that it is not lost when a particular employee leaves the company. One best practice is to establish lists of approved suppliers known to provide goods of acceptable quality (control 8.1). Purchase orders should be reviewed to ensure that only these approved suppliers are being used (control 8.2). In addition, the accounting information system should collect detailed product quality data (control 8.3). For example, AOE can measure the quality of a supplier's products by tracking how often its items fail to pass inspection in the receiving department and the amount of production that has to be reworked or scrapped because of substandard materials. The purchasing manager should regularly review that data to maintain and revise the list of approved suppliers. Finally, purchasing managers should be held accountable for the total cost of purchases (control 8.4), which includes not only the purchase price but also the quality-related costs of rework and scrap. Doing this requires designing the system to track the latter costs so that they can be allocated back to the purchasing department.

As the introductory case demonstrated, another potential problem is unreliable performance by suppliers (threat 9 in Table 15-2). One way to reduce the risk of problems with supplier dependability is to require that suppliers be certified as meeting international quality standards such as ISO 9000 (control 9.1). However, the accounting information system should also be designed to capture and track information about supplier performance (control 9.2). For example, AOE can track actual delivery dates versus those promised. Indeed, the ERP system can be configured to automatically generate reports of purchase orders that have not been delivered within the promised time period. Some large retailers, like Wal-Mart, regularly track supplier on-time delivery performance and "fine" suppliers who fail to meet established targets by subtracting a prespecified percentage from invoices related to late deliveries.

Purchasing from unauthorized suppliers (threat 10) can result in numerous problems. Items may be of inferior quality or overpriced. The purchase may even cause legal problems. Various government agencies, such as the Office of Foreign Assets Control and the Bureau of Industry and Security in the Department of Commerce, maintain lists of individuals and companies with whom it is illegal to transact business. Payments to entities on such lists can result in substantial fines and, sometimes, imprisonment. Consequently, ERP systems should be configured to prevent issuing purchase orders to suppliers not in the approved master file (control 10.1). All purchase orders should be reviewed to ensure that only approved suppliers are used (control 10.2). It is especially important to restrict access to the approved supplier list and to periodically review the list for any unauthorized changes.

Using EDI for purchase orders requires additional control procedures. Access to the EDI system should be controlled and limited to authorized personnel through the use of passwords, user IDs, access control matrices, and physical access controls. Procedures to verify and authenticate EDI transactions also are needed. Most EDI systems are programmed to send an acknowledgment for each transaction, which provides a rudimentary accuracy check. Further protection against transmission problems, which can result in the loss of orders, is provided by time-stamping and numbering all EDI transactions. Companies should maintain and periodically review a log of all EDI transactions to ensure that all have been processed and that established policies are being followed. Encryption can ensure the privacy of EDI transactions, which is especially important for competitive bids. Digital signatures should be used to ensure the authenticity of transactions.

Numerous policy-related threats also arise with EDI, each of which must be covered in the trading agreement. Examples of these types of issues include the following:

- At what point in the process can the order be canceled?
- Which party is responsible for the cost of return freight if contract terms are not followed?
- Which party is responsible for errors in bar codes, RFID tags, and labels?
- What happens if errors in the purchasing company's sales system cause additional errors in the amount of goods that suppliers provide?
- Can suppliers ship more inventory than ordered if doing so reduces total freight costs because it results in a full, rather than partial, truckload?

kickbacks - Gifts given by suppliers to purchasing agents for the purpose of influencing their choice of suppliers.

Table 15-2 shows that **kickbacks**, which are gifts from suppliers to purchasing agents for the purpose of influencing their choice of suppliers, are another threat. For the kickback to make economic sense, the supplier must find some way to recover the money spent on the bribe. This usually is accomplished by inflating the price of subsequent purchases or by substituting goods of inferior quality. Even if neither of these problems occurs, kickbacks impair the buyer's objectivity.

FOCUS 15-1 Supplier Audits: A Means to Control Purchasing

Supplier audits may be one of the best tools for assessing the effectiveness of expenditure cycle controls. They entail having an internal auditor visit a supplier's office to check its records. The objective is to identify suppliers likely to be associated with problems such as kickbacks. Red flags that indicate potential problems include:

1. A large percentage of the supplier's gross sales was to the company conducting the supplier audit.
2. The supplier's pricing methods differ from standard industry practice.
3. The supplier does not own the equipment it rents but is itself renting that equipment from a third party.
4. Entertainment expenses are high in terms of a percentage of the supplier's gross sales.
5. The supplier submits altered or fictitious third-party invoices.
6. The supplier's address on its invoices is fictitious.

Supplier audits can yield substantial returns. One company recovered more than $250,000 for such problems as duplicate billings. Supplier audits also often uncover violations of the company's conflict of interest policy. Interestingly, many suppliers support the idea of supplier audits because the process gives them a "good excuse" for not offering purchasing agents gifts or entertainment. Nevertheless, organizations should include a "right to audit" clause in all purchase orders and contracts with suppliers to ensure the ability to use this powerful detective control.

To prevent kickbacks, companies should prohibit purchasing agents from accepting any gifts (control 11.1) from potential or existing suppliers. (Trinkets that are clearly of inconsequential value may be allowed.) These policies should apply not only to gifts of tangible goods, but also to services. For example, meeting planners should be informed that it is against company policy to accept frequent-traveler points from hotels for booking the company's meetings there. Training employees how to respond to unsolicited "gifts" from suppliers is also important because many kickback schemes are initiated when unethical suppliers send such "tokens of appreciation," usually in the form of cash, to unwary employees. Once the employee accepts the gift, the supplier threatens to disclose the payment to a supervisor unless the employee makes additional purchases from that supplier.

Job rotation (control 11.2) is another important control to reduce the risk of kickbacks: Purchasing agents should not deal with the same suppliers indefinitely because doing so increases the risk that they may succumb to the constant temptations offered by an unethical supplier. If the organization is too small to rotate job duties across different purchasing agents, it should periodically conduct a detailed audit of the purchasing agent's activities. Purchasing agents should also be required to take their allotted vacation time each year because many frauds are discovered when the perpetrator is absent and unable to continue covering up the illicit activity. Finally, purchasing agents should be required to sign annual conflict of interest statements, (control 11.3) disclosing any financial interests they may have in current or potential suppliers.

Kickbacks are difficult to prevent, so detective controls are also necessary. Focus 15-1 discusses one particularly effective detection control: the supplier audit (control 11.4).

Receiving

The second major business activity in the expenditure cycle (circle 2.0 in Figure 15-2) is the receipt and storage of ordered items. Figure 15-8 shows these two steps as distinct processes because each is performed by a different organizational function. The receiving department is responsible for accepting deliveries from suppliers. It usually reports to the warehouse manager, who in turn reports to the vice president of manufacturing. The inventory stores department, which also reports to the warehouse manager, is responsible for storage of the goods. Information about the receipt of ordered merchandise must be communicated to the inventory control function to update the inventory records.

FIGURE 15-8
Level 1 Data Flow Diagram: Receiving (annotated to include threats)

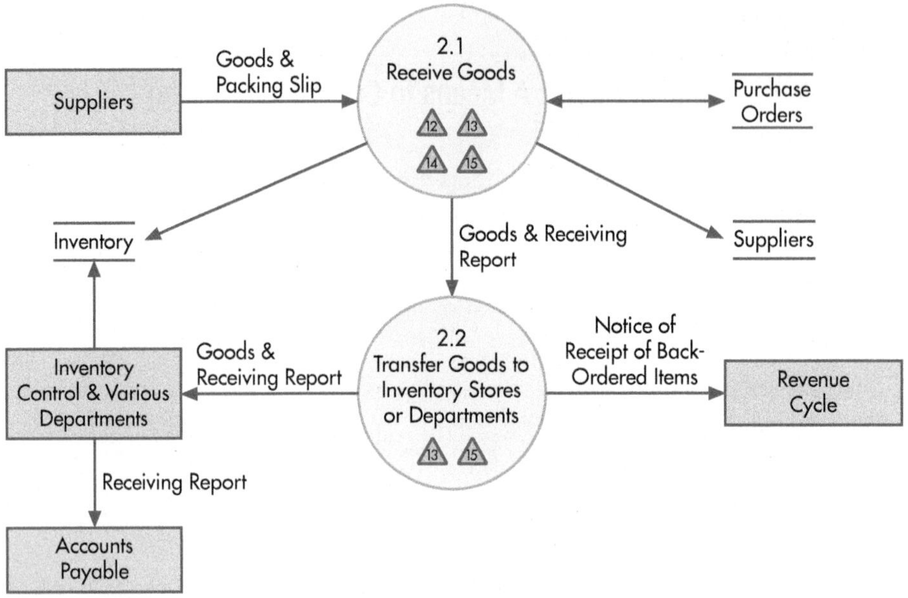

PROCESS

receiving report - A document that records details about each delivery, including the date received, shipper, supplier, and quantity received.

When a delivery arrives, a receiving clerk compares the purchase order number referenced on the supplier's packing slip with the open purchase order file to verify that the goods were ordered. The receiving clerk then counts the quantity of goods delivered and inspects for signs of obvious damage. The receiving clerk documents everything on a **receiving report**, including the date received, shipper, supplier, and purchase order number (Figure 15-9). For each item received, the receiving report shows the item number, description, unit of measure, and quantity. The receiving report also contains space to identify the persons who received and inspected the goods as well as for remarks concerning the quality of the items received.

debit memo - A document used to record a reduction to the balance due to a supplier.

The three possible exceptions to this process are (1) receiving a quantity of goods different from the amount ordered, (2) receiving damaged goods, or (3) receiving goods of inferior quality that fail inspection. In all three cases, the purchasing department must resolve the situation with the supplier. Usually the supplier will give the buyer permission to correct the invoice for any discrepancies in quantity. In the case of damaged or poor-quality goods, a document called a debit memo is prepared after the supplier agrees to take back the goods or to grant a price reduction. The **debit memo** records the adjustment being requested. One copy of the debit memo is sent to the supplier, who subsequently creates and returns a credit memo in acknowledgment. The accounts payable department is notified and adjusts the account balance owed to that supplier. A copy of the debit memo accompanies the goods to the shipping department to authorize their return to the supplier.

FIGURE 15-9
Example of a Receiving Report Data Entry Screen

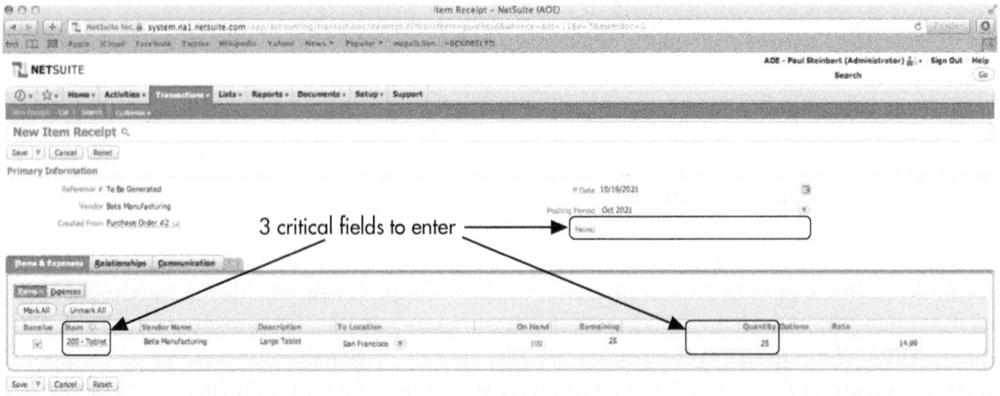

Source: 2010 © NetSuite Inc.

Counting and recording inventory deliveries is a labor-intensive task. One way for companies such as AOE to improve the efficiency of this process is to require suppliers to barcode or affix RFID tags to their products. Either approach streamlines the counting of items received but does not eliminate the need to inspect the quality.

EDI and satellite technology provide another way to improve the efficiency of inbound logistics. EDI advance shipping notices inform companies when products have been shipped. By using shipping companies whose trucks are equipped with data terminals linked to satellites, a business can track the exact location of all incoming shipments and ensure that adequate staff will be there to unload the trucks. Truck drivers also can be directed to pull up to specific loading docks closest to the place where the goods will be used.

THREATS AND CONTROLS

Accepting delivery of unordered goods (threat 12) results in costs associated with unloading, storing, and later returning those items. The best control procedure to mitigate this threat is to instruct the receiving department to accept only deliveries for which there is an approved purchase order (control 12.1). That is why Figure 15-8 shows the receiving department needs access to the open purchase orders file.

Another threat is making mistakes in counting items received. Correctly counting the quantity received is crucial for maintaining accurate perpetual inventory records. It also ensures that the company pays only for goods actually received. To encourage the receiving clerk to accurately count what was delivered, many companies design the inquiry processing system so that when reviewing open purchase orders, receiving-dock workers do not see the quantity ordered (control 13.1). (If paper documents are still used, the quantity-ordered field is blacked out on the receiving department's copy of the purchase order.) Nevertheless, the receiving clerk still knows the expected quantity of goods because suppliers usually include a packing slip with each order. Consequently, there is a temptation to do just a quick visual comparison of quantities received with those indicated on the packing slip, to quickly route the goods to where they are needed. Therefore, companies must clearly communicate to receiving clerks the importance of carefully and accurately counting all deliveries. An effective means of communication is to require receiving clerks not only to record the quantity received but also to sign the receiving report or enter their employee ID numbers in the system (control 13.2). Such procedures indicate an assumption of responsibility, which usually results in more diligent work. Some companies also offer bonuses (control 13.3) to receiving clerks for catching discrepancies between the packing slip and actual quantity received before the delivery person leaves. Wherever feasible, use of bar codes and RFID tags (control 13.4) can significantly reduce accidental mistakes in counting. Finally, the ERP system should be configured to automatically flag discrepancies between receiving counts and order quantities that exceed a predetermined tolerance level so that they can be promptly investigated (control 13.5).

Thus far, the discussion has centered on the purchase of inventory items. Different procedures are needed to control the purchase of services, such as painting or maintenance work. The major challenge in this area is establishing that the services were actually performed (threat 14), which may be difficult. For example, visual inspection can indicate whether a room has been painted; it does not reveal, however, whether the walls were appropriately primed, unless the inspection was done during the painting process, which may not always be feasible.

One way to control the purchase of services is to hold the appropriate supervisor accountable for all such costs incurred by that department. The supervisor is required to acknowledge receipt of the services, and the related expenses are then charged to accounts for which he or she is responsible. Actual versus budgeted expenses should be routinely compared and any discrepancies investigated (control 14.1).

It is difficult to prevent fraudulent billing for services. Therefore, detective controls are also needed. One of the most effective techniques is for the internal audit function to periodically conduct detailed reviews of contracts for services (control 14.2), including audits of supplier records, as discussed in Focus 15-1.

Theft of inventory is another threat. Several control procedures can be used to safeguard inventory against loss. First, inventories should be stored in secure locations with restricted access (control 15.1). Second, all transfers of inventory within the company should be documented (control 15.2). For example, both the receiving department and the inventory stores department should acknowledge the transfer of goods from the receiving dock into inventory. Similarly, both the inventory stores and the production departments should acknowledge the release of inventory into production. This documentation provides the necessary information for establishing accountability for any shortages, thereby encouraging employees to take special care to record all inventory movements accurately. Third, it is important to periodically count the inventory on hand, reconcile those counts with the inventory (control 15.3), and investigate material discrepancies.

Finally, proper segregation of duties (control 15.4) can further help minimize the risk of inventory theft. Employees who are responsible for controlling physical access to inventory should not be able to adjust inventory records without review and approval. Neither the employees responsible for custody of inventory nor those authorized to adjust inventory records should be responsible for the receiving or shipping functions.

Approving Supplier Invoices

The third main activity in the expenditure cycle is approving supplier invoices for payment (circle 3.0 in Figure 15-2).

PROCESS

The accounts payable department approves supplier invoices for payment. A legal obligation to pay suppliers arises at the time goods are received. For practical reasons, however, most companies record accounts payable only after receipt and approval of the supplier's invoice. This timing difference is usually not important for daily decision making, but it does require making appropriate adjusting entries to prepare accurate financial statements at the end of a fiscal period.

voucher package - The set of documents used to authorize payment to a supplier. It consists of a purchase order, receiving report, and supplier invoice.

nonvoucher system - A method for processing accounts payable in which each approved invoice is posted to individual supplier records in the accounts payable file and is then stored in an open invoice file. Contrast with *voucher system*.

When a supplier's invoice is received, the accounts payable department is responsible for matching it with a corresponding purchase order and receiving report. This combination of the supplier invoice and associated supporting documentation creates what is called a **voucher package**. Figure 15-10 shows an example of a data entry screen for approving a supplier invoice. Once the approver has verified that the company received what it had ordered and that the invoice is accurate, the invoice is approved for payment.

There are two ways to process supplier invoices, referred to as nonvoucher or voucher systems. In a **nonvoucher system**, each approved invoice (along with the supporting documentation) is posted to individual supplier records in the accounts payable file and is then stored in an open-invoice file. When a check is written to pay for an invoice, the voucher package is

FIGURE 15-10
Example of Supplier Invoice Approval Screen

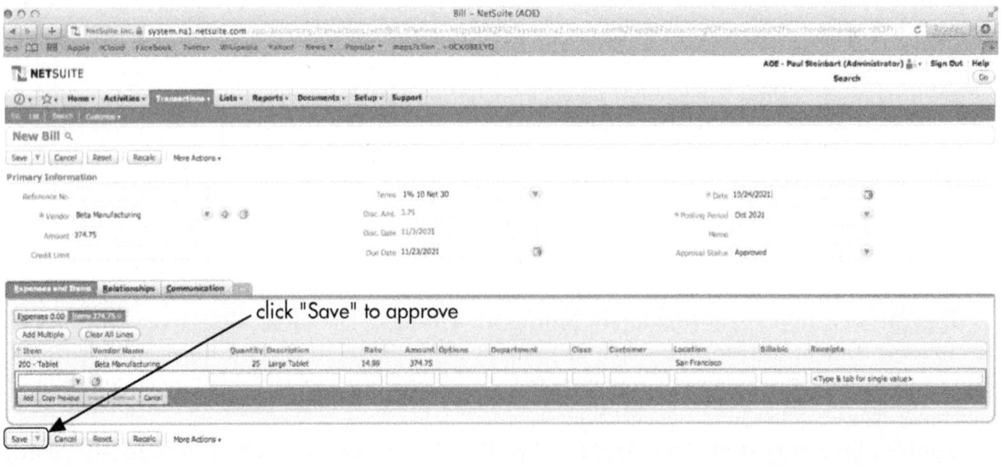

Source: 2010 © NetSuite Inc.

FOCUS 15-2 Applying Manufacturing Process Improvement Principles to Accounts Payable

Medtronic, Inc., a global medical technology company, is demonstrating that process improvement principles originally developed to improve manufacturing activities can also be successfully adopted to improve the accounts payable function. Like many manufacturers, Medtronic had successfully used both Six Sigma and Lean principles to streamline its work-flow activities and improve product quality. Six Sigma is a philosophy that focuses on improving quality by reducing mistakes. Lean analysis seeks to improve efficiency by eliminating bottlenecks and redundancies. Medtronic decided to try to apply these same techniques used in manufacturing to its accounts payable function. The initial motivation for doing so was the insight that financial transactions, just like manufacturing a product, involved moving an item (e.g., a supplier invoice) through a sequence of steps.

Medtronic initiated a series of intensive five-day projects, called *kaizen*, to apply Six Sigma and Lean principles to improve accounts payable. On day 1, a team consisting of accounts payable employees and manufacturing process improvement experts carefully studied how supplier invoices were processed, beginning with the time when mail was first opened all the way through printing and mailing checks. On day 2, the team measured the time it took to perform each step of the process and the volume of transactions passing through each step. On days 3 and 4, the team diagrammed the physical flow of all accounts payable documentation. They then rearranged cubicles and desks and added new wheeled carts and paper bins to slash the physical distance a supplier invoice traveled from 1,464 to 165 feet. They also modified the image-scanning process to be able to merge all supplier invoices (those for inventory purchases, with associated purchase orders, and those without purchase orders) into one queue. On day 5, the team walked the entire department through the reengineered work-flow process.

Medtronic's application of process improvement techniques yielded a dramatic improvement in the efficiency and effectiveness of its accounts payable function:

- The time required to open the mail and to sort, process, and record supplier invoices dropped from three days to one day.
- The number of invoices for which discounts for prompt payment were taken increased by 15%.
- Payment processing times were cut by 50%.

It is important to note that these benefits were obtained with the same employees who had been working in accounts payable prior to the reengineering effort. This shows that when companies are seeking to improve results, they should focus first on fixing the process, rather than on replacing the people who perform it.

removed from the open-invoice file, the invoice is marked paid, and then the voucher package is stored in the paid-invoice file. In a **voucher system**, an additional document called a disbursement voucher is also created when a supplier invoice is approved for payment. The **disbursement voucher** identifies the supplier, lists the outstanding invoices, and indicates the net amount to be paid after deducting any applicable discounts and allowances.

Voucher systems offer three advantages over nonvoucher systems. First, they reduce the number of checks that need to be written because several invoices may be included on one disbursement voucher. Second, because the disbursement voucher is an internally generated document, it can be prenumbered to simplify tracking all payables. Third, because the voucher provides an explicit record that a supplier invoice has been approved for payment, it facilitates separating the time of invoice approval from the time of invoice payment. This makes it easier to schedule both activities to maximize efficiency.

The accounts payable process, which matches supplier invoices to purchase orders and receiving reports, is a prime candidate for automation. Large global companies can process over a million supplier invoices each year. As Focus 15-2 shows, reengineering the process and automating as many steps as possible can yield significant savings.

One way to improve efficiency is to ask suppliers to submit their invoices via EDI and configure the system to automatically match those invoices to the appropriate purchase orders and receiving reports. Only those supplier invoices that fail this matching process need be processed manually.

Another option is to eliminate supplier invoices. After all, for most recurring purchases, companies know the prices of goods and services at the time they are ordered. Thus, as soon as

voucher system - A method for processing accounts payable in which a disbursement voucher is prepared instead of posting invoices directly to supplier records in the accounts payable subsidiary ledger. The disbursement voucher identifies the supplier, lists the outstanding invoices, and indicates the net amount to be paid after deducting any applicable discounts and allowances. Contrast with *nonvoucher system*.

disbursement voucher - A document that identifies the supplier, lists the outstanding invoices, and indicates the net amount to be paid after deducting any applicable discounts and allowances.

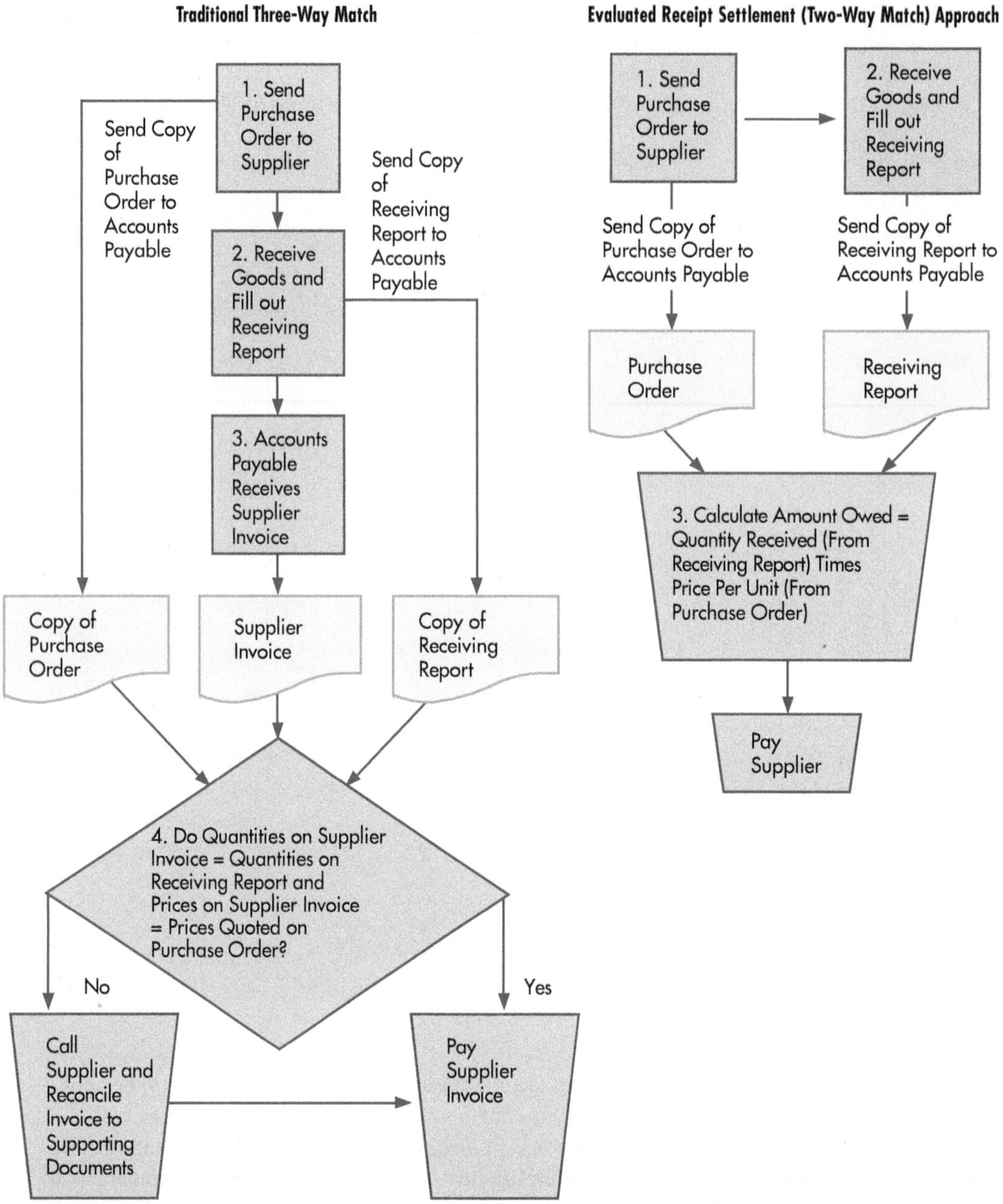

FIGURE 15-11
Comparison of Traditional Three-Way Match for Accounts Payable with the Two-Way Match used by Evaluated Receipt Settlement (ERS) Systems

evaluated receipt settlement (ERS) - An invoiceless approach to accounts payable that replaces the three-way matching process (supplier invoice, receiving report, and purchase order) with a two-way match of the purchase order and receiving report.

receipt of the goods or services is verified, all the information required to pay the supplier is already known. This "invoiceless" approach is called **evaluated receipt settlement (ERS)**. ERS replaces the traditional three-way matching process (supplier invoice, receiving report, and purchase order) with a two-way match of the purchase order and receiving report (Figure 15-11). ERS saves time and money by reducing the number of documents that need to be matched and, hence, the number of potential mismatches. In fact, ERS systems are often configured to automate the two-way matching process and automatically generate payments; manual review is necessary only when there are discrepancies between the receiving report and purchase order. ERS also saves suppliers the time and expense of generating and tracking invoices. This is an example of how improvements in one company's expenditure cycle processes provide benefits to another company's revenue cycle processes.

Noninventory purchases for supplies provide perhaps the biggest opportunity to improve the efficiency of accounts payable and cash disbursements. Noninventory purchases typically account for a large proportion of accounts payable *transactions* but represent a small percentage of the total dollar value of all purchases. For example, an AICPA-sponsored survey found that over 60% of all invoices processed by accounts payable departments were for amounts under $2,000. Procurement cards provide one way to eliminate the need for accounts payable to process many such small invoices. A **procurement card** is a corporate credit card that employees can use only at designated suppliers to purchase specific kinds of items. Spending limits can be set for each card. In addition, the account numbers on each procurement card can be mapped to specific general ledger accounts, such as office supplies. Procurement cards simplify accounts payable because the company receives one monthly statement that summarizes noninventory purchases by account category. Procurement cards also improve the efficiency of the cash disbursement process because the company only has to make one payment for all noninventory purchases during a given time period, instead of making separate payments to various suppliers.

procurement card - A corporate credit card that employees can use only at designated suppliers to purchase specific kinds of items.

THREATS AND CONTROLS

Table 15-2 indicates that one threat is errors on supplier invoices, such as discrepancies between quoted and actual prices charged or miscalculations of the total amount due. Consequently, the mathematical accuracy of supplier invoices must be verified (control 16.1) and the prices and quantities listed therein compared with those indicated on the purchase order and receiving report. For procurement card purchases, users should be required to keep receipts (control 16.2) and verify the accuracy of the monthly statement. Adopting the ERS approach (control 16.3) eliminates the potential for errors in supplier invoices because companies pay by matching counts of what they receive with prices quoted when the goods were ordered.

Even with ERS, freight expenses require special consideration because their complexity creates numerous opportunities for mistakes to occur. The best way to reduce freight-related threats is to provide the purchasing and accounts payable staffs with adequate training on transportation practices and terminology. For example, if the purchase contract says "full freight allowed," then the supplier is responsible for the freight costs. When the purchasing organization is responsible for freight expenses, using a designated carrier for all incoming shipments can reduce costs. The discounts will only be realized, however, if suppliers comply with requests to use that carrier. Therefore, an important detective control is to have internal audit periodically verify the accuracy of freight bills and invoices to ensure that the company is not being charged for transportation costs that the supplier is supposed to pay (control 16.4).

Mistakes in recording and posting payments to suppliers (threat 17) result in erroneous financial and performance reports that, in turn, can contribute to poor decision making. The data entry and processing controls to ensure processing integrity that were discussed in Chapter 13 (control 17.1) are necessary to prevent these types of problems. One such control is to compare the difference in supplier account balances with the total amount of invoices processed—before and after processing checks. The total of all supplier account balances (or unpaid vouchers) also should be reconciled periodically with the amount of the accounts payable control account in the general ledger (control 17.2).

Cash Disbursements

The final activity in the expenditure cycle is paying suppliers (circle 4.0 in Figure 15-2).

PROCESS

The cashier, who reports to the treasurer, is responsible for paying suppliers. This segregates the custody function, performed by the cashier, from the authorization and recording functions, performed by the purchasing and accounts payable departments, respectively. Payments are made when accounts payable sends the cashier a voucher package. Although the use of EFT and FEDI is increasing, many payments continue to be made by check.

THREATS AND CONTROLS

Failing to take advantage of purchase discounts for prompt payment (threat 18) can be costly. For example, a 1% discount for paying within 10 days instead of 30 days represents a savings of 18% annually. Proper filing can significantly reduce the risk of this threat. Approved invoices should be filed by due date, and the system should be designed to track invoice due dates and print a periodic list of all outstanding invoices (control 18.1). A cash flow budget (control 18.2) that indicates expected cash inflows and outstanding commitments also can help companies plan to utilize available purchase discounts. The information in this budget comes from a number of sources. Accounts receivable provides projections of future cash collections. The accounts payable and open purchase order files indicate the amount of current and pending commitments to suppliers, and the human resources function provides information about payroll needs.

Another threat is paying for goods not received. The best control to prevent this threat is to compare the quantities indicated on the supplier invoice with the quantities entered by the inventory control person, who accepts the transfer of those goods from the receiving department. Many companies require the inventory control department to verify the quantities on the receiving report before it can be used to support payment of a supplier invoice (control 19.1). Verification that services (e.g., cleaning or painting) were performed in the manner billed is more difficult. Therefore, most companies rely on budgetary controls and careful review of departmental expenses (control 19.2) to indicate potential problems that need investigation.

Reimbursement of employees' travel and entertainment expenses warrants special attention because this is an area in which fraud often occurs and technological trends have made it easier for employees to submit fraudulent claims. For example, most airlines now encourage travelers to print their boarding passes at home. This saves the traveler time at check-in, but it also reduces the value of a boarding pass as supporting documentation for a claimed expense because the document can be altered by the traveler or printed but never used. Electronic receipts are also easy to alter or forge. Consequently, many organizations require employees to submit additional evidence, such as a conference agenda that identifies attendees, to prove that they actually took a trip (control 19.3). Another potential threat is for an employee to book multiple flights or hotels, cancel all but the cheapest ones, but submit a reimbursement claim for the most expensive option. The best way to prevent this problem is to require all employees to use corporate credit cards for travel (control 19.4), as this ensures that the organization will receive a complete audit trail of all charges *and* credits to the account.

Duplicate payments (threat 20) can happen for a variety of reasons. It may be a duplicate invoice that was sent after the company's check was already in the mail, or it may have become separated from the other documents in the voucher package. Although the supplier usually detects a duplicate payment and credits the company's account, it can affect a company's cash flow needs. In addition, the financial records will be incorrect, at least until the duplicate payment is detected.

Several related control procedures can mitigate this threat. First (control 20.1), invoices should be approved for payment only when accompanied by a complete voucher package (purchase order and receiving report). Second, only the *original* copy of an invoice should be paid (control 20.2). Payment should never be authorized for a photocopy of an invoice. Third, when an invoice is paid, the invoice and the voucher package should be canceled (marked "paid") in a manner that would prevent their resubmission (control 20.3). Although ERS eliminates vendor invoices entirely, it is still important to mark all receiving reports as paid to avoid duplicate payments. Finally, because preventive controls are never 100% effective, it is important to regularly audit all payments to suppliers to timely detect duplicate payments and initiate corrective actions.

Probably the most serious threat associated with the cash disbursements function is theft or misappropriation of funds (threat 21). Because cash is the easiest asset to steal, access to cash, blank checks, and the check-signing machine should be restricted (control 21.1). Checks should be sequentially numbered and periodically accounted for (control 21.2) by the cashier.

EFT, either by itself or as part of FEDI, requires additional control procedures. Strict access controls over all outgoing EFT transactions (control 21.3) are important. Passwords and user IDs should be used to specifically identify and monitor each employee authorized to initiate EFT transactions. The location of the originating terminal should also be recorded. EFT transactions above a certain threshold should require real-time supervisory approval. There should also be limits on the total dollar amount of transactions allowed per day per individual. All EFT transmissions should be encrypted to prevent alteration. In addition, all EFT transactions should be time-stamped and numbered to facilitate subsequent reconciliation. Special programs, called *embedded audit modules*, can be designed into the system to monitor all EFT transactions and identify any that possess specific characteristics. A report of those flagged transactions then can be given to management and internal audit for review and, if necessary, more detailed investigation.

Online banking transactions require constant monitoring. Timely detection of suspicious transactions and prompt notification of the bank are necessary for recovering any funds that are fraudulently disbursed. A serious threat is that keystroke-logging software could infect the computer used for online banking and provide criminals with the organization's banking credentials. Indeed, in recent years criminals have directed spear phishing attacks (see Chapter 9) at treasurers to attempt to do this. The best way to mitigate this threat is to designate a specific computer to be used for online banking (control 21.4), to restrict access to that computer to the treasurer or whoever is responsible for authorizing payments, and to use that computer *only* for online banking and no other activity. Otherwise, if the treasurer uses the same computer for both e-mail and online banking and falls victim to a spear phishing attack, criminals can install keylogging software, use it obtain the organization's banking credentials, and then steal the organization's funds. Companies should also consider placing Automated Clearing House (ACH) blocks, which instruct banks to not allow ACH debits (outflows) from specific accounts. For example, if a company makes all payments to its suppliers only from its main operating checking account, it may wish to instruct the bank to block all ACH debits from any of its other bank accounts (control 21.5).

Fraudulent disbursements, particularly the issuance of checks to fictitious suppliers, are a common type of fraud. Proper segregation of duties (control 21.6) can significantly reduce the risk of this threat. The accounts payable function should authorize payment, including the assembling of a voucher package; however, only the treasurer or cashier should sign checks. To ensure that checks are sent to the intended recipients, the cashier should mail the signed checks rather than return them to accounts payable. The cashier also should cancel all documents in the voucher package to prevent their being resubmitted to support another disbursement. Checks in excess of a certain amount, such as \$5,000 to \$10,000, should require two signatures (control 21.7), thereby providing yet another independent review of the expenditure. Finally, someone who did not participate in processing either cash collections or disbursements should reconcile all bank accounts (control 21.8). This control provides an independent check on accuracy and prevents someone from misappropriating cash and then concealing the theft by adjusting the bank statement.

Access to the approved supplier list should be restricted (control 21.9), and any changes to that list should be carefully reviewed and approved. It is especially important to independently verify any e-mail (or telephone) messages purportedly from suppliers that request changes to the bank accounts to which payments are to be wired because such messages are often fraudulent (e.g., such e-mails are part of the Business E-mail Compromise scam discussed in Chapter 9). Failure to verify instructions to change supplier bank accounts costs U.S. businesses hundreds of millions of dollars annually. It is also important to restrict the ability to create one-time suppliers (control 21.10) and process invoices so that the same employee cannot both create a new supplier and issue a check to that supplier.

When possible, expenditures should be made by check or EFT because doing so provides an audit trail. Nevertheless, it is often more convenient to pay for minor purchases, such as coffee or donuts, in cash. A petty cash fund (control 21.11), managed by an employee who has no other cash-handling or accounting responsibilities, should be established to handle such expenditures. The petty cash fund should be set up as an imprest fund. An **imprest fund** has two characteristics: It is set at a fixed amount, such as \$100, and it requires that the person managing the fund retain receipts for every disbursement. At all times, the sum of cash plus receipts should equal the preset fund balance. When the fund balance gets low, the receipts are presented to accounts payable to justify replenishing the fund. After accounts payable authorizes this transaction, the cashier then writes a check to restore the petty cash fund to its designated level. As with the supporting documents used for regular purchases, the receipts used to support replenishment of the petty cash fund should be canceled at the time the fund is restored to its preset level.

imprest fund - A cash account with two characteristics: (1) It is set at a fixed amount, such as \$100; and (2) vouchers are required for every disbursement. At all times, the sum of cash plus vouchers should equal the preset fund balance.

The operation of an imprest petty cash fund technically violates the principle of segregation of duties because the same person who has custody of the cash also authorizes disbursements from the fund and maintains a record of the fund balance. The threat of misappropriation is more than offset, however, by the convenience of not having to process small miscellaneous purchases through the normal expenditure cycle. Moreover, the risk of misappropriation can be mitigated by making periodic unannounced counts of the fund balance and receipts and by holding the person in charge of the petty cash fund accountable for any shortages discovered during those surprise audits (control 21.12).

Theft can also occur through check alteration (threat 22). Check-protection machines (control 22.1) can reduce the risk of this threat by imprinting the amount in distinctive colors, typically a combination of red and blue ink. Using special inks that change colors if altered and printing checks on special papers (control 22.2) that contain watermarks can further reduce the probability of alteration. Many banks also provide special services to help protect companies against fraudulent checks. One such service, called Positive Pay (control 22.3), involves sending a daily list of all legitimate checks and EFT transactions to the bank, which will then clear only checks and ACH transactions appearing on that list. Reconciling bank accounts every month is an important detective control for identifying check fraud. It is important to reconcile bank accounts in a timely manner because many banks will cover bad-check losses only if a company notifies them promptly of any such checks it discovers.

Finally, it is important to plan and monitor expenditures in order to avoid cash flow problems (threat 23). A cash flow budget (control 23.1) is the best way to mitigate this threat.

Summary and Case Conclusion

The basic business activities performed in the expenditure cycle include ordering materials, supplies, and services; receiving materials, supplies, and services; approving supplier invoices for payment; and paying for goods and services.

The efficiency and effectiveness of these activities can significantly affect a company's overall performance. For example, deficiencies in requesting and ordering necessary inventory and supplies can create production bottlenecks and result in lost sales due to stockouts of popular items. Problems in the procedures related to receiving and storing inventory can result in a company's paying for items it never received, accepting delivery and incurring storage costs for unordered items, and experiencing a theft of inventory. Problems in approving supplier invoices for payment can result in overpaying suppliers or failing to take available discounts for prompt payment. Weaknesses in the cash disbursement process can result in the misappropriation of cash.

IT can help improve the efficiency and effectiveness with which expenditure cycle activities are performed. In particular, EDI, bar-coding, RFID, and EFT can significantly reduce the time and costs associated with ordering, receiving, and paying for goods. Proper control procedures, especially segregation of duties, are needed to mitigate various threats such as errors in performing expenditure cycle activities and the theft of inventory or cash.

At the next executive meeting, Ann Brandt and Elizabeth Venko presented to Linda Spurgeon their recommendations for improving AOE's expenditure cycle business activities. Elizabeth Venko stated that she was working to increase the number of suppliers who either bar-code or RFID tag their shipments. This would improve both the efficiency and accuracy of the receiving process and also the accuracy of AOE's inventory records, thereby providing possible additional reductions in inventory carrying costs. In addition, Elizabeth wants to encourage more suppliers to either send invoices via EDI or agree to ERS, which should improve the efficiency and accuracy of processing invoices and reduce the costs associated with handling and storing paper invoices. Concurrently, Elizabeth plans to increase EFT as much as possible to further streamline the cash disbursements process and reduce the costs associated with processing payments by check. She also explains that any requests by suppliers to change their banking information will be independently verified before being made.

Ann indicates that LeRoy Williams's plan to conduct more frequent physical counts of key raw materials components will increase the accuracy of the database and reduce the likelihood of future stockouts at the Wichita plant. She also designed a query to produce a daily supplier performance report that will highlight any negative trends before they become the types of problems that disrupted production at the Dayton plant. Ann also indicated that it would be possible to link AOE's inventory and production planning systems with major suppliers to better manage AOE's inventory levels. As the meeting draws to a close, LeRoy Williams asks if Elizabeth and Ann can meet with him to explore additional ways to improve how AOE's new system tracks manufacturing activities.

KEY TERMS

expenditure cycle 469
economic order quantity (EOQ) 477
reorder point 477
materials requirements planning (MRP) 478
just-in-time (JIT) inventory system 478
purchase requisition 478
purchase order 480
blanket purchase order or blanket order 480
vendor-managed inventory (VMI) 481
kickbacks 482
receiving report 484
debit memo 484
voucher package 486
nonvoucher system 486
voucher system 487
disbursement voucher 487
evaluated receipt settlement (ERS) 488
procurement card 489
imprest fund 491

AIS in Action

CHAPTER QUIZ

1. Which of the following inventory control methods is most likely to be used for a product for which sales can be reliably forecast?
   a. JIT b. EOQ c. MRP d. ABC
2. Which of the following matches is performed in evaluated receipt settlement (ERS)?
   a. the vendor invoice with the receiving report
   b. the purchase order with the receiving report
   c. the vendor invoice with the purchase order
   d. the vendor invoice, the receiving report, and the purchase order
3. Which of the following is true?
   a. It is easier to verify the accuracy of invoices for purchases of services than invoices for purchases of raw materials.
   b. Setting up petty cash as an imprest fund violates segregation of duties.
   c. The EOQ formula is used to identify when to reorder inventory.
   d. A voucher package usually includes a debit memo.
4. Which document is used to establish a contract for the purchase of goods or services from a supplier?
   a. vendor invoice
   b. purchase requisition
   c. purchase order
   d. disbursement voucher
5. Which method would provide the greatest efficiency improvements for the purchase of noninventory items such as miscellaneous office supplies?
   a. bar-coding
   b. EDI
   c. procurement cards
   d. EFT
6. Which of the following expenditure cycle activities can be eliminated through the use of IT or reengineering?
   a. ordering goods
   b. approving vendor invoices
   c. receiving goods
   d. cash disbursements
7. What is the best control procedure to prevent paying the same invoice twice?
   a. Segregate check-preparation and check-signing functions.
   b. Prepare checks only for invoices that have been matched to receiving reports and purchase orders.
   c. Require two signatures on all checks above a certain limit.
   d. Cancel all supporting documents when the check is signed.
8. For good internal control, who should sign checks?
   a. cashier
   b. accounts payable
   c. purchasing agent
   d. controller

9. Which of the following procedures is designed to prevent the purchasing agent from receiving kickbacks?
   a. maintaining a list of approved suppliers and requiring all purchases to be made from suppliers on that list
   b. requiring purchasing agents to disclose any financial investments in potential suppliers
   c. requiring approval of all purchase orders
   d. prenumbering and periodically accounting for all purchase orders

10. Which document is used to record adjustments to accounts payable based on the return of unacceptable inventory to the supplier?
   a. receiving report
   b. credit memo
   c. debit memo
   d. purchase order

DISCUSSION QUESTIONS

15.1 In this chapter and in Chapter 14, the controller of AOE played a major role in evaluating and recommending ways to use IT to improve efficiency and effectiveness. Should the company's chief information officer make these decisions instead? Should the controller be involved in making these types of decisions? Why, or why not?

15.2 Companies such as Walmart have moved beyond JIT to vendor-managed inventory (VMI) systems. Discuss the potential advantages and disadvantages of this arrangement. What special controls, if any, should be developed to monitor VMI systems?

15.3 Procurement cards are designed to improve the efficiency of small noninventory purchases. What controls should be placed on their use? Why?

15.4 In what ways can you apply the control procedures discussed in this chapter to paying personal debts (e.g., credit card bills)?

15.5 Should every company switch from the traditional three-way matching process (purchase orders, receiving reports, and supplier invoices) to the two-way match (purchase orders and receiving reports) used in evaluated receipt settlement (ERS)? Why, or why not?

15.6 Should companies allow purchasing agents to start their own businesses that produce goods the company frequently purchases? Why? Would you change your answer if the purchasing agent's company were rated by an independent service, such as *Consumer Reports*, as providing the best value for price? Why?

PROBLEMS

15.1 Which internal control procedure would be most cost-effective in dealing with the following expenditure cycle threats?
   a. A purchasing agent orders materials from a supplier he partially owns.
   b. Receiving-dock personnel steal inventory and then claim the inventory was sent to the warehouse.
   c. An unordered supply of laser printer paper delivered to the office is accepted and paid for because the "price is right." After all of the laser printers are jammed, however, it becomes obvious the "bargain" paper is of inferior quality.
   d. The company fails to take advantage of a 1% discount for promptly paying a vendor invoice.
   e. A company is late in paying a particular invoice. Consequently, a second invoice is sent, which crosses the first invoice's payment in the mail. The second invoice is submitted for processing and paid.
   f. Inventory records show an adequate supply of copy paper should be in stock, but none is available on the supply shelf.
   g. The inventory records are incorrectly updated when a receiving-dock employee enters the wrong product number at the terminal.
   h. A clerical employee obtains a blank check and writes a large amount payable to a fictitious company. The employee then cashes the check.

i. A fictitious invoice is received and a check is issued to pay for goods never ordered or delivered.
j. The petty cash custodian confesses to having "borrowed" $12,000 over the last five years.
k. A purchasing agent adds a new record to the supplier master file. The company does not exist. Subsequently, the purchasing agent submits invoices from the fake company for various cleaning services. The invoices are paid.
l. A clerk affixes a price tag intended for a low-end flat-panel TV to a top-of-the-line model. The clerk's friend then purchases that item, which the clerk scans at the checkout counter.
m. A receiving dock employee notices a delivery has four cases of iPads but the purchase order only requested three cases, so the employee set aside the fourth box and took it home.
n. A purchasing agent regularly orders from particular suppliers who pay the employee kickbacks in order to win orders.

15.2 Match the terms with their definitions:

____ **1.** economic order quantity (EOQ)	a. Document that creates a legal obligation to buy and pay for goods or services
____ **2.** materials requirements planning (MRP)	b. Method used to maintain the cash balance in the petty cash account
____ **3.** just-in-time (JIT) inventory system	c. The time to reorder inventory triggered when the quantity on hand falls to a predetermined level
____ **4.** purchase requisition	d. Document used to authorize a reduction in accounts payable because merchandise has been returned to a supplier
____ **5.** imprest fund	e. Inventory control system that triggers production based upon actual sales
____ **6.** purchase order	f. Inventory control system that triggers production based on forecasted sales
____ **7.** kickbacks	g. Document used only internally to initiate the purchase of materials, supplies, or services
____ **8.** procurement card	h. Process for approving supplier invoices based on a two-way match of the receiving report and purchase order
____ **9.** blanket purchase order	i. Process for approving supplier invoices based on a three-way match of the purchase order, receiving report, and supplier invoice
____ **10.** evaluated receipts settlement (ERS)	j. Method of maintaining accounts payable in which each supplier invoice is tracked and paid for separately
____ **11.** disbursement voucher	k. Method of maintaining accounts payable that generates one check to pay for a set of invoices from the same supplier
____ **12.** receiving report	l. Combination of a purchase order, receiving report, and supplier invoice that all relate to the same transaction
____ **13.** debit memo	m. Document used to list each invoice being paid by a check

____ **14.** vendor-managed inventory	n. Inventory control system that seeks to minimize the sum of ordering, carrying, and stockout costs
____ **15.** voucher package	o. System whereby suppliers are granted access to point-of-sale (POS) and inventory data in order to automatically replenish inventory levels
____ **16.** nonvoucher system	p. Agreement to purchase set quantities at specified intervals from a specific supplier
____ **17.** voucher system	q. Document used to record the quantities and condition of items delivered by a supplier
	r. Special-purpose credit card used to purchase supplies
	s. Fraud in which a supplier pays a buyer or purchasing agent in order to sell its products or services

15.3 Excel Project: Using Benford's Law to Detect Potential Disbursements Fraud.*

REQUIRED

a. Read the article "Using Spreadsheets and Benford's Law to Test Accounting Data," by Mark G. Simkin in the *ISACA Journal*, 2010, Vol. 1, available at www.isaca.org.

b. Download the spreadsheet for this problem and follow the steps in the article to analyze whether the invoice data conforms to Benford's Law. Your spreadsheet should:

1. Display the first digit for each invoice amount (Hint: You may need to use the Value and Left functions).
2. Complete the columns for "Expected #" and "Actual #" for the data set.
3. Use a formula in cell F13 that calculates the sample size.
4. Use a formula in cell G15 to calculate the chi-square test value comparing the actual and expected distribution of leading digits of invoice amounts.
5. Create a chart that compares the actual and expected frequencies for the leading digits for invoice amounts.

Invoice Number	Amount
2725	$8,745
2726	$9,277
2727	$3,195
2728	$4,355
2729	$7,733
2730	$4,155
2731	$2,639
2732	$5,273
2733	$8,162
2734	$9,133
2735	$5,731
2736	$4,400
2737	$8,522
2738	$9,725
2739	$1,200
2740	$2,856
2741	$8,163
2742	$3,375
2743	$2,621
2744	$7,199

* Life-long learning opportunity: see pp. xxiii–xxiv in preface.

Invoice Number	Amount
2745	$4,150
2746	$9,725
2747	$8,239
2748	$5,188
2749	$2,267
2750	$8,790
2751	$9,745
2752	$1,724
2753	$3,911
2754	$7,419

15.4 Match the threats in the left column to appropriate control procedures in the right column. More than one control may be applicable.

Threat	Control Procedure
___ 1. Failing to take available purchase discounts for prompt payment	a. Accept only deliveries for which an approved purchase order exists.
___ 2. Recording and posting errors in accounts payable	b. Document all transfers of inventory.
___ 3. Paying for items not received	c. Restrict physical access to inventory.
___ 4. Kickbacks	d. File invoices by due date.
___ 5. Theft of inventory	e. Maintain a cash budget.
___ 6. Paying the same invoice twice	f. Conduct an automated comparison of total change in cash to total changes in accounts payable.
___ 7. Stockouts	g. Adopt a perpetual inventory system.
___ 8. Purchasing items at inflated prices	h. Require purchasing agents to disclose financial or personal interests in suppliers.
___ 9. Misappropriation of cash	i. Require purchases to be made only from approved suppliers.
___ 10. Purchasing goods of inferior quality	j. Restrict access to the supplier master data.
___ 11. Wasted time and cost of returning unordered merchandise to suppliers	k. Restrict access to blank checks.
___ 12. Accidental loss of purchasing data	l. Issue checks only for complete voucher packages (receiving report, supplier invoice, and purchase order).
___ 13. Disclosure of sensitive supplier information (e.g., banking data)	m. Cancel or mark "Paid" supporting documents in voucher package when check is issued.
	n. Carry out a regular backup of expenditure cycle database.
	o. Train employees in how to properly respond to gifts or incentives offered by suppliers.
	p. Hold purchasing managers responsible for costs of scrap and rework.
	q. Ensure that someone other than the cashier reconciles bank accounts.

15.5 Use Table 15-2 to create a questionnaire checklist that can be used to evaluate controls for each of the basic activities in the expenditure cycle (ordering goods, receiving, approving supplier invoices, and cash disbursements).

REQUIRED

a. For each control issue, write a Yes/No question such that a "No" answer represents a control weakness. For example, one question might be "Are supporting documents, such as purchase orders and receiving reports, marked 'paid' when a check is issued to the vendor?"

b. For each Yes/No question, write a brief explanation of why a "No" answer represents a control weakness.

15.6 Research Problem: Payments Frauds

1. Visit the website of the Association of Finance Professionals (afponline.org) and write a report that includes the following:
   a. The proportion of B2B payments still made by check and the trend over the past five years
   b. The size of payments frauds and trends in the amount of payments frauds
   c. Frauds experienced with paying by check and solutions to mitigate those threats
   d. Frauds encountered when paying by ACH transfer and solutions to mitigate those threats
   e. Frauds encountered when paying by wire transfer and solutions to mitigate those threats
2. Visit the website of the Association of Certified Fraud Examiners (acfe.com) and write a report that includes the following:
   a. The size of payments frauds and trends in the amount of payment frauds
   b. Methods used to commit payments frauds and suggested solutions to prevent those threats
   c. Source of detecting payments frauds

15.7 The following table presents the results of using a CAAT tool to interrogate the XYZ Company's ERP system for expenditure cycle activities. It shows the number of times each employee performed a specific task.

	Order Inventory	Maintain Supplier Master File (Add, Delete, Edit)	Receive Inventory	Approve Supplier Invoices for Payment	Pay Suppliers Via EFT	Sign Checks	Mail Checks	Reconcile Bank Account
Employee A	150			5				
Employee B					100	100	100	
Employee C		7		10				
Employee D				10	10	10		
Employee E			425					
Employee F						150	125	1
Employee G				400			25	
Employee H	306							
Employee I			300					

REQUIRED

Identify three examples of improper segregation of duties and explain the nature of each problem you find.

15.8 The following list identifies several important control features. For each control, (1) describe its purpose, and (2) explain how it could be best implemented in an integrated ERP system.

a. Cancellation of the voucher package by the cashier after signing the check
b. Separation of duties of approving invoices for payment and signing checks
c. Prenumbering and periodically accounting for all purchase orders
d. Periodic physical count of inventory
e. Requiring two signatures on checks for large amounts

f. Requiring that a copy of the receiving report be routed through the inventory stores department prior to going to accounts payable
g. Requiring a regular reconciliation of the bank account by someone other than the person responsible for writing checks
h. Maintaining an approved supplier list and checking that all purchase orders are issued only to suppliers on that list

15.9 For good internal control, which of the following duties can be performed by the same individual?

1. Request purchases of inventory
2. Approve purchase orders
3. Count quantity received
4. Approve supplier invoices for payment
5. Cancel supporting documents in the voucher package
6. Sign checks
7. Mail checks
8. Reconcile the bank account

15.10 Last year the Diamond Manufacturing Company purchased over $10 million worth of office equipment under its "special ordering" system, with individual orders ranging from $5,000 to $30,000. Special orders are for low-volume items that have been included in a department manager's budget. The budget, which limits the types and dollar amounts of office equipment a department head can requisition, is approved at the beginning of the year by the board of directors. The special ordering system functions as follows.

Purchasing A purchase requisition form is prepared and sent to the purchasing department. Upon receiving a purchase requisition, one of the five purchasing agents (buyers) verifies that the requester is indeed a department head. The buyer next selects the appropriate supplier by searching the various catalogs on file. The buyer then phones the supplier, requests a price quote, and places a verbal order. A prenumbered purchase order is processed, with the original sent to the supplier and copies to the department head, receiving, and accounts payable. One copy is also filed in the open requisition file. When the receiving department verbally informs the buyer that the item has been received, the purchase order is transferred from the open to the filled file. Once a month, the buyer reviews the unfilled file to follow up on open orders.

Receiving The receiving department gets a copy of each purchase order. When equipment is received, that copy of the purchase order is stamped with the date, and, if applicable, any differences between the quantity ordered and the quantity received are noted in red ink. The receiving clerk then forwards the stamped purchase order and equipment to the requisitioning department head and verbally notifies the purchasing department that the goods were received.

Accounts Payable Upon receipt of a purchase order, the accounts payable clerk files it in the open purchase order file. When a vendor invoice is received, it is matched with the applicable purchase order, and a payable is created by debiting the requisitioning department's equipment account. Unpaid invoices are filed by due date. On the due date, a check is prepared and forwarded to the treasurer for signature. The invoice and purchase order are then filed by purchase order number in the paid-invoice file.

Treasurer Checks received daily from the accounts payable department are sorted into two groups: those over and those under $10,000. Checks for less than $10,000 are machine signed. The cashier maintains the check signature machine's key and signature plate and monitors its use. Both the cashier and the treasurer sign all checks over $10,000.

REQUIRED

a. Describe the weaknesses relating to purchases and payments of "special orders" by the Diamond Manufacturing Company.
b. Recommend control procedures that must be added to overcome weaknesses identified in part a.

c. Describe how the control procedures you recommended in part b should be modified if Diamond reengineered its expenditure cycle activities to make maximum use of current IT (e.g., EDI, EFT, bar-code scanning, and electronic forms in place of paper documents). *(CPA Examination, adapted)*

d. Draw a BPMN diagram that depicts Diamond's reengineered expenditure cycle.

15.11 The ABC Company performs its expenditure cycle activities using its integrated ERP system as follows:

- Employees in any department can enter purchase requests for items they note as either out of stock or in small quantity.
- The company maintains a perpetual inventory system.
- Each day, employees in the purchasing department process all purchase requests from the prior day. To the extent possible, requests for items available from the same supplier are combined into one larger purchase order to obtain volume discounts. Purchasing agents use the Internet to compare prices in order to select suppliers. If an Internet search discovers a potential new supplier, the purchasing agent enters the relevant information in the system, thereby adding the supplier to the approved supplier list. Purchase orders above $10,000 must be approved by the purchasing department manager. EDI is used to transmit purchase orders to most suppliers, but paper purchase orders are printed and mailed to suppliers who are not EDI capable.
- Receiving department employees have read-only access to outstanding purchase orders. Usually, they check the system to verify existence of a purchase order prior to accepting delivery, but sometimes during rush periods they unload trucks and place the items in a corner of the warehouse where they sit until there is time to use the system to retrieve the relevant purchase order. In such cases, if no purchase order is found, the receiving employee contacts the supplier to arrange for the goods to be returned.
- Receiving department employees compare the quantity delivered to the quantity indicated on the purchase order. Whenever a discrepancy is greater than 5%, the receiving employee sends an e-mail to the purchasing department manager. The receiving employee uses an online terminal to enter the quantity received before moving the material to the inventory stores department.
- Inventory is stored in a locked room. During normal business hours, an inventory employee allows any employee wearing an identification badge to enter the storeroom and remove needed items. The inventory storeroom employee counts the quantity removed and enters that information in an online terminal located in the storeroom.
- Occasionally, special items are ordered that are not regularly kept as part of inventory from a specialty supplier who will not be used for any regular purchases. In these cases, an accounts payable clerk creates a one-time supplier record.
- All supplier invoices (both regular and one-time) are routed to accounts payable for review and approval. The system is configured to perform an automatic three-way match of the supplier invoice with the corresponding purchase order and receiving report.
- Each Friday, approved supplier invoices due within the next week are routed to the treasurer's department for payment. The cashier and treasurer are the only employees authorized to disburse funds, either by EFT or by printing a check. Checks are printed on a dedicated printer located in the treasurer's department, using special stock paper stored in a locked cabinet accessible only to the treasurer and cashier. The paper checks are sent to accounts payable to be mailed to suppliers.
- Monthly, the treasurer reconciles the bank statements and investigates any discrepancies with recorded cash balances.

REQUIRED

a. Identify weaknesses in ABC's existing expenditure cycle procedures, explain the problem, and suggest a solution. Present your answer in a three-column table with these headings: Weakness, Problem, Solution.

b. Draw a BPMN diagram that depicts ABC's expenditure cycle process redesigned to incorporate your answer to step a.

15.12 Figure 15-12 depicts the basic activities performed in Lexsteel's expenditure cycle. The following additional information supplements that figure:

- Because of cash flow problems, Lexsteel always pays suppliers on the last possible day before incurring a penalty for late payment. Supplier invoices are processed and paid weekly. Every Friday, the accounts payable clerk reviews and approves all invoices with a due date the following week.
- The purchasing manager reviews and approves all purchases prior to e-mailing them to suppliers.
- After counting and inspecting incoming deliveries, the receiving clerk enters the following information into the system:
  - Quantities received for each inventory item
  - Date and time received
  - Supplier number
- After entering that information, the receiving clerk takes the inventory to the inventory control department for storage.
- Access to the inventory control department is restricted.
- Inventory is only released to production when a properly authorized request is received. When the inventory is released, the inventory control clerk updates the perpetual inventory system.
- Physical counts of inventory are taken every three months. Discrepancies between the counts and recorded quantities on hand are investigated. Upon resolution of the investigation, the plant manager authorizes adjustments to the perpetual inventory records to change them to the amount actually on hand.

REQUIRED

Identify at least three control weaknesses in Lexsteel's expenditure cycle. For each weakness, explain the threat and suggest how to change the procedures to mitigate that threat.

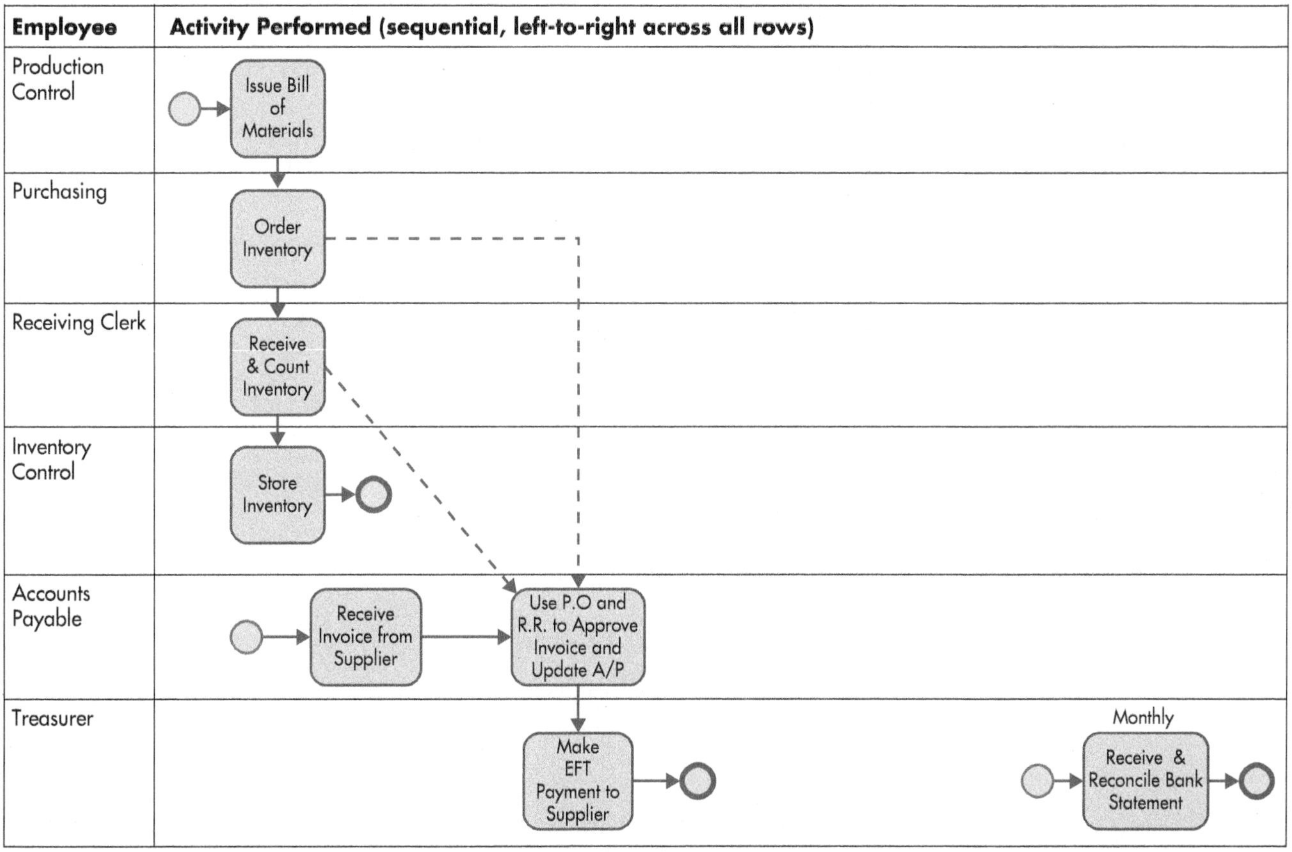

FIGURE 15-12

Lexsteel Expenditure Cycle Procedures

15.13 Excel Problem

REQUIRED

Download the spreadsheet for this problem from the course website and use the Filter and Sort functions to identify the following warning signs of potentially fraudulent supplier invoices:

1. Suppliers that have multiple different names but the same address
2. Different suppliers with the same PO Box for an address
3. Suppliers who submit sequentially numbered invoices
4. Invoices just below a threshold requiring approval; for example, invoices below $10,000
5. Duplicate invoice numbers from the same supplier
6. Invoices without a number

15.14 Answer the following multiple-choice questions:

1. The control procedure of comparing a voucher package to vendor invoices is designed to reduce the risk of ______.
   a. failure to take advantage of discounts for prompt payment
   b. mistakes in posting to accounts payable
   c. paying for items not received
   d. theft of inventory
   e. making duplicate payments

2. Which of the following statements are true?
   a. Issuing employees procurement cards is an example of the control procedure referred to as "general authorization."
   b. Organizations can reduce the risk of fraudulent disbursements by sending their bank a list of all checks issued, a process referred to as "Positive Pay."
   c. Both of the statements above are true.
   d. None of the statements above are true.

3. The control procedure of prohibiting employees from accepting gifts is designed to reduce the risk of ______.
   a. theft of inventory
   b. kickbacks
   c. fraudulent cash disbursements
   d. stockouts
   e. none of the above

4. The control procedure of cancelling the documents in a voucher package is designed to reduce the risk of ______.
   a. making duplicate payments
   b. paying for items not received
   c. fraudulent cash disbursements
   d. failure to take advantage of discounts for prompt payment
   e. theft of inventory

5. Which of the following control procedures is designed to reduce the risk of check alteration fraud?
   a. ACH blocks on accounts not used for payments
   b. use of dedicated computer and browser for online banking
   c. establishing "Positive Pay" arrangements with banks
   d. access controls for EFT terminals
   e. prenumbering all checks

6. Which of the following control procedures is designed to reduce the risk of theft of inventory?
   a. restriction of physical access to inventory
   b. periodic physical counts of inventory and reconciliation to recorded quantities on hand
   c. documentation of all transfers of inventory between employees
   d. All of the above
   e. None of the above

7. Which of the following control procedures is designed to reduce the risk of ordering unneeded inventory?
   a. tracking and monitoring product quality by supplier
   b. purchasing only from approved suppliers
   c. holding purchasing managers responsible for rework and scrap costs
   d. All of the above
   e. None of the above

8. Which of the following documents is no longer needed if a company uses the evaluated receipts system (ERS) with its suppliers?
   a. purchase order
   b. receiving report
   c. supplier invoice
   d. debit memo
   e. None of the above

9. Kickbacks are a problem because they increase the risk of ______.
   a. purchasing inventory that is not needed
   b. purchasing inferior quality items
   c. purchasing at inflated prices
   d. all of the above
   e. none of the above

10. Which threat is most likely to result in the largest losses in a short period of time?
   a. alteration of checks or EFT payments
   b. theft of inventory
   c. duplicate payments to suppliers
   d. All of the above
   e. None of the above

CASE 15-1 Group Case Analysis: School District Expenditure Fraud

Read the case titled "The Rosslyn School District Fraud: Improving School District Internal Control and Financial Oversight" available from your instructor, and write a report that answers the following questions:

1. What internal control weaknesses allowed the fraud to occur?
2. How would the establishment of an audit committee and six hours of training on financial oversight responsibilities (part of the Five Point Plan) reduce the risk of a similar fraud occurring again?
3. How would the recommended changes in claims processing affect the risk of a similar fraud occurring again?

CASE 15-2 Anatomy of a Multi-Million Dollar Embezzlement at ING Bank

REQUIRED:

It is instructive to study in detail how payment frauds work. Read the article "Lessons from an $8 Million Fraud" by Mark J. Nigrini and Nathan J. Mueller, published in the *Journal of Accountancy* (August 2014), pp. 32–37, and write a report that answers the following questions:

1. What misconfiguration error in the ERP system enabled the fraud to occur?
2. What security best practices were not followed and, therefore, facilitated the fraud? What access controls should have been in place to prevent or reduce the risk of the fraud?
3. What segregation of duties violations allowed the fraud to occur?
4. What detective controls failed, thereby allowing the fraud to continue?
5. How was the fraud finally uncovered?
6. What aspects of the internal environment element of the COSO framework could have prevented or reduced the likelihood of the fraud occurring?
7. How could the fraud have been detected earlier?

AIS in Action Solutions

QUIZ KEY

1. Which of the following inventory control methods is most likely to be used for a product for which sales can be reliably forecast?
   a. JIT [Incorrect. JIT seeks to minimize inventory by making purchases only after sales.] It is used primarily for products for which it is hard to forecast demand.]
   b. EOQ [Incorrect. EOQ represents the optimal amount of inventory to purchase to minimize the sum of ordering, carrying, and stockout costs.]
   ▶ c. MRP [Correct. MRP forecasts sales and uses that information to purchase inventory to meet anticipated needs.]
   d. ABC [Incorrect. ABC is a method for stratifying inventory according to importance and scheduling more frequent inventory counts for the more important items.]

2. Which of the following matches is performed in evaluated receipt settlement (ERS)?
   a. the vendor invoice with the receiving report [Incorrect. ERS eliminates the vendor invoice.]
   ▶ b. the purchase order with the receiving report [Correct. ERS eliminates the vendor invoice and schedules payments based on matching the purchase order and receiving report.]
   c. the vendor invoice with the purchase order [Incorrect. ERS eliminates the vendor invoice.]
   d. the vendor invoice, the receiving report, and the purchase order [Incorrect. ERS eliminates the vendor invoice.]

3. Which of the following is true?
   a. It is easier to verify the accuracy of invoices for purchases of services than invoices for purchases of raw materials. [Incorrect. It is easier to verify invoices for purchases of raw materials because you can compare to receiving reports. Receiving reports normally do not exist for purchase of services.]
   ▶ b. Setting up petty cash as an imprest fund violates segregation of duties. [Correct. Technically, setting up petty cash as an imprest fund violates segregation of duties because the same person has custody of the asset—cash—authorizes its disbursement, and maintains records.]
   c. The EOQ formula is used to identify when to reorder inventory. [Incorrect. The EOQ formula is used to determine how much to order. The reorder point identifies when to reorder inventory.]
   d. A voucher package usually includes a debit memo. [Incorrect. Voucher packages consist of the purchase order, receiving report, and vendor invoice, if one is received; debit memos are used to record adjustments of accounts payable.]

4. Which document is used to establish a contract for the purchase of goods or services from a supplier?
   a. vendor invoice [Incorrect. The vendor invoice is a bill.]
   b. purchase requisition [Incorrect. A purchase requisition is an internal document.]
   ▶ c. purchase order [Correct. A purchase order is an offer to buy goods.]
   d. disbursement voucher [Incorrect. A disbursement voucher is used to specify which accounts to debit when paying vendor invoices.]

5. Which method would provide the greatest efficiency improvements for the purchase of noninventory items such as miscellaneous office supplies?
   a. bar-coding [Incorrect. Bar-coding improves accuracy of counting inventory items. The biggest efficiency-related problem with noninventory purchases is the time and effort required to generate a purchase order, create a voucher package, and make payments for a large number of small-dollar amount purchases.]
   b. EDI [Incorrect. EDI is seldom used for miscellaneous purchases.]
   ▶ c. procurement cards [Correct. Procurement cards were designed specifically for purchase of noninventory items.]
   d. EFT [Incorrect. EFT improves the efficiency of payments, but does not improve the efficiency of ordering and approving supplier invoices.]

6. Which of the following expenditure cycle activities can be eliminated through the use of IT or reengineering?
   a. ordering goods [Incorrect. Even with vendor-managed inventory, the vendor's system must initiate the ordering process.]
► **b.** approving vendor invoices [Correct. ERS systems eliminate vendor invoices.]
   c. receiving goods [Incorrect. Ordered goods must always be received and moved to the appropriate location.]
   d. cash disbursements [Incorrect. IT can change the method used to make cash disbursements, such as by EFT instead of by check, but the function must still be performed.]

7. What is the best control procedure to prevent paying the same invoice twice?
   a. Segregate check-preparation and check-signing functions. [Incorrect. This is a good control procedure, but its purpose is to ensure payments are valid.]
   b. Prepare checks only for invoices that have been matched to receiving reports and purchase orders. [Incorrect. This is a good control procedure, but its purpose is to ensure that organizations pay only for goods ordered and received.]
   c. Require two signatures on all checks above a certain limit. [Incorrect. This is a good control procedure, but its purpose is to better control large outflows of cash.]
► **d.** Cancel all supporting documents when the check is signed. [Correct. This ensures that the supporting documents cannot be resubmitted to pay the same invoice again.]

8. For good internal control, who should sign checks?
► **a.** cashier [Correct. The cashier is responsible for managing cash and reports to the treasurer.]
   b. accounts payable [Incorrect. Accounts payable maintains vendor records.]
   c. purchasing agent [Incorrect. The purchasing agent authorizes acquisition of goods.]
   d. controller [Incorrect. The controller is in charge of accounting, the record-keeping function.]

9. Which of the following procedures is designed to prevent the purchasing agent from receiving kickbacks?
   a. maintaining a list of approved suppliers and requiring all purchases to be made from suppliers on that list [Incorrect. The purpose of this control is to minimize the risk of purchasing inferior goods at inflated prices or violating regulations.]
► **b.** requiring purchasing agents to disclose any financial investments in potential suppliers [Correct. The purpose of such disclosure is to minimize the risk of conflicts of interest that could result in kickbacks.]
   c. requiring approval of all purchase orders [Incorrect. This control is designed to ensure that only goods that are really needed are ordered and that they are ordered from approved vendors.]
   d. prenumbering and periodically accounting for all purchase orders [Incorrect. This control procedure is designed to ensure that all valid purchase orders are recorded.]

10. Which document is used to record adjustments to accounts payable based on the return of unacceptable inventory to the supplier?
   a. receiving report [Incorrect. This document records quantities of goods received.]
   b. credit memo [Incorrect. This document is used in the revenue cycle to adjust a customer's account.]
► **c.** debit memo [Correct. This document is used to adjust accounts payable.]
   d. purchase order [Incorrect. This document establishes a legal obligation to purchase goods.]

CHAPTER

16 The Production Cycle

LEARNING OBJECTIVES

1. Describe the major business activities and key decisions that must be made in the production cycle, the threats to accomplishing production cycle objectives, and the controls that can mitigate those threats.
2. Explain the key decisions and information needs in *product design*, the threats to those activities, and the controls that can mitigate those threats.
3. Explain the key decisions and information needs in *planning and scheduling* production, the threats to those activities, and the controls that can mitigate those threats.
4. Explain the key decisions and information needs in *production operations*, the threats to those activities, and the controls that can mitigate those threats.
5. Explain the key decisions and information needs for accurate *cost accounting*, threats to those activities, and the controls that can mitigate those threats.

INTEGRATIVE CASE Alpha Omega Electronics

LeRoy Williams, vice president for manufacturing at Alpha Omega Electronics (AOE), is concerned about problems associated with the company's change in strategic mission. Two years ago, AOE's top management decided to shift the company from its traditional position as a low-cost producer of consumer electronic products to a product differentiation strategy. Since then, AOE has increased the variety of sizes, styles, and features within each of its product lines.

To support this shift in strategic focus, AOE has invested heavily in factory automation. Top management also endorsed LeRoy's decision to adopt lean manufacturing techniques, with the goal of dramatically reducing inventory levels of finished goods. AOE's cost accounting system has not been changed, however. For example, manufacturing overhead is still allocated based on direct labor hours, even though automation has drastically reduced the amount of direct labor used to manufacture a product. Consequently, investments in new equipment and machinery have resulted in dramatic increases in manufacturing overhead rates. This situation has created the following problems:

1. Production supervisors complain that the accounting system makes no sense and that they are being penalized for making investments that improve overall efficiency. Indeed,

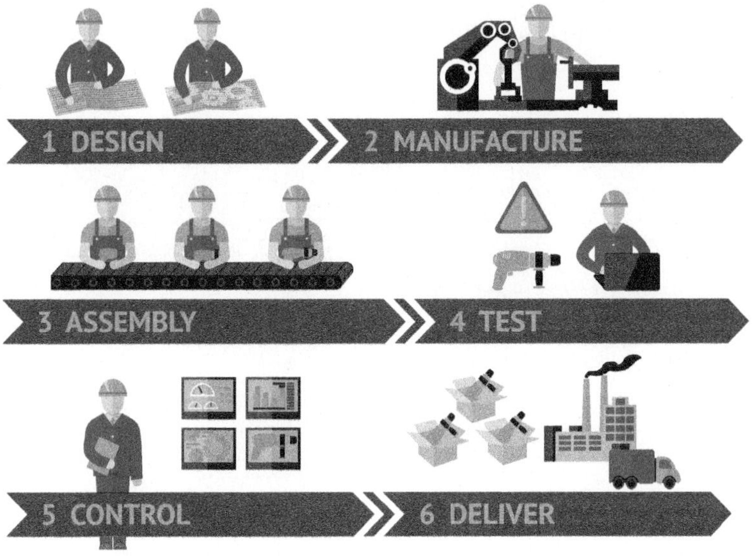

Macrovector/Shutterstock

according to the system, some products now cost more to produce using state-of-the-art equipment than they did before the new equipment was purchased. Yet the new equipment has increased production capacity while simultaneously reducing defects.

2. The marketing and product design executives have all but dismissed the system's product cost figures as useless for setting prices or determining the potential profitability of new products. Indeed, some competitors have begun to price their products below what AOE's cost accounting system says it costs to produce that item.
3. Although a number of steps have been taken to improve quality, the cost accounting system does not provide adequate measures to evaluate the effect of those steps and to indicate areas that need further improvement. As a result, LeRoy is frustrated by his inability to quantify the effects of the quality improvements that have occurred.
4. Performance reports continue to focus primarily on financial measures. Line managers in the factory, however, complain that they need more accurate and timely information on physical activities, such as units produced, defect rates, and production time.
5. LeRoy is frustrated because the move to lean manufacturing was successful in markedly reducing inventory levels this past year, but the traditional GAAP-based financial reports show that this has significantly lowered profitability.

LeRoy expressed these concerns to Linda Spurgeon, AOE's president, who agreed that the problems are serious. Linda then called a meeting with LeRoy; Ann Brandt, AOE's vice president of information systems; and Elizabeth Venko, AOE's controller. At the meeting, Elizabeth and Ann agreed to study how to modify the cost accounting system to more accurately reflect AOE's new production processes. To begin this project, LeRoy agreed to take Elizabeth and Ann on a factory tour so they could see and understand how the new technology has affected production cycle activities.

As this case suggests, deficiencies in the information system used to support production cycle activities can create significant problems for an organization. As you read this chapter, think about how the introduction of new technology in the production cycle may require corresponding changes in a company's cost accounting system.

Introduction

The **production cycle** is a recurring set of business activities and related information processing operations associated with the manufacture of products. Figure 16-1 shows how the production cycle is linked to the other subsystems in a company's information system.

production cycle - The recurring set of business activities and related data processing operations associated with the manufacture of products.

FIGURE 16-1
Context Diagram of the Production Cycle

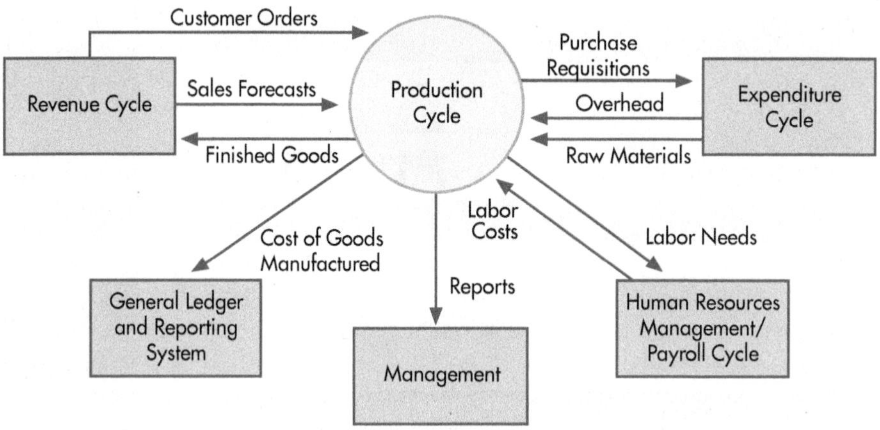

The revenue cycle information system (see Chapter 14) provides the information (customer orders and sales forecasts) used to plan production and inventory levels. In return, the production cycle information system sends the revenue cycle information about finished goods that have been produced and are available for sale. Information about raw materials needs is sent to the expenditure cycle information system (see Chapter 15) in the form of purchase requisitions. In exchange, the expenditure cycle system provides information about raw material acquisitions and about other expenditures included in manufacturing overhead. Information about labor needs is sent to the human resources cycle (see Chapter 17), which in return provides data about labor costs and availability. Finally, information about the cost of goods manufactured is sent to the general ledger and reporting information system (see Chapter 18).

Figure 16-2 depicts the four basic activities in the production cycle: product design, planning and scheduling, production operations, and cost accounting. Although accountants are

FIGURE 16-2
Level 0 Data Flow Diagram of the Production Cycle (annotated to include threats)

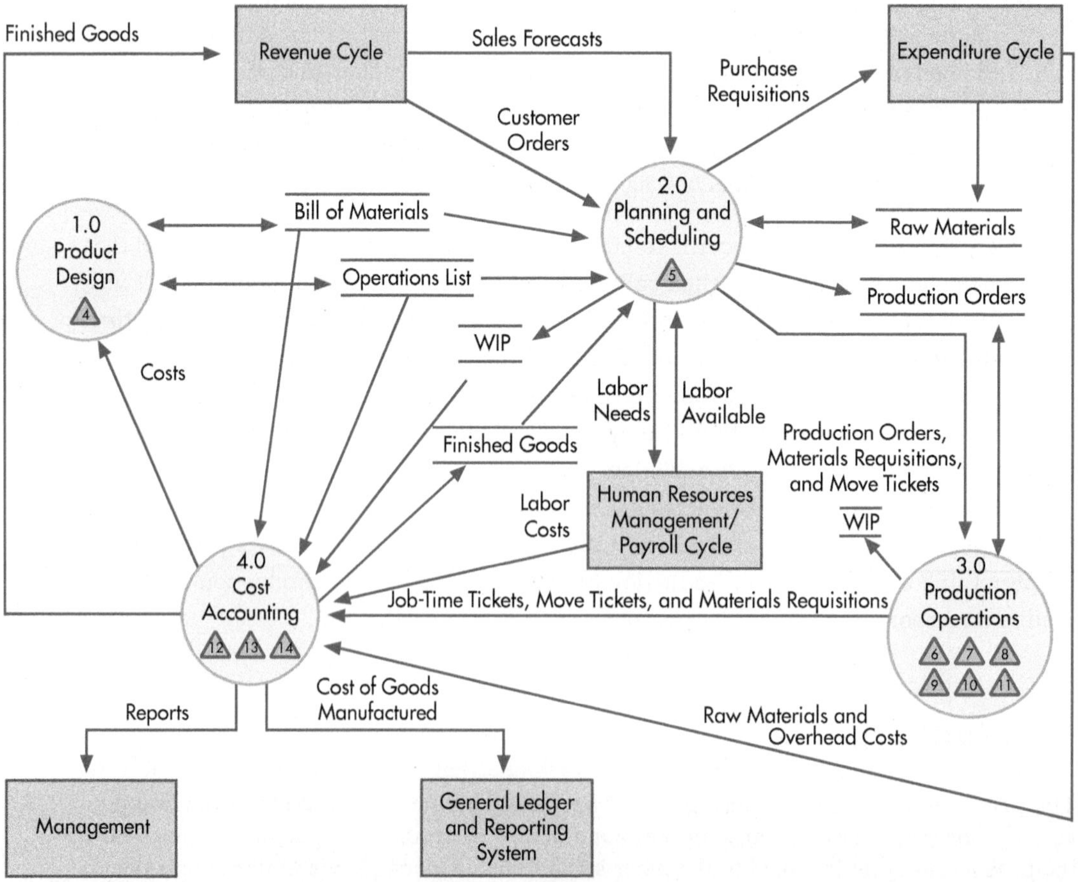

involved primarily in the fourth step, cost accounting, they must understand the other three processes to be able to design reports that provide management with the information needed to manage the production cycle activities of a modern manufacturing company. For example, one popular approach to improving manufacturing performance, called Six Sigma, begins with careful measurement and analysis of current processes in order to find ways to improve them. Accountants should participate in such efforts by helping to design accurate measures; their ability to do so, however, requires that they understand the production activities being measured.

This chapter explains how an organization's information system supports each of the production cycle activities. We begin by describing the design of the information system and the basic controls necessary to ensure that it provides management with reliable information to assess the efficiency and effectiveness of production cycle activities. We then discuss in detail each of the four basic production cycle activities. For each activity, we describe how the information needed to perform and manage those activities is collected, processed, and stored. We also explain the controls necessary to ensure not only the reliability of that information but also the safeguarding of the organization's resources.

Production Cycle Information System

Figure 16-3 presents the portion of the enterprise resource planning (ERP) that supports an organization's production cycle.

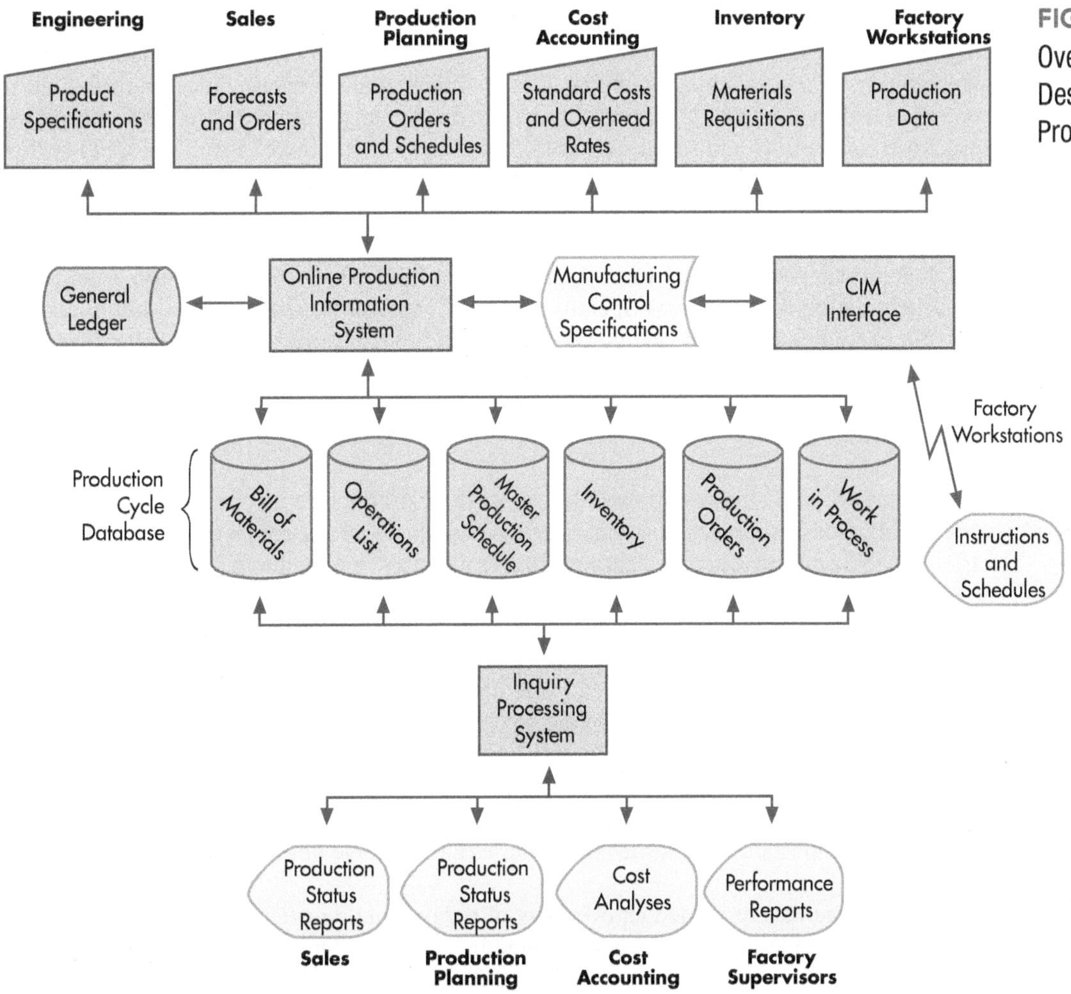

FIGURE 16-3
Overview of ERP System Design to Support the Production Cycle

PROCESS

Notice how the production cycle information system integrates both operational and financial data from many sources. The bill of materials file stores information about product components, and the operations list file contains information about how to manufacture each product. The engineering department accesses both files to develop product specifications and to design similar products. It also accesses the general ledger and inventory files for information needed to calculate the costs of alternative product designs. The sales department enters information about sales forecasts and customer orders. The production planning department uses that information, plus data about current inventory levels, to develop the master production schedule and create new records in the production order file to authorize the production of specific goods. At the same time, new records are added to the work-in-process file to accumulate cost data. Materials requisitions are sent to the inventory stores department to authorize the release of raw materials. The computer-integrated manufacturing (CIM) interface sends detailed instructions to factory workstations. The CIM interface also collects cost and operational data used to update the work-in-process and production order files, respectively.

THREATS AND CONTROLS

As Figure 16-3 shows, the production cycle activities depend on and update the integrated database that contains master data about product specifications and inventory (both finished goods and raw materials). Therefore, the first threat listed in Table 16-1 is the risk of inaccurate or invalid master data. Inaccurate data about factory operations can result in incorrect costing of products and valuation of inventory. Inaccurate inventory records can result in either failure to timely manufacture finished goods or unnecessary production. Errors in product specifications (bills of materials and operations lists) can result in poorly designed products. The various processing integrity controls discussed in Chapter 13 (control 1.1) can reduce the risk of inaccurate data entry. It is also important to restrict access to production cycle master data (control 1.2) to prevent unauthorized changes to production data. Enforcing proper access controls and segregation of duties requires that the controller or CFO review and suggest appropriate configuration of user rights in integrated ERP systems. The default installation of such systems typically provides every employee with far too much power. Therefore, it is important to modify user permissions to ensure that employees are assigned only those privileges necessary to perform their specified job duties. In addition to multifactor authentication of employees, location-based access controls on devices should also be used. For example, the system should be programmed to reject any attempts to alter inventory records from a terminal located in the engineering department. Finally, logs of all activities, especially any actions involving managerial approval, such as requests for additional raw materials or overtime, should be recorded and maintained for later review (control 1.3) as part of the audit trail.

Another threat is the unauthorized disclosure of production information, such as trade secrets and process improvements that provide a company with a competitive advantage. The various access controls discussed earlier provide one way to mitigate this threat (control 2.1). In addition, sensitive data, such as the precise procedures to follow in manufacturing a given product, should be encrypted (control 2.2) both while in storage and during transmission over the Internet to manufacturing plants and business partners.

The third general threat listed in Table 16-1 is the loss or destruction of production data. The production cycle database must be protected from either intentional or accidental loss or damage. As discussed in Chapter 13, regular backing up of all data files is imperative (control 3.1). Additional copies of key master files, such as open production orders and raw materials inventory, should be stored off-site. To reduce the possibility of accidental erasure of important files, all disks and tapes should have both external and internal file labels.

Now that we have provided an overview of the production cycle information system, let us examine each of the basic activities depicted in Figure 16-2 in more detail.

TABLE 16-1 Threats and Controls in the Production Cycle

Activity	Threat	Controls (first number refers to the corresponding threat)
General issues throughout entire production cycle	1. Inaccurate or invalid master data 2. Unauthorized disclosure of sensitive information 3. Loss or destruction of data	1.1 Data processing integrity controls 1.2 Restriction of access to master data 1.3 Review of all changes to master data 2.1 Access controls 2.2 Encryption 3.1 Backup and disaster recovery procedures
Product design	4. Poor product design resulting in excess costs	4.1 Accounting analysis of costs arising from product design choices 4.2 Analysis of warranty and repair costs
Planning and scheduling	5. Over- and underproduction	5.1 Production planning systems 5.2 Review and approval of production schedules and orders 5.3 Restriction of access to production orders and production schedules
Production operations	6. Theft of inventory 7. Theft of fixed assets 8. Poor performance 9. Suboptimal investment in fixed assets 10. Loss of inventory or fixed assets due to fire or other disasters 11. Disruption of operations	6.1 Physical access controls 6.2 Documentation of all inventory movement 6.3 Segregation of duties—custody of assets from recording and authorization of removal 6.4 Restriction of access to inventory master data 6.5 Periodic physical counts of inventory and reconciliation of those counts to recorded quantities 7.1 Physical inventory of all fixed assets 7.2 Restriction of physical access to fixed assets 7.3 Maintaining detailed records of fixed assets, including disposal 8.1 Training 8.2 Performance reports 9.1 Proper approval of fixed-asset acquisitions, including use of requests for proposals to solicit multiple competitive bids 10.1 Physical safeguards (e.g., fire sprinklers) 10.2 Insurance 11.1 Backup and disaster recovery plans 11.2 Network and logical access controls
Cost accounting	12. Inaccurate cost data 13. Inappropriate allocation of overhead costs 14. Misleading reports	12.1 Source data automation 12.2 Data processing integrity controls 13.1 Time-driven activity-based costing 14.1 Innovative performance metrics (e.g., throughput)

Product Design

The first step in the production cycle is product design (circle 1.0 in Figure 16-2). The objective is to create a product that meets customer requirements in terms of quality, durability, and functionality while simultaneously minimizing production costs. These criteria often conflict with one another, making product design a challenging task.

PROCESS

The product design activity creates two outputs. The first, a **bill of materials** (Figure 16-4), specifies the part number, description, and quantity of each component used in a finished product. The second is an **operations list** (Figure 16-5), which specifies the sequence of steps to follow in making the product, which equipment to use, and how long each step should take.

bill of materials - A document that specifies the part number, description, and quantity of each component used in a product.

operations list - A document that specifies the sequence of steps to follow in making a product, which equipment to use, and how long each step should take.

Tools such as product life-cycle management (PLM) software can help improve the efficiency and effectiveness of the product design process. PLM software consists of three key components: computer-aided design (CAD) software to design new products, digital manufacturing software that simulates how those products will be manufactured, and product data management software that stores all the data associated with products. CAD software enables manufacturers to design and test virtual 3-D models of products, thereby

FIGURE 16-4
Example of a Bill of Materials

FINISHED PRODUCT: BLU-RAY PLAYER

Part Number	Description	Quantity
105	Control Unit	1
125	Back Panel	1
148	Side Panel	2
155	Top/Bottom Panel	2
173	Timer	1
195	Front Panel	1
199	Screw	6

FIGURE 16-5
Example of an Operations List

OPERATIONS LIST FOR: CREATE SIDE PANEL

Operation Number	Description	Machine Number	Standard Time (minutes:seconds)
105	Cut to Shape	ML15-12	2:00
106	Corner Cut	ML15-9	3:15
124	Turn and Shape	S28-17	4:00
142	Finish	F54-5	7:10
155	Paint	P89-1	9:30

eliminating the costs associated with creating and destroying physical prototypes. CAD software facilitates collaboration by design teams dispersed around the globe and eliminates the costs associated with exchanging static copies of product designs. Digital manufacturing software allows companies to determine labor, machine, and process requirements to optimally produce items in different facilities across the globe in order to minimize costs. Product data management software provides easy access to detailed engineering specifications

FOCUS 16-1 Using PLM Software to Improve Product Design: The Need for Management Involvement

The potential benefits of PLM software are enormous. For example, General Motors estimates that it costs approximately $500,000 to run crash tests with real cars and hopes that CAD software can reduce the number of such tests by 85%. As Airbus learned, however, PLM software also has pitfalls. Production of the A380 superjumbo airliner was delayed by about two years, costing Airbus approximately $6 billion in lost profits. The problem? Use of different versions of the same CAD software by design teams in Germany and France resulted in incompatibilities between the front and rear fuselages. Each A380 contains over 300 miles of wires and more than 40,000 connectors to power everything in both the customer cabin and the cockpit. When workers tried to assemble the front and rear fuselages, they discovered that the wiring could not be properly connected.

How could using two editions of the same software create such problems? The answer is that each version treated drawings in different ways, resulting in different models. Engineers using the older version at the German plant had to manually tinker with the drawings to indicate where conduits should be placed, whereas the newer version of the software used at the French plant did this automatically. In addition, many technical notes containing key information about product specifications and units of measurement were lost when drawings were converted between the two versions of the software.

The experience of Airbus is not unique. A survey found that almost 50% of companies using CAD software had to redesign products because of incompatibilities between CAD software used by different design teams. Airbus executives did not force engineers at different plants to use the same versions of CAD software. This decision initially saved money by avoiding the need to purchase new software and the associated time and costs of retraining engineers. But those short-term savings were more than offset by the subsequent loss of profits due to production delays. This underscores the importance of management involvement and support whenever companies implement complex software such as PLM.

and other product data to facilitate product redesign, modification, and post-sale maintenance. Although PLM can dramatically improve both the efficiency and effectiveness of product design, Focus 16-1 shows that reaping its full benefits requires careful supervision by senior management.

THREATS AND CONTROLS

Poor product design (threat 4 in Table 16-1) drives up costs in several ways. Using too many unique components when producing similar products increases the costs associated with purchasing and maintaining raw materials inventories. It also often results in inefficient production processes because of excessive complexity in changing from the production of one product to another. Poorly designed products are also more likely to incur high warranty and repair costs.

To mitigate this threat, accountants should participate in the product design activity (control 4.1) because 65% to 80% of product costs are determined at this stage of the production process. Accountants can analyze how the use of alternative components and changes to the production process affect costs. In addition, accountants can use information from the revenue cycle about repair and warranty costs (control 4.2) associated with existing products to identify the primary causes of product failure and suggest opportunities to redesign products to improve quality.

Planning and Scheduling

The second step in the production cycle is planning and scheduling (circle 2.0 in Figure 16-2). The objective is to develop a production plan efficient enough to meet existing orders and anticipated short-term demand while minimizing inventories of both raw materials and finished goods.

PRODUCTION PLANNING METHODS

Two common methods of production planning are manufacturing resource planning and lean manufacturing. **Manufacturing resource planning (MRP-II)** is an extension of materials requirements planning (discussed in Chapter 15) that seeks to balance existing production capacity and raw materials needs to meet forecasted sales demands. MRP-II systems are often referred to as *push manufacturing* because goods are produced in expectation of customer demand.

manufacturing resource planning (MRP-II) - An extension of materials requirements planning that seeks to balance existing production capacity and raw materials needs to meet forecasted sales demands. Also referred to as push manufacturing because goods are produced in expectation of customer demand.

Just as MRP-II is an extension of MRP inventory control systems, **lean manufacturing** extends the principles of just-in-time inventory systems (discussed in Chapter 15) to the entire production process. The goal of lean manufacturing is to minimize or eliminate inventories of raw materials, work in process, and finished goods. Lean manufacturing is often referred to as *pull manufacturing* because goods are produced in response to customer demand. Theoretically, lean manufacturing systems produce only in response to customer orders. In practice, however, most lean manufacturing systems develop short-run production plans. For example, Toyota develops monthly production plans so that it can provide a stable schedule to its suppliers. This strategy enables the suppliers to plan their production schedules so that they can deliver their products to Toyota at the exact time they are needed.

lean manufacturing - Extends the principles of just-in-time inventory systems to the entire production process to minimize or eliminate inventories of raw materials, work in process, and finished goods. Lean manufacturing is often referred to as pull manufacturing because goods are produced in response to customer demand.

Thus, both MRP-II and lean manufacturing systems plan production in advance. They differ, however, in the length of the planning horizon. MRP-II systems may develop production plans for up to 12 months in advance, whereas lean manufacturing systems use much shorter planning horizons. If demand for a company's product is predictable and the product has a long life cycle, then an MRP-II approach is justified. In contrast, a lean manufacturing approach is more appropriate if a company's products are characterized by short life cycles and unpredictable demand.

KEY DOCUMENTS AND FORMS

Information about customer orders, sales forecasts, and inventory levels of finished goods is used to determine production levels. The result is a **master production schedule (MPS)**,

master production schedule (MPS) - Specifies how much of each product is to be produced during the planning period and when that production should occur.

FIGURE 16-6
Sample of a Master Production Schedule (MPS)

MASTER PRODUCTION SCHEDULE								
Product Number	120			**Description:**	Blu-Ray Player			
Lead time:[a]	**Week Number**							
1 week	**1**	**2**	**3**	**4**	**5**	**6**	**7**	**8**
Quantity on hand	500	350[b]	350	300	350	300	450	300
Scheduled production	150[c]	300	250	300	250	400	250	300
Forecasted sales	300	300	300	250	300	250	400	250
Net available	350[d]	350	300	350	300	450	300	350

[a]*Time to manufacture product (1 week for Blu-ray player).*
[b]*Ending quantity on hand (net available) from prior week.*
[c]*Calculated by subtracting quantity on hand from sum of this week's and next week's forecasted sales, plus a 50-unit buffer stock. For example, begin week 1 with 500 units. Projected sales for weeks 1 and 2 total 600 units. Adding 50-unit desired buffer inventory yields 650 units needed by end of week 1. Subtracting beginning inventory of 500 units results in planned production of 150 units during week 1.*
[d]*Beginning quantity on hand plus scheduled production less forecasted sales.*

which specifies how much of each product is to be produced during the planning period and when that production should occur (Figure 16-6). Although the long-range part of the MPS may be modified in response to changes in market conditions, production plans for many products must be frozen a few weeks in advance to provide sufficient time to procure the necessary raw materials, supplies, and labor resources.

The complexity of scheduling increases dramatically as the number of factories grows. For example, large manufacturing companies such as Intel and General Motors must coordinate production at many different plants in different countries. Some of those plants produce basic components, and others assemble the final products. The production information system must coordinate these activities to minimize bottlenecks and the buildup of partially completed inventories.

The MPS is used to develop a detailed timetable that specifies daily production and to determine raw materials purchases. To do this, it is necessary to "explode" the bill of materials to determine the immediate raw materials requirements for meeting the production goals listed in the MPS (see Table 16-2). These requirements are compared with current inventory levels, and if additional materials are needed, purchase requisitions are generated and sent to the purchasing department to initiate the acquisition process.

production order - A document authorizing the manufacture of a specified quantity of a particular product.

materials requisition - Authorizes the removal of the necessary quantity of raw materials from the storeroom.

move tickets - Documents that identify the internal transfer of parts, the location to which they are transferred, and the time of the transfer.

Figure 16-2 shows that the planning and scheduling activity produces three other documents: production orders, materials requisitions, and move tickets. A **production order** (Figure 16-7) authorizes the manufacture of a specified quantity of a particular product. It lists the operations that need to be performed, the quantity to be produced, and the location where the finished product should be delivered. It also collects data about each of those activities. A **materials requisition** (Figure 16-8) authorizes the removal of the necessary quantity of raw materials from the storeroom to the factory location where they will be used. This document contains the production order number, date of issue, and, based on the bill of materials, the part numbers and quantities of all necessary raw materials. Subsequent transfers of raw materials throughout the factory are documented on **move tickets**, which identify the parts being transferred, the location to which they are transferred, and the time of transfer (Figure 16-9 shows an example of an inventory transfer data entry screen used to capture this data).

Notice that many of the documents used in the production cycle track the movement and usage of raw materials. The use of bar-coding and RFID tags provides opportunities to improve the efficiency and accuracy of these materials handling activities by eliminating the need for manual entry of data. RFID also facilitates locating specific inventory because the scanning devices are not limited to reading only those items directly in line-of-sight. This can be especially useful in large warehouse and storage facilities, where items may get moved around to make room for new shipments.

TABLE 16-2 Example of "Exploding" a Bill of Materials

Step 1: Multiply the component requirements for ONE product by the number of products to be produced next period (from the MPS).

Components in Each Blu-Ray Player

PART NO.	DESCRIPTION	QUANTITY	NUMBER OF BLU-RAY PLAYERS	TOTAL REQUIREMENTS
105	Control Unit	1	2,000	2,000
125	Back Panel	1	2,000	2,000
148	Side Panel	4	2,000	8,000
173	Timer	1	2,000	2,000
195	Front Panel	1	2,000	2,000
199	Screw	6	2,000	12,000
135	Top Panel	1	2,000	2,000
136	Bottom Panel	1	2,000	2,000

Components in Each CD Player

PART NO.	DESCRIPTION	QUANTITY	NUMBER OF CD PLAYERS	TOTAL REQUIREMENTS
103	Control Unit	1	3,000	3,000
120	Front Panel	1	3,000	3,000
121	Back Panel	1	3,000	3,000
173	Timer	1	3,000	3,000
190	Side Panel	4	3,000	12,000
199	Screw	4	3,000	12,000
135	Top Panel	1	3,000	3,000
136	Bottom Panel	1	3,000	3,000

Step 2: Calculate total component requirements by summing products.

PART NO.	BLU-RAY PLAYER	CD PLAYER	TOTAL
103	0	3,000	3,000
105	2,000	0	2,000
120	0	3,000	3,000
121	0	3,000	3,000
125	2,000	0	2,000
148	8,000	0	8,000
173	2,000	3,000	5,000
190	0	12,000	12,000
195	2,000	0	2,000
199	12,000	12,000	24,000
135	2,000	3,000	5,000
136	2,000	3,000	5,000

Step 3: Repeat steps 1 and 2 for each week during planning horizon.

PART NO.	WEEK 1	WEEK 2	WEEK 3	WEEK 4	WEEK 5	WEEK 6
103	3,000	2,000	2,500	3,000	2,500	3,000
105	2,000	2,000	2,500	2,500	2,000	3,000
120	3,000	2,000	2,500	3,000	2,500	3,000
121	3,000	2,000	2,500	3,000	2,500	3,000
125	2,000	2,000	2,500	2,500	2,000	3,000
148	8,000	8,000	10,000	10,000	8,000	12,000
173	5,000	4,000	5,000	5,500	4,500	6,000
190	12,000	12,000	10,000	12,000	10,000	12,000
195	2,000	2,000	2,500	2,500	2,000	3,000
199	24,000	20,000	25,000	27,000	22,000	30,000
135	5,000	5,000	5,000	5,000	5,000	5,000
136	5,000	5,000	5,000	5,000	5,000	5,000

Finally, accurate production planning requires integrating information about customer orders (from the revenue cycle) with information about purchases from suppliers (from the expenditure cycle), along with information about labor availability (from the HR/payroll cycle). Figure 16-10 illustrates how an ERP system provides this integration. The system first checks

FIGURE 16-7
Sample Production Order for Alpha Omega Electronics

Alpha Omega Engineering **PRODUCTION ORDER**							4587
Order No. 2289	**Product No.** 4430	**Description:** Cabinet Side Panel			**Production Quantity** 1000		
Approved by: PJS	**Release Date:** 02/24/2020	**Issue Date:** 02/25/2020		**Completion Date:** 03/09/2020	**Deliver To:** Assembly Department		

Work Station No.	Product Operation No.	Quantity	Operation Description	Start Date & Time		Finish Date & Time	
MH25	100	1,003	Transfer from stock	02/28	0700	02/28	0800
ML15-12	105	1,003	Cut to shape	02/28	0800	02/28	1000
ML15-9	106	1,002	Corner cut	02/28	1030	02/28	1200
S28-17	124	1,002	Turn & shape	02/28	1300	02/28	1700
F54-5	142	1,001	Finish	03/01	0800	03/01	1100
P89-1	155	1,001	Paint	03/01	1300	03/02	1300
QC94	194	1,001	Inspect	03/02	1400	03/02	1600
MH25	101	1,000	Transfer to assembly	03/02	1600	03/02	1700

Explanation of numbers in Quantity column:

1. *Total of 1,003 sheets of raw material used to produce 1,000 good panels and 3 rejected panels.*
2. *One panel not cut to proper shape, thus only 1,002 units had operations 106 and 124 performed on them.*
3. *One panel not properly turned and shaped; hence only 1,001 panels finished, painted, and received final inspection.*
4. *One panel rejected during final inspection; thus only 1,000 good panels transferred to assembly department.*

inventory on hand to determine how much needs to be produced to fill the new order. It then calculates labor needs and determines whether there is a need to schedule overtime or hire temporary help in order to meet the promised fill date. At the same time, information in the bill of materials is used to determine what components, if any, need to be ordered. Any necessary purchase orders are sent to suppliers via electronic data interchange (EDI). The MPS is then adjusted to include the new order. Notice how this sharing of information across the revenue, production, and expenditure cycles in the manner just described enables companies to efficiently manage inventories by timing their purchases to meet actual customer demand.

FIGURE 16-8
Sample Materials Requisition for Alpha Omega Electronics

MATERIALS REQUISITION				No. 2345
Issued To: Assembly	**Issue Date:** 08/15/2020		**Production Order Number:** 62913	

Part Number	Description	Quantity	Unit Cost $	Total Cost $
115	Calculator Unit	2,000	2.95	5,900.00
135	Lower Casing	2,000	.45	900.00
198	Screw	16,000	.02	320.00
178	Battery	2,000	.75	1,500.00
136	Upper Casing	2,000	.80	1,600.00
199	Screw	12,000	.02	240.00
Issued by: **AKL**				10,460.00
Received by: GWS		Costed by: ZBD		

Note: Cost information is entered when the materials requisition is turned in to the cost accounting department. Other information, except for signatures, is printed by the system when the document is prepared.

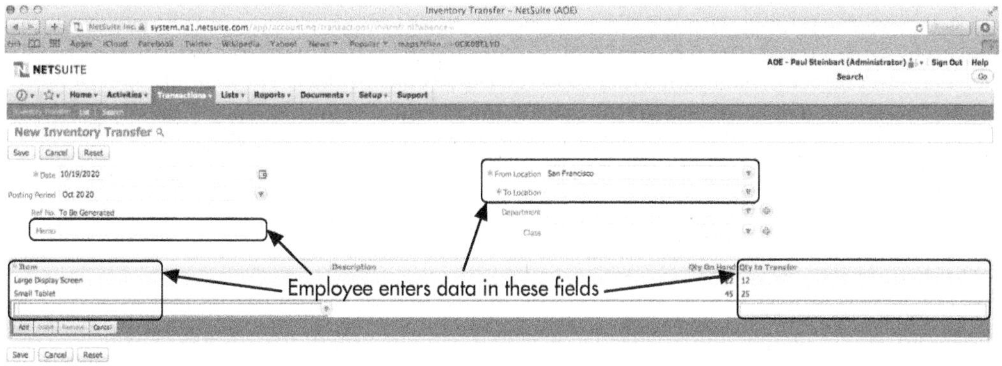

FIGURE 16-9
Example of Inventory Transfer Screen

Source: 2010 © NetSuite Inc.

THREATS AND CONTROLS

Table 16-1 shows that the primary threat in the planning and scheduling activity is over- or underproduction. Overproduction can result in a supply of goods in excess of short-run demands, thereby creating potential cash flow problems because resources are tied up in inventory. Overproduction also increases the risk of carrying inventory that becomes obsolete. Conversely, underproduction can result in lost sales and customer dissatisfaction because of lack of availability of desired items.

Production planning systems (control 5.1) can reduce the risk of over- and underproduction. Improvement requires accurate and current sales forecasts and data about inventory stocks, information that the revenue and expenditure cycle systems can provide. In addition to improved forecasts, information about production performance, particularly concerning trends in total time to manufacture each product, should be regularly collected. These data sources should be used periodically to review and adjust the MPS.

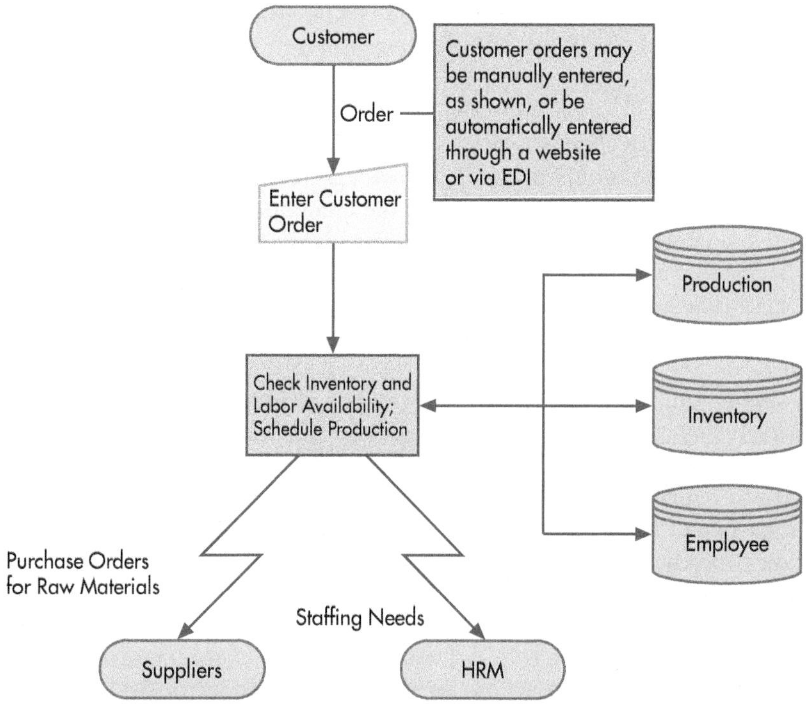

FIGURE 16-10
Illustration of How ERP Systems Integrate Production Cycle Information with Data from Other Cycles

Proper approval and authorization of production orders (control 5.2) is another control to prevent over- or underproduction of specific items. Careful review and approval also ensure that the correct production orders are released (control 5.2). The risk of unauthorized production orders can be reduced by restricting access to the production scheduling program (control 5.3).

Production Operations

The third step in the production cycle is the actual manufacture of products (circle 3.0 in Figure 16-2). The manner in which this activity is accomplished varies greatly across companies, differing according to the type of product being manufactured and the degree of automation used in the production process.

computer-integrated manufacturing (CIM) - A manufacturing approach in which much of the manufacturing process is performed and monitored by computerized equipment, in part through the use of robotics and real-time data collection of manufacturing activities.

Using various forms of information technology (IT) in the production process, such as robots and computer-controlled machinery, is referred to as **computer-integrated manufacturing (CIM)**. CIM can significantly affect the production process. For example, 3-D printing dramatically reduces both the time and cost to make products. 3-D printing also makes it possible to build products that could not be made using traditional manufacturing processes. The ability to attach sensors to every piece of equipment (part of what is sometimes called the Industrial Internet of Things) makes it easier to ensure that preventive maintenance is done, thereby avoiding costs and delays due to breakdowns.

Accountants need not be experts on every facet of CIM, but they must understand how it affects both operations and cost accounting. One operational effect of CIM is a shift from mass production to custom-order manufacturing. This capability requires redesign of inventory management systems and work flows to facilitate quick changes in production. As we will discuss in the final section of this chapter, such flexibility in manufacturing operations also has implications for the design of cost accounting systems.

THREATS AND CONTROLS

Theft of inventories (threat 6) and fixed assets (threat 7) are major concerns (see Table 16-1). In addition to the loss of assets, thefts also result in overstated asset balances, which can lead to erroneous analyses of financial performance and underproduction.

To reduce the risk of inventory loss, physical access to inventories should be restricted (control 6.1), and all internal movements of inventory should be documented (control 6.2). Thus, materials requisitions should be used to authorize the release of raw materials to production. Both the inventory control clerk and the production employee receiving the raw materials should sign the requisition to acknowledge release of the goods to production. Requests for additional materials in excess of the amounts specified in the bill of materials should be documented and authorized by supervisory personnel. Move tickets should be used to document subsequent movement of inventory through various stages of the production process. The return of any materials not used in production also should be documented. Wherever feasible, RFID tags or bar codes should be used to automate the tracking of inventories.

Proper segregation of duties (control 6.3) is important to safeguard inventory. Maintaining physical custody of the raw materials and finished goods inventories is the responsibility of the inventory stores department. Department or factory supervisors have primary responsibility for work-in-process inventories. RFID equipment, bar-code scanners, and online terminals can be used to record movement of inventory, thereby maintaining accurate perpetual inventory records. The authorization function, represented by the preparation of production orders, materials requisitions, and move tickets, is the responsibility of the production planners or, increasingly, of the production information system itself. Consequently, proper access controls and compatibility tests are important to ensure that only authorized personnel have access to those records (control 6.4). Finally, an employee without any custodial responsibility should periodically count inventory on hand (control 6.5). Any discrepancies between these physical counts and recorded amounts should be investigated.

Similar controls are needed to safeguard fixed assets. First, all fixed assets must be identified and recorded (control 7.1) so that managers can be assigned responsibility and accountability for fixed assets under their control. RFID tags provide a cost-effective way to monitor the location of fixed assets. As with inventory, security measures should be in place to control physical access to fixed assets (control 7.2). Because manufacturing machinery and equipment are often replaced before they are completely worn out, it is important to formally approve and accurately record their sale or disposal (control 7.3). A report of all fixed-asset transactions should be printed periodically and sent to the controller, who should verify that each transaction was properly authorized and executed. The cost accounting system also needs to maintain accurate records of acquisition cost, any improvements, and depreciation in order to properly calculate the gain or loss arising from such transactions.

Poor performance is another threat to production operations. Training (control 8.1) is one way to mitigate this threat. Indeed, surveys of manufacturing companies report a direct relationship between time spent on training and overall productivity. It is also important to regularly prepare and review reports on performance (control 8.2) in order to identify when additional training is needed.

Another threat associated with production cycle activities is suboptimal investment in fixed assets. Overinvesting in fixed assets can create excess costs; underinvestment can impair productivity. Both problems reduce profitability. Thus, proper authorization of fixed-asset transactions (control 9.1) is important.

Acquisitions of fixed assets represent a special type of expenditure and follow the same basic processes (order the fixed asset, receive it, and pay for it) and control procedures discussed in Chapter 15. Nonetheless, the size of most fixed-asset transactions necessitates some modifications of the processes used to acquire inventory and miscellaneous supplies. A supervisor or manager, who provides details about expected cash flows and other costs and benefits of the proposed expenditure, should first recommend large capital expenditures. All such recommendations should be reviewed by a senior executive or by an executive committee and the various projects ranked by priority. Smaller capital expenditures (e.g., those costing $10,000 or less) usually can be purchased directly out of departmental budgets, which avoids a formal approval process. Holding managers accountable for their department's return on the fixed assets provides incentive to control such expenditures.

Another difference is that orders for machinery and equipment almost always involve a formal request for competitive bids by potential suppliers. A document called a **request for proposal (RFP)**, which specifies the desired properties of the asset, is sent to each prospective supplier. The capital investments committee should review the responses and select the best bid. Once a supplier has been selected, the acquisition of the asset may be handled through the regular expenditure cycle process, as described in Chapter 15. Specifically, a formal purchase order is prepared, receipt of the asset is formally documented using a receiving report, and a disbursement voucher is used to authorize payment to the supplier. The same set of processing controls and edit checks employed for other purchases also should be used for fixed-asset acquisitions (for details, refer back to the discussion in Chapter 15).

request for proposal (RFP) - A request by an organization or department for suppliers to bid to supply a fixed asset that possesses specific characteristics.

Another threat noted in Table 16-1 is that both inventories and fixed assets are subject to loss due to fire or other disasters. Physical safeguards (control 10.1), such as fire suppression systems, are designed to prevent such disasters. However, because preventive controls are never 100% effective, organizations also need to purchase adequate insurance (control 10.2) to cover such losses and provide for replacement of those assets.

A related concern is disruption of production activities (threat 11). The high level of automation in production cycle activities means that disasters, such as power outages, not only interrupt the functioning of information systems but can also disrupt manufacturing activities. Backup power sources (control 11.1), such as generators, and uninterruptible power supply devices should be acquired to ensure that critical equipment and machinery is not damaged by sudden unexpected loss of power and that important production processes can continue on schedule. Companies also need to investigate the disaster preparedness of key suppliers and identify alternative sources for critical components. This is especially important for companies that practice lean manufacturing; they maintain low inventories of both raw materials and finished goods, so any disruptions to either their manufacturing activities or those of their suppliers can quickly result in lost sales.

Production activities can also be disrupted by cyberattacks, which exploit security weaknesses in the Industrial Internet of Things. Indeed, as the Stuxnet incident that affected Iran's nuclear program showed, cyberattacks can even destroy manufacturing equipment. Consequently, the various network and logical access controls described in Chapter 11 need to be extended to production cycle networks (control 11.2).

Cost Accounting

The final step in the production cycle is cost accounting (circle 4.0 in Figure 16-2). The three principal objectives of the cost accounting system are (1) to provide information for planning, controlling, and evaluating the performance of production operations; (2) to provide accurate cost data about products for use in pricing and product mix decisions; and (3) to collect and process the information used to calculate the inventory and cost of goods sold values that appear in the company's financial statements.

To successfully accomplish the first objective, the cost accounting system must be designed to collect real-time data about the performance of production activities so that management can make timely decisions. The proliferation of smart sensors, part of the Industrial Internet of Things, increases both the quantity and quality of such data. To accomplish the other two objectives, the cost accounting system must classify costs by various categories and then assign those costs to specific products and organizational units. This requires careful coding of cost data during collection because often the same costs may be allocated in multiple ways, for several different purposes. For example, factory supervisory costs may be assigned to departments for performance evaluation purposes but to specific products for pricing and product mix decisions.

PROCESS

job-order costing - A cost system that assigns costs to specific production batches or jobs.

process costing - A cost system that assigns costs to each process, or work center, in the production cycle, and then calculates the average cost for all units produced.

Most companies use either job-order or process costing to assign production costs. **Job-order costing** assigns costs to specific production batches, or jobs, and is used when the product or service being sold consists of discretely identifiable items. For example, construction companies use job-order costing for each house being built. Similarly, public accounting and law firms use job-order costing to account for the costs of individual audits or cases, respectively. AOE currently uses job-order costing.

In contrast, **process costing** assigns costs to each process, or work center, in the production cycle, and then calculates the average cost for all units produced. Process costing is used when similar goods or services are produced in mass quantities and discrete units cannot be readily identified. For example, breweries accumulate the costs associated with the various processes (e.g., mashing, primary fermentation, filtering, and bottling) in producing a batch of a particular kind of beer and then compute the average total unit cost for that product. Similarly, mutual funds accumulate the costs associated with handling customer deposits and withdrawals and then compute the per-unit costs of those transactions.

The choice of job-order or process costing affects only the method used to *assign* costs to products, not the methods used to collect that data. Let us now examine how data about raw materials used, labor hours expended, machine operations performed, and manufacturing overhead are collected.

RAW MATERIALS USAGE DATA When production is initiated, the issuance of a materials requisition triggers a debit to work in process for the raw materials sent to production. If additional materials are needed, another debit is made to work in process. Conversely, work in process is credited for any materials not used and returned to inventory. Many raw materials can be tracked by bar codes and RFID tags. However, data about some types of inventory, such as liquids and gases, must still be manually recorded.

DIRECT LABOR COSTS In the past, AOE and other manufacturers used a paper document called a **job-time ticket** to collect data about labor activity. This document recorded the amount of time a worker spent on each specific job task. Now, as shown in Figure 16-3, workers enter this data using online terminals at each factory workstation. To further improve the efficiency of this process, AOE is considering switching to coded identification cards, which workers would run through a badge reader or bar-code scanner when they start and finish any task. The time savings associated with using bar-coding to automate data collection can be significant. For example, Consolidated Diesel Company found that using bar-code scanners to capture data about materials usage and labor operations saved about 12 seconds per workstation, per activity. Although this may not seem like much, when multiplied by the hundreds of workstations and multiple activities performed daily by hundreds of employees, the change resulted in a permanent 15% increase in productivity.

job-time ticket - A document used to collect data about labor activity by recording the amount of time a worker spent on each specific job task.

MACHINERY AND EQUIPMENT USAGE As companies implement CIM to automate the production process, an ever larger proportion of product costs relate to the machinery and equipment used to make that product. Data about machinery and equipment usage are collected at each step in the production process, often in conjunction with data about labor costs. For example, when workers record their activities at a particular workstation, the system can also record information identifying the machinery and equipment used and the duration of such use. Until recently, this data was collected by wiring the factory so that each piece of equipment was linked to the computer system. This limited the ability to quickly and easily redesign the layout of the shop floor to improve production efficiency. Consequently, many manufacturing companies are replacing such wired connections with wireless technology. Doing so enables them to use new 3-D simulation software to evaluate the effects of modifying shop-floor layout and workflow and to easily and quickly implement beneficial changes.

MANUFACTURING OVERHEAD COSTS Manufacturing costs not economically feasible to trace directly to specific jobs or processes are considered **manufacturing overhead**. Examples include the costs of water, power, and other utilities; miscellaneous supplies; rent, insurance, and property taxes for the factory plant; and the salaries of factory supervisors. Most of these costs are collected by the expenditure cycle information system (see Chapter 15), with the exception of supervisory salaries, which are processed by the human resources cycle information system (see Chapter 17).

manufacturing overhead - All manufacturing costs not economically feasible to trace directly to specific jobs or processes.

Accountants can play a key role in controlling overhead costs by carefully assessing how changes in product mix affect total manufacturing overhead. They should go beyond merely collecting such data, however, and identify the underlying factors that drive the changes in total costs. This information then can be used to adjust production plans and factory layout to maximize efficiency and profitability. As the AOE case illustrates, to do this effectively requires that the cost accounting system be redesigned to collect and report costs in a manner consistent with the production planning techniques of the company. For example, lean manufacturing emphasizes working in teams and seeks to maximize the efficiency and synergy of all teams involved in making a particular product. Consequently, Elizabeth Venko realizes that collecting and reporting labor variances at the individual or team level may create dysfunctional incentives to maximize local performance at the expense of plant-wide performance. Therefore, she plans to redesign AOE's cost accounting system so that it collects and reports costs in a manner that highlights the *joint* contributions of all teams that make a particular product.

THREATS AND CONTROLS

As the AOE case illustrated, inaccurate cost data (threat 12 in Table 16-1) can diminish the effectiveness of production scheduling and undermine management's ability to monitor and control manufacturing operations. For example, inaccurate cost data can result in inappropriate decisions about which products to make and how to set current selling prices. Errors in inventory records can lead to either over- or underproduction of goods. Overstated fixed assets increase expenses through extra depreciation and higher property taxes. Understated fixed assets also can cause problems; for example, inaccurate counts of the number of personal computers in use can cause a company to unknowingly violate software license requirements. Inaccuracies in financial statements and managerial reports can distort analyses of past performance and the desirability of future investments or changes in operations.

The best control procedure to ensure that data entry is accurate is to automate data collection (control 12.1) using RFID technology, bar-code scanners, badge readers, and other devices. When this is not feasible, online terminals should be used for data entry and should employ the various data entry edit controls discussed in Chapter 13 (control 12.2). For example, check digits and closed-loop verification should be used to ensure that information about the raw materials used, operations performed, and employee number is entered correctly. Validity checks, such as comparing part numbers of raw materials to those listed in the bill of materials file, provide further assurance of accuracy. Finally, to verify the accuracy of database records, periodic physical counts of inventories and fixed assets should be made and compared with recorded quantities (control 12.3).

Accurate cost data are not sufficient, however. As the AOE case showed, poorly designed cost accounting systems misallocate costs to products (threat 13) and produce misleading reports about production cycle activities (threat 14), both of which can lead to erroneous decisions and frustration. The following two subsections explain how activity-based costing systems and innovative performance metrics can mitigate these problems.

IMPROVED CONTROL WITH ACTIVITY-BASED COSTING SYSTEMS Traditional cost systems use volume-driven bases, such as direct labor or machine hours, to apply overhead to products. Many overhead costs, however, do not vary directly with production volume. Setup and materials handling costs, for example, vary with the number of different batches that are run, not with the total number of units produced. Thus, allocating these types of overhead costs to products based on output volume overstates the costs of products manufactured in large quantities. It also understates the costs of products manufactured in small batches.

In addition, allocating overhead based on direct labor input can distort costs across products. As investments in factory automation increase, the amount of direct labor used in production decreases. Consequently, the amount of overhead charged per unit of labor increases dramatically. As a result, small differences in the amount of labor used to produce two products can result in significant differences in product costs.

activity-based costing - A cost system designed to trace costs to the activities that create them.

Activity-based costing[1] (control 13.1) can refine and improve cost allocations under both job-order and process cost systems by tracing costs to the activities that create them, such as grinding or polishing, and only subsequently allocating those costs to products or departments. An underlying objective of activity-based costing is to link costs to corporate strategy. Corporate strategy results in decisions about what goods and services to produce. Activities must be performed to produce these goods and services, which in turn incur costs. Thus, corporate strategy determines costs. Consequently, by measuring the costs of basic activities, such as materials handling or processing purchase orders, activity-based costing provides information to management for evaluating the consequences of its strategic decisions.

Activity-based costing systems differ from conventional cost accounting systems in three important ways:

1. Using advances in IT to trace a larger proportion of overhead costs to products. For example, RFID technology and bar-coding facilitate tracking the exact quantities of

[1]In this section, we provide an overview of activity-based costing, its effects on the cost accounting system, and its benefits. For additional details on the mechanics of activity-based costing, see any cost accounting textbook.

miscellaneous parts used in each product or process stage. When implementing activity-based costing systems, accountants observe production operations and interview factory workers and supervisors to obtain a better understanding of how manufacturing activities affect costs.

2. Using a greater number of cost pools to accumulate indirect costs (manufacturing overhead). Whereas most traditional cost systems lump all overhead costs together, activity-based costing systems distinguish three separate categories of overhead:
   - **Batch-related overhead.** Examples include setup costs, inspections, and materials handling. Activity-based cost systems accumulate these costs for a batch and then allocate them to the units produced in that batch. Thus, products produced in large quantities have lower batch-related overhead costs per unit than products produced in small quantities.
   - **Product-related overhead.** These costs are related to the diversity of the company's product line. Examples include research and development, expediting, shipping and receiving, environmental regulations, and purchasing. Activity-based cost systems try to link these costs to specific products when possible. For example, if a company produces three product lines, one of which generates hazardous waste, an activity-based cost system would charge only that one set of products for all the costs of complying with environmental regulations. Other costs, such as purchasing raw materials, might be allocated across products based on the relative number of purchase orders required to make each product.
   - **Companywide overhead.** This category includes such costs as rent or property taxes. These costs apply to all products. Thus, activity-based cost systems typically allocate them using departmental or plant rates.
3. Attempting to rationalize the allocation of overhead to products by identifying cost drivers. A **cost driver** is anything that has a cause-and-effect relationship on costs. For example, the number of purchase orders processed is one cost driver of purchasing department costs; that is, the total costs of processing purchase orders (e.g., purchasing department salaries, postage) vary directly with the number of purchase orders processed. As in this example, cost drivers in activity-based cost systems are often nonfinancial variables. In contrast, traditional costing systems often use financial variables, such as dollar volume of purchases, as the bases for allocating manufacturing overhead.

cost driver - Anything that has a cause-and-effect relationship to costs.

ERP systems make it easier to implement activity-based costing because they provide detailed information about the steps required to process a transaction. For example, the time (and therefore the cost) of requisitioning the raw materials needed to manufacture a product depends upon the number of components in the finished product. Accountants and engineers can observe and calculate the average time it takes to retrieve one component from inventory. That time measure can then be multiplied by the number of line items in a production order (automatically recorded by the ERP system) to calculate the materials requisition costs for each different finished product.

Proponents of activity-based costing argue that it provides two important benefits: More accurate cost data result in better product mix and pricing decisions, and more detailed cost data improve management's ability to control and manage total costs.

Better Decisions. Traditional cost systems tend to apply too much overhead to some products and too little to others because too few cost pools are used. This leads to two types of problems, both of which AOE experienced. First, companies may accept sales contracts for some products at prices below their true cost of production. Consequently, although sales increase, profits decline. Second, companies may overprice other products, thereby inviting new competitors to enter the market. Ironically, if more accurate cost data were available, companies would find that they could cut prices to keep competitors out of the market and still make a profit on each sale. Activity-based cost systems avoid these problems because overhead is divided into three categories and applied using cost drivers that are causally related to production. Therefore, product cost data are more accurate.

Activity-based costing also makes better use of production data to improve product design. For example, the costs associated with processing purchase orders can be used to

TABLE 16-3 Comparison of Reports Based on Activity-Based and Traditional Cost Systems

Traditional Cost Reports, Based on General Ledger Account Categories

	Budget	Actual	Variance
Salaries	$386,000	$375,000	$11,000
Computer software	845,000	855,000	(10,000)
Travel	124,000	150,000	(26,000)
Supplies	25,000	20,000	5,000
Total	$1,380,000	$1,400,000	($20,000)

Activity-Based Costing Analysis

	Budget	Actual	Variance
Systems analysis	$200,000	$210,000	($10,000)
Coding	440,000	400,000	40,000
Testing	235,000	250,000	(15,000)
Maintenance	250,000	275,000	(25,000)
User support	90,000	50,000	40,000
Reports	87,000	75,000	12,000
Training	78,000	140,000	(62,000)
Total	$1,380,000	$1,400,000	($20,000)

calculate the purchasing-related overhead associated with each component used in a finished product. Engineering can use this information, along with data on relative usage of components across products, to identify unique components that could be replaced by lower-cost, more commonly used parts.

Finally, activity-based cost data improve managerial decision making by providing information about the costs associated with specific activities, instead of classifying those costs by financial statement category. Table 16-3 shows an example of how this rearrangement of data can improve managerial analysis by focusing attention on key processes. Notice how the traditional cost report draws attention to the fact that travel and software costs are above budget. The activity-based cost report, in contrast, shows which *activities* (training, testing, maintenance, and systems analysis) are running over budget, and which are not.

Improved Cost Management. Proponents argue that another advantage of activity-based costing is that it clearly measures the results of managerial actions on overall profitability. Whereas traditional cost systems only measure spending to acquire resources, activity-based cost systems measure both the amount spent to acquire resources and the consumption of those resources. This distinction is reflected in the following formula:

Cost of activity capability = Cost of activity used + Cost of unused capacity

To illustrate, consider the receiving function at a manufacturing firm such as AOE. The total monthly employee cost in the receiving department, including salaries and benefits, represents the cost of providing this function—receiving shipments from suppliers. Assume that the salary expense of the receiving department is $100,000, and assume that the number of employees is sufficient to handle 500 shipments. The cost per shipment would be $200. Finally, assume that 400 shipments are actually received. The activity-based cost system would report that the cost of the receiving activity used is $80,000 ($200 × 400 shipments) and that the remaining $20,000 in salary expense represents the cost of unused capacity.

In this way, performance reports that activity-based cost systems generate help direct managerial attention to how policy decisions made in one area affect costs in another area. For example, a purchasing department manager may decide to increase the minimum size of orders to obtain larger discounts for bulk purchases. This would reduce the number of incoming shipments that the receiving department must handle, thereby increasing its unused capacity. Similarly, actions taken to improve the efficiency of operations, such as requiring vendors to send products in bar-coded containers, increase practical capacity and create additional unused capacity. In either case, activity-based cost performance reports highlight this excess capacity for managerial attention. Management can then try to improve profitability by applying that unused capacity to other revenue-generating activities.

IMPROVED CONTROL WITH INNOVATIVE PERFORMANCE METRICS Modern approaches to production, such as lean manufacturing, differ significantly from traditional mass production. One major difference is a marked reduction in inventory levels of finished goods because production is scheduled in response to customer demand instead of projections based on prior years. Although this is beneficial in the long run, it often creates a short-term decline in reported profitability. The reason: Traditional financial accounting treats inventory as an asset. Thus, the costs of producing inventory are not recognized until the products are sold. When a company switches from mass production to lean manufacturing, it reduces existing inventory levels, with the result that costs incurred in prior periods to create that inventory are now expensed. In addition, because lean manufacturing seeks to minimize the creation of additional inventories, almost all labor and overhead costs are expensed in the current period, instead of being allocated to inventory and thereby treated as an asset and deferred to future periods. The combined effect of these changes often results in a marked increase in expenses in the year of transitioning to lean accounting. Although this effect is only temporary, it can create significant concern among managers, particularly if their performance evaluations are based primarily on the company's reported financial statements.

To address these problems, CPAs who work for and with companies that have adopted lean manufacturing techniques advocate supplementing traditional financial reports based on Generally Accepted Accounting Principles (GAAP) with additional reports based on lean-accounting[2] principles. One suggested change involves assigning costs to product lines instead of departments. For example, all the costs incurred to design, produce, sell, deliver, process customer payments, and provide post-sales support are grouped by product. Another change involves reporting overhead costs as a separate item, rather than including them in the calculation of the cost of goods sold. Lean-accounting reports also identify the change in inventory as a separate expense item, to more clearly reveal the effect of inventory levels on reported profits.

In addition to changing the structure of performance reports, accountants should also develop and refine new measures designed to focus on issues important to production cycle managers (control 14.1). Two particularly important issues are the level of usable output produced per unit of time and measures of quality control.

Throughput: A Measure of Production Effectiveness. **Throughput** represents the number of good units produced in a given period of time. It consists of three factors, each of which can be separately controlled, as shown in the following formula:[3]

throughput - A measure of production efficiency representing the number of "good" units produced in a given period of time.

$$\text{Throughput} = (\text{Total units produced} / \text{Processing time}) \times (\text{Processing time} / \text{Total time}) \times (\text{Good units} / \text{Total units})$$

Productive capacity, the first term in the formula, shows the maximum number of units that can be produced using current technology. Productive capacity can be increased by improving labor or machine efficiency, by rearranging the factory-floor layout to expedite the movement of materials, or by simplifying product design specifications. *Productive processing time*, the second term in the formula, indicates the percentage of total production time used to manufacture the product. Productive processing time can be improved by improving maintenance to reduce machine downtime or by more efficient scheduling of material and supply deliveries to reduce wait time. *Yield*, the third term in the formula, represents the percentage of good

[2]The introductory material in this section is based on an article by Karen M. Kroll, "The Lowdown on Lean Accounting," *Journal of Accountancy* (July 2004): 69–76.

[3]This formula was developed by Carole Cheatham in "Measuring and Improving Throughput," *Journal of Accountancy* (March 1990): 89–91.

(nondefective) units produced. Using better-quality raw materials or improving worker skills can improve yield.

Quality Control Measures. Information about quality costs can help companies determine the effects of actions taken to improve yield and identify areas for further improvement. Quality control costs can be divided into four areas:

1. *Prevention costs* are associated with changes to production processes designed to reduce the product defect rate.
2. *Inspection costs* are associated with testing to ensure that products meet quality standards.
3. *Internal failure costs* are associated with reworking, or scrapping, products identified as being defective prior to sale.
4. *External failure costs* result when defective products are sold to customers. They include such costs as product liability claims, warranty and repair expenses, loss of customer satisfaction, and damage to the company's reputation.

The ultimate objective of quality control is to "get it right the first time" by manufacturing products that meet customer specifications. This often requires trade-offs among the four quality cost categories. For example, increasing prevention costs can lower inspection costs as well as internal and external failure costs. Indeed, many companies have found that increased spending to prevent defects reduces the sum of inspection, internal failure, and external failure costs. In addition, improved quality control can also help companies become "greener." For example, when the Subaru plant in Indiana redesigned its manufacturing process, it reduced the amount of electricity required to produce a car by 14% and totally eliminated waste sent to landfills.

Summary and Case Conclusion

The production cycle consists of four basic activities: product design, production planning and scheduling, production operations, and cost accounting. Companies are continually investing in IT to improve the efficiency of the first three activities. However, for a business to reap the full benefit of these changes, corresponding modifications must also be made to the cost accounting system. In addition, accountants need to modify financial reports and develop new measures that more accurately reflect and measure manufacturing performance.

After completing her tour of the factory, Elizabeth Venko was convinced that some major changes were required in AOE's cost accounting system. For example, although AOE's production operations were highly automated, manufacturing overhead was still being allocated based on direct labor hours. This resulted in distorted product costs due to small differences in the amount of direct labor used to assemble each item. Elizabeth decided that the solution was to do more than merely change the allocation base. Instead, AOE would implement activity-based costing. A number of different pools would be used to accumulate overhead costs, and the appropriate cost drivers would be identified for use in assigning those costs to specific products. Based on her research, including conversations with a controller at another company that had recently implemented an activity-based costing system, Elizabeth believed that these changes would solve AOE's problems with product pricing and mix decisions and more accurately reflect the effects of investments in factory automation.

Elizabeth also decided that three other major changes were needed in the reports the production cycle information system produced. First, data about all the costs associated with quality control, not just those involving rework and scrap, should be collected and reported. Second, performance reports should include nonfinancial measures, such as throughput, in addition to financial measures. Third, lean accounting principles, rather than GAAP, could be used to create financial reports intended for internal use. She discussed with LeRoy the likely behavioral effects of these changes. They agreed that identifying the different components of quality control costs should encourage continued investments that would be likely to improve the overall yield rate. Further, separately showing the effect of changes in inventory levels on profits would make it easier to reward efforts to reduce inventory levels. They also agreed on the need to closely monitor the effects of any new performance reports and make appropriate modifications to them.

Ann Brandt realized that Elizabeth's proposed changes would necessitate a redesign of AOE's production cycle database. In addition, the desire for more timely and accurate information would require additional investments in RFID technology to replace the use of bar codes wherever feasible.

Elizabeth and Ann presented their plans at the next executive meeting. LeRoy Williams was satisfied that the changes would indeed address his complaints about AOE's current production cycle information system. Linda Spurgeon supported the proposal and agreed to fund the necessary changes. She then told Elizabeth and Ann that their next task was to look at ways to improve AOE's HR and payroll process.

KEY TERMS

production cycle 507
bill of materials 511
operations list 511
manufacturing resource planning (MRP-II) 513
lean manufacturing 513
master production schedule (MPS) 513
production order 514
materials requisition 514
move tickets 514
computer-integrated manufacturing (CIM) 518
request for proposal (RFP) 519
job-order costing 520
process costing 520
job-time ticket 521
manufacturing overhead 521
activity-based costing 522
cost driver 523
throughput 525

AIS in Action

CHAPTER QUIZ

1. Most costs are locked in at which stage in the production cycle?
a. product design
b. production planning
c. production operations
d. cost accounting

2. Which of the following is an advantage of bar-coding over RFID?
a. speed
b. accuracy
c. cost
d. safety

3. Which document lists the components needed to manufacture a specific product?
a. operations list
b. master production schedule
c. bill of materials
d. production order

4. Which document captures information about labor used in production?
a. move ticket
b. job-time ticket
c. operations list
d. bill of materials

5. An increase in which component of quality costs is most likely to result in a decrease in the other three components?
a. prevention costs
b. inspection costs
c. internal failure costs
d. external failure costs

6. Activity-based costing can be used to refine which of the following?
a. job-order costing
b. process costing
c. both job-order and process costing
d. neither job-order nor process costing

7. Which system is most likely to be used by a company that mass-produces large batches of standard items in anticipation of customer demand?
   a. MRP-II
   b. lean manufacturing
   c. activity-based costing
   d. throughput

8. The development of an MPS would be most effective in preventing which of the following threats?
   a. recording and posting errors
   b. loss of inventory
   c. production of poor-quality goods
   d. excess production

9. Which control procedure is probably *least* effective in reducing the threat of inventory loss?
   a. limiting physical access to inventory
   b. documenting all transfers of inventory within the company
   c. regular materials usage reports that highlight variances from standards
   d. periodically counting inventory and investigating any discrepancies between those counts and recorded amounts

10. What is the number of good units produced in a given period of time called?
   a. productive capacity
   b. productive processing time
   c. yield
   d. throughput

DISCUSSION QUESTIONS

16.1 When activity-based cost reports indicate that excess capacity exists, management should either find alternative revenue-enhancing uses for that capacity or eliminate it through downsizing. What factors influence management's decision? What are the likely behavioral side effects of each choice? What implications do those side effects have for the long-run usefulness of activity-based cost systems?

16.2 Why should accountants participate in product design? What insights about costs can accountants contribute that differ from the perspectives of purchasing managers and engineers?

16.3 Some companies have eliminated the collection and reporting of detailed analyses on direct labor costs broken down by various activities. Instead, first-line supervisors are responsible for controlling the total costs of direct labor. The justification for this argument is that labor costs represent only a small fraction of the total costs of producing a product and are not worth the time and effort to trace to individual activities. Do you agree or disagree with this argument? Why?

16.4 Typically, McDonald's produces menu items in advance of customer orders based on anticipated demand. In contrast, Burger King produces menu items only in response to customer orders. Which system (MRP-II or lean manufacturing) does each company use? What are the relative advantages and disadvantages of each system?

16.5 Some companies have switched from a "management by exception" philosophy to a "continuous improvement" viewpoint. The change is subtle, but significant. Continuous improvement focuses on comparing actual performance to the ideal (i.e., perfection). Consequently, all variances are negative (how can you do better than perfect?). The largest variances indicate the areas with the greatest amount of "waste," and, correspondingly, the greatest opportunity for improving the bottom line. What are the advantages and disadvantages of this practice?

PROBLEMS

16.1 Match the terms with their definitions.

Term	Definition
____ 1. bill of materials	a. Factor that causes costs to change
____ 2. operations list	b. Measure of the number of good units produced in a period of time
____ 3. master production schedule	c. List of the raw materials used to create a finished product
____ 4. lean manufacturing	d. Document used to authorize removal of raw materials from inventory
____ 5. production order	e. Cost accounting method that assigns costs to products based on specific processes performed
____ 6. materials requisition	f. Cost accounting method that assigns costs to specific batches or production runs and is used when the product or service consists of uniquely identifiable items
____ 7. move ticket	g. Cost accounting method that assigns costs to each step or work center and then calculates the average cost for all products that passed through that step or work center
____ 8. job-time ticket	h. Document that records labor costs associated with manufacturing a product
____ 9. job-order costing	i. Document that tracks transfer of inventory from one work center to another
____ 10. cost driver	j. Document that authorizes manufacture of a finished good
____ 11. throughput	k. Document that lists the steps required to manufacture a finished good
____ 12. computer-integrated manufacturing	l. Document that specifies how much of a finished good is to be produced during a specific time period
	m. Production planning technique that is an extension of the just-in-time inventory control method
	n. Production planning technique that is an extension of the materials requirement planning inventory control method
	o. Use of robots and other IT techniques as part of the production process

16.2 What internal control procedure(s) would best prevent or detect the following problems?

a. A production order was initiated for a product that was already overstocked in the company's warehouse.
b. A production employee stole items of work-in-process inventory.
c. The "rush-order" tag on a partially completed production job became detached from the materials and lost, resulting in a costly delay.
d. A production employee entered a materials requisition form into the system in order to steal $300 worth of parts from the raw materials storeroom.
e. A production worker entering job-time data on an online terminal mistakenly entered 3,000 instead of 300 in the "quantity-completed" field.

f. A production worker entering job-time data on an online terminal mistakenly posted the completion of operation 562 to production order 7569 instead of production order 7596.
g. A parts storeroom clerk issued parts in quantities 10% lower than those indicated on several materials requisitions and stole the excess quantities.
h. A production manager stole several expensive machines and covered up the loss by submitting a form to the accounting department indicating that the missing machines were obsolete and should be written off as worthless.
i. The quantity-on-hand balance for a key component shows a negative balance.
j. A factory supervisor accessed the operations list file and inflated the standards for work completed in his department. Consequently, future performance reports show favorable budget variances for that department.
k. A factory supervisor wrote off a robotic assembly machine as being sold for salvage but actually sold the machine and pocketed the proceeds.
l. Overproduction of a slow-moving product resulted in excessive inventory that had to eventually be marked down and sold at a loss.

16.3 Use Table 16-1 to create a questionnaire checklist that can be used to evaluate controls for each of the basic activities in the production cycle (product design, planning and scheduling, production operations, and cost accounting).

REQUIRED

a. For each control issue, write a Yes/No question such that a "No" answer represents a control weakness.
b. For each Yes/No question, write a brief explanation of why a "No" answer represents a control weakness.

16.4 You have recently been hired as the controller for a small manufacturing firm that makes high-definition televisions. One of your first tasks is to develop a report measuring throughput.

REQUIRED

Describe the data required to measure throughput and the most efficient and accurate method of collecting that data.

16.5 The Joseph Brant Manufacturing Company makes athletic footwear. Processing of production orders is as follows: At the end of each week, the production planning department prepares a master production schedule (MPS) that lists which shoe styles and quantities are to be produced during the next week. A production order preparation program accesses the MPS and the operations list (stored in a permanent disk file) to prepare a production order for each shoe style to be manufactured. Each new production order is added to the open production order master file stored on disk.

Each day, parts department clerks review the open production orders and the MPS to determine which materials need to be released to production. All materials are bar-coded. Factory workers work individually at specially designed U-shaped work areas equipped with several machines to assist them in completely making a pair of shoes. Factory workers scan the bar codes as they use materials. To operate a machine, the factory workers swipe their ID badge through a reader. This results in the system automatically collecting data identifying who produced each pair of shoes and how much time it took to make them.

Once a pair of shoes is finished, it is placed in a box. The last machine in each work cell prints a bar-code label that the worker affixes to the box. The completed shoes are then sent to the warehouse.

REQUIRED

a. Prepare a data flow diagram of all operations described.
b. What control procedures should be included in the system?

16.6 Excel Problem*

The XYZ Manufacturing Company is evaluating options for spending on product quality and wants to find the optimal amount to spend on changing its processes to improve prevention of defects. Its engineers have developed the following estimates:

---

*Life-long learning opportunity: see pp. xxiii–xxiv in preface.

- The current defect rate is 10%. If it invests an additional $10 per unit in prevention costs, the defect rate will drop to 6%; spending $20 per unit on prevention drops the defect rate to 3%; spending $30 per unit drops the defect rate to 1.5%; and investing $40 per unit on prevention reduces the defect rate to 1%.
- Inspection costs are $5 per unit. Inspection is successful at detecting 98% of defective units; the remaining 2% of defective products are sold and eventually returned for warranty repairs or replacement at no cost to the customer.
- Internal failure costs are $400 per defective unit detected.
- External failure costs are $1,000 per unit returned.
- Current production level is 1 million units.

REQUIRED

a. Create and submit a spreadsheet that calculates total quality costs for the existing process and for each of the four options for investing in additional prevention.
b. Use conditional formatting to highlight the cell with minimum total quality costs. Important: If you change the prevention costs, your conditional formatting should automatically switch to the cell that has the new minimum total costs.

16.7 Excel Problem*

REQUIRED

a. Create a spreadsheet that calculates throughput for the following combinations:
   - Productive capacity = 1,000 units per hour
   - Productive processing time ranges from 90% to 98%, increasing in increments of 2%
   - Yield ranges from 91% to 99%, increasing in increments of 2%
   - Costs of productive processing time:
     - 90% = $100
     - 92% = $150
     - 94% = $250
     - 96% = $400
     - 98% = $600
   - Costs of yield rates:
     - 91% = $10
     - 93% = $20
     - 95% = $35
     - 97% = $60
     - 99% = $100
b. a formula that displays in a labeled cell the maximum throughput.
c. Create a cell range that displays the total costs for the various combinations of yield and productive processing time.
d. Below the cell range created in step 3, write a statement explaining whether the company should focus on changing productive processing time or yield to minimize total costs for the same amount of throughput.

16.8 Excel Problem*

Acme Manufacturing currently employs 13 people in its receiving department. Each receiving dock clerk earns $50,000 per year. Each employee can unload up to 200 pallets of inventory per day. It currently receives on average 2450 pallets per day.

Acme is considering two options to improve productivity of its receiving dock employees. Option 1 (Automation) involves investing $200,000 in automation equipment that would enable each employee to unload up to 350 pallets of inventory per day. Option 2 (RFID) involves investing $50,000 in RFID equipment that would enable each employee to unload up to 275 pallets per day.

For both options, Acme plans to keep total costs of the receiving function the same as they currently are by eliminating some workers. Four workers would be eliminated if Acme chooses option 1 (automation) and one worker would be eliminated if it chooses option 2 (RFID).

---

*Life-long learning opportunity: see pp. xxiii–xxiv in preface.

REQUIRED

a. Download the spreadsheet from the course website and complete it by creating formulas to calculate:
   i. Receiving capacity
   ii. Cost per pallet received (Note: standard cost equals total costs divided by maximum capacity)
   iii. Cost of receiving capability used
   iv. Cost of unused receiving capability

b. Acme now wishes to further downsize its operations under options 1 and 2, but without impairing its ability to receive and process incoming shipments. Thus, it desires to keep enough employees to be able to process at least 2600 pallets per day. Management realizes it cannot employ a fraction of a worker, thus there will continue to be some excess capacity with both options.

Complete the remainder of the spreadsheet to show:
   i. Number of employees required under all three options
   ii. Actual receiving capability under all three options
   iii. Cost per pallet received (Note: standard cost equals total costs divided by maximum capacity)
   iv. Cost of receiving capability used
   v. Cost of unused receiving capability

16.9 Excel Problem*

REQUIRED

Download the spreadsheet for problem 16.9 from the website for this textbook. Write formulas to calculate the total depreciation expense and to display the correct values in the following three columns: Age, Depreciation Rate, and Depreciation Expense. (*Hint:* You will need to use the VLOOKUP and MATCH functions to do this. You may also want to read the article "Double-Teaming in Excel," by Judith K. Welch, Lois S. Mahoney, and Daniel R. Brickner, in the November 2005 issue of the *Journal of Accountancy*, from which this problem was adapted.)

16.10 Answer all of the following multiple-choice questions.

1. In terms of quality control measures, scrap and rework costs are part of ________.
   a. prevention costs
   b. inspection costs
   c. internal failure costs
   d. external failure costs

2. Which part of the throughput formula provides information about the impact of equipment downtime on overall productivity?
   a. productive capacity
   b. productive processing time
   c. yield
   d. None of the above

3. Which of the following is most likely the cost driver for accounts payable expenses associated with processing supplier invoices?
   a. number of different parts purchased
   b. total price of purchases
   c. number of suppliers used
   d. number of purchases made
   e. All of the metrics listed above

*Life-long learning opportunity: see pp. xxiii–xxiv in preface.

4. Move tickets are a control procedure designed to reduce the risk of ________.
   a. loss or destruction of production data
   b. theft of inventory
   c. disruption of operations
   d. inappropriate allocation of overhead costs

5. At which stage of the production process can accountants contribute to significantly reducing the cost of goods sold?
   a. product design
   b. planning and scheduling
   c. production operations
   d. None of the above

6. MRP-II would most likely be used by a company that produces ________.
   a. different grades of milk (e.g., whole, 2%, and skim)
   b. toner cartridges for laser printers
   c. toys based on a new movie
   d. All of the above
   e. None of the above

7. In terms of quality control measures, the costs associated with issuing credit memos to customers who return defective products is part of ________.
   a. prevention costs
   b. inspection costs
   c. internal failure costs
   d. external failure costs
   e. None of the above

8. Which control procedure would be most effective in reducing the risk of over- or under-production?
   a. reviewing all changes to master data
   b. activity-based costing
   c. production planning systems
   d. computer-integrated manufacturing
   e. reports that highlight the components of throughput

CASE 16-1 The Accountant and CIM

Examine issues of the *Journal of Accountancy, Strategic Finance*, and other business magazines for the past three years to find stories about current developments in factory automation. Write a brief report that discusses the accounting implications of one development: how it affects the efficiency and accuracy of data collection and any new opportunities for improving the quality of performance reports. Also discuss how the development affects the risks of various production cycle threats and the control procedures used to mitigate those risks.

AIS in Action Solutions

QUIZ KEY

1. Most costs are locked in at which stage in the production cycle?
▶ a. product design [Correct. Decisions made during product design determine the majority of costs.]
   b. production planning [Incorrect. Decisions made during product design determine the majority of costs.]

c. production operations [Incorrect. Decisions made during product design determine the majority of costs.]
d. cost accounting [Incorrect. Decisions made during product design determine the majority of costs.]

2. Which of the following is an advantage of bar-coding over RFID?
a. speed [Incorrect. RFID technology can read information from multiple items at the same time, whereas bar-code scanners can read only one item at a time. In addition, employees spend time aligning the bar codes on each item with the reader.]
b. accuracy [Incorrect. In certain applications, RFID is more accurate than bar-coding. For example, in retail stores, when checking out items that are similar but not identical—for example, different flavors of soda—clerks frequently enter the bar code for one item and then enter a quantity of, say, 7, rather than scanning the bar codes of each item; an RFID reader, in contrast, would identify which seven specific products were sold.]
▶ **c.** cost [Correct. Bar-coding is currently less expensive than RFID.]
d. safety [Incorrect. There is no difference in the safety of bar-coding and RFID.]

3. Which document lists the components needed to manufacture a specific product?
a. operations list [Incorrect. This document lists the sequence of steps to manufacture the product.]
b. master production schedule [Incorrect. This document is used to plan production activities.]
▶ **c.** bill of materials [Correct. The bill of materials lists the components of a finished product.]
d. production order [Incorrect. This document authorizes production activities.]

4. Which document captures information about labor used in production?
a. move ticket [Incorrect. The move ticket documents movement of materials.]
▶ **b.** job-time ticket [Correct. The job-time ticket records time spent on each activity.]
c. operations list [Incorrect. The operations list specifies the sequence of steps to manufacture a product.]
d. bill of materials [Incorrect. The bill of materials identifies the components used to manufacture a product.]

5. An increase in which component of quality costs is most likely to result in a decrease in the other three components?
▶ **a.** prevention costs [Correct. Increases in prevention costs often reduce the time and cost of inspecting products, as well as the proportion of defective products.]w
b. inspection costs [Incorrect. Increases in inspection costs do not necessarily reduce the other three quality control costs.]
c. internal failure costs [Incorrect. Increases in internal failure costs do not have any effect on prevention or inspection costs.]
d. external failure costs [Incorrect. Increases in external failure costs do not reduce other components of quality costs.]

6. Activity-based costing can be used to refine which of the following?
a. job-order costing [Incorrect. Activity-based costing can be used with either job-order or process costing.]
b. process costing [Incorrect. Activity-based costing can be used with either job-order or process costing.]
▶ **c.** both job-order and process costing [Correct. Activity-based costing can be used with either job-order or process costing.]
d. neither job-order nor process costing [Incorrect. Activity-based costing can be used with either job-order or process costing.]

7. Which system is most likely to be used by a company that mass-produces large batches of standard items in anticipation of customer demand?

▶ **a.** MRP-II [Correct. MRP-II is a push form of manufacturing appropriate for mass production of standardized items for which demand is predictable.]

b. lean manufacturing [Incorrect. Lean manufacturing seeks to minimize inventories by producing only in response to customer orders.]

c. activity-based costing [Incorrect. Activity-based costing is a cost allocation system, not a production planning technique.]

d. throughput [Incorrect. Throughput is a measure of efficiency.]

8. The development of an MPS would be most effective in preventing which of the following threats?

a. recording and posting errors [Incorrect. Data validation and processing controls would best minimize recording and posting errors.]

b. loss of inventory [Incorrect. Access controls and frequent physical counts of inventory would best reduce the risk of inventory theft.]

c. production of poor-quality goods [Incorrect. Product design addresses this issue.]

▶ **d.** excess production [Correct. An MPS schedules production to satisfy demand and, therefore, reduces the chance of overproduction.]

9. Which control procedure is probably *least* effective in reducing the threat of inventory loss?

a. limiting physical access to inventory [Incorrect. Physical access controls are an important method for reducing the risk of inventory theft.]

b. documenting all transfers of inventory within the company [Incorrect. Adequate documentation is an important control to reduce the risk of inventory theft.]

▶ **c.** regular materials usage reports that highlight variances from standards [Correct. Although variances could indicate theft, they are more likely to reflect changes in efficiency.]

d. periodically counting inventory and investigating any discrepancies between those counts and recorded amounts [Incorrect. Periodic counts of inventory are an important control for reducing the risk of inventory theft.]

10. What is the number of good units produced in a given period of time called?

a. productive capacity [Incorrect. Productive capacity is a component of throughput that represents the total number of units, both good and bad, produced per unit of time.]

b. productive processing time [Incorrect. Productive processing time is the component of throughput that measures the proportion of time actually spent producing output.]

c. yield [Incorrect. Yield is the component of throughput that measures the proportion of good units produced per batch.]

▶ **d.** throughput [Correct. Throughput is the measure of the number of good units produced per unit of time.]

CHAPTER

17

The Human Resources Management and Payroll Cycle

LEARNING OBJECTIVES

After studying this chapter, you should be able to:

1. Describe the major business activities, key decisions, and information needs in the HRM/payroll cycle, the general threats to those activities, and the controls that can mitigate those threats.
2. Explain the payroll cycle activities, key decisions and information needs, the threats to those activities, and the controls that can mitigate those threats.
3. Discuss and evaluate the options for outsourcing HRM/payroll cycle activities.

INTEGRATIVE CASE Alpha Omega Electronics

Like many companies, Alpha Omega Electronics (AOE) did not fully implement all modules of its new enterprise resource planning (ERP) system at the same time. It focused first on integrating the revenue and expenditure cycles with the production cycle while continuing to use its existing payroll and HRM systems. Thus, like many companies, AOE currently has separate HRM and payroll systems. The payroll system, which is under the accounting department's control, produces employee paychecks and maintains the related records as required by government regulations. The payroll system uses batch processing because employees are paid biweekly. The HRM system, which the human resources department runs, maintains files on employee job history, skills, and benefits; these files are updated weekly. Each system maintains its own separate files, sometimes storing the same data, such as pay rates, in different formats. This practice makes it difficult for accounting personnel to prepare reports that combine HRM and payroll data.

Peter Wu, the new vice president for human resources at AOE, wants to address several problems with AOE's payroll and HRM activities. Payroll processing costs have risen, and employees are unhappy with the lengthy delays required to obtain information about their benefits and retirement plans. In addition, the current HRM system makes it difficult to accurately track employee skill development, which impedes evaluating the effectiveness of AOE's investment in training and continuing education. Consequently, employees find it difficult and time-consuming to obtain approval to attend professional training classes. In addition, managers have tended to hire externally to meet new staffing needs, rather than

Gary Arbach/123RF

promoting or transferring existing employees. These practices have hurt employee morale. Peter thinks that implementing the payroll and HRM modules of the ERP system will solve these problems.

Peter meets with Elizabeth Venko and Ann Brandt to discuss the process of migrating from AOE's current stand-alone payroll and HRM systems to integration of those functions in the new ERP system. Elizabeth and Ann agree that such a conversion would improve both the efficiency of payroll processing and the effectiveness of HRM. They begin developing a detailed timetable for the system conversions. As you read this chapter, think about the relationships between HRM and payroll activities and how an integrated database can make both functions more efficient and effective.

Introduction

The **human resources management (HRM)/payroll cycle** is a recurring set of business activities and related data processing operations associated with effectively managing the employee workforce. The more important tasks include the following:

human resources management (HRM)/payroll cycle - The recurring set of business activities and data processing operations associated with effectively managing the employee workforce.

1. Recruiting and hiring new employees.
2. Training.
3. Job assignment.
4. Compensation (payroll).
5. Performance evaluation.
6. Discharge of employees due to voluntary or involuntary termination.

Tasks 1 and 6 are performed only once for each employee, whereas tasks 2 through 5 are performed repeatedly for as long as an employee works for the company. In most companies, these six activities are split between two separate systems. Task 4, compensating employees, is the payroll system's primary function. (In addition, as discussed in Chapter 16, the payroll system also allocates labor costs to products and departments for use in product pricing and mix decisions.) The HRM system performs the other five tasks. In many companies, these two systems are organizationally separate: The HRM system is usually the responsibility of the director of human resources, whereas the controller manages the payroll system. However, as Figure 17-1 shows, ERP systems integrate the two sets of activities.

This chapter focuses primarily on the payroll system because accountants have traditionally been responsible for this function. We begin by describing the design of the integrated HRM/payroll system and discuss the basic controls necessary to ensure that it provides management with reliable information and complies with government regulations. We then describe in detail each of the basic payroll cycle activities. We conclude with a discussion of options for outsourcing both payroll and HRM functions.

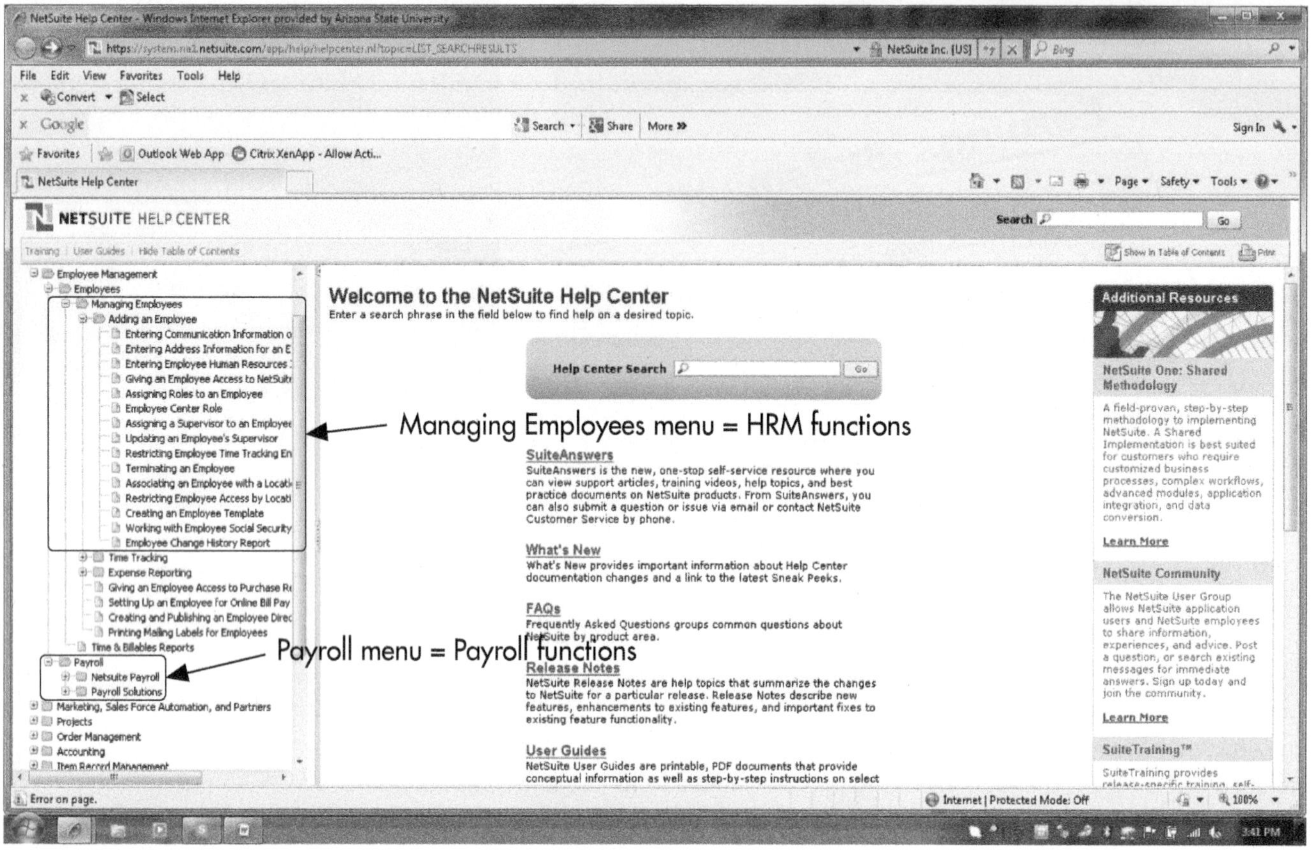

FIGURE 17-1

Integration of HRM and Payroll Functions in Typical ERP System
Source: 2010 © NetSuite Inc.

HRM/Payroll Cycle Information System

Figure 17-2 depicts the portion of an ERP system that supports the HRM/payroll cycle. The HRM-related activities (information about hiring, firing, transfers, training, etc.) and the collection of information about the use of employee time occur daily. The actual processing of payroll, however, occurs only periodically because in most organizations employees are paid on a weekly, biweekly, or monthly basis rather than every day. Thus, payroll is one application that continues to be processed in batch mode.

OVERVIEW OF HRM PROCESS AND INFORMATION NEEDS

Organizational success depends on skilled and motivated employees because their knowledge and skills affect the quality of the goods and services provided to customers. Indeed, in professional service organizations, such as accounting and law firms, employees' knowledge and skills *are* the principal component of the company's product, and labor costs represent the major expense incurred in generating revenues. Even in manufacturing firms, where direct labor costs represent only a fraction of total direct costs, employees are a key cost driver in that the quality of their work affects both overall productivity and product defect rates. Thus, it is not surprising to find that some stock analysts believe that employee skills and knowledge may be worth several times the value of a company's tangible assets, such as inventory, property, and equipment.

To effectively utilize the organization's employees, the HRM/payroll system must collect and store the information managers need to answer the following kinds of questions:

- How many employees does the organization need to accomplish its strategic plans?
- Which employees possess specific skills?

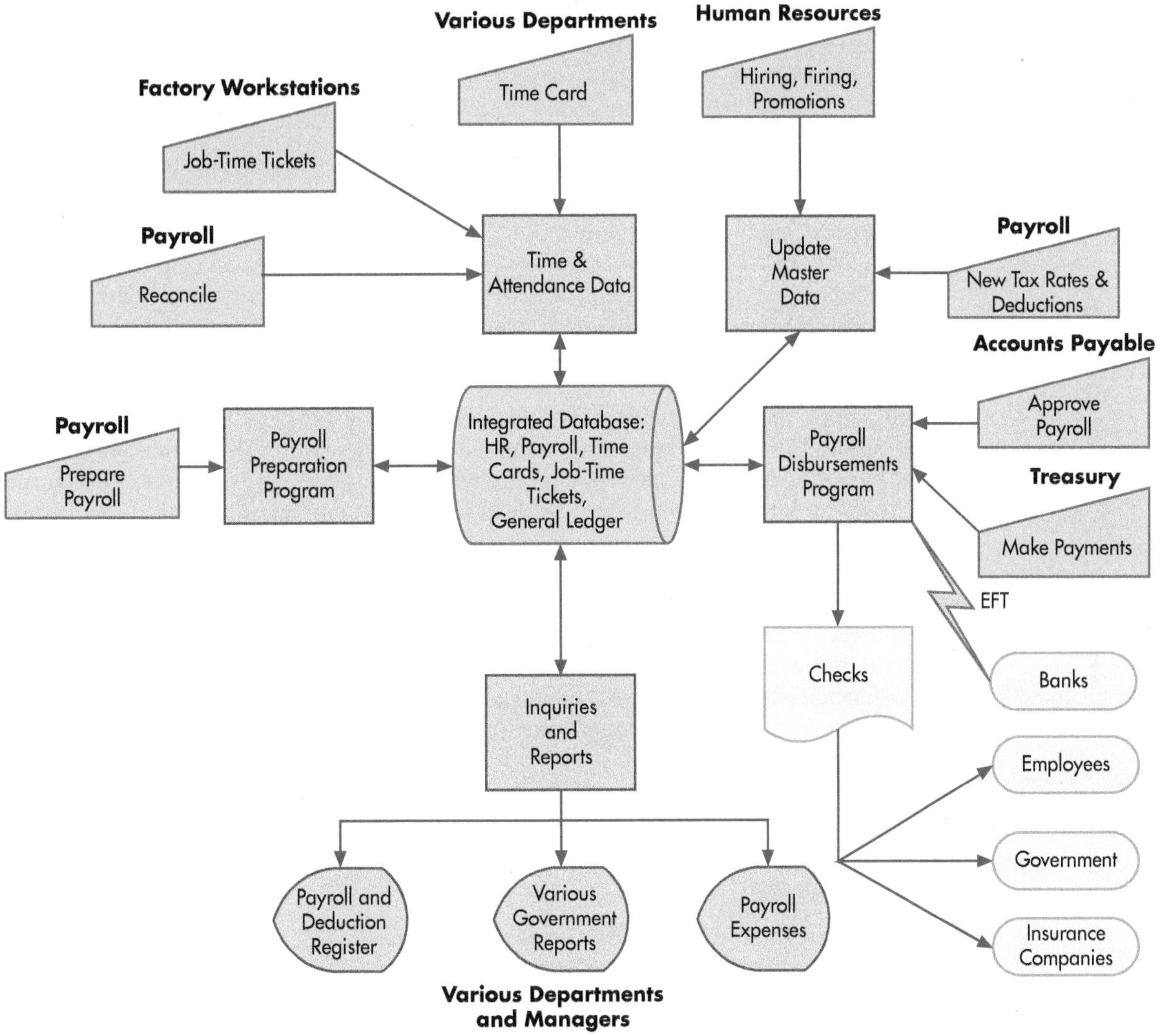

FIGURE 17-2

Portion of ERP System That Supports Human Resources Management and Payroll

- Which skills are in short supply? Which skills are in oversupply?
- How effective are current training programs in maintaining and improving employee skill levels?
- Is overall performance improving or declining?
- Are there problems with turnover, tardiness, or absenteeism?

The HRM/payroll master database (Figure 17-2) provides some of the information needed to answer those questions. However, it typically contains only descriptive information, such as which employees possess which skills and who has attended various training programs. Although such information enables managers to make staffing-related decisions, it does not help leverage the specific knowledge and expertise possessed by their employees.

To more effectively use employees' knowledge and skills, many organizations have invested in knowledge management systems. **Knowledge management systems** not only serve as a directory identifying the areas of expertise possessed by individual employees but also capture and store that knowledge so that it can be shared and used by others. Knowledge management systems can significantly improve productivity. For example, professional consulting firms often provide similar services to many different clients. Knowledge management software enables consultants to store their solutions to specific problems in a shared database. Oftentimes, those solutions can be used as a template to address the needs of other clients.

knowledge management systems - Software that stores and organizes expertise possessed by individual employees so the knowledge can be shared and used by others.

Such reuse of knowledge saves time on future engagements. Access to the shared database also enables employees to learn from geographically dispersed colleagues who have had prior experience in addressing a particular issue.

Recognizing the value of employees' knowledge and skills can help companies better understand the true costs associated with excessive turnover. In addition to the direct expenses associated with the hiring process (advertising, background checks, interviewing candidates, etc.), there are also the costs associated with hiring temporary help, training new employees, and the reduced productivity of new employees until they fully learn how to perform their tasks. Thus, estimates place the total costs to replace an employee at about 1.5 times the annual salary. Consequently, organizations that experience below-industry-average turnover rates reap considerable cost savings compared to rivals with higher turnover rates. For example, consider two companies, each with 1,500 employees earning on average $50,000. One company experiences 20% annual turnover, the other only 8%. The company with 20% annual turnover would incur costs of $22.5 million (300 employees times $75,000) to replace employees, compared to only $9 million (120 employees times $75,000) for the company experiencing only 8% annual turnover. Of course, some turnover will always occur and may even be desirable. For example, professional consulting organizations have traditionally encouraged some level of turnover because they believe it provides an important source of new ideas. The key is to control and manage turnover rates so that they are not excessive.

Employee morale is also important. Low employee morale creates financial costs when it results in turnover. Conversely, there is increasing evidence that high employee morale provides financial benefits because it improves the quality of service provided to customers. Indeed, research has found a positive correlation between employee attitudes and financial performance, particularly in highly competitive industries.[1] Thus, it is not surprising that many companies take steps like those described in Focus 17-1 to improve working conditions and morale.

THREATS AND CONTROLS

Figure 17-2 shows that all HRM/payroll cycle activities depend on the integrated database that contains information about employees, payroll, and use of employee time. Therefore, the first general threat listed in Table 17-1 is inaccurate or invalid master data. Inaccurate employee master data could result in over- or understaffing. It can also create inefficiencies due to assigning employees to perform tasks for which they are not fully qualified. Inaccurate payroll master data that results in errors in paying employees can create significant morale issues. In addition, the organization may incur fines for errors made in paying payroll taxes. Errors in data about use of employee time can result in inaccurate performance evaluations and mistakes in calculating the costs of the organization's products and services.

One way to mitigate the threat of inaccurate or invalid master data is to use the various processing integrity controls discussed in Chapter 13 to minimize the risk of data input errors (control 1.1). It is also important to restrict access to that data and configure the system so that only authorized employees can make changes to master data (control 1.2). This requires changing the default configurations of employee roles in ERP systems to appropriately segregate incompatible duties. For example, consider the situation where a payroll clerk types in the name of an employee who is not currently in the database. The default configurations of most integrated ERP systems would respond by asking whether the clerk wants to create a new employee record. This violates segregation of duties by permitting the person who does the recording (payroll) to also authorize the creation of new accounts. Similarly, the default configurations of many systems permit payroll staff not only to read but also to change the salary information in the employee payroll master file. These examples are just some of the many areas that the controller or CFO needs to review to ensure that various employees

[1] Alex Edmans, "Does the Stock Market Fully Value Intangibles? Employee Satisfaction and Equity Prices" (June 2010), SSRN.com/abstract=985735; Rajiv D. Banker and Raj Mashruwala, "The Moderating Role of Competition in the Relationship between Nonfinancial Measures and Future Financial Performance," Contemporary Accounting Research (24:3, Fall 2007): pp. 763–793.

FOCUS 17-1 The Value of Understanding Employee Jobs and Attitudes

Companies are implementing a number of initiatives to improve employee morale because it can reduce costs and improve productivity. One common technique that can be used whenever output can be clearly measured is to provide employees with more flexibility in terms of when and where they work. For example, Wilkin & Guttenplan PC, a mid-sized firm in New Jersey, has embraced flexible work arrangements and has been listed as one of the top places to work in New Jersey for years. Flexibility works best, however, when performance evaluations are based on results-based measures (e.g., number of tasks completed) rather than time-based measures (e.g., hours billed).

Another morale-boosting action is to improve the transparency of pay-for-performance compensation schemes by publishing the formulas and criteria used to determine raises. Such transparency reduces misunderstandings that can hurt morale and increase turnover. Firms are also eliminating antiquated policies that prohibit employees from discussing their salaries. However, few companies disclose each employee's compensation, especially when the work requires a high degree of collaboration and team effort, because most people grossly overestimate their own contributions and underestimate that of others.

Another innovation is encouraging employees to take paid time off without fear that doing so will harm career progression. For example, High Rock Accounting, a small firm in Tempe, Arizona, offers financial incentives to encourage staff to take vacations. The firm reimburses employees up to $1,000 for personal travel, but only if the employee "unplugs" by turning off work email during their time off. The firm benefits by having happier and more motivated staff, which translates into overall increases in productivity. Having everyone take time off also forces staff to learn new skills so that they can cover for one another.

are assigned only those privileges necessary to perform their specified job duties. Although the procedures for modifying configurations vary across different software packages, knowing what changes need to be made requires only a sound understanding of proper segregation of duties for different business processes. However, since such preventive controls can never be 100% effective, Table 17-1 also indicates that an important detective control is to regularly produce a report of all changes to master data and review them to verify that the database remains accurate (control 1.3).

A second general threat in the HRM/payroll cycle is unauthorized disclosure of sensitive information, such as salary and performance evaluations for individual employees. Such disclosures can create morale problems if employees learn that their pay differs significantly from co-workers. In addition, unauthorized disclosure of performance evaluations or reasons for firing an employee may subject the organization to lawsuits. The best control procedure for reducing the risk of unauthorized disclosure of payroll data is using multifactor authentication and physical security controls to restrict access to HRM/payroll master data to only those employees who need such access to perform their jobs (control 2.1). It is also important to configure the system to limit employees' ability to use the system's built-in query capabilities to indirectly infer sensitive information. For example, queries about salary averages should be allowed only if the query set is sufficiently large. Otherwise, someone could infer another employee's salary by writing a query that calculates the average salary for two people: the query writer and the employee of interest. Encrypting the database (control 2.2) provides additional protection by making the information unintelligible to anyone who succeeds in obtaining unauthorized access to the database. Encryption also prevents information technology (IT) employees who do not have access to the ERP system from using operating system utilities to view sensitive information. Tokenization (control 2.3) of employee IDs or Social Security Numbers further protects payroll data from "snooping" by the employees who are authorized to run payroll.

A third general threat in the HRM/payroll cycle concerns the loss or destruction of master data. The best way to mitigate the risk of this threat is to employ the backup and disaster recovery procedures (control 3.1) that were discussed in Chapter 13.

A fourth general threat in the HRM/payroll cycle is hiring unqualified or larcenous employees. Hiring unqualified employees can increase production expenses, and hiring

TABLE 17-1 Threats and Controls in the Payroll/HRM Cycle

Activity	Threat	Controls (first number refers to the corresponding threat)
General issues throughout entire HRM/ payroll cycle	1. Inaccurate or invalid master data 2. Unauthorized disclosure of sensitive information 3. Loss or destruction of data 4. Hiring unqualified or larcenous employees 5. Violations of employment laws	1.1 Data processing integrity controls 1.2 Restriction of access to master data 1.3 Review of all changes to master data 2.1 Access controls 2.2 Encryption 2.3 Tokenization 3.1 Backup and disaster recovery procedures 4.1 Sound hiring procedures, including verification of job applicants' credentials, skills, references, and employment history 4.2 Criminal background investigation checks of all applicants for finance-related positions 5.1 Thorough documentation of hiring, performance evaluation, and dismissal procedures 5.2 Continuing education on changes in employment laws
Update payroll master data	6. Unauthorized changes to payroll master data 7. Inaccurate updating of payroll master data	6.1 Segregation of duties: HRM department updates master data, but only payroll department issues paychecks 6.2 Access controls 7.1 Data processing integrity controls 7.2 Regular review of all changes to master payroll data
Validate time and attendance data	8. Inaccurate time and attendance data	8.1 Source data automation for data capture 8.2 Biometric authentication 8.3 Segregation of duties (reconciliation of job-time tickets to time cards) 8.4 Supervisory review
Prepare payroll	9. Errors in processing payroll	9.1 Data processing integrity controls: batch totals, cross-footing of the payroll register, use of a payroll clearing account and a zero-balance check 9.2 Supervisory review of payroll register and other reports 9.3 Issuing earnings statements to employees 9.4 Review of IRS guidelines to ensure proper classification of workers as either employees or independent contractors
Disburse payroll	10. Theft or fraudulent distribution of paychecks	10.1 Restriction of physical access to blank payroll checks and the check signature machine 10.2 Restriction of access to the EFT system 10.3 Prenumbering and periodically accounting for all payroll checks and review of all EFT direct deposit transactions 10.4 Require proper supporting documentation for all paychecks 10.5 Use of a separate checking account for payroll, maintained as an imprest fund 10.6 Segregation of duties (cashier versus accounts payable; check distribution from hiring/firing; independent reconciliation of the payroll checking account) 10.7 Restriction of access to payroll master database 10.8 Verification of identity of all employees receiving paychecks 10.9 Redepositing unclaimed paychecks and investigating cause
Disburse payroll taxes and miscellaneous deductions	11. Failure to make required payments 12. Untimely payments 13. Inaccurate payments	11.1 Configuration of system to make required payments using current instructions from IRS (Publication Circular E) 12.1 Same as 11.1 13.1 Processing integrity controls 13.2 Supervisory review of reports 13.3 Employee review of earnings statement

a larcenous employee can result in the theft of assets. Both problems are best dealt with by appropriate hiring procedures (control 4.1). Skill qualifications for each open position should be stated explicitly in the position control report. Candidates should be asked to sign a statement on the job application form that confirms the accuracy of the information being submitted and provides their consent to a thorough background check of their credentials and employment history. Independent verification of an applicant's credentials is important because résumés often contain false or embellished information. For example, the *Wall Street Journal* has reported a number of cases where résumés for senior executives at companies contained information that could not be verified; in some cases, the executive resigned or was fired. To reduce the risk of hiring larcenous employees, organizations should hire a professional firm to perform thorough background checks (control 4.2) of all applicants for positions that involve access to financial data and assets to identify applicants with a prior criminal record.

The fifth general threat in the HRM/payroll cycle is violation of applicable laws and regulations concerning the proper hiring and dismissal of employees. The government imposes stiff penalties on firms that violate provisions of employment law. In addition, organizations can also be subject to civil suits by alleged victims of employment discrimination. Table 17-1 shows that the best control procedure to mitigate these potential problems is to carefully document all actions relating to advertising for, recruiting, and hiring new employees and to the dismissal of employees (control 5.1); this will demonstrate compliance with the applicable government regulations. Continued training (control 5.2) to keep current with employment law is also important.

Payroll Cycle Activities

Figure 17-3 presents a context diagram of the payroll system. It shows that there are five major sources of inputs to the payroll system. The HRM department provides information about hirings, terminations, and pay-rate changes due to raises and promotions. Employees initiate changes in their discretionary deductions (e.g., contributions to retirement plans). The various departments provide data about actual hours employees work. Government agencies provide tax rates and instructions for meeting regulatory requirements. Similarly, insurance companies and other organizations provide instructions for calculating and remitting various withholdings.

Figure 17-3 shows that checks (which may be electronic) are the payroll system's principal output. Employees receive individual *paychecks* in compensation for their services. A *payroll check* is sent to the bank to transfer funds from the company's regular accounts to its payroll account. Checks also are issued to government agencies, insurance companies, and other organizations to meet company obligations (e.g., taxes, insurance premiums). In addition, the payroll system produces a variety of reports, which we discuss later, for internal and external use.

Figure 17-4 shows the basic activities performed in the payroll cycle. We now discuss each of those activities. For each activity, we describe how the information needed to perform and manage the activity is collected, processed, and stored. We also explain the controls necessary to ensure not only the reliability of that information but also the safeguarding of the organization's resources.

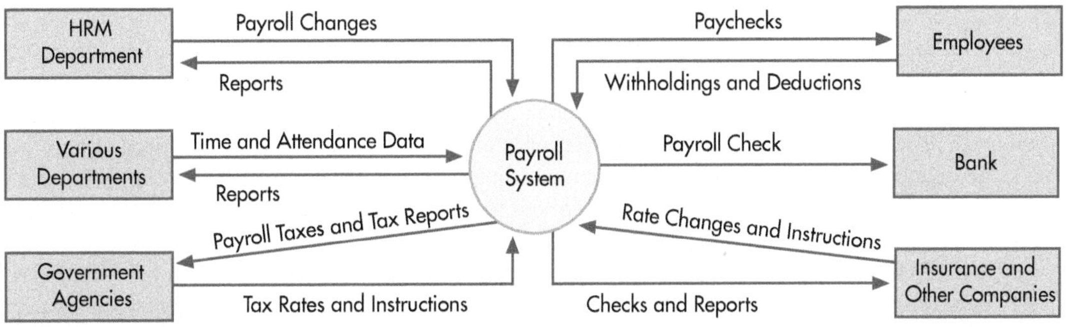

FIGURE 17-3
Context Diagram of the Payroll Portion of the HRM/Payroll Cycle

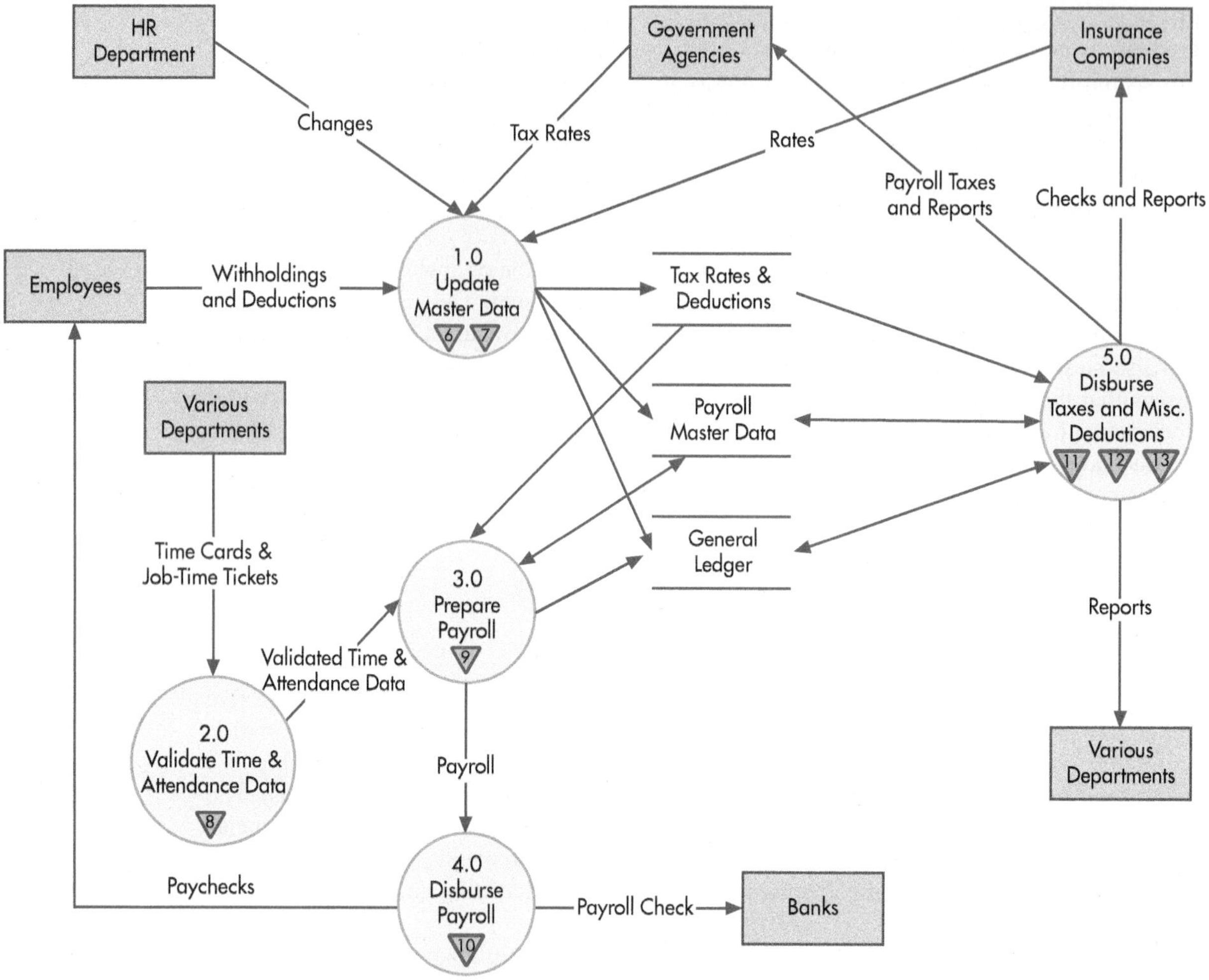

FIGURE 17-4
Level 0 Data Flow Diagram for the Payroll Cycle

UPDATE PAYROLL MASTER DATABASE

The first activity in the HRM/payroll cycle involves updating the payroll master database to reflect various types of internally initiated changes: new hires, terminations, changes in pay rates, or changes in discretionary withholdings (circle 1.0 in Figure 17-4). In addition, periodically the master data needs to be updated to reflect changes in tax rates and deductions for insurance.

PROCESS Figure 17-2 shows that the HRM department is responsible for updating the payroll master database for internally initiated changes related to employment, whereas the payroll department updates information about tax rates and other payroll deductions when it receives notification of changes from various government units and insurance companies. Although payroll is processed in batch mode, the HRM department has online access to update the payroll master database so that all payroll changes are entered in a timely manner and are properly reflected in the next pay period. Records of employees who quit or are fired should not be deleted immediately, however, because some year-end tax reports, including W-2 forms, require data about all employees who worked for the organization at any time during the year.

THREATS AND CONTROLS Unauthorized changes to payroll master data (threat 6 in Table 17-1) can result in increased expenses from unjustified payments to employees. Proper segregation of duties (control 6.1) is the key control procedure for dealing with this threat. As shown in Figure 17-2, only the HRM department should be able to update the payroll master file for hirings, firings, pay raises, and promotions. HRM department employees in turn should not directly participate in payroll processing or paycheck distribution. This segregation of duties prevents someone with access to paychecks from creating fictitious employees or altering pay rates and then intercepting those fraudulent checks. In addition, all changes to the payroll master file should be reviewed and approved by someone other than the person recommending the change. To facilitate this review, the system should be configured to produce a report listing all payroll-related changes and send the report to each affected department supervisor for review.

Controlling access to the payroll system (control 6.2) is also important. The system should be configured to compare user IDs and passwords with an access control matrix that (1) defines what actions each employee is allowed to perform and (2) confirms what files each employee is allowed to access.

Another threat is inaccurate updating of payroll master data, which can result in errors in paying employees and fines for not remitting proper amounts of payroll taxes to the government. To mitigate this threat, appropriate processing integrity controls discussed in Chapter 13, such as validity checks on employee number and reasonableness tests for the changes being made, should be applied to all payroll change transactions (control 7.1). In addition, having department managers review (control 7.2) reports of all changes to employees in their department provides a timely way to detect errors.

VALIDATE TIME AND ATTENDANCE DATA

The second step in the payroll cycle is to validate each employee's time and attendance data (circle 2.0 in Figure 17-4).

PROCESS How employee time and attendance data is collected differs depending on the employee's pay status. For employees paid on an hourly basis, many companies use a **time card** to record the employee's daily arrival and departure times. Employees who earn a fixed salary (e.g., managers and professional staff) seldom record their labor efforts on time cards. Instead, their supervisors informally monitor their presence on the job.

time card - A document that records the employee's arrival and departure times for each work shift.

As discussed in Chapter 16, manufacturing companies also use job-time tickets to record detailed data about how employees use their time (i.e., which jobs they perform). The job-time ticket data are used to allocate labor costs among various departments, cost centers, and production jobs. Professionals in such service organizations as accounting, law, and consulting firms similarly track the time they spend performing various tasks and for which clients, recording that data on a **time sheet** (see Figure 17-5 for an example of a data entry screen to track time). Their employers use the time sheets to assign costs and accurately bill clients for services provided.

time sheet - A data entry screen (or paper document) used by salaried professionals to record how much time was spent performing various tasks for specific clients.

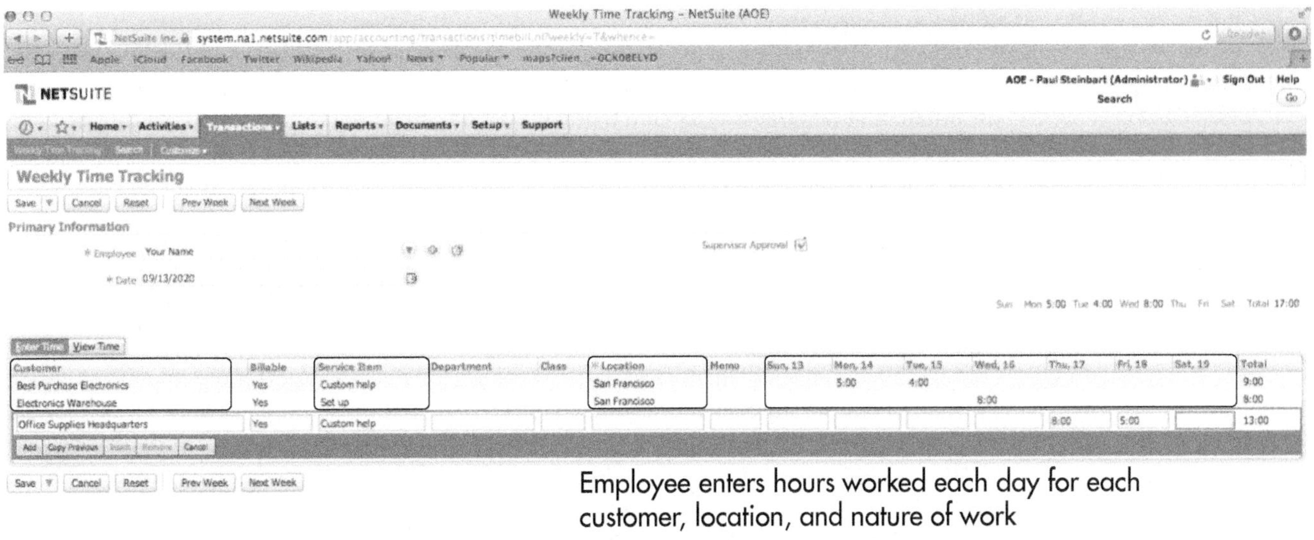
Employee enters hours worked each day for each customer, location, and nature of work

FIGURE 17-5

Example of Data Entry Screen to Track Time (Time Sheet)

Source: 2010 © NetSuite Inc.

Sales staff often are paid either on a straight commission or on a salary plus commission basis. This requires the staff to carefully record the amount of their sales. In addition, some sales staff are paid bonuses for exceeding targets. An increasing number of companies in the United States are extending such incentive bonuses to employees other than sales staff, to motivate employees to improve their productivity and work quality. For example, Nucor Corporation, one of the largest steel producers in the United States, pays its steelworkers an hourly rate plus a bonus based on the tons of steel they produce and ship. Companies have long used stock options to reward executives; in recent years, many companies have extended this practice to their nonexecutive employees as well. The argument is that stock options motivate employees to actively look for ways to improve service and cut costs so that the value of their compensation package rises.

Using incentives, commissions, and bonuses requires linking the payroll system and the information systems of sales and other cycles to collect the data used to calculate bonuses. Moreover, the bonus/incentive schemes must be properly designed with realistic, attainable goals that can be objectively measured. It is also important that goals be congruent with corporate objectives and that managers monitor goals to ensure that they continue to be appropriate. Indeed, poorly designed incentive pay schemes can result in undesirable behavior. For example, an auto repair business experienced unintended negative effects from implementing a new incentive plan that paid its repair staff a commission based on the amount of parts sold and number of hours worked. The intent was to focus employees' attention on how their efforts affected the company's bottom line. The result, however, was a scandal in which it was alleged that employees recommended unnecessary repairs to boost their own pay. The alleged abuses reduced public trust in the company and led to lower revenues. Although the company discontinued use of this incentive system, it took years to fully regain the consumer trust it had lost. Besides the possibility of creating unintended and undesirable behaviors, poorly designed incentive pay schemes can also run afoul of legal, tax, and regulatory requirements. For example, members of the Board of Directors compensation committee may not understand all the details of tax regulations, such as the Employee Retirement Income Security Act (ERISA), which limit the allowable differences between the benefit packages offered to executives and those offered to other employees. Thus, accountants should be involved in reviewing a company's compensation practices.

THREATS AND CONTROLS The main threat to this payroll activity is inaccurate time and attendance data. Inaccuracies in time and attendance records can result in increased labor expenses and erroneous labor expense reports. Moreover, inaccuracies can either hurt employee morale (if paychecks are incorrect or missing) or result in payments for labor services not rendered.

Source data automation (control 8.1) can reduce the risk of *unintentional* errors in collecting time and attendance data. For example, badge readers can be used to collect job-time data for production employees and automatically feed the data to the payroll processing system. Using technology to capture time and attendance data can also improve productivity and cut costs. For example, the retail chain Meijer, Inc. installed fingerprint readers at its cash registers so that employees could log in and immediately begin working. The company estimates that this eliminated several minutes of wasted time spent walking from the time clock in the back of the store to the register. Saving a few minutes per employee may not sound dramatic, but when multiplied across thousands of employees in an industry with a profit margin of less than 1%, the effect on the bottom line can be significant. Source data automation can also be used to collect time and attendance data for professional service staff. For example, AT&T's internal service staff uses touch-tone telephones to log in time spent on various tasks, thereby eliminating the use of paper time sheets. Various data processing integrity checks discussed in Chapter 13, such as a limit check on hours worked and a validity check on employee number, ensure the accuracy of that information.

IT can also reduce the risk of *intentional* inaccuracies in time and attendance data. For example, some manufacturing companies now use biometric authentication techniques (control 8.2), such as hand scans, to verify the identity of the employee who is clocking in and out

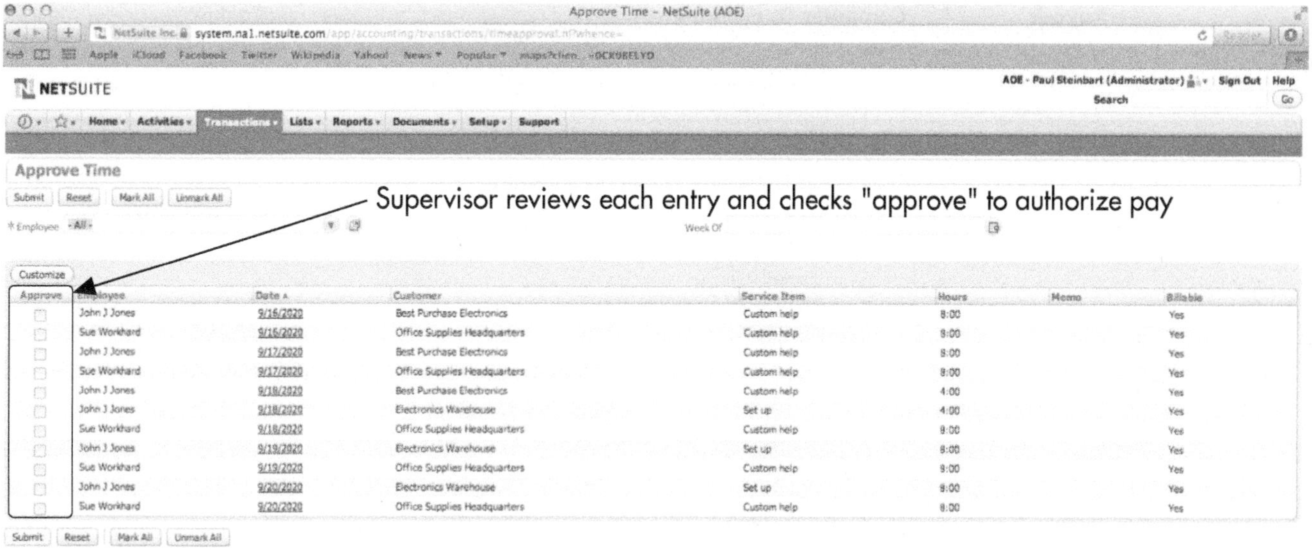

FIGURE 17-6

Example of Supervisory Approval of Time Worked Screen
Source: 2010 © NetSuite Inc.

of work. The objective is to prevent an employee from leaving work early but having a friend falsely record that person as being at work. Segregation of duties (control 8.3) is also important. Time card data, used for calculating payroll, should be reconciled to the job-time ticket data, used for costing and managerial purposes, by someone not involved in generating that data. The total time spent on all tasks, as recorded on the job-time tickets, should not exceed the attendance time indicated on an employee's time card. Conversely, all time spent at work should be accounted for on the job-time tickets.

In addition, requiring departmental supervisors to review and approve time cards and job-time tickets (see Figure 17-6, which illustrates one way to implement control 8.4) provides a detective control on the accuracy of time and attendance data. Supervisory review is particularly important for employees who telecommute. Analysis of system logs can provide assurance that telecommuters are truly working the amount of time for which they are getting paid and that they are not operating a personal business on the side, using company-provided assets.

PREPARE PAYROLL

The third step in the payroll cycle is preparing payroll (circle 3.0 in Figure 17-4).

PROCESS Figure 17-7 shows the sequence of activities in processing payroll. First, payroll transaction data is edited, and the validated transactions are then sorted by employee number. If the organization is processing payrolls from several divisions, each of these payroll transaction files must also be merged. The sorted payroll transactions file is then used to prepare employee paychecks. For each employee, the payroll master file record and corresponding transaction record are read, and gross pay is calculated. For hourly employees, the number of hours worked is multiplied by the wage rate, and then any applicable premiums for overtime or bonuses are added. For salaried employees, gross pay is a fraction of the annual salary, where the fraction reflects the length of the pay period. For example, salaried employees paid monthly would receive one-twelfth of their annual salary each pay period. Any applicable commissions, bonuses, and other incentives are also included in calculating gross pay.

Next, all payroll deductions are summed, and the total is subtracted from gross pay to obtain net pay. Payroll deductions fall into two broad categories: payroll tax withholdings and

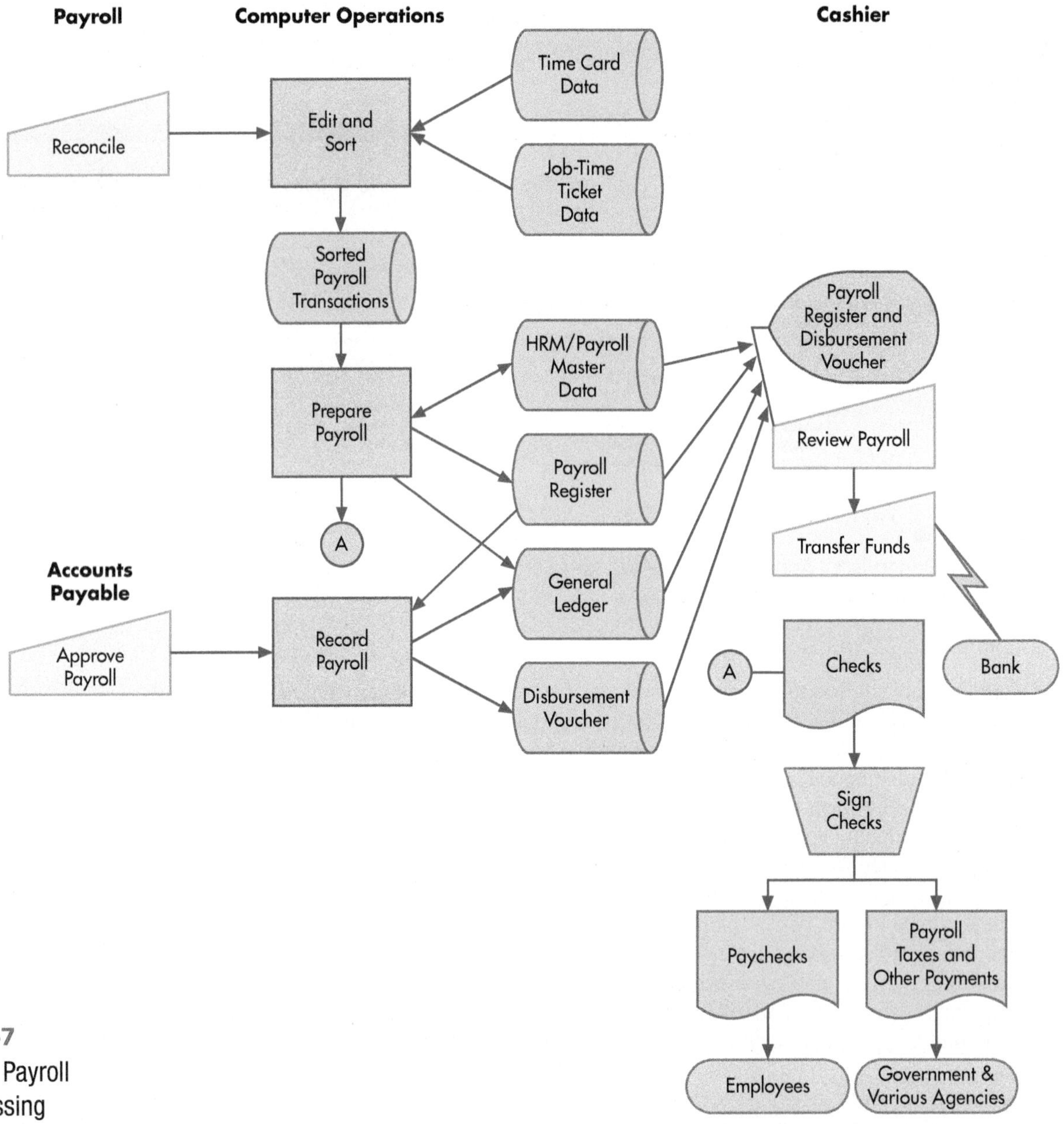

FIGURE 17-7
Flowchart of Payroll Batch Processing

voluntary deductions. The former includes federal, state, and local income taxes, as well as Social Security taxes. Voluntary deductions include contributions to a pension plan; premiums for group life, health, and disability insurance; union dues; and contributions to various charities.

Once net pay is calculated, the year-to-date fields for gross pay, deductions, and net pay in each employee's record in the payroll master file are updated. Maintaining accurate cumulative earnings records is important for two reasons. First, because Social Security tax withholdings and other deductions have cutoffs, the company must know when to cease deductions for individual employees. Second, this information is needed to ensure that the appropriate amounts of taxes and other deductions are remitted to government agencies, insurance companies, and various charitable organizations. This information also must be included in the various reports filed with those agencies.

payroll register - A listing of payroll data for each employee for a payroll period.

deduction register - A report listing the miscellaneous voluntary deductions for each employee.

Next, the payroll and deduction registers are created. The **payroll register** lists each employee's gross pay, payroll deductions, and net pay in a multicolumn format. It also serves as the supporting documentation to authorize transferring funds to the organization's payroll checking account. The **deduction register** lists the miscellaneous voluntary deductions for each employee. Figure 17-8 presents examples of these two reports.

Alpha Omega Electronics			PAYROLL REGISTER					Period Ended 12/03/2020	
					Deductions				
Employee No.	Name	Hours	Pay Rate	Gross Pay	Fed. Tax	FICA	State Tax	Misc.	Net Pay
37884	Jarvis	40.0	6.25	250.00	35.60	18.75	16.25	27.60	151.80
37885	Burke	43.6	6.50	295.10	42.40	22.13	19.18	40.15	171.24
37886	Lincoln	40.0	6.75	270.00	39.20	20.25	17.55	27.90	165.10
37887	Douglass	44.2	7.00	324.10	46.60	24.31	21.07	29.62	202.50

Alpha Omega Electronics			DEDUCTION REGISTER			Period Ended 12/03/2020	
		Miscellaneous Deductions					
Employee No.	Name	Health Ins.	Life Ins.	Retirement	Union Dues	Savings Bond	Total Misc.
37884	Jarvis	10.40	5.50	7.50	4.20	0.00	27.60
37885	Burke	11.60	5.50	8.85	4.20	10.00	40.15
37886	Lincoln	10.40	5.20	8.10	4.20	0.00	27.90
37887	Douglass	10.20	5.50	9.72	4.20	0.00	29.62

FIGURE 17-8
Examples of Payroll and Deduction Registers

Finally, the system prints employee paychecks (or facsimiles, in the case of direct deposit). These also typically include an **earnings statement**, which lists the amount of gross pay, deductions, and net pay for the current period and year-to-date totals for each category.

earnings statement - A report listing the amount of gross pay, deductions, and net pay for the current period and the year-to-date totals for each category.

As each payroll transaction is processed, the system also allocates labor costs to the appropriate general ledger accounts by checking the code on the job-time ticket record. The system maintains a running total of these allocations until all employee payroll records have been processed. These totals, and the column totals in the payroll register, form the basis for the summary journal entry, which is posted to the general ledger after all paychecks have been printed.

The payroll system also produces a number of detailed reports. Table 17-2 describes the content of the most common reports. Some of these are for internal use, but many are required by various government agencies. Consequently, as Figure 17-9 shows, the HRM/payroll portion of ERP systems provides extensive support for meeting the reporting requirements of federal, state, and local governments.

THREATS AND CONTROLS The complexity of payroll processing, especially the various tax law requirements, makes it susceptible to errors (threat 9 in Table 17-1). Errors obviously can hurt employee morale, particularly if paychecks are late. In addition to incorrect payroll expense records and reports, processing errors can lead to penalties if the errors result in failure to remit the proper amount of payroll taxes due the government. Similarly, failure to accurately implement garnishments on employees' wages and remit those funds to the appropriate party can also lead to financial penalties.

Table 17-1 lists three types of data processing integrity controls (control 9.1) that can mitigate the threat of payroll errors:

1. ***Batch totals.*** Even advanced HRM/payroll systems continue to use batch processing for payroll. Consequently, batch totals should be calculated at the time of data entry and then checked against comparable totals calculated during each stage of processing. Hash totals of employee numbers, for example, are particularly useful. If the original and subsequent hash totals of employee numbers agree, it means that (1) all payroll records have been processed, (2) data input was accurate, and (3) no bogus time cards were entered during processing. If the batch totals do not agree, the organization has timely evidence of a payroll error (most likely a failure to generate a paycheck for an employee) so that the problem can be promptly corrected.

TABLE 17-2 Contents and Purpose of Commonly Generated HRM/Payroll Reports

Report Name	Contents	Purpose
Cumulative earnings register	Cumulative year-to-date gross pay, net pay, and deductions for each employee	Used for employee information and annual payroll reports
Workforce inventory	List of employees by department	Used in preparing labor-related reports for government agencies
Position control report	List of each authorized position, job qualifications, budgeted salary, and position status (filled or vacant)	Used in planning future workforce needs
Skills inventory report	List of employees and current skills	Useful in planning future workforce needs and training programs
Form 941	Employer's quarterly federal tax return (showing all wages subject to tax and amounts withheld for income tax and FICA)	Filed quarterly to reconcile monthly tax payments with total tax liability for the quarter
Form W-2	Report of wages and withholdings for each employee	Sent to each employee for use in preparing individual tax returns; due by January 31
Form W-3	Summary of all W-2 forms	Sent to federal government along with a copy of all W-2 forms; due by February 28
Form 1099-Misc.	Report of income paid to independent contractors	Sent to recipients of income for use in filing their income tax returns; due by January 31
Various other reports to government agencies	Data on compliance with various regulatory provisions, state and local tax reports, etc.	To document compliance with applicable regulations

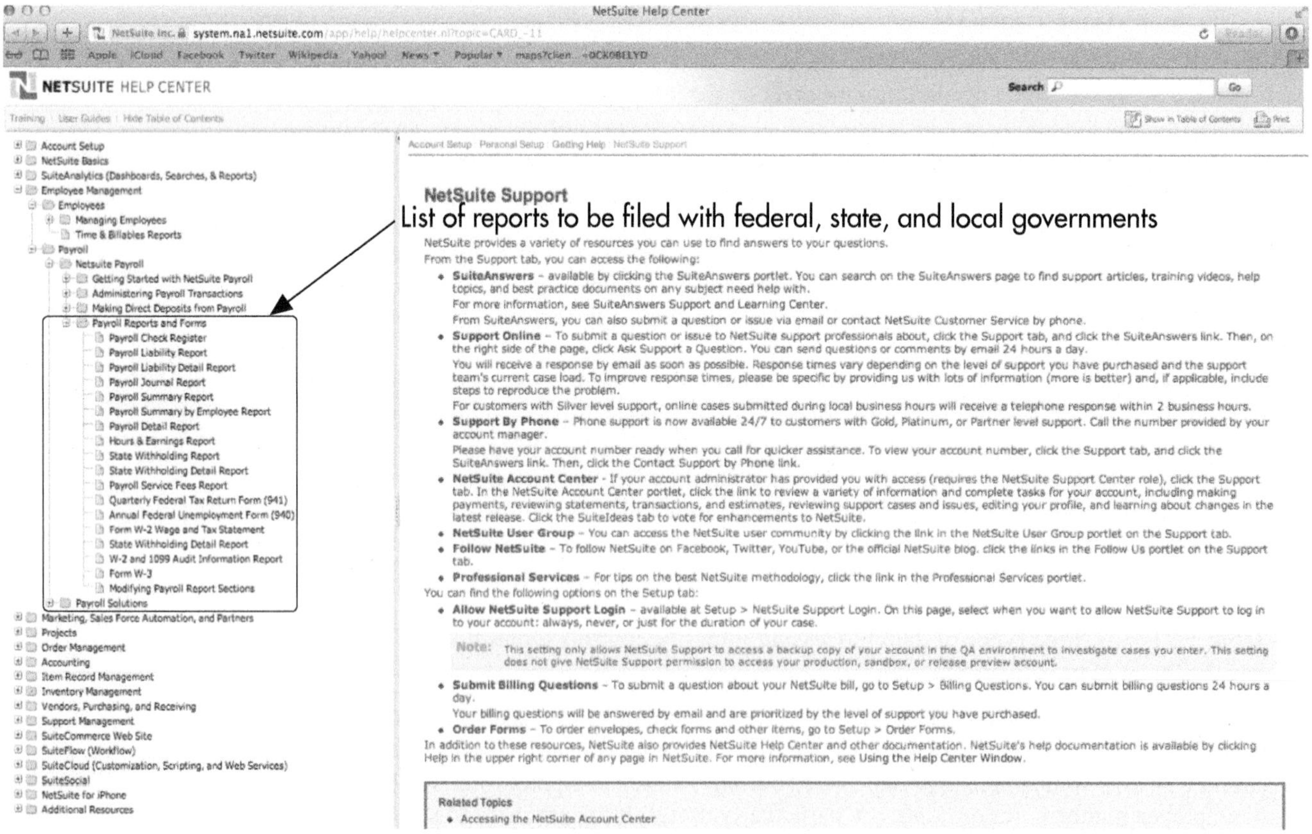

FIGURE 17-9

Screenshot Showing Typical ERP System Support for Payroll-Related Reports Required for Federal, State, and Local Governments

Source: 2010 © NetSuite Inc.

2. ***Cross-footing the payroll register.*** The total of the net pay column should equal the total of gross pay less total deductions. If it does not, an error occurred in processing that needs to be promptly investigated and corrected.
3. ***A payroll clearing account.*** The **payroll clearing account** is a general ledger account used in a two-step process to check the accuracy and completeness of recording payroll costs and their subsequent allocation to appropriate cost centers. First, the payroll clearing account is debited for the amount of gross pay; cash is credited for the amount of net pay, and the various withholdings are credited to separate liability accounts. Second, the cost accounting process distributes labor costs to various expense categories and credits the payroll clearing account for the sum of these allocations. The amount credited to the payroll clearing account should equal the amount that was previously debited when net pay and the various withholdings were recorded. This particular internal check is an example of a *zero-balance check* (discussed in Chapter 13) because the payroll clearing account should equal zero once both entries have been posted.

payroll clearing account - A general ledger account used to check the accuracy and completeness of recording payroll costs and their subsequent allocation to appropriate cost centers.

In addition, supervisory review (control 9.2) of the payroll register and other reports serves as a detective control to identify payroll processing errors. Issuing employees an earnings statement (control 9.3) provides another layer of detective controls because employees are likely to report obvious errors.

It is also important to properly classify workers as either employees or independent contractors because misclassification can cause companies to owe substantial back taxes, interest, and even penalties. This issue often arises when department managers attempt to circumvent a general hiring freeze by using independent contractors. The HRM department always should review any decisions to hire temporary or outside help. The Internal Revenue Service (IRS) provides a checklist of questions that can be used to determine whether a worker should be classified as an employee or an independent contractor (control 9.4).

DISBURSE PAYROLL

The next step is the actual disbursement of paychecks to employees (circle 4.0 in Figure 17-4). Most employees are paid either by check or by direct deposit of the net pay amount into their personal bank account. Unlike cash payments, both methods provide a means to document the amount of wages paid.

PROCESS After paychecks have been prepared, accounts payable reviews and approves the payroll register. A disbursement voucher is then prepared to authorize the transfer of funds from the company's general checking account to its payroll bank account. The disbursement voucher is then used to update the general ledger.

After reviewing the payroll register and disbursement voucher, the cashier then prepares and signs a check (or initiates an electronic funds transfer [EFT] transaction) transferring funds to the company's payroll bank account. If the organization still issues paper checks, the cashier also reviews, signs, and distributes the employee paychecks. The cashier promptly redeposits any unclaimed paychecks in the company's bank account. A list of unclaimed paychecks is then sent to the internal audit department for further investigation.

Direct deposit is one way to improve the efficiency and reduce the costs of payroll processing. Employees who are paid by direct deposit generally receive a copy of the paycheck indicating the amount deposited along with an earnings statement. The payroll system must generate a series of payroll deposit files, one for each bank through which payroll deposits are made. Each file contains a record for each employee whose account is maintained at a particular bank. Each record includes the employee's name, Social Security number, bank account number, and net pay amount. These files are sent electronically to each participating bank. The funds are then electronically transferred from the employer's bank account to the employee's account. Direct deposit thus eliminates the need for the cashier to sign individual payroll checks. The cashier does, however, still have to authorize the release of funds from the organization's regular checking account.

Direct deposit provides savings to employers by eliminating the cost of purchasing, processing, and distributing paper checks. It also reduces bank fees and postage expenses. Consequently, most companies now offer their employees the option of direct deposit payment and encourage them to elect this form of payment. Some employees, however, may not have bank accounts and, therefore, cannot elect direct deposit. Organizations can still eliminate the need to issue paper payroll checks by paying such employees with payroll debit cards. Payroll debit cards are stored value cards that cannot be overdrawn, but they can be replenished with additional funds each payday. Employees can use payroll debit cards to make purchases and can withdraw available cash at ATM machines.

THREATS AND CONTROLS As Table 17-1 indicates, another major threat in the payroll process is the theft of paychecks or the issuance of paychecks to fictitious or terminated employees. This can result in increased expenses and the loss of cash.

Applying to payroll the controls related to other cash disbursements, discussed in Chapter 15, can mitigate this threat. Specifically:

- Access to blank payroll checks and to the check signature machine should be restricted (control 10.1). Similarly, ability to authorize EFT transactions should be restricted (control 10.2) and controlled through the use of strong multifactor authentication.
- All payroll checks should be sequentially prenumbered and periodically accounted for (control 10.3). If payroll is made via direct deposit, all EFT transactions should be reviewed.
- The cashier should sign all payroll checks only when supported by proper documentation (the payroll register and disbursement voucher—control 10.4).

In addition, payroll checks should not be drawn on the organization's regular bank account. Instead, for control purposes, a separate payroll bank account should be used (control 10.5). Doing so limits the company's loss exposure to the amount of cash in the separate payroll account. It also makes it easier to reconcile payroll and to detect paycheck forgery. Like petty cash, the payroll account should be operated as an imprest fund. Each payday, the amount of the check written (or EFT funds transfer) to replenish the payroll checking account should equal the amount of net pay for that period. Thus, when all paychecks have been cashed, the payroll account should have a zero balance. A separate payroll checking account also makes it easier to spot any fraudulent checks when the account is reconciled. As with the other cash disbursements discussed in Chapter 15, segregation of duties (control 10.6) is another important control. Thus, accounts payable has responsibility for recording payroll, but the cashier is responsible for distributing paychecks. It is also important that the person who distributes paychecks or authorizes EFT transactions for direct deposit has no other payroll or HRM-related duties. To see why this segregation of duties is so important, assume that the person responsible for hiring and firing employees also distributes paychecks. This combination of duties could enable that person to conveniently "forget" to report an employee's termination and subsequently keep that employee's future paychecks. In addition, the payroll bank account should be reconciled by someone who performs no other payroll or HRM duties.

Use of multifactor authentication and other controls to restrict access to the payroll master database (control 10.7) reduces the risk of creating checks for nonexistent employees. In addition, the person responsible for distributing paychecks should be required to positively identify each person picking up a paycheck (control 10.8). Further control is provided by having the internal audit department periodically observe, on a surprise basis, the paycheck distribution process to verify that all paychecks are picked up by valid employees. Internal audit should also use data analytics to identify signs of payroll fraud. For example, "ghost" (i.e., fake) employees typically have no deductions for taxes or other withholdings because if the firm remitted those monies to the government or insurance entity, the recipient would inform the company that it does not have a record of that person. Publicizing that such tests are regularly applied may deter fraudsters from attempting to create such employees.

Special procedures should be used to handle unclaimed paychecks because they indicate the possibility of a problem, such as a nonexistent or terminated employee. Unclaimed paychecks should be returned to the treasurer's office for prompt redeposit (control 10.9). They should then be traced back to time records and matched against the employee payroll master file to verify that they are indeed legitimate.

CALCULATE AND DISBURSE EMPLOYER-PAID BENEFITS, TAXES, AND VOLUNTARY EMPLOYEE DEDUCTIONS

The final payroll activity is to calculate and remit payroll taxes and employee benefits to the appropriate government or other entity (circle 5.0 in Figure 17-4).

PROCESS Employers must pay Social Security taxes in addition to the amounts withheld from employee paychecks. Federal and state laws also require employers to contribute a specified percentage of each employee's gross pay, up to a maximum annual limit, to federal and state unemployment compensation insurance funds.

In addition to mandatory tax-related disbursements, employers are responsible for ensuring that other funds deducted from employee paychecks are correctly calculated and remitted in a timely manner to the appropriate entity. Such deductions include court-ordered payments for alimony, child support, or bankruptcy. Many employers also contribute some or all of the amounts to pay for their employees' health, disability, and life insurance premiums as well as making matching contributions to retirement plans.

Many employers also offer their employees **flexible benefits plans**, under which each employee chooses some minimum coverage in medical insurance, retirement plans, and charitable contributions. Flexible benefit plans place increased demands on a company's HRM/payroll system. For example, the HRM staff of a large company with thousands of employees can spend a considerable amount of time just responding to 401(k) plan inquiries. Moreover, employees want to be able to make changes in their investment decisions on a timely basis. Organizations can satisfy employee demands for such services without increasing costs by providing access to HRM/payroll information on the company's intranet.

flexible benefits plans - Plans under which each employee receives some minimum coverage in medical insurance and pension contributions, plus additional benefit "credits" that can be used to acquire extra vacation time or additional health insurance. These plans are sometimes called *cafeteria-style benefit plans* because they offer a menu of options.

THREATS AND CONTROLS The primary threats in this activity are failing to make the necessary remittances, untimely remittances, or errors in those remittances (threats 11–13 in Table 17-1). These problems can result in fines from government agencies and employee complaints if the errors adversely affect their retirement or other benefits.

Circular E, *Employer's Tax Guide*, published by the IRS, provides detailed instructions about an employer's obligations for withholding and remitting payroll taxes and for filing various reports. To mitigate the threats of omitted or untimely remittances, the information in Circular E should be used to configure the payroll system to automatically disburse the funds when payroll is processed (controls 11.1 and 12.1). Processing integrity controls (control 13.1), such as cross-footing checks and batch totals, minimize the risk of inaccuracies. Regular supervisory review (control 13.2) of payroll reports provides a detective control. In addition, providing employees with earnings statements (control 13.3) enables them to timely detect and report any problems.

Outsourcing Options: Payroll Service Bureaus and Professional Employer Organizations

In an effort to reduce costs, many organizations outsource their payroll and HRM functions to payroll service bureaus and professional employer organizations. A **payroll service bureau** maintains the payroll master data for each of its clients and processes payroll for them. A **professional employer organization (PEO)** not only processes payroll but also provides HRM services such as employee benefit design and administration. Because they provide a narrower range of services, payroll service bureaus are generally less expensive than PEOs.

payroll service bureau - An organization that maintains the payroll master file for each of its clients and performs their payroll processing activities for a fee.

professional employer organization (PEO) - An organization that processes payroll and also provides human resource management services such as employee benefit design and administration.

When organizations outsource payroll processing, they send time and attendance data along with information about personnel changes to the payroll service bureau or PEO at the end of each pay period. The payroll service bureau or PEO then uses that data to prepare employee paychecks, earnings statements, and a payroll register. The payroll processing service also periodically produces employee W-2 forms and other tax-related reports.

Payroll service bureaus and PEOs are especially attractive to small and midsized businesses for the following reasons:

- ***Reduced costs.*** Payroll service bureaus and PEOs benefit from the economies of scale associated with preparing paychecks for a large number of companies. They can charge fees that are typically less than the cost of doing payroll in-house. A payroll service bureau or PEO also saves money by eliminating the need to develop and maintain the expertise required to comply with the constantly changing tax laws.
- ***Wider range of benefits.*** PEOs pool the costs of administering benefits across all their clients. Consequently, a PEO enables smaller companies to offer the same wide range of benefits that large companies typically provide.
- ***Freeing up of computer resources.*** A payroll service bureau or PEO eliminates one or more accounting information system (AIS) applications (payroll and benefits management). The freed-up computing resources can then be used to improve service in other areas, such as sales order entry.

As the basis for competitive advantage increasingly hinges on employees' skills and knowledge, the effective and efficient management of the payroll and HRM functions becomes increasingly important. Outsourcing may provide a way to reduce costs. However, companies need to be sure to carefully monitor service quality to ensure that the outsourced system effectively integrates HRM and payroll data in a manner that supports effective management of employees.

Summary and Case Conclusion

The HRM/payroll cycle information system consists of two related, but separate, subsystems: HRM and payroll. The HRM system records and processes data about the activities of recruiting, hiring, training, assigning, evaluating, and discharging employees. The payroll system records and processes data used to pay employees for their services.

The HRM/payroll system must be designed to comply with a myriad of government regulations related to both taxes and employment practices. In addition, adequate controls must exist to prevent (1) overpaying employees due to invalid (overstated) time and attendance data and (2) disbursing paychecks to fictitious employees. These two threats can be best minimized by proper segregation of duties, specifically by having the following functions performed by different individuals:

1. Authorizing and making changes to the payroll master file for such events as hirings, firings, and pay raises.
2. Recording and verifying time worked by employees.
3. Preparing paychecks.
4. Distributing paychecks.
5. Reconciling the payroll bank account.

Although the HRM and payroll systems have traditionally been separated, many companies, including AOE, are trying to integrate them to manage their human resources more effectively and to provide employees with better benefits and service. Elizabeth Venko and Ann Brandt showed Peter Wu how AOE's new ERP system would facilitate integrating these two functions. Peter was impressed with how easily he could retrieve data about employee skills and attendance at training classes from this database. He agreed that this would satisfy the needs of department managers for quick and easy access to such information. Peter also realized that the HRM staff could similarly use this query capability to provide a quick response to employee requests for information about their benefits, deductions, or retirement plans. He was even more impressed when Elizabeth and Ann explained that another recently implemented add-on feature would also allow employees to make direct changes in their retirement savings allocations, medical plan choices, and other benefit options. Peter realized that freeing the HRM staff from these routine clerical tasks would allow them to devote more time to helping him organize the information needed to make strategic decisions, such as planning for future workforce needs, career counseling, employee development, and negotiations with service providers to improve benefits.

Elizabeth explained that payroll processing itself could continue to be performed in batch mode because there is no need for online processing (employees would continue to be paid only at periodic intervals). However, she wants to require employees to either sign up for direct deposit of their paychecks or receive payroll debit cards, thereby eliminating the need to issue paychecks. An access control matrix would be created to maintain adequate segregation of duties in the new system and protect the integrity of the HRM/payroll database. For example, only HRM employees would add new employees, and only from terminals located in the HRM department.

Linda Spurgeon was pleased with Elizabeth and Ann's work on improving the company's HRM/payroll systems. She indicated that their next task would be to work with Stephanie Cromwell, AOE's chief financial officer, to improve the financial closing process and to help develop reports that would provide better insight into AOE's performance.

KEY TERMS

human resources management (HRM)/payroll cycle 537
knowledge management systems 539
time card 545
time sheet 545
payroll register 548
deduction register 548
earnings statement 549
payroll clearing account 551
flexible benefits plans 553
payroll service bureau 553
professional employer organization (PEO) 553

AIS in Action

CHAPTER QUIZ

1. Traditionally, accountants have been most involved with which portion of the HRM/payroll cycle?
   a. hiring
   b. payroll
   c. training
   d. performance evaluation

2. Which of the following statements is true?
   a. Financial statements report the value of employee knowledge and skills.
   b. Turnover and absenteeism are costly.
   c. All employees must fill out time cards.
   d. Default configurations of ERP packages typically provide good segregation of duties.

3. Which document lists the current amount and year-to-date totals of gross pay, deductions, and net pay for one employee?
   a. payroll register
   b. time card
   c. paycheck
   d. earnings statement

4. Online processing is most useful for which of these tasks?
   a. preparing payroll checks
   b. reconciling job-time tickets and time cards
   c. paying payroll tax obligations
   d. making changes in employee benefit choices

5. Use of a payroll service bureau or a PEO provides which of the following benefits?
   a. fewer staff needed to process payroll
   b. lower cost of processing payroll
   c. less need for developing and maintaining payroll tax expertise
   d. All of the above

6. Which control procedure would be most effective in detecting the failure to prepare a paycheck for a new employee *before* paychecks are distributed?
   a. validity checks on the employee number on each time card
   b. record counts of time cards submitted and time cards processed
   c. zero-balance check
   d. use of a separate payroll bank account

7. Which department should have responsibility for authorizing pay-rate changes?
   a. timekeeping
   b. payroll
   c. HRM
   d. accounting

8. To maximize effectiveness of internal controls over payroll, which of the following persons should be responsible for distributing employee paychecks?
   a. departmental secretary
   b. payroll clerk
   c. controller
   d. departmental supervisor

9. Where should unclaimed paychecks be returned?
   a. HRM department
   b. cashier
   c. payroll department
   d. absent employee's supervisor

10. Which of the following is an important supporting document to authorize the transfer of funds to the payroll bank account?
   a. earnings statement
   b. time card
   c. payroll register
   d. W-2 form

DISCUSSION QUESTIONS

17.1 Should CPA firms continue to use time sheets for their employees? Why, or why not?

17.2 Some accountants have advocated that a company's human assets be measured and included directly in the financial statements. For example, the costs of hiring and training an employee would be recorded as an asset that is amortized over the employee's expected term of service. Do you agree or disagree? Why?

17.3 You are responsible for implementing a new employee performance measurement system that will provide factory supervisors with detailed information about each of their employees on a weekly basis. In conversation with some of these supervisors, you are surprised to learn they do not believe these reports will be useful. They explain that they can already obtain all the information they need to manage their employees simply by observing the shop floor. Comment on that opinion. How could formal reports supplement and enhance what the supervisors learn by direct observation?

17.4 One of the threats associated with having employees telecommute is that they may use company-provided resources (laptop, printer, etc.) for a side business. What are some other threats? What controls can mitigate the risk of these threats?

17.5 How would you respond to the treasurer of a small charity who tells you that the organization does not use a separate checking account for payroll because the benefits are not worth the extra monthly service fee?

17.6 This chapter discussed how the HR department should have responsibility for updating the HRM/payroll database for hiring, firing, and promotions. What other kinds of changes may need to be made? What controls should be implemented to ensure the accuracy and validity of such changes?

PROBLEMS

17.1 Match the terms with their definitions.

___ **1.** payroll service bureau	a. List of each employee's gross pay, payroll deductions, and net pay in a multicolumn format
___ **2.** payroll clearing account	b. Records activities performed by a salaried professional for various clients
___ **3.** earnings statement	c. Records time worked by an hourly-wage employee
___ **4.** payroll register	d. Organization that processes payroll and provides other HRM services
___ **5.** time card	e. Organization that processes payroll
___ **6.** time sheet	f. List of all the deductions for each employee
	g. Document given to each employee that shows gross pay and net pay and itemizes all deductions for the current pay period and for the year-to-date
	h. Special general ledger account for payroll processing

17.2 What internal control procedure(s) would be most effective in preventing the following errors or fraudulent acts?

a. An inadvertent data entry error caused an employee's wage rate to be overstated in the payroll master file.
b. A fictitious employee payroll record was added to the payroll master file.
c. During data entry, the hours worked on an employee's time card for one day were accidentally entered as 80 hours, instead of 8 hours.
d. A computer operator used an online terminal to increase her own salary.
e. A factory supervisor failed to notify the HRM department that an employee had been fired. Consequently, paychecks continued to be issued for that employee. The supervisor pocketed and cashed those paychecks.
f. A factory employee punched a friend's time card in at 1:00 P.M. and out at 5:00 P.M. while the friend played golf that afternoon.
g. A programmer obtained the payroll master file and increased his salary.
h. Some time cards were lost during payroll preparation; consequently, when paychecks were distributed, several employees complained about not being paid.
i. A large portion of the payroll master file was destroyed when the disk pack containing the file was overwritten when used as a scratch file for another application.
j. The organization was fined $5,000 for making a late quarterly payroll tax payment to the IRS.

17.3 You have been hired to evaluate the payroll system for the Skip-Rope Manufacturing Company. The company processes its payroll in-house. Use Table 17-1 as a reference to prepare a list of questions to evaluate Skip-Rope's internal control structure as it pertains to payroll processing for its factory employees. Each question should be phrased so that it can be answered with either a yes or a no; all "no" answers should indicate potential internal control weaknesses. Include a third column listing the potential problem that could arise if that particular control were not in place. (*CPA Examination, adapted*)

17.4 Although most medium and large companies have implemented sophisticated payroll and HRM systems like the one described in this chapter, many smaller companies still maintain separate payroll and HRM systems that employ many manual procedures.

Typical of such small companies is the Kowal Manufacturing Company, which employs about 50 production workers and has the following payroll procedures:

- The factory supervisor interviews and hires all job applicants. The new employee prepares a W-4 form (Employee's Withholding Exemption Certificate) and gives it to the supervisor. The supervisor writes the hourly rate of pay for the new employee in the corner of the W-4 form and then gives the form to the payroll clerk as notice that a new worker has been hired. The supervisor verbally advises the payroll department of any subsequent pay raises.
- A supply of blank time cards is kept in a box near the entrance to the factory. All workers take a time card on Monday morning and fill in their names. During the week they record the time they arrive and leave work by punching their time cards in the time clock located near the main entrance to the factory. At the end of the week the workers drop the time cards in a box near the exit. A payroll clerk retrieves the completed time cards from the box on Monday morning. Employees are automatically removed from the payroll master file when they fail to turn in a time card.
- The payroll checks are manually signed by the chief accountant and then given to the factory supervisor, who distributes them to the employees. The factory supervisor arranges for delivery of the paychecks to any employee who is absent on payday.
- The payroll bank account is reconciled by the chief accountant, who also prepares the various quarterly and annual tax reports.

REQUIRED

a. Identify weaknesses in current procedures, and explain the threats that they may allow to occur.
b. Suggest ways to improve the Kowal Manufacturing Company's internal controls over hiring and payroll processing.
c. Draw a BPMN diagram that shows Kowal Manufacturing Company's payroll process redesigned to implement your suggestions in step b. (*CPA Examination, adapted*)

17.5 Arlington Industries manufactures and sells engine parts for large industrial equipment. The company employs more than 1,000 workers for three shifts, and most employees work overtime when necessary. Figure 17-10 depicts the procedures followed to process payroll. Additional information about payroll procedures follows:

- The HRM department determines the wage rates of all employees. The process begins when a form authorizing the addition of a new employee to the payroll master file is sent to the payroll coordinator for review and approval. Once the information about the new employee is entered in the system, the computer automatically calculates the overtime and shift differential rates for that employee.
- A local accounting firm provides Arlington with monthly payroll tax updates, which are used to modify the tax rates.
- Employees record their time worked on time cards. Every Monday morning, the previous week's time cards are collected from a bin next to the time clock, and new time cards are left for employees to use. The payroll department manager reviews the time cards to ensure that hours are correctly totaled; the system automatically determines whether overtime has been worked or a shift differential is required.
- The payroll department manager performs all the other activities depicted in Figure 17-10.
- The system automatically assigns a sequential number to each payroll check. The checks are stored in a box next to the printer for easy access. After the checks are printed, the payroll department manager uses an automatic check-signing machine to sign the checks. The signature plate is kept locked in a safe. After the checks have been signed, the payroll manager distributes the paychecks to all first-shift employees. Paychecks for the other two shifts are given to the shift supervisor for distribution.
- The payroll master file is backed up weekly, after payroll processing is finished.

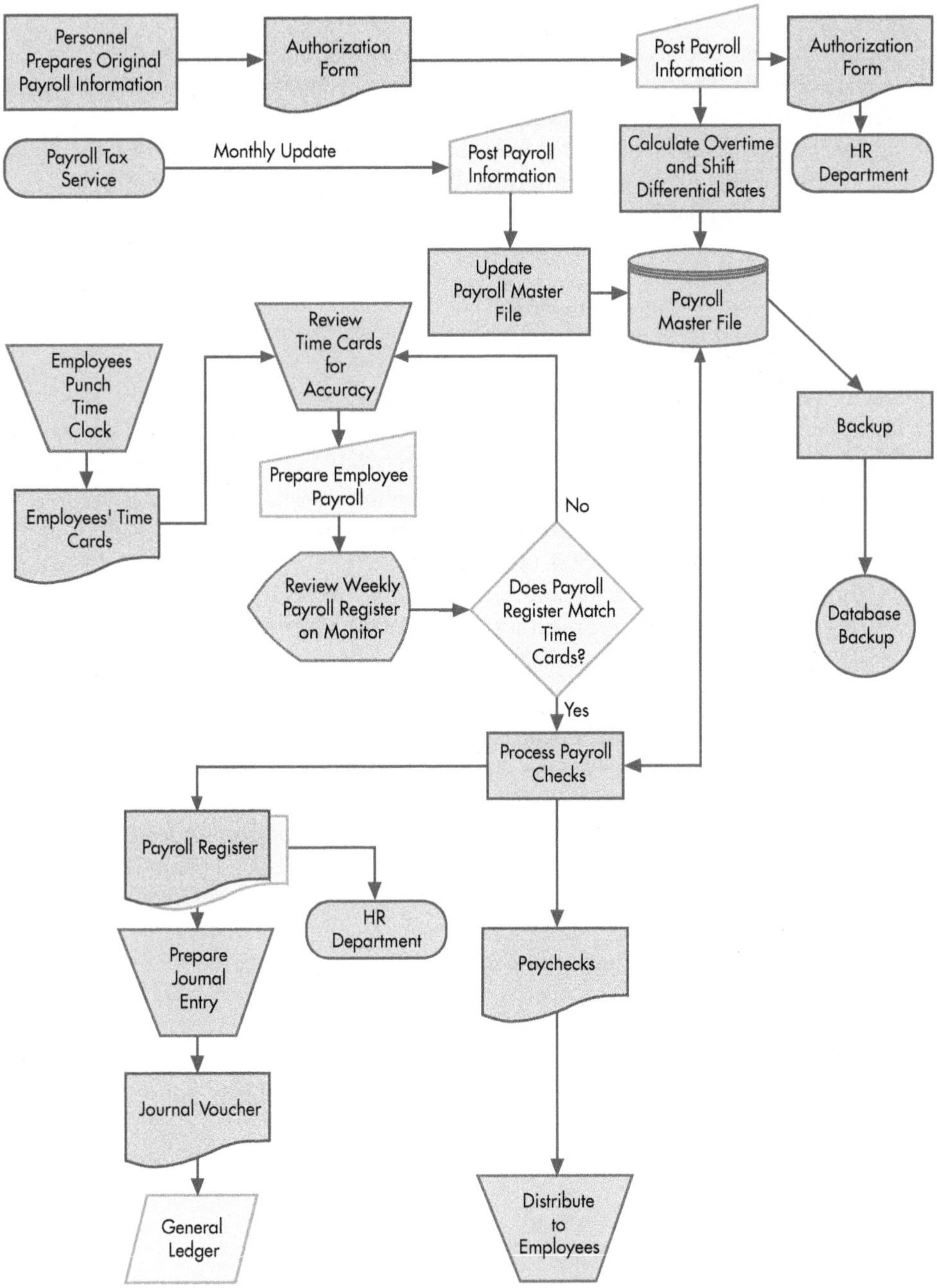

FIGURE 17-10
Arlington Industries Flowchart for Problem 17.5

REQUIRED

a. Identify and describe at least three weaknesses in Arlington Industries' payroll process.
b. Identify and describe at least two different areas in Arlington's payroll processing system where controls are satisfactory. (*CMA Examination, adapted*)

17.6 Excel Problem*

Objective: Learn how to find and correct errors in spreadsheets used for payroll.

*Life-long learning opportunity: see pp. xxiii–xxiv in preface.

REQUIRED

a. Download the worksheet for this problem from the website.
b. Create formulas in columns K–O that would display an error message if that payroll record violated any of the following rules:
   1. All employees must be paid at least the minimum wage of $15.
   2. Overtime only exists if the employee has worked 40 hours of regular time.
   3. Maximum regular hours is 40.
   4. Net pay does not equal gross pay minus all deductions (overtime pay is 1.5 times regular pay rate).
   5. An employee has zero deductions.

17.7 Excel Problem*

Objective: Learn how to use VLOOKUP.

REQUIRED

a. Download the worksheet for this problem from the website.
b. Create a formula to calculate taxes, using the following rate table:
   - If gross pay is less than $500, taxes are 12%.
   - If gross pay is at least $500 and less than $750, taxes are 15%.
   - If gross pay is at least $750 but less than $1,000, taxes are 20%.
   - If gross pay is greater than $1,000, taxes are 28%.

17.8 The local community feels that secondary school education is a necessity and that lack of education leads to a number of social problems. As a result, the local school board has decided to take action to reverse the rising dropout rate. The board has voted to provide funds to encourage students to remain in school and earn their high school diplomas. The idea is to treat secondary education like a job and pay students. The board, however, could not agree on the details for implementing this new plan. Consequently, you have been hired to devise a system to compensate students for staying in school and earning a diploma.

As you devise your compensation scheme, be sure it meets the following general control objectives for the payroll cycle:

- All transactions are properly authorized.
- Everyone is assigned to do productive work, and they do it efficiently and effectively.
- All transactions are accurately recorded and processed.
- Accurate records are maintained.
- All disbursements are proper.

REQUIRED

Write a proposal that addresses these five questions:

a. How should the students be compensated (e.g., for attendance, grades)?
b. How and by whom will the payments be authorized?
c. How will the payments be processed?
d. How should the payments be made (e.g., in cash or other means)?
e. When will the payments be made?

(Adapted from Carol F. Venable, "Development of Diversity Awareness and Critical Thinking," Proceedings of the Lilly Conference on Excellence in College and University Teaching—West [Lake Arrowhead, Calif., March 1995]; and American Accounting Association Teaching and Curriculum Demonstration Session [Orlando, Fla., August 1995]. Reprinted with permission of Dr. Carol Venable.)

---

* Life-long learning opportunity: see pp. xxiii–xxiv in preface.

17.9 What is the purpose of each of the following control procedures (i.e., what threats is it designed to mitigate)?

a. Comparison of a listing of current and former employees to the payroll register.
b. Reconciliation of labor costs (based on job-time ticket data) with payroll (based on time card data).
c. Direct deposit of paychecks.
d. Validity checks on Social Security numbers of all new employees added to the payroll master file.
e. Cross-footing the payroll register.
f. Limit checks on hours worked for each time card.
g. Use of a fingerprint scanner for employees to record the time they started and the time they quit working each day.
h. Encryption of payroll data both when it is electronically sent to a payroll service bureau and while at rest in the HR/payroll database.
i. Establishing a separate payroll checking account and funding it as an imprest account.
j. Comparison of hash totals of employee numbers created prior to transmitting time-worked data to payroll provider with hash totals of employee numbers created by payroll provider when preparing paychecks.
k. Periodic reports of all changes to payroll database sent to each department manager.
l. Providing employees with earnings statements every pay period.
m. Check for paychecks with no social security or income tax witholding.
n. Check for multiple direct deposits to the same bank account in a single pay period.

17.10 Excel Problem*

Objective: Learn how to use text and array formulas to locate potential payroll problems.

REQUIRED

a. Download the spreadsheet for this problem from the course website.
b. In column I, under the label "Ghost Employee?" write a function that compares the employee# in the time cards column to the employee# in the payroll master data column and displays the message: "Time card employee# does not exist in master data" for any employee in the time cards column who is not listed in the payroll master data column. The function should leave the cell blank if the employee# in the time cards worksheet does exist in the payroll master file worksheet or if that row in the time card column is blank. (*Hint:* Use the ISNA and MATCH functions.)
c. In column L, titled "Invalid SSN?" write a function to identify invalid Social Security numbers. Assume that Social Security numbers that begin with the digit 0 or that have the digits 99 for the middle two numbers are invalid. Your function should display a message that flags either of these two conditions or that displays nothing otherwise. (*Hint:* There are text functions that examine specific portions of a string, such as the left three characters, and there are also functions that convert text to numeric values.)
d. In column P, titled "Missing Paycheck?" write a function to check whether a time card exists for each employee in the master payroll data section of the worksheet. The formula should either return the message "No paycheck created for this employee" or display nothing.

---

* Life-long learning opportunity: see pp. xxiii–xxiv in preface.

17.11 Answer all of the following multiple-choice questions.

1. Tokenization is a control that mitigates the risk of ________.
a. inaccurate or invalid master data
b. unauthorized disclosure of sensitive data
c. unauthorized changes to payroll master data
d. inaccurate time and attendance data
e. theft of fraudulent distribution of paychecks

2. Which of the following controls reduce the risk of issuing paychecks to a "phantom" or "ghost" employee?
a. restrict physical access to blank paychecks
b. prenumber all payroll checks
c. use an imprest account to clear payroll checks
d. All of the above
e. None of the above

3. To implement proper segregation of duties, who should have the ability to create new records in the employee master file used for processing payroll?
a. a payroll clerk
b. someone in HR
c. the new employee's supervisor
d. Any of the three people listed above could perform this task
e. None of the three people listed above should perform this task

4. An application control that compares the amount of an employee's raise to that employee's existing salary is called a ________.
a. limit check
b. range test
c. reasonableness test
d. check digit verification
e. size check

5. The purpose of issuing earnings statements to employees is to mitigate the risk of ________.
a. unauthorized changes to payroll master data
b. errors in processing payroll
c. theft or fraudulent distribution of paychecks
d. untimely payments

6. The use of biometrics as part of employee authentication is designed primarily to reduce the risk of which threat?
a. inaccurate updating of the master payroll file
b. inaccurate time and attendance data
c. failure to make required payroll tax payments
d. errors in processing payroll

7. Which of the following control procedures is designed to reduce the risk of theft of paychecks or fraudulent distribution of paychecks?
a. restriction of access to blank payroll checks
b. prenumbering and periodically accounting for all paychecks
c. redepositing all unclaimed paychecks and investigating the reasons why the paychecks were not claimed
d. All of the above
e. None of the above

8. Use of a separate checking account for payroll is designed to reduce the risk of the threat of ________.
a. unauthorized changes to the payroll master file
b. errors in processing payroll
c. theft or fraudulent disbursement of paychecks
d. failure to make required payments to government tax agencies
e. loss or destruction of payroll data

CASE 17-1 Excel Project*: Sorting and Grouping Data

Download the spreadsheet for this case from the website. The spreadsheet contains performance data by region and by employee for multiple time periods.

REQUIRED

1. Copy the raw data to a second sheet in the same workbook and use the subtotals function to group the data by employee so that you can either display the full details for various employees or just the totals by each employee by region.
2. Copy the raw data to a third sheet in the same workbook and create a PivotTable to group the data by employee and region so that you can display each employee's performance.
3. Open a fourth sheet in the same workbook and title it "Preferences." On that sheet, state which approach (SubTotals or PivotTable) you prefer and explain why.

AIS in Action Solutions

QUIZ KEY

1. Traditionally, accountants have been most involved with which portion of the HRM/payroll cycle?
   a. hiring [Incorrect. This has traditionally been handled by the HR department.]
   ▶ b. payroll [Correct. The payroll system has traditionally been the part of the HRM/payroll system used by accountants.]
   c. training [Incorrect. This has traditionally been handled by the HR department.]
   d. performance evaluation [Incorrect. This has traditionally been handled by supervisors.]

2. Which of the following statements is true?
   a. Financial statements report the value of employee knowledge and skills. [Incorrect. Costs associated with acquiring the use of employees' skills and knowledge have traditionally been recognized as an expense on the income statement.]
   ▶ b. Turnover and absenteeism are costly. [Correct. Turnover costs 1.5 times the departing employee's salary, and absenteeism increases overtime and short-term hiring costs.]
   c. All employees must fill out time cards. [Incorrect. Hourly employees typically fill out time cards to record hours worked. Salaried professionals, however, do not because their periodic pay is a set fraction of their annual salary. Salaried employees in professional services firms, however, do record the time spent performing various activities for different clients on time sheets so their employers can accurately assign costs and bill clients for services rendered.]
   d. Default configurations of ERP packages typically provide good segregation of duties. [Incorrect. Default configurations of ERP systems typically provide users with far too much authority.]

3. Which document lists the current amount and year-to-date totals of gross pay, deductions, and net pay for one employee?
   a. payroll register [Incorrect. The payroll register lists this information for all employees.]
   b. time card [Incorrect. Time cards collect data about time worked during a specific pay period.]
   c. paycheck [Incorrect. The paycheck is a means of transferring funds.]
   ▶ d. earnings statement [Correct. The earnings statement attached to each paycheck provides the information listed.]

---

* Life-long learning opportunity: see pp. xxiii–xxiv in preface.

4. Online processing is most useful for which of these tasks?
   a. preparing payroll checks [Incorrect. Because paychecks are issued only periodically, batch processing is appropriate.]
   b. reconciling job-time tickets and time cards [Incorrect. Because this occurs only when payroll is calculated, batch processing is appropriate.]
   c. paying payroll tax obligations [Incorrect. Payment is periodic, so batch processing is appropriate.]
▶ **d.** making changes in employee benefit choices [Correct. Employees want to be able to have access to this information and make changes whenever desired.]

5. Use of a payroll service bureau or a PEO provides which of the following benefits?
   a. fewer staff needed to process payroll [Incorrect. Outsourcing not only typically reduces staffing requirements, but also lowers costs (answer b) and reduces the need for in-house expertise (answer c).]
   b. lower cost of processing payroll [Incorrect. Outsourcing usually not only reduces costs, but also requires fewer staff (answer a) and reduces the need for in-house expertise (answer c).]
   c. less need for developing and maintaining payroll tax expertise [Incorrect. Outsourcing does reduce the need to maintain in-house payroll tax expertise, but it also provides the benefits listed in answers a and b.]
▶ **d.** All of the above [Correct.]

6. Which control procedure would be most effective in detecting the failure to prepare a paycheck for a new employee before paychecks are distributed?
   a. validity checks on the employee number on each time card [Incorrect. This control is designed to ensure that only valid employees are paid.]
▶ **b.** record counts of time cards submitted and time cards processed [Correct. Batch totals, such as record counts, would identify failure to process all transaction records.]
   c. zero-balance check [Incorrect. This control is designed to verify the accuracy of payroll disbursements.]
   d. use of a separate payroll bank account [Incorrect. This control is designed to limit the amount of cash that could be lost as a result of forged or altered paychecks.]

7. Which department should have responsibility for authorizing pay-rate changes?
   a. timekeeping [Incorrect. Timekeeping is a recording function.]
   b. payroll [Incorrect. Payroll calculates the pay for the current period and should not also authorize changes.]
▶ **c.** HRM [Correct. HRM has no other role in the payroll process.]
   d. accounting [Incorrect. Accounting maintains records related to payroll and should not authorize changes in pay rates.]

8. To maximize effectiveness of internal controls over payroll, which of the following persons should be responsible for distributing employee paychecks?
▶ **a.** departmental secretary [Correct. This person has no other payroll duties and so cannot conceal theft of paychecks.]
   b. payroll clerk [Incorrect. The payroll clerk prepares and records the checks and so could create checks for nonexistent employees and cash them.]
   c. controller [Incorrect. The controller is in charge of the recording function and should not have custody of checks.]
   d. departmental supervisor [Incorrect. The supervisor authorizes payment by reviewing time cards and should not also have custody of assets.]

9. Where should unclaimed paychecks be returned?
   a. HRM department [Incorrect. Unclaimed checks should be returned to the cashier for redeposit.]
▶ **b.** cashier [Correct. This permits funds to be quickly redeposited.]
   c. payroll department [Incorrect. Unclaimed checks should be returned to the cashier for redeposit.]
   d. absent employee's supervisor [Incorrect. Unclaimed checks should be returned to the cashier for redeposit.]

10. Which of the following is an important supporting document to authorize the transfer of funds to the payroll bank account?

a. earnings statement [Incorrect. This is the stub attached to each paycheck, providing the employee with YTD information about pay and various deductions.]

b. time card [Incorrect. This document records time worked.]

▶ c. payroll register [Correct. This document summarizes the amount to be paid to each employee and is sent to the accounts payable department for use in preparing a disbursement voucher to authorize the transfer of funds to the payroll account.]

d. W-2 form [Incorrect. This is a year-end statement given to each employee summarizing net pay, taxes withheld, and other deductions.]

CHAPTER

18

General Ledger and Reporting System

LEARNING OBJECTIVES

After studying this chapter, you should be able to:

1. Describe the activities, information needs, and key decisions made in the general ledger and reporting system, explain the general threats in the cycle, and describe the controls that can be used to mitigate those threats.
2. Explain the process for ***updating the general ledger***, the threats to that process, and the controls that can be used to mitigate those threats.
3. Explain the purpose and nature of ***posting adjusting entries***, the threats to that process, and the controls that can be used to mitigate those threats.
4. Explain the process of ***preparing financial statements***, the threats to that process, the controls that can be used to mitigate those threats, and how IT developments such as XBRL can improve the efficiency and effectiveness of preparing financial statements.
5. Describe the process for ***producing various managerial reports***, the threats to that process, and how tools like responsibility accounting and the balanced scorecard can help mitigate those threats.

INTEGRATIVE CASE Alpha Omega Electronics

Linda Spurgeon, president and CEO of Alpha Omega Electronics (AOE), is not satisfied with the reporting capabilities of AOE's new enterprise resource planning (ERP) system. Although the monthly closing process now takes less than two days, the system only provides management with timely information about the firm's financial performance. Linda wants a report that integrates financial information with operational measures about how the firm is doing. She is also concerned about how to prepare AOE to transition from U.S. Generally Accepted Accounting Principles (GAAP) to International Financial Reporting Standards (IFRS).

Linda calls a meeting with Stephanie Cromwell, AOE's chief financial officer, Elizabeth Venko, AOE's controller, and Ann Brandt, AOE's vice president of information systems, to discuss these issues. Stephanie mentions that she has been reading about something called a balanced scorecard that might provide the kind of multidimensional report Linda desires.

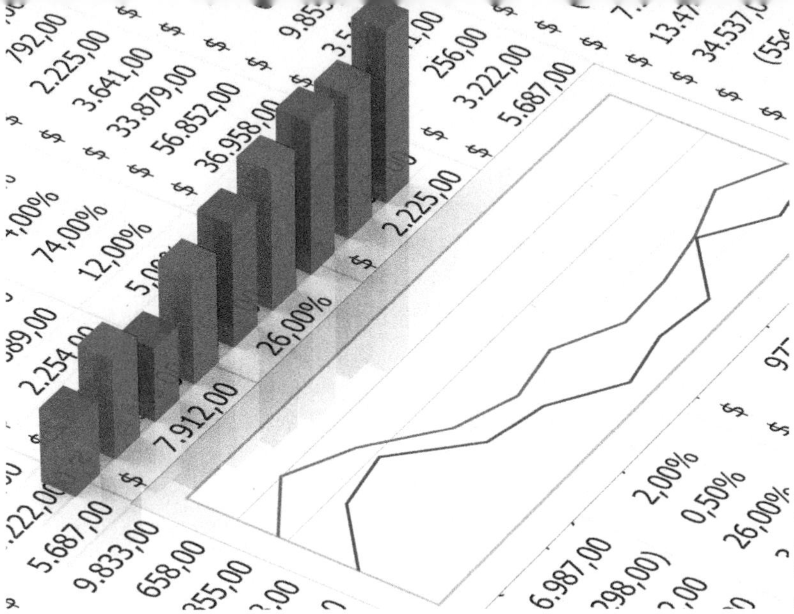

Cico/Shutterstock

Ann and Elizabeth agree to research the balanced scorecard and investigate how AOE's new ERP system could be configured to produce one. Stephanie asks them to also look at how AOE could make better use of the reporting and graphing capabilities of its new ERP system. In addition, they will report back on what needs to be done to prepare for IFRS and how to use XBRL to streamline its external reporting requirements. As you read this chapter, think about how both technological and regulatory changes affect the design and operation of an organization's general ledger and reporting systems.

Introduction

This chapter discusses the information processing operations involved in updating the general ledger and preparing reports that summarize the results of an organization's activities. As shown in Figure 18-1, the general ledger and reporting system plays a central role in a company's accounting information system. Its primary function is to collect and organize data from the following sources:

- Each of the accounting cycle subsystems described in Chapters 14 through 17 provides information about regular transactions. (Only the principal data flows from each subsystem are depicted, to keep the figure uncluttered.)
- The treasurer provides information about financing and investing activities, such as the issuance or retirement of debt and equity instruments and the purchase or sale of investment securities.
- The budget department provides budget numbers.
- The controller makes adjusting entries.

Figure 18-2 shows the basic activities performed in the general ledger and reporting cycle. The first three activities represent the basic steps in the accounting cycle, which culminate in the production of the traditional set of financial statements. The fourth activity indicates that, in addition to financial reports for external users, an organization's accounting system produces a variety of reports for internal management.

We begin by describing the design of a typical general ledger and reporting system and discuss the basic controls necessary to ensure that it provides management and various external stakeholders with reliable information. We then discuss in detail each of the basic general ledger and reporting cycle activities depicted in Figure 18-2. For each activity, we describe how the information needed to perform and manage the activity is collected, processed, and stored. We also explain the controls necessary to ensure not only the reliability of that information but also the safeguarding of the organization's resources. In addition, we discuss the impact of regulatory and technological changes, such as the proposed switch from GAAP to IFRS and the SEC's mandate to use XBRL for electronic filing, on the design and operation

FIGURE 18-1
Context Diagram of the General Ledger and Reporting System

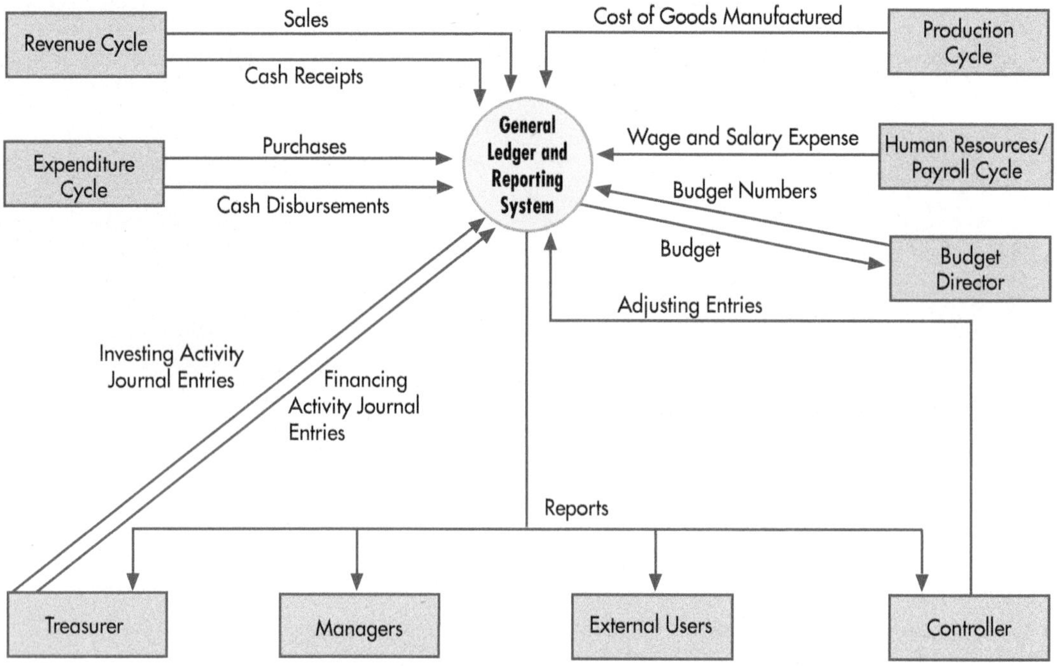

of the general ledger and reporting system. We also explore how tools such as responsibility accounting and balanced scorecards can improve the quality of information provided to managers.

General Ledger and Reporting System

Figure 18-3 shows the typical design of an online general ledger and reporting system.

FIGURE 18-2
Level 0 Data Flow Diagram of the General Ledger and Reporting Cycle (annotated to include threats)

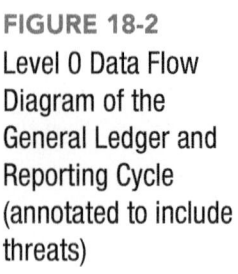

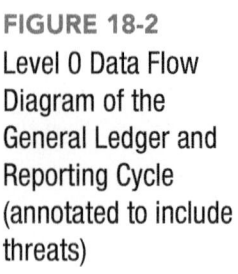

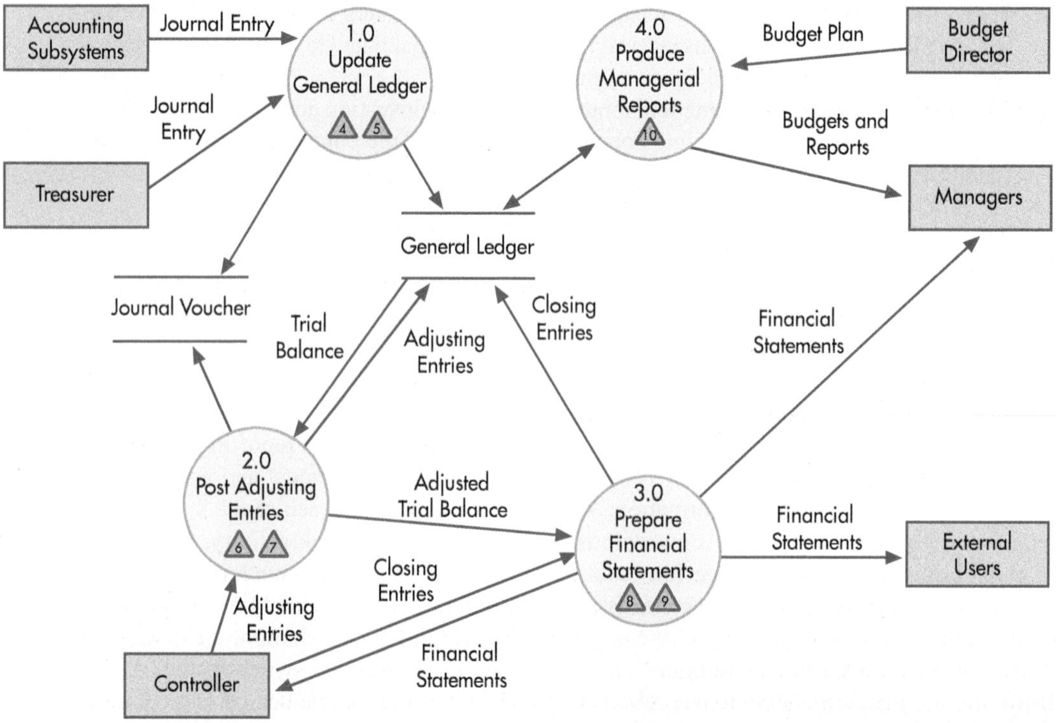

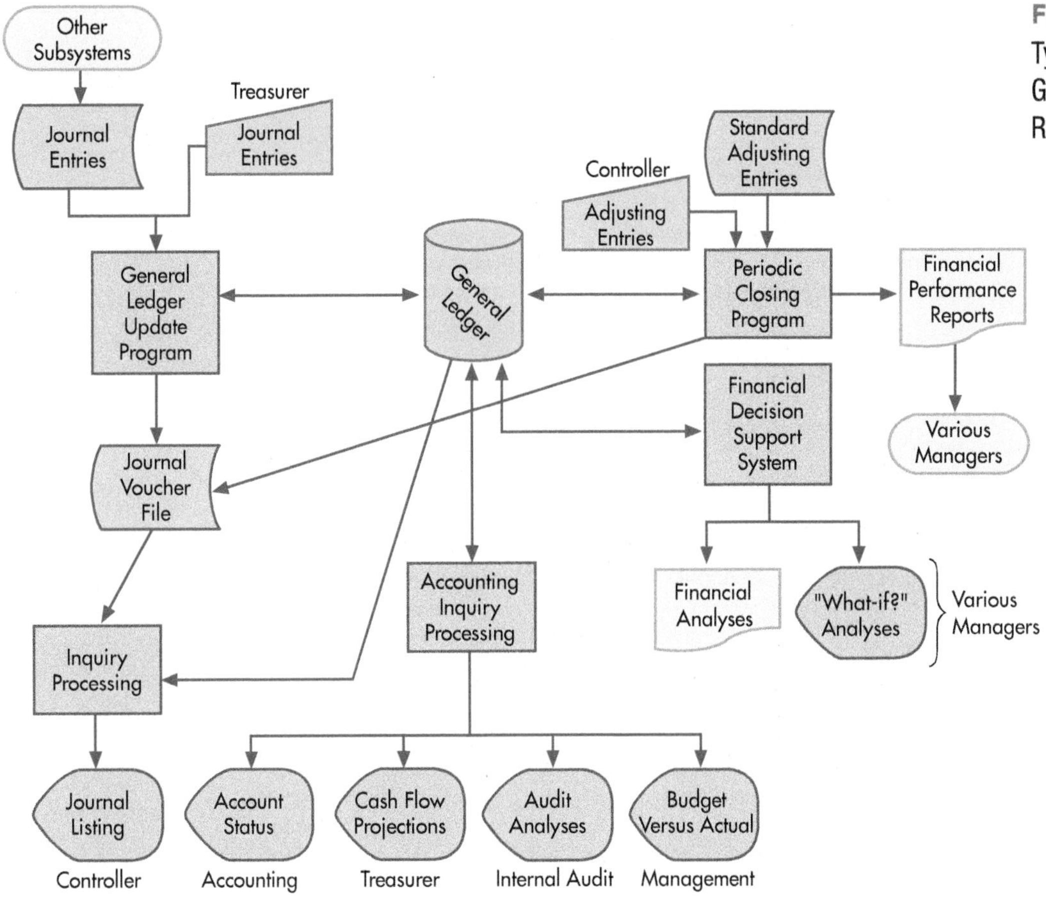

FIGURE 18-3
Typical Design of Online General Ledger and Reporting System

PROCESS

The centralized database must be organized in a manner that facilitates meeting the varied information needs of both internal and external users. Managers need timely detailed information about the results of operations in their particular area of responsibility. Investors and creditors want periodic financial statements and timely updates to help them assess the organization's performance. Various government agencies also mandate specific information requirements. To satisfy these multiple needs, the general ledger and reporting system not only produces periodic reports but also supports online inquiries.

THREATS AND CONTROLS

Figure 18-3 shows that all general ledger and reporting cycle activities depend on the integrated database. Therefore, the first general threat listed in Table 18-1 is inaccurate or invalid general ledger data. Inaccurate general ledger data can result in misleading reports that cause managers to make erroneous decisions. Similarly, errors in financial statements provided to creditors, investors, and government agencies can cause those stakeholders to make wrong decisions. In addition, errors in financial statements and reports provided to external stakeholders can also result in fines and negative reactions from the capital markets.

One way to mitigate the threat of inaccurate or invalid general ledger data is to use the various processing integrity controls discussed in Chapter 13 to minimize the risk of data input errors when the treasurer and controller make direct journal entries (control 1.1). It is also important to restrict access to the general ledger and configure the system so that only authorized employees can make changes to master data (control 1.2). Thus, multifactor authentication should be used to restrict access to the general ledger. In addition, authorization controls (an access control matrix and compatibility tests) should also be used to limit the functions that each legitimate user may perform. For example, most managers should be given read-only access to the general ledger, as depicted at the bottom of Figure 18-3. Otherwise,

TABLE 18-1 Threats and Controls in the General Ledger and Reporting System

Activity	Threat	Controls (First Number Refers to the Corresponding Threat)
General issues throughout entire general ledger and reporting cycle	1. Inaccurate or invalid general ledger data 2. Unauthorized disclosure of financial statement 3. Loss or destruction of data	1.1 Data processing integrity controls 1.2 Restriction of access to general ledger 1.3 Review of all changes to general ledger data 2.1 Access controls 2.2 Encryption 3.1 Backup and disaster recovery procedures
Update general ledger	4. Inaccurate updating of general ledger 5. Unauthorized journal entries	4.1 Data entry processing integrity controls 4.2 Reconciliations and control reports 4.3 Audit trail creation and review 5.1 Access controls 5.2 Reconciliations and control reports 5.3 Audit trail creation and review
Post adjusting entries	6. Inaccurate adjusting entries 7. Unauthorized adjusting entries	6.1 Data entry processing integrity controls 6.2 Spreadsheet error protection controls 6.3 Standard adjusting entries 6.4 Reconciliations and control reports 6.5 Audit trail creation and review 7.1 Access controls 7.2 Reconciliations and control reports 7.3 Audit trail creation and review
Prepare financial statements	8. Inaccurate financial statements 9. Fraudulent financial reporting	8.1 Processing integrity controls 8.2 Use of packaged software 8.3 Training and experience in applying IFRS and XBRL 8.4 Audits 9.1 Audits
Produce managerial reports	10. Poorly designed reports and graphs	10.1 Responsibility accounting 10.2 Balanced scorecard 10.3 Training on proper graph design

an unscrupulous manager can conceal theft of assets or poor performance by altering the information in the general ledger. Moreover, it is also important to carefully restrict read-only privileges to only those specific portions of the system relevant to that manager. In addition, the access control matrix should also be designed to limit the functions that can be performed at various terminals. Adjusting entries, for example, should be allowed only from terminals in the controller's office. However, because such preventive controls can never be 100% effective, Table 18-1 also indicates that an important detective control is to regularly produce a report of all changes to the general ledger and review them to verify that the database remains accurate (control 1.3).

A second general threat in the general ledger and reporting cycle is unauthorized disclosure of financial information. In particular, it is important not to prematurely release financial statements; doing so is likely to result in fines from various regulatory agencies and possible shareholder lawsuits. The best control procedure for reducing the risk of unauthorized disclosure of financial statements is to use multifactor authentication and physical security controls to restrict access to the general ledger (control 2.1) to only those employees who need such access to perform their jobs. Encrypting the database (control 2.2) provides additional protection by making the information unintelligible to anyone who succeeds in obtaining unauthorized access to the database. Encryption also prevents IT employees who do not have access to the ERP system from using operating system utilities to view sensitive information. In addition, general ledger data should be encrypted when it is transmitted over the Internet to other corporate offices, analysts, or government agencies.

A third general threat in the general ledger and reporting cycle concerns the loss or destruction of master data. The best way to mitigate the risk of this threat is to employ the backup and disaster recovery procedures (control 3.1) that were discussed in Chapter 13.

Update General Ledger

As shown in Figure 18-2, the first activity in the general ledger system (circle 1.0) is updating the general ledger.

PROCESS

Updating consists of posting journal entries that originate from two sources:

1. ***Accounting subsystems.*** Each of the accounting subsystems described in Chapters 14 through 17 creates a journal entry to update the general ledger. In theory, the general ledger could be updated for each individual transaction. In practice, however, the various accounting subsystems usually update the general ledger by means of summary journal entries that represent the results of all transactions that occurred during a given period of time (day, week, or month). For example, the revenue cycle subsystem would generate a summary journal entry debiting accounts receivable and cash and crediting sales for all sales made during the update period. Similarly, the expenditure cycle would generate summary journal entries to record the purchase of supplies and inventories and to record cash disbursements in payment for those purchases.
2. ***Treasurer.*** The treasurer's office provides information for journal entries to update the general ledger for nonroutine transactions such as the issuance or retirement of debt, the purchase or sale of investment securities, or the acquisition of treasury stock. Figure 18-4 shows an example of a typical journal entry screen for an ERP system.

Figure 18-3 shows that the individual journal entries used to update the general ledger are stored in the **journal voucher file**. The journal voucher file contains the information that would be found in the general journal in a manual accounting system: the date of the journal entry, the accounts debited and credited, and the amounts. Note, however, that the journal voucher file is a by-product of, not an input to, the posting process. As we will explain later,

journal voucher file - A file that stores all journal entries used to update the general ledger.

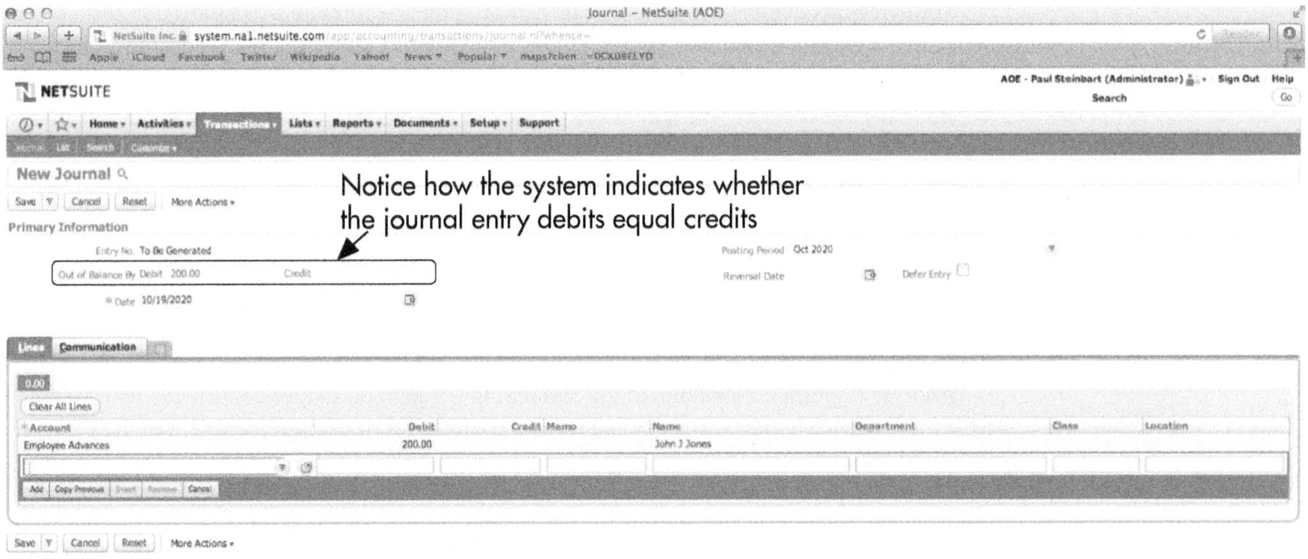

FIGURE 18-4

Example of Journal Entry Input Screen

Source: 2010 © NetSuite Inc.

the journal voucher file forms an important part of the audit trail, providing evidence that all authorized transactions have been accurately and completely recorded.

THREATS AND CONTROLS

Table 18-1 shows that two related threats at this stage are inaccurate and unauthorized journal entries to update the general ledger. Both can lead to poor decision making based on erroneous information in financial performance reports.

As Figure 18-3 shows, there are two sources of journal entries for updating the general ledger: summary journal entries from the other AIS cycles and direct entries made by the treasurer. The former are the output of a series of processing steps, each of which was subject to a variety of application control procedures designed to ensure accuracy and completeness, as described in the preceding four chapters. Consequently, the primary input edit control for summary journal entries from the other cycles is configuring the system to verify that the entries represent activity for the most recent time period.

Journal entries made by the treasurer, however, are original data entry. Consequently, the following types of input edit and processing controls discussed in Chapter 13 are needed to ensure they are accurate and complete (control 4.1):

1. A *validity check* to ensure that general ledger accounts exist for each account number referenced in a journal entry.
2. *Field (format) checks* to ensure that the amount field in the journal entry contains only numeric data.
3. A *zero-balance check* to verify that total debits equal total credits in a journal entry. (Figure 18-4 shows feedback from this control.)
4. A *completeness test* to ensure that all pertinent data are entered, especially the source of the journal entry.
5. *Closed-loop verification* matching account numbers with account descriptions, to ensure the correct general ledger account is accessed.
6. A *sign check* of the general ledger account balance, once updating is completed, to verify that the balance is of the appropriate nature (debit or credit).
7. Calculating *run-to-run totals* to verify the accuracy of journal voucher batch processing. (The computer calculates the new balance of the general ledger account, based on its beginning balance and the total debits and credits applied to that account, then compares that with the actual account balance in the updated general ledger. Any discrepancies indicate a processing error that must be investigated.)

Strong access controls, including multifactor authentication and compatibility tests based on access control matrices, reduce the risk of unauthorized journal entries (control 4.1). In addition to these preventive controls, Table 18-1 lists two types of detective controls that should be used to identify inaccurate and unauthorized journal entries: reconciliations and control reports (controls 4.2 and 5.2), and maintenance of an adequate audit trail (controls 4.3 and 5.3).

trial balance - A report listing the balances of all general ledger accounts.

RECONCILIATIONS AND CONTROL REPORTS Reconciliations and control reports can detect whether any errors were made during the process of updating the general ledger. One form of reconciliation is the preparation of a trial balance. The **trial balance** is a report that lists the balances for all general ledger accounts (see Figure 18-5). Its name reflects the fact that if all activities have been properly recorded, the total of all debit balances in various accounts should equal the total of all credit balances; if not, a posting error has occurred.

Another important reconciliation is comparing the general ledger control account balances to the total balance in the corresponding subsidiary ledger. For example, the sum of the balances of individual customer accounts should equal the amount of the accounts receivable control account in the general ledger. If these two totals do not agree, the difference must be investigated and corrected. It is also important to examine all transactions occurring near the end of an accounting period to verify that they are recorded in the proper time period.

At the end of a fiscal period, it is also important to verify that any temporary "suspense" or "clearing" accounts have zero balances. Clearing and suspense accounts provide a means to ensure that the general ledger is always in balance. To illustrate how these types of special accounts are used, assume that one clerk is responsible for recording the release of inventory to

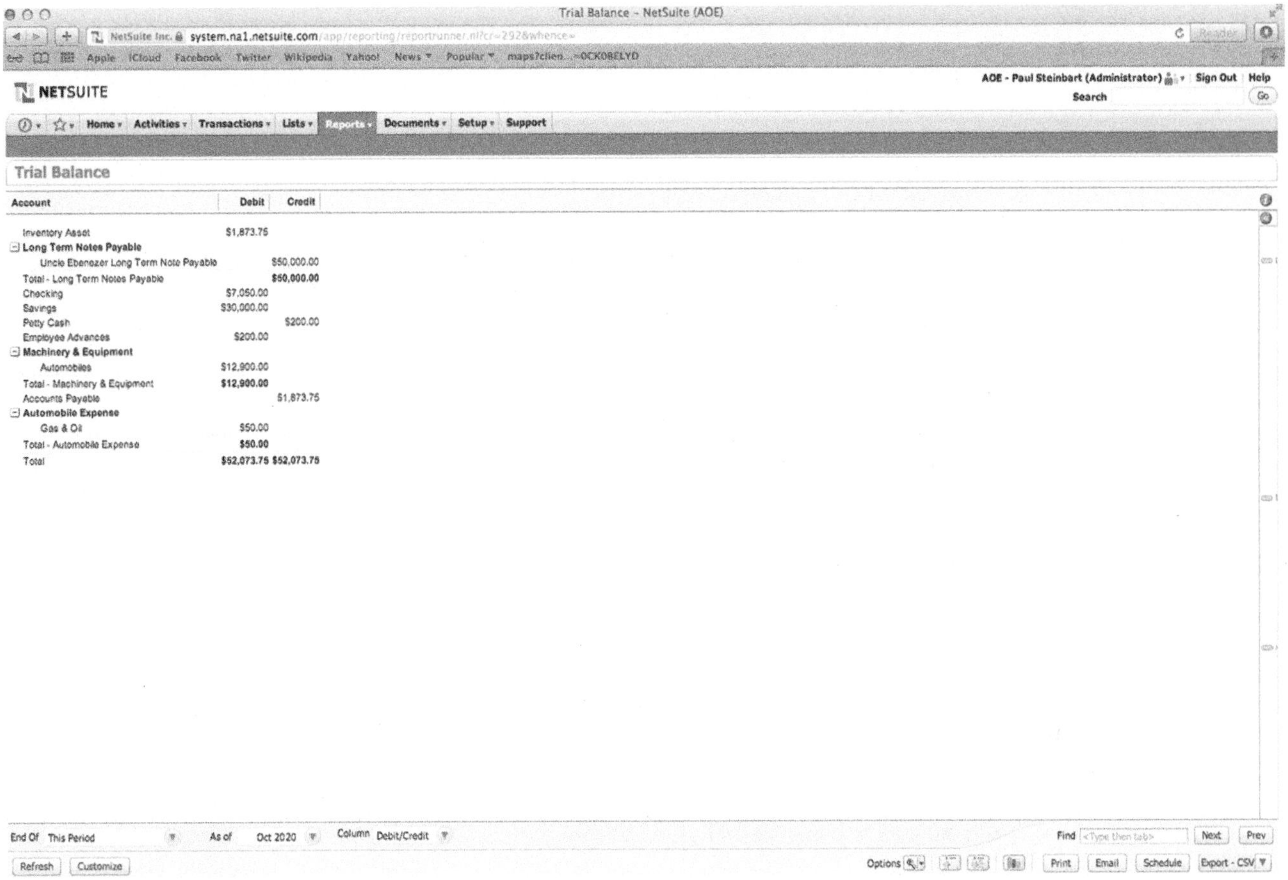

FIGURE 18-5
Example Portion of Trial Balance
Source: 2010 © NetSuite Inc.

customers and that another clerk is responsible for recording the billing of customers. (Neither clerk has custody of inventory.) The first clerk would make the following journal entry:

Unbilled shipments	xxx	
Inventory		xxx

The second clerk would make this entry:

Cost of Goods Sold	xxx	
Accounts Receivable	yyy	
Unbilled Shipments		xxx
Sales		yyy

Once both entries have been completed, the special clearing account, unbilled shipments, should have a zero balance. If not, an error has been made and must be investigated and corrected.

Figure 18-6 is an example of one of the many kinds of control reports that ERP systems provide to help identify the source of any errors that occurred in the general ledger update process. Listing journal vouchers by general account number facilitates identifying the cause of errors affecting a specific general ledger account. Listing the journal vouchers by numerical sequence, date, and account number can indicate the absence of any journal entry postings. These reports often include totals to show whether total debits and credits posted to the general ledger were equal.

THE AUDIT TRAIL As explained in Chapter 2, the audit trail is a traceable path that shows how a transaction flows through the information system to affect general ledger account balances (see Figure 2-2). It is an important detective control that provides evidence about the causes of changes in general ledger account balances.

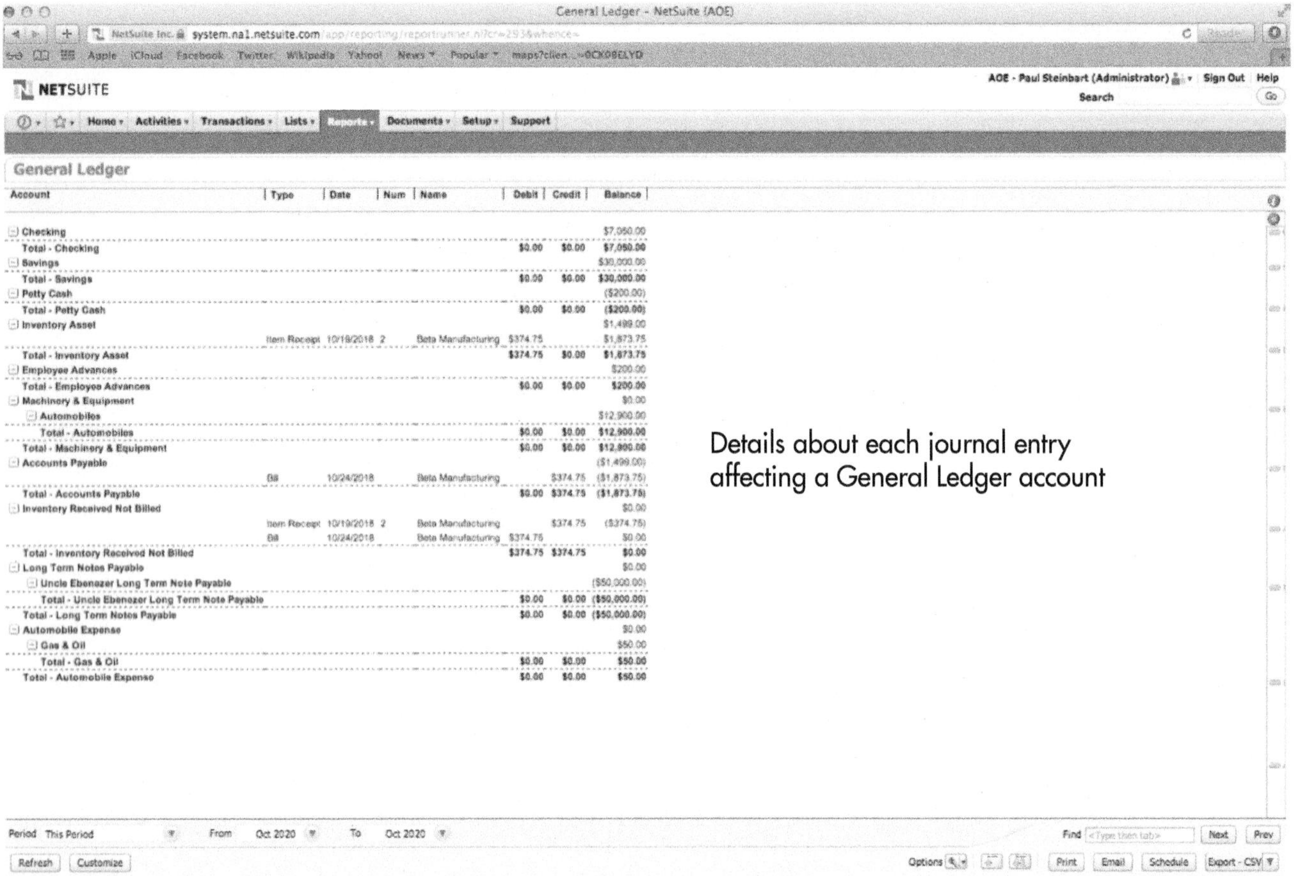

FIGURE 18-6

Example of Control Report Providing Details About Changes to a General Ledger Account Balance

Source: 2010 © NetSuite Inc.

A properly designed audit trail provides the ability to perform the following tasks:

1. Trace any transaction from its original source document (whether paper or electronic) to the journal entry that updated the general ledger and to any report or other document using that data. This provides a means to verify that all authorized transactions were recorded.
2. Trace any item appearing in a report back through the general ledger to its original source document (whether paper or electronic). This provides a means to verify that all recorded transactions were indeed authorized and that they were recorded correctly.

In legacy accounting systems, the journal voucher file is an important part of the audit trail, providing information about the source of all entries made to update the general ledger. The same capability is provided by the business workflow features in ERP systems, which make it easy to trace every step performed in processing a transaction. The usefulness of the audit trail depends on its integrity. Therefore, it is important to periodically make backups of all audit trail components and to control access to them to ensure that they cannot be altered. Thus, as Figure 18-7 shows, access to the audit trail is typically restricted. In addition, ERP systems provide built-in tools to ensure the integrity of the audit trail. SAP, for example, creates prenumbered records (called documents) for every action performed. These documents cannot be deleted; thus, enabling this built-in feature ensures that SAP creates and maintains a secure audit trail.

Post Adjusting Entries

The second activity in the general ledger system is posting various adjusting entries (circle 2.0 in Figure 18-2).

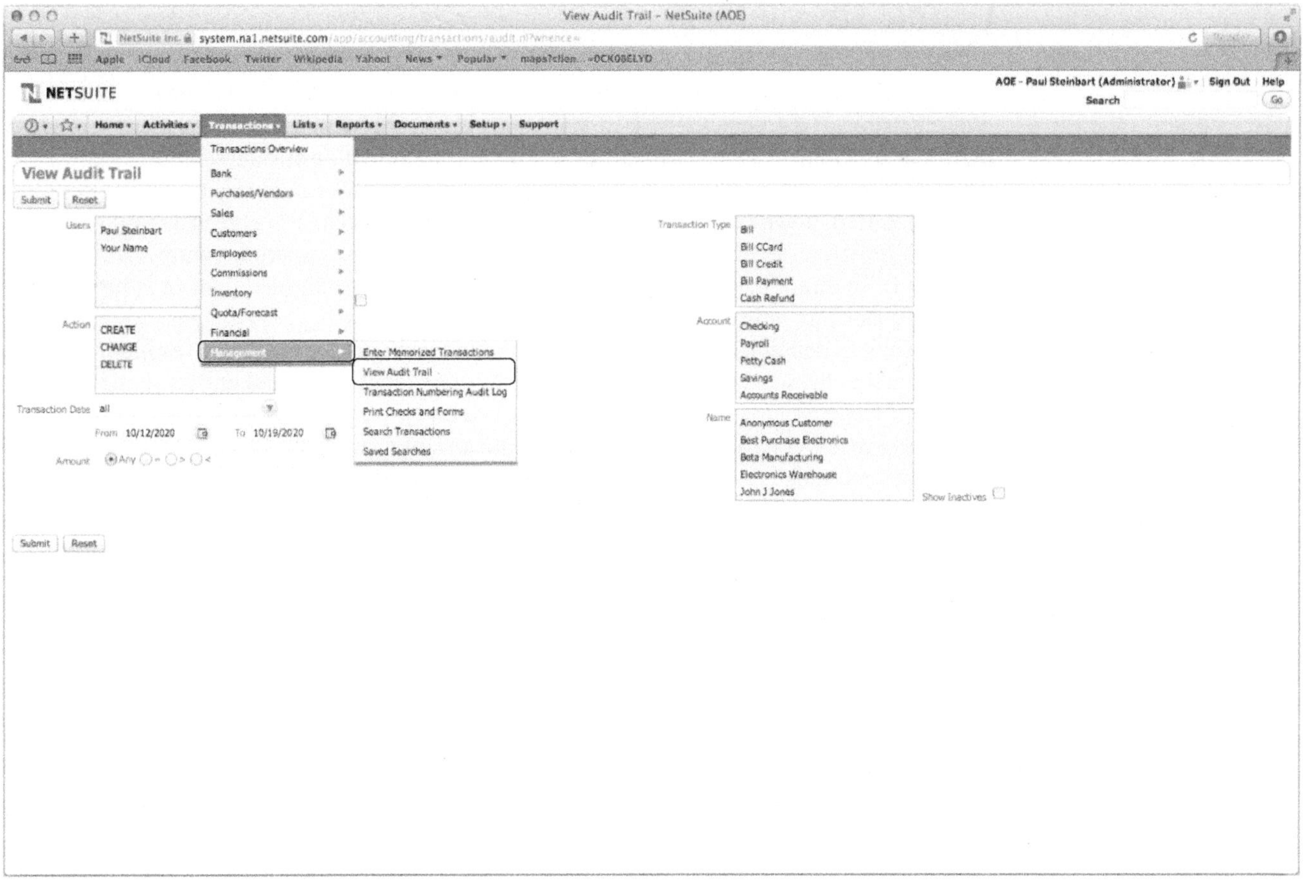

FIGURE 18-7
Illustration of How Access to Audit Trail Is Restricted to Managers
Source: 2010 © NetSuite Inc.

PROCESS

Adjusting entries originate from the controller's office, after the initial trial balance has been prepared. Adjusting entries fall into five basic categories:

1. *Accruals* are entries made at the end of the accounting period to reflect events that have occurred but for which cash has not yet been received or disbursed. Examples include the recording of interest revenue earned and wages payable.
2. *Deferrals* are entries made at the end of the accounting period to reflect the exchange of cash prior to performance of the related event. Examples include recognizing advance payments from customers as a liability and recording certain payments (e.g., rent, interest, and insurance) as prepaid assets.
3. *Estimates* are entries that reflect a portion of expenses expected to occur over a number of accounting periods. Examples include depreciation and bad-debt expenses.
4. *Revaluations* are entries made to reflect either differences between the actual and recorded value of an asset or a change in accounting principle. Examples include a change in the method used to value inventory, reducing the value of inventory to reflect obsolescence, or adjusting inventory records to reflect the results noted during a physical count of inventory.
5. *Corrections* are entries made to counteract the effects of errors found in the general ledger.

As shown in Figure 18-3, information about these adjusting entries is also stored in the journal voucher file. After all adjusting entries have been posted, an adjusted trial balance is prepared. The adjusted trial balance serves as the input to the next step in the general ledger and financial reporting cycle, the preparation of financial statements.

THREATS AND CONTROLS

As Table 18-1 shows, inaccurate and unauthorized adjusting journal entries are threats that need to be addressed because they can produce erroneous financial statements that lead to poor decisions. To reduce the risk of erroneous input, the same types of data entry processing integrity controls discussed earlier to prevent the threat of erroneous journal entries by the treasurer should also be applied to adjusting journal entries made by the controller (control 6.1). Often, however, adjusting journal entries are calculated in spreadsheets. Therefore, it is also important to employ the various spreadsheet error protection controls discussed in Chapter 13 to minimize the risk of mistakes (control 6.2). Additional control is provided by creating a standard adjusting entry file (control 6.3) for recurring adjusting entries made each period, such as depreciation expense. A standard adjusting entry file improves input accuracy by eliminating the need to repeatedly key in the same types of journal entries. It also reduces the risk of forgetting to make a recurring adjusting entry, thereby ensuring input completeness.

Strong access controls (control 7.1) reduce the risk of unauthorized adjusting entries. In addition to the preceding preventive controls, periodic reconciliations (controls 6.4 and 7.2) and audit trails (controls 6.5 and 7.3) provide a means to detect unauthorized or inaccurate adjusting entries.

Prepare Financial Statements

The third activity in the general ledger and reporting system is preparing financial statements (circle 3.0 in Figure 18-2).

PROCESS

Most organizations "close the books" to produce financial statements monthly, quarterly, and annually. A closing journal entry zeroes out all revenue and expense accounts in the adjusted trial balance and transfers the net income (or loss) to retained earnings. We now discuss two important recent regulatory and technological developments that significantly affect the process of preparing financial statements: the proposed upcoming change from U.S. GAAP to IFRS and the mandatory use of XBRL to submit reports to the SEC.

TRANSITION FROM GAAP TO IFRS Although the effective date continues to be pushed back, the SEC maintains that it is committed to requiring American companies to switch from U.S.-based GAAP to IFRS as the basis for preparing financial statements. Therefore, companies need to begin planning for the transition now because it will likely require extensive changes to their general ledger and reporting systems.

IFRS differs from GAAP in several ways that affect the design of a company's general ledger and reporting systems. One major difference concerns accounting for fixed assets. Under GAAP, most major fixed assets are recorded and depreciated on a composite basis. For example, the entire cost of a new corporate headquarters building would be recorded as one asset and depreciated over its estimated useful life, which, for buildings, is typically 40 years. In contrast, IFRS generally requires componentization of fixed assets, to recognize the fact that different elements (components) may have different economic lives. In terms of a corporate headquarters building, that would mean that the costs of the roof and of the heating and air conditioning systems would be recorded separately from the building itself because they are not likely to last 40 years. Componentization will require companies to dig through their databases to identify and disaggregate the costs of many fixed assets. For large companies that may have tens of thousands of fixed assets, componentization will be a major undertaking that carries the risk of classification and recording errors as they change the structure of their general ledgers.

Another difference involves accounting for research and development (R&D) costs. IFRS permits capitalization of development costs at an earlier stage of the process than does GAAP. Consequently, American companies may need to improve the way that they collect and record R&D related costs so that they can properly decide which costs must be expensed and which can be capitalized. At a minimum, this process will require creating additional fields in data records to capture information about the stage of the R&D process when costs were incurred. In turn, this will necessitate careful modification and testing of existing programs to ensure that they correctly process the redesigned transaction records.

A third difference is that IFRS does not permit use of the last-in first-out (LIFO) method of accounting for inventory. Consequently, companies that use LIFO will have to modify their cost accounting systems and the calculations used to value inventory. Those changes will need to be carefully reviewed and tested to minimize the risk of errors.

XBRL: REVOLUTIONIZING THE REPORTING PROCESS **XBRL** stands for e**X**tensible **B**usiness **R**eporting **L**anguage; it is a programming language designed specifically to facilitate the communication of business information. To understand the revolutionary nature of XBRL, examine Figure 18-8. The top portion shows that prior to XBRL, preparers had to manually create reports in various formats for different users. Although those reports were then sent electronically to users, regardless of format (text, spreadsheet, HTML, PDF, etc.), the reports were humanly readable but the recipients then had to reenter the data into their own systems in order to manipulate it. The entire process was inefficient and prone to error.

XBRL - eXtensible Business Reporting Language is a variant of XML (eXtensible Markup Language) specifically designed for use in communicating the content of financial data.

The bottom portion of Figure 18-8 shows how XBRL improves the reporting process. Preparers use XBRL to encode the data with machine-readable tags that explain what each

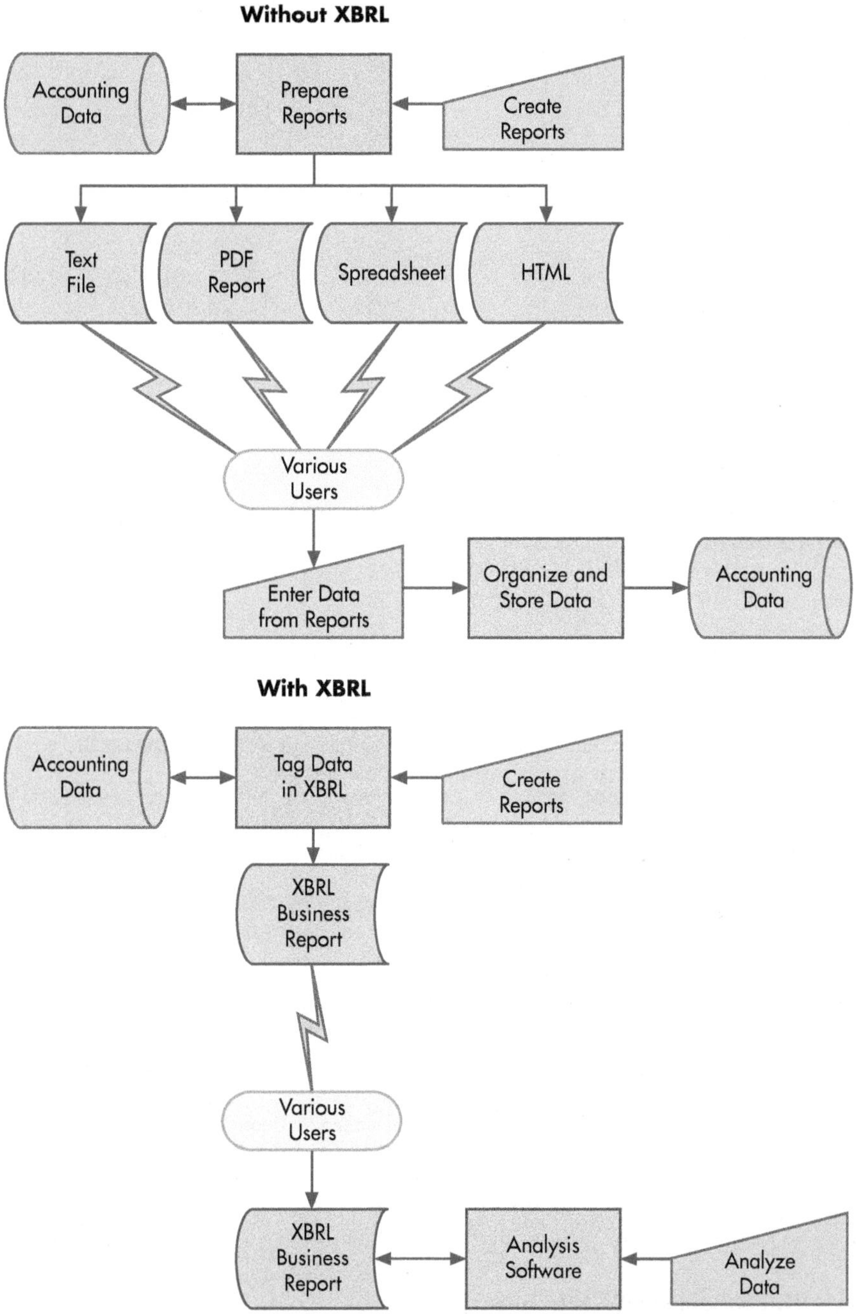

FIGURE 18-8
How XBRL Transforms the Reporting Process

data item means and then transmit it electronically in various formats to users. Thus, XBRL saves time and reduces the chances for data entry errors.

To illustrate, Figure 18-9 shows how XBRL can annotate a number in a spreadsheet to indicate that it represents sales for a particular time period, following U.S. GAAP and measured in U.S. dollars. The top portion of Figure 18-9 shows the spreadsheet that most users would see; the XBRL code in the bottom portion is intended for use by software, although it can be viewed by programmers, auditors, or anyone who needs or wants to see it.

inline XBRL (iXBRL) - An open standard that merges HTML and XBRL tags so that the same document is simultaneously human-readable in a browser yet also contains structured data that is machine-readable.

Inline XBRL (iXBRL) merges HTML and XBRL so that the same document is human-readable in a browser yet also contains structured machine-readable data that can be automatically processed by various analytics tools without requiring any manual input. Public companies must use iXBRL when submitting documents to the SEC. The top panel of

Panel A: Portion of XBRL-Encoded Spreadsheet

Statement of Income Alternative (USD $) (in Millions, except per share data)	12 Months Ended Dec. 31, 2021	Dec. 31, 2020	Dec. 31, 2019
Sales (Q)	26,901	29,280	28,950
Cost of goods sold (exclusive of expenses below)	22,175	22,803	21,955
Selling, general administrative, and other expenses	1,167	1,444	1,372
Research and development expenses	246	238	201
Provision for depreciation, depletion, and amortization	1,234	1,244	1,252
Restructuring and other charges (D)	939	268	507
Interest expense (V)	407	401	384
Other income, net (O)	−59	−1,920	−236
Total costs and expenses	26,109	24,478	25,435
Income from continuing operations before taxes on income	792	4,802	3,515
Provision for taxes on income (T)	342	1,623	853
Income from continuing operations before minority interests' share	450	3,179	2,662
Minority interests	221	365	436
Income from continuing operations (Statement [Line Items])	229	2,814	2,226
(Loss) income from discontinued operations (B)	-303	-250	22
Net (Loss) Income (Statement [Line Items])	−74	2,564	2,248
Income from continuing operations (Basic)	0.28	3.27	2.56
(Loss) income from discontinued operations (Basic)	−0.37	−0.29	0.03
Net (loss) income (Basic)	−0.09	2.98	2.59
Income from continuing operations (Diluted)	0.28	3.23	2.54
(Loss) income from discontinued operations (Diluted)	−0.37	−0.28	0.03
Net (loss) income (Diluted)	−0.09	2.95	2.57

Panel B: Portion of XBRL Code

```
<us-gaap:ResearchAndDevelopmentExpense contextRef="eol_0001193125-09-029469_STD_p12m_20191231_0"
    decimals="-6" unitRef="USD">201000000</us-gaap:ResearchAndDevelopmentExpense>
<us-gaap:RestructuringCharges contextRef="eol_0001193125-09-029469_STD_p12m_20191231_0" decimals="-6"
    unitRef="USD">507000000</us-gaap:RestructuringCharges>
<us-gaap:SalesRevenueGoodsNet contextRef="eol_0001193125-09-029469_STD_p12m_20191231_0" decimals="-6"
    unitRef="USD">28950000000</us-gaap:SalesRevenueGoodsNet>
<us-gaap:SellingGeneralAndAdministrativeExpense contextRef="eol_0001193125-09-029469_STD_p12m_20191231_0"
    decimals="-6" unitRef="USD">1372000000</us-gaap:SellingGeneralAndAdministrativeExpense>
```

Explanation:

The spreadsheet shows that the company had sales of $28,950,000,000 for the year ended December 31, 2019. The XBRL code reveals that:

- The number 28,950 appearing on the spreadsheet is based on US-GAAP (the element begins with <usgaap: SalesRevenueGoodsNet and closes with </us-gaap:SalesRevenueGoodsNet>).
- The context is the SEC Edgar Online filing (eol) for a 12-month period (p12m) ending on December 31, 2019.
- The numbers on the spreadsheet are rounded to the nearest million (decimals = -6, raw value = 28950000000).
- The value is in U.S. dollars ("USD").

FIGURE 18-9

Example of an Instance Document Showing XBRL Tags

FIGURE 18-10
Example Screenshots Using the SEC's iXBRL Viewer

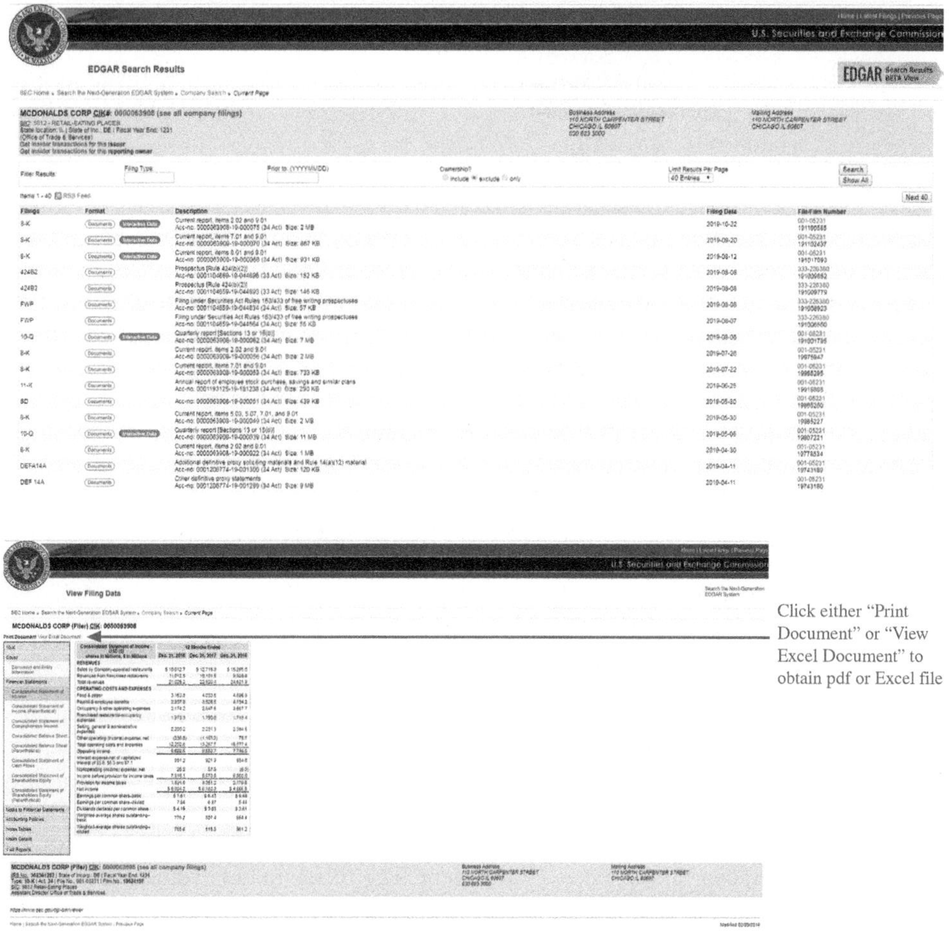
EDGAR Search Results
View Filing Data
Click either "Print Document" or "View Excel Document" to obtain pdf or Excel file

Figure 18-10 shows the various documents the SEC's EDGAR database has for McDonalds Corporation; clicking the button labeled *Interactive Data* in the row for its 10-K displays the iXBRL version of McDonalds Corporation's Consolidated Statement of Income shown in the bottom panel of Figure 18-10. Notice how the data in the lower panel is human-readable and looks like an extract from an Excel spreadsheet. Indeed, if the viewer clicks on the red words *View Excel Document*, the browser will download an XBRL-tagged spreadsheet with that data. If instead the view clicks on the black words *Print Document*, the browser will download a PDF version of that income statement.

XBRL PROCESS AND TERMINOLOGY Figure 18-11 provides a high-level view of the basic steps in preparing and delivering iXBRL reports (hereafter our discussion refers to iXBRL because the SEC now requires public companies to use it; however, the same process that we now describe also applies to XBRL). The iXBRL file containing the tagged data delivered to users is called an **instance document**. The instance document contains facts about specific financial statement line items, including their values and contextual information such as the measurement unit (dollars, euros, yuans, etc.) and whether the value is for a specific point in time (e.g., a balance sheet item) or a period of time (e.g., an income statement item). Each specific data item in an iXBRL document is called an **element**. An element's specific value is displayed in an instance document between tags. Angle brackets are used to identify tags. Two tags are used for each element. The first tag presents the element name inside a pair of angle brackets; the second tag also uses a pair of angle brackets but precedes the element name with a slash. Additional information is needed to properly interpret that value, such as the monetary units used to measure net sales and the time period during which those sales occurred. That context information is also presented in the instance document between tags. Panel B of Figure 18-9 provides a detailed example for the element "Net Sales."

instance document - An iXBRL file that contains tagged data.

element - A specific data item in an iXBRL instance document, such as a financial statement line item.

FIGURE 18-11
Electronic Reporting with XBRL

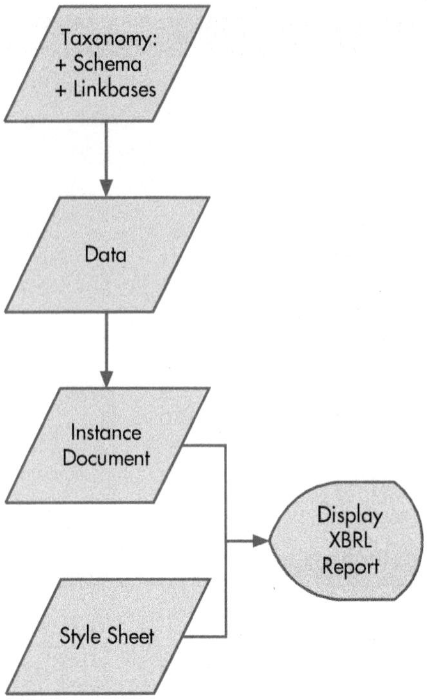

taxonomy - A set of XBRL files that defines elements and the relationships among them.

schema - An XBRL file that defines every element that appears in a specific instance document.

An instance document is created by applying a taxonomy to a set of data. A **taxonomy** is a set of files that defines the various elements and the relationships between them. One part of the taxonomy is called the **schema**, which is a file that contains the definitions of every element that could appear in an instance document. The following are some of the basic attributes used to define each element:

- A unique identifying *name* used by the software.
- A *description* that can be used to correctly interpret the element.
- The element's *data type* (monetary unit, text, date, etc.).
- The element's normal *balance type* (debit or credit).
- The element's *period type* (one point in time, called an instant, or a period of time, called a duration).

Attribute information is enclosed within tags. Thus, to continue our example, the schema would contain the following portion of a definition of the *Net Sales* element:

> *<element name="NetSales" description="Sales net of returns and allowances" type=monetaryItemType balance="credit" periodType="duration"</element>*

linkbases - One or more XBRL files that define the relationships among elements found in a specific instance document.

The taxonomy also includes a set of files called **linkbases**, which define the relationships among elements in a specific instance document. Important linkbases include the following:

- The *Reference* linkbase identifies relevant authoritative pronouncements (e.g., U.S.-GAAP, IFRS) for that element.
- The *Calculation* linkbase specifies how to combine elements (e.g., that "Current Assets" equals the sum of Cash, Accounts Receivable, and Inventory).
- The *Definition* linkbase indicates hierarchical relationships among elements (e.g., that "Current Assets" is a subset of "Assets").
- The *Presentation* linkbase describes how to group elements (e.g., Assets, Liabilities, and Equities).
- The *Label* linkbase associates human-readable labels with elements.

As Figure 18-11 shows, the information in an XBRL taxonomy is used to tag the data and create an instance document. The same taxonomy is usually used to create a set of separate instance documents, one for each reporting year. Instance documents, however, contain only the data values. Another document, called the **style sheet**, provides the instructions on how to appropriately display (render) the content of an instance document, either on a computer screen or in a printed report. The top panel of Figure 18-12 shows that all of these files are available in the SEC's EDGAR database (see list of XBRL files in the Data Files window). Panel B shows a portion of McDonalds' schema document and Panel C shows a portion of the company's Instance Document.

style sheet - An XBRL file that provides instructions on how to display (render) an instance document on either a computer screen or printed report.

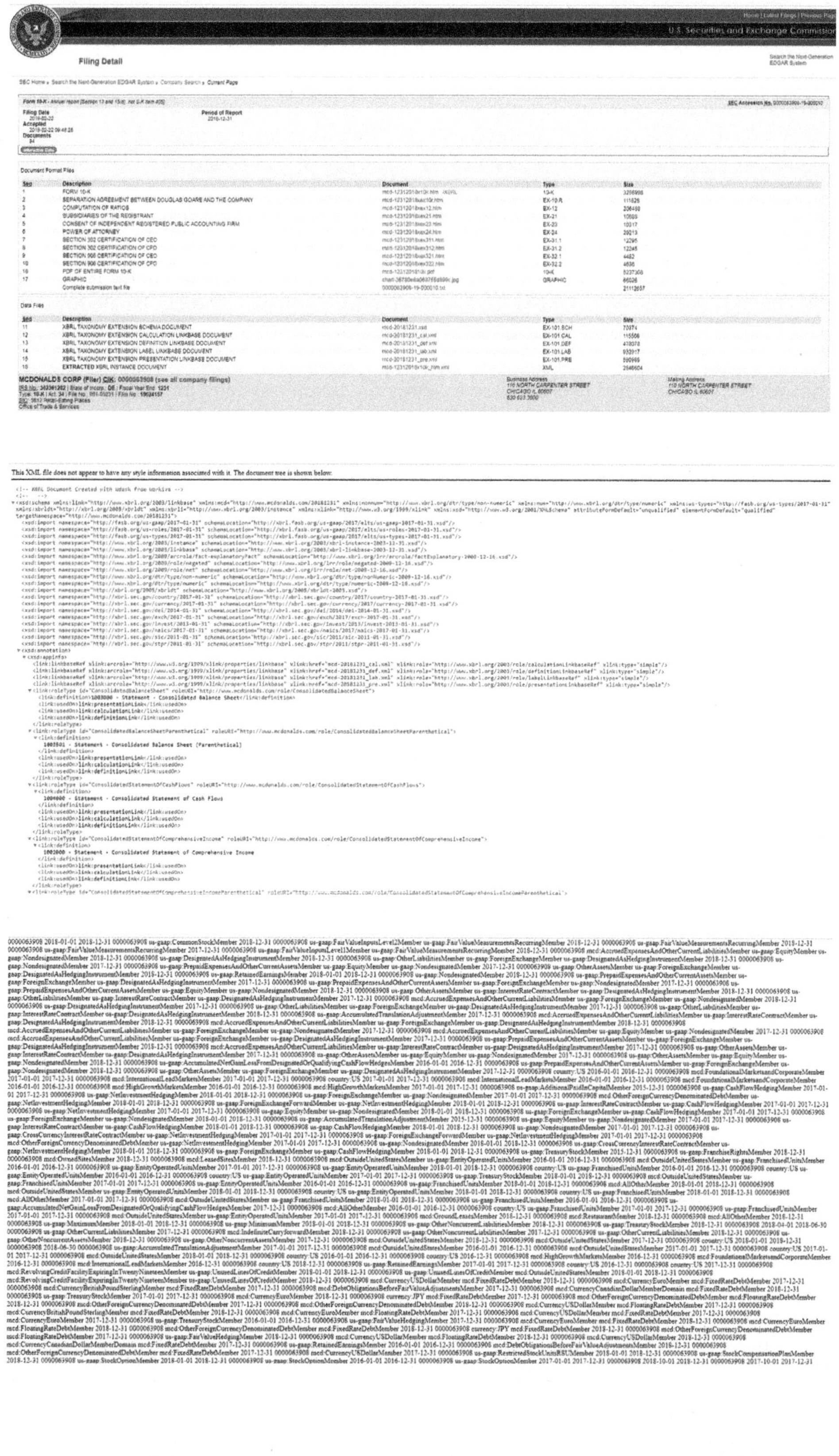

FIGURE 18-12
Finding XBRL Documents in the SEC's EDGAR Database

THE ACCOUNTANT'S ROLE The benefits of XBRL are not limited to its use for external reporting. Internal reporting will also benefit because data can be exported from the basic ERP system in a format that managers can import directly into a variety of applications, saving time and eliminating the errors arising from having to manually reenter data. Therefore, accountants can, and should, play a major role in all phases of producing XBRL reports, beginning with the selection of an appropriate taxonomy. To ensure comparability across XBRL reports produced by different organizations, standard taxonomies have been developed for many different countries and industries. Accountants use their knowledge of the organization's business practices plus general accounting principles to select the standard taxonomy that best fits the organization. They then map each data item in the organization's accounting system to its corresponding element in the taxonomy.

However, standard taxonomies cannot cover every possible situation. Sometimes, an organization needs to record financial information in a different manner or level of detail to reflect its unique way of doing business. In such cases, accountants can create new tags to more accurately present information about the organization's business activities. These new tags create what is called an **extension taxonomy**. This ability to modify XBRL is why it is referred to as an *extensible* language. Viewers can read about the taxonomies used by a company by clicking on a data element in an iXBRL instance document. For example, Figure 18-13 shows that McDonalds uses the standard U.S. GAAP taxonomy for the element labeled revenues (panel A) but that the element labeled Occupancy and Other Operating Expenses (panel B) is a customized extension.

extension taxonomy - A set of custom XBRL tags to define elements unique to the reporting organization that are not part of the standard generally accepted taxonomies for that industry.

Accountants should also use software to apply the taxonomy (and any extensions) to tag their organization's data, create instance documents, and then validate those instance documents before they are submitted. Accountants will also typically participate in creating style sheets to ensure that the information is displayed appropriately.

Not only do accountants use XBRL; as Focus 18-1 explains, the accounting profession played a major role in its creation. XBRL is a work in process. You should bookmark and regularly visit both the xbrl.org and sec.gov websites to stay abreast of continued developments in this important reporting tool.

FOCUS 18-1 The Accounting Profession's Role in XBRL

The origins of XBRL can be traced back to the early 1990s. At that time, a software engineer named Jon Bosak recognized that a critical shortcoming of HTML is its inability to describe the content of the data presented. Bosak convinced the World Wide Web Consortium (W3C) to sponsor the development of a language with this capability. That project resulted in Bosak and two other software engineers creating a programming language called XML, which stands for extensible markup language. XML is a general-purpose tool that can tag any data with identifying markers.

XML was a step in the right direction. Charlie Hoffman, a CPA who worked for a local accounting firm in Tacoma, Washington, realized, however, that XML did not go far enough to be a general-purpose language for communicating financial information. What was needed was the ability not only to identify each piece of data but also how to process it and how to relate it to other data items. Hoffman started work on adding the desired capabilities to XML but realized that the project required additional support. He sought and obtained the AICPA's help to pursue the development of a prototype set of XML-enhanced financial statements.

As the work progressed, the results were shared with major software companies, who recognized the value of such a common business language and joined the project. Eventually, many leading software companies, and important user groups, cooperated in the venture with the AICPA. The result: XBRL. The continued development and maintenance of XBRL is now overseen by a nonprofit international organization (XBRL International). Vendors are currently working on making a wide range of financial and decision support software capable of supporting XBRL. Industry-specific coding taxonomies have been developed in many countries. XBRL is on its way to becoming the global computer language for communicating financial data. And it all started with one CPA who was looking for a better way to disseminate financial data on the Internet!

Postscript: In December 2006, the AICPA formally recognized Charlie Hoffman's pioneering work in developing XBRL with a special achievement award.

- Definition
Amount of revenue recognized from goods sold, services rendered, insurance premiums, or other activities that constitute an earning process. Includes, but is not limited to, investment and interest income before deduction of interest expense when recognized as a component of revenue, and sales and trading gain (loss).

- References
Reference 1: http://www.xbrl.org/2003/role/presentationRef
-Publisher FASB
-Name Accounting Standards Codification
-Topic 225
-SubTopic 10
-Section S99
-Paragraph 2
-Subparagraph (SX 210.5-03.1)
-URI http://asc.fasb.org/extlink&oid=63488584&loc=d3e20235-122688

- Details

Name:	us-gaap_Revenues
Namespace Prefix:	us-gaap_
Data Type:	xbrli:monetaryItemType
Balance Type:	credit
Period Type:	duration

- Definition
Cost of rent for ground and top leases to third party owners of land and/or buildings of which company-operated restaurants are operated, as well as the depreciation of tangible assets (equipment, signs, seating, decor and leasehold improvements), company-operated restaurant buildings/leaseholds and the amortization of reacquired franchise rights, and the cost of advertising, promotion, operating supplies, maintenance and repair, insurance, taxes and licenses, credit/debit card processing fees, etc.

- References
No definition available.

- Details

Name:	mcd_OccupancyAndOtherOperatingExpenses
Namespace Prefix:	mcd_
Data Type:	xbrli:monetaryItemType
Balance Type:	debit
Period Type:	duration

FIGURE 18-13
Taxonomy Information for Elements in an iXBRL Instance Document

THREATS AND CONTROLS

Table 18-1 shows that one threat is the creation of inaccurate financial statements (threat 8). The data processing integrity controls for journal entries discussed earlier (control 8.1) combined with the use of packaged software (control 8.2) to produce the financial statements minimizes the risk of numerical errors in the data. However, because both IFRS and XBRL require numerous judgments about how to classify information, there is a risk that financial statements may not accurately represent the results of operations. For example, mistakes in componentizing fixed assets can result in inaccurate depreciation expenses for IFRS financial statements. XBRL standard taxonomies offer many fine-grained choices (e.g., more than 20 elements define the concept "Cash and Cash Equivalents"), which can result in selecting an inappropriate tag unless the person doing the mapping has extensive knowledge both about the organization's business practices and the XBRL taxonomies. Unnecessarily creating taxonomy extensions instead of using a standard tag is another potential problem because it eliminates one of the major advantages of XBRL (standardization, which enables automatic comparisons across companies). Training (control 8.3) and experience will likely reduce the risk of making such mistakes. In addition, an independent external audit (control 8.4) is necessary as a detective control.

Fraudulent financial reporting (threat 9) is another potential problem. Financial statement fraud often involves journal entries by upper-level management that cause the organization's financial statements to either overstate revenues or understate liabilities. It is difficult to prevent such journal entries because upper-level management inherently has the ability to override most internal controls. Therefore, the best control (control 9.1) to mitigate the threat of financial statement fraud is an independent review (audit) of all special journal entries to the general ledger (i.e., all entries other than the summary journal entries automatically generated by the various cycles discussed in Chapters 14 to 17). Although external auditors routinely "test the appropriateness of journal entries recorded in the general ledger and other adjustments," internal auditors should also regularly review all adjustments to the general ledger. To be effective, however, such testing requires proper configuration of the accounting system, so that every change to general ledger accounts is captured and recorded as part of the audit trail.

Produce Managerial Reports

The final activity in the general ledger and reporting system (circle 4.0 in Figure 18-2) is to produce various managerial reports, including budgets.

PROCESS

ERP systems like the one depicted in Figure 18-3 can produce a number of budgets to help managers plan and evaluate performance. An operating budget depicts planned revenues and expenditures for each organizational unit. A capital expenditures budget shows planned cash inflows and outflows for each capital project. Cash flow budgets compare estimated cash inflows from operations with planned expenditures and are used to determine borrowing needs.

In addition to budgets, the inquiry processing capabilities of ERP systems enable managers to easily create an almost unlimited number of performance reports. For example, sales can be broken down by products, by salesperson, and by customer. Displaying the data in graphs can help managers quickly identify important trends and relationships, as well as areas in need of more detailed analysis. Accountants should understand how to use the flexible reporting and graphing capabilities of ERP systems so that they can add value by suggesting alternative ways to organize and analyze data about business processes.

THREATS AND CONTROLS

Poorly designed reports and graphs (threat 10 in Table 18-1) can cause managers to make biased or erroneous decisions. The following subsections discuss two important controls to mitigate that threat: the use of responsibility accounting and flexible budgets to design performance reports (control 10.1) and the balanced scorecard (control 10.2). The principles of proper graph design (control 10.3) were discussed in Chapter 7.

RESPONSIBILITY ACCOUNTING AND FLEXIBLE BUDGETING To properly evaluate performance, reports should highlight the results that can be directly controlled by the person or unit evaluated. **Responsibility accounting** does this by producing a set of correlated reports that break down the organization's overall performance by the specific subunits which can most directly control those activities, as shown in Figure 18-14. Note how each report shows actual costs and variances from budget for the current month and the year to date, but only for those items that the manager of that subunit controls. Note also the hierarchical nature of the reports: The total cost of each individual subunit is displayed as a single line item on the next-higher-level report.

responsibility accounting - A system of reporting financial results on the basis of managerial responsibilities within an organization.

It is also important to design the budget so that its content matches the nature of the unit evaluated. For example, the performance reports depicted in Figure 18-14 focus on costs because production departments are usually treated as cost centers. In contrast, sales departments are often evaluated as revenue centers. Consequently, their performance reports should compare actual to forecasted sales, broken down by appropriate product and geographic

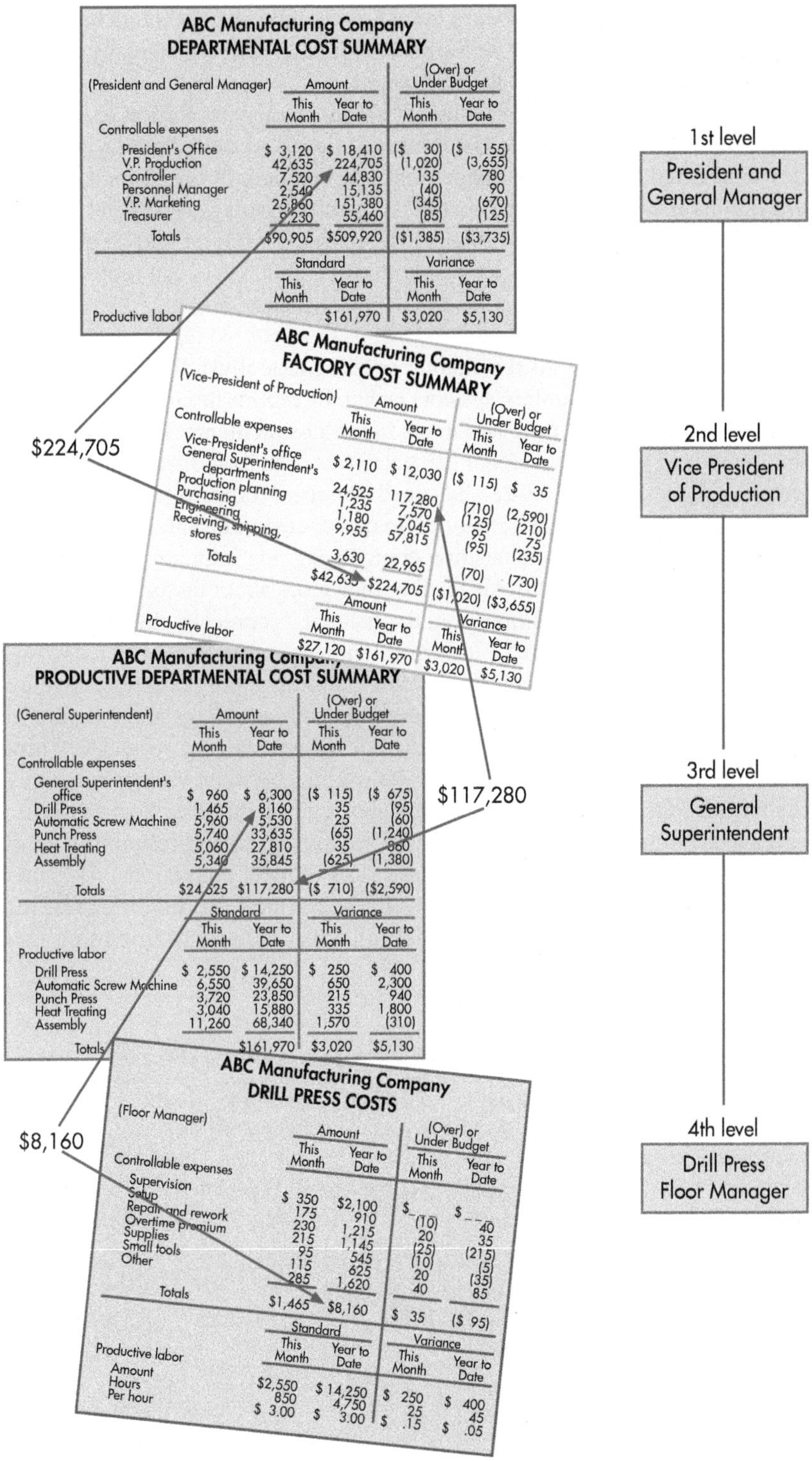

FIGURE 18-14
Sample Set of Reports to Illustrate Responsibility Accounting

categories. Similarly, reports for departments treated as profit centers should include both revenues and expenses.

No matter which basis is used to prepare a unit's budgetary performance report, the method used to calculate the budget standard is crucial. The easiest approach is to establish fixed targets for each unit, store those figures in the database, and compare actual performance with those preset values. A major drawback to this approach is that the budget number is static and does not reflect unforeseen changes in the operating environment. Consequently, individual managers may be penalized or rewarded for factors beyond their control. For example, assume that the budgeted amounts in Figure 18-14 for the general superintendent are based on planned output of 2,000 units. If, however, actual production is 2,200 units because of greater-than-anticipated sales, then the negative variances for each expense category may indicate not inefficiency, but rather the increased level of output.

flexible budget - A budget in which the amounts are stated in terms of formulas based on actual level of activity.

A **flexible budget**, in which the budgeted amounts vary in relation to some measure of organizational activity, mitigates such problems. In terms of our previous example, flexible budgeting would entail dividing the budget for each line item in the general superintendent's department into its fixed and variable cost components. In this way, budget standards would be automatically adjusted for any unplanned increases (or decreases) in production. Thus, any differences between these adjusted standards and actual costs can more appropriately be interpreted.

balanced scorecard - A management report that measures four dimensions of organizational performance: financial, internal operations, innovation and learning, and customer perspectives.

THE BALANCED SCORECARD As the chapter opening case illustrated, one problem with the reports produced by many accounting systems is that the reports too narrowly focus on just one dimension of performance: that reflected in the financial statements. The **balanced scorecard**, a report that provides a multidimensional perspective of organizational performance, addresses that problem. As shown in Table 18-2, a balanced scorecard[1] contains measures reflecting four perspectives on organizational performance: financial, customer, internal operations, and innovation and learning. The financial section contains lagging indicators of past performance, whereas the other three sections provide leading indicators about factors likely to affect future financial performance. For each dimension, the balanced scorecard shows the organization's goals and specific measures that reflect performance in attaining those goals. Together, the four dimensions of the balanced scorecard provide a much more comprehensive overview of organizational performance than that provided by financial measures alone. Let us now examine Table 18-2 to see how the four parts of the balanced scorecard reflect key aspects of an organization's strategy and important causal relationships between various measures.

AOE's top management, like many companies, agreed on three key financial goals: increased revenue streams through sales of new products, increased profitability as reflected in return on equity, and maintaining adequate cash flow to meet obligations. As shown in Table 18-2, specific measures and targets were developed to track the attainment of those goals. Both the choice of key metrics and the setting of target values are important management

TABLE 18-2 Example of a Balanced Scorecard

Dimension Goals	Measure	Target	2021	2020	2019
Financial					
New revenue streams	Sales of new products (000s)	104	103	100	98
Improve profitability	Return on equity (%)	12.5%	12.6%	12.2%	12.1%
Positive cash flow	Cash from operations (000s)	156	185	143	164
Customer					
Improve satisfaction	Rating (0–100)	95	93	92	90
Be a preferred supplier	Percentage of key customers' electronics purchases made from us	20%	20%	18%	17%
Internal Operations					
Service quality	Orders filled without error (%)	98%	97%	95%	94%
Speed of delivery	Order cycle time (days)	10.4	10.5	11.2	11.5
Process efficiency	Defect rate	1.0%	1.1%	1.05%	1.02%
Innovation and Learning					
New products	Number of new products	4	4	3	3
Employee learning	Personnel attending advanced training courses (%)	10%	25%	9%	5%

[1]This section is based on two articles by Robert S. Kaplan and David P. Norton: "The Balanced Scorecard—Measures That Drive Performance," *Harvard Business Review* (January–February 1992): 71–79; and "Using the Balanced Scorecard as a Strategic Management System," *Harvard Business Review* (January–February 1996): 75–85. Additional information about the balanced scorecard can be found at www.balancedscorecard.org.

decisions. Many organizations make the mistake of setting targets that reflect industry benchmark values. The problem with such an approach is that the organization's aspirations and, hence, its performance are limited by its competitors' performance. Although industry benchmarks may provide a useful reference point, management should set targets that take into consideration the organization's unique strengths and weaknesses.

For every organization, customers are the key to achieving financial goals. Accordingly, the customer perspective of AOE's balanced scorecard contains two key goals: Improve customer satisfaction and become the preferred supplier for key customers. In turn, meeting those customer-oriented goals requires efficiently and effectively performing internal business processes. Consequently, the internal operations perspective portion of AOE's balanced scorecard focuses on those activities most likely to directly affect customer perceptions: service quality, speed of delivery, and process efficiency. Finally, AOE's top management acknowledged the importance of developing new products and training its workforce to continuously improve service and results. Therefore, measures of those two items are included in the innovation and learning perspective of AOE's balanced scorecard.

Note that the preceding discussion implied a number of hypotheses about cause-and-effect relationships. For example, increased employee training is expected to improve service quality, as reflected in the percentage of customer orders filled correctly. In turn, improved service quality is expected to result in increased customer satisfaction and in more purchases from key customers. Finally, increased customer satisfaction is expected to result in improved profitability and cash flow. Thus, the measures in the innovation and learning, internal operations, and customer perspective portions of the balanced scorecard are hypothesized to be leading indicators of financial measures. Analyzing trends in the actual measures allows AOE's management to test the validity of those hypotheses. If improvements in one perspective do not generate expected improvements in other areas in subsequent time periods, top management must reevaluate and probably revise hypotheses about the determinants of organizational success. Indeed, this ability to test and refine strategy is one of the major benefits the balanced scorecard provides.

Accountants and systems professionals should participate in the development of a balanced scorecard. Top management's role is to specify the goals to be pursued in each dimension. Accountants and information systems professionals can then help management choose the most appropriate measures for tracking achievement of those goals. In addition, they can provide input concerning the feasibility of collecting the data that would be required to implement various proposed measures.

Although the balanced scorecard was initially developed as a strategic management tool, it can also be used as a vehicle to better manage enterprise risk by incorporating appropriate risk-based goals and measures in the various dimensions. For example, an organization might want to increase information security awareness among employees. One way to motivate attention to that objective is to explicitly list increased security awareness as one of the goals in the Innovation and Learning section of the scorecard and then measure employee knowledge about security best practices. Similarly, listing reduced inventory shrinkage as one of the Internal Operations Process goals and measuring it can help focus attention on reducing the risk of employee theft. External threats, such as loss of market share, can likewise be addressed by including appropriate measures (e.g., sales to repeat customers, number of new customers) in the Customer and Financial sections of the balanced scorecard. Thus, the balanced scorecard can be used as one tool to monitor and evaluate an organization's controls and risk management program.

The balanced scorecard, like all scorecards, is created periodically and provides management with a means to evaluate past performance. But, as the chapter-opening case explains, management also needs real-time reports that can be used to take corrective action in a timely manner. Such information is provided in **dashboards**, which are typically interactive displays of real-time measures of key indicators of operating performance.

dashboards - Interactive real-time displays of key indicators of operating performance.

Finally, although a number of different scorecards, dashboards, and other reports are necessary to support effective management, organizations should monitor the total number of reports and the costs associated with producing them. For example, one useful metric is to divide the total number of reports by the total number of employees. High scores may indicate that the company is producing a large number of reports used by very few individuals and therefore could reduce costs by eliminating some of those reports. Another useful metric is the number of reports in which each general ledger account is used. Low scores may indicate unnecessary accounts which, if eliminated, could speed up the closing process and thereby provide more timely financial statements.

Summary and Case Conclusion

The general ledger and financial reporting system integrates and summarizes the results of the various accounting subsystems for the revenue, expenditure, production, and human resources cycles. The general ledger is the central master file in the accounting system. Consequently, it is important to implement control procedures to ensure its accuracy and security. Important controls include data processing integrity checks of the journal voucher records posted to the general ledger, access controls, an adequate audit trail, and appropriate backup and disaster recovery procedures.

The outputs produced by the general ledger system fall into two primary categories: financial statements and managerial reports. The former are prepared periodically in accordance with regulatory frameworks (GAAP or IFRS) and are distributed to both internal and external users. The latter are prepared for internal use only and therefore often include comparisons between actual and budgeted performance. The usefulness of these reports, whether presented in the form of tables or graphs, is affected by how well they are designed.

Organizations must provide information to a wide variety of users, including government agencies, industry analysts, financial institutions, and individual decision makers. XBRL provides a mechanism for improving the efficiency of generating such information, as well as for using information obtained from external sources.

Elizabeth Venko and Ann Brandt explained that AOE's new integrated transaction processing database provides much of the data needed to create a balanced scorecard. They told Linda Spurgeon that they could help her design a balanced scorecard that included metrics that would reflect AOE's strategic goals. Linda and Stephanie agreed with those suggestions. Linda also approved Elizabeth and Ann's request for two accountants and two IS staff to be assigned to begin work on reconfiguring AOE's new ERP system to generate financial statements in accordance with IFRS.

This chapter concludes our examination of the various cycles in an integrated accounting system. This chapter and the previous four explained how an accounting system should be designed: (1) to process transactions for accountability purposes, (2) to maintain adequate controls to ensure the integrity of the organization's data and the safeguarding of its assets, and (3) to provide information to support decision making. One other theme that appears throughout this book is the need for accountants to move beyond the traditional role of scorekeeper and actively seek to add value to their organization. Accountants should participate in decisions about adopting new technology and implementing new information systems because they have the training to properly evaluate the relative costs and benefits, as well as the economic risks, underlying such investments. Effectively participating in decisions concerning technology, however, requires accountants not only to keep abreast of current accounting developments but also to stay informed about advances in IT. Thus, as an accountant, you must make a commitment to lifelong learning. We wish you well in this endeavor.

KEY TERMS

journal voucher file 571
trial balance 572
XBRL 577
inline XBRL (iXBRL) 578
instance document 579
element 579
taxonomy 580
schema 580
linkbases 580
style sheet 581
extension taxonomy 582
responsibility accounting 584
flexible budget 586
balanced scorecard 586
dashboards 587

AIS in Action

CHAPTER QUIZ

1. From where do adjusting entries usually come?
   a. treasurer
   b. controller
   c. various accounting cycle subsystems, such as sales order entry
   d. unit managers

2. Preparing performance reports that contain data only about items that a specific organizational unit controls is an example of which of the following?
   a. flexible budget system
   b. responsibility accounting system
   c. closing the books
   d. management by exception

3. The definition of an XBRL element, including such information as whether its normal account balance is a debit or a credit, is found in which of the following?
   a. linkbase
   b. instance document
   c. schema
   d. style sheet

4. Which of the following shows the implied causal linkages among the portions of the balanced scorecard?
   a. Financial → Internal → Innovation and learning → Customer
   b. Innovation and learning → Internal → Customer → Financial
   c. Customer → Financial → Internal → Innovation and learning
   d. Internal → Customer → Innovation and learning → Financial

5. Which of the following XBRL documents contains the actual data values for a company's net income for a particular year?
   a. style sheets
   b. schema
   c. linkbases
   d. instance document

6. The number of orders shipped per warehouse worker each day is a metric that would most likely appear in which part of the balanced scorecard?
   a. innovation and learning
   b. customer
   c. internal operations
   d. financial

7. Which of the following is an important part of the audit trail?
   a. journal vouchers
   b. flexible budgets
   c. trial balance
   d. data warehouse

8. An adjusting journal entry to record interest revenue that has been earned but not yet received is an example of which of the following?
   a. accrual
   b. deferral
   c. estimate
   d. revaluation

9. Which of the following is designed primarily to improve the efficiency of financial reporting?
   a. XML
   b. XBRL
   c. IFRS
   d. the balanced scorecard

10. Which of the following provides real-time data about key measures of operating performance ?
    a. XBRL
    b. the balanced scorecard
    c. dashboards
    d. a flexible budget

DISCUSSION QUESTIONS

18.1 Although XBRL facilitates the electronic exchange of financial information, some external users do not think it goes far enough. They would like access to the entire general ledger, not just to XBRL-tagged financial reports that summarize general ledger accounts. Should companies provide external users with such access? Why, or why not?

18.2 How can responsibility accounting and flexible budgets improve morale?

18.3 Why is the audit trail an important control?

18.4 The balanced scorecard measures organizational performance along four dimensions. Is it possible that measures on the customer, internal operations, and innovation and learning dimensions could be improving without any positive change in the financial dimension? If so, what are the implications of such a pattern?

18.5 The "X" in XBRL (and iXBRL) stands for extensible, which means companies can create customized tags for financial statement elements. This capability allows companies to present financial information in a manner that reflects their unique business practices. However, some critics argue that many companies abuse this privilege, creating unnecessary extensions and thereby undermining one of the benefits of XBRL (structured machine-readable data) because the use of extensions requires human intervention to properly compare data across companies. How should the accounting profession respond to this criticism?

PROBLEMS

18.1 Match the terms with their definitions:

Term	Definition
____ **1.** journal voucher file	a. Individual financial statement item
____ **2.** instance document	b. Evaluating performance based on controllable costs
____ **3.** XBRL element	c. Evaluating performance by computing standards in light of actual activity levels
____ **4.** balanced scorecard	d. Set of journal entries that updated the general ledger
____ **5.** XBRL extension taxonomy	e. Set of files that defines XBRL elements and specifies the relationships among them
____ **6.** dashboards	f. Multidimensional performance report
____ **7.** XBRL taxonomy	g. File that defines relationships among XBRL elements
____ **8.** XBRL linkbase	h. File that defines the attributes of XBRL elements
____ **9.** XBRL schema	i. Detective control that can be used to trace changes in general ledger account balances back to source documents
____ **10.** XBRL style sheet	j. File that explains how to display an XBRL instance document
____ **11.** responsibility accounting	k. File that contains specific data values for a set of XBRL elements for a specific time period or point in time
____ **12.** flexible budget	l. File containing a set of customized tags to define new XBRL elements that are unique to a specific organization
	m. A real-time report containing key operating performance metrics

18.2 Which control procedure would be most effective in addressing the following problems?

a. When entering a journal entry to record issuance of new debt, the treasurer inadvertently transposes two digits in the debit amount.
b. The spreadsheet used to calculate accruals had an error in a formula. As a result, the controller's adjusting entry was for the wrong amount.
c. The controller forgot to make an adjusting entry to record depreciation.
d. A sales manager tipped off friends that the company's financial results, to be released tomorrow, were unexpectedly good.
e. The general ledger master file is stored on disk. For some reason, the disk is no longer readable. It takes the accounting department a week to reenter the past month's transactions from source documents in order to create a new general ledger master file.
f. The controller sent a spreadsheet containing a preliminary draft of the income statement to the CFO by e-mail. An investor intercepted the e-mail and used the information to sell his stock in the company before news of the disappointing results became public.
g. A company's XBRL business report was incorrect because the controller selected the wrong element from the taxonomy.
h. Instead of a zero, an employee entered the letter o when typing in data values in an XBRL instance document.

18.3 Explain the components of an audit trail for verifying changes to accounts payable. Your answer should specify how those components can be used to verify the accuracy, completeness, and validity of all purchases, purchase returns, purchase discounts, debit memos, and cash disbursements.

18.4 As manager of a local automobile repair shop, you want to develop a balanced scorecard so you can more effectively monitor the shop's performance.

REQUIRED

a. Propose at least two goals for each dimension, and explain why those goals are important to the overall success of the repair shop. One goal should be purely performance oriented, and the other should be risk related.
b. Suggest specific measures for each goal developed in part a.
c. Explain how to gather the data needed for each measure developed in part b.

18.5 Use Table 18-1 to create a questionnaire checklist that can be used to evaluate controls in the general ledger and reporting cycle.

a. For each control issue, write a Yes/No question such that a "No" answer represents a control weakness. For example, one question might be, "Is access to the general ledger restricted?"
b. For each Yes/No question, write a brief explanation of why a "No" answer represents a control weakness.

18.6 Excel Problem.*

Objective: Enhancing Tabular Displays in Excel.

REQUIRED

a. Improve tabular displays of information by shading alternate rows. Download the spreadsheet for this problem from the textbook website and use conditional formatting to shade alternating rows so that even numbered rows are in standard white, but odd numbered rows are in a light shade of blue, beginning with row 3.
b. Improve tabular displays by adding colored arrows (red, yellow, and green) in column A (next to the name of the row) to indicate status in terms of "red" = definitely a negative trend, "yellow" = warning, and "green" = definitely a positive trend. Use the following rules:
   1. For sales: Green means that this year's sales are larger than last year's; yellow means this year's sales are less than last year's but more than two years ago; red otherwise.
   2. For net sales: Green means net sales are more than 97% of sales; yellow means between 95% and 97% of sales; red means net sales are less than 95% of sales.

---

* Life-long learning opportunity: see pp. xxiii–xxiv in preface.

3. For gross profit, green means more than last year; yellow means less than last year but more than two years ago; red otherwise.

c. Insert a row between Operating Expenses and Income tax, with the label "Income before tax." Your solution at this point should look like Figure 18-15 below.

HINTS

- The formula mod(row(),2) returns the remainder of dividing the row number by two.
- Choose classic style for row shading; choose icon sets and then search for the colored arrows for "labeling" the trends of sales, net sales, and gross profits.
- You may want to check the "reverse icon" box for some of the rows where you are placing your icon.

18.7 Answer all of the following multiple-choice questions.

1. The theory underlying the Balanced Scorecard is that improvements in the _____ section will lead to improvements in the _____ section, leading to improvements in the _____ section, ultimately creating better results in the financial section.
 a. customer, learning & innovation, internal
 b. learning & innovation, internal, customer
 c. internal, customer, learning & innovation

2. Journal entries made by either the treasurer or controller should be subject to input edit and processing controls. A data entry application control designed to ensure that the total debits in a journal entry equal the total credits is called a(n) _____.
 a. sign check
 b. equality check
 c. reasonableness check
 d. zero-balance check

3. Which section of the Balanced Scorecard would benefit most from collecting data from external parties rather than relying on internally generated data?
 a. financial
 b. customer
 c. internal operations
 d. innovation and learning

4. Fraudulent financial reporting is a concern in the GL/reporting cycle. The best control to deal with that potential problem is _____.
 a. proper segregation of duties
 b. processing integrity controls such as validity checks
 c. an independent audit of all adjusting entries
 d. requiring mandatory vacations for all managers
 e. prenumbering of all documents

FIGURE 18-15

Example of Solution to Problem 18.6

		2021	2020	2019	2018	2017
Sales	●	935,000	944,000	925,000	930,000	910,000
Sales returns	●	25,000	31,000	33,000	36,000	39,000
Net Sales		910,000	913,000	892,000	894,000	871,000
Cost of Goods Sold		742,000	727,000	713,000	715,000	700,000
Gross Profit		168,000	186,000	179,000	179,000	171,000
Operating Expenses	○	143,000	142,000	141,000	138,000	135,000
Income Taxes		6,250	11,000	9,500	10,250	9,000
Net Income		18,750	33,000	28,500	30,750	27,000

5. Creation and review of an audit trail is a detective control that can enable organizations to find and correct problems arising from ________.
   a. inaccurate updating of the general ledger
   b. unauthorized adjusting entries
   c. both a and b
   d. neither a nor b

6. An adjusting entry to record bad debt expense is an example of a(n) ________.
   a. accrual
   b. deferral
   c. estimate
   d. revaluation
   e. correction

7. Which of the following XBRL components contains information about which items should be summed to create a category total (e.g., which items comprise current liabilities)?
   a. instance document
   b. style sheet
   c. taxonomy
   d. linkbase
   e. schema

8. Which of the following XBRL components can, if used too much, limit the potential benefits of comparability across organizations?
   a. presentation linkbases
   b. taxonomy extensions
   c. style sheets
   d. schemas

18.8 Excel Problem.*

Objective: Learn how to use the camera feature to create a dashboard.

REQUIRED

a. Download the spreadsheet for this problem.
b. Format the data to display sales and income before tax as currency, with no decimals.
c. Format the rest of the data to display commas for the thousands, with no decimals.
d. Create a column chart (or bar chart, whichever you prefer) that shows the trend in sales and net sales.

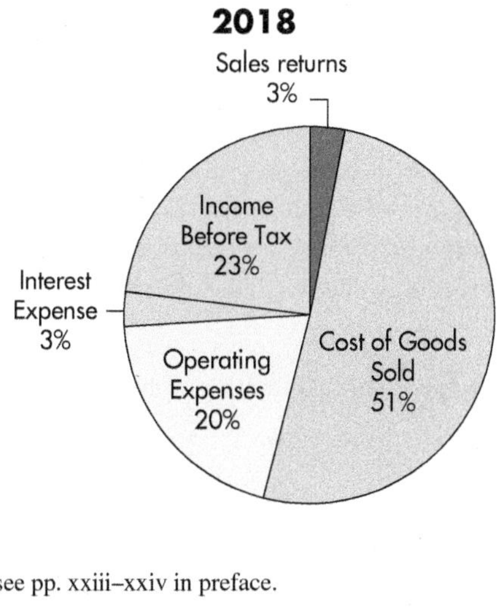

FIGURE 18-16
Sample Pie Chart for Problem 18.8

* Life-long learning opportunity: see pp. xxiii–xxiv in preface.

e. Create four pie charts, one for each year, to show the relative size of sales returns, cost of goods sold, operating expenses, interest expense, and income before tax expressed as percentages of total sales (see Figure 18-16 on previous page for an example).
f. Create a line chart that shows the trend in sales and income before tax.
g. Label this entire worksheet, with the 3 charts, as "Source Data."
h. Open a new blank worksheet and label it "Dashboard."
i. Use the camera tool to insert the charts from the "Source Data" worksheet on the "Dashboard" worksheet.
j. Resize and rearrange the charts on the Dashboard page in any manner you think is most interesting.

HINTS

- You may need to load the camera tool onto your toolbar. Search the Internet for tips on how to do this.
- You may need to move your charts around so they do not share any cells in the spreadsheet because you may have to select the cells in which the chart is located, not the chart itself, to be able to use the camera tool.

18.9 XBRL Problem*

Objective: Practice examining iXBRL financial statements to identify use of extension taxonomies.

REQUIRED

a. Access the iXBRL reports from the SEC for two companies in the same industry (your instructor may specifically assign companies and industries or leave the choice to you—the key is that both companies must be in the same industry). Use the SEC's iXBRL viewer (or another iXBRL viewer of your choice) to explore the iXBRL Consolidated Statement of Income for each company, and submit a document that completes the following table:

	Name of Company 1	Name of Company 2
Number of iXBRL elements in the Consolidated Statement of Income based on a standard taxonomy (US GAPP, IFRS, etc.)		
Number of iXBRL elements in the Consolidated Statement of Income based on an extension taxonomy		

b. Attach screenshots of all iXBRL elements that use an extension taxonomy.
c. How do you explain any differences you find between the two companies? For example, given that they are in the same industry, why do you think one company created a special extension taxonomy for one or more elements but the other company did not and instead used the standard U.S. GAPP taxonomy?

18.10 Excel Problem*

Objective: How to do what-if analysis with graphs.

* Life-long learning opportunity: see pp. xxiii–xxiv in preface.

REQUIRED

a. Read the article "Tweaking the Numbers," by Theo Callahan in the June 2001 issue of the *Journal of Accountancy* (available at www.aicpa.org). Follow the instructions in the article to create a spreadsheet with graphs that do what-if analysis.

b. Now create a spreadsheet to do graphical what-if analysis for the "cash gap." Cash gap represents the number of days between when a company has to pay its suppliers and when it gets paid by its customers. Thus,

Cash gap = Inventory days on hand + Receivables collection period
− Accounts payable period

The purpose of your spreadsheet is to display visually what happens to cash gap when you "tweak" policies concerning inventory, receivables, and payables. Thus, you will create a spreadsheet that looks like Figure 18-17.

c. Set the three spin buttons to have the following values:

	Spin Button for Inventory	Spin Button for Receivables	Spin Button for Payables
Linked cell	C2	C3	C4
Maximum	120	120	90
Minimum	0	30	20
Value	30	60	20
Small change	10	10	10

d. The article "Analyzing Liquidity: Using the Cash Conversion Cycle" by C. S. Cagle, S. N. Campbell, and K. T. Jones in the *Journal of Accountancy* (May 2013), pp. 44–48, calls the "Cash Gap" the "Currency Conversion Cycle" and explains that bigger values are bad because they indicate less liquidity (because cash needed to pay suppliers is tied up in receivables and inventory). Indeed, the "cash gap" can even be negative for companies, like Dell, that collect payment from customers in advance and stretch out payments to suppliers as long as possible. Given that background, collect the information from annual reports needed to calculate the "cash gap"

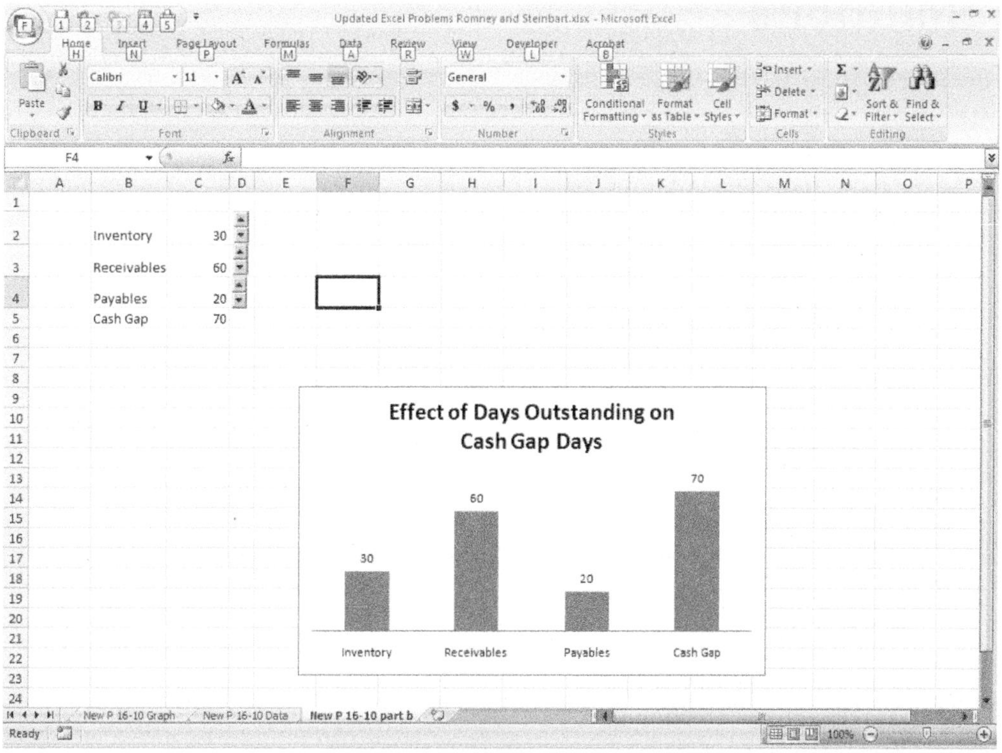

FIGURE 18-17
Spreadsheet for Problem 18.10, part b

for at least 3 years for Dell, Walmart, Home Depot, and McDonalds. Enter that data in a spreadsheet and create a graph that best highlights the trend in cash gap across the different companies.

CASE 18-1 Exploring iXBRL Viewers*

The SEC provides a free iXBRL viewer. Another free viewer is available at edgardashboard.xbrlcloud.com. Use those two iXBRL viewers (and any others your professor assigns) to examine the iXBRL filings by a specific company, and write a report that compares them in terms of ease of use and features. Attach screen shots to support your analyses.

CASE 18-2 Evaluating a General Ledger Package*

Magazines such as *Journal of Accountancy* and *Strategic Finance* periodically publish reviews of accounting software. Obtain a copy of a recent software review article, and read its comments about a general ledger package to which you have access. Using the software, write a report that indicates whether, and why, you agree or disagree with the review's opinions about the following features:

a. Ease of installation
b. Flexibility of the initial setup of the chart of accounts
c. Ease of modifying the chart of account
d. Control procedures available to restrict access
e. Control procedures available to ensure accuracy of input and processing
f. Report flexibility (how easy it is to design reports, etc.)
g. Adequacy and control of the audit trail (e.g., what reference data are automatically provided versus how much of the audit trail has to be manually constructed)

AIS in Action Solutions

QUIZ KEY

1. From where do adjusting entries usually come?
   a. treasurer [Incorrect. Adjusting entries are entered by the controller after the trial balance has been prepared. The treasurer makes regular journal entries to record financing activities, such as issuing or retiring debt.]
   ▶ b. controller [Correct. Adjusting entries are entered by the controller after the trial balance has been prepared.]
   c. various accounting cycle subsystems, such as sales order entry [Incorrect. Subsystems send summary regular journal entries, not adjusting entries, to the general ledger.]
   d. unit managers [Incorrect. Unit managers should not make any journal entries.]

2. Preparing performance reports that contain data only about items that a specific organizational unit controls is an example of which of the following?
   a. flexible budget system [Incorrect. Flexible budgets adjust targets based on actual inputs.]
   ▶ b. responsibility accounting system [Correct. This is the essence and purpose of responsibility accounting.]
   c. closing the books [Incorrect. Closing the books is a process performed at the end of a fiscal period to prepare financial statements.]
   d. management by exception [Incorrect. Management by exception is a reporting technique that focuses on unusual variations from standards.]

* Life-long learning opportunity: see pp. xxiii–xxiv in preface.

3. The definition of an XBRL element, including such information as whether its normal account balance is a debit or a credit, is found in which of the following?
   a. linkbase [Incorrect. The linkbase files in the taxonomy provide information about relationships among elements.]
   b. instance document [Incorrect. The instance document contains the value of an element and contextual information, but not its full definition.]
   ▶ c. schema [Correct. The schema file in the taxonomy contains definitions of XBRL elements.]
   d. style sheet [Incorrect. The style sheet specifies how to display an instance document on either a computer screen or on a printed report.]

4. Which of the following shows the implied causal linkages among the portions of the balanced scorecard?
   a. Financial → Internal → Innovation and learning → Customer [Incorrect.]
   ▶ b. Innovation and learning → Internal → Customer → Financial [Correct. The theory underlying the balanced scorecard is that learning and innovation will improve internal measures of performance, which will in turn improve customer satisfaction, which will then be reflected in better financial performance.]
   c. Customer → Financial → Internal → Innovation and learning [Incorrect.]
   d. Internal → Customer → Innovation and learning → Financial [Incorrect.]

5. Which of the following XBRL documents contains the actual data values for a company's net income for a particular year?
   a. style sheets [Incorrect. Style sheets provide information about how to display the information in an instance document.]
   b. schema [Incorrect. Schemas define elements of financial statements, such as net income, but do not provide actual data values for those elements.]
   c. linkbases [Incorrect. Linkbases describe relationships among taxonomy elements.]
   ▶ d. instance document [Correct. An instance document contains specific values for financial statement elements.]

6. The number of orders shipped per warehouse worker each day is a metric that would most likely appear in which part of the balanced scorecard?
   a. innovation and learning [Incorrect. The proposed metric is a measure of process efficiency and, therefore, would appear in the internal operations section of the balanced scorecard.]
   b. customer [Incorrect. The proposed metric is a measure of process efficiency and, therefore, would appear in the internal operations section of the balanced scorecard.]
   ▶ c. internal operations [Correct.]
   d. financial [Incorrect. The proposed metric is a measure of process efficiency and, therefore, would appear in the internal operations section of the balanced scorecard.]

7. Which of the following is an important part of the audit trail?
   ▶ a. journal vouchers [Correct. Journal vouchers provide information concerning the source of changes to the general ledger accounts.]
   b. flexible budgets [Incorrect. Flexible budgets are a performance evaluation tool.]
   c. trial balance [Incorrect. The trial balance is a step in the preparation of financial statements.]
   d. data warehouse [Incorrect. A data warehouse is used for business intelligence.]

8. An adjusting journal entry to record interest revenue that has been earned but not yet received is an example of which of the following?
   ▶ a. accrual [Correct.]
   b. deferral [Incorrect. A deferral would involve postponing recognition of an event for which cash has already been exchanged in advance of performing the event.]
   c. estimate [Incorrect. An estimate is an entry used to record the results of judgmental analysis.]
   d. revaluation [Incorrect. A revaluation entry is used to correct a prior error.]

9. Which of the following is designed primarily to improve the efficiency of financial reporting?
   a. XML [Incorrect. XML is a general-purpose language but is not designed for financial reporting.]
   ▶ b. XBRL [Correct. The eXtensible Business Reporting Language was developed, in part, by accountants to facilitate business reporting.]
   c. IFRS [Incorrect. IFRS is an alternative to GAAP.]
   d. The balanced scorecard [Incorrect. The balanced scorecard is a multidimensional performance report.]

10. Which of the following provides real-time data about key measures of operating performance?
   a. XBRL [Incorrect. XBRL is a tool used to produce financial statements.]
   b. the balanced scorecard [Incorrect. The balanced scorecard is a periodic report that summarizes performance for a period of time.]
   ▶ c. dashboards [Correct. Dashboards present real-time measures of key operating performance data.]
   d. a flexible budget [Incorrect. Flexible budgets are designed to help managers more accurately interpret variances from plans. However, like the balanced scorecard, they do not present real-time data but are only prepared periodically and summarize performance for a period of time.]

The REA Data Model

PART

V

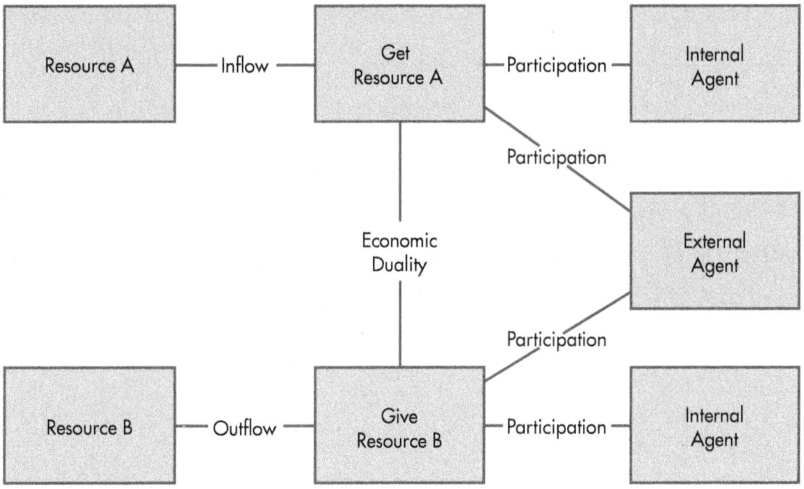

CHAPTER **19**

Database Design Using the REA Data Model

CHAPTER **20**

Implementing an REA Model in a Relational Database

CHAPTER **21**

Special Topics in REA Modeling

CHAPTER 19

Database Design Using the REA Data Model

LEARNING OBJECTIVES

After studying this chapter, you should be able to:

1. Discuss the steps for designing and implementing a database system.
2. Explain the nature and use of Entity-Relationship (E-R) diagrams.
3. Explain the content and purpose of the REA data model.
4. Use the REA data model to design an AIS database.
5. Read an REA diagram and explain what it reveals about the business activities and policies of the organization modeled.

INTEGRATIVE CASE Fred's Train Shop

Fred Smith is frustrated. Business in his model train shop is booming. But the simple accounting software that he uses to run the business has only limited reporting capabilities. Consequently, he often has to manually review transaction data to prepare custom reports. The process is time consuming and prone to error. For example, Fred spent the past weekend poring over sales records for the prior three months, trying to identify which combinations of items were most frequently purchased together. He plans to use the information to offer a special sales promotion but is concerned about the quality of his analysis.

At lunch, Fred explains his frustrations to his CPA, Paul Stone. Paul mentions he has just completed a training course on database design. He suggests that he could create a relational database for Fred that would interface with his accounting software and provide Fred with the ability to easily design reports to analyze his business. Fred likes the idea and hires Paul to design a relational database for his train store.

Introduction

Chapter 4 covered the fundamental principles of relational databases. The three chapters in this section will teach you how to design and document a relational database for an accounting information system. Although not all of you may become consultants who, like Paul Stone in the chapter opening case, design a database for clients, every accounting professional needs to understand

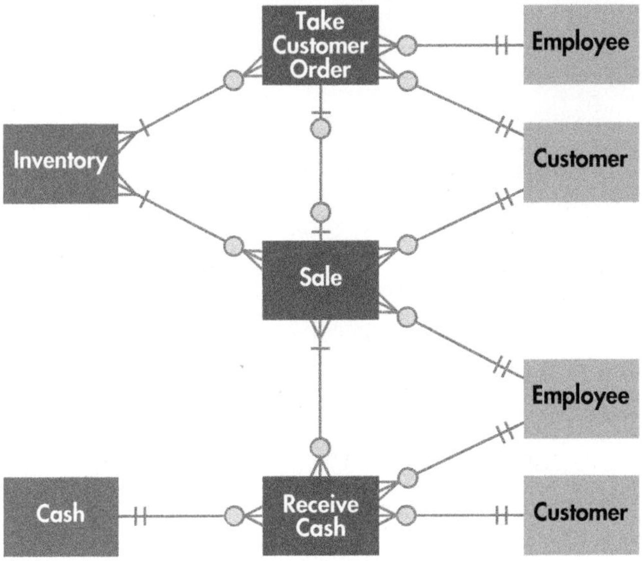

how to document a database and use such documentation as a guide for retrieving information. Auditors (both internal and external) often need to obtain audit evidence from relational databases. Corporate accountants also need to query their organization's databases to retrieve relevant data for cost analysis and tax planning, as well as to produce useful and relevant managerial reports.

This chapter introduces the topic of data modeling. We demonstrate how to use a tool called the REA (resources, events, and agents) data model to design and document an Accounting Information system (AIS). We also explain how the REA data model provides auditors with valuable information about an organization's business activities and policies. Chapter 20 describes how to implement an REA data model in a database management system and how to use it to query the resulting database to retrieve information relevant to managers and auditors. Chapter 21 concludes this three-chapter section by examining a number of advanced data modeling and database design issues.

Database Design Process

Figure 19-1 shows the five basic steps in database design. The first stage (systems analysis) consists of initial planning to determine the need for and feasibility of developing a new system. This stage includes preliminary judgments about the proposal's technological and economic feasibility. It also involves identifying user information needs, defining the scope of the proposed new system, and using information about the expected number of users and transaction volumes to make preliminary decisions about hardware and software requirements. The second stage (conceptual design) includes developing the different schemas for the new system at the conceptual, external, and internal levels. The third stage (physical design) consists of translating the internal-level schema into the actual database structures that will be implemented in the new system. This is also the stage when new applications are developed. The fourth stage (implementation and conversion) includes all the activities associated with transferring data from existing systems to the new database AIS, testing the new system, and training employees how to use it. The final stage is using and maintaining the new system. This includes carefully monitoring system performance and user satisfaction to determine the need for making system enhancements and modifications. Eventually, changes in business strategies and practices or significant new developments in information technology prompt the company to begin investigating the feasibility of developing a new system, and the entire process starts again (note the arrow returning to the systems analysis stage).

Accountants can and should participate in every stage of the database design process, although the level of their involvement is likely to vary across stages. During the systems analysis phase, accountants help evaluate project feasibility and identify user information needs. In the conceptual design stage, accountants participate in developing the logical schemas, designing the data dictionary, and specifying important controls. Accountants with good database skills may directly participate in implementing the data model during the physical design

FIGURE 19-1
Data Modeling in the Database Design Process

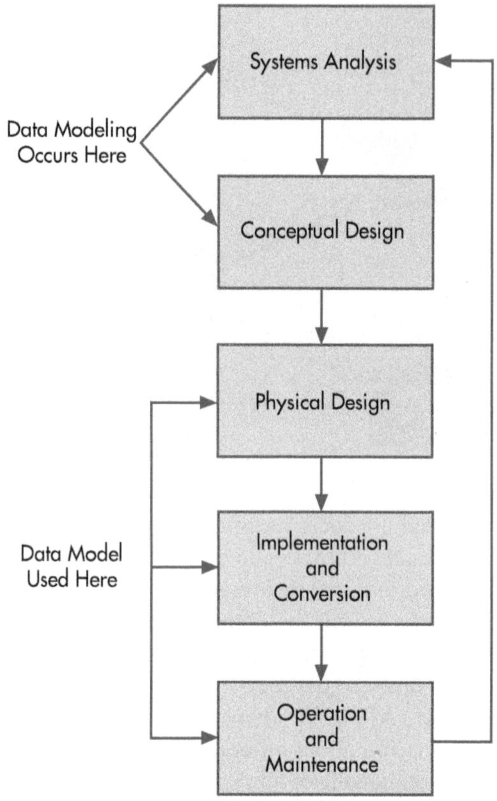

stage. During the implementation and conversion stage, accountants should be involved in testing the accuracy of the new database and the application programs that will use that data, as well as assessing the adequacy of controls. Finally, many accountants are regular users of the organization's database and sometimes even have responsibility for its management.

data modeling - Defining a database to faithfully represent all key components of an organization's environment. The objective is to explicitly capture and store data about every business activity the organization wishes to plan, control, or evaluate.

Accountants may provide the greatest value to their organizations by participating in data modeling. **Data modeling** is the process of defining a database to faithfully represent all aspects of the organization, including its interactions with the external environment. As shown in Figure 19-1, data modeling occurs during both the systems analysis and conceptual design stages of database design. Next, we discuss two important tools accountants can use to perform data modeling: entity-relationship diagramming and the REA data model.

Entity-Relationship Diagrams

entity-relationship (E-R) diagram - A graphical depiction of a database's contents showing the various entities modeled and the important relationships among them.

entity - Anything about which an organization wants to collect and store information.

An **entity-relationship (E-R) diagram**[1] is a graphical technique for portraying a database schema. It is called an E-R diagram because it shows the various *entities* modeled and the important *relationships* among them. An **entity** is anything about which the organization wants to collect and store information. For example, Fred's Train Shop's database would include entities for employees, customers, suppliers, inventory, and business events such as sales to customers and deliveries from suppliers. In a relational database, separate tables would be created to store information about each distinct entity; in an object-oriented database, separate classes would be created for each distinct entity.

In an E-R diagram, entities are depicted as rectangles. Unfortunately, however, there are no industry standards for other aspects of E-R diagrams. Some data modelers and authors use diamonds to depict relationships (Figure 19-2, panel A) whereas others do not (Figure 19-2, panel B). Sometimes the attributes associated with each entity are depicted as named ovals connected to each rectangle (Figure 19-2, panel C), whereas other times the attributes

[1]The material in this section is based on P. Chen, "The Entity Relationship Model—Toward a Unified View of Data," *Transactions on Database Systems* (1:1, March 1976): pp. 9–36.

FIGURE 19-2
E-R Diagram Variations

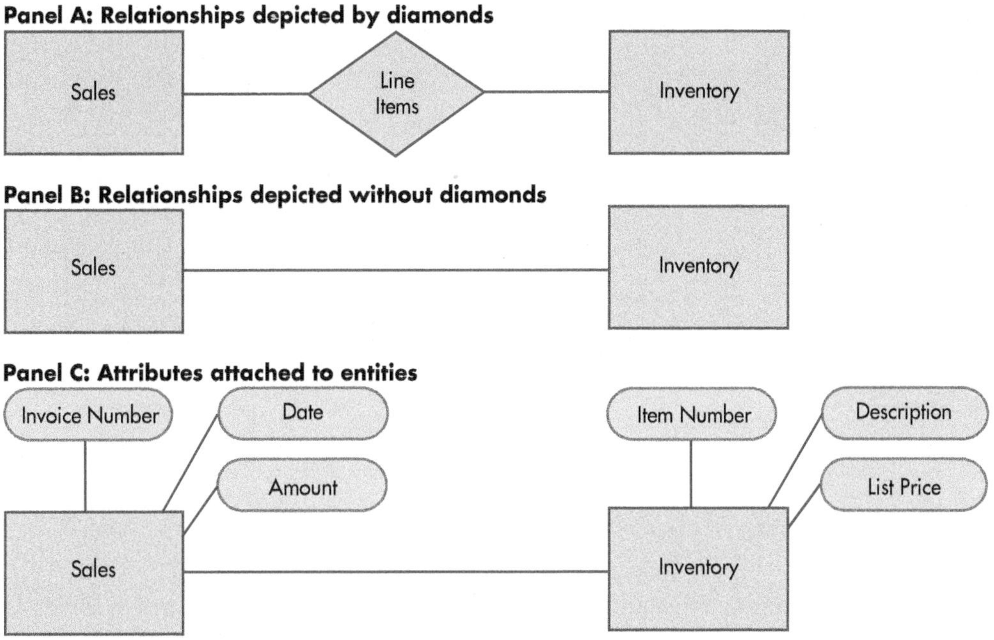

Panel D: Attributes listed in separate table

Entity Name	Attributes
Sales	Invoice number, date, amount
Inventory	Item number, description, list price

associated with each entity are listed in a separate table (Figure 19-2, panel D). In this book, we will create E-R diagrams with a large number of entities and relationships. Therefore, to reduce clutter and improve readability, we omit the diamonds for relationships and list the attributes associated with each entity in a separate table. Thus, our diagrams look like a combination of panels B and D in Figure 19-2.

E-R diagrams can be used to represent the contents of any kind of database. For example, the E-R diagram of an intramural sports database might include students, teams, and leagues as entities, whereas an E-R diagram for a school might include students, teachers, and courses as entities. In this book, our focus is on databases designed to support an organization's business activities. Consequently, we will show how E-R diagrams can be used not only to design databases but also to document and understand existing databases and to redesign business processes. Business process management is covered in Part VI; in this chapter, we focus on using E-R diagrams for database design and for understanding the contents of existing databases.

As noted, E-R diagrams can include many different kinds of entities and relationships among those entities. An important step in database design, therefore, entails deciding which entities need to be modeled. The REA data model is useful for making that decision.

The REA Data Model

The **REA data model**[2] was developed specifically for use in designing AIS. The REA data model focuses on the business semantics underlying an organization's value-chain activities. It provides guidance for database design by identifying what entities should be included in the

REA data model - A data model used to design AIS databases. It contains information about three fundamental types of entities: resources, events, and agents.

[2]The material in this section is adapted from William E. McCarthy, "An Entity-Relationship View of Accounting Models," *The Accounting Review* (October 1979): pp. 667–686; William E. McCarthy, "The REA Accounting Model: A Generalized Framework for Accounting Systems in a Shared Data Environment," *The Accounting Review* (July 1982): pp. 554–578; and Guido L. Geerts and W. E. McCarthy, "An Ontological Analysis of the Primitives of the Extended-REA Enterprise Information Architecture," *International Journal of Accounting Information Systems* (3, March 2002): pp. 1–16.

FIGURE 19-3
Basic Elements of an REA Diagram

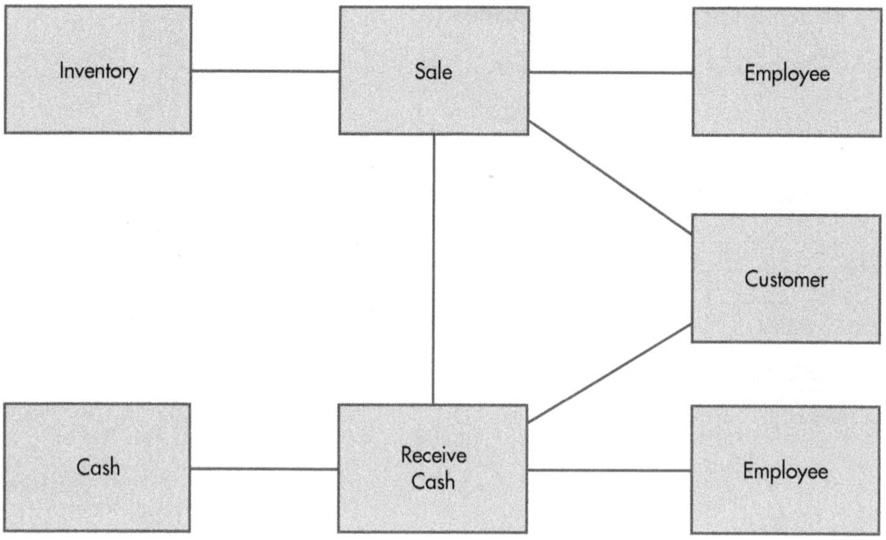

AIS database and by prescribing how to structure relationships among the entities in that database. REA data models are usually depicted in the form of E-R diagrams. Consequently, in the remainder of this chapter and throughout the book, we will refer to E-R diagrams developed according to the REA data model as REA diagrams.

THREE BASIC TYPES OF ENTITIES

The REA data model is so named because it classifies entities into three distinct categories: the ***r***esources the organization acquires and uses, the ***e***vents (business activities) in which the organization engages, and the ***a***gents participating in these events.[3] Figure 19-3 provides examples of these three types of entities.

resources - Things that have economic value to an organization such as cash, inventory, supplies, factories, and land.

events - Business activities about which management wants to collect information for planning or control purposes.

agents - The people and organizations who participate in events and about whom information is desired.

Resources are things that have economic value to the organization. Figure 19-3 includes two resource entities: Cash and Inventory. **Events** are the various business activities about which management wants to collect information for planning or control purposes.[4] There are two event entities in Figure 19-3: Sale and Receive Cash. **Agents** are the people and organizations that participate in events and about whom information is desired for planning, control, and evaluation purposes. Figure 19-3 includes two types of agent entities: Employees and Customers.

STRUCTURING RELATIONSHIPS: THE BASIC REA TEMPLATE

The REA data model prescribes a basic pattern for how the three types of entities (resources, events, and agents) should relate to one another. Figure 19-4 presents this basic pattern. The essential features of the pattern are as follows:

1. Each event is linked to at least one resource that it affects.
2. Each event is linked to at least one other event.
3. Each event is linked to at least two participating agents.

[3]Some REA data modelers have proposed a fourth type of entity, which they call locations. Stores and warehouses would be examples of this fourth type of entity. However, such "location" entities are usually also resources controlled by the organization. Therefore, the authors of this text see no compelling reason to create yet another type of entity and model locations as resources. If an organization does not want or need to store information about locations except to identify where an event occurred, location can be an attribute for each event.

[4]The discussion of events in this section is based on the work of Julie Smith David, "Three 'Events' That Define an REA Methodology for Systems Analysis, Design, and Implementation," Working Paper, Arizona State University, August 1997; and Guido L. Geerts and W. E. McCarthy, "An Ontological Analysis of the Primitives of the Extended-REA Enterprise Information Architecture," *International Journal of Accounting Information Systems* (3, March 2002): pp. 1–16.

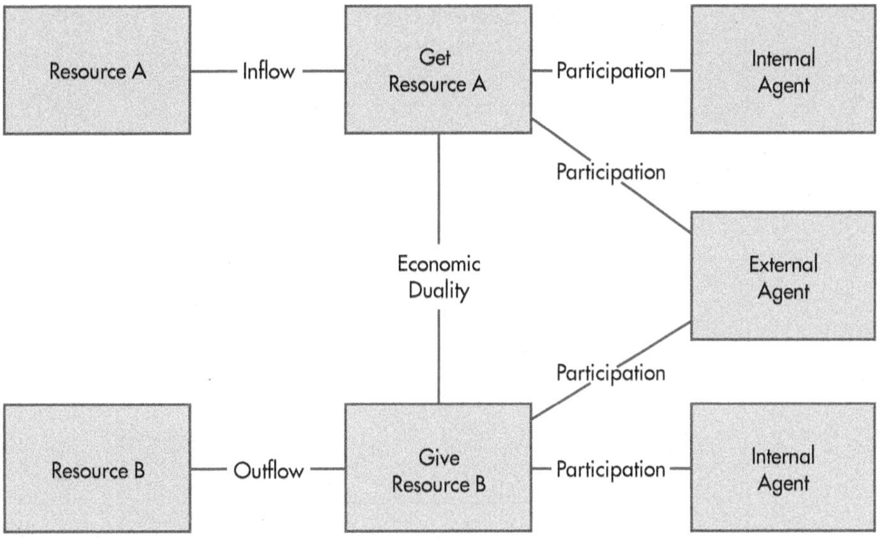

The names on the lines describe the nature of the relationship. Agents participate in events. The economic duality relationship between the "get" event and the "give" event reflects the fact that organizations must give up one resource (e.g., cash) in order to get some other resource (e.g., inventory). The stockflow relationships between an event and a resource represent either inflows or outflows of a resource.

FIGURE 19-4
Standard REA Template

RULE 1: EVERY EVENT ENTITY MUST BE LINKED TO AT LEAST ONE RESOURCE ENTITY Events *must* be linked to at least one resource that they affect. Some events, such as the one labeled "Get Resource A" in Figure 19-4, increase the quantity of a resource. Common examples of such "Get" events include the receipt of goods from a supplier (which increases the quantity on hand of inventory) and the receipt of payment from a customer (which increases the amount of cash). Other events, such as the one labeled "Give Resource B" in Figure 19-4, directly decrease the quantity of a resource. Common examples of such "Give" events include paying suppliers and selling merchandise, which decrease the amount of cash and quantity on hand of inventory, respectively.

Relationships that affect the quantity of a resource are sometimes referred to as *stockflow* relationships because they represent either an inflow or outflow of that resource. Not every event directly alters the quantity of a resource, however. For example, orders from customers represent commitments that will eventually result in a future sale of merchandise, just as orders to suppliers represent commitments that will eventually result in the subsequent purchase of inventory. For simplicity, Figure 19-4 does not include any such commitment events. Organizations do, however, need to track the effects of such commitments, both to provide better service and for planning purposes. For example, customer orders reduce the quantity available of the specific inventory items ordered. Sales staff need to know this information to be able to properly respond to subsequent customer inquiries and orders. Manufacturing companies may use information about customer orders to plan production. Later in the chapter we will see how to add commitment events to the basic pattern shown in Figure 19-4.

RULE 2: EVERY EVENT ENTITY MUST BE LINKED TO AT LEAST ONE OTHER EVENT ENTITY Figure 19-4 also shows that the Get Resource A event is linked to the Give Resource B event in what is labeled as an economic duality relationship. Such give-to-get duality relationships reflect the basic business principle that organizations typically engage in activities that use up resources only in the hopes of acquiring some other resource in exchange. For example, the Sale event, which requires giving up (decreasing) inventory, is related to the Receive Cash event, which involves getting (increasing) the amount of cash. Figure 19-5 shows that each accounting cycle can be described in terms of such give-to-get economic duality relationships. The bottom portion of the figure also shows that sometimes one event can be linked to several other events.

Not every relationship between two events represents a give-to-get economic duality, however. Commitment events are linked to other events to reflect sequential cause–effect

FIGURE 19-5
An AIS Viewed as a Set of Give-to-Get Exchanges

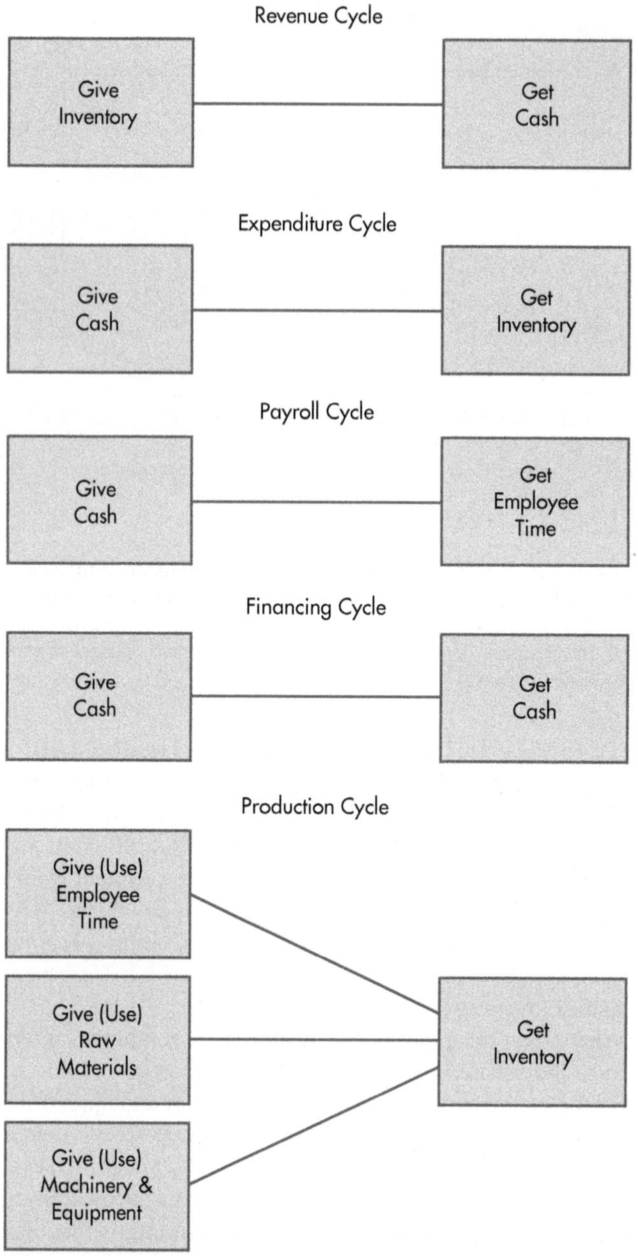

relationships. For example, the Take Customer Order event would be linked to the Sale event to reflect the fact that such orders precede and result in sales. Similarly, the Order Inventory (purchase) event would be linked to the Receive Inventory event to reflect another sequential cause–effect relationship.

RULE 3: EVERY EVENT ENTITY MUST BE LINKED TO AT LEAST TWO PARTICIPATING AGENTS For accountability, organizations need to be able to track the actions of employees. Organizations also need to monitor the status of commitments and economic duality exchanges engaged in with outside parties. Thus, Figure 19-4 shows each event linked to two participating agent entities. For events that involve transactions with external parties, the internal agent is the employee who is responsible for the resource affected by that event, and the external agent is the outside party to the transaction. For internal events, such as the transfer of raw materials from the storeroom to production, the internal agent is the employee who is giving up responsibility for or custody of the resource, and the external agent is the employee who is receiving custody of or assuming responsibility for that resource.

Developing an REA Diagram

This chapter focuses on developing an REA diagram for a single business cycle. In the next chapter, we will learn how to integrate REA diagrams for individual business cycles to create one enterprise-wide REA diagram.

Developing an REA diagram for a specific business cycle consists of the following three steps:

1. Identify the events about which management wants to collect information.
2. Identify the resources affected by each event and the agents who participate in those events.
3. Determine the cardinalities of each relationship.

Let us follow these three steps to see how Paul developed Figure 19-6 to model the revenue cycle of Fred's Train Shop.

STEP 1: IDENTIFY RELEVANT EVENTS

The first step in developing an REA model of a single business cycle is to identify the events of interest to management. At a minimum, every REA model must include the two events that represent the basic give-to-get economic exchange performed in that particular business cycle (see Figure 19-5). Usually there are other events that management is interested in planning, controlling, and monitoring; they also need to be included in the REA model.

A solid understanding of activities performed in each business cycle (see Chapters 14–18) is needed to identify which events comprise the basic give-to-get economic duality relationships. For example, Chapter 14 explained that the revenue cycle typically consists of four sequential activities:

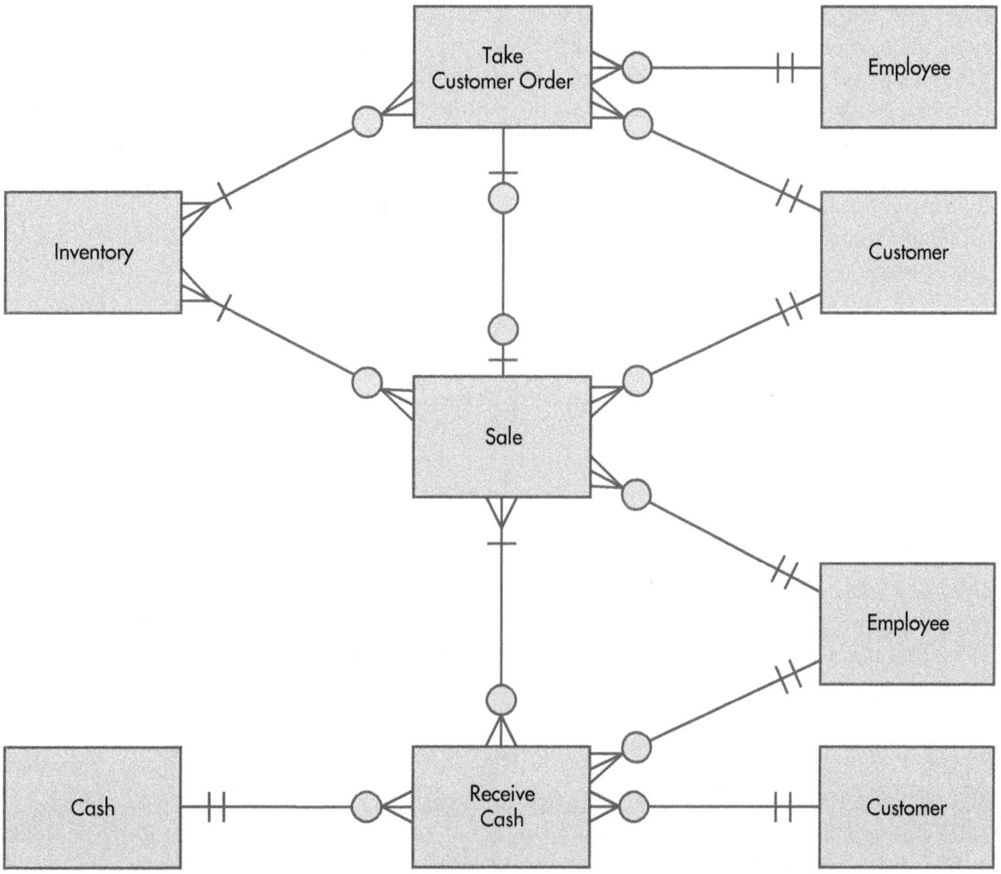

FIGURE 19-6
Partial REA Diagram for Fred's Train Shop Revenue Cycle

1. Take customer orders.
2. Fill customer orders.
3. Bill customers.
4. Collect payment from customers.

Analysis of the first activity, taking customer orders, indicates that it does not involve either the acquisition of resources from or provision of resources to an external party. It is only a commitment to perform such actions in the future. The second activity, fill customer orders, does reduce the organization's stock of a resource that has economic value (inventory) by delivering it to an external party (the customer). Thus, it represents an example of the prototypical Give Resource event depicted in Figure 19-4. The third activity, billing customers, involves the exchange of information with an external party but does not directly increase or decrease the quantity of any economic resource. Finally, analysis of the fourth activity, collect payments from customers, indicates that it results in an increase in the organization's supply of an economic resource (the entity labeled Cash in Figure 19-6) as a result of receiving it from an external party (the customer). Thus, it is an example of the prototypical Get Resource event depicted in Figure 19-4. Consequently, analysis of the basic business activities performed in the revenue cycle indicates that the basic give-to-get economic exchange consists of two events: fill customer orders (usually referred to as the Sale event) and collect payments from customers (often called the Receive Cash event).

In drawing an REA diagram for a single business cycle, it is useful to divide the paper into three columns, one for each type of entity. Use the left column for resources, the center column for events, and the right column for agents. Readability is further enhanced if the event entities are drawn from top to bottom corresponding to the sequence in which they occur. Thus, Paul begins to draw Figure 19-6 by placing the Sale event entity above the Receive Cash event entity in the center column of the paper.[5]

After the economic exchange events are identified, it is necessary to determine which other business activities should be represented as events in the REA model. This, too, requires understanding what each activity entails because only those activities that involve the acquisition of new information need to be included in the model. Returning to our example, Paul notes that the economic duality of Sale and Receive Cash accurately reflects most in-store sales transactions in which the customer selects one or more items and pays for them. Sometimes, however, customers call the store and ask if specific items can be set aside for pickup later that week. To ensure that he reorders popular items on a timely basis, Fred needs not only to set those items aside but also to record such orders in the system. Therefore, Paul decides to add the commitment event Take Customer Order to the REA diagram, placing it above the Sale event because customer orders precede the Sales event.

Paul then considers the other revenue cycle business activity, billing customers. He knows that in-store sales are paid for immediately and, therefore, do not involve a separate "billing" step. But Fred also sells model trains to shopping centers, hotels, and other institutions that want to set up seasonal displays for their customers. Such sales are made on credit, and Fred does subsequently prepare and mail invoices to those customers. However, printing and mailing invoices does not directly increase or decrease any economic resource. Nor does the billing activity represent a commitment to a future economic exchange: The customer's legal obligation to pay arises from the delivery of the merchandise, not from the printing of an invoice. Consequently, as noted in Chapters 14 and 15, many organizations are beginning to realize that billing is a non-value-added activity that can be eliminated entirely. Moreover, the activity of printing an invoice does not add any new information to the database. The prices and quantities of items sold were recorded at the time of the sale, at which time the terms of payment were also agreed on. Thus, the billing activity is simply an information processing event that merely *retrieves* information from the database, similar to writing a query or printing an internal report. Since such information retrieval events do not alter the contents of the database, they need not be modeled as events in an REA diagram. For all the foregoing

[5]Placement conventions, such as the use of columns and sequential ordering of events, are not *required* to use the REA model to design a database. We suggest these rules only because following them often simplifies the process of drawing an REA diagram and produces REA diagrams that are easy to read.

reasons, Paul realizes that he does not need to include a billing event in his revenue cycle REA diagram for Fred's Train Shop.

But what about accounts receivable? If there is no billing event, how can Fred's Train Shop monitor this balance sheet item? The solution lies in understanding that accounts receivable is merely a timing difference between the two components of the basic economic exchange in the revenue cycle: sales and the receipt of payment. In other words, accounts receivable simply equals all sales for which customers have not yet paid. Consequently, accounts receivable can be calculated and monitored by simply collecting information about Sale and Receive Cash events. The next chapter will illustrate several different ways for extracting information about accounts receivable from a database built using the REA data model.

Finally, notice that there are no events that pertain to the entry of data. The reason for this is that the REA data model is used to design transaction processing databases. The objective is to model the basic value-chain business activities of an organization: what it does to generate revenues and how it spends cash and uses its other resources. Entering data about those events and about the resources and agents associated with them is not usually considered a primary value-chain activity. Thus, just like writing queries and printing reports, data entry activities are not considered important events about which detailed data needs to be collected. Moreover, as discussed in the preceding five chapters, there is a continuous trend to use technology to eliminate routine clerical information processing activities, including data entry. Thus, it is possible to conceive of business events (such as the sale of merchandise) performed without the need for any separate data entry activities. Indeed, much data entry already occurs as a byproduct of performing business events included in the REA diagram. For example, whenever a sale, purchase, receipt of cash, or payment occurs, information about that event is entered in the database. Thus, what gets modeled in the REA diagram is the business event (e.g., the sale transaction) and the facts that management wants to collect about that event, not the entry of that data.

STEP 2: IDENTIFY RESOURCES AND AGENTS

Once the relevant events have been specified, the resources affected by those events need to be identified. This involves answering three questions:

1. What economic resource is reduced by the "Give" event?
2. What economic resource is acquired by the "Get" event?
3. What economic resource is affected by a commitment event?

Again, a solid understanding of business processes makes it easy to answer these questions. To continue our example, Paul has observed that the Sale event involves giving inventory to customers and that the Receive Cash event involves obtaining payments (whether in the form of money, checks, credit card, or debit card) from customers. Therefore, he adds an Inventory resource entity to the REA diagram and links it to the Sale event entity. The Inventory entity stores information about each product that Fred sells. Then Paul adds a Cash resource entity to the diagram. Although organizations typically use multiple accounts to track cash and cash equivalents (e.g., operating checking account, petty cash, and short-term investments), these are all summarized in one balance sheet account called Cash. Similarly, the Cash resource contains information about every individual cash account. Thus, in a relational database, the "Cash" table would contain a separate row for each specific account (e.g., petty cash, checking account). Paul then links the Cash resource entity to the Receive Cash event entity. Finally, the Take Customer Order event involves setting aside merchandise for a specific customer. To maintain accurate inventory records, and to facilitate timely reordering to avoid stockouts, each Take Customer Order event should result in reducing the quantity available of that particular inventory item. Therefore, Paul adds a link between the Inventory resource entity and the Take Customer Order event entity in the REA diagram he is developing for Fred's Train Shop's revenue cycle.

In addition to specifying the resources affected by each event, it is also necessary to identify the agents who participate in those events. There will always be at least one internal agent (employee) and, in most cases, an external agent (customer or vendor) who participate in each event. In the case of Fred's Train Shop's revenue cycle, a customer and a salesperson participate

TABLE 19-1 Graphical Symbols for Representing Cardinality Information

Symbol	Cardinalities	Example	Meaning
─○┼─	Minimum = 0; Maximum = 1	Entity A ——○┼—— Entity B	Each instance of entity A may or may not be linked to any instances of entity B, but can be linked to at most one instance of entity B.
─┼┼─	Minimum = 1; Maximum = 1	Entity A ——┼┼—— Entity B	Each instance of entity A must be linked to an instance of entity B, and can only be linked to at most one instance of entity B.
─○<─	Minimum = 0; Maximum = many	Entity A ——○<—— Entity B	Each instance of entity A may or may not be linked to any instances of entity B, but could be linked to more than one instance of entity B.
─┼<─	Minimum = 1; Maximum = many	Entity A ——┼<—— Entity B	Each instance of entity A must be linked to at least one instance of entity B, but can be linked to many instances of entity B.

in each Sale event. The customer and a cashier are the two agents participating in each Receive Cash event. Both the salesperson and the cashier are employees of Fred's. Thus, both revenue cycle economic exchange events involve the same two general types of agents: employees (the internal party) and customers (the external party). The Take Customer Order event also involves both customers and employees. Therefore, Paul adds both types of agents to the diagram and draws relationships to indicate which agents participated in which events. To reduce clutter, he sometimes links one copy of a particular agent entity to two adjacent event entities.[6]

STEP 3: DETERMINE CARDINALITIES OF RELATIONSHIPS

The final step in drawing an REA diagram for one transaction cycle is to add information about relationship cardinalities. **Cardinalities** describe the nature of the relationship between two entities by indicating how many instances of one entity can be linked to each specific instance of another entity. Consider the relationship between the Customer agent entity and the Sale event entity. Each entity in an REA diagram represents a set. For example, the Customer entity represents the set of the organization's customers, and the Sale entity represents the set of individual sales transactions that occur during the current fiscal period. Each individual customer or sales transaction represents a specific instance of that entity. Thus, in a relational database, each row in the Customer table would store information about a particular customer, and each row in the Sales table would store information about a specific sales transaction. Cardinalities define how many sales transactions (instances of the Sale entity) can be associated with each customer (instance of the Customer entity) and, conversely, how many customers can be associated with each sales transaction.

No universal standard exists for representing information about cardinalities in REA diagrams. In this text, we use the graphical "crow's feet" notation style for representing cardinality information because it is becoming increasingly popular and is used by many software design tools. Table 19-1 explains the meanings of the symbols used to represent cardinality information, and Focus 19-1 compares the notation used in this book with other commonly used conventions.

cardinalities - Describe the nature of a database relationship indicating the number of occurrences of one entity that may be associated with a single occurrence of the other entity. Three types of cardinalities are one-to-one, one-to-many, and many-to-many.

[6]Deciding how many copies of the same entity to include in an REA diagram is a matter of personal taste. Including too many copies clutters the diagram with redundant rectangles, but too few copies can result in a confusing tangled web of lines connecting entities to one another.

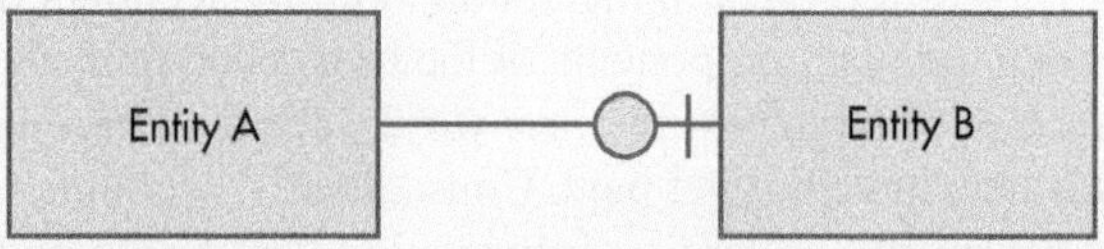

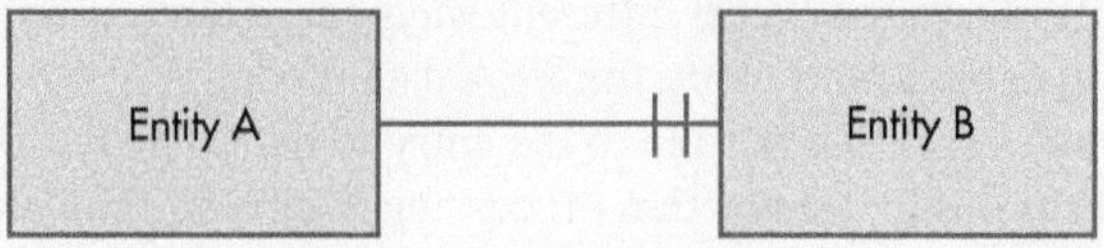

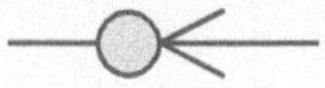

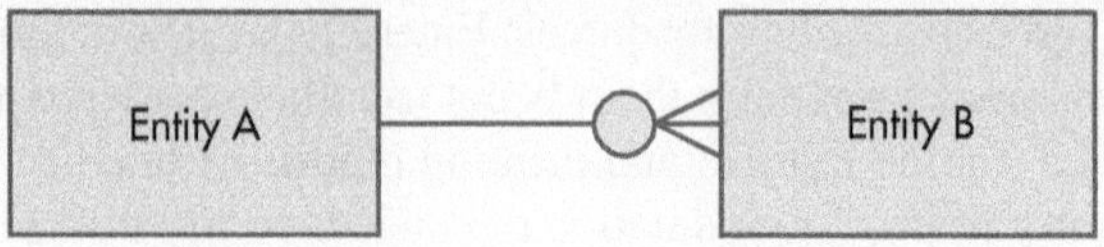

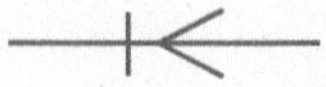

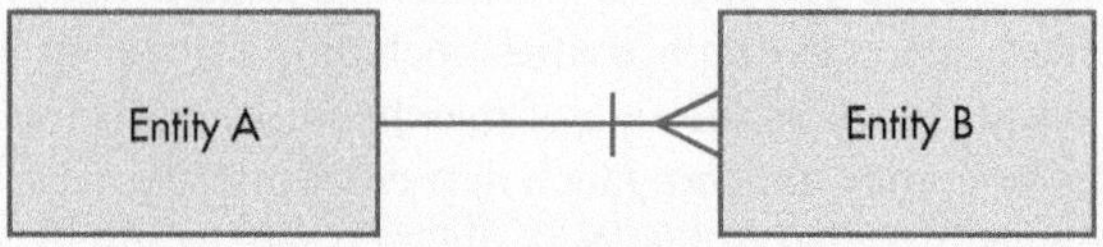

FOCUS 19-1 Alternative Methods to Represent Cardinality Information

A number of different notations exist for depicting minimum and maximum cardinalities. Some of the more common alternatives to the crow's feet used in this text are shown here.

NOTATION | **EXPLANATION** | **EXAMPLE**

(Min, Max)

A pair of alphanumeric characters inside parentheses:
(0,1) means minimum = 0, maximum = 1
(1,1) means minimum = 1; maximum = 1
(0,N) means minimum = 0; maximum = many
(1,N) means minimum = 1; maximum = many

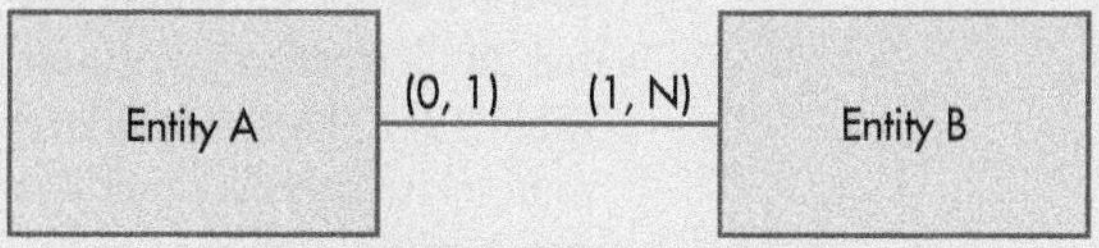

Each instance of entity A must be linked to at least one instance of entity B but may be linked to many instances of entity B; each instance of entity B may or may not be linked to an instance of entity A but can only be linked to at most one instance of entity A. **Note:** *Some authors and consultants flip which side of the relationship the cardinality pair appears on! So when you see an REA diagram with cardinality pairs in parentheses, ask which pair refers to which entity.*

UML

One or two alphanumeric characters separated by two periods:
0..1 means minimum = 0; maximum = 1
1 means minimum = 1; maximum = 1
* means minimum = 0; maximum = many
1..* means minimum = 1; maximum = many

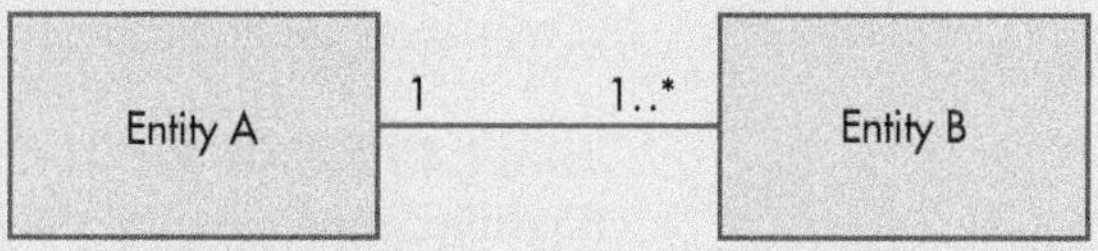

Each instance of entity A must be linked to at least one instance of entity B but may be linked to many instances of entity B; each instance of entity B must be linked to an instance of entity A and can only be linked to at most one instance of entity A.

Maximums only (Microsoft Access)

One alphanumeric character to represent the maximum cardinality in that relationship: 1 means 1; the infinity symbol (∞) means many

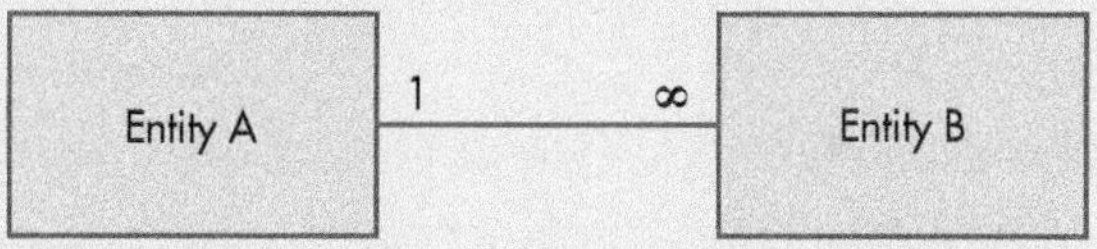

Each instance of entity A may be linked to many instances of entity B; each instance of entity B can only be linked to at most one instance of entity A.

As shown in Table 19-1, cardinalities are represented by the pair of symbols next to an entity. The four rows in Table 19-1 depict the four possible combinations of minimum and maximum cardinalities. The **minimum cardinality** can be either zero (0) or one (1), depending on whether the relationship between the two entities is optional (the minimum cardinality is zero; see rows one and three) or mandatory (the minimum cardinality is one, as in rows two and four). The **maximum cardinality** can be either one or many (the crow's feet symbol), depending on whether each instance of entity A can be linked to at most one instance (as in the top two rows) or potentially many instances of entity B (as in the bottom two rows).

minimum cardinality - The minimum number of instances an entity can be linked to the other entity in the relationship. Only two options: 0 and 1.

maximum cardinality - The maximum number of instances an entity can be linked to the other entity in the relationship. Only two options: 1 or many.

Let us now use the information in Table 19-1 to interpret some of the cardinalities in Figure 19-6. Look first at the Sale-Customer relationship. The minimum and maximum cardinalities next to the Customer entity are both one. This pattern is the same as that in row two in Table 19-1. Thus, the minimum cardinality of one next to the Customer entity in Figure 19-6 indicates that each sale transaction (entity A) *must* be linked to some specific customer (entity B). The maximum cardinality of one means each sale transaction can be linked to at most *only one* specific customer. This reflects normal business practices: only one legally identifiable customer (which could be an individual or a business) is held responsible for a sale and its subsequent payment. Now look at the cardinality pair next to the Sale entity. As in row three in Table 19-1, the minimum cardinality is zero, and the maximum cardinality is many. The zero minimum cardinality means the relationship is optional: A customer does not have to be associated with any specific sale transaction. This allows Fred's Train Shop to enter information about prospective customers to whom it can send advertisements before they have ever purchased anything. The maximum cardinality is many, indicating that a specific customer may, and Fred hopes will, be associated with multiple sale transactions (i.e., become a loyal customer who makes repeated purchases from Fred's Train Shop). Now notice that the cardinality pairs next to the Inventory entity in Figure 19-6 have a minimum of one and a maximum of many for every relationship. This is the same pattern as in row four in Table 19-1. This means every customer order or sale transaction *must* involve at least one inventory item (you cannot sell "nothing") but *may* involve multiple different items (e.g., a customer could purchase both a locomotive and a rail car in the same transaction). Finally, notice that the cardinality pair next to the Sale entity in its relationship with the Take Customer Order entity is like the pattern in row one of Table 19-1. The minimum cardinality of zero reflects that an order may not *yet* have been turned into an actual sale transaction. The maximum cardinality of one indicates that Fred's Train Shop fills all customer orders in full rather than making a number of partial deliveries.

You should be able to interpret the rest of Figure 19-6 by following the same process just presented by comparing the cardinality pairs next to each entity to the four patterns in Table 19-1. Let us now examine what the various types of relationships mean and what they reveal about an organization's business practices.

THREE TYPES OF RELATIONSHIPS Three basic types of relationships between entities are possible, depending on the *maximum* cardinality associated with each entity (the minimum cardinality does not matter):

one-to-one (1:1) relationship - A relationship between two entities where the maximum cardinality for each entity is 1.

1. ***A one-to-one (1:1) relationship*** exists when the maximum cardinality for each entity in that relationship is 1 (see Figure 19-7, panel A).

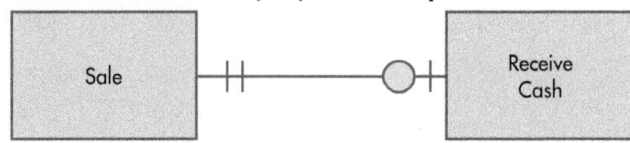

FIGURE 19-7
Examples of Different Types of Relationships

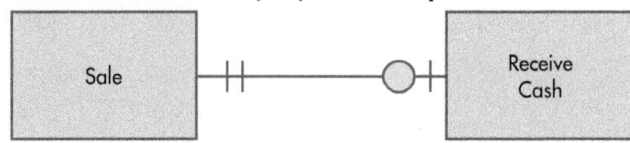

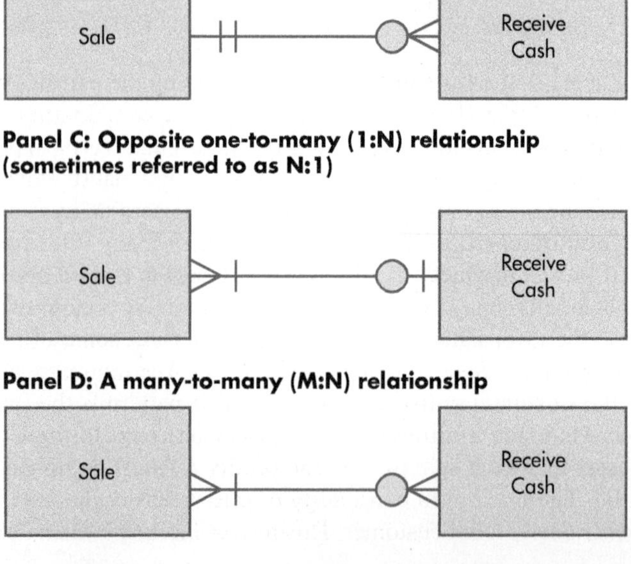

2. ***A one-to-many (1:N) relationship*** exists when the maximum cardinality of one entity in the relationship is 1 and the maximum cardinality for the other entity in that relationship is many (see Figure 19-7, panels B and C).
3. ***A many-to-many (M:N) relationship*** exists when the maximum cardinality for both entities in the relationship is many (Figure 19-7, panel D).

one-to-many (1:N) relationship - A relationship between two entities where the maximum cardinality for one of the entities is 1, but the other entity has a maximum cardinality of many.

many-to-many (M:N) relationship - A relationship between two entities where the maximum cardinality of both entities is many.

Figure 19-7 shows that any of these possibilities *might* describe the relationship between the Sale and Receive Cash events. The data modeler or database designer cannot arbitrarily choose which of these three possibilities to use when depicting various relationships. Instead, the cardinalities *must* reflect the organization's business policies. Let us now examine what each of the possibilities depicted in Figure 19-7 means. Figure 19-7, panel A, depicts a one-to-one (1:1) relationship between the Sale and Receive Cash events. The maximum cardinality of 1 associated with the Receive Cash entity means that each Sale event (transaction) can be linked to *at most* one Receive Cash event. This would be appropriate for an organization that had a business policy of not allowing customers to make installment payments. At the same time, the maximum cardinality of 1 associated with each Sale event means each payment a customer submits is linked to *at most* one sales event. This would be appropriate for an organization that had a business policy of requiring customers to pay for each sales transaction separately. Thus, the 1:1 relationship depicted in Figure 19-7, panel A, represents the typical revenue cycle relationship for business-to-consumer retail sales: Customers must pay, in full, for each sales transaction before they are allowed to leave the store with the merchandise they purchased. Note that it does not matter *how* customers pay for each sales transaction (e.g., with cash, check, credit card, or debit card). Regardless of the method used, there is one, and only one, payment linked to each sales transaction and, conversely, every sales transaction is linked to one, and only one, payment from a customer (payments made by debit and credit cards also involve the card issuer; for simplicity, that transfer agent is not included in Figure 19-6). If management is interested in tracking the frequency of how customers choose to pay, payment method might be recorded as an attribute of the Receive Cash event.

Panels B and C of Figure 19-7 depict two ways that one-to-many (1:N) relationships can occur. Panel B shows that each Sale event may be linked to *many* Receive Cash events. This indicates that the organization has a business policy that allows customers to make installment payments *to the selling organization.* If the customer uses a third-party source of credit, the selling organization receives *one* payment in full from that third party for that particular sales transaction; the customer may be making installment payments to the credit agency, but those payments would not be modeled in an REA diagram for the selling organization. (Think about it: The selling organization has no way of tracking when one of its customers pays a portion of a credit card bill or makes a monthly payment on a bank loan). The situation depicted in Figure 19-7, panel B, does not, however, mean that *every* sales transaction is paid for in installments: The maximum cardinality of N simply means that some sales transactions may be paid in installments. Panel B of Figure 19-7 also shows that each Receive Cash event is linked to *at most* one Sale event. This indicates that the organization has a business policy that requires customers to pay for each sales transaction separately and are not allowed to build up an account balance over a period of time. Thus, Figure 19-7, panel B, represents the revenue cycle of an organization that probably sells big-ticket items. Should a customer return and make another purchase, a separate set of installment payments would be created to separately track how much has been paid for each sales transaction.

Figure 19-7, panel C, shows another type of 1:N relationship between the Sale and Receive Cash events. In this case, each Sale event can be linked to *at most* one Receive Cash event. This indicates the organization has a business policy that does not permit customers to make installment payments. Figure 19-7, panel C, also shows that each Receive Cash event *may* be linked to many different Sale events. This indicates the existence of a business policy allowing customers to make a number of purchases during a period of time (e.g., a month) and then pay off those purchases with one payment. The situation depicted in Figure 19-7, panel C, is quite common, especially for business-to-business sales of nondurable goods.

Figure 19-7, panel D, depicts a many-to-many (M:N) relationship between the Sale and Receive Cash events. It shows that each Sale event may be linked to *one or more* Receive Cash events and that each Receive Cash event may in turn be linked to *one or more* Sale events.

This reflects an organization that has business policies that allow customers to make installment payments and permits customers to accumulate a balance representing a set of sales transactions over a period of time. Keep in mind, however, that maximum cardinalities of N do not represent mandatory practices: Thus, for the relationship depicted in panel D, some sales transactions may be paid in full in one payment and some customers may pay for each sales transaction separately. The situation depicted in Figure 19-7, panel D, is quite common.

What an REA Diagram Reveals About an Organization

BUSINESS MEANING OF CARDINALITIES

REA diagrams can be used not only to design an AIS but also to understand the organization's business processes.

As noted, the choice of cardinalities is not arbitrary but reflects facts about the organization modeled and its business practices. This information is obtained during the systems analysis and conceptual design stages of the database design process. Thus, Paul Stone had to clearly understand how Fred's Train Shop conducts its business activities to ensure that Figure 19-6 was correct.

Let us now examine Figure 19-6 to see what it reveals about Fred's Train Shop's revenue cycle processes. First, note that all of the agent–event relationships are 1:N. This is typical for most organizations: A particular agent often participates in many events. For example, organizations expect that over time a given employee will repeatedly perform a particular task. Organizations also desire their customers to make repeat orders and purchases, just as they typically place orders with the same suppliers. However, for accountability purposes, events are usually linked to a specific internal agent and a specific external agent; hence, the maximum cardinality on the agent side of the agent–event relationships in Figure 19-6 is always 1. If, however, a particular event required the cooperation of a team of employees, the maximum cardinality on the agent side of the relationship would be many.

The minimum cardinalities associated with the agent–event relationships in Figure 19-6 also reflect typical business processes followed by most organizations. The figure shows that each event *must* be linked to an agent (a sale must involve a customer, a payment must come from a customer, etc.); hence the minimum cardinality of 1 on the agent side of the relationship. In contrast, Figure 19-6 shows that the minimum cardinality on the event side of the agent–event relationship is 0. There are several reasons why a particular agent need not have participated in any events. The organization may wish to store information about potential customers and alternate suppliers with whom it has not yet conducted any business. Information about newly hired employees will exist in the database prior to their first day on the job. Finally, there is a fundamental difference in the nature of agent entities and event entities. Organizations usually desire to maintain information about agents indefinitely but typically store information only about events that have occurred during the current fiscal year. Thus, agent entities are analogous to master files, whereas event entities are analogous to transaction files. At the end of a fiscal year, the contents of event entities are typically archived, and the next fiscal year begins with no instances of that event. Thus, at the beginning of a new fiscal year, agents are not linked to any current events.

Figure 19-6 depicts M:N relationships between the Inventory resource and the various events that affect it. This is the typical situation for organizations, like Fred's Train Shop, that sell mass-produced items. Most organizations track such inventory by an identifier such as part number, item number, or stock-keeping unit (SKU) number and do not attempt to track each physical instance of that product. When a sale occurs, the system notes which product number(s) were sold. Thus, the same inventory item may be linked to many different sales events. For example, Fred's Train Shop uses product number 15734 to refer to a particular model of a steam locomotive. At a given point in time, it may have five of those locomotives in stock. If, during the course of a weekend, five different customers each purchased one of those locomotives, the system would link product number 15734 to five separate sales events. Hence, the maximum cardinality on the event side of the relationship is many. Of course, Fred's Train Shop, like most organizations, permits (and desires) that customers purchase many different products at the same time. For example, a customer who purchases a steam locomotive (product number 15734) may also purchase a box of curved track (product number 3265). Thus, the system would link one Sale event to multiple inventory items; hence the maximum cardinality on the Inventory side of the relationship is also many.

But what if an organization sells unique, one-of-a-kind inventory, such as original artwork? Such items can only be sold one time; consequently, the maximum cardinality on the event side of the Inventory–Sale relationship would be 1. The maximum cardinality on the Inventory side of the relationship would still be many, however, because most organizations will be happy to sell as many different one-of-a-kind items as a customer wants and can afford to buy.

The minimum cardinalities on each side of the Inventory–event relationships depicted in Figure 19-6 also reflect typical business practices. Fred's Train Shop, like many retail organizations, only sells physical inventory. Therefore, every order or sales event *must* be linked to at least one inventory item; hence, the minimum cardinality on the Inventory side of the Inventory–event relationships is 1. The minimum cardinality on the event side of those relationships, however, is 0, for the same reasons that it is 0 in agent–event relationships.

Now consider the relationship between the Cash resource and the Receive Cash event. Figure 19-6 depicts this as a 1:N relationship, which reflects a best practice followed by most organizations with good internal controls. Each cash receipt from a customer is deposited into one cash account, usually the organization's general checking account. The treasurer subsequently transfers money from that account to other cash accounts (e.g., payroll, checking, investments) as necessary. The minimum cardinalities on each side of this relationship are also typical. Each customer payment must be deposited into some account; hence the minimum cardinality is 1 on the resource side of the relationship. Conversely, the minimum cardinality on the event side of the relationship is 0 for the same reasons that it is 0 in the agent–event and inventory–event relationships discussed previously.

Finally, let us examine the event–event relationships depicted in Figure 19-6. Fred's Train Shop ships each business customer order individually and waits until all items are in stock before filling an order. Thus, each order is linked to only one sales transaction, and each sales transaction is related to only one order. Therefore, Paul has modeled the relationship between the Take Customer Order and Sale events as 1:1. The minimum cardinality on the Sale side of the relationship is 0, meaning that orders may exist which are not linked to sales. This reflects the temporal sequence between the two events: Orders precede sales, so at any given point in time, Fred's Train Shop may have orders that it has not yet filled. Fred's Train Shop does not, however, require that every sale be preceded by an order; indeed, while many sales to corporate customers are preceded by orders, walk-in sales to consumers are not. Therefore, Paul Stone has modeled the minimum cardinality on the Take Customer Order side of the Sale–Take Customer Order relationship as 0.

Paul also has learned that Fred's Train Shop extends credit to its business customers and mails them monthly statements listing all unpaid purchases. He also has found out that many business customers send Fred one check to cover all their purchases during a given time period. Thus, one Receive Cash event could be linked to many different Sale events. However, Fred's Train Shop also allows its business customers to make installment payments on large purchases; thus, a given Sale event could be connected to more than one Receive Cash event. That is why Paul has modeled the relationship between the Sale and Receive Cash events as many-to-many.

Because Fred's Train Shop extends credit to some of its customers, at any point in time there can be Sale events not yet linked to any Receive Cash events. Therefore, Figure 19-6 shows the minimum cardinality on the Receive Cash side of the relationship as 0. Paul also has learned that Fred's Train Shop never requires customers to pay in advance for special orders. Thus, every Receive Cash event must be linked to a previous Sale event; consequently, Figure 19-6 shows the minimum cardinality on the sales side of the Sale–Receive Cash relationship is 1.

UNIQUENESS OF REA DIAGRAMS

The preceding discussion indicates that each organization will have its own unique REA diagram. At a minimum, because business practices differ across companies, so will relationship cardinalities. In fact, an REA diagram for a given organization will have to change to reflect changes to existing business practices. For example, if Fred's Train Shop decides to begin making partial shipments to fill customer orders, then Figure 19-6 would have to be changed to show the relationship between the Take Customer Order and Sale events as 1:N,

FOCUS 19-2 Why Should Users Participate in Data Modeling?

Data modeling is not an easy task, as Hewlett-Packard learned when it began designing a new database for its accounting and finance function. A major problem was that the same term meant different things to different people. For example, accounting used the term *orders* to refer to the total dollar amount of orders per time period, whereas the sales department used the term to refer to individual customer orders. Moreover, such confusions existed even within the accounting and finance function. For example, the reporting group used the term *product* to refer to any good currently sold to customers. Thus, the primary key for this entity was product number. In contrast, the forecasting group used the term *product* to refer to any good that was often still in the planning stage and had no product number assigned yet.

To solve these problems, Hewlett-Packard asked the different user groups to actively participate in the data modeling process. The first step was to convince all users of the need for and benefits of creating a data model for their function. Then it was necessary to carefully define the scope of the modeling effort. Hewlett-Packard found that the time invested in these early steps was worthwhile because it facilitated the activities of clarifying definitions and developing attribute lists that took place later in the process. The latter activity was iterative and included many revisions. Documentation was critical to this process. Each member of the modeling team and user groups had copies of the proposed lists, which made it easier to spot inconsistencies in definitions.

Hewlett-Packard credits the data modeling approach as contributing significantly to the project's overall success. Data modeling allowed the participants to concentrate first on understanding the essential business characteristics of the new system, instead of getting bogged down in specifying the contents of relational database tables. This helped them to identify and resolve conflicting viewpoints early in the process and paved the way for eventual acceptance of the resulting system. The key step, however, was in getting the different user groups to actively participate in the data modeling process. Otherwise, the resulting data model would not have been as accurate or widely accepted.

instead of the 1:1 relationship currently depicted. Similarly, if Fred's Train Shop also decided to adopt a policy of combining several orders from one customer into one large shipment, then Figure 19-6 would have to be modified to depict the relationship between those two events as M:N. Sometimes, differences in business practices can result in different entities modeled. For example, if Fred's Train Shop only made sales to walk-in customers and did not take any orders from businesses, then Figure 19-6 would not need to include the Take Customer Order commitment event.

Although the development of the REA diagram for Fred's Train Shop's revenue cycle may seem to have been relatively straightforward and intuitive, data modeling is usually a complex and repetitive process. Frequently, data modelers develop an initial REA diagram that reflects their understanding of the organization's business processes, only to learn when showing it to intended users that they had omitted key dimensions or misunderstood some operating procedures. Thus, it is not unusual to erase and redraw portions of an REA diagram several times before finally producing an acceptable model. One common source of misunderstanding is the use of different terminology by various subsets of the intended user groups. Focus 19-2 highlights the importance of involving the eventual users of the system in the data modeling process so that terminology is consistent.

Summary and Case Conclusion

The database design process has five stages: systems analysis, conceptual design, physical design, implementation and conversion, and operation and maintenance. Because of their extensive knowledge of transaction processing requirements and general business functions, accountants should actively participate in every stage.

One way to perform the activities of systems analysis and conceptual design is to build a data model of the AIS. The REA accounting data model is developed specifically for designing a database to support an AIS. The REA model classifies entities into three basic categories: resources, events, and agents. An REA model can be documented in the form of an entity-relationship (E-R) diagram, which depicts the entities about which data are collected as rectangles and represents the important relationships between entities by connecting lines. The cardinalities of the relationships depicted in REA diagrams specify the minimum and maximum number of times an instance of one entity can be linked to an instance of the other entity participating in that relationship. Cardinalities also provide information about the basic business policies an organization follows.

Developing an REA diagram involves three steps. First, identify the basic events of interest (any activity about which management wants to collect information in order to plan, control, and evaluate performance). Second, identify the resources affected by and the agents who participate in those events. Third, use knowledge about the organization's business practices to add relationship cardinality information to the diagram.

Paul Stone followed these steps to develop an REA diagram for Fred's Train Shop's revenue cycle. He interviewed Fred to understand the store's business policies and used his general knowledge of revenue cycle activities to draw Figure 19-6. Paul showed the diagram to Fred and explained what each portion represents. Fred indicated that the diagram correctly reflects his store's revenue cycle activities. Paul then explained that he will proceed to use the model to design a relational database that Fred can use to automate the analyses he currently does by hand.

KEY TERMS

data modeling 602
entity-relationship (E-R) diagram 602
entity 602
REA data model 603
resources 604
events 604
agents 604
cardinalities 610
minimum cardinality 611
maximum cardinality 611
one-to-one (1:1) relationship 612
one-to-many (1:N) relationship 613
many-to-many (M:N) relationship 613

AIS in Action

CHAPTER QUIZ

1. Accounts Receivable would appear in an REA diagram as an example of which kind of entity?
   a. resource
   b. event
   c. agent
   d. None of the above
2. Which of the following is not likely to be depicted as an entity in the REA data model?
   a. customers
   b. sales
   c. invoices
   d. delivery trucks
3. In most cases, the relationship between agent entities and event entities is ______.
   a. 1:1
   b. 1:N
   c. M:N
   d. 0:N
4. If customers pay for each sales transaction with a separate check and are not permitted to make installment payments on any sales, then the relationship between the Sale and Receive Cash events would be modeled as which of the following?
   a. 1:1
   b. 1:N
   c. M:N
   d. 0:N

5. Which of the following most accurately models the sales of low-cost, mass-produced items by a retail store?

a.
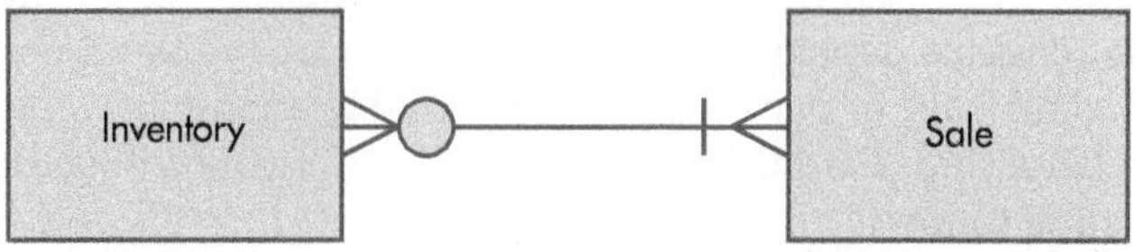

b.
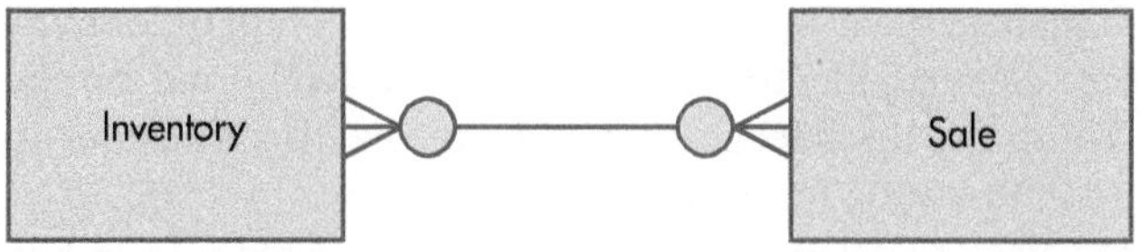

c.
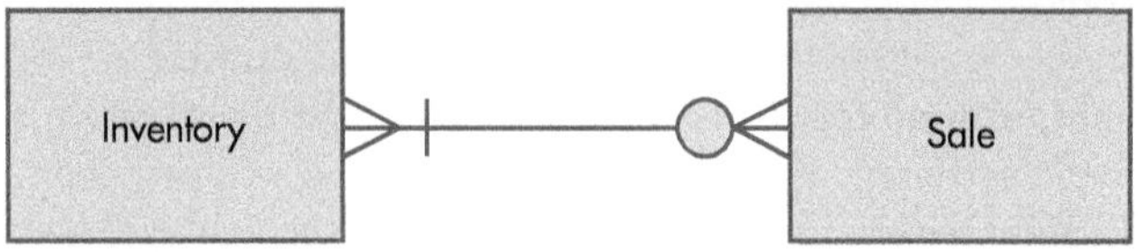

d.
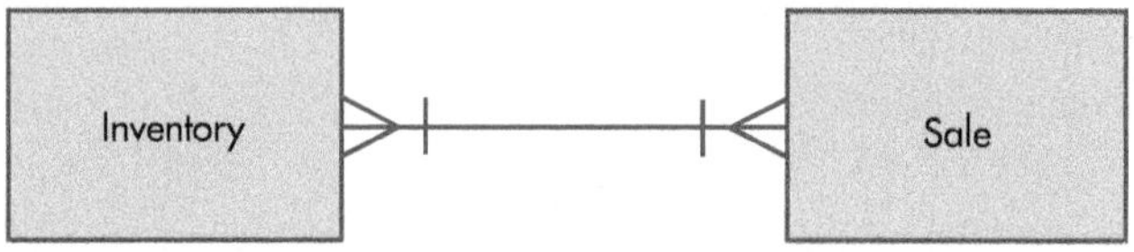

6. Data modeling occurs during which stages of database design?
   a. systems analysis and physical design
   b. systems analysis and conceptual design
   c. conceptual design and implementation and conversion
   d. physical design and implementation and conversion

7. A company has five different cash accounts (checking, money market, petty cash, payroll, and investments). It deposits all payments received from customers into its checking account. Which of the following accurately depicts the relationship between the Cash entity and the Receive Cash event?

a.

b.
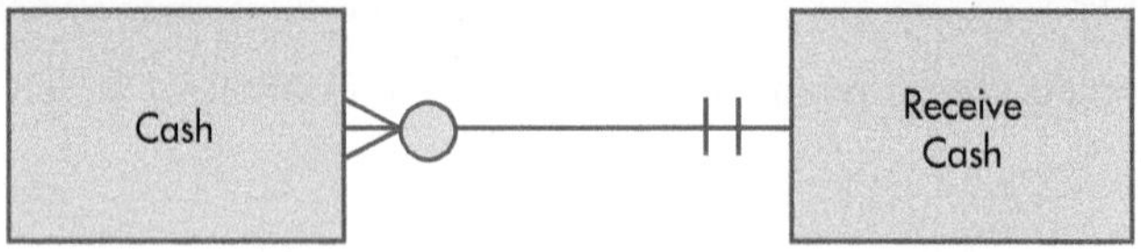

c.
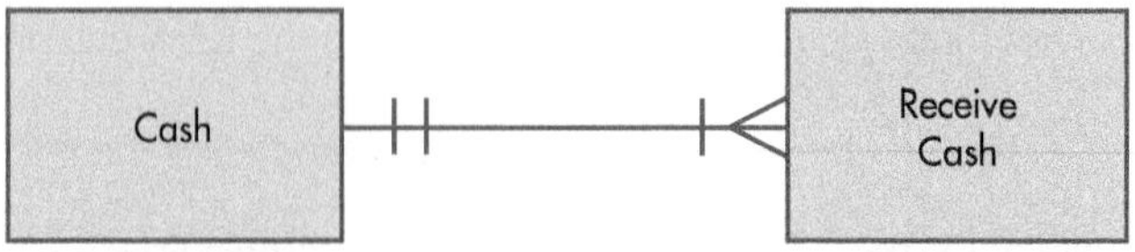

d.
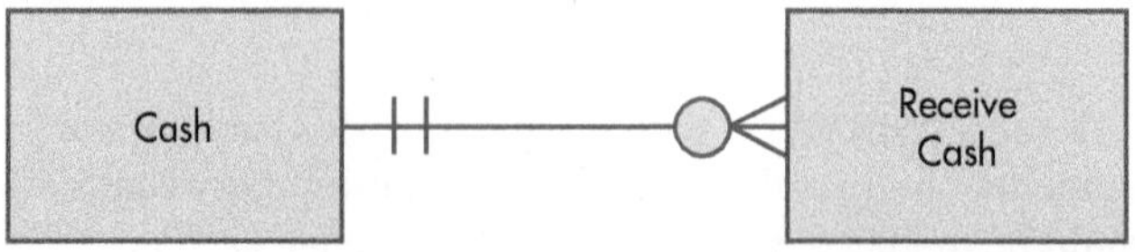

8. EZ Construction Company builds residential houses. It sells only homes that it built. Most of its homes are sold to individuals, but sometimes an investor may purchase several homes and hold them for subsequent resale. Which of the following is the correct way to model the relationship between Sale and Inventory for EZ Construction Company?

a. 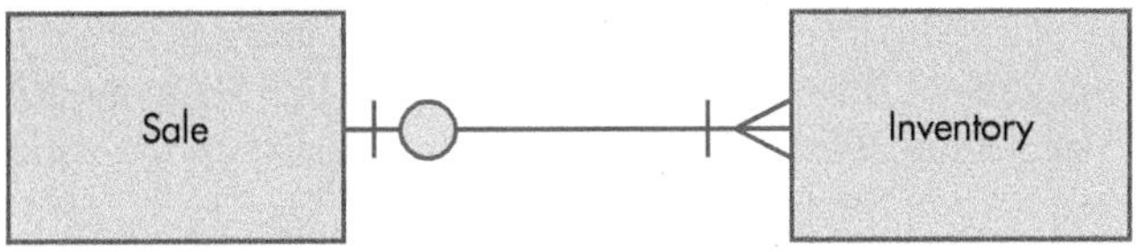

b. 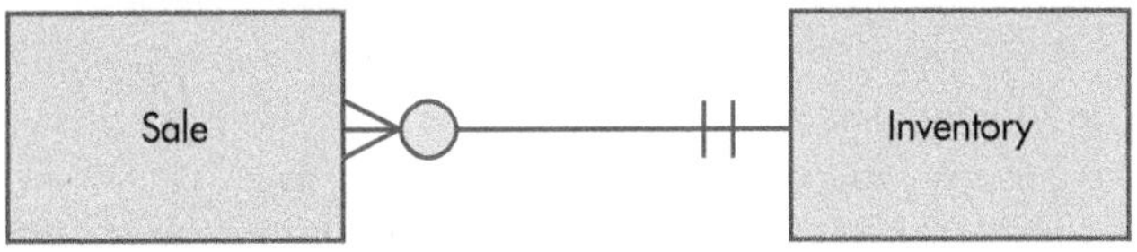

c. 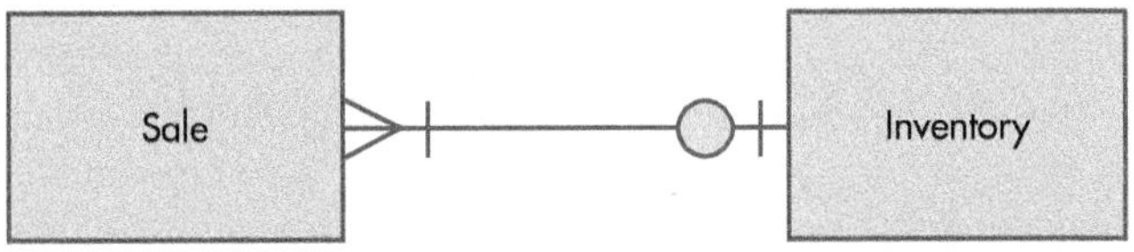

d. 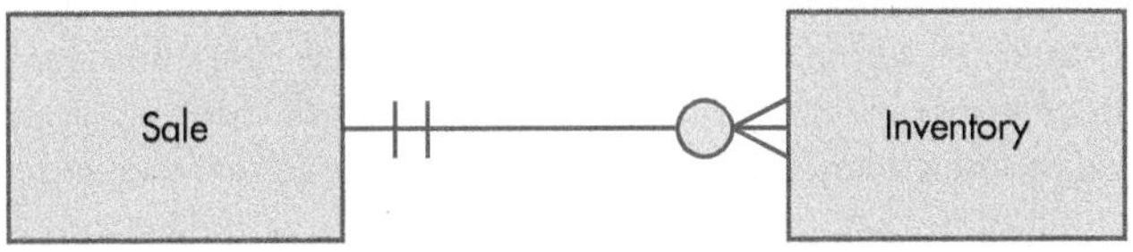

9. Which of the following statements about the REA data model is true?

a. Every event must be linked to at least two agents.
b. Every resource must be linked to at least one agent.
c. Every event must be linked to at least two resources.
d. Every agent must be linked to at least two events.

10. A business operates by always collecting payments for the entire amount of the sale from customers in advance. It then orders the items from its suppliers, and when they all arrive it ships the entire order to the customer. Which of the following describes the relationship between the Sale and Receive Cash events for this company?

a. 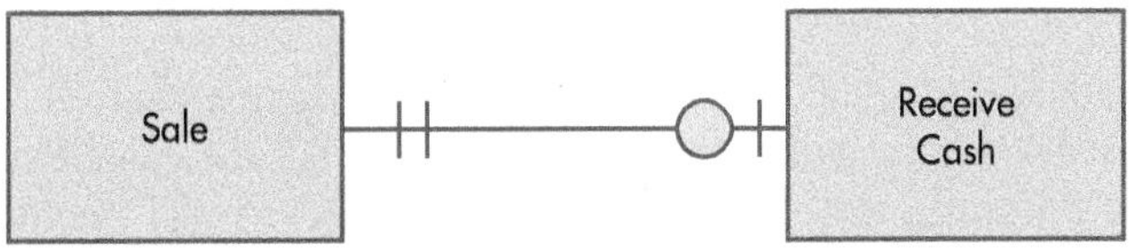

b. 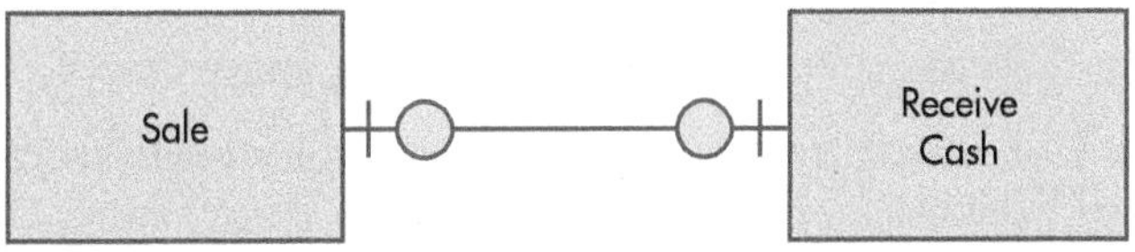

c. 

d. 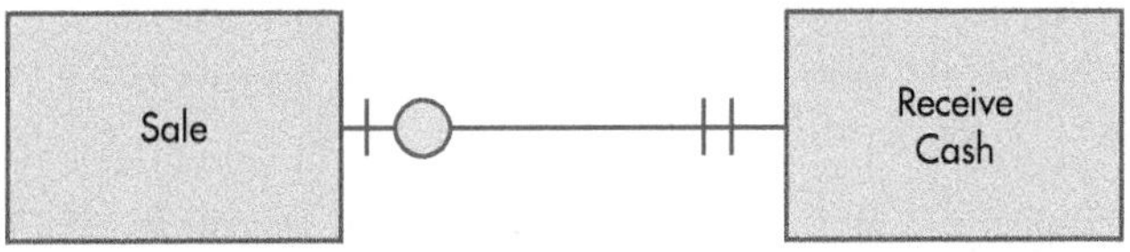

COMPREHENSIVE PROBLEM

Expenditure Cycle for Fred's Train Shop

In order for Fred to sell trains and train accessories, he first needs to have inventory to sell. Thus, as part of his overall engagement, Paul Stone has also prepared an REA model for the expenditure cycle of Fred's Train Shop. The following paragraph describes the expenditure cycle business processes of Fred's Train Shop:

> *Fred deals with more than one supplier and often places orders for multiple items at the same time. Fred takes inventory and places orders every Monday. Fred's suppliers strive to provide outstanding service. Therefore, they never consolidate multiple orders into one shipment, but always ship merchandise the day after receiving an order. Usually, Fred's suppliers can fill his entire order in one shipment. Occasionally, however, a supplier may be temporarily out of stock of a particular item. In such cases, the supplier ships as much of the order as possible and then ships the out-of-stock item separately as soon as it becomes available. Fred pays for each order in full at one time; that is, he does not make partial payments on orders received. Some suppliers offer discount terms for early payments; Fred always takes advantage of such offers, paying individual invoices, in full, on the appropriate date. Suppliers who do not offer such discounts send Fred monthly statements listing all orders placed the prior month. Fred pays the entire balance indicated on the statement in one check by the specified due date.*

REQUIRED

Prepare an REA diagram for Fred's Train Shop's expenditure cycle.

DISCUSSION QUESTIONS

19.1 Why is it not necessary to model activities such as entering information about customers or suppliers, mailing invoices to customers, and recording invoices received from suppliers as events in an REA diagram?

19.2 The basic REA template includes links between two events and links between events and resources and between events and agents. Why do you think the basic REA template does not include direct links between (a) two resources, (b) two agents, or (c) between resources and agents?

19.3 How can REA diagrams help an auditor understand a client's business processes?

19.4 Which parts of Figure 19-6 would accurately depict almost every organization's revenue cycle? Which parts would change?

19.5 What is the relationship between the things that would be represented as resources in an REA diagram and the different categories of assets found on an organization's balance sheet? (*Hint:* Are there any assets that would not be modeled as resources? Are any resources in an REA diagram not listed as assets on a balance sheet?)

19.6 How would accounts payable be reflected in an REA diagram? Why?

19.7 What are the five stages of the database design process? In which stages should accountants participate? Why?

19.8 What is the difference between an Entity-Relationship (E-R) diagram and an REA diagram?

PROBLEMS

19.1 Joe's is a small ice-cream shop located near the local university's baseball field. Joe's serves walk-in customers only. The shop carries 26 flavors of ice cream. Customers can buy cones, sundaes, or shakes. When a customer pays for an individual purchase, a sales transaction usually includes just one item. When a customer pays for a family or group purchase, however, a single sales transaction includes many different items. All sales must be paid for at the time the ice cream is served. Joe's maintains several banking accounts but deposits all sales receipts into its main checking account.

REQUIRED

Draw an REA diagram, complete with cardinalities, for Joe's revenue cycle.

19.2 Joe, the owner of the ice-cream shop, purchases ice cream from two vendors. Over the years, he has developed good relationships with both vendors, and they allow Joe to pay them biweekly for all purchases made during the preceding two-week period. Joe calls in ice-cream orders on Mondays and Thursdays. The orders are delivered the next day. Joe buys ice-cream toppings from one of several local stores and pays for each such purchase at the time of sale with a check from the company's main checking account.

REQUIRED

Draw an REA diagram, complete with cardinalities, for Joe's expenditure cycle.

19.3 Sue's Gallery sells original paintings by local artists. All sales occur in the store. Sometimes customers purchase more than one painting. Individual customers must pay for purchases in full at the time of sale. Corporate customers, such as hotels, however, may pay in installments if they purchase more than 10 paintings. Although Sue's Gallery has several bank accounts, all sales monies are deposited intact into the main checking account.

REQUIRED

Draw an REA diagram for the gallery's revenue cycle. Be sure to include cardinalities.

19.4 Sue's Gallery only purchases finished paintings (it never commissions artists). It pays each artist 50% of the agreed price at the time of purchase, and the remainder after the painting is sold. All purchases are paid by check from Sue's main checking account.

REQUIRED

Draw an REA diagram, complete with cardinalities, of the gallery's expenditure cycle.

19.5 Develop a data model of Fred's Train Shop's expenditure cycle activities related to the acquisition of office equipment and other fixed assets. Fred sometimes orders multiple pieces of equipment. Vendors usually ship the entire order but sometimes are out of stock of some items. In such cases, they immediately ship to Fred what they have in stock and then send a second shipment when they obtain the other items. Conversely, several orders placed within a short time period with the same vendor might be filled with one delivery. Assume that Fred makes installment payments for most fixed-asset acquisitions but occasionally pays for some equipment in full at the time of purchase.

REQUIRED

Draw an REA diagram of your data model. Be sure to include cardinalities.

19.6 Provide an example (in terms of companies with which you are familiar) for each of the business situations described by the following relationship cardinalities:

a.
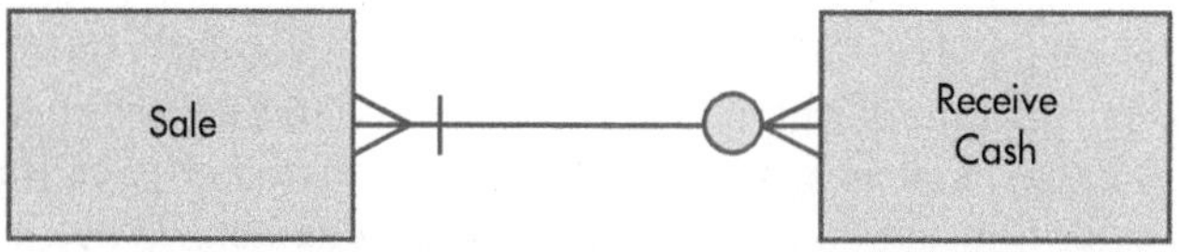

b.

c.
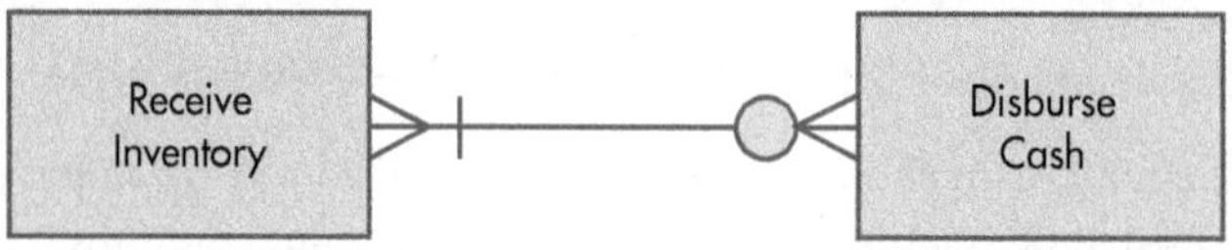

d.
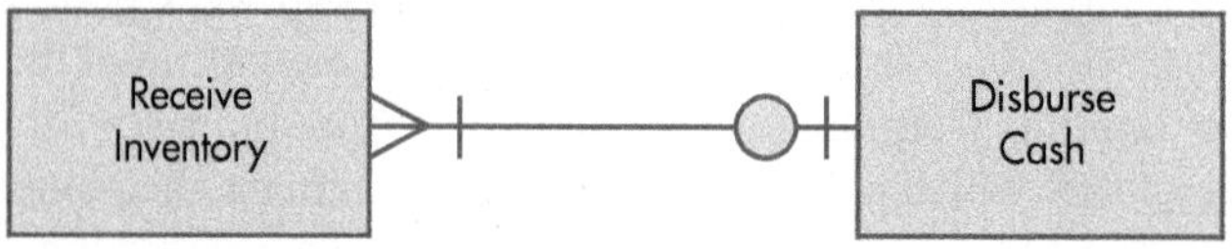

e.
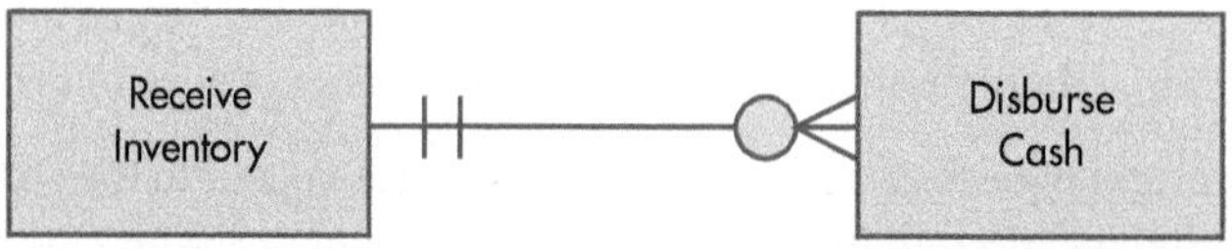

f.
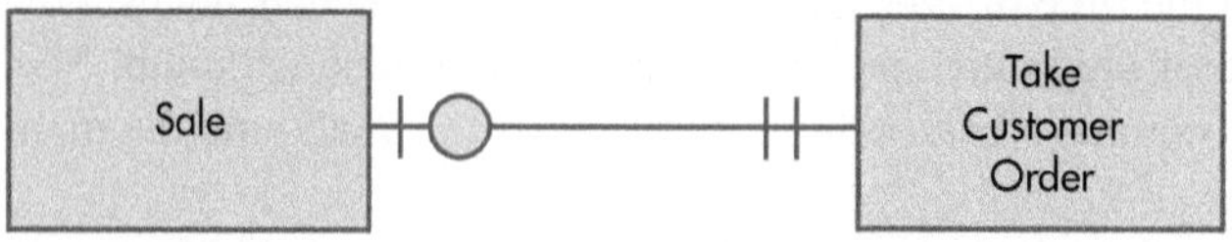

g.
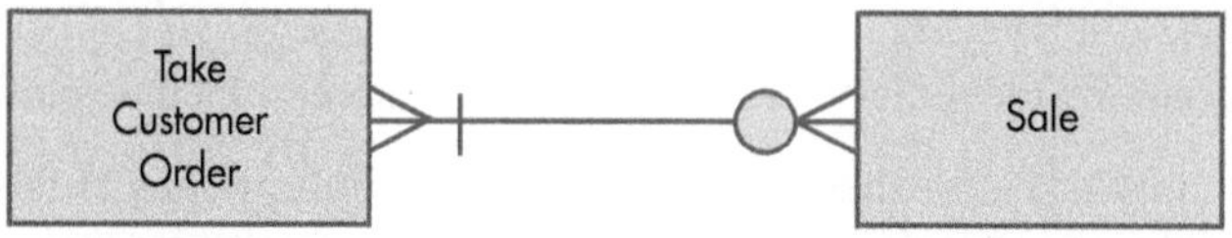

h.
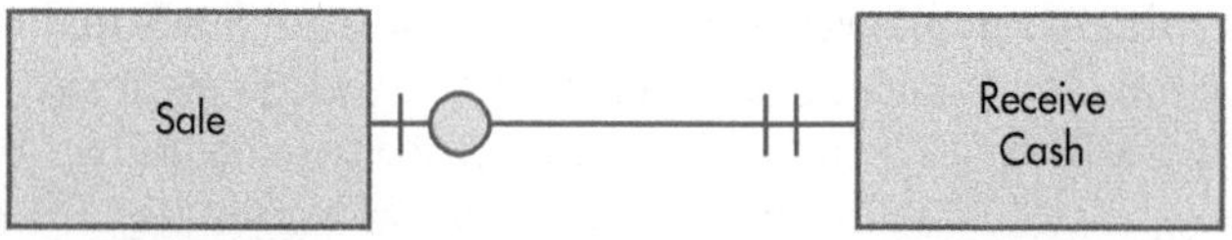

i.
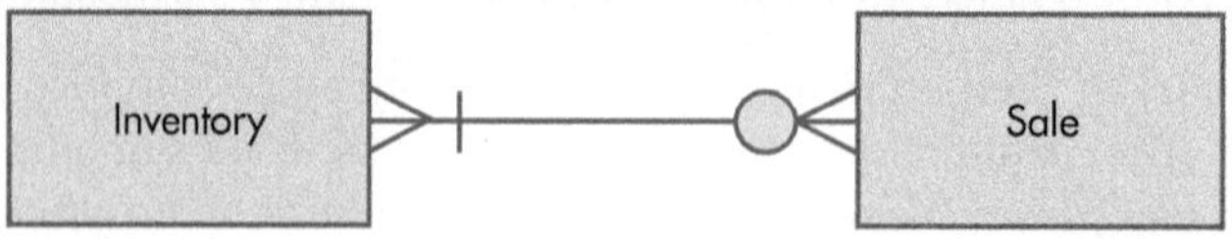

j.
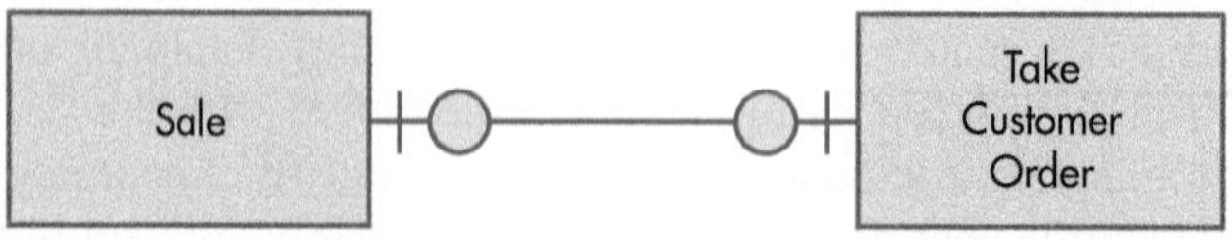

19.7 Model the cardinalities of the following business policies:

a. The relationship between the Sale and Receive Cash events for installment sales.

b. The relationship between the Sale and Receive Cash events at a convenience store.

c. The Take Customer Order–Sale relationship in a situation when occasionally several shipments are required to fill an order because some items were out of stock.

d. The Sale–Inventory relationship for a custom homebuilder.
e. The relationship between the Sale and Receive Cash events for Dell computers, which requires customers to pay the entire amount of their purchase in advance, prior to Dell shipping the merchandise.
f. The relationship between the Sale and Receive Cash events for a retail store that has some in-store sales paid in full by customers at the time of the sale but that also makes some in-store sales to customers on credit, billing them later and permitting them to make installment payments.
g. The relationship between the Receive Inventory and Disburse Cash events in the case where suppliers require payment in advance, in full.
h. The relationship between the Call on Customers event (i.e., the visit by a salesperson to a potential customer) and the Take Customer Order event for a business that is only conducted door-to-door (e.g., kitchen knives, certain books) so that the only way to order the items is when a salesperson visits the customer. (*Hint:* Do you think every call results in an order?)
i. The relationship between the Call on Customers and Take Customer Orders events for a manufacturer which also accepts orders on its website.
j. The relationship between the Receive Inventory and Disburse Cash events for a company which receives monthly bills from its suppliers for all purchases made the previous month; some suppliers require payment of the entire bill, in full, within 30 days or they will not accept any subsequent orders, but other suppliers accept installment payments.

19.8 The Computer Warehouse sells computer hardware, software, and supplies (such as paper). Individual customers just walk into the store, select merchandise, and must pay for their purchases in full before leaving the store. Corporate customers, however, call in orders in advance, so that the items are waiting to be picked up. Corporate customers may charge their purchases to their account. The Computer Warehouse mails corporate customers monthly statements that summarize all purchases made the prior month. Corporate customers pay the entire balance, as listed on the monthly statement, with one check or EFT transaction.

REQUIRED

Draw an REA diagram of the Computer Warehouse's revenue cycle, complete with cardinalities.

19.9 The Computer Warehouse purchases its inventory from more than a dozen different vendors. Orders are placed via telephone, fax, or on the supplier's website. Most orders are delivered the next day. Most orders are filled completely in one shipment, but sometimes a supplier is out of stock of a particular item. In such situations, the bulk of the order is shipped immediately and the out-of-stock item is shipped separately as soon as it arrives (such shipments of back orders are never combined with any new orders placed by the Computer Warehouse). The Computer Warehouse pays for some of its purchases C.O.D. but usually pays by the 10th of the month for all purchases made the prior month. None of its suppliers allow it to make installment payments.

REQUIRED

Draw an REA diagram of the Computer Warehouse's expenditure cycle, complete with cardinalities.

19.10 Stan's Southern Barbeque Supply Store orders mass-produced barbecue products from various suppliers. Stan's maintains information about a contact person at each supplier along with all required address information. Each purchase order has the order number, date, tax, and total. Purchase orders also contain the following information for each product ordered: stock number, description, and price. The manager of Stan's places orders by fax several times a day, whenever he notices that an item is running low. Some suppliers fill each individual order separately. Others, however, consolidate orders and fill all of them in one weekly delivery. Stan's suppliers never make partial shipments; if they are out of stock of a certain item, they wait until they obtain that item and then ship the entire order. Some suppliers require payment at the time of delivery, but others send Stan's a monthly statement detailing all purchases during the current period. Two suppliers allow Stan's to make installment payments for any individual purchase orders that exceed $20,000.

REQUIRED

Draw an REA diagram with cardinalities for the expenditure cycle of Stan's Southern Barbeque Supply Store.

19.11 Answer the following multiple-choice problems.

1. Which of the following steps in the revenue cycle would appear as event entities in an REA diagram?
a. Sales Order Entry
b. Shipping
c. Billing
d. Cash Collections

2. Which of the following steps in the expenditure cycle would appear as event entities in an REA diagram?
a. Ordering
b. Receiving
c. Approve Supplier Invoices
d. Cash Disbursements

3. Customers are sent monthly statements that list and total all sales transactions during the preceding month. Customers must pay the entire balance owed in full with one check. Given this set of facts, the relationship between the Sale and Receive Cash events would be modeled as ________.
a. 1:1
b. 1:N
c. N:1
d. M:N

4. ABC company has a checking account, savings account, and payroll account with the XYZ bank. ABC company deposits all customer payments into its checking account. The relationship between Cash and Receive Cash would be modeled as ________.
a. 1:1
b. 1:N
c. N:1
d. M:N

5. The REA diagram for the revenue cycle of a pet store would represent the relationship between Sales and Inventory as ________.
a. 1:1
b. 1:N
c. N:1
d. M:N

6. An art museum only purchases and displays original pieces of art. It sometimes purchases several works of art from the same artist at the same time. The REA diagram for the art museum's expenditure cycle would model the relationship between Purchases and Inventory as ________.
a. 1:1
b. 1:N
c. N:1
d. M:N

7. A company's suppliers send it separate invoices for each purchase. It also sends the company a monthly statement that summarizes all transactions during the preceding calendar month. Sometimes a supplier offers a discount if a specific invoice is paid in full within 15 days; in such cases, the company takes advantage of the discount. Otherwise, the company pays the full amount listed on the monthly statement within seven days of receiving the statement. Given this set of facts, the relationship between the Disburse Cash and Purchase events in the company's expenditure cycle REA diagram would be modeled as ______.

a. 1:1
b. 1:N
c. N:1
d. M:N

8. A grocery store sells to individuals and groups, such as the local fire department and a college fraternity. Given this set of facts, the grocery store's revenue cycle REA diagram would model the relationship between Sales and Customers as ______.

a. 1:1
b. 1:N
c. N:1
d. M:N

9. ABC company has a checking account, savings account, and payroll account with the XYZ bank. The REA diagram for ABC's expenditure cycle would model the relationship between Disburse Cash and Cash as ______.

a. 1:1
b. 1:N
c. N:1
d. M:N

CASE 19-1 REA Data Modeling Extension

An important analytical and problem-solving skill is the ability to adapt and transfer patterns learned in one setting to other situations. This chapter explained how to develop an REA diagram for a business that sells tangible inventory. Yet some businesses provide only a service. For example, the following narrative describes Sparky's Amusement Park's revenue cycle.

Sparky's Amusement Park is an entertainment park run by recent college graduates. It caters to young people and others who are young at heart. The owners are very interested in applying what they have learned in their information systems and marketing classes to operate a park better than any other in the area.

To accomplish these goals, guests of the park are given a personal "membership card" as they enter. This card will be used to identify each guest. Assume that a new card is issued each time a guest comes to the park. As a result, the system does not have to track one person over a period of time.

As at other parks, guests pay a flat fee for the day and then are able to ride all of the attractions (such as a double-looping roller coaster and the merry-go-round) for no extra charge. The owners, however, want to track the rides each guest takes and the attractions the guests use. They plan to have guests swipe their membership card through a computerized card reader, which automatically enters information into the computer system. This should allow the owners to gather data about the following:

- Number of people who use each piece of equipment. (How many people rode the Ferris wheel today?)
- Number of times each piece of equipment is operated daily.
- Times of day the attraction is busy or slow. (When was the carousel the busiest?)
- Number of attractions each guest uses. (How many different pieces of equipment did customer 1122 ride?)
- Number of rides each guest enjoys. (How many different rides did customer 1122 enjoy? Did each guest go on any rides more than once?)

REQUIRED

Draw an REA diagram for Sparky's *revenue* cycle only. Be sure to include cardinalities. State any assumptions you had to make.

Source: Adapted from one developed for classroom use by Dr. Julie Smith David at Arizona State University.

AIS in Action Solutions

QUIZ KEY

1. Accounts Receivable would appear in an REA diagram as an example of which kind of entity?
   a. resource [Incorrect. Accounts Receivable is not a resource as defined in the REA model, but simply equals the difference between the Sales and Receive Cash events.]
   b. event [Incorrect. Accounts Receivable is not an event, but represents the difference between two events.]
   c. agent [Incorrect. Agents are people or organizations.]
   ▶ **d.** none of the above [Correct. Accounts Receivable would not appear as an entity in an REA diagram because it represents the difference between two events.]

2. Which of the following is not likely to be depicted as an entity in the REA data model?
   a. customers [Incorrect. Customers are an agent entity.]
   b. sales [Incorrect. Sales are an event entity.]
   ▶ **c.** invoices [Correct. Invoices are paper outputs of a database—they do not meet the definition of a resource, an event, or an agent and, therefore, are not modeled as an entity in an REA diagram.]
   d. delivery trucks [Incorrect. Delivery trucks are an economic resource entity.]

3. In most cases, the relationship between agent entities and event entities is ______.
   a. 1:1 [Incorrect. Over time, agents can participate in many events.]
   ▶ **b.** 1:N [Correct. Over time, agents usually participate in many events. Usually, for accountability purposes, an event is linked to only one specific internal agent and one specific external agent. Occasionally, a complex task may be linked to a team of internal agents, but this is not the norm.]
   c. M:N [Incorrect. This pattern may occasionally occur, but it is not the norm.]
   d. 0:N [Incorrect. There is no such thing as a 0:N relationship.]

4. If customers pay for each sales transaction with a separate check and are not permitted to make installment payments on any sales, then the relationship between the Sale and Receive Cash events would be modeled as which of the following?
   ▶ **a.** 1:1 [Correct. Each sales transaction is linked to only one payment (no installments) and each payment is linked to only one sales transaction (separate checks).]
   b. 1:N [Incorrect. This indicates that each sale event could be linked to multiple cash receipts, implying installment payments.]
   c. M:N [Incorrect. This not only indicates the possibility of installment payments but also the use of one check to pay for multiple sales.]
   d. 0:N [Incorrect. There is no such thing as a 0:N relationship.]

5. Which of the following most accurately models the sales of low-cost, mass-produced items by a retail store?

a. 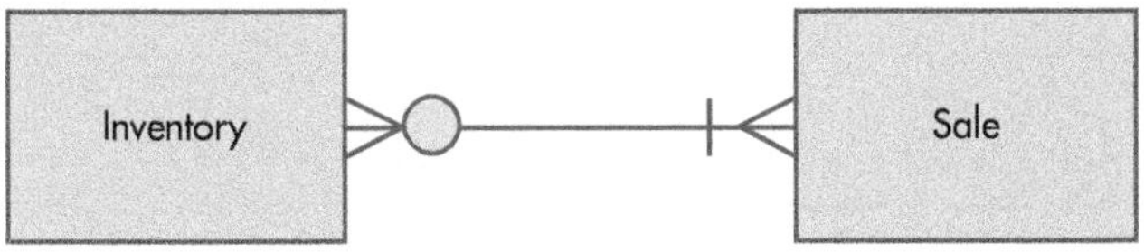

[Incorrect. This indicates that every inventory item must be linked to at least one sale, but that a sales transaction may consist of no inventory.]

b. 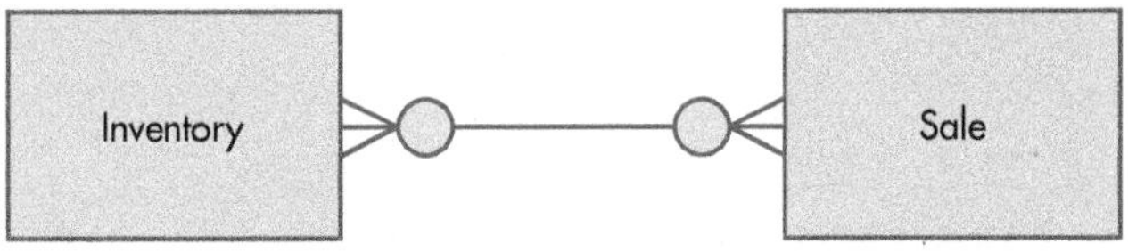

[Incorrect. This shows that a sales transaction can consist of no inventory items.]

▶ c. 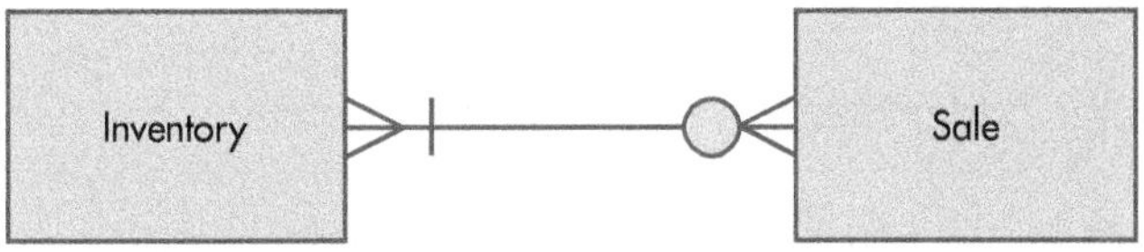

[Correct. Each sale must involve at least one item of inventory, but possibly many; conversely, each inventory item may not be linked to any sales transaction, but a given item could be linked to many sale events.]

d. 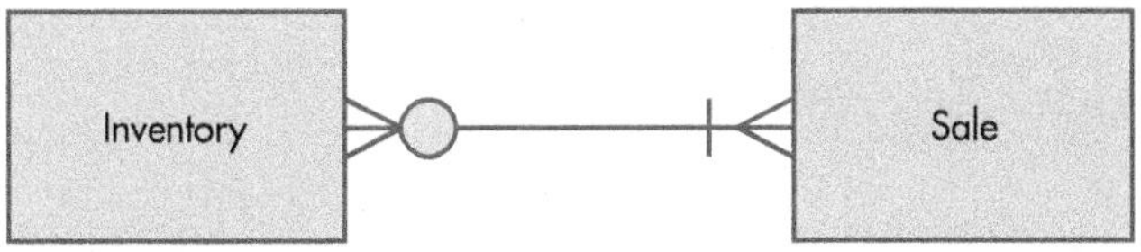

[Incorrect. This says every inventory item must be linked to at least one sales transaction—this is not true at the beginning of a fiscal year and precludes storing information about new products prior to being sold.]

6. Data modeling occurs during which stages of database design?

a. system analysis and physical design [Incorrect. Data modeling occurs during the system analysis and conceptual design stages of the database design process.]

▶ **b.** system analysis and conceptual design [Correct.]

c. conceptual design and implementation and conversion [Incorrect. Data modeling occurs during the system analysis and conceptual design stages of the database design process.]

d. physical design and implementation and conversion [Incorrect. Data modeling occurs during the system analysis and conceptual design stages of the database design process.]

7. A company has five different cash accounts [checking, money market, petty cash, payroll, and investments]. It deposits all payments received from customers into its checking account. Which of the following accurately depicts the relationship between the Cash entity and the Receive Cash Event?

a. 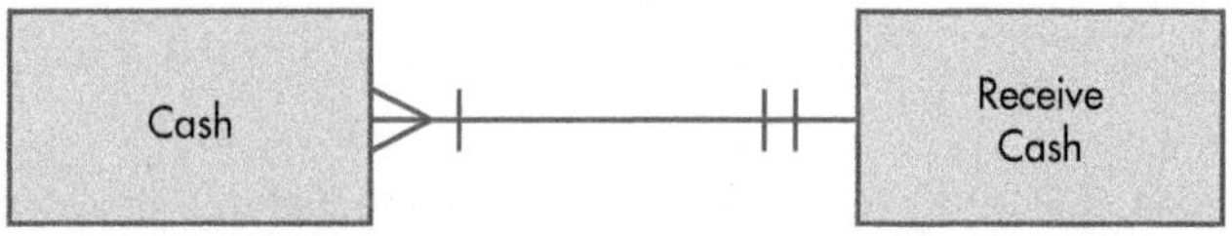

[Incorrect. This says that every Cash account must be linked to at least one Receive Cash event and that a Receive Cash event could be linked to multiple cash accounts.]

b. 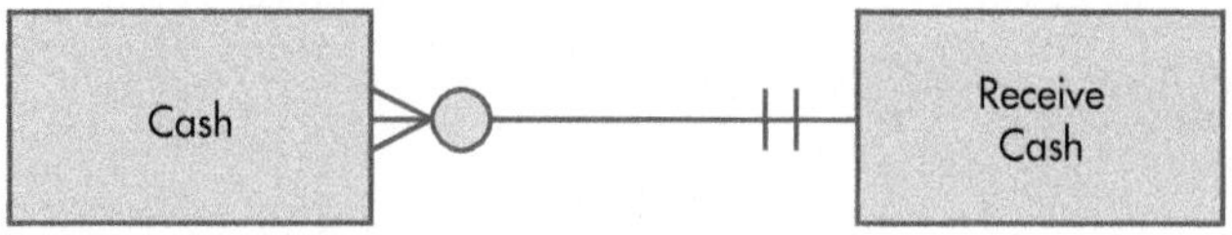

[Incorrect. Same problems as in a.]

c. 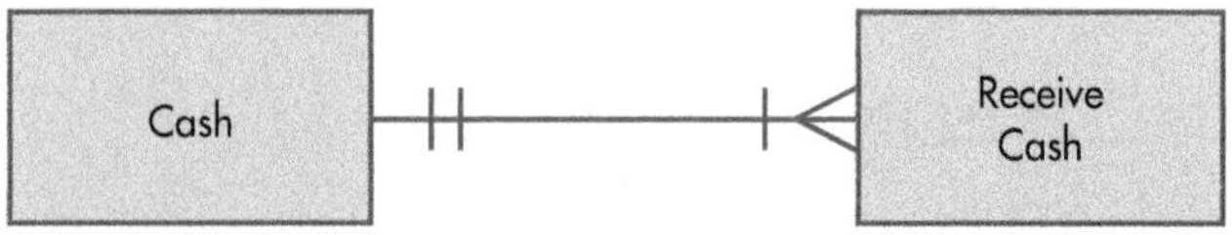

[Incorrect. This says that every Cash account must be linked to at least one Receive Cash event, which is not true: At the beginning of a new fiscal year, there are no Receive Cash events and four of the company's five Cash accounts never directly receive funds collected from customers.]

▶ **d.** 

[Correct. This shows that some Cash accounts may not be linked to any Receive Cash events, whereas others may be linked to many events. Conversely, this shows that each Receive Cash event must be linked to a Cash account, and to only one Cash account.]

8. EZ Construction Company builds residential houses. It sells only homes that it has built. Most of its homes are sold to individuals, but sometimes an investor may purchase several homes and hold them for subsequent resale. Which of the following is the correct way to model the relationship between Sale and Inventory for EZ Construction Company?

▶ a. 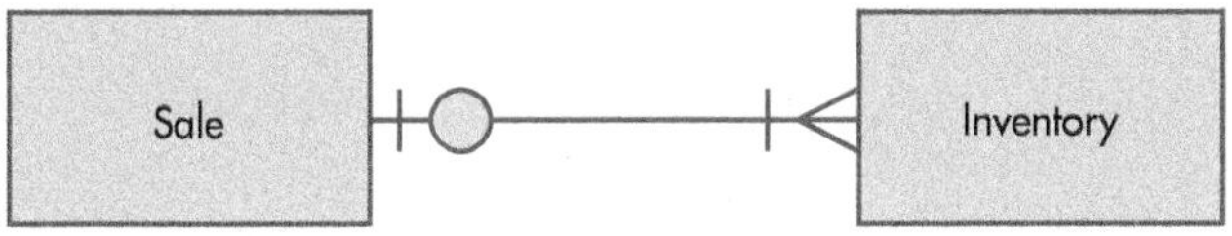

[Correct. Each sale must involve at least one home from inventory but could involve many; conversely, each home may or may not be sold (yet) but can be sold at most one time.]

b. 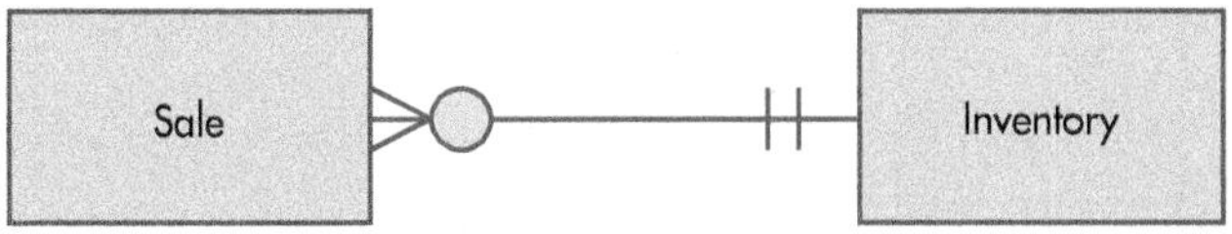

[Incorrect. This shows that a sale can only involve at most one home from inventory and it shows that a given home can be sold multiple times.]

c. 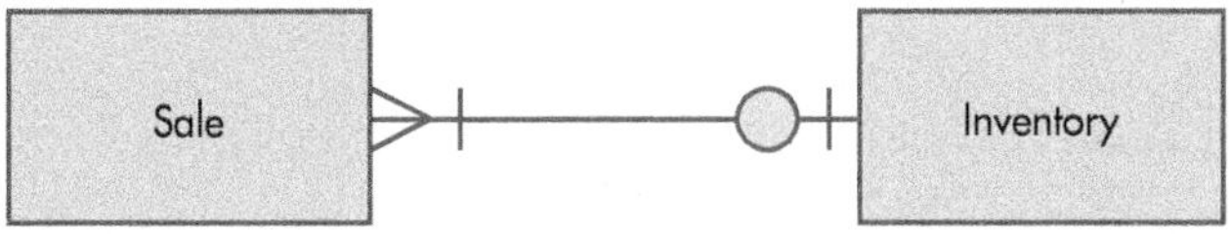

[Incorrect. This shows that a sale could involve no homes or at most one home, and it shows that every home must be sold but could be sold more than once.]

d. 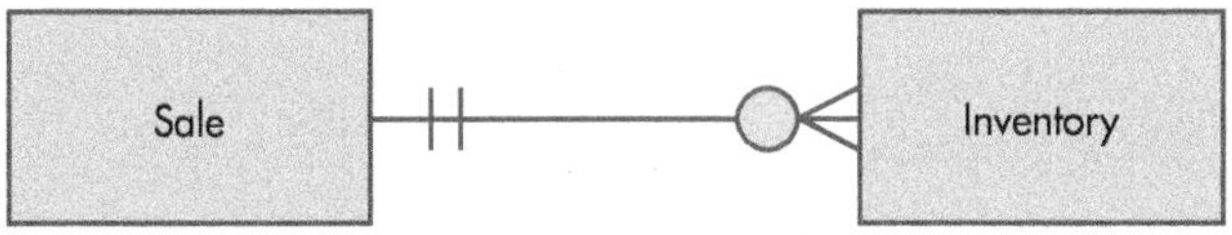

[Incorrect. This shows that every home must be sold and it also shows that a sale could involve no homes.]

9. Which of the following statements about the REA data model is true?

▶ a. Every event must be linked to at least two agents. [Correct.]

b. Every resource must be linked to at least two agents. [Incorrect. Resources and agents are not usually directly linked to one another.]

c. Every event must be linked to at least two resources. [Incorrect. Every event must be linked to at least one resource.]

d. Every agent must be linked to at least two events. [Incorrect. Some agents may only need to be linked to one event.]

10. A business operates by always collecting payments for the entire amount of the sale from customers in advance. It then orders the items from its suppliers, and when they all arrive it ships the entire order to the customer. Which of the following describes the relationship between the Sale and Receive Cash events for this company?

a. 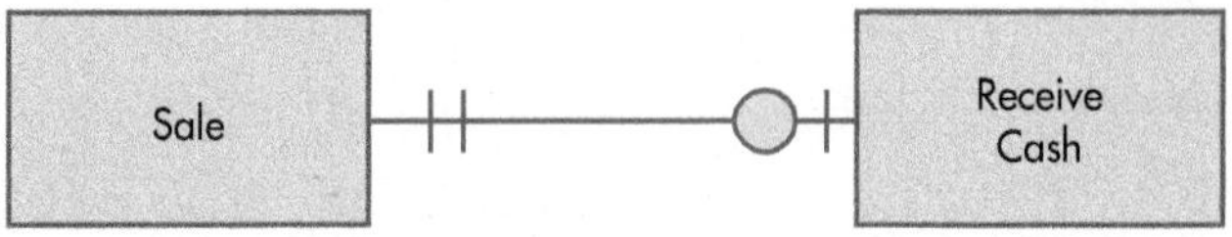

[Incorrect. This shows that a Sale event might not be linked to any Receive Cash events, which means that the merchandise is delivered prior to the customer's payment. Another problem is that this shows that every Receive Cash event must be linked to a Sale event, but the company receives payment prior to delivering the merchandise.]

b. 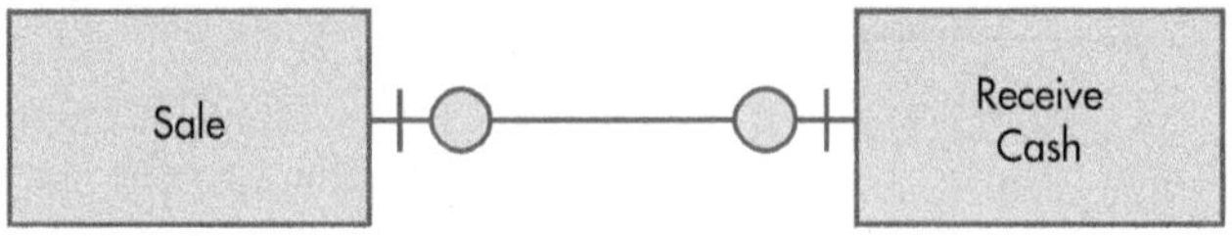

[Incorrect. Same problems as in a.]

c. 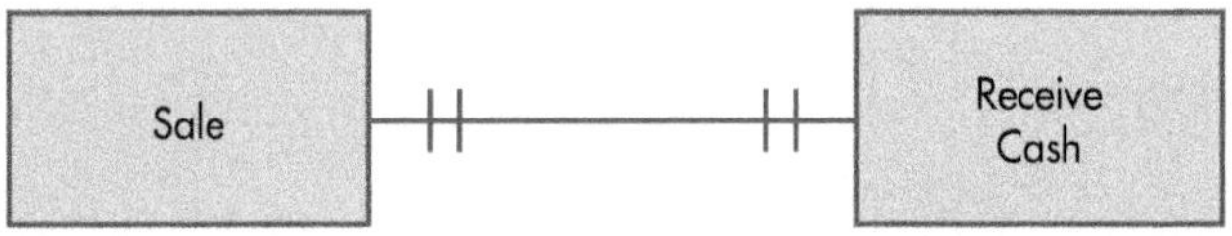

[Incorrect. This shows that every Receive Cash event must be linked to a Sale event, but this is not true because the company receives cash prior to shipping the merchandise.]

▶ d. 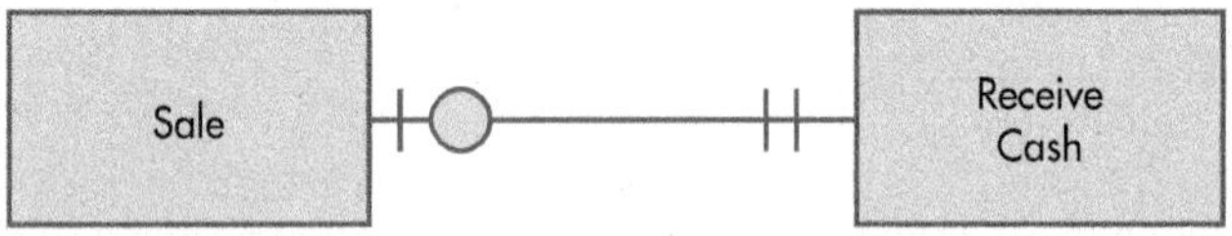

[Correct. This shows that each Sale event must be linked to a prior Receive Cash event but that a Receive Cash event may not (yet) be linked to any Sale event.]

COMPREHENSIVE PROBLEM SOLUTION

REA DIAGRAM OF EXPENDITURE CYCLE FOR FRED'S TRAIN SHOP

To create an entity-relationship diagram using the REA model, follow the three basic steps outlined in the chapter.

1 IDENTIFY EVENTS

As explained in the chapter, the first step is to identify all relevant events or transactions using the basic "give-to-get" exchange. After talking to Fred about how he buys the inventory he needs, Paul identifies three basic events that occur:

1. Order Inventory.
2. Receive Inventory.
3. Pay for Inventory, which Paul decides to call "Disburse Cash".

2 IDENTIFY RESOURCES AND AGENTS

Next, identify the resources involved with these events. Paul determines that there are two resources involved with these events:

1. Inventory.
2. Cash.

Then identify the agents or people needed to make these events happen, remembering that there are usually two agents for each event, one internal to Fred's store (e.g., an employee) and one external to Fred's store (e.g., the supplier).

Paul lists the following agents as involved in the Order Inventory event:

1. Purchasing Clerk.
2. Supplier.

The following are the agents involved in the Receive Inventory event:

1. Receiving Clerk.
2. Supplier.

The following are the agents involved in the Disburse Cash event:

1. Supplier.
2. Cashier.

3 DETERMINE CARDINALITIES OF RELATIONSHIPS

After all events, resources, and agents are identified, the next step is to determine how all of these entities interact by determining the cardinalities of all of the relationships between and among the entities. This involves three steps:

1. Specify cardinalities of event–agent relationships.
2. Specify cardinalities of event–resource relationships.
3. Specify cardinalities of event–event relationships.

Step 1: Specify Event–Agent Relationship Cardinalities

After talking with Fred, Paul understands that any employee can order merchandise from suppliers. However, one and only one employee is involved in each order event. Similarly, any employee can check in deliveries from suppliers. Because model train merchandise is not heavy or bulky, each delivery is checked in by only one employee. Fred, or his wife, signs all checks to suppliers, and only one signature is ever required. Thus, the *maximum* cardinality on the agent side of relationships between events and internal agents (employees) is always 1. Obviously, an employee must participate in each event: There must be some employee who places an order, there must be some employee who checks in a delivery, and either Fred or his wife must sign each check. Thus, the *minimum* cardinality on the agent side of relationships between events and internal agents is also 1.

Orders, receipts of inventory, and payments all involve suppliers. Each event must be linked to a particular supplier: A purchase order must identify and be sent to a supplier, a delivery comes from some supplier, and a payment is made to some identifiable supplier. Moreover, each event can be linked to *only one* supplier: Each order is placed with a *specific* supplier, each delivery comes from a *specific* supplier, and each payment is made to a *specific* supplier (e.g., each check is made payable to one, and only one, supplier). Thus, the minimum and maximum cardinalities on the agent side of relationships between events and external agents is 1.

Paul also knows that information about both internal and external agents is maintained indefinitely but that information about events is maintained only for the current fiscal year. Therefore, at the beginning of each fiscal period, no internal agent and no external agent are linked to any order, inventory receipt, or payment events. Thus, the *minimum* cardinality on the event side of relationships between events and agents is 0. During the course of the year, however, the same employee may place many different orders or may check in many different deliveries of merchandise. In addition, both Fred and his wife will sign many different checks sent to suppliers. Conversely, during the year many orders may be placed with the same supplier; many deliveries may be received from the same supplier; and many payments may be made to the same supplier. Thus, the *maximum* cardinality on the event side of relationships between events and agents is N.

Step 2: Specify Event–Resource Relationship Cardinalities

Each order must involve at least one inventory item but could be for many different items. Similarly, each delivery of merchandise from a supplier must involve at least one inventory item but may include many different items. Consequently, Paul depicts the minimum cardinality as 1 and the maximum cardinality as N on the inventory side of all relationships between the inventory resource and various events.

Information about inventory is maintained indefinitely, but only orders and inventory receipts that occurred during the current fiscal year are maintained in the database. Thus, at the beginning of each fiscal year the inventory entity is not linked to any order or receive inventory events. During the course of the year, however, a particular inventory item may be ordered and received many times. Thus, Paul depicts the minimum cardinality as 0 and the maximum cardinality as N on the event side of all relationships between the Inventory resource and various events affecting it.

Each payment must be made from some general ledger cash account. In addition, each payment can be made from only one specific account. For example, a check can be linked to either the operating checking account or the payroll checking account, but it cannot be linked to both accounts. Therefore, Paul sets the minimum and maximum cardinalities to 1 on the resource side of the relationship between the Cash resource and the Disburse Cash event.

Information about the various cash accounts in the general ledger (operating checking, payroll, investment, etc.) is maintained indefinitely, but the Disburse Cash event entity contains information only about payments made during the current fiscal year. Therefore, at the beginning of each fiscal year, the cash resource is not linked to any Disburse Cash events. During the course of the year, however, a given cash account may be linked to many different Disburse Cash events. Thus, the minimum cardinality is 0 and the maximum cardinality is N on the event side of the relationship between the Cash resource and the Disburse Cash event.

Step 3: Specify Event–Event Relationship Cardinalities

Orders occur before deliveries. Some orders, however, may include items that are out of stock; when that happens, the merchandise in stock is sent immediately, and one or more additional shipments are made for any items that the supplier had to back order. Thus, one order can be linked to multiple Receive Inventory events. Consequently, Paul assigns a minimum cardinality of 0 and a maximum cardinality of N on the Receive Inventory side of the relationship between the Order Inventory and Receive Inventory events.

Fred's employees have been trained to accept only deliveries for which a valid purchase order exists. Thus, each Receive Inventory event must be linked to an order. Fred's suppliers never consolidate multiple orders into one delivery; thus, each Receive Inventory event can be linked to at most one order event. Therefore, Paul depicts the minimum and maximum cardinalities on the Order Inventory side of the relationship between the Receive Inventory and Order Inventory events as 1.

Often, Fred pays for deliveries in the following month. Thus, there may be Receive Inventory events not yet linked to any Disburse Cash events. Fred always pays for deliveries in full; he never makes installment payments. Therefore, each Receive Inventory event is linked to at most one Disburse Cash event. Consequently, Paul assigns a minimum cardinality of 0 and a maximum cardinality of 1 to the Disburse Cash side of the relationship between the Receive Inventory and Disburse Cash events.

Fred's only pays for deliveries after the merchandise has been received and inspected. Thus, every Disburse Cash event must be linked to a preceding Receive Inventory event. Oftentimes, Fred or his wife will write one check to pay for several deliveries received during the preceding month. Therefore, Paul draws the minimum cardinality as 1 and the maximum cardinality as N on the Receive Inventory side of the relationship between the Receive Inventory and Disburse Cash events.

After completing the three steps, Paul created the REA diagram of the expenditure cycle of Fred's Train Shop that appears on the next page.

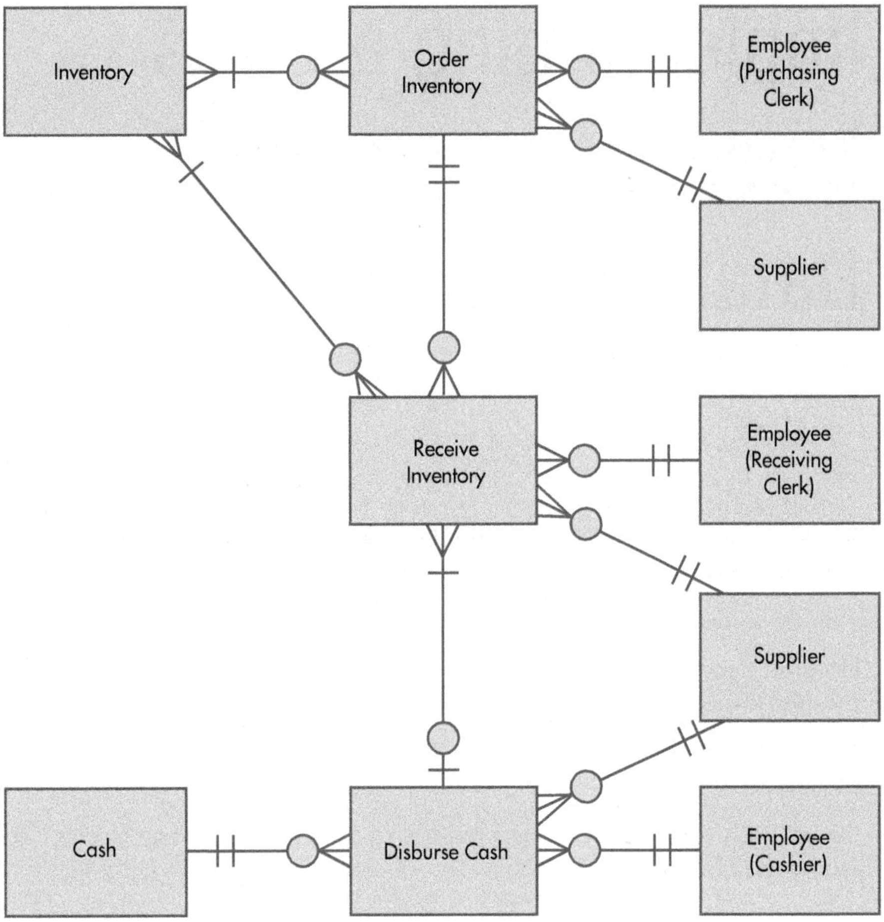
Inventory
Order Inventory
Employee (Purchasing Clerk)
Supplier
Receive Inventory
Employee (Receiving Clerk)
Supplier
Cash
Disburse Cash
Employee (Cashier)

CHAPTER

20

Implementing an REA Model in a Relational Database

LEARNING OBJECTIVES

After studying this chapter, you should be able to:

1. Integrate separate REA diagrams for individual business cycles into a single, comprehensive, organization-wide REA diagram.
2. Build a set of tables to implement an REA model of an AIS in a relational database.
3. Use the REA data model to write queries to retrieve information from an AIS relational database.

INTEGRATIVE CASE Fred's Train Shop

Paul Stone shows Fred the set of REA diagrams he developed to model the business activities for the revenue, expenditure, and payroll cycles of Fred's Train Shop. Fred verifies that Paul correctly represented his company's business processes. He then says that although the diagrams "look nice," he wondered why Paul spent so much time developing them, instead of building Fred the database he promised. Paul responds that the time spent up front in thoroughly understanding Fred's Train Shop's business processes is necessary to properly design a database that will satisfy Fred's needs.

Paul asks Fred whether he has a database program. Fred replies that a relational database was part of the "business applications" he purchased as part of an office productivity package. Fred says that although he knows how to use the program, he has not been able to figure out how to import data to it from his AIS and store it in a manner that will allow him to analyze his store's business activities. Paul says he will create a useful database for Fred by following these steps:

1. First, he will integrate the separate REA diagrams he developed into a single, comprehensive, enterprise-wide data model.
2. Second, he will use the integrated data model to design a set of relational database tables.
3. Third, he will show Fred how he can query the resulting database to generate both traditional financial statements as well as any custom performance reports.

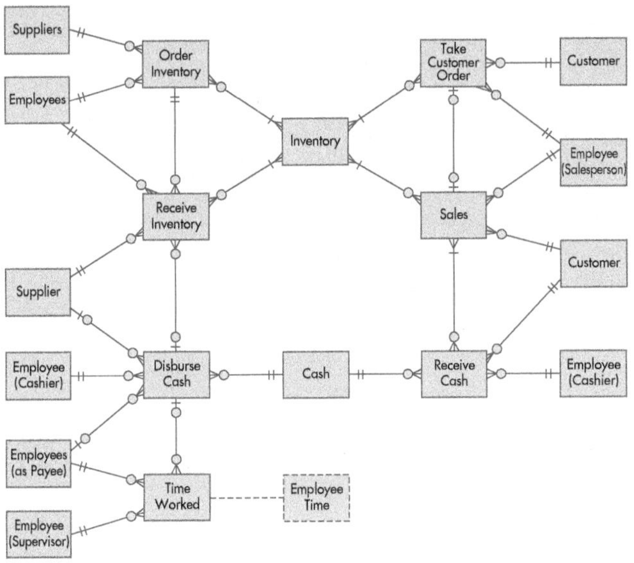

Introduction

The previous chapter introduced the topic of REA data modeling and explained how to develop REA diagrams for an individual business cycle. This chapter shows how to implement an REA diagram in a database. We focus on relational databases because they are commonly used to support transaction processing systems and are likely familiar to most business students. Nevertheless, REA data modeling is not limited for use only in designing relational databases; it can also be used to design object-oriented databases.

We begin by showing how to integrate separate REA diagrams developed for individual business cycles into a single, comprehensive, enterprise-wide data model. Next, we explain how to implement the resulting model in a relational database. We then describe how to use the REA diagram to query the database to produce traditional financial statements as well as a variety of management reports.

Integrating REA Diagrams Across Cycles

Figures 20-1, 20-2, and 20-3 present REA diagrams of Fred's Train Shop's revenue, expenditure, and payroll cycles, respectively. These separate diagrams should be integrated to provide a single, comprehensive, enterprise-wide model of the organization. Doing so requires understanding what the cardinalities in each separate diagram reveal about the organization's business policies and activities. Figures 20-1 and 20-2 were explained in Chapter 19 (see discussion of Figures 19-6 and the comprehensive end-of-chapter problem, respectively), so we focus here on Figure 20-3.

Figure 20-3 depicts the payroll portion of Fred's Train Shop's HR/payroll cycle activities. The basic economic exchange involves acquiring the use of each employee's time and skills in exchange for which the employee receives a paycheck. Like many small businesses, Fred's Train Shop uses an electronic time clock to record the hours worked by each employee each day. Thus, each Time Worked event records the time an employee began and ended working on a specific day. Each such event must be linked to a particular employee and his or her supervisor; each employee or supervisor, however, may be linked to many different events. Similarly, a paycheck is issued to a particular employee and signed by a particular cashier, but each employee and cashier may be associated with many different Disburse Cash events over time. Hence, Figure 20-3 depicts the relationships between agents and events as 1:N. The minimum cardinality on the agent side of those relationships is always 1 because each event *must* be linked to a specific employee. (For example, Fred would not want to issue a paycheck and leave the payee name blank.) The minimum cardinality on the event side of the relationships is always 0 in order to accommodate storing data about new employees prior to their beginning work and because the event entities are empty at the beginning of each new fiscal year.

FIGURE 20-1
Fred's Train Shop
Revenue Cycle

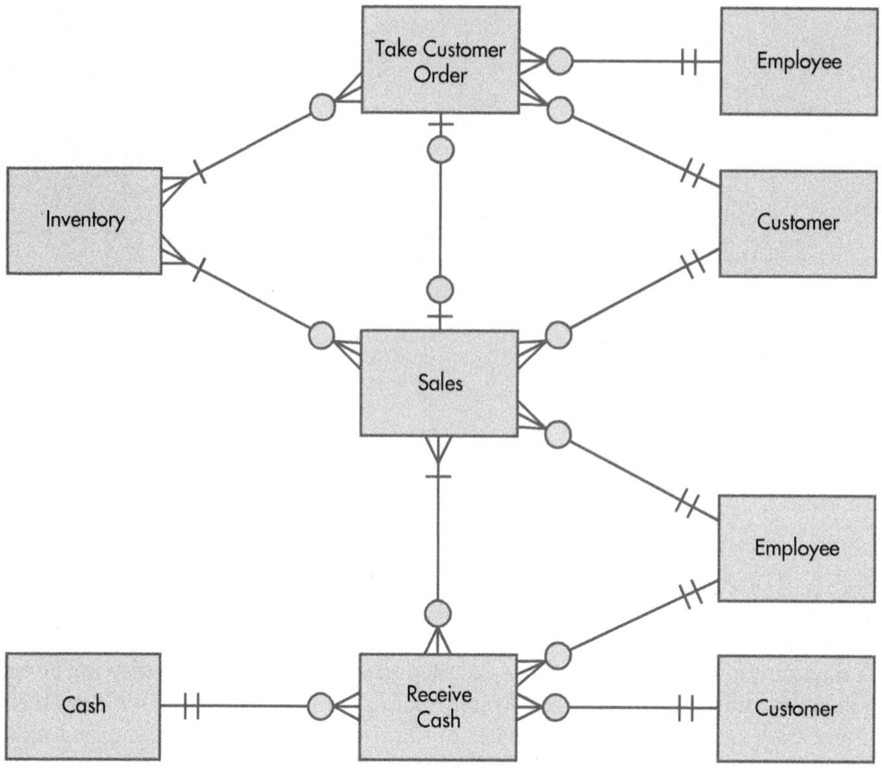

FIGURE 20-2
Fred's Train Shop
Expenditure Cycle

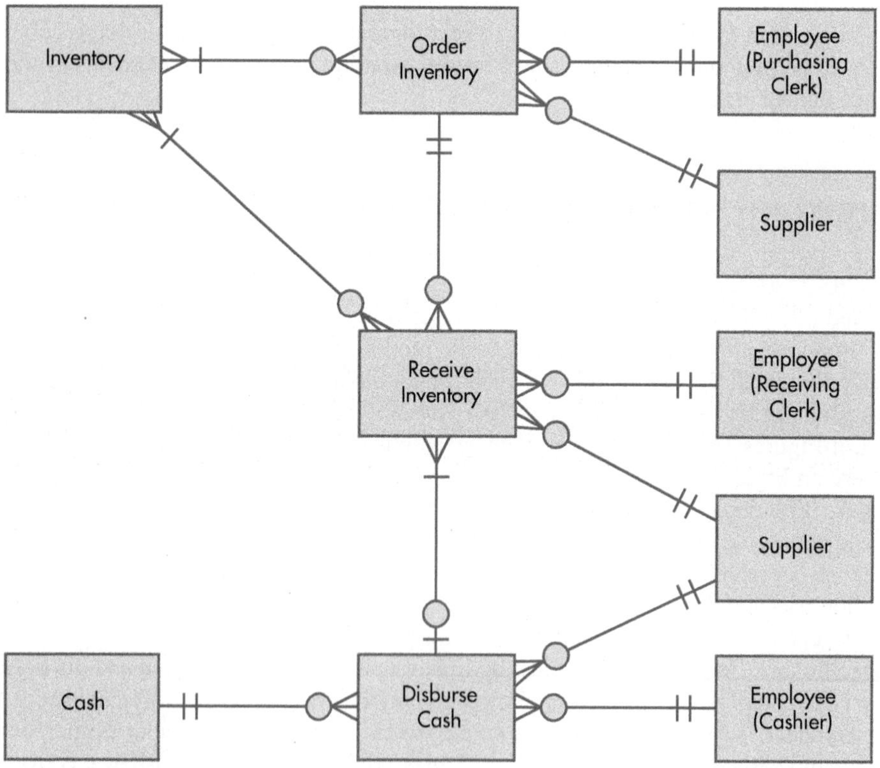

The relationship between the Time Worked and Disburse Cash events reflects the basic economic exchange of getting the use of an employee's time and paying for it. Figure 20-3 shows that the relationship between these two events is 1:N. This is because Fred's Train Shop, like most businesses, pays employees periodically but records their time worked daily. Thus, each Disburse Cash event is linked to many daily Time Worked events. Like most businesses,

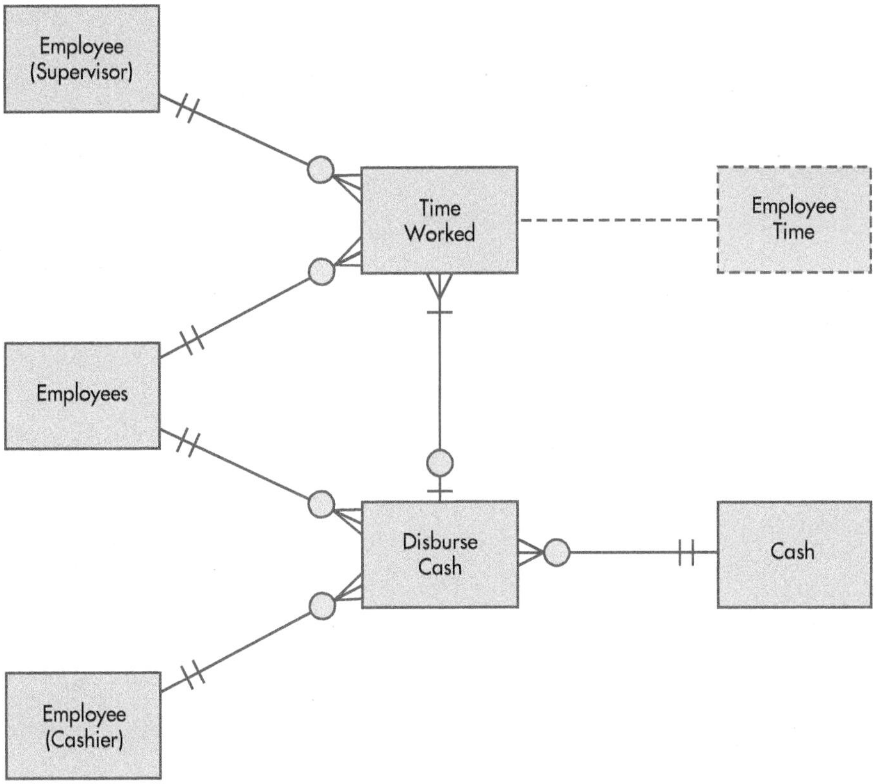

FIGURE 20-3
Fred's Train Shop Payroll Cycle

however, Fred's Train Shop does not divide one day into two different pay periods, nor does it pay employees in installments; thus, each Time Worked event is linked to only 1 Disburse Cash event. The minimum cardinalities on each side of the relationship reflect the normal business practice of paying employees after they have worked, rather than in advance.

The Employee Time entity requires some explanation. It represents the fact that the resource acquired by the Time Worked event is the use of an employee's skills and knowledge for a particular period of time. Time, however, is different from inventory, cash, and other tangible resources, as well as from intangible resources like trade secrets or other forms of intellectual property, in that it cannot be stored. In addition, there are only a few relevant attributes about employee time: the hours worked and how that time was used. Every organization needs to monitor how much time each employee works in order to calculate payroll. The Time Worked event, which is an example of a "Get" resource event, serves this purpose. Chapter 21 will discuss how some organizations, such as manufacturers and professional services firms (e.g., law firms, consulting organizations, and accounting firms) also collect detailed records of how employees use their time, which is an example of a "Give" resource event, in order to properly bill clients for those services. These two events (Time Worked and Time Used) capture all of the information about employee time that is practical to collect and monitor. Consequently, the Employee Time resource entity is almost never implemented in an actual database. Therefore, it is depicted with dotted lines in Figure 20-3.

Finally, the cardinalities of the relationship between the Disburse Cash event and the Cash resource are identical to those in the expenditure cycle (Figure 20-2): Each check or electronic funds transfer must be linked to at least one cash account and can be linked to only one cash account, whereas the same cash account may be linked to many Disburse Cash events.

Now that we understand the business policies underlying Figures 20-1, 20-2, and 20-3, we can proceed to merge them into one integrated REA diagram. You have probably noticed that Figures 20-1, 20-2, and 20-3 each contain some of the same entities. For example, the Inventory resource appears in both Figures 20-1 and 20-2. The Disburse Cash event appears in both Figures 20-2 and 20-3. Both the Employee agent and the Cash resource appear in all three diagrams. Such redundancies provide the basis for combining REA diagrams depicting individual business cycles into a single, comprehensive, enterprise-wide REA model.

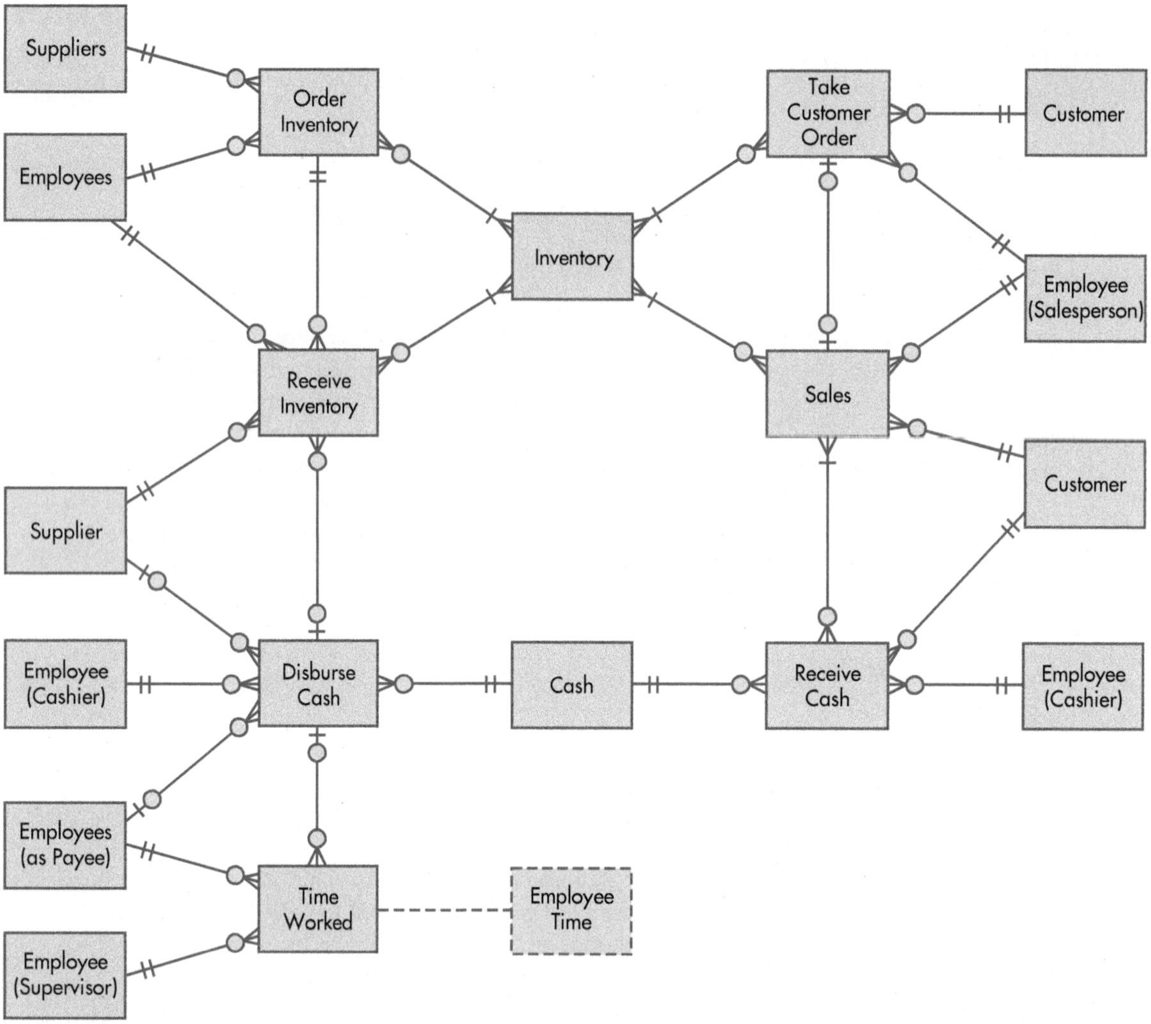

FIGURE 20-4

Integrated REA Diagram for Fred's Train Shop

Figure 20-4 shows such a model for Fred's Train Shop. Notice that the integrated diagram merges multiple copies of resource and event entities but retains multiple copies of agent entities. This maximizes the legibility of the comprehensive REA diagram by avoiding the need to have relationship lines cross one another. Let us now examine how to combine redundant resource and event entities.

MERGING REDUNDANT RESOURCE ENTITIES

Recall that REA diagrams for individual business cycles are built around basic give-to-get economic exchanges. Such economic duality relationships explain why a resource is either acquired or disposed of. They provide only a part of the story about each resource, however. For example, Figure 20-1 shows that inventory is reduced (the Sales event) in exchange for cash (the Receive Cash event). But Figure 20-1 does not show how that inventory was initially acquired. Nor does it show how the organization uses the cash it receives from customers. Conversely, Figure 20-2 shows how inventory was acquired (the Receive Inventory event) by giving up cash (the Disburse Cash event). Yet, Figure 20-2 does not show what the organization does with the inventory or how it acquired the cash used to pay suppliers.

Thus, REA diagrams for individual business cycles provide only partial information about the resources controlled by an organization. The complete picture would show how each resource is acquired and how it is used. As shown in Figure 20-4, this can be done by redrawing an REA diagram to place common resources between the events that affect them. Doing so reflects another important duality that must be depicted in a complete REA model of any organization: Every resource must be connected to at least one event that increases that resource and to at least one event that decreases it.

MERGING REDUNDANT EVENT ENTITIES

REA diagrams for individual business cycles may include some events that also appear in the REA diagrams of another cycle. For example, Figures 20-2 and 20-3 both contain the Disburse Cash event entity. As was the case with resources, merging these multiple occurrences of the same event improves the legibility of the resulting comprehensive REA diagram. Thus, Figure 20-4 shows that the Disburse Cash event is linked to both the Receive Inventory and the Time Worked events.

Close examination of Figure 20-4 reveals an important difference, however, between merging redundant events and merging redundant resources: Merging redundant resources does not affect any cardinalities, but merging redundant events alters the minimum cardinalities associated with the other events related to the merged event. Thus, in Figure 20-4 the cardinalities between the Inventory resource and each of the four events to which it is related are the same as those depicted in Figures 20-1 and 20-2. In contrast, the cardinalities between the Disburse Cash event and the other events with which it is linked are different in Figure 20-4 than in Figures 20-2 and 20-3.

The reason for this difference lies in the underlying semantics about the nature of the relationship between the merged entity and other entities. An instance of a resource entity can be, and usually is, linked to multiple events. For example, a given inventory item carried by Fred's Train Shop can be linked not only to a Receive Inventory event, when it is acquired from a supplier, but also to a Sales event, when it is sold to a customer. In other words, the resource entity is linked to event entities in one business cycle *and* to event entities in the other cycle. Because both links are possible, none of the cardinalities in the individual REA diagrams needs to change.

The situation is different when merging an event across business cycles. The event that appears in both individual business cycle REA diagrams may be linked to *either* an event that is part of one business cycle *or* to an event that is part of another cycle *but cannot be linked to both* events. For example, in Figure 20-4, a particular Disburse Cash event (i.e., a particular check or EFT transaction) could be associated with a prior receipt of inventory from a supplier or with time worked by an employee, but the same check (or EFT transaction) cannot be used *both* to pay a supplier for receipt of inventory *and* to pay an employee for working the previous week. Consequently, the minimum cardinality associated with the other events *must* be 0 in the integrated REA diagram, regardless of what it was in each of the individual transaction cycle REA diagrams. To understand why, recall that a minimum of 1 means that each instance of that entity has to be associated with at least one instance of the other entity. In terms of cash disbursements in Figure 20-4, retaining the minimum 1 with the Time Worked event, for example, would mean that every Disburse Cash must be linked to a Time Worked event—which is clearly not true because Fred may make a cash disbursement to pay a supplier. For similar reasons, the minimum cardinality from the Disburse Cash event to the Receive Inventory event must also be 0.

Merging two transaction cycles on a common event may also affect the minimum cardinalities between the merged event and the agents participating in that event. For example, in Figure 20-4 the minimum cardinality between the Disburse Cash event and the Supplier entity is now 0, instead of 1, as it was in Figure 20-2. The reason is that a given check (cash disbursement) may be written *either* to a supplier as payee or to an employee as payee, but the same check *cannot* be written to *both* agents simultaneously. That is why the minimum cardinality between the Disburse Cash event and the Employee (payee) agent is also 0. Thus, whenever a merged event involves different agents in each of the individual business cycles being merged, the minimum cardinalities between that event and those agents change from the usual 1 to 0 because the event may now be linked to either of the two types of agents, but not both.

VALIDATING THE ACCURACY OF INTEGRATED REA DIAGRAMS

Chapter 19 presented three basic principles for drawing REA diagrams for individual business cycles; the preceding discussion for combining such diagrams into a single, comprehensive, enterprise-wide model adds three more rules. Thus, a correctly drawn, integrated REA diagram must satisfy these six rules:

1. Every event must be linked to at least one resource.
2. Every event must be linked to two agents who participate in that event.
3. Every event that involves the disposition of a resource must be linked to an event that involves the acquisition of a resource. (This reflects the economic duality underlying "give-to-get" economic exchanges.)
4. Every resource must be linked to at least one event that increments that resource and to at least one event that decrements that resource.
5. If event A can be linked to more than one other event, but cannot be linked simultaneously to all of those other events, then the REA diagram should show that event A is linked to a minimum of 0 of each of those other events.
6. If an event can be linked to any one of a set of agents, but cannot be simultaneously linked to all those agents, then the REA diagram should show that event is linked to a minimum of 0 of each of those agents.

Notice that these six rules can be used not only to develop an integrated REA diagram but also as "check figures" to validate the accuracy of a completed REA diagram. Technically, Figure 20-4 is not complete because rule 4 is not satisfied for the Employee Time resource. We will correct this shortcoming in Chapter 21. For now, let us ignore it and proceed to the next step in the database design process: implementation of an REA data model in a relational database.

Implementing an REA Diagram in a Relational Database

Once an REA diagram has been developed, it can be used to design a well-structured relational database. In fact, creating a set of tables from an REA diagram automatically results in a well-structured relational database that is not subject to the update, insert, and delete anomaly problems discussed in Chapter 4.

There are three steps to implementing an REA diagram in a relational database:

1. Create a table for each *distinct* entity in the diagram and for each many-to-many relationship.
2. Assign attributes to appropriate tables.
3. Use foreign keys to implement one-to-one and one-to-many relationships.

Recall that even though REA diagrams for different organizations may include the same entities, differences in business policies are likely and will result in differences in relationship cardinalities. For example, the REA diagram for one organization may show a 1:1 relationship between the Sales and Receive Cash events, whereas the REA diagram for another organization may model that same pair of events as involved in an M:N relationship. Thus, the design of a database (number of tables, placement of attributes) is specific to the organization being modeled.

STEP 1: CREATE TABLES FOR EACH DISTINCT ENTITY AND M:N RELATIONSHIP

A properly designed relational database has a table for each distinct entity and for each many-to-many relationship in an REA diagram. Figure 20-4 has 13 distinct entities, but as previously discussed, one, Employee Time, will not be implemented in the database. The remaining 12 distinct entities depicted in Figure 20-4 need to be implemented as tables in a relational database. Seven tables will represent the event entities in the diagram: Order Inventory, Receive Inventory, Disburse Cash, Time Worked, Take Customer Order, Sales, and Receive Cash. There are two tables for resource entities: Inventory and Cash. Three tables are needed to implement the distinct agent entities: Employees, Customers, and Suppliers (supervisors are labeled separately to make the diagram easier to read, but are themselves employees).

Figure 20-4 also depicts five M:N relationships. Three are from the revenue cycle: Take Customer Orders–Inventory, Sales–Inventory, and Sales–Receive Cash. Two others are from the expenditure cycle: Inventory–Order Inventory and Inventory–Receive Inventory. Therefore, the 17 tables listed in Table 20-1 must be created to accurately implement Figure 20-4 in a relational database. Notice that the suggested table names in Table 20-1 correspond to the names of entities in the REA diagram or, in the case of tables for M:N relationships, are

TABLE 20-1 Table Names and Attribute Placement for Figure 20-4

		Attributes	
Tables	**Primary Key**	**Foreign Keys**	**Other Attributes**
Order Inventory	Purchase order number	Supplier number, employee number	Date, time, reason
Receive Inventory	Receiving report number	Supplier number, employee number, purchase order number, check number	Date, time, remarks, vendor invoice number
Disburse Cash	Check number	Supplier number, employee number (payee), employee number (signer), account number	Amount, description, date
Take Customer Order	Sales order number	Customer number, employee number	Date, time, special remarks
Sales	Invoice number	Customer number, employee number, sales order number	Date, time, invoice sent (Y/N)
Receive Cash	Remittance number	Customer number, employee number, account number	Date, time, method of payment
Time Worked	Timecard number	Employee number, supervisor number, paycheck number	Date, time in, time out
Inventory	Product number		Description, list price, standard cost, beginning quantity-on-hand, beginning quantity-available, reorder quantity, reorder point
Cash	Account number		Beginning-balance, type of account
Employees	Employee number		Name, date hired, date of birth, pay rate, job title
Customers	Customer number		Name, address,[a] beginning account balance, credit limit
Suppliers	Supplier number		Name, address,[a] beginning account balance, performance rating
Order Inventory–Inventory	Purchase order number, product number		Quantity ordered, actual unit cost
Receive Inventory–Inventory	Receiving report number, product number		Quantity received, condition
Take Customer Order–Inventory	Sales order number, product number		Quantity ordered
Sales–Inventory	Invoice number, product number		Quantity sold, actual sale price
Sales–Receive Cash	Invoice number, remittance number		Amount applied to invoice

[a]Actually, only the street address and zip code would be stored in these tables. In both tables zip code would be a foreign key. Zip code would also be the primary key of an "address table," which would also include city and state as other attributes.

hyphenated concatenations of the entities involved in the relationship. This makes it easier to verify that all necessary tables have been created and to use the REA diagram as a guide when querying the database.

STEP 2: ASSIGN ATTRIBUTES TO EACH TABLE

The next step is to determine which attributes should be included in each table.[1] The database designer needs to interview users and management to identify which facts need to be included in the database. The database designer must use the REA diagram to help determine in which table(s) to place those facts, depending upon whether that fact is a primary key or is just a descriptive attribute.

IDENTIFY PRIMARY KEYS As explained in Chapter 4, every table in a relational database must have a primary key, consisting of an attribute, or combination of attributes, that uniquely identifies each row in that table. Companies often create numeric identifiers for specific resources, events, and agents. These numeric identifiers are good candidates for primary keys. For example, Table 20-1 shows that Fred's Train Shop uses invoice number as the primary key of the sales table and customer number as the primary key of the customer table.

Usually the primary key of a table representing an entity is a single attribute. The primary key for M:N relationship tables, however, always consists of two attributes that represent the primary keys of each entity linked in that relationship. For example, the primary key of the Sales–Inventory table consists of both the invoice number (the primary key of the sales entity) and product number (the primary key of the inventory entity). Such multiple-attribute primary keys are called **concatenated keys**.

concatenated keys - Two or more primary keys of other database tables that, together, become the unique identifier or primary key of an M:N relationship table.

ASSIGN OTHER ATTRIBUTES TO APPROPRIATE TABLES Additional attributes besides the primary key are included in each table to satisfy transaction processing requirements and management's information needs. As discussed in Chapter 4, any other attribute included in a relational database table must either be a fact about the object represented by the primary key or a foreign key. Thus, information about customers, such as their name and address, belongs in the Customer table because those attributes describe the object represented by the primary key (customer number) of the Customer table. Those attributes do not belong in the Sales table because they do not describe some property of the object represented by the primary key (invoice number) of that table.

Table 20-1 shows some of the attributes that Paul Stone has assigned to the various tables he has created to implement Figure 20-4 in a relational database. Some of these attributes, such as the date of each sale and the amount remitted by a customer, are necessary for complete and accurate transaction processing and the production of financial statements and managerial reports. Other attributes are stored because they facilitate the effective management of an organization's resources, events, and agents. For example, Fred can use data about the time of day when each sales transaction occurs to design staff work schedules.

Table 20-1 also includes other attributes in some of the M:N relationship tables. Let us examine the placement of these attributes in some of the M:N tables to see why they must be stored in those particular tables. Consider first the Sales–Receive Cash table. Recall that Fred's Train Shop allows its customers to make multiple purchases on credit and to make installment payments on their outstanding balances. Thus, one customer payment may need to be applied to several different invoices (sales transactions). Therefore, the attribute "amount applied" cannot be placed in the Receive Cash table because it could take on more than one value (one for each invoice paid), thereby violating the basic requirement of relational databases that every attribute in every row be single-valued (i.e., the requirement that every table be a flat file). Nor can the attribute "amount applied" be placed in the Sales table because the possibility of installment payments also creates a situation in which that attribute can have multiple values (i.e., one entry for each installment payment related to that particular sale). Thus, analysis of the underlying business process indicates that the

[1]As explained in Chapter 19, some designers prefer to include attributes as part of the REA diagram itself. We choose to list them in a separate table to reduce the clutter on the diagram.

attribute "amount applied" is a fact about both a specific customer payment (remittance) and a specific sales transaction and, therefore, belongs in the M:N table linking those two events.

Now examine the Sales–Inventory table. Each row in this table contains information about a line item in an invoice. Although many customers of Fred's Train Shop buy just one of each kind of product it sells, some sales to customers involve larger quantities. For example, a department store may buy five identical coal cars (product number 31125) for its window display. Consequently, Fred's Train Shop must record the quantity sold of each item. Each sales event, however, may include more than one inventory item. Thus, the attribute "quantity sold" may have several values on a single sales invoice, one for each different item (product number) sold. Consequently, the attribute "quantity sold" cannot be placed in the Sales table because there can be more than one "quantity sold" value associated with a given invoice number. In addition, recall that Fred's Train Shop, like most retail stores, tracks inventory by kinds of items, each of which is identified by product number, not by specific identification. Therefore, a given item, such as an orange diesel locomotive, product number 14887, may be sold as part of many different sales transactions. Consequently, "quantity sold" cannot be an attribute in the Inventory table because it can take on multiple values. Instead, the preceding analysis makes it clear that the attribute "quantity sold" pertains to a specific product number on a specific sales invoice. Therefore, it belongs in the M:N relationship table that links the inventory and sales entities.

Price and Cost Data. In Table 20-1, notice that information about prices and costs are stored as an attribute in several different tables. For example, the Inventory table stores the suggested list price for the item, which generally remains constant for a given fiscal period. The Sales table stores the actual sales price, which varies during the course of the year as a result of sales promotions. Similarly, the standard and actual purchase costs of each item are stored in different tables. The general rule is that time-independent data should be stored as an attribute of a resource or agent, but data that varies across time should be stored with event entities or M:N relationships that link a resource and an event.

Cumulative and Calculable Data. Notice that Table 20-1 does not contain cumulative data, such as "quantity-on-hand" in the inventory table, or calculable data, such as "total amount of sale" in the sales table. The reason is that neither type of data item is needed because those values can be derived from other attributes that are stored. For example, the quantity-on-hand of a given inventory item equals the quantity-on-hand at the beginning of the current fiscal period (an attribute of the Inventory table) plus the total quantity purchased this period (which is itself calculated by summing the quantity received attribute in the Inventory–Receive Inventory table) minus the total quantity sold (which is calculated by summing the quantity sold attribute in the Sales–Inventory table) in this period. Similarly, the total amount of a sales transaction can be calculated by multiplying the quantity sold by the actual sale price of each item sold and summing that result for every row in the Sales–Inventory table that has the same invoice number.

STEP 3: USE FOREIGN KEYS TO IMPLEMENT 1:1 AND 1:N RELATIONSHIPS

Although 1:1 and 1:N relationships also can be implemented as separate tables, it is usually more efficient to implement them by means of foreign keys. Recall from Chapter 4 that a foreign key is an attribute of one entity that is itself the primary key of another entity. For example, the attribute "customer number" might appear in both the Customer and the Sales tables. It would be the primary key of the Customer table, but a foreign key in the Sales table.

USING FOREIGN KEYS TO IMPLEMENT 1:1 RELATIONSHIPS In a relational database, 1:1 relationships between entities can be implemented by including the primary key of either entity as a foreign key in the table representing the other entity. For purposes of designing a well-structured database, the choice of which table to place the foreign key in is arbitrary. Careful analysis of the minimum cardinalities of the relationship, however, may suggest which approach is likely to be more *efficient*.

Consider the case of a 1:1 relationship between sales and customer payments (see Figure 19-7, panel A). The minimum cardinality for the Receive Cash event is 0, indicating the existence of credit sales, and the minimum cardinality for the Sale event is 1, indicating that customer payments only occur after a sale has been made (e.g., there are no advance deposits). In this case, including invoice number (the primary key of the sales event) as a foreign key in the Receive Cash event may be more efficient because then only that one table would have to be accessed and updated when processing each customer payment. Moreover, for 1:1 relationships between two sequential events, including the primary key of the event that occurs first as a foreign key in the event that occurs second may improve internal control. This is because the employee given access to update the table containing data about the second event need not access the table used to store information about the first event. However, the internal control benefits of doing this must be weighed against a possible increase in difficulty of querying the database.

USING FOREIGN KEYS TO IMPLEMENT 1:N RELATIONSHIPS As with 1:1 relationships, 1:N relationships also should be implemented in relational databases with foreign keys. There is only one way to do this: The primary key of the entity that can be linked to multiple instances of the other entity *must* become a foreign key in that other entity. Thus, in Table 20-1, the primary keys of the Salesperson and Customer tables are included as foreign keys in the Sales table. Similarly, the primary keys of the Cash, Customer, and Cashier tables are included as foreign keys in the Receive Cash table. Reversing this procedure would violate one of the fundamental rules of relational database design. For example, placing invoice number as a foreign key in the Customer table would not work because it can have more than one value (i.e., a given customer may be, and one hopes is, associated with multiple invoice numbers because of participation in many sales transactions).

Note that this is why M:N relationships *must* be implemented as separate tables: Since each entity can be linked to multiple occurrences of the entity on the other side of the relationship, it is not possible to make either entity's primary key a foreign key in the other entity. Consider the M:N relationship between the Sales event and the Inventory resource. Each Sales event may be linked to many different inventory items. Therefore, product number cannot be used as a foreign key in the Sales table because it would be multivalued. Conversely, each product may be involved in many different sales transactions. Therefore, invoice number cannot be used as a foreign key in the Inventory table because it would be multivalued. Thus, the only way to link the Sales and Inventory tables is to create a new table that has separate rows for each actual combination of invoice number and product number. Notice that in the resulting M:N table a particular invoice number (e.g., 787923) will appear in many different rows, one for each different item that was part of that sales transaction. Conversely, a particular product number (e.g., 12345) will appear in many different rows, once for each different sales transaction in which it was sold. Thus, neither attribute, by itself, uniquely identifies a given row. However, there will be only one row that contains the combination of a particular invoice number and product number (e.g., invoice number 787923 and product number 12345); thus, both attributes together can serve as a primary key for the M:N table.

COMPLETENESS CHECK

The list of attributes that users and management want included in the database provides a means to check and validate the implementation process. Every attribute in that list should appear in at least one table, as either a primary key or "other" attribute.

Checking this list against the table column names may reveal not only the fact that a particular attribute has not been assigned to the appropriate table in the database but may even indicate the need to modify the REA diagram itself. For example, when Paul Stone double-checked the list of desired attributes, he found that he did not have any table in which to place the attribute "product discussed during sales call." In such a situation, the database designer needs to revisit users and management to understand the purpose for collecting that particular attribute. In this case, Fred explains that he plans to have one of his employees call on corporate customers to set up sample displays. Fred wants to collect information about such demonstrations to evaluate their effectiveness.

Paul realizes that this necessitates creating another event entity, Call on Customers, which would be linked to both the Customer and Employee agent tables, the Inventory table, and the Take Customer Order table (see Figure 21-1 on p. 660). The primary key of this new event would be "appointment number." Employee number and customer number would be foreign keys in the table, which would also include attributes for the date and time of the demonstration, along with a text field for comments. Because each demonstration could involve multiple items and each item could be demonstrated in many different calls, there would be an M:N relationship between the Call on Customer event and the Inventory table. The set of rows in that table with the same appointment number would identify which products were shown during a particular sales call. Some calls would result in orders, but others would not. In addition, some orders would occur without any sales call (e.g., because the customer saw an advertisement). Therefore, the minimum cardinality is 0 on each side of the relationship between the Call on Customer and Take Customer Order events. The maximum cardinality on each side of the relationship is 1 to simplify tracking the effect of sales calls.

Paul's need to modify his REA diagram to accommodate additional facts is not unusual. Indeed, it is often useful to create tables and assign attributes to them even before completely finishing an REA diagram. This helps clarify exactly what each entity represents, which often resolves dilemmas about the correct cardinalities for various relationships. The database designer can then modify and refine the REA diagram to include additional entities and relationships to accommodate other facts that are supposed to be in the database but that have not yet been assigned to existing tables.

Once all attributes have been assigned to tables, the basic requirements for designing well-structured relational databases that were discussed in Chapter 4 can be used as a final accuracy check:

1. Every table must have a primary key.
2. Other nonkey attributes in each table must be either a fact about the thing designated by the primary key or foreign keys used to link that table to another table.
3. Every attribute in every table is single-valued (i.e., each table is a flat file).

Note how the set of relational tables listed in Table 20-1 satisfy these three basic requirements. Moreover, they also correspond to Figure 20-4 and, therefore, reflect Fred's Train Shop's business policies. This correspondence also facilitates using the REA diagram to guide the design of queries and reports to retrieve and display information about the organization's business activities.

Using REA Diagrams to Retrieve Information from a Database

Thus far, we have shown how to use the REA data model to guide the design of an AIS that will efficiently store information about an organization's business activities. In this section we refer to Figure 20-4 and Table 20-1 to show how to use completed REA diagrams to facilitate the retrieval of that information to evaluate performance.

CREATING JOURNALS AND LEDGERS

At first glance, it may appear that a number of elements found in traditional AIS, such as journals, ledgers, and information about receivables and payables, are missing. We will see that such information, although not explicitly represented as entities in an REA diagram, can be obtained through appropriate queries. These queries need only be created once and can then be stored and rerun whenever desired.

DERIVING JOURNALS FROM QUERIES Journals provide a chronological listing of transactions. In a relational database designed according to the REA data model, event entities store information about transactions. Thus, the information normally found in a journal is contained in the tables used to record data about events. For example, the Sales and Sales–Inventory tables contain information about a particular sales transaction. Thus, a sales journal can be produced by writing a query that references both tables to calculate the amount of sales made during a given period.

Doing so, however, would not necessarily create the traditional sales journal because it would produce a list of *all* sales transactions, including both credit and cash sales. Traditionally, however, sales journals record only *credit* sales. In a relational database built on the REA model, such as the one in Figure 20-4, customer payments are recorded in the Receive Cash event table. Consequently, a query to produce a traditional sales journal (i.e., listing only those sales made on credit) would have to also include both the Receive Cash and the Sales–Receive Cash tables. A database built on the REA model would create a row in the Sales table for each sale of merchandise to a customer and a row in the Receive Cash table to record receipt of payment from a customer. For cash sales, both rows would have the same values in the date and customer number columns. Therefore, the logic of a query to produce a traditional sales journal would restrict the output to display only those sales *not* linked to a corresponding customer payment event (i.e., the same customer number appears in both tables, and the amount of the Receive Cash event equals the amount of the sale) that occurred *on the same day* as the Sales event. (Rows in the Receive Cash table with dates later than the date of the corresponding sales transaction represent payments on credit sales.) Similar processes can be followed to write queries to produce other special journals, such as all credit purchases or all cash disbursements not related to payroll.

LEDGERS Ledgers are master files that contain cumulative information about specific accounts. In a relational database designed according to the REA data model, resource entities contain permanent information that is carried over from one fiscal year to the next. Thus, much of the information about an organization's assets that is traditionally recorded in ledgers is stored in resource tables in an REA-based relational database. For example, each row in the Equipment resource table would contain information about a specific piece or class of machinery, such as its acquisition cost, useful life, depreciation method, and estimated salvage value. Similarly, each row in the Cash resource table contains information about a specific account that holds the organization's cash and cash equivalents, and each row in the Inventory resource table stores information about a specific inventory item.

Each of these resource accounts is affected by increment and decrement events: Equipment is purchased and used; cash is received and disbursed; inventory is purchased and sold. Thus, queries to display the current cumulative balance for these accounts must reference not only the appropriate table for that resource entity but also the event tables that affect it. For example, a query to display the current balance in a specific bank account would reference not only the Cash resource table, to identify the account number and the balance as of the beginning of the current fiscal period, but also the Receive Cash and Disburse Cash tables, to find the inflows and outflows affecting that account during the current fiscal period.

GENERATING FINANCIAL STATEMENTS

A completed REA diagram can also be used to guide the writing of queries to produce the information that would be included in financial statements. Many financial statement accounts, such as Cash, Inventory, and Fixed Assets, are represented as resources in the REA model. An important exception, however, is claims: Figure 20-4 includes neither an entity called Accounts Receivable nor one called Accounts Payable. As explained in Chapter 19, the reason is that both of these accounts merely represent an imbalance between two related events. Accounts receivable represents sales transactions for which customer payments have not yet been received, and accounts payable represents purchases from suppliers that have not yet been paid for. Therefore, neither accounts receivable nor accounts payable needs to be explicitly stored as a separate table in an REA database. Instead, those claims can be derived from a set of queries against the relevant agent and event tables. For example, three queries can be used to calculate total Accounts Receivable.[2] First, sum the total beginning balances in every customer account. Second, calculate total new sales this period by writing a query against the M:N Sales–Inventory relationship table to sum the product of quantity sold times unit price. Third, determine the total cash received from customers this period by summing the amount column in the Receive Cash table. Total Accounts Receivable equals beginning Accounts Receivable (query 1) plus new sales (query 2) minus cash receipts (query 3). A similar set of queries will produce total Accounts Payable.

CREATING MANAGERIAL REPORTS

The REA data model facilitates creating a wide variety of managerial reports because it integrates nonfinancial and financial data. For example, Table 20-1 shows that the Sales entity in Figure 20-4 includes an attribute to record the *time* that the sale occurred. Fred can use this data to track sales activity during different times of the day to better plan staffing needs at the train shop. Other useful nonfinancial attributes could be included in other tables. For example, the Customer table could be modified to include an attribute that identifies whether a customer has an indoor or outdoor train layout. If Fred can collect this information from his customers, he may be able to better target his advertising to meet each individual customer's interests. In addition, Table 20-1 can be modified easily to integrate data from external sources. For example, to better evaluate the creditworthiness of business customers, Fred may decide to collect information from a credit rating agency, such as Dun & Bradstreet. This information could be added to the database by creating an additional column in the Customer table to store the customer's credit rating. A similar process could be used to store information about suppliers that could be used in the vendor selection process.

Summary and Case Conclusion

REA diagrams for individual business cycles depict basic give-to-get economic duality relationships but usually provide only a partial view of resources, showing either how they are acquired or how they are used, but not both. Therefore, individual business cycle REA diagrams need to be combined in order to provide a comprehensive enterprise-wide data model. This is usually done by merging resource and event entities that appear in two or more individual REA diagrams. Merging two or more REA diagrams that contain the same resource entity does not require any changes to the cardinality pairs in the individual diagrams. Merging two or more diagrams that contain a common event entity, however, often requires changing the minimum cardinalities associated with the other events to 0 to reflect the fact that the merged event may be connected to any one of several different events but not to all of them simultaneously. The minimum cardinalities associated with the agents participating in those merged events may also have to be changed to 0.

A data model documented in an REA diagram can be implemented in a relational database in three steps. First, create tables for all unique entities and M:N relationships in the REA diagram. Second, assign primary keys and nonkey attributes to each table. Third, use foreign keys to implement 1:1 and 1:N relationships.

Paul Stone follows these steps to implement a database AIS for Fred's Train Shop based on Figure 20-4. He first creates separate tables for each of the 12 distinct entities and 5 M:N relationships in the figure. Next, Paul identifies primary keys for each table and uses some of them as foreign keys to implement the 1:1 and 1:N relationships in Figure 20-4. He then assigns the remaining attributes that Fred wants to monitor to the appropriate tables. Paul then demonstrates how easy it is to write queries to retrieve a variety of managerial reports and financial statements from the relational DBMS. Fred is quite impressed and immediately begins to use the new system to provide detailed information about the business activities of Fred's Train Shop.

---

[2]To calculate the account balance for an individual customer, follow a similar process but restrict the queries to just those Sales and Receive Cash events that have a specific customer number as a foreign key.

KEY TERM

concatenated keys 642

AIS in Action

CHAPTER QUIZ

1. Which of the following types of entities must become a separate table in a relational database?
   a. resources
   b. events
   c. agents
   d. All of the above

2. How many tables are needed to implement an REA data model that has seven distinct enities, three M:N relationships, and five 1:N relationships in a relational database?
   a. 7
   b. 10
   c. 12
   d. 15

3. Which type of relationship cardinality must be implemented in a relational database as a separate table?
   a. 1:1 relationship
   b. 1:N relationship
   c. M:N relationship
   d. All of the above

4. Combining two REA diagrams typically does not involve merging which type of entity?
   a. resources
   b. events
   c. agents
   d. All of the above

5. Which of the following elements of a traditional AIS can be derived from queries of an REA database?
   a. journals
   b. ledgers
   c. claims (receivables and payables)
   d. All of the above

6. Which of the following tables would most likely have a concatenated primary key?
   a. Inventory
   b. Sales
   c. Inventory–Sales
   d. None of the above

7. An REA diagram contains four instances of the Employee entity. How many tables does this require in a relational database?
   a. 1
   b. 2
   c. 3
   d. 4

8. A business orders mass-produced merchandise frequently throughout the year. In which table should the attribute "quantity ordered" appear?
   a. Order Inventory
   b. Inventory
   c. Order Inventory–Inventory
   d. None of the above

9. Which of the following statements is true only about an integrated REA data model?
   a. Every event must be linked to at least two agents.
   b. Every increment (Get) event must be linked to a decrement (Give) event.
   c. Every resource must be linked to at least one increment event and at least one decrement event.
   d. Every resource must be linked to at least one agent.

10. In a relational database designed according to the REA data model, information traditionally stored in ledgers can be obtained by querying which of the following?
    a. resources
    b. events
    c. M:N relationship tables between resources and events
    d. a set of queries involving all of the above

COMPREHENSIVE PROBLEM

TRAILSPAN TRAVEL CLUB

The Trailspan Travel Club markets travel books across the United States and Canada. Members of the travel club place orders online through Trailspan's website, over the phone by calling an 800 number, or by mail. Online orders are entered into the club computer system automatically. Telephone and mail orders are entered into Trailspan's computer system by the club's sales representatives. Once the orders have been entered, an order notification is sent to the shipping department. A shipping clerk retrieves the ordered items from inventory and then packs and ships each order. Trailspan only ships complete orders; if an item is temporarily out of stock, it notifies the customer that the entire shipment will be delayed. Once an order has been shipped, the computer system sends an invoice to the member and sends a notification to accounts receivable. Members who do not pay within 30 days are charged 6% interest on their outstanding balance. When making payments, members may pay part or all of their remaining balance. A clerk in the cash receipts department processes all cash receipts and makes deposits into the company's bank account.

When a particular inventory item meets its reorder point, Trailspan's computer system generates a purchase order and the purchasing agent sends the purchase order to the appropriate vendor. Suppliers fill each order individually; sometimes, however, they are out of stock of an item. In such cases, they immediately ship what is in stock and then make a second delivery for items that they had to back order. Once an inventory order is received by the receiving clerk, it is counted and sent to inventory. The cash disbursements clerk pays all vendor invoices individually as they become due to take advantage of any purchase discounts.

REQUIRED

a. Prepare an integrated REA diagram for the revenue and expenditure cycles of Trailspan Travel Club.
b. Prepare a set of tables to implement your data model in a relational database. Assign every attribute mentioned in the narrative to the appropriate table(s).

DISCUSSION QUESTIONS

20.1 How would the process of generating a cash disbursements journal from the REA data model presented in Figure 20-4 and Table 20-1 differ from the process for creating a sales journal?

20.2 Why take the time to develop separate REA diagrams for each business cycle if the ultimate objective is to combine them into one integrated enterprise-wide data model? Why not just focus on the integrated model from the start?

20.3 Building separate tables for every relationship (1:1, 1:N, and M:N) does not violate any of the rules for building a well-structured database. Why then do you think that REA data modelers recommend building separate tables only for M:N relationships and using foreign keys to implement 1:1 and 1:N relationships?

20.4 Assume that there exists a 1:1 relationship between the Receive Inventory and Disburse Cash events. How does the manner in which the relationship between the two events is implemented (i.e., in which table a foreign key is placed) affect the process used to record payments made to suppliers?

20.5 Refer to Figure 20-4 and Table 20-1. How would you determine the amount of cash that Fred's Train Shop has at any point in time?

20.6 Why does Figure 20-4 show only one Disburse Cash entity if Fred's Train Shop uses a general operating checking account for purchases of inventory, supplies, and operating expenses such as rent but also uses a separate checking account for payroll?

20.7 Examine Figure 20-4 and Table 20-1. Why do the Inventory, Customers, and Suppliers tables all have an attribute that contains data about the balance at the beginning of the current fiscal period?

PROBLEMS

20.1 Refer to Problems 19.1 and 19.2 for information about the revenue and expenditure cycle activities for Joe's ice-cream shop in order to draw an integrated REA diagram of both cycles.

20.2 Develop a set of tables to implement the integrated REA diagram you developed in Problem 20.1 for Joe's ice-cream shop in a relational database. Specify a primary key for each table, and suggest at least one other attribute that should be included in each table.

20.3 Refer to Problems 19.3 and 19.4 for information about the revenue and expenditure cycle activities of Sue's Gallery in order to draw an integrated REA diagram of both cycles.

20.4 Develop a set of tables to implement the integrated REA diagram you developed in Problem 20.3 for Sue's Gallery in a relational database. Specify a primary key for each table, and suggest at least one other attribute that should be included in each table.

20.5 The following tables and attributes exist in a relational database:

Table	Attributes
Vendor	Vendor #, name, street address, city, state
Purchases	P.O. #, date, amount, vendor #, purchasing agent #
Inventory Receipts	Receiving report #, date, receiving clerk #, remarks, P.O. #
Disburse Cash	Check #, date, amount
Inventory Receipts–Disburse Cash	Check #, receiving report #, amount applied to invoice

REQUIRED

Draw an REA diagram for this database. State any additional assumptions you need to make about cardinalities.

20.6 Refer to Problems 19.8 and 19.9 for information about the revenue and expenditure cycles for the Computer Warehouse and use that information to draw an integrated REA diagram for both cycles.

20.7 Develop a set of tables to implement the integrated REA diagram you developed in Problem 20.6 for the Computer Warehouse in a relational database. Specify a primary key for each table, and suggest at least one other attribute that should be included in each table.

20.8 Explain how to calculate the total amount of accounts payable.

20.9 Refer to Figure 20-4 and Table 20-1 to write the query logic needed to answer the following questions. (Optional: If requested by your instructor, write your queries in SQL or a Query-By-Example graphical interface.) Some answers may require more than one query—try to write the most efficient queries possible.

a. Accounts payable for all suppliers in Arizona
b. Total amount of sales to a customer named Smith
c. Total wage expense
d. Total wages payable
e. Net increase (decrease) in quantity-on-hand for a particular inventory item
f. The proportion of sales made to walk-in customers (i.e., no order)
g. The salesperson who made the largest amount of sales in October
h. The salesperson who made the most sales in October
i. The most popular item, in terms of total units sold

20.10 Refer to Problem 19.10 and develop a set of tables to implement the REA diagram you developed for Stan's Southern Barbeque Supply Store. Identify the primary and foreign keys for each table, and don't forget to address any M:N relationships.

20.11 Answer the following multiple-choice problems.

1. Which of the following types of relationships in an REA diagram must be implemented as a separate table in a relational database?
a. 1:1
b. 1:N
c. N:1
d. M:N

2. When implementing a revenue cycle REA diagram in a relational database, the relationship between customers and sales would be implemented by ______.
a. placing the customer number attribute as a foreign key in the sales table
b. placing the sales invoice number as a foreign key in the customer table
c. either approach is equally acceptable

3. When merging REA diagrams from two different cycles, it is not necessary to change the minimum cardinality for ______ that appear in both of the separate REA diagrams.
a. resources
b. agents
c. events

4. ABC Company sells original manuscripts of Broadway plays. ABC pays for all its purchases in full with one check. It allows customers to make installment payments on sales that exceed $33,000. However, a customer cannot make another purchase until all prior purchases have been paid for. The REA diagram for ABC company depicts seven Employee entities, each labeled for the role played by that type of employee (e.g., cashier, salesperson, shipping clerk, accountant, etc.). The REA diagram also contains two resource entities (Inventory and Cash) and the following events: Purchases, Disburse Cash, Sales, and Receive Cash. The REA diagram also contains two instances of the Customer entity and three instances of the Supplier entity. Implementing the integrated REA diagram for the revenue and expenditure cycles of the ABC company in a relational database requires how many tables?
a. 5
b. 7
c. 9
d. 15
e. 18

5. The XYZ Company sells sports equipment. The actual sales price of a given item varies throughout the year due to sales events. The actual sales price should be stored as an attribute in the ________ table.
   a. Sales
   b. Inventory
   c. Sales–Inventory

6. In an integrated REA diagram for both the revenue and expenditure cycles, the quantity on hand during the middle of the year for an inventory item would be stored as an attribute in the ________ table.
   a. Inventory
   b. Sales–Inventory
   c. Purchases–Inventory
   d. None of the three tables

CASE 20-1 Practical Database Design

Hands-on practice in database design is important. Use a relational DBMS to implement the integrated REA data model presented in this chapter, or one of the integrated data models from the homework problems, or a model provided by your instructor. Then, perform the following tasks:

1. Write a query to calculate total accounts receivable.
2. Write a query to calculate accounts receivable for a specific customer.
3. Create a sales invoice form that references the appropriate tables and inputs data about attributes into the proper tables.
4. Write queries to calculate as many financial statement items as possible from the data model you implement.
5. Design appropriate input controls to ensure the validity of data entered in the form created in step 3.

AIS in Action Solutions

QUIZ KEY

1. Which of the following types of entities must become a separate table in a relational database?
   a. resources [Incorrect. All three types of entities become separate tables.]
   b. events [Incorrect. All three types of entities become separate tables.]
   c. agents [Incorrect. All three types of entities become separate tables.]
   ► d. all of the above [Correct. All three types of entities become separate tables.]

2. How many tables are needed to implement an REA data model that has seven distinct entities, three M:N relationships, and five 1:N relationships in a relational database?
   a. 7 [Incorrect. There must be 10 tables, one for each distinct entity and one for each M:N relationship.]
   ► b. 10 [Correct. There must be 10 tables, one for each distinct entity and one for each M:N relationship.]
   c. 12 [Incorrect. There must be 10 tables, one for each distinct entity and one for each M:N relationship.]
   d. 15 [Incorrect. There must be 10 tables, one for each distinct entity and one for each M:N relationship.]

3. Which type of relationship cardinality must be implemented in a relational database as a separate table?
   a. 1:1 relationship [Incorrect. Only M:N relationships must be implemented as separate tables in a relational database. Foreign keys can be used to implement 1:N and 1:1 relationships.]
   b. 1:N relationship [Incorrect. Only M:N relationships must be implemented as separate tables in a relational database. Foreign keys can be used to implement 1:N and 1:1 relationships.]
   ► c. M:N relationship [Correct. Only M:N relationships must be implemented as separate tables in a relational database. Foreign keys can be used to implement 1:N and 1:1 relationships.]
   d. all of the above [Incorrect. Only M:N relationships must be implemented as separate tables in a relational database. Foreign keys can be used to implement 1:N and 1:1 relationships.]

4. Combining two REA diagrams typically does not involve merging which type of entity?
   a. resources [Incorrect. Combining two REA diagrams often involves merging resource entities that appear on both individual diagrams.]
   b. events [Incorrect. Combining two REA diagrams often involves merging event entities that appear on both individual diagrams.]
   ► c. agents [Correct. Combining two REA diagrams often involves merging resource and event entities that appear on both individual diagrams but usually retains multiple copies of agent entities to minimize the number of criss-crossing relationships.]
   d. all of the above [Incorrect. Combining two REA diagrams often involves merging resource and event entities that appear on both individual diagrams, but not agent entities.]

5. Which of the following elements of a traditional AIS can be derived from queries of an REA database?
   a. journals [Incorrect. Journals, ledgers, and claims can all be derived from queries of an REA database.]
   b. ledgers [Incorrect. Journals, ledgers, and claims can all be derived from queries of an REA database.]
   c. claims (receivables and payables) [Incorrect. Journals, ledgers, and claims can all be derived from queries of an REA database.]
   ▶ d. all of the above [Correct. Journals, ledgers, and claims can all be derived from queries of an REA database.]

6. Which of the following tables would most likely have a concatenated primary key?
   a. Inventory [Incorrect. Although any entity may have a concatenated key, few do except for M:N relationships, which must have concatenated primary keys.]
   b. Sales [Incorrect. Although any entity may have a concatenated key, few do except for M:N relationships, which must have concatenated primary keys.]
   ▶ c. Inventory–Sales [Correct. Although any entity may have a concatenated key, few do except for M:N relationships, which must have concatenated primary keys.]
   d. none of the above [Incorrect. Although any entity may have a concatenated key, few do except for M:N relationships, which must have concatenated primary keys.]

7. An REA diagram contains four instances of the Employee entity. How many tables does this require in a relational database?
   ▶ a. 1 [Correct. Multiple occurrences of the same entity in an REA diagram improve readability, but only one table is needed for each distinct entity.]
   b. 2 [Incorrect. Multiple occurrences of the same entity in an REA diagram improve readability, but only one table is needed for each distinct entity.]
   c. 3 [Incorrect. Multiple occurrences of the same entity in an REA diagram improve readability, but only one table is needed for each distinct entity.]
   d. 4 [Incorrect. Multiple occurrences of the same entity in an REA diagram improve readability, but only one table is needed for each distinct entity.]

8. A business orders mass-produced merchandise frequently throughout the year. In which table should the attribute "quantity ordered" appear?
   a. Order Inventory [Incorrect. The attribute "quantity ordered" is a fact about a specific order for a specific item. It cannot appear in the Order Inventory table because a purchase order can include more than one inventory item. It cannot be included in the Inventory table because a given item can be ordered many times.]
   b. Inventory [Incorrect. The attribute "quantity ordered" is a fact about a specific order for a specific item. It cannot appear in the Order Inventory table because a purchase order can include more than one inventory item. It cannot be included in the Inventory table because a given item can be ordered many times.]
   ▶ c. Order Inventory–Inventory [Correct. The attribute "quantity ordered" is a fact about a specific order for a specific item. It cannot appear in the Order Inventory table because a purchase order can include more than one inventory item. It cannot be included in the Inventory table because a given item can be ordered many times.]
   d. none of the above [Incorrect. M:N relationships have concatenated primary keys that consist of the primary key of each entity participating in that relationship.]

9. Which of the following statements is true only about an integrated REA data model?
   a. Every event must be linked to at least two agents. [Incorrect. This is true of any REA model.]
   b. Every increment (Get) event must be linked to a decrement (Give) event. [Incorrect. This is true of any REA diagram.]
   ▶ c. Every resource must be linked to at least one increment event and at least one decrement event. [Correct. This is a unique feature of, and is the reason for, integrating multiple REA diagrams.]
   d. Every resource must be linked to at least one agent. [Incorrect. This is not true of any REA diagram.]

10. In a relational database designed according to the REA data model, information traditionally stored in ledgers can be obtained by querying which of the following?

a. resources [Incorrect. To obtain the information traditionally found in a ledger often involves querying not only resource tables but also event tables and any M:N relationships between those two entities.]

b. events [Incorrect. To obtain the information traditionally found in a ledger often involves querying not only resource tables but also event tables and any M:N relationships between those two entities.]

c. M:N relationship tables between resources and events [Incorrect. To obtain the information traditionally found in a ledger often involves querying not only resource tables but also event tables and any M:N relationships between those two entities.]

▶ **d.** A set of queries involving all of the above [Correct. To obtain the information traditionally found in a ledger often involves querying not only resource tables but also event tables and any M:N relationships between those two entities.]

COMPREHENSIVE PROBLEM SOLUTION

Part a Prepare an integrated REA diagram for Trailspan Travel Club's revenue and expenditure cycles.

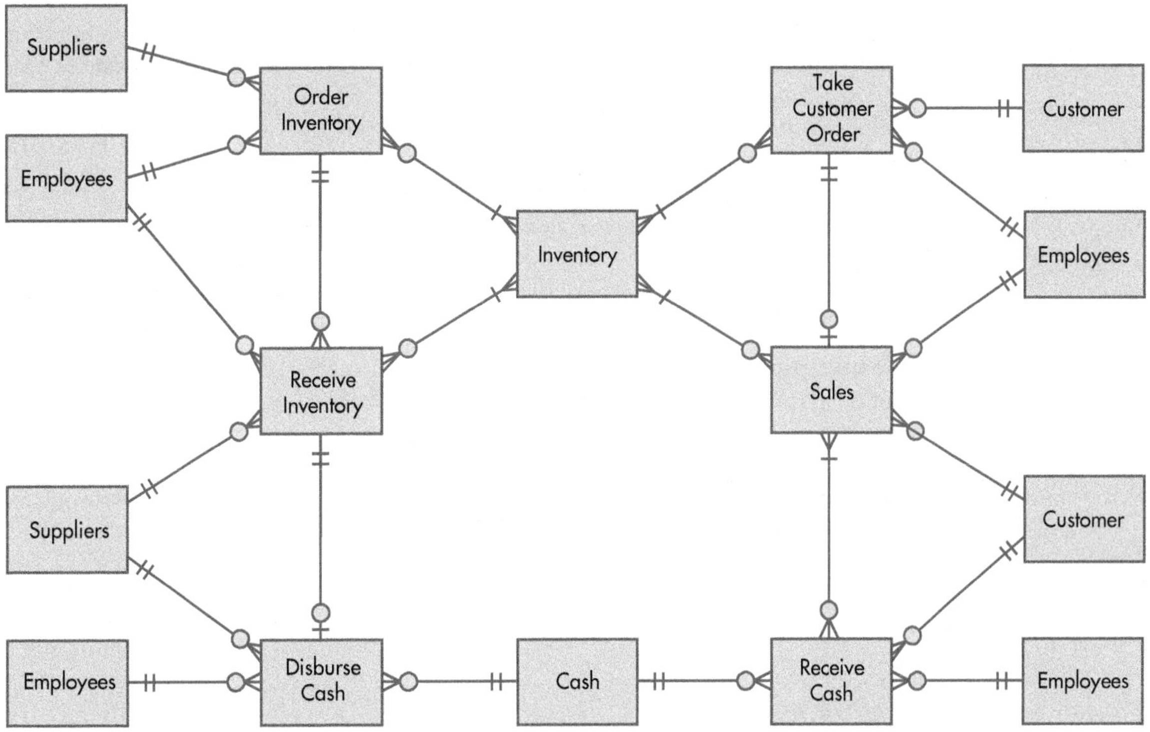

EXPLANATION OF RELATIONSHIPS AND CARDINALITIES

The relationships between the agent and event entities are all modeled as 1:N with 0 minimums on the event side and 1 minimum on the agent side. This reflects standard practice: Every event must involve at least one agent, but a given agent may or may not be involved in any particular event. Moreover, for accountability purposes, every event is linked to only one specific internal and one specific external agent, but both types of agents may be linked to many different events.

The cardinalities of the relationships between the Cash resource and the Disburse Cash and Receive Cash events are also standard. Each event must be linked to a cash account (hence the minimum of 1) and for accountability purposes is linked to only one cash account (hence the maximum of 1). Conversely, some cash accounts may never be linked to any Disburse Cash or Receive Cash events (hence the minimum cardinality is 0), but other cash accounts may be linked to many such events (hence the maximum cardinality is N).

The cardinalities of the relationships between the Inventory resource and the four events that affect it are also standard for retail organizations that sell mass-produced goods: They are all M:N. This reflects the fact that a given product number may be linked to many different events, and any given event may involve multiple products. The minimums are 0 going to the event entities for two reasons: (1) to allow the organization to add information about new products prior to engaging in any transactions involving those products and (2) because the event tables are empty at the beginning of each new fiscal year. The minimum cardinalities are 1 in the reverse direction because every event must involve at least one inventory item.

The relationship between the Order Inventory and Receive Inventory events is 1:N because Trailspan's suppliers sometimes are out of items ordered and therefore must make more than one delivery to fill a particular order. Trailspan's suppliers do not hold and aggregate its orders, however, which is why each Receive Inventory event is linked to at most one Order event. The minimum cardinalities reflect the fact that orders precede deliveries from suppliers.

The relationship between the Receive Inventory and Disburse Cash events is 1:1 because Trailspan's policy is to pay for each vendor invoice separately, in order to take advantage of discounts for prompt payment. Thus, it cuts separate checks for each delivery received, and each check pays for only one specific delivery. The minimum cardinalities reflect the fact that Trailspan does not pay for its purchases in advance.

The relationship between Take Customer Orders and Sales is 1:1 because Trailspan fills each customer order separately but does not do so until it can completely fill each order. The minimum cardinalities reflect the fact that orders precede sales.

The relationship between the Sales and Receive Cash events is M:N because Trailspan allows its customers to make installment payments on any given sale and to periodically pay for multiple sales transactions that occurred during the prior months. The minimum cardinalities reflect the fact that Trailspan does not require customers to ever pay in advance for sales.

Part b Prepare tables for each entity. The following tables must be created to implement the REA diagram developed in part a into a relational database.

Table	Primary Key	Foreign Keys	Other Attributes
Employee	Employee number		Name, address, date hired
Customer	Customer number		Name, address, credit limit, account balance beginning current period
Supplier	Supplier number		Name, address, account balance beginning current period
Order Inventory	Purchase order number	Supplier number, employee number	Date, comments
Receive Inventory	Receiving report number	Supplier number, employee number, purchase order number	Remarks, supplier's invoice number
Disburse Cash	Check number	Supplier number, employee number, account number, receiving report number	Amount, description

continued

Table	Primary Key	Foreign Keys	Other Attributes
Inventory	Item number		Description, list price, beginning quantity-on-hand, beginning quantity-available
Cash	Account number		Balance beginning current period, type of account
Take Customer Order	Sales order number	Customer number, employee number	Date, comments
Sales	Invoice number	Customer number, employee number, sales order number	Date, time
Receive Cash	Remittance number	Customer number, employee number, account number	Date, total amount
Inventory–Order Inventory	Item number, purchase order number		Quantity ordered
Inventory–Receive Inventory	Item number, receiving report number		Quantity received, condition
Inventory–Take Customer Order	Item number, sales order number		Quantity ordered, price
Inventory–Sales	Item number, invoice number		Quantity sold
Sales–Receive Cash	Invoice number, remittance number		Amount applied to invoice

CHAPTER

21

Special Topics in REA Modeling

LEARNING OBJECTIVES

After studying this chapter, you should be able to:

1. Create REA data models for the revenue and expenditure cycles of other types of organizations besides retail.
2. Extend REA diagrams to include information about employee roles, M:N agent-event relationships, locations, and relationships between resources and agents.
3. Understand and create an REA diagram for the production cycle.
4. Understand and create an REA diagram for the HR/payroll cycle.
5. Understand and create an REA diagram for the financing cycle.

INTEGRATIVE CASE Paul Stone, Consulting

Paul Stone has enjoyed designing a database for Fred's Train Shop so much that he decides he wants to do similar work for other local businesses. First, however, he realizes that he needs to acquire some additional skills. Although he feels confident of his ability to model the activities of retail businesses like Fred's Train Shop, Paul knows that he needs to learn more about how to model other types of businesses, such as manufacturers, distributors, and service providers.

Paul begins searching the Internet for information about data modeling and database design. He finds a link to a workshop on REA data modeling offered by the American Accounting Association. After reading about it, Paul is certain that it is exactly what he is looking for. He registers for the class. He then prepares a list of questions about the situations that he wants to learn how to model:

1. How do you model the revenue cycle activities of a business that provides services, such as computer or automotive repairs? What about a business that rents items instead of selling them?
2. How do you model the production cycle activities of a manufacturer?
3. How do you integrate payroll activities with other HR processes, such as hiring and training employees?
4. How do you model financing transactions, such as the issuance of stock or debt?

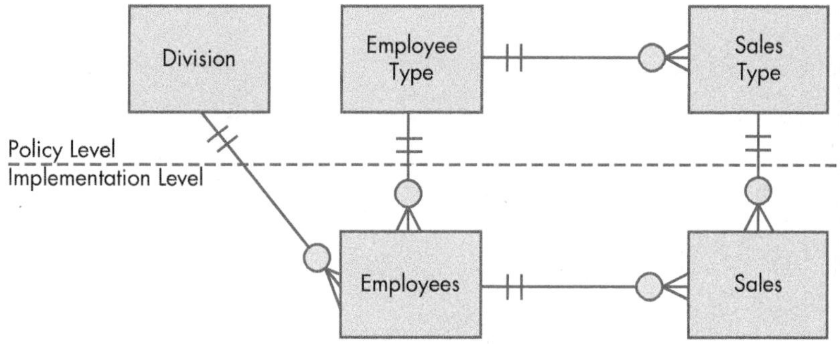

Introduction

The previous two chapters introduced the topic of REA data modeling and explained how to implement an REA model in a relational database. Both chapters focused primarily on the revenue and expenditure cycle activities for a typical retail organization. This chapter extends those basic concepts to a variety of other types of businesses and business cycles. We begin by examining more complex models of the revenue and expenditure cycles, including some additional activities typically performed by manufacturers and distributors and other special situations. Then we discuss several additions to the basic REA model. Next we explain how to model basic business activities in the production, human resources (HR), and financing cycles. We conclude by presenting a comprehensive integrated REA model that incorporates many of the topics presented in this chapter.

Additional Revenue and Expenditure Cycle Modeling Topics

Figures 21-1 and 21-2 present REA diagrams that include additional events for the revenue and expenditure cycles, respectively. Tables 21-1 and 21-2 show how to implement these models in a relational database.

ADDITIONAL REVENUE CYCLE EVENTS AND ATTRIBUTE PLACEMENT

Many of the entities and relationships depicted in Figure 21-1 have already been discussed in previous chapters, so we will focus only on those aspects that are new. Figure 21-1 separates the warehouse activity of filling an order from the activity of actually shipping or delivering that order to the customer. Thus, each instance of the Fill Customer Order event represents the picking and packing of an order by a warehouse employee. The meaning of the cardinality pairs between that event and the Inventory resource and participating agents should be understood from discussions in the previous two chapters. The relationship between the Take Customer Order and Fill Customer Order events is represented as one-to-many (1:N). The minimum cardinalities reflect the fact that two events occur sequentially. The maximum cardinalities reflect the fact that sometimes the company may be out of stock of one or more items that were ordered. Therefore, it may take multiple warehouse activities to completely fill a particular order. Each customer order has to be individually picked and packed, however. The relationship between the Fill Customer Order and Ship Order events is 1:1. The minimum cardinalities reflect the fact that the two events are sequential. The maximum cardinalities are

FIGURE 21-1
Extended Partial Revenue Cycle REA Diagram

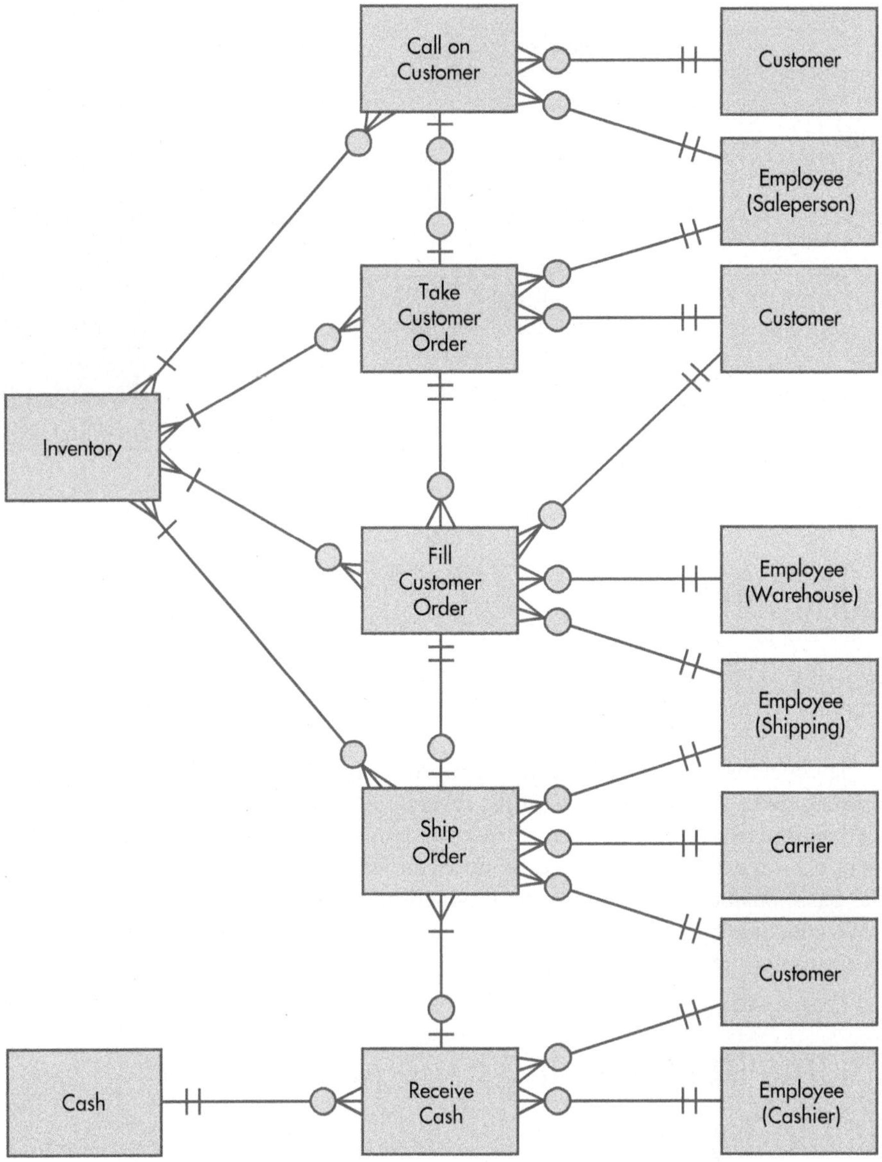

typical best practices followed by most companies. Once all the items that were ordered and in stock have been picked and packed, that entire package is shipped intact to the customer. Note that the Ship Order event occurs when the merchandise is given to the customer (i.e., it is the Sales event depicted in Figure 20-1). Thus, if formal sales invoices are prepared, there would be a separate invoice for each filled order. For proper accountability, each Ship Order event is linked to one, and only one, Fill Customer Order event. It is true that oftentimes many different orders are placed on the same truck or railroad car. However, producing accurate financial records requires tracking each individual "shipment" (sale) on that truckload/carload separately.

Table 21-1 shows that the primary key of the Ship Order event is the shipment number. The bill-of-lading number is another attribute, but it is not the primary key because it may be null for deliveries made using the company's own trucks. Sales invoice number is another attribute of the shipment event. It is not the primary key, however, because as discussed in Chapters 14 and 15, many companies are moving to eliminate the printing of paper invoices and even the creation of electronic ones. Moreover, even when invoices are still used, they may not be generated at the time the merchandise is shipped. Therefore, if invoice number were the primary key, information about the shipment could not be recorded until the invoice was generated. For companies that do still use invoices, however, the invoice number attribute serves an important internal control function: Examination of the value of this attribute provides

TABLE 21-1 Attributes for Relational Tables in Figure 21-1

Table Name	Primary Key	Foreign Keys	Other Attributes
Inventory	Product number		Description, unit standard cost, unit list price, weight, reorder point, beginning quantity-on-hand
Cash	General ledger account number		Name, beginning balance
Call on customer	Call number	Customer number, salesperson employee number	Date, time, purpose
Take customer order	Sales order number	Customer number, salesperson employee number, call number	Date, time, terms, desired delivery date
Fill customer order	Picking ticket number	Sales order number, customer number, warehouse employee number, shipping employee number	Date, time, comments
Ship order	Shipment number	Picking ticket number, customer number, shipping employee number, carrier number, remittance number	Date, time, bill-of-lading number, invoice number
Receive cash	Remittance number	Customer number, employee number, cash account number	Date, time, amount received
Employees	Employee number		Name, date hired, date of birth, number of dependents, pay rate, other tax/withholding information, job title
Customers	Customer number		Name, address, credit limit, beginning balance
Carriers	Carrier number		Name, contact phone
Inventory–Call on Customers	Product number, call number		Comments
Inventory–Take Customer Order	Product number, sales order number		Quantity ordered, price per unit
Inventory–Fill Order	Product number, picking ticket number		Quantity picked
Inventory–Ship Order	Product number, shipment number		Quantity shipped

an easy means of verifying whether all shipments have indeed been billed and recorded (a null value means that an invoice has not yet been prepared).

Also notice that Table 21-1 shows that information about prices and costs is stored in several places. The Inventory table contains information about the standard (list) price and standard cost of each item because those values are typically constant for the entire fiscal year. The Inventory–Take Customer Order table, however, contains information about not only the quantity ordered but also the actual price and accounting cost assigned to each item. This reflects the fact that companies may change prices several times during the year. Thus, although the list price is constant, the actual sales price depends on when the sale occurs. Similarly, although the standard cost for each item is constant during the year, the calculated cost of goods sold (which may be determined using either FIFO, LIFO, weighted-average, or specific identification) will vary throughout the year, especially if a perpetual inventory system is used.

ADDITIONAL EXPENDITURE CYCLE EVENTS AND ATTRIBUTE PLACEMENT

Most of the entities and relationships depicted in Figure 21-2 have been explained in the previous two chapters. The one new entity is the Request Inventory event. Many larger organizations want to formally approve requests to purchase goods; the Request Inventory event provides a

FIGURE 21-2
Extended REA Diagram for Expenditure Cycle

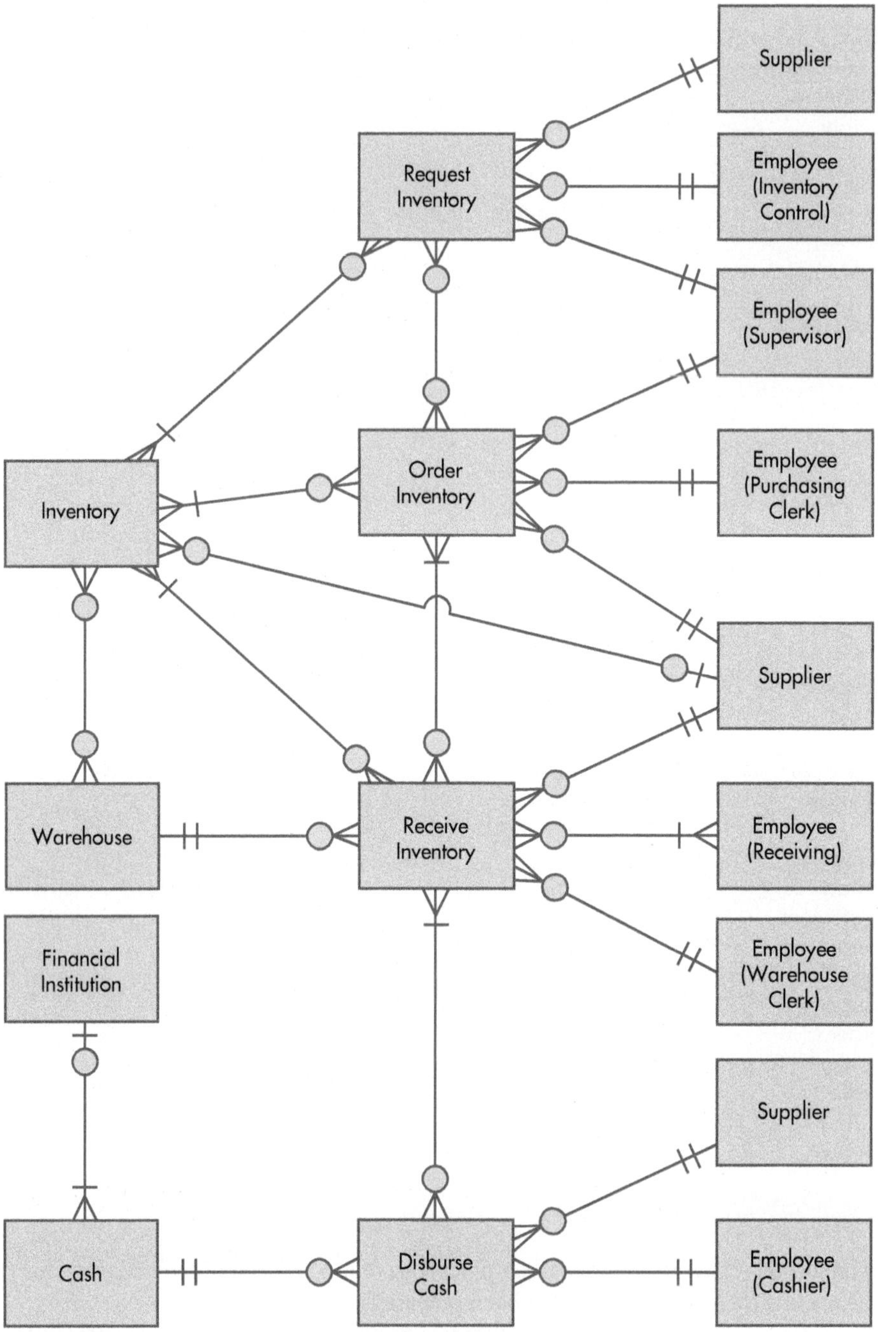

way to collect data about such activities. Each instance of this event represents a request to purchase one or more items. The M:N relationship between the Request Inventory and the Order Inventory events has a minimum cardinality of 0 in both directions. The 0 minimum associated with the Order Inventory event reflects the fact that requests occur before actual orders; in addition, some requests are denied and thus are never linked to an order. The 0 minimum associated with the Request Inventory event reflects the fact that some orders are generated automatically by the inventory control system rather than as a result of a specific request. The maximum associated with the Order Inventory event is many because some requests may be for several different items, each of which may be normally obtained from different sources. Separate purchase orders are needed for each different supplier. Therefore, an approved request may be linked to several different orders. The maximum cardinality associated with the Request Inventory event is many to reflect the common practice of combining different requests for items provided by the same supplier into one larger order to obtain better terms.

Table 21-2 shows that cost information is stored in several tables. Standard cost is stored as an attribute of the Inventory table because it is the same for all units of a given inventory item for a fiscal year. In contrast, the actual cost of inventory is stored in the Inventory–Order_Inventory table. This reflects the fact that purchase prices can vary over time. By storing the cost of each order with the quantity purchased, the system can calculate the actual cost of ending inventory and the cost of goods sold according to any accepted inventory valuation method (LIFO, FIFO, weighted-average, or specific identification). If, on the other hand, actual cost were stored as an attribute of the Inventory table,

TABLE 21-2 Attributes for Relational Tables in Figure 21-2

Table Name (Entity)	Primary Key	Foreign Keys	Other Attributes
Inventory	Product number		Description, unit standard cost, unit list price, weight, reorder point, beginning quantity-on-hand
Warehouse	Warehouse number		Name, address, capacity
Financial institution	Institution number		Name, contact phone
Cash	General ledger account number	Financial institution number	Name, beginning balance
Request inventory	Purchase requisition number	Supplier number, inventory control employee number, supervisor employee number	Date, reason
Order inventory	Purchase order number	Supplier number, purchasing clerk employee number, supervisor employee number	Date, comments
Receive inventory	Receiving report number	Warehouse number, supplier number, warehouse employee number	Date, time, remarks, supplier's invoice number
Disburse cash	Check number	Supplier number, employee number, cash account number	Date, amount, memo
Suppliers	Supplier number		Name, contact phone, rating, beginning balance
Employees	Employee number		Name, date hired, date of birth, number of dependents, pay rate, other tax/withholding information, job title
Inventory– Request_Inventory	Product number, purchase requisition number		Quantity requested
Inventory– Order_Inventory	Product number, purchase order number		Quantity ordered, cost per unit
Inventory– Receive_Inventory	Product number, receiving report number		Quantity received, condition
Inventory–Warehouse	Product number, warehouse number		Quantity stored
Request_Inventory–Order_Inventory	Purchase requisition number, purchase order number		
Order_Inventory–Receive_Inventory	Purchase order number, receiving report number		
Receive_Inventory–Disburse_Cash	Receiving report number, check number		Amount applied to invoice
Receive_Inventory–Employee	Receiving report number, employee number		
Inventory–Supplier	Product number, supplier number		Type (preferred, alternate)

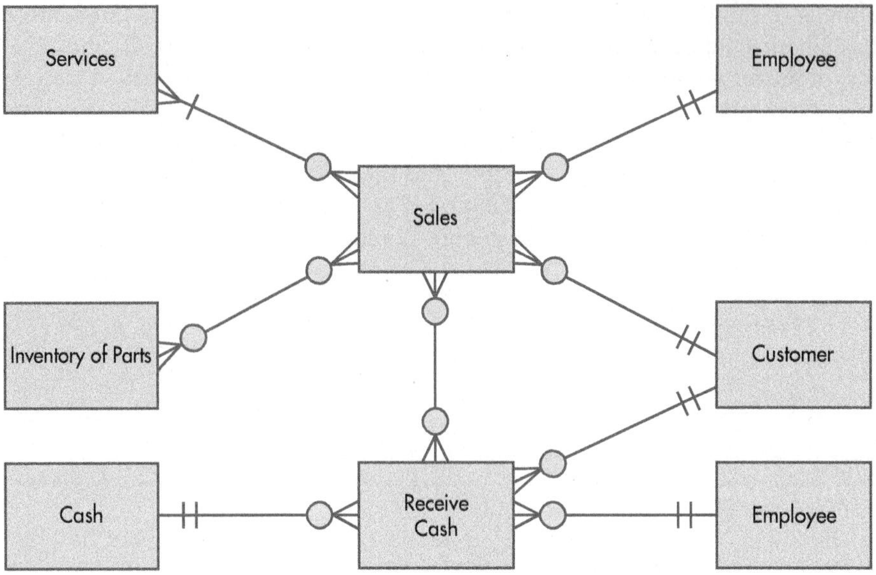

FIGURE 21-3
Partial Revenue Cycle for Sale of Services

it would necessitate using the weighted-average method because all units of a given inventory item would be assigned the same cost. In addition, cost data would be available only in this format; it would be impossible to compute alternative values for inventory because the detailed data about the cost associated with each purchase would not be stored in the database.

SALE OF SERVICES

Thus far, all our modeling examples have focused on businesses that sell tangible inventory. Businesses like automotive repair shops, however, generate revenue from both the sale of products and the provision of services. Figure 21-3 presents a partial REA model of the revenue cycle for such a company.

The Services entity in Figure 21-3 contains information about the organization's revenue-generating activities. Each row identifies a specific type of service the company provides. For example, the Services table for an automotive repair shop might include individual rows for oil changes and brake replacement. Each row would include information about the standard ("book") time it should take to complete the service and the standard (regular) price charged for that type of repair.

Figure 21-3 includes relationships between the Sales event and both the Services and Inventory Resource entities. The nature of the cardinality of those relationships depends on the specific business, but usually both relationships will be modeled as M:N because most businesses provide the same types of services to many different customers, using standard mass-produced parts. The minimum and maximum cardinalities in Figure 21-3 are typical for businesses like automotive and appliance repairs. For such businesses, every sales transaction must involve at least one specific type of service but may include several services (e.g., a customer may require an oil change and brake repairs). However, some repair services, such as fixing a flat tire, may not involve the use of any identifiable inventory parts, requiring only labor.

ACQUISITION OF INTANGIBLE SERVICES

In addition to purchasing inventory, equipment, and buildings, organizations also acquire various intangible services, such as Internet access, telephone service, and utilities. Figure 21-4 shows how to model such activities.

The basic give-to-get economic exchange involves acquiring various services and paying for them. Payments for those services are included in the Disburse Cash table. A separate

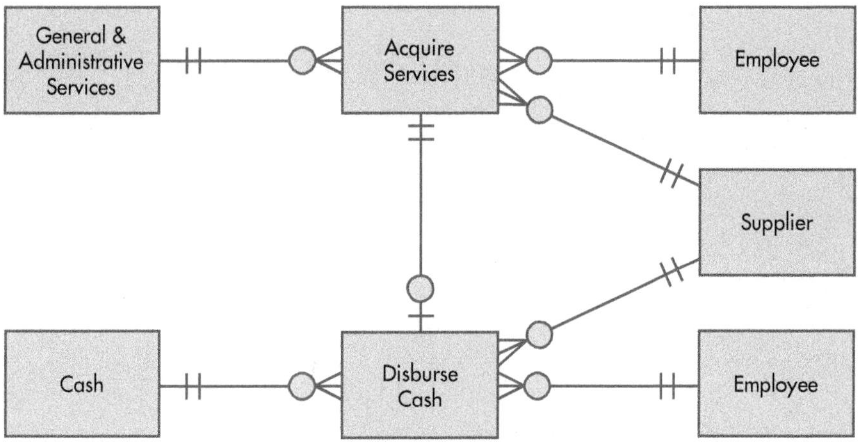

FIGURE 21-4
Partial Expenditure Cycle for Acquisition of Services

event, Acquire Services, is used to collect data about the acquisition of those services. This event entity stores information about the actual amount of the service consumed and the actual price charged. In Figure 21-4, this event is linked to a resource labeled "General and Administrative Services" that reflects the financial accounting treatment for these items. That resource entity includes information about the intangible resource, such as the length of the contract, if any, its starting date, the budgeted cost for that service, the budgeted or standard amount provided each period, and a description of any limitations or special requirements associated with its use.

The relationship between the acquisition event and the resource entity is modeled as 1:N in Figure 21-4 because in most cases each service (telephone, electricity, etc.) is acquired separately, usually from a different supplier. The relationship between the Acquire Services and Disburse Cash events is modeled as 1:1 to reflect the common situation in which the organization obtains the use of a specific service for a particular period of time and makes a payment each month for the services it acquired and used that month.

DIGITAL ASSETS

What about digital assets? Companies that sell software, music, or digital photographs over the Internet give up a digital copy of those resources, but not the actual resource itself. How does this affect the REA models of the revenue and expenditure cycles? It doesn't. Such companies still need to collect information about their purchase of and payment for those digital assets, as well as tracking orders for and delivery of those digital assets, along with receipt of payments from their customers. Those companies also need an Inventory table so that customers can see what digital products are available for sale. The structure of that Inventory table is almost identical to that of mass-produced merchandise. The only difference is that because sales involve only a digital copy of the resource, there is no need for attributes such as quantity-on-hand, quantity-available, reorder point, and standard reorder quantity. However, the Inventory table will still include information about the standard list price of each item and its description.

RENTAL TRANSACTIONS

Some businesses generate revenue through rental transactions, rather than sales. Thus, the basic give-to-get economic exchange involves the temporary use of a resource in return for both the receipt of cash and the subsequent return of the resource rented. Figure 21-5 shows how to model such transactions.

Businesses that rent equipment or other resources want to track each physical item separately. Therefore, the primary key for the Rental Inventory table is some kind of unique serial number, rather than a part number. Each Rent Item event records information about the rental of one specific item, such as the date and time it was rented, the rental price, and any specific terms of the agreement. If a customer rents multiple items, the system treats this as a set of

FIGURE 21-5
Partial Revenue Cycle for Rental Transactions

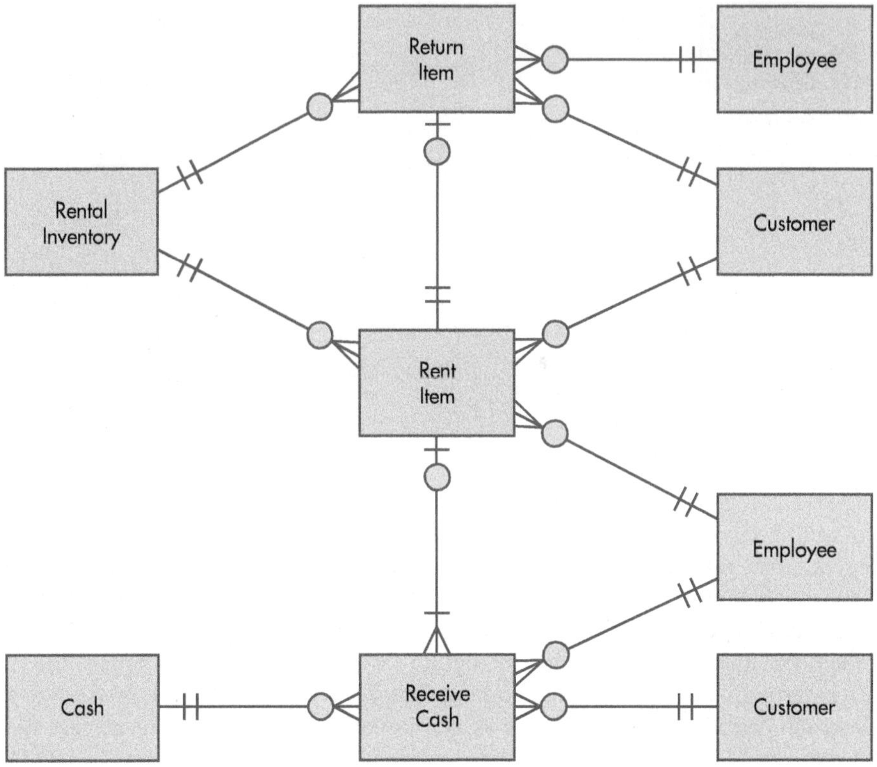

rental events, each for one particular inventory item. This facilitates tracking the status of each piece of Rental Inventory. For example, a query to determine whether an item is still outstanding needs to reference only the Rental and Return events; in contrast, if the rental of five items had been recorded as one event, then the preceding query would also have to include the M:N relationship table linking the Rental event and Rental Inventory entity. (*Note:* This is transparent to the customer. The customer simply completes the required paperwork and pays the specified amount and neither knows, nor cares, that the system created several rows in the database, instead of one, to record the transaction.)

Figure 21-5 shows that the Rent Item event is linked to both the Receive Cash and Return Item events. Examine the relationship from the Rent Item to the Receive Cash event. The minimum cardinality of 1 reflects the fact that customers typically pay first, prior to taking possession of the item. The maximum cardinality is many because there may be additional charges imposed when the item is returned. The cardinality pair associated with the Rent Item event has a 0 minimum and 1 maximum because the Receive Cash event occurs first and is linked to one, and only one, specific rental event. The relationship between the Rent Item and Return Item events is 1:1 to reflect the fact that the rental of each specific item is individually tracked, as is its return; moreover, each item rented can be returned at most one time. The minimum cardinalities on each side of the relationship reflect the temporal sequence of the two events (i.e., an item is rented before it is returned).

Organizations sometimes rent, rather than purchase, resources. For example, many organizations rent office spaces and warehouses. The basic economic give-to-get exchange involves payments to the supplier for the right to use a resource for a specific period of time. Information about the Payment event is included in the Disburse Cash table. A separate Rent Resource event may be created to represent the acquisition of the resource because that event will probably collect information about different attributes than those relevant to the receipt of inventory. Although it is rented and not owned, the resource itself would also be included in the model as a separate entity because organizations will likely need to maintain much of the same kind of information (e.g., location, description) about rented resources as they do for resources that are owned. Rented and owned resources may be represented in separate entities, however, because each may contain a number of attributes not relevant to the other (e.g., information about rental contract terms, acquisition cost, depreciation method). In addition, if the rented resource must be returned (e.g., rental of equipment), then another event will need to be included in the REA diagram to record that activity. In that case, the Rent Resource event would be linked to two events: Disburse Cash and Return Rented Resource forming a mirror image of the REA model of the renting organization's revenue cycle activities discussed earlier.

Additional REA Features

Figures 21-1 and 21-2 depict several new additional elements of REA data models not discussed in the prior two chapters: employee roles, M:N agent–event relationships, locations, and relationships between resources and agents.

EMPLOYEE ROLES

Figures 21-1 and 21-2 identified the role played by an employee (e.g., salesperson, warehouse clerk). This information enriches the REA diagram and can be used to verify whether job functions are properly segregated. However, Tables 21-1 and 21-2 still show that there is only one employee entity. Information about job roles is simply another attribute (job title) in the Employee table.

M:N AGENT–EVENT RELATIONSHIPS

Figure 21-2 depicts the relationship between the Receive Inventory event and employees as M:N. This reflects the fact that many deliveries are so large that several employees must work together to unload and store the items. M:N agent–event relationships occur whenever an activity is performed by more than one employee, yet management wants to retain the ability to monitor each individual's performance.

LOCATIONS

Figure 21-2 introduces two new entities: Warehouses and Financial Institutions. These entities store information about the location where resources are stored and where certain events take place. Many companies have multiple warehouses. The cardinality pairs linking the Warehouse and Inventory entities reflect several common situations. A warehouse can, occasionally, be empty but usually stores many different inventory items. Conversely, the same inventory items may be stored in several different warehouses. Sometimes companies may also want to maintain information about inventory that they do not normally carry.

Note also that linking the Receive Inventory event to the Warehouse entity makes it possible to evaluate performance at different locations. Events, such as Receive Inventory, can only occur at a specific location; conversely, many events can occur at the same location. Therefore, Figure 21-2 depicts the relationship between Warehouses and Receive Inventory as 1:N.

Examination of Table 21-2 shows that the Financial Institution entity clarifies the nature of the Cash entity. Each row in the Cash table corresponds to a specific general ledger account aggregated in the balance sheet under the heading "Cash and Cash Equivalents." The cardinality pairs associated with the Financial Institution and Cash entities reflect common business practices. A specific cash account can only be located at one financial institution and some accounts, such as "Petty Cash," are not on deposit anywhere. Companies also typically only keep information about financial institutions with which they have accounts but may have more than one account at the same financial institution.

RELATIONSHIPS BETWEEN RESOURCES AND AGENTS

Figure 21-2 also includes a M:N relationship between the Inventory entity (a Resource) and the Supplier entity (an Agent). This relationship reflects the common best practice of identifying preferred and alternative suppliers for specific inventory items. Similar relationships between resources and employees can be used to model responsibility and accountability.

Production Cycle REA Model

Figure 21-6 is a data model for the basic production cycle activities of a manufacturing company, and Table 21-3 lists the tables required to implement that model in a relational database, along with the placement of various attributes. Accurate product cost management and performance evaluation of production cycle activities require collecting detailed information about the use of raw materials, labor, and machinery to produce finished products. Thus, there are four main events of interest included in a typical production cycle REA diagram:

1. Issuance of raw materials.
2. Use of labor in production.
3. Use of machinery and equipment in production.
4. Production of new finished products, represented by the work-in-process event.

ADDITIONAL ENTITIES—INTELLECTUAL PROPERTY

Figure 21-6 includes three special types of entities—the Bill of Materials, the Job Operations List, and the Machine Operations List—that store important portions of a manufacturing company's intellectual property. The Bill of Materials entity contains information about the raw materials used to make a finished product. As Table 21-3 shows, this includes data about the *standard* quantity of each raw material that should be used to make that product. Thus, the bill of materials can be thought of as the list of ingredients in a recipe. By itself, however, such a list is not sufficient to manufacture a product—instructions concerning how to combine those components, including the proper sequence of steps, are also needed. The Job Operations List entity stores the instructions concerning labor activities, and the Machine Operations List entity stores the instructions for actions to be performed using various pieces of equipment. Both entities also store data about the *standard* time it should take to perform those operations.

FIGURE 21-6
Partial REA Diagram for Production Cycle

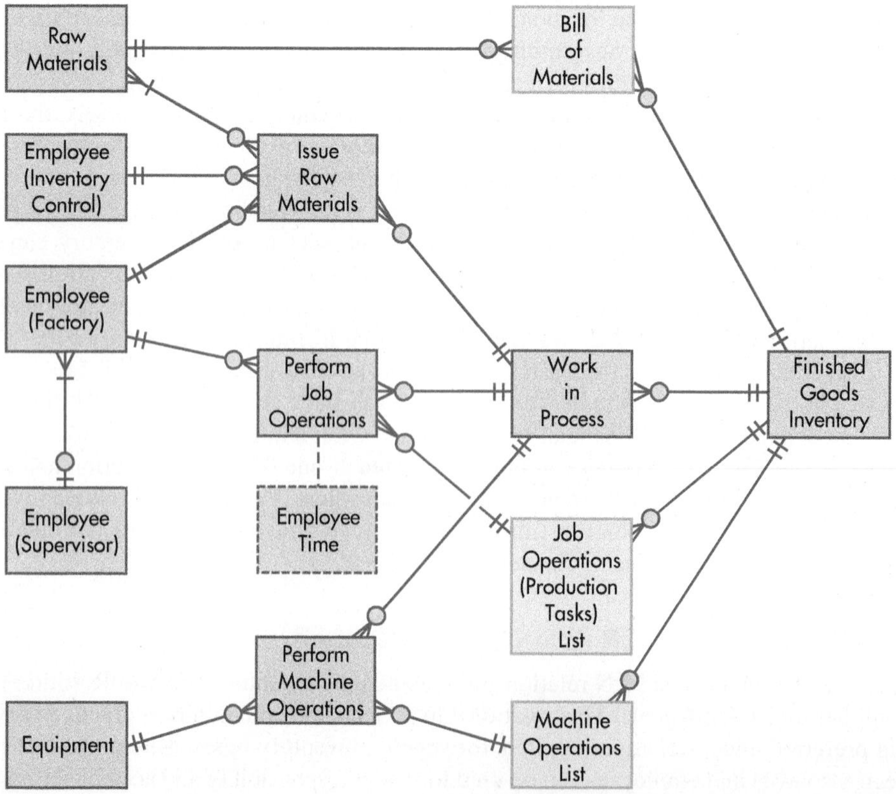

TABLE 21-3 Attributes for Relational Tables in Figure 21-6

Table Name (Entity)	Primary Key	Foreign Keys	Other Attributes
Raw materials[a]	RM item number		Description, standard unit cost, reorder point, beginning quantity-on-hand
Employees	Employee number		Name, date hired, date of birth, number of dependents, pay rate, other tax/withholding information, job title
Equipment	Equipment ID number		Description, acquisition cost, depreciation method, depreciation life, salvage value
Issue raw materials	RM issue number	Inventory control employee number, factory employee number, WIP job number	Date, time, comments
Perform job operations	Job operation number	Employee number, WIP job number, job operations list number	Date, time started, time finished
Perform machine operations	Machine operation number	Equipment ID number, WIP job number, machine operations list number	Date, time started, time finished
Bill of materials	Bill of materials number	Finished good product number, raw materials item number	Standard quantity needed
Work in process	WIP job number	Finished good product number	Date/time started, date/time completed, target completion date, quantity ordered, quantity produced, production order number
Job operations list	Job operations list number	Finished good product number	Instructions, standard time for operation
Machine operations list	Machine operations list number	Finished good product number	Instructions, standard time for operation
Finished goods inventory[a]	Product number		Description, unit standard cost, unit list price, weight, beginning quantity-on-hand
Raw materials–issue raw materials	RM item number, RM issue number		Quantity issued

[a]Some organizations may combine Finished Goods and Raw Materials into one inventory table.

Figure 21-6 shows 1:N relationships between the Bill of Materials entity and both the Raw Materials and Finished Goods inventory entities. Each row in the Bill of Materials entity specifies how much of a specific raw material is needed to make a particular finished good; thus, each row represents the information that would be found on one line of a Bill of Materials list. This reflects the fact that the same raw material (e.g., 12-gauge wire) may be used in five different products, with a different amount used to make each product. The relationship between the Raw Materials entity and the Issue Raw Materials event is M:N because the same raw materials can be related to many different events of issuing that raw material; conversely, often all of the different materials needed to manufacture a product are issued at the same time; hence, one Issue Raw Materials event can be linked to many different lines in the Raw Materials table.

The relationships between the Finished Goods Inventory resource and both the Job Operations List and Machine Operations List entities are 1:N. This reflects the fact that each row in the list entities represents information about a specific activity required to make a specific product. For example, there would be separate rows for polishing brass for each product that included brass parts; each row would store information about the standard time it should take to polish the brass when making a particular product. Often, multiple steps are required to make a single product. Thus, one finished good would be linked to many different rows in the Job Operations List and Machine Operations List entity tables.

Figure 21-6 also includes an entity labeled "Employee Time." As explained in Chapter 20, this entity is seldom instantiated as a table in a relational database. Hence, it is represented with dashed lines in Figure 21-6 and does not appear as an entity in Table 21-3.

PRODUCTION CYCLE EVENTS

Data about *actual* raw materials used in production is stored in the Issue Raw Materials entity. Similarly, information about the *actual* labor and machine operations performed, including the actual amount of time each activity took, is stored in the Perform Job Operations and Perform Machine Operations entities, respectively. Performance can be evaluated by comparing the data in these three event entities with the information about standards stored in the corresponding information entities (Bill of Materials, Job Operations List, and Machine Operations List).

The Perform Job Operations event entity is an example of a Give Resource event: It records the use of employee time. Each row in that table records information about how much time an employee spent working on a particular job. Thus, there can be many rows in this table for each employee every day. For example, on July 7, employee 727 may spend three hours on WIP job 2234, two hours on WIP job 2235, and three hours on WIP job 2236. Collecting this kind of detailed information about how factory employees use their time enables manufacturing companies to accurately assign labor costs to different production batches and product lines.

The Perform Machine Operations event is similar to the Perform Job Operations event, except that it records information about the use of a specific piece of machinery or equipment. This information is useful not only to assign costs to products but also for scheduling maintenance. Note that the Perform Machine Operations event is *not* used to record depreciation. Depreciation expenses seldom correspond to actual use of the equipment. Depreciation is not modeled as an event in the REA diagram because it is an accounting concept that arbitrarily allocates the cost of an acquired resource to different fiscal periods. Periodic depreciation is simply a calculation based on a formula (depreciation method) and a set of assumptions (estimated useful life, salvage value, etc.). Information about the formula and assumptions is stored in the resource entity for use in calculating periodic depreciation charges, but the calculation process itself is not an event, just as the processes of calculating the total amount of a particular sales transaction or the amount of an employee's paycheck are not modeled as events.

Figure 21-6 models the relationships between the Perform Job Operations event and the Job Operations List entity, and between the Perform Machine Operations event and the Machine Operations List entity, as being 1:N. The list entities store information about the standard time it should take to perform each individually identifiable activity; the operations events record the actual time used to perform that activity. Thus, each actual event can be linked to only one entry in the standards table, but each entry in the standards table is likely to be linked to many actual performances of that activity.

The Work-in-Process entity is used to collect and summarize data about the raw materials, labor, and machine operations used to produce a batch of goods. The relationships between Work-in-Process and those three event entities are all 1:N, reflecting the fact that each production run may involve a number of raw materials issuances, labor operations, and machine operations. Each of those activities, however, is linked to a specific production run. These links reflect an internal give-to-get exchange that is the essence of the production cycle: Raw materials, labor, and equipment are all used in order to produce finished goods inventory. Thus, three Give Resource events are related to one Get Resource event.

NEW REA FEATURE

Notice that Figure 21-6 differs from previous REA diagrams in that it shows only one agent associated with the Perform Job Operations (and Perform Machine Operations) events. These internal events differ from the other events discussed throughout this book in that they do not involve an exchange or transfer of resources. Instead, they represent the consumption or use of individual resources, such as a specific employee's time or the use of a specific piece of equipment. Therefore, the event is linked to that agent (employee or piece of machinery) for which management wants to collect information for product costing and performance evaluation purposes.

Figure 21-6 also depicts a 1:N relationship between employees and supervisors. This reflects the typical situation where each employee is assigned to a specific supervisor, but each supervisor is responsible for many employees. In contrast, a matrix style of organization, where each employee reports to several supervisors, would be modeled as an M:N relationship between factory employees and supervisors. Relationships between internal agents may be created to model lines of responsibility. Relationships between internal and external agents can also occur. For example, some organizations that primarily provide services, such as banks and insurance companies, may assign customers to specific employees who are responsible for effectively managing the overall quality of the ongoing association with each customer. Relationships between external agents are rare but may sometimes be implemented to satisfy the requirements for a well-structured database. For example, if an insurance company needed to collect and maintain detailed information about each of a customer's dependents, it could do so by creating a separate entity called "Dependents" and establishing a 1:N relationship between that entity and the Customer entity.

Combined HR/Payroll Data Model

Figure 21-7 integrates payroll and HR activities. The Time Worked event is necessary to calculate payroll. The Time Used event is used for cost accounting, to properly assign labor costs (in manufacturing companies, this event entity is often called "Job Operations"). All of the other events represent important HR activities.

HR CYCLE ENTITIES

Notice that in Figure 21-7 the Employee entity is linked to almost every other entity in the diagram, reflecting the importance of employees to the organization. The Employee entity stores much of the data typically found in the employee (payroll) master file: name, date hired, date of birth, pay rate, job title, supervisor, number of dependents, withholding allowances, and information about any voluntary deductions, such as 401(k) plans.

The Skills entity contains data about the different job skills of interest to the organization. There would be a row in this table for each major job skill. For example, a software developer may list different programming languages and application programs in this table. The relationship between Skills and Employees is modeled as being M:N because one employee may possess a number of job skills (e.g., one programmer may be proficient in several different languages) and, conversely, several employees may possess the same skill.

The Training event entity represents the various workshops, training programs, and other opportunities provided for employees to develop and maintain their skills. Thus, this entity stores data that can be used to evaluate the effectiveness and cost of training and development efforts. The relationship between the Employees and Training entities is M:N because a given employee will, over time, attend numerous training courses and, conversely, several employees may attend the same specific training class. The relationship between the Skills and Training entities is 1:N because each course is designed to develop a specific skill, but each skill may be taught many different times.

The Recruiting event entity stores data about activities performed to notify the public of job openings. The data recorded in this entity are useful for documenting compliance with employment laws and for evaluating the effectiveness of various methods used to announce job opportunities. The M:N relationship between Skills and Recruiting reflects the fact that each advertisement may seek several specific skills and that, over time, there may be several advertisements for a given skill. The relationship between the Recruiting event and Job Applicants is modeled as being M:N because many people typically apply for each job opening, but a given individual may also respond to more than one recruiting event. Also, more than one employee may participate in each recruiting event, and, over time, a given employee may participate in many such events.

The Interview event stores detailed data about each job interview. It is linked to the Hire Employees event in a 1:N relationship. This reflects the fact that the Hiring event occurs only once but may result from either one or a number of preceding interviews.

TRACKING EMPLOYEES' TIME

The section on the Production Cycle discussed the use of a Perform Job Operations event to track how factory workers spent their time so that labor costs can be allocated to products. Professional services firms, such as law firms, consulting organizations, and accounting firms, similarly need to track how their members use their time in order to accurately bill each client. Figure 21-7 uses the Time Used event for this purpose. The structure of this table is similar to that of the Perform Job Operations table described earlier (we use a different name here because "perform job operations" has a manufacturing connotation). Thus, each row in this table includes the following attributes: the employee, the job (client) to which that employee's time should be charged, a description of the task performed (e.g., prepare will, telephone consultation, court appearance), and the time when that task was started and ended. Information about the nature of the task needs to be collected in order to evaluate performance and because sometimes the rate billed for a particular employee may vary depending on the task being performed.

It is instructive to compare the information provided by the Time Used event to that provided by linking specific business events to the employee agent who performed that task. Regular event–agent relationships, such as that between sales and employees, collect data that can be used to answer such questions as "How much did salesperson X sell this week?" or "How many sales did each salesperson make?" In contrast, the Time Used event provides the information needed to answer such questions as "How much time did a particular salesperson spend calling on customers, as opposed to providing customer service support via the telephone?" Each instance of a regular event entity (e.g., each row in the Call on Customer, Sales,

FIGURE 21-7
Integrated REA Diagram for HR/Payroll Cycles

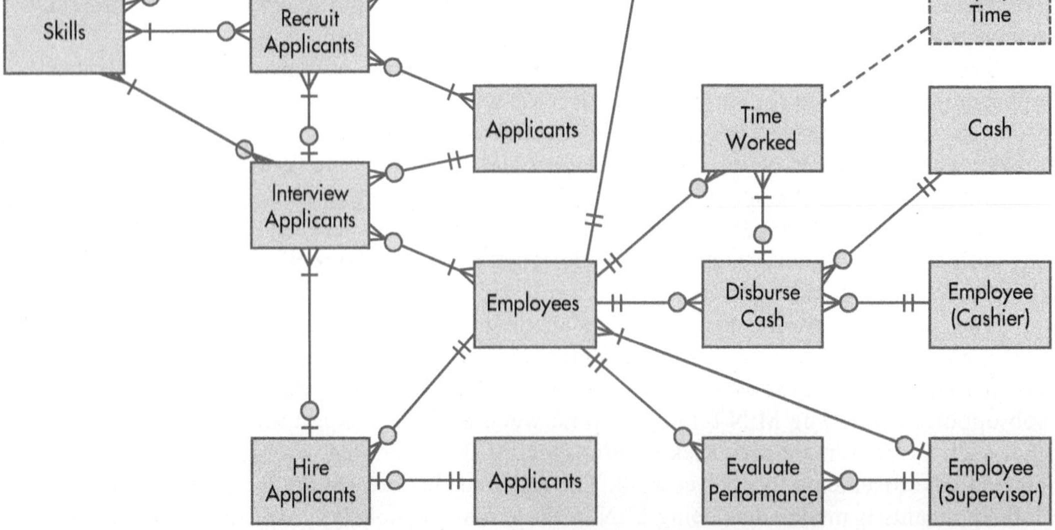

or Provide Customer Support tables) captures data about discrete activities, such as a particular sales transaction. In contrast, each row in the Time Used event captures data about what an employee did during a block of time. Hence, each row in the Time Used table can be, and often is, linked to many rows in a Business Event table. For example, employee 007 may spend five hours making sales calls to customers, during which time she visited five customers. That would be represented as one row in the Track Time Used table but five separate rows in the call on customer table. Thus, there is a 1:N relationship between the two types of events. It is not necessary to link the Time Used entity to specific business events, however, but doing so facilitates evaluating performance at a very detailed level (i.e., to answer questions such as during which block of time on which days of the week is a particular salesperson most effective).

It is also instructive to compare the "Time Used" and "Time Worked" entities. The former collects data to answer questions about how employees use their time, and thus helps managers assess performance. In contrast, the "Time Worked" entity merely records the total time for which an employee is to be paid and is used to process payroll.

Not every organization collects detailed data about their employees' use of time, in which case there is no need for a Time Used entity. Moreover, even when such an event is included, the resource used (Employee Time) is seldom implemented as a table in the database because there are no meaningful attributes to describe it. Hence, the resource entity "Employee Time" is depicted with dashed lines in Figure 21-7.

Financing Activities Data Model

Most organizations issue stock and debt to finance their operations. Figure 21-8 is an REA diagram of these two financing activities.

The event Issue Debt is a special kind of cash receipt; hence, it is connected to the Cash resource entity. It is often modeled as a separate event entity distinct from "Receive Cash" because it contains different attributes from those associated with cash receipts that arise from the Sales event, such as the face amount of debt issued, total amount received, date issued, maturity date, and interest rate. Usually, most companies do not deal directly with individual creditors. Instead, they sell their debt instruments through a financial intermediary, which is depicted in Figure 21-8 as the Transfer Agent. The transfer agent maintains the

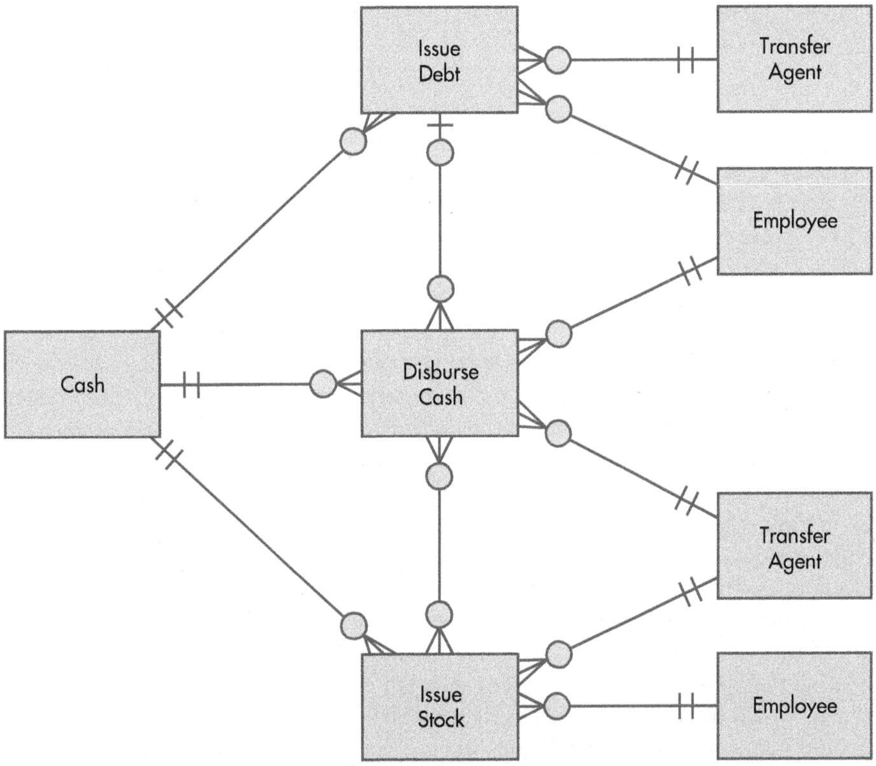

FIGURE 21-8
Partial Financing Activities Diagram

necessary information about individual creditors to properly direct both the periodic interest payments and eventual repayment of principal. Therefore, each occurrence of an Issue Debt event contains data about the *aggregate* amount received from issuing a set of debt instruments. For example, the issuance of $10,000,000 of 5% bonds, which were ultimately purchased by several thousand different individuals for a total of $9,954,000, constitutes one Issue Debt event.

Debt-related payments (whether periodic interest payments or repayment of principal at maturity) are cash disbursements. Usually, the organization writes one check for the total amount of interest owed for a particular bond or note and sends that to the transfer agent, who then handles the distribution of individual checks to each creditor. Thus, to continue our example, the company would send $125,000 to the transfer agent to make the first quarterly payment on that $10,000,000 of bonds. The transfer of funds would be recorded as *one* row in the Disburse Cash table. Note that if a company has issued different series of bonds at different points in time, it would normally make separate transfers of funds to the transfer agent for payments linked to each debt issue. Thus, Figure 21-8 shows each Disburse Cash event linked to a maximum of 1 Issue Debt events. The minimum cardinality is 0 because a particular Disburse Cash event may be linked to either an Issue Debt event or an Issue Stock event.

Equity transactions are modeled in a manner similar to debt transactions. The Issue Stock event is a special kind of cash receipt associated with the issuance of stock, and the dividend payments are another type of cash disbursement. As with debt, most companies do not deal directly with individual stockholders. Thus, Figure 21-8 shows that both types of equity transactions involve participation by an employee (the treasurer) and the external transfer agent. The relationship between the Disburse Cash and Issue Stock events is modeled as M:N because each stock issuance may be linked to many dividend payments and, conversely, a particular dividend payment may be related to multiple different issuances of stock (i.e., *all* shareholders, regardless of which issue they bought, will receive a portion of each dividend). The minimum cardinalities are 0 in both directions because there is a temporal sequence between the two events and because a given Disburse Cash event might be linked to an Issue Debt event instead of to an Issue Stock event.

The issuance of stock and debt does not occur very often. Moreover, the information associated with these events (par value, actual cash received, etc.) needs to be retained for years in order to track equity and debt accounts to prepare financial statements. Therefore, information about these two events is maintained indefinitely rather than erased at the end of the fiscal period as are other events.

Summary and Case Conclusion

Figure 21-9 presents an integrated enterprise-wide data model that includes most of the situations discussed in this and the previous two chapters. Note how the figure shows the linkages among different subsystems of the organization's AIS. For example, a customer order for finished goods may, if there is insufficient inventory on hand to fill the order, trigger the scheduling of a production run to produce those goods. In turn, this production run may necessitate ordering additional raw materials. Enterprise Resource Planning (ERP) systems are designed to automatically trigger these types of related actions across subsystems by linking each subsystem to a common enterprise-wide database. Thus, even though the databases used in many ERP systems may not be explicitly based on the REA data model, a model like that depicted in Figure 21-9 provides useful documentation about the business activities supported by the ERP system.

Indeed, one of the benefits of an integrated enterprise-wide data model like Figure 21-9 is that auditors can use it to guide the development of queries to validate the completeness and accuracy of transaction processing. To illustrate the possibilities, let us examine the process for validating the updates to the sales account in the general ledger. Referring to Figure 21-9, the first step would be writing queries against the data model for the revenue cycle. One such query would sum the amount of all sales during the time period of interest. Other queries

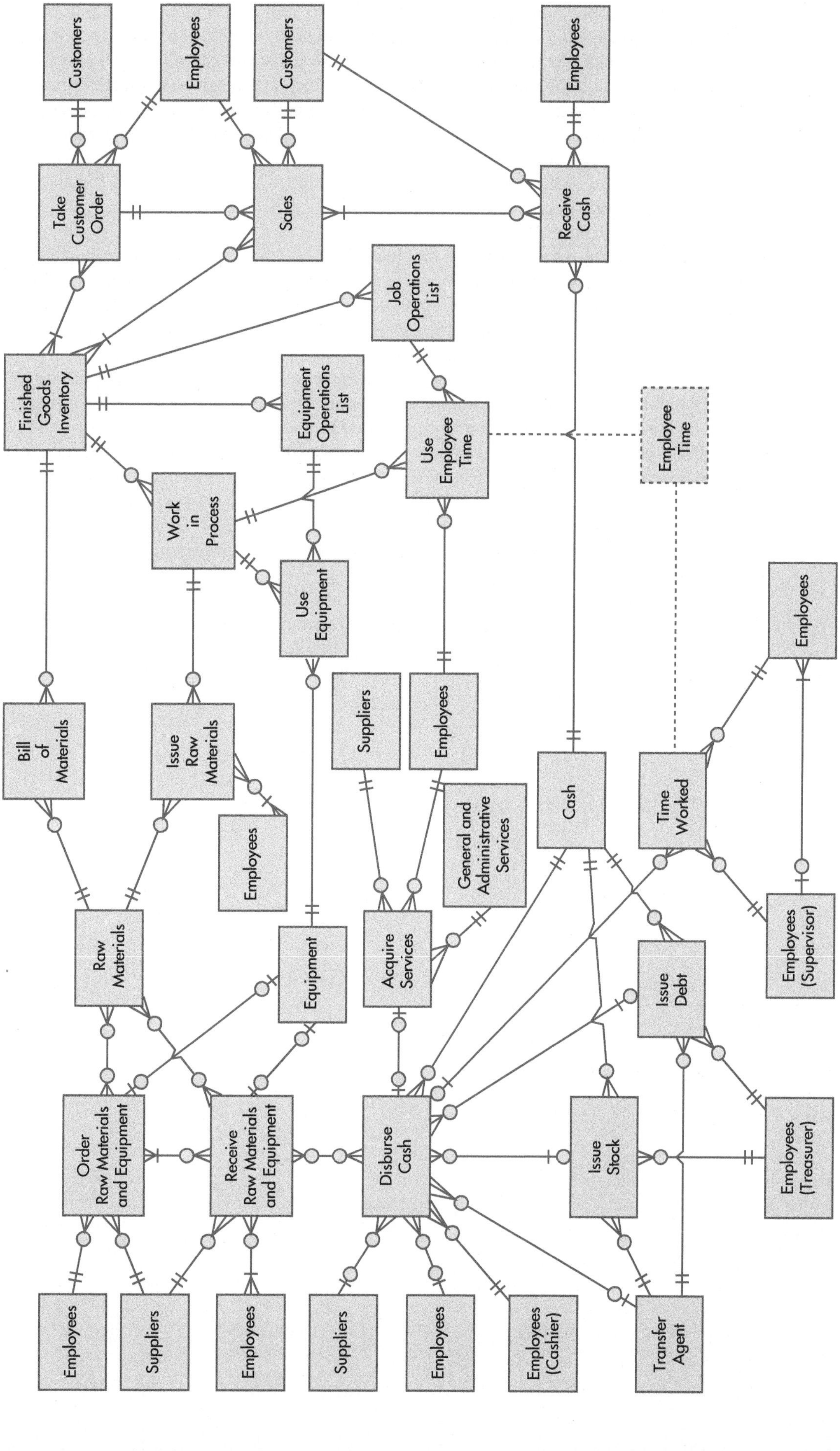

FIGURE 21-9
Integrated, Enterprise-wide REA Diagram

would link the Sales and Take Customer Order tables to verify the completeness and validity of all recorded sales. Additional queries could be written to trace sales to specific customers and sales staff. In fact, the number of such cross-table links that can be easily generated is limited only by the auditor's imagination. In addition, the system can be configured to create extensive log files that make it possible to identify who authorized a transaction. Thus, integrated data models make it possible to write a set of queries that creates a rich, complex audit trail of an organization's business activities.

An integrated enterprise-wide data model like that depicted in Figure 21-9 can also significantly improve the support provided for managerial decision making. Managers can write queries to assess operational efficiency. For example, queries that link the "Use Employee Time" event to various other events can provide information about the relative productivity of various employees. Moreover, the REA model's inherent flexibility makes it easy to collect new information items to evaluate performance, often simply by adding new attributes to existing tables. As Focus 21-1 explains, this flexibility not only facilitates managerial decisions, but can also provide tax benefits.

Creating an integrated, enterprise-wide data model also facilitates the amalgamation of financial and nonfinancial information in the same database, which can improve internal reporting. Traditionally, internal reports have focused primarily on financial performance measures. Effective management of an organization, however, requires measuring performance on multiple dimensions because no single measure is sufficient. Instead, top management must have reports that provide a multidimensional perspective on performance. An integrated, enterprise-wide data model like that depicted in Figure 21-9 facilitates the development of multidimensional performance reports, such as the balanced scorecard discussed in Chapter 18.

Paul Stone reflects on what he has learned at the REA workshop. He realizes that although a number of different types of businesses and transactions were covered, he is likely to encounter clients with yet other situations. Nevertheless, he feels confident that he now understands a wide enough variety of situations that he can use that knowledge to develop solutions to enable him to model almost any type of business activity he is likely to encounter. After all, as a CPA, Paul's entire career has involved continuous learning and refinement of his skills.

FOCUS 21-1 Tax Benefits of Well-Designed Databases

A well-designed database efficiently and effectively supports an organization's transaction processing requirements while also providing management with easy access to the information it needs to plan, control, and evaluate performance. A properly designed database can also yield tax benefits. This can be illustrated easily when considering business travel and entertainment expenses.

The IRS generally allows organizations to deduct 50% of the meals and entertainment expenses incurred when dealing with customers or prospective customers. Many organizations simply accumulate all meal and entertainment expenses in one general ledger account. This makes it easy to calculate the tax deduction at the end of the year: Just multiply the total amount in the meals and entertainment account by 50%. Although this approach is simple, efficient, and logical, it can cause an organization to miss out on additional tax deductions. The IRS has established several exceptions in which meals and entertainment expenses are 100% deductible. To take advantage of these exceptions, organizations need to design their databases to be able to identify tax-relevant characteristics of specific meals and entertainment expenses. This can be as simple as adding another attribute to the table used to record those expenses.

Is it worth the effort? Consider the following examples: (a) Four tickets to an NBA game, plus refreshments, can cost over $400; (b) four tickets to a concert by a major symphony with dessert and coffee afterwards can cost over $300. When you multiply such examples by the number of times your sales staff entertains clients during the course of a year, the potential tax benefits of deducting an additional 50% of such costs can be huge.

AIS in Action

CHAPTER QUIZ

1. Which of the following represents the "get" side of the basic give-to-get economic exchange for a business that rents equipment and machinery for use by others?
   a. Rent Equipment
   b. Receive Cash
   c. Return Rented Equipment
   d. Return Rented Equipment and Receive Cash

2. Which resource in the HR/payroll cycle is seldom implemented in a database?
   a. Skills
   b. Employee Time
   c. Applicants
   d. Disburse Cash

3. Joe's Computers makes service calls to repair computer equipment. Some calls involve only labor charges, and others involve both labor and parts. Which of the following correctly models the relationship between the Service Calls event and Parts Inventory?

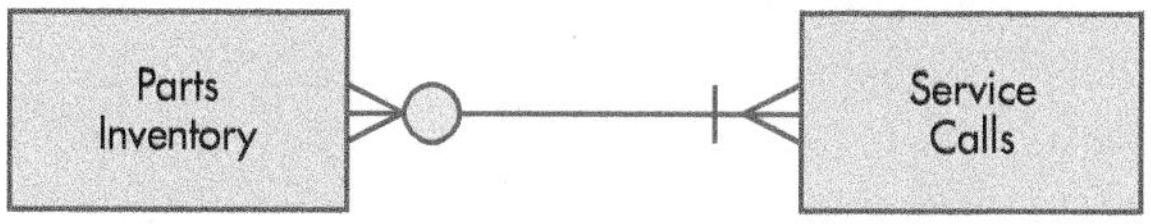

a.

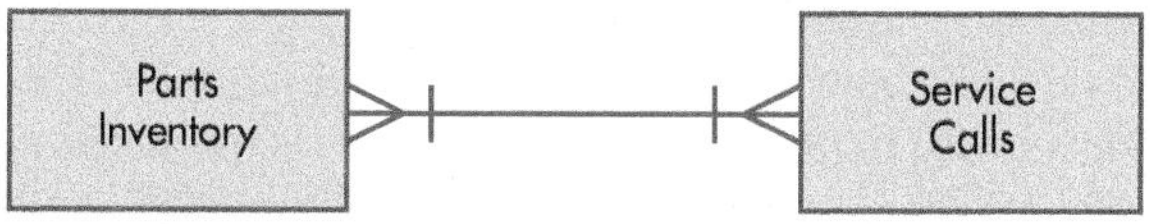

b.

c.

d.

4. Which entity contains information about the components used to manufacture a particular product?
   a. Inventory
   b. Job Operations List
   c. Bill of Materials
   d. Machine Operations List

5. Which of the following production cycle events involves the *acquisition* of a resource (i.e., is a Get event)?
   a. Perform Machine Operations
   b. Perform Job Operations
   c. Work in Process
   d. Issue Raw Materials

6. Which production cycle event collects the data used to calculate payroll?
   a. Perform Job Operations
   b. Time Worked
   c. Time Used
   d. Disburse Cash

7. The give-to-get economic exchange associated with debt financing involves which two events?
   a. Issue Debt and Receive Cash
   b. Issue Debt and Disburse Cash
   c. Receive Cash and Disburse Cash
   d. None of the above

8. Acme Manufacturing tracks information about customer calls by sales representative. Although many calls involve demonstrations of products, some are purely to build relationships. What is the correct way to model the relationship between Inventory and the Call on Customers event?

a. 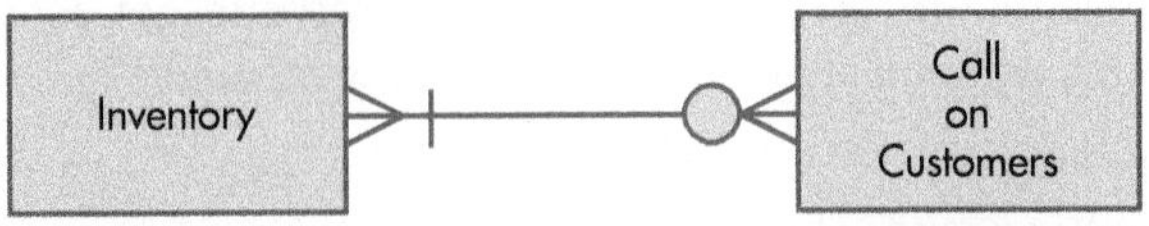

b. 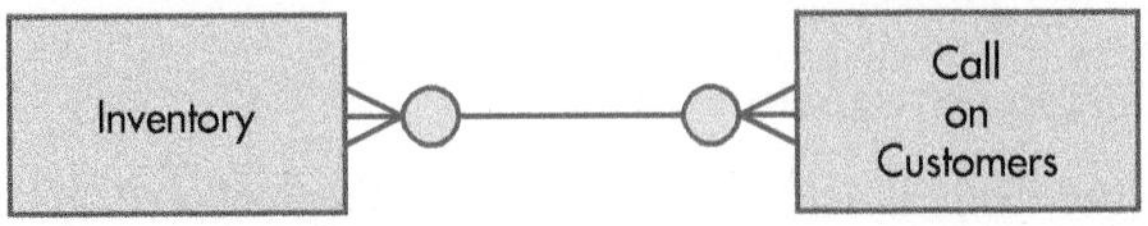

c. 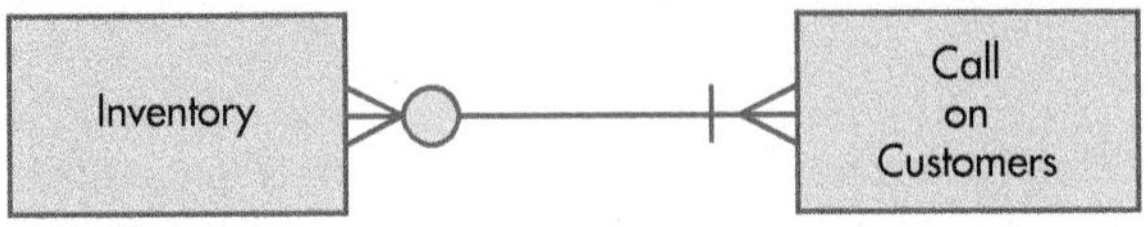

d. 

9. Acme manufacturing wants to track post-sales customer service by collecting information about each customer service call: who called, when the call happened, which customer service representative handled the call, how long the call lasted, which sales transaction prompted the call, and which inventory items were discussed. The relationship between the Sales and Post-sales Service Call events should most likely be modeled as which of the following?
   a. 1:1
   b. 1:N
   c. M:N
   d. 0:N

10. Which of the following additions to the basic REA template are sometimes needed?
   a. relationships between two resources
   b. relationships between two agents
   c. relationships between a resource and an agent
   d. All of the above

DISCUSSION QUESTIONS

21.1 Often, it takes several sales calls to obtain the first order from a new customer. Why then does Figure 21-1 depict the relationship between the Call on Customer and Take Customer Orders events as 1:1?

21.2 How could an automobile dealer model the use of loaner cars, which it gives to customers for free whenever they drop off a vehicle for maintenance that will take longer than one day to complete?

21.3 In what situations would you expect to model a relationship between an agent and a resource?

21.4 Why is depreciation not represented as an event in the REA data model?

21.5 How would you model the acquisition of a digital asset, such as the purchase of software online (the software is downloaded and then installed on the purchaser's computer)?

21.6 How are the similarities and differences between the purchase of services, such as telephone service, and the purchase of raw materials reflected in an REA data model?

21.7 How would you modify the expenditure cycle REA diagram depicted in Figure 21-4 to include the return of defective products to suppliers for credit?

PROBLEMS

21.1 We-Fix-Computers, Inc., provides spare parts and service for a wide variety of computers. Customers may purchase parts to take home for do-it-yourself repairs, or they may bring their systems in for repair, in which case they pay for both the parts and the labor associated with the type of service required. Some services do not include any new parts, just a labor charge for that service. Individual customers must pay for all parts purchases in full at the time of sale. Individual customers must pay 50% down when they bring their computers in for servicing and pay the balance at pickup. Corporate customers, however, are billed monthly for all sales (parts or service). Although We-Fix-Computers, Inc., has several different banking accounts, all sales are deposited intact into its main checking account.

We-Fix-Computers, Inc. purchases its inventory of parts from more than a dozen different vendors. Orders are usually delivered the next day; sometimes, however, suppliers ship only partial orders. We-Fix-Computers pays for some of its purchases C.O.D., but usually pays by the 10th of the month for all purchases made the prior month. None of its suppliers allows it to make installment payments.

REQUIRED

Draw an integrated REA diagram for We-Fix-Computers' revenue and expenditure cycles.

21.2 The Mesa Veterinary Hospital is run by Dr. Brigitte Roosevelt. She has two employees in the office and has asked you to develop a database to help better track her data.

Dr. Roosevelt currently uses her personal computer only for word processing, but she is interested in also using it to maintain pet histories and accounting information. She is excited about the transition and is counting on you to help her through the process. She describes her daily activities as follows:

When new customers come to Mesa Veterinary Hospital, the "owners" of the pets are required to complete an introductory form. This form includes the following:

- *Owner name*
- *Address*
- *Day phone*
- *Night phone*

They are also required to provide the following information about each pet, as some people own many pets:

- *Pet name*
- *Breed*
- *Color*
- *Birth date*

Dr. Roosevelt would like to enter this information once, and then have the system retrieve it for all subsequent visits.

When customers call to make appointments, one of the office clerks asks what kind of services they require (e.g., is it a routine exam, a surgery). Dr. Roosevelt sees only one pet during each appointment. If she is going to see one owner's two pets, then two separate appointments are necessary (but scheduled back-to-back). For each appointment, Dr. Roosevelt records the pet's weight, notes the reason for the appointment, and records her diagnosis. Depending on the diagnosis, the doctor will possibly prescribe any number of medications to cure the pet. Owners are charged $125 for each appointment and must pay additionally for any medications prescribed for their pets. Dr. Roosevelt requires all pets to be brought back for another examination prior to refilling any prescriptions. Customers must pay for services and medication in full at the conclusion of their visits.

You also learn that Dr. Roosevelt orders drugs and medications from several different suppliers. She places orders weekly, on Fridays. Suppliers usually make one shipment to fill each order, but sometimes have to make additional shipments if they are currently out of stock of one or more items. In such cases, they always ship the back-ordered item as soon as they receive it from the manufacturer; they never combine such back orders with subsequent orders by Dr. Roosevelt. Suppliers bill Dr. Roosevelt monthly and expect payment in full by the 15th of the following month. A few suppliers do permit Dr. Roosevelt to make installment payments. The prices charged by suppliers for a given product may change several times during the year, so it is important to accurately store the cost of each item each time it is purchased.

Dr. Roosevelt concludes the interview by requesting that in addition to the facts mentioned, she wants the system to store the following attributes:

- Number of pets owned by each customer
- Total charge for the appointment
- Prescription price
- Drug name
- Length of appointment
- Diagnosis
- Date of appointment
- Service requested

REQUIRED

a. Given this brief overview, draw an integrated REA diagram for the Mesa Veterinary Hospital and include cardinalities.
b. As directed by your instructor, either draw the tables necessary to implement the integrated REA diagram you developed for the Mesa Veterinary Hospital or build the tables in a relational DBMS to which you have access. Be sure to include all attributes from the narrative plus the additional ones explicitly listed by Dr. Roosevelt at the conclusion of the interview. Create additional attributes only if necessary.

(This problem is adapted from one created by Dr. Julie Smith David for classroom use at Arizona State University.)

21.3 Your university hires you to implement a database system for the library network. You have interviewed several librarians, and the following summarizes these discussions:

- The library's main goal is to provide students and professors with access to books and other publications. The library, therefore, maintains an extensive collection of materials available to anyone with a valid university identification card.
- The standard procedure for lending materials is that the student or faculty member comes to one of the three campus libraries and locates the book or journal on the shelves.
- Each book is assigned three unique numbers. First, the book is assigned a number by the publisher, called the International Standard Book Number (ISBN). This number allows the publishers to track each title, and the number changes with each new edition. The second number is the Dewey decimal number, which is assigned to the title and written on the outside spine of the book. This number is used to organize the library shelves and is thus helpful to the students and faculty. It is therefore critical that this number be available to users on the online inquiry screens. The last number is a university book ID number. A different number is assigned to every book received so the library can track all copies of each book. This number is different from the other two numbers such that if the library has three copies of one book, each will have a unique university book ID number.
- When students or faculty check out books, the system must be able to track the specific copy borrowed. Each book has a magnetic strip inserted in its spine, which is used as a security measure. If someone tries to take a book without checking it out, an alarm sounds.
- In general, students and faculty have equal clout in the library. Both are able to check out most books and to check out several books at one time. No one is allowed to remove periodicals from any library. The length of time that the book may be borrowed varies, however, depending on who checks it out. Students are allowed to check out a book for several weeks; faculty may borrow books for several months.

- When patrons check out books, they take their materials to the circulation desk. At that time, the librarian scans in each item's university book ID number and the borrower's ID number. The system records a separate loan event for each book checked out, assigning each a separate loan number. At this time, each book's due date is calculated and marked on a slip located inside each book's front cover. Simultaneously, the magnetic strip is deactivated so the book may be removed from the library.
- After borrowers check out a book, they are expected to return it by its due date. In reality, everyone is allowed 30 days after the due date recorded on the checkout slip before the book is officially overdue. At that point, the book must be returned, and the borrower is assessed a $10 fine. If the book is permanently lost, then the borrower is fined $75 for the book's replacement. All fines must be paid in cash, in full. Students are not allowed to enroll for subsequent semesters until all library fines are paid; they also do not receive a diploma until all library fines are paid. Faculty must pay all outstanding fines by June 30 of each year.
- When a book is returned, the return must be entered into the system, and a unique return number is used to log the transaction. At that time, the loan record is updated to show that the book has been returned.

The following attributes have been identified as critical for the new system:

University book ID	Borrower phone number	Type of borrower (faculty or student)
Book publisher	Cash account number	
Due date	Librarian name	Librarian college degree
Loan number	Book status (on the shelf or checked out)	Actual return date
Checkout date		Borrower ID
Borrower name	Borrower's fine balance owed	Library borrowed from
Book title		Librarian number
Fine receipt number	ISBN number	Account balance
Amount received	Book return number	Total number of books in a specific library
Library name	Dewey decimal number	
Amount of fine	Borrower address	Loan status (still outstanding, or returned)
Default library where book is shelved	Book copyright date	
	Borrower e-mail address	Author name

REQUIRED

a. Draw an REA diagram for the library system. Remember to include cardinalities.

b. As directed by your instructor, either create the tables on paper that would be required to implement your REA diagram or actually build those tables in a relational DBMS to which you have access. Only use the attributes listed, unless others are absolutely necessary.

(This problem is adapted from one developed by Dr. Julie Smith David for classroom use at Arizona State University.)

21.4 Assume that Stained Glass Artistry, a new shop that specializes in making stained glass artwork, has hired you to design an integrated database that will provide the owners with the accounting information they need to effectively manage the business. Stained Glass Artistry makes a wide variety of stained glass windows for sale in its store.

A unique job order is assigned to each production run, which includes creating multiple copies of the same basic design. When raw materials are issued to employees, the issuance is documented on a prenumbered raw material issue form. The different kinds of glass needed for the product, and other materials such as copper foil or lead, are issued at one time, so that employees can efficiently produce the design.

Creating a piece of stained glass art involves several different steps, including cutting, foiling, and soldering. The owners want to track how much time each employee spends each day performing each of those various tasks.

The owners have developed raw material and direct labor standards for each design they offer. They want their AIS to track actual costs and standard costs so that they can generate reports that provide price and quantity variance information.

The owners also have provided you with the following list of facts that they want stored in the database. (*Note:* You must create appropriate primary keys for each table; this is the list of other attributes.)

Attributes in Standard Glass Artistry AIS

Date hired	Time started task	Time completed task
Style of glass (name or description)	Quantity on hand	Color of glass
Design name	Quantity to be produced	Actual cost of design
Standard hours to make design	Standard quantity of glass to use in design	Quantity issued
Wage rate	Date design produced	Standard cost of design
	Employee name	Date of birth
		Standard cost of glass

REQUIRED

a. Draw an integrated REA diagram for Stained Glass Artistry. Include both minimum and maximum cardinalities.

b. Create the set of relational tables required to implement your REA diagram for Stained Glass Artistry in a relational database.

21.5 The XYZ Company sells tools and parts to automotive repair shops. Shops call in orders; all orders received by noon are delivered the same day. Between 12:00 and 1:00, the system prints out schedules. From 1:00 to 5:00, drivers make deliveries according to the printed schedules. Typically, each driver makes between 25 and 30 deliveries each day. Each delivery is signed for by a repair shop manager; the portable laptop then uses wireless communications to transmit information about the delivery back to the XYZ company and the information is recorded as another row in the sales event table. The XYZ Company uses its own trucks to make local deliveries to its customers. It wants to track information about the use of those trucks: which employee drove which truck, to which customers did a particular truck make deliveries, which deliveries are made on which days, what was the starting and stopping mileage each day?

REQUIRED

a. Draw a partial REA diagram of the XYZ Company's revenue cycle to model these events: Taking Customer Orders, Deliveries, and the Use of Vehicles. Be sure to include cardinalities.

b. Create a set of tables (either on paper or in a relational DBMS to which you have access) to implement the REA model you developed for the XYZ Company.

21.6 Bernie's Pet Store sells pet food, toys, and supplies. Bernie, the owner, is the only person who places orders with suppliers. He is also the only person who writes checks. Suppliers ship each order individually; if they are out of an item, they back order it and ship it separately as soon as it arrives. Bernie pays each supplier monthly for all purchases made the previous month. Suppliers do not allow him to make installment payments.

Bernie has eight employees, each of whom can check in materials received from suppliers and sell merchandise to customers. Bernie pays his employees weekly from a separate checking account used only for payroll purposes.

All sales are made in-store and are paid for immediately by cash, check, or credit card.

When employees are not working the cash register or checking in merchandise, they restock shelves and clean up the premises. Bernie does not want to track each *individual* restock or clean-up event, but does want to know how much time each employee spends each day doing those tasks. He also wants to track how much time each employee spends each day receiving inventory and how much time they spend working at the cash register. He wants to be able to write queries that would show time spent by job task (restocking, cleaning, receiving, or sales) for each employee. It is not practical, however, to try to measure the time spent on individual tasks (e.g., Bernie does not want employees to track the time they start and finished unloading a shipment from supplier X, then repeat for supplier Y; similarly, he does not want to track how long it takes to ring up each individual customer at the cash register). All he wants is to know how much time each day (e.g., 3.75 hours) each employee spent performing each different type of job.

REQUIRED

Draw an integrated REA diagram for Bernie's Pet Shop. Be sure to include both payroll processing and the ability to track how employees use their time.

21.7 At Big Time University (BTU) students are allowed to purchase two basketball tickets for each home game. Each ticket contains the date of the game and the seat information, such as section, row, and individual seat number. Students pay for each game individually; that is, student sporting event passes are not used at BTU. BTU deposits the proceeds from each game into its bank.

REQUIRED

a. Prepare an REA diagram with cardinalities for the revenue cycle for BTU's basketball games. State any assumptions you may have to make concerning BTU's business policies and practices.
b. Implement your model in a set of relational tables. Be sure to specify primary keys, foreign keys, and identify at least one other attribute that should be included in each table.

21.8 Small contractors often rent special equipment for specific jobs. They need to track the equipment rented, when it is returned, and payments made to the rental company.

REQUIRED

a. Draw a partial REA diagram for the acquisition, payment, and return of rental equipment. Be sure to include cardinalities and state any assumptions you made when specifying those cardinalities.
b. Create a set of tables (either on paper or in a relational DBMS to which you have access) to implement the REA model you developed.

21.9 Answer the following multiple-choice problems.

1. The ABC Company services residential pools. Each week it comes out and cleans the pool. If necessary, it also replaces any broken equipment. The REA diagram for ABC's revenue cycle would show that each service call is linked to ____.
   a. a minimum of zero services and a minimum of zero parts
   b. a minimum of zero services and a minimum of one part
   c. a minimum of one service and a minimum of zero parts
   d. a minimum of one service and a minimum of one part

2. The ABC Company rents bicycles. Customers pay a deposit. Upon return, the bike is checked for damage and customers may be assessed additional fees. If the customer fails to return the bicycle, ABC charges the cost to replace the bicycle to the same credit card used to rent the bicycle. The revenue cycle REA diagram for ABC would show that each rental event is linked to ____.
   a. a minimum of zero return events and a minimum of zero receive cash events
   b. a minimum of zero return events and a minimum of one receive cash event
   c. a minimum of one return event and a minimum of zero receive cash events
   d. a minimum of one return event and a minimum of one receive cash event

3. The ABC Company maintains the following financial accounts: checking, savings, and investments. It has accounts in several different financial institutions. It does not have a "Petty Cash" account. ABC Company only maintains information about financial institutions where it has accounts. The REA diagram for ABC company would model the relationship between the Cash and Financial Institution entities as having ____.
   a. a minimum of zero on both sides of the relationship
   b. a minimum of zero on the Cash side of the relationship and a minimum of one on the Financial Institution side of the relationship
   c. a minimum of one on the Cash side of the relationship and a minimum of zero on the Financial Institution side of the relationship
   d. a minimum of one on both sides of the relationship
4. In an REA diagram, the employee entity can be linked to ____.
   a. Event entities
   b. Resource entities
   c. another employee entity
   d. All of the above
5. Which Production Cycle entity stores the information about the time employees spend making products?
   a. Work in Process
   b. Job Operations List
   c. Perform Job Operations
   d. None of the three tables

CASE 21-1 Practical Database Assignment

This case involves creating a database from an integrated REA diagram and then using the REA diagram to guide the writing of queries to prepare financial statements.

REQUIRED

a. Create the tables necessary to implement Figure 21-9 in a relational database. Be sure to include primary keys and other relevant attributes in each table.
b. Write the query, or set of queries, necessary to generate as many elements of financial statements as possible. For example, write the query or set of queries that would be used to calculate the amount of cash on hand, the total of accounts receivable, the total value of raw materials inventory on hand.

AIS in Action Solutions

QUIZ KEY

1. Which of the following represents the "get" side of the basic give-to-get economic exchange for a business that rents equipment and machinery?
   a. Rent Equipment [Incorrect. The Give event (Rent Equipment) is linked to two Get events: Return Rented Equipment and Receive Cash.]
   b. Receive Cash [Incorrect. The Give event (Rent Equipment) is linked to two Get events: Return Rented Equipment and Receive Cash.]
   c. Return Rented Equipment [Incorrect. The Give event (Rent Equipment) is linked to two Get events: Return Rented Equipment and Receive Cash.]
   ▶ **d.** Return Rented Equipment and Receive Cash [Correct. The Give event (Rent Equipment) is linked to two Get events: Return Rented Equipment and Receive Cash.]

2. Which resource in the HR/payroll cycle is seldom implemented in a database?
   a. Skills [Incorrect. Information about skills is important to record.]
   ▶ b. Employee Time [Correct. The employee time represents the right to use an employee's time—but time is a noninventoriable asset and is consumed when it is acquired, so this resource is seldom, if ever, implemented as a table in a database.]
   c. Applicants [Incorrect. Applicants are agents and information about them must be recorded.]
   d. Disburse Cash [Incorrect. Cash disbursements is an event about which information must be recorded.]

3. Joe's Computers makes service calls to repair computer equipment. Some calls involve only labor charges, and others involve both labor and parts. Which of the following correctly models the relationship between the Service Calls event and Parts Inventory?

   a. 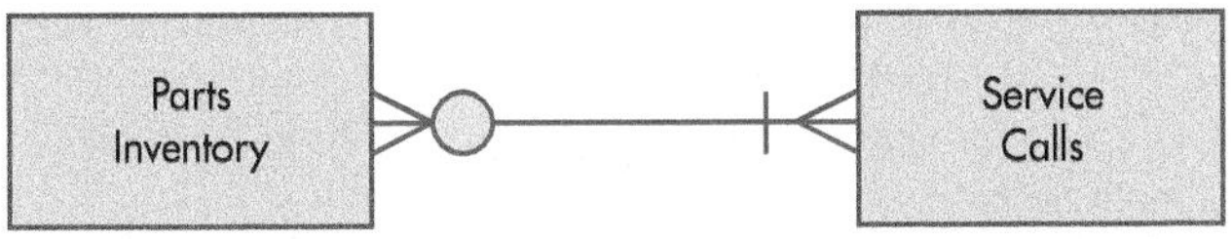

   [Incorrect. This shows that every part must be linked to use on at least one service call.]

   b. 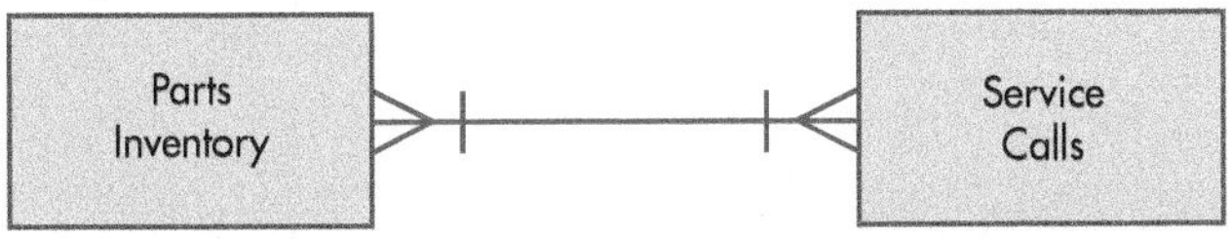

   [Incorrect. This shows that every part must be linked to at least one service call and that every service call must involve use of at least one part.]

   ▶ c. 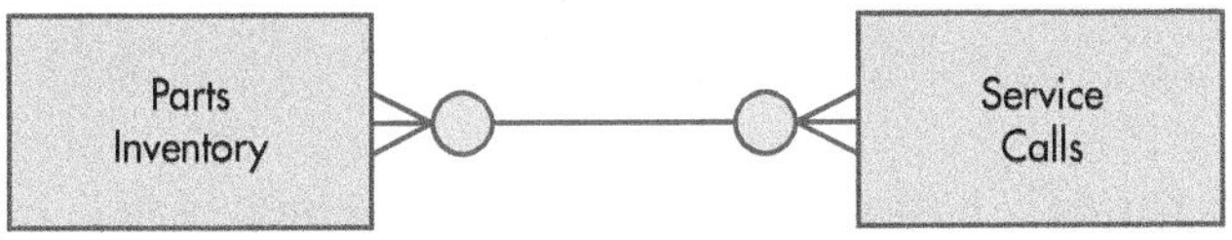

   [Correct. This shows that some parts may not be linked to any service call, but others could be linked to many service calls. It also shows that some service calls do not involve the use of any parts, although other service calls may involve the use of multiple parts.]

   d. 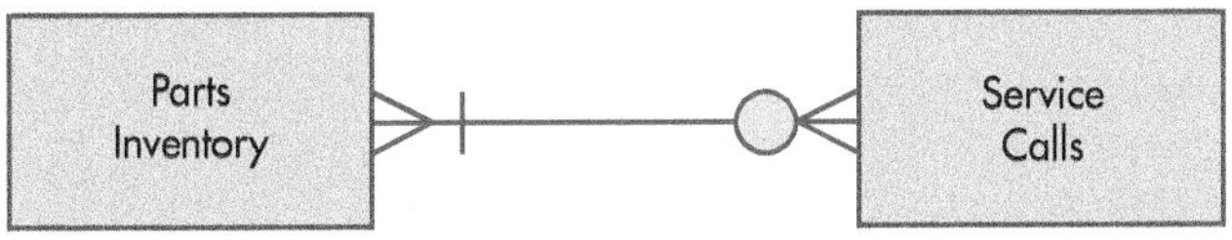

   [Incorrect. This shows that every service call must involve the use of at least one part.]

4. Which entity contains information about the components used to manufacture a particular product?
   a. Inventory [Incorrect. The Bill of Materials entity stores the list of ingredients (components) used to manufacture a given product.]
   b. Job Operations List [Incorrect. The Job Operations list entity identifies the steps required to manufacture the product, but the list of components used is stored in the Bill of Materials entity.]
   ▶ c. Bill of Materials [Correct. The Bill of Materials entity stores the list of components used to manufacture a given product.]
   d. Machine Operations List [Incorrect. The Machine Operations List entity stores the steps and processes involving machinery used to manufacture a product.]

5. Which of the following production cycle event involves the *acquisition* of a resource (i.e., it is a Get event)?

a. Perform Machine Operations [Incorrect. The Perform Machine Operations event records information about the use of machinery and equipment; i.e., it is a Give event.]

b. Perform Job Operations [Incorrect. The Perform Job Operations event records information about the use of labor to manufacture a product; i.e., it is a Give event.]

▶ c. Work in Process [Correct. The Work in Process event collects and aggregates all the costs associated with creating a finished product.]

d. Issue Raw Materials [Incorrect. The Issue Raw Materials event records information about the raw materials used to manufacture a product; it is an example of a Give event.]

6. Which production cycle event collects data used to calculate payroll?

a. Perform Job Operations [Incorrect. The Perform Job Operations event collects data about the use of labor; it is used to calculate product costs.]

▶ b. Time Worked [Correct. This event captures the acquisition of time from employees, in return for which they must be paid.]

c. Time Used [Incorrect. This event collects data about the use of labor; it is used to calculate product costs.]

d. Disburse Cash [Incorrect. This event records the paying of wages, but not their calculation.]

7. The give-to-get economic exchange associated with debt financing involves which two events?

a. Issue Debt and Receive Cash [Incorrect. The Issue Debt is a special instance of the Receive Cash Event.]

▶ b. Issue Debt and Disburse Cash [Correct. Issuing debt results in receipt of cash and subsequent repayments of that debt.]

c. Receive Cash and Disburse Cash [Incorrect. The Issue Debt event is used to record the facts about borrowing events, which differ from the facts collected about cash receipts for sales.]

d. None of the above [Incorrect.]

8. Acme manufacturing tracks information about customer calls by sales representative. Although many calls involve demonstrations of products, some are purely to build relationships. What is the correct way to model the relationship between Inventory and the Call on Customer event?

a. 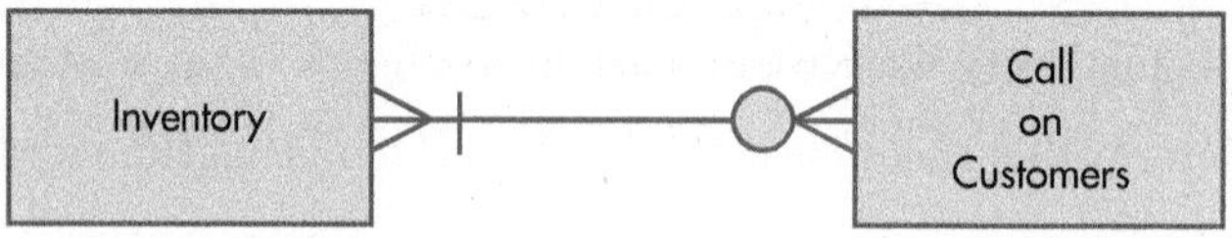

[Incorrect. This shows that every call must involve demonstration of at least one product.]

▶ b. 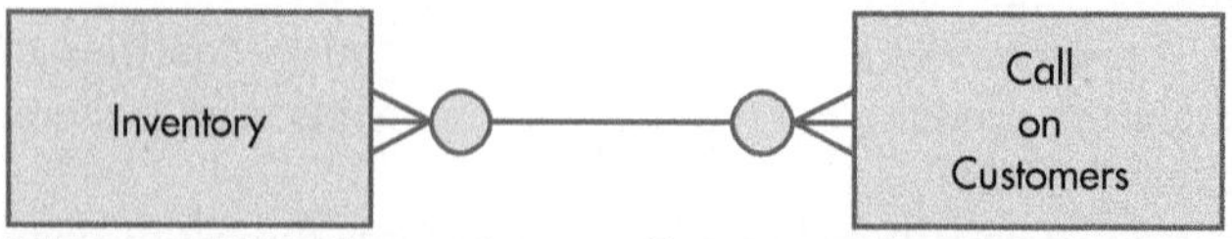

[Correct. This shows that a call may not involve the demonstration of any products, although it could demonstrate multiple products. At the same time, it correctly shows that some products may not be linked to any sales calls, whereas others may be linked to many different sales calls.]

c. 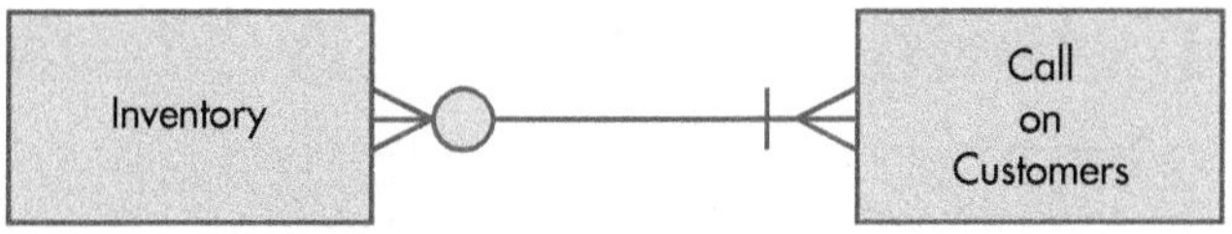

[Incorrect. This shows that every product must be linked to a sales call.]

d. 

[Incorrect. This both shows that every product must be linked to a sales call and that every sales call must involve the demonstration of at least one product.]

9. Acme manufacturing wants to track post-sales customer service by collecting information about each customer service call: who called, when the call happened, which customer service representative handled the call, how long the call lasted, which sales transaction prompted the call, and which inventory items were discussed. The relationship between the Sales and Post-Sales Service Call events should most likely be modeled as which of the following?

a. 1:1 [Incorrect. Some customers may make more than one service call related to a specific sales transaction and they may also discuss several sales transactions during the same service call.]

b. 1:N [Incorrect. Some customers may make more than one service call related to a specific sales transaction and they may also discuss several sales transactions during the same service call.]

▶ **c.** M:N [Correct. Some customers may make more than one service call related to a specific sales transaction and they may also discuss several sales transactions during the same service call.]

d. 0:N [Incorrect. There is no such thing as a 0:N relationship.]

10. Which of the following additions to the basic REA template are sometimes needed?

a. relationships between two resources [Incorrect. This chapter introduced an example of this to model location information, but it also introduced examples of relationships between two agents and between a resource and an agent.]

b. The relationship between two agents [Incorrect. This chapter introduced an example of this to model information about supervisors, but it also introduced examples of relationships between two resources and between a resource and an agent.]

c. The relationship between a resource and an agent [Incorrect. This chapter introduced an example of this to model responsibility for a resource, but it also introduced examples of relationships between two resources and between two agents.]

▶ **d.** All of the above [Correct. Examples of each of the above were introduced in this chapter.]

Appendix: Extending the REA Model to Include Information About Policies

Chapters 19–21 explained how the REA model can be used to describe the contents of a database used to support an organization's transaction processing requirements. The various REA diagrams presented in those three chapters depicted the actual resources, events, and agents involved in carrying out the organization's business processes. The basic rules presented for developing an REA diagram are designed to ensure the accurate recording of things that exist, the events that occurred, and the specific agents who participated in those events. The REA model can be extended to also explicitly represent information about an organization's business policies. Doing so provides the opportunity to model information about such things as standards and internal controls. This Appendix provides a brief introduction to this topic.

Extending the REA model to incorporate information about policies[1] that represent what should, could, or must happen involves the use of two new data modeling concepts: Type and Group entities. Type entities are used to depict "is-a-kind-of" relationships and Group entities are used to represent "is-a-member-of" relationships. Table 21A-1 shows that both kinds of entities exist at the policy level and that they are mapped to entities at the operational level. For example, each individual sales transaction represents a specific type of sale (Internet, In-store, Mail Order, etc.). Similarly, each individual employee is linked to one, and only one, specific class of employees (buyers, cashiers, salespeople, etc.); in other words, each individual employee is a type of employee. In addition, Figure 21A-1 shows that employees are also assigned to (members of) specific divisions in the organization.

Type and Group entities are similar in that both are abstractions that represent sets of objects. They differ in terms of semantics and attributes. Type entities contain attributes that apply to every individual entity of that type. For example, Table 21A-1 shows that the Employee Type entity contains the attributes Role, Base Pay, and Salary Range and the Sales Type entity contains attributes about whether to charge for shipping, sales tax, and so on. In contrast, Group entities contain attributes that apply to the set as a whole and are often derived values. Thus, Table 21A-1 shows that the Group entity called Division contains attributes such as average salary and the number of employees, which represent properties of the entire set calculated from the values of every entity that belongs to that group.

The attributes of Type entities provide a way to specify policy information (e.g., valid salary ranges, shipping charges) so that the system can enforce and validate adherence to the organization's business policies. For example, an individual employee's salary can be compared to the permissible salary range for that class of employee. Similarly, the system can decide whether to collect sales tax on a particular sales transaction by checking the stated policy

TABLE 21A-1 Policy-Level Entities and Relationships

Policy-Level Entities	**Primary Key**	**Foreign Keys**	**Other Attributes**
Division	Division number		Budgeted sales this period average salary, number of employees
Employee type	Employee type number		Role, base pay, permissible salary range
Sales type	Sales type number	Employee type number	Venue (Internet, mail-order, in-store, etc.), collect sales tax, shipping charges (Y/N)
Operational-Level Entities	**Primary Key**	**Foreign Keys**	**Other Attributes**
Employees	Employee number	Division number, employee type number	Name, date hired, salary, etc.
Sales	Invoice number	Employee number, sales type number	Date, time, comments

[1] The material in this Appendix is based on the article, "Policy-Level Specification in REA Enterprise Information Systems" by Guido L. Geerts and William E. McCarthy, in the *Journal of Information Systems* (20:2, Fall 2006): pp. 37–63.

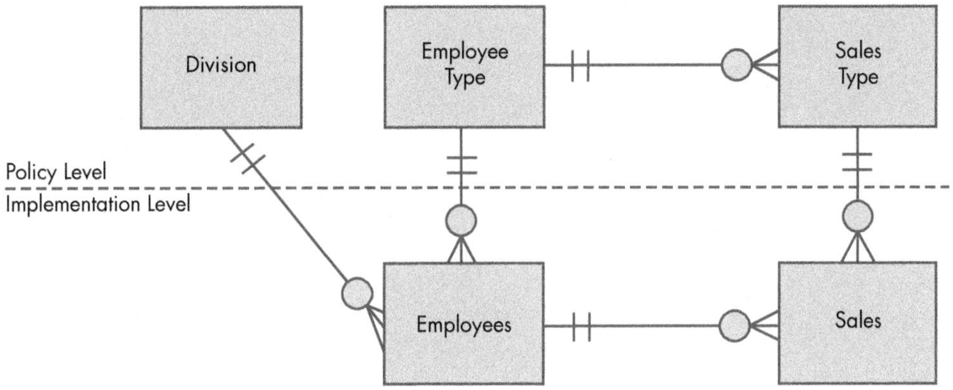

FIGURE 21A-1
Extending the REA Model to Include Policy-Level Information

for that type of sale. The attributes of Group entities provide a way to represent budgetary information, such as sales goals for each division, in a manner that facilitates creating reports that compare actual results (data stored in the operational-level entities) with plans (data stored in the policy-level entities).

Finally, Figure 21A-1 also shows that there can be relationships among Type entities. This provides another means to specify business policies and internal controls. For example, including Employee Type as an attribute in the Sales Type entity provides a mechanism for specifying that only sales staff can make sales to customers; similar linkages can be used to specify that only buyers can order inventory from suppliers, that only cashiers can write checks, and so on.

The objective of this Appendix was to provide an introduction to how the REA model can be extended to incorporate information about organizational policies and internal controls. If you take a database course, you will learn more about abstractions like Type and Group entities and the concepts of typification, generalization, and aggregation. You may also learn more about policy-level REA issues on your own by reading the article cited as the reference source for this Appendix.

The Systems Development Process

PART

VI

Andrea Danti/123RF

CHAPTER **22**

Introduction to Systems Development and Systems Analysis

CHAPTER **23**

AIS Development Strategies

CHAPTER **24**

Systems Design, Implementation, and Operation

CHAPTER

22

Introduction to Systems Development and Systems Analysis

LEARNING OBJECTIVES

After studying this chapter, you should be able to:

1. Explain the five phases of the systems development life cycle, and discuss the people involved in systems development and the roles they play.
2. Explain the importance of systems development planning, and describe the types of plans and planning techniques used.
3. Discuss the various types of feasibility analysis, and calculate economic feasibility using capital budgeting techniques.
4. Explain why system changes trigger behavioral reactions, what form this resistance to change takes, and how to avoid or minimize the resulting problems.
5. Discuss the key issues, objectives, and steps in systems analysis.

INTEGRATIVE CASE Shoppers Mart

Ann Christy is the new controller of Shoppers Mart, a rapidly growing chain of discount stores. To assess how she can better serve Shoppers Mart, she held meetings with top management and visited with store managers and employees. Her findings are as follows:

1. Store managers cannot obtain information other than what is contained in periodic, preformatted reports. If they request information from several functional areas, the system bogs down.
2. Because timely information about product sales is not available, stores are often out of popular items and overstocked with products customers are not buying.
3. Management is concerned about losing market share to rivals with better prices and selection. The current system cannot provide the information management needs to solve this problem.

Ann is convinced that Shoppers Mart needs a new information system that is flexible, efficient, and responsive to user needs. Ann knows the new system will not be successful without management's complete support. Before asking for approval and funding for the new system, Ann met with systems development to ask the following questions:

Dusit/Shutterstock

1. What process must be followed to obtain and implement a new system?
2. What planning is necessary to ensure the system's success? Who will be involved, and how? Do special committees need to be formed? What resources are needed? How should the planning be documented?
3. How will employees react to a new system? What problems might this change cause, and how can they be minimized?
4. How should the new system be "sold" to top management? How can expected costs and benefits be quantified to determine whether the system will be cost-effective?

Introduction

Because we live in a highly competitive and ever-changing world, at any given time most organizations are improving or replacing their information systems. It is estimated that each year corporate America spends more than $300 billion on more than 200,000 software projects. Companies change their systems for the following reasons:

- ***Changes in user or business needs.*** Increased competition, business growth or consolidation, downsizing operations, mergers and divestitures, or new regulations can alter an organization's structure and purpose. To remain responsive, the system must change.
- ***Technological changes.*** As technology advances and becomes less costly, organizations adopt new technologies. For example, a New York utility downsized from a mainframe to a client/server system and eliminated 100 clerical positions. The new system does much more than the old one, including handling workflow management, user contact, database queries, automatic cash processing, and voice/data integration.
- ***Improved business processes.*** Many companies change their systems to improve inefficient business processes. At Nashua, an office supply manufacturer, processing a customer's telephone order took up to two days because three separate systems had to be accessed. The new system requires three minutes.
- ***Competitive advantage.*** Companies invest heavily in technology to increase the quality, quantity, and speed of information; to improve products or services; to lower costs; and to provide other competitive advantages.
- ***Productivity gains.*** Information systems can automate clerical tasks, decrease task performance time, and provide employees with specialized knowledge. Carolina Power and Light eliminated 27% of its information systems staff with a system that significantly outperformed the old one.
- ***Systems integration.*** Organizations with incompatible systems integrate them to remove incompatibilities and to consolidate databases. The U.S. Department of Defense (DOD) is trying to integrate more than 700 separate systems.

- ***Systems age and need to be replaced.*** As systems age and are updated numerous times, they become less stable and eventually need to be replaced. Focus 22-1 describes how the Internal Revenue Service is trying to replace its aged information system.

Developing quality, error-free software is a difficult, expensive, and time-consuming task. Most software development projects deliver less, cost more, and take longer than expected. A study by Standish Group found that 70% of software development projects were late, 54% were over budget, 66% were unsuccessful, and 30% were canceled before completion. An American Management Systems study revealed that 75% of all large systems are not used, are not used as intended, or generate meaningless reports or inaccurate data. Nike implemented a forecasting system that did not work and had to take a multimillion-dollar inventory write-down. The system told Nike to order $90 million of shoes that did not sell, while it had $100 million of orders on popular models that it could not meet.

Skipping or skimping on systems development processes causes runaways that consume time and money and produces no usable results, as illustrated by the following examples:

- Pacific Gas & Electric pulled the plug on a system that was five years in development. It was a financial disaster with no usable product.
- When jeweler Shane Co. upgraded its enterprise resource planning (ERP) system, cost and deadline overruns pushed the cost from $10 million to more than $36 million and caused inventory problems that, combined with a faltering economy, resulted in bankruptcy.
- California's Department of Motor Vehicles attempted to overhaul its system. Developed in 1965, it was so difficult to maintain that it took 18 programmers working an entire year to add a Social Security number file to the drivers' license and vehicle registration system. After seven years, $44 million, and not a single usable application, the project was canceled.

This chapter discusses five topics. The first is the systems development life cycle, the process followed to obtain and implement a new accounting information system (AIS). The second is the planning activities needed during development. The third is preparing a feasibility analysis. The fourth is the behavioral aspects of change that must be dealt with to implement a new system. The fifth topic is systems analysis, the first step in the systems development life cycle.

FOCUS 22-1 The IRS Attempts to Replace Its Aging Information System

The IRS recognizes that it needs to modernize its 40-year-old system to provide better customer service, improve compliance with the nation's tax laws, and reduce the volume of paper tax returns. The system processes and stores all taxpayer records and takes in more than $2 trillion a year.

Critics claim the fragile and antiquated system has been updated so many times that a software meltdown is a very real possibility. In a worst-case scenario, the IRS would not know who had paid taxes, hundreds of billions of dollars of revenue would not be collected, and the government would have to borrow money to meet its obligations, throwing the financial markets into a panic.

The need to modernize is no secret; the IRS has been trying for some time. Years ago, the IRS spent $3.3 billion on an upgrade effort that failed. More recently, the IRS embarked on an $8 billion effort called the Business Systems Modernization (BSM) program. This program involves more than 20,000 major tasks and scores of organizations and is one of the largest and most complex information system challenges in history. At the same time, the IRS is trying to change its management culture and the way it is organized; some critics claim both are more out of date than its information system.

The IRS cannot change the entire system at once; instead, it will occur in stages over 15 to 20 years. The effort has been compared to rebuilding all New York City buildings, streets, sewers, and communication and transportation systems, all while its inhabitants do not notice the changes as they go about their daily lives.

How is the IRS doing? Reports are not encouraging. The BSM spent almost $4 million on a project that was canceled. The effort has had a number of significant cost overruns, management delays, performance shortfalls, and missed project completion dates. One report indicates the project runs a "significant risk of not succeeding."

Systems Development

This section discusses the systems development life cycle and the people involved in systems development.

THE SYSTEMS DEVELOPMENT LIFE CYCLE

Ann Christy asked the manager of systems development to explain the process Shoppers Mart uses to design and implement a new system. He sketched the five-step **systems development life cycle (SDLC)** shown in Figure 22-1 and briefly explained here.

systems development life cycle (SDLC) - A five-step process used to design and implement a new system.

SYSTEMS ANALYSIS The first step in systems development is **systems analysis**, where the information needed to purchase, develop, or modify a system is gathered. To better use limited resources, development requests are screened and prioritized. If a decision is made to move forward, the nature and scope of the proposed project is identified, the current system is surveyed to identify its strengths and weaknesses, and the feasibility of the proposed project is determined. If the proposed project is feasible, the information needs of system users and managers are identified and documented. These needs are used to develop and document the systems requirements used to select or develop a new system. A systems analysis report is prepared and submitted to the information systems steering committee.

systems analysis - First SDLC step where the information needed to purchase, develop, or modify a system is gathered.

CONCEPTUAL DESIGN During **conceptual design**, the company decides how to meet user needs. The first task is to identify and evaluate appropriate design alternatives, such as buying software, developing it in-house, or outsourcing system development to someone else. Detailed specifications outlining what the system is to accomplish and how it is to be controlled are developed. This phase is complete when conceptual design requirements are communicated to the information systems steering committee.

conceptual design - Second SDLC step where analysts decide how to meet user needs, identify and evaluate design alternatives, and develop detailed specifications for what the system is to accomplish and how it is to be controlled.

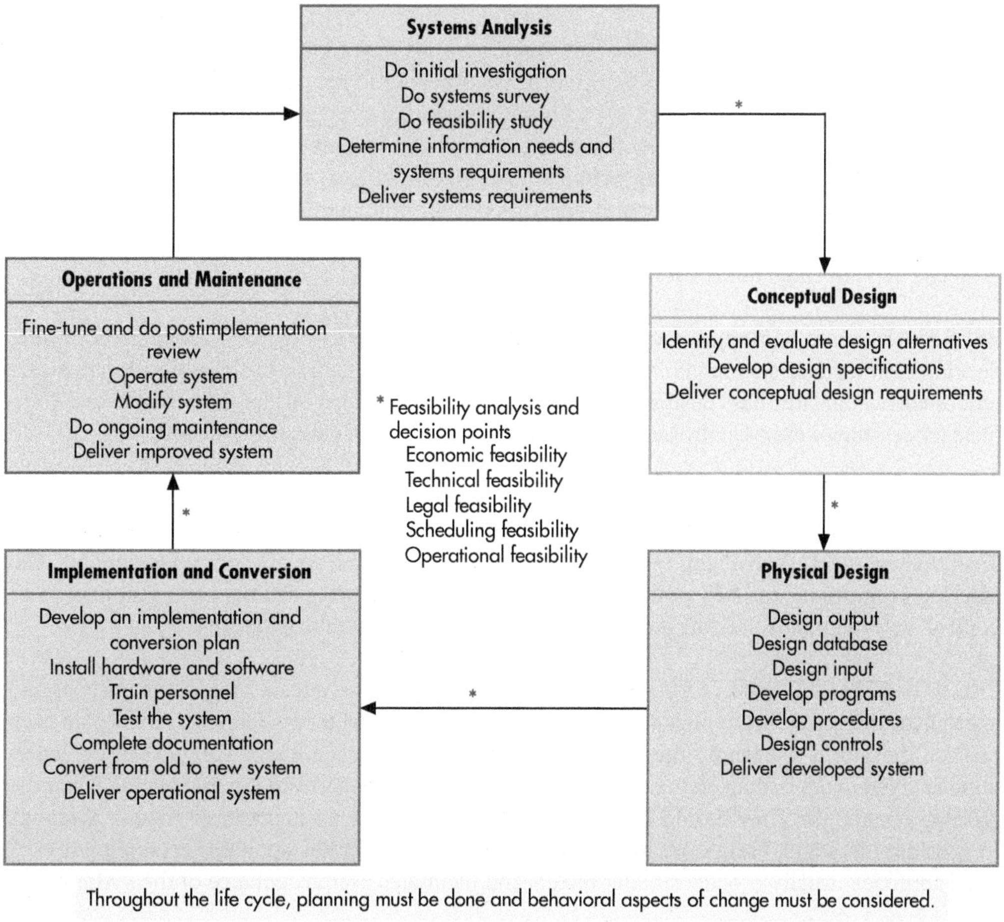

FIGURE 22-1
The Systems Development Life Cycle

physical design - Third SDLC step where broad, user-oriented conceptual design requirements are translated into the detailed specifications used to code and test software, design input/output, create files/databases, develop procedures, and implement controls.

PHYSICAL DESIGN During **physical design**, the company translates the broad, user-oriented conceptual design requirements into the detailed specifications used to code and test computer programs, design input and output documents, create files and databases, develop procedures, and build controls into the new system. This phase is complete when the results of the physical system design are communicated to the information systems steering committee.

implementation and conversion - Fourth SDLC step where the company hires and trains employees, tests and modifies procedures, establishes standards and controls, completes documentation, moves to the new system, and detects and corrects design deficiencies.

IMPLEMENTATION AND CONVERSION All the elements and activities of the system come together in the **implementation and conversion** phase. An implementation and conversion plan is developed and followed, new hardware and software are installed and tested, employees are hired and trained or existing employees relocated, and processing procedures are tested and modified. Standards and controls for the new system are established and system documentation completed. The organization converts to the new system and dismantles the old one, makes needed adjustments, and conducts a postimplementation review to detect and correct design deficiencies. When the operational system is delivered, system development is complete. A final report is prepared and sent to the information systems steering committee.

operations and maintenance - Fifth SDLC step where the system is periodically reviewed and necessary modifications and improvements are made.

OPERATIONS AND MAINTENANCE During **operations and maintenance**, the new system is periodically reviewed and modifications are made as problems arise or as new needs become evident. Eventually, a major modification or system replacement is necessary, and the SDLC begins again.

In addition to these five phases, three activities (planning, managing behavioral reactions to change, and assessing the ongoing feasibility of the project) are performed throughout the life cycle. These three activities, as well as systems analysis, are discussed in this chapter. The different approaches to obtaining an AIS are discussed in Chapter 23. The last four SDLC phases are explained in Chapter 24.

THE PLAYERS

A number of people must cooperate to successfully develop and implement an AIS.

MANAGEMENT Management's most important systems development roles are to emphasize the importance of involving users in the process, to provide support and encouragement for development projects, and to align systems with corporate strategies. Other key roles include establishing system goals and objectives, selecting system department leadership and reviewing their performance, establishing policies for project selection and organizational structure, and participating in important system decisions. User management determines information requirements, assists analysts with cost and benefit estimates, assigns staff to development projects, and allocates funds for development and operation.

USERS AIS users communicate their information needs to system developers. As project development team or steering committee members, they help manage systems development. As requested, accountants help design, test, and audit the controls that ensure the accurate and complete processing of data. Control issues are discussed in depth in Chapters 8 through 13.

information systems steering committee - High-level management who plan and oversee the IS function, setting IS policies that govern the AIS, ensuring top-management guidance and control, and coordinating and integrating systems activities.

INFORMATION SYSTEMS STEERING COMMITTEE An executive-level **information systems steering committee** plans and oversees the information systems function. It consists of high-level management, such as the controller and systems and user-department management. The steering committee sets AIS policies; ensures top-management participation, guidance, and control; and facilitates the coordination and integration of systems activities.

PROJECT DEVELOPMENT TEAM Each development project has a team of systems analysts and specialists, managers, accountants, and users to guide its development. Team members plan each project, monitor it to ensure timely and cost-effective completion, make sure proper consideration is given to the human element, and communicate project status to top management and the steering committee. They should communicate frequently with users and hold regular meetings to consider ideas and discuss progress so that there are no surprises upon project completion. A team approach usually produces better results and facilitates user acceptance of the system.

SYSTEMS ANALYSTS AND PROGRAMMERS **Systems analysts** help users determine their information needs, study existing systems and design new ones, and prepare the specifications used by computer programmers. Analysts interact with employees throughout the organization to bridge the gap between the user and technology. Analysts are responsible for ensuring that the system meets user needs.

Computer programmers write and test programs using the specifications developed by systems analysts. They also modify and maintain existing computer programs.

systems analysts - People who help users determine their information needs, study existing systems and design new ones, and prepare specifications used by computer programmers.

computer programmers - People who write and test programs using the specifications developed by the analysts and modify and maintain existing computer programs.

EXTERNAL PLAYERS Customers, vendors, external auditors, and governmental entities play a role in systems development. For example, Walmart vendors are required to implement and use electronic data interchange (EDI).

Planning Systems Development

This section discusses the planning performed throughout the SDLC (see Figure 22-1).

Imagine that you built a two-bedroom house. Over the years, you add two bedrooms, a bathroom, a family room, a recreation room, a deck, and a two-car garage, and you expand the kitchen. Without a long-range plan, your house will end up as a poorly organized and costly patchwork of rooms surrounding the original structure. This scenario also applies to an AIS; the result is a costly and poorly integrated system that is difficult to operate and maintain.

Planning has distinct advantages. It enables the system's goals and objectives to correspond to the organization's overall strategic plan. Systems are more efficient, subsystems are coordinated, and there is a sound basis for selecting new applications for development. The company remains abreast of the ever-present changes in information technology (IT). Duplication, wasted effort, and cost and time overruns are avoided. The system is less costly and easier to maintain. Finally, management is prepared for resource needs, and employees are prepared for the changes that will occur.

When development is poorly planned, a company must often return to a prior phase and correct errors and design flaws, as shown in Figure 22-2. This is costly and results in delays, frustration, and low morale.

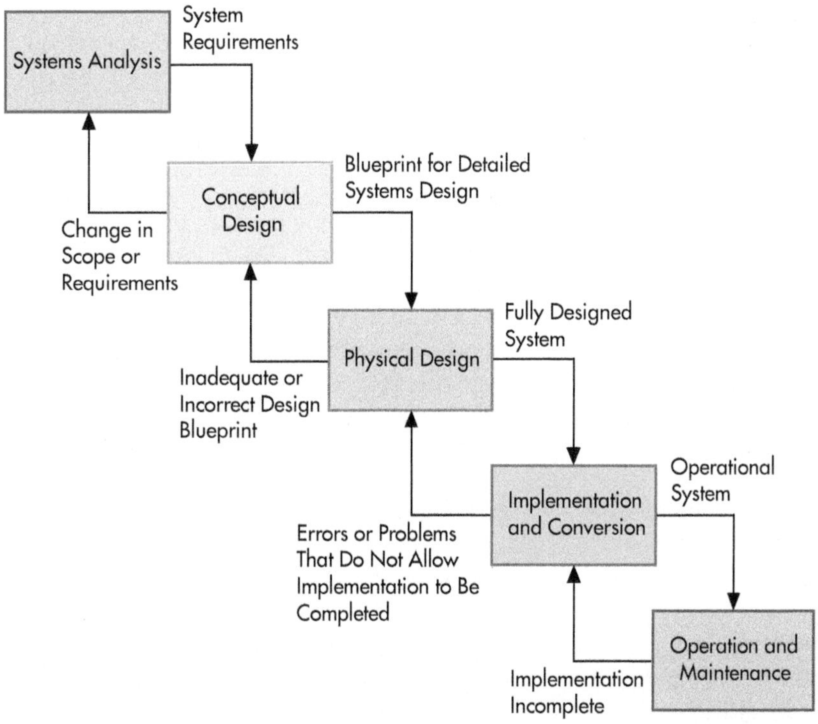

FIGURE 22-2
Reasons for Returning to a Prior SDLC Phase

project development plan - Document showing project requirements (people, hardware, software, and financial), a cost–benefit analysis, and how a project will be completed (modules or tasks to be performed, who will perform them, and completion dates).

master plan - Describes what a system will consist of, how it will be developed, who will develop it, when it will be developed, how needed resources will be acquired, the status of projects in process, the prioritization of planned projects, and the prioritization criteria.

Two systems development plans are needed:

1. ***Project development plan.*** A **project development plan**, prepared by the project team, contains a cost–benefit analysis, developmental and operational requirements (people, hardware, software, and financial), and a schedule of the activities required to develop and operate the new application.
2. ***Master plan.*** A long-range **master plan**, prepared by the information systems steering committee, specifies what the system will consist of, how it will be developed, who will develop it, how needed resources will be acquired, and where the AIS is headed. It describes the status of projects in process, prioritizes planned projects, describes the criteria used for prioritization, and provides development timetables. Projects with the highest priority are developed first. A three-year planning horizon is common, with the plan updated quarterly or monthly. Table 22-1 shows the master plan components at Shoppers Mart.

As explained in Focus 22-2, inadequate planning was one reason why Electronic Data Systems (EDS) lost a significant amount of money in its contract with the U.S. military.

TABLE 22-1 Components of the Master Plan at Shoppers Mart

Organizational Goals and Objectives	**Status of Systems Being Developed**
Company mission statement and goals	Proposed systems priorities
Information systems strategic plan and goals	Approved systems development
Organizational constraints	Proposals under consideration
Organizational approach to AIS	Development timetables and schedules
Organizational and AIS priorities	**Forecast of Future Developments**
Inventory and Assessments	Forecasts of information needs
Current systems	Technological forecasts
Approved systems	Environmental/regulatory forecasts
Current hardware	Audit and control requirements
Current software	External user needs
Current AIS staff	
Assessment of strengths and weaknesses	

FOCUS 22-2 EDS Loses Billions in Its Contract with the Navy

The U.S. military hired Electronic Data Systems (EDS) to develop a secure network to link 350,000 computers at 4,000 Navy sites. The $10 billion contract resulted in significant headaches and estimated losses of $1.7 billion. EDS made the following mistakes:

- With little military experience, EDS did not plan for their delays and requests. Congress delayed the project for 18 months by asking for network-performance tests EDS was not used to handling. EDS also failed to plan for the 200 technical hurdles the military imposed.
- EDS did not verify Navy estimates, such as the 5,000 software programs to be installed on the new PCs; in reality, there were 67,000. EDS underestimated cost and time requirements to customize individual computers. They also had to revamp the Navy's old software before it could be installed.
- EDS did not plan and coordinate project tasks. When EDS went to Navy bases to install the computers, they did not have proper military clearances and some sailors and officers were busy or overseas.
- EDS did not give the Navy adequate instructions.
- EDS could not complete an order without a service member's rank, but EDS did not tell the Navy to send the rank.
- EDS did not track computer inventory. Some servicemen ordered PCs and then changed their orders to laptops. EDS did not require them to cancel the first order, so two computers were prepared. Duplicate and incomplete orders sat in warehouses for months.

To get the project back on track, EDS made some changes. Rather than installing computers at many different locations simultaneously, it installed computers at the largest bases first, reused expensive hardware, installed the warehoused computers before buying new ones, and customized computers by job function rather than by individual.

PLANNING TECHNIQUES

PERT and Gantt charts are techniques for scheduling and monitoring systems development activities. The **program evaluation and review technique (PERT)** requires that all activities and the precedent and subsequent relationships among them be identified. The activities and relationships are used to draw a PERT diagram, which is a network of arrows and nodes representing project activities that require an expenditure of time and resources and the completion and initiation of activities. Completion time estimates are made, and the **critical path**—the path requiring the greatest amount of time—is determined. If any activity on the critical path is delayed, then the whole project is delayed. If possible, resources can be shifted to critical path activities to reduce project completion time.

program evaluation and review technique (PERT) - A way to plan, develop, coordinate, control, and schedule systems development activities; all activities, and precedent and subsequent relationships among activities, are identified and shown on a PERT diagram.

critical path - The PERT path requiring the greatest amount of time to complete a project; if a critical path activity is delayed, the whole project is delayed.

A **Gantt chart** (Figure 22-3) is a bar chart with project activities on the left-hand side and units of time across the top. For each activity, a bar is drawn from the scheduled starting date to the ending date, thereby defining expected project completion time. As activities are completed, they are recorded on the Gantt chart by filling in the bar; thus, at any time it is possible to determine which activities are on schedule and which are behind. The primary advantage of the Gantt chart is the ability to show graphically the entire schedule for a large, complex project, including progress to date and status. A disadvantage is that the charts do not show the relationships among project activities.

Gantt chart - A bar graph used for project planning. It shows project activities on the left, units of time across the top, and the time each activity is expected to take as a horizontal bar.

Feasibility Analysis

As shown in Figure 22-1, a **feasibility study** (or business case) is prepared during systems analysis and updated as necessary during the SDLC. The extent varies; for a large-scale system, it is generally extensive, whereas one for a desktop system might be informal. The feasibility study is prepared with input from management, accountants, systems personnel, and users.

feasibility study - An investigation to determine whether it is practical to develop a new application or system.

At major decision points, the steering committee reassess feasibility to decide whether to terminate a project, proceed unconditionally, or proceed if specific problems are resolved. Early go/no-go decisions are particularly important because each subsequent SDLC step requires more time and monetary commitments. The further along a development project is, the less likely it is to be canceled if a proper feasibility study has been prepared and updated.

Although uncommon, systems have been scrapped after implementation because they did not work or failed to meet an organization's needs. Bank of America, for example, hired a software firm to replace a 20-year-old system used to manage billions of dollars in institutional trust accounts. After two years of development, the new system was implemented despite warnings that it was not adequately tested. Ten months later the system was scrapped, top executives resigned, and the company took a $60 million write-off. The company lost

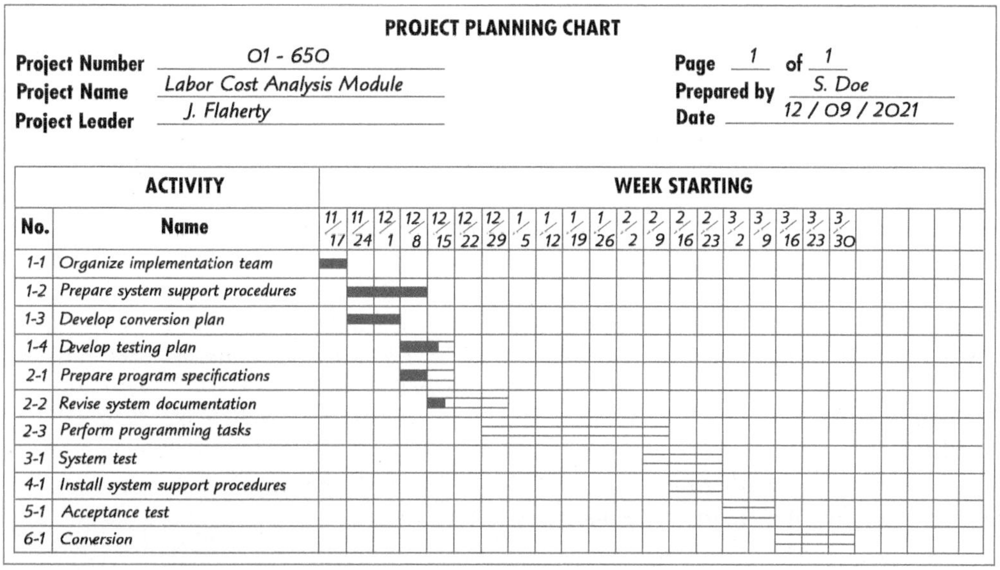

FIGURE 22-3
Sample Gantt Chart

100 institutional accounts with $4 billion in assets. Focus 22-3 describes a Blue Cross/Blue Shield project that was scrapped after six years and a $120 million investment.

There are five important aspects to be considered during a feasibility study:

economic feasibility - Determining whether system benefits justify the time, money, and resources required to implement it.

technical feasibility - Determining if a proposed system can be developed given the available technology.

legal feasibility - Determining if a proposed system will comply with all applicable federal and state laws, administrative agency regulations, and contractual obligations.

scheduling feasibility - Determining if a proposed system can be developed and implemented in the time allotted.

operational feasibility - Determining if the organization has access to people who can design, implement, and operate the proposed system and if employees will use the system.

1. ***Economic feasibility.*** Will system benefits justify the time, money, and resources required to implement it?
2. ***Technical feasibility.*** Can the system be developed and implemented using existing technology?
3. ***Legal feasibility.*** Does the system comply with all applicable federal and state laws, administrative agency regulations, and contractual obligations?
4. ***Scheduling feasibility.*** Can the system be developed and implemented in the time allotted?
5. ***Operational feasibility.*** Does the organization have access to people who can design, implement, and operate the proposed system? Will people use the system?

Economic feasibility is now discussed in greater depth. Ann's feasibility analysis for Shoppers Mart is shown in Table 22-8 at the end of this chapter.

CAPITAL BUDGETING: CALCULATING ECONOMIC FEASIBILITY

During systems design, alternative approaches to meeting system requirements are developed. Too often, companies overspend on technology because IT costs and payoffs are not measured and evaluated like other corporate investments. Merrill Lynch overcame significant philosophical and bureaucratic obstacles to implement a return-on-investment program for IT expenditures. Merrill Lynch now requires a 15% cash return on equity investment within five years, and all IT purchases are made by business, finance, and IT professionals working together.

capital budgeting model - A return-on-investment technique used to compare estimated benefits and costs to determine whether a system is cost beneficial.

Many organizations now use capital budgeting return-on-investment techniques to evaluate the economic merits of the alternatives. In a **capital budgeting model**, benefits and costs are estimated and compared to determine whether the system is cost beneficial. Benefits and costs not easily quantifiable are estimated and included. If they cannot be accurately estimated, they are listed, and their likelihood and expected impact on the organization evaluated. Tangible and intangible benefits include cost savings, improved customer service, productivity increases, improved data processing, better decision making, greater management control, increased job satisfaction, and increased employee morale. Initial outlay and operating costs are shown in Table 22-2. Between 65% and 75% of yearly systems-related expenditures are for maintaining current systems.

FOCUS 22-3 Blue Cross/Blue Shield Abandons Runaway

Blue Cross/Blue Shield of Massachusetts had high hopes for its new information system. After six years and $120 million, however, the System 21 project was behind schedule and way over budget.

Although system failures of this magnitude are unusual, KPMG found that 35% of major information system projects become a runaway—a project millions of dollars over budget and months or years behind schedule. Other surveys show that almost every Fortune 200 company has had at least one runaway.

One reason for the problems was that Blue Cross hired an independent contractor to develop the software but neglected to appoint an in-house person to coordinate and manage the project. Nor did management establish a firm set of priorities regarding essential features and the sequence of application development.

The developers presented claims processing software to Blue Cross, but managers and users were not happy and requested numerous changes. As a result, the whole project was delayed. This led to ever-increasing cost overruns. By the time System 21 was launched, Blue Cross had fallen far behind its competitors' ability to process an ever-swelling paperwork load. During the six-year period, it lost 1 million subscribers and came close to bankruptcy.

Blue Cross learned a painful lesson. It abandoned the system it spent six years building and turned its hardware over to EDS. Fortunately, although the system died, the patient survived.

TABLE 22-2 Initial Outlay and Operating Costs

Hardware
- Central processing unit
- Peripherals
- Communications hardware
- Special input/output devices
- Replacement, upgrade, expansion costs

Software
- Application, system, general-purpose, utility, and communications software
- Updated versions of software
- Application software design, programming, modification, testing, and documentation

Staff
- Supervisors
- Analysts and programmers
- Computer operators
- Input (data conversion) personnel
- Hiring, training, and relocating staff
- Consultants

Supplies and Overhead
- Preprinted forms
- Data storage devices
- Supplies (paper, toner)
- Utilities and power

Maintenance/Backup
- Hardware/software maintenance
- Backup and recovery operations
- Power supply protection

Documentation
- Systems documentation
- Training program documentation
- Operating standards and procedures

Site Preparation
- Air-conditioning, humidity, dust controls
- Physical security (access)
- Fire and water protection
- Cabling, wiring, and outlets
- Furnishings and fixtures

Installation
- Freight and delivery charges
- Setup and connection fees

Conversion
- Systems testing
- File and data conversions
- Parallel operations

Financial
- Finance charges
- Legal fees
- Insurance

The following are three commonly used capital budgeting techniques:

1. ***Payback period.*** The **payback period** is the number of years required for the net savings to equal the initial cost of the investment. The project with the shortest payback period is usually selected.
2. ***Net present value (NPV).*** All estimated future cash flows are discounted back to the present, using a discount rate that reflects the time value of money. The initial outlay costs are deducted from the discounted cash flows to obtain the **net present value (NPV)**. A positive NPV indicates the alternative is economically feasible. The highest positive NPV is usually selected.
3. ***Internal rate of return (IRR).*** The **internal rate of return (IRR)** is the effective interest rate that results in an NPV of zero. A project's IRR is compared with a minimum acceptable rate to determine acceptance or rejection. The proposal with the highest IRR is usually selected.

Payback, NPV, and IRR are illustrated in the feasibility analysis shown in Table 22-8.

payback period - A return-on-investment technique used to calculate the number of years required for the net savings of a system to equal its initial cost.

net present value (NPV) - A return-on-investment technique that discounts all estimated future cash flows back to the present using a discount rate that reflects the time value of money.

internal rate of return (IRR) - A return-on-investment technique that calculates the interest rate that makes the present value of total costs equal to the present value of total savings.

Behavioral Aspects of Change

Individuals participating in systems development are change agents who are continually confronted by resistance to change. The **behavioral aspects of change** are crucial because the best system will fail without the support of the people it serves. Niccolo Machiavelli discussed resistance to change more than 400 years ago:

> *It must be considered that there is nothing more difficult to carry out, nor more doubtful of success, nor more dangerous to handle, than to initiate a new order of things. For the reformer has enemies in all those who could profit by the old order, and only lukewarm defenders in all those who could profit by the new order. This*

behavioral aspects of change - The positive and negative ways people react to change; managing these behavioral reactions is crucial to successfully implementing a new system.

lukewarmness arises partly from fear of their adversaries, who have the laws in their favor, and partly from the incredulity of mankind, who do not truly believe in anything new until they have had an actual experience of it.[1]

Organizations must be sensitive to and consider the feelings and reactions of persons affected by change. This section discusses the type of behavioral problems that can result from change.

WHY BEHAVIORAL PROBLEMS OCCUR

An individual's view of change, as either good or bad, usually depends on how that individual is personally affected by it. Management views change positively if it increases profits or reduces costs. Employees view the same change as bad if their jobs are terminated or adversely affected.

To minimize adverse behavioral reactions, one must understand why resistance takes place. Some of the more important factors include the following:

- ***Fear.*** People fear the unknown, losing their jobs, losing respect or status, failure, technology and automation, and the uncertainty accompanying change.
- ***Top-management support.*** Employees who sense a lack of top-management support for change wonder why they should endorse it.
- ***Experience with prior changes.*** Employees who had a bad experience with prior changes are more reluctant to cooperate.
- ***Communication.*** Employees are unlikely to support a change unless the reasons behind it are explained.
- ***Disruptive nature of change.*** Requests for information and interviews are distracting and place additional burdens on people, causing negative feelings toward the change that prompted them.
- ***How change is introduced.*** Resistance is often a reaction to the methods of instituting change rather than to change itself. The rationale used to sell the system to top management may not be appropriate for lower-level employees. The elimination of menial tasks and the ability to advance and grow are often more important to users than increasing profits and reducing costs.
- ***Biases and emotions.*** People with emotional attachments to their duties or coworkers may not want to change if those elements are affected.
- ***Personal characteristics and background.*** Generally speaking, the younger and more highly educated people are, the more likely they are to accept change. Likewise, the more comfortable people are with technology, the less likely they are to oppose changes.

HOW PEOPLE RESIST CHANGE

Behavioral problems begin when people find out a change is being considered. Initial resistance is often subtle, manifested by failure to provide developers with information, tardiness, or subpar performance. Major behavioral problems often occur when the new system is implemented and the change becomes a reality. Focus 22-4 explains the resistance the DOD experienced.

Resistance often takes one of three forms: aggression, projection, or avoidance.

aggression - Resistance to change intended to destroy, cripple, or weaken system effectiveness, such as increased error rates, disruptions, or deliberate sabotage.

AGGRESSION **Aggression** is behavior that destroys, cripples, or weakens system effectiveness, such as increased error rates, disruptions, or deliberate sabotage. After one organization introduced an online AIS, data input devices had honey poured on them, were run over by forklifts, or had paper clips inserted in them. Employees also entered erroneous data into the system. In another organization, disgruntled workers punched in to an unpopular supervisor's department and worked in other areas. This adversely affected the supervisor's performance evaluation because he was charged for hours that did not belong to him.

projection - Resistance to change that blames anything and everything on the new system, such that it becomes the scapegoat for all real and imagined problems and errors.

PROJECTION **Projection** is blaming the new system for everything that goes wrong. The system becomes the scapegoat for all real and imagined problems and errors. If these criticisms are not controlled or answered, system integrity can be damaged or destroyed.

---

[1] Niccolo Machiavelli, *The Prince*, translated by Luigi Rice, revised by E.R.P. Vincent (New York: New American Library, 1952).

FOCUS 22-4 Resistance to Change at the Department of Defense

The U.S. Department of Defense (DOD) has a budget of $417 billion, 3.3 million employees, and more than $1 trillion in assets. It also has one of the most antiquated and inefficient information systems in the world and cannot produce accurate accounting information or get a clean audit. Only a few of their 4,000 systems communicate effectively with other systems. Most systems require data that are transferred between systems to be manually reentered.

The DOD has been trying to modernize its AIS for more than 20 years, at a cost of more than $35 billion. After three notable failures, it is trying a fourth time. The Business Management Modernization Project's (BMMP) goal is to integrate DOD systems and business processes and produce a user-transparent system. Unfortunately, many people would rather not see the DOD realize this transparency. Past reforms failed because system developers could not break through the barriers DOD agencies created to protect their processes, procedures, and chains of command.

Users resist integration because what is optimal for one user is often suboptimal for the DOD. Government bureaucrats resist because an integrated, transparent system will reveal many unnecessary or obsolete programs that further personal agendas. For example, managers are often promoted for their ability to generate, receive funding for, and operate programs, regardless of their effectiveness. Senators and congressional representatives resist because a new system could adversely affect their ability to steer spending to constituents and thereby get reelected.

To overcome these behavioral problems, the DOD is trying to convince the armed forces to rid themselves of their "program protection" mindset. In one notable success, the Air Force now promotes personnel based on actions that improve the Air Force as a whole, rather than on actions that defend a specific turf or program.

AVOIDANCE **Avoidance** is ignoring a new AIS in the hope that the problem (the system) will eventually go away. Davis Controls, a struggling manufacturer, processed its orders using e-mail, but pertinent information was frequently lost or forgotten. Davis invested $300,000 in software that efficiently captured customer information, properly handled purchase orders, helped managers make better daily decisions, and made it possible to process four times as many transactions. Employees avoided it, even though the CEO explained the system's benefits and told them the company's survival and their jobs were at stake. Finally, the CEO disabled the uncooperative employees' e-mail accounts and terminated the employees who continued to avoid the system.

avoidance - Resistance to change where users ignore a new IS in the hope that the new system will eventually go away.

PREVENTING BEHAVIORAL PROBLEMS

The human element, which is often the most significant problem a company encounters in implementing a system, can be improved by observing the following guidelines:

- ***Obtain management support.*** Appoint a champion who can provide resources and motivate others to assist and cooperate with systems development.
- ***Meet user needs.*** It is essential that the system satisfy user needs.
- ***Involve users.*** Those affected by the system should participate in its development by making suggestions and helping make decisions. To avoid misunderstandings, users should be told which suggestions are being used and how, and which are not and why. Participation is ego enhancing, challenging, and intrinsically satisfying. Users who participate in development are more knowledgeable, better trained, and more committed to using the system.
- ***Allay fears, and stress new opportunities.*** Users are vitally interested in how system changes affect them personally. Address their concerns and provide assurances (to the extent possible) that job losses and responsibility shifts will not occur—for example, through relocation, attrition, and early retirement. If employees are terminated, provide severance pay and outplacement services. Emphasize that the system may provide advancement opportunities and greater job satisfaction because the job has become more interesting and challenging.

- ***Avoid emotionalism.*** When logic vies with emotion, it rarely stands a chance. Emotional issues should be allowed to cool, they should be handled in a nonconfrontational manner, or they should be sidestepped.
- ***Provide training.*** Effective use and support are not possible if users do not understand the system. User training needs are often underestimated.
- ***Reexamine performance evaluation.*** Performance standards and criteria should be reevaluated to ensure that they are congruent with the new system.
- ***Keep communication lines open.*** Everyone affected by systems development should have an attitude of trust and cooperation. If employees become hostile, it is difficult to change their attitude and to implement the system. As soon as possible, employees should be told what changes are being made and why and be shown how the new system benefits them. This helps employees identify with the company's efforts and feel they are key players in the company's future goals and plans. It also helps prevent rumors and misunderstandings. Employees should be told whom they can contact if they have questions or concerns.
- ***Test the system.*** The system should be properly tested prior to implementation to minimize initial bad impressions.
- ***Keep the system simple, and humanize it.*** Avoid complex systems that cause radical changes. Make the change as simple as possible by conforming to existing organizational procedures. The new system is unlikely to be accepted if individuals believe the computer is controlling them or has usurped their positions.
- ***Control users' expectations.*** A system is sold too well if users have unrealistic expectations of its capabilities and performance. Be realistic when describing the merits of the system.

These guidelines are time-consuming and expensive, and workers may skip them to speed systems development and installation. However, the problems caused by not following the guidelines are usually more expensive and time-consuming to fix than to prevent.

Systems Analysis

request for systems development - A written request for a new or improved system that describes the current system's problems, the reasons for the change, and the proposed system's objectives, benefits, and costs.

When a new or improved system is needed, a written **request for systems development** is prepared. The request describes the current problems, the reasons for the change, the proposed system's objectives, and its anticipated benefits and costs. The five steps in the analysis phase and their objectives are shown in Figure 22-4 and discussed in this section.

INITIAL INVESTIGATION

initial investigation - A preliminary investigation to determine whether a proposed new system is both needed and feasible.

An **initial investigation** is conducted to screen the requests for systems development. The exact nature of the problem(s) must be determined. In some instances, the perceived problem is not the real problem. A government accountant once asked a consultant to develop an AIS to produce the information he needed regarding fund expenditures and available funds. An investigation showed that the system provided the information, and he did not understand the reports he received.

The project's scope (what it should and should not accomplish) is determined. Scope creep (adding additional requirements to the scope after it has been agreed to) is a real problem. Because of scope creep, a plan to have Census Bureau employees compile and transmit 2010 census information to headquarters with handheld computers was scrapped after two years of work. After spending $595 million on handhelds, the Census Bureau reverted back to pen-and-paper census taking.

A new AIS is useful when problems result from lack of information, inaccessibility of data, and inefficient data processing. A new AIS is not the answer to organizational problems. Likewise, if a manager lacks organizational skills, or if failure to enforce existing procedures causes control problems, a new AIS is not the answer. The initial investigation should also

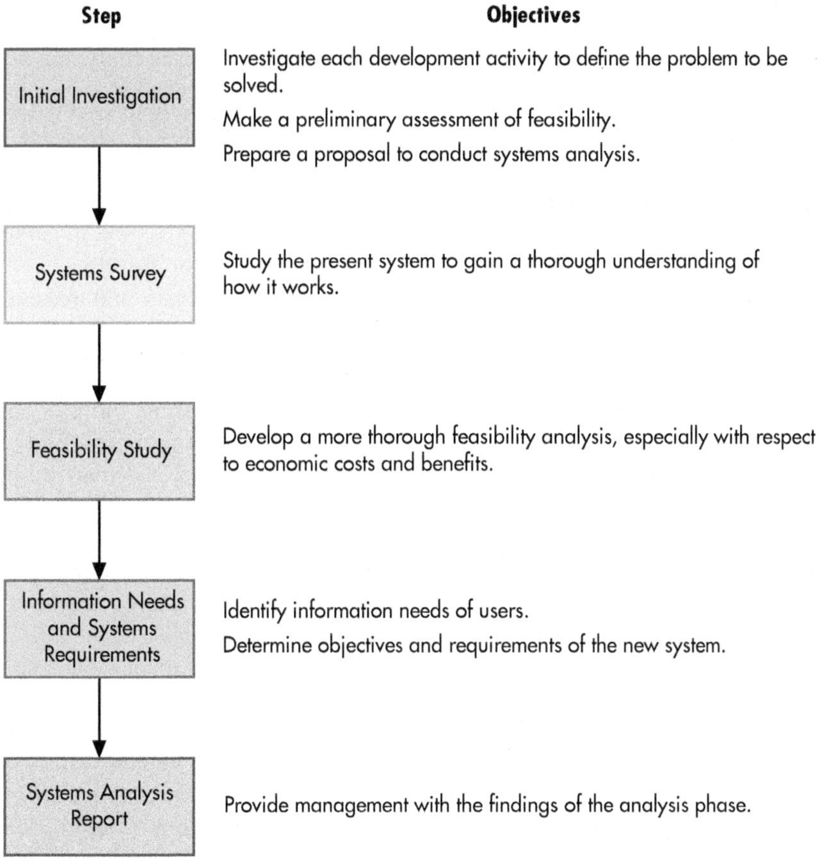
Step
Objectives
Initial Investigation
Investigate each development activity to define the problem to be solved.
Make a preliminary assessment of feasibility.
Prepare a proposal to conduct systems analysis.
Systems Survey
Study the present system to gain a thorough understanding of how it works.
Feasibility Study
Develop a more thorough feasibility analysis, especially with respect to economic costs and benefits.
Information Needs and Systems Requirements
Identify information needs of users.
Determine objectives and requirements of the new system.
Systems Analysis Report
Provide management with the findings of the analysis phase.

FIGURE 22-4
Steps in Systems Analysis

determine a project's viability and preliminary costs and benefits, and it should recommend whether to initiate the project as proposed, modify it, or abandon it.

A **proposal to conduct systems analysis** is prepared for approved projects. The project is assigned a priority and added to the master plan. Table 22-3 shows the information contents of a proposal to conduct systems analysis.

proposal to conduct systems analysis - A request to complete the systems analysis phase for a project that makes it through the initial investigation.

TABLE 22-3 Table of Contents for Reports Prepared During Systems Analysis at Shoppers Mart

Proposal to Conduct Systems Analysis	Systems Survey Report	Systems Analysis Report
Table of Contents	**Table of Contents**	**Table of Contents**
i. Executive Summary ii. System Problems and Opportunities iii. Goals and Objectives of Proposed System iv. Project Scope v. Anticipated Costs and Benefits vi. Participants in Development Project vii. Proposed System Development Tasks and Work Plan viii. Recommendations	i. Executive Summary ii. System Goals and Objectives iii. System Problems and Opportunities iv. Current System Operations A. Policies, Procedures, and Practices Affecting System B. System Design and Operation (Intended and Actual) C. System Users and Their Responsibilities D. System Outputs, Inputs, and Data Storage E. System Controls F. System Strengths, Weaknesses, and Constraints G. Costs to Operate System v. User Requirements Identified	i. Executive Summary ii. System Goals and Objectives iii. System Problems and Opportunities iv. Project Scope v. Relationship of Project to Overall Strategic Information Systems Plan vi. Current System Operations vii. User Requirements viii. Feasibility Analysis ix. System Constraints x. Recommendations for New System xi. Proposed Project Participants and Work Plan xii. Summary xiii. Approvals xiv. Appendix of Documents, Tables, Charts, Glossary

SYSTEMS SURVEY

systems survey - An extensive study of the current AIS.

A **systems survey** is an extensive study of the current AIS that has the following objectives:

- Gain an understanding of company operations, policies, procedures, and information flow; AIS strengths and weaknesses; and available hardware, software, and personnel.
- Make preliminary assessments of current and future processing needs, and determine the extent and nature of the changes needed.
- Develop working relationships with users, and build support for the AIS.
- Collect data that identify user needs, conduct a feasibility analysis, and make recommendations to management.

Data about the current AIS is gathered from employees and from documentation such as organizational charts and procedure manuals. External sources include consultants, customers and suppliers, industry associations, and government agencies. The advantages and disadvantages of four common methods of gathering data are summarized here and in Table 22-4.

An *interview* gathers answers to "why" questions. Care must be taken to ensure that personal biases, self-interest, or a desire to say what the employee thinks the interviewer wants to hear does not produce inaccurate information. Ann's Shoppers Mart interviews were successful because of her approach and preparation. For each interview, Ann made an appointment, explained the purpose beforehand, indicated the amount of time needed, and arrived on time. Before each session, Ann studied the interviewee's responsibilities and listed points she wanted to cover. Ann put each interviewee at ease by being friendly, courteous, and tactful. Her questions dealt with the person's responsibilities, how she interacted with the AIS, how the system might be improved, and the person's information needs. Ann let the interviewee do most of the talking and paid special attention to nonverbal communication because subtle overtones and body language can be as significant as direct responses to questions. Ann took notes, augmented them with detailed impressions shortly after the interview, and asked permission to tape especially important interviews.

Questionnaires are used when the amount of information to be gathered is small and well defined, is obtained from many people or from those who are located elsewhere, or is intended to verify data from other sources. Questionnaires take relatively little time to administer, but developing a quality questionnaire can be challenging and requires significant time and effort.

TABLE 22-4 Advantages and Disadvantages of Data-Gathering Methods

	Advantages	Disadvantages
Interviews	Can answer "why" questions Interviewer can probe and follow up Questions can be clarified Builds positive relationships with interviewee Builds acceptance and support for new system	Time-consuming Expensive Personal biases or self-interest may produce inaccurate information
Questionnaires	Can be anonymous Not time-consuming Inexpensive Allows more time to think about responses	Does not allow in-depth questions or answers Cannot follow up on responses Questions cannot be clarified Impersonal; does not build relationships Difficult to develop Often ignored or completed superficially
Observation	Can verify how system actually works, rather than how it should work Results in greater understanding of the system	Time-consuming Expensive Difficult to interpret properly Observed people may alter behavior
Systems Documentation	Describes how system should work Written form facilitates review, analysis	Time-consuming May not be available or easy to find

Observation is used to verify information gathered using other approaches and to determine how a system actually works, rather than how it should work. It is difficult to interpret observations because people may change their normal behavior or make mistakes when they know they are being observed. Identifying what is to be observed, estimating how long it will take, obtaining permission, and explaining what will be done and why can maximize the effectiveness of observation. The observer should not make value judgments and should document notes and impressions as soon as possible.

Systems documentation describes how the system is intended to work. Throughout the survey, the project team should be alert to differences between intended and actual systems operation as they provide important insights into problems and weaknesses.

Systems analysis work is documented so it can be used throughout the development project. Documentation consists of questionnaire copies, interview notes, memos, document copies, and models. **Physical models** illustrate *how* a system functions by describing document flow, computer processes performed, the people performing them, and the equipment used. **Logical models** focus on essential activities (*what* is being done) and the flow of information, not on the physical processes of transforming and storing data. Table 22-5 lists analysis and design tools and techniques used to create an AIS and identifies the chapter where each is discussed.

Once data gathering is complete, the team evaluates the AIS's strengths and weaknesses to develop ideas for designing and structuring the new AIS. When appropriate, strengths are retained and weaknesses corrected.

The systems survey culminates with a **systems survey report**. Table 22-3 shows the table of contents for the Shoppers Mart systems survey report. The report is supported by documentation such as memos, interview and observation notes, questionnaire data, file and record layouts and descriptions, input and output descriptions, copies of documents, E-R diagrams, flowcharts, and data flow diagrams.

systems documentation - A complete description of how the system is supposed to work, including questionnaire copies, interview notes, memos, document copies, and models.

physical models - Descriptions of how systems function by describing document flow, computer processes performed, the people performing them, and the equipment used.

logical models - System descriptions that focus on what essential activities are performed and the flow of information irrespective of how the flow is actually accomplished.

systems survey report - A report that summarizes all the activities that took place during the systems survey, including all relevant documentation.

FEASIBILITY STUDY

At this point, the thorough feasibility analysis discussed earlier in the chapter is conducted to determine the project's viability. The feasibility analysis is updated regularly as the project proceeds and costs and benefits become clearer.

INFORMATION NEEDS AND SYSTEMS REQUIREMENTS

Once a project is deemed feasible, the company identifies the information needs of users and documents systems requirements. Table 22-6 is an example of systems requirements.

Determining information needs is a challenging process because of the sheer quantity and variety of information that must be specified. In addition, it may be difficult for employees to articulate their information needs, or they may identify them incorrectly. According to *CIO* magazine, 70% of project failures are due to insufficient, inaccurate, or outdated systems requirements. Figure 22-5 is a humorous view of the types of communication problems associated with this process.

When Corning Corporation investigated the ophthalmic pressings it manufactures, it found that 35% of its drafting documents contained errors. Drafting errors are increasingly

TABLE 22-5 Systems Analysis and Design Tools and Techniques

Agile methodologies (Chapter 23)	Forms design checklist (Chapter 24)
Business process diagrams (Chapter 3)	Gantt charts (Chapter 22)
CASE (Chapter 23)	PERT charts (Chapter 22)
Data dictionary (Chapter 4)	Prototyping (Chapter 23)
Data flow diagrams (Chapter 3)	REA data models (Chapter 19)
E-R diagrams (Chapter 19)	Record layouts (Chapter 4)
Flowcharts (Chapter 3)	

TABLE 22-6 Possible Contents of System Requirements

Processes	Business process descriptions, including what is to be done and by whom
Data elements	The name, size, format, source, and significance of required data elements
Data structure	How the data elements will be organized into logical records
Outputs	Description of the purpose, frequency, and distribution of system outputs
Inputs	Description of contents, source, and person responsible for system inputs
Documentation	How the new system and each subsystem will operate
Constraints	Deadlines, schedules, security requirements, staffing limitations, and statutory or regulatory requirements
Controls	Controls to ensure the accuracy and reliability of inputs, outputs, and processing
Reorganizations	Organizational reorganization needed to meet users' information needs, such as increasing staff levels and adding new job functions

more expensive to correct at each subsequent manufacturing stage: \$250 before toolmakers cut the tools, \$20,000 before production begins, and \$100,000 after the tools are sold. Several corrective actions reduced the error rates from 35% to 0.2%. The same cost relationships exist in systems development; error correction costs increase as development proceeds through the SDLC.

System objectives, such as those shown in Table 22-7, are the elements most vital to an AIS's success. It is difficult for a system to satisfy every objective. For example, designing adequate internal controls is a trade-off between the objectives of economy and reliability.

Because organizational constraints make it difficult to develop all AIS components simultaneously, the system is divided into modules that are developed and installed independently. When changes are needed, only the affected module is changed. The modules must be properly integrated into a workable system.

A system's success often depends on the ability to cope with organizational constraints. Common constraints include governmental agency requirements, management policies, lack of qualified staff, user capabilities and attitudes, technology, and limited finances. To maximize system performance, these constraints must be minimized.

FIGURE 22-5
Communication Problems in Systems Analysis and Design

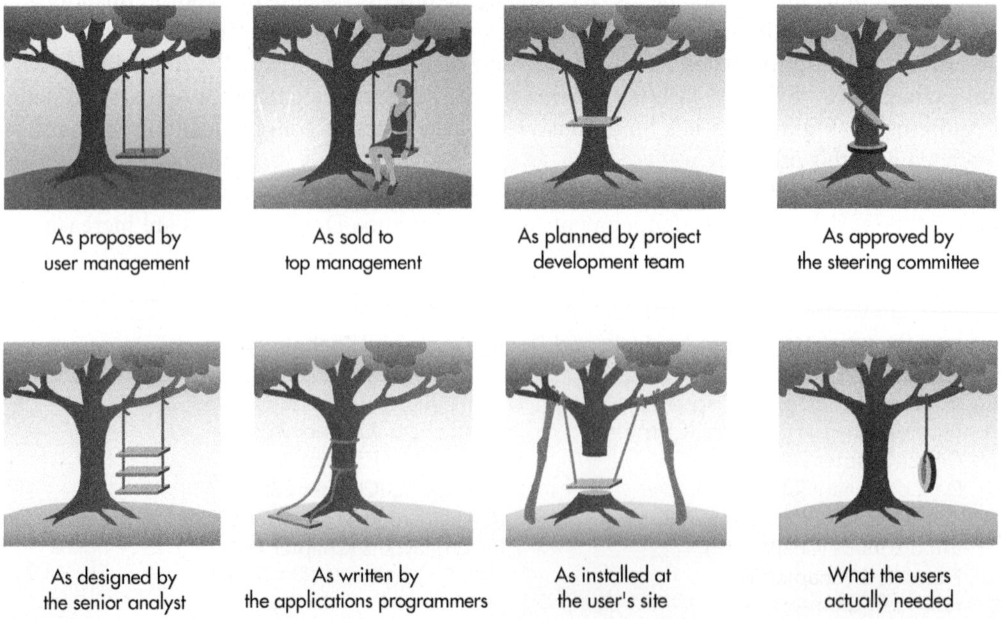

TABLE 22-7 AIS Objectives

Usefulness	Information output should help management and users make decisions.
Economy	System benefits should exceed the cost.
Reliability	System should process data accurately and completely.
Availability	Users should be able to access the system at their convenience.
Timeliness	Crucial information is produced first, less important items as time permits.
Customer service	Customer service must be courteous and efficient.
Capacity	System capacity must be sufficient to handle periods of peak operation and future growth.
Ease of use	System should be user-friendly.
Flexibility	System should be able to accommodate reasonable requirement changes.
Tractability	System is easily understood and facilitates problem solving and future development.
Auditability	Auditability is built into the system from the beginning.
Security	Only authorized users are granted access to or allowed to change system data.

The following four strategies are used to determine AIS requirements:

1. ***Ask users what they need.*** This is the simplest and fastest strategy, but many people do not understand their needs. They know their job but may be unable to break it down into the individual information elements they use. It is sometimes better to ask what decisions they make and what processes they are involved in and then design systems to address their answers. Users must think beyond current information needs so that new systems do not simply replicate current information in improved formats.
2. ***Analyze external systems.*** If a solution already exists, do not "reinvent the wheel."
3. ***Examine existing systems.*** Determine if existing modules are used as intended, may be augmented by manual tasks, or may be avoided altogether. This approach helps determine whether a system can be modified or must be replaced.
4. ***Create a prototype.*** When it is difficult to identify requirements, a developer can quickly rough out a system for users to critique. Users identify what they like and dislike about the system and request changes. This iterative process of looking at what is developed and improving it continues until users agree on their needs. Prototyping is discussed in Chapter 23.

Detailed AIS requirements that explain exactly what the system is to produce are created and documented. The requirements are supported by sample input and output forms, as well as charts, so users can conceptualize the system. A nontechnical summary of important user requirements and development efforts to date is often prepared for management. The project team meets with the users, explains the requirements, and obtains their approval. When an agreement is reached, user management signs the system requirements documents to indicate approval.

SYSTEMS ANALYSIS REPORT

The concluding step in systems analysis is preparing a **systems analysis report** to summarize and document analysis activities. The Shoppers Mart systems analysis report, shown in Table 22-3, shows the information typically contained in the report.

systems analysis report - Comprehensive report summarizing systems analysis that documents the findings of analysis activities.

A go/no-go decision is made up to three times during systems analysis: first, during the initial investigation, to determine whether to conduct a systems survey; second, at the end of the feasibility study, to determine whether to proceed to the information requirements phase; and third, at the completion of the analysis phase, to decide whether to proceed to conceptual systems design. The remaining phases in the SDLC are discussed in the next two chapters.

Summary and Case Conclusion

After an extensive analysis of Shoppers Mart's current system and core business processes, Ann Christy has proposed some changes. She has asked the corporate office to produce daily sales data for each store to help them adapt quickly to customer needs and to help suppliers avoid stockouts and overstocking. Shoppers Mart will coordinate buying at the corporate office to minimize inventory levels and negotiate lower wholesale prices. Stores will electronically send daily orders to the corporate office. Based on store orders and warehouse inventory, the corporate office will send purchase orders to suppliers. Suppliers will process orders and ship goods to regional warehouses or directly to the stores the day orders are received. Each store will have the flexibility to respond to local sales trends and conditions by placing local orders. Accounts payable will be centralized so payments can be made electronically.

Ann reviews the proposed system with the legal department and the AIS staff. She is told it complies with all legal considerations and is technologically feasible. Top management and the information systems steering committee will decide how to allocate time and resources for the project and will communicate all staff assignments to systems management and personnel.

Ann's team conducts an economic feasibility study (see Table 22-8) and determines that the project makes excellent use of funds. The team estimates that initial outlay costs for the system are $5 million. The team estimates recurring operating costs and expected savings for years 1 through 6, which are expected to rise from year to year. Ann calculates the net annual savings and then calculates the after-tax cash savings for each year.

Payback occurs in the fourth year when the savings net of taxes of $6,266,800 exceed the costs of $5,000,000.

TABLE 22-8 Economic Feasibility of Shoppers Mart's New Information System

	Initial Outlay	Year 1	Year 2	Year 3	YEAR 4	Year 5	Year 6
Initial Outlay Costs							
Hardware	$2,000,000						
Software	400,000						
Training	200,000						
Site preparation	200,000						
Initial systems design	2,000,000						
Conversion	200,000						
Total initial outlays	$5,000,000						
Recurring Costs							
Hardware expansion			$260,000	$300,000	$340,000	$380,000	$400,000
Software			150,000	200,000	225,000	250,000	250,000
Systems maintenance		$60,000	120,000	130,000	140,000	150,000	160,000
Personnel costs		500,000	800,000	900,000	1,000,000	1,100,000	1,300,000
Communication charges		100,000	160,000	180,000	200,000	220,000	250,000
Overhead		300,000	420,000	490,000	560,000	600,000	640,000
Total costs		$960,000	$1,910,000	$2,200,000	$2,465,000	$2,700,000	$3,000,000
Savings							
Clerical cost savings		$600,000	$1,200,000	$1,400,000	$1,600,000	$1,800,000	$2,000,000
Working capital savings		900,000	1,200,000	1,500,000	1,500,000	1,500,000	1,500,000
Profits from sales increases			500,000	900,000	1,200,000	1,500,000	1,800,000
Warehousing efficiencies			400,000	800,000	1,200,000	1,600,000	2,000,000
Total savings		$1,500,000	$3,300,000	$4,600,000	$5,500,000	$6,400,000	$7,300,300
Savings Minus Recurring Costs		$540,000	$1,390,000	$2,400,000	$3,035,000	$3,700,000	$4,300,000
Less income taxes (34% rate)		(183,600)	(472,600)	(816,600)	(1,031,900)	(1,258,000)	(1,462,000)
Cash savings (net of tax)		356,400	917,400	1,584,000	2,003,100	2,442,000	2,838,000
Savings on taxes (due to depreciation deduction)		340,000	544,000	326,400	195,500	195,500	98,600
Net savings	($5,000,000)	$696,400	$1,461,400	$1,910,400	$2,198,600	$2,637,500	$2,936,600

Net Present Value (Interest Rate of 10%):		**Depreciation on Initial Investment of $5,000,000:**			
	($5,000,000)	Tax Rate 34%			
		Year	Rate (%)	Depreciation	Tax Savings
696,400 x 0.9091 =	633,097	1	20.00	$1,000,000	$340,000
1,461,400 x 0.8265 =	1,207,847	2	32.00	1,600,000	544,000
1,910,400 x 0.7513 =	1,435,284	3	19.20	960,000	326,400
2,198,600 x 0.6830 =	1,501,644	4	11.50	575,000	195,500
2,637,500 x 0.6209 =	1,637,624	5	11.50	575,000	195,500
2,936,600 x 0.5645 =	1,657,711	6	5.80	290,000	98,600
Net present value is	$3,073,207				
Internal rate of return is	25.04%				

The $5 million system can be depreciated over its six-year expected life. Because the company does not have to pay taxes on the $1 million depreciation in year 1, it ends up saving an additional $340,000. Finally, Ann calculates the net savings for each year.

Ann uses Shoppers Mart's 10% cost of capital rate to calculate the NPV of the investment, which is more than $3 million. The IRR is a lofty 25%, and payback occurs in the fourth year. Ann realizes how advantageous it would be for the company to borrow the money (at a 10% interest rate) to produce a 25% return.

Ann presents the system to management and describes its objectives. Challenges to her estimates are plugged into her spreadsheet model to show their effect. Even the stiffest challenges to Ann's numbers show a positive return. Top management votes to support the new system, requests some changes, and tells Ann to proceed.

Ann has found management's enthusiastic support crucial to the system's success. Several employees with vested interests in the current system are critical of her ideas. Some employees remember the problems Shoppers Mart had when the current system was implemented years ago. Ann concludes that people resisting the new system are afraid of the change's effect on them personally. To counter negative behavioral reactions, Ann takes great pains to explain how the new system would benefit employees individually and how it will affect the company as a whole. With management's approval, she assures employees they will not lose their jobs and that all affected employees will be retrained. She involves the two most vocal opponents in planning activities, and they soon become two of the new system's biggest advocates.

Ann invites the managers of all affected departments to be on a steering committee. A master plan for developing the system is formulated, and the system is broken down into manageable projects. The projects are prioritized, and project teams are formed to begin work on the highest-priority projects. Documentation standards are developed and approved.

KEY TERMS

systems development life cycle (SDLC) 695
systems analysis 695
conceptual design 695
physical design 696
implementation and conversion 696
operations and maintenance 696
information systems steering committee 696
systems analysts 697
computer programmers 697
project development plan 698
master plan 698
program evaluation and review technique (PERT) 699
critical path 699
Gantt chart 699
feasibility study 699
economic feasibility 700
technical feasibility 700
legal feasibility 700
scheduling feasibility 700
operational feasibility 700
capital budgeting model 700
payback period 701
net present value (NPV) 701
internal rate of return (IRR) 701
behavioral aspects of change 701
aggression 702
projection 702
avoidance 703
request for systems development 704

initial investigation 704
proposal to conduct systems analysis 705
systems survey 706
systems documentation 707
physical models 707
logical models 707
systems survey report 707
systems analysis report 709

AIS in Action

CHAPTER QUIZ

1. Which of the following is not a reason why companies make changes to their AIS?
a. gain a competitive advantage
b. increase productivity
c. keep up with business growth
d. downsize company operations
e. All of the above are reasons why companies change an AIS.

2. Which of the following is the planning technique that identifies implementation activities and their relationships, constructs a network of arrows and nodes, and then determines the critical path through the network?
a. Gantt chart
b. PERT diagram
c. physical model
d. data flow diagram

3. The purchasing department is designing a new AIS. Who is best able to determine departmental information requirements?
a. steering committee
b. controller
c. top management
d. purchasing department

4. Which of the following is the correct order of the steps in systems analysis?
a. initial investigation, determination of information needs and system requirements, feasibility study, system survey
b. determination of information needs and system requirements, system survey, feasibility study, initial investigation
c. system survey, initial investigation, determination of information needs and system requirements, feasibility study
d. initial investigation, system survey, feasibility study, determination of information needs and system requirements

5. Which of the following is the long-range planning document that specifies what the system will consist of, how it will be developed, who will develop it, how needed resources will be acquired, and its overall vision?
a. steering committee agenda
b. master plan
c. systems development life cycle
d. project development plan

6. Resistance is often a reaction to the methods of instituting change rather than to change itself.
a. true
b. false

7. Increased error rates, disruptions, and sabotage are examples of which of the following?
a. aggression
b. avoidance
c. projection
d. payback

8. What is often the most significant problem a company encounters in designing, developing, and implementing a system?
a. the human element
b. technology
c. legal challenges
d. planning for the new system

9. Determining whether the organization has access to people who can design, implement, and operate the proposed system is referred to as which of the following?
a. technical feasibility
b. operational feasibility
c. legal feasibility
d. scheduling feasibility
e. economic feasibility

10. Which of the following is not one of the tangible or intangible benefits a company might obtain from a new system?

a. cost savings
b. improved customer service and productivity
c. improved decision making
d. improved data processing
e. All are benefits of a new system.

COMPREHENSIVE PROBLEM

Riverbend Software Support Administrators (RSSA) provides online and telephone help desk services. Because RSSA's labor costs have steadily increased, it is outsourcing its call center. RSSA's executive-level committee, who oversees the information systems (IS) function, selected a project development team to create a system to move the help desk and manage it from corporate headquarters.

Two incidents delayed the help desk conversion date by 15 days. A server was damaged when an unidentified employee put a hot coffee pot on it, and several backup tapes were found floating in a restroom sink.

The five-year contract requires an initial payment of $1,750,000 and yearly payments of $525,000. Each year, the contract will save $750,000 in salary, benefits, and equipment costs. There is a $150,000 one-time charge for breaking the current call center's building lease, but doing so will save $360,000 a year. RSSA's cost of capital is 11%.

REQUIRED

a. What is the executive-level committee commonly called, who typically serves on it, and what is its primary function?
b. Who typically serves on the project development team?
c. What steps would the development team take during system analysis?
d. Why do you think the server and data tapes were damaged?
e. Calculate the following capital budgeting metrics for RSSA's outsourcing plan:
   1. payback period
   2. net present value (NPV)
   3. internal rate of return (IRR)

DISCUSSION QUESTIONS

22.1 The approach to long-range AIS planning described in this chapter is important for large organizations with extensive investments in computer facilities. Should small organizations with far fewer information systems employees attempt to implement planning programs? Why, or why not? Be prepared to defend your position to the class.

22.2 You are a consultant advising a firm on the design and implementation of a new system. Management has decided to let several employees go after the system is implemented. Some have many years of company service. How would you advise management to communicate this decision to the affected employees? To the entire staff?

22.3 While reviewing a list of benefits from a computer vendor's proposal, you note an item that reads, "Improvements in management decision making—$50,000 per year." How would you interpret this item? What influence should it have on the economic feasibility and the computer acquisition decision?

22.4 For the following, discuss which data-gathering method(s) are most appropriate and why:

a. examining the adequacy of internal controls in the purchase requisition procedure
b. identifying the controller's information needs
c. determining how cash disbursement procedures are actually performed

d. surveying employees about the move to a total quality management program
e. investigating an increase in uncollectible accounts

22.5 The following problems occurred in a manufacturing firm. What questions should you ask to understand the problem?

- Customer complaints about product quality have increased.
- Accounting sees an increase in the number and dollar value of bad-debt write-offs.
- Operating margins have declined each of the past four years because of higher-than-expected production costs from idle time, overtime, and reworking products.

22.6 Give some examples of systems analysis decisions that involve a trade-off between each of the following pairs of objectives:

a. economy and usefulness
b. economy and reliability
c. economy and customer service
d. simplicity and usefulness
e. simplicity and reliability
f. economy and capacity
g. economy and flexibility

22.7 For years, Jerry Jingle's dairy production facilities have led the state in sales volume, but recent declines worry him. Customers are satisfied with his products but are troubled by the dairy's late deliveries and incomplete orders. Production employees (not the cows) are concerned about bottlenecks in milk pasteurization and homogenization due to poor job scheduling, mix-ups in customers' orders, and improperly labeled products. How should Jerry address the problems? What data-gathering techniques would be helpful at this early stage?

22.8 A manufacturing firm needed a specialized software program to identify and monitor cost overruns. After an extensive analysis, the company purchased prepackaged software and assigned three programmers to modify it to meet its individual circumstances and processes. After six months of work, during final testing, the company told the programmers to stop all work until further notice. While reading the software vendor's sales agreement, the manufacturing manager found a clause stating that the software could not be changed without the prior written consent of the vendor. The firm had to pay the software vendor an additional fee so it could use the modified software in its manufacturing process. Which aspect(s) of feasibility did the manufacturing firm fail to consider prior to purchasing the software?

22.9 Ajax Manufacturing installed a new bar-code-based inventory tracking system in its warehouse. To close the books each month on a timely basis, the six people who work in the warehouse must scan each item in a 36-hour period while still performing their normal duties. During certain months, when inventory expands to meet seasonal demands, the scan takes as many as 30 hours to complete. In addition, the scanners do not accurately record some inventory items that require low operating temperatures. A recent audit brought to management's attention that the inventory records are not always accurate. Which aspect(s) of feasibility did Ajax fail to consider prior to installing the inventory tracking system?

PROBLEMS

22.1 Match the terms with their definitions:

____	**1.** systems analysis	a.	Process of deciding how to meet user needs, identifying and evaluating design alternatives, and developing detailed system specifications
____	**2.** conceptual design	b.	Describes a system's contents; how it's developed, by whom, and when; and how needed resources will be acquired
____	**3.** physical design	c.	Description of a system's document flow, computer processes and people performing them, and equipment used

____ **4.** implementation and conversion	d. Resisting change by destroying, crippling, or weakening system effectiveness such as increased error rates or sabotage
____ **5.** IS steering committee	e. Bar graph that shows project activities on the left, units of time on the top, and activity time requirements as a horizontal bar
____ **6.** systems analysts	f. Resisting change by ignoring a new IS and hoping the new system will go away
____ **7.** master plan	g. Document showing project requirements, a cost–benefit analysis, and how a project will be completed
____ **8.** PERT diagram	h. High-level management that plans and oversees the IS function, sets policies to govern the AIS, ensures control, and coordinates activities
____ **9.** critical path	i. Calculation of the number of years required for the net savings of an investment to equal its initial cost
____ **10.** Gantt chart	j. Calculating the interest rate that makes the present value of total costs equal to the present value of total savings
____ **11.** feasibility study	k. System description that focuses on activities performed and information flow regardless of how the flow is accomplished
____ **12.** economic feasibility	l. People who help users determine their information needs, study existing systems, and design new ones
____ **13.** technical feasibility	m. SDLC step of gathering information needed to purchase, develop, or modify a system
____ **14.** operational feasibility	n. PERT path requiring the greatest amount of time to complete a project; if any activity is delayed, the whole project is delayed
____ **15.** payback period	o. Way to coordinate, control, and schedule systems development activities; a diagram shows the relationships among activities
____ **16.** NPV	p. Determining if system benefits justify the time, money, and resources required to implement it
____ **17.** IRR	q. Return-on-investment technique that compares estimated benefits and costs to determine if a system is cost beneficial
____ **18.** aggression	r. Detailed specifications are used to code and test software, design input/output, and create files/databases, and implement controls
____ **19.** avoidance	s. Process in which procedures are tested and modified, controls are established, documentation is completed, and employees are trained on a new system
____ **20.** initial investigation	t. Determining if a company needs the people to design, implement, and operate the proposed system and if employees will use it

____ **21.** systems survey	u. Determining if a proposed system can be developed given the available technology
____ **22.** logical model	v. Preliminary investigation to determine whether a proposed new system is both needed and feasible
	w. Extensive study of the current AIS
	x. Resisting change by blaming everything on the new system so it becomes the scapegoat for all problems and errors
	y. Investigation to determine if it is practical to develop a new application or system
	z. Discounting estimated future cash flows back to the present using a discount rate that reflects the time value of money

22.2 Mary Smith is the bookkeeper for Dave's Distributing Company, a distributor of soft drinks and juices. Because the company is rather small, Mary performs all daily accounting tasks herself. Dave, the owner of the company, supervises the warehouse/delivery and front office staff, but he also spends much of his time jogging and skiing.

For several years, profits were good, and sales grew faster than industry averages. Although the accounting system was working well, bottlers were pressuring Dave to computerize. With a little guidance from a CPA friend and with no mention to Mary, Dave bought a new computer system and some accounting software. Only one day was required to set up the hardware, install the software, and convert the files. The morning the vendor installed the computer system, Mary's job performance changed dramatically. Although the software company provided two full days of training, Mary resisted learning the new system. As a result, Dave decided she should run both the manual and computer systems for a month to verify the new system's accuracy.

Mary continually complained that she lacked the time and expertise to update both systems by herself. She also complained that she did not understand how to use the new computer system. To keep accounts up to date, Dave spent two to three hours a day running the new system himself. Dave found that much of the time spent running the system was devoted to identifying discrepancies between the computer and manual results. When the error was located, it was usually in the manual system. This significantly increased Dave's confidence in the new system.

At the end of the month, Dave was ready to scrap the manual system, but Mary said she was not ready. Dave went back to skiing and jogging, and Mary went on with the manual system. When the computer system fell behind, Dave again spent time catching it up. He also worked with Mary to try to help her understand how to operate the computer system.

Months later, Dave was very frustrated because he was still keeping the computer system up to date and training Mary. He commented, "I'm sure Mary *knows* how to use the system, but she doesn't seem to *want* to. I can do all the accounting work on the computer in two or three hours a day, but she can't even do it in her normal eight-hour workday. What should I do?"

REQUIRED

a. What do you believe is the real cause of Mary's resistance to computers?
b. What events may have contributed to the new system's failure?
c. In retrospect, how should Dave have handled the accounting system computerization?
d. At what point in the decision-making process should Mary have been informed? Should she have had some say in whether the computer was purchased? If so, what

should have been the nature of her input? If Mary had not agreed with Dave's decision to acquire the computer, what should Dave have done?

e. A hard decision must be made about Mary. Significant efforts have been made to train her, but they have been unsuccessful. What would you recommend at this point? Should she be fired? Threatened with the loss of her job? Moved somewhere else in the business? Given additional training?

22.3 A large city created a powerful new information system that made it possible for its detectives and police officers to use powerful criminal databases and a slew of new data analytics tools to give officers and detectives the information they need to fight crime more effectively. The detectives can access criminal history and arrest records; the modus operandi of crimes and criminals; and the ownership of weapons based on their serial number, manufacturer, and caliber. They also have powerful data analytics tools that mine multiple databases to find crimes of a similar nature and relationships between seemingly unrelated data. These tools are accessible by computer, tablet, and mobile phones.

Many of the longer-tenured detectives have little or no experience using the new data analytics tools and believe their experience and gut instincts are better tools to fight crime. They have not been responsive to calls to combine their experience and instincts with the new analytics tools. You suspect that at least some of the resistance is due to them not feeling comfortable with the new tools and to the changes to the way they interface with the system. After months of complaints about the new system, the police chief decided he had to do something.

REQUIRED

a. Identify as many system analysis and design problems as you can.
b. What principles of system analysis and design were violated in this case?
c. Explain why employees resist organizational change.
d. How can companies alleviate employee resistance to change?
e. What is a steering committee, and how could it have helped the police department design a new system?

22.4 The controller of Tim's Travel (TT) is deciding between upgrading the company's existing computer system or replacing it with a new one. Upgrading the four-year-old system will cost \$97,500 and extend its useful life for another seven years. The book value is \$19,500, although it would sell for \$24,000. Upgrading will eliminate one employee at a salary of \$19,400; the new computer will eliminate two employees. Annual operating costs are estimated at \$15,950 per year. Upgrading is expected to increase profits 3.5% above last year's level of \$553,000.

The BetaTech Company has quoted a price of \$224,800 for a new computer with a useful life of seven years. Annual operating costs are estimated to be \$14,260. The average processing speed of the new computer is 12% faster than that of other systems in its price range, which would increase TT's profits by 4.5%.

Tim's present tax rate is 35%, and the cost of financing is 11%. After seven years, the salvage value, net of tax, would be \$12,000 for the new computer and \$7,500 for the present system. For tax purposes, computers are depreciated over five full years (six calendar years; a half year the first and last years), and the depreciation percentages are as follows:

Year	Percent (%)
1	20.00
2	32.00
3	19.20
4	11.52
5	11.52
6	5.76

REQUIRED

Using a spreadsheet package, prepare an economic feasibility analysis to determine whether TT should rehabilitate the old system or purchase the new computer. As part of the analysis, compute the after-tax cash flows for years 1 through 7 and the payback, NPV, and IRR of each alternative.

22.5 Rossco is considering the purchase of a new computer with the following estimated costs: initial systems design, $54,000; hardware, $74,000; software, $35,000, one-time initial training, $11,000; system installation, $20,000; and file conversion, $12,000. A net reduction of three employees is expected, with average yearly salaries of $40,000. The system will decrease average yearly inventory by $150,000. Annual operating costs will be $30,000 per year.

The expected life of the machine is four years, with an estimated salvage value of zero. The effective tax rate is 40%. All computer purchase costs will be depreciated using the straight-line method over its four-year life. Rossco can invest money made available from the reduction in inventory at its cost of capital of 11%. All cash flows, except for the initial investment and start-up costs, are at the end of the year. Assume 365 days in a year.

REQUIRED

Use a spreadsheet to perform a feasibility analysis to determine whether Rossco should purchase the computer. Compute the following as part of the analysis: initial investment, after-tax cash flows for years 1 through 4, payback period, net present value, and internal rate of return.

22.6 Joanne Grey, a senior consultant, and David Young, a junior consultant, are conducting a systems analysis for a client to determine the feasibility of integrating and automating clerical functions. Joanne had previously worked for the client, but David was a recent hire.

The first morning on the job, Joanne directed David to interview a departmental supervisor and learn as much as possible about department operations. David introduced himself and said, "Your company has hired us to study how your department works so we can make recommendations on how to improve its efficiency and lower its cost. I would like to interview you to determine what goes on in your department."

David questioned the supervisor for 30 minutes but found him to be uncooperative. David gave Joanne an oral report on how the interview went and what he learned about the department.

REQUIRED

Describe several flaws in David's approach to obtaining information. How should this task have been performed?

22.7 The following list presents specific project activities and their scheduled starting and completion times:

Activity	Starting Date	Ending Date
A	Jan. 5	Feb. 9
B	Jan. 5	Jan. 19
C	Jan. 26	Feb. 23
D	Mar. 2	Mar. 23
E	Mar. 2	Mar. 16
F	Feb. 2	Mar. 16
G	Mar. 30	Apr. 20
H	Mar. 23	Apr. 27

REQUIRED

a. Using a format similar to that in Figure 22-3, prepare a Gantt chart for this project. Assume each activity starts on a Monday and ends on a Friday.
b. Assume today is February 16 and activities A and B have been completed, C is half completed, F is a quarter completed, and the other activities have not commenced. Record this information on your Gantt chart. Is the project behind schedule, on schedule, or ahead of schedule? Explain.
c. Discuss the relative merits of the Gantt chart and PERT as project planning and control tools.

22.8 Businesses often modify or replace their financial information system to keep pace with their growth and take advantage of improved IT. This requires a substantial time and resource commitment. When an organization changes its AIS, a systems analysis takes place.

REQUIRED

a. Explain the purpose and reasons for surveying an organization's existing system.
b. Explain the activities commonly performed during systems analysis.
c. Systems analysis is often performed by a project team composed of a systems analyst, a management accountant, and other knowledgeable and helpful people. What is the management accountant's role in systems analysis? *(CMA Examination, adapted)*

22.9 Managers at some companies face an ongoing systems development problem: IS departments develop systems that businesses cannot or will not use. At the heart of the problem is a gap that separates the world of business and the world of IS that many departments are unable or ready to cross.

One reason for the crisis is that many companies are looking for ways to improve existing, out-of-date systems or to build new ones. Another is high user expectations that IS departments are not meeting. Users seek more powerful applications than are available on many older systems.

The results can be devastating. An East Coast chemical company spent more than $1 million on a budgeting and control system that was never used. The systems department's expertise was technical excellence, not budgets. As a result, the new system completely missed the mark when it came to meeting business needs.

In another instance, a Midwestern bank used an expensive computer-aided software engineering (CASE) tool to develop a system that users ignored because there had been no design planning. A senior analyst for the bank said, "They built the system right; but unfortunately, they didn't build the right system."

REQUIRED

a. What causes this gap?
b. What would you suggest to solve this problem?
c. Discuss the roles a systems designer, business manager, and end user can take to narrow this gap.
d. Who plays the most vital role in the effective development of the system?

22.10 Focus 22-1 described the IRS's attempts to replace its aging information systems. Many other governmental agencies have similar problems. News reports indicate that the U.S. government is spending billions to keep antiquated computer systems running. Other reports describe how some governmental agencies still use floppy disks to store data. Conduct a search (using written materials, the Internet, electronic databases, etc.) for information on how governmental agencies need to replace its aging legacy systems. Per your professor's instructions, prepare an oral or written summary reporting your findings.

22.11 Select the correct answer for each of the following multiple-choice questions.

1. In which SDLC step does the company translate broad, user-oriented systems requirements into the detailed specifications used to create a fully developed system?
   a. physical design
   b. systems analysis
   c. conceptual design
   d. implementation and conversion
   e. operations and maintenance

2. Who in the organization is responsible for planning individual system development projects and monitoring the project to ensure timely and cost-effective completion?
   a. management
   b. project development team
   c. users
   d. information systems steering committee
   e. systems analysts

3. There are several different types of feasibility analysis. Which type of analysis seeks to answer the question: "Does the system comply with all applicable federal and state laws, administrative agency regulations, and contractual obligations?"
   a. legal feasibility
   b. economic feasibility
   c. technical feasibility
   d. scheduling feasibility
   e. operational feasibility

4. When a new or improved system is needed, which document describes the problem, explains the need for a change, lists the proposed system's objectives, and explains its anticipated benefits and costs?
   a. request for initial investigation
   b. request for systems analysis
   c. request for systems development
   d. request for feasibility analysis

5. A systems survey is an extensive study of the current AIS that has a number of objectives. Which of the following is not one of those objectives?
   a. Gain an understanding of company operations, policies, and procedures
   b. Make preliminary assessments of current and future processing needs
   c. Develop working relationships with users, and build support for the AIS
   d. Develop a blueprint for detailed systems design that can be given to management
   e. Collect data that identify user needs and conduct a feasibility analysis

6. At the end of the systems analysis process, systems developers need to do all of the following except ______________.
   a. create and document detailed system requirements that explain exactly what the system will produce.
   b. explain the requirements to users, obtain their approval, and have user management sign system requirements documents to indicate their approval.
   c. prepare a detailed and technical document of all user requirements for top management.
   d. prepare a systems analysis report to summarize and document all analysis activities.

7. In which SDLC step do all the elements and activities of the system come together to form a completed operational system?
   a. systems analysis
   b. conceptual design
   c. physical design
   d. operations and maintenance
   e. implementation and conversion

8. Who in the organization is responsible for planning and overseeing the information systems function?
   a. management
   b. users
   c. project development team
   d. systems analysts
   e. information systems steering committee

9. There are several different types of feasibility analysis. The analysis that seeks to answer the question "Can the system be developed and implemented using existing technology?" is called ____________ feasibility.
   a. economic
   b. legal
   c. scheduling
   d. technical
   e. operational

10. With respect to an initial investigation, which of the following statements is false?
   a. A project's scope is a description of what a development project should and should not accomplish.
   b. A new AIS is often the answer to organizational problems because it provides needed structures and processes.
   c. A new AIS is useful when the identified problem is a result of the lack of information or inefficient data processing.
   d. The initial investigation should determine a project's viability and recommend it be initiated as proposed, modified, or abandoned.
   e. Approved projects should be assigned a priority and added to the organization's master plan.

11. Which of the following statements is false?
   a. When data gathering is complete, the current system's strengths and weaknesses are evaluated to generate ideas for how to design and structure the new system.
   b. Determining information needs is a relatively easy task because most employees can adequately explain their information needs.
   c. A feasibility analysis is updated regularly as a project proceeds and costs and benefits become clearer.
   d. When a project is deemed feasible, user needs are identified and system requirements are documented.

12. Which approach to gathering data about an organization's existing information system can help verify how a system operates?
   a. interviews
   b. questionnaires
   c. systems documentation
   d. observation

13. Which of the following strategies for determining system requirements is least likely to be successful?
   a. Ask management what information their employees need.
   b. Examine existing systems to find what is working well in the current system.
   c. Analyze external systems so you do not have to "reinvent the wheel."
   d. Create a prototype so users can identify what they like and dislike about the system.

CASE 22-1 Audio Visual Corporation

Audio Visual Corporation (AVC) manufactures and sells visual display equipment. Headquartered in Boston, it has seven sales offices with nearby warehouses that carry its inventory of new equipment and replacement parts. AVC has a departmentalized manufacturing plant with assembly, maintenance, engineering, scheduling, and cost accounting departments as well as several component parts departments.

When management decided to upgrade its AIS, they installed a mainframe at headquarters and local area networks at each sales office. The IS manager and four systems analysts were hired shortly before they integrated the new computer and the existing AIS. The other IS employees have been with the company for years.

During its early years, AVC had a centralized decision-making organization. Top management formulated all plans and directed all operations. As the company expanded, decision making was decentralized, although data processing was highly centralized. Departments coordinated their plans with the corporate office but had the freedom to develop their own sales programs. However, information problems developed, and the IS department was asked to improve the company's information processing system once the new equipment was installed.

Before acquiring the new computer, the systems analysts studied the existing AIS, identified its weaknesses, and designed applications to solve them. In the 18 months since the new equipment was acquired, the following applications were redesigned or developed: payroll, production scheduling, financial statement preparation, customer billing, raw materials usage, and finished goods inventory. The departments affected by the changes were rarely consulted until the system was operational.

Recently the president stated, "The systems people are doing a good job, and I have complete confidence in their work. I talk to them frequently, and they have encountered no difficulties in doing their work. We paid a lot of money for the new equipment, and the systems people certainly cost enough, but the new equipment and new IS staff should solve all our problems."

Two additional conversations regarding the new AIS took place.

BILL TAYLOR, IS MANAGER, AND JERRY ADAMS, PLANT MANAGER

JERRY: Bill, you're trying to run my plant for me. I'm the manager, and you keep interfering. I wish you would mind your own business.

BILL: You've got a job to do, and so do I. As we analyzed the information needed for production scheduling and by top management, we saw where we could improve the workflow. Now that the system is operational, you can't reroute work and change procedures because that would destroy the value of the information we're processing. And while I'm on that subject, we can't trust the information we're getting from production. The documents we receive from production contain a lot of errors.

JERRY: I'm responsible for the efficient operation of production. I'm the best judge of production efficiency. The system you installed reduced my workforce and increased the workload of the remaining employees, but it hasn't improved anything. In fact, it might explain the high error rate in the documents.

BILL: This new computer cost a lot of money, and I'm trying to make sure the company gets its money's worth.

JERRY ADAMS, PLANT MANAGER AND TERRY WILLIAMS, HUMAN RESOURCES MANAGER

JERRY: My best production assistant, the one I'm grooming to be a supervisor, told me he was thinking of quitting. When I asked why, he said he didn't enjoy the work anymore. He's not the only one who is unhappy. The supervisors and department heads no longer have a voice in establishing production schedules. This new computer system took away the contribution we made to company planning and direction. We're going back to when top management made all the decisions. I have more production problems now than I ever had. It boils down to my management team's lack of interest. I know the problem is in my area, but I thought you could help me.

TERRY: I have no recommendations, but I've had similar complaints from purchasing and shipping. We should explore your concerns during tomorrow's plant management meeting.

ANSWER THE FOLLOWING QUESTIONS:

1. Identify the problems the new computer system created, and discuss what caused them.
2. How could AVC have avoided the problems? How can they prevent them in the future?

(CMA Examination, adapted)

AIS in Action Solutions

QUIZ KEY

1. Which of the following is not a reason why companies make changes to their AIS?
   a. gain a competitive advantage [AIS changes can help a company increase the quality, quantity, and speed of information, which leads to improved decision making and a greater competitive advantage.]
   b. increase productivity [Using computers in an AIS can automate repetitive tasks, which allows more work to be done in the same amount of time. This increases productivity.]
   c. keep up with business growth [As a company grows, its old system will likely not be able to handle the increase in demand and thus will require changes to the AIS to accommodate the growth.]
   d. downsize company operations [A smaller company requires a smaller AIS. For instance, downsizing may prompt a company to move from centralized decision making to decentralized decision making. As a result, the AIS would most likely shift from using a mainframe computer to a set of networked workstations.]
   ▶ e. All of the above are reasons why companies change an AIS. [Correct.]

2. Which of the following is the planning technique that identifies implementation activities and their relationships, constructs a network of arrows and nodes, and then determines the critical path through the network?
   a. Gantt chart [Incorrect. A Gantt chart is a bar chart that displays dates and stages of completion for each project task. See Figure 22-3.]
   ▶ b. PERT diagram [Correct.]
   c. physical model [Incorrect. A physical model illustrates how a system functions. It describes document flows, computer processes, equipment used, and other physical elements of the system.]
   d. data flow diagram [Incorrect. A data flow diagram is used to document a system with four basic symbols—i.e., squares, circles, parallel lines, and arrows.]

3. The purchasing department is designing a new AIS. Who is best able to determine departmental information requirements?
   a. steering committee [Incorrect. The steering committee is a high-level executive committee that oversees the function of the information system; they probably do not understand the purchasing department's information requirements.]
   b. controller [Incorrect. The controller is the manager of the accounting department and probably does not understand all of the purchasing department's information requirements.]
   c. top management [Incorrect. Top management in such cases should provide direction and resources, not analysis of the purchasing department's information requirements.]
   ▶ d. purchasing department [Correct. The people who will actually be using the new system are in the best position to determine the system's information requirements.]

4. Which of the following is the correct order of the steps in systems analysis?
   a. initial investigation, determination of information needs and system requirements, feasibility study, system survey [Incorrect. See Figure 22-4.]
   b. determination of information needs and system requirements, system survey, feasibility study, initial investigation [Incorrect. See Figure 22-4.]
   c. system survey, initial investigation, determination of information needs and system requirements, feasibility study [Incorrect. See Figure 22-4.]
   ▶ d. initial investigation, system survey, feasibility study, determination of information needs and system requirements [Correct. See Figure 22-4.]

5. Which of the following is the long-range planning document that specifies what the system will consist of, how it will be developed, who will develop it, how needed resources will be acquired, and its overall vision?

a. steering committee agenda [Incorrect. The steering committee's agenda would involve discussing all aspects of the information system, not just system development.]
▶ b. master plan [Correct.]
c. systems development life cycle [Incorrect. The systems development life cycle is not a long-range planning document but a conceptual framework that applies to systems development in general.]
d. project development plan [Incorrect. The project development plan is used for individual projects. It includes such items as cost–benefit analyses, developmental and operational requirements, and a schedule of activities for developing and operating the new system.]

6. Resistance is often a reaction to the methods of instituting change rather than to change itself.
▶ a. true [Correct. Although change is generally difficult, the way change is instituted can either facilitate the change or hinder the change.]
b. false [Incorrect.]

7. Increased error rates, disruptions, and sabotage are examples of which of the following?
▶ a. aggression [Correct. These are classic symptoms of aggression as a reaction to change.]
b. avoidance [Incorrect. Avoidance is best illustrated by the statement that if a person does not use the new system, maybe it will go away.]
c. projection [Incorrect. Projection refers to blaming all problems on the new system.]
d. payback [Incorrect. Payback is an economic feasibility metric.]

8. What is often the most significant problem a company encounters in designing, developing, and implementing a system?
▶ a. the human element [Correct. A system will fail without the support of the people it is designed to serve—for a variety of reasons, including fear of change, poor communication and training, disruption of work, and lack of top-management support.]
b. technology [Incorrect. The technology a system employs is normally tested for functionality prior to its implementation in a new system.]
c. legal challenges [Incorrect. With proper system planning and design, systems can meet all laws and regulations.]
d. planning for the new system [Incorrect. Proper planning can actually prevent problems from occurring.]

9. Determining whether the organization has access to people who can design, implement, and operate the proposed system is referred to as which of the following?
a. technical feasibility [Incorrect. Technical feasibility refers to whether the system can be developed and implemented with existing technology.]
▶ b. operational feasibility [Correct. Operational feasibility refers to whether the organization and its people can actually design, implement, and operate the system.]
c. legal feasibility [Incorrect. Legal feasibility refers to whether the system complies with all applicable laws and regulations.]
d. scheduling feasibility [Incorrect. Scheduling feasibility refers to whether the system can be analyzed, planned, designed, and implemented in the time allocated.]
e. economic feasibility [Incorrect. Economic feasibility refers to whether the system's benefits outweigh its costs.]

10. Which of the following is not one of the tangible or intangible benefits a company might obtain from a new system?
a. cost savings [Although this answer is correct, there are other correct answers. Automated systems can reduce clerical costs as well as other related costs.]
b. improved customer service and productivity [Although this answer is correct, there are other correct answers. New systems can integrate data from several sources to provide fast, reliable information to assist customers and increase productivity.]

c. improved decision making [Although this answer is correct, there are other correct answers. Better information greatly increases the likelihood of better decisions.]
d. improved data processing [Although this answer is correct, there are other correct answers. Better-designed systems using newer technology improve data processing and reduce the likelihood of human error.]
▶ e. All are benefits of a new system. [Correct.]

COMPREHENSIVE PROBLEM SOLUTION

a. *What is the executive-level committee commonly called, who typically serves on it, and what is its primary function?*

An information systems steering committee, which plans and oversees the IS function, consists of high-level management people, such as the controller and systems and user-department management. The committee sets IS policies; ensures top-management participation, guidance, and control; and facilitates the coordination and integration of systems activities.

b. *Who typically serves on the project development team?*

The project development team includes systems analysts, systems specialists, managers, accountants, systems auditors, and users.

c. *What steps would the development team take during system analysis?*

RSSA's development team will do an initial assessment of management's plans for moving the help desk. They will survey the existing system to determine what it does, what the company should continue to use, and what should be changed for the new system. They will complete a feasibility analysis to determine the technical, operational, legal, scheduling, and economic feasibility of the new system. Then the team will determine the system's information needs and requirements. Lastly, the team will prepare a systems analysis report.

d. *Why do you think the server and data tapes were damaged?*

Change is usually difficult for people and organizations. When operations are outsourced, employees can lose their jobs. Apparently, some employees exhibited aggressive behavior toward the new system.

e. *Calculate the following capital budgeting metrics for RSSA's outsourcing plan:*
   1. payback period
   2. net present value (NPV)
   3. internal rate of return (IRR)

Table 22-9 summarizes the cash spent or saved each year of RSSA's proposed project. The initial contract payment and the lease cancellation penalty occur at the beginning of the project, referred to as year 0. For simplicity's sake, we assume cash flows

TABLE 22-9 Cash Flows for RSSA

Year	0	1	2	3	4	5
Cash Outflows						
Initial contract	−$1,750,000					
Lease cancellation penalty	−$150,000					
Center operations cost		−$525,000	−$525,000	−$525,000	−$525,000	−$525,000
Total cash outflow	−$1,900,000	−$525,000	−$525,000	−$525,000	−$525,000	−$525,000
Cash inflows						
Personnel savings		$750,000	$750,000	$750,000	$750,000	$750,000
Lease cancellation savings		$360,000	$360,000	$360,000	$360,000	$360,000
Total cash inflows	$0	$1,110,000	$1,110,000	$1,110,000	$1,110,000	$1,110,000
Net Cash Flows	−$1,900,000	$585,000	$585,000	$585,000	$585,000	$585,000

take place at the end of the year. For years 1 through 5, the $525,000 expenditure for operations, the $750,000 personnel savings, and the $360,000 lease cancellation savings are entered. The last line of Table 22-9 shows the net cash flows for each period, which are total cash inflows less total cash outflows.

1 PAYBACK

The payback period is when cash inflows equal cash outflows. Table 22-10, which shows cumulative net cash flow totals, indicates that breakeven occurs during year 4. To determine how far into year 4, divide year-3 negative cumulative cash flows of $145,000 by year-4 net cash flows of $585,000. It took 25% of the year (145,000/585,000), or 3.25 years, to get to payback.

2 NET PRESENT VALUE

Payback period does not take into consideration the time value of money (a dollar received today is worth more than the same dollar received a year from now). The net present value (NPV) techniques take the time value of money into consideration by using the company's cost of capital, called its discount rate. This rate is the company's average cost of borrowing capital.

Net present value is calculated by multiplying each year's net cash flow by a discount factor calculated using the formula $1/(1+r)n$, where r = the company's discount rate and n = the number of time periods between time 0 and the designated cash flow. For example, if the cash flow occurred at the end of year 4, n would equal 4. The discount factor is calculated for each time period and multiplied by the net cash flow for that period. When all net cash flows have been discounted to their present value, they are totaled to determine the project's NPV.

As a practical matter, most people do not use the formula to make the calculations, but rather use a business calculator or the NPV function in Microsoft Excel.

Projects with a positive NPV earn an estimated return in excess of the company's discount rate and are financially feasible. Projects with a negative NPV are usually rejected. As shown in Table 22-11, RSSA's NPV is $262,103 and the project would likely be acceptable to management.

TABLE 22-10 Payback for RSSA's Proposed Project

Year	0	1	2	3	4	5
Net cash flows	–$1,900,000	$585,000	$585,000	$585,000	$585,000	$585,000
Cumulative cash flows	–$1,900,000	–$1,315,000	–$730,000	–$145,000	$440,000	$1,025,000
Payback	3.25 years or 3 years, 3 months					

3 INTERNAL RATE OF RETURN

The NPV calculation does not calculate an estimated rate of return. This limitation is resolved by calculating an internal rate of return (IRR), which is the discount rate that produces an NPV of zero. Calculating an IRR is a trial-and-error process of changing the discount rate until NPV equals zero. Because this is so tedious, IRR is usually calculated using a business calculator or the IRR function in a spreadsheet program. The internal rate of return for this project is 16.35% (rounded).

TABLE 22-11 The Net Present Value of RSSA's Proposed Project

Net cash flows	–$1,900,000	$585,000	$585,000	$585,000	$585,000	$585,000
Present value factors	1	0.9009	0.8116	0.7312	0.6587	0.5935
Present value amounts	–$1,900,000	$527,027	$474,786	$427,752	$385,340	$347,198
Net present value	$262,103					
IRR	16.35%					

CHAPTER

23

AIS Development Strategies

LEARNING OBJECTIVES

After studying this chapter, you should be able to:

1. Describe how organizations purchase application software, vendor services, and hardware.
2. Explain how information system departments develop custom software.
3. Explain why organizations outsource their information systems, and evaluate the benefits and risks of this strategy.
4. Explain how business process management, prototyping, agile development, and computer-aided software engineering can help improve system development.

INTEGRATIVE CASE Shoppers Mart

Ann Christy is elated that the system Shoppers Mart (SM) so badly needed was approved and that she and her team have accurately assessed company needs. Now Ann needs to determine whether to purchase the software, develop it in-house, or outsource system development and operation. More specifically, she needs answers to these questions:

1. Can Ann buy the software she needs? If so, how should she buy hardware and software and select a vendor?
2. How do companies develop software in-house? Is this the best approach for SM?
3. How extensively should SM use end-user-developed software?
4. Should SM improve its existing system or redesign its business processes and develop a system to support them?
5. Is outsourcing the information system a viable alternative to obtaining a new system? Do the benefits of outsourcing outweigh its risks?
6. If SM decides to develop the system in-house, should it use technologies such as business process management, agile development, prototyping, or computer-assisted software engineering?

Ann decided to investigate design alternatives to determine the best course of action for Shoppers Mart.

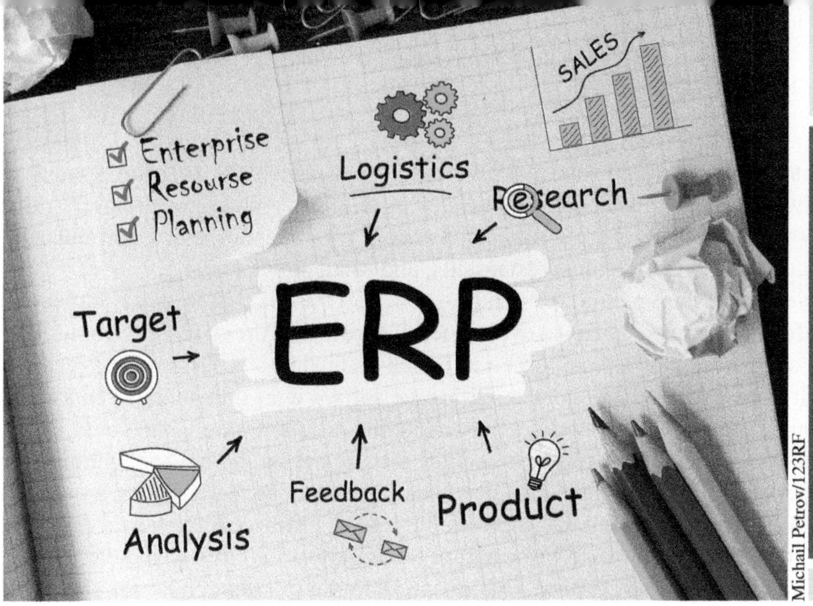

Michail Petrov/123RF

Introduction

Companies have experienced the following difficulties when developing an accounting information system (AIS):

- Development requests are so numerous that projects are backlogged for years.
- Users discover that the new AIS does not meet their needs. This occurs because users find it hard to visualize how the AIS will operate by reviewing design documentation and because developers who do not understand business or user needs find it hard to make meaningful suggestions for improvement.
- Development takes so long the system no longer meets company needs. Fannie Mae spent eight years and $100 million developing the world's largest loan accounting system. Unfortunately, it no longer met many of Fannie Mae's needs.
- Users do not adequately specify their needs because they do not know what they need or they cannot communicate the needs to systems developers.
- Changes are difficult to make after requirements are frozen. If users keep changing requirements, the AIS may take forever to finish.

In this chapter, you learn three ways to obtain an information system: purchasing software, developing software in-house, and hiring a company to develop and operate the system. You also learn four ways to improve the development process: business process redesign, prototyping, agile development technologies, and computer-aided software engineering tools.

Purchasing Software

In the early days of computers, it was difficult to buy software that met user needs. That is no longer the case. A Deloitte & Touche survey found that most chief information officers expect to replace their current systems with commercially available software packages. Many organizations, especially larger ones, purchase Enterprise Resource Planning (ERP) packages that integrate all aspects of a company's organizations. Chapter 2 discusses ERP systems in more depth.

Consider the following examples:

- Hard Rock Cafe purchased customer relationship software and mailed promotional offers to 225,000 customers. A year later, profits from the increased traffic paid for the new system.
- WellPoint Health Networks installed payroll, benefits, and human resources software so employees could manage their benefits, saving $400,000 a year.
- Pacific Gas & Electric responded to California's power deregulation by spending three years and $204 million installing the largest customer information system in the utility industry.

commercial software - Programs for sale on the open market to a broad range of users with similar needs.

turnkey system - Software and hardware sold as a package such that the vendor installs the system and the user "turns on the key"; often written by vendors who specialize in a particular industry.

Software-as-a-Service (SaaS) providers - Companies that rent cloud-based software applications that customers can access using the Internet.

Commercial software is sold to users with similar requirements.A **turnkey system** is software and hardware sold as a package. The vendor installs the system and the user "turns on the key." Many turnkey systems are written by vendors who specialize in a particular industry, such as doctors, auto repair shops, restaurants, and retail stores.

A major problem with commercial, or off-the-shelf, software is that it may not meet all of a company's information needs. This is overcome by modifying the software. About 90% of Dow Chemical's software has been modified to match its business processes. The rest was written in-house. It is best when the vendor modifies the software, as unauthorized modifications may not be supported by the vendor and may make the program unreliable.

Software as a Service (SaaS) providers, provide cloud-based software applications that customers can access using the Internet. This provides scalability as the business grows and global access to information. It automates software upgrades, allows companies to focus on core financial competencies rather than information technology (IT) issues, and can reduce software costs and administrative overhead.This is one example of cloud computing services described in Chapters 11 and 13.

Companies that buy AIS software follow the normal systems development life cycle (SDLC) except for the following:

- During conceptual systems design, companies determine whether software that meets AIS requirements is available and, if so, whether to buy it or create their own.
- Some physical design and implementation and conversion steps can be omitted. For example, the company usually does not need to design, code, and test program modules or document the computer program.

SELECTING A VENDOR

Hardware, service, maintenance, and other AIS resource decisions can be made independently of the decision to make or purchase software, although they may depend on the software decision.

Vendors are found by referrals, at conferences, in industry magazines, and on the Internet. Choosing must be done carefully because vendors with little experience, insufficient capital, or a poor product go out of business and leave their customers and products with no support or recourse. Problems can occur even when established vendors are selected. For example, when Texas selected IBM to consolidate data centers across the state, service levels dropped dramatically, and routine tasks took far too long to perform. The problem was attributed to poor project requirements and selecting the vendor with the lowest bid. IBM almost lost the contract after it failed to back up critical systems.

ACQUIRING HARDWARE AND SOFTWARE

request for proposal (RFP) - A request for vendors to bid on a system to meet a company's specified needs.

Companies that buy large or complex systems send vendors a **request for proposal (RFP)**, asking them to propose a system that meets their needs. The best proposals are investigated to verify that company requirements can be met. Using an RFP is important because it:

1. ***Saves time.*** The same information is provided to all vendors, eliminating repetitive interviews and questions.
2. ***Simplifies the decision-making process.*** All responses are in the same format and based on the same information.
3. ***Reduces errors.*** The chances of overlooking important factors are reduced.
4. ***Avoids potential for disagreement.*** Both parties possess the same expectations, and pertinent information is captured in writing.

RFPs for exact hardware and software specifications have lower total costs and require less time to prepare and evaluate, but they do not permit the vendor to recommend alternative technology. Requesting a system that meets specific performance objectives and requirements leaves technical issues to the vendor but is harder to evaluate and often results in more costly bids.

The more information a company provides vendors, the better their chances of receiving a system that meets its requirements. Vendors need detailed specifications, including required applications, inputs and outputs, files and databases, frequency and methods of file updating and inquiry, and unique requirements. It is essential to distinguish mandatory requirements from desirable features.

EVALUATING PROPOSALS AND SELECTING A SYSTEM

Proposals that lack important information, fail to meet minimum requirements, or are ambiguous are eliminated. Proposals passing this preliminary screening are compared with system requirements to determine whether all mandatory requirements are met and how many desirable requirements are met. Top vendors are invited to demonstrate their system using company-supplied data to measure system performance and validate vendor's claims. Table 23-1 presents hardware, software, and vendor evaluation criteria.

System performance can be compared several ways. A **benchmark problem** is an input, processing, and output task typical of what the new AIS will perform. **Point scoring** assigns

benchmark problem - Comparing systems by executing an input, processing, and output task on different computer systems and evaluating the results.

point scoring - Evaluating the overall merits of vendor proposals by assigning a weight to each evaluation criterion based on its importance.

TABLE 23-1 Hardware, Software, and Vendor Evaluation Criteria

Hardware Evaluation	Are hardware costs reasonable, based on capabilities and features? Are processing speed and capabilities adequate for the intended use? Are secondary storage capabilities adequate? Are the input and output speeds and capabilities adequate? Is the system expandable? Is the hardware based on old technology that will soon to be out of date? Is the hardware available now? If not, when? Is the hardware compatible with existing hardware, software, and peripherals? How do performance evaluations compare with competitors? What are the availability and cost of support and maintenance? What warranties come with the system? Is financing available (if applicable)?
Software Evaluation	Does the software meet all mandatory specifications? How well does the software meet desirable specifications? Will program modifications be required to meet company needs? Does the software have adequate control capabilities? Is the performance (speed, accuracy, reliability) adequate? How many companies use the software? Are they satisfied? Is documentation adequate? Is the software compatible with existing software? Was the software demonstration/test-drive adequate? Does the software have an adequate warranty? Is the software flexible, easily maintained, and user-friendly? Is online inquiry of files and records possible? Will the vendor keep the software up to date?
Vendor Evaluation	How long has the vendor been in business? Is the vendor financially stable and secure? How experienced is the vendor with the hardware and software? Does the vendor stand behind its products? How good is its warranty? Does the vendor regularly update its products? Does the vendor provide financing? Will the vendor put promises in a contract? Will the vendor supply a list of customer references? Does the vendor have a reputation for reliability and dependability? Does the vendor provide timely support and maintenance? Does the vendor provide implementation and installation support? Does the vendor have high-quality, responsive, and experienced personnel? Does the vendor provide training?

a weight to each evaluation criterion based on its importance. For each criterion, vendors are scored based on how well their proposals meet the requirement, and the weighted score totals are compared. In Table 23-2, vendor 3 offers the best system because its system scored 190 points more than vendor 2 did.

requirement costing - Comparing systems based on the cost of all required features; when software does not meet all requirements, the cost of developing unavailable features is estimated and added to its cost.

A **requirement costing** estimates the cost of purchasing or developing unavailable features. Total AIS costs, which is the cost of acquiring the system and the cost of developing the unavailable features, provides an equitable basis for comparing systems.

Because neither point scoring nor requirements costing is totally objective, the final choice among vendor proposals is not clear-cut. Point-scoring weights and scores are assigned subjectively, and dollar estimates of costs and benefits are not included. Requirement costing overlooks intangible factors such as reliability and vendor support.

Once the best AIS is identified, the software is thoroughly test-driven, other users are contacted to determine their satisfaction with the choice, vendor personnel are evaluated, and proposal details are confirmed to verify that the best AIS on paper is the best in practice. The lessons Geophysical Systems learned from its vendor selection highlight the importance of a thorough vendor evaluation (see Focus 23-1).

TABLE 23-2 Point-Scoring Evaluation of Vendor Proposals

		Vendor 1		Vendor 2		Vendor 3	
Criterion	**Weight**	**Score**	**Weighted Score**	**Score**	**Weighted Score**	**Score**	**Weighted Score**
Hardware compatibility	60	6	360	7	420	8	480
Hardware speed	30	6	180	10	300	5	150
Memory expansion	60	5	300	7	420	8	480
Hardware current	30	9	270	9	270	6	180
Software compatibility	90	7	630	7	630	9	810
Online inquiry capabilities	40	9	360	10	400	8	320
Controls	50	7	350	6	300	9	450
Positive references	40	10	400	8	320	6	240
Documentation	30	9	270	8	240	7	210
Easily maintained; updated regularly	50	7	350	8	400	9	450
Network capabilities	50	8	400	7	350	8	400
Vendor support	70	6	420	9	630	10	700
Totals			**4,290**		**4,680**		**4,870**

FOCUS 23-1 A Software Purchase That Went Awry

Geophysical Systems Corporation (GSC) developed a sonar device to analyze the production potential of oil and gas discoveries. GSC needed software to analyze the data generated by the sonar device and paid Seismograph Service $20 million to create it. When the Seismograph system could not accurately process the massive volume of data and perform the complex computations needed, GSC clients canceled their contracts. GSC went from yearly sales of $40 million and profits of $6 million to filing for bankruptcy two years later.

GSC sued, claiming Seismograph's system did not perform as promised and that Seismograph knew that before it began development. The jury awarded GSC $48 million for lost profits and the cost of the computer system. Seismograph appealed, claiming its system did work and that GSC's decline resulted from a slump in oil prices.

GSC's experience is common; many systems development projects do not produce the intended results.

Development by In-House Information Systems Departments

Organizations develop **custom software** when doing so provides a significant competitive advantage. There is little benefit to a custom-written payroll or accounts receivable system, whereas there may be significant benefits to sophisticated, just-in-time inventory management or product manufacturing software.

custom software - Software developed and written in-house to meet the unique needs of a particular company.

The hurdles that must be overcome to develop quality software are the significant amounts of time required, the complexity of the system, poor requirements, insufficient planning, inadequate communication and cooperation, lack of qualified staff, and poor top-management support.

Custom software is created in-house or by an outside company hired to write the software or assemble it from its inventory of program modules. When using an outside developer, a company maintains control over the development process as follows:

- Carefully select a developer that has experience in the company's industry and an in-depth understanding of how the company conducts its business.
- Sign a contract that rigorously defines the relationship between the company and the developer, places responsibility for meeting system requirements on the developer, and allows the project to be discontinued if key conditions are not met.
- Plan the project in detail and frequently monitor each step in the development.
- Communicate frequently and effectively.
- Control all costs and minimize cash outflows until the project is accepted.

There is no single right answer to the build-or-buy decision. Different companies come to different conclusions. After developing its own software, Gillette decided to purchase commercial software when possible to gain a greater competitive advantage from deciding *how* software should be used rather than determining *what* software should be used and then creating it. If commercial software does not meet all of Gillette's needs, it is modified using high-level development tools.

Pepsi moved in the opposite direction. It bought most of its mainframe software but, after moving to a client/server architecture, it could not find software sophisticated enough to meet its needs. Although Pepsi still buys software when it can find it, it has created most of its software.

Chapter 22 discusses in more depth the process used to develop custom software.

END-USER-DEVELOPED SOFTWARE

After the automobile was introduced, a famous sociologist predicted that the automobile market would not exceed 2 million cars because only that many people would be willing to serve as chauffeurs. It was once predicted that the telephone system would collapse because the geometric growth in calls would require everyone to be telephone operators. Instead, equipment was developed that automated operator functions.

After the introduction of computers, an expert claimed that the demand for information systems would grow so astronomically that almost everyone would have to become a programmer. Does this sound familiar? The solution is to help end users meet their own information needs. As with telephones, technology is being developed to automate much of the process for us. Just as most people have learned to drive automobiles, so will inexpensive PCs, a wide variety of powerful and inexpensive software, increased computer literacy, easier-to-use programming tools, and the Internet allow most organizations and people to meet their information needs.

End-user computing (EUC) is the hands-on development, use, and control of computer-based information systems by users. EUC is people using IT to meet their information needs rather than relying on systems professionals. For example, a savings and loan in California wanted a system to track loan reserve requirements. When the information systems (IS) department said the system would take 18 months to develop, the loan department used a PC and a database program to develop a functional program in one day. Enhancing the program took several more days. The loan department not only cut the development time from 18 months to a few days, but also got the exact information it needed because users developed the system themselves.

end-user computing (EUC) - The hands-on development, use, and control of computer-based information systems by users.

The following are examples of appropriate end-user development:

- Retrieving information from company databases to produce simple reports or to answer one-time queries.
- Performing "what-if," sensitivity, or statistical analyses.
- Developing applications using software such as a spreadsheet or a database system.
- Preparing schedules, such as depreciation schedules and loan amortizations.

End-user development is inappropriate for complex systems, such as those that process a large number of transactions or update database records. Therefore, it is not used for processing payroll, accounts receivables and payables, general ledger, or inventory.

As end users meet their information needs, they realize they can use computers to meet more and more information needs. Increased access to data also creates many new uses and information needs. The result is a tremendous ongoing growth in EUC.

The growth in EUC has altered the information system staff's role. They continue to develop and maintain transaction processing systems and companywide databases. In addition, they provide users with technical advice and operational support and make as much information available to end users as possible. Although this has created more work for the IS staff, it is counterbalanced by a decreased demand for traditional services. If the trend in EUC continues, it will represent 75% to 95% of all information processing by the end of the next decade.

ADVANTAGES AND DISADVANTAGES OF END-USER COMPUTING

EUC offers the following advantages:

- ***User creation, control, and implementation.*** Users, rather than the IS department, control the development process. Users decide whether a system should be developed and what information is important. This ownership helps users develop better systems.
- ***Systems that meet user needs.*** Systems developed by end users are more likely to meet user needs. Users discover flaws that IS people do not catch. Many of the user-analyst-programmer communication problems in traditional program development are avoided.
- ***Timeliness.*** Much of the lengthy delay inherent in traditional systems development is avoided, such as time-consuming cost–benefit analyses, detailed requirements definitions, and the delays and red tape of the approval process.
- ***Freeing up of systems resources.*** The more information needs users meet, the more time the IS department can spend on other development and maintenance activities. This reduces both the visible and the invisible backlog of systems development projects.
- ***Versatility and ease of use.*** Most EUC software is easy to understand and use. Users can change the information they produce or modify their application any time their requirements change. With a laptop computer, employees can complete work at home, on a plane—almost anywhere.

However, there are significant drawbacks to EUC and to eliminating the involvement of analysts or programmers in the development process.

- ***Logic and development errors.*** With little experience in systems development, end users are more likely to make errors and less likely to recognize when errors have occurred. They may solve the wrong problem, poorly define system requirements, apply an inappropriate analytical method, use the wrong software, use incomplete or outdated information, use faulty logic, or incorrectly use formulas or software commands. An oil and gas company developed a complex spreadsheet that showed that a proposed acquisition was profitable. When their CPA firm tested the model and agreed with it, a board of directors meeting was scheduled to propose the acquisition. Shortly before the meeting, a presenter tested the model so that he could understand how it worked and answer tough questions. He discovered formulas that distorted the projections, so he called in the creator and the CPA firm. The corrected formulas showed a significant loss on the acquisition. The board presentation was canceled, and the spreadsheet creator and CPA firm were fired.

- ***Inadequately tested applications.*** Users are less likely to test their applications rigorously, either because they do not recognize the need to do so or because of the difficulty or time involved. One Big Four CPA firm found that 90% of the spreadsheet models it tested had at least one calculation error.
- ***Inefficient systems.*** Most end users are not programmers nor are they trained in systems development. As a result, their systems are not always efficient. One bank clerk spent three weeks developing a program that examined each cell in a spreadsheet and changed its value to zero if it was a negative amount. When the 60-page program began returning a "too many nested ifs" error message, the clerk called in a consultant. Within five minutes, the consultant developed a finished application using a built-in spreadsheet function.
- ***Poorly controlled and documented systems.*** Many end users do not implement controls to protect their systems. User-created systems are often poorly documented because the user considers the task boring or unimportant. Users fail to realize that without documentation, others cannot understand how their system works.
- ***System incompatibilities.*** Companies that add end-user equipment without considering the technological implications have a diversity of hardware and software that is difficult to support or network. Aetna Life & Casualty spent more than $1 billion a year on IT to gain a competitive advantage. The result was 50,000 PCs from a few dozen manufacturers, 2,000 servers, 19 incompatible e-mail systems, and 36 different communications networks. Aetna finally realized it needed to shift its emphasis from owning the latest technology to the effective use of technology. Aetna standardized its systems and now uses only a few different PCs, Microsoft software, two e-mail systems, and one network. The result is compatibility across all systems and significantly less cost.
- ***Duplication of systems and data; wasted resources.*** End users are typically unaware that other users have similar information needs, resulting in duplicate systems. Inexperienced users may take on more development than they are able to accomplish. Both of these problems end up wasting time and resources.
- ***Increased costs.*** A single PC purchase is inexpensive; buying hundreds or thousands is costly. So is updating the hardware and software every few years. EUC has a high opportunity cost if it diverts users' attention from their primary jobs. It also increases time and data demands on corporate information systems.

It is possible to achieve the proper balance between the benefits and risks of end-user systems by training users, using systems analysts as advisers, and requiring user-created systems to be reviewed and documented prior to use.

MANAGING AND CONTROLLING END-USER COMPUTING

Organizations must manage and control EUC. Giving the IS department control discourages EUC and eliminates its benefits. However, if the organization maintains no controls over end users, such as what EUC tools are purchased or how they are used, it is likely to lead to significant problems. It is best to provide enough guidance and standards to control the system yet allow users the flexibility they need.

A **help desk** supports and controls end-user activities. The 60 help desk analysts and technicians at Schering-Plough handle 9,000 calls a month. Front-line analysts use expert system software to find scripted answers to user questions. Second-line technicians handle queries that are more complicated. Other companies use multimedia software with animation or videos to help staffers walk callers through a complicated process.

help desk - Analysts and technicians who answer employee questions with the purpose of encouraging, supporting, coordinating, and controlling end-user activity.

Help desk duties include resolving problems, disseminating information, evaluating new hardware and software products and training end users how to use them, assisting with application development, and providing technical maintenance and support. Help desks also develop and implement standards for hardware and software purchases, documentation, application testing, and security. Lastly, the help desk controls access to and sharing of corporate data among end users, while ensuring that the data are not duplicated and that access to confidential data remains restricted.

Outsourcing the System

outsourcing - Hiring an outside company to handle all or part of an organization's data processing activities.

Outsourcing is hiring an outside company to handle all or part of an organization's data processing activities. In mainframe outsourcing agreements, outsourcers buy client computers, hire the client's IS employees, operate and manage the system on the client's site, or migrate the system to the outsourcer's computers. Many outsourcing contracts are in effect for up to 10 years and cost millions of dollars a year. In a client/server or a PC outsourcing agreement, a service, function, or segment of business is outsourced. Most Fortune 500 companies outsource their PC support function. Royal Dutch Shell, the international oil company, has 80,000 PCs worldwide and outsources its installation, maintenance, training, help desk, and technical support.

Outsourcing was initially used for standardized applications such as payroll and accounting or by companies who wanted a cash infusion from selling their hardware. In 1989, Eastman Kodak surprised the business world by hiring IBM to run its data processing operations, DEC to run its telecommunications functions, and Businessland to run its PC operations. Kodak retained its IS strategic planning and development role, but outsourcers performed the implementation and operation responsibilities. The results were dramatic. Computer expenditures fell 90%. Operating expenses decreased 10% to 20%. Annual IS savings during the 10-year agreement were expected to be $130 million. Several years later, Xerox signed what was then the largest outsourcing deal in history: a $3.2 billion, 10-year contract with EDS to outsource its computing, telecommunications, and software management in 19 countries.

In one survey, 73% of companies outsourced some or all of their information systems, and most outsourced to several companies to increase flexibility, foster competition, and reduce costs. Most companies do not, however, outsource strategic IT management, business process management, or IT architecture.

Many smaller companies outsource. One company with annual revenues of $1 million outsources all accounting functions to a local CPA. Whenever they want, the owners can view all their transactions on the CPA's website and produce a myriad of reports. They also outsourced all IT processes, including website design and maintenance.

ADVANTAGES AND DISADVANTAGES OF OUTSOURCING

There are a number of significant advantages to outsourcing:

- ***A business solution.*** Outsourcing is a viable strategic and economic business solution that allows companies to concentrate on core competencies. Kodak focused on what it does best and left data processing to qualified computer companies. Kodak treats its outsourcers as partners and works closely with them to meet strategic and operational objectives.
- ***Asset utilization.*** Organizations improve their cash position and reduce expenses by selling assets to an outsourcer. Health Dimension outsourced data processing at its four hospitals so it could use its limited monetary resources to generate revenue.
- ***Access to greater expertise and better technology.*** Del Monte Foods turned to outsourcing because the cost and time involved in staying at the cutting edge of technology were rising significantly.
- ***Lower costs.*** IBM outsources programming to Chinese companies, whose labor costs are 30% of those in the United States. Outsourcers lower costs by standardizing user applications, buying hardware at bulk prices, splitting development and maintenance costs between projects, and operating at higher volumes. Continental Bank will save $100 million during its 10-year contract. However, Occidental Petroleum rejected outsourcing as costing more than internal AIS development and operation.
- ***Less development time.*** Experienced industry specialists develop and implement systems faster and more efficiently than in-house staff. Outsourcers also help cut through systems development politics.
- ***Elimination of peaks-and-valleys usage.*** Seasonal businesses require significant computer resources part of the year, and little the rest of the year. From January to March, W. Atlee Burpee's computers operated at 80% capacity processing seed and gardening

orders and at 20% the rest of the time. Outsourcing cut Burpee's processing costs in half by paying based on how much the system is used.

- ***Facilitation of downsizing.*** Companies that downsize often have an unnecessarily large AIS function. General Dynamics downsized dramatically because of reductions in defense industry spending. It signed a $3 billion, 10-year outsourcing contract even though its IS function was rated number one in the aerospace industry. It sold its data centers to CSC for $200 million and transferred 2,600 employees to CSC.

However, not all outsourcing experiences have been successful. Between 25% and 50% of outsourcing agreements fail or are major disappointments. In one survey, company executives labeled 17% of them disasters and almost 50% were brought back in-house. There have been a number of significant outsourcing failures, including the problems EDS has had with its U.S. Navy contract (see Focus 22-2). Another is JPMorgan Chase's cancellation of its $5 billion, seven-year deal with IBM.

Outsourcing failures are caused by failure to prepare properly, lukewarm company buy-in, blind imitation of competitors, thinking that outsourcing will solve deeper problems, shifting responsibility for a bad process to someone else, and entering into ill-defined agreements that do not meet expectations. Finally, many companies do not realize that systems development is a more complex management challenge when performed by outsiders.

Companies that outsource often experience some of the following drawbacks:

- ***Inflexibility.*** Many contracts are for 10 years. If a company is dissatisfied or has structural changes, the contract is difficult or costly to break. Before they merged, Integra Financial and Equimark had contracts with different outsourcers. Canceling one of them cost $4.5 million.
- ***Loss of control.*** A company runs the risk of losing control of its system and its data. For that reason, Ford's outsourcing agreement prevents CSC from working with other automobile manufacturers.
- ***Reduced competitive advantage.*** Companies may lose sight of how their AIS produces competitive advantages. Outsourcers are not as motivated as their clients to meet competitive challenges. Companies can mitigate this problem by outsourcing standard business processes (payroll, cash disbursements, etc.) and customizing those that provide competitive advantages.
- ***Locked-in system.*** It is expensive and difficult to reverse outsourcing. A company may have to buy new equipment and hire a new data processing staff, often at prohibitive costs. When Blue Cross of California decided to end its agreement, it knew virtually nothing about its system and could not afford to discharge EDS. In contrast, LSI Logic brought its system back in-house at significant dollar and personnel savings when it installed an enterprise resource planning (ERP) system.
- ***Unfulfilled goals.*** Critics claim some outsourcing benefits, such as increased efficiency, are a myth. USF&G canceled its $100 million contract with Cigna Information Services after 18 months when Cigna could not make the system work properly.
- ***Poor service.*** Common complaints are that responsiveness to changing business conditions is slow or nonexistent and migration to new technologies is poorly planned.
- ***Increased risk.*** Outsourcing business processes can expose a company to significant operational, financial, technology, strategy, personnel, legal, and regulatory risks.

Methods for Improving Systems Development

The systems analysis and design process has evolved considerably since computer programming began in the 1950s with programs developed in machine language or assembly language. Third generation languages were introduced in the 1960s, database management systems in the 1970s, and fourth generation languages in the 1980s. The 1990s brought visual development technologies and integrated enterprise resource planning systems (ERP). By the 2000s, the development of Internet-based web systems and the use of mobile devices, cloud computing, and resource sharing systems were in full swing. The coming years will undoubtedly produce more improvements and changes.

Information system development is a complex and difficult process, fraught with many failures. As time has evolved, the software industry has developed a number of techniques to simplify, improve, and speed up the development process. This section of the chapter discusses some of the more important ones, including business process management, prototyping, agile technologies, and computer-aided software engineering.

BUSINESS PROCESS MANAGEMENT

business process reengineering (BPR) - The thorough analysis and redesign of business processes and information systems to achieve dramatic performance improvements; often a drastic, one-time event.

business process management (BPM) - A systematic approach to continuously improving and optimizing business processes; a more gradual improvement facilitated by technology.

As organizations seek to improve their information systems and comply with legal and regulatory reforms, they are paying greater attention to their business processes. **Business process reengineering (BPR)** is a drastic, one-time-event approach to improving and automating business processes. However, it has had a low success rate. With further improvements, BPR has evolved into **business process management (BPM)**, a systematic approach to continuously improving and optimizing an organization's business processes. BPM is a more gradual and ongoing business process improvement supported and enabled by technology. As a result, BPM is a good way to introduce both a human and a technological change capability into an organization.

Some of the important principles underlying BPM are the following:

- ***Business processes can produce competitive advantages.*** Innovative processes that help business respond to changing consumer, market, and regulatory demands faster than competitors create competitive advantages. Good business process design is vital to an organization's success. For example, if a competitive bidding process is time sensitive and requires coordination between multiple functions, a poorly designed bid process can handicap the process so much that effective and profitable bids are not prepared.
- ***Business processes must be managed end to end.*** BPM views business processes as strategic organizational assets that should be understood, managed, and improved. Even if each part of a multifunctional business process functions well independently, the entire process may be suboptimal if there is inadequate communication and coordination among functional units (sales, production, etc.). Managing business processes from inception to completion can control such problems. A process owner is designated, performance standards are set, and control and monitoring processes are established.
- ***Business processes should be agile.*** Organizations must continuously improve and adapt their business processes to compete. This requires flexibility and business process automation technology that supports rapid modifications.
- ***Business processes must be aligned with organizational strategy and needs.*** To be effective and efficient, a company must align its business processes with its business strategy.

business process management systems (BPMS) - Systems that automate and facilitate business process improvements throughout the SDLC.

Business process management systems (BPMS) automate and facilitate business process improvements. A BPMS can improve communication and collaboration, automate activities, and integrate with other systems and with other partners in the value chain. Some people claim that BPMS is the bridge between IT and business. Many companies worldwide are successfully implementing BPMS-based processes.

Like enterprise resource planning (ERP) systems, BPMS are enterprise-wide systems that support corporate activities. However, ERP systems are data-centered and BPMS are process-centered. Most manufactures of ERP systems are now integrating BPM into their systems.

A BPMS has the following four major components:

- A process engine to model and execute applications, including business rules.
- Business analytics to help identify and react to business issues, trends, and opportunities.
- Collaboration tools to remove communication barriers.
- A content manager to store and secure electronic documents, images, and other files.

INTERNAL CONTROLS IN A BUSINESS PROCESS MANAGEMENT SYSTEM A BPMS can improve internal controls. In event-based (as opposed to process-based) systems, users are granted access only to certain activity types. When authorization is granted using other parameters, such as dollar amounts, system developers have to include complex and expensive authorization restrictions. A BPMS uses the organization's business process rules to determine the correct person to perform a task and authorizes that person to perform it.

Segregation of duties can also be improved in a BPMS. In many event-based systems, the procedures for obtaining management approvals lengthen the business process and add additional costs. BPMS reduces the delays and costs by instantaneously transferring items needing approval to the manager. Within a few minutes, the manager can inspect and authorize the electronic form and transfer it to the next step in the process. BPMS have several other innovative authorization mechanisms, such as delegating authority to co-managers and creating a pool of authorizing managers to reduce bottlenecks when managers are overburdened or unavailable.

Application controls are also strengthened by a BPMS. In event-based systems, users identify what actions must be done, such as billing a customer when goods are shipped. If the action is not taken, an error occurs, such as doing something twice, not doing it at all, or doing the wrong thing. A BPMS uses a proactive process management approach that eliminates such problems. Users do not have to decide whether to take action and then decide which action is correct. The BPMS, using the company's business rules, decides what action must take place and forwards the task to the appropriate person's task list, where it remains until it is executed. The person gets an e-mail informing them that the task awaits their attention. This process prevents errors because it prevents procedures from being circumvented, prevents users from performing a different action, prevents items from being removed from the task list before they are accomplished, and sends additional reminder messages until the task is performed.

Another control advantage of BPMS is its built-in audit trail. The process monitoring and tracking systems, which document and link all actions and process steps in the order they occur in a process log, make it easy to track everything that takes place. This allows the auditor to continuously audit the business processes while they are active and afterward.

PROTOTYPING

Prototyping is a systems design approach in which a simplified working model of a system is developed. Developers who use prototyping still go through the SDLC discussed in Chapter 22, but prototyping allows them to condense and speed up some analysis and design tasks. Prototyping helps capture user needs and helps developers and users make conceptual and physical design decisions.

prototyping - An approach to systems design in which a simplified working model, or prototype, of an IS is developed.

UNUM Life Insurance wanted to use image processing to link systems and users. When top management had a hard time getting middle managers to understand how the system would work and the issues involved in the change, they had a prototype prepared. After using it, the managers grasped the possibilities and issues. Up to that point, they thought image processing meant replacing file cabinets.

As shown in Figure 23-1, a prototype is developed using four steps. The first is to meet with users to agree on the size and scope of the system and to decide what the system should and should not include. Developers and users also determine decision-making and transaction processing outputs as well as the inputs and data needed to produce the outputs. The emphasis is on *what* output should be produced rather than *how* it should be produced. The developer must ensure that users' expectations are realistic and that their basic information requirements can be met. The designer uses the information requirements to develop cost, time, and feasibility estimates for alternative AIS solutions.

The second step is to develop an initial prototype. The emphasis is on low cost and rapid development. Nonessential functions, controls, exception handling, input validation, and processing speed are ignored in the interests of simplicity, flexibility, and ease of use. Users need to see and use tentative data entry screens, menus, and source documents; respond to prompts; query the system; judge response times; and issue commands. The developer demonstrates the finished prototype and asks users to provide feedback on what they like and dislike, which is much easier to do than imagining what they want in a system. Even a simple system that is not fully functional demonstrates features better than diagrams, drawings, or verbal explanations.

In the third step, developers use the feedback to modify the system and return it to the users. Trial usage and modification continues until users are satisfied that the system meets their needs. A typical prototype goes through four to six iterations.

FIGURE 23-1
The Steps for Developing a System from a Prototype

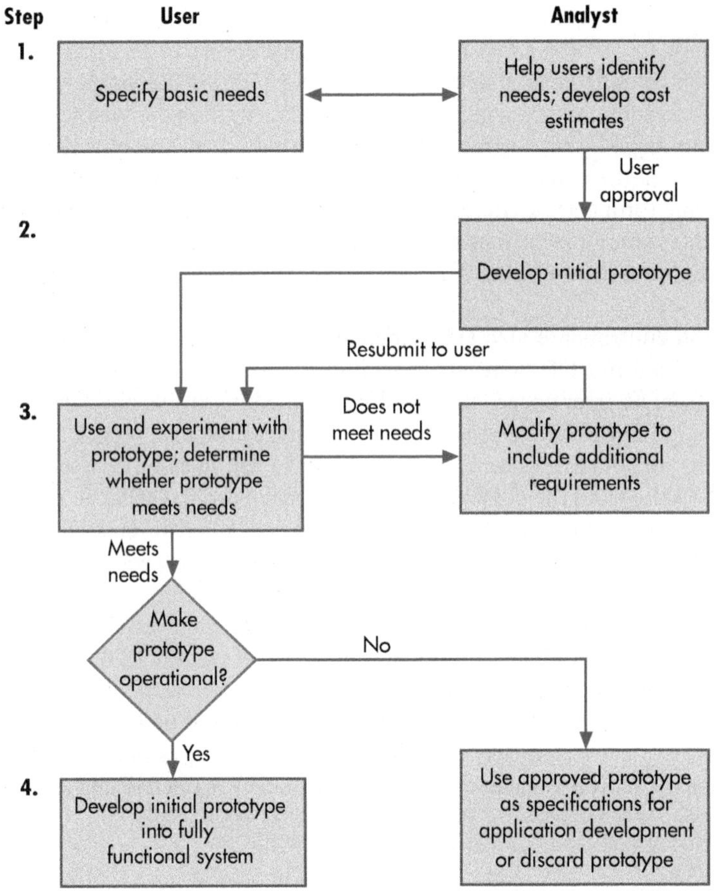

operational prototypes - Prototypes that are further developed into fully functional systems.

nonoperational (throwaway) prototypes - Prototypes that are discarded, but the system requirements identified from the prototypes are used to develop a new system.

The fourth step is to use the system. An approved prototype is typically used in one of two ways. Half of all prototypes are turned into fully functional systems, referred to as **operational prototypes**. To make the prototype operational, the developer incorporates the things ignored in step one, provides backup and recovery, and integrates the prototype with other systems. **Nonoperational (throwaway) prototypes** are used several ways. System requirements identified during prototyping can be used to develop a new system. The prototype can be used as the initial prototype for an expanded system designed to meet the needs of many different users. When an unsalvageable prototype is discarded, the company potentially saves itself years of development work and lots of money by avoiding the traditional SDLC process.

WHEN TO USE PROTOTYPING Prototyping is appropriate when there is a high level of uncertainty, it is unclear what questions to ask, the AIS cannot be clearly visualized, or there is a high likelihood of failure. Good candidates for prototyping include decision support systems, executive information systems, expert systems, and information retrieval systems. Prototyping is less appropriate for large or complex systems that serve major organizational components or cross-organizational boundaries or for developing standard AIS components, such as accounts receivable or inventory management. Table 23-3 shows the conditions that make prototyping an appropriate design methodology.

ADVANTAGES OF PROTOTYPING Prototyping has the following advantages:

- ***Better definition of user needs.*** Prototyping generally requires intensive involvement from end users, resulting in well-defined user needs.
- ***Higher user involvement and satisfaction.*** Because users' requirements are met, there is less risk that the AIS will not be used. Early user involvement helps to build a climate of acceptance rather than skepticism and criticism.

TABLE 23-3 Conditions That Favor the Use of Prototyping

Users' needs are not understood, change rapidly, or evolve as the system is used.
System requirements are hard to define.
System inputs and outputs are not known.
The task to be performed is not well structured.
Designers are uncertain about what technology to use.
The system is crucial and needed quickly.
The risk associated with developing the wrong system is high.
User reactions are especially important development considerations.
Many design strategies must be tested.
The design staff has little experience developing the system or application.
The system will be used infrequently (processing efficiency is not a major concern).

- ***Faster development time.*** Prototypes are often functioning after a few days or weeks, allowing users to immediately evaluate the system. John Hancock Mutual Life Insurance developed an executive information system prototype in one month, as described in Focus 23-2.
- ***Fewer errors.*** The users test each version of the prototype, so errors are detected and eliminated early. It is also easier to identify and terminate infeasible systems before a great deal of time and expense is incurred.
- ***More opportunity for changes.*** Users can suggest changes until the system is exactly what they want.
- ***Less costly.*** Prototype systems can be developed for 20% of the cost of traditional systems. One utility company claimed a 13-to-1 improvement in development time over traditional methods when prototyping was used to develop 10 major applications.

DISADVANTAGES OF PROTOTYPING Prototyping has the following disadvantages:

- ***Significant user time.*** Users must devote significant time to working with the prototype and providing feedback. It may require more involvement and commitment than users are willing to give.
- ***Less efficient use of system resources.*** Prototype development does not always achieve resource efficiency, sometimes resulting in poor performance and reliability as well as high maintenance and support costs.
- ***Inadequate testing and documentation.*** Developers may shortchange testing and documentation because users are testing the prototype during development.
- ***Negative behavioral reactions.*** These can occur when requests for improvements are not made, there are too many iterations, or a prototype that users are invested in is thrown away.
- ***Never-ending development.*** This occurs when prototyping is not managed properly and the prototype is never completed due to recurring iterations and revision requests.

AGILE METHODOLOGIES

One of the problems with the traditional SDLC approach, often called the waterfall approach, is that it assumes requirements do not change as a system is designed. Figure 22-2 shows the waterfall nature of this development and the reasons why a developer would return to a prior SDLC phase. However, the reality is that in many systems development projects, requirements do change because users often do not understand all the things they want the software to do. That is, they discover more and different requirements as the software development process proceeds. Furthermore, as technology changes so fast, more things can be accomplished with technology. These rapid changes in requirements and technology created the need for shorter product life cycles that were often not compatible with traditional software development methodologies.

What many system developers wanted was a more iterative development methodology—one that embraced changes in requirements rather than restricted them and that was better agile development - A guiding philosophy and a set of principles for developing information systems in an unknown, rapidly changing environment.

scrum methodology - A software development methodology where a team works together in an intense but relatively short iterative and incremental scrum process to reach a common development goal, with team members meeting daily in face-to-face communication, until development is concluded.

scrum development - A process that embraces customers frequently changing their minds about what they need or want. Scrum development focuses on flexibility, responding to new requirements, adapting to evolving changes in technology, and quickly delivering a system the customer can evaluate.

product owner - The customer who is responsible for making sure the scrum team produces what is needed. They write the user stories and prioritize backlog items so the scrum team knows what to develop next.

user stories - A description of something a user wants to include in the system written by the product owner.

product backlog - Items waiting to be developed that are prioritized by the product owner.

scrum team - A small group of up to 9 cross-functional developers responsible for developing, testing, and delivering software at the end of a scrum sprint. The team determines a sprint's major goals and deliverables.

sprint - A pre-determined time period where the team works on high priority items in the product backlog. A sprint's scope is frozen and desired changes are added to the product backlog. Sprints begin with a planning event to determine goals and deliverables and ends with a review to see if they were achieved. The incremental software developed is presented to the customer.

scrum master - Scrum facilitator who makes sure scrum practices are followed, promotes self-organization within the team, holds daily team meetings, works with the product owner to make sure the product backlog is properly maintained, and removes any impediments that affect the team's ability to achieve its goals and produce the sprint's deliverables.

able to deal with a lack of predictability in software development. They wanted a development process designed to produce frequent versions of a working system, with each succeeding iteration including more subsets of what users wanted in their system. In other words, they wanted to embrace smaller, incremental changes rather than a one-time, massive change in the software. These new processes require users and developers to work closely together with frequent feedback between the two groups to produce the desired system.

In 2001, proponents of a more iterative development process met and came up with **agile development**, a guiding philosophy and a set of principles for developing information systems in an unknown, rapidly changing environment. According to the agile development philosophy, it is more important to:

1. Respond to change than to follow a plan or predefined schedule.
2. Emphasize individuals and interactions than processes, tools, and development controls.
3. Emphasize customer collaboration than contract negotiations.
4. Produce quality software than to produce good software documentation.

There are a number of development methodologies that make use of agile development principles. Three of the most important are discussed here: Scrum, Extreme Programming, and the Unified Process.

SCRUM Scrum's name is derived from the game of rugby. After a penalty, players from both teams line up across from each other in a tightly-packed formation and the ball is thrown into the gap between the teams. What follows is an intense and relatively short struggle between the two teams in order to gain possession of the ball. Like the rugby scrum, the **scrum methodology** involves a software development team that works together in an intense but relatively short process to reach a common development goal. The iterative and incremental scrum process continues to repeat itself, with team members meeting daily in face-to-face communication, until development is concluded.

Those involved in **scrum development** embrace the fact that the intended users, called the client or customer, will frequently change their minds about what they need or want. They accept the unpredictability associated with the customer not fully understanding or being able to define all their system needs. Instead, they focus on flexibility, responding to new requirements, adapting to evolving changes in technology and market conditions, and quickly delivering a system that the customer can evaluate.

In the scrum process there are three main roles: product owner, team members, and scrum master. The **product owner** is the customer who is responsible for making sure the scrum team produces what is needed. The product owner works with system users and writes **user stories** (a description of something a user wants to include in the system), places them in the **product backlog** (items waiting to be developed), and prioritizes the backlog items so the team knows what to develop next. The product owner spends much of his or her time focusing on the business side of the development project, working with users to identify their business needs, and serving as the communication bridge between the users and the scrum team.

The **scrum team** is a small group of up to 9 cross-functional developers responsible for developing, testing, and delivering software at the end of a scrum sprint. A **sprint** is a pre-determined time period, usually between one and four weeks, that the team works on one or more high priority items in the product backlog. A sprint's scope is frozen and anyone desiring changes must ask the product owner to add them to the product backlog. Each sprint begins with a planning event where the team determines the sprint's goals and deliverables and ends with a sprint review to see if they were achieved and to determine how to improve the next sprint. The incremental software developed during the sprint is presented to the customer.

The **scrum master** is the scrum facilitator that ensures scrum practices are followed and helps the team self-organize. She acts as a buffer between the team and any distracting influences by removing impediments that affect the team's ability to achieve its goals and produce the sprint's deliverables. The scrum master works with the product owner to make sure the product backlog is properly maintained. The scrum master holds a brief daily scrum meeting with all team members where they report the progress made the day before, what they will work on that day, and what help they need from the scrum master to remove an impediment.

EXTREME PROGRAMMING **Extreme programming (XP)** is a software development methodology designed to produce higher-quality software more productively by taking the beneficial elements and best practices of traditional software development to "extreme" levels. Some of the more important characteristics of XP include.

extreme programming (XP) - A software development methodology designed to produce higher-quality software more productively by taking the beneficial elements and best practices of traditional software development to "extreme" levels.

- Uses two-person programming teams.
- Recognizes that changes to systems requirements are a normal and accepted occurrence in software development that should be expected and planned for as time passes and system needs are better understood. XP embraces changes and abandons the idea that a stable set of requirements can be produced during the initial planning phase of development.
- Uses short development cycles, culminating in frequent software releases, so that there are many checkpoints that allow new customer requirements to be introduced. Makes many small, incremental changes, rather than a few big changes, allowing the customer more control over the software development process. It reduces the cost of changes and improves development productivity.
- Starts with the simplest solution and only adds extra functionality as needed. Trying to design and code uncertain or complex future requirements might delay crucial features and risks spending resources on features that might not be needed or desired.
- Uses code to communicate thoughts about complex or hard to understand programming problems. Often, clear and concise code can better explain a problem than a written or oral description of the problem. Other programmers can give feedback on this code by coding their thoughts about the problem.
- Requires programmers to listen to customer needs and understand their business processes so they can provide customer feedback about the technical aspects of how a problem can or cannot be solved.
- Tests extensively every piece of code written before developing additional features to eliminate as many coding flaws as possible. Programmers create as many automated tests as possible to try to break the code. **Unit tests** help determine whether a given feature works as intended. **Acceptance tests** are used to verify that code satisfies the customer's actual requirements. System-wide **integration tests** are used to check for incompatible interfaces between code segments.
- Requires frequent and prompt communication and feedback between customers, developers, and testers. Customers communicate their needs and help develop the acceptance tests that occur every few weeks so they can easily correct design flaws and steer development. Developers estimate the costs and the time required to implement new requirements and communicate them to customers. Developers need feedback from testers to correct errors or weaknesses found during testing.
- Organizes system logic to prevent system dependencies so that changes in one part of the system will not affect other parts of the system.

unit tests - Help determine whether a given feature works as intended.

acceptance tests - Used to verify that code satisfies the customer's actual requirements.

integration tests - Used to check for incompatible interfaces between code segments.

UNIFIED PROCESS The **Unified Process** is a software development framework with four phases: inception, elaboration, construction, and transition. The last three phases are divided into a series of iterations of a predetermined length. Each incremental iteration contains additional functions or an improved version of the previously developed software. There are several versions, including Agile Unified Process, OpenUP, and the most popular—the Rational Unified Process.

Unified Process - A development framework with four phases: inception, elaboration, construction, and transition. The last three phases are divided into a series of iterations of a predetermined length. Each incremental iteration contains additional functions or an improved version of the previously developed software.

Inception is the shortest phase; if it takes too long it usually indicates that there are too many or too detailed up-front specifications. In the inception phase, analysts define the project's scope, identify preliminary key requirements and risks, determine the project's feasibility, and make the business case for developing the project.

In the elaboration phase, which is the second longest and considered by some to be the most important, analysts do most of the analysis and design activities for the project. They develop detailed user requirements and determine how to address known risk factors, with the executable architecture baseline - A partial implementation of the system that includes all significant architecture components and demonstrates that the architecture supports key system functionality and will produce the desired performance and scalability at an acceptable cost.

most important risks addressed first. They determine the system's architecture and validate it using an **executable architecture baseline**, which is a partial implementation of the system that includes all significant architecture components and demonstrates that the architecture supports key system functionality and will produce the desired performance and scalability at an acceptable cost. The phase concludes with a plan for the Construction phase.

Construction, the longest phase, is where the system is coded and built, using the foundation created in the elaboration phase. The system is built and implemented in a series of short iterations, each of which results in an executable software release. Each new iteration is based on a use case. The construction phase ends with a beta version of the software that will be deployed during the transition phase.

In the transition phase, the system is made available to system users. System conversions and user training also take place during transition. The transition phase often includes several iterations, and user feedback during the initial transition phases is used to refine the system in the later transition phases. The transition phase is complete when the system meets user expectations and acceptance test criteria are satisfied.

COMPUTER-AIDED SOFTWARE ENGINEERING

computer-aided software (or systems) engineering (CASE) - Integrated package of tools that skilled designers use to help plan, analyze, design, program, and maintain an IS.

Computer-aided software (or systems) engineering (CASE) is an integrated package of tools that skilled designers use to help plan, analyze, design, program, and maintain an information system. CASE software typically has tools for strategic planning, project and system management, database design, screen and report layout, and automatic code generation. Many companies use CASE tools. Florida Power's $86 million customer information system was created using Accenture's CASE tool.

CASE tools provide a number of important advantages:

- ***Improved productivity.*** CASE can generate bug-free code from system specifications and can automate repetitive tasks. A programmer at Baptist Medical System used CASE to develop a system in one week that was estimated to take four months. Sony reported that CASE increased their productivity by 600%.
- ***Improved program quality.*** CASE tools simplify the enforcement of structured development standards, check the internal accuracy of the design, and detect inconsistencies.
- ***Cost savings.*** Savings of 80% to 90% are reported. At DuPont, an application estimated to require 27 months at a cost of $270,000 was finished in 4 months for $30,000. More than 90% of the code was generated directly from design specifications.
- ***Improved control procedures.*** CASE tools encourage system controls, security measures, and system auditability and error-handling procedures early in the design process.
- ***Simplified documentation.*** CASE automatically documents the system as the development progresses.

FOCUS 23-2 Prototyping at John Hancock

John Hancock Mutual Life Insurance was dissatisfied with the traditional development process. Too often, after development the typical user reaction was, "I may have said this is what I wanted, but it isn't." To counter this problem, Hancock used prototyping to develop an executive information system (EIS) that would obtain data quickly and easily from the existing system.

The development team included IBM consultants, users, systems analysts, and programmers. The prototyping process was highly interactive, and continual user involvement eliminated many misunderstandings. Programming started immediately, preparing sample screens for the first user interviews. Developers showed the users how the system would work and gave them a chance to try the screens. Almost immediately, users could determine whether what they said they wanted was what they needed.

The EIS prototype, which took a month to build, allowed top management to query current and historical financial data and measurements. Top managers who were skeptical when the project began were impressed by how much the team was able to accomplish in a single month.

Some of the more serious problems with CASE technology include the following:

- ***Incompatibility.*** Some CASE tools do not interact effectively with other systems.
- ***Cost.*** CASE technology is expensive, putting it out of the reach of many small companies.
- ***Unmet expectations.*** A Deloitte & Touche survey indicated that only 37% of CIOs using CASE believe they achieved the expected benefits.

Summary and Case Conclusion

A company can use different strategies to obtain a new AIS. First, as the quality and quantity of vendor-written software increases, more companies are purchasing it. Second, IS departments develop the software or allow end users to develop it. Third, some companies buy software and modify it themselves or ask the vendor to modify it so it meets company needs. Fourth, companies outsource data processing activities.

There are many ways to speed up or improve the development process. One way is business process management, which is a systematic approach to continuously improving and optimizing an organization's business processes.

A second way is to design a prototype, a simplified working model of a system. A prototype is quickly and inexpensively built and is given to users to "test-drive" so they can decide what they like and dislike about the system. Their reactions and feedback are used to modify the system, which is again given to the users to test. This iterative process of trial usage and modification continues until the users are satisfied that the system adequately meets their needs.

A third way to improve the development process is to use CASE tools to plan, analyze, design, program, and maintain an information system. They are also used to enhance the efforts of managers, users, and programmers in understanding information needs.

Ann considered the different strategies and eliminated several of them. She decided against outsourcing because she believes her team can do a better and faster job developing the system than an outsourcer could. Ann does not think prototyping would be effective because Shoppers Mart needs a large and complex system that would serve the needs of many users in many functional areas. Ann narrowed her options down to purchasing a system or designing one in-house. If Shoppers Mart develops its own software, Ann will investigate the various CASE and BPMS packages on the market to see whether they will add value to the development process.

No matter which approach she chooses, Ann wants to facilitate as much end-user development as is practical and useful. Ann will make the final decision during the conceptual design phase (Chapter 24). To gather the information she needs to decide whether to purchase software, Ann prepares and sends an RFP to vendors asking them to propose software and hardware to meet the company's needs identified during systems analysis.

KEY TERMS

commercial software 730
turnkey system 730
Software-as-a-Service (SaaS) providers 730
request for proposal (RFP) 730
benchmark problem 731
point scoring 731
requirement costing 732
custom software 733
end-user computing (EUC) 733
help desk 735
outsourcing 736
business process reengineering (BPR) 738
business process management (BPM) 738
business process management systems (BPMS) 738
prototyping 739
operational prototypes 740
nonoperational (throwaway) prototypes 740
agile development 742
scrum methodology 742
scrum development 742
product owner 742
user stories 742
product backlog 742
scrum team 742
sprint 742
scrum master 742
extreme programming (XP) 743
unit tests 743
acceptance tests 743
integration tests 743
Unified Process 743
executable architecture baseline 744
computer-aided software (or systems) engineering (CASE) 744

AIS in Action

CHAPTER QUIZ

1. Which of the following is not one of the difficulties software developers have experienced using the traditional systems development life cycle?
   a. AIS development projects are backlogged for years.
   b. Changes are usually not possible after requirements have been frozen.
   c. The AIS developed may not meet their needs.
   d. All are difficulties with the traditional SDLC.

2. Companies that buy rather than develop an AIS must still go through the systems development life cycle.
   a. true
   b. false

3. Which of the following statements is false?
   a. As a general rule, companies should buy rather than develop software if they can find commercial software that meets their needs.
   b. As an AIS increases in size and complexity, there is a greater likelihood that commercial software can be found that meets user needs.
   c. A company should not attempt to develop its own custom software unless experienced, in-house programming personnel are available and the job can be completed less expensively on the inside.
   d. As a general rule, a company should develop custom software only when it will provide a significant competitive advantage.

4. When a company is buying large and complex systems, vendors are invited to submit systems for consideration. What is such a solicitation called?
   a. request for quotation
   b. request for system
   c. request for proposal
   d. good-faith estimate

5. To compare system performance, a company can create a data processing task with input, processing, and output jobs. This task is performed on the systems under consideration, and the processing times are compared. The AIS with the lowest time is the most efficient. What is this process called?
   a. benchmarking
   b. requirements costing
   c. point scoring
   d. performance testing

6. Which of the following statements is true?
   a. Because the AIS is so crucial, companies never outsource parts of the AIS.
   b. Most mainframe outsourcing contracts are for two to three years and cost thousands of dollars a year.
   c. Outsourcers often buy the client's computers and hire all or most of its information systems employees.
   d. Only companies struggling to survive and wanting a quick infusion of cash from selling their hardware use outsourcing.

7. Which of the following is not a benefit of outsourcing?
   a. It offers a great deal of flexibility because it is relatively easy to change outsourcers.
   b. It can provide access to the expertise and special services provided by outsourcers.
   c. It allows companies to move to a more sophisticated level of computing at a reasonable cost.
   d. It is a cost-effective way to handle the peaks and valleys found in seasonal businesses.

8. Which of the following is a true statement about prototyping?
   a. In the early stages of prototyping, system controls and exception handling may be sacrificed in the interests of simplicity, flexibility, and ease of use.
   b. A prototype is a scaled-down, first-draft model that is quickly and inexpensively built and given to users to evaluate.

c. The first step in prototyping is to identify system requirements.
d. All of the statements are true.

9. Which of the following is not an advantage of prototyping?
a. better definition of user needs
b. adequately tested and documented systems
c. higher user involvement and satisfaction
d. faster development time

10. When is it most appropriate to use prototyping?
a. when there is little uncertainty about the AIS
b. when it is clear what users' needs are
c. when the final AIS cannot be clearly visualized because the decision process is still unclear
d. when there is a very low likelihood of failure

COMPREHENSIVE PROBLEM

In 1991, telemarketers placed 18 million calls per day; by 2003, it was 104 million. President Bush announced the Do Not Call Registry by saying, "Unwanted telemarketing calls are intrusive, they are annoying, and they're all too common. When Americans are sitting down to dinner, or a parent is reading to his or her child, the last thing they need is a call from a stranger with a sales pitch." Congress appropriated $18.1 million to fund the program, which made it a federal offense for telemarketers to call anyone on the list. Within 72 hours, more than 10 million phone numbers were added to the Do Not Call list when people accessed the donotcall.gov website or called the toll-free number. The Do Not Call Registry was hailed as one the most successful IT projects in the history of government.

Identify the benefits and risks of the FTC purchasing a prewritten software system, developing the system in-house, and outsourcing the system to an external vendor. What approach do you think the FTC should have used?

(*Source:* Adapted from Alice Dragoon, "How the FTC Rescued the Dinner Hour," *CIO* [June 1, 2004]: 59–64.)

DISCUSSION QUESTIONS

23.1 What is the accountant's role in the computer acquisition process? Should the accountant play an active role, or should all the work be left to computer experts? In what aspects of computer acquisition might an accountant provide a useful contribution?

23.2 In a Midwest city of 45,000, a computer was purchased, and in-house programmers began developing programs. Four years later, only one incomplete and poorly functioning application had been developed, none of the software met users' minimum requirements, and the hardware and the software frequently failed. Why do you think the city was unable to produce quality, workable software? Would the city have been better off purchasing commercial software? Could the city have found commercial software that met its needs? Why, or why not?

23.3 You are a systems consultant for Ernst, Price, and Deloitte, CPAs. At your country club's annual golf tournament, Frank Fender, an automobile dealer, describes a proposal from Turnkey Systems and asks for your opinion. The commercial software system will handle inventories, receivables, payroll, accounts payable, and general ledger accounting. Turnkey personnel would install the $40,000 system and train Fender's employees. Identify the major themes you would touch on in responding to Fender. Identify the advantages and disadvantages of using a turnkey system with commercial software for the organization's accounting system.

23.4 Sara Jones owns a rapidly growing retail store that faces stiff competition due to poor customer service, late and error-prone billing, and inefficient inventory control. For the company's growth to continue, its AIS must be upgraded, but Sara is not sure what the company wants the AIS to accomplish. Sara has heard about prototyping but does not know what it is or whether it would help. How would you explain prototyping to Sara? Include an explanation of its advantages and disadvantages as well as when its use is appropriate.

23.5 Clint Grace has been in business more than 30 years and has definite ideas about how his 10 retail stores should be run. He is financially conservative and is reluctant to make expenditures that do not have a clear financial payoff. Store profitability has declined sharply, and customer dissatisfaction is high. Store managers never know how much inventory is on hand and when purchases are needed until a shelf is empty. Clint asks you to determine why profitability has declined and to recommend a solution. You determine that the current AIS is inefficient and unreliable and that company processes and procedures are out-of-date. You believe the solution is to redesign the systems and business processes using BPM. What are some challenges you might face in redesigning the system? How will you present your recommendations to Clint?

PROBLEMS

23.1 Match the terms with their definitions:

____	**1.** scrum master	a.	Software and hardware sold as a package; the user can begin using the system after the vendor installs it
____	**2.** turnkey system	b.	Company that rents cloud-based software applications that customers can access via the Internet
____	**3.** executable architecture baseline	c.	Document that asks vendors to bid on a system to meet specified needs
____	**4.** scrum development	d.	Comparing systems by executing input, processing, and output tasks on different computer systems and evaluating the results
____	**5.** nonoperational prototypes	e.	Evaluating the overall merits of vendor proposals by assigning a weight to each evaluation criterion based on its importance
____	**6.** integration tests	f.	Hands-on development, use, and control of computer-based information systems by users
____	**7.** unified process	g.	Hiring an outside company to handle an organization's data processing activities
____	**8.** point scoring	h.	Systematic approach to gradually and continuously improving business processes
____	**9.** prototyping	i.	Systems design approach where a simplified working model of an AIS is developed
____	**10.** user stories	j.	Prototype is discarded, but the system requirements identified are used to develop a new system
____	**11.** Software-as-a-Service	k.	Philosophy and principles for IS development in an unknown, rapidly changing environment
____	**12.** unit tests	l.	Development focus is flexibility, responding to new requirements, adapting to changes, and quickly delivering a system to evaluate
____	**13.** business process reengineering	m.	Customer is responsible for making sure the scrum team produces what is needed

____**14.** product owner	n.	Description of what a product owner wants to include in the system
____**15.** business process management	o.	Pre-determined time period where the team works on high priority items in the product backlog
____**16.** sprint	p.	Person who makes sure scrum practices are followed, holds daily team meetings, and works with product owners
____**17.** scrum methodology	q.	Produces higher quality software by taking best software development practices to very high levels
____**18.** outsourcing	r.	Helps determine whether a given feature works as intended
____**19.** benchmark problem	s.	Checks for incompatible interfaces between code segments
____**20.** extreme programming	t.	Development framework with four phases: inception, elaboration, construction, and transition
____**21.** agile development	u.	Partial system implementation that includes all significant architecture components
____**22.** request for proposal	v.	Integrated package of tools that skilled designers use to plan, analyze, design, program, and maintain an IS
	w.	Thorough analysis and redesign of business processes and systems to achieve dramatic improvements; often a drastic, one-time-event
	x.	Prototypes that are further developed into fully functional systems
	y.	Development methodology where teams work in an intense, short, iterative, incremental process to reach a common development goal
	z.	Items waiting to be developed; prioritized by the product owner

23.2 This chapter describes several different agile methodologies for system development. Select one of the methodologies and conduct a search (using written materials, the Internet, electronic databases, etc.) for one or more companies that successfully used that methodology to develop an information system. Per your professor's instructions, prepare an oral or written summary of the successful implementation. Include in your summary the nature of the system, the approach used to develop the system, and a description of what it does and how it has helped the company that developed it.

23.3 Search written materials, the Internet, and electronic databases for successful and failed information system implementations. Prepare an oral or written summary of a successful and a failed implementation. Include the approach used to acquire or develop the system.

23.4 Mark Mitton, the liaison to the IS department, has eliminated all but the best three systems. Mark developed a list of required features, carefully reviewed each system, talked to other users, and interviewed appropriate systems representatives. Mark used a point-scoring system to assign weights to each requirement. Mark developed Table 23-4 to help him select the best system.

REQUIRED

a. Use a spreadsheet to develop a point-scoring matrix and determine which system Mark should select.

TABLE 23-4 An Evaluation Matrix

Selection Criteria	Weight	System 1	System 2	System 3
Software				
Fulfillment of business needs	100	6	8	9
Acceptance in marketplace	30	6	7	6
Quality of documentation	50	7	9	8
Quality of warranty	50	4	8	7
Ease of use	80	7	6	5
Control features	50	9	7	9
Flexibility	20	4	5	9
Security features	30	4	4	8
Modularity	30	8	5	4
Integration with other software	30	8	9	6
Quality of support utilities	50	9	8	5
Vendor				
Reputation and reliability	10	3	9	6
Experience with similar systems	20	5	5	6
Installation assistance	70	9	4	6
Training assistance	35	4	8	6
Timeliness of maintenance	35	5	4	4
Hardware				
Internal memory size (RAM)	70	5	6	8
Hard-drive capacity	40	9	9	5
Graphics capabilities	50	7	7	8
Processing speed	30	8	8	5
Overall performance	40	9	4	4
Expandability	50	7	2	5
Support for network technology	30	3	4	7

b. Susan Shelton did not agree with Mark's weightings and suggested the following changes:

Flexibility	60
Reputation and reliability	50
Quality of support utilities	10
Graphics capability	10

When the changes are made, which vendor should Mark recommend?

c. Mark's manager suggested the following changes to Susan's weightings:

Reputation and reliability	90
Installation assistance	40
Experience with similar systems	40
Training assistance	65
Internal memory size	10

Will the manager's changes affect the decision about which system to buy?

d. What can you conclude about point scoring from the changes made by Susan and Mark's manager? Develop your own weighting scale to evaluate the commercial software. What other selection criteria would you use? Be prepared to discuss your results with the class.

e. What are the weaknesses of the point-scoring method?

23.5 Nielsen Marketing Research (NMR), with operations in 29 countries, produces and disseminates marketing information. Nielsen has been the primary supplier of decision support information for more than 70 years. NMR's most recognizable product is the Nielsen television ratings. Nielsen is one of the largest users of computer capacity in the United States. Its information system consistently ranks above average in efficiency for its industry. NMR hired IBM to evaluate outsourcing its information processing. NMR wanted to know whether outsourcing would allow it to concentrate on giving its customers value-added services and insights, increase its flexibility, promote rapid growth, and provide it with more real-time information.

REQUIRED

What are the benefits and risks of outsourcing for NMR? Do the benefits outweigh the risks? Explain your answer.

23.6 A large organization had 18 months to replace its old customer information system with a new one that could differentiate among customer levels and provide appropriate products and services on demand. The new system, which cost $1 million and was installed by the IS staff on time, did not work properly. Complex transactions were error-prone, some transactions were canceled and others were put on hold, and the system could not differentiate among customers. The system was finally shut down, and transactions were processed manually. New IS management was hired to build a new system and mend the strained relationship between operations and IS.

So what went wrong? IS couldn't—or wouldn't—say no to all the requests for systems enhancements. Eager to please top management, IS management ignored the facts and assured them they could build a scalable system that was on time and within budget. Another big mistake was a strict project schedule with little flexibility to deal with problems and unforeseen challenges. Developers never spoke up about any glitches they encountered along the way. More than a dozen people (including the CIO) lost their jobs because of their roles in this disaster.

REQUIRED

a. What could IS management have done differently to make this project successful?
b. What in-house development issues are demonstrated in this case?
c. How could the in-house issues have been addressed to prevent the system's failure?
d. Can we conclude from this case that organizations should not have custom software written for them? Explain your answer.

23.7 Meredith Corporation publishes books and magazines, owns and operates television stations, and has a real estate marketing and franchising service. Meredith has 11 different systems that do not communicate with each other. Management wants an executive information system that provides them with the correct and timely information they need to make good business decisions. Meredith has decided to use prototyping to develop the system.

REQUIRED

a. Identify three questions you would ask Meredith personnel to determine systems requirements. What information are you attempting to elicit from each question?
b. Explain how prototyping works. What would system developers do during the iterative process? Why would you want the fewest iterations possible?
c. Would you want the prototype to be operational or nonoperational? Why? If it were an operational prototype, what would have to happen? If it were a nonoperational prototype, how could the prototype be used?
d. Suppose the company decides the prototype system is not practical, abandons it, and takes some other approach to solving its information problem. Does that mean prototyping is not a valid systems development approach? Explain your answer.

23.8 Norcom, a division of a large manufacturer, needed a new distribution and customer service system. The project was estimated to take 18 months and cost $5 million. The project team consisted of 20 business and IT staff members. After two years, the CIO was fired, and the company hired a CIO with expertise in saving troubled projects. The new CIO said three grave errors were committed.

1. IT picked the wrong software using a very naïve request for proposal process.
2. IT did not formulate a project plan.
3. No one "owned" the project. The IT staff assumed the users owned the project, the users believed the IT staff owned it, and management believed the vendor owned it.

The CIO developed a 2,000-line plan to rescue the project. Three months later, the system failed, even with IT staff and consultants working on it day and night. The failed system was to have been the company's preeminent system, but it could not even process customer orders correctly, resulting in complaints about late shipments and receiving the wrong goods.

After three years and $4 million, the new CIO polled the staff anonymously. Only two said the project could be saved, and they had staked their careers on the project. The message that the project was not worth saving was very hard for the CIO to give. It was likewise hard for the division president to receive it; he could not accept the idea of killing a project that cost so much money. He finally accepted the decision and all the ramifications involved, including corporate IT taking control of all IT operations at his division.

REQUIRED

a. List the primary components of an RFP.
b. Identify possible components or deficiencies in Norcom's RFP that could have led the new CIO to claim that it was naïve or insufficient.
c. Identify possible approaches Norcom could have used to evaluate RFP responses.

23.9 Quickfix is rapidly losing business, and management wants to redesign its computer repair processes and procedures to decrease costs and increase customer service. Currently, a customer needing help calls one of five regional service centers. A customer service representative records the relevant customer information, finds the closest qualified technician, and calls the technician's cell phone to see whether the repair fits into his or her schedule. If not, the representative finds the next closest technician. When a technician is located, customer repair information is texted or e-mailed to the technician. The technician calls the customer and arranges to pick up the computer and replace it with a loaner. Making these arrangements takes one to two days and sometimes more if technicians are not available or do not promptly return calls.

If a broken computer cannot be quickly repaired, it is sent to a repair depot. These repairs take another four to seven days. If problems arise, it can take up to two weeks for an item to be repaired. When a customer calls to see whether the computer is ready, the service representative calls the technician to find out the status and calls the customer back. The repair process usually takes five phone calls between the customer, the service representative, and the technician.

Several problems with this process led to a significant drop in business: (1) it is time-consuming; (2) it is inconvenient for a customer to have a computer removed, a new one installed, and then the old one reinstalled; and (3) service representatives do not have immediate access to information about items being repaired. Quickfix decides to use BPM principles to redesign its business processes.

REQUIRED

a. Identify the repair processes that occur, and decide which should be redesigned.
b. Describe how the repair process can be redesigned to solve the problems identified.
c. What benefits can Quickfix achieve by redesigning the repair process?

CASE 23-1 Wong Engineering Corp.

Wong Engineering Corp (WEC) operates in 25 states and three countries. WEC faced a crucial decision: choosing network software that would maximize functionality, manageability, and end-user acceptance of the system. WEC developed and followed a four-step approach:

Step 1. *Develop evaluation criteria.* WEC organized a committee that interviewed users and developed the following evaluation criteria:

- Ease of use
- Scope of vendor support
- Ease of network management and administration
- Cost, speed, and performance
- Ability to access other computing platforms
- Security and control
- Fault tolerance and recovery abilities
- Ability to connect workstations to the network
- Global naming services

CASE 23-1 Continued

- Upgrade and enhancement options
- Vendor stability

WEC organized the criteria into the following four categories and prioritized them. Criteria vital to short-term and long-term business goals were given a 5. "Wish list" criteria were weighted a 3. Inapplicable criteria were given a 1.

1. Business criteria: overall business, economic, and competitive issues
2. Operational criteria: tactical issues and operating characteristics
3. Organizational criteria: networks' impact on the information systems structure
4. Technical criteria: hardware, software, and communications issues

Step 2. *Define the operating environment.* Several data-gathering techniques were used to collect information from which an information systems model was developed. The model revealed the need to share accounting, sales, marketing, and engineering data at three organizational levels: district, division, and home office. District offices needed access to centralized financial information to handle payroll. WEC needed a distributed network that allowed users throughout the organization to access company data.

Step 3. *Identify operating alternatives.* Using the criteria from step 1, committee members evaluated each commercial software package and then compared notes during a roundtable discussion.

Step 4. *Test the software.* The highest-scoring products were tested, and the product that fit the organization's needs the best was selected.

REQUIRED

Discuss the committee's role in the selection process. How should committee members be selected? What are the pros and cons of using a committee to make the selection?

a. What data-gathering techniques could WEC use to assess user needs? To select a vendor?
b. What is the benefit of analyzing the operating environment before selecting the software? What data-gathering techniques help a company understand the operating environment?
c. In selecting a system using the point-scoring method, how should the committee resolve scoring disputes? List at least two methods.
d. Should a purchase decision be made on the point-scoring process alone? What other procedure(s) should the committee employ in making the final selection?

AIS in Action Solutions

QUIZ KEY

1. Which of the following is not one of the difficulties software developers have experienced using the traditional systems development life cycle?
   a. AIS development projects are backlogged for years. [Incorrect. This is one of the difficulties accountants have experienced using the traditional SDLC, but there is more than one correct answer.]
   b. Changes are usually not possible after requirements have been frozen. [Incorrect. This is one of the difficulties accountants have experienced using the traditional SDLC, but there is more than one correct answer.]
   c. The AIS developed may not meet their needs. [Incorrect. This is one of the difficulties accountants have experienced using the traditional SDLC, but there is more than one correct answer.]
   ▶ **d.** All are difficulties with the traditional SDLC. [Correct.]

2. Companies that buy rather than develop an AIS must still go through the systems development life cycle.
   ▶ **a.** true [Correct. Purchasing a system still requires a company to follow the systems development life cycle of analyzing, designing (conceptual and physical), and implementing a new system. Otherwise, the company risks not purchasing the right system for its needs.]
   b. false [Incorrect.]

3. Which of the following statements is false?
   a. As a general rule, companies should buy rather than develop software if they can find commercial software that meets their needs. [Incorrect. This is a true statement, not a false statement. Purchasing software is generally less expensive than developing software in-house.]
   ▶ b. As an AIS increases in size and complexity, there is a greater likelihood that commercial software can be found that meets user needs. [Correct. This is a false statement. Large and complex systems need greater customization than smaller systems and thus are less likely to lend themselves to the one-size-fits-all approach of commercial software.]
   c. A company should not attempt to develop its own custom software unless experienced, in-house programming personnel are available and the job can be completed less expensively on the inside. [Incorrect. This is a true statement, not a false statement. Skilled in-house programmers and the promise of lower costs are essential if companies decide to develop their own custom software.]
   d. As a general rule, a company should develop custom software only when it will provide a significant competitive advantage. [Incorrect. This is a true statement, not a false statement. According to Arthur Little, companies should pursue custom software only when it provides a distinct competitive advantage.]

4. When a company is buying large and complex systems, vendors are invited to submit systems for consideration. What is such a solicitation called?
   a. request for quotation [Incorrect. A request for quotation asks for dollar bids on proposed systems or their components.]
   b. request for system [Incorrect. A request for system is not the terminology used to refer to inviting vendors to submit systems for consideration.]
   ▶ c. request for proposal [Correct. A request for proposal invites vendors to propose solutions to a company's needs.]
   d. good-faith estimate [Incorrect. A good-faith estimate provides a vendor's best guess on the cost of a proposal based on reliable parameters.]

5. To compare system performance, a company can create a data processing task with input, processing, and output jobs. This task is performed on the systems under consideration and the processing times are compared. The AIS with the lowest time is the most efficient. What is this process called?
   ▶ a. benchmarking [Correct. Benchmarking measures system performance by comparing processing times.]
   b. requirements costing [Incorrect. Requirement costing estimates the costs of purchasing or developing features that are not present in a particular AIS.]
   c. point scoring [Incorrect. Point scoring measures system performance by comparing each system based on weighted criteria.]
   d. performance testing [Incorrect. Performance testing is a general term applied to many types of comparison testing.]

6. Which of the following statements is true?
   a. Because the AIS is so crucial, companies never outsource parts of the AIS. [Incorrect. AIS functions are routinely outsourced.]
   b. Most mainframe outsourcing contracts are for two to three years and cost thousands of dollars a year. [Incorrect. Most mainframe outsourcing contracts are longer term (averaging 10 years) and cost hundreds of thousands to millions of dollars.]
   ▶ c. Outsourcers often buy the client's computers and hire all or most of its information systems employees. [Correct. Many large outsourcing deals involve purchasing the client's hardware and hiring the client's employees.]
   d. Only companies struggling to survive and wanting a quick infusion of cash from selling their hardware use outsourcing. [Incorrect. Many large and financially sound companies use outsourcing as a way to decrease costs and become even more profitable.]

7. Which of the following is not a benefit of outsourcing?

▶ **a.** It offers a great deal of flexibility because it is relatively easy to change outsourcers. [Correct. This is not a benefit of outsourcing. Because contracts are long term, outsourcers can be very inflexible as well as difficult and costly to change.]

b. It can provide access to the expertise and special services provided by outsourcers. [Incorrect. This is a benefit of outsourcing. Many companies cannot afford to retain information systems expertise on their payroll; therefore, outsourcing provides a less expensive way to acquire that expertise.]

c. It allows companies to move to a more sophisticated level of computing at a reasonable cost. [Incorrect. This is a benefit of outsourcing. Many companies cannot afford to maintain the most effective and sophisticated hardware; therefore, outsourcing provides a less expensive way to gain access to that hardware.]

d. It is a cost-effective way to handle the peaks and valleys found in seasonal businesses. [Incorrect. This is a benefit of outsourcing. For companies in cyclical industries, outsourcing provides an effective way to meet company needs during the busy times and to lower costs during the slow times of their business cycle.]

8. Which of the following is a true statement about prototyping?

a. In the early stages of prototyping, system controls and exception handling may be sacrificed in the interests of simplicity, flexibility, and ease of use. [Incorrect. This is a true statement. Prototyping provides simplicity, flexibility, and ease of use by sacrificing controls and exception handling. However, this is not the only true statement.]

b. A prototype is a scaled-down, first-draft model that is quickly and inexpensively built and given to users to evaluate. [Incorrect. This is a true statement. Prototypes are essentially rough-draft models. However, this is not the only true statement.]

c. The first step in prototyping is to identify system requirements. [Incorrect. This is a true statement. The first step in prototyping is to identify system requirements. However, this is not the only true statement.]

▶ **d.** All of the statements are true. [Correct.]

9. Which of the following is not an advantage of prototyping?

a. better definition of user needs [Incorrect. This is an advantage of prototyping. Because users can test-drive the model, they can give better feedback to the developers regarding their needs and requirements.]

▶ **b.** adequately tested and documented systems [Correct. This is not an advantage of prototyping. Because prototypes are developed so quickly, developers often neglect documentation and a full testing before the system becomes operational.]

c. higher user involvement and satisfaction [Incorrect. This is an advantage of prototyping. Prototyping success depends on high user involvement, which generally leads to greater user satisfaction.]

d. faster development time [Incorrect. This is an advantage of prototyping. Prototypes can be developed in a matter of days or weeks, whereas a more traditional approach can take a year or longer.]

10. When is it most appropriate to use prototyping?

a. when there is little uncertainty about the AIS [Incorrect. Prototyping is more effective when there is substantial uncertainty about how an AIS should work.]

b. when it is clear what users' needs are [Incorrect. Prototyping is more effective when users are uncertain of their needs and benefit from working on models to help them identify and solidify their needs.]

▶ **c.** when the final AIS cannot be clearly visualized because the decision process is still unclear [Correct. Prototyping is more effective when there is substantial uncertainty about how an AIS should work, look, and feel.]

d. when there is a very low likelihood of failure [Incorrect. Prototyping is the most effective when there is substantial uncertainty about whether a new system will work.]

COMPREHENSIVE PROBLEM SOLUTION

Identify the benefits and risks of the three courses of action facing the FTC: purchasing a prewritten software system, developing the system in-house, and outsourcing the system to an external vendor.

PURCHASING SOFTWARE

The primary benefit of purchasing software is greater availability and lower cost; because the product is sold to many companies, it can be sold at a lower price. The downside is that because the software is designed for as wide an audience as possible, it may not meet all the needs of the purchaser. In addition, software support is a problem if the vendor goes out of business.

DEVELOPING THE SYSTEM IN-HOUSE

The primary benefit of in-house development is that the system should meet the entity's needs. The drawbacks are that it occupies significant time and resources, it is usually a very complex process, and problems—such as poor requirements planning, insufficient staff, poor top-management support, inadequate communication, and a lack of cooperation between the developers and users—can easily derail a project.

OUTSOURCING THE SYSTEM

Outsourcing allows entities to devote time and resources to their core competencies instead of diverting attention to systems development. It also gives companies access to expertise at a much lower cost. Outsourcing can save 15% to 30% in overall systems development costs because of quicker development time, smoothing usage peaks and valleys, and facilitating corporate restructuring (downsizing). The risks involve a loss of control over the project, inflexible outsourcing contracts, and poor service. Entities can also lose their competitive advantage by not maintaining proprietary systems.

WHAT THE FTC DID

Given the short timeframe to implement such a large task, the FTC could not have built this system on its own. Instead, they outsourced it to AT&T, which had the expertise and staff to handle the system's analysis, design, and implementation. With AT&T's help, the project became one of the government's most successful IT projects.

CHAPTER

24 Systems Design, Implementation, and Operation

LEARNING OBJECTIVES

After studying this chapter, you should be able to:

1. Discuss the conceptual systems design process and the activities in this phase.
2. Discuss the physical systems design process and the activities in this phase.
3. Discuss the systems implementation process and the activities in this phase.
4. Discuss the systems conversion process and the activities in this phase.
5. Discuss the systems operation and maintenance process and the activities in this phase.

INTEGRATIVE CASE Shoppers Mart

Ann Christy received permission to develop a new AIS (Chapter 22 conclusion) for Shoppers Mart (SM). Ann is concerned because many development projects bog down during the design and implementation phases, and she does not want a runaway project that she cannot control. She wants to plan the rest of the project so that it is completed correctly, and her first task is to determine what type of system will best meet SM's needs. She scheduled a meeting with the head of systems development to discuss the following questions:

1. Should her team develop what it considers the best approach to meeting SM's needs, or should they develop several approaches?
2. How can she ensure that system output will meet user needs? When and how should input be captured, and who should capture it? Where should AIS data be stored, and how should it be organized and accessed?
3. How should SM convert from its current to its new AIS? How much time and effort will be needed to maintain the new AIS? In what capacity should Ann's accounting staff participate?

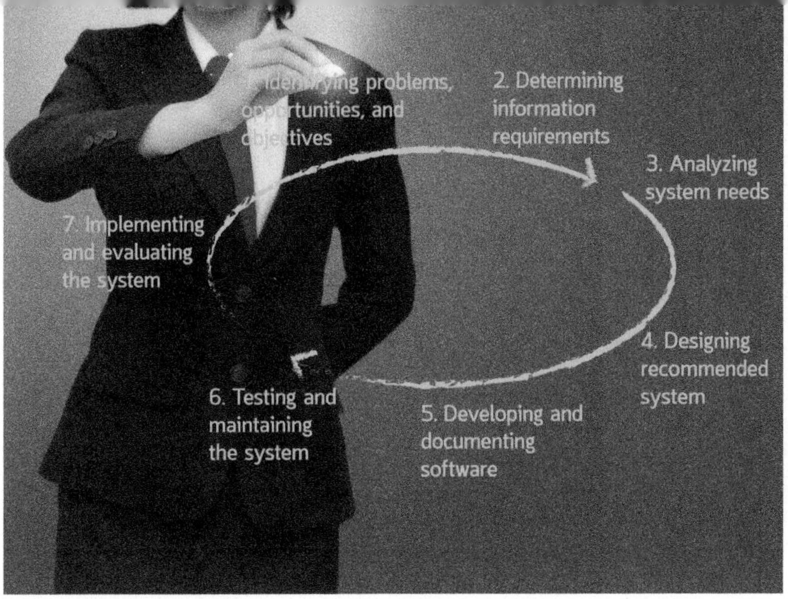

A. Singkham/123RF

Introduction

Effective systems analysis and design can help developers correctly define business problems and create a system to solve those problems. As discussed in Chapter 22, system requirements are defined during systems analysis. This chapter discusses the other four systems development life cycle (SDLC) steps (see Figure 22-1): conceptual systems design, physical systems design, systems implementation and conversion, and operation and maintenance. Chapter 23 discusses how some SDLC steps can be shortened or made more effective.

Conceptual Systems Design

In conceptual design, the developer creates a general framework for implementing user requirements and solving the problems identified in the analysis phase. Figure 24-1 shows the conceptual design steps: evaluating design alternatives, preparing design specifications, and preparing the conceptual systems design report.

EVALUATE DESIGN ALTERNATIVES

There are many ways to design an AIS, so systems designers must make many design decisions. For example, should SM mail hard-copy purchase orders, use electronic data interchange (EDI), or enter orders over the Internet? Should SM have a large centralized mainframe and database or distribute computer power to the stores using a network of servers and PCs? Should data entry be by keyboard, optical character recognition, point-of-sale devices, barcodes, radio-frequency identification (RFID) tags, the Internet, or some combination?

There are many ways SM can approach the systems development process. It can purchase software, ask in-house information systems (IS) staff to develop it, or hire an outside company to develop and manage the system. The company could modify existing software or redesign its business processes and develop software to support the new processes. These conceptual design alternatives are discussed in Chapter 23.

The following standards should be used to evaluate design alternatives: (1) how well it meets organizational and system objectives, (2) how well it meets user needs, (3) whether it is economically feasible, and (4) how advantages weigh against disadvantages. The steering committee evaluates the alternatives and selects the one that best meets the organization's needs.

Table 24-1 summarizes design considerations and alternatives.

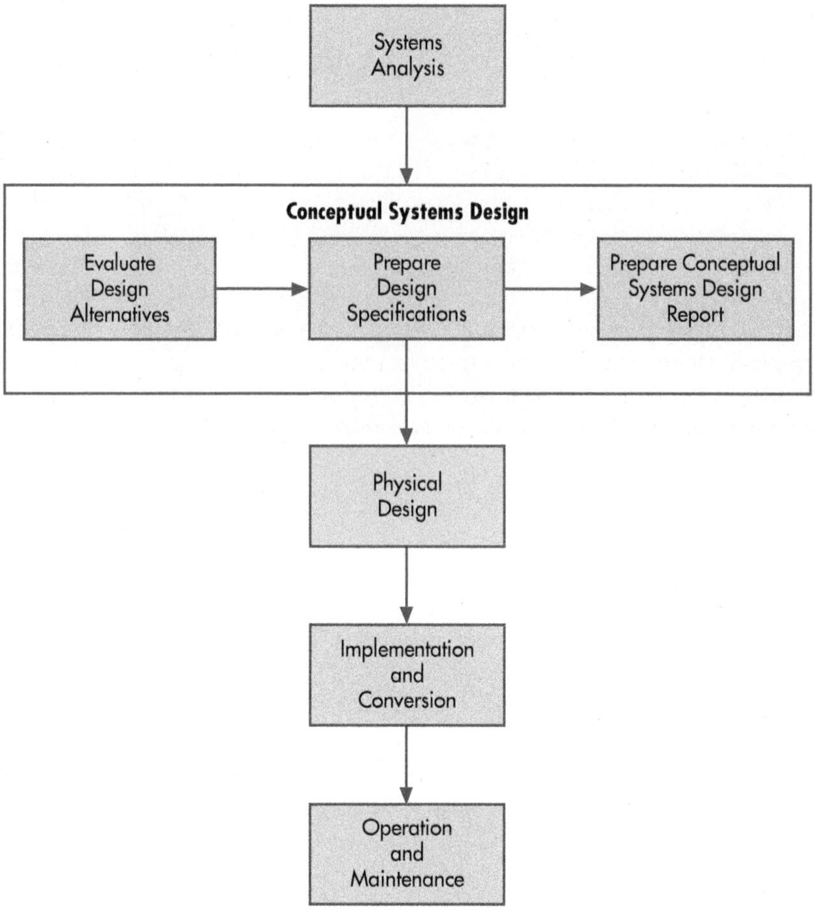

FIGURE 24-1 Conceptual Systems Design Activities

TABLE 24-1 Design Considerations and Alternatives

Design Considerations	Design Alternatives
Communications channels	Telephone, Internet, cable, fiber optics, or satellite
Communications network	Centralized, decentralized, distributed, or local area
Data storage medium	Server, hard or disk drive, cloud storage, flash drive, tape, CD, or paper
Data storage structure	Files or database
File organization and access	Random, sequential, or indexed-sequential access
Input medium	Keying, optical character recognition (OCR), magnetic ink character recognition (MICR), point-of-sale (POS), EDI, or voice
Input format	Source document, turnaround document, source data automation, or screen
Operations	In-house or outsourcing
Output and update frequency	Instantaneous, hourly, daily, weekly, or monthly
Output medium	Paper, screen, voice, CD, or microfilm
Output scheduling	Predetermined times or on demand
Output format	Narrative, table, graph, file, or electronic
Printed output format	Preprinted forms or system-generated forms
Processing mode	Manual, batch, or real time
Processor	Personal computer, server, or mainframe
Software acquisition	Canned, custom, or modified
Transaction processing	Batch or online

PREPARE DESIGN SPECIFICATIONS AND REPORTS

Once a design alternative is selected, **conceptual design specifications** are created for the following elements:

conceptual design specifications - Requirement specifications for systems output, data storage, input, processing procedures, and operations.

1. ***Output.*** Because the system is designed to meet user information needs, output specifications are prepared first. To evaluate store sales, SM must decide (a) how often to produce a sales analysis report, (b) what the report should contain, (c) what it will look like, and (d) whether it is a hard-copy or screen (or both) output.
2. ***Data storage.*** Data storage decisions include which data elements must be stored to produce the sales report, how they should be stored, and what type of file or database to use.
3. ***Input.*** Input design considerations include which sales data to enter; sale location and amount; and where, when, and how to collect the data.
4. ***Processing procedures and operations.*** Design considerations include how to process the input and stored data to produce the sales report and in which sequence the processes must be performed.

A **conceptual systems design report** summarizes conceptual design activities, guides physical design activities, communicates how all information needs will be met, and helps the steering committee assess feasibility. The main component is a description of one or more recommended system designs. Table 24-8, just before the chapter summary, shows what this report contains.

conceptual systems design report - Summarizes conceptual design activities, guides physical design activities, communicates how all information needs will be met, and helps the steering committee assess feasibility.

Physical Systems Design

During physical design, the broad, user-oriented AIS requirements of conceptual design are translated into detailed specifications used to code and test the computer programs. Figure 24-2 shows the physical system design phases described below in detail.

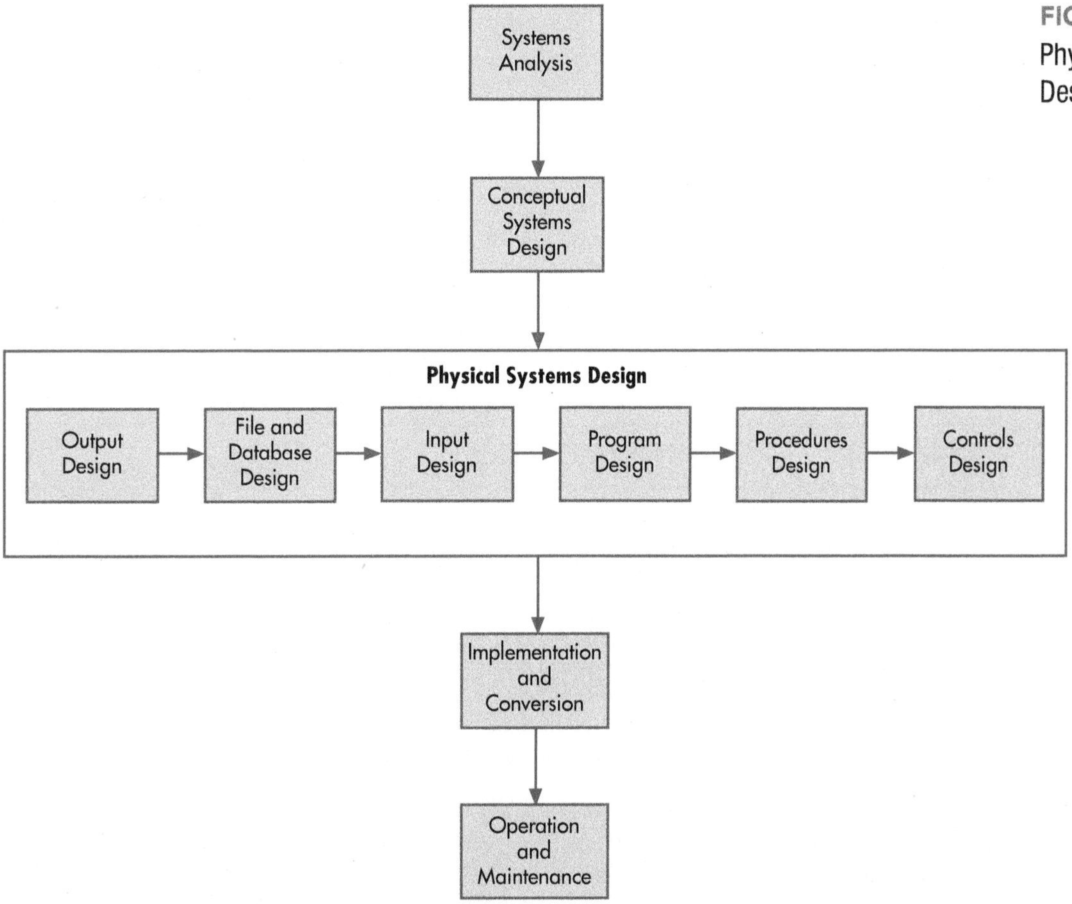

FIGURE 24-2
Physical Systems Design Activities

Failing to take sufficient time on conceptual and physical design can cause problems. A rush to implement an enterprise resource planning (ERP) package at Overstock.com caused early design problems. The result was a mistake-laden Oracle implementation. The ERP package was out of sync with the accounting software, causing the order tracking system to go down for a week. Ultimately, five years of earnings had to be restated, with revenue reduced by $12.9 million and increased losses of $10.3 million.

OUTPUT DESIGN

The objective of output design is to determine the nature, format, content, and timing of reports, documents, and screen displays. Tailoring the output to user needs requires cooperation between users and designers. Important output design considerations are summarized in Table 24-2.

Output usually fits into one of the following four categories:

scheduled reports - Reports prepared on a regular basis, with a pre-specified content and format.

special-purpose analysis reports - Reports with no pre-specified content, format, or schedule; usually prepared in response to a management request.

triggered exception reports - Reports with a pre-specified content and format, prepared only in response to abnormal conditions.

demand reports - Reports with a pre-specified content and format, prepared only on request.

1. **Scheduled reports** have a prespecified content and format and are prepared on a regular basis. Examples include monthly performance reports, weekly sales analyses, and annual financial statements.
2. **Special-purpose analysis reports** have no prespecified content or format and are not prepared on a regular schedule. They are prepared in response to a management request to evaluate an issue, such as which of three new products would provide the highest profits.
3. **Triggered exception reports** have a prespecified content and format but are prepared only in response to abnormal conditions. Excessive absenteeism, cost overruns, inventory shortages, and situations requiring immediate corrective action trigger such reports.
4. **Demand reports** have a prespecified content and format but are prepared only on request. Both triggered exception reports and demand reports can be used effectively to facilitate the management process.

Designers often prepare sample outputs and ask users to evaluate whether they are complete, relevant, and useful. Unacceptable output is modified and reviewed again as many times as necessary to make it acceptable. To avoid expensive time delays later in the SDLC, many organizations require users to sign a document stating that the output form and content are acceptable.

FILE AND DATABASE DESIGN

Data in various company units should be stored in compatible formats to help avoid the problem AT&T faced: 23 business units, a jumble of incompatible systems and data formats, and an inability to communicate and share data with other units. AT&T spent five years creating a "single view" of each customer so customer data could be shared across business units.

Chapter 4 discusses files and databases and how to design them. Important file and database design considerations are summarized in Table 24-3.

TABLE 24-2 Output Design Considerations

Consideration	Concern
Use	Who will use the output, why and when do users need it, and what decisions will they make based on it?
Medium	Use paper, screen, voice, e-mail, or some combination?
Format	Will narrative, table, or graphic format best convey information?
Preprinted	Use preprinted forms? Turnaround documents?
Location	Where should output be sent?
Access	Who should have access to hard-copy and screen output?
Detail	Should a summary or table of contents be included with lengthy output?
	Should headings organize data and highlight important items?
	Should detailed information be placed in an appendix?
Timeliness	How often should output be produced?

TABLE 24-3 File and Database Design Considerations

Consideration	Concern
Medium	Store data on hard drive, disk, CD, tape, or paper?
Processing mode	Use manual, batch, or real-time processing?
Maintenance	What procedures are needed to maintain data effectively?
Size	How many records will be stored in the database, how large will they be, and how fast will the number of records grow?
Activity level	What percentage of the records will be updated, added, or deleted each year?

INPUT DESIGN

Input design considerations include what types of data will be input and the optimal input method. Considerations for input design are shown in Table 24-4.

FORM DESIGN Although systems are moving away from paper documents and toward source data automation, form design is still an important topic. Form design principles are summarized in Table 24-5.

COMPUTER SCREEN DESIGN It is more efficient to enter data directly into the computer than onto paper for subsequent entry. Computer input screens are most effective when these procedures are followed:

- Organize the screen so data can be entered quickly, accurately, and completely. Minimize data input by retrieving as much data as possible from the system. For example, entering a customer number could cause the system to retrieve the customer's name, address, and other key information.
- Enter data in the same order as displayed on paper forms that capture the data.
- Group logically related data together. Complete the screen from left to right and top to bottom.
- Design the screen so users can jump from one data entry location to another or use a single key to go directly to screen locations.
- Make it easy to correct mistakes. Clear and explicit error messages consistent across all screens are essential. There should be a help feature to provide online assistance.
- Restrict the data or the number of menu options on a screen to avoid clutter.

TABLE 24-4 Input Design Considerations

Consideration	Concern
Medium	Enter data using a keyboard, OCR, MICR, POS terminal, barcodes, RFID tags, EDI, or voice input?
Source	Where do data originate (computer, customer, remote location, etc.), and how does that affect data entry?
Format	What format (source or turnaround document, screen, source data automation) efficiently captures the data with the least effort and cost?
Type	What is the nature of the data?
Volume	How much data are to be entered?
Personnel	What are data entry operators' abilities, functions, and expertise? Is additional training necessary?
Frequency	How often must data be entered?
Cost	How can costs be minimized without adversely affecting efficiency and accuracy?
Error detection and correction	What errors are possible, and how can they be detected and corrected?

TABLE 24-5 Principles of Good Form Design

General Considerations
- Are preprinted data used as much as possible?
- Are the weight and grade of the paper appropriate for the planned use?
- Do bold type, lines, and shading highlight different parts of the form?
- Is the form a standard size?
- Is the form size consistent with filing, binding, or mailing requirements?
- If the form is mailed, will the address show in a window envelope?
- Are copies printed in different colors to facilitate proper distribution?
- Do clear instructions explain how to complete the form?

Introduction
- Does the form name appear at the top in bold type?
- Is the form consecutively prenumbered?
- Is the company name and address preprinted on forms sent to external parties?

Main Body
- Is logically related information (e.g., customer name, address) grouped together?
- Is there sufficient room to record each data item?
- Is data entry consistent with the sequence in which the data are acquired?
- Are codes or check-offs that are used instead of written entries adequately explained?

Conclusion
- Is space provided to record the final disposition of the form?
- Is space provided for a signature(s) to indicate transaction approval?
- Is space provided to record the approval date?
- Is space provided for a dollar or numeric total?
- Is the distribution of each copy of the form clearly indicated?

PROGRAM DESIGN

Program development, one of the most time-consuming SDLC activities, takes place in the eight steps shown below. Step 1 is part of the systems analysis phase. Step 2 begins in conceptual systems design and may carry over to physical design. Most of steps 3 and 4 are done during systems design and are completed during systems implementation. Steps 5 and 6 are begun in systems design, but most of the work is done during systems implementation. Step 7 is done during systems implementation and conversion. Step 8 is part of operation and maintenance.

1. ***Determine user needs.*** Systems analysts consult with users and reach an agreement on user needs and software requirements.
2. ***Create and document a development plan.***
3. ***Write program instructions (computer code).*** Program preparation time may range from a few days to a few years, depending on program complexity. Programming standards (rules for writing programs) contribute to program consistency, making them easier to read and maintain. Computer programs should be subdivided into small, well-defined modules to reduce complexity and enhance reliability and modifiability, a process called **structured programming**. Modules should interact with a control module rather than with each other. To facilitate testing and modification, each module should have only one entry and exit point.
4. ***Test the program.*** **Debugging** is the process of discovering and eliminating program errors. A program is tested for logic errors using test data that simulate as many real processing situations and input data combinations as possible. Large programs are often tested in three stages: individual program modules, the linkages between modules and a control module, and interfaces with other application programs.

   It is important to find errors as soon as possible during the development process. The Gartner Group estimates that bugs discovered later in the SDLC cost 80% to 1,000% more to fix than those discovered earlier. Focus 24-1 discusses the difficulty of testing software and the consequences of releasing software with undetected errors. Between

structured programming - A modular approach to programming in which each module performs a specific function and is coordinated by a control module.

debugging - The process of discovering and eliminating program errors.

FOCUS 24-1 Software Bugs Take Their Toll

An $18.5 million rocket explodes seconds after liftoff. Because of three missing digits in several million lines of programming code, telephone networks crash, leaving 10 million customers without service. A nuclear plant releases hundreds of gallons of radioactive water near Lake Huron. A device that uses X-rays to treat cancer victims delivered a radiation overdose, killing one patient and leaving two others deeply burned and partly paralyzed. A software error prevented a Patriot missile from destroying an incoming Iraqi Scud missile that killed 28 people.

These events have one disturbing fact in common. They were caused by program errors called bugs. The term *bug* was coined during World War II when a researcher, puzzled by a computer shutdown, removed a moth stuck between two electric relays. A program containing bugs can work adequately for quite some time until, with no warning, the bug triggers something, and the computer goes haywire. One incorrect letter—even a missing period—can cause a computer to issue an incorrect command or no command at all.

Bugs exist in most software, and it is almost impossible to eliminate all of them. The sheer volume of software code in a complex program makes finding bugs difficult. There are more than 2.5 million lines of code in systems that check for cracks in the engine wheel of the space shuttle and 12 million in a phone company's call-switching computer. Finding a flaw in this code is as difficult as looking for one misspelled name in the New York City phone book. It is estimated that flawed or bug-ridden software costs businesses worldwide more than $175 billion last year.

Programmers go to great pains to detect and eliminate bugs, but no one has the time or money to find every bug or to simulate every situation the program will encounter in the real world. Instead, software is tested with assumptions about how it will be used and what processing volumes it must handle.

One product manager estimated that his company often found 5,000 bugs in each product. They fixed serious flaws and ignored minor flaws that were unlikely to cause a problem. If developers took the time to find and correct every flaw, they would risk not getting their product to market on a timely basis and losing market share.

Software developers also cannot predict whether computer users will work faster than the software itself. The linear accelerators that killed and maimed cancer patients were controlled by an operator who typed extremely fast. She accidentally selected the X-ray mode and then switched to the electron beam. The software was not quick enough to recognize the change, and the machine beamed radiation at full power to a tiny spot on the patients' bodies. The bug was so subtle it took programmers a year to detect and eliminate it.

20% and 30% of software development costs should be allocated to testing, debugging, and rewriting software.

5. ***Document the program.*** Documentation explains how programs work and is used to correct errors. Program documentation includes flowcharts, data flow diagrams, E-R diagrams, data models, record layouts, and narrative descriptions. These items are stored in a documentation manual.
6. ***Train program users.*** Program documentation is often used to train users.
7. ***Install the system.*** All system components, including the programs and the hardware, are combined, and the company begins to use the system.
8. ***Use and modify the system.*** Factors that require existing programs to be revised, referred to as **program maintenance**, include requests for new or revised reports; changes in input, file content, or values such as tax rates; error detection; and conversion to new hardware.

program maintenance - Updating a computer program due to changed user needs, fixing bugs, legal or regulatory changes, or to make use of new technology.

PROCEDURES AND CONTROLS DESIGN

Everyone who interacts with a system needs procedures that answer the who, what, when, where, why, and how questions related to IS activities. Procedures should cover input preparation, transaction processing, error detection and correction, controls, reconciliation of balances, database access, output preparation and distribution, and computer operator instructions. Procedures documentation and training may take the form of system manuals, user instruction classes, training materials, or online help screens. Developers, users, or teams representing both groups may write procedures.

The adage "garbage in, garbage out" emphasizes that improperly controlled input, processing, and data storage functions produce unreliable information. Controls must be built into an AIS to ensure its effectiveness, efficiency, and accuracy. They should minimize errors as well as detect and correct them when they occur. Accountants play a vital role in this area. Important control concerns are summarized in Table 24-6. Controls are discussed in detail in Chapters 10 through 13.

Failing to produce good policies and procedures and failing to implement controls can be devastating. Nonexistent governance kept Kaiser Kidney Transplant Center from developing good policies and procedures. As a result, hundreds of patients did not receive life-saving transplant surgeries, and the transplant center was forced to close two years after opening. Inadequate controls at Heartland Payment Systems, a credit card processor, allowed hackers to steal sensitive information from more than 100 million credit card accounts.

physical systems design report - Summarizes what was accomplished in physical design; used to determine whether or not to proceed to the implementation phase.

A **physical systems design report** summarizes what was accomplished and serves as the basis for management's decision whether or not to proceed to the implementation phase. Table 24-8 shows a table of contents for the report prepared at Shoppers Mart.

Systems Implementation

systems implementation - The process of installing hardware and software and getting the IS up and running.

Systems implementation is the process of installing hardware and software and getting the AIS up and running. Implementation processes are shown in Figure 24-3 and described below. Focus 24-2 describes the improvements the state of Virginia made to its AIS.

IMPLEMENTATION PLANNING AND SITE PREPARATION

implementation plan - A written plan showing how the new system will be implemented; specifies when the project should be complete and the IS operational, including a completion timetable, cost estimates, task milestones, and who is responsible for each activity.

An **implementation plan** consists of implementation tasks, expected completion dates, cost estimates, and who is responsible for each task. The plan specifies when the project should be complete and when the AIS is operational. The implementation team identifies factors that decrease the likelihood of successful implementation, and the plan contains a strategy for coping with each factor.

AIS changes may require adjustments to a company's existing organizational structure. New departments may be created, existing ones may be eliminated or downsized, or the IS department itself may change. Technical staff at Blue Cross and Blue Shield of Wisconsin who did not understand the company's business or vision contracted for a $200 million system that did not work properly. It sent checks to a nonexistent town, made $60 million in overpayments, and resulted in the loss of 35,000 clients. One reason the system failed was that its implementation should have included an organizational restructuring.

Site preparation is a lengthy process and should begin well in advance of the installation date. A large computer may require extensive changes, such as additional electrical outlets, data

TABLE 24-6 Controls Design Considerations

Consideration	Concern
Validity	Are system interactions valid (e.g., all cash disbursements are made to legitimate vendors)?
Authorization	Are input, processing, storage, and output activities authorized by the appropriate managers?
Accuracy	Is input verified to ensure accuracy? Are data processed and stored accurately?
Security	Is the system protected against (a) unauthorized physical and logical access to prevent the improper use, alteration, destruction, or disclosure of information and software and (b) the theft of system resources?
Numerical control	Are documents prenumbered to prevent errors and fraud and to detect when documents are misused, missing, or stolen?
Availability	Is the system available at times set forth in service-level agreements? Can users enter, update, and retrieve data during the agreed-upon times?
Maintainability	Can the system be modified without affecting system availability, security, and integrity? Are only authorized, tested, and documented changes made? Are resources available to manage, schedule, document, and communicate the changes?
Integrity	Is data processing complete, accurate, timely, and authorized? Is data processing free from unauthorized or inadvertent system manipulation?
Audit trail	Can transactions be traced from source documents to final output?

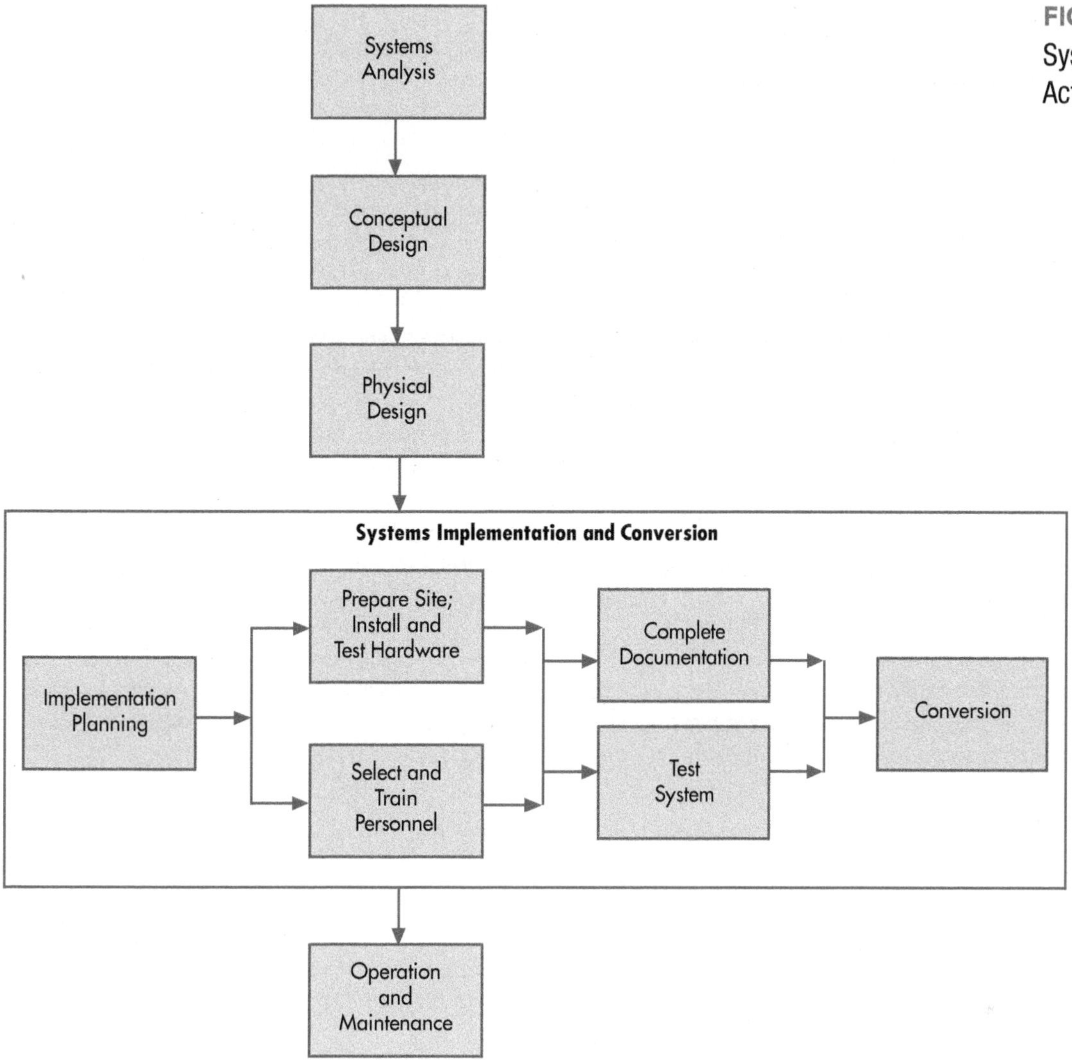

FIGURE 24-3
Systems Implementation Activities

communications facilities, raised floors, humidity controls, special lighting, air conditioning, fire protection, and an emergency power supply. Space is needed for equipment, storage, and offices.

SELECTING AND TRAINING PERSONNEL

Employees are hired from outside the company or transferred internally, which often is the less costly alternative because they already understand the firm's business and operations. Transferring employees who are displaced because of the new system could boost employee loyalty and morale.

When users are not adequately trained, the company will not achieve the expected benefits and return on its investment. Companies provide insufficient training because it is time-consuming and expensive. The hidden cost of inadequate training is that users turn for help to coworkers who have mastered the system, decreasing the productivity of coworkers and increasing company costs.

Employees must be trained on the hardware, software, and any new policies and procedures. Training should be scheduled for just before systems testing and conversion. Many training options are available, such as vendor training, self-study manuals, computer-assisted instruction, videotape presentations, role-playing, case studies, and experimenting with the system under the guidance of experienced users.

Boots the Chemists, a British pharmacy chain with more than 1,000 stores, developed a novel approach to training employees nervous about a forthcoming system. They were invited to a party at a store where a new POS system had been installed. They were invited to try to harm the system by pushing the wrong buttons or fouling up a transaction. Employees quickly found they could not harm the system and that it was easy to use.

FOCUS 24-2 STARS Saves Virginia $80 Million

Most Virginia taxpayers receive tax refunds within a week of filing (instead of the usual two to three months) thanks to Jane Bailey, director of AIS at the Department of Taxation. Jane managed the development of the State Tax Accounting and Reporting System (STARS), a multisystem project that took nine years to complete. STARS was so successful that the IRS, 27 states, and a Canadian province sent teams to Richmond to see whether STARS could improve their systems development and implementation efforts.

The state's IT group had strongly recommended outside contractors for the job, saying Jane's six-person staff was far too small and unsophisticated to overhaul the state's disjointed manual and batch systems. Jane insisted on going with an inside job. She was able to convince management by stating that she would maintain the system and respond quickly to tax law changes.

Jane insisted on hiring first-rate people, and her staff eventually swelled to 45 employees. If she could not hire the experts and specialists she needed, she retained them as consultants and used them to train her staff. She recruited five management analysts to redesign business processes, write user documentation, and train users. Ten people from her staff are management analysts who work full-time on user procedures and issues. Seeing user involvement as crucial, Jane succeeded in getting six managers from user areas assigned full-time to the project.

Over the years, STARS expanded to encompass more functions and more users, and its budget climbed from $3 million to $11 million. A new piece of software was installed every three to six months. Users had to adapt, often getting 15 new screens at a time. The megaproject eventually involved putting together 1,500 programs, 40 IBM databases, and 350 online screens in 25 applications for 1,800 users.

The state asked for a Chevrolet and got a Cadillac; the payoff has been impressive. STARS users estimate that it saved the state $80 million over five years, most of it from added collections from would-be tax cheats.

COMPLETE DOCUMENTATION

Three types of documentation must be prepared for new systems:

1. ***Development documentation*** describes the new AIS. It includes a system description; copies of output, input, and file and database layouts; program flowcharts; test results; and user acceptance forms.
2. ***Operations documentation*** includes operating schedules; files and databases accessed; and equipment, security, and file-retention requirements.
3. ***User documentation*** teaches users how to operate the AIS. It includes a procedures manual and training materials.

TESTING THE SYSTEM

Inadequate system testing was another reason for the Blue Cross and Blue Shield system failure. The developers underestimated system complexity and promised an unrealistic delivery time of 18 months. One shortcut they took to meet the deadline was to deliver an untested system. Documents and reports, user input, controls, operating and processing procedures, capacity limits, recovery procedures, and computer programs should all be tested in realistic circumstances. Following are three common forms of testing:

walk-throughs - Step-by-step reviews of procedures or program logic to find incorrect logic, errors, omissions, or other problems.

processing test data - Processing valid and erroneous transactions to determine if a program operates as designed and that valid transactions are handled properly and errors are detected and dealt with appropriately.

acceptance tests - Tests of a new system using real transactions to determine if user-developed acceptance criteria are met.

1. **Walk-throughs** are step-by-step reviews of procedures or program logic to find incorrect logic, errors, omissions, or other problems. The development team and system users attend walk-throughs early in system design. The focus is on the input, files, outputs, and data flows of the organization. Subsequent walk-throughs, attended by programmers, address logical and structural aspects of program code.
2. **Processing test data**, including all valid transactions and all possible error conditions, is performed to determine whether a program operates as designed; that is, valid transactions are handled properly and errors are detected and dealt with appropriately. To evaluate test results, the correct system response for each test transaction must be specified in advance.
3. **Acceptance tests** use copies of real transactions and files rather than hypothetical ones. Users develop the acceptance criteria and make the final decision whether to accept the AIS.

Chemical Bank did not adequately test an ATM upgrade, and customers who withdrew cash had their accounts debited twice. More than 150,000 withdrawals with a total value of $8 million were posted twice. Thousands of small accounts were overdrawn or emptied, which annoyed and angered customers. Chemical Bank lost a great deal of customer credibility because of the glitch.

Even software purchased from an outside vendor must be tested thoroughly before being installed. As soon as Kane Carpets installed an AIS custom tailored to the floor-covering industry, its inventory control system told salespeople that orders could not be filled when the product was available, and vice versa. As a result, Kane lost many of its customers.

Systems Conversion

Conversion is changing from the old to the new AIS. Many elements must be converted: hardware, software, data files, and procedures. The process is complete when the new AIS is a routine, ongoing part of the system. Four conversion approaches are used:

conversion - The process of changing from an old computer system or format to a new one.

- **Direct conversion** terminates the old AIS when the new one is introduced. For example, SM could discontinue its old system on Saturday night and use its new AIS on Monday morning. Direct conversion is appropriate when a new system is so different that comparisons between the two are meaningless. The approach is inexpensive, but it provides no backup AIS. Unless a system has been carefully developed and tested, direct conversion carries a high risk of failure. Focus 24-3 discusses the problems at Sunbeam, caused in part by attempting a direct conversion.

direct conversion - Changing from an old system to a new one by terminating the old IS when the new one is introduced.

- **Parallel conversion** operates the old and new systems simultaneously for a period. For example, SM could process transactions with both systems, compare the output, reconcile the differences, correct problems, and discontinue the old system after the new system proves itself. Parallel processing protects companies from errors, but it is costly and stressful to process transactions twice. Because companies often experience problems during conversion, parallel processing has gained widespread popularity.

parallel conversion - Changing from an old system to a new one by operating both systems simultaneously until the organization is confident the new system is functioning correctly.

FOCUS 24-3 Sunbeam and the Price of Direct Conversion

Sunbeam hired CEO Al Dunlap to turn the company around. While turning Scott Paper around, Al made such drastic cost cuts that he was nicknamed Chainsaw Al. At Sunbeam, Al also made drastic cost-cutting moves, many of which went too far and ended up hurting the company much more than they helped. He eliminated 87% of the company's products and half of its 6,000 employees, including outsourcing the IS staff. Terminated computer personnel making $35,000 a year were replaced with contract workers paid significantly more than $35,000. Ironically, some of the contract workers turned out to be terminated employees.

To minimize costs during an IS modernization, Sunbeam used a direct conversion approach that did not work. Because there was no backup system, the entire system was down for months. The result was total chaos. Orders were lost, and customers did not receive their shipments, received their orders two or three times, or received the wrong order. Sunbeam had no way to respond to upset customers because employees could not track orders or shipments. Customers could not be billed automatically, and Sunbeam had to bill its customers manually.

Because of poor management and no AIS for a long time, Sunbeam's stock plummeted. Al Dunlap was fired, shareholder lawsuits were filed, and governmental entities investigated the company. The SEC claimed that Al perpetrated an accounting fraud because $62 million of Sunbeam's $189 million in income in 1997 did not comply with accounting rules. Sunbeam filed for Chapter 11 bankruptcy protection, and several Sunbeam executives paid fines to settle charges of participating in a scheme to inflate the worth of the company. Al Dunlap agreed to a $500,000 fine without admitting or denying the SEC's accusations. Arthur Andersen, their auditors, paid $110 million in damages to settle a shareholder class-action suit. Phillip Harlow, the Andersen partner in charge of Sunbeam's 1997 year-end financial audit, was barred from practicing public accounting before the SEC for three years in exchange for having fraud charges against him dropped.

phase-in conversion - Changing from an old to a new system by gradually replacing elements of the old with the new until the old system has been entirely replaced.

pilot conversion - Changing from an old to a new system by implementing a system in one location, using it until all problems are resolved, and then implementing it in the rest of the organization.

- **Phase-in conversion** gradually replaces elements of the old AIS with the new one. For example, SM could implement its inventory system, then disbursements, then sales collection, and so forth, until the whole system is functional. Gradual changes allow data processing resources to be acquired over time. The disadvantages are the cost of creating the temporary interfaces between the old and the new AIS and the time required to make the gradual changeover.
- **Pilot conversion** implements a system in one part of the organization, such as a branch location. For example, SM could install its new POS system at one of its stores using a direct, parallel, or phase-in approach. When problems with the system are resolved, the new system could be implemented at the remaining locations. This localizes conversion problems and allows training in a live environment. The disadvantages are the long conversion time and the need for interfaces between the old and the new systems, which coexist until all locations have been converted. Owens-Corning Fiberglass implemented its accounts payable, travel expense, and payroll systems by getting the system up and running in one plant and then moving it to all the others.

Data conversion can be time-consuming, tedious, and expensive; its difficulty and magnitude are easily underestimated. Data files may need to be modified in three ways. First, files may be moved to a different storage medium—for example, from tapes to disks. Second, data content may be changed—for example, fields and records may be added or deleted. Third, file or database format may be changed.

The first step in data conversion is to decide which data files need to be converted. Then the data are checked for completeness and errors, and inconsistencies are removed. Following data conversion, the new files are validated to ensure data were not lost during conversion. If data conversion is lengthy, the new files must be updated with the transactions that occurred during data conversion. Once the files and databases have been converted and tested for accuracy, the new system is functional. The system should be monitored for a time to make sure it runs smoothly and accurately. The final activity is to document the conversion activities.

postimplementation review - Review made after a new system has been operating for a brief period to ensure that the new system is meeting its planned objectives, identify the adequacy of system standards, and review system controls.

postimplementation review report - A report that analyzes a newly delivered system to determine if the system achieved its intended purpose and was completed within budget.

Operation and Maintenance

The final SDLC step is to operate and maintain the new system. A **postimplementation review** is conducted to determine whether the system meets its planned objectives. Important review considerations are listed in Table 24-7. Problems uncovered during the review are brought to the attention of management, and the necessary adjustments are made. Table 24-8 illustrates what the **postimplementation review report** should contain. User acceptance of the report is the final activity in the systems development process.

TABLE 24-7 Factors to Investigate During Postimplementation Review

Factors	Questions
Goals and objectives	Does the system help the organization meet its goals, objectives, and overall mission?
Satisfaction	Are users satisfied? What would they like changed or improved?
Benefits	How have users benefited? Were the expected benefits achieved?
Costs	Are actual costs in line with expected costs?
Reliability	Is the system reliable? Has it failed? If so, what caused its failure?
Accuracy	Does the system produce accurate and complete data?
Timeliness	Does the system produce information on a timely basis?
Compatibility	Are hardware, software, data, and procedures compatible with existing systems?
Controls and security	Is the system safeguarded against errors, fraud, and intrusion?
Errors	Do adequate error-handling procedures exist?
Training	Are systems personnel and users trained to support and use the system?
Communications	Is the communications system adequate?
Organizational changes	Are organizational changes beneficial or harmful? If harmful, how can they be resolved?
Documentation	Is system documentation complete and accurate?

TABLE 24-8 Table of Contents for Shoppers Mart Reports

Conceptual Systems Design Report	Physical Systems Design Report	Postimplementation Review Report
Table of Contents	**Table of Contents**	**Table of Contents**
I. Executive Summary of Conceptual Systems Design	I. Executive Summary of Physical Systems Design	I. Executive Summary of Postimplementation Review
II. Overview of Project Purpose and Summary of Findings to Date	II. Overview of Project Purpose and Summary of Findings to Date	II. Overview of Development Project
III. Recommended Conceptual Design(s)	III. Physical Design Recommendations	III. Evaluation of the Development
A. Overview of Recommended Design(s)	A. Output Design	A. Degree to Which System Objectives Were Met
B. Objectives to Be Achieved by Design(s)	B. Input Design	B. Analysis of Actual Versus Expected Costs and Benefits
C. Impact of Design(s) on Information System and Organization	C. Database Design	C. User Reactions and Satisfaction
D. Expected Costs and Benefits of Design(s)	D. Software Design	IV. Evaluation of Project Development Team
E. Audit, Control, and Security Processes and Procedures	E. Hardware Design	V. Recommendations
F. Hardware, Software, and Other Resource Requirements	F. Controls Design	A. Recommendations for Improving the New System
G. Processing Flows: Relationships of Programs, Databases, Inputs, and Outputs	G. Procedures Design	B. Recommendations for Improving the System Development Process
H. Description of System Components (Programs, Databases, Inputs, and Outputs)	IV. Assumptions and Unresolved Problems	VI. Summary
IV. Assumptions and Unresolved Problems	V. Summary	
V. Summary	VI. Appendixes, Glossary	
VI. Appendixes, Glossary		

Control of the AIS is passed to the data processing department, but work on the new system is not finished. Over the life of a typical system, 30% of the work takes place during development, and 70% is spent on software modifications and updates. At Hartford Insurance Group, 70% of its personnel resources are devoted to maintaining an inventory of 34,000 program modules containing 24 million lines of code. The job is even more difficult because changes in insurance regulations and business strategies reduced the structure of the code and increased its complexity.

Summary and Case Conclusion

Ann Christy tackles the sales processing system first. She gives the project development team her systems analysis report and accompanying data. During conceptual systems design, the team visits stores with similar operations and identifies ways to meet AIS requirements. Alternative approaches are discussed with users, management, and the steering committee. They are narrowed down to Ann's original approach. Ann has considered buying software but does not find a package that accomplishes what she and the company want. The team develops conceptual design specifications for the output, input, processing, and data storage elements.

The company decides to use screen-based output and to capture data electronically using point-of-sale (POS) devices. Data that cannot be captured electronically will be entered using PCs. Each store will have a network that connects its PCs and POS devices to a local database. The POS cash registers will capture and feed sales data electronically to this database. Each store will be linked to the central office using a wide area network. All sales data, store orders, and other summary-level information will be uploaded to the corporate database daily. The corporate database will download the information needed to manage the store. The central office will use electronic data interchange to order goods and pay suppliers.

During physical design, the development team designs each report identified during conceptual design. Users and designers rework the reports until everyone is satisfied. The team designs all files, databases, and input screens. Then they design the software programs that collect and process data and produce the output. The team develops new procedures for handling data and operating the AIS. The accountants and the internal audit staff are especially helpful during the design of the controls needed to protect the system against errors and fraud.

Implementation planning starts early. A location for the new mainframe is identified, and site preparation begins during the design phase. The hardware and software are installed and tested and then the entire AIS is tested. The new AIS is staffed with existing employees who are trained as the system is tested. System documentation is completed before data from the old AIS are converted to the new one.

For the corporate system, the new and old systems are operated in parallel for a month, and the results compared. The bugs are ironed out, and the old AIS is discontinued. For the store systems, a pilot approach is used. The AIS is installed at three stores, and all problems are resolved before the system is implemented at the remaining stores. Conversion requires a fair amount of overtime and duplicate processing. After a few months, Ann and her staff conduct a postimplementation review and make some adjustments to enhance the high user acceptance of the new AIS.

Ann makes a final presentation to top management after the AIS is installed and operating. She is widely congratulated and even hears the president mention that she "is worth keeping an eye on" for even more responsibility in the firm. Table 24-8 is a summary of the contents of the conceptual, physical, and postimplementation reports.

KEY TERMS

- conceptual design specifications 761
- conceptual systems design report 761
- scheduled reports 762
- special-purpose analysis reports 762
- triggered exception reports 762
- demand reports 762
- structured programming 764
- debugging 764
- program maintenance 765
- physical systems design report 766
- systems implementation 766
- implementation plan 766
- walk-throughs 768
- processing test data 768
- acceptance tests 768
- conversion 769
- direct conversion 769
- parallel conversion 769
- phase-in conversion 770
- pilot conversion 770
- postimplementation review 770
- postimplementation review report 770

AIS in Action

CHAPTER QUIZ

1. The developers of your new system have proposed two different AIS designs and have asked you to evaluate them. This evaluation process is most likely to be a part of which SDLC step?
   a. systems analysis
   b. conceptual design
   c. physical design
   d. implementation and conversion
   e. operation and maintenance

2. What is the purpose of the conceptual systems design report?
   a. to guide physical systems design activities
   b. to communicate how management and user information needs are met
   c. to help the steering committee assess system feasibility
   d. a and b
   e. a, b, and c

3. Which of the following is the correct order of the steps in physical systems design?
   a. input, file and database, output, controls, procedures, program
   b. file and database, output, input, procedures, program, controls
   c. output, input, file and database, procedures, program, controls
   d. output, file and database, input, program, procedures, controls

4. A monthly payroll register showing all hourly employees, the number of hours they worked, their deductions, and their net pay is most likely which of the following?
   a. scheduled report
   b. special-purpose analysis
   c. triggered exception report
   d. demand report

5. Which of the following is not a consideration in input design?
   a. Which errors are possible, and how can they be detected and corrected?
   b. How can data be entered (keyboards, OCR, or POS terminal)?
   c. Which format efficiently captures the input data with the least effort and cost?
   d. How often should the system produce reports?

6. Which of the following is most likely to help improve program development?
   a. physical model
   b. IT strategic plan
   c. walk-through
   d. record layout

7. Which of the following statements is true?
   a. The Gartner Group estimates that programming bugs not found until later in the SDLC cost 25% to 30% more to correct than if they had been found earlier in the SDLC.
   b. Direct system conversion is the least risky of the system conversion methods.
   c. Many software developers state that 5% to 10% of software development costs should be allocated to testing, debugging, and rewriting software.
   d. Over the life of a system, only 30% of information systems work takes place during development; the remaining 70% is spent maintaining the system.

8. Which of the following describes the systems testing approach that uses real transactions and files rather than hypothetical ones?
   a. walk-through
   b. processing of test transactions
   c. acceptance test
   d. parallel conversion test

9. What is the process of discontinuing an old system as soon as a new one is introduced?
   a. direct conversion
   b. parallel conversion
   c. phase-in conversion
   d. pilot conversion

10. Which of the following describes designing a program from the top-down to more detailed levels?
   a. hierarchical program design
   b. top-down program design
   c. parallel program design
   d. unstructured program design

COMPREHENSIVE PROBLEM

Halloween is the biggest candy season of them all, with $1.8 billion in sales. For Hershey's, Halloween 1999 was the scariest of all time. Hershey's had planned to implement a $112 million ERP system in 48 months. Instead, it was implemented in an accelerated 30-month time frame. Hershey's "flipped the switch" in July 1999, right during its busiest ordering season. Issues with inventory and ordering processes promptly gummed up the order-distribution system. By August 1999, Hershey's was 15 days behind in shipping orders. Many distributors who placed orders in September were still waiting for their shipment at Halloween. Hershey had plenty of candy in inventory; it just could not move the candy from its warehouses to its customers. The implementation problem contributed to a 19% drop in revenue. It took a full year for the company to bounce back.

The new ERP system employed more than 5,000 PCs, network hubs, and servers. The ERP software was supplied by three firms and implemented by a large consulting firm. Despite the system's size and complexity, Hershey's chose to implement most of it in one step called the "big bang."

REQUIRED

What could Hershey's have done to properly design, implement, and operate this new ERP?

DISCUSSION QUESTIONS

24.1 Prism Glass is converting to a new information system. To expedite and speed up implementation, the CEO asked your consulting team to postpone establishing standards and controls until after the system is fully operational. How should you respond to the CEO's request?

24.2 When a company converts from one system to another, many areas within the organization are affected. Explain how conversion to a new system will affect the following groups, both individually and collectively.

a. personnel
b. data storage
c. operations
d. policies and procedures
e. physical facilities

24.3 During which of the five SDLC stages is each task, labeled (a) through (m), performed? More than one answer may apply for each activity.

____ **1.** systems analysis

____ **2.** conceptual (general) systems design

____ **3.** physical (detailed) systems design

____ **4.** implementation and conversion

____ **5.** operation and maintenance

a. Writing operating procedure manuals
b. Developing program and process controls
c. Identifying alternative systems designs
d. Developing a logical model of the system
e. Identifying external and administrative controls
f. Testing the system
g. Training personnel
h. Evaluating the existing system
i. Analyzing the achievement of systems benefits
j. Modifying and altering programs
k. Analyzing total quality management (TQM) performance measures
l. Conducting a feasibility analysis
m. Aligning AIS development plans with business objectives

24.4 In which phase of the systems development cycle would each of the following positions be most actively involved? Justify your answers.

a. managerial accountant
b. programmer
c. systems analyst
d. financial vice president
e. information systems manager
f. internal auditor

PROBLEMS

24.1 Match the terms with their definitions:

Term	Definition
____ **1.** direct conversion	a. Requirement specifications for systems output, data storage, input, processing procedures, and operations
____ **2.** conceptual design specifications	b. Summarizes conceptual design, guides physical design, and communicates how information needs will be met
____ **3.** scheduled report	c. Output prepared on a regular basis, with a pre-specified content and format
____ **4.** acceptance test	d. Output with no pre-specified content, format, or schedule; usually prepared at management request
____ **5.** postimplementation review	e. Output with pre-specified content and format; prepared in response to abnormal conditions
____ **6.** processing test data	f. Output with a pre-specified content and format; prepared only on request
____ **7.** pilot conversion	g. Modular programming approach; each module performs specific function and is coordinated by a control module
____ **8.** program maintenance	h. Process of discovering and eliminating program errors
____ **9.** structured programming	i. Updating a computer program due to changed user needs, fixing bugs, or legal or regulatory changes
____**10.** postimplementation review report	j. Summarizes what was accomplished in physical design; used to determine whether to proceed to implementation
____**11.** demand report	k. Process of installing hardware and software and getting the IS up and running
____**12.** parallel conversion	l. Written plan showing how new system will be implemented and when the project is complete and the IS operational
____**13.** walk-throughs	m. Step-by-step reviews of program logic to find incorrect logic, errors, omissions, or other problems
____**14.** physical systems design report	n. Processing valid and erroneous transactions to see if a program operates as designed and errors are detected and corrected
____**15.** phase-in conversion	o. Using real transactions to determine if user-developed acceptance criteria are met
____**16.** triggered exception report	p. Process of changing from an old computer system to a new one
____**17.** systems implementation	q. Changing from an old to a new system by terminating the old when the new is introduced
____**18.** special-purpose analysis report	r. Changing from an old to a new system by operating both simultaneously until confident the new system functions correctly

_____**19.**	implementation plan	s.	Gradually replacing elements in an old system with new elements until the old system is replaced
_____**20.**	debugging	t.	Implementing a new system in one location, resolving its problems, and then implementing it in the rest of the organization
		u.	Review of new system after operating for a brief period to ensure it meets planned objectives and to review system controls
		v.	Report that analyzes a new system to determine if it achieved its intended purpose

24.2 Wang Lab's tremendous growth left the company with a serious problem. Customers would often wait months for Wang to fill orders and process invoices. Repeated attempts by Wang's understaffed IS department to solve these problems met with failure. Finally, Wang hired a consulting firm to solve its revenue tracking problems and expedite prompt receipt of payments. The 18-month project turned into a doubly long nightmare. After three years and $10 million, the consultants were dismissed from the unfinished project.

The project failed for many reasons. The systems development process was so dynamic that the failure to complete the project quickly became self-defeating as modifications took over the original design. Second, management did not have a clear vision of the new AIS and lacked a strong support staff. As a result, a number of incompatible tracking systems sprang from the company's distributed computer system. Third, the project was too large and complex for the consulting firm, who had little experience with the complex database at the heart of the new system. Finally, the project had too many applications. Interdependencies among subprograms left consultants with few completed programs. Every program was linked to several subprograms, which in turn were linked to several other programs. Programmers eventually found themselves lost in a morass of subroutines with no completed program.

The IS department finally developed a system to solve the problem, but their revenue tracking system suffered quality problems for years.

REQUIRED

Wang asked you to write a memo explaining the failure of the systems development project.

a. Why did the development project fail? What role did the consultants play in the failure?
b. Identify the organizational issues that management must address in the future.
c. Recommend steps the company could take to guarantee consulting service quality.

24.3 Tiny Toddlers, a manufacturer of children's toys and furniture, is designing and implementing a distributed system to assist its sales force. Each of the 10 sales offices in Canada and 20 in the United States maintains its own customers and is responsible for granting credit and collecting receivables. Electronic data input forms used by each sales office to maintain the customer master file and to enter the daily sales orders are shown in Figures 24-4 and 24-5.

REQUIRED

Evaluate the electronic data input forms shown in Figures 24-4 and 24-5 using the following format:

Weakness	Explanation	Recommendation(s)

(SMAC Examination, adapted)

24.4 Mickie Louderman is the new assistant controller of Pickens Publishers. She was the controller of a company in a similar industry, where she was in charge of accounting and had considerable influence over computer center operations. Pickens wants to revamp its information system, placing increased emphasis on decentralized data access

CUSTOMER MAINTENANCE FORM

New Customer?	❑ Yes
	☑ No 24671
Name	The Little Ones Furniture Store
New Address	5 St. Antoine Street N. Quebec City
Old Address	305 St. Antoine Street S. Quebec City
Salesperson #	02
Requested Credit Limit	50,000
Sales Office	Eastern Canada
Pricing Code	25
Estimated Sales	300,000
Credit Limit	10,000
Currency	U.S.A. ❑, Canada ❑
Bank	Canadian Credit Bank 50 St. Antoine Street Quebec City
Bank Line	
Rating	Satisfactory
Sales Manager	
Credit Manager	

FIGURE 24-4
Customer Maintenance Form for Tiny Toddlers

and online systems. John Richards, the controller, is near retirement. He has put Mickie in charge of developing a new system that integrates the company's accounting-related functions. Her promotion to controller will depend on the success of the new AIS.

Mickie uses the same design characteristics and reporting format she used at her former company. She sends details of the new AIS to the departments that interface with accounting, including inventory control, purchasing, human resources, production control, and marketing. If they do not respond with suggestions by a prescribed date, she will continue the development process. Mickie and John have established a new schedule for many of the reports, changing the frequency from weekly to monthly. After a meeting with the director of IS, Mickie selects a programmer to help her with the details of the new reporting formats.

Most control features of the old system are maintained to decrease the installation time, with a few new ones added for unusual situations. The procedures for maintaining the controls are substantially changed. Mickie makes all the AIS control change and program-testing decisions, including screening the control features related to payroll, inventory control, accounts receivable, cash deposits, and accounts payable.

As each module is completed, Mickie has the corresponding department implement the change immediately to take advantage of the labor savings. Incomplete instructions accompany these changes, and specific implementation responsibility is not assigned to departmental personnel. Mickie believes operations people should learn as they go, reporting errors as they occur.

Accounts payable and inventory control are implemented first, and several problems arise. The semimonthly payroll runs, which had been weekly under the old system, have abundant errors, requiring numerous manual paychecks. Payroll run control totals take hours to reconcile with the computer printout. To expedite matters, Mickie authorizes the payroll clerk to prepare payroll journal entries.

The new inventory control system fails to improve the carrying level of many stock items. This causes critical stock outs of raw material that result in expensive rush orders. The new system's primary control procedure is the availability of ordering and

FIGURE 24-5
Sales Order Form for Tiny Toddlers

SALES ORDER FORM

Customer: 24671 Date: ________
The Little Ones Furniture Store
5 St. Antoine Street N.
Quebec City

Product Code	Description	Quantity
24571	Crib	4
M0002	Mattress	102
HG730	High chair—white	32
HG223	High chair—natural wood	22
CT200	Changing table	300
D0025	Desk—modern design	2
C9925	Chair—modern design	5
BP809	Bumper pads	1200

Salesperson No.: ________

Entered by: ________

user information. The information is available to both inventory control and purchasing personnel so that both departments can issue timely purchase orders. Because the inventory levels are updated daily, Mickie discontinues the previous weekly report.

Because of these problems, system documentation is behind schedule, and proper backup procedures have not been implemented. Mickie has requested budget approval to hire two systems analysts, an accountant, and an administrative assistant to help her implement the new system. John is disturbed by her request because her predecessor had only one part-time assistant.

REQUIRED

a. List the steps Mickie should have taken while designing the AIS to ensure that end-user needs were satisfied.
b. Identify and describe three ways Mickie violated internal control principles during the AIS implementation.
c. Identify and describe the weaknesses in Mickie's approach to implementing the new AIS. How could you improve the development process for the remaining parts of the AIS? *(CMA Examination, adapted)*

24.5 Ryon Pulsipher, manager of Columbia's property accounting division, has had difficulty responding to the following departmental requests for information about fixed assets.

1. The controller has requested individual fixed assets schedules to support the general ledger balance. Although Ryon has furnished the information, it is late. The way the records are organized makes it difficult to obtain information easily.
2. The maintenance manager wants to verify the existence of a punch press that he thinks was repaired twice. He has asked Ryon to confirm the asset number and the location of the press.
3. The insurance department wants data on the cost and book values of assets to include in its review of current insurance coverage.
4. The tax department has requested data to determine whether Columbia should switch depreciation methods for tax purposes.
5. The internal auditors have spent significant time in the property accounting division to confirm the annual depreciation expense.

Ryon's property account records, kept in an Excel spreadsheet, show the asset acquisition date, its account number, the dollar amount capitalized, and its estimated useful life for depreciation purposes. After many frustrations, Ryon realizes his records are inadequate and that he cannot supply data easily when requested. He discusses his problems with the controller, Gig Griffith.

RYON: Gig, something has to give. My people are working overtime and can't keep up. You worked in property accounting before you became controller. You know I can't tell the tax, insurance, and maintenance people everything they need to know from my records. Internal auditing is living in my area, and that slows down the work. The requests of these people are reasonable, and we should be able to answer their questions and provide the needed data. I think we need an automated property accounting system. I want to talk with the AIS people to see if they can help me.

GIG: I think that's a great idea. Just be sure you are personally involved in the design of any system so you get all the info you need. Keep me posted on the project's progress.

REQUIRED

a. Identify and justify four major objectives Columbia's automated property accounting system should possess to respond to departmental requests for information.
b. Identify the data that should be included in the database for each asset. *(CMA Examination, adapted)*

24.6 A credit union is developing a new AIS. The internal auditors suggest planning the systems development process in accordance with the SDLC concept. The following nine items are identified as major systems development activities that will have to be completed.

1. System test
2. User specifications
3. Conversion
4. Systems survey
5. Technical specifications
6. Post-implementation planning
7. Implementation planning
8. User procedures and training
9. Programming

REQUIRED

a. Arrange the nine items in the sequence in which they should logically occur.
b. One major activity is to convert data files from the old system to the new one. List three types of file conversion documentation that would be of particular interest to an auditor. *(CMA Examination, adapted)*

24.7 MetLife, an insurance company, spent $11 billion to acquire Travelers Life and Annuity from Citicorp in one of the largest insurance company acquisitions of all time. The Metlife CIO estimated it would take three years to integrate the two systems. Because the integration project was especially critical, he figured he could accomplish the integration in 18 months if he pulled out all the stops. The MetLife CEO gave him nine months to complete the task. To pull off the integration in nine months, he had to:

- Integrate more than 600 IS applications, all with their own infrastructure and business processes. The new systems had to comply with "One MetLife," a company policy that all information systems had to have a common look and feel companywide and be able to function seamlessly with other MetLife systems.
- Work with more than 4,000 employees located in 88 offices scattered all over the globe.
- Supervise an oversight team and 50 integration teams in seven project management offices.
- Work with hostile, uncooperative Travelers employees for the six months it took to get regulatory approval and close the deal. The systems had to be integrated three months after the deal closed.
- Identify integration deliverables (144 in total) and manage the process to deliver them.
- Negotiate with Citicorp for hundreds of transition services that would not be immediately converted to MetLife's systems

REQUIRED

a. What tasks would MetLife have to perform to integrate the Travelers systems into MetLife's?
b. Search the Internet for articles that describe the integration process. Write a two-page summary of the problems and successes that MetLife experienced while integrating the two systems.

24.8 During final testing, just before launching a new payroll system, the project manager at Reutzel Legal Services found that the purchased payroll system was doing the following:

- Writing checks for negative amounts
- Printing checks with names and employee numbers that did not match
- Making errors; for example, \$8 per hour became \$800 per hour if a decimal point was not entered
- Writing checks for amounts greater than a full year's salary

Fortunately, payroll was still installed on time, and only 1.5% of the checks had to be manually reissued every payday until the problem was solved.

Other problems were that no one had made sure the new system was compatible with the existing payroll database, and there appeared to be no formal transition between the development of the project and the implementation of the project. The system was never run in parallel.

Although the programming manager lost his job, the payroll problems helped raise awareness of the company's growing dependence on IT. Lacking a major problem, there was a perception that the information system did not affect operations.

REQUIRED

a. What does "the system was never run in parallel" mean?
b. If the company had run the system in parallel, what should have occurred?
c. What other testing methodologies could have been used by the firm?
d. What other types of problems are evident from reading the case?

24.9 A new program at Jones and Carter Corporation (JCC) was supposed to track customer calls. Unfortunately, the program took 20 minutes to load on a PC, and it crashed frequently. The project did not have a traditional reporting structure, and it appeared that no one was actually in charge. The lead project manager quit halfway through the project, the in-house programmers were reassigned to other projects or let go, and two layers of management loosely supervised the systems analyst.

Management hired consultants to fix the application, but after three months and \$200,000, the project was discontinued. JCC did not check the references of the consulting firm it hired to create the new system. The consultants, who were located two states away, made many programming errors. Although the systems analyst caught some of the consultant's mistakes, they grew increasingly distant and difficult to work with. They would not even furnish the source code to the project managers, most likely because they were afraid of revealing their incompetence.

REQUIRED

a. Identify potential causes for the system implementation failure.
b. What steps should JCC have taken to successfully design and implement the call tracking system?

24.10 This chapter describes several different systems conversion approaches. Select one of the approaches and conduct a search (using written materials, the Internet, electronic databases, etc.) for one or more companies that successfully used the approach to convert from an older system to a newer system. Per your professor's instructions, prepare an oral or written summary of the successful conversion. Include in your summary the nature of the system, the approach used to convert the system, and a description of how successful the conversion was, including what worked well and what did not.

CASE 24-1 Citizen's Gas Company

Citizen's Gas Company (CGC) provides natural gas service to 200,000 customers. The customer base is divided into the following three revenue classes:

Class	Customers	Sales in Cubic Feet	Revenues
Residential	160,000	80 billion	$160 million
Commercial	38,000	15 billion	$ 25 million
Industrial	2,000	50 billion	$ 65 million
Totals		145 billion	$250 million

Residential customer gas usage is highly correlated with the weather. Commercial customer usage is partially weather dependent. Industrial customer usage is governed almost entirely by business factors.

The company buys natural gas from 10 pipeline companies in the amounts specified in contracts that run for 5 to 15 years. For some contracts, the supply is in equal monthly increments; for other contracts, the supply varies according to the heating season. Supply over the contract amounts is not available, and some contracts contain take-or-pay clauses. That is, the company must pay for the gas volume specified in the contract, regardless of the amount used.

To match customer demand with supply, gas is pumped into a storage field when supply exceeds customer demand. Gas is withdrawn when demand exceeds supply. There are no restrictions on the gas storage field except that the field must be full at the beginning of each gas year (September 1). Consequently, when the contractual supply for the remainder of the gas year is less than that required to satisfy projected demand and fill the storage field, CGC curtails service to industrial customers (except for heating quantities). The curtailments must be carefully controlled to prevent either an oversupply at year-end or a curtailing of commercial or residential customers so the storage field can be filled at year-end.

In recent years, CGC's planning efforts have not been able to control the supply during the gas year or provide the information needed to establish long-term contracts. Customer demand has been projected only as a function of the total number of customers. Commercial and industrial customers' demand for gas has been curtailed. This has resulted in lost sales and caused an excess of supply at the end of the gas year.

To correct the problems, CGC has hired a director of corporate planning. She is presented with a conceptual design for an information system that will help analyze gas supply and demand. The system will provide a monthly gas plan for the next five years, with particular emphasis on the first year. The plan will provide detailed reports that assist in the decision-making process. The system will use actual data during the year to project demand for the year. The president has indicated that she will base her decisions on the effect alternative plans have on operating income.

REQUIRED

1. Discuss the criteria to consider in specifying the structure and features of CGC's new system.
2. Identify the data that should be incorporated into CGC's new system to provide adequate planning capability. Explain why each data item is important and the level of detail needed for the data to be useful. *(CMA Examination, adapted)*

AIS in Action Solutions

QUIZ KEY

1. The developers of your new system have proposed two different AIS designs and have asked you to evaluate them. This evaluation process is most likely to be a part of which SDLC step?
   a. systems analysis [Incorrect. During systems analysis, analysts identify user requirements and establish objectives and specifications for the design phases of the SDLC.]
   ▶ b. conceptual design [Correct. During conceptual design, users develop and evaluate appropriate design alternatives.]
   c. physical design [Incorrect. During physical design, the company translates the broad, user-oriented requirements of the conceptual design into detailed specifications used to develop and test computer programs.]
   d. implementation and conversion [Incorrect. During implementation and conversion, the company installs and tests hardware, software, and procedures as well as converts from the old system to the new system.]

e. operation and maintenance [Incorrect. During operation and maintenance, the company runs the system and performs ongoing maintenance and minor modifications.]

2. What is the purpose of the conceptual systems design report?

a. to guide physical systems design activities [Incorrect. The conceptual design report also includes communicating how management and users' needs are met and helping the steering committee assess system feasibility.]

b. to communicate how management and user information needs are met [Incorrect. The conceptual design report also includes guiding physical systems design activities and helping the steering committee assess system feasibility.]

c. to help the steering committee assess system feasibility [Incorrect. The conceptual design report also includes communicating how management and users' needs are met and guiding physical systems design activities.]

d. a and b [Incorrect. The conceptual design report also includes helping the steering committee assess system feasibility.]

▶ **e.** a, b, and c [Correct. The conceptual design report guides physical systems design activities, communicates how management and users' needs are met, and helps the steering committee assess system feasibility.]

3. Which of the following is the correct order of the steps in physical systems design?

a. input, file and database, output, controls, procedures, program [Incorrect. See Figure 24-2.]

b. file and database, output, input, procedures, program, controls [Incorrect. See Figure 24-2.]

c. output, input, file and database, procedures, program, controls [Incorrect. See Figure 24-2.]

▶ **d.** output, file and database, input, program, procedures, controls [Correct. See Figure 24-2.]

4. A monthly payroll register showing all hourly employees, the number of hours they worked, their deductions, and their net pay is most likely which of the following?

▶ **a.** scheduled report [Correct. Scheduled reports have a specified content, format, and delivery time. A monthly payroll register exhibits these characteristics.]

b. special-purpose analysis [Incorrect. A special-purpose analysis has no specified content, format, or delivery schedule.]

c. triggered exception report [Incorrect. A triggered exception report has specified content and format, but it is generated only if a certain event occurs.]

d. demand report [Incorrect. A demand report has specified content and format, but it is generated only on request.]

5. Which of the following is not a consideration in input design?

a. Which errors are possible, and how can they be detected and corrected? [Incorrect. Error identification and correction should be considered during input design. See Table 24-4.]

b. How can data be entered (keyboards, OCR, or POS terminal)? [Incorrect. Data entry methods should be considered during input design. See Table 24-4.]

c. Which format efficiently captures the input data with the least effort and cost? [Incorrect. Data format should be considered during input design. See Table 24-4.]

▶ **d.** How often should the system produce reports? [Correct. Report generation frequency is not normally considered during input design. See Table 24-4.]

6. Which of the following is most likely to help improve program development?

a. physical model [Incorrect. A physical model is most commonly used to describe the physical characteristics of a database.]

b. IT strategic plan [Incorrect. An entity's strategic plan provides a roadmap for achieving long-range goals.]

▶ **c.** walk-through [Correct. During walk-throughs, people associated with designing the project review it step-by-step so any problems can be identified and corrected.]

d. record layout [Incorrect. A record layout illustrates how data items are stored in a file.]

7. Which of the following statements is true?

a. The Gartner Group estimates that programming bugs not found until later in the SDLC cost 25% to 30% more to correct than if they had been found earlier in the SDLC. [Incorrect. The correct estimate is 80% to 1,000% more.]

b. Direct system conversion is the least risky of the system conversion methods. [Incorrect. Direct conversion is the most risky rather than the least risky method for converting from an old system to a new system.]

c. Many software developers state that 5% to 10% of software development costs should be allocated to testing, debugging, and rewriting software. [Incorrect. Software developers recommend that 20% to 30% of software development costs be allocated to testing, debugging, and rewriting software.]

▶ **d.** Over the life of a system, only 30% of information systems work takes place during development; the remaining 70% is spent maintaining the system. [Correct.]

8. Which of the following describes the systems testing approach that uses real transactions and files rather than hypothetical ones?

a. walk-through [Incorrect. Walk-throughs are step-by-step reviews of procedures or programs so any problems can be identified and corrected.]

b. processing of test transactions [Incorrect. Processing of test transactions uses valid and erroneous data to test for the proper handling of transactions as well as the proper detection and handling of errors.]

▶ **c.** acceptance test [Correct. An acceptance test uses real transaction data to test a new system.]

d. parallel conversion test [Incorrect. Parallel conversion is a system conversion method, not a testing method.]

9. What is the process of discontinuing an old system as soon as a new one is introduced?

▶ **a.** direct conversion [Correct. In direct conversion, the old system is discontinued as soon as the new one is activated.]

b. parallel conversion [Incorrect. A parallel conversion involves operating both the old and the new system in parallel until the users accept the new system.]

c. phase-in conversion [Incorrect. Phase-in conversion gradually replaces elements of the old system with the new one.]

d. pilot conversion [Incorrect. A pilot conversion activates and tests the new system in one or a few locations.]

10. Which of the following describes designing a program from the top-down to more detailed levels?

▶ **a.** hierarchical program design [Correct. Hierarchical program design is the process of programming from the general level to the detailed level.]

b. top-down program design [Incorrect. This is not a program design method described in the text.]

c. parallel program design [Incorrect. This is not a program design method described in the text.]

d. unstructured program design [Incorrect. This is not a program design method described in the text.]

COMPREHENSIVE PROBLEM SOLUTION

To properly design, implement, and operate this new ERP system, Hershey's could have taken the following steps.

CONCEPTUAL DESIGN

In designing its new ERP system, Hershey's should have looked at all possible designs, evaluated their strengths and weaknesses, and selected the best one. Once the system was selected, Hershey's needed to address the design specifications, such as what distribution output is needed to meet customer demands, how to store order and shipping data, how to input order and shipping data, and how to process the inputs and data to produce the outputs. Hershey's should have prepared a detailed report to guide the physical design phase and communicate with management and the steering committee the project's progress, requirements, and feasibility.

PHYSICAL DESIGN

Once the conceptual design was approved, physical design should have been planned. During this design phase, the following should have been created: order and shipment output documents, reports, files and databases; and the input forms and computer screens needed to capture order and shipment data. Hershey's needed to choose which ERP modules to implement and to decide how to structure and modify those modules to meet its needs. Hershey's also needed to decide how employees would interact with the system and to develop policies and procedures to formalize that interaction. Controls should have been designed to make sure those procedures and the system in general performed as intended and to prevent fraud and abuse. All of the physical design elements also should have been put into a report to guide Hershey's in the actual implementation of the system.

SYSTEMS IMPLEMENTATION

Once the new ERP system had been designed and created, the actual hardware, software, procedures, and controls should have been implemented. An installation plan includes all tasks needed to prepare the physical location of the new ERP system, train managers and users to operate the ERP system, document the system, and test it. Based on the information in the case, it appears that Hershey's failed to test its new ERP system adequately before converting from the old system.

SYSTEM CONVERSION

Of the four primary system conversion approaches, Hershey's chose direct conversion—the highest-risk approach. Hershey's called the approach the "big bang"—and the big bang that was heard was a drop in market capitalization (stock price) and a damaged reputation due to the loss of orders and the loss of supplier confidence. In hindsight, Hershey's should have used one of the other three approaches—parallel, phase-in, or pilot—with the parallel approach probably being the most effective. If Hershey's had been able to convert to the new ERP system more successfully, it could have then focused on operating and maintaining the new system and making improvements to make it more effective and efficient.

Glossary

A

acceptance tests Tests of a new system using real transactions to determine if user-developed acceptance criteria are met.

access control lists (ACLs) Sets of IF-THEN rules used to determine what to do with arriving packets.

access control matrix A table used to implement authorization controls.

access rights Permissions granted to create, read, update, and delete data, database records, or data files.

accounting The systematic and comprehensive recording of an organization's financial transactions, including summarizing, analyzing, and reporting these transactions to all users.

accounting information system (AIS) A system that collects, records, stores, and processes data to produce information for decision makers. It includes people, procedures and instructions, data, software, information technology infrastructure, and internal controls and security measures.

accounts receivable aging report A report listing customer account balances by length of time outstanding. The report provides useful information for evaluating current credit policies, for estimating bad debts, and for deciding whether to increase the credit limit for specific customers.

activity-based costing A cost system designed to trace costs to the activities that create them.

adware Spyware that causes banner ads to pop up on a monitor, collects information about the user's web-surfing and spending habits, and forwards it to the adware creator, often an advertising or media organization. Adware usually comes bundled with freeware and shareware downloaded from the Internet.

agents In the REA data model, the people and organizations who participate in events and about whom information is desired.

aggregate data The presentation of data in a summarized form.

aggression Resistance to change intended to destroy, cripple, or weaken system effectiveness, such as increased error rates, disruptions, or deliberate sabotage.

agile development A guiding philosophy and a set of principles for developing information systems in an unknown, rapidly changing environment.

alternative hypothesis A proposed explanation worded in the form of an inequality, meaning that one of the two concepts, ideas, or groups will be greater or less than the other concept, idea, or group.

analytical review The examination of the relationships between different sets of data; abnormal or unusual relationships and trends should be further investigated.

analytics mindset A way of thinking that centers on the correct use of data and analysis for decision making.

application controls Controls that prevent, detect, and correct transaction errors and fraud in application programs. They are concerned with the accuracy, completeness, validity, and authorization of the data captured, entered into the system, processed, stored, transmitted to other systems, and reported. Contrast with *general controls*.

archive A copy of a database, master file, or software retained indefinitely as a historical record, usually to satisfy legal and regulatory requirements.

artificial intelligence (AI) The use of computer systems to simulate human intelligence processes such as learning, reasoning, and self-improvement.

asymmetric encryption systems Encryption systems that use two keys (one public, the other private); either key can encrypt, but only the other matching key can decrypt.

attributes The properties, identifying numbers, and characteristics of interest of an entity stored in a database. Examples are employee number, pay rate, name, and address.

audit committee The outside, independent board of director members responsible for financial reporting, regulatory compliance, internal control, and hiring and overseeing internal and external auditors.

audit trail A path that allows a transaction to be traced through a data processing system from point of origin to output or backwards from output to point of origin. It is used to check the accuracy and validity of ledger postings and to trace changes in general ledger accounts from their beginning balance to their ending balance.

authentication Verifying the identity of the person or device attempting to access the system.

authorization The process of restricting access of authenticated users to specific portions of the system and limiting what actions they are permitted to perform.

automation The application of machines to automatically perform a task once performed by humans.

avoidance Resistance to change where users ignore a new IS in the hope that the new system will eventually go away.

B

back order A document authorizing the purchase or production of items that is created when there is insufficient inventory to meet customer orders.

background check An investigation of a prospective or current employee that involves verifying their educational and work experience, talking to references, checking for a criminal record or credit problems, and examining other publicly available information.

balance-forward method Method of maintaining accounts receivable in which customers typically pay according to the amount shown on a monthly statement, rather than by individual invoices. Remittances are applied against the total account balance, rather than specific invoices.

balanced scorecard A management report that measures four dimensions of organizational performance: financial, internal operations, innovation and learning, and customer perspectives.

batch processing Accumulating transaction records into groups or batches for processing at a regular interval such as daily or weekly. The records are usually sorted into some sequence (such as numerically or alphabetically) before processing.

batch totals The sum of a numerical item for a batch of documents, calculated prior to processing the batch, when the data are entered, and subsequently compared with computer-generated totals after each processing step to verify that the data was processed correctly.

behavioral aspects of change The positive and negative ways people react to change; managing these behavioral reactions is crucial to successfully implementing a new system.

belief system System that describes how a company creates value, helps employees understand management's vision, communicates company core values, and inspires employees to live by those values.

benchmark problem Comparing systems by executing an input, processing, and output task on different computer systems and evaluating the results.

big data Data sets characterized by huge amounts (volume) of frequently updated data (velocity) in various formats (variety), for which the quality may be suspect (veracity).

bill of lading A legal contract that defines responsibility for goods while they are in transit. It identifies the carrier, source, destination, shipping instructions, and the party (customer or vendor) that must pay the carrier.

bill of materials A document that specifies the part number, description, and quantity of each component used in a product.

biometric identifier A physical or behavioral characteristic used as an authentication credential.

blanket purchase order or blanket order A commitment to purchase specified items at designated prices from a particular supplier for a set time period, often one year.

block code Blocks of numbers reserved for specific categories of data, thereby helping to organize the data. An example is a chart of accounts.

blockchain Individual digital records, called blocks, linked together using cryptography in a single list, called a chain. The blockchain isn't stored in a single location. Instead, it is a distributed ledger of hashed documents that functions as a decentralized database. Each computer in the distributed peer-to-peer network maintains a copy of the ledger to prevent a single point of failure.

bluebugging Taking control of someone else's phone to make or listen to calls, send or read text messages, connect to the Internet, forward the victim's calls, and call numbers that charge fees.

bluesnarfing Stealing (snarfing) contact lists, images, and other data using flaws in Bluetooth applications.

border router A device that connects an organization's information system to the Internet.

bot Autonomous computer program designed to perform a specific task.

bot herder The person who creates a botnet by installing software on PCs that responds to the bot herder's electronic instructions. This control over the PCs allows the bot herder to mount a variety of Internet attacks.

botnet A network of powerful and dangerous hijacked computers that are used to attack systems or spread malware.

boundary system System that helps employees act ethically by setting boundaries on employee behavior. Instead of telling employees exactly what to do, they are encouraged to creatively solve problems and meet customer needs while meeting minimum performance standards, shunning off-limit activities, and avoiding actions that might damage their reputation.

brute force attack Trial-and-error method that uses software to guess information, such as the user ID and the password, needed to gain access to a system.

buffer overflow attack When the amount of data entered into a program is greater than the amount of the input buffer. The input overflow overwrites the next computer instruction, causing the system to crash. Hackers exploit this by crafting the input so that the overflow contains code that tells the computer what to do next. This code could open a back door into the system.

business continuity plan (BCP) A plan that specifies how to resume all business processes in the event of a major calamity.

business intelligence Analyzing large amounts of data for strategic decision making. There are two main business intelligence techniques: online analytical processing (OLAP) and data mining.

business process A set of related, coordinated, and structured activities and tasks, performed by a person, a computer, or a machine, that helps accomplish a specific organizational goal.

business process diagram (BPD) A visual way to describe the different steps or activities in a business process, providing a reader with an easily understood pictorial view of what takes place in a business process.

business process management (BPM) A systematic approach to continuously improving and optimizing business processes; a more gradual improvement facilitated by technology.

business process management systems (BPMS) Systems that automate and facilitate business process improvements throughout the SDLC. It can improve communication and collaboration, automate activities, and integrate with other systems and with other partners in the value chain.

business process reengineering (BPR) The thorough analysis and redesign of business processes and information systems to achieve dramatic performance improvements; often a drastic, one-time event.

business processes or transaction cycles The major give-get exchanges that occur frequently in most companies.

C

caller ID spoofing Displaying an incorrect number on the recipient's caller ID display to hide the caller's identity.

capital budgeting model A return-on-investment technique used to compare estimated benefits and costs to determine whether a system is cost beneficial.

cardinalities Describe the nature of a database relationship indicating the number of occurrences of one entity that may be associated with a single occurrence of the other entity. Three types of cardinalities are one-to-one, one-to-many, and many-to-many.

carding Activities performed on stolen credit cards, including making a small online purchase to determine whether the card is still valid and buying and selling stolen credit card numbers.

cash flow budget A budget that shows projected cash inflows and outflows for a specified period.

categorical data Data items that take on a limited number of assigned values to represent different groups.

certificate authority An organization that issues public and private keys and records the public key in a digital certificate.

change management Process of making sure changes are made smoothly and efficiently and do not negatively affect the system.

chart of accounts A listing of all the numbers assigned to balance sheet and income statement accounts. The account numbers allow transaction data to be coded, classified, and entered into the proper accounts. They also facilitate financial statement and report preparation.

check digit ID numbers (such as inventory item number) can contain a check digit computed from the other digits.

check digit verification Recalculating a check digit to verify that a data entry error has not been made.

check kiting Creating cash using the lag between the time a check is deposited and the time it clears the bank. Suppose an account is opened in banks A, B, and C. The perpetrator "creates" cash by depositing a $1,000 check from bank B in bank C and withdrawing the funds. If it takes two days for the check to clear bank B, he has created $1,000 for two days. After two days, the perpetrator deposits a $1,000 check from bank A in bank B to cover the created $1,000 for two more days. At the appropriate time, $1,000 is deposited from bank C in bank A. The scheme continues—writing checks and making deposits as needed to keep the checks from bouncing—until the person is caught or he deposits money to cover the created and stolen cash.

checksum A data transmission control that uses a hash of a file to verify accuracy.

chief compliance officer (CCO) An employee responsible for all the compliance tasks associated with SOX and other laws and regulatory rulings.

chipping Planting a small chip that records transaction data in a legitimate credit card reader. The chip is later removed or electronically accessed to retrieve the data recorded on it.

ciphertext Plaintext transformed into unreadable gibberish using encryption.

classification analyses Techniques that identify various groups and then try to classify new observations into one of those groups.

click fraud Manipulating the number of times an ad is clicked on to inflate advertising bills. Companies advertising online pay from a few cents to over $10 for each click on their ads.

closed-loop verification An input validation method that uses data entered into the system to retrieve and display other related information so that the data entry person can verify the accuracy of the input data.

cloud computing Using a browser to remotely access software, data storage, hardware, and applications.

coding (1) The systematic assignment of numbers or letters to items to classify and organize them. (2) Writing program instructions that direct a computer to perform specific data processing tasks.

cold site A disaster recovery option that relies on access to an alternative facility prewired for necessary telephone and Internet access, but does not contain any computing equipment.

collusion Cooperation between two or more people in an effort to thwart internal controls.

commercial software Programs for sale on the open market to a broad range of users with similar needs.

Committee of Sponsoring Organizations (COSO) A private-sector group consisting of the American Accounting Association, the AICPA, the Institute of Internal Auditors, the Institute of Management Accountants, and the Financial Executives Institute.

compatibility test Matching the user's authentication credentials against the access control matrix to determine whether that employee should be allowed to access that resource and perform the requested action.

completeness check (or test) An edit check that verifies that all data required have been entered.

computer-aided software (or systems) engineering (CASE) Integrated package of tools that skilled designers use to help plan, analyze, design, program, and maintain an IS.

computer forensics specialists Computer experts who discover, extract, safeguard, and document computer evidence such that its authenticity, accuracy, and integrity will not succumb to legal challenges.

computer fraud Any type of fraud that requires computer technology to perpetrate.

computer incident response team (CIRT) A team responsible for dealing with major security incidents.

computer-integrated manufacturing (CIM) A manufacturing approach in which much of the manufacturing process is performed and monitored by computerized equipment, in part through the use of robotics and real-time data collection of manufacturing activities.

computer operators People who operate the company's computers. They ensure that data are input properly, processed correctly, and that needed output is produced.

computer programmers People who write and test programs using the specifications developed by the analysts and modify and maintain existing computer programs.

computer security officer (CSO) An employee independent of the information system function who monitors the system, disseminates information about improper system uses and their consequences, and reports to top management.

concatenated keys Two or more primary keys of other database tables that, together, become the unique identifier or primary key of an M:N relationship table.

conceptual design Second SDLC step where analysts decide how to meet user needs, identify and evaluate design alternatives, and develop detailed specifications for what the system is to accomplish and how it is to be controlled.

conceptual design specifications Requirement specifications for systems output, data storage, input, processing procedures, and operations.

conceptual-level schema The organization-wide view of the entire database that lists all data elements and the relationships between them. Contrast with *external-level schema* and *internal-level schema*.

conceptual systems design report Summarizes conceptual design activities, guides physical design activities, communicates how all information needs will be met, and helps the steering committee assess feasibility.

concurrent update controls Controls that lock out users to protect individual records from errors that could occur if multiple users attempted to update the same record simultaneously.

confirmatory data analysis Testing a hypothesis and providing statistical evidence of the likelihood that the evidence refutes or supports a hypothesis.

context diagram Highest-level DFD; a summary-level view of a system, showing the data processing system, its input(s) and output(s), and their sources and destinations.

control account A title given to a general ledger account that summarizes the total amounts recorded in a subsidiary ledger. For example, the accounts receivable control account in the general ledger represents the total amount owed by all customers. The balances in the accounts receivable subsidiary ledger indicate the amount owed by each specific customer.

control activities Policies, procedures, and rules that provide reasonable assurance that control objectives are met and risk responses are carried out.

control environment The company culture that is the foundation for all other internal control components, as it influences how organizations establish strategies and objectives; structure business activities; and identify, assess, and respond to risk.

Control Objectives for Information and Related Technology (COBIT) A security and control framework that allows (1) management to benchmark the security and control practices of IT environments, (2) users of IT services to be assured that adequate security and control exist, and (3) auditors to substantiate their internal control opinions and advise on IT security and control matters.

conversion The process of changing from an old computer system or format to a new one.

cookie A text file created by a website and stored on a visitor's hard drive. Cookies store information about who the user is and what the user has done on the site.

corrective controls Controls that identify and correct problems as well as correct and recover from the resulting errors, such as maintaining backup copies of files, correcting data entry errors, and resubmitting transactions for subsequent processing.

corruption Dishonest conduct by those in power which often involves actions that are illegitimate, immoral, or incompatible with ethical standards. Examples include bribery and bid rigging.

cost driver Anything that has a cause-and-effect relationship to costs. For example, the number of purchase orders processed is a purchasing department cost driver.

credit limit The maximum allowable credit account balance for each customer, based on past credit history and ability to pay.

credit memo A document, approved by the credit manager, authorizing the billing department to credit a customer's account. Usually issued for sales returns, for allowances granted for damaged goods kept by the customer, or to write off uncollectible accounts.

critical path The PERT path requiring the greatest amount of time to complete a project; if a critical path activity is delayed, the whole project is delayed. If possible, resources are shifted to critical path activities to reduce project completion time.

cross-footing balance test A processing control that verifies accuracy by comparing two alternative ways of calculating the same total.

cross-site scripting (XSS) A vulnerability in dynamic web pages that allows an attacker to bypass a browser's security mechanisms and instruct the victim's browser to execute code, thinking it came from the desired website.

cryptic data values Data items that have no meaning without understanding a coding scheme.

cryptocurrency fraud Defrauding investors in a variety of cryptocurrency-related fraud schemes, such as fake initial coin offerings and fake exchanges and wallets.

custom software Software developed and written in-house to meet the unique needs of a particular company.

customer relationship management (CRM) systems Software that organizes information about customers in a manner that facilitates efficient and personalized service.

cyber-bullying Using computer technology to support deliberate, repeated, and hostile behavior that torments, threatens, harasses, humiliates, embarrasses, or otherwise harms another person.

cyber-extortion Threatening to harm a company or a person if a specified amount of money is not paid.

cycle billing Producing monthly statements for subsets of customers at different times. For example, each week monthly statements would be prepared for one-fourth of the customers.

D

dark data Information the organization has collected and stored that would be useful for analysis but is not analyzed and is thus generally ignored.

dashboards Interactive real-time displays of key indicators of operating performance.

data Facts that are collected, recorded, stored, and processed by an information system.

data analytics Use of software and algorithms to find and solve problems and improve business performance.

data cleaning The process of updating data to be consistent, accurate, and complete.

data concatenation The combining of data from two or more fields into a single field.

data consistency The principle that every value in a field should be stored in the same way.

data contradiction errors An error that exists when the same entity is described in two conflicting ways.

data control People who ensure that source data is approved, monitor the flow of work, reconcile input and output, handle input errors, and distribute systems output.

data dashboard Interactive real-time display of key indicators of operating performance; display of important data points, metrics, and key performance indicators in easily understood data visualizations such as line or bar charts, tables, or gauges.

data deception A graphical depiction of information, designed with or without an intent to deceive, that may create a belief about the message and/or its components, which varies from the actual message.

data de-duplication The process of analyzing data and removing two or more records that contain identical information.

data definition language (DDL) DBMS language that builds the data dictionary, creates the database, describes logical views, and specifies record or field security constraints.

data destination The entity that receives data produced by a system.

data dictionary Information about the structure of the database, including a description of each data element.

data entry errors All types of errors that come from inputting data incorrectly.

data filtering The process of removing records or fields of information from a data source.

data flow The movement of data among processes, stores, sources, and destinations.

data flow diagram (DFD) A graphical description of the flow of data within an organization, including data sources/destinations, data flows, transformation processes, and data storage.

data imputation The process of replacing a null or missing value with a substituted value.

data lake Collection of structured, semi-structured, and unstructured data stored in a single location.

data loss prevention (DLP) Software that works like antivirus programs in reverse, blocking outgoing messages (e-mail, instant messages, etc.) that contain key words or phrases associated with intellectual property or other sensitive data the organization wants to protect.

data manipulation language (DML) DBMS language that changes database content, including data element creations, updates, insertions, and deletions.

data marts Data repositories that hold structured data for a subset of an organization.

data masking Protecting privacy by replacing sensitive personal information with fake data. Also called tokenization.

data mining Using sophisticated statistical analysis to "discover" unhypothesized relationships in the data.

data model An abstract representation of database contents.

data modeling Defining a database to faithfully represent all key components of an organization's environment. The objective is to explicitly capture and store data about every business activity the organization wishes to plan, control, or evaluate.

data ordering The intentional arranging of visualization items in a way to produce emphasis.

data overfitting When a model is designed to fit training data very well but does not predict well when applied to other datasets.

data owner The person or function in the organization who is accountable for the data and can give permission to access and analyze the data.

data parsing Separating data from a single field into multiple fields.

data pivoting A technique that rotates data from rows to columns.

data processing cycle The four operations (data input, data storage, data processing, and information output) performed on data to generate meaningful and relevant information.

data processing schedule A schedule that shows when each data processing task should be performed.

data query language (DQL) High-level, English-like, DBMS language that contains powerful, easy-to-use commands that enable users to retrieve, sort, order, and display data.

data source The entity that produces or sends the data entered into a system.

data standardization The process of standardizing the structure and meaning of each data element so it can be analyzed and used in decision making.

data store The place or medium where system data is stored.

data storytelling The process of translating often complex data analyses into more easy to understand terms to enable better decision making.

data structuring The process of changing the organization and relationships among data fields to prepare the data for analysis.

data swamps Data repositories that are not accurately documented so that the stored data cannot be properly identified and analyzed.

data threshold violations Data errors that occur when a data value falls outside an allowable level.

data validation The process of analyzing data to make certain the data has the properties of high-quality data: accuracy, completeness, consistency, timeliness, and validity.

data value The actual value stored in a field. It describes a particular attribute of an entity. For example, the customer name field would contain "ZYX Company" if that company were a customer.

data variety The different forms data can take.

data velocity The pace at which data is created and stored.

data veracity The quality or trustworthiness of data.

data visualization Use of a graphical representation of data to convey meaning.

data volume The amount of data created and stored by an organization.

data warehouse Very large databases containing detailed and summarized data for a number of years used for analysis rather than transaction processing.

database A set of interrelated, centrally controlled data files stored with as little data redundancy as possible. A database consolidates records previously stored in separate files into a common pool and serves a variety of users and data processing applications.

database administrator (DBA) The person responsible for coordinating, controlling, and managing the database.

database management system (DBMS) The program that manages and controls the data and the interfaces between the data and the application programs that use the data stored in the database.

database system The database, the DBMS, and the application programs that access the database through the DBMS.

debit memo A document used to record a reduction to the balance due to a supplier.

debugging The process of discovering and eliminating program errors.

decryption Transforming ciphertext back into plaintext.

deduction register A report listing the miscellaneous voluntary deductions for each employee.

deduplication A process that uses hashing to identify and backup only those portions of a file or database that have been updated since the last backup.

deep packet inspection A process that examines the data in the body of a TCP packet to control traffic, rather than looking only at the information in the IP and TCP headers.

defense-in-depth Employing multiple layers of controls to avoid a single point-of-failure.

delete anomaly Improper organization of a database that results in the loss of all information about an entity when a row is deleted. If customer addresses are stored in the sales table, then deleting the row where the only sale to a customer is stored results in the loss of all information for that customer. The solution is to have a sales table and a customer table and link the two tables.

delimiter Character, or series of characters, that marks the end of one field and the beginning of the next field.

demand reports Reports with a pre-specified content and format, prepared only on request.

demilitarized zone (DMZ) A separate network located outside the organization's internal information system that permits controlled access from the Internet.

denial-of-service (DoS) attack A computer attack in which the attacker sends so many e-mail bombs or web page requests, often from randomly generated false addresses, that the Internet service provider's e-mail server or the web server is overloaded and shuts down.

descriptive analytics Information that results from the examination of data to understand the past, answers the question "what happened?"

detective controls Controls designed to discover control problems that were not prevented, such as duplicate checking of calculations and preparing bank reconciliations and monthly trial balances.

diagnostic analytics Information that attempts to determine causal relationships, answers the question "why did this happen?"

diagnostic control system System that measures, monitors, and compares actual company progress to budgets and performance goals; feedback helps management adjust and fine-tune inputs and processes so future outputs more closely match goals.

dictionary attack Software that generates user ID and password guesses using information about the targeted company and a dictionary of possible user IDs and passwords to reduce the number of guesses required.

differential backup A type of partial backup that involves copying all changes made since the last full backup. Thus, each new differential backup file contains the cumulative effects of all activity since the last full backup.

digital certificate An electronic document that certifies the identity of the owner of a particular public key and contains that party's public key.

digital signature A hash encrypted with the hash creator's private key.

digital watermark Code embedded in documents that enables an organization to identify confidential information that has been disclosed.

direct conversion Changing from an old system to a new one by terminating the old IS when the new one is introduced (also known as "burning the bridges" or "crash conversion").

dirty data Data that is inconsistent, inaccurate, or incomplete.

disaster recovery plan (DRP) A plan to restore an organization's IT capability in the event its data center is destroyed.

disbursement voucher A document that identifies the supplier, lists the outstanding invoices, and indicates the net amount to be paid after deducting any applicable discounts and allowances.

document flowcharts Illustrate the flow of documents and data among areas of responsibility within an organization, from cradle to grave; shows where each document originates, its distribution, its purposes, and its ultimate disposition.

documentation Narratives, flowcharts, diagrams, and other written materials that explain how a system works.

documents Records of transaction or other company data. Examples include checks, invoices, receiving reports, and purchase requisitions.

dummy variable or dichotomous variable A data field that contains only two responses, typically 0 or 1.

E

earnings statement A report listing the amount of gross pay, deductions, and net pay for the current period and the year-to-date totals for each category.

eavesdropping Listening to private communications or tapping into data transmissions intended for someone else. One way to intercept signals is by setting up a wiretap.

economic espionage Theft of information, trade secrets, and intellectual property.

economic feasibility Determining whether system benefits justify the time, money, and resources required to implement it.

economic order quantity (EOQ) The optimal order size to minimize the sum of ordering, carrying, and stockout costs. Ordering costs are expenses associated with processing purchase transactions. Carrying costs are the costs associated with holding inventory. Stockout costs, such as lost sales or production delays, result from inventory shortages.

effect size A quantitative measure of the magnitude of the effect.

electronic data interchange (EDI) The use of computerized communications and a standard coding scheme to submit business documents electronically in a format that can be automatically processed by the recipient's information system.

electronic funds transfer (EFT) The transfer of funds through use of online banking software.

electronic lockbox A lockbox arrangement (see *lockbox*) in which the bank electronically sends the company information about the customer account number and the amount remitted as soon as it receives payments.

element A specific data item in an iXBRL instance document, such as a financial statement line item.

e-mail spoofing Making a sender address and other parts of an e-mail header appear as though the e-mail originated from a different source.

e-mail threats Threats sent to victims by e-mail. The threats usually require some follow-up action, often at great expense to the victim.

emphasis In design, assuring the most important message is easily identifiable.

encryption The process of transforming normal text, called *plaintext*, into unreadable gibberish, called *ciphertext*. Encryption is particularly important when confidential data is being transmitted from remote terminals because data transmission lines can be electronically monitored without the user's knowledge.

end-user computing (EUC) The hands-on development, use, and control of computer-based information systems by users.

endpoints Collective term for the workstations, servers, printers, and other devices that comprise an organization's network.

enterprise resource planning (ERP) systems Systems that integrate all aspects of an organization's activities—such as accounting, finance, marketing, human resources, manufacturing, inventory management—into one system. An ERP system is modularized; companies can purchase the individual modules that meet their specific needs. An ERP facilitates information flow among the company's various business functions and manages communications with outside stakeholders.

entity Anything about which an organization wants to collect and store information. Examples include an employee, an inventory item, and a customer.

entity integrity rule A nonnull primary key ensures that every row in a table represents something and that it can be identified.

entity-relationship (E-R) diagram A graphical depiction of a database's contents showing the various entities modeled and the important relationships among them. An entity is any class of objects about which data are collected, such as the resources, events, and agents that comprise the REA data model.

ethical data presentation Avoiding the intentional or unintentional use of deceptive practices that can alter the user's understanding of the data being presented.

ETL process A set of procedures for blending data. The acronym stands for extract, transform, and load data.

evaluated receipt settlement (ERS) An invoiceless approach to accounts payable that replaces the three-way matching process (supplier invoice, receiving report, and purchase order) with a two-way match of the purchase order and receiving report.

events (1) Business activities about which management wants to collect information for planning or control purposes. (2) A positive or negative incident or occurrence from internal or external sources that affects the implementation of strategy or the achievement of objectives. (3) Any potential adverse occurrence or unwanted event that could be injurious to either the AIS or the organization; also referred to as a *threat*.

evil twin A wireless network with the same name *(Service Set Identifier)* as a legitimate wireless access point. Users are connected to the twin because it has a stronger wireless signal or the twin disrupts or disables the legitimate access point. Users are unaware that they connect to the evil twin and the perpetrator monitors the traffic looking for confidential information.

executable architecture baseline A partial implementation of the system that includes all significant architecture components and demonstrates that the architecture supports key system functionality and will produce the desired performance and scalability at an acceptable cost.

expected loss The mathematical product of the potential dollar loss that would occur should a threat become a reality (called *impact* or *exposure*) and the risk or probability that the threat will occur (called *likelihood*).

expenditure cycle A recurring set of business activities and related data processing operations associated with purchasing inventory or raw materials in exchange for cash or a future promise to pay cash.

exploit A program designed to take advantage of a known vulnerability.

exploratory data analysis An approach to examining data that seeks to explore the data without testing formal models or hypotheses.

exposure/impact The potential dollar loss if a particular threat becomes a reality.

extension taxonomy A set of custom XBRL tags to define elements unique to the reporting organization that are not part of the standard generally accepted taxonomies for that industry.

external-level schema An individual user's view of portions of a database; also called a subschema. Contrast with *conceptual-level schema* and *internal-level schema*.

extrapolation beyond the range A process of estimating a value beyond the range of the data used to create the model.

extreme programming (XP) A software development methodology designed to produce higher-quality software more productively by taking the beneficial elements and best practices of traditional software development to "extreme" levels.

F

factoring Selling accounts receivable at a discount to a firm that specializes in collections of past-due accounts.

fault tolerance The capability of a system to continue performing when there is a hardware failure.

feasibility study An investigation to determine whether it is practical to develop a new application or system.

field The portion of a data record where the data value for a particular attribute is stored. For example, in a spreadsheet, each row might represent a customer and each column an attribute of the customer. Each cell in a spreadsheet is a field.

field check An edit check that tests whether the characters in a field are of the correct field type (e.g., numeric data in numeric fields).

file A set of logically related records, such as the payroll records of all employees.

financial electronic data interchange (FEDI) The Combination of EFT and EDI that enables both remittance data and funds transfer instructions to be included in one electronic package.

financial total A type of batch total that equals the sum of a field that contains monetary values.

financing cycle Activities associated with raising money by selling shares in the company to investors and borrowing money as well as paying dividends and interest.

firewall A special-purpose hardware device or software running a general-purpose computer that controls both inbound and outbound communication between the system behind the firewall and other networks.

flat file Text file that contains data from multiple tables or sources and merges that data into a single row.

flexible benefits plans Plans under which each employee receives some minimum coverage in medical insurance and pension contributions, plus additional benefit "credits" that can be used to acquire extra vacation time or additional health insurance. These plans are sometimes called *cafeteria-style benefit plans* because they offer a menu of options.

flexible budget A budget in which the amounts are stated in terms of formulas based on actual level of activity.

flowchart An analytical technique that uses a standard set of symbols to describe pictorially some aspect of an IS in a clear, concise, and logical manner; used to record how business processes are performed and how documents flow through an organization.

Foreign Corrupt Practices Act (FCPA) Legislation passed to prevent companies from bribing foreign officials to obtain business; also requires all publicly owned corporations maintain a system of internal accounting controls.

foreign key An attribute in a table that is also a primary key in another table; used to link the two tables.

forensic investigators Individuals who specialize in fraud, most of whom have specialized training with law enforcement agencies such as the FBI or IRS or have professional certifications such as Certified Fraud Examiner (CFE).

fraud Any and all means a person uses to gain an unfair advantage over another person.

fraud hotline A phone number employees can call to anonymously report fraud and abuse.

fraudulent financial reporting Intentional or reckless conduct, whether by act or omission, that results in materially misleading financial statements.

full backup Exact copy of an entire database.

G

Gantt chart A bar graph used for project planning. It shows project activities on the left, units of time across the top, and the time each activity is expected to take as a horizontal bar.

general authorization The authorization given employees to handle routine transactions without special approval.

general controls Controls designed to make sure an organization's information system and control environment is stable and well managed, such as security; IT infrastructure; and software acquisition, development, and maintenance controls. Contrast with *application controls*.

general journal A journal used to record infrequent or nonroutine transactions, such as loan payments and end-of-period adjusting and closing entries.

general ledger A ledger that contains summary-level data for every asset, liability, equity, revenue, and expense account of the organization.

general ledger and reporting system Information-processing operations involved in updating the general ledger and preparing reports for both management and external parties.

give-get exchange Transactions that happen a great many times, such as giving up cash to get inventory from a supplier and giving employees a paycheck in exchange for their labor.

goal conflict When a subsystem's goals are inconsistent with the goals of another subsystem or the system as a whole.

goal congruence When a subsystem achieves its goals while contributing to the organization's overall goal.

group codes Two or more subgroups of digits used to code an item. A group code is often used in conjunction with a block code.

H

hacking Unauthorized access, modification, or use of an electronic device or some element of a computer system.

hardening The process of modifying the default configuration of endpoints to eliminate unnecessary settings and services.

hash Plaintext transformed into short code.

hash total A type of batch total generated by summing values for a field that would not usually be totaled.

hashing Transforming plaintext of any length into a short code called a hash.

header record Type of internal label that appears at the beginning of each file and contains the file name, expiration date, and other file identification information.

help desk Analysts and technicians who answer employee questions with the purpose of encouraging, supporting, coordinating, and controlling end-user activity.

hijacking Gaining control of someone else's computer to carry out illicit activities, such as sending spam without the computer user's knowledge.

honeypot A decoy system used to provide early warning that an insider or outsider is attempting to search for confidential information.

hot site A disaster recovery option that relies on access to a completely operational alternative data center not only prewired but also contains all necessary hardware and software.

human resources management (HRM)/payroll cycle The recurring set of business activities and data processing operations associated with effectively managing the employee workforce.

human resources/payroll cycle Activities associated with hiring, training, compensating, evaluating, promoting, and terminating employees.

I

identity theft Assuming someone's identity, usually for economic gain, by illegally obtaining confidential information such as a Social Security number or a bank account or credit card number.

implementation and conversion Fourth SDLC step where the company hires and trains employees, tests and modifies procedures, establishes standards and controls, completes documentation, moves to the new system, and detects and corrects design deficiencies.

implementation plan A written plan showing how the new system will be implemented; specifies when the project should be complete and the IS operational, including a completion timetable, cost estimates, task milestones, and who is responsible for each activity.

imprest fund A cash account with two characteristics: (1) It is set at a fixed amount, such as $100; and (2) vouchers are required for every disbursement. At all times, the sum of cash plus vouchers should equal the preset fund balance.

incremental backup A type of partial backup that involves copying only the data items that have changed since the last partial backup. This produces a set of incremental backup files, each containing the results of one day's transactions.

information Data that have been organized and processed to provide meaning and improve decision making.

information overload Exceeding the amount of information a human mind can absorb and process, resulting in a decline in decision-making quality and an increase in the cost of providing information.

information rights management (IRM) Software that offers the capability not only to limit access to specific files or documents but also to specify the actions (read, copy, print, download, etc.) that individuals granted access to that resource can perform. Some IRM software even has the capability to limit access privileges to a specific period of time and to remotely erase protected files.

information system The people and technologies in an organization that produce information. It is an organized way of collecting, processing, managing, and reporting information so that an organization can achieve its objectives and goals. Formal information systems have an explicit responsibility to produce information. An informal information system meets a need that is not satisfied by a formal channel and operates without formal designation of responsibility.

information systems steering committee High-level management who plan and oversee the IS function, setting IS policies that govern the AIS, ensuring top-management guidance and control, and coordinating and integrating systems activities.

information technology (IT) The computers and other electronic devices used to store, retrieve, transmit, and manipulate data.

inherent risk The susceptibility of a set of accounts or transactions to significant control problems in the absence of internal control.

initial investigation A preliminary investigation to determine whether a proposed new system is both needed and feasible.

inline XBRL (iXBRL) An open standard that merges HTML and XBRL tags so that the same document is simultaneously human-readable in a browser yet also contains structured data that is machine-readable.

insert anomaly Improper database organization that results in the inability to add records to a database.

instance document An iXBRL file that contains tagged data.

integration tests Used to check for incompatible interfaces between code segments.

interactive control system System that helps managers to focus subordinates' attention on key strategic issues and to be more involved in their decisions; system data are interpreted and discussed in face-to-face meetings of superiors, subordinates, and peers.

internal control flowchart Used to describe, analyze, and evaluate internal controls, including identifying system strengths, weaknesses, and inefficiencies.

Internal Control—Integrated Framework (IC) A COSO framework that defines internal controls and provides guidance for evaluating and enhancing internal control systems; widely accepted authority on internal controls incorporated into policies, rules, and regulations used to control business activities.

internal controls The processes and procedures implemented to provide reasonable assurance that control objectives are met.

internal-level schema A low-level view of the entire database describing how the data are actually stored and accessed; it includes information about record layouts, definitions, addresses, and indexes. Contrast with *external-level schema* and *conceptual-level schema.*

internal rate of return (IRR) A return-on-investment technique that calculates the interest rate that makes the present value of total costs equal to the present value of total savings.

Internet auction fraud Using an Internet auction site to defraud another person.

Internet misinformation Using the Internet to spread false or misleading information.

Internet of Things (IoT) Embedding sensors in devices so they can connect to the Internet.

Internet pump-and-dump fraud Using the Internet to pump up the price of a stock and then sell it.

intrusion detection systems (IDSs) Systems that create logs of all network traffic that was permitted to pass the firewall and then analyze those logs for signs of attempted or successful intrusions.

intrusion prevention systems (IPS) Software or hardware that monitors patterns in the traffic flow to identify and automatically block attacks.

investment fraud Misrepresenting or leaving out facts in order to promote an investment that promises fantastic profits with little or no risk. Examples include Ponzi schemes and securities fraud.

IP address spoofing Creating Internet Protocol packets with a forged IP address to hide the sender's identity or to impersonate another computer system.

J

job-order costing A cost system that assigns costs to specific production batches or jobs.

job-time ticket A document used to collect data about labor activity by recording the amount of time a worker spent on each specific job task.

journal voucher file A file that stores all journal entries used to update the general ledger.

just-in-time (JIT) inventory system A system that minimizes or virtually eliminates inventories by purchasing and producing goods only in response to actual, rather than forecasted, sales.

K

key escrow The process of storing a copy of an encryption key in a secure location.

keylogger Software that records computer activity, such as a user's keystrokes, e-mails sent and received, websites visited, and chat session participation.

kickbacks Gifts given by suppliers to purchasing agents for the purpose of influencing their choice of suppliers.

knowledge management systems Software that stores and organizes expertise possessed by individual employees so the knowledge can be shared and used by others.

L

lapping Concealing the theft of cash by means of a series of delays in posting collections to accounts receivable. For example, a perpetrator steals customer A's accounts receivable payment. Funds received at a later date from customer B are used to pay off customer A's balance. Funds from customer C are used to pay off B's balance, and so forth.

lean manufacturing Extends the principles of just-in-time inventory systems to the entire production process to minimize or eliminate inventories of raw materials, work in process, and finished goods. Lean manufacturing is often referred to as *pull manufacturing* because goods are produced in response to customer demand.

Lebanese looping Inserting a sleeve into an ATM that prevents it from ejecting the card. The perpetrator pretends to help the victim, tricking the person into entering the PIN again. Once the victim gives up, the thief removes the card and uses it and the PIN to withdraw money.

legal feasibility Determining if a proposed system will comply with all applicable federal and state laws, administrative agency regulations, and contractual obligations.

likelihood/risk The probability that a threat will come to pass.

limit check An edit check that tests a numerical amount against a fixed value.

linkbases One or more XBRL files that define the relationships among elements found in a specific instance document.

lockbox A postal address to which customers send their remittances. This Post Office box is maintained by the participating bank, which picks up the checks each day and deposits them to the company's account. The bank sends the remittance advices, an electronic list of all remittances, and digital copies of all checks to the company.

log analysis The process of examining logs to identify evidence of possible attacks.

logical models System descriptions that focus on what essential activities are performed and the flow of information irrespective of how the flow is actually accomplished.

logical view How people conceptually organize, view, and understand the relationships among data items. Contrast with *physical view*.

M

machine learning An application of artificial intelligence that allows computer systems to improve and update prediction models without explicit programming.

machine-readable Data in a format that can be read and processed by a computer.

malware Any software that is used to do harm.

man-in-the-middle (MITM) attack A hacker placing himself between a client and a host to intercept communications between them; also called *session hijacking*.

manufacturing overhead All manufacturing costs not economically feasible to trace directly to specific jobs or processes.

manufacturing resource planning (MRP-II) An extension of materials requirements planning that seeks to balance existing production capacity and raw materials needs to meet forecasted sales demands. Also referred to as *push manufacturing* because goods are produced in expectation of customer demand.

many-to-many (M:N) relationship A relationship between two entities where the maximum cardinality of both entities is many. For example, each inventory item can be sold to many different customers and each customer can order many different inventory items.

masquerading/impersonation Gaining access to a system by pretending to be an authorized user. This requires that the perpetrator know the legitimate user's ID and passwords.

master file A permanent file of records that stores cumulative data about an organization. As transactions take place, individual records within a master file are updated to keep them current.

master plan Describes what a system will consist of, how it will be developed, who will develop it, when it will be developed, how needed resources will be acquired, the status of projects in process, the prioritization of planned projects, and the prioritization criteria.

master production schedule (MPS) Specifies how much of each product is to be produced during the planning period and when that production should occur.

materials requirements planning (MRP) An approach to inventory management that seeks to reduce required inventory levels by improving the accuracy of forecasting techniques to better schedule purchases to satisfy production needs.

materials requisition Authorizes the removal of the necessary quantity of raw materials from the storeroom.

maximum cardinality The maximum number of instances an entity can be linked to the other entity in the relationship. Only two options: 1 or many.

metadata Data that describes other data.

mindset A mental attitude, a way of thinking, or a frame of mind.

minimum cardinality The minimum number of instances an entity can be linked to the other entity in the relationship. Only two options: 0 and 1.

misappropriation of assets Theft of company assets by employees.

misfielded data values Data values that are correctly formatted but not listed in the correct field.

mnemonic codes Letters and numbers interspersed to identify an item. The mnemonic code is derived from the description of the item and is usually easy to memorize. For example, Dry300W could represent a dryer (Dry), model number 300, that is white (W).

monthly statement A document listing all transactions that occurred during the past month and informing customers of their current account balance.

move tickets Documents that identify the internal transfer of parts, the location to which they are transferred, and the time of the transfer.

multifactor authentication The use of two or more types of authentication credentials in conjunction to achieve a greater level of security.

multimodal authentication The use of multiple authentication credentials of the same type to achieve a greater level of security.

N

narrative description Written, step-by-step explanation of system components and how they interact.

net present value (NPV) A return-on-investment technique that discounts all estimated future cash flows back to the present using a discount rate that reflects the time value of money.

network managers People who ensure that the organization's networks operate properly.

neural networks Computing systems that imitate the brain's learning process by using a network of interconnected processors that perform multiple operations simultaneously and interact dynamically.

nonce A random number; used in the mining process to validate a new block in a blockchain.

nonoperational (throwaway) prototypes Prototypes that are discarded, but the system requirements identified from the prototypes are used to develop a new system.

nonrepudiation Creating legally binding agreements that cannot be unilaterally repudiated by either party.

nonvoucher system A method for processing accounts payable in which each approved invoice is posted to individual supplier records in the accounts payable file and is then stored in an open invoice file. Contrast with *voucher system*.

normalization Following relational database creation rules to design a relational database that is free from delete, insert, and update anomalies.

null hypothesis A proposed explanation worded in the form of an equality, meaning that one of the two concepts, ideas, or groups will be no different than the other concept, idea, or group.

O

one-to-many (1:N) relationship A relationship between two entities where the maximum cardinality for one of the entities is 1, but the other entity has a maximum cardinality of many.

one-to-one (1:1) relationship A relationship between two entities where the maximum cardinality for each entity is 1.

online analytical processing (OLAP) Using queries to investigate hypothesized relationships among data; one of two main techniques used in business intelligence.

online transaction processing database (OLTP) Database containing detailed current transaction data, usually in third normal form. Focuses on throughput, speed, availability, concurrency, and recoverability. Often used concurrently by hundreds of users.

open-invoice method Method for maintaining accounts receivable in which customers typically pay according to each invoice.

operational feasibility Determining if the organization has access to people who can design, implement, and operate the proposed system and if employees will use the system.

operational prototypes Prototypes that are further developed into fully functional systems.

operations and maintenance Fifth SDLC step where the system is periodically reviewed and necessary modifications and improvements are made.

operations list A document that specifies the sequence of steps to follow in making a product, which equipment to use, and how long each step should take.

opportunity The condition or situation that allows a person or organization to commit and conceal a dishonest act and convert it to personal gain.

opt-in Referred to as explicit consent because organizations cannot collect and use customers' personal information unless they explicitly agree to allow such actions.

opt-out Referred to as implicit consent because companies can assume it is okay to collect and use customers' personal information unless they explicitly object.

outlier A data point, or a few data points, that lie an abnormal distance from other values in the data.

outsourcing Hiring an outside company to handle all or part of an organization's data processing activities.

P

packet filtering A process that uses various fields in a packet's IP and TCP headers to decide what to do with the packet.

packet sniffers Programs that capture data from information packets as they travel over the Internet or company networks. Captured data is sifted to find confidential or proprietary information.

packing slip A document listing the quantity and description of each item included in a shipment.

parallel conversion Changing from an old system to a new one by operating both systems simultaneously until the organization is confident the new system is functioning correctly.

parity bit An extra bit added to every character; used to check transmission accuracy.

parity checking A data transmission control in which the receiving device recalculates the parity bit to verify accuracy of transmitted data.

password cracking Recovering passwords by trying every possible combination of upper- and lower-case letters, numbers, and special characters and comparing them to a cryptographic hash of the password.

patch Code released by software developers that fixes a particular vulnerability.

patch management The process of regularly applying patches and updates to software.

payback period A return-on-investment technique used to calculate the number of years required for the net savings of a system to equal its initial cost.

payroll clearing account A general ledger account used to check the accuracy and completeness of recording payroll costs and their subsequent allocation to appropriate cost centers.

payroll register A listing of payroll data for each employee for a payroll period.

payroll service bureau An organization that maintains the payroll master file for each of its clients and performs their payroll processing activities for a fee.

penetration test An authorized attempt to break into the organization's information system.

pharming Redirecting website traffic to a spoofed website.

phase-in conversion Changing from an old to a new system by gradually replacing elements of the old with the new until the old system has been entirely replaced.

phishing Sending an electronic message pretending to be a legitimate company, usually a financial institution, and requesting information or verification of information and often warning of a consequence if it is not provided. The request is bogus, and the information gathered is used to commit identity theft or to steal funds from the victim's account.

phreaking Attacking phone systems to obtain free phone line access; use phone lines to transmit malware; and to access, steal, and destroy data.

physical design Third SDLC step where broad, user-oriented conceptual design requirements are translated into the detailed specifications used to code and test software, design input/output, create files/databases, develop procedures, and implement controls.

physical models Descriptions of how systems function by describing document flow, computer processes performed, the people performing them, and the equipment used.

physical systems design report Summarizes what was accomplished in physical design; used to determine whether or not to proceed to the implementation phase.

physical view The way data are physically arranged and stored in the computer system. Contrast with *logical view*.

picking ticket A document that lists the items and quantities ordered and authorizes the inventory control function to release that merchandise to the shipping department. The picking ticket is often printed so that the item numbers and quantities are listed in the sequence in which they can be most efficiently retrieved from the warehouse.

piggybacking (1) Tapping into a communications line and electronically latching onto a legitimate user who unknowingly carries the perpetrator into the system. (2) The clandestine use of a neighbor's Wi-Fi network. (3) An unauthorized person following an authorized person through a secure door, bypassing physical security controls.

pilot conversion Changing from an old to a new system by implementing a system in one location, using it until all problems are resolved, and then implementing it in the rest of the organization.

plaintext Normal text that has not been encrypted.

podslurping Using a small device with storage capacity (iPod, flash drive) to download unauthorized data from a computer.

point scoring Evaluating the overall merits of vendor proposals by assigning a weight to each evaluation criterion based on its importance.

policy and procedures manual A document that explains proper business practices, describes needed knowledge and experience, explains document procedures, explains how to handle transactions, and lists the resources provided to carry out specific duties; it includes the chart of accounts, copies of forms and documents, and is a helpful on-the-job reference and training tool.

posing Creating a seemingly legitimate business, collecting personal information while making a sale, and never delivering the product.

postimplementation review Review made after a new system has been operating for a brief period to ensure that the new system is meeting its planned objectives, identify the adequacy of system standards, and review system controls.

postimplementation review report A report that analyzes a newly delivered system to determine if the system achieved its intended purpose and was completed within budget.

predictive analytics Information that results from analyses that focus on predicting the future, answers the question, "what might happen in the future?"

prescriptive analytics Information that results from analyses to provide a recommendation of what should happen, answers the question "what should be done?"

pressure A person's incentive or motivation for committing fraud.

pretexting Using an invented scenario (the pretext) that creates legitimacy in the target's mind in order to increase the likelihood that a victim will divulge information or do something.

preventive controls Controls that deter problems before they arise, such as hiring qualified accounting personnel; appropriately segregating employee duties; and effectively controlling physical access to assets, facilities, and information.

primary activities Value chain activities that produce, market, and deliver products and services to customers and provide post-delivery service and support.

primary key Database attribute, or combination of attributes, that uniquely identifies each row in a table; used to distinguish, order, and reference records in a database.

private key One of the keys used in asymmetric encryption systems. It is kept secret and known only to the owner of that pair of public and private keys.

process costing A cost system that assigns costs to each process, or work center, in the production cycle, and then calculates the average cost for all units produced.

processes Actions that transform data into other data or information.

processing test data Processing valid and erroneous transactions to determine if a program operates as designed and that valid transactions are handled properly and errors are detected and dealt with appropriately.

procurement card A corporate credit card that employees can use only at designated suppliers to purchase specific kinds of items.

product backlog Items waiting to be developed that are prioritized by the product owner.

product owner The customer who is responsible for making sure the scrum team produces what is needed. They write the user stories and prioritize backlog items so the scrum team knows what to develop next.

production cycle The recurring set of business activities and related data processing operations associated with using labor, raw materials, and equipment to produce finished goods. Also called *conversion cycle*.

production order A document authorizing the manufacture of a specified quantity of a particular product. It lists the operations to be performed, the quantity to be produced, and the location to which the finished product is to be delivered.

professional employer organization (PEO) An organization that processes payroll and also provides human resource management services such as employee benefit design and administration.

program evaluation and review technique (PERT) A way to plan, develop, coordinate, control, and schedule systems development activities; all activities, and precedent and subsequent relationships among activities, are identified and shown on a PERT diagram.

program flowchart Illustrates the sequence of logical operations performed by a computer in executing a program; describes the specific logic to perform a process shown on a system flowchart.

program maintenance Updating a computer program due to changed user needs, fixing bugs, legal or regulatory changes, or to make use of new technology.

programmers People who use the analysts' design to create and test computer programs.

project development plan Document showing project requirements (people, hardware, software, and financial), a cost–benefit analysis, and how a project will be completed (modules or tasks to be performed, who will perform them, and completion dates).

project milestones Points where progress is reviewed and actual and estimated completion times are compared.

projection Resistance to change that blames anything and everything on the new system, such that it becomes the scapegoat for all real and imagined problems and errors.

prompting An online data entry completeness check that requests each required item of input data and then waits for an acceptable response before requesting the next required item.

proposal to conduct systems analysis A request to complete the systems analysis phase for a project that makes it through the initial investigation.

prototyping An approach to systems design in which a simplified working model, or prototype, of an IS is developed. The users experiment with the prototype to determine what they like and do not like about the system. The developers make modifications until the users are satisfied with the system.

Public Company Accounting Oversight Board (PCAOB) A board created by SOX that regulates the auditing profession; created as part of SOX.

public key One of the keys used in asymmetric encryption systems. It is widely distributed and available to everyone.

public key infrastructure (PKI) The system for issuing pairs of public and private keys and corresponding digital certificates.

purchase order A document that formally requests a supplier to sell and deliver specified products at designated prices. It is also a promise to pay and becomes a contract once the supplier accepts it.

purchase requisition A document or electronic form that identifies the requisitioner; specifies the delivery location and date needed; identifies the item numbers, descriptions, quantity, and price of each item requested; and may suggest a supplier.

Q

query A request for the database to provide the information needed to deal with a problem or answer a question. The information is retrieved, displayed or printed, and/or analyzed as requested.

R

range check An edit check that tests whether a data item falls within predetermined upper and lower limits.

ransomware Software that encrypts programs and data until a ransom is paid to remove it.

rationalization The excuse that fraud perpetrators use to justify their illegal behavior.

REA data model A data model used to design AIS databases. It contains information about three fundamental types of entities: resources, events, and agents. Resources represent identifiable objects that have economic value to the organization. Events represent an organization's business activities. Agents represent the people or organizations about which data are collected.

real-time mirroring Maintaining complete copies of a database at two separate data centers and updating both copies in real time as each transaction occurs.

real-time processing The computer system processes data immediately after capture and provides updated information to users on a timely basis.

reasonableness test An edit check of the logical correctness of relationships among data items.

receiving report A document that records details about each delivery, including the date received, shipper, supplier, and quantity received.

record A set of fields whose data values describe specific attributes of an entity, such as all payroll data relating to a single employee. An example is a row in a spreadsheet.

record count A type of batch total that equals the number of records processed at a given time.

record layout Document that shows the items stored in a file, including the order and length of the data fields and the type of data stored.

recovery point objective (RPO) The amount of data the organization is willing to reenter or potentially lose.

recovery time objective (RTO) The maximum tolerable time to restore an organization's information system following a disaster, representing the length of time that the organization is willing to attempt to function without its information system.

redundant arrays of independent drives (RAID) A fault tolerance technique that records data on multiple disk drives instead of just one to reduce the risk of data loss.

referential integrity rule Foreign keys which link rows in one table to rows in another table must have values that correspond to the value of a primary key in another table.

relational data model A two-dimensional table representation of data; each row represents a unique entity (record) and each column is a field where record attributes are stored. Foreign keys can contain null values; when customers pay cash, Customer # in the sales table can be blank.

relational database A database built using the relational data model.

remittance advice A copy of the sales invoice returned with a customer's payment that indicates the invoices, statements, or other items being paid.

remittance list A document listing names and amounts of all customer payments received in the mail.

reorder point Specifies the level to which the inventory balance of an item must fall before an order to replenish stock is initiated.

report writer DBMS language that simplifies report creation; users specify which data elements they want to print, and the elements are printed in the user-specified format.

reports System output organized in a meaningful fashion used by employees to control operational activities, by managers to make decisions and design strategies, and by investors and creditors to understand a company's business activities.

request for proposal (RFP) A request for vendors to (1) bid on a system to meet a company's specified needs or (2) supply a fixed asset that possesses specific characteristics.

request for systems development A written request for a new or improved system that describes the current system's problems, the reasons for the change, and the proposed system's objectives, benefits, and costs.

requirement costing Comparing systems based on the cost of all required features; when software does not meet all requirements, the cost of developing unavailable features is estimated and added to its cost.

residual risk The risk that remains after management implements internal controls or some other response to risk.

resources Things that have economic value to an organization such as cash, inventory, supplies, factories, and land.

response time How long it takes for a system to respond, such as the amount of time that elapses between making a query and receiving a response.

responsibility accounting A system of reporting financial results on the basis of managerial responsibilities within an organization.

revenue cycle The recurring set of business activities and data processing operations associated with selling goods and services in exchange for cash or a future promise to receive cash.

risk appetite The amount of risk a company is willing to accept to achieve its goals and objectives. To avoid undue risk, risk appetite must be in alignment with company strategy.

robotic process automation (RPA) Computer software that can be programmed to automatically perform tasks across applications just as human workers do.

rootkit A means of concealing system components and malware from the operating system and other programs; can also modify the operating system.

round-down fraud Instructing the computer to round down all interest calculations to two decimal places. The fraction of a cent rounded down on each calculation is put into the programmer's account. Most frequently found in financial institutions that pay interest.

routers Special purpose devices designed to read the source and destination address fields in IP packet headers to decide where to send (route) the packet next.

S

sabotage An intentional act where the intent is to destroy a system or some of its components.

salami technique Stealing tiny slices of money from many different accounts.

sales invoice A document notifying customers of the amount of a sale and where to send payment.

sales order The document created during sales order entry listing the item numbers, quantities, prices, and terms of the sale.

Sarbanes–Oxley Act (SOX) Legislation intended to prevent financial statement fraud, make financial reports more transparent, provide protection to investors, strengthen internal controls at public companies, and punish executives who perpetrate fraud.

scareware Malicious software of no benefit that is sold using scare tactics.

scavenging/dumpster diving Searching documents and records to gain access to confidential information. Scavenging methods include searching garbage cans, communal trash bins, and city dumps.

scheduled reports Reports prepared on a regular basis, with a prespecified content and format.

scheduling feasibility Determining if a proposed system can be developed and implemented in the time allotted.

schema (1) A description of the data elements in a database, the relationships among them, and the logical model used to organize and describe the data. (2) An XBRL file that defines every element that appears in a specific instance document.

scrum development A process that embraces customers frequently changing their minds about what they need or want. Scrum development focuses on flexibility, responding to new requirements, adapting to evolving changes in technology, and quickly delivering a system the customer can evaluate.

scrum master Scrum facilitator who makes sure scrum practices are followed, promotes self-organization within the team, holds daily team meetings, works with the product owner to make sure the product backlog is properly maintained, and removes any impediments that affect the team's ability to achieve its goals and produce the sprint's deliverables.

scrum methodology A software development methodology where a team works together in an intense but relatively short iterative and incremental scrum process to reach a common development goal, with team members meeting daily in face-to-face communication, until development is concluded.

scrum team A small group of up to 9 cross-functional developers that is responsible for developing, testing, and delivering software at the end of a scrum sprint. The team determines a sprint's major goals and deliverables.

security management People who make sure systems are secure and protected from internal and external threats.

segregation of accounting duties Separating the accounting functions of authorization, custody, and recording to minimize an employee's ability to commit fraud.

segregation of systems duties Implementing control procedures to clearly divide authority and responsibility within the information system function.

semantic data modeling Using knowledge of business processes and information needs to create a diagram that shows what to include in a fully normalized database (in 3NF).

semi-structured data Data that has some organization but is not fully organized to be inserted into a relational database.

sequence check An edit check that determines if a transaction file is in the proper numerical or alphabetical sequence.

sequence codes Items are numbered consecutively so that gaps in the sequence code indicate missing items that should be investigated. Examples include prenumbered checks, invoices, and purchase orders.

sexting Exchanging sexually explicit text messages and revealing pictures with other people, usually by means of a phone.

shoulder surfing When perpetrators look over a person's shoulders in a public place to get information such as ATM PIN numbers or user IDs and passwords.

sign check An edit check that verifies that the data in a field have the appropriate arithmetic sign.

simplification In design, making a visualization easy to interpret and understand.

size check An edit check that ensures the input data will fit into the assigned field.

skimming Double-swiping a credit card in a legitimate terminal or covertly swiping a credit card in a small, hidden, handheld card reader that records credit card data for later use.

smart contract A regular contract with the terms and agreed upon details built into the blockchain. The organization using the blockchain establishes the rules that govern the blockchain's interaction with users. An organization can automate the execution of a smart contract based on external triggers.

SMS spoofing Using short message service (SMS) to change the name or number a text message appears to come from.

social engineering The techniques or psychological tricks used to get people to comply with the perpetrator's wishes in order to gain physical or logical access to a building, computer, server, or network. It is usually to get the information needed to obtain confidential data.

Software-as-a-Service (SaaS) providers Companies that rent cloud-based software applications that customers can access using the Internet.

software piracy The unauthorized copying or distribution of copyrighted software.

source data automation The collection of transaction data in machine-readable form at the time and place of origin. Examples are point-of-sale terminals and ATMs.

source documents Documents used to capture transaction data at its source – when the transaction takes place. Examples include sales orders, purchase orders, and employee time cards.

spamming Simultaneously sending the same unsolicited message to many people, often in an attempt to sell them something.

special-purpose analysis reports Reports with no pre-specified content, format, or schedule; usually prepared in response to a management request.

specialized journal A journal used to record a large number of repetitive transactions such as credit sales, cash receipts, purchases, and cash disbursements.

specific authorization Special approval an employee needs in order to be allowed to handle a transaction.

spoofing Altering some part of an electronic communication to make it look as if someone else sent the communication in order to gain the trust of the recipient. Many things are spoofed, such as email addresses, caller IDs, IP addresses, address resolution protocols, SMS messages, web pages, and domain name systems.

sprint A pre-determined time period where the team works on high priority items in the product backlog. A sprint's scope is frozen and desired changes are added to the product backlog. Sprints begin with a planning event to determine goals and deliverables and ends with a review to see if they were achieved. The incremental software developed is presented to the customer.

spyware Software that secretly monitors computer usage, collects personal information about users, and sends it to someone else, often without the computer user's permission.

SQL injection (insertion) attack Inserting a malicious SQL query in input such that it is passed to and executed by an application program. This allows a hacker to convince the application to run SQL code that it was not intended to execute.

steering committee An executive-level committee to plan and oversee the information systems function; it typically consists of management from systems and other areas affected by the information systems function.

steganography program A program that can merge confidential information with a seemingly harmless file, password protect the file, and send it anywhere in the world, where the file is unlocked and the confidential information is reassembled. The host file can still be heard or viewed because humans are not sensitive enough to pick up the slight decrease in image or sound quality.

strategic master plan A multiple-year plan of the projects the company must complete to achieve its long-range goals.

structured data Data that is highly organized and fits into fixed fields.

structured programming A modular approach to programming in which each module performs a specific function and is coordinated by a control module.

structured query language (SQL) Standardized commercial programming language designed for managing data in relational database systems. Even though it is standardized, variations exist among different database systems.

style sheet An XBRL file that provides instructions on how to display (render) an instance document on either a computer screen or printed report.

subschema A subset of the schema; the way the user defines the data and the data relationships.

subsidiary ledger A ledger used to record detailed data for a general ledger account with many individual subaccounts, such as accounts receivable, inventory, and accounts payable.

supply chain An extended system that includes an organization's value chain as well as its suppliers, distributors, and customers.

support activities Value chain activities such as firm infrastructure, technology, purchasing, and human resources that enable primary activities to be performed efficiently and effectively.

symmetric encryption systems Encryption systems that use the same key both to encrypt and to decrypt.

system (1) Two or more interrelated components that interact to achieve a goal, often composed of subsystems that support the larger system. (2) The equipment and programs that comprise a complete computer installation. (3) The detailed methods, procedures, and routines that carry out specific activities, perform a duty, achieve goals or objectives, or solve one or more problems.

system flowchart Depicts the relationships among system input, processing, storage, and output.

system performance measurements Ways to evaluate and assess a system. Common measurements include throughput (output per unit of time), utilization (percentage of time the system is being productively used), and response time (how long it takes the system to respond).

systems administrators People responsible for making sure a system operates smoothly and efficiently.

systems analysis First SDLC step where the information needed to purchase, develop, or modify a system is gathered.

systems analysis report Comprehensive report summarizing systems analysis that documents the findings of analysis activities.

systems analysts People who help users determine their information needs, study existing systems and design new ones, and prepare specifications used by computer programmers.

systems development life cycle (SDLC) A five-step process used to design and implement a new system: systems analysis, conceptual design, physical design, implementation and conversion, and operation and maintenance.

systems documentation A complete description of how the system is supposed to work, including questionnaire copies, interview notes, memos, document copies, and models.

systems implementation The process of installing hardware and software and getting the IS up and running.

systems integrator An outside party hired to manage a company's systems development effort.

systems survey An extensive study of the current AIS.

systems survey report A report that summarizes all the activities that took place during the systems survey, including all relevant documentation such as memos; interview and observation notes; questionnaire data; file and record layouts and descriptions; input and output descriptions; and copies of documents, E-R diagrams, flowcharts, and data flow diagrams.

T

taxonomy A set of XBRL files that defines elements and the relationships among them.

technical feasibility Determining if a proposed system can be developed given the available technology.

test dataset A subset of data not used for the development of a model but used to test how well the model predicts the target outcome.

text qualifier Two characters that indicate the beginning and ending of a field and tell the program to ignore any delimiters contained between the characters.

threat Any potential adverse occurrence or unwanted event that could injure the AIS or the organization. Also referred to as an *event*.

throughput (1) The total amount of useful work performed by a computer system during a given period of time. (2) The number of "good" units produced in a given period of time.

time-based model of information security Implementing a combination of preventive, detective, and corrective controls that protect information assets long enough to enable an organization to recognize that an attack is occurring and take steps to thwart it before any information is lost or compromised.

time bomb/logic bomb A program that lies idle until some specified circumstance or a particular time triggers it. Once triggered, the program sabotages the system by destroying programs or data.

time card A document that records the employee's arrival and departure times for each work shift. The time card records the total hours worked by an employee during a pay period.

time sheet A data entry screen (or paper document) used by salaried professionals to record how much time was spent performing various tasks for specific clients.

tokenization Another word for data masking.

torpedo software Software that destroys competing malware. This sometimes results in "malware warfare" between competing malware developers.

trailer record Type of internal label that appears at the end of a file; in transaction files, the trailer record contains the batch totals calculated during input.

training dataset A subset of data used to train a model for future prediction.

transaction An agreement between two entities to exchange goods or services, such as selling inventory in exchange for cash; any other event that can be measured in economic terms by an organization.

transaction file A file that contains the individual business transactions that occur during a specific fiscal period. A transaction file is conceptually similar to a journal in a manual AIS.

transaction processing Process of capturing transaction data, processing it, storing it for later use, and producing information output, such as a managerial report or a financial statement.

transposition error An error that results when numbers in two adjacent columns are inadvertently exchanged (for example, 64 is written as 46).

trap door/back door A set of computer instructions that allows a user to bypass the system's normal controls.

trial balance A report listing the balances of all general ledger accounts. It is used to verify that the total debit balances in various accounts equal the total credit balances in other accounts.

triggered exception reports Reports with a pre-specified content and format, prepared only in response to abnormal conditions.

Trojan horse A set of unauthorized computer instructions in an authorized and otherwise properly functioning program.

tuple A row in a table that contains data about a specific item in a database table. For example, each row in the inventory table contains data (i.e., name description, price) about a particular inventory item.

turnaround documents Records of company data sent to an external party and then returned to the system as input. Turnaround documents are in machine-readable form to facilitate their subsequent processing as input records. An example is a utility bill.

turnkey system Software and hardware sold as a package such that the vendor installs the system and the user "turns on the key"; often written by vendors who specialize in a particular industry.

type I error The incorrect rejection of a true null hypothesis.

type II error The failure to reject a false null hypothesis.

typosquatting/URL hijacking Setting up similarly named websites so that users making typographical errors when entering a website name are sent to an invalid site.

U

Unified Process A development framework with four phases: inception, elaboration, construction, and transition. The last three phases are divided into a series of iterations of a predetermined length. Each incremental iteration contains additional functions or an improved version of the previously developed software.

uninterruptible power supply (UPS) An alternative power supply device that protects against the loss of power and fluctuations in the power level by using battery power to enable the system to operate long enough to back up critical data and safely shut down.

unit tests Help determine whether a given feature works as intended.

universal payment identification code (UPIC) A number that enables customers to remit payments via an ACH credit without requiring the seller to divulge detailed information about its bank account.

unstructured data Data that has no uniform structure.

update anomaly Improper database organization where a non-primary key item is stored multiple times; updating the item in one location and not the others causes data inconsistencies.

user stories A description of something a user wants to include in the system written by the product owner.

users People who record transactions, authorize data processing, and use system output.

utilization The percentage of time a system is used.

V

validity check An edit test that compares the ID code or account number in transaction data with similar data in the master file to verify that the account exists.

value chain Linking all primary and support activities in a business. Value is added as a product passes through the chain.

value of information The benefit provided by information minus the cost of producing it.

vendor-managed inventory (VMI) Practice in which manufacturers and distributors manage a retail customer's inventory using EDI. The supplier accesses its customer's point-of-sale system in order to monitor inventory and automatically replenish products when they fall to agreed-upon levels.

violated attribute dependencies Errors that occur when a secondary attribute in a row of data does not match the primary attribute.

virtual private network (VPN) Using encryption and authentication to securely transfer information over the Internet, thereby creating a "virtual" private network.

virtualization Running multiple systems simultaneously on one physical computer.

virus A segment of executable code that attaches itself to a file, program, or some other executable system component. When the hidden program is triggered, it makes unauthorized alterations to the way a system operates.

vishing Voice phishing; it is like phishing except the victim enters confidential data by phone.

visual inspection Examining data using human vision to see if there are problems.

visual weight In design, the amount of attention an element attracts.

visualization Any visual representation of data, such as a graph, diagram, or animation; called a viz for short.

voucher package The set of documents used to authorize payment to a supplier. It consists of a purchase order, receiving report, and supplier invoice.

voucher system A method for processing accounts payable in which a disbursement voucher is prepared instead of posting invoices directly to supplier records in the accounts payable subsidiary ledger. The disbursement voucher identifies the supplier, lists the outstanding invoices, and indicates the net amount to be paid after deducting any applicable discounts and allowances. Contrast with *nonvoucher system*.

vulnerabilities Software program flaws that a hacker can exploit to either crash a system or take control of it.

vulnerability scanners Automated tools designed to identify whether a given system possesses any unused and unnecessary programs that represent potential security threats.

W

walk-throughs Step-by-step reviews of procedures or program logic to find incorrect logic, errors, omissions, or other problems.

war dialing Programming a computer to dial thousands of phone lines searching for dialup modem lines. Hackers hack into the PC attached to the modem and access the network to which it is connected.

war driving Driving around looking for unprotected home or corporate wireless networks.

web-page spoofing See *phishing*.

white-collar criminals Typically, businesspeople who commit fraud. White-collar criminals usually resort to trickery or cunning, and their crimes usually involve a violation of trust or confidence.

worm Similar to a virus, except that it is a program rather than a code segment hidden in a host program. A worm also copies itself automatically and actively transmits itself directly to other systems.

X

XBRL eXtensible Business Reporting Language is a variant of XML (eXtensible Markup Language) specifically designed for use in communicating the content of financial data. It does this by creating tags for each data item that look much like the tags used by HTML.

Z

zero-balance test A processing control that verifies that the balance of a control account equals zero after all entries to it have been made.

zero-day attack An attack between the time a new software vulnerability is discovered and "released into the wild" and the time a software developer releases a patch to fix the problem.

zombies Hijacked computers, typically part of a botnet, that are used to launch a variety of Internet attacks.

Index

A

Abercrombie & Fitch, 20
Accenture, 316
acceptance tests, 743
access control lists (ACLs), 348–349
access control matrix, 345
access controls, 341–342
access rights, 98
accountants, 138–139
accounting, 10–11, 312–314
  double-entry accounting, 318
  future of and database systems, 114–115
accounting firms, 149
accounting information system (AIS), 3, 10–13
  agile methodologies, 741–744
  business process management (BPM), 738–739
  business process management systems (BPMS), 738
  business process reengineering (BPR), 738
  computer-aided software (or systems) engineering (CASE), 744–745
  corporate strategy and, 18–19
  custom software, 733
  data, 11, 93
  data processing cycle, 32–41
  data storage, 33–38
  difficulties developing, 729
  equipment malfunctions, 225
  firm infrastructure, 20
  fraud, 227–242
  human resources, 20
  inbound logistics, 19
  information technology (IT), 11, 18, 19
  in-house information systems department development, 733–735
  marketing, 19
  methods for improving system development, 737–745
  natural and political disasters, 223–225
  operations, 19
  organizational culture, 18
  outbound logistics, 19
  outsourcing accounting information system (AIS), 736–737
  primary activities, 19–20
  primary purpose of, 318
  prototyping, 739–741
  purchasing software, 729–732
  relational databases, 92–135
  sales, 19
  service, 19
  software errors, 225
  technology, 20
  as transaction processing system, 42
  value chain, 19–20
  virtualization, 18
accounts payable department, 486–488
accounts receivable, 448–450
  aging report, 437–438
  projections of future cash collections, 490
accruals, 575
ACFE. *See* Association of Certified Fraud Examiners
ACLs. *See* access control lists
Acquire Services event, 665
activity-based costing systems, 522–526
  enterprise resource planning (ERP) systems, 523
Adelphia, 299
advertising, 6
adware, 272
AES, 377
Aetna Life & Casualty, 735
agent-event relationship, 614
agents, 604
  identifying, 609–610
  relationship with resources, 667
aggregate data, 165–166
aggression, 702
agile development, 742
agile methodologies, 741–744
AI. *See* artificial intelligence
AICPA. *See* American Institute of Certified Public Accountants
Airbus, 512
airlines, 14, 138
AIS. *See* accounting information system
algorithm encryption, 377
Amazon AI, 12
Amazon.com, 13, 193, 259, 435, 442
American Accounting Association, 302
American Express, 269
American Institute of Certified Public Accountants (AIPCA), 12, 138, 299, 302
  Audit Data Standards, 139–140
  data standards, 168
  Generally Accepted Privacy Principles (GAPP), 373–376
American Management Systems, 693
America Online, 317
analytical reviews, 318
AND operator, 106
Anonymous, 226
antimalware controls, 346–351
antivirus software, 276–277
antivirus software vendors, 271
application controls, 298
archives, 406
area chart, 198
Arthur Andersen, 299
artificial intelligence (AI), 12–13, 194
AS alias operator, 106
assets, 316–318
Association of Certified Fraud Examiners (ACFE)
  asset misappropriation, 229
  Report to the Nation on Occupational Fraud and Abuse, 227
asymmetric encryption, 377, 378–379
Atlantic Richfield, 310
AT&T, 546
attacks, 353–356
attendance validation, 545–547
attributes, 38
audit committee, 306
Audit Data Standards, 142, 144
auditors, 60, 137, 229–230
audits, 320
audit trail, 37–38, 318, 573–574
The Australian newspaper, 269
authentication, 343–345
authentication controls, 370
  access control matrix, 345
  antimalware controls, 346
  authorization controls, 345–346
  biometric identifiers, 343
  information technology (IT) solutions, 346–353
  MAC addresses, 345
  multifactor authentication, 343–344
  multimodal authentication, 343
  passwords, 343–344
  perimeter defense, 347–350
  personal identification numbers (PINs), 343
  smart cards, 343
authority, 306–307
authorization, 311–314, 345

authorization controls, 345–346, 370, 432
Automated Clearing House (ACH) blocks, 491
automation, 148–150
  accounts payable department, 487
  bot, 148–149
  data dashboard, 149
  human element, 149–150
  robotic process automation (RPA) software, 148–149, 157–158
Automation Anywhere, 148
avoidance, 703

B

background checks, 307
back order, 438
BackOrifice, 274
backup procedures, 405–406
balanced scorecard, 586–587
balance-forward method, 448, 449
Bank of America, 93, 95, 270
banks
  blockchain, 17
  electronic data interchange (EDI), 451–453
  information technology (IT), 215–218
  lockbox, 451
Baptist Medical System, 744
bar charts, 196, 202
bar codes, 439, 472
bar-coding
  cost accounting, 521
  ordering materials, supplies, and services, 479
batch processing, 39, 399
batch-related overhead, 523
batch totals, 399
beating the system, 231
behavioral aspects of change, 701–704
belief system, 299
benchmark problem, 731
Benford, Frank, 236
Benford's Law, 236, 341–342
Big 4 accounting firms, 145, 148, 236
big data, 138
billing, 445–450, 608
bill of lading, 444
bill of materials, 511, 514–516
biometric identifiers, 343
blanket purchase order, 480
block attacks, 350
blockchains, 14–17, 41–42
  altering, 383
  documentation, 60
  hashing, 383–385
  nonce, 383
  output controls, 401
  root hash, 383
  smart contracts, 42
  three-step procedure, 383, 385
block codes, 34
blogs, 440
Bloomberg, Michael, 238
bluebugging, 276–277
Blue Cross/Blue Shield, 309, 700, 737, 766
BluePrism, 148
bluesnarfing, 276
Bluetooth, 276
board of directors, 306–307
Boots the Chemists, 767
border router, 347
Bosak, Jon, 582
Boston Medical Center, 193
bot, 148–149
bot herder, 258
botnets, 258–259, 271
boundary system, 299
boxplot, 198
BPD. *See* business process diagram
BPM. *See* business process management
BPMS. *See* business process management systems
BPR. *See* business process reengineering
Bredolab botnet, 258
browsers, 383
brute force attacks, 259–260
buffer overflow attacks, 262, 352
bullet graph, 196
Burger King, 225
business activities, 32
business continuity plan (BCP), 407–408
Business E-mail Compromise scam, 491
businesses
  artificial intelligence (AI), 12
  data, 3
  give-get exchanges, 7
business intelligence, 95
Businessland, 736
Business Management Modernization Project (BMMP), 703
business policies, 612–613
business process diagrams (BPD), 59, 60–62
business processes, 5–10
business process management (BPM), 738–739
business process management systems (BPMS)
  internal controls, 738–739
  segregation of duties, 346
Business Process Modeling Initiative Notation Working Group, 60
business process reengineering (BPR), 738
Business Software Alliance, 266
Business Systems Modernization (BSM) program, 693

C

California Consumer Privacy Act (CCPA), 373
California Department of Motor Vehicles, 693
California Power and Light, 692
caller ID spoofing, 260–261
Canadian Institute of Chartered Accountants (CICA), 373–376
capital budgeting model, 700–701
CAQ. *See* Center for Audit Quality
cardinalities, 610
  agent-event relationship, 614
  business meaning of, 614–615
  maximum cardinality, 611–612, 615
  minimum cardinality, 611–612, 614, 615, 637
  reflecting organization's business policies, 613
carding, 268
Cargill, 13
carrying costs, 477
cash collections, 451–454
cash disbursements, 488–492
cash flow budget, 453–454
Cash Resource entity, 673
categorical data, 193
causation, 146–147
CCO. *See* chief compliance officer
CCPA. *See* California Consumer Privacy Act
cell phones
  antivirus software, 277
  caller ID spoofing, 260–261
  malware, 276–277
  navigation, 168
  protecting information resources, 342
Center for Audit Quality (CAQ), 138–139
CEO. *See* chief executive officer
certificate authority, 383
Certified Public Accountants (CPAs), 11, 30
  CITP (Certified Information Technology Professional) designation, 12
change
  behavioral aspects of, 701–704
  controls, 356–357
change management, 315–316, 356–357
chart of accounts, 35–36
chat bots, 440
check digit verification, 398–399
check kiting, 233
checksums, 401
Chemical Bank, 769
Chevron, 297
chief compliance officer (CCO), 320
chief executive officer (CEO), 356
chief information officer (CIO), 356
chief information security officer (CISO), 355–356
chief operating officer (COO), 356
chipping, 270
CICA. *See* Canadian Institute of Chartered Accountants
Cigna Information Services, 737
CIM. *See* computer-integrated manufacturing
CIO (Chief Information Officer), 18
CIO Magazine, 18, 403
ciphertext, 376
CIRT. *See* computer incidence response team
Cisco, 237
CISO. *See* chief information security officer
Citibank, 258
Citigroup, 226
CITP (Certified Information Technology Professional) designation, 12
classification analysis, 194
click fraud, 265
closed-loop verification, 399
cloud computing, 18
  effects on systems, 409–410
  implications of, 357
  unauthorized access to sensitive information, 372
CloudNine, 259
CNN, 259
COBIT. *See* Control Objectives for Information and Related Technology
Code Red worm, 262
coding techniques, 34–35
cold site, 407
collusion, 313–314
combined human resources (HR)/ payroll data model, 671–672
commercial software, 730
Committee of Sponsoring Organizations (COSO), 302–303

communication systems, 318
companies
  audit committee, 306
  auditors, 60
  background check on employees, 233
  corporate honesty, 233
  employees' personal relationships with customers and suppliers, 234
  prosecuting those who perpetrate fraud, 233
  risk appetite, 305
  unclear policies and procedures, 233
  valuing employees' knowledge and skills, 540
company-wide overhead, 523
comparison visualizations, 196
compatibility test, 345
competence, 305–306
completeness check (or test), 398
computer-aided design (CAD) software, 511–512
computer-aided software (or systems) engineering (CASE), 744–745
computer attacks and abuse
  bot herder, 258
  botnets, 258–259
  brute force attacks, 259–260
  buffer overflow attacks, 262
  caller ID spoofing, 260–261
  click fraud, 265
  Code Red worm, 262
  covering tracks, 258
  credential recycling, 260
  cross-site scripting (XSS), 261–262
  cryptocurrency fraud, 265
  cyber-bullying, 264
  denial-of-service (DoS) attack, 259
  dictionary attack, 260
  economic espionage, 264
  e-mail spoofing, 260
  e-mail threats, 264
  executing attack, 258
  Flash, 261
  hacking, 258
  hijacking, 258
  HTML, 261
  Internet auction fraud, 264–265
  Internet misinformation, 264
  Internet pump-and-dump fraud, 265
  IP address spoofing, 261
  JavaScript, 261
  malicious scripts, 262
  man-in-the-middle (MITM) attack, 262–263
  masquerading/impersonation, 263
  MyDoom virus, 259
  password cracking, 260
  phreaking, 263–264
  piggybacking, 263
  podslurping, 264
  reconnaissance, 257
  research, 258
  round-down fraud, 264
  salami technique, 264
  scanning and mapping target, 258
  sexting, 264
  short message service (SMS) spoofing, 261
  social engineering, 257–258, 266–270
  software piracy, 265–266
  software programs vulnerabilities, 261
  spamming, 260
  spoofing, 260–261
  SQL injection (insertion) attack, 262
  techniques, 277–279
  tracking down computer criminals, 259
  Trojan horse, 258, 261
  war dialing, 263
  war driving, 263
  Web-page spoofing, 261
  zero-day attack, 261
  Zeus malware, 259
  zombies, 258
computer-based storage concepts, 38
computer forensics specialists, 320
computer fraud
  access points, 235
  Benford's law, 236
  classifications, 236–238
  computer instructions fraud, 237
  corporate databases, 235
  cybercriminals, 230, 256–257
  cybersecurity personnel, 256–257
  cyber sleuths, 236
  data fraud, 237–238
  employees stealing data, 237–238
  input fraud, 236–237
  insecure networks, 236
  law enforcement and, 236
  malware, 270–279
  modifying programs illegally, 235
  output fraud, 238
  perpetrators, 230, 236
  personal computers (PCs), 235
  processor fraud, 237
  undetected, 235
  unreported, 236
computer incidence response team (CIRT), 355
computer instructions fraud, 237
computer-integrated manufacturing (CIM), 510, 518
computer operators, 315
computer programmers, 697
computers
  antivirus software, 276
  digital signatures, 312
  vulnerability, 235
computer security chief (CSO), 320
Computing Technology Industry Association, 225
concatenated keys, 642
conceptual design, 695, 761
conceptual-level schema, 97
conceptual systems design, 759–761
conceptual systems design report, 761
Conficker worm, 276
confidentiality
  information technology (IT), 335
  intellectual property, 369
  protecting, 369–372
confirmation bias, 147
confirmatory data analysis, 1910192
context diagram, 71
Continental Bank, 736
control account, 34
control activities
  change management controls, 316
  design and use of documents and records, 316
  independent checks on performance, 317–318
  project development and acquisition controls, 315
  proper authorization of transactions and activities, 311–312
  safeguarding assets, records, and data, 316–317
  segregation of duties, 312–315
control environment
  assigning authority and responsibility, 306–307
  external influences, 308
  human resources standards, 307–308
  integrity, ethical values, and competence, 306
  organizational structure, 306
  oversight by board of directors, 306
  philosophy, operating style, and risk management, 305
control frameworks, 300–304
  Committee of Sponsoring Organizations (COSO), 302
  Control Objectives for Information and Related Technology (COBIT), 300–301
Control Objectives for Information and Related Technology (COBIT), 300–301, 335
  identifying organization's culture and ethics for information security, 338
  IT-related controls contributing to systems reliability, 335–336
  security awareness training, 338–339
control processes
  chief compliance officer (CCO), 320
  communicating information about, 318
  computer forensics specialists, 320
  computer security chief (CSO), 320
  effective supervision, 319
  forensic investigators, 320
  fraud detection software, 320–321
  fraud hotline, 321
  internal control evaluations, 319
  monitoring system activities, 319
  periodic audits, 320
  responsibility accounting systems, 319
  tracking software and mobile devices, 319
control reports, 572–573
conversion, 8, 769
COO. *See* chief operating officer
cookies, 226, 373–374
Coordinated Universal Time (UTC), 171
Corning Corporation, 707–708
corporate accountants, 137
corporate strategy, 18–19
corrective controls, 298, 309
correlation, 146–147, 196–197
corruption, 228
cost accounting
  activity-based costing systems, 522–525
  bar coding, 521
  direct labor costs, 521
  errors in inventory records, 522
  inaccurate cost data, 521–522
  job-time ticket, 521
  machinery and equipment usage, 521
  manufacturing overhead costs, 521
  overstating fixed assets, 522
  principle objectives, 520
  process, 520–521
  production cycle, 520–526
  raw materials usage data, 520
  traditional cost systems, 522
cost drivers, 523

cost management, 524–525
costs
 blockchain, 16
 corporate strategy determining, 522
 hiring, 540
Coughlin, Thomas, 232
CPAs. *See* Certified Public Accountants
Crate & Barrel, 442
credential recycling, 260
credit approval, 436–438
credit limit, 436
credit memo, 449
credit sales processing, 401–402
critical path, 699
cross-footing balance test, 400
cross-functional analysis, 96
cross-site scripting (XSS), 261–262
CRUD (creating records, reading data, updating data, deleting data), 39
cryptocurrency, 42
cryptocurrency fraud, 265
CSO. *See* computer security chief
current update controls, 400
customer accounts, 449
customer inquiries, 439–441
customer relationship management (CRM) systems, 440
customer service, 440
custom software, 733
cyber attacks, 224
cyber-bullying, 264
cybercriminals, 226, 230, 256–258
cyber-extortion, 273
cybersecurity personnel, 256–257
cycle billing, 449
cyphertext, 380

D

dark data, 141
dashboard. *See* data dashboard
data, 3, 138
 accuracy, 33, 95
 aggregate data, 165–166
 appropriate use of, 137–138
 auditing sample, 175
 available, 140–142
 backup procedures, 405–406
 batch processing, 39
 big data, 138
 blockchain, 317
 cleaning, 95
 csv format, 140
 data dictionary, 141
 data owner, 142
 deduplication, 405–406
 defining, 140
 deleting, 39
 differential backup, 405
 dirty, 163–164
 ETL (extracting, transforming, and loading) process, 139–145
 extracting, 140–143
 extrapolation beyond the range, 195
 formatting, 144–145
 full backup, 405
 inconsistencies, 96
 incremental backup, 405
 independence, 96
 information, 139
 JSON format, 140, 144
 loading, 144–145
 logical and physical views of, 96–97
 machine-readable format, 4, 33
 organizing, 140
 petabytes (quadrillion bytes), 14
 policies and procedures, 317
 proliferation, 137
 reading, 39
 real-time processing, 39
 record creation, 39
 redundancies, 41, 93–94, 96, 101
 referential integrity, 144
 relational databases, 93
 safeguarding, 316–317
 semi-structured data, 140
 storing in one table, 101
 streamed data, 140
 stripping out or standardizing formatting, 145
 structured data, 140
 text file with delimiters, 144
 theft, 316–317
 transforming, 162–176
 trends, patterns, anomalies, and exceptions in, 340
 unnormalized to relational tables, 132–135
 unstructured data, 140
 updating, 39
 XBRL (eXtensible Business Reporting Language), 33, 144
 xml format, 140
data analysis
 descriptive analytics, 189–191
 diagnostic analytics, 191–193
 GIGO (garbage in, garbage out), 194
 predictive analytics, 193–194
 prescriptive analytics, 194
data analytics, 13, 95
 anomaly detection, 341
 automation, 148–150
 Benford's Law, 341–342
 causation, 146–147
 common problems with, 194–195
 contemporary coding languages, 145
 correlation, 146–147
 data analysis, 189–195
 data dashboard, 13
 data overfitting, 195
 data presentation, 196–208
 data storytelling, 147
 data visualization, 147–148
 decision making, 13–14
 defining data, 140
 descriptive analytics, 145, 189–191
 diagnostic analytics, 145, 191–193
 ETL (extracting, transforming, and loading) process, 139–145
 extracting data, 140–143
 GIGO (garbage in, garbage out), 194
 interpreting results, 146–147
 legacy technologies, 145–146
 loading data, 144–145
 misuse of, 195
 outlier detection, 341
 predictive analytics, 145, 193–194
 prescriptive analytics, 145, 194
 preventing and detecting fraud, 240–241
 regression analysis, 341
 semantic modeling, 341
 sharing results, 147–148
 SMART (specific, measurable, achievable, relevant, and timely) objectives, 139
 structured and unstructured databases, 146
 testing all kinds of data, 341
 transforming data, 143–144, 162–176
database administrator (DBA), 94, 97
database management system (DBMS), 94, 114–115, 116
 data definition language (DDL), 100
 data dictionary, 98–100
 data manipulation language (DML), 100
 relational data model, 100
 report writer, 100
 structured query language (SQL), 100
databases, 38, 41
 access rights, 98
 aggregate data, 165
 computer fraud, 235
 cross-functional analysis, 96
 cryptic data values, 169–170
 database administrator (DBA), 94
 database management system (DBMS), 94
 data independence, 96
 data integration, 95
 data sharing, 96
 data warehouses, 95
 disaggregated data, 165
 entity-relationship diagramming, 93
 files, 93
 good data, 96
 information about entities, 93
 information about structure of, 98–100
 online transaction processing database (OLTP), 95
 queries, 41
 REA data model, 93
 reconciling records, 400–401
 redundancy and data inconsistencies, 93–94, 96
 structured and unstructured, 146
database systems, 94
 advantages, 95–96
 data dictionary, 98–100
 future of accounting and, 114–115
 logical view, 97
 physical view, 97
 record layout, 96
 schemas, 97–98
data cleaning, 172–174
data concatenation, 169
data consistency, 170–171
data contradiction errors, 173
data controls, 315, 398
data dashboards, 13, 147, 587
 color, 204
 updating, 149
data deception, 205–208
data deduplication, 172
data definition language (DDL), 100
data destination, 70
data dictionary, 98–100, 141–142, 145
data entry, 314
data entry controls, 398–399
data entry errors, 174
data filtering, 172–173

data flow diagram (DFD), 59, 62
  context diagram, 71
  data destination, 70
  data flows, 70
  data source, 70
  data store, 70
  guidelines, 73–74
  processes, 70
  subdividing, 71–72
  symbols, 69
data flows, 70
data formatting, 170–171
data fraud, 237–238
data imputation, 173
data input, 32–33
data integration, 95
data joining, 166
data lakes, 140–141
data loss prevention (DLP) software, 371
data manipulation language (DML), 100
data marts, 140–141
data masking programs, 371
data matching, 399
data mining, 95
data modeling, 100, 602, 616
data normalization
  first normal form (1NF), 132–133
  second normal form (2NF), 132, 133–134
  third normal form (3NF), 132, 133, 134–135
data ordering, 205
data overfitting, 193, 195
data owner, 142
data parsing, 167–169
data pivoting, 166–167
data presentation
  choosing right visualization, 196–198
  designing high-quality visualizations, 199–208
data processing, 39
data processing cycle
  data input, 32–33
  data processing, 39
  data storage, 33–38
  information output, 39–41
data processing schedule, 316
data query language (DQL), 100
data sharing, 96
data source, 70
data standardization, 167–171
data storage, 315
  audit trail, 37–38
  chart of accounts, 35–36
  coding techniques, 34–35
  computer-based storage concepts, 38
  control account, 34
  general ledger, 34
  journals, 36–37
  ledgers, 34
  subsidiary ledger, 34
data store, 70
data storytelling, 147
data structuring
  aggregate data, 165–166
  data joining, 166
  data pivoting, 166–167
data swamps, 141
data threshold violations, 173
data validation, 95, 174–176
data value, 38
data variety, 138
data veracity, 138
data visualization, 147–148
data volume, 138
data warehouses, 95, 140–141
Davis Controls, 703
DBA. *See* database administrator
DBMS. *See* database management system
DDL. *See* data definition language
DDoS. *See* distributed denial of service attacks
debit memo, 484
debugging, 764–765
decision making, 3, 12–14
decryption, 376, 380
deduction register, 548
deduplication, 405–406
Deep Blue, 149
deep packet inspection, 349–350
defense-in-depth, 340
deferrals, 575
delete anomaly, 101
delimiters, 142
Del Monte Foods, 736
Deloitte & Touche, 17, 729, 745
demand reports, 762
demilitarized zone (DMZ), 347
denial-of-service (DoS) attack, 259
depreciation, 670
descriptive analytics, 145, 189–191
detecting attacks, 353–354
detective controls, 298, 309
Deutsche Bank, 258
device and software hardening controls, 351–353
DFD. *See* data flow diagram
diagnostic analytics, 145, 191–193
diagnostic control system, 299
dichotomous variables, 170
dictionary attack, 260
differential backup, 405
Digicert, 383
digital assets, 665
digital certificates, 382–383
digital manufacturing software, 511, 512
digital signatures, 312, 381–382
digital watermark, 371
Dillards, 442
direct conversion, 769
direct labor costs, 521
dirty data, 163–164, 172
disaster recovery plan (DRP), 407–408
disbursement voucher, 487, 551
disburse payroll, 551–553
Discover Card, 269
discussion boards, 440
distributed denial of service attacks (DDoS), 224
distribution visualizations, 197–198
DML. *See* data manipulation language
documentation, 59–60
documentation tools
  business process diagram (BPD), 60–62
  data flow diagram (DFD), 69–74
  flowcharts, 63–68
  systems development process, 60
document flowcharts, 59, 64
documents, 39–40, 316–317
double-entry accounting, 318
Dow Chemical, 730
Dow Jones Industrial Average, 208
DQL. *See* data query language
drive-by downloading, 271
DriveCleaner, 273
drop services, 271
DRP. *See* disaster recovery plan
Drug Enforcement Administration, 273
dummy variables, 170
DuPont, 744
Duronio, Roger, 274

E

earnings statement, 549
Eastman Kodak, 736
eavesdropping, 270
eBay, 259, 269
economic espionage, 264
economic feasibility, 700–701
economic order quantity (EOQ), 477
EDI. *See* electronic data interchange
EDI over the Internet (EDINT), 481
EDS. *See* Electronic Data Systems
efficiency, 11, 16
EFT. *See* electronic funds transfer
Egerstad, Dan, 274
electronic data interchange (EDI), 435, 470
  accounts payable department, 487
  banks, 451–453
  controlling access to, 482
  encryption, 482
  expenditure cycle information system, 470–472
  improving purchasing process, 481
Electronic Data Systems (EDS), 698, 737
electronic funds transfer (EFT), 451–453, 473
  cash disbursements, 490–491
electronic warfare, 224–225
elements, 579–580
Eli Lilly, 374
e-mail
  archiving, 406
  backups, 406
  phishing, 268
  sales order entry, 435
  spam, 260
e-mail spoofing, 260
Employee entity, 671
employee roles, 667
employees
  audits, 320
  background checks, 307
  changes in discretionary deductions, 543
  compensating, 307
  confidentiality agreements, 308
  data theft, 316–317
  discharging, 308
  evaluating, 307
  flexibility of where and when they work, 541
  hiring and training, 6, 307, 540
  information security, 338–339
  job-time tickets, 545
  key cost driver, 538
  knowledge and skills, 540
  morale, 540–541
  paid time off, 541
  pay-for-performance compensation, 541

employees (*Continued*)
- paying, 6
- promoting, 307
- prosecuting and incarcerating perpetrators, 308
- recording use of time, 670
- reimbursement of travel and entertainment expenses, 490
- sales order entry, 435
- security awareness training, 338–339
- segregation of duties, 346
- time card, 545
- tracking time, 672–673
- understanding jobs and attitudes, 541
- unintentional threats, 317
- vacations, 308

Employee Type entity, 688
employer-paid benefits, 553
encryption, 353
- AES, 377
- algorithm, 377
- asymmetric encryption, 377, 378–379
- ciphertext, 376, 380
- data warehouses, 95
- decryption, 376, 380
- encryption keys, 377–378
- key escrow, 378
- key length, 377
- plaintext, 376
- private key, 377
- protecting sensitive information, 370
- public key, 377
- symmetric encryption, 377–378
- types of systems, 377–379
- virtual private networks (VPNs), 379–380

endpoints, 351–352
end-user computing (EUC), 733–735
end-user-developed software, 733–734
Enron, 299
enterprise data structure, 95
Enterprise Resource Planning (ERP) software, 729
enterprise resource planning (ERP) systems, 42–45
- activity-based costing, 523
- advantages, 43–44
- centralized database, 42
- consulting companies, 43
- coordinating and managing data, business processes, and resources, 42
- disadvantages, 44
- general ledger accounts, 450
- management and, 44
- modular design, 42–43
- production cycle information system, 509–511
- proper configuration, 43–44
- reporting capabilities, 475
- revenue cycle information systems, 430–433
- segregation of duties, 437, 453
- up-to-date information, 42

Enterprise Risk Management-Integrated Framework (ERM) *versus* Internal Control-Integrated Framework (IC), 303
Enterprise Risk Management-Integrating with Strategy and Performance, 303
entities, 602
- attributes, 38
- information about, 93
- REA data model, 604
- relationship between, 610–614

entity integrity rule, 103
entity-relationship (E-R) diagram, 93, 602–603
EOQ. *See* economic order quantity
Equimark, 737
equipment
- acquiring, 6
- instructions to be performed with, 668
- malfunctions, 224–225

ERM. *See* Enterprise Risk Management-Integrated Framework
Ernst & Young Foundation, 145–146
ERP. *See* enterprise resource planning (ERP) systems
error log, 399
ErrorSafe, 273
ERS. *See* evaluated receipt settlement
ESG. *See* Improving Organizational Resiliency: New Guidance Addresses Environmental, Social, and Governance-Related Risks
ESM, 306
estimates, 575
Ethernet headers, 348
ETL (extracting, transforming, and loading) process, 139–145
- data, 140
- data joining, 166

E-trade, 238
European Union's General Data Privacy Regulation (GDPR), 335, 372–373
Europol, 292
evaluated receipt settlement (ERS), 488
events, 604
- relationships, 615

evil twin, 269
Excel, 63
executable architecture baseline, 744
expenditure cycle, 8–9, 469–470
- acquisition of intangible services, 664–665
- approving supplier invoices, 486–489
- cash disbursements, 489–492
- digital assets, 665
- events and attribute placement, 661–664
- exchange of information with suppliers, 470
- identifying what, when, and how much to purchase, 477–479
- ordering materials, supplies, and services, 477–483
- receiving, 483–486
- rental transactions, 665–667
- sale of services, 664

expenditure cycle information system
- access controls, 475
- batch processing, 473
- electronic data interchange (EDI), 470–472
- electronic funds transfer (EFT), 473
- encrypting sensitive information, 475
- entering data, 472
- financial electronic data interchange (FEDI), 473
- inaccurate or invalid data, 473
- integrity controls, 473
- inventory master data, 473
- inventory master file, 471
- loss or destruction of master data, 475
- open-invoice file, 473
- process, 470–473
- purchase order, 471
- purchase request, 471
- raw materials, 508
- remittance data, 473
- reports to better manage inventory, 476
- segregation of duties, 473, 476

Experian, 163
exploding bill of materials, 514–515
exploit, 351–352
exploratory data analysis, 190
exposure/impact, 298
eXtensible Business Reporting Language (XBRL)
- accountant's role, 582
- elements, 579–580
- extension taxonomy, 582
- instance document, 579–580
- linkbases, 580
- process, 579–581
- schema, 580
- style sheet, 581
- taxonomy, 580
- terminology, 579–581

extension taxonomy, 582
external failure costs, 526
extracting data
- back processing controls, 142–143
- documenting what was done, 142–143
- flat files, 142
- text qualifier, 142
- understanding data needs and data available, 140–142
- verifying quality, 142–143

extrapolation beyond the range, 195
extreme programming (XP), 743
EY accounting firm, 139

F

Facebook, 225, 259, 261, 272
- data warehouse, 140
- fraud and security risks, 267

factoring, 453
false acceptance rate, 343
false rejection rate, 343
Fannie Mae, 729
FAQs. *See* frequently asked questions
Farmer, Dan, 236
FASB. *See* Financial Accounting Standards Board
fault tolerance, 404
FBI, 96, 264, 308
FCPA. *See* Foreign Corrupt Practices Act
feasibility analysis, 699–701
Federal Trade Commission, 273
FedEx, 39
FEDI. *See* financial electronic data interchange
Fiat Chrysler, 261
fidelity bond insurance, 308
Fidelity's Magellan fund, 172
field check, 398
fields, 38
file and database design, 762–763
files, 38
- databases, 93
- labels, 399–400

Fill Customer Order event, 659, 660
finance and artificial intelligence (AI), 13

Financial Accounting Standards Board (FASB), 308
financial electronic data interchange (FEDI), 452–453, 473
Financial Executives Institute, 302
financial pressures, 230–231
financial reports, 525
Financial Services Modernization Act (Gramm-Leach-Bliley Act), 373
financial statements
  eXtensible Business Reporting Language (XBRL), 577–579
  fraudulent financial reporting, 584
  generating from relational databases, 646–647
  inline XBRL (iXBRL), 578–579
  preparing, 576–584
  transitioning from GAAP to IFRS, 576–577
  unauthorized disclosure of financial information, 560
  XBRL (eXtensible Business Reporting Language), 4
financial total, 399
financing activities data model, 673–674
financing cycle, 8, 10
Finished Goods inventory entity, 669
firewalls, 347–350
first normal form (1NF), 132–133
5 Why's principle, 191
fixed assets, 518–519, 522
Flash, 261
flat files, 142
flexible benefits plans, 553
flowcharts
  document flowcharts, 59, 64
  guidelines for preparing, 64
  internal control flowcharts, 64–65
  program flowcharts, 59, 68
  symbols, 63–64
  system flowcharts, 59, 68
Ford, 737
Foreign Corrupt Practices Act (FCPA), 299–300
foreign keys, 103
forensic investigators, 320
forms design, 397
Forrester Research, 225
fraud
  adaptive crime, 340
  auditors, 229–230
  background check on employees, 233
  beating the system, 231
  Benford's Law, 341–342
  charging stolen item to expense accounts, 233
  check kiting, 233
  collusion, 313–314
  committing, 232
  computer fraud, 235–238
  concealing, 232–233
  converting theft or misrepresentation to personal gain, 233
  corporate honesty, 233
  corruption, 228
  data analytics and, 240–241
  detection methods, 239
  emotional pressure, 231
  false statement, 227
  financial pressures, 230–231
  fraud triangle, 230–235
  fraudulent financial reporting, 229
  greed, ego, pride, or ambition, 232
  impact of, 309
  inattention or carelessness by management, 233
  injury or loss, 227
  intent to deceive, 227
  investment fraud, 228
  justifying illegal behavior, 234
  lapping scheme, 233
  malicious software, 230
  management misrepresenting financial statements, 232
  material fact, 227
  misappropriation of assets, 228–229
  mutually beneficial personal relationships with customers and suppliers, 234
  neural networks, 320–321
  opportunities, 232–234
  perpetrators, 227–228, 230–235
  person's lifestyle, 232
  phantom controller, 233
  pressures, 230–232
  preventing and detecting, 235, 238–242
  prosecuting and incarcerating perpetrators, 233, 308
  rationalizations, 234–235
  red flags, 340
  risk of, 309
  theft of assets, 232
  trends, patterns, anomalies, and exceptions in data, 340
  unclear policies and procedures, 233
  white-collar criminals, 228, 230
fraud detection software, 320–321
fraud hotline, 321
fraud triangle, 230–235
fraudulent financial reporting, 229
frequently asked questions (FAQs), 440
Fukushima Daichi nuclear reactor (Japan), 195
full backup, 405

G

gamification, 215–218
Gantt chart, 699
Gap, 442
GAPP. *See* Generally Accepted Privacy Principles
Gartner Group, 764
Gates, Bill, 264
GDPR. *See* General Data Privacy Regulation
General and Administrative Services resource, 665
general authorization, 312
General Data Privacy Regulation (GDPR), 335, 372–373
General Dynamics, 737
general journal, 36
general ledger, 9, 34
  account codes, 36
  accounting subsystems, 571
  accruals, 575
  audit trail, 573–574
  authorization controls, 569–570
  chart of accounts, 35–36
  closed-loop verification, 572
  comparing control account balances to total balance in subsidiary ledger, 572
  control account, 34
  control reports, 572–573
  corrections, 575
  deferrals, 575
  encrypting data, 570
  estimates, 575
  field (format) checks, 572
  inaccurate or invalid data, 569, 572
  journal voucher file, 571–572
  limiting functions that can be performed, 570
  loss of master data, 571
  post adjusting entries, 574–576
  process, 571–572
  read-only privileges, 570
  reconciliation, 400, 572–573
  reevaluations, 575
  restricting access to, 569
  run-to-run totals, 572
  suspending or clearing accounts with zero balances, 572–573
  treasurer's office, 571
  trial balance, 572
  updating, 571–574
  validity check, 572
  zero-balance check, 572
general ledger and reporting system, 568–571
Generally Accepted Accounting Principles (GAAP)
  financial reports, 525
  fixed assets, 576
  transition to IFRS, 576–577
Generally Accepted Privacy Principles (GAPP), 373–374
General Motors, 512
Geophysical Systems Corporation (GSC), 732
Get resource event, 637
GIGO (garbage in, garbage out), 194
give-get exchanges, 7
Global Communications, 264
Global Crossing, 299
Global Payments, 226
Gonzalez, Albert, 262
Google, 261, 269
  AlphaGo, 149
  Gmail accounts, 273
  web apps, 168
Google AI, 12
Google Transit, 168
Gramm-Leach-Bliley Act. *See* Financial Services Modernization Act
GROUP BY clause, 106, 111, 114
group codes, 34
Group entity, 688
Grum botnet, 258
guarantors, 271

H

hacking, 258
Hadoop, 146
Hard Rock Cafe, 729
hardwiring, 403
Hartford Insurance Group, 770
hash, 380–381, 399
hashing
  blockchains, 383–385
  digital certificates, 382–383
  digital signatures, 381–382
  hash, 380–381

hashing (*Continued*)
hashing algorithms, 380
nonrepudiation, 381–382
public key infrastructure (PKI), 383
SHA-256 algorithm, 380
header record, 400
healthcare
artificial intelligence (AI), 13
blockchain, 17
Health Dimension, 736
Health Information Technology for Economic and Clinical Health (HITECH), 335, 373
Health Insurance Portability and Accountability Act (HIPAA), 335, 373
Heartland Payment Systems, 270
heat maps, 197
help desk, 735
Hewlett-Packard (H-P), 267, 616
High Rock Accounting, 541
hijacking, 258
HIPAA. *See* Health Insurance Portability and Accountability Act
hiring, 307, 540
histograms, 198
HITECH. *See* Health Information Technology for Economic and Clinical Health
Hoffman, Charlie, 582
Hollywood Presbyterian Medical Center, 273
Homeland Security, 292
honeypots, 354
HotLan Trojan, 273
hot site, 407
HTML, 261–262
human resources (HR), 307–308
accounting information service (AIS), 20
cycle entities, 671–672
tracking employees' time, 672–673
Human Resources (HR)/ payroll cycle activities
integrating REA diagram across cycles, 635–640
payroll portion, 635
human resources management (HRM), 543
human resources management (HRM)/ payroll cycle, 537
human resources management (HRM)/ payroll cycle information system
hiring unqualified employees, 541–543
inaccurate master data, 540
larcenous employees, 541–543
loss or destruction of master data, 541
overview of process and information needs, 538–540
payroll master database, 539
segregating incompatible duties, 540–541
unauthorized disclosure of sensitive information, 541
violation of laws and regulations in hiring and dismission employees, 543
human resources/payroll cycle, 8–10

I

IBM, 96, 163, 316, 730, 736, 737, 744
Watson, 12, 149
IC. *See* Internal Control-Integrated Framework
ID badges, 343
ID codes, 398
identity theft, 266–267, 375
IDSs. *See* intrusion detection systems
IFRS, 576–577
IM. *See* instant messaging
impersonation, 263
implementation plan, 766–767
imprest fund, 491
Improving Organizational Resiliency: New Guidance Addresses Environmental, Social, and Governance-Related Risks (ESG), 303
incremental backup, 405
independent review, 318
Industrial Internet of Things, 520
information, 3
access restricted, 4
accounting information system (AIS), 11
availability, 403–409
communicating about control processes, 318
controlling access to sensitive information, 370–372
decrypting to process, 370
encryption, 370
entities, 93
how it is transmitted on Internet, 347–348
identifying and classifying for protection, 370
protecting resources, 341–353
transforming data into, 139
value of, 4–5
information needs, 5–10
information output, 39–41
information overload, 4
information rights management (IRM) software, 370–371
information security
defense-in-depth, 340
employee skills and competencies, 338
fundamental concepts, 336–340
management issue, not just technology issue, 336–338
multiple functions involved in, 337
organization's culture and ethics, 338
security awareness training, 338–339
time-based model of information security, 339–340
information systems, 5
changing, 692–693
communicating about control processes, 318
competitive advantage, 692
expenditure cycle, 470–476
productivity gains, 692
revenue cycle, 430–433
systems integration, 692
technology changes, 692
information systems steering committee, 696
information technology (IT), 4
analyzing gamified training in, 215–218
antimalware controls, 346
authentication controls, 346–353
availability, 336
capabilities and risks, 298
computer-integrated manufacturing (CIM), 518
confidentiality, 335
developments, 18, 19
electronic data interchange (EDI), 435
electronic funds transfer (EFT), 451–453
electronic lockbox, 451
infrastructure, 11
IT-related controls, 335–336
network access controls, 346–351
perimeter defense, 347–350
privacy, 336
processing integrity, 336
redesigning supply chain with, 20
security, 335
InfraGard, 259
in-house information systems department development, 733–735
initial investigation, 704–705
Inline eXtensible Business Reporting Language (iXBRL), 60
inline XBRL (iXBRL), 578–579
innovative performance metrics, 525–526
input controls
accuracy and, 397
cancellation and storage of source documents, 397
credit sales processing, 401–402
data entry controls, 398–399
source documents, 397
turnaround documents, 397
input design, 763–764
input fraud, 236–237
inspection costs, 526
instance document, 579–580
instant messaging (IM), 435, 440
Institute of Internal Auditors, 302
intangible services, 664–665
Integra Financial, 737
integration tests, 743
integrity, commitment to, 305–306
integrity controls
expenditure cycle information system, 473
revenue cycle information systems, 432
Intel, 238
intellectual property, 369
Intentia, 316
intentional acts, 224
interactive control system, 299
internal control flowcharts, 64–65
Internal Control-Integrated Framework (IC), 302
components and principals, 305
versus Enterprise Risk Management-Integrated Framework (ERM), 303
internal controls, 11–12, 298
internal failure costs, 526
internal-level schema, 97
internal rate of return (IRR), 701
Internal Revenue Service (IRS), 693
Internet
how information is transmitted on, 347–348
impact on people and businesses, 41
misinformation, 264
retailers, 435
Internet of Things (IoT), 18, 137, 357
Internet Protocol (IP), 261, 348
Internet pump-and-dump fraud, 265
interviews, 706
intrusion detection systems (IDSs), 354
intrusion prevention systems (IPS), 347–350
inventory
acquiring, 6
checking availability, 438–439
documenting internal movement of, 518
on hand, 516
loss from fire or disasters, 519
production operations, 518–519
radio frequency identification (RFID) tags, 518

reports to better manage, 476
restricted access to, 518
segregation of duties, 518
theft, 442, 518
investment advisors, 138
investment fraud, 228
invoices, 660–661
invoicing
billing errors, 447–448
controls, 447–448
invoiceless billing, 446
maintaining accounts receivable, 448–450
sales invoice, 446–447
IoT. *See* Internet of Things
IP address spoofing, 261
IPS. *See* intrusion prevention systems
IPSec, 379
IRR. *See* internal rate of return
IRS's phishing@irs.gov website, 268
Israel Defense Forces, 270
IT. *See* information technology
iXBRL. *See* Inline eXtensible Business Reporting Language

J

James, Jonathan, 274
Japan's Fukushima Daichi nuclear reactor, 195
Java, 145
JavaScript, 261
Jennings, Ken, 149
job-time tickets, 521, 545
John Hancock Mutual Life, 744
JOIN linkage, 106
Journal of Accountancy, 342
journals, 36–37
deriving from relational database queries, 645–646
journal voucher file, 571–572
JPMorgan Chase, 737
just-in-time (JIT) inventory system, 478

K

Kaggle, 172
kaizen, 487
Kasparov, Garry, 149
key escrow, 378
keylogger, 273
keystroke-logging software, 491
kickbacks, 482–483
Kinko's, 272
knowledge management systems, 539–540
Koenig, Mark, 270
Kozlowski, Dennis, 232

L

labor
information about, 670
instructions concerning activities, 668
lapping scheme, 233, 452
laptops, 342
Laurie, Adam, 276
lean manufacturing, 513
Lebanese looping, 270
ledgers, 34, 646
legacy accounting systems, 574
legal feasibility, 700
Lewis University, 260
likelihood/risk, 298
limit check, 398
Limited Brands, 20
line chart, 198
linkbases, 580
Liszewski, Robert W., 307
loading data, 144–145
lockbox, 451
log analysis, 353–354
logical models, 707
logical view, 97
LSI Logic, 737

M

MAC addresses, 345
Machiavelli, Niccolo, 701–702
machine learning, 194
machine operations, 670
machine-readable format, 4, 33
machinery and equipment usage, 521, 670
malicious software, 230
malware
adware, 272
antivirus software vendors, 271
bluebugging, 276–277
bluesnarfing, 276
botnet owners, 271
cell phones, 276–277
cyber-extortion, 273
drop services, 271
guarantors, 271
HotLan Trojan, 273
identity fraudsters, 271
identity intermediaries, 271
keylogger, 273
malware owners, 271
malware writers, 271
mobile devices, 270
packet sniffers, 274
personal electronic devices, 276–277
PlaceRaider app, 270–271
ransomware, 273
rootkit, 274–275
scareware, 272–273
spyware, 271–272
steganography program, 274
time bomb/logic bomb, 274
torpedo software, 272
trap door/back door, 274
Trojan horse, 273–274
viruses, 275–276
worms, 275–276
malware owners, 271
malware writers, 271
management
assigning authority and responsibility, 306–307
change management, 315
data control, 315
Generally Accepted Privacy Principles (GAPP), 373
identifying and assessing threats, 309
improving information security, 338
network managers, 315
penalties against employees violating security policies, 339
philosophy, operating style, and risk management, 305
planning and preparing for succession, 307
security awareness training, 339
security management, 315
segregation of duties, 315
support for employees following security policies, 339
systems administrators, 315
systems development life cycle (SDLC), 696
user accounts, 352
managerial reports, 647
balanced scorecard, 586–587
capital expenditures budget, 584
cash flow budgets, 584
cause-and-effect relationships, 587
dashboards, 587
flexible budgeting, 586
operating budgets, 584
responsibility accounting, 584–585
threats and controls, 584–588
man-in-the-middle (MITM) attack, 262–263
Mantovani, Andrew, 292
man-traps, 341, 342
manufacturing companies
automation, 148
blockchain, 17
overhead, 521
manufacturing process improvement principles, 487
manufacturing resource planning (MRP-II), 513
many-to-many relationship, 613–614, 664
many-to-one relationship, 662
MapMyFitness, 13
Mariposa botnet, 258
marketing, 6, 19
masquerading, 263
MasterCard, 320–321
master files, 38, 41
master plan, 698
master production schedule (MPS), 513–516
Match.com, 193
material fact, 227
materials
ordering, 477–483
requisition, 514
materials requirements planning (MRP), 478
maximum cardinality, 611–612, 615, 659–660, 662
McAfee, 226, 270
McDonald's, 264
McHugh, Bibiana, 168
mean, 190
median, 190
MediaWiki, 261
medical identity theft, 375
Medtronic, Inc., 487
Meijer, Inc., 546
Mellon Bank, 320–321
Merrill Lynch, 700
metadata, 141–142
Microsoft, 258, 259
Hotmail accounts, 273
Malicious Software Removal Tool, 272
Patch Tuesday, 261
Microsoft Access, 105, 142, 145
Microsoft Cognitive Services, 12
Microsoft Excel, 142, 145, 170

Microsoft Internet Explorer, 275
Microsoft Outlook, 275
Milano, Albert, 228
mindset, 139
"Mindset, Behaviors, Knowledge & Skills Building a Roadmap for the Auditor of the Future," 138
minimum cardinality, 611–612, 614–615, 637, 659, 662, 666
misappropriation of assets, 228–229
Mizuho Securities, 225
mnemonic codes, 34
mobile devices, 270, 319
MongoDB, 146
monthly statement, 448–449
Morris, Robert T., 276
MPS. *See* master production schedule
MRP-II. *See* manufacturing resource planning
multifactor authentication, 343–344
multimodal authentication, 343
MyDoom virus, 259, 275
MySpace, 261, 276

N

Nakamoto, Satoshi, 14
narrative description, 59
NASA, 164–165, 195
NASDAQ, 409
Nashua, 692
National City Bank, 276
National Commission on Fraudulent Financial Reporting (Treadway Commission), 229
National Security Agency, 226
NCR Corporation, 41
Nelson, John, 307
Netbus, 274
net present value (NPV), 701
network access controls, 346–351
network diagrams, 198
network managers, 315
networks, 236, 350
neural networks, 320–321
Nevada Gaming Control Board, 402
New York Police Department, 263
New York University School of Law, 205
Nike, 693
nonce, 383
noninventory purchases, 488
nonoperational (throwaway) prototypes, 740
nonrepudiation, 381
nonvoucher system, 486–487
normalization, 105
NPV. *See* net present value
Nucor Corporation, 546
null hypothesis, 192
null values, 172–173

O

Obama, Barack, 224
observation, 707
Office of Foreign Assets Control, 482
OLAP. *See* online analytical processing
OLTP. *See* online transaction processing database
one-to-many relationship, 613–614, 665
one-to-one relationship, 612–615, 636
online analytical processing (OLAP), 95
online transaction processing database (OLTP), 95
open-invoice method, 448, 449
operational feasibility, 700
operational prototypes, 740
operations, 315
  accounting information system (AIS), 19
  management, 696
operations list, 511
opt-in, 373
opt-out, 373
Oracle Corporation, 44, 260, 269
ordering costs, 477
ordering materials, supplies, and services
  bar-coding, 479
  carrying costs, 477
  choosing suppliers, 479–483
  counting inventory on hand, 479
  economic order quantity (EOQ), 477
  identifying what, when, and how much to purchase, 477–479
  inaccurate inventory records, 478
  just-in-time (JIT) inventory system, 478
  materials requirements planning (MRP), 478
  ordering costs, 477
  production scheduling, 478
  purchase requisition, 478
  purchasing agents (buyers), 479
  purchasing items not currently needed, 479
  radio frequency identity (RFID) tags, 479
  reorder point, 477
  request to purchase, 478
  stockout costs, 477
organizational goals, 3
organizational structure, 306
organizations
  below-industry turnover rates, 540
  decision making, 5–6
  integrity, ethical values, and competence, 305–306
  policy and procedures manual, 306–307
  renting resources, 666
  security-aware culture, 338
  selling one-of-a-kind inventory, 615
  success and employees, 538
  what REA diagram reveals about, 614–616
outliers, 190
output controls, 400–402
output fraud, 238
outsourcing
  accounting information system (AIS), 736–737
  advantages and disadvantages, 736–737
  payroll cycle activities, 553–554
overhead costs, 522
Overstock.com, 17, 762

P

Pacific Gas & Electric, 693, 729
Pacific Telephone, 269
packets, controlling access by filtering, 348–350
packet sniffers, 274
packing slip, 443–444
Panetta, Leon E., 224
parallel conversion, 769
parity bit, 401
parity checking, 401
part-to-whole visualizations, 198
PASSUR Aerospace, 138
password cracking, 260
passwords, 343–344
patches, 261
patch management, 352
pattern recognition, 167–168
payback period, 701
Payment Card Industry Data Security Standards (PCI-DSS), 335
payments, 6
PayPal, 269
payroll
  batch totals, 549
  cross-footing payroll register, 551
  deduction register, 548
  deductions, 547–548
  disbursing, 551–553
  earnings statement, 549
  hourly employees, 547
  master file, 548
  payroll clearing account, 551
  payroll register, 548
  preparing, 547–551
  processing errors, 549
  salaried employees, 547
  transaction files, 547
payroll clearing account, 551
payroll cycle activities
  changes in employee discretionary deductions, 543
  checks, 543
  disburse payroll, 551–553
  employer-paid benefits, 553
  inaccurate time and attendance data, 546
  information about hirings, terminations, and pay-rate changes, 543
  outsourcing, 553–554
  payroll service bureau, 553–554
  preparing payroll, 547–551
  professional employer organization (PEO), 553–554
  segregation of duties, 547
  source data automation, 546
  taxes, 553
  updating payroll master database, 544–545
  validating time and attendance data, 545–547
  voluntary employee deductions, 553
payroll master database, 544–545
payroll register, 548, 551
payroll service bureau, 553–554
PCI-DSS. *See* Payment Card Industry Data Security Standards
PCs. *See* personal computers
penetration testing, 356
Pentagon, 235
PEO. *See* professional employer organization
people
  accounting information system (AIS), 11
  information security, 338–339
  participating in activity, 32
perimeter defense
  access control lists (ACLs), 348–349
  border router, 347
  defense-in-depth to restrict network access, 350
  demilitarized zone (DMZ), 347

filtering packets, 348–350
firewalls, 347–350
intrusion prevention systems, 347–350
routers, 347–350
Perini Corp., 317
perpetrators of fraud, 230
perpetual inventory method, 439
personal computers (PCs), 235
personal electronic devices and malware, 276–277
personal identification numbers (PINs), 343–344
PERT. *See* program evaluation and review technique
petabytes (quadrillion bytes), 14
Petrobras, 299
phantom controller, 233
pharming, 268–269
phase-in conversion, 770
Philip Crosby Associates (PCA), 307
phishing, 268
See also Web-page spoofing
phishing@irs.gov website, 268
phreaking, 263–264
physical design, 696
physical inventory worksheet report, 439
physical models, 707
physical security, 341–342
physical systems design
computer screen design, 763
debugging, 764–765
demand reports, 762
file and database design, 762–763
form design, 763
input design, 763–764
output design, 762
physical systems design report, 766
procedures and controls design, 765–766
program design, 764–765
program maintenance, 765
scheduled reports, 762
special-purpose analysis reports, 762
structured programming, 764
triggered exception reports, 762
physical systems design report, 766
physical view, 97
picking and packing order, 441–443
pie charts, 198
piggybacking, 263, 339
pilot conversion, 770
PINs. *See* personal identification numbers
pipe delimiter, 142
PKI. *See* public key infrastructure
PlaceRaider app, 270–271
plaintext, 376
planning and scheduling
approval or authorization of production orders, 518
information about labor availability, 515, 516
integrating information about customer orders, 515
inventory on hand, 516
key documents and forms, 513–516
lean manufacturing, 513
manufacturing resource planning (MRP-II), 513
master production schedule (MPS), 513–516
materials requisition, 514
movement and usage of raw materials, 514
move tickets, 514
over- or underproduction, 517
production cycle, 513–518
production order, 514
production planning methods, 513
pull manufacturing, 513
push manufacturing, 513
planning systems development, 697–699
PLM. *See* product life-cycle management
podslurping, 264
point scoring, 731–732
policy and procedures manual, 306–307
Ponzi schemes, 265
porn websites, 267
Positive Pay, 492
postimplementation review, 316, 770
PowerPoint, 63
pre-award audit, 481
predictive analytics, 145, 193–194
prescriptive analytics, 145, 194
pressures, 230–232
pretexting, 267
preventing behavioral problems, 703–704
prevention costs, 526
preventive controls, 298, 309
PricewaterhouseCoopers (PwC), 145–146
primary key, 101, 103, 132–134, 642
printers, 342
privacy
California Consumer Privacy Act (CCPA), 373
European Union's General Data Privacy Regulation (GDPR), 372–373
Financial Services Modernization Act (Gramm-Leach-Bliley Act), 373
Generally Accepted Privacy Principles (GAPP), 373–376
Health Information Technology for Economic and Clinical Health (HITECH), 373
Health Insurance Portability and Accountability Act (HIPPA), 373
identity theft, 375
information technology (IT), 336
protecting, 369–372
regulations, 372–375
United States laws, 372–373
Privacy Foundation, 319
private key, 377
processing controls, 399–400, 402
processing integrity, 336
credit sales processing, 401–402
electronic voting, 402
input controls, 397–399
output controls, 400–401
processing controls, 399–400
spreadsheets, 403
processing test data, 768
processor fraud, 237
procurement card, 489
product backlog, 742
product data management software, 511, 512–513
product design, 511–513
production cycle, 8, 10
cost accounting, 520–526
events, 670
planning and scheduling, 513–518
product design, 511–513
production operations, 518–520
revenue cycle information system, 508
production cycle information system, 509–511
production cycle REA model, 668–671
production operations
computer-integrated manufacturing (CIM), 518
disruption of production activities, 519–520
fixed assets, 518–519
inventory, 518–519
poor performance, 519
production cycle, 518–520
request for proposal (RFP), 519
training, 519
production order, 514
production planning methods, 513
productive capacity, 525–526
productive processing time, 525
product life-cycle management (PLM), 511–513
product owner, 742
product-related overhead, 523
products, 11
professional employer organization (PEO), 553–554
program design, 764–765
program evaluation and review technique (PERT), 699
program flowchart, 59
program maintenance, 765
programmers, 314
programming, 314
programs, 351–352
project development, 316
project development and acquisition controls, 315
project development plan, 315–316, 698
project development team, 696
projection, 702
project milestones, 315–316
property rights, 17
proposal to conduct systems analysis, 705
protecting information resources
access controls, 341–342
cell phones, 342
device and software hardening controls, 351–353
laptops, 342
man-traps, 341, 342
physical access, 341
physical security, 341–342
printers, 342
tablets, 342
user access controls, 342–346
prototyping, 739–741, 744
Provide Customer Support tables, 673
Public Company Accounting Oversight Board (PCAOB), 299, 308
public key, 377
public key infrastructure (PKI), 383
pull manufacturing, 513
purchase order, 480–481
purchase requisition, 478
purchasing, 20
purchasing software, 729–732
push manufacturing, 513
PwC. *See* PricewaterhouseCoopers
Python, 145

Q

Qlikview, 146
QR codes, 435
queries, 41
  description and quantity of inventory sold in specific time, 111
  invoice numbers, dates, salesperson for sale to customer, 105, 108
  query-by-example (QBE) query, 105, 108–109
  sale date, description, and quantity for transactions, 108–110
  sale date and invoice total in specific time, 113–114
  structured query language (SQL), 105–114
query-by-example (QBE) query, 105, 108–109

R

radio frequency identification (RFID) tags, 400, 439
  ordering materials, supplies, and services, 479
  picking and packing order, 441–442
  suppliers, 472
RAID. *See* redundant arrays of independent drives
range check, 398
ransomware, 273
raw materials
  expenditure cycle information system, 508
  movement and usage of, 514
  usage data, 520
  used to make finished product, 668–670
REA data model, 93, 603–606
  accounts receivable, 609
  acquisition of intangible services, 664–665
  additional expenditure cycle events and attribute placement, 661–664
  additional revenue and expenditure cycle modeling topics, 659–667
  agent-event relationships, 667
  agents, 604
  basic template, 604–606
  billing, 608–609
  business activities as events, 608
  digital assets, 665
  employee roles, 667
  entities, 604
  events, 604, 607–609
  extending to include information about policies, 688–689
  implementing in relational databases, 635–647
  locations, 667
  new feature, 670–671
  production cycle, 668–671
  relationships between resources and agents, 667
  rental transactions, 665–667
  resources, 604
  sale of services, 664
  structuring relationships, 604–606
Reader's Digest, 228
REA diagrams
  agent-event relationship, 614
  assigning attributes to each table, 642–643
  business cycles, 607–608
  cardinalities of relationships, 610–615
  completeness check, 644–645
  development, 607–614
  foreign keys, 643
  integrating across cycles, 635–640
  merging redundant event entities, 639
  merging redundant resource entities, 638–639
  relationships, 612–614
  relevant events, 607–609
  resources and agents, 609–610
  retrieving information from database, 645–647
  tables for each distinct entity and many-to-one relationship, 640–642
  uniqueness, 615–616
  validating accuracy, 640
  what it reveals about organization, 614–616
real-time mirroring, 407
real-time processing, 39
reasonableness test, 398
receiving
  accepting delivery of unordered goods, 485
  counting and recording inventory, 485
  debit memo, 484
  expenditure cycle, 483–486
  mistakes in counting items received, 485
  purchase of services, 485
  receiving report, 484
  segregation of duties, 486
  theft of inventory, 485–486
receiving report, 484
reconciliations, 572–573
  independently maintained records, 318
records, 38, 93
  creating, 39
  design and use of, 316
  protecting, 317
  reconciliation of independently maintained, 318
  safeguarding, 316–317
recovery point objective (RPO), 404, 407
recovery time objective (RTO), 404, 407
redundant arrays of independent drives (RAID), 404
reevaluations, 575
referential integrity, 103, 144
regression analysis, 341
relational databases, 100–150
  adding new data, 104
  assigning attributes to each table, 642–643
  attributes, 101
  basic requirements, 103–104
  completeness check, 644–645
  conceptual design, 601
  cumulative and calculable data, 643
  data, 93
  data modeling, 602
  delete anomaly, 101
  deriving journals from queries, 645–646
  designing, 101–103, 105, 600–602
  efficient use of space, 104
  entities, 602–603
  entity integrity rule, 103
  entity-relationship (E-R) diagram, 602–603
  extracting data from, 106
  foreign keys, 103, 643
  generating financial statements, 646–647
  implementation and conversion, 601
  insert anomaly, 101
  ledgers, 646
  managerial reports, 647
  nonkey attributes, 103
  normalization, 105
  physical design, 601
  price and cost data, 643
  primary key, 101, 103
  problems with invoice data, 101
  queries, 105–114
  REA data model, 93, 603–606, 635–647
  REA diagram development, 607–614
  redundant data, 101, 103
  referential integrity rule, 103
  related tables, 103
  relationships, 602–603
  retrieving information from, 645–647
  semantic data modeling, 105
  storing all data in one table, 101
  structured query language (SQL), 105, 108
  systems analysis, 601
  tables, 100, 640–642
  third normal form (3NF), 105
  update anomaly, 101
  using and maintaining, 601
  varying number of columns for repeating items, 101, 103
relational data model, 100
relationships, 602–603
  cardinalities of, 610–614
  between entities, 610–614
  event-agent relationship, 672
  event-event relationship, 615
  many-to-many relationship, 613–614
  many-to-one relationship, 664
  minimum cardinality, 637
  one-to-many relationship, 613–614, 665
  one-to-one relationship, 612–613, 615, 636
  between resources and agents, 667
  types of, 612–614
relevant information, 4
ReliaStar Financial, 320
remittance advice, 448
remittance list, 451
Remote Deposit Capture software, 451
Rental event, 666
Rental Inventory table, 665–666
rental transactions, 665–667
reorder point, 477
reporting system, 9
  managerial reports, 584–588
  preparing financial statements, 576–584
reports, 40–41
  physical inventory worksheet report, 439
Report to the Nation on Occupational Fraud and Abuse (ACFE), 227
report writer, 100
reputable information, 4
request for proposal (RFP), 519, 730
request for systems development, 704
Request Inventory event, 661–662
requirement costing, 732
resources, 604
  affected by activity, 32
  identifying, 609–610
  relationship with agents, 667
responding to attacks, 355–356
response time, 316
responsibility, 306–307
responsibility accounting, 586
responsibility accounting systems, 319
revenue cycle, 7, 9, 428, 607–608
  accounts receivable aging report, 437–438
  additional events, 659–661

attribute placement, 659–661
billing, 445–450
bill-of-lading attribute, 660
cash collections, 451–454
credit approval, 436–438
credit limit, 436
information about activities, 428
production cycle information system, 508
sales order entry, 433–441
shipping, 441–445
revenue cycle information systems, 430–433
authorization controls, 432
customer master data errors, 432
enterprise resource planning (ERP) system, 430–433
integrity controls, 432
inventory master data errors, 432
loss or destruction of master data, 432–433
pricing master data errors, 432
process, 430
production cycle, 508
unauthorized disclosure of sensitive information, 432
reverse auctions, 481
RFID. *See* radio frequency identification
RFP. *See* request for proposal
risk, 309, 311
risk analysis and management software, 319
risk appetite, 305
risk assessment, 309–311
risk response, 309–311
robotic process automation (RPA) software, 148–149, 157–158
robots, 442
rootkit, 274–275
round-down fraud, 264
routers, 347–350
Royal Canadian Mounted Police, 292
RPO. *See* recovery point objective
R program, 146
RTO. *See* recovery time objective

S

sabotage, 226
salami technique, 264
sales
accounting information system (AIS), 19
data, 3
sales invoice, 446–447
sales order entry
checking inventory availability, 438–439
customers, 435
electronic data interchange (EDI), 435
e-mail, 435
employees, 435
instant messaging (IM), 435
missing or inaccurate data, 436
process, 435
responding to customer inquiries, 439–441
retention performance, 440
revenue cycle, 433–441
sales orders, 434–436
sales orders, 434–346
sales staff, 546
sample sales journal, 36–37
San Diego Padres, 308
Sankey diagrams, 198
SAP, 44
Sarbanes-Oxley Act (SOX), 60, 96, 299–301, 306, 335
SATAN, 236
scareware, 272–273
scatterplot, 196–197
scavenging/dumpster diving, 269
scheduled reports, 762
scheduling feasibility, 700
schemas, 97–98, 580
Schneider, Jerry, 269
scrum, 742–743
SDLC. *See* systems development life cycle
second normal form (2NF), 132, 133–134
Securities and Exchange Commission (SEC), 299, 308
inline XBRL (iXBRL), 578–579
management mandates, 300
security
blockchain, 16
Generally Accepted Privacy Principles (GAPP), 374
information technology (IT), 335
management, 315
monitoring and revising security solutions, 356–357
virtualization, cloud computing, and Internet of Things, 357
security life cycle, 336–337
Sedol, Lee, 149
segregation of duties, 312–315
semantic modeling, 105, 341
semi-structured data, 140
services, 351
accounting information service (AIS), 19
fraudulent billing, 485
improving quality, 11
ordering, 477–483
purchase of, 485
reducing costs, 11
Service Set Identifier (SSID), 269, 351
7-Eleven, 5
sexting, 264
SHA-256 algorithm, 380
Shadowcrew, 292
Shalika Foundation, 258
Shane Co., 693
sharing results, 147–148
shipping order to customer, 441–445
short message service (SMS) spoofing, 261
shoulder surfing, 269–270
Simons, Robert, 299
Six Sigma, 487
skimming, 270
smart cards, 343
smart contracts, 42
smartphones, 435
SMART (specific, measurable, achievable, relevant, and timely) objectives, 139
Smith, C. Arnold, 308
Sobig virus, 226
social engineering, 257–258
carding, 268
chipping, 270
eavesdropping, 270
evil twin, 269
identity theft, 266–267
Lebanese looping, 270
pharming, 268–269
phishing, 268
piggybacking, 339
posing, 268
pretexting, 267
scavenging/dumpster diving, 269
security awareness training, 339
shoulder surfing, 269–270
skimming, 270
spear phishing, 339
typosquatting/URL hijacking, 269
vishing (voice phishing), 268
social media, 440
fraud and security risks, 267
software
accounting information system (AIS), 11
design, 352–353
documentation, 60
errors, 224, 225
patch, 261
purchasing, 729–732
tracking, 319
vulnerabilities, 261
zero-day attack, 261
Software as a Service (SaaS) providers, 730
software piracy, 265–266
software-sharing websites, 267
Sony, 275, 744
Sony Playstation, 258
source data automation, 33
source documents, 32–33, 397
South Dakota v. Wayfair, 448
Southland Corporation, 5
SOX. *See* Sarbanes-Oxley Act
Space Shuttle Challenger, 195
spamming, 260
spear phishing, 268, 339
special-purpose analysis reports, 762
spoofing, 260–261
spreadsheets, 403
spyware, 271–272
SQL. *See* structured query language
SQL injection (insertion) attack, 262, 352–353
SSID. *See* Service Set Identifier
Standish Group, 693
Statement on Auditing Standards (SAS) No. 99 *Consideration of Fraud in a Financial Statement*, 229–230
State Tax Accounting and Reporting System (STARS), 768
static graphics, 196
statistic courses, 146
steering committee, 315
Steffen, Roswell, 308
steganography program, 274
strategic master plan, 315
structured programming, 764
structured query language (SQL), 100, 106–107, 109–111, 113–114, 146
queries, 105–114
Stuxnet virus, 224
style sheet, 581
subschemas, 97, 98
SubSeven, 274
subsidiary ledger, 34, 36
subsystems, 3
Sunbeam, 769
supplier invoices, 486–489

suppliers
  auditing, 483
  bar codes, 472
  blanket purchase order or blanket order, 480
  budgets and, 481
  competitive bids, 481
  dependability, 480
  evaluating, 480
  exchange of information with, 470
  formal bids by competitive, 519
  inferior-quality products, 481–482
  kickbacks, 482–483
  ordering materials, supplies, and services, 479–483
  potential alternative, 480
  pre-award audit, 481
  price lists, 481
  process, 480–481
  product inventory master record, 480
  purchase order, 480–481
  purchasing items at inflated prices, 481
  radio frequency identification (RFID) tags, 472
  reverse auctions, 481
  unauthorized, 482
  unreliable performance by, 482
  vendor-managed inventory (VMI), 481
supplies, ordering, 477–483
supply chain, 11, 20
Swartz, Mark, 232
Swedish Stock Exchange, 316
Symantec, 226, 383
symmetric encryption, 377–378
system flowcharts, 59, 68
system performance measurements, 316
system requirements, 707–709
systems, 3
  availability, 403–409
  business continuity plan (BCP), 407–408
  data backup procedures, 405–406
  data centers, 404
  disaster recovery plan (DRP), 407–408
  documentation, 707
  duties, 314
  fault tolerance, 404
  minimizing risk of downtime, 403–404
  preventive maintenance, 403–404
  recovery and resumption of normal operations, 404–409
  recovery point objective (RPO), 404, 407
  recovery time objective (RTO), 404, 409
  redundant arrays of independent drives (RAID), 404
  training, 404
  uninterruptible power supply (UPS), 404
  virtualization and cloud computing effects, 409–410
systems administrators, 315
systems analysis, 695, 704–709
  feasibility study, 707
  information needs, 707–709
  initial investigation, 704–705
  logical models, 707
  physical models, 707
  proposal to conduct systems analysis, 705
  scope creep, 704
  system requirements, 707–709
  systems analysis report, 709
  systems documentation, 707
  systems survey, 706–707
systems analysis report, 709
systems analysts, 314, 697
systems conversion, 769–770
systems development life cycle (SDLC)
  behavioral aspects of change, 701–704
  computer programmers, 697
  conceptual design, 695
  conceptual systems design, 759–761
  external players, 697
  feasibility analysis, 699–701
  implementation and conversion phase, 696
  information systems steering committee, 696
  management, 696
  operation and maintenance, 770–771
  operations and management, 696
  physical design, 696
  physical systems design, 761–766
  planning, 697–699
  players, 696–697
  project development team, 696
  request for systems development, 704
  systems analysis, 695, 704–709
  systems analysts, 697
  systems conversion, 769–770
  systems implementation, 766–769
  users, 696
systems implementation
  acceptance tests, 768–769
  completing documentation, 768
  implementation plan, 766
  processing test data, 768
  selecting and training personnel, 767
  testing system, 768–769
  walk-throughs, 768
systems integrator, 316
systems survey, 706–707
systems survey report, 707

T

Tableau, 149
Tableau SpotFire, 146
tables
  adding data, 104
  assigning attributes, 642–643
  columns for repeating items, 101, 103
  cumulative and calculable data, 643
  data concatenation, 169
  data consistency, 170–171
  data joining, 166
  data pivoting, 166–167
  for distinct entity and many-to-one relationship, 640–642
  duplicate data, 172
  first normal form (1NF), 132–133
  foreign keys, 103
  formatting data, 170–171
  misfielded data values, 170
  missing or empty values, 172–173
  nonkey attributes, 103
  price and cost data, 643
  primary key, 101, 103, 132–133, 134, 642
  querying, 106
  relational databases, 100
  second normal form (2NF), 132, 133–134
  selecting field, 106
  set of related tables, 103
  storing all data in, 101
  third normal form (3NF), 105, 132, 133, 134–135
  tuple, 100
tablets, 342
taxes, 6, 553
tax identity theft, 375
taxonomy, 580
tax professionals, 137
technical feasibility, 700
technology
  accounting information service (AIS), 20
  capturing time and attendance data, 546
  intentional errors in collecting data, 546–547
  unintentional errors in collecting data, 546
test dataset, 193
text qualifier, 142
theft
  cash collections, 451
  cash disbursements, 490, 491–492
  fixed assets, 518
  inventory, 442, 518
  laptops, 342
third normal form (3NF), 105, 132, 133, 134–135
throughput, 316, 525–526
time-based model of information security, 339–340
time bomb/logic bomb, 274
time card, 545
Time magazine, 235
time sheet, 545
TimesOnline, 276
time validation, 545–547
tokenization, 371
top-level reviews, 317
torpedo software, 272
Toys 'R' Us, 40
traditional cost systems, 522–523, 525
training
  production operations, 519
  protecting confidentiality and privacy, 372
  systems, 404
training dataset, 193–194
transaction cycles
  conversion cycle, 8
  expenditure cycle, 8, 9
  financing cycle, 8, 10
  human resources/payroll cycle, 8, 9–10
  production cycle, 8, 10
  revenue cycle, 7, 9
transaction files, 38
transaction log, 399
transaction processing, 7
  blockchains, 41–42
transactions, 7
  Internet, 41
  nonrepudiation, 381
  proper authorization, 311–312
Transfer Agent entity, 673
transforming data, 162–176
  data cleaning, 172–174
  data requirements, 144
  data standardization, 167–171
  data structuring, 165–167
  data validation, 174–176
  dirty data, 163–164
  documenting process, 144

high-quality data attributes, 164–165
poor quality data, 163
standardizing, structuring, and cleaning data, 144
understanding data and desired outcome, 144
validating data quality, 144
Transmission Control Protocol (TCP), 348, 401
transposition error, 400
trap door/back door, 274
treemaps, 198
trial balance, 572
triggered exception reports, 762
Trojan horse, 258, 261, 273–274
Trust Services Framework, 335, 338
tuple, 100
turnaround documents, 32–33, 397
turnkey system, 730
Twitter, 272
Tyco International, 232, 299
Type 2 System and Organization Controls (SOC) 2 report, 357
typosquatting/URL hijacking, 269

U

U.S. Cyber Command, 224–225
U.S. Department of Commerce
Bureau of Industry and Security, 482
U.S. Department of Defense (DOD), 235, 274, 692, 702, 703
U.S. Department of Veterans Affairs, 238
U.S. Justice Department, 292
U.S. Navy Warfare Center, 270
U.S. Secret Service, 292
Ubiquity Networks, 263
Uconnect, 261
UIPath, 148
unauthorized suppliers, 482
Under Armour, 13
Unified Process, 743–744
unintentional acts, 224
unintentional errors, 225–226
uninterruptible power supply (UPS), 404
United Parcel Service (UPS), 194, 226
United States' laws about privacy, 372–373
unit tests, 743
universal payment identification code (UPIC), 453
University of Michigan Medicine, 226
Unix epoch time, 170–171
UNUM Life Insurance, 739
update anomaly, 101
Update (U) access right, 98
UPIC. *See* universal payment identification code
UPS. *See* uninterruptible power supply
UPS. *See* United Parcel Service
USA Today, 274
USB Paine Webber, 274
user access controls, 342–346
user accounts, 352
user stories, 742
USF&G, 737
Usher, Albert, 264
UTC. *See* Coordinated Universal Time
utilization, 316

V

validity check, 398
value chain, 19–20, 441
vendor-managed inventory (VMI), 481
Veteran Affairs (VA) Department, 317
Veteran's Memorial Coliseum, 237
Victoria's Secret, 20
violated attribute dependencies, 174
virtualization, 18
effects on systems, 409–410
implications of, 357
unauthorized access to sensitive information, 372
virtual private networks (VPNs), 379–380
viruses, 275–276
Visa, 320–321
vishing (voice phishing), 268
Visio, 63
visual inspection, 175
visualizations, 191
area chart, 198
bar chart, 196
bar charts, 202
boxplot, 198
bullet graph, 196
choosing right, 196–198
color, 202–204
combining, 198
comparison, 196
correlation, 196–197
data deception, 205–208
data ordering, 205
designing, 199–208
distance, 200–201
distribution, 197–198
emphasis, 199, 202–205
ethical data presentation, 199, 205–208
formats, 200
heat maps, 197
highlighting, 202–203
histograms, 198
information overload, 200
labels, arrows, and graphics, 203
line chart, 198
maps with data overlays, 198
network diagrams, 198
orientation, 201–202
part-to-whole, 198
pie charts, 198
quantity, 200
Sankey diagrams, 198
scatterplot, 196–197
shading, 203
simplification, 199–202
static graphics, 196
too much or too little information, 200
treemaps, 198
trend evaluation, 198
visual weight, 204
visual weight, 204
VKontakte, 259
VMI. *See* vendor-managed inventory
voice over Internet protocol (VoIP), 372
VoIP. *See* voice over Internet protocol
voluntary employee deductions, 553
voucher package, 486–487
voucher system, 487
VPNs. *See* virtual private networks
vulnerability scanners, 351

W

W. Atlee Burpee, 736–737
Walgreens, 442
walk-throughs, 768
Wall Street Journal, 543
Walmart, 14, 41, 232, 297
Walmart Labs data analytics team, 14
Walton, Sam, 232
war dialing, 263
war driving, 263
warehouses
robots, 442
staffing to process incoming shipments, 472
wireless technology, 441
Warner, Gary, 259
web-based retailers, 13
Web-page spoofing, 261
websites, 440
customer interaction on, 435
fraud and security risks, 267
instant messaging (IMs), 440
spoofed websites, 268–269
WellPoint Health Networks, 729
Westpac Banking, 316
white-collar criminals, 228, 230
Wilkin & Guttenplan PC, 541
WinAntivirus, 273
WinFixer, 273
wireless devices, 350–351
Wireshark, 348
Wood's Amazing Woods Inc. (Wood's), 157–158
Word, 63
Worldcom, 299
worms, 275–276
write-protection mechanisms, 400

X

XBRL. *See* eXtensible Business Reporting Language
XBRL (eXtensible Business Reporting Language), 4, 33, 60, 144
Xerox, 299, 736
XML (extensible markup language), 582
XP. *See* extreme programming
XP Antivirus, 273
XSS. *See* cross-site scripting

Y

Yahoo, 259, 261, 264
YouTube, 272

Z

Zappos, 226
zero-balance test, 400
zero-day attack, 261
Zeus malware, 259
zombies, 258